B

D1350581

061551

**Editor:** Eddie Dyja

**Project Manager:** David Sharp
**Production:** Tom Cabot

**Statistics Research:**
Research & Statistics Unit - UK Film Council
Phil Wickham - *bfi* Information Unit

**Additional Research/Editorial Assistance**
Nigel Arthur, Sean Delaney, Jose de Esteban, Allen
Eyles, Patrick Fahy, Christie Quinn, Matt Ker, Ayesha
Khan, Elena Marcarini, Lavinia Orton, Nathalie
Sergent, David Sharp
**Database Consultant:** Lavinia Orton
**Marketing:** Hannah Hamed, Claire Milburn
**Cover Design:** Jethro Clunies–Ross
**Advertising Consultant:** Ronnie Hackston

**Website:** www.bfi.org.uk/handbook

Stills courtesy of British Film Institute
For rapid access to the bfi's collection of over four
million film and television images call 0207 957 4797 or
email requests to stills.films@bfi.org.uk

Many thanks to: Andrew Beck, United International
Pictures (UK)

Thanks to those who also assisted with images: BBC,
Buena Vista International, Carlton, Channel 4 Television,
Columbia TriStar, Entertainment Film Distributors,
Granada, Icon, Miramax, Momentum Pictures, Pathé
Distribution, Twentieth Century Fox, United
International Pictures (UK), The Walt Disney Company,
Warner Bros, Yash Raj, Yorkshire Television

© **British Film Institute 2004**
21 Stephen Street
London W1T 1LN

Printed in Great Britain by Bath Press, Bath

A catalogue record for this book is available from the
British Library.

**ISBN** 1 844570 428

**Price:** £23.99

# Contents

# ACKNOWLEDGMENTS

For this year's edition I would like to start with a special mention to my Library colleagues. Without the Library there would have been no *bfi* Film and Television Handbook. Every member of Library staff contributes in one way or another to the information that makes its way into these pages. It is perhaps fitting that after 70 years of service, Library staff past and present should be thanked for imparting their knowledge and enthusiasm and for the professional way that they have carried out their duties.

Coming back to the present day I'd like to thank the following for taking up the baton and assisting me in compiling some of the sections in the directory: Sean Delaney, Jose de Esteban, Allen Eyles, Matt Ker, Ayesha Khan, Elena Marcarini, Lavinia Orton, Christie Quinn, and Nathalie Sergent.

And let us not forget our indexer Linda Wood, who has completed the final most furious dash to the line over the past few years with fleet footed efficiency.

The bulk of the statistics were compiled by the UK Film Council's Research Unit. I would like to thank Jim Barratt and Steve Perkins in particular for the swift way that they dispatched figures to me.

It would be doing a great department a disservice by not acknowledging the support that I have been given by my colleagues in the *bfi*'s Information Unit. Many thanks go Phil Wickham who continued to provide an authoritative view about film production in the UK. Thanks also go to Peter Todd, Erinna Mettler, David Reeve, Ian O'Sullivan and Matt Ker (again) for updating me with new information whenever it came to hand.

I offer a special thanks to all my colleagues in Publishing who have experienced a topsy turvy kind of year. I naturally have to single out Tom Cabot for his unflinching dedication to the cause. His gentle methods of ensuring that the Handbook was delivered on time are very much appreciated.

Thanks also to Claire Milburn for keeping up to date with the latest news on how well the Handbook is doing.

Beyond the printed pages I have to thank Danny Birchall Danny Birchall, Gareth de Walters and Matt Ker for spreading Handbook information to all corners of the *bfi* website and even on the Handbook web page itself.

The *bfi* Stills department but in particular the unflappable Nigel Arthur also deserve a big ovation this year for cheerfully providing me with a useful selection of images to add a little bit of colour to the pages.

Speaking of images, many thanks to designer Jethro Clunies–Ross who produced the magnificent cover artwork and can now call himself an expert in pop corn kernels.

In a quiet corner of the *bfi* works our ad man Ronnie Hackston who has managed to juggle working on Sight and Sound and the Handbook with a commendable amount of dexterity.

The following honourable mentions are for the intangible day to day, week in week out, month after month moral support. Top of the list this year goes to David Sharp who has given me tremendous encouragement and empathy during this difficult year.

Thanks go to all of the people that I have mentioned up to now and also to Nina Bishop, Maureen Brown, Karen Cattini, Sophie Contento, Christophe Dupin, Eugene Finn, Hannah Hamed, Guy Hinton, Richard Holford, Alex Hogg, Alison Kirwan, Tina McFarling, Ivan Mowse, Mandy Rosencrown, Lucy Skipper, Emma Smart, Sara Squire and Tise Vahimagi.

I would like to thank the continued loyal support from Nielsen EDI Ltd, Screen Finance, Screen International, British Videogram Association (BVA), European Audio-visual Observatory and the UK Film Council for allowing me to dip in and out of their resources.

Thanks also go to the following organisations who have helped us produce the Handbook over the years – The Arts Council of Wales, The Arts Council of Northern Ireland, the BBC, The British Council Film and Literature Department, the British Film Commission (BFC), Central Statistical Office (CSO), the Cinema Advertising Association (CAA), the Department for Culture, Media and Sport (DCMS), Media +, Scottish Screen, UK Media Desk, TaRiS Taylor Nelson Sofres.

**Eddie Dyja, Handbook Editor, August 2004**

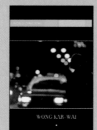

# 70 Years of the *bfi* National Library

On 7th July 2004 the bfi National Library celebrated the 70th anniversary of the appointment of Ernest Lindgren as the first Head of Information Section, by hosting an Open Evening in its Reading Room. Below is a brief chronological look back over the past 70 years featuring a Library timeline, selected highlights from Special Collections for each decade and a very selective listing of some books and periodicals.

## 1930s

1933    bfi founded, with information service among its initial functions.

1934    first Head of Information Section appointed (Ernest Lindgren)

1935    details of 2,000 films have been collected (the foundations of SIFT)

1939    described as "... the best centre of information on cinema in Europe."

Researchers can explore the work of the Film Society in Britain throughout the thirties by reading their meeting agendas and minutes. The Ivor Montagu Collection also covers the filmmaker's work with the Society, and includes items relating to the BBFC, letters and sketches from Sergei M Eisenstein, and documentation referring to many films such as Hitchcock's THE MAN WHO KNEW TOO MUCH (1934) and THE SECRET AGENT (1936).

### Film
*Film technique; five essays and two addresses*/Pudovkin (1933)
First bfi annual report (1933)
*Monthly Film Bulletin, Amateur Cine World*,(1934)
Catalogue of the National Film Library / National Film Library (1936)
*Sketch book* /Disney (1938)

### Television
*The kingdom of the camera*/Baker (1934)
*Television; a guide for the amateur*, Sydney A. Moseley and Herbert McKay (1936)
*The cinema and television* /Legg (March of time) (1939)

## 1940s

1940    premises in Great Russell St suffer bomb damage

The Carol Reed Collection houses material from all stages of the director's career, treasures from the forties include the annotated scripts of THE ODD MAN OUT (1947) and THE THIRD MAN (1949). Both the Michael Powell and Emeric Pressburger collections illustrate the complex process of filmmaking-there are papers from various stages of production for I KNOW WHERE I'M GOING! (1945), BLACK NARCISSUS (1947) and THE RED SHOES (1948). Researchers can also

explore the working papers for many unrealised projects the pair developed together.

### Film
*One of our aircraft is missing* /Pressburger (1942)
*Book list; being a list of books of special interest available to students of the cinema in the library of the Institute*/ BFI(1943)
Film form by Sergei Eisenstein (1949)

### Television
*Ariel and all his quality: an impression of the B.B.C. from within*, by Richard S. Lambert (1940)
*Four thousand years of television* / Hubbell (1946)
*Muffin the Mule*, by Annette Mills (1949)

## 1950's

1950s    information department "... relegated to the smelly basement at 164 Shaftesbury Avenue"

1955    Brenda Davies appointed as Head of Information and Documentation Dept

1959    Information Dept and Book Library merged into National Film Archive

The British public was ready for more Ealing comedies in the fifties and they were not disappointed when films such as THE LAVENDER HILL MOB (1951), THE MAN IN THE WHITE SUIT (1951) and THE LADYKILLERS (1955) were released. The work

that went into these films can be explored through the Michael Balcon, Robert Hamer, Charles Crichton and T.E.B Clarke Collections. Other items of special interest from the fifties include Dirk Bogarde's annotated scripts from his early career, and Peter Sellers scrapbooks.

### Film
*Films in Review* (1950)
*Cahiers du Cinema* (1951)
NFT Programmes (1957)

### Television
*TV Guide* (1952)
*TV Times* (1955)

## 1960s

1963    Library serving 3,500 users, double the previous year's figure

Interesting items from this decade include production files in the Gerald (Carry On) Thomas collection, a scrapbook compiled by THE WITCHFINDER GENERAL (1968) director Michael Reeves, and letters from the BBFC in the Hammer Films Collection concerning various 'Dracula' projects. Key figures in sixties television such as Troy Kennedy Martin, John McGrath, Irene Shubik and Julia Jones have donated their working papers to bfi Special Collections.

**Film**
*Hitchcock's films* / Wood (1965)
*I lost it at the movies* / Kael(1965)
*The New Wave* / Graham(1968)
*Filmgoers' Companion*/Halliwell (1965)
**Television**
*The BBC book of That Was The Week That Was* / Campey
*Birth of Broadcasting (History of Broadcasting in the United Kingdom, v.1)*, by Asa Briggs

### 1970's

1974   Library and Information Dept separated from Archive
1977   move to Charing Cross Road

Joseph Losey's career in the seventies resulted in films such as THE GO-BETWEEN (1971) and THE ROMANTIC ENGLISHWOMAN (1975). In addition to the detailed production notes and script drafts, the Losey Collection contains correspondence with some of the stars the director worked with- Elizabeth Taylor, Richard Burton, Julie Christie, and Dirk Bogarde to name but a few. Derek Jarman's notebooks, sketches, and draft scripts are held for many of his films, including JUBILEE (1978) and THE TEMPEST (1979).
**Film**
*Great movie stars* / Shipman (1970)
*Hollywood, England: the British film industry in the sixties* / Walker (1974)
*Hollywood Babylon* / Anger (1975)
*Film Dope Index on Censorship*
**Television**
Television: the critical view (1sted),ed by Horace Newcomb (1976)

### 1980's

1980   Gillian Hartnoll succeeds Brenda Davies as Head of Library Services
1987   move to 21 Stephen Street
Material in the David Puttnam Collection shows how Colin Welland's novel 'Runners' was turned into the Oscar winning film CHARIOTS OF FIRE (1981). Items include treatments and various script drafts, location reports, information about distribution, and press cuttings from around the world. There is a collection named after Peter Greenaway's film THE DRAUGHTSMAN'S CONTRACT (1982) containing daily reports and Polaroid continuity shots.

**Film**
*International Film Encyclopedia*/Katz (1980)
BFI Dossiers first appear (1980)
*Psychoanalysis and cinema: the imaginary signifier*, by Christian Metz (1982)
*British Cinema History* /Curran & Porter (1983)
BFI Film and Television Yearbook (1983)
**Television**
*On television* (1st ed), by Stuart Hood (1980)
*Popular culture: past and present,*
ed.Tony Bennett et al. (1982)
*Television sitcom* (bfi Dossier n.17), ed by Jim Cook (1982)

### 1990's

1990   Library serving over 10,000 visitors
1992   SIFT goes live in Reading Room
1993   new paperstore opened, to house Library's Special Collections
1995   Reading Room extension opened
1997   new Head (Ray Templeton) and new title: bfi National Library
1998   Library serving 17,500 visitors and 41,000 telephone/written enquiries.
Following a recent donation of production files from Skreba films researchers can now access casting ideas, call sheets, and scripts for popular films such as BLUE JUICE (1995), SLAB BOYS (1997), and LAND GIRLS (1998). Character actor Roger Ashton-Griffiths has also donated many of his scripts from his film and television work in the nineties, including copies of THE DARLING BUDS OF MAY (1991-3), THE MADNESS OF KING GEORGE (1994), RESTORATION (1995) and THE PORTRAIT OF A LADY (1996).
**Film**
*Psychoanalysis and cinema*, ed by Ann E. Kaplan (1990)
*Arrows of desire: the films* of Michael Powell and Emeric Pressburger, by Ian Christie (rev. def. ed) (1994)
*Black looks: race and representation* / Bell Hooks (1992)
*Easy riders, raging bulls..*/Peter Biskind (1998)
*Black Film Bulletin*
**Television**
*Popular television in Britain*, ed by John Corner
*The Guinness book of classic British TV*, by Cornell, Day & Topping
*L!ve tv: tellybrats and topless darts: the uncut story of topless television* / Nathan & Horrie (1999)

### 2000 – 2004

2000   Library catalogue available on bfi website
2002   collections of the ITC Library received for incorporation
2004   bfi seeks partnership with academic institution for a joint initiative to develop and establish a new centre for learning and research on film and television
**Film**
*Which lie did I tell? More adventures in the screen trade* /William Goldman (2000)
*A long hard look at Psycho*, Raymond Durgnat's last work (2002)
**Television**
*Big brother: the unseen story*/Richie (2000)
*The television genre book* / Creeber (2001)

# INTRODUCTION

**by Amanda Nevill**
**Director of the British Film Institute**

we can create, contribute to and inform debates about film and TV in the UK.

Everyone at the *bfi* has a passion for the moving image. We all want to increase knowledge about, and simplify rich and meaningful access to, the widest possible range of film and television culture. As a public body, our duty to the nation is to ensure that all of the moving image media are understood, enjoyed and valued by everyone — and that we fulfil our duty as effectively and cost-efficiently as possible.

Our renewed commitment to reaching wider audiences across the UK is demonstrated through two forthcoming flagship projects, the Mitchell & Kenyon Collection and Black World.

The Mitchell & Kenyon Collection provides a fascinating social record of early 20th Century British life. This remarkable collection of some 800 films from 1900-1913 showing ordinary people in everyday situations was commissioned by travelling showmen to screen at local fairgrounds or other locations across the UK. The films feature almost all parts of the UK outside South East England - but particularly Lancashire, Yorkshire, the North East, the Midlands, and Scotland.

The *bfi* is, quite simply, unique. There is no other film culture and heritage organisation like it in the world. As such, it is admired and envied across the globe.

Following a review of the *bfi* which was reported in April 2004, we are now in the busy process of implementing a series of new projects and initiatives.

Our new strategic direction does not change the organisation's core values or principles. We are on a mission to champion moving image culture in all its richness and diversity to as diverse an audience as possible and hopefully, by engaging with our audiences

Discovered in a shop basement in Blackburn by businessman and historian Peter Worden, the films had been stored in sealed barrels for many decades. In the skillful hands of *bfi* archive staff, the films then underwent painstaking restoration and preservation work as part of a four-year Arts and Humanities Research Board project by the British Film Institute in partnership with the National Fairground Archive at University of Sheffield.

Now preserved, identified, catalogued and contextualised, the collection can be rediscovered through a programme of events and activities. The *bfi* is organising a nationwide tour of the films, as well as releasing a DVD and publishing accompanying books. We have also been working with the BBC on a three-part BBC2 documentary on the films due for transmission in 2004-5.

Looking ahead, preparations are underway for Black World 2005. Offering a celebration and critical evaluation of black cinema in Britain, the six-month programme will consist of film seasons, events, workshops and critical debates designed to engage a diverse range of British communities, but specifically targeting young people across the UK.

The project aims to consolidate sustainable networks and organisations working to support, preserve and inspire black filmmaking.

We have a range of new initiatives designed to develop our UK-wide remit and establish closer working relationships with regional and national colleagues to promote film culture.

One initiative will create, with partners, a network of Archive Portals - or mediatheques - across the UK. These are facilities, probably sites in existing destinations, where anyone and everyone can access informally – for fun – digitised materials from both the *bfi* National Film Archive and Regional Archive – access to material which simply could not be available otherwise.

We are also committed to developing Virtual *bfi*. We plan to develop the range of resources currently available on our website. Ideas include making our legendary filmographic database available online, webcasts of key events from the National Film Theatre and the creation of an online "debating chamber".

We re-affirm our commitment to achieving a flagship home for film in the UK; a vibrant meeting place where people will come together to experience film in all its richness. This is a long-term project which will require patience, perseverence and pursuasion before it becomes a reality. Surely film, like every other major art form, should have a major national home with an international reach?

In the meantime we are making productive use of the currently unoccupied space at the South Bank. The vision for this site is to create an exciting destination with an extensive and innovative range of film and television related activities designed to excite and challenge audiences of all ages and interests. Due to open in autumn 2005, the key elements will include an exhibition space for artists working in film, video and new media; a mediatheque, providing access to archive material.

And of course, these new projects are all in addition to our usual range of activities, where work continues apace. This year alone we have had 550,000 admissions in the UK in 520 venues of films from Distribution and Archival Collections (65 per cent from outside London), we have released 32 DVDs, and have enabled access to over 7,000 titles from the *bfi*'s collections. We also provided research access to 5,320 titles to more than 1,500 students and researchers.

# UK FILM, TELEVISION AND DVD/VIDEO: OVERVIEW

### by Eddie Dyja

It has been another paradoxical year for the British film industry. On the one hand we saw a record-breaking production boom which filled UK film studios with films such as *Troy, Thunderbirds* and *Harry Potter and the Prisoner of Azkaban*, while on the other hand we witnessed the Government tightening up loopholes in the tax system which had an immediate impact on dozens of British films which were about to start shooting. We learned that while the top ten British films, which included *Love Actually, Calendar Girls* and *Johnny English*, burst the £1billion mark at the worldwide box office, British films in general made little impact at Cannes or at the Oscars. So, in other words, it was a typically topsy turvy year, where talking up the British film industry was as easy as writing it off. In the end the real story about the year in British film was rather familiar. British box office successes were generally bankrolled with American money and know how. Hollywood dominated the domestic and global box office, while defining the Britishness of British films was open to several interpretations.

## Is there a British Film Industry?

Way back in September 2003, The Culture, Media and Sport Committee published its report on the state of the British film industry. The inquiry posed, and attempted to answer, the thorny, perennial question: 'is there a British film industry?'

The Committee concluded that there is a British film industry, but then qualified this statement by saying: "The nature of the British film industry is perhaps not what we would wish it to be. Ideally, we would prefer the main activity to be indigenous production of films about Britain, a substantial proportion of which break out to achieve success in the global market."

It identified three clearly distinct areas in which the British film industry currently operates.

*The most popular British film in 2003 was Love Actually*

1. The British film industry provides lucrative provision of services for the major Hollywood studios – attracted by UK talent, facilities and tax regimes – to make high-budget and technically-demanding motion pictures.

2. It produces indigenous, usually distinctively British, films shot in the UK. This however, was described to the Committee as "an under-capitalised 'cottage' industry based around entrepreneurial individuals driving single-project vehicles."

3. It produces films shot abroad under co-production treaties.

The Committee noted how the British film industry has concentrated on production with insufficient emphasis on distribution. Furthermore, the majority of British productions tend to exist as entities in themselves. Any successes, expected or otherwise, do not reap rewards to fund further projects.

The Committee's conclusions and recommendations to the Government provided no radical solutions to the problems of distribution in Britain. Instead it re-emphasised the importance of tax relief: "We regard the existing level of tax relief for film production as absolutely essential to the health of the industry."

Nevertheless, the Committee was delighted by progress made by the UK Film Council and other agencies in attempting to identify and rectify the chronic longstanding problems that have thwarted the British film industry from becoming a more easily identifiable and self-sufficient organ.

In November 2003, as a first step in its review of international co-production treaties, the Government published updated guidelines clarifying the criteria for international co-productions for films in an effort to tighten up loopholes. It was thought that some producers were exaggerating how much of a film's budget was spent in the UK in order to qualify for tax reliefs.

The first new agreement stipulated that a minimum 40 per cent of the film budget in any bilateral UK/Canada co-production must be spent in the UK – up from 20 per cent. A similar alteration was marked out for agreements with France, Italy, Denmark and Iceland. They too had to spend 40 per cent of their budgets in the UK to qualify for tax relief – up from 30 per cent.

At the beginning of 2004, the UK Film Council provided a welcome good news story when statistics showed that spending on UK films in 2003 had risen by well over 50 per cent and passed the £1 billion barrier. A month later the UK production sector seemed less robust when the Inland Revenue set about closing some tax loopholes after fears that some crafty tax partnerships were exploiting the system.

Out of the blue the Inland Revenue put its foot down and sought to take action against tax avoidance schemes that exploited relief for trading losses through partnerships. From 10 February 2004 the amount of loss relief available in partnerships was limited to the amount invested.

The legal tax-avoidance partnership schemes operated under what are termed Generally Accepted Accounting Principles (GAAP). Explaining the decision to close the loophole, Dawn Primarolo, the paymaster general, said: "the schemes manipulate tax relief to create claims for

# Tax incentives for filmmakers

## Sale and Leaseback

Sale and leaseback is currently the mechanism through which the UK's tax breaks for British qualifying feature films are channelled. A producer or production company can reduce its borrowing (approximately 10-15 per cent of the budget) by selling the rights to the film to a UK purchaser, who can claim tax relief on the purchase price while leasing the rights back to the seller.

Sale and leaseback may only be used for British qualifying feature films intended for theatrical release.

## Section 48 up to July 2005

The Government introduced its Section 48 tax break in 1997 to help small independent film makers. Section 48 allows benefits for films with budgets of less than £15 million. Tax relief allows a 100 per cent write-off of production and acquisition expenditure on films.

Section 48 is due to expire in July 2005 and the Government has recently announced plans for a new tax credit to take its place. At the time of writing the exact details have not been finalised. However, check the contact details below for updates.

## Section 42

Section 42 usually allows benefits for films with budgets greater than £15 million. Tax relief allows a 100 per cent write-off of production and acquisition expenditure over a period of three years.

The Government announced that Section 42 would remain intact, and this scheme does not have an end date.

## Further details
**Department Media for Culture and Sport**
www.culture.gov.uk
**UK Film Council**
www.ukfilmcouncil.org.uk
**British Council Films and Television Department**
www.britfilms.com

*Calling International Rescue. We need help to make our films*

losses in excess of the capital at risk…schemes like this undermine the true purpose of tax relief and we are determined to take all appropriate action to counter them."

However, when the Inland Revenue closed the GAAP loophole it threatened to knock the funding out of dozens of UK co-productions and nearly closed down high profile productions such as *The Libertine* starring Johnny Depp – and did close down *Tulip Fever*, the adaptation of the novel by Deborah Moggach. Producers immediately had to look elsewhere to finance productions about to start filming.

What caused further consternation was that the move by the Inland Revenue had taken everyone by surprise. By closing tax loopholes and causing panic within the British film industry, the Government inadvertently exposed some fragile aspects of production in the UK. Yet, despite this flurry of excitement, and the prospect of the Section 48 tax incentive scheme being reformed in 2005, there were reasons to be optimistic about film production in the UK.

## Film Production

Last year's Handbook anticipated the boom in UK film production with UK film studios housing blockbusters such as *Troy, Thunderbirds* and the ubiquitous *Harry Potter and the Prisoner of Azkaban*.   Andrew Lloyd Webber's Really Useful Group also managed to make *The Phantom of the Opera* one of the UK's highest budget productions. If you add Oliver Stone's big budget *Alexander* into the list, then  the production sector in the UK had a  phenomenally successful year in 2003 with spending to the tune of £1.17 billion.

Post production too enjoyed a boom time in Britain with productions such as Terry Gilliam's *Brothers Grimm* and Antoine Fuqua's *King Arthur* all benefiting from British special effects expertise. But perhaps the real excitement of the boom was the genuine anticipation that the films made in the UK, were making, and would make an impact at the box office.

Everywhere down the list of UK titles there seemed to be potential box office hits such as Gurinder Chadha's *Bride and Prejudice*, Aardman Animation's *Curse of the Wererabbit*, the re-make of *Alfie* starring Jude Law, the second Bridget Jones film,  and *Valiant*, an  animation film about a carrier pigeon in the Second World War.

The industry buzz about British films was typically misunderstood and misinterpreted by the Press, who relished the challenge of being the first to run with the perennial "the British are Coming" stories.

Stewart Till, CBE who replaced Sir Alan Parker as Chairman of the UK Film Council in 2004,  struck a cautious note when he said: "Despite all the advances, the financing of the British film industry is a precarious hand-to-hand process. There   are not as many significant independent British distributors as there are in other European countries and the ones that exist no longer enjoy the muscle and backing of the former corporate structures of PolyGram and FilmFour."

The continuing fact remains that Harry Potter films have reaped millions for Warner Brothers in the US despite being made in the UK. Similarly Working Title (whose

*American actress Renée Zellweger stars as Bridget Jones*

recent British hits include *Love Actually* and *Bridget Jones*) depend on their success with an essential link to Universal. In fact, behind most successful British films the profits are counted out in dollars rather than sterling. For some filmmakers this is not problematic, and in fact they embrace the relationship as many of those dollars are reinvested in new projects using British creativity and crews. For others the financial relationship with our American cousins sits uneasily with the promulgation of an indigenous film industry.

In an interview to *Time Out* in February 2004 Sir Alan Parker put the position as bluntly as he could: "Our studios wouldn't exist without American movies. Would it be a healthier film industry if all the camera assistants had to go back to being mini-cab drivers as they did in the '80s? The inward investment creates an infrastructure, it absolutely does."

Those mourning the loss of an indigenous film industry point to the fact that the Hollywood studios ultimately call the shots. Some feel that too many compromises are made in order to keep the US producers happy.

Many critics pointed out that the *Thunderbirds* movie had more in common with *Spy Kids* than Gerry Anderson's original Supermarionation classic. While the crafts were authentically replicated and given resplendent life via state of the art CGI, the film seemed to have an American audience first and foremost on its mind.

The top three British films of last year – *Love Actually, Calendar Girls* and *Johnny English* – were all essentially British stories but each ensured that they contained a nod to their US partners. News that the re-make of *Alfie* is being set in New York brings back memories of how *High Fidelity,* the adaptation *of* Nick Hornby's book set in North London, also received an Atlantic crossing. Also, it is worth noting that the transatlantic tennis romance, *Wimbledon,* was released just after the US Open Tennis Championship had completed, rather than just after Wimbledon tennis fortnight. The Americanization of British cultural themes is the price British producers have to pay for aspiring to compete on the global stage.

It was also interesting to note the defensive reaction that some Amercians gave to *Cold Mountain,* Anthony Minghella's faithful adaptation of Charles Frazier's novel set during the American Civil War. It prompted the director to say: "A few people in the US believe that we – a British director and his international team – have stolen this essentially American story."

*Cold Mountain – an essentially American story?*

However, it should also be pointed out that in recent years British films have managed the remarkable trick of producing hit films which show distinctively British themes, with distinctively British regional accents and displaying British cultural diversity. Recently, films such as *24 Hour Party People* and *Shaun of the Dead* have demonstrated that the Brits can still make entertaining films with a British tone. Furthermore, the box office success of films like *East is East* and *Bend it Like Beckham* and the critically acclaimed *Dirty Pretty Things* showed the type of films which reflect and acknowledge the multi-cultural nature of Britain.

Nevertheless, it still came as a surprise to learn that the release of *Emotional Backgammon*, directed by Leon Herbert was the first feature film in 12 years to be written, produced and directed by a black person. It highlighted the infrequency of homegrown Black cinema in the UK. In this respect the neurosis of targeting and selling homegrown films in the UK persists.

It is also startling to see the paucity of women directors represented in UK films. In 2003 the number of women directing UK films was 12 out of 109 titles. The "male gaze" dominates film in the UK, as it does the global arena.

Elsewhere in the production sector a scheme to encourage apprenticeship in the film industry was launched by the UK Film Council and Skillset. *A Bigger Future* was heralded as the first national training plan for the UK film industry. The scheme is designed to meet the industry's skills needs entering the bottom rung of the ladder and working their way up.

UK Film Council Chairman Stewart Till said: "At the moment, if you want a career in the film industry….it is

*No British stars? What's that all about – Alfie?*

very hard to know where to start because the entry points are illogical and irrational."

Indeed, many young potential film-makers will testify to the sweatshop mentality of working on some films. The pay-off is not financial – many trying to get on the bottom rung of the ladder work for nothing on these films – but it is to gain a few lines of experience on their CV's. The UK Film Council and Skillset are trying to set up some formal, less painful, way for those wanting to get into movie making, as well as those already working in the industry looking to progress their skills.

The rollercoaster process of putting a film together and hoping to get people in the industry interested has left many casualties along the way. Whilst researching UK film productions I stumbled upon a website for a UK film called *Living in Hope* which was made in 2002 (www.fluidityfilms.com). It contains a personalised diary section charting the making of the film, and in doing so paints a vivid, amusing and often painful picture of the endless round of hoops and obstacles that need to be negotiated before the film first, can be made, and second, can find a distributor.

### Seeing Stars

Film financing, tax incentives and film distribution – three key issues that seem to have dominated recent debates about the British film industry were given a new issue to ponder when US Director Quentin Tarantino, the president of the 2004 Cannes film festival jury, made a far simpler pronouncement about the British film industry.

"People go to films to see stars," he said. "When countries

had their own stars, they had an industry. There are only three countries in the world now with sustainable film industries – America, India and Hong Kong. What do they have in common? These countries have stars whom the public want to see."

Tarantino's controversial quote gave some pause for thought and raised a few questions. Who are the 'A' list stars in British cinema today? Why do actresses like Keira Knightly migrate in Hollywood? Does the nationality of the actor really make such a difference as the esteemed director suggests?

The three genuine British hits in 2003 – *Love Actually, Calendar Girls* and *Johnny English* all made it into the Top 10 UK films at the box office. The first two films were awash with British stars including Hugh Grant, Liam Neeson, Alan Rickman, Colin Firth, Bill Nighy, Keira Knightly, Emma Thompson, Helen Mirren, Julie Waters, Celia Imre, Geraldine James. Furthermore, *Johnny English* was essentially a vehicle for Rowan Atkinson's comic creation. It was apparent that UK audiences did turn up to see these films on the basis of the predominantly British casts.

Nevertheless, there may be some iron in Tarantino's words, when viewed in terms of global box office appeal.

The more pressing problem facing the industry is how to convert the investment that has led to a boom time for film production in the UK into the dividends which come from success at the box office and via other media such as pay-TV and DVD.s

At present the UK is dominated by the big five major US distributors – 20th Century Fox, Buena Vista International, Warner, UIP, Columbia TriStar. Of the

*Calendar Girls proved to be a popular picture*

independent distributors, only Entertainment is in the same league.

The rest of the UK Distribution sector is made up of about a dozen distributors who issue at least 12 films per year and a raft of between 30 and 40 distributors who issue between a handful to just one film per year.

The fact remains that out of the 400 odd films released each year in the UK, the majority lose money. For Hollywood companies the flops are offset by the hits. Every year the majors can point to one or two films within their stable which keep the other films afloat. In Britain, we cannot sustain our flops because our own hits cannot be guaranteed. At present the success of films like *Bend it Like Beckham*, *28 Days Later* and *Touching the Void* still get labelled as surprises whereas critical and commercial flops such as *SW9* and *Shoreditch*, are sadly shrugged off as typically poor low budget British fare.

*Documentaries such as Touching the Void reached big audiences*

Perhaps in the current global climate three entries in the domestic Top 10 should be regarded as a success. Nevertheless, it will be interesting to see whether next year the bountiful seeds sewn in the production sector of the UK film industry will provide a bumper crop of box office hits.

## Cinema

The explanations given for the slight dip in cinema attendances in 2003 (the first drop for 12 years) ranged from blaming a sweltering British summer to the abundance of uninspiring sequels.

The quality in the marketing of movies now seems to have overtaken the content of some of the films – particularly at the blockbuster end of the market. The breathless anticipation of each new film and the compliant way the Press tends to welcome these excesses all spell box office bonanzas for the big studios. But even the big studios are aware that there is a limit to the amount of hype and cross-promotion an audience will accept. At the end of the day cinema audiences want to see good movies rather than good trailers. The diminishing law of returns applies to the majority of sequels. If the market is flooded with films that "weren't as good as the first one", then there is a real danger that the dip in cinema attendances may become a slide.

However, 2003 could also be seen a year where new and surprising trends developed away from the traditional 15-24 demographic.

At the time of writing Michael Moore's highly publicised film *Fahrenheit 9/11* was breaking all sorts of box office records for a documentary (not to mention picking up the Palme d'Or at Cannes). However, the previous box office record holder had been the UK's *Touching the Void* (directed by Kevin Macdonald which was released in 2003). These documentary hits follow hard on the heels of Moore's other high-profile film, the Oscar winning *Bowling for Columbine*. Other documentaries of note which have gone on general release include *Capturing the Friedmans* and *Super Size Me*. Michael Winterbottom's *In This World* might also be grouped into this list. His film is essentially semi-fiction and semi-documentary but most importantly it tells a real story about real people.

The gentle rise of the documentary film must come as a surprise to those making feature films that end up being endorsed by Macdonald's and Burger King. Elsewhere, there were some developments in the exhibition sector that were worth tracking.

### At a cinema near you

The bold steps in launching easyCinema aimed at producing cheap no thrills cinema tickets continued with varying support from the top six film distributors. The Office of Fair Trading was brought into the fray at one stage but by then the tensions had eased when 20th Century Fox allowed the easyCinema the rights to show *Down With Love* in its first run. Some punters at the easyCinema payed as little as 50p to see *Charlie's Angels* with the most expensive ticket coming in at £2.35. It will

*This Not a Love Song – simultaneous online and cinema premier*

be interesting to see if the easyCinema model is repeated in other towns in Britain, or whether the idea proves to be commercially unviable.

In the past year a growing disenchantment with the current dearth of cinemas showing non-commercial films have left some film enthusiasts frustrated. It is not surprising that each year there is a call in the Press (usually from a writer in the 35 plus age group) for multiplexes to devote more screens to arthouse films. Their calls have been largerly ignored and it is still harder to see a wide range of films in your local multiplex.

As a result film clubs and film societies are springing up to cater for those audiences hankering for a bit of cerebral action, whether it be of the *Battleship Potemkin* variety or of the short film showcase type. It would be hard to imagine a local multiplex setting aside a screen to show British Avant Garde Film from the Sixties. Instead, the role of specialised exhibition increasingly seems to be finding outlets in art galleries such as Tate Modern.

It should be noted that UGC cinemas have been more experimental in their programming and have devoted some screens to less obviously mainstream films such as, *Goodbye Lenin! Whale Rider* and *Spirited Away*. Also, news of the formation of the UK Film Council's Digital Screen Network – an initiative designed to get a broader range of films, including film classics to audiences across the UK – should provide something to cheer up the grumpy old man brigade.

The gradual advances in Digital Cinema may lead eventually to a shake up of what gets shown at your local multiplex. The potential to show sharp quality films via satellite, over the internet or by a disk, may lead to a leveller playing field where the number of screens devoted to titles will not be purely dependent on the number of prints available.

An early example of what a difference a format can make has been in the recent upturn in fortunes for IMAX cinemas. Two years ago IMAX introduced DMR (Digital Re-Mastering) a process which made it possible to customise 35mm live-action features for IMAX without any loss of picture quality.

The digitally re-mastered version of The Matrix Reloaded made its way to the IMAX screen and proved the sceptics that there was an audience curious enough to try out the feature length IMAX experience. In the same year that the IMAX in Birmingham closed, the *bfi*'s IMAX, which showed *the Matrix,* reported its best year ever.

The problem facing IMAX cinemas is that the educational programming which seems to have been the mainstay of the IMAX remit might make way for crowd pleasing blockbusters. James Cameron's *Ghosts of the Abyss*, about the salvage operation around the wreck of the Titanic, was more in keeping with the IMAX

*Harry Potter was an even bigger hit at the IMAX*

corporations output. However, it is clear that in order to keep IMAX cinemas afloat they will have to keep dipping into the DMR formats.

All indications show that the public prefer watching their films on big screens in cinemas. In September 2003 *This is Not a Love Song* made its premiere on four cinema screens, but more significantly was streamed from the internet from the www.thisisnotalovesong.co.uk website.

The revolutionary premiere was not without its hitches with the computer system unable to cope with the number of people attempting to watch the film.

With more and more people switching to Broadband the likelihood of other ventures is possible. However, it is hard to see the public swapping the communal big screen experience for the slightly nerdy isolated internet screen.

As for the next big thing? There have been reports that boffins are currently working on providing 3D cinema which doesn't depend on glasses. If this becomes achieveable then expect 3D images on your home computer. The future may well be holographic.

## DVD/Video
An article in the Economist in February 2004 reported that. "In 2003, Americans spent $22.5 billion on DVDs and video cassettes compared with $9.2 billion at the box office." Home entertainment systems have improved to the degree that people can have a cinematic experience in their own homes.

More importantly, people can choose what films they wish to have in their personal collections. While it is easy to predict, and therefore market, households with shelves containing *Finding Nemo* or the next Harry Potter, the same is less true about those wishing to collect box sets of their all-time favourite films or TV programmes.

TV companies are busily trying to work out the complicated area of rights and copyright in order to be reissue classics. Horror stories have emerged about how the BBC wiped many programmes deemed unlikely to ever be watched again in order to make storage space available. As archivists will testify, what seems disposal today may become the treasure chest of tomorrow. In June 2004 the *bfi*'s Missing Believed Wiped project unearthed some lost episodes of Peter Cook and Dudley Moore's *Not Only But Also* series. Audiences who may feel alienated from the incessant pandering to the 15-24 audiences at the cinema and on their TV screens, have

found DVDs an area of visual entertainment that is timeless and not totally reliant on the latest, greatest biggest thing.

One thing is certain, that the boom in DVD sales is set to continue, however this success has come with a worrying price for the industry.

The desire to own DVDs as opposed to rent them, as in the good old days of VHS, has seen the rental market see total transactions falling to their lowest level for over 10 years. Independent video stores have been hit the hardest by this trend. Even Blockbuster, the largest rental chain in the UK, was devising two nights for the price of one schemes to keep their business afloat, while also offering more opportunities for users to purchase DVDs. Another development in the rental business was the appearance of internet DVD rental sites.

With sales of DVD players up and continuing to rise, pre-recorded VHS video tapes looked increasingly like a format belonging to the distant past.

## Piracy
Novelties to the cinema-going experience over the past year have included the request for mobile phones to be switched off and a reminder to patrons that filming of the feature presentation is a crime.

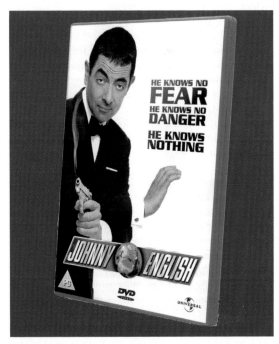

*The boom in DVD sales brought some unwelcome problems*

The booming trade in bootleg films has been made easier with the wide availability of digital technology. The bootleggers are cashing in on consumer's insatiable appetite by making it cheaper and quicker to produce black market copies of films.

In the kingdom of mass consumption, where we are encouraged by cleverly-targeted marketing campaigns to want the latest product immediately, the bootlegger is king. The bootlegger allows us to quench our thirst to be first. Under these circumstances, it is understandable why the consumer might have little sympathy with the big corporations who are worried about the impact that piracy has on their profits.

It is an interesting dilemma facing the video industry. It is only too aware of what has happened in the music industry which has seen CD sales fall dramatically. Online piracy, and CD burners all contributed to making piracy simple.

The interesting response of the music industry was to say: "If you can't beat them, join them." Record companies realised that their consumers were downloading music off the internet and so they responded by making it easier to download music legitimately. The new musical marketing mix now includes downloading music online.

The DVD/Video industry may not be able to come up with the same response since download time for feature films is still too long. Instead, hefty fines and tighter legislation may be the road that it chooses to take to tackle the pirates. In any case, organisations such as the Federation Against Copyright Theft and the Alliance Against Counterfeiting and Piracy are all combining forces in order to counter what is known as Intellectual Property Crime.

There has been an interesting knock on effect of all this illegal activity. A few years ago it was common practice for films to open earlier in the US. Indeed, British cinema audiences often had to endure second-hand prints of films that had already done the rounds in the States. As a result films were being copied within a matter of hours and the bootleggers enacted their own form of global capitalism. Now there are more simultaneous release dates for films.

The major studios also tried to ban "screeners", DVDs that were sent free to voters of the Oscars, BAFTAs and Golden Globes. Twitchy studio bosses thought that the freebies enabled criminal gangs to flood the market with pirate copies. The ban on freebies has also led to a knock on effect, especially in the UK with owners of preview theatres noticing an upturn of business for preview screenings.

## UK Films on UK Television

Movies are still an essential ingredient of the terrestrial channel output. Gone are the days when the terrestrial channels could roll out a premier of a blockbuster in the knowledge that the majority of the TV audience had not seen it.

There is a significant catalogue of titles, ITV's perennial James Bond seasons spring to mind, that are pretty much guaranteed to attract a good audience whenever they are shown. However, when push comes to shove TV executives plump for the appeal of Hollywood films in their primetime slots.

The UK Film Council reported that during the period between Christmas Eve and New Year's Day in 2003 only around 5 per cent of the films screened on terrestrial were UK films made within the last eight years. The UK Film Council were rightly frustrated that the failure of TV companies to buy and distribute British film.

It is worth recalling the list of successful British film-makers who got their start in British television – Ken Loach, Mike Leigh, Michael Apted, Chris Menges, Stephen Frears and Richard Curtis. The strength of the UK television production sector used to feed the film industry with talent.

Sadly, the advent of the Reality TV boom and the insatiable lust for ratings and the cash cow revenue stream from texting has been largely to the detriment of original dramas on TV. The apprenticeship which bore such film talent is in danger of being seen as a thing of the past.

Thanks to lobbying by the UK Film Council, the Communications Act now insists that UK films become an essential item of terrestrial broadcasting schedules. It seems that broadcasters are already shunting British films into the late night slots that once were allocated to foreign language films. While hit UK films such as *Billy Elliot* are afforded decent time slots, films which struggled to get onto UK cinema screens do well if they are shown before midnight.

## Local or global

*Calendar Girls*, based on a true story, was an essentially

British film set amongst the characters of the Women's Institute and around the picturesque backdrop of the Yorkshire dales. For two-thirds of the film the audience is treated to a poignant comedy featuring British manners, traditions, and mores. The campaign to produce a nude calendar is triggered by the death from leukaemia by the husband of one of the women. However, in the film when the calendar achieves its success and becomes a global phenomena the action switches from North Yorkshire to the perceived glamour and glitz of Los Angeles – a move which some critics felt made the film lose some of its charm.

There is a danger when pandering to a global imperative that the essence of what makes a film interesting and engaging is blown up and distorted. On the one hand you don't wish to bite the hand that feeds you, on the other hand you want to retain some semblance of integrity.

The British film industry has benefited in recent years from the support of the Government and the creation of film agencies to ensure some continuity in producing homegrown films. It is clear that strategic bodies can have a profound influence on how the British film industry is regarded, locally and globally.

Yet, in reality despite enjoying our successes the truth remains that Hollywood calls the shots. To attempt to compete on a global stage without a secure infrastructure in place is rather like attempting to do a high wire act without a safety net – you are all right until you fall.

It seems obvious that in order for a truly vibrant film industry to flourish and thrive, it is important not to lose sight of the cultural identity of where the film derives its inspiration. It is equally important to present and embrace new ideas.

In an era where sequels, and remakes of old TV shows for the big screen seem to be in vogue, the global film industry is in danger of becoming like a worn out 45 record which continues to play the same tune over and over again. Even the most gullible of audiences will eventually start voting with their feet if they are not given something new.

It is apparent that creative new ideas are like gold dust. More emphasis should be placed on nurturing creative talent, whether it is in front or behind the camera. It is also the case that filmmakers should be encouraged to have the courage of their own convictions. At present, it is hard to envisage a creative renaissance in British cinema – a new British wave. Sadly, it seems improbable that any new, exciting or original material is likely to emerge when the industry seems so heavily indebted to taxmen, accountants and marketeers.

*Calendar Girls go global*

| **① Number and Value of UK Films\*** <br> **1981-2003** | | | |
|---|---|---|---|
| **Year** | **Titles produced** | **Current prices (£m)** | **Production cost (£m) (2004 prices\*)** |
| 1981 | 24 | 61.2 | 151.30 |
| 1982 | 40 | 141.1 | 310.22 |
| 1983 | 51 | 251.1 | 531.09 |
| 1984 | 53 | 270.4 | 507.70 |
| 1985 | 54 | 269.4 | 511.91 |
| 1986 | 41 | 165.8 | 305.90 |
| 1987 | 55 | 195.3 | 344.73 |
| 1988 | 48 | 175.2 | 298.11 |
| 1989 | 30 | 104.7 | 166.06 |
| 1990 | 60 | 217.4 | 307.27 |
| 1991 | 59 | 243.2 | 322.83 |
| 1992 | 47 | 184.9 | 236.62 |
| 1993 | 67 | 224.1 | 286.13 |
| 1994 | 84 | 455.2 | 567.25 |
| 1995 | 78 | 402.4 | 497.74 |
| 1996 | 128 | 741.4 | 885.50 |
| 1997 | 116 | 562.8 | 656.83 |
| 1998 | 88 | 509.3 | 575.28 |
| 1999 | 100 | 549.2 | 601.84 |
| 2000 | 98 | 804.3 | 868.17 |
| 2001 | 96 | 592.3 | 620.90 |
| 2002 | 105 | 536.7\*\* | 619.5\*\* |
| 2003 | 109 | 1,116.64\*\* | 1,116.90\*\* |

\*UK films are defined here as films produced in the UK or with a UK financial involvement, they include majority and minority co-productions
\* based on calendar year inflation figure of 3 per cent
\*\* Figure includes estimated budgets

**Source: Screen Finance/bfi**

*The Phantom of the Opera – a big budget British production*

# Film Production

Spending on UK film production burst through the £1 billion barrier in 2003 making it a record year for the industry. Big budgets were spent on films such as *Harry Potter and the Prisoner of Azkaban*, *Troy*, *the Phantom of the Opera* and *Thunderbirds*. The figures are up by over 50 per cent compared to the last year's total of £536.7m (Table 1). The total is made more remarkable by the modest increase of UK films which went up from 105 to 109 in 2003. It is far cry from the bad old days in the 1980s when in 1981 the UK film industry mustered a mere 24 titles all for the relative price of £151.3m.

It was not just UK film studios that were busy, UK expertise was used to great effect with UK post-production facilities experiencing a boom time. We have continued to define UK films via five broad categories. There are endless debates to be had as to the actual involvement UK producers have in the film titles listed in these pages. As always, our categories are intended as a guide through the complicated world of film production. Where possible we have tried to define UK films as films produced in the UK or with some direct financial involvement. In this respect our analysis differs slightly from our colleagues in the UK Film Council (for example we do not list short films made in the UK) whose exhaustive statistical research into all aspects of the UK film industry is recommended reading.

With such an increase in investment it is interesting to try to see where the money has come from. The first change comes in our Category A productions which can be defined as our homegrown films. In previous years the wholly UK films market has seen on average 40 films produced each year, many of which rarely make it onto the big screen. In 2003, the 31 productions (Table 2) were down by 13 films compared with 2002. Significantly, the average cost rose from £2.5m in 2002 to £4.5m in 2003. This figure is undeniably bolstered by *The Phantom of the Opera's* big budget of £48m. The other big budget film in this section is the animated film *Valiant* which has a budget of £27.5m. While it is true that these two films carry well over half the total of £135.06m, it is worth noting that the call for fewer, better targetted UK films may have been answered.

Audiences have already been treated to two extremes from this section. On the one hand there was the spoof horror yarn *Shaun of the Dead*, which received favourable views. On the other hand there was the universally lambasted comedy *Sex Lives of the Potato Men*, which was

## UK Film Production 2003 - Category A

Feature films where the cultural and financial impetus is from the UK and where the majority of personnel are British.

| Title | Production company(ies) | Production cost (£m) |
| --- | --- | --- |
| Bullet Boy | Shine Limited/UK Film Council | n/a* |
| Closer to the Sun | Global Films/ /Mnemoics/Edgelimagebank | 0.6 |
| Cold and Dark | Future Film Group/Cold Films | 2.4 |
| Dead Man's Shoes | Warp Films/FilmFour/East Midlands Media Initiative | 1.5 |
| Dear Frankie | Scorpio Films/Pathe/UK Film Council/Scottish Screen | 3.2 |
| Enduring Love | Free Range Films/Film Four/Pathe/UK Film Council/Inside Track | 3.0 |
| Fat Slags | Artists Independent Network/Entertainment Films | 3.5 |
| Frozen | Liminal Films/RS Productions/Shoreline Films/Freedonia Films | 1.4 |
| Hello You | Fecund Films | 0.6 |
| How to Film Your Neighbour | Mad as Hell Films | 1.0 |
| Ladies in Lavender | Scala Productions/UK Film Council/Baker Street Media Finance | 3.6 |
| Map of the Universe 2: The Memos | Global Films | 0.6 |
| Map of the Universe 3: In and Out of Planet Earth | Global Films | 0.6 |
| Millions | Mission Pictures/BBC Films/Pathe/UK Film Council | 5.0 |
| My Summer of Love | Apocalypso Pictures/BBC Films/Film Consortium/UK Film Council/ Baker Street Media | 1.6 |
| Nine Songs | Revolution Films | 1.0 |
| The Phantom of the Opera | Really Useful Company/Scion Films | 48.0 |
| The Purifiers | Vestry Films/Bill Kenwright Films/Scottish Screen/First Choice | n/a* |
| Red Rose | Palm Tree | 2.5 |
| The Rulers, the Dealers and the Losers | RDL Productions | 0.7 |
| School for Seduction | Ipso Facto Films/Her Films/'UK Film Services | 3.0 |
| Sex Lives of the Potato Men | Devotion Films/UK Film Council | 1.8 |
| Shaun of the Dead | WT2/Big Talk Productions | 3.76 |
| Spivs | Carnaby Productions/EIS | 2.4 |
| Things to Do Before You're 30 | Samuelson Productions/Momentum/Isle of Man Film Fund/First Choice | 3.0 |
| Valiant | Vanguard Animation/Ealing studios/UK Film Council/Baker Street Media | 27.5 |
| Vera Drake | Thin Man Films/UK Film Council | 5.0 |
| A Way of Life | Awol Films/UK Film Council/Arts Council of Wales/HTV | 2.0 |
| Yasmin | Parallax/Channel 4 | n/a* |
| Yes | Adventure Pictures/UK Film Council | 1.3 |

| | | | |
| --- | --- | --- | --- |
| **TOTAL NUMBER OF FILMS** | **31** | | |
| **TOTAL COST OF KNOWN BUDGETS** | **£130.56m  (28 films)** | **ApproximateTotal Cost** | **£135.06m*** |
| **AVERAGE COST** | **£4.21m (28 films)** | **Average Cost** | **£4.35m** |

\* Where budgets are not available an approximate amount has been estimated based on an average total of £1.5m per film

**Source: Screen Finance/Screen International/British Council/UK Film Council/bfi**

described as the worst British film ever made (a label once carried by *Rancid Aluminium*).

There were 18 majority UK co-productions produced in 2003, the same number as in 2002 (Table 3). Again the difference in average cost was up from £5.25m to £8.27m..

The biggest budget at £30m belonged to the Irish co-production *Tristan and Isolde*. In terms of potential UK hit films the titles to watch out for include Ken Loach's *Ae Fond Kiss*, *Churchill: the Hollywood Years* (from Peter Richardson of the Comic Strip fame) and *Stage Beauty*. Trying to predict which films will succeed and which ones will fail based on cast, director and funding is a precarious business, and yet, these are just some of the criteria that are used in determining the funding of British films. The ingredient missing from this mix is the script and many will agree the worst aspects of British films in recent years have been the quality of scripts.

## UK Film Production 2003 - Category B

Majority UK Co-Productions. Films in which, although there are foreign partners, there is a UK cultural content and a significant amount of British finance and personnel.

| Title | Production companies/participating countries | Production cost (£m) |
|---|---|---|
| Ae Fond Kiss | Sixteen Films/Bianca Films/EMC/Tornasol/Scottish Screen/Azure/ Glasgow Film Office (Italy/Germany/Spain) | 3.00 |
| Asylum | Seven Arts Films/Woodfall Films/Samson Films/Future Film Group (Republic of Ireland) | 15.00 |
| Beyond the Sea | Archer Street/Quality International/trigger Street/ Filmboard Berlin-Brandenburg (Germany/USA) | 14.00 |
| Blind Flight | Parallax/Partisan Films/Makar Productions/Samson Films/Network Movie/ZDF/Irish Film Board/Glasgow Film Office/Scottish Screen/UK Film Council/Arts Council of Northern Ireland/Matrix(Republic of Ireland/Germany) | 2.30 |
| The Bridge of San Luis Rey | Spice Factory/Pembridge Pictures/Kanzaman/Davis Film/Movision/Scion (Republic of Ireland/Spain/France) | 13.40 |
| Churchill: The Hollywood Years | Little Bird/Pathe/UK Film Council/Isle of Man Dfilm and TV Fund/B Sky B (Republic of Ireland) | 10.00 |
| Compleat Film Stage Beauty | Qwerty Films/BBC Films/N1 European Filmproducktion/Tribeca (Germany/USA) | 9.00 |
| Creep | Dan Films/UK Film Council/Zero West/Filmstiftung NRW/Artisan Ent(Germany/USA) | 3.30 |
| Dead Fish | SE8 Group/Orange Pictures/IMF (Germany) | 8.00 |
| Inside I'm Dancing | WT2/ Octagon Films/Irish Film Board (Republic of Ireland) | 3.60 |
| Jonjo Mickeybo | WT2/New Moon/Irish Film Board/ Northern Ireland Film and TV Commission (Republic of Ireland) | 3.00 |
| Man About Dog | Pot Boiler Productions/Treasure Entertainment/Irish Film Board/Section 481 | 1.50 |
| Omagh | Tiger Aspect/Channel 4/Hell's Kitchen/Irish Film Board/RTE (Republic of Ireland) | n/a* |
| Out on A Limb | Theta Films/Out on a Limb (South Africa) | 1.0 |
| The Queen of Sheba's Pearls | AKA Pictures/Sweetwater/Swedish Film Institute/ TV4(Sweden) | n/a* |
| Red Light Runners | Nu Creation Film Group (Republic of Ireland) | 8.00 |
| Sons of the Wind | Dan Films/UGC/Mate Productions/Ingenious(France/Spain) | 12.90 |
| Tristan and Isolde | Scott Free/Matrix Film Finance/ Section 481 (Republic of Ireland) | 30.00 |

| | | | |
|---|---|---|---|
| **TOTAL NUMBER OF FILMS** | **18** | | |
| **TOTAL COST OF KNOWN BUDGETS** | **£138m (16 films)** | **ApproximateTotal Cost** | **£149m\*** |
| **AVERAGE COST** | **£8.62m (16 films)** | **Average Cost** | **£8.27m** |

\* Where budgets are not available an approximate total has been estimated based on an average total of £3m per film

**Source: Screen Finance/Screen International/British Council/UK Film Council/bfi**

There were six more minority co-productions made in 2003 with an increased average cost of £5.40m compared with £3.9m in 2002 (Table 4). Of these, four films were made with budgets over £11m, with *Resident Evil* (the sequel of the film based on the computer game) easily coming out on top with a hefty £25m budget.

It is only when we reach the US/UK productions that we can see where the next British blockbusters are likely to come from (Table 5). The success of films such as *Calendar Girls, Die Another Day, Johnny English, Love Actually* and *Tomb Raider 2* have helped to make the UK an attractive proposition for US film producers.

This is reflected in the rise of titles: 29 were produced in 2003 compared with 19 in 2002. The average cost of these films has climbed from £17.88m to £19.81m.

*Stage Beauty offered audiences a costume comedy*

# UK Film Production 2003 - Category C

Minority UK Co-productions. Foreign (non US) films in which there is a small UK involvement in finance or personnel.

| Title | Production company(ies)/participating countries | Production cost (£m) |
|---|---|---|
| Being Julia | Myriad Pictures/Serendipity Point/ISL Films/First Choice/Astral Media/Corus Entertainment/Telefilm Canada (Canada/Hungary) | 11.00 |
| Blackout Journey | Towers of London/Epo-Film/Film-Line/Raymaxxfilm (Germany/Austria) | n/a* |
| Bride of Ice | Marloo Media/UKI Films (Germany) | 0.63 |
| Bye Bye Blackbird | Ipso Facto/Samsa/Reverse Angle Factory/Dor Films/FilmFund Lux/Osterriche Film/MFG/NRW/Great British Films(Luxembourg/Austria/Germany) | 4.70 |
| Deadline: Beirut | Psychology News/Film Consortium/UK Film Council/Baker Street MediaRaphael Films/Cinetelefilms (France/Tunisia) | n/a* |
| Dear Wendy | Zoma Films/Lucky Punch/Liberator 2/Pain Unlimited/TV2/ZDF/Canal Plus/Danish Film Institute/Nordic Film and TV Fund//Nordisk Film/NRW(Denmark/Germany/France) | 4.60 |
| A Different Loyalty | Spice Factory/Forum Films/Movision (Canada) | 9.50 |
| Fateless | Renegade Films/Magic Media/EuroArts/Hungarian Cultural Ministry/MDR/MDM/MFG (Hungary/Germany) | 7.00 |
| Head in the clouds | Dakota Films/Spice Factory/Tusk/Remstar/Movision (Canada) | 11.60 |
| Hollywood Flies | Studio Eight/GFT/Movieweb (Italy/Canada) | 3.28 |
| In my Father's Den | Little Bird/T.H.E/UK Film Council/Visionview/NZ on Air (New Zealand) | 3.00 |
| Innocence | Blue Light/UK Film Council/Ex Nihilo/Love Streams (France) | n/a* |
| Jet Lag | Visionary Films/Balagan Productions (China) | 2.70 |
| The Last Sign | Spice Factory/Transfilm/Carrere(France/Canada) | 7.2 |
| Lila Says | Passion Pictures/UK Film Council/Huit et Demi/Zeal/France 2/Pyramide(France) | n/a* |
| Mother Theresa | Spice Factory -Blue Spice/Lux Vide (Italy/Sri Lanka) | 8.10 |
| Mouth to Mouth | MJW (Germany/Portugal) | n/a* |
| My Brother is a Dog | F&ME/Tradewind Pictures/Bos Bros/Film and TV Production/WDR/NRW/MDM/FFA/Dutch Film Fund/Invicta Capital (Germany/Netherlands) | 3.10 |
| Niceland | F&ME/Zik Zak/ Tradewind Pictures/Nimbus Films/NRW/Danish Film Institute/Nordic Film and TV Fund/Iceland Film Fund/Hamburg Film Fund/Eurimages/Invicta Capital (Iceland/Denmark/Germany) | 1.75 |
| Oh Happy Days! | Ugly Duckling/Fine and Mellow/Nordisk/Matrix Film Finance/Danish Film Institute(Denmark) | 1.88 |
| The Oyster Farmer | Oyster Farmer Films/Little Wing/Anthony Buckley Films/Australian Film Finance corpatioon/NSW FilmOffice/Showtime/Future Film Group/Ocean Dendy (Australia) | 3.00 |
| The Preacher | David.P.Kelly Productions/Theorama Films/Dutch Film Fund/Samsa Films/NOS/VARA (Netherlands) | 2.30 |
| Rabbit on the Moon | Headgear Films/Beanca Films/Calle Cruzada/Fidicine Fund (Spain/Germany) | 1.80 |
| Resident Evil | Impact Pictures/Constantin Film/Davis Films (Germany/France) | 2500 |
| The Statement | Company Pictures/Spice Factory/SerendipityPoint/Odessa Films/Movision (France/Canada) | 11.20 |
| Strings | F&ME/Bald Films/Bob Film/Nordisk Film/DR/NRK/SVT/Danish Film Institute/Nordic Film Fund/Swedish Film Institute/Sandrew Metronome (Sweden/Denmark/Norway) | 2.40 |
| That Touch of Pink | Martin Pope Productions/Sienna Films/ChumTV/Movie Central/Movie Network/Canadian TV Fund/Astral Media/Telefilm Canada/Greenburg Fund (Canada) | 3.00 |
| Wild Side | Zephyr Films/Maia Films/Alligator Films/Lancelot Films (France/Belgium) | n/a* |
| The Wooden Camera | Tall Stories/UK Film Council/Richard Green and Associates/Odelion (South Africa) | n/a* |

| | | | |
|---|---|---|---|
| **TOTAL NUMBER OF FILMS** | 29 | | |
| **TOTAL COST OF KNOWN BUDGETS** | £128.74 (22 films) | **ApproximateTotal Cost** | £156.74m* |
| **AVERAGE COST** | £5.858m (22 films) | **Average Cost** | £5.40m |

* Where budgets are not available an approximate total has been estimated based on an average total of £4m per film

**Source: Screen Finance/Screen International/British Council/UK Film Council/bfi**

# UK Film Production 2003 - Category D

American financed or part-financed films made in the UK. Most titles have a British cultural content.

| Title | Production company(ies) | Production cost (£m) |
|---|---|---|
| Agent Cody Banks 2: Destination London | Splendid Pictures/Maverick Films/Dylan Sellars/MGM-UA | 16.00 |
| Alfie | Paramount | 20.00 |
| Bride and Prejudice | Bride Productions/Pathe/Miramax | 15.00 |
| Bridget Jones: The Edge of Reason | Working Title/Universal | 18.00 |
| Chasing Liberty | Alcon Entertainment/Warner Brothers | 14.00 |
| Code 46 | Revolution Films/BBC Films/UK Film Council/United Artists | 4.50 |
| Country of My Skull | Studio Eight/Merlin Films/Chartoff Productions/Phoenix Pictures/ Morula Pictures/Film Afrika Worlwide/Ingenious/ Ind.Dev.Corp of South Africa | 9.39 |
| Curse of the Wererabbit | Aardman Animation/Dreamworks SKG | 25.00 |
| Danny the Dog | Europa Corporation/Current Entertainment/Twentieth Century Fox | 26.25 |
| De-Lovely | Cloud Nine/Winkler Films | 15.00 |
| Five Children and It | Capitol Films/Endgame/Jim Henson Company/UK Film Council/ Isle of Man Film Fund | 12.30 |
| A Good Woman | Meltemi Entertainment/International Arts Entertainment/ Lighthouse Entertainment/Buskin Film (Italy)/ Kanzaman (Spain)/Magic Hour Finance/Matrix Film Finance | 7.00 |
| Harry Potter and the Prisoner of Azkaban | Heyday Films/Warner Brothers | 100.00 |
| Layer Cake | Ska Films/Columbia Tristar | 5.00 |
| The Life and Death of Peter Sellers | HBO | 15.00 |
| The Merchant of Venice | Spice Factory/Movision/Avenue Pictures/UK Film Council/ Instito Luce/Delux/Scotts Atlantic/Navidi Wilde | 18.00 |
| Piccadilly Jim | Mission pictures/Inside Track/Myriad Pictures | 9.00 |
| Proof | Hart Sharp/Miramax/Endgame entertainment | 12.00 |
| Sky Captain and the World of Tomorrow | Natural Nylon/Brooklyn Films | 38.00 |
| Something Borrowed | Gold Circle Film/26 Films | n/a* |
| Thunderbirds | Working Title/Universal | 41.00 |
| Tooth | Redbus Pictures/Archangel Prods/ | 7.50 |
| Trauma | Little Bird/Ministry of Fear/BBC Films/Isle of Man Film Fund/First Choice | 8.00 |
| Troy | Warner Brothers | 62.00 |
| The Upside of Anger | Media 8/VIP 2+3/Zephyr Films | n/a* |
| Vanity Fair | Granada Films/Tempesta Films/Focus Features | 14.20 |
| A Way Through the Woods | Celador/DNA Films/Fox Searchlight/UK Film Council | 5.00 |
| White on White | Cinerenta/Lakeshore Entertainment | 12.50 |
| Wimbledon | Working Title/Universal/Inside Track | 25.00 |

| **TOTAL NUMBER OF FILMS** | **29** | | |
|---|---|---|---|
| **TOTAL COST OF KNOWN BUDGETS** | **£554.64 (27 films)** | **ApproximateTotal Cost** | **£574.64m*** |
| **AVERAGE COST** | **£20.54m (27 films)** | **Average Cost** | **£19.81m** |

* Where budgets are not available an approximate total has been estimated based on an average total of £10m per film

Note: The following films shot for two weeks or less in the UK- under 25% of the shoot. **New France** (Canada)**The Lazurus Child** (Italy/Germany/Canada)**Bobby Jones: Stroke of Genius** (US)

**Source: Screen Finance/Screen International/British Council/UK Film Council/bfis**

### UK Film Production 2003 - Category E

American Films with some British financial involvement.

| Title | Production Companies | Production Cost (£m) |
|---|---|---|
| Alexander | Intermedia/Pacifica Film | 100.00 |
| The Hillside Strangler | Tartan Films/Constant Howling Production | 1.20 |

| | |
|---|---|
| **NUMBER OF FILMS** | 2 |
| **TOTAL COST** | £101.20m |
| **AVERAGE COST** | £50.60m |

**Source: Screen Finance/Screen International/British Council/UK Film Council/bfi**

### Types of Release for UK films 1984-2002

Proportion of films with a UK involvement which achieved;

a) Wide release. Opening or playing on 30 or more screens around the country within a year of production

b) Limited release, mainly in art house cinemas or a short West End run within a year of release.

c) Unreleased a year after production

| Year | wide% | limited% | unreleased% |
|---|---|---|---|
| 1984 | 50.00 | 44.00 | 6.00 |
| 1985 | 52.80 | 35.90 | 11.30 |
| 1986 | 55.80 | 41.90 | 2.30 |
| 1987 | 36.00 | 60.00 | 4.00 |
| 1988 | 29.50 | 61.20 | 9.30 |
| 1989 | 33.30 | 38.90 | 27.80 |
| 1990 | 29.40 | 47.10 | 23.50 |
| 1991 | 32.20 | 37.30 | 30.50 |
| 1992 | 38.30 | 29.80 | 31.90 |
| 1993 | 25.40 | 22.40 | 52.20 |
| 1994 | 31.00 | 22.60 | 46.40 |
| 1995 | 23.10 | 34.60 | 42.30 |
| 1996 | 19.00 | 14.00 | 67.00 |
| 1997 | 15.50 | 19.00 | 65.50 |
| 1998 | 22.70 | 21.60 | 55.70 |
| 1999 | 30.00 | 10.00 | 60.00 |
| 2000 | 22.50 | 12.20 | 65.30 |
| 2001 | 24.50 | 10.60 | 64.50 |
| 2002 | 18.10 | 10.48 | 69.52 |

**Source: Screen Finance/Nielsen EDI/bfi**

19/105 – wide release = 18.09%

11/105 – limited release = 10.47%

73/105 – Unreleased after a year = 67.62%

64/105 – Unreleased = 60.95%

9 /105 – Released in 2004 = 8.57%

39/105 – Released at 1 June 2004 = 37.14%

13/105 – over 100 screns = 12.38%

7/105 – over 300 screens = 6.66%

Top of the class is *Harry Potter and the Prisoner of Azkaban* with an enormous budget of £100m. However, the success of the Harry Potter brand is undeniable and will no doubt continue to enhance the reputation of the UK film industry for a few years to come.

At the time of writing, audiences have already had a chance to see *Troy* and *Thunderbirds* (the former of which has performed better than the latter at the UK box office). However on the horizon lurk some potential big British hits; namely *Bridget Jones: The Edge of Reason* (which reunites the principle players of Renée Zellweger, Hugh Grant and Colin Frith), Gurinder Chadha's *Bride and Prejudice*, and Aardman's *Curse of Wererabbit* to name just three.

Oliver Stone's big budget film, *Alexander* which was filmed in Britain, has been placed in the anomalous table which represents mainly American titles that have some British financial involvement (Table 6). Its inclusion in our list helps to boost the production totals of UK films to the tune of £100m.

It cannot be denied that inward investment into the British film industry has been phenomenal in 2003. However, the debate as to just how British, some of the so-called British films are will probably never be satisfactorily resolved. Nevertheless to build on the record-breaking success the infrastructure needs to be in place to improve the distribution of British films, not only in the UK but also abroad. This represents the next real challenge for the UK film industry.

The worrying statistic shows that of the 105 UK films made in 2002 an uncomfortable 69.52 per cent remained unreleased a year after production (Table 7). This figure has shown a steady rise since 1997. The paradox of the 1980s is that fewer films were made but relatively few unreleased. Only seven out 105 UK films were released

# What Happened to 2002 UK Films?

Distribution of 2002 UK productions and foreign films made in the UK up to 1 June 2004. Where appropriate the number of screens that the film opened on is shown beside the title

### Released theatrically in 2002/2003

| | |
|---|---|
| The Actors | 270 |
| AKA | 3 |
| American Cousins | 6 |
| Blackball | 304 |
| Bright Young Things | 192 |
| Calendar Girls | 1* |
| Cold Mountain | 135 |
| Devil's Gate | 2 |
| Die Another Day | 430 |
| Hoover Street Revival | 9 |
| I'll Be There | 78 |
| Intermission | 28 |
| In This World | 5 |
| Johnny English | 445 |
| Live Forever | 12 |
| Love Actually | 447 |
| The Mother | 21 |
| Ned Kelly | 213 |
| Nicholas Nickleby | 204 |
| Octane | 24 |
| Pure | 8 |
| S Club Seeing Double | 395 |
| Shanghai Knights | 371 |
| Song for a Raggy Boy | 37 |
| The Swimming Pool | 37 |
| To Kill a King | 53 |
| Tomb Raider 2 | 449 |
| Touching the Void | 29 |
| What a Girl Wants (Amercian Girls) | 250 |
| Wilbur Wants to Kill Himself | 31 |
| Young Adam | 133 |

### Released theatrically at 1 June 2004

| | |
|---|---|
| The Calcium Kid | |
| The Dreamers | 34 |
| Emile | |
| The Football Factory | |
| Girl with a Pearl Earring | |
| I'll Sleep When I'm Dead | |
| Kiss of Life (Helen of Peckham) | |
| Living in Hope | |
| Leo | 15 |
| Man Dancin' | 8 |
| The Night We Called It a Day | |
| One Last Chance (The Bum's Rush) | 18 |
| Suzie Gold | 24 |
| Sylvia | 67 |
| Wondrous Oblivion | |

### Awaiting release at 1 June 2004

Absolon
Ashes & Sand
Baltic Storm
Bitter Sweet
Bl,.m
The Blue Butterfly
The Bone Hunter
Chaos and Cadavers
Cheeky
Cloud Cuckoo Land
The Day I Will Never Forget
Day of the Sirens
Dot the I
This Little Life (Entering Blue Zone)
Fallen Angels
Fakers
Finding Fortune
Lighthouse Hill (A Flight of Fancy)
Gladiatress
The Great Goose Caper
I Am David
If Only
The I Inside
Jericho Mansions
The Last Horror Movie – 25 June
LD50
Loving Glances
Luger
Luminal

The Magic Roundabout
Mrs Ritchie
Neil's Party
JM Barrie's Neverland (Neverland)
Nine Lives
Masked & Anonymous
The Motorcycle Diaries
One for the Road          2 July 2004
One Love
Piazza of the Five Moons
The Poet
The Prodigal
The Republic of Love
Rivers and Tides ? (2003 release?)
Sandmother
16 Years of Alcohol
Skaggerak
Solid Air
Stella Street          21 March 2004 TV
Team One
Three Blind Mice
The Tulse Luper Suitcase:
The Early Years
Virgin of Liverpool
Wanted (Crime Spree)
The Water Giant

20/105 – wide release =
12/105 – limited release =
62/105 – Unreleased = 60.95%
10 /105 – Released in 2004 = 8.57%
40/105 – Released at 1 June 2004 =
14/105 – over 100 screens =
7/105 – over 300 screens = 6.66%

Titles in paranthesis indicate former title of film

**Source: bfi/Nielsen EDI/Screen Finance**

on 300 screens or more. The Handbook still defines a wide release as being 30 screens or more. Only 19 UK films manage a wide range. Unfortunately, this is not a great news story for the British film industry but the natural consequence of producing films is that they should be seen.

The whole list of UK films is provided in Table 8. It should be emphasised that there is absolutely no value judgement based on those films that are still awaiting release. Just because a film isn't released doesn't mean to say that it is unworthy.

It will be interesting to observe over the next couple of years whether the UK Film Council's efforts in relation to expanding the opportunities for audiences to see a broader range of films has the desired knock-on effect on prompting an increase in  the distribution of greater numbers of UK titles. It would be great to report next year about a record-breaking year for UK films at the box office, but until then Hollywood will dominate the UK Distribution and Exhibition sector.

*Bride and Prejudice – Jane Austen, Bollywood style*

**9**   **Number of UK Feature Films Produced 1912-2003**

| Year | Number | Year | Number |
|------|--------|------|--------|
| 1912 | 2 | 1960 | 122 |
| 1913 | 18 | 1961 | 117 |
| 1914 | 15 | 1962 | 114 |
| 1915 | 73 | 1963 | 113 |
| 1916 | 107 | 1964 | 95 |
| 1917 | 66 | 1965 | 93 |
| 1918 | 76 | 1966 | 82 |
| 1919 | 122 | 1967 | 83 |
|  |  | 1968 | 88 |
| 1920 | 155 | 1969 | 92 |
| 1921 | 137 |  |  |
| 1922 | 110 | 1970 | 97 |
| 1923 | 68 | 1971 | 96 |
| 1924 | 49 | 1972 | 104 |
| 1925 | 33 | 1973 | 99 |
| 1926 | 33 | 1974 | 88 |
| 1927 | 48 | 1975 | 81 |
| 1928 | 80 | 1976 | 80 |
| 1929 | 81 | 1977 | 50 |
|  |  | 1978 | 54 |
| 1930 | 75 | 1979 | 61 |
| 1931 | 93 |  |  |
| 1932 | 110 | 1980 | 31 |
| 1933 | 115 | 1981 | 24 |
| 1934 | 145 | 1982 | 40 |
| 1935 | 165 | 1983 | 51 |
| 1936 | 192 | 1984 | 53 |
| 1937 | 176 | 1985 | 54 |
| 1938 | 134 | 1986 | 41 |
| 1939 | 84 | 1987 | 55 |
|  |  | 1988 | 48 |
| 1940 | 50 | 1989 | 30 |
| 1941 | 46 |  |  |
| 1942 | 39 | 1990 | 60 |
| 1943 | 47 | 1991 | 59 |
| 1944 | 35 | 1992 | 47 |
| 1945 | 39 | 1993 | 67 |
| 1946 | 41 | 1994 | 84 |
| 1947 | 58 | 1995 | 78 |
| 1948 | 74 | 1996 | 128 |
| 1949 | 101 | 1997 | 116 |
|  |  | 1998 | 88 |
| 1950 | 125 | 1999 | 100 |
| 1951 | 114 | 2000 | 98 |
| 1952 | 117 | 2001 | 96 |
| 1953 | 138 | 2002 | 105 |
| 1954 | 150 | 2003 | 109 |
| 1955 | 110 |  |  |
| 1956 | 108 | **Source: Screen** |  |
| 1957 | 138 | **Digest/Screen** |  |
| 1958 | 121 | **Finance/bfi** |  |
| 1959 | 122 |  |  |

# National Lottery

It is an interesting notion that everyone who buys a Lottery ticket can claim to be stakeholders in Lottery funded films. To follow this analogy the prize for your Lottery ticket should be money invested into the type of film that you would want to watch. In the end you buy your Lottery ticket and then you buy your cinema ticket and keep your fingers crossed that you will have bought winning tickets for both.

Funding of UK films via Lottery money is dispersed via the UK Film Council and via Scottish Screen, Sgrin, Wales, and the Northern Ireland Film and Television Commission.

Some commentators remain sceptical as to whether public funds should be allocated into film production. The memory of a potentially damaging era for UK films is still fresh in their minds. During this time Lottery grants were dished out like confetti from the Arts Council of England, and millions of pounds of Lottery money was wasted on underachieving, poorly conceived UK films (not including Billy Elliot).

The restructuring of Lottery grant allocation in 2000 via the UK Film Council was much needed and a far more coherent approach was adopted. On top of three key production funds that were established – the Premiere Fund (for bigger budget films), the New Cinema Fund (for less mainstream projects) and the Development Fund (for the development of innovative and commercially viable screenplays) – the UK Film Council has added First Light, aimed at encouraging children and young people to experience filmmaking using digital technology.

Although not directly concerned with UK film production, the UK Film Council's international

**10**    ## Top 25 All-time Lottery Funded List by UK Box Office

| | Title | Award (£m) | Budget (£m) | Box Office (£) |
|---|---|---|---|---|
| 1 | Billy Elliot | 0.85 | 2.83 | 18,386,715 |
| 2 | Gosford Park | 2.00 | 13.50 | 12,259,248 |
| 3 | Bend it like Beckham | 0.95 | 2.70 | 11,551,538 |
| 4 | 28 Days Later | 3.23 | 10.40 | 6,296,734 |
| 5 | Shooting Fish | 0.98 | 2.90 | 4,023,825 |
| 6 | The 51st State | 2.00 | 16.34 | 3,789,865 |
| 7 | This Year's Love | 0.75 | 2.75 | 3,600,636 |
| 8 | Mike Bassett: England Manager | 1.20 | 3.50 | 3,568,492 |
| 9 | The Importance of Being Earnest | 1.32 | 10.50 | 3,519,574 |
| 10 | The Parole Officer | 2.00 | 5.99 | 3,283,870 |
| 11 | An Ideal Husband | 1.00 | 6.50 | 2,893,170 |
| 12 | Plunkett and Macleane | 0.95 | 9.30 | 2,779,315 |
| 13 | Touching the Void | 0.34 | 2.00 | 2,441,185 |
| 14 | The Hole | 1.50 | 4.16 | 2,302,381 |
| 15 | Intermission | 0.57 | 2.50 | 2,142,126 |
| 16 | The Magdalene Sisters | 0.62 | 1.60 | 2,138,934 |
| 17 | Thunderpants | 2.05 | 5.00 | 1,983,879 |
| 18 | Anita and Me | 0.68 | 2.98 | 1,888,362 |
| 19 | Long Time Dead | 1.00 | 3.27 | 1,774,552 |
| 20 | Land Girls | 1.50 | 5.50 | 1,573,783 |
| 21 | A Christmas Carol - the Movie | 1.18 | 6.85 | 1,462,329 |
| 22 | Topsy Turvy | 2.00 | 13.50 | 1,177,542 |
| 23 | Bright Young Things | 3.00 | 7.60 | 1,085,470 |
| 24 | Hilary and Jackie | 0.95 | 4.90 | 1,040,788 |
| 25 | 24 Hour Party People | 2.00 | 4.20 | 1,036,879 |

**Source: Nielsen EDI/Film Council/Screen Finance/bfi**

## 11    Funding of Film Productions by National Lottery Awards 2003/04

This table represents the principle film production awards granted by the UK Film Council. It does not include awards granted for short films, specialised p&a, distribution, equipment, training or film publications

## Premiere Fund

| Project Title | Organisation Name | Grant Amount |
|---|---|---|
| Chemins de Traverse | Holy Cow Films | 0.00 |
| Code 46 - Disability Access Materials | Code 46 Films Ltd | 10,799.00 |
| Creep | Dan Films Ltd. | 1,260,000.00 |
| Creep - Digital Grade | Creep Films Ltd | 48,000.00 |
| Five Children and It | Sandfairy Productions Ltd | 2,100,000.00 |
| Ladies in Lavender | Scala Productions Ltd | 1,101,775.00 |
| Ladies in Lavender - Additional Funding music overcosts | Ladies in Lavender Ltd | 10,000.00 |
| Ladies In Lavender - Award increase | Scala Productions Ltd | 868,075.00 |
| Little Trip To Heaven | Zik Zak Filmworks | 250,000.00 |
| Love and Hate (aka Northern Soul) | Ruby Films Ltd | 802,903.00 |
| Only Human (Seres Queridos) | Greenpoint Films Ltd | 285,000.00 |
| Only Human (shortfall) | Greenpoint Films Limited | 13,723.72 |
| Pobby & Dingan | Academy Productions Ltd | 900,000.00 |
| Sex Lives of the Potato Men - music costs | Devotion Films | 26,922.50 |
| Sex Lives of The Potato Men (re shoot/extra scenes) | Devotion Films | 120,294.00 |
| Sylvia - additional costs | Ariel Films Ltd | 37,643.00 |
| The Libertine | Odyssey Entertainment Ltd | 0.00 |
| The Merchant of Venice | Shylock Trading Ltd | 604,720.00 |
| The Rising | Kaleidoscope UK Ltd | 0.00 |
| Young Adam - Disability - Access Materials | Recorded Picture Company Ltd | 1,955.00 |
| **Total** | | **8,441,810.22** |

## New Cinema Fund

| Project Title | Organisation Name | Grant Amount |
|---|---|---|
| A Changed Man - additional costs | Stink Ltd | 3,850.00 |
| A Way of Life | AWOL Films Ltd | 422,000.00 |
| A.K.A. - additional funds | Third Rock Ltd | 104,045.00 |
| Blind Flight - Disability Access Material | Parallax (Blind Flight) Limited | 10,480.00 |
| Blind Flight - re-edit costs | Parallax (Blind Flight) Limited | 9,743.00 |
| Diameter of the Bomb | Diameter Productions Limited | 138,447.00 |
| Diameter of the Bomb - Additional Insurance | Diameter Productions Limited | 4,550.00 |
| Diameter of the Bomb - additional request | Diameter Productions Limited | 38,006.00 |
| Game Over: Kasparov and the Machine - additional funds | Gambit Films Ltd | 16,333.00 |
| In My Father's Den | Little Bird (U.K.) | 393,095.00 |
| Kiss of Life - additional funds | Wild Horses Film Company | 7,112.87 |
| Lila Says | Passion Pictures | 400,000.00 |
| Managing Company for Short Film Programme | Lifesize Pictures Limited | 114,477.00 |
| One For the Road - additional funds | One For the Road Films Ltd | 11,100.00 |
| Pilot - The Story of _____ | Magnet Films Ltd. | 10,000.00 |
| School (aka L'Ecole) | Ex Nihilo | 397,330.00 |
| Taste of Rain - Pilot (aka Dust) | Potboiler Productions Ltd | 10,000.00 |
| The Boys (aka Bullet Boy) | Shine Entertainment | 450,000.00 |
| The Piano Tuner of Earthquakes | Koninck Studios Ltd | 275,862.00 |
| The Truth About Love | Lex Filmed Entertainment | 544,104.00 |
| This is not a Love Song - Disability Provision | This Is Not a Company Ltd | 9,995.00 |
| This is not a Love Song - online distribution costs | This Is Not a Company Ltd | 44,541.43 |
| Touching the Void - hearing impaired provision | Touching the Void Ltd | 7,348.00 |
| Yes | Adventure Pictures | 355,000.00 |
| Yes - enhancement funding | Adventure Pictures (Yes) Limited | 94,500.00 |
| **Total** | | **3,871,919.30** |

## Development Fund

| Project Title | Organisation Name | Grant Amount |
| --- | --- | --- |
| A Green and Quiet River | The Bureau Film Company | 31,532.00 |
| A Way of Life | AWOL Films Ltd | 10,000.00 |
| A Woman in Winter | Vestry Films Ltd | 31,500.00 |
| Balance of Power | Scarlet Pictures Ltd | 4,500.00 |
| Balance of Power | Scarlet Pictures Ltd | 49,700.00 |
| Balance of Power | Scarlet Pictures Ltd | 3,500.00 |
| Being Me | Suzie Smith | 9,282.00 |
| Belly Dance | Samuelson Productions Ltd. | 8,500.00 |
| Black Ice | Cougar Films | 9,660.00 |
| Bob's Ark | George Webster | 1,000.00 |
| Champagne Breakfast (previously 'The Richmond Project') | Holy Cow Films | 3,000.00 |
| Chance | Celtic Films Entertainment Ltd / AV Pictures Ltd | 36,750.00 |
| Chasing Heaven | Ice Productions | 32,500.00 |
| Clever (aka Sweet Milk) | Crab Apple Films Ltd | 7,878.00 |
| Clever (aka Sweet Milk) - additional | Crab Apple Films Ltd | 375.00 |
| Crossed Wires | Tigerlily Films Limited | 33,200.00 |
| Dan Leno and the Limehouse Golem | Number 9 Films | 142,425.00 |
| Deja Vu | Liverpool Film Consortium | 8,500.00 |
| Du Cane's Boys (aka Du Quesne's Boys) | Scala Productions Ltd | 15,800.00 |
| Du Cane's Boys (Du Quesne's Boys) | Scala Productions Ltd | 12,706.00 |
| Friends Forever | Ice Productions / Greenroom Digital | 15,000.00 |
| Happy Birthday Lubna | Rule 8 Productions Ltd. | 95,300.00 |
| Hendrix (aka Cross Town Traffic) | Number 9 Films | 2,500.00 |
| Hoyland Common vs. Italy | Sixteen Films | 19,275.00 |
| Jean Lee | Cougar Films | 50,416.00 |
| Kidulthood | Stealth Films Ltd | 0.00 |
| Kidulthood | Stealth Films Ltd | 10,000.00 |
| Little Ashes | APT Films | 12,000.00 |
| Little Sisters | Oscar Films Ltd | 3,500.00 |
| Mermaids | The Hub Film Company | 23,500.00 |
| My Soul To Keep | Prospect Entertainment | 250.00 |
| Nightfall | Juggernaut Pictures Ltd | 26,500.00 |
| Noir | Trademark Films | 27,750.00 |
| Northern Soul (aka My Soul to Keep) | Prospect Entertainment | 12,500.00 |
| One Wish (working title) | Coded Pictures | 5,000.00 |
| Outpost | Northmen Productions | 52,000.00 |
| Passengers (aka Mexico) | Picture Farm Ltd | 8,000.00 |
| Passengers (aka Mexico) | Picture Farm Ltd | 8,575.00 |
| Passengers (aka Mexico) | Picture Farm Ltd | 17,340.00 |
| Passengers (aka Mexico) | Picture Farm Ltd | 4,566.00 |
| Patrick Robertson | Litmus Productions | 52,000.00 |
| Patrick Robertson | Litmus Productions | 395.00 |
| Peacock (The Peacock Manifesto) | Samuelson Productions Ltd. | 2,500.00 |
| Perfect Host (aka Rent - A - Wife) | The Agency | 10,000.00 |
| Perrier's Bounty | Number 9 Films | 45,150.00 |
| Property Ladder | Seymour Films Ltd | 40,400.00 |
| Raising the Necessary | Liverpool Film Consortium | 8,500.00 |
| Reputation | Cougar Films | 82,897.16 |
| Run | Hanthum Films | 0.00 |
| Skin | Elysian Films | 31,000.00 |
| Slow Motion Explosion | Hot Property Films Ltd | 18,500.00 |
| Solid | Fiesta Productions Ltd. | 46,350.00 |
| Ssshhh | Magnet Films Ltd. | 13,000.00 |
| Steer Wood | Ice Productions / Greenroom Digital | 11,250.00 |
| Stones In His Pockets | Stones in his Pockets Ltd | 5,000.00 |
| Storage | Midfield Films Ltd | 19,750.00 |
| Straightheads | Straightheads Limited | 11,875.00 |
| Straightheads | Suspect Device | 3,000.00 |
| Stupid Cupid | Scorpio Films | 14,000.00 |
| Tashkent Girls | Big Talk Productions Ltd | 12,500.00 |
| The Bell | The Mob Film Company Ltd. | 14,500.00 |
| The Box of Delights | 50 Canon Entertainment UK | 10,000.00 |

| Project Title | Organisation Name | Grant Amount |
|---|---|---|
| The Dark | Impact Pictures | 15,675.00 |
| The Darkest Hour | Crab Apple Films Ltd | 7,878.00 |
| The Darkest Hour - additional | Crab Apple Films Ltd | 375.00 |
| The Describer (aka Meera Syal Untitled) | Starfield Productions | 5,000.00 |
| The Devil's Assassin | Samuelson Productions Ltd. | 1,333.00 |
| The Edge Chronicles | Jigsaw Films Ltd | 36,150.00 |
| The Festival | Pirate Productions | 28,300.00 |
| The Handsomest Sons in the World | Cougar Films | 22,080.00 |
| The Legendeer | Jigsaw Films Ltd | 98,050.00 |
| The Legendeer | Sarah Radclyffe Productions Ltd | 0.00 |
| The Mutes | Lotus Films | 27,000.00 |
| The Pear Tree | Scorpio Films | 59,750.00 |
| The Prince of Dalston | Carlton Television Limited | 22,000.00 |
| The Prince of Dalston | Carlton Television Limited | 17,000.00 |
| The Rose of Tralee | Feelgood Fiction | 6,000.00 |
| The Scholar | Cofe Ltd | 35,325.00 |
| The Stand-In | 50 Canon Entertainment UK | 81,875.00 |
| The Third Day | Rubicon Pictures | 9,350.00 |
| The Third Day | Rubicon Pictures | 750.00 |
| The Truth About Love | The Truth About Love Ltd | 20,000.00 |
| This is Your Life | Icon Entertainment International | 23,250.00 |
| Three Way Split | Martin Pope Productions | 54,000.00 |
| Thylacine | Tiger Aspect Pictures Ltd | 43,715.00 |
| Underground | Impact Pictures | 29,250.00 |
| Water Warriors | Silver Fox Films | 0.00 |
| You Are Here (aka Monsieur Hire Remake) | Taxi Productions Ltd. | 73,000.00 |
| Young Santa | Jigsaw Films Ltd | 23,850.00 |
| **Total** | | **2,085,803.16** |

## Franchises

| Project Title | Organisation Name | Grant Amount |
|---|---|---|
| A Way Through The Woods | DNA Films Limited | 1,455,489.00 |
| A Way Through the Woods | DNA Films Limited | 19,146.00 |
| Clean | The Film Consortium | 370,300.00 |
| Enduring Love | Pathé Pictures Ltd | 1,799,000.00 |
| Guy X - resubmission | The Film Consortium | 920,000.00 |
| Millions | Pathé Pictures Ltd | 2,000,000.00 |
| My Summer of Love (Additional Application - Overcost) | The Film Consortium | 74,755.00 |
| My Summer of Love - Production | The Film Consortium | 412,000.00 |
| Pride and Prejudice: The Bollywood Musical | Pathé Pictures Ltd | 2,000,000.00 |
| River Queen | The Film Consortium | 1,348,009.00 |
| River Queen | The Film Consortium | 1,006,379.00 |
| The Magic Roundabout - Additional Production | Pathé Pictures Ltd | 500,000.00 |
| A Woman of No Importance | The Film Consortium | 15,000.00 |
| Concrete Slippers | The Film Consortium | 13,200.00 |
| Development Overhead Contribution | DNA Films Limited | 200,000.00 |
| Getting and Spending | Pathé Pictures Ltd | 29,147.54 |
| Guy X - Development Funding | The Film Consortium | 10,000.00 |
| The Battle of Hastings | The Film Consortium | 6,000.00 |
| The Best Man - Additional award | The Film Consortium | 10,000.00 |
| Bugs! | The Film Consortium | 18,750.00 |
| Bugs! | The Film Consortium | 15,000.00 |
| **Total** | | **12,222,175.54** |

**Source: UK Film Council**

For the most recent funding decisions by other public funds check the following websites:
Northern Ireland Film Commission: www.nifc.co.uk
Scottish Screen: www.scottishscreen.com/
Sgrin: www.sgrin.co.uk
UK Film Council www.ukfilmcouncil.org.uk

## MEDIA Plus Funding: UK Beneficiaries - 2003

### Development

#### Single Project Company Awards

| | Region | Award (Euros) |
|---|---|---|
| John Cary Studios | England | 50,000 |
| Living Doll | Wales | 50,000 |
| Lupus Entertainment | England | 50,000 |
| Arcimboldo Productions | England | 20,000 |
| Crinkle Cut Motion Pictures | England | 15,000 |
| Element Productions | Wales | 30,000 |
| Moonbeam Films | England | 10,000 |
| Poseidon Film Distributors | England | 20,000 |
| 50 Cannon Entertainment | England | 50,000 |
| Company Films | England | 50,000 |
| Cowboy Films | England | 40,000 |
| De Facto Films | N. Ireland | 50,000 |
| Fiesta Productions | England | 40,000 |
| Flagmile | England | 30,000 |
| Gorilla Entertainment | England | 50,000 |
| Hotbed Media | England | 30,000 |
| La Belle Allee Productions | Scotland | 20,000 |
| Loud Mouse Productions | England | 40,000 |
| Scarlet Pictures | England | 50,000 |
| Tiger Aspect Pictures | England | 50,000 |
| Utah Films | England | 30,000 |
| Wild Films | Wales | 20,000 |

#### Slate Company Awards

| | | |
|---|---|---|
| Optical Image | England | 30,000 |
| Pesky | England | 10,000 |
| Two Sides TV | England | 90,000 |
| Blackwatch Productions | Scotland | 90,000 |
| Brook Lapping Productions | England | 90,000 |
| Cheeky Productions | England | 90,000 |
| Cyclops Vision | England | 40,000 |
| Dan Films | England | 125,000 |
| Deem | Wales | 90,000 |
| Fiction Factory | Wales | 90,000 |
| Fragile Films | England | 125,000 |
| Gruber Films | England | 100,000 |
| QI | England | 90,000 |
| Random Harvest Pictures | England | 125,000 |
| Scala Productions | England | 125,000 |
| Sixteen Films | England | 125,000 |
| Slate Films | England | 100,000 |
| Steve Walsh Productions | England | 125,000 |
| The Bureau Film Company | England | 100,000 |
| Film and Music Entertainment | England | 110,000 |
| Recorded Picture Company | England | 125,000 |
| **Total** | | **2,790,000** |

### Distribution Selective Scheme

| company | film title | amount |
|---|---|---|
| Optimum Releasing | Nirgendwo in Afrika | 25,000 |
| Pathe Distribution | It's All About Love | 85,000 |
| Artificial Eye | Le temps du loup | 35,000 |
| Artificial Eye | Noi Albinoi | 25,000 |
| UGC Films | Good Bye, Lenin! | 60,000 |
| UGC Films | Swimming Pool | 100,000 |
| ICA Projects | Kitchen Stories | 19,000 |
| Parasol Peccadillo Releasing | Son frere | 20,000 |
| Axiom Films | Any Way the Wind Blows | 20,000 |
| Soda Pictures | La Finestra di Fronte | 17,000 |
| Winchester Film Distribution | Los Lunes al Sol | 45,000 |
| UGC Films | Mieux que la vie (aka Jeux d'enfants) | 78,000 |
| Soda Pictures | Reconstruction | 20,000 |
| Soda Pictures | Rezervni Deli | 9,000 |
| UGC Films | Tais-toi! (aka Les Tourtereaux) | 74,000 |
| **Total** | | **632,000** |

### Distribution Automatic Scheme

| company | amount |
|---|---|
| Tartan Films | 35,287 |
| Optimum Releasing | 71,575 |
| Pathe Distribution | 225,924 |
| Artificial Eye | 94,153 |
| UGC Films | 37,757 |
| Cinefrance | 5,572 |
| **Total** | **470,268** |

### Festivals

| festival | amount |
|---|---|
| Cinemagic World Screen Festival for Young People | 7,000 |
| Sheffield International Documentary Festival | 10,000 |
| Brief Encounters International Short Film Festival | 10,000 |
| Leeds International Film Festival | 50,000 |
| Onedotzero | 10,000 |
| **Total** | **87,000** |

### Training

| training provider | amount |
|---|---|
| Moonstone International: Screen Labs | 300,000 |
| The Script Factory: Scene Insiders | 175,000 |
| Draft Zero: The European Development Network | 176,302 |
| **Total** | **651,302** |

#### i2i Growth & Audiovisual

| company | amount |
|---|---|
| Haystack Productions | 50,000 |
| Scala Productions | 50,000 |
| **Total** | **100,000** |

## TV Broadcasting

| company | programme title | UK nation | amount |
|---|---|---|---|
| TV4C | Space Lunies | England | 340,000 |
| Kirk Productions | Kirk | Wales | 300,000 |
| Boomerang Television | The Chosen Seven | Wales | 240,000 |
| Teledu Opus Television | The Normans | Wales | 110,000 |
| Wild Dream Films | The Map Makers | England | 182,000 |
| Mosaic Films | Athens through the Hoops | England | 68,000 |
| The Canning Factory | Ebb & Flo | England | 168,000 |
| Mentorn | Ancient Cataclysms | England | 252,000 |
| Brook Lapping | The Iraq War - One Year On | England | 220,000 |
| Faction Films | Aphrodite's Drop | England | 56,000 |
| Wark Clements | Storm in the East | Scotland | 120,000 |
| Charlotte Street Films | Why We Fight | England | 150,000 |
| **Total** | | | **2,206,000** |

The UK MEDIA Desk calculates results based on the relevant deadline date. The results for a particular year include monies allocated to all deadlines falling within that year.

department has been set up to encourage inward investment from producers outside the UK and to export production strategies for promoting British talent and films abroad.

Critics of Lottery funding for film argue that the returns at the UK box office do not justify the amount of grants donated. The UK Film Council scored successive hits with *Gosford Park*, *Bend it Like Beckham* and *28 Days Later* (Table 10). Not only did these films perform well at the UK box office, they also gained global box office appeal.

Caught between a rock and a hard place the UK Film Council is committed to investing its funds in less mainstream films as well as hit films, although our table of the all-time 25 Lottery funded films shows no change to the top 12 films. The new entries *Touching the Void*, *Intermission*, and *The Magdalene Sisters*, represent an interesting cross section of UK film styles. Ironically, the performance of *Bright Young Things*, which appeared to have more mainstream prospects, was less impressive.

However, there is no magic formula to guarantee box office success. The UK Film Council is faced with a conundrum in promoting the UK film industry, which it does with a certain amount of gusto, it is mindful that the UK's recent big box office hits *Johnny English*, *Calendar Girls*, and Harry Potter were all made without public funding via the Lottery. As well as wishing to nurture emerging talent by investing in more risky films, the UK Film Council is also mindful of the need to support films which will offer some sort of box office return. It will be interesting to see how potential hits like *Vera Drake*, *The Merchant of Venice* and *In My Father's Den* will perform.

One senses that the UK Film Council would like another big box office hit under its belt to keep the critics, who slated *Sex Lives of the Potato Men*, at bay.

It should also be noted that The UK Film Council and the other Lottery bodies provide public funding for a range of initiatives supporting film development, training, education, distribution and exhibition. Indeed, it is likely that having established a solid structure for film production, the UK Film Council will increasingly be turning its attention to distribution and exhibition – arguably the harder nut to crack.

### European Funding

The European Commission runs a MEDIA Programme to encourage the audiovisual industry within the European Union. This is called MEDIA Plus and there are UK bases at the UK Film Council, Scottish Screen, Sgrîn and the Northern Ireland Film and Television Commission.

MEDIA Plus provides funding to two main areas. As with the National Lottery, production funding is now based largely around development – there is also a growing concentration on slate funding, hoping to build up sustainable companies that can nurture a range of projects. There are also funds available for distribution and exhibition. The distribution awards are to ensure that films from other European countries can reach audiences when Hollywood blockbusters dominate the market-place. British films receive the same assistance in other territories.

A wider audience for works that otherwise would not be seen is also encouraged by the funding support for a range of films which cover such unsung areas as documentary, short films and children's films.

## ⑬ Cinema Admissions 1933–2003 (millions)

| Year | Admissions | Year | Admissions |
|---|---|---|---|
| 1933 | 903.00 | 1970 | 193.00 |
| 1934 | 950.00 | 1971 | 176.00 |
| 1935 | 912.33 | 1972 | 156.60 |
| 1936 | 917.00 | 1973 | 134.20 |
| 1937 | 946.00 | 1974 | 138.50 |
| 1938 | 987.00 | 1975 | 116.30 |
| 1939 | 990.00 | 1976 | 103.90 |
| | | 1977 | 103.50 |
| 1940 | 1,027.00 | 1978 | 126.10 |
| 1941 | 1,309.00 | 1979 | 111.90 |
| 1942 | 1,494.00 | | |
| 1943 | 1,541.00 | 1980 | 101.00 |
| 1944 | 1,575.00 | 1981 | 86.00 |
| 1945 | 1,585.00 | 1982 | 64.00 |
| 1946 | 1,635.00 | 1983 | 65.70 |
| 1947 | 1,462.00 | 1984 | 54.00 |
| 1948 | 1,514.00 | 1985 | 72.00 |
| 1949 | 1,430.00 | 1986 | 75.50 |
| | | 1987 | 78.50 |
| 1950 | 1,395.80 | 1988 | 84.00 |
| 1951 | 1,365.00 | 1989 | 94.50 |
| 1952 | 1,312.10 | | |
| 1953 | 1,284.50 | 1990 | 97.37 |
| 1954 | 1,275.80 | 1991 | 100.29 |
| 1955 | 1,181.80 | 1992 | 103.64 |
| 1956 | 1,100.80 | 1993 | 114.36 |
| 1957 | 915.20 | 1994 | 123.53 |
| 1958 | 754.70 | 1995 | 114.56 |
| 1959 | 581.00 | 1996 | 123.80 |
| | | 1997 | 139.30 |
| 1960 | 500.80 | 1998 | 135.50 |
| 1961 | 449.10 | 1999 | 139.75 |
| 1962 | 395.00 | 2000 | 142.50 |
| 1963 | 357.20 | 2001 | 155.91 |
| 1964 | 342.80 | 2002 | 176.00 |
| 1965 | 326.60 | 2003 | 167.30 |
| 1966 | 288.80 | | |
| 1967 | 264.80 | | |
| 1968 | 237.30 | | |
| 1969 | 214.90 | | |

Source: Screen Digest/
CAA/Nielsen
EDI/Screen Finance

## ⑭ UK Box Office 2000–2003

| | 2000 | 2001 | 2002 | 2003 |
|---|---|---|---|---|
| Admissions (millions) | 142.5 | 155.91 | 176 | 167.3 |
| Total cinema sites | 686 | 692 | 668 | 678 |
| Total cinema screens | 2,954 | 3,164 | 3,258 | 3,318 |
| Total multiplex sites | 209 | 224 | 222 | 234 |
| Total multiplex screens | 2.003 | 2,170 | 2,215 | 2,362 |
| Box office gross (millions) | £577 | £692 | £755 | £742 |
| Average ticket price | £4.00 | £4.14 | £4.29 | £4.43 |

Source: CAA, Dodona Research, Nielsen EDI

## Cinema

Having embraced the good news about the rise in UK film production it came as a bit of a disappointment to hear the bad news that cinema admissions actually went down by 8.7 million in 2003 (Table 13). Most commentators felt that this was a mere blip rather than the beginning of a downward trend. Indeed, many preferred to point to the fact that admissions were the second highest since 1971. Nevertheless the box office gross was down by £13m (which was roughly equivalent to the box office receipts for 8 Mile). So, in other words the UK box office was short of one reasonable blockbuster.

What is also revealing is that 2003 saw a slight rise in cinema sites (10 new sites) and a definite increase of cinema screens up to 3,318 (Table 14). There were also 12 new multiplex sites introduced raising the number of multiplex screens to 2,362. Admissions may have been down but the number of seats were definitely up, as was the average price of a ticket which rose to £4.43.

It comes as no surprise to learn that the most enthusiastic cinema goers are aged between 15-24 (Tables 16 & 17). This group of young people are more likely to be at the head of the cinema queue since they are the age group that tend to go to the cinema once a month or more. The 35 plus audience, representing 31.73 million people are the least likely to go once a month. In fact, the 35 plus audience continues to be marganalised when it comes to the majority of releases. Whereas all the other age groups have shown modest rises in the frequency of cinema going. The split between male and females is roughly even – which might not be reflected in the type of films on offer. The dominant demographic remains the young male.

*S Club 7 were released in 2003*

**15** 
## UK Sites and Screens
## 1984-2003

| Yea | Total Sites | Total Screens |
|---|---|---|
| 1984 | 660 | 1,271 |
| 1985 | 663 | 1,251 |
| 1986 | 660 | 1,249 |
| 1987 | 648 | 1,215 |
| 1988 | 699 | 1,416 |
| 1989 | 719 | 1,559 |
| 1990 | 737 | 1,685 |
| 1991 | 724 | 1,789 |
| 1992 | 735 | 1,845 |
| 1993 | 723 | 1,890 |
| 1994 | 734 | 1,969 |
| 1995 | 743 | 2,019 |
| 1996 | 742 | 2,166 |
| 1997 | 747 | 2,383 |
| 1998 | 759 | 2,564 |
| 1999 | 692 | 2,758 |
| 2000 | 686 | 2,954 |
| 2001 | 692 | 3,164 |
| 2002 | 668 | 3,258 |
| 2003 | 678 | 3,318 |

**Source: Dodona Research**

There were few surprises in the Top 20 films at the UK Box Office. The concluding chapter of the Lord of the Rings trilogy was by far the most popular film in the UK (Table 18). It had made £60,666,284 at the box office while Finding Nemo was in second place with takings of £37,364,251. There was some excellent news for the UK film industry with three films – *Love Actually, Calendar Girls* and *Johnny English* making it into the Top Ten.

However, British films on the whole had a slightly more modest success rate at the box office than in 2002. In that year the top 6 UK films all burst through the £10m mark. In 2003, only the top three had passed that figure, with Cold Mountain still on release coming in at around £9m (Table 19).

*Love Actually* came out as the most popular British film. The US/UK production is the closest that British cinema gets to a guaranteed winning formula. This basically relies on the combined talents of Working Title, Richard Curtis, Hugh Grant, and the clout of Universal to push and promote the film.

*S Club 7 Seeing Double* by comparison was the most successful homegrown feature film topping a typically

**16** 
## Frequency of Cinema-going 2003

| Age Group | 4 to 14 | 15 to 24 | 25 to 34 | 35+ | ABC1 | C2DE | Male | Female | Total |
|---|---|---|---|---|---|---|---|---|---|
| No. of people (millions) | 8.02 | 7.13 | 8.03 | 31.73 | 29.43 | 25.47 | 26.74 | 28.16 | 54.90 |
| Once a month or more | 33% | 52% | 33% | 14% | 28% | 21% | 25% | 24% | 25% |
| Less than once a month but at least twice a year | 47% | 34% | 40% | 34% | 43% | 30% | 36% | 38% | 37% |
| Once a year or less | 14% | 10% | 19.5% | 26% | 17.5% | 25.5% | 20% | 22% | 21% |
| Total who ever go to the cinema | 94% | 96% | 92.5% | 74% | 88.5% | 76.5% | 81% | 84% | 83% |

**Source: CAA/CAVIAR 21**

**17** 
## Cinemagoing - 19 Year Trends

| | 1984 | 1987 | 1990 | 1993 | 1996 | 1997 | 1998 | 1999 | 2000 | 2001 | 2002 | 2003 |
|---|---|---|---|---|---|---|---|---|---|---|---|---|
| **People who ever go to the cinema** | | | | | | | | | | | | |
| 7+ | 38% | 58% | 64% | 69% | 72% | 75% | 83% | 78% | 86% | 82% | 82% | 83% |
| 7 to 14 | 73% | 88% | 85% | 93% | 95% | 95% | 97% | 955% | 97% | 97% | 98% | 91% |
| 15 to 34 | 55% | 74% | 83% | 86% | 90% | 94% | 96% | 93% | 95% | 94% | 94% | 87% |
| 35+ | 21% | 42% | 49% | 535% | 58% | 60% | 74% | 66% | 79% | 73% | 74% | 60% |
| **Regular Cinemagoers** | | | | | | | | | | | | |
| 7+ | 5% | 8% | 11% | 14% | 15% | 22% | 24% | 25% | 24% | 25% | 26% | 25% |
| 7 to 14 | 10% | 12% | 18% | 22% | 25% | 34% | 39% | 37% | 32% | 38% | 37% | 38% |
| 15-34 | 10% | 17% | 23% | 26% | 27% | 42% | 42% | 46% | 41% | 38% | 42% | 41.5% |
| 35+ | 1% | 1% | 3% | 5% | 6% | 10% | 11% | 12% | 14% | 15% | 17% | 14% |

Regular cinemagoers are defined as those that go to the cinema once a month or more

**Source: CAA/CAVIAR 21**

**18**

# Top 20 Films at the UK Box Office 2003

| Title | Distributor | Country of Origin | Box Office Gross (£m) |
|---|---|---|---|
| 1 Lord of the Rings: Return of the King* | Entertainment | US/NZ | 60,666,284 |
| 2 Finding Nemo | Buena Vista | US | 37,364,251 |
| 3 Love Actually | UIP | UK/US | 36,450,860 |
| 4 The Matrix Reloaded | Warner Bros | US | 33,423,117 |
| 5 The Pirates of the Caribbean | Buena Vista | US | 28,171,721 |
| 6 Bruce Almighty | Buena Vista | US | 23,642,290 |
| 7 X-Men 2 | 20th Century Fox | US | 20,660,229 |
| 8 Calendar Girls | Buena Vista | UK/US | 20,427,788 |
| 9 Johnny English | UIP | UK/US | 19,650,225 |
| 10 Terminator 3: Rise of the Machines | Columbia TriStar | US/Germany | 18,909,904 |
| 11 The Matrix Revolutions | Warner Bros | US | 17,992,877 |
| 12 American Pie: The Wedding | UIP | US | 17,093,190 |
| 13 Chicago | Buena Vista | US/Canada | 16,419,445 |
| 14 Elf | Entertainment | US | 16,344,883 |
| 15 Catch Me If You Can | UIP | US | 15,044,459 |
| 16 Two Weeks Notice | Warner Bros | US | 13,651,822 |
| 17 8 Mile | UIP | US/Germany | 13,254,612 |
| 18 Charlie's Angels: Full Throttle | Columbia TriStar | US | 12,355,642 |
| 19 Kill Bill – Volume 1 | Buena Vista | US | 11,621,761 |
| 20 Gangs of New York | Entertainment | US | 10,563,616 |

Box office gross = cumulative total up to 22 March 2004. Films with asterisk (*) were still being exhibited on 22 March 2004

**Source: Nielsen EDI/UK Film Council analysis**

**19**

# Top 20 UK Films at the UK Box Office 2003

| Title | Distributor | Country of Origin | Box Office Gross (£m) |
|---|---|---|---|
| 1 Love Actually | UIP | UK/US | 36,450,860 |
| 2 Calendar Girls | Buena Vista | UK/US | 20,427,788 |
| 3 Johnny English | UIP | UK/US | 19,650,225 |
| 4 Cold Mountain* | Buena Vista | UK/US/Romania/Italy | 9,118,817 |
| 5 Tomb Raider 2 | UIP | UK/US/Japan/Germany | 5,297,335 |
| 6 The Hours | Buena Vista | UK/US | 4,697,689 |
| 7 Underworld | Entertainment | UK/US | 4,391,553 |
| 8 Veronica Guerin | Buena Vista | UK/US/Ireland | 3,304,231 |
| 9 The Pianist | Pathé | UK/France/Germany/Poland | 2,972,334 |
| 10 S Club Seeing Double | Col/TriStar | UK | 2,317,357 |
| 11 Touching the Void* | Pathé | UK | 2,217,479 |
| 12 Intermission | Buena Vista | UK/Ireland | 2,142,126 |
| 13 In America | 20th Century Fox | UK/Ireland | 1,900,096 |
| 14 Evelyn | Pathé | UK/Ireland | 1,445,396 |
| 15 Nicholas Nickleby | 20th Fox | UK | 1,244,263 |
| 16 Buffalo Soldiers | Pathé | UK/Germany | 1,098,522 |
| 17 Bright Young Things | Icon | UK | 1,085,470 |
| 18 I Capture the Castle | Momentum | UK | 1,043,230 |
| 19 Ripley's Game | Entertainment | UK | 1,011,364 |
| 20 Blackball | Icon | UK | 889,238 |

Box office gross = cumulative total up to 22 March 2004. Films with asterisk (*) were still being exhibited on 22 March 2004

**Source: Nielsen EDI/UK Film Council analysis**

**20**    ## UK Box Office for UK Feature Films released in 2003 - UK Films

| | Title | Distributor | Country of Origin | Box Office Gross (£m) |
|---|---|---|---|---|
| 1 | S Club Seeing Double | Columbia Tristar | UK | 2,317,357 |
| 2 | Touching The Void | Pathe Distribution Ltd. | UK | 2,217,479 |
| 3 | Bright Young Things | Icon Film Dist. | UK | 1,085,470 |
| 4 | I Capture The Castle | Momentum Pictures | UK | 1,043,230 |
| 5 | Blackball | Icon Film Dist. | UK | 889,238 |
| 6 | The Mother | Momentum Pictures | UK | 280,494 |
| 7 | In This World | ICA Projects | UK | 147,623 |
| 8 | In The Name Of Buddha | Miracle Communications | UK | 50,500 |
| 9 | Bollywood Queen | Redbus | UK | 50,246 |
| 10 | Revenger's Tragedy | Metro Tartan | UK | 42,278 |
| 11 | Steal | Redbus | UK | 40,331 |
| 12 | Pure | Artificial Eye | UK | 26,947 |
| 13 | American Cousins | Bard | UK | 24,054 |
| 14 | Live Forever | Helkon Sk | UK | 22,066 |
| 15 | Mrs. Caldicot's Cabbage War | Arrow Films | UK | 16,415 |
| 16 | Bodysong | Pathe Distribution Ltd. | UK | 12,933 |
| 27 | Aileen: Life And Death Of A... | Optimum Rel. | UK | 12,702 |
| 18 | Nine Dead Gay Guys | Guerilla Films | UK | 12,685 |
| 19 | Concert For George | Pathe Distribution Ltd. | UK | 11,413 |
| 20 | Citizen Verdict | Georgia Films | UK | 9,593 |
| 21 | Mr In-Between | Verve Picture | UK | 7,846 |
| 22 | The Late Twentieth | Timeless Picture | UK | 4,442 |
| 23 | Devil's Gate | Independent Uk | UK | 2,908 |
| 24 | Shoreditch | Georgia Films | UK | 2,272 |
| 25 | The Draughtman's Contract (Re) | ICA Projects | UK | 1,741 |
| 26 | This Is Not A Love Song | Soda Pictures | UK | 1,709 |
| 27 | The Boy David Story | Ratpack | UK | 1,444 |
| 28 | Otherworld | Miracle Communications | UK | 1,272 |
| 29 | Emotional Backgammon | Buccaneer | UK | 1,046 |

**Total**    **8,337,734**

## UK Box Office for UK Feature Films released in 2003 - Other UK Co-productions

| | Title | Distributor | Country of Origin | Box Office Gross (£m) |
|---|---|---|---|---|
| 1 | Tomb Raider 2 | United Intl. Pictures | UK/US/Germany/Japan/Netherlands | 5,297,335 |
| 2 | Underworld | Entertainment | UK/US/Germany/Hungary | 4,391,553 |
| 3 | Veronica Guerin | Buena Vista Intl. | UK/US/Ireland | 3,304,231 |
| 4 | The Pianist | Pathe Distribution Ltd. | UK/France/Germany/Poland | 2,972,334 |
| 5 | Intermission | Buena Vista Intl. | UK/Ireland | 2,142,126 |
| 6 | In America | Twentieth Century Fox | UK/Ireland | 1,900,096 |
| 7 | Evelyn | Pathe Distribution Ltd. | UK/US/Germany/Ireland/Netherlands | 1,445,396 |
| 8 | Nicholas Nickleby | Twentieth Century Fox | UK/US/Germany/Netherlands | 1,244,263 |
| 9 | Buffalo Soldiers | Pathe Distribution Ltd. | UK/US/Germany | 1,098,522 |
| 10 | In The Cut | Pathe Distribution Ltd. | US/Australia/UK | 1,051,871 |
| 11 | Ripley's Game | Entertainment | UK/US/Italy | 1,011,364 |
| 12 | Young Adam | Warner Bros. | UK/France | 836,788 |
| 13 | Swimming Pool | Ugc Films | UK/France | 715,155 |
| 14 | Ned Kelly | United Intl. Pictures | UK/Australia | 524,022 |

| | Title | Distributor | Country of Origin | Box Office Gross (£m) |
|---|---|---|---|---|
| 15 | Song For A Raggy Boy | Abbey Home Entertainment | UK/Ireland/Denmark/Spain | 479,243 |
| 16 | The Actors | Momentum Pictures | UK/US/Ireland | 458,220 |
| 17 | L'homme Du Train | Pathe Distribution Ltd. | UK/France /Germany | 437,681 |
| 18 | Spin The Bottle | Buena Vista Intl. | UK/Ireland | 362,842 |
| 19 | Spider | Helkon Sk | UK/France/Canada/Japan | 326,414 |
| 20 | The Good Thief | Momentum Pictures | UK/France/Canada/Ireland | 325,514 |
| 21 | To Kill A King | Pathe Distribution Ltd. | UK/ Germany | 262,102 |
| 22 | The Heart Of Me | Pathe Distribution Ltd. | UK/Germany | 239,779 |
| 23 | Max | Pathe Distribution Ltd. | UK/Canada/Germany /Hungary | 133,309 |
| 24 | Summer Things | Ugc Films | UK/France/Italy | 132,238 |
| 25 | Wilbur Wants To Kill Himself | Icon Film Dist. | UK/Denmark/Sweden/France | 127,340 |
| 26 | Noi Albinoi | Artificial Eye | Iceland/Germany/UK/Denmark | 115,510 |
| 27 | The One And Only | Pathe Distribution Ltd. | UK/France | 113,150 |
| 28 | Petites Coupures | Artificial Eye | France/UK | 73,897 |
| 29 | The Hard Word | Metrodome Dist. | Australia/UK | 67,912 |
| 30 | The Shape Of Things | Momentum Pictures | US/France/UK | 60,006 |
| 31 | Feardotcom | Columbia Tristar | UK/Germany/Luxemborug/US | 57,931 |
| 32 | The Last Great Wilderness | Feature Film Co. | UK/Denmark | 27,672 |
| 33 | Octane | Buena Vista Intl. | UK/Luxembourg | 19,061 |
| 34 | Hoover Street Revival | Metro Tartan | UK/France | 14,075 |
| 35 | Mystics | Momentum Pictures | UK/Ireland | 12,666 |
| 36 | Taking Sides | Guerilla Films | UK/France/Germany/Austria | 9,576 |
| 37 | Miranda | Pathe Distribution Ltd. | UK/Germany | 8,641 |
| 38 | Innocence | Capers Matcine | UK/Australia | 6,058 |
| 39 | Puckoon | Guerilla Films | UK/Ireland/Germany | 5,991 |
| 40 | Most Fertile Man In Ireland | Ian Rattray Films | UK/Ireland | 4,799 |
| 41 | Ten Minutes Older: Cello | Blue Dolphin | UK/Germany | 1,615 |
| 42 | Fogbound | Blue Dolphin | UK/Netherlands | 1,033 |
| 43 | That Girl From Rio | Helkon Sk | UK/Spain | 488 |

**Total**                                                       **31,819,819**

## UK Box Office for UK Feature Films released in 2003 - US/UK Co-productions

| | Title | Distributor | Country of Origin | Box Office Gross (£m) |
|---|---|---|---|---|
| 1 | Love Actually | United Intl. Pictures | UK/US | 36,450,860 |
| 2 | Calendar Girls | Buena Vista Intl. | UK/US | 20,427,788 |
| 3 | Johnny English | United Intl. Pictures | UK/US | 19,650,225 |
| 4 | Cold Mountain | Buena Vista Intl. | UK/US | 9,118,817 |
| 5 | The Italian Job | United Intl. Pictures | US/UK | 7,713,411 |
| 6 | The Hours | Buena Vista Intl. | UK/US | 4,697,689 |
| 7 | The Core | United Intl. Pictures | US/UK | 1,591,786 |
| 8 | Hope Springs | Buena Vista Intl. | US/UK | 1,062,100 |
| 9 | What A Girl Wants | Warner Bros. | UK/US | 873,699 |
| 10 | Alien - Director's Cut | Twentieth Century Fox | US/UK | 543,350 |
| 11 | Thirteen | United Intl. Pictures | US/UK | 276,411 |
| 12 | Four Feathers | Buena Vista Intl. | US/UK | 164,725 |
| 13 | Heartlands | Buena Vista Intl. | US/UK | 72,228 |
| 14 | I'll Be There | Warner Bros. | UK/US | 30,688 |
| 15 | The Safety Of Objects | Entertainment | US/UK | 8,231 |

**Total**                                                       **102,682,008**
**Total Box Office Gross**                                **143,039,561**

Box office gross = cumulative total up to 22 March 2004

**Source: Nielsen EDI, UK Film Council analysis**

# Top 20 EU Films at the UK Box Office 2003

| Title | Distributor | Country of Origin | Box Office Gross (£m) |
|---|---|---|---|
| 1  Terminator 3: Rise Of Machines | Columbia Tristar | US/Germany | 18,909,904 |
| 2  8 Mile | United Intl. Pictures | US/Germany | 13,254,612 |
| 3  Far From Heaven | Entertainment | US/France | 1,853,941 |
| 4  Wrong Turn | Pathe Distribution Ltd. | US/Germany | 1,569,243 |
| 5  Whale Rider | Icon Film Dist. | New Zealand/Germany | 1,517,346 |
| 6  Confessions Of Dangerous Mind | Buena Vista Intl. | US/Canada/Germany | 1,457,769 |
| 7  Confidence | Momentum Pictures | US/Canada/Germany | 1,189,939 |
| 8  Good Bye, Lenin! | UGC Films | Germany | 1,151,696 |
| 9  The Rules Of Attraction | Icon Film Dist. | US/Germany | 1,130,854 |
| 10  The Little Polar Bear | Warner Bros. | Germany | 784,162 |
| 11  Belleville Rendezvous | Metro Tartan | France/Belgium/Canada | 740,726 |
| 12  The Transporter | Twentieth Century Fox | US/France | 715,561 |
| 13  Etre Et Avoir | Metro Tartan | France | 708,116 |
| 14  The Good Girl | Twentieth Century Fox | US/Germany/Netherlands | 523,393 |
| 15  Russian Ark | Artificial Eye | Russia/Germany | 471,505 |
| 16  Respiro | Metro Tartan | Italy/France | 359,413 |
| 17  The Leopard (Re) | BFI | Italy/France | 346,807 |
| 18  Sin Eater | Twentieth Century Fox | US/Germany | 328,039 |
| 19  The In-Laws | Warner Bros. | US/Germany | 324,408 |
| 20  Intacto | Momentum Pictures | Spain | 299,743 |

Box office gross = cumulative total up to 22 March 2004. Films exclude UK and UK co-productions

**Source: Nielsen EDI/UK Film Council analysis**

# Top 20 Foreign Language Films Released in the UK 2003

| Title | Distributor | Country of Origin | Box Office Gross (£) |
|---|---|---|---|
| 1  City Of God | Buena Vista | Brazil | 2,372,951 |
| 2  Kal Ho Naa Ho | Yash Raj Films | India | 1,671,690 |
| 3  Good Bye, Lenin! | UGC Films | Germany | 1,151,696 |
| 4  Spirited Away | Optimum Rel. | US/Japan | 973,037 |
| 5  The Little Polar Bear | Warner Bros. | Germany | 784,162 |
| 6  Chalte Chalte | Eros | India | 775,552 |
| 7  Baghban | Eros | India/UK | 748,028 |
| 8  Belleville Rendezvous | Metro Tartan | France/Belgium/Canada | 740,726 |
| 9  Etre Et Avoir | Metro Tartan | France | 708,116 |
| 10  Koi...Mil Gaya | Yash Raj Films | India | 647,035 |
| 11  Main Prem Ki Diwani Hoon | Yash Raj Films | India | 547,245 |
| 12  Russian Ark | Artificial Eye | Russia/Germany | 471,505 |
| 13  Dil Ka Rishtaa | Venus Films | India | 446,480 |
| 14  L'Homme du Train | Pathé | UK/France/Germany | 437,681 |
| 15  Respiro | Metro Tartan | Italy/France | 359,413 |
| 16  The Leopard | bfi | Italy/France | 346,807 |
| 17  Andaaz | Tip Top | India | 317,530 |
| 18  Armaan | Eros | India | 316,524 |
| 19  Intacto | Momentum | Spain | 299,743 |
| 20  Kuch Naa Kaho | Eros | India | 266,705 |

Figures as at 22 March 2004

**Source: Nielsen EDI/BBFC/UK Film Council analysis**

**Breakdown of UK Box Office by Country of Origin 2003**

| Territories | No. of Titles | Box office | % |
|---|---|---|---|
| USA solo | 133 | 512.31 | 61.7 |
| USA co-productions (other) | 53 | 164.74 | 19.9 |
| UK and UK co-productions | 59 | 20.55 | 2.50 |
| USA/UK | 16 | 109.56 | 13.2 |
| Europe | 66 | 7.85 | 0.90 |
| India | 56 | 8.13 | 1.00 |
| Rest of the world | 40 | 6.58 | 0.80 |
| **Total** | **423** | **829.71** | **100** |

Box office gross = cumulative total up to 22 March 2004

**Source: Nielsen EDI/UK Film Council analysis**

**24** **Top 10 UK Films Released in the US in 2003 by US Box Office Revenue**

| | Title | Distributor (US) | Country of Origin | Box Office Gross ($m) |
|---|---|---|---|---|
| 1 | Cold Mountain | Miramax | UK/US/Romania/Italy | 95,313,718 |
| 2 | Lara Croft Tomb Raider 2: The Cradle Of Life | Paramount | UK/US/Japan/Germany | 65,660,196 |
| 3 | Love Actually | Universal | UK/US | 59,393,405 |
| 4 | Underworld | Sony Pictures | UK/US/Germany/Hungary | 51,483,949 |
| 5 | 28 Days Later | Fox Searchlight | UK/Netherlands/US | 45,064,915 |
| 6 | What A Girl Wants | Warner Bros. | UK/US | 36,017,014 |
| 7 | Bend It Like Beckham | Fox Searchlight | UK/Germany | 32,543,449 |
| 8 | Calendar Girls | Buena Vista | UK/US | 31,011,616 |
| 9 | Johnny English | Universal | UK/US | 28,082,366 |
| 10 | In America | Fox Searchlight | UK/Ireland | 15,436,796 |

**Source: Neilsen EDI/UK Film Council analysis**

*City of God (Cidade de Deus) from Brazil, was the top foreign language film released in 2003*

## 25    Top 20 of Admissions of Films Distributed in the European Union in 2003

| | Title | Country of Origin | Admissions |
|---|---|---|---|
| 1 | Finding Nemo | US | 37,714,270 |
| 2 | The Matrix Reloaded | US | 31,903,696 |
| 3 | Pirates of the Caribbean: Black Pearl | US | 28,990,197 |
| 4 | The Lord of the Rings: The Two Towers* | US/New Zealand | 27,343,536 |
| 5 | The Lord of the Rings: The Return of the King | USA/New Zealand | 27,221,839 |
| 6 | Bruce Almighty | US | 22,015,534 |
| 7 | The Matrix Revolutions | US | 18,349,309 |
| 8 | Terminator 3: Rise of the Machines | US /Germany | 17,267,985 |
| 9 | Catch Me If You Can | US | 16,432,648 |
| 10 | American Wedding | US/Germany | 14,095,363 |
| 11 | Johnny English | UK/US | 13,779,900 |
| 12 | X2: X-Men United | US | 13,547,808 |
| 13 | 8 Mile | US | 13,304,095 |
| 14 | Love Actually | UK/US | 12,566,125 |
| 15 | The Jungle Book 2 | US/Australia | 11,913,646 |
| 16 | Bad Boys 2 | US | 10,429,492 |
| 17 | The Ring** | US/ Japan | 9,785,243 |
| 18 | Chicago *** | US | 9,774,108 |
| 19 | Two Weeks Notice | US | 9,709,159 |
| 20 | Gangs of New York | US | 9,483,666 |

*25 611 709 admissions in Europe in 2002. **303 792 admissions in Europe in 2002. ***24 865 admissions in Europe in 2002
Based on data from 21 European countries

**Source : European Audiovisual Observatory/LUMIERE**

*Finding Nemo made a big splash across the countries of the European Union*

## Top 20 of Admissions of European Films Distributed in the European Union in 2003

| Title | Country of Origin | Admissions |
|---|---|---|
| 1　Johnny English | UK /US | 13,779,900 |
| 2　Love Actually | UK /US | 12,566,125 |
| 3　Good Bye, Lenin! | Germany | 9,209,683 |
| 4　Taxi 3 | France | 7,378,194 |
| 5　Die Another Day * | UK /US | 6,048,188 |
| 6　Calendar Girls | UK | 5,103,315 |
| 7　La gran aventura de Mortadelo y Filemón | Spain | 4,979,991 |
| 8　Chouchou | France | 3,989,163 |
| 9　Tais-toi | France | 3,472,059 |
| 10　The Pianist** | France /Germany /UK /Poland | 3,266,755 |
| 11　Das Wunder von Bern | Germany | 3,253,216 |
| 12　Natale in India | Italy | 2,594,918 |
| 13　28 Days Later*** | UK | 2,517,056 |
| 14　Días de fútbol | Spain | 2,424,949 |
| 15　Luther | Germany | 2,342,972 |
| 16　La beuze | France | 2,042,933 |
| 17　La finestra di fronte | Italy/ Portugal | 1,967,024 |
| 18　Das Fliegende Klassenzimmer | Germany | 1,870,041 |
| 19　Ricordati di me | Italy /France /UK | 1,868,152 |
| 20　Il paradiso all'improvviso | Italy | 1,829,916 |

*19 757 094 admissions in Europe in 2002
** 4 920 127 admissions in Europe in 2002
***1 362 045 admissions in Europe (UK) in 2002
Based on data from 21 European countries

**Source : European Audiovisual Observatory/LUMIERE**

eclectic chart with a box office total of £2,317,357 (Table 20). The critically acclaimed documentary, the Lottery-funded, *Touching the Void* came an impressive second in this table, and emphasised the public's apparent growing appreciation of documentary films.

The top EU film at the UK Box Office is *Terminator 3: Rise of Machines* on basis of its US/Germany production input (Table 21). In fact, Germany funded 13 out of the top 20 EU films.

If the EU film table looks to have a suspiciously Hollywood flavour then Table 22, representing Foreign Language Films, shows that only the top three titles – *City of God* (Brazil), *Kal Ho Naa Ho* (India), and *Goodbye Lenin!* (Germany) broke through the £1m mark at the box office.

A truer picture of the USA's global domination can be seen in the breakdown of box office by country (Table 23). If you add all the totals which involve US input then you discover that the USA makes up an astonishing 94.8

per cent of the total UK box office market. Doing the same sums with UK involvement brings a modest figure of just 15.7 per cent. In other words only 75 out of the 423 films released in the UK are British. European films make up 0.9 per cent of the market while Indian films fare slightly better eking out 1 per cent. The rest of the world cinema in the UK is represented by 0.8 per cent of the market (40 films out 423). Meanwhile the US alone takes 61.7 per cent of the UK market. This is no Rosetta Stone type of discovery. The US film industry dominates all the countries in Europe in a similar fashion (with the possible exception of France). In relative terms the British film industry does reasonably well in terms of its homegrown product.

Conversely, British films make a modest impact on the US Box office (Table 24) and doesn't quite mirror the UK's own box office appreciation of its home products. Sure enough the Top 10 contains the UK's top three hits *Love Actually, Calendar Girls* and *Johnny English* but topping the table is *Cold Mountain* followed by Lara *Croft Tomb Raider2: The Cradle of Life*. The table also contains

**27**   **Breakdown of UK Box Office by Distributor in 2003**

| Distributor | Titles | Box Office |
|---|---|---|
| Buena Vista Intl. | 39 | 224,605,319 |
| United Intl. Pictures | 29 | 195,763,176 |
| Warner Bros. | 17 | 81,665,144 |
| Columbia Tristar | 31 | 80,026,369 |
| Twentieth Century Fox | 24 | 69,310,342 |
| **Total Majors** | **140** | **651,370,350** |
| Entertainment | 17 | 115,515,057 |
| Pathe Distribution Ltd. | 22 | 17,925,974 |
| Momentum Pictures | 20 | 9,585,811 |
| Icon Film Dist. | 8 | 5,532,683 |
| Redbus | 5 | 4,143,872 |
| Metro Tartan | 20 | 3,734,332 |
| Eros International Ltd. | 17 | 3,033,707 |
| Yash Raj Films | 3 | 2,865,970 |
| Optimum Rel. | 20 | 2,515,211 |
| Helkon Sk | 5 | 2,349,619 |
| UGC Films | 3 | 1,999,089 |
| Winchester Films | 4 | 1,986,893 |
| Artificial Eye | 21 | 1,332,599 |
| Metrodome Dist. | 5 | 937,759 |
| BFI | 10 | 704,722 |
| Venus Entertainment | 11 | 561,695 |
| Abbey Home Entertainment | 1 | 479,243 |
| ICA Projects | 8 | 454,584 |
| Venus Films | 1 | 446,480 |
| Tip Top Entertainment | 3 | 423,731 |
| Tartan Films | 5 | 215,361 |
| Bollywood Films | 8 | 187,274 |
| Gurpreet Video Intl. | 6 | 163,200 |
| Twenty First Century Film | 1 | 151,987 |
| Soda Pictures | 6 | 150,550 |
| Shree Krishna Film | 2 | 139,352 |
| Spark Ent. | 4 | 121,946 |
| Miracle Communications | 3 | 83,028 |
| City Screen | 2 | 55,838 |
| Movie Box | 1 | 54,610 |
| Eclipse Pictures | 1 | 53,101 |
| Maiden Voyage Pictures | 1 | 50,351 |
| Peccadillo Pictures | 3 | 46,961 |
| Himalayan Motion Pictures | 1 | 46,461 |
| Rio Dist. | 2 | 41,841 |
| Medusa | 1 | 40,026 |
| Guerilla Films | 3 | 28,252 |
| Feature Film Co. | 1 | 27,672 |
| Bard | 1 | 24,054 |
| Axiom Films | 2 | 20,388 |
| Arrow Films | 2 | 17,494 |
| Palm Pictures | 1 | 12,632 |
| Georgia Films | 2 | 11,865 |
| Cinefrance | 1 | 9,471 |
| Circuit Film | 1 | 9,026 |

| Distributor | Titles | Box Office |
|---|---|---|
| Verve Picture | 1 | 7,846 |
| Metropolis Films | 1 | 6,263 |
| Capers Matcine | 1 | 6,058 |
| Ian Rattray Films | 1 | 4,799 |
| Timeless Picture | 1 | 4,442 |
| Mandrake Media | 1 | 3,367 |
| Independent Uk | 1 | 2,908 |
| Blue Dolphin | 2 | 2,648 |
| Millivres | 2 | 2,513 |
| Gala | 1 | 1,932 |
| Ratpack | 1 | 1,444 |
| Park Circus Films | 1 | 1,134 |
| Buccaneer | 1 | 1,046 |
| Hyde Park Pictures Ltd. | 1 | 901 |
| P-Kino | 1 | 285 |
| Rafu Miah | 1 | 282 |
| **Total Independents** | **282** | **178,439,640** |
| **Total** | **423** | **829,709,990** |

Box Office gross for period 3 January 2003 to 22 March 2004

**Source: Nielsen EDI**

a couple of anomalies such as *Underworld* and *In America*. Neither of these two films made a big impact on the UK box office (Tables 18 & 19).

Proof of the USA's domination of Europe is illustrated by the table showing admissions of films in the European Union (Table 25). The entire table consists of American products with the exception of two UK films – *Love Actually* and *Johnny English*.

Even with nine countries joining the European Union in 2004 it is unlikely that this table will change in years to come. American films dominate all European territories.

Table 26 shows the most popular European films within the European Union. The UK was involved in seven of the top 20 productions with *Love Actually* and *Johnny English* leading way. Very few foreign language films seem to make an impact on these tables. We are nearing a time when all the top films across Europe will be spoken in English.

Back in Britain the bulk of the distribution sector is dominated by five American major distributors and one independent company Entertainment. The fierce competition at the top provides year on year changes at the top of the table. Buena Vista made it to the top of the chart with four films of the Top 10 films at the UK Box

**28**

# UK Cinema Circuits 1984-2003
## s (sites) scr (screens)

| | ABC | | UGC *(ex-Virgin) | | Cine UK | | Odeon** | | Showcase | | UCI | | Vue (ex-Warner Village) | | Small Chains | | Independents | |
|---|---|---|---|---|---|---|---|---|---|---|---|---|---|---|---|---|---|---|
| | s | scr | s | scr | s | scr | s | scr | s | scr | s | scr | s | scr | s | scr | s | scr |
| 1985 | - | - | 158 | 403* | - | - | 76 | 194 | - | - | 3 | 17 | 1 | 5 | - | - | - | - |
| 1986 | - | - | 173 | 443* | - | - | 74 | 190 | - | - | 3 | 17 | 1 | 5 | - | - | - | - |
| 1987 | - | - | 154 | 408* | - | - | 75 | 203 | - | - | 5 | 33 | 1 | 5 | - | - | - | - |
| 1988 | - | - | 140 | 379* | - | - | 73 | 214 | 7 | 85 | 12 | 99 | 1 | 5 | - | - | - | - |
| 1989 | - | - | 142 | 388* | - | - | 75 | 241 | 7 | 85 | 18 | 156 | 3 | 26 | - | - | - | - |
| 1990 | - | - | 142 | 411* | - | - | 75 | 266 | 7 | 85 | 21 | 189 | 5 | 48 | - | - | - | - |
| 1991 | - | - | 136 | 435* | - | - | 75 | 296 | 8 | 97 | 23 | 208 | 6 | 57 | - | - | - | - |
| 1992 | - | - | 131 | 422* | - | - | 75 | 313 | 9 | 109 | 25 | 219 | 7 | 64 | - | - | - | - |
| 1993 | - | - | 125 | 408* | - | - | 75 | 322 | 10 | 127 | 25 | 219 | 9 | 84 | - | - | - | - |
| 1994 | - | - | 119 | 402* | - | - | 76 | 327 | 11 | 141 | 26 | 232 | 10 | 93 | - | - | 437 | 631 |
| 1995 | - | - | 116 | 406* | - | - | 71 | 320 | 11 | 143 | 26 | 232 | 12 | 110 | - | - | 469 | 716 |
| 1996 | 92 | 244 | 24 | 162* | 2 | 24 | 73 | 362 | 14 | 181 | 26 | 232 | 16 | 143 | 58 | 139 | 437 | 679 |
| 1997 | 80 | 225 | 29 | 213* | 5 | 66 | 73 | 362 | 15 | 197 | 26 | 263 | 17 | 152 | 68 | 166 | 434 | 739 |
| 1998 | 81 | 234 | 34 | 290* | 10 | 116 | 79 | 415 | 15 | 199 | 29 | 287 | 22 | 200 | 73 | 100 | 416 | 633 |
| 1999 | 58 | 180 | 36 | 312 | 13 | 146 | 79 | 415 | 16 | 221 | 31 | 320 | 28 | 200 | 55 | 170 | 376 | 794 |
| 2000 | | | 41 | 363 | 20 | 219 | 118 | 634 | 19 | 244 | 35 | 345 | 33 | 331 | 54 | 159 | 366 | 659 |
| 2001 | | | 41 | 386 | 25 | 276 | 103 | 597 | 19 | 244 | 35 | 355 | 41 | 364 | 81 | 209 | 351 | 733 |
| 2002 | | | 43 | 405 | 30 | 333 | 97 | 608 | 19 | 244 | 39 | 375 | 42 | 405 | 72 | 252 | 326 | 636 |
| 2003 | | | 41 | 389 | 32 | 357 | 98 | 604 | 19 | 243 | 35 | 352 | 45 | 426 | | | 408 | 947 |

**Total: Sites: 678 Screens:3,318**

**Source: Dodona Research**      * figures from 1985 to 1998 indicate Virgin Cinemas
** Odeon bought up the ABC chain in 2000

*The Lord of the Rings The Return of the King was by far the most popular film with UK cinema audiences in 2003*

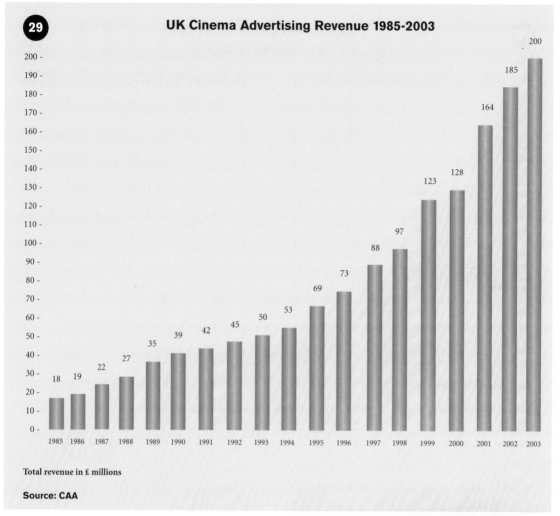

**29**

# UK Cinema Advertising Revenue 1985-2003

| Year | Revenue |
|------|---------|
| 1985 | 18 |
| 1986 | 19 |
| 1987 | 22 |
| 1988 | 27 |
| 1989 | 35 |
| 1990 | 39 |
| 1991 | 42 |
| 1992 | 45 |
| 1993 | 50 |
| 1994 | 53 |
| 1995 | 69 |
| 1996 | 73 |
| 1997 | 88 |
| 1998 | 97 |
| 1999 | 123 |
| 2000 | 128 |
| 2001 | 164 |
| 2002 | 185 |
| 2003 | 200 |

Total revenue in £ millions

Source: CAA

*Troy (left) and Harry Potter and the Prisoner of Azkaban (right), two films that made it into the all-time top twenty table.*

**30**      ## All-time Top 20 UK Films at the UK Box Office

| Title | Year of Release | Box Office Gross (£) |
| --- | --- | --- |
| 1  Harry Potter and the Philosopher's Stone | 2001 | 66,096,060 |
| 2  Harry Potter and the Chamber of Secrets | 2002 | 54,780,731 |
| 3  The Full Monty | 1997 | 52,232,058 |
| 4  Bridget Jones's Diary | 2001 | 42,007,008 |
| 5  Harry Potter and the Prisoner of Azkaban | 2003 | 45,217,254 |
| 6  Love Actually | 2003 | 36,800,418 |
| 7  Die Another Day | 2002 | 36,044,960 |
| 8  Notting Hill | 1999 | 31,006,109 |
| 9  Chicken Run | 2000 | 29,514,237 |
| 10  The World is not Enough | 1999 | 28,576,504 |
| 11  Four Weddings and a Funeral | 1994 | 27,762,648 |
| 12  Shakespeare in Love | 1999 | 20,814,996 |
| 13  Calendar Girls | 2003 | 20,427,788 |
| 14  Tomorrow Never Dies | 1997 | 19,884,412 |
| 15  Johnny English | 2002 | 19,064,424 |
| 16  Billy Elliott | 2000 | 18,386,715 |
| 17  Goldeneye | 1995 | 18,245,572 |
| 18  Bean | 1997 | 17,972,562 |
| 19  Troy | 2003 | 17,964,967 |
| 20  About a Boy | 2002 | 16,935,159 |

Box office gross up to 1 August 2004

**Source: Nielsen EDI, UK Film Council analysis**

N.B. Star Wars Episode 1 The Phantom Menace (1999 £51,063,81; The Mummy Returns (2002 £20,390,060 were partially produced in the UK, but for these purposes have been treated as US films)

*Love Actually had all the ingredients required to make the perfect British box office hit*

**31**     **Top 10 Indian Movies in the UK**

| | Title | Distributor | Year of Release | Total Box Office (£) |
|---|---|---|---|---|
| 1 | Kabhi Khushi Kabhie Gham | Yash Raj | 2001 | 2,498,281 |
| 2 | Kuch Kuch Hota Hai | Yash Raj | 1998 | 1,750,000 |
| 3 | Devdas | Eros | 2002 | 1,742,553 |
| 4 | Kal Ho Naa Ho | Yash Raj | 2003 | 1,671,690 |
| 5 | Mohabbatein | Yash Raj | 2000 | 1,100,000 |
| 6 | Dil To Pagal Hai | Yash Raj | 1997 | 990,000 |
| 7 | Mujse Dosti Karoge! | Yash Raj | 2002 | 831,000 |
| 8 | Chalte Chalte | Eros | 2003 | 775,552 |
| 9 | Baghban | Eros | 2003 | 748,028 |
| 10 | Hum Tumhare Hain Sanam | Eros | 2002 | 671,215 |

Box office gross up to 22 March 2004

**Source: Nielsen EDI**

Office – *Finding Nemo, Pirates of the Caribbean, Bruce Almighty* and *Calendar Girls*. Despite these successes it should be noted that Buena Vista distributed the most number of titles – 39 in all.

UIP follows in second place with its two biggest hits being the UK hits *Love Actually* and *Johnny English*. This is a result of the distribution deal that Working Title has with Universal and undeniably accounts for recent success British films have had. Nevertheless it is worth noting that in the list of Distributors in Table 20 for homegrown UK products  out of all the majors only Columbia TriStar appears with its release of *S Club 7 Seeing Double*.

With 17 releases Entertainment's performance in the Distributors chart is the most impressive. Entertainment landed the big one when it took on *The Lord of the Rings*. This title alone has ensured a healthy box office figure.

The biggest slide has been that of Twentieth Century Fox who were top of the table last year and have slipped down to sixth place in 2003 with just one title in the Top 20 – *X Men 2*.

The entire box office total from all the independent distributors of £178,439,640 is surpassed by both Buena Vista £224,605,319  UIP. Of the top ten independents there is little change behind Entertainment with Pathé, Momentum, Icon, Redbus and Metro Tartan maintaining their share of the market.

The two major Indian Distributors follow as the most successful Distributors for in their own product. This is emphasised in Table 31 of the Top 10 Indian Movies in the UK of all time. *Kai No Naa Ho* is this year's top entry with the top five films all breaking the £1m mark at the box office.

As for list of the best British films in the UK there have been four new entries (at the time of writing) in the Top 20 from 2003 – *Harry Potter and the Prisoner of Azkaban, Love Actually, Calendar Girls* and *Troy*. Perhaps the biggest surprise is that the third Harry Potter film didn't join the first two Harry Potter films at the top of the chart.

Despite the slight fall in attendances it is clear that the British public enjoy  their movies. It is also obvious that the comfort of multiplexes and the American blockbusters that they offer are what the majority of cinema goers expect. In the end the majority of cinema goers expect to be entertained.

Those wishing to see a more evenly balanced set of programming featuring more British films, or even a spread of more culturally diverse movies, are in the minority. It is unlikely that cinema-going trends will change overnight without the sort of impetus that the USA brought to the UK in 1980s when they invested in building multiplexes and then filling them with films which had mass appeal. Nevertheless, the indications are that there is a desire to attempt to instigate a more varied selection on our cinema menus. The big question is whether cinema audiences will recognise, or even respond to the potential changes.

# DVD/Video

To say that the video industry is at the strongest point in its history would be no understatement. It is clear, with sales of DVD players up by a remarkable 71 per cent in 2003, that the public has embraced the medium. However, the continued growth of the DVD has come as a double-edged sword to the industry. On the one hand the take up of the format by the consumer has been spectacular. In 2002 DVD sales exceeded VHS sales for the first time and that trend continued into 2003. On the other hand the whole industry has been trying to devise ways to combat the equally spectacular growth in DVD piracy. It is likely to prove quite a battle in which the consumer will be encouraged more and more not to remain neutral by rejecting pirated copies.

DVD/Videos, particularly in retail terms, do give us a sense of longevity of a film. The re-consumption of a film from the cinema screen to the DVD/video player at home enables us to see which films or programmes are destined for repeat plays and viewings.

In just five years, since DVDs were introduced, the number of DVDs bought has rocketed up from 4 million in 1999 to an astonishing 145 million units in 2003. The value of DVDs will surely burst through the £2 billion

**32**    **BBFC Video Classification in 2003**

| Certificate | Number of Films Submitted | Number of Films Passed After Cuts |
|---|---|---|
| Uc | 152 | 0 |
| U | 2084 | 13 |
| PG | 2280 | 13 |
| 12 | 1685 | 14 |
| 15 | 2244 | 18 |
| 18 | 980 | 112 |
| R18 | 1405 | 259 |
| **Total** | **10833** | **429** |
| Rejected | 3 | |

**Source: BBFC**

barrier in 2005. It is not surprising that VHS sales have begun a decline from an all high figure of 114 million units in 2000 to 63 million units in 2003. Perhaps at last we can begin to write our farewells to the VHS format.

The VHS format particularly took a hammering in rental transactions, with a fall of 50 million in 2003. It was interesting to see that while DVD rentals took a 30

**33**    **The UK Video/DVD Market 1986-2003**

| Year | Retail Transactions (million) | | Value (£m) | | Rental Transactions (millions) | | Value (£m) | |
|---|---|---|---|---|---|---|---|---|
| 1986 | 6 | | 55 | | 233 | | 284 | |
| 1987 | 12 | | 110 | | 251 | | 326 | |
| 1988 | 20 | | 184 | | 271 | | 371 | |
| 1989 | 38 | | 345 | | 289 | | 416 | |
| 1990 | 40 | | 374 | | 277 | | 418 | |
| 1991 | 45 | | 440 | | 253 | | 407 | |
| 1992 | 48 | | 506 | | 222 | | 389 | |
| 1993 | 60 | | 643 | | 184 | | 350 | |
| 1994 | 66 | | 698 | | 167 | | 339 | |
| 1995 | 73 | | 789 | | 167 | | 351 | |
| 1996 | 79 | | 803 | | 175 | | 382 | |
| 1997 | 87 | | 858 | | 161 | | 369 | |
| 1998 | 100 | | 940 | | 186 | | 437 | |
| 1999 | 96 | (4.0) | 882 | (68) | 174 | | 408 | |
| 2000 | 114 | (16.6) | 1104 | (264) | 186 | | 444 | |
| 2001 | 93.5 | (41.3) | 844 | (646) | 162 | (24.6) | 399 | (65) |
| 2002 | 79 | (90.0) | 745 | (1,305) | 119 | (57.0) | 312 | (164) |
| 2003 | 63 | (145.0) | 537 | (1,884) | 69 | (87.0) | 191 | (259) |

DVD retail/rental transactions in parentheses

**Source: BVA/Official Charts Company**

## 34　Top 20 Rental VHS Titles in the UK 2003

| | Title | Distributor | Country |
|---|---|---|---|
| 1 | My Big Fat Greek Wedding (PG) | EV | US |
| 2 | Signs (12) | Buena Vista | US |
| 3 | The Bourne Identity (12) | Universal | US |
| 4 | Catch Me If You Can (12) | Universal | US |
| 5 | Road to Perdition (15) | Fox Pathé | US |
| 6 | Men In Black II (PG) | Columbia TriStar | US |
| 7 | Gangs of New York (18) | EV | US |
| 8 | Minority Report (12) | Fox Pathé | US |
| 9 | The Ring (15) | Universal | US |
| 10 | 28 Days Later (18) | Fox Pathé | UK/US/NL |
| 11 | xXx (12) | Columbia TriStar | US |
| 12 | Insomnia (15) | Buena Vista | US |
| 13 | About a Boy (12) | Universal | UK/US |
| 14 | One Hour Photo (15) | Fox Pathé | US |
| 15 | The Sum of all Fears (12) | Paramount | US |
| 16 | Reign of Fire (12) | Buena Vista | UK/Ire/US |
| 17 | Johnny English (PG) | Universal | UK/US |
| 18 | Two Weeks Notice (12) | Warner | US |
| 19 | Phone Booth (15) | Fox Pathé | US |
| 20 | Mr. Deeds (12) | Columbia TriStar | US |

**Source: Rental Monitor/BVA**

## 35　Top 20 Rental DVD Titles in the UK 2003

| | Title | Distributor | Country |
|---|---|---|---|
| 1 | Signs (12) | Buena Vista | US |
| 2 | Catch Me If You Can (12) | Universal | US |
| 3 | The Bourne Identity (12) | Universal | US |
| 4 | My Big Fat Greek Wedding (PG) | EV | US |
| 5 | The Ring (15) | Universal | US |
| 6 | Phone Booth (15) | Fox Pathé | US |
| 7 | 28 Days Later (18) | Fox Pathé | UK/US/Neth |
| 8 | Road to Perdition (15) | Fox Pathé | US |
| 9 | Gangs of New York (18) | EV | US |
| 10 | xXx (12) | Columbia TriStar | US |
| 11 | Johnny English (PG) | Universal | UK/US |
| 12 | Bruce Almighty (12) | Buena Vista | US |
| 13 | Changing Lanes (15) | Paramount | US |
| 14 | Pirates of the Caribbean (12) | Buena Vista | US |
| 15 | Red Dragon (15) | Universal | US |
| 16 | One Hour Photo (15) | Fox Pathé | US |
| 17 | Two Weeks Notice (12) | Warner | US |
| 18 | Mr. Deeds (12) | Columbia TriStar | US |
| 19 | Men In Black II (PG) | Columbia TriStar | US |
| 20 | The Matrix Reloaded (15) | Warner | US |

**Source: Rental Monitor/BVA**

*Signs was the top rental film in 2003*

## 36　Top 20 Rental Videos VHS & DVD in the UK 2003

| | Title | Distributor | Country |
|---|---|---|---|
| 1 | Signs (12) | Buena Vista | US |
| 2 | My Big Fat Greek Wedding (PG) | EV | US |
| 3 | The Bourne Identity (12) | Universal | US |
| 4 | Catch me if you can (12) | Universal | US |
| 5 | Road to Perdition (15) | Fox Pathé | US |
| 6 | The Ring (15) | Universal | US/Jap |
| 7 | Gangs of New York (18) | EV | US |
| 8 | 28 Days Later (18) | Fox Pathé | UK/US/Neth |
| 9 | Phone Booth (15) | Fox Pathé | US |
| 10 | xXx (12) | Columbia TriStar | US |
| 11 | Men in Black II (PG) | Columbia TriStar | US |
| 12 | Johnny English (PG) | Universal | UK/US |
| 13 | One Hour Photo (15) | Fox Pathé | US |
| 14 | Two Weeks Notice (12) | Warner | US |
| 15 | Changing Lanes (15) | Paramount | US |
| 16 | Insomnia (15) | Buena Vista | US |
| 17 | Reign of Fire (12) | Buena Vista | UK/US/Ire |
| 18 | Mr. Deeds (12) | Columbia TriStar | US |
| 19 | Red Dragon (15) | Universal | US |
| 20 | Bruce Almighty (12) | Buena Vista | US |

**Source: Rental Monitor/BVA**

## 37 Top 20 Retail VHS Titles in the UK 2003

| | Title | Distributor | Country |
|---|---|---|---|
| 1 | Harry Potter and the Chamber of Secrets (PG) | Warner | UK/US |
| 2 | The Lord of the Rings - The Two Towers (12) | EV | US/NZ |
| 3 | Lilo & Stitch (U) | Buena Vista | US |
| 4 | Stuart Little 2 (U) | Columbia TriStar | US |
| 5 | Ice Age (U) | 20th Century Fox | US |
| 6 | Pirates of the Caribbean - The Curse of the Black Pearl (12) | Buena Vista | US |
| 7 | Spiderman (12) | Columbia TriStar | US |
| 8 | Snow Dogs (PG) | Buena Vista | US |
| 9 | Bridget Jones's Diary (15) | Universal | UK/US |
| 10 | Bedknobs and Broomsticks (U) | Buena Vista | US |
| 11 | Mickey's Magical Christmas - Snowed In (U) | Buena Vista | US |
| 12 | Stuart Little (U) | Columbia TriStar | US |
| 13 | Signs (12) | Buena Vista | US |
| 14 | The Lord of the Rings - The Fellowship of the Ring (PG) | EV | US/NZ |
| 15 | Die Another Day | MGM | UK/US |
| 16 | Dirty Dancing (15) | Columbia TriStar | US |
| 17 | Grease (PG) | Paramount | US |
| 18 | Peter Kay - Live at the Bolton Albert Halls (15) | Universal | UK |
| 19 | The Matrix (15) | Warner | US |
| 20 | Willy Wonka & the Chocolate Factory (U) | Warner | US |

Source: Rental Monitor/BVA

## 38 Top 20 Retail DVD Titles in the UK 2003

| | Title | Distributor | Country |
|---|---|---|---|
| 1 | The Lord of the Rings - The Two Towers (12) | EV | US/NZ |
| 2 | Pirates of the Caribbean - The Curse of the Black Pearl (12) | Buena Vista | US |
| 3 | Harry Potter and the Chamber of Secrets (PG) | Warner | UK/US |
| 4 | The Matrix Reloaded (15) | Warner | US |
| 5 | The Lord of the Rings - The Fellowship of the Ring (PG) | EV | US/NZ |
| 6 | Bruce Almighty (12) | Buena Vista | US |
| 7 | Peter Kay - Live at the Bolton Albert Halls (15) | Universal | UK |
| 8 | Die Another Day (12) | MGM | UK/US |
| 9 | X-Men 2 (12) | 20th Century Fox | US |
| 10 | The Lion King (U) | Buena Vista | US |
| 11 | The Matrix (15) | Warner | US |
| 12 | 8 Mile (15) | Universal | US |
| 13 | xXx (12) | Columbia TriStar | US |
| 14 | The Office - The Complete Second Series (-) | BBC | UK |
| 15 | Spiderman (12) | Columbia TriStar | US |
| 16 | Terminator 3 - Rise of the Machines (12) | Columbia TriStar | US |
| 17 | Chicago (12) | Buena Vista | US/Can |
| 18 | Lilo & Stitch (U) | Buena Vista | US |
| 19 | Ocean's Eleven (12) | Warner | US |
| 20 | Signs (12) | Buena Vista | US |

Source: Rental Monitor/BVA

million upward leap, the overall total transactions of 156 million were the lowest for 10 years. The BVA reported that its research had found that some consumers prefer to own DVDs rather than rent them. If this is a trend then it is quite a remarkable one and may spell danger for the whole DVD/Video rental sector. It will be interesting to see to what lengths the rental sector will take to woo consumers back to their stores.

The number of videos requiring cuts by the British Board of Film Classification (BBFC) rose slightly in 2003 from 3.6 per cent to 4 per cent (Table 32). The explanation for this rise came in the increase of R18 videos now under scrutiny. The three rejected titles were *Video Voyeur*; hidden camera footage of a men's changing room which did not have any consent of its participants, *Spy of Darkness*; a Japanese manga animation depicting sexual violence to women, and finally, the depiction of exploitation of vulnerable homeless people in *Bumfights – A Cause For Concern*. A

*The Lord of the Rings towered above the rest in the retail chart*

**39    Top 20 Retail Videos VHS & DVD in the UK 2003**

| | Title | Distributor | Country |
|---|---|---|---|
| 1 | The Lord of the Rings - The Two Towers (12) | EV | US/NZ |
| 2 | Harry Potter and the Chamber of Secrets (PG) | Warner | UK/US |
| 3 | Pirates of the Caribbean - The Curse of the Black Pearl (12) | Buena Vista | US |
| 4 | The Matrix Reloaded (15) | Warner | US |
| 5 | The Lord of the Rings - The Fellowship of the Ring (PG) | EV | US/NZ |
| 6 | Peter Kay - Live at the Bolton Albert Halls (15) | Universal | UK |
| 7 | Lilo & Stitch (U) | Buena Vista | US |
| 8 | Die Another Day (12) | MGM | UK/US |
| 9 | Bruce Almighty (12) | Buena Vista | US |
| 10 | Spiderman (12) | Columbia TriStar | US |
| 11 | The Matrix (15) | Warner | US |
| 12 | The Lion King (U) | Buena Vista | US |
| 13 | 8 Mile (15) | Universal | US |
| 14 | X-Men 2 (12) | 20th Century Fox | US |
| 15 | Signs (12) | Buena Vista | US |
| 16 | Chicago (12) | Buena Vista | US/Can |
| 17 | Staurt Little 2 (U) | Columbia TriStar | US |
| 18 | Ice Age (U) | 20th Century Fox | US |
| 19 | Terminator 3 - Rise of the Machines (12) | Columbia TriStar | US |
| 20 | The Office - the Complete Second Series (-) | BBC | UK |

**Source: Rental Monitor/BVA**

**40    All Time Top 20 Rental Video in the UK 2003**

| | Title | Distributor | Country |
|---|---|---|---|
| 1 | Four Weddings and a Funeral | Columbia TriStar | UK/US |
| 2 | Dirty Dancing | First Independent | US |
| 3 | Basic Instinct | Guild | US |
| 4 | Crocodile Dundee | Fox | USA/Aus |
| 5 | Gladiator | Universal/Columbia | US |
| 6 | Sister Act | Buena Vista | US |
| 7 | Forrest Gump | CIC | US |
| 8 | The Sixth Sense | Buena Vista | US |
| 9 | Home Alone | Fox | US |
| 10 | Ghost | CIC | US |
| 11 | The Green Mile | Universal/Warner | US |
| 12 | Speed | Fox Video | US |
| 13 | Pretty Woman | Buena Vista | US |
| 14 | Braveheart | Fox Guild | US |
| 15 | Jurassic Park | CIC | US |
| 16 | Pulp Fiction | Buena Vista | US |
| 17 | The Silence of the Lambs | Columbia TriStar | US |
| 18 | Bridget Jones's Diary | Universal | US |
| 19 | Robocop | VVL | US |
| 20 | A Fish Called Wanda | MGM | UK/US |

**Source: BVA/Rental Monitor**

TV programme about the last video was nevertheless screened on Five in May 2004, in a typical ploy to cash in on the exploitation.

The BBFC also spent the year embarking on a consultation with members of the public, in order to check that the current guidelines are clear and relevant to modern day users.

As DVD becomes the dominant home entertainment media of choice for the consumer, it is harder to spot any real differences in consumer preferences.

Nevertheless, we are still providing VHS and DVD charts. Fifteen titles are common to both Tables 34 and 35. Both charts are similar with the VHS chart putting *My Big Fat Greek Wedding* at the top instead of *Signs*, which makes it to the top of the DVD Rental chart. The combined table of VHS/DVD tables are quite a fair gauge as to the most popular titles in the Rental market. In this case *Signs* comes out as the most popular Rental film behind *My Big Fat Greek Wedding*. What perhaps is notable about these two titles is to check their relative performance at the UK Box Office in 2002. Both films made it into the lower half of the Top 20 with *Signs* positioned at number 13 and *My Big Fat Greek Wedding* at 15.

Only three British films make it into the combined video and DVD charts – *28 Days Later, Johnny English* and *Reign of Fire*, with *About a Boy* also representing British interests in the VHS chart.

The box office successes of *Harry Potter and the Chamber of Secrets* and *The Lord of the Rings – The Two Towers* are replicated in the Retail charts. Harry Potter topping the VHS and the Lord of the Rings topping the DVD charts. This also repeats the same trend as last year when *Harry*

### 41   All Time Top 20 Retail Video in the UK 2003

| | Title | Distributor | Country |
|---|---|---|---|
| 1 | Titanic | 20th Century Fox | US |
| 2 | Lord of the Rings: Fellowship of the Ring | EV | US/NZ |
| 3 | The Jungle Book | Buena Vista | US |
| 4 | The Lion King | Buena Vista | US |
| 5 | Snow White and the Seven Dwarfs | Buena Vista | US |
| 6 | Shrek | Universal | US |
| 7 | Gladiator | Universal/Columbia | US |
| 8 | Toy Story | Buena Vista | US |
| 9 | The Matrix | Warner | US |
| 10 | Lord of the Rings: The Two Towers | EV | US/NZ |
| 11 | Harry Potter and the Philosopher's Stone | Warner | UK/US |
| 12 | Beauty and the Beast | Buena Vista | US |
| 13 | Dirty Dancing | Columbia TriStar | US |
| 14 | Bridget Jones's Diary | Universal/Columbia | UK/US |
| 15 | Harry Potter and the Chamber of Secrets | Warner | UK/US |
| 16 | The Full Monty | 20th Century Fox | UK/US |
| 17 | Fantasia | Buena Vista | US |
| 18 | 101 Dalmatians | Buena Vista | US |
| 19 | Star Wars | 20th Century Fox | US |
| 20 | Grease | Paramount | US |

**Source: BVA/Official UK Charts**

### 42   Distributors' Share of UK Rental Transactions (%) 2003

| | Distributor | % share |
|---|---|---|
| 1 | Fox Pathé/MGM | 19.28 |
| 2 | Universal | 16.08 |
| 3 | Buena Vista | 15.92 |
| 4 | Columbia TriStar | 13.66 |
| 5 | EV | 9.92 |
| 6 | Warner/Icon/Redbus | 9.90 |
| 7 | Paramount | 5.97 |
| 8 | Momentum | 3.02 |
| 9 | High Fliers/DEJ | 1.55 |
| 10 | Redbus | 1.40 |

Includes DVD and VHS
**Source: Rental Monitor/BVA**

### 43   Video Retail Company Market Share by Volume (%) 2003

| | Distributor | % share |
|---|---|---|
| 1 | Warner | 17.1 |
| 2 | Buena Vista | 13.6 |
| 3 | Universal | 11.2 |
| 4 | 20th Century Fox | 10.2 |
| 5 | Columbia TriStar | 9.9 |
| 6 | EV | 6.1 |
| 7 | Paramount | 5.8 |
| 8 | VCI | 5.2 |
| 9 | MGM | 4.8 |
| 10 | BBC | 3.3 |

Includes DVD and VHS
**Source: BVA/Official UK Charts**

Potter and the Philosophers Stone topped the VHS chart and the Lord of the Rings – The Fellowship of the Ring topped the DVD chart.

Again British film interest boils down to just three titles – Harry Potter and the Chamber of Secrets, Die Another Day (in the DVD and VHS tables) and Bridget Jones's Diary which made it into the chart in VHS format.

Two British comedy videos also break into the Top 20 list. Peter Kay – Live at the Bolton Albert Halls is evident in both formats while those wishing to own The Office – The Complete Second Series preferred the DVD format.

The all-time Retail Chart shows some changes with Titanic finally overtaking The Jungle Book as the most purchased DVD/VHS. There are four new entries in this chart – The Lord of the Rings The Two Towers, Bridget Jones's Diary, Harry Potter and the Chamber of Secrets,

and Grease, which made it back into the chart on the strength of a 25th Anniversary repacking. Look out for more such reissued DVDs in the coming years.

In terms of Distributor's share of the respective markets Fox-Pathe/MGM again led the Rental market with a share of 19.28 per cent featuring titles such as Road to Perdition, 28 Days Later and Phone Booth.

The success of Harry Potter films helped Warner to take a 17.1 per cent share at the top of the Retail market which also showed Buena Vista leaping from an 8.1 per cent share in 2002 up to 13.6 per cent in 2003, helped on its way with the swashbucking family favourite – Pirates of the Caribbean.

## 44     Top 25 Programmes for all Terrestrial Channels 2003

Only top rated episodes of each series are included

| | Title | Channel | TX date | Audience (m) |
|---|---|---|---|---|
| 1 | Coronation Street | ITV1 | 24/02/03 | 19.4 |
| 2 | Eastenders | BBC1 | 29/09/03 | 16.7 |
| 3 | Only Fools and Horses | BBC1 | 25/12/03 | 16.4 |
| 4 | Millionaire Tonight Special | ITV1 | 21/04/03 | 16.1 |
| 5 | Michael Jackson Tonight Special | ITV1 | 03/02/03 | 15.3 |
| 6 | Heartbeat | ITV1 | 12/01/03 | 12.8 |
| 7 | I'm a Celebrity – Get Me Out of Here! | ITV1 | 12/05/03 | 12.7 |
| 8 | Billy Elliot | BBC1 | 01/01/03 | 12.7 |
| 9 | A Touch of Frost | ITV1 | 03/03/03 | 12.2 |
| 10 | The Royal | ITV1 | 19/01/03 | 12.0 |
| 11 | Emmerdale | ITV1 | 10/02/03 | 11.9 |
| 12 | Comic Relief | BBC1 | 14/03/03 | 11.7 |
| 13 | Rosemary and Thyme | ITV1 | 31/08/03 | 11.1 |
| 14 | Pop Idol | ITV1 | 20/12/03 | 11.0 |
| 15 | Cold Feet | ITV1 | 16/03/03 | 10.7 |
| 16 | Prime Suspect 6 | ITV1 | 09/11/03 | 10.5 |
| 17 | UEFA Champions League Live | ITV1 | 23/04/03 | 10.5 |
| 18 | Children in Need | BBC1 | 21/11/03 | 10.5 |
| 19 | The Bill | ITV1 | 30/10/03 | 10.4 |
| 20 | Ten O'Clock News | BBC1 | 21/11/03 | 10.3 |
| 21 | Antiques Roadshow | BBC1 | 09/02/03 | 10.2 |
| 22 | My Family | BBC1 | 04/04/03 | 10.2 |
| 23 | Pompeii – The Last Day | BBC1 | 20/10/03 | 10.1 |
| 24 | Midsomer Murders | ITV1 | 02/11/03 | 10.0 |
| 25 | Casualty | BBC1 | 01/03/03 | 10.0 |

Only the top rated episode of each series is included

**Source: TARiS Taylor Nelson Sofres/BARB**

# Television

Although the emphasis of this year's Handbook is based on the film industry we have included some TV tables, in order to preserve some continuity and in order to assess the terrestrial channels' commitment to UK films.

In the past few years the one-off Christmas special of *Only Fools and Horses* has taken the top honours as the most watched terrestrial TV programme. In 2003 *Coronation Street* took top honours with its grisly serial killer story line featuring Richard Hillman wreaking implausible havoc in Springfield (Table 44). The February episode which saw him plunge himself and his family into a canal, attracted 19.4 million viewers and a 62 per cent audience share. While the family survived, Richard Hillman died in the accident and viewers saw him zipped up into a body bag, presumbably never to return again – but then again in Soaps anything is possible. This was proved by *Eastenders* when 16.7 millions were glued to their sets to see Dirty Den make his unlikely return to the BBC1 soap. This shot *Eastenders* into second spot.

In the end 2003 proved to be a good year for ITV1, with the commercial network taking up 15 positions out of the top 25 programmes.

*Billy Elliot*, screened by the BBC1 on New Year's Day, was the only feature film to make it into the top 20 programme list. It took a big audience of 12.7 million viewers – easily the highest rating amongst the feature films on TV.

ITV1 also dominated the Top Original Drama table building on its usual favourites such as *Heartbeat, A Touch of Frost* and *The Bill*, with the introduction of

**45**

# Top 25 Original Drama Productions 2003

Includes Soap Operas, Series, Serials and UK TV Movies. Audience figures are for highest rated episodes of each production

| | Title | Channel | Producer | Tx date | Audience(m) |
|---|---|---|---|---|---|
| 1 | Coronation Street | ITV1 | Granada | 24/02/03 | 19.4 |
| 2 | Eastenders | BBC1 | BBC | 29/09/03 | 16.7 |
| 3 | Heartbeat | ITV1 | Yorkshire | 12/01/03 | 12.8 |
| 4 | A Touch of Frost | ITV1 | Yorkshire | 03/03/03 | 12.2 |
| 5 | The Royal | ITV1 | Yorkshire | 19/01/03 | 12.0 |
| 6 | Emmerdale | ITV1 | Yorkshire | 10/2/03 | 11.9 |
| 7 | Rosemary and Thyme | ITV1 | Carnival Films | 31/08/03 | 11.1 |
| 8 | Cold Feet | ITV1 | Carlton | 16/03/03 | 10.7 |
| 9 | Prime Suspect 6 | ITV1 | Granada | 09/11/03 | 10.5 |
| 10 | The Bill | ITV1 | Fremantle | 30/10/03 | 10.4 |
| 11 | Midsomer Murders | ITV1 | Bentley Productions | 02/11/03 | 10.0 |
| 12 | Casualty | BBC1 | BBC | 01/03/03 | 10.0 |
| 13 | Jonathan Creek | BBC1 | BBC | 08/03/03 | 9.9 |
| 14 | Holby City | BBC1 | BBC | 16/12/03 | 9.8 |
| 15 | Foyle's War | ITV1 | Greenlit Productions | 07/12/03 | 9.7 |
| 16 | The Booze Cruise | ITV1 | Yorkshire | 07/09/03 | 9.7 |
| 17 | William and Mary | ITV1 | Meridian | 27/04/03 | 9.6 |
| 18 | Monarch of the Glen | BBC1 | Ecosse Films | 28/09/03 | 9.2 |
| 19 | Blue Murder | ITV1 | Granada | 18/05/03 | 8.9 |
| 20 | The Lost Prince | BBC1 | Fremantle | 26/01/03 | 8.9 |
| 21 | Danielle Cable - Eye Witness | ITV1 | Granada | 14/04/03 | 8.6 |
| 22 | Suspicion | ITV1 | Granada | 08/09/03 | 8.6 |
| 23 | Silent Witness | BBC1 | BBC | 25/10/03 | 8.5 |
| 24 | Waking The Dead | BBC1 | BBC | 06/10/03 | 8.4 |
| 25 | Henry VIII | ITV1 | Granada | 12/10/03 | 8.4 |

**Source:TARiS Taylor Nelson Sofres/BARB**

programmes such as *Heartbeat* spin-off *The Royal*, and the unlikely gardening sleuths, *Rosemary and Thyme*. BBC1 offered viewers little in original dramas relying on programmes such as *Casualty* and *Holby City* on the one hand and *Silent Witness* and *Waking the Dead* on the other. The Top 25 demonstrates a dearth of originality in terrestrial TV – in between the Soaps and Reality TV shows lurk hospital dramas, murder mysteries, and detectives of all shapes and sizes.

Certainly, drama on TV is going through a barren patch. US shows (all produced by HBO) such as the *West Wing*, the *Sopranos* and *Six Feet Under*, merely serve as a reminder of how inarticulate and unimaginative our own drama output has become.

One observation over the past few years about low-budget British films is that they would have been more successful as made-for TV dramas. The reluctance of terrestrial broadcasters to show these films have promoted the UK Film Council to lobby for voluntary quotas of British films to be screened and called for broadcasters to become more involved in film production.

The list of TV premieres of feature films funded by terrestrial broadcasters throws up an interesting selection of titles. Many of these may not have been strong enough to compete at the cinema box office but deserve a better outing on the small screen. Sadly, the majority of these features are consigned to late night schedules with primetime film slots being allotted to Hollywood blockbusters or the perennial James Bond season on ITV1.

Beyond *Billy Elliot* the BBC1's most successful screening was *New Tricks* which attracted an audience of 6.7 million, while *Little Voice* proved to be the most popular film shown on BBC2.

# UK TV Films Premiered 2003

British TV films, single dramas and drama documentaries shown on UK terrestrial TV during 2003. Single feature length films shown on British television and transmissions of feature films funded by UK broadcasters which may have had a previous theatrical release are marked by *

| Title | Tx date | Audience (m) | Writer | Director |
|---|---|---|---|---|
| **BBC1** | | | | |
| Billy Elliot* | 1-Jan | 12.7 | Lee Hall | Stephen Daldry |
| The Gathering Storm | 5-Jan | 4.2 | Larry Ramin, Hugh Whitemore | Richard Loncraine |
| Up'n'Under* | 23-Feb | 1.8 | John Godber | John Godber |
| New Tricks | 27-Mar | 6.7 | Nigel McCrery, Roy Mitchell | Graham Theakston |
| Kevin and Perry Go Large* | 17-May | 5.5 | Dave Cummings, Harry Enfield | Ed Bye |
| Arthur's Dyke* | 23-Aug | 2.7 | Robb Stringle | Gerry Poulson |
| Enemy at the Gates* | 29-Nov | 3.9 | Jean-Jacques Annaud, Alain Godard | Jean-Jacques Annaud |
| The Young Visiters | 26-Dec | 3.9 | Partick Barlow | David Yates |
| **BBC2** | | | | |
| Little Voice* | 2-Jan | 5.8 | Jim Cartwright, Mark Herman | Mark Herman |
| Wild About Harry* | 15-Jan | 2.1 | Colin Bateman | Declan Lowney |
| Bedrooms and Hallways* | 26-Jan | 0.4 | Robert Farrar | Rose Troche |
| Among Giants* | 1-Feb | 0.9 | Simon Beaufoy | Sam Miller |
| GMT Greenwich Mean Time* | 23-Feb | 0.3 | Simon Mirren | John Strickland |
| This Little Life | 19-Mar | 1.5 | Rosemary Kay | Sarah Gavron |
| When Brendan Met Trudy | 22-Mar | 1.1 | Roddy Doyle | Kieron J Walsh |
| Rehab | 26-Mar | 0.9 | Rona Munro | Antonia Bird |
| The Other Boleyn Girl | 28-Mar | 2.7 | Philippa Gregory, Philippa Lowthorpe | Philippa Lowthorpe |
| Ordinary Decent Criminal* | 22-Jun | 1.1 | Gerard Stembridge | Thaddeus O'Sullivan |
| Love Again | 26-Jul | 1.6 | Richard Cottan | Susanna White |
| Felicia's Journey* | 3-Aug | 0.8 | William Trevor, Atom Egoyan | Atom Egoyan |
| Eroica | 4-Oct | 1.6 | Nick Dear | Simon Cellan Jones |
| The Trench* | 2-Nov | 0.5 | William Boyd | William Boyd |
| Iris* | 20-Dec | 3.1 | John Bayley, Richard Eyre, Charles Wood | Richard Eyre |
| **ITV1** | | | | |
| Pollyanna | 1-Jan | 7.5 | Eleanor H. Porter, Simon Nye | Sarah Harding |
| B Monkey* | 14-Jan | 0.8 | Andrew Davies, Chloe King, Michael Radford, Michael Thomas | Michael Radford |
| Unconditional Love | 20-Jan | 7.5 | Chris Lang | Ferdinand Fairfax |
| Loving You | 24-Feb | 7.4 | Matthew Hall, Margaret Leroy | Jean Stewart |
| Lucky Jim | 11-Apr | 4.2 | Kingsley Amis, Jack Rosenthal | Robin Sheppard |
| Danielle Cable - Eye Witness | 14-Apr | 8.6 | Kate Brooke, Terry Winsor | Adrian Shergold |
| Watermelon | 16-Apr | 5.9 | Marian Keyes | Kieron J. Walsh |
| The Booze Cruise | 7-Sep | 9.7 | Brian Leveson, Paul Minett | Paul Seed |
| Carla | 15-Sep | 7.3 | Joanna Hines, Barbara Machin | Diarmuid Lawrence |
| Margery and Gladys | 21-Sep | 7.9 | John Flanagan, Andrew McCulloch | Geoffrey Sax |
| Boudica | 28-Sep | 5.4 | Andrew Davies | Bill Anderson |
| Sparkling Cyanide | 5-Oct | 6.6 | Agatha Christie, Laura Lamson | Tristram Powell |
| Gifted | 29-Oct | 6.2 | Kay Mellor | Douglas Mackinnon |
| Reversals | 19-Nov | 4.9 | Tim Loane | David Evans |
| Up on the Roof* | 10-Dec | 0.7 | Simon Moore, Jane Prowse | Simon Moore |
| The Crooked Man | 17-Dec | 5.7 | Philip Davison | David Drury |
| Promoted to Glory | 21-Dec | 8.0 | Rob Heyland | Richard Spence |
| The Return | 30-Dec | 9.1 | Kate O'Riordan | Dermot Boyd |
| The Brides in the Bath | 31-Dec | 5.4 | Glenn Chandler | Harry Bradbeer |
| **Channel 4** | | | | |
| Tea With Mussolini* | 1-Jan | 2.2 | Franco Zeffirelli, John Mortimer | Franco Zeffirelli |
| The Match* | 23-Feb | 0.2 | Mick Davis | Mick Davis |
| Sexy Beast* | 30-Mar | 2.2 | Louis Mellis, David Scinto, Andrew Michael Jolley | Jonathan Glazer |
| Rancid Aluminium* | 7-Apr | 0.2 | James Hawes | Edward Thomas |
| My Life So Far* | 14-Jun | 0.2 | Denis Forman, Simon Donald | Hugh Hudson |
| Do I Love You? | 30-Jul | 0.2 | Lisa Gornick | Lisa Gornick |
| Straw Dogs* | 10-Aug | 1.7 | Gordon Williams, David Zelag Goodman, Sam Peckinpah | Sam Peckinpah |
| Don't Go Breaking My Heart* | 7-Sep | 0.2 | Geoff Morrow | Willi Patterson |
| The Deal | 28-Sep | 1.5 | Peter Morgan | Stephen Frears |
| Adult at 14: Pleasureland | 16-Nov | 2.6 | Helen Blakeman | Brian Percival |
| Orphans* | 17-Nov | 0.3 | Peter Mullan | Peter Mullan |
| Little Otik* | 25-Nov | 0.2 | Jan Svankmajer | Jan Svankmajer |
| Get Real* | 2-Dec | 0.4 | Patrick Wilde | Simon Shore |
| Gregory's Two Girls* | 8-Dec | 0.3 | Bill Forsyth | Bill Forsyth |
| Late Night Shopping* | 27-Dec | 0.2 | Jack Lothian | Saul Metzstein |
| **Five** | | | | |
| Greenfingers* | 3-Jul | 1.4 | Joel Hershman | Joel Hershman |
| Snatch* | 1-Oct | 2.2 | Guy Ritchie | Guy Ritchie |
| Hear the Silence | 15-Dec | 1.3 | Tim Prager, Andrew Wakefield | Tim Fywell |
| Jim's Gift | 23-Dec | 0.1 | Tony Clarke | Bob Keen |

## 47 Top 25 Feature Films Shown on Terrestrial TV 2003

| | Title | Country | Year | Channel | Audience (m) |
|---|---|---|---|---|---|
| 1 | Billy Elliot | UK/France | 2000 | BBC1 | 12,655.3 |
| 2 | Cast Away | US | 2000 | BBC1 | 9,599.2 |
| 3 | The Sixth Sense | US | 1999 | ITV1 | 9,054.5 |
| 4 | Indiana Jones and the Last Crusade | US | 1989 | BBC1 | 8,792.6 |
| 5 | Dr. Dolittle | US | 1998 | ITV1 | 8,213.1 |
| 6 | The World is Not Enough | UK/US | 1999 | ITV1 | 7,825.6 |
| 7 | The Thomas Crown Affair | US | 1999 | BBC1 | 7,655.4 |
| 8 | The Full Monty | UK/US | 1997 | ITV1 | 7,569.6 |
| 9 | Goldeneye | UK/US | 1995 | ITV1 | 7,455.4 |
| 10 | Meet the Parents | US | 2000 | BBC1 | 7,400.2 |
| 11 | X-Men | US | 2000 | ITV1 | 7,220.1 |
| 12 | Tomorrow Never Dies | UK/US | 1997 | ITV1 | 7,177.5 |
| 13 | Independence Day | US | 1996 | BBC1 | 7,128.3 |
| 14 | Billy Elliot | UK/France | 2000 | BBC1 | 7,066.9 |
| 15 | Double Jeopardy | US | 1999 | ITV1 | 6,895.4 |
| 16 | Kindergarten Cop | US | 1990 | ITV1 | 6,893.4 |
| 17 | The Bone Collector | US | 2000 | BBC1 | 6,844.2 |
| 18 | Chicken Run | UK/US | 2000 | BBC1 | 6,828.2 |
| 19 | Raiders of the Lost Ark | US | 1981 | BBC1 | 6,778.9 |
| 20 | Men in Black | US | 1997 | BBC1 | 6,775.8 |
| 21 | Mission: Impossible II | US | 2000 | ITV1 | 6,772.1 |
| 22 | Kiss the Girls | US | 1998 | BBC1 | 6,717.6 |
| 23 | Tomorrow Never Dies | UK/US | 1997 | ITV1 | 6,701.3 |
| 24 | Indiana Jones and the Temple of Doom | US | 1984 | BBC1 | 6,695.7 |
| 25 | The Whole Nine Yards | US | 2000 | ITV1 | 6,637.8 |

Source:TARiS Taylor Nelson Sofres/BARB

The Booze Cruise proved to be ITV1's top feature film with an audience of 9.7 million. Channel 4 offered an interesting variety of films from the underestimated Sexy Beast, to the infamous Rancid Alluminum. Meanwhile, Five who didn't show a single recent British film in 2002 made up for lost time with four TV premieres, the most watched being Snatch which drew an audience of 2.2 million.

One interesting observation about the Top 25 Feature films shown on Terrestrial TV in 2003 was the double showings over the year of Billy Elliot (with audiences of 12.6 million and 7 million) and Tomorrow Never Dies (with audiences of 7.1 million and 6.7 million). Five films from last year (including all the Indiana Jones films) appeared in last year's top 25 which demonstrates the enduring audience appeal of Hollywood blockbusters.

Billy Elliot – so popular that they screened it twice in one year

# Further Reading

Statistical sources for film, television, video/dvd cannot be found, alas, in one single encyclopaedic source. They are renowned for their disparate and partially submerged nature. In some cases they have not even been collated, let alone re-packaged for ravenous researchers and deadline led students.

Searching techniques can be nothing more insightful than ploughing through the 'Three Screens' of Screen International, Screen Digest and Screen Finance, the main UK trade journals for the film industry, for their statistical bone marrow.

Below are some of the most authoritative well used and, needless to say, expensive sources, which have been consulted to compile the tables in the above section. They are based on the holdings of the bfi National Library and the hard won experience of its staff. Some are available for free and even online. It also contains some further reading suggestions to complement the annual commentary. Compiled by Sean Delaney

## Statistics Sources

### British Films Catalogue 2004
British Council.
This annual listing of features, documentary, short, and animation films is a vital tool in calculating the notoriously sensitive number of British films produced in a year. Regularly updated online at: www.britfilms.com

### BVA Yearbook 2004
London: British Video Association, 2004
Outside expensive reports and the trade journals, the only source for UK video/DVD data on sales, market share, genre etc. Also includes amusing pictures of their Christmas party. Some data online at: www.bva.org.uk

### Cinemagoing 12
Leicester: Dodona Research, 2004
Now in its 12th edition, this is the key report on the UK (& Ireland) exhibition sector. It contains a market overview, company profiles with an abundance of tables. Dodona Research publishes similarly well-regarded reports for Europe and the rest of the world. www.dodona.co.uk

## Film in the UK 2002

### Statistical Yearbook
UK Film Council, 2003.
UKFC Compilation of 'BFI Handbook' style statistics for the UK film industry.

### GB Cinema exhibitors
National Statistics, 2001.
These statistics are now online at www.statistics.gov.uk
Enter exhibitors in search field to get tot GB Cinemas Inquiry 1950-2001 (http://www.statistics.gov.uk/CCI/SearchRes.asp?term=exhibitors)

## International Service Transactions of the Film & Television Industries, 2002
National Statistics, 2003.
Available at www.statistics.gov.uk
(Formerly known as "Overseas transactions of the film and television industry").

### Nielsen/EDI Database Reports
London: Nielsen/EDI.
The primary source used by the *bfi* National Library for UK and US Box Office data since the 1980s. Updated weekly.

### Yearbook: film, television, video and multimedia in Europe
European Audiovisual Observatory, 2002
Five volume set offers covering a range of data on the European audiovisual industries including film production, distribution, admissions, etc. (Formerly known as: Statistical Yearbook: cinema, television and new media in Europe).

## Web Based Sources

### Arts Council of England annual report 2003
www.artscouncil.org.uk/information/publications_title.php

### British Board of Film Classification annual report 2003
www.bbfc.co.uk

### British Film Institute annual review 2002/2003
www.bfi.org.uk/about/review/

bfi Facts on Film - Statistics
www.bfi.org.uk/facts/stats/index.html
Features film and television statistics collated by the bfi Information Service for the bfi Handbook.

bfi Film Links Gateway
www.bfi.org.uk/gateway
Film Links Gateway provides links to
the most useful and interesting
websites relating to film

## British Video Association
www.bva.org.uk
Lists DVD and Video charts &
releases plus a useful listing of video
distributors and statistical
information.

## European cinema yearbook 2003
Milan: MEDIA Salles, 2004
Now available on web only:
www.mediasalles.it/yearbook.htm

## Eurostat
www.europa.eu.int/comm/eurostat
European Information service
offering a variety of free and paid
services. The keyword 'Film' retrieves
recent statistics on cinema
attendance, audiovisual services, the
European TV broadcasting market
etc.

## Film Distributors' Association
www.launchingfilms.com
Contains current & forthcoming
releases, current top 10 films, and
recent film statistics, which include
top 50 UK films for all time.

## Hollywood Reporter
www.hollywoodreporter.com/thr/ind
ex.jsp
Headline and limited article content
available for free, but users will need
to subscribe for full stories. Box office
grosses are made available every
Sunday. Includes the Hollywood
Reporter Film 500

## Screendaily
www.screendaily.com/
Daily on-line news service for the
film industry. It features global news,
film reviews and box office info from
every major territory. Free of charge
and with a useful keyword search
facility.

## UK Film Council Annual Review 2002/03
www.ukfilmcouncil.org.uk/
filmindustry/

## Variety
www.variety.com
Holds box office information on
current top 60 US films and current
news and reviews.

# Other Sources from the bfi

**Guide to the Annuals Collection,
by Christophe Dupin**
Excellent guide to these sources held
in the bfi National Library.
(Available at:www.bfi.org.uk/library/
collections/ annuals )

**European film industries, by Anne
Jackel**
British Film Institute, 2003.
ISBN 0851709478

**Genre and contemporary
Hollywood, by Steve Neale**
British Film Institute, 2002
ISBN 0851708862

**Global Hollywood, by Toby Miller,
et. al.**
British Film Institute, 2001.
ISBN 0851708463  (revised edition
due out November 2004)

**Global Media Atlas, by  Mark
Balnaves & Donald James**
British Film Institute, 2001.
ISBN 0851708609

**Hollywood abroad: audiences and
cultural exchange, by Melvyn Stokes
and Richard Maltby**
British Film Institute, July 2004.
ISBN 1844570517

**Odeon Cinemas 2: from J. Arthur
Rank to the multiplex, by Allen Eyles**
British Film Institute, due October
2004.
ISBN 1844570487

**Producing the Goods? UK film
production since 1991: an
information briefing, by
Phil Wickham.**
bfi National Library, 2003.
ISBN 1844570045
New survey of the British film
industry in the 1990s with very useful
statistics.

**The stats: an overview of the film,
television, video and DVD
industries in the UK 1990-2001,** by
Erinna Mettler and Philip Wickham
with Matt Ker
*bfi* National Library, 2003.
ISBN 1844570177
Compilation of statistics and tables
from the *bfi* Film and Television
Handbook.

# UK Film Council Documents

(All available at:www.ukfilmcouncil.
org.uk/ filmindustry )

**A bigger future: the UK film Skills
Strategy**
UKFC/Skillset, 2003.

**Building a sustainable UK film
industry: a presentation to the UK
film industry, a presentation by Alan
Parker**
(5th November 2002).

**Developing UK film talent: a
comprehensive skills survey of the
UK film industry**
Skillset/ UK Film Council, 2003.

**Film Council specialised exhibition
and distribution strategy**
UK Film Council, 2001.

**Film in England: a development
strategy for film and the moving
image in the English regions**
Film Council, 2000.

**Post-Production in the UK**
UK Film Council, 2003.

**The Relph report: a study for the
Film Council examining the costs of
lower budget UK films and their
value in the world market.**
UK Film Council, 2002.

**Success through diversity and
inclusion**
UK Film Council, 2003.

**Three years on: a consultation on
our funding and policy priorities,
April 2004 to March 2007**
UK Film Council, 2003.

**Towards a Sustainable UK Film
Industry**
Film Council, 2000.

**Working together, making a
difference: the work of the public
film agencies in the UK**
UK Film Council, 2002.

# Suggested further reading and other useful sources

**Always look on the bright side of life** [the story of Handmade Films], by Robert Sellers
Metro Publishing, 2003.
ISBN 1843580640

**Art of the deal: the essential guide to business affairs for television, film and new media producers** (3rd ed), by Dorothy Viljeon.
PACT, 2002.
ISBN 0952958635

**The British Film Industry, Sixth Report of Session 2002-03** (3 vols.) [HC 667- I;II;III]
House of Commons Culture, Media and Sport Committee (Chair: Gerald Kaufman), 2003.

**British Film Industry: Government Response to the Select Committee Report on the British Film Industry**
Session 2002-2003.
DCMS, 2003.

**The British film business**, by Bill Baillieu and John Goodchild
Chichester: John Wiley & Sons, 2002.
ISBN 0471499188
Useful introduction on the workings of the British film industry since 1896.

**Creative Industries Mapping Document 2001**
Department for Culture, Media and Sport, 2002.

**Dazzled by Disney?: the global Disney audiences project**, edited by Janet Wasko et. al.
Leicester University Press, 2001.
ISBN 0718502604

**Digital cinema factbook**, by Katharine Wright
Dodona Research, 2004.

**Entertainment industry economics: a guide for financial analysis** (5th ed), by Harold L. Vogel.
Cambridge University Press, 2001.
ISBN 0521792649

**Film Council: improving access to, and education about, the moving image through the British Film Institute**, Forty-seventh report of Session 2002/3. House of Commons Committee of Public Accounts [HC 685], 2003.

**Films in theatres: the theatrical market for films in the United States and Europe**, by Karsten Grummitt and Sarah Brown
Dodona, 2003.
Analysis of European films & co-productions in US and Europe and other markets.

**Global culture: media, arts, policy, and globalization**, edited by Diana Crane et. al.
Routledge, 2002.
ISBN 0415932300

**Global Film: Exhibition & Distribution** (6th ed), by Andy Thomas & Simon Dyson
Informa Media Group, 2003.
Report covering forecasts, digital cinema and overviews for major territories

**Hollywood economics: how extreme uncertainty shapes the film industry**, by Arthur De Vany
Routledge, 2004.
ISBN 0415312612

**How Hollywood works**, by Janet Wasko
Sage, 2003
ISBN 0761968148

**Listening to the past, speaking to the future: report of the Archives Task Force**
Museums, Libraries and Archives Council, 2004.
ISBN 1903743494

**The movie game: the film business in Britain, Europe and America**, by Martin Dale
Cassell, 1997.
ISBN 0304333875

**My first movie**, edited by Stephen Lowenstein
Faber, 2000.
ISBN 0571196691

**Screen Digest report on the implication of digital technology for the film industry.**
Department for Culture, Media & Sport/Screen Digest, 2002.

**Screen traffic: movies, multiplexes, and global culture**, by Charles R.
Acland
Duke University Press, 2003.
ISBN 0822331632

**Understanding media economics**, by Gillian Doyle
Sage, 2002.
ISBN 076196875X

# Key Periodicals

Hollywood Reporter (Int'l ed), (US, weekly)
PACT magazine (UK, monthly)
Screen Digest (UK, monthly)
Screen Finance (UK, fortnightly)
Screen International (UK, weekly)
Sight and Sound (UK, monthly)

The latest listing of current periodicals held by the bfi National Library (May 2004) is available at: www.bfi.org.uk/library/collections/periodicals

# ARCHIVES AND FILM LIBRARIES

Compiled by Nathalie Sergent

## International Organisations

### FIAF
### (International Federation of Film Archives)
1 Rue Defacqz
1000 Brussels
Tel: (32) 2 538 3065
Fax: (32) 2 534 4774
email: info@fiafnet.org
Website: www.fiafnet.org
Christian Dimitriu, Senior Administrator
Founded in 1938, FIAF (Federation Internationale des Archives du Film) is a collaborative association of the world's leading film archives whose purpose is to ensure the proper preservation and showing of motion pictures. More than 130 archives in over 60 countries collect, restore, and exhibit films and cinema documentation spanning the entire history of film. It also publishes handbooks on film archiving practice which can be obtained from the above address

### FIAT/IFTA
### (International Federation of Television Archives)
email: office@fiatifta.org
Website: www.fiatifta.org
IFTA was set up in Rome in 1977, by ARD (Germany), BBC (UK), INA (France) and RAI (Italy). Gathering 180 members coming from over 70 countries, FIAT/IFTA is presently the most important professional organisation in the field of broadcasting archives. Its membership is drawn from public and commercial broadcasters, national audiovisual archives and technical companies catering to the broacasting industry. Key areas of professional concern are preservation; migration policies to the digital environment: metadata, cataloguing and documentation; media management, provision for access to archived materials; commercial exploitation of these archives; encouragement of audiovisual production based on archives; addressing of related issues such as Rights and Intellectual Property Rights

## European Archives

Below are some European Film Archives of countries in the European Union. For more specialised information consult *Film and Television Collections in Europe – The MAP-TV Guide* published by Blueprint

### AUSTRIA

**Filmarchiv Austria**
Audiovisuelles Zentrum Wien
Obere Augartenstraße 1
1020 Wien
Tel: (43) 1 216 13 10
Fax: (43) 1 216 1300-100
email: augarten@filmarchiv.at
Website: www.filmarchiv.at
Mag. Ernst Kieninger, Head of Archive

### BELGIUM

**Cinematheque Royale de Belgique/Koninklijk Belgisch Filmarchief (Royal Film Archives)**
Palais des Beaux-Arts (2nd Floor)
Rue Ravenstein, 23
1000 Bruxelles
Tel: (32) 02 507 83 70
Fax: (32) 02 513 12 72
email: cinematheque@ledoux.be
Website: www.ledoux.be
Gabrielle Claes, Curator

### CYPRUS

Website: www.hri.org/cypio
At present being set up and organised by the Ministry of the Interior

### CZECH REPUBLIC

**Narodni filmovy archiv**
Malesicka 12
Prague 3, 130 00
email: film.historici@nfa.cz
Website: www.nfa.cz

### DENMARK

**Der Danske Filminstitut**
Bibliotek e Filmarkivet
Gothersgade 55

1123 Copenhagen K
Tel: (45) 33 74 34 00
Fax: (45) 33 74 34 03
email: dfi@dfi.dk
Website: www.dfi.dk

## ESTONIA

### Estonian Filmarchive

Ristiku 84
Tallinn 10318
Tel: (372) 693 8613
Fax: (372) 693 8611
email: filmiarhiiv@ra.ee
Website: www.filmi.arhiiv.ee

## FINLAND

### Suomen Elokuva-Arkisto

Pursimiehenkatu 29-31A
00151 Helsinki
Tel: (358) 9 615 400
Fax: (358) 9 615 402 42
email: sea@sea.fi
Website: www.sea.fi

## FRANCE

### Archives du Film du Centre National de la Cinematographie

7 bis rue Alexandre Turpault
78390 Bois d'Arcy Cedex
Tel: (33) 1 34 14 80 00
Fax: (33) 1 34 60 52 25
email: michelle.aubert@cnc.fr
Website: www.cnc.fr
Michelle Aubert, Curator

## GERMANY

### Bundesarchiv-Filmarchiv

Furstenwalder Allee 401
12589 Berlin
Tel: (49) 1888 7770 920
Fax: (49) 1888 7770 999
email: filmarchiv@barch.bund.de
Website: www.bundesarchiv.de
Hans Gunter Voigt, Access

## GREECE

### Teniothiki Tis Elladas

1 Kanari Street
Athens 10671
Tel: (30) 1 361 2046
Fax: (30) 1 362 8468
email: tain@otenet.gr
Website: www.tte.gr

## HUNGARY

### Magyar Nemzeti Filmarchivum

Hungarian National Film Archives
1021 Budapest, Budakeszi ut 51/E
Tel: (361) 394-1322 / 394-1018

email: filmintezet@ella.hu
Website: www.filmintezet.hu

## IRELAND

### Irish Film Archive

6 Eustace Street
Temple Bar Dublin 2
Tel: (353) 1 679 5744
Fax: (353) 1 677 8755
email: info@irishfilm.ie
Website: www.irishfilm.ie
Kasandra O'Connell, Head of Archives

## ITALY

### Cineteca Nazionale

Centro Sperimentale di Cinematografia
Via Tuscolana 1524
00173 Roma
Tel: (39) 06 722 941
Fax: (39) 06 7211619
email: info@snc.it
Website: www.snc.it/fondazione/contatti.asp

## LATVIA

### Latvia State Archive of Audiovisual Documents

Smerla iela 5
1006, Rīga
Tel: (371) 7529 855
Fax: (371) 7529954
email: fonds@parks.lv
Websites: www.latfilma.lv
www.arhivi.lv/engl/en-lvas-frame.htm

## LITHUANIA

### Lithuania Theatre, Music and Cinema

Cinema Department and Collections
4 Vilniaus str.
2001 Vilnius
Tel: (370) 226 224 06
email: itmkm@tikas.lt
Website: http://teatras.mch.mii.lt

## LUXEMBOURG

### Cinemathèque Municipale de Luxembourg

Ville de Luxembourg
10 rue Eugène Ruppert
2453 Luxembourg
Tel: (352) 4796 2644
Fax: (352) 407 519
email: cinematheque@vdl.lu
Claude Bertemes, Curator

## NETHERLANDS

### Nederlands Filmmuseum

Vondelpark 3
Postbus 74782
1070 BT Amsterdam
Tel: (31) 20 589 1400
Fax: (31) 20 683 3401
email: info@filmmuseum.nl
Website: www.filmmuseum.nl

## POLAND

### Archiwum Dokumentacji Mechanicznej

ul. Swietojerska 24
00-202 Warszawa
Tel/fax: (48) 22 831-1736
Website:
www.piasa.org/polisharchives/warsaw
avr.html

## PORTUGAL

### Cinemateca Portuguesa – Museu do Cinemateca

Rua Barata Salgueiro, 39
1269-059 Lisbon
Tel: (351) 21 359 62 00
Fax: (351 )21 352 31 80
email: cinemateca@cinemateca.pt
Website: www.cinemateca.pt

## SLOVAK REPUBLIC

### Slovensky filmovy ustav Slovak Film Institute

Grosslingova 32
81109 Bratislava
Tel: (421) 571 015 25
Fax: (21) 527 332 14
email: filmsk@sfu.sk
Website: www.filmsk.sk
www.sfu.sk

## SLOVENIA

### Arhiv Republike Slovenije

Slovene Film Archive
Zvezdarska 1 p.p.21
1127 Ljubljana
Tel: (386) 1 241 4229
Fax: (386) 1 241 4269
Alojz Trsan, Head of Archive
Website: www.sigov.si/ars

## SPAIN

### Filmoteca Espanola

Magdalena 10
28012 Madrid
Tel: (34) 91 467 26 00
Fax: (34) 91 467 26 11
email: filmoteca@filmoteca.mcu.es
Website:
www.cultura.mecd.es/cine/film/filmot

eca.jsp
Jose Maria Prado, Director

## SWEDEN

### Svenska Filminstitutet - Cinemateket
Filmhuset
Borgvagen 1-5
10252 Stockholm
Tel: (46)  8 665 11 00
Fax: (46) 8 661 18 20
email: info@sfi.se
Website: www.sfi.se
Jan-Erik Billinger, Head of Cinemateket

# National Archives

### British Film Institute (Incorporating The National Film and Television Archive)
British Film Institute
J. Paul Getty Jnr. Conservation Centre
Kingshill Way
Berkhamsted
Herts HP4 3TP
Tel: 01442 876301
Fax: 01442 289112
Website: www.bfi.org.uk
Heather Stewart, Head of Access
David Pierce, Curator NFTVA
The National Film and Television Archive contains more than 275,000 films and 210,000 TV programmes, dating from 1895. Related collections of stills, posters, designs, scripts and printed ephemera such as marketing materials, technology, props and costumes have been assembled alongside the software to give added context and meaning

### Imperial War Museum
Film and Video Archive
Lambeth Road
London SE1 6HZ
Tel: 020 7416 5320
Fax: 020 7416 5374
email: filmcommercial@iwm.org.uk
email: film@iwm.org.uk (non-commercial enquiries)
Website: www.iwm.org.uk
www.iwmcollections.org.uk (databases)
The national museum of modern conflict, illustrating and recording all aspects of modern war. The Archive reflects these terms of reference with an extensive collection of film and video material, which is widely used by historians and by film and television companies

### Scottish Screen Archive
1 Bowmont Gardens
Glasgow G12 9LR
Tel: 0141 337 7400
Fax: 0141 337 7413
email: archive@scottishscreen.com
Website:
www.scottishscreen.com/archive
Janet McBain: Curator
Enquiries  Tel: 0141 337 7400 (or email)
Almost exclusively non-fiction film, the collection dates from 1896 to the present day and concerns aspects of Scottish social, cultural and industrial history. Available to broadcasters, programme makers, educational users and researchers. Access charges and conditions available on request

### National Screen and Sound Archive of Wales
The National Library of Wales
Aberystwyth
Ceredigion SY23 3BU
Tel: 01970 632828
Fax: 01970 632544
email: agssc@llgc.org.uk
Website:
www.screenandsound.llgc.org.uk
Contact: Iestyn Hughes
The Archive locates, preserves and catalogues film and video material relating to Wales. The collection is made accessible where possible for research and viewing. The Archive is part of The National Library of Wales, Aberystwyth

# Regional Archives

## East Anglian Film Archive
The Archive Centre
Martineau Lane
Norwich NR1 2DQ
Tel: 01603 592 664
Fax: 01603 593475
email: eafa@uea.ac.uk
Website: www.uea.ac.uk/eafa
David Cleveland, Director
Jane Alvey, Deputy Director
Phil Butcher, Film Archivist
Established in 1976, EAFA was the
first regional film archive in the UK.
Preserving both fiction and non-
fiction, amateur and professional
films, television and video material
showing life and work in
Bedfordshire, Cambridgeshire, Essex,
Hertfordshire, Norfolk and Suffolk.
Expertise in the repair, conservation,
printing and telecine of small gauge
film, up to 16mm. EAFA also teaches
future film archivists on its MA in
Film Archiving, in conjunction with
English and American Studies at UEA

## North West Film Archive
Manchester Metropolitan University
Minshull House
47-49 Chorlton Street
Manchester M1 3EU
Tel: 0161 247 3097
Fax: 0161 247 3098
email: n.w.filmarchive@mmu.ac.uk
Website: www.nwfa.mmu.ac.uk
Marion Hewitt, Acting Director
Enquiries:  Jo Abley
Preserves moving images showing life
in the North West and operates as a
public regional archive. Urban and
industrial themes are particularly well
illustrated. Online film and video
catalogue at the Archive's websiteThe
Archive cares for over 29,000 items
from the pioneer days of film in the
mid 1890s to video production of the
present day.

## Northern Region Film and Television Archive
c/o Tyne and Wear Archives Service
Blanford House
Blanford Square
Newcastle upon Tyne NE1 4JA
Tel: 0191 2772250
Fax: 0191 230 2614
email: isa@nrfta.org.uk
Website: www.nrfta.org.uk
Middlesbrough Office:
Northern Region Film and
Television Archive
c/o School of Arts and Media

University of Teesside
Middlesbrough
Tees Valley TS1 3BA
Tel: 01642 384022
Fax:  01642 384099
Contact: For access enquiries and
depositing material
contact Lisa Bond
Tel: 0191 2772250
email: lisa@nrfta.org.uk
The NRFTA was founded in 1998 in
order to collect, preserve and provide
access to moving images of historical,
social and cultural relevance to an
area covering Tyneside, Teesside,
Cumbria, Northumberland and
County Durham.  The bulk of its
current holdings (almost entirely
non-fiction) consist of BBC North-
East news footage from 1958-72, the
news and documentary output of
Tyne-Tees and Border Television and
the productions of Trade Films, a
Newcastle-based unit whose output is
concerned with industry, in
particular coal mining and its
community

## South East Film & Video Archive
University of Brighton
Faculty of Arts and Architecture
Grand Parade
Brighton BN2 0JY
Tel: 01273 643213
Fax: 01273 643214
email: sefva@brighton.ac.uk
Website: www.bton.ac.uk/sefva/
Ine van Dooren, Moving Image
Archivist
Established in 1992, SEFVA collects,
preserves and promotes films,
videotapes and digital material made
in the four counties of Surrey, Kent,
East Sussex and West Sussex and the
Unitary Authorities of Brighton &
Hove and Medway. SEFVA mounts
over 60 presentations each year,
organised for fim and video clubs,
specialist societies, museums,
educaton centres and record offices.

## South West Film and Television Archive
Melville Building
Royal William Yard
Stonehouse
Plymouth
Devon PL1 3RP
Tel: 01752 202650
Fax: 01752 205025
email: enquiries@tswfta.co.uk
Website: www.tswfta.co.uk
Holds south western film material

and includes three television
collections covering the period 1961
to 1992 - Westward Television,
Television South West and BBC
South West

## Wessex Film and Sound Archive
Hampshire Record Office
Sussex Street
Winchester SO23 8TH
Tel: 01962 847742
Fax: 01962 878681
email: david.lee@hants.gov.uk
Website: www.hants.gov.uk/record-
office/film
David Lee, Film and Sound Archivist
WFSA was set up in 1988 by
Hampshire Archives Trust. Preserves
and makes publicly accessible for
research, films, video and sound
recordings of local interest to central
southern England

## Yorkshire Film Archive
York St John College
Lord Mayor's Walk
York YO31 7EX
Tel: 01904 716550
Fax: 01904 716552
email: yfa@yorksj.ac.uk
Website:
www.yorkshirefilmarchive.com
http://www.movinghistory.ac.uk/arch
ives/ya/collection.html
Exists to locate, preserve and show
film about the Yorkshire region.
Material dates from 1897 and
includes newsreels, documentaries,
advertising and amateur films

# Newsreel, Production and Stock Shot Libraries

## Archive Film Agency
49 South Croxted Road
West Dulwich
London SE21 8AZ
Tel: 020 8670 3618
Fax: 020 8670 3618
email: acrchivefilmagency@email.com
Website: www.archivefilmagency.com
Bob Geoghegan
Film from 1898, including a current worldwide stock shot library. Specialists in early fiction, newsreel, documentary, Music Hall, Midlands, Yorkshire, British 1930s stills. Cassette services

## Associated Press Television News (APTN)
The Interchange
Oval Road
Camden Lock
London NW1 7DZ
Tel: 020 7482 7400
Fax: 020 7413 8302
email: aptnbookings@ap.org
Website: www.aptn.com
Leading supplier of worldwide video news content launched in 1994

## BBC Information & Archives - Television Archive
Wood Lane
London W12 7RJ
Tel: 0208 433 2861/2
email: Research-Central@bbc.co.uk
email: ukls@bbcfootage.com
Website: ww.bbcresearchcentral.com
The largest collection of broadcast programmes in the world reflecting the whole range of BBC output

## bfi Archival Footage Sales
21 Stephen Street
London W1T 1LN
Tel: 020 7957 4842
Fax: 020 7436 4014
email: footage.films@bfi.org.uk
Website:
www.bfi.org.uk/collections/afs
bfi Archival Footage Sales is the gateway for programme and film-makers to the unrivalled wealth of materials held in the bfi's National Film and Television Archive. The remarkable variety of footage available ranges from the earliest films to documentaries, fiction, home movies, animation and classic and contemporary television. Core collections include British Transport

Films, the National Coal Board, ETV and the silent newsreel, Topical Budget. New collections are constantly being added, and our commitment to increasing the range and amount of materials available ensures we are the most comprehensive and diverse source of film and television in the UK

## Boulton-Hawker Films
Hadleigh
Ipswich
Suffolk IP7 5BG
Tel: 01473 822 235
Fax: 01473 824 519
email: sales@boultonhawker.co.uk
Educational films and videos: health education, social welfare, home economics, P.S.E., P.E., Maths, biology, physics, chemistry, geography

## British Artists' Film and Video Study Collection
Central Saint Martins College of Art and Design
Southampton Row
London WC1B 4AP
Tel: 020 7514 8159
email: info@studycollection.org.uk
Website: www.studycollection.org.uk
The Study Collection contains:
- a library of more than 2,000 individual British artists' titles on tape and DVD;
- a large collection of publications, posters, fliers and programme notes relating to British Artists' film and video;
- more than 500 files of paper documentation containing published and unpublished writings by and about artists, and other ephemera (letters, promotional cards, etc);
- a large collection of still images;
- an expansive collection of documentation tracing the institutional history of British artists' film and video, including material on The London Filmmakers Co-op, the LUX, the IFA, and Arts Council and BFI funding of artists. The website hosts a comprehensive database of information about British artists' film and video, online exhibitions of material from the Study Collection, extensive bibliographies and research papers, and is regularly updated with new research resources

## British Defence Film Library
Services Sound & Vision
Corporation
Chalfont Grove
Narcot Lane

Chalfont St. Peter
Gerrards Cross
Bucks SL9 8TN
Tel: 01494 878 278
Fax: 01494 878 007
email: robert.dungate@ssvc.com
Website: www.ssvc.com
Robert Dungate, Library Manager
SSVC has many years experience in providing both entertainment and support for the military. The British Defence Film Library (BDFL) is an independent department within SSVC which holds and distributes audio visual training materials for use by the armed forces which have been specifically commissioned by the Ministry of Defence. The Library also supplies this footage to the film and television industry offering a unique collection of British military material

## British Movietonews
Denham Media Park
Denham UB9 5HQ
Tel: 01895 833 071
Fax: +44 (0)1895 834 893
email: library@mtone.co.uk
Website: www.movietone.com
One of the world's major film archives featuring high quality cinema newsreels from the turn of the century, with an emphasis on 1929-1979. The library now represents on an exclusive basis the TV-AM News Library with over 1,100 hours of British and World news covering the period 1983-1991. This material is available on re-mastered digital tape

## British Pathé Plc
New Pathé House
57 Jameston Road
London NW1 7DB
Tel: 020 7424 3650/020 7424 3636
Fax: 020 7485 3606
email:
larry.mckinna@britishpathe.com
Website: www.britishpathe.com
Larry McKinna, Chief Librarian
50 million feet of newsreel and social documentary from 1896 to 1970. Rapid research and sourcing through computerised catalogue. Footage sales now managed by ITN Archive

## Canal + Image UK Ltd
Pinewood Studios
Pinewood Road, Iver
Bucks SL0 0NH
Tel: 01753 631 111
Fax: 01753 655 813
Feature films, TV series, stock shots and stills, b/w and colour, 35mm,

from 1925 to present day. Includes material produced by Associated British, British Lion and Ealing Studios

## Chain Production Ltd
2 Clanricarde Gardens
London W2 4NA
Tel: 020 7229 4277
Fax: 020 7229 0861
email: garwindavidson@chainproduction.com
Website: www.chainproduction.com
Specialist in European films and world cinema, cult classics, handling European Film Libraries with all rights to over 1,000 films - also clip rights and clip search

## Channel Four Clip Library
c/o ITN Archive
Channel 4 Television
124 Horseferry Road
London SW1P 2TX
Tel: 020 7306 8490
Fax: 020 7306 8366
email: clipsales@channel4.co.uk
Website: www.4clipsales.com
Paul McAllister
Programme and film clips from the Channel 4 archive, spanning the channel's output since its launch 20 years ago, available alongside ITN Archive. Includes documentaries, entertainment, youth programmes produced for Channel 4 and E4, as well as feature films made by Film Four

## Clips & Footage
2nd Floor
80a Dean Street
London W1V 5AD
Tel: 020 7287 7287
Fax: 020 7439 4886
email: clipsetc@easynet.co.uk
Website: www.clipsandfootage.com
Supplies historical and modern colour footage of every description to broadcast, commercial and corporate producers. Special collections include B-movies, feature film trailers, newsreels, 35mm stock shots and timelapse. Free research.

## COI Footage File
2 The Quadrant
135 Salusbury Road
London NW6 6RJ
Tel: 020 7624 3388
Fax: 020 7624 3377
email: research@film-images.com.
Website: www.film-images.com
Tony Dykes, Researcher
Crown copyright films produced for

the British Government spanning the last 75 years featuring a number of film greats such as John Grierson, Humphrey Jennings, Alfred Hitchcock and Richard Massingham. The COI Footage File collection has been managed by Film Images since 1997 and a full on-line catalogue is available

## Contemporary Films
24 Southwood Lawn Road
Highgate
London N6 5SF
Tel: 0208 340 5715
Fax: 0208 348 1238
email: inquiries@contemporaryfilms.com
Website: www.contemporaryfilms.com
Documentaries on China, USSR, Cuba, Nazi Germany, South Africa. The library also covers areas like the McCarthy witch hunts in the '50s, the civil rights movements of the '60s, hippie culture, feminism

## Editions Audiovisuel Beulah
66 Rochester Way
Crowborough TN6 2DU
Tel: 01892 652 413
Fax: 01892 652 413
email: foot@eavb.co.uk
Website: www.eavb.co.uk/library
Beulah publishes videos on the Royal Navy, Military Transport, Yesterday's Britain, operates a stock shot and sound effects library, and provides film and video restoration services

## Environmental Investigation Agency
62-63 Upper Street
London N1 ONY
Tel: 020 7354 7960
Fax: 020 7354 3961
email: communications@eia-international.org
Website: www.eia-international.org
The Environmental Investigation Agency is a non-profit organisation dedicated to fighting environmental crime. By recording its investigations worldwide the Environmental Investigation Agency has established a dynamic documentary archive. All fees generated help fund future campaigns

## Film and Video Umbrella
52 Bermondsey Street
London SE1 3UD
Tel: 020 7407 7755
Fax: 020 7407 7766
email: info@fvu.co.uk
Website: www.fvumbrella.com

Steve Bode, Director
Curates and produces film, video and new media projects by artists which are commissioned and presented in collaboration with galleries and venues across England

## Film Images
2 The Quadrant
135 Salusbury Road
London NW6 6RJ
Tel: 020 7624 3388
Fax: 020 7624 3377
email: research@film-images.com
Website: www.film-images.com
Thousands of hours of classic and contemporary film images from hundreds of different sources around the world. All fully catalogued and immediately available for viewing on VHS or U-Matic. Suppliers include Central Office of Information and Overseas Film and Television

## Film Research & Production Services
PO Box 28045
London SE27 9WZ
Tel: 0208 670 2959
Fax: 0208 670 1793
email: frps@aol.com
Website: www.filmresearch.co.uk
Amanda Dunne, James Webb
FRPS provides both contemporary and archive moving footage and stills sourced from all genres including:- news, sport, wildlife, feature films and television programmes. Footage is supplied for use in all media production formats, including:- commercials, feature films, corporate films, pop promos, documentaries and television series

## Fred Goodland Archives, Video & Record Collections
81 Farmilo Road
London E17 8JN
Tel: 0208 539 4412
Fax: 0208 539 4412
Fred Goodland MBKS
An eclectic collection of actuality and entertainment subjects on high quality film prints, NTSC video laserdiscs and broadcast format video (1890s-2000). The Film Archive includes a wide range of often rare musical material (1920s-1960s), plus examples of early sound and colour film systems, personalities, vintage fashion, animation, amateur footage, adverts and trailers. VHS preview tapes with BITC are available to researchers. Broadcast format

transfers are personally supervised. The Sound Archive, containing thousands of recordings on shellac, vinyl and tape, reproduces many musical styles of the 20th century. Transfers for professional use are available on CDR

## Fremantle Archive Sales
1 Stephen Street
London W1T 1AL
Tel: 020 7691 6000
Fax: 020 7691 6100
email: archive@fremantlemedia.com
Website: www.fremantlemedia.com
One of the most comprehensive television archives worldwide with moving images from 1950's. Includes light entertainment, drama, game shows, documentaries and current affairs

## GB Associates
7 Marion Grove
Woodford Green
Essex 9TA
Tel: 0208 504 6340
Fax: 0208 505 1850
email: filmview@dial.pipex.com
Malcolm Billingsley
An extensive collection, mainly on 35mm, of fact and fiction film from the turn of the century. The collection is particularly strong in vintage trailers, the early sound era, early colour systems and adverts

## Granada Visual
48 Leicester Square
London WC2H 7FB
Tel: 020 7633 2700
Fax: 020 7633 2701
email: granada.visual@granadamedia.com
Website: www.granadamedia.com/visual
Amanda Deadman - General Manager
Granada Visual represents an ever increasing catalogue of over 100,000 hours of diverse programming and materials covering every genre, from entertainment and music to drama and documentaries or news and personalities to wildlife and stockshots. Granada Visual provides access to footage from the libraries of Anglia TV, Border TV, Granada TV, Granada Wild, HTV Network, LWT, Meridian, Tyne Tees TV and Yorkshire TV

## Huntley Film Archives
191 Wardour Street
London W1F 8ZE
Tel: 020 7287 8000
Fax: 020 7287 8001
email: films@huntleyarchives.com
Website: www.huntleyarchives.com

Amanda Huntley
Archive film library for broadcast, corporate and educational purposes, specialising in documentary footage 1900-1980

## Index Stock Shots
Highgate Business Centre
33 Greenwood Place
London NW5 1LD
Tel: 020 7482 1953
Fax: 020 7482 1967
email: info@indexstockshots.com
Website: www.indexstockshots.com
Unique stock footage on 35mm film and tape. Including time-lapse and aerial photography, cities, landmarks, aviation, wildlife

## ITN Archive
200 Gray's Inn Road
London WC1X 8XZ
Tel: 020 7430 4480
Fax: 020 7430 4453
email: sales@itn.co.uk
Website: www.itnarchive.com
One of the largest commercial archives in the world, providing access to high quality news and feature material dating back to 1986. The holdings also comprise all ITN's output, including award-winning reports and selected rushes since 1955. ITN Archive has exclusive world rights to the entire Reuters Television Archive which includes historical newsreel such as British Paramount News, Empire News Bulletin , Gaumont Graphic and Gaumont British.The entire full integrated database is available free on-line and much of the material is grouped into themed collections to aid research

## London Film Archive
78 Mildmay Park
Islington
London N1 4PR
Tel: 020 7923 4074
Fax: 020 7241 4929
email: info@londonfilmarchive.org
Website: www.londonfilmarchive.org
Dedicated to the acquisition and preservation of film relating to the Greater London region. The collection consists of material from 1895 and represents professional and amateur produced features and documentary films

## London Jewish Cultural Centre
The Old House
c/o King's College London
Kidderpore Avenue

London NW3 7SZ
Tel: 020 7431 0345
Fax: 020 7431 0361
email: admin@ljcc.org.uk
Website: www.ljcc.org.uk
The LJCC is an educational organisation with an extensive library of feature, documentary and Israeli film containing rare and previously unseen documentary footage, educational compilation tapes, and a vast archive of material on the Holocaust. It offers some consultancy services to researchers and producers working in this field and organises regular showings of films from the collection

## Medi Scene
32-38 Osnaburgh Street
London NW1 3ND
Tel: 020 7387 3606
Fax: 020 7387 9693
Wide range of accurately catalogued medical and scientific shots available on film and video

## Moving Image Communications
Maidstone Studios
Vinters Park
Maidstone ME14 5N2
Tel: 01622 684 569
Fax: 01622 687 444
email: mail@milibrary.com
Website: www.milibrary.com
Nathalie Banaigs, Marketing & Sales
Provides a comprehensive footage resource with images ranging from silent movies to celebrity chat shows and from newsreels to travelogues.

## Nova Film and Video Library
62 Ascot Avenue
Cantley
Doncaster DN4 6HE
Tel: 0870 765 1094
Fax: 0870 169 2982
email: info@novaonline.co.uk
Website:
www.novaonline.co.uk/library.html
An extensive and unrivalled collection of unique archive material of Britain and the world. The Library holds a huge selection of amateur cine film documenting the changing social life of Britain dating back to 1944 and has a dedicated collection of transport footage from 1949. Also holds a wide selection of specially shot modem footage and interviews

## Olympic Television Archive Bureau
4th Floor

McCormack House
Burlington Lane
London W4 2TH
Tel: 0208 233 5353
Fax: 0208 233 5354
email: webmaster@otab.com
Website: www.otab.com
OTAB was established in 1995 by the International Olympic Committee in order to streamline the commercial management of the audiovisual library of the Olympic Games. The archive contains imagery from the first Olympic Games of the Modern Era, Athens 1896, through to comprehensive coverage of the most recent Olympic Games

## Oxford Scientific Films
Ground Floor
Network House
Station Yard
Thame OX9 3UH
Tel: 01844 262 370
Fax: 01844 262 380
email: film.library@osf.uk.com
Website: www.osf.uk.com
Stock footage on 16mm, 35mm film and video. Wide range of wildlife, special effects, timelapse, slow motion, medicine, industry, scenics, world locations, macro, micro etc. Catalogue and showreel available. Extensive stills library

## Reuters Television Library
(Managed and Distributed by ITN Archive)
200 Grays Inn Road
London WC1X 8XE
Tel: 020 7430 4480
Fax: 020 7430 4453
email: archive.sales@itn.co.uk
Website: www.itnarchive.com
Original newsreel, television news and feature footage from 1896 to present day. Special Collections. Online database (free access) and expert researchers. See ITN Archive

## Ronald Grant Archive
The Cinema Museum
The Master's House
2 Dugard Way
London SE11 4TH
Tel: 020 7840 2200
Fax: 020 7840 2299
email: pixdesk@rgapix.com
15 million feet of fact and fiction film, mainly 35mm, from 1896 on. Also 1 million film stills, posters, programmes, scripts and information. The museum is a FIAF subscriber

## Royal Mail Film and Video Archive
PO Box 145
Sittingbourne
Kent ME10 1NH
Tel: 01795 426 465
Fax: 01795 437 988
email: info@edist.co.uk
Holds a representative selection of documentary programmes made by the GPO Film Unit, including the classic Night Mail, together with programmes produced from 1970s onwards

## RSPB Film Collection, Newsplayer Ltd
Portland House
4 Great Portland Street
London W1W 8QJ
Tel: 020 7927 6699
Fax: 020 7927 6698
email: greg@newsplayer.com
Website: www.rspb.org.uk/films
Greg Owen
The RSPB Film Unit was established in 1953 and contains both finished films and raw footage. Its collection is an invaluable resource for professional filmmakers of all types who require clips of birds in their natural habitat whether nesting, feeding, in combat or soaring in flight

## Sky News Library Sales
British Sky Broadcasting Ltd
6 Centaurs Business Park
Grant Way
Isleworth
Middlesex TW7 5QD
Tel: 020 7705 3132
Fax: 020 7705 3201
email: libsales@bskyb.com
Website:
www.sky.com/skynewslibsales
Ben White, Susannah Owen
Extensive round the clock news and current affairs coverage since 1989. Entire library held on Beta SP on site. Library operates 24 hours a day

## TWI Archive
Trans World International
McCormack House
Burlington Lane
London W4 2TH
Tel: 0208 233 5500
Fax: 0208 233 6476
email: twiarchive@imgworld.com
Website: www.twiarchive.com
TWI Archive is one of the leading sporting and non-sporting archives, represents over 60 of the most prestigious federations in the World.

Combining professional sales expertise, consultancy, acquisitions and archive management with state-of-the-art storage facilities, TWI Archive provides a one-stop service for its clients and customers

## Undercurrents Archive
Old Telephone Exchange
Pier Street
Swansea SA1 1RY
Wales
Tel: 01792 455 900
Fax: 0870 316103
email: info@undercurrents.org
Website: www.undercurrents.org
Undercurrents is an archive of grassroots environmental and social protest and dissent and community issues from 1990 to present day

## World Backgrounds Film Production Library
Millennium Studios
Elstree Way
Borehamwood WD6 1SF
Tel: 0208 236 0011
Fax: 0208 953 6633
email: films@worldbackgrounds.com
Website:
www.worldbackgrounds.com
Video library portal serving the film and television industry with stock footage for the last 50 years. Specialises in scenes for features, TV commercials, television productions, pop promos and corporate videos

# Photographic Libraries

## BBC Photograph Library
B116 Television Centre
Wood Lane
London W12 7RJ
Tel: 0208 225 7193
Fax: 0208 576 7020
email: Research-Central@bbc.co.uk
Website: www.bbcresearchcentral.com
The BBC's unique archive of radio and television programme stills, equipment, premises, news and personalities dating from 1922. B/w and colour. Visits by appointment

## BFI Stills, Posters & Designs
21 Stephen Street
London W1T 1LN
Tel: 020 7957 4797
Fax: 020 7323 9260
Website: www.bfi.org.uk/stills
The world's most comprehensive collection of film and television stills, posters & designs, capturing both on and off-screen moments. The collection illustrates every aspect of the development of world cinema and television - featuring scene stills, star portraits and behind-the-scenes - in addition to original movie posters and designs. Rapid access is available by photographic and digital reproduction or visits by appointment

## Bridgeman Art Library
17-19 Garway Road
London W2 4PH
Tel: 020 7727 4065
Fax: 020 7792 8509
email: london@bridgeman.co.uk
Website: www.bridgeman.co.uk
The world's leading source of fine art images for reproduction. From iconic classics to contemporary art, all styles and periods are represented. Images can be viewed and ordered online and a free printed catalogue is available

## Corbis
111 Salusbury Road
London NW6 6RG
Tel: 020 7644 7644
Fax: 020 7644 7645
email: info@corbis.com
Website: www.corbis.com
Photographic stills agency/library

## FremantleMedia Stills Library
Teddington Studios
Broom Road
Teddington
Middlesex TW11 9NT
Tel: 0208 781 2789
Fax: 0208 614 2250
email: stills.library@fremantlemedia.com
Website: www.fremantlemediastills.com
The Library contains over a million images available in all formats including digital. Classic comedy images can be found in the Library's large archive, incorporating programmes both old and new made by some of the biggest names in television production; Thames (Morecambe and Wise, Benny Hill, Pop Idol, The Bill), Grundy (Neighbours) and Talkback ( House Doctor, They Think It's All Over)

## Getty Images Film
101 Bayham Street
London NW1 0AG
Tel: +44 (0) 800 376 7977
Fax: +44 (0) 207 267 8988
email: sales@gettyimages.co.uk
Website: www.gettyimages.com

## Hulton Archive - Getty Images
Unique House
21-31 Woodfield Road
London W9 2BA
Tel: 0800 376 7977
Fax: 020 7266 2660
email: sales@getty-images.com
Website: www.gettyimages.com
One of the world's largest stills archives with over 40 million photographs, prints and engravings covering the entire history of photojournalism

## Image Bank Film
17 Conway Street
London W1T 6EE
Tel: 0800 279 9255
Fax: 020 7391 9123
email: motion.sales@gettyimages.com
Website: www.gettyimages.com

## Image Diggers Picture and Tape Library
618b Finchley Road
London NW11 7RR
Tel: 0208 455 4564
Fax: 0208 455 4564
email: ziph@macunlimited.net
Website: www.imagediggers.netfirms.com
A varied collection of pictures, 35mm transparencies, ephemera, memorabilia, clippings, recording, stills, postcards, sheet music, magazine and book material for hire. Cinema, theatre and literature clippings archive. Audio/visual tape resources in performing arts and other areas, plus theme research

## image.net
1 Hardwick Street
London, EC1R 4RB
Tel: 020 7841 0550
email: sales@image.net
Website: www.image.net
Exclusive on-line access to pre-release publicity material on behalf of leading entertainment companies

## Imperial War Museum
Photograph Archive
All Saints Annexe
Austral Street
London SE11 4SL
Tel: 020 7416 5333/8
Fax: 020 7416 5355
email: photos@iwm.org.uk
Website: www.iwm.org.uk
www.iwmcollections.org.uk (databases)
David Bell
A collection of some 6 million images illustrating all aspects of 20th century warfare. Film stills can also be made from material held by the IWM's Film & Video Archive, by prior arrangement

## Institute of Contemporary History & Wiener Library
4 Devonshire Street
London W1W 5BH
Tel: 020 7636 7247
Fax: 020 7436 6428
email: Library@Wienerlibrary.co.uk
Website: www.wienerlibrary.co.uk
The Wiener Library is a private research library and institute specialising in contemporary European and Jewish history, especially the rise and fall of the Third Reich, Nazism and fascist movements, anit-Semitism, the Holocaust and post-war Germany. It holds Britain's largest collection of documents, testimonies, books and videos on the Holocaust. The photographic archive contains stills, postcards, posters and portraits, illustrated books, approx. 2,000 videos and recordings

## Joel Finler Collection
7A Belsize Square
London NW3 4HT
Tel: 020 7794 7175
Fax: 020 7813 2965
Joel Finler
Large selection of film stills, posters, slides and transparencies covering the entire history of world cinema, with a

special emphasis on colour, Hollywood, production and behind-the-scenes shots of film-makers and stars

## Kobal Collection
2 The Quadrant
135 Salusbury Road
London NW6 6RJ
Tel: 020 7624 3300
Fax: 020 7624 3311
email: info@picture-desk.com
Website: www.picture-desk.com
One of the world's leading film photo archives in private ownership. Film stills and portraits, lobby cards and posters, from the earliest days of the cinema to modern times

## Mckenzie Heritage Picture Archive
Studio 226
Station House
49 Greenwich High Road
London SE10 8JL
Tel: 0208 469 2000
Fax: 0208 469 2000
email: info@mckenziehpa.com
Website: www.mckenziehpa.com
Provides publishers, broadcasters and organisations with photos and other images of African, Asian and Carribban people, cultures and communities spanning the 19th and 20th centuries

## Moviestore Collection Ltd
2nd Floor North
Chartwell Buildings
61-65 Paulet Road
London SE5 9HW
Tel: 020 7733 9990
email: sales@moviestorecollection.com
Website: www.moviestorecolllection.com
Provider of film and television imagery to all aspects of the media publishing industry

## Retrograph Nostalgia Archive
10 Hanover Crescent
Brighton BN2 9SB
Tel: 01273 687 554
email: retropix1@aol.com
Website: www.retrograph.com
Jilliana Ranicar-Breese
Vintage worldwide consumer advertising. Decorative labels, magazine advertisements, posters and prints. Commercial and Fine Art (1860-1960). Supplier to CD, film and TV companies. Transparencies, slides, high resolution colour lasers or digital images either by email or CD supplied. Search and service fees. Free colour literature on request

# Museums

## Bill Douglas Centre for the History of Cinema and Popular Culture
University of Exeter
The Old Library
Prince of Wales Road
Exeter EX4 4PX
Tel: 01392 264 321
Fax: 01392 263 871
email: info@billdouglas.org
Website: www.billdouglas.org
Dr Hester Higton
The core of the Centre's collection was assembled over many years by film-maker Bill Douglas and his friend Peter Jewell. Since the original donation, important additions have come from film-makers Roy Fowler, Don Boyd, James Mackay and Gavrik Losey and from cinematographer Ossie Morris. The collections comprise an extensive range of books, periodicals, programmes, posters, sheet music, cards, toys and games related to the cinema, in addition to 19th century pre-cinema artefacts such as zoetropes, magic lanterns, panoramas, peepshows and other optical toys and devices. A comprehensive online catalogue is available on the website.

## Cinema Museum
c/o Ronald Grant Archive
The Master's House
2 Dugard Way
London SE11 4TH
Tel: 020 7840 2200
Fax: 020 7840 2299
email: pixdesk@rgapix.com
15 million feet of fact and fiction film, mainly 35mm, from 1896 on. Also 1 million film stills, posters, programmes, scripts and information

## Imperial War Museum Film and Video Archive
Lambeth Road
London SE1 6HZ
Tel: 020 7416 5291/5292
Fax: 020 7416 5299
email: film@iwm.org.uk
Website: www.iwm.org.uk
Paul Sargent/Jane Fish
The national museum of modern conflict, illustrating and recording all aspects of modern war. The Archive reflects these terms of reference with an extensive collection of film and video material, which is widely used by historians and by film and television companies

## Laurel and Hardy Museum
4C Upper Brook Street
Ulverston
Cumbria LA12 7BQ
Tel: 01229 582 292
email: info@laurel-and-hardy.co.uk
Website: www.laurel-and-hardy-museum.co.uk
Everything you want to know about the comedy duo can be found at the museum at Ulverston, where Stan was born in June 1890. The collection of memorabilia includes letters, photographs, personal items and furniture, and is believed to be the largest in the world. A small cinema shows films and documentaries throughout the day.

## National Museum of Photography, Film & Television
Bradford BD1 1NQ
Tel: 0870 70 10 200
Fax: 01274 723 155
email: talk.nmpft@nmsi.ac.uk
Website: www.nmpft.org.uk
Founded in 1983 as part of the National Museum of Science and Industry (NMSI), this museum is devoted to still and moving pictures, their technology and history. Features Britain's first giant IMAX film system; the world's only public Cinerama; interactive galleries and 'TV Heaven', reference library of programmes and commercials

# Film Awards 2003

This section features some of the principal film festival prizes and awards from 1 January 2003 to 31 December 2003. Compiled by Christie Quinn

## BAFTA FILM AWARDS

The Orange British Academy Awards
Awarded on 23 February 2003 at The Odeon Leicester Square, London

### BAFTA

195 Piccadilly
London W1V OLN
Tel: 020 7734 0022
Fax: 020 7734 1792
Website: www.bafta.org
**Best Film:**
THE PIANIST (France/Poland/Germany/UK/US) Dir Roman Polanski
**Academy Fellowship:**
Saul Zaentz
**Michael Balcon Award For Outstanding British Contribution to Cinema:**
David Tomblin and Michael Stevenson
**Alexander Korda Award For Outstanding British Film of the Year:**
THE WARRIOR (UK/France) Dir Asif Kapadia
**David Lean Award For Achievement in Direction:**
Roman Polanksi THE PIANIST (France/Poland/Germany/UK/US)
**Best Screenplay (Original):**
Pedro Almodóvar for HABLE CON ELLA (Spain) Dir Pedro Almodóvar
**Best Screenplay (Adapted):**
Charlie Kaufman/Donald Kaufman for ADAPTATION (US) Dir Spike Jonze
**Performance by an Actress in a Leading Role:**
Nicole Kidman for THE HOURS (US/UK) Dir Stephen Daldry
**Performance by an Actor in a Leading Role:**
Daniel Day-Lewis for GANGS OF NEW YORK (US) Dir Martin Scorsese
**Performance by an Actress in a Supporting Role:**
Catherine Zeta-Jones for CHICAGO (US) Dir Rob Marshall
**Performance by an Actor in a Supporting Role:**
Christopher Walken for CATCH ME IF YOU CAN (US) Dir Steven Spielberg
**Film Not in the English Language:**
HABLE CON ELLA (Spain) Dir Pedro Almodóvar
**Anthony Asquith Award For Achievement in Film Music:**
Philip Glass for THE HOURS (US/UK) Dir Stephen Daldry
**Carl Foreman Award For Most Promising Newcomer to British Film:**
Asif Kapadia Director/Co-Writer: THE WARRIOR

(UK/France)
**Best Cinematography:**
Conrad L. Hall for ROAD TO PERDITION (US) Dir Sam Mendes
**Best Production Design:**
Dennis Gassner for ROAD TO PERDITION (US) Dir Sam Mendes
**Best Costume Design:**
Ngila Dickson and Richard Taylor for The LORD OF THE RINGS THE TWO TOWERS (US/New Zealand) Dir Peter Jackson
**Best Editing:**
Daniel Rezende for CIDADE DE DEUS (Brazil/Germany) Dir Fernando Meirelles
**Best Sound:**
Michael Minkle, Dominick R.Tavella, David Lee and Maurice Schell for
CHICAGO (US/Germany) Dir Rob Marshall
**Achievement in Special Visual Effects:**
Jim Rygiel, Joe Letteri, Alex Funke, Randall William Cook for THE LORD OF THE RINGS THE TWO TOWERS (US/New Zealand) Dir Peter Jackson
**Best Make Up/Hair:**
Judy Chin, Beatrice De Alba, John Jackson, Regina Reyes for FRIDA (US) Dir Julie Taymor
**Best Short Film:**
MY WRONGS 8245-8249 AND 117 (UK) Dir Chris Morris
**Best Short Animation:**
FISH NEVER SLEEP (UK) Dir Gaëlle Dennis
**Orange Audience Award:**
THE LORD OF THE RINGS THE TWO TOWERS (US/New Zealand) Dir Peter Jackson

## 53rd BERLIN INTERNATIONAL FILM FESTIVAL

Held 6-16 February 2003, Berlin
Internationale Filmfestspiele Berlin

### Berlin International Film Festival

Potsdamer Strafle 5
D-10785 Berlin
Tel: (49) 030 25 920
Fax: (49) 030 25 920 299
email: info@berlinale.de
Website: www.berlinale.de

**INTERNATIONAL JURY**
**Golden Berlin Bear:**
IN THIS WORLD (UK) Dir Michael Winterbottom
**Jury Grand Prix, Silver Berlin Bear:**
ADAPTATION (US) Dir Spike Jonze
**Silver Berlin Bear for the Best Director:**
Patrice Chereau for SON FREREhis film LUNDI MATIN (France)
**Silver Berlin Bear for the Best Actress:**
Meryl Streep, Nicole Kidman and Julianne Moore for THE HOURS (US/UK) Dir Stephen Daldry
**Silver Berlin Bear for the Best Actor:**

Sam Rockwell for CONFESSIONS OF A DANGEROUS MIND Dir George Clooney
**Silver Berlin Bear for an individual artistic contribution:**
Li Yang as screenwriter and director for MANG JING (Blind Shaft) (Hong Kong/China/Germany)
**Silver Berlin Bear for best film music:**
Majoly, Serge Fiori, Mamadou Diabaté for MADAME BROUETTE (Canada/Senegal/France) Dir Moussa Sene Absa
**AGICOA Blue Angel award for best European film:**
GOOD BYE LENIN (Germany) Dir Wolfgang Becker
**The Alfred Bauer Prize:**
YING XIONG (Hero) (China/Hong Kong) Dir Zhang Yimou

**INTERNATIONAL SHORT FILM JURY**
Golden Berlin Bear for Best Short Film:
(A)TORZIJA (Slovenia) Dir Stefan Arsenijevic
Jury Prize, Silver Berlin Bear:
EN AUSENCIA (Argentina) Dir Lucia Cedron
ISCHOV TRAMWAI No.9 (Ukraine) Dir Stepan Koval

**OTHER AWARDS**
**Prize of the Churches of the Ecumenical Jury**
IN THIS WORLD (UK) Dir Michael Winterbottom
**The award for a film screened in the Panorama:**
KNAFAYIM SHVUROT (Broken Wings) (Israel) Dir Nir Bergman
**Award for a film screened in the Forum:**
EDI (Poland) Dir Piotr Trzaskalski
**FIPRESCI prizes**
**Prize for a film screened in Competition:**
LICHTER (Germany) Dir Hans-Christian Schmid
**Prize for a film screened in the Panorama:**
WOLFSBURG (Germany) Dir Christian Petzold
**Prize for a film screened in the Forum:**
EDI (Poland) Dir Piotr Trzaskalski
**Prize of the Guild of German Art House Cinemas**
MY LIFE WITHOUT ME Dir Isabel Coixet
**Readers' Prize of The Berliner Morgenpost**
THE HOURS (US/UK) Dir Stephen Daldry
**C.I.C.A.E. Prize**
**Prize for a film screened in the Panorama:**
KNAFAYIM SHVUROT (Broken Wings) (Israel) Dir Nir Bergman
**Special Mention:**
POLIGONO SUR (Spain/France) Dir Dominique Abel
Prize for a film screened in the Forum:
AMARELO MANGA (Brazil) Dir Claudio Assis
**Special Mention:**
POWER TRIP (US) Dir Paul Devlin
**Prix UIP Berlin**
(A)TORZIJA (Solvenia) Dir Stefan Arsenijevic
**LVT – Manfred Salzgeber Prize:**
PURE (UK) Dir Gillies MacKinnon
**Special mention for acting:**
Harry Eden for PURE (UK) Dir Gillies MacKinnon
**Panorama Short Film Award**
**Best Short Film:**
MISDEMEANOR (US) Dir Jonathan LeMond
New York Film Academy Scholarship:
MOGLEM BYC CZLOWIEKIEM (I Could Have Been Human) (Poland) Dir Barbara Medajska
**Special Mention:**
UNDERDOG by Eran Merav
**Panorama Audience Prize**
KNAFAYIM SHVUROT (Broken Wings) (Israel) Dir Nir Bergman

**Prize of the Deutsches Kinderhilfswerk**
**Grand Prix for Best Feature:**
KALD MIG BARE AKSEL (Denmark) Dir Pia Bovin
**Special Mention:**
ELINA – SOM OM JAG INTE FANNS (Sweden/Finaland) by Klaus Haro
DRENGEN DER VILLE GORE DET UMULIGE (The Boy Who Wanted to Be a Bear) (France/Denmark/Norway) by Jannik Hastrup
**Special Prize for Best Short film:**
LE TROP PETIT PRINCE (France) Dir Zoia Trofimova
**Special Mention:**
HOUDINS HUND by Sara Johnsen
**Crystal Bear**
**Crystal Bear for best feature film of the Kinderfilmfest:**
ELINA – SOM OM JAG INTE FANNS (Sweden/Finland) Dir Klaus Haro
**Special Mention:**
MISS ENTEBBE ( Israel) Dir Omri Levy
**EL VIAJE DE CAROL (Carol's Journey) by Imanol Uribe**
**Crystal Bear for best short film:**
LE TROP PETIT PRINCE (France) Dir Zoia Trofimova
**Special Mention: BIRJU by Heeraz Marfatia**
**Peace Film Prize**
IN THIS WORLD (UK) Dir Michael Winterbottom
**Teddy 2003**
**Teddy for best feature film:**
MIL NUBES DE PAZ CERCAN EL CIELO, AMOR, JAMAS ACABARAS DE SER AMOR (Mexico) Dir Julián Hernández
**Teddy for best documentary:**
ICH KENN KEINEN – ALLEIN UNTER HETEROS (Gemany) Dir Jochen Hick
**Teddy for best short film:**
FREMRAGENDE TIMER (Precious Moments) (Norway) Dir Lars Daniel Krutzkoff and Jan Dalchow
**Special Teddy:**
Friedrich Wilhelm Murnau (1888-1931)
Readers' Prize of The Siegessaule
THE EVENT (Canada/US) Dir Thom Fitzgerald
**Wolfgang Staudte Award 2003**
RENGETEG (Forest) (Hungary) Dir Benedek Fliegauf
**Caligari Film Prize 2003**
**SALT (Iceland/US) Dir Bradley Rust Gray**
**NETPAC Prize**
KOUFUKU NO KANE (The Blessing Bell) (Japan) Dir Sabu
**Special Mention:**
AKU INGIN MENCIUMMU SEKALI SAJA (Bird-Man Tale) (Indonesia) Dir Garin Nugroho
**Don Quixote Prize of the International Federation of Film Societies**
**EDI (Poland) Dir Piotr Trzaskalski**
**Readers' Prize of The Berliner Zeitung**
POWER TRIP (US) Dir Paul Devlin

# BLACK FILMMAKERS MAGAZINE (BFM) FILM AND TELEVISION AWARDS
**See Screen Nation Film and Television Awards**

## 5th BRITISH INDEPENDENT FILM AWARDS

Awarded 4 November 2003, London

### British Independent Film Awards

81 Berwick Street
London WLF 8TW
Tel: 020 7287 3833
Fax: 020 7439 2243
email: info@bifa.org.uk
Website: www.bifa.org.uk

**Best British Independent Film:**
DIRTY PRETTY THINGS (US/UK) Dir Stephen Frears
**Best Foreign Film:**
CITY OF GOD (Brazil/Germany/France) Dir Fernando Meirelles
**Most Promising Newcomer:**
Harry Eden for PURE (UK) Dir Gillies MacKinnon
**The Douglas Hickox Award (Debut Director):**
Richard Jobson for 16 YEARS OF ALCHOHOL (UK/Netherlands)
**Best Technical Achievement:**
Peter Christelis for editing IN THIS WORLD (UK) Dir Michael Winterbottom
**Special Jury Prize:**
Jeremy Thomas
**Best Screenplay:**
Steve Knight for DIRTY PRETTY THINGS (US/UK) Dir Stephen Frears
**Best Actor:**
Chiwetel Ejiofor in DIRTY PRETTY THINGS (US/UK) Dir Stephen Frears
**Best Documentary:**
BODYSONG (UK) Dir Simon Pummell
**Best Short Film:**
DAD'S DEAD (UK) Dir Chris Shepherd
**British Airways Bursary:**
Lenka Clayton
**Best Actress:**
Olivia Williams in THE HEART OF ME (UK/France) Dir Thaddeus O'Sullivan
**Best Ensemble Performance:**
THE MAGDALENE SISTERS (UK/Ireland) Dir Peter Mullan
**Best Director:**
Stephen Frears for DIRTY PRETTY THINGS (US/UK)
**The Variety UK Personality Award:**
Sir Ian McKellen

## 56th CANNES FESTIVAL

Held in Cannes, 14-25 May 2003

### Festival International du Film de Cannes

Departement Films
3, rue Amelie
F-75007 Paris
Tel: (33) 1 53 59 61 20
Fax: (3)3 1 53 59 61 24
email residence@festival-cannes.fr
Website: www.festival cannes.org

**Feature Film Palme d'Or:**
ELEPHANT (US) Dir Gus Van Sant
**Grand Prize:**
UZAK (Turkey) Dir Nuri Bilge Ceylan
**Best Director Award:**
Gus Van Sant for ELEPHANT (US)

**Jury Prize:**
FIVE IN THE AFTERNOON (Iran) Dir Samira Makhmalbaf
**Best Screenplay:**
BARBARIAN INVASIONS (Canada) Dir Denys Arcand
**Best Actress Award:**
Marie Josée Croze for BARBARIAN INVASIONS (Canada) Dir Denys Arcand
**Best Actor Award:**
Muzaffer Ozdemir and Mehmet Emin Toprak for UZAK (Turkey) Dir Nuri Bilge Ceylan
**Camera d'Or:**
RECONSTRUCTION (Denmark) Dir Christoffer Boe
**Special Mention:**
OSAMA (Afghanistan) Dir Sedigh Barmak
**Cinéfondation Award (First Prize):**
BEZI ZEKO BEZI (RUN RABBIT RUN) (Serbia) Dir Pavle Vuckov
**Cinéfondation Award (Second Prize):**
STORY OF THE DESERT (Spain) Dir Celia Galan Julve
**Cinéfondation Award (Third Prize):**
TV CITY (Germany) Dirs Alberto Couceiro and Alejandra Tomel
(Ex-aequo) AT THAT POINT (Mexico) Dir Luciana Jauffred Gorostiza

## 27th CÉSARS

Selected by L'Académie des Arts et Techniques du Cinéma. Awarded in Paris, 22 February 2003

### Académie Des Arts et Technique du Cinéma

19, rue Lauriston
75116 Paris
Tél. : +33 1 53 64 05 25
Fax. : +33 1 53 64 05 24
email: info@lescesarducinema.com
Website: www.lescesarducinema.com

**Best French Film:**
LE PIANIST (France/Poland/Germany/UK/US)  Dir Roman Polanski
**Best Actor:**
Adrien Brody for THE PIANIST (France/Poland/Germany/UK/US)  Dir Roman Polanski
**Best Actress:**
Isaballe Carre for SE SOUVENIR DES BELLES CHOSES (France) Dir Zabou Breitman
**Best Supporting Actor:**
Bernard Le Coq for SE SOUVENIR DES BELLES CHOSES (France) Dir  Zabou Breitman
**Best Supporting Actress:**
Karin Viard for EMBRASSEZ QUI VOUS VOUDREZ (France/UK/ Italy) Dir Michel Blanc
**Best Director:**
Roman Polanski for THE PIANIST (France/Poland/Germany/UK/US)
**Best Foreign Film:**
BOWLING FOR COLUMBINE   (Canada/Germany/US) Dir Michael Moore
**Best European Union Film:**
HABLE CON ELLA (Spain) Dir Pedro Almodóvar
**Best First Feature Film:**
Se Souvenir Des Belles Choses (France) Dir Zabou Breitman
**Best Short Film:**
PEAU DE VACHE Dir Gerald Hustache-Mathieu
**Best Original or Adapted Screenplay:**
Costa-Gavras, Jean-Claude Grumberg for AMEN

(France/Germany) Dir Costa-Gavras
**Best Art Direction:**
Allan Starski for THE PIANIST
(France/Poland/Germany/UK/US)
Dir Roman Polanski
**Best Cinematography:**
Pawel Edelman for THE PIANIST
(France/Poland/Germany/UK/US)
Dir Roman Polanski
**Best Costume Design:**
Philippe Guillotel, Tanino Liberatore, Florence Sadaune for
ASTERIX ET OBELIX: MISSION CLEOPATRA
(France/Germany) Dir Alain Chabet
**Best Editing:**
Nicolas Philibert for ETRE ET AVOIR (France) Dir
Nicholas Philibert
**Best Music:**
Wojciech Kilar for THE PIANIST
(France/Poland/Germany/UK/US)
Dir Roman Polanski
**Best Sound:**
Jean-Marie Blondel, Gerard Hardy, Dean Humphreys for
THE PIANIST (France/Poland/Germany/UK/US) Dir
Roman Polanski
**Best Newcomer, Actor:**
Jean-Paul Rouve for MONSIEUR BATIGNOLE (France)
Dir Gerard Jugnot
**Best Newcomer, Actress:**
Cecile de France for L'AUBERGE ESPAGNOLE (France)
Dir Cédric Klapisch
**Honorary Cesars:**
Berndadette Laffont, Spike Lee and Meryl Streep

## EDINBURGH INTERNATIONAL FILM FESTIVAL
Held in Edinburgh, 13-24 August 2003

### Edinburgh International Film Festival
Filmhouse
88 Lothian Road
Edinburgh EH3 9BZ
Tel: (44) 131 228 4051
Fax: (44) 131 229 5501
email: info@edfilmfest.org.uk
Website: www.edfilmfest.org.uk

**The Michael Powell Award for Best New British Feature:**
YOUNG ADAM (UK/France) Dir David MacKENZIE
**Saltire Society Grierson Award for Short Documentary
supported by BAILLIE GIFFORD:**
SHE TOON CITY OF BINGO (UK) Dir Craig Collinson
**The Guardian New Director's Award:**
AMERICAN SPLENDOR (US) Dirs Shari Berman, Robert
Pulcini
**The Standard Life Audience Award:**
AFTERLIFE (UK) Dir Alison Peebles
**The Kodak Dazzle Award for Best British Short Film:**
LOVE ME OR LEAVE ME ALONG (UK) Dir Duane
Hopkins
**Best European Short Film Award:**
SMALL AVALANCHES (Denmark) Dir Brigitte
Staermose
**The McLaren Animation Award for New British
Animation:**
PULLIN' THE DEVIL BY THE TAIL (UK) Dir Stephen
McCullum

## EMPIRE FILM AWARDS
Held at the Dorchester Hotel, London, 5 February 2003

### Empire Magazine
4th Floor
Mappin House
4 Winsley Street
London W1W 8HF
Tel: 020 7437 9011
Fax: 020 7859 8613
email: empire@ecm.emap.com
Website: www.empireonline.co.uk/magazine

**Best Film:**
THE LORD OF THE RINGS THE FELLOWSHIP OF
THE RING (US/New Zealand) Dir Peter Jackson
**Best British Actor:**
Hugh Grant for ABOUT A BOY
(Germany/US/France/UK) Dir Paul Weitz
**Best British Actress:**
Samantha Morton for MINORITY REPORT (US) Dir
Steven Spielberg
**Sky Movies Best British Film:**
28 DAYS LATER (UK) Dir Danny Boyle
**Best Newcomer:**
Rosamund Pike for DIE ANOTHER DAY (UK/US) Dir Lee
Tamahori
**Best Actor:**
Tom Cruise for MINORITY REPORT (US) Dir Steven
Spielberg
**Best Actress:**
Kirsten Dunst for SPIDER-MAN (US) Dir Sam Raimi
**Best Director:**
Steven Spielberg for MINORITY REPORT (US)
**Independent Spirit Award:**
Michael Winterbottom and Andrew Eaton, director and
producer of 24 HOUR PARTY PEOPLE (UK)
**Sony Ericsson Scene of the Year:**
Yoda's duel in STAR WARS EPISODE II ATTACK OF THE
CLONES (US)
**The Empire Lifetime Achievement Award:**
Dustin Hoffman

## EUROPEAN FILM AWARDS
16th European Film Awards
Awarded in Berlin, 6 December 2003

### European Film Academy
Kurfürstendamm 225
107 19 Berlin
Tel: 49 (30) 887 167 0
Fax: 49 (30) 887 167 77
Website: www.europeanfilmacademy.org

**European Film:**
GOOD BYE, LENIN! (Germany) Dir Wolfgang Becker
**European Director:**
Lars von Trier for DOGVILLE (Denmark)
**European Actor:**
Daniel Brühl for GOOD BYE, LENIN! (Germany) Dir
Wolfgang Becker
**European Actress:**
Charlotte Rampling for SWIMMING POOL (France) Dir
François Ozon
**European Screenwriter:**
Bern Lichtenberg for GOOD BYE, LENIN! (Germany) Dir
Wolfgang Becker
**European Cinematographer:**

Anthony Dod Mantle for 28 DAYS LATER (UK) Dir Danny Boyle and DOGVILLE (Denmark) Dir Lars von Trier
**Screen International Award - for a non-European Film:**
LES INVASIONS BARBARES (Canada) Dir Denis Arcand
**European Discovery - Fassbinder Award:**
VOZVRASCHENIE (The Return) (Russia) Dir Andrei Zvyagintsev
Special Mention:
GORI VATRA (Bosnia Herzegovina) Dir Pjer Zalica
**European Short Film Award - Prix UIP:**
(A) TORZIJA (Slovenia) Dir Stefan Arsenijevic
**European Documentary Award - Prix Arte:**
S21, LA MACHINE DE MORT KHMERE ROUGE (France) Dir Rithy Panh
**European Achievement in World Cinema:**
Carlo di Palma, Italy
**European Film Academy Lifetime Achievement Award:**
Claude Chabrol, France
**European Critics' Award - Prix Fipresci:**
BUONGIORNO, NOTTE (Italy) Dir Marco Bellocchio
**The Jameson People's Choice Awards
(voted for by film fans across Europe):**
**Best European Director:**
Wolfgang Becker for GOOD BYE, LENIN! (Germany)
Best European Actor:
Daniel Brühl for GOOD BYE, LENIN! (Germany) Dir Wolfgang Becker
**Best European Actress:**
Katrin Sass for GOOD BYE, LENIN! (Germany) Dir Wolfgang Becker

# EVENING STANDARD BRITISH FILM AWARDS
Awarded in London, 5 February 2003

## Evening Standard
Northcliffe House
2 Derry Street
London W8 5EE

Tel: 020 7938 600
Website: www.thisislondon.co.uk

**Best Film:**
DIRTY PRETTY THINGS (US/UK) Dir Stephen Frears
Best Actor: Chiwetel Ejiofor Hunter
**Peter Sellers Award for Comedy:**
LOST IN LA MANCHA (UK) Dir (Keith Fulton)
**The Carlton Television Most Promising Newcomer:**
Asif Kapadia for directing THE WARRIOR (UK/France)
Technical Achievement: Eve Stuart for production design of ALL OR NOTHING (UK/France) Dir (Mike Leigh)
**Special Award:**
Barbara Broccoli and Michael G. Wilson for 40 years of James Bond

# 60th GOLDEN GLOBE AWARDS
Awarded in Los Angeles, 19 January 2003

## Golden Globes
Hollywood Foreign Press Association
646 North Robertson Boulevard
West Hollywood
California 90069
Tel: (310) 657 1731
Fax: (310) 657 5576
email: hfpa95@aol.com
Website: www.hfpa.com

**Best Motion Picture - Drama:**
THE HOURS (US/UK) Dir Stephen Daldry
**Best Motion Picture - Musical or Comedy:**
CHICAGO (US/Germany) Dir Rob Marshall
**Best Director:**
Martin Scorsese for GANGS OF NEW YORK (US)
**Best Foreign Language Film:**
HABLE CON ELLA (Talk to Her) (Spain) Dir Pedro Almodóvar
**Best Performance by an Actor in a Motion Picture - Drama:**
Jack Nicholson for ABOUT SCHMIDT (US) Dir Alexander Payne
**Best Performance by an Actor in a Motion Picture - Comedy or Musical:**
Richard Gere in CHICAGO (US/Germany) Dir Rob Marshall
**Best Performance by an Actor in a Supporting Role in a Motion Picture:**
Chris Cooper in ADAPTATION (US) Dir Spike Jonze
**Best Performance by an Actress in a Motion Picture - Drama:**
Nicole Kidman for THE HOURS (US/UK) Dir Stephen Daldry
**Best Performance by an Actress in a Motion Picture - Comedy or Musical:**
Renée Zellweger in CHICAGO (US/Germany) Dir Rob Marshall
**Best Performance by an Actress in a Supporting Role in a Motion Picture:**
Meryl Streep in ADAPTATION (US) Dir Spike Jonze
**Best Screenplay - Motion Picture:**
Alexander Payne and Jim Taylor for ABOUT SCHMIDT (US) Dir Alexander Payne
**Best Original Score - Motion Picture:**
Elliott Goldenthal for FRIDA (US) Dir Julie Taymor
**Best Original Song - Motion Picture:**
THE HANDS THAT BUILT AMERICA  Music and Lyrics: U2 from GANGS OF NEW YORK (US) Dir Martin Scorsese
**Cecil B. DeMille Award:**
Gene Hackman

# INDIAN INTERNATIONAL FILM ACADEMY AWARDS
Awarded 17 May 2003, Johannesburg, South Africa

Indian International Film Academy
Website: www.iifa.com

**Best Picture:**
DEVDAS
**Best Director:**
Sanjay Leela Bhansali for DEVDAS
**Actor in a Leading Role**
Shah Rukh Khan for DEVDAS Dir Sanjay Leela Bhansali
**Actress in a Leading Role:**
Aishwarya Rai for DEVDAS Dir Sanjay Leela Bhansali
**Actor in a Supporting Role:**
Mohanlal for COMPANY Dir Ram Gopal Verma
**Actress in a Supporting Role:**
Kiron Kher for DEVDAS Dir Sanjay Leela Bhansali
**Lyrics:**
Nusrat Badr for DOLA RE DOLA
**Performance in a Negative Role:**
Akshaye Khanna for HUMRAAZ  Dir Abbas-Mustan
**Performance in a Comic Role:**
Mahesh Manjrekar for KAANTE  Dir Sanjay Gupta

**Composer:**
A.R. Rahman for SAATHIYA Dir Shaad Ali
**Male Playback Singer:**
Sonu Nigam for SAATHIYA Dir Shaad Ali
**Female Playback Singer:**
Shreya Ghosal and Kavita Krishnamurthi for DOLA RE DOLA
**Best Story:**
Jaideep Sahni for COMPANY Dir Ram Gopal Verma
**Sound Recording:**
Jitendra Chowdhary, Vikram Motwane, Kunal Sharma for DEVEDAS Dir Sanjay Leela Bhansali
**Costume Designer:**
Neeta Lulla, Abu Jani, Sandeep Khosla, Reza Sharifi for DEVDAS Dir Sanjay Leela Bhansali
**Song Recording:**
Daman Sood, Bishwadeep Chattarjee, Tanay Gajjar for DEVDAS Dir Sanjay Leela Bhansali
**Art Direction:**    Nitin Chandrakant Desai for DEVDAS Dir Sanjay Leela Bhansali
**Dialogue:**
Prakash Kapadia for DEVDAS Dir Sanjay Leela Bhansali
**Choreography:**
Saroj Khan for DEVDAS Dir Sanjay Leela Bhansali
**Cinematography:**
Binod Pradhan for DEVDAS Dir Sanjay Leela Bhansali
**Background Score:**
A.R. Rahman for SAATHIYA Dir Shaad Ali
**Editing:**
Chandan Arora for COMPANY Dir Ram Gopal Verma
**Screenplay:**
Mahesh Bhatt for RAAZ Dir Vikram Bhatt
**Sound Re - recording:**
Leslie Fernandes for DEVDAS Dir Sanjay Leela Bhansali
**Make-up:**
Arun Pillai, Jaywant Parab, Pradeep Nahate for DEVDAS Dir Sanjay Leela Bhansali
**Special Effects:**
Prime Focus for KAANTE Dir Sanjay Gupta
**Action:**
Allan Amin for COMPANY Dir Ram Gopal Verma
**Outstanding Indian Contribution to International Cinema:**
Aparna Sen
**Lifetime Achievement Award:**
Dev Anand
**Special Diva Award:**
Rekha
**Samsung Style Icon Award:**
Fardeen Khan
**Sony Face of the Year:**
Esha Deol and John Abraham

# 38TH KARLOVY VARY INTERNATIONAL FILM FESTIVAL

**Held 4-12 July 2003 at Karlovy Vary, Czech Republic.**
**Film Servis Festival Karlovy Vary**
**Panská 1110 00 Prague**
Tel: (420) 221 411 011
Fax: (420) 221 411 033
email: festival@iffkv.cz
Website:www.iffkv.cz

**Grand Prix – Crystal Globe:**
LA FINESTRA DI FRONTE (Facing Window) (Italy/UK/Turkey/Portugal) Dir Ferzan Ozpetek

Special Jury Prize: BABUSJA (Russia/France) Dir Lidia Bobrova
**Best Director Award:**
Ferzan Ozpetek for LA FINESTRA DI FRONTE (Facing Window) (Italy/UK/Turkey/Portugal **Best Actress Award (Ex-Aequo):**
Sylvie Testud for STUPEUR ET TREMBLEMENTS (France/Japan) Dir Alain Corneau
Giovanna Mezzogiorne for LA FINESTRA DI FRONTE (Facing Window) (Italy/UK/Turkey/Portugal) Dir Ferzan Ozpetek
**Best Actor Award:**
Björn Kjellman for SE TIL VENSTRE, DER ER EN SVENSKER (Denmark) Dir Natasha Arthy
**Special Jury Mentions:**
STUPEUR ET TREMBLEMENTS (France/Japan) Dir Alain Corneau (for best screenplay)
A RÓZSA ÉNEKEI (Hungary) Dir Andor Szilágyi (for best debut feature and its cinematography)

**DOCUMENTARY FILMS IN COMPETITION**
**Best Documentary Film Above 30 Minutes in Length:**
JESUS, DU WEISST (Austria) Dir Ulrich Seidl
**Best Documentary Film Lasting 30 Minutes or Less:**
ZONEN (Sweden) Dir Esaias Baitel
**Special Mention:**
VAVERAGROGH (Armenia) Dir Harutyun Khachatryan
KROPPIN MIN (Norway) Dir Margreth Olin
**PORTRET (Russia) Dir Sergey Loznitsa**

**OTHER PRIZES AWARDED AT THE FESTIVAL**
**Award for Outstanding Artistic Contribution to World Cinema:**
Stephen Frears, United Kingdom
Ji?í Menzel, Czech Republic
Morgan Freeman, USA
**Prize of the Town of Karlovy Vary:**
HAENSUN (The Coast Guard)(Korea) Dir Kim-Ki-duk
**Mladá Fronta Dnes Audience Prize:**
BUDDY (Norway) Morten Tyldum

**NON STATUTORY AWARDS**
**The Philip Morris Film Award:**
KOKTEBEL (Russia) Dir Boris Khlebnikov, Alexei Popogrebsky
EDI (Poland) Dir Piotr Trzaskalski
**Award of International Film Critics (FIPRESCI)**
HAEANSUN (The Coast Guard) (Korea) Dir Kim Ki-duk
**The Don Quijote Prize (FICC - International Federation of Film Societies)**
BABUSJA (Russia/France) Dir Lidia Bobrova
**Ecumenical Jury Award:**
**BABUSJA (Russia/France) Dir Lidia Bobrova**
**NETPAC AWARD**
HAEANSUN (The Coast Guard) (Korea) Dir Kim Ki-duk

**STUDENT FILMS**
**Best Student Film:**
LET'S GO FOR A WALK ((Russia) Dir Julia Kolesnik
**Special Prizes:**
HINH BONG (Germany)Dir Robin van Hardenberg
ORPHÉE (France) Dir Kamen Kalu
**Best collection of student films:**
FAMU, Czech Republic

## 56TH LOCARNO INTERNATIONAL FILM FESTIVAL

Held 6-16 August 2003, at Locarno, Switzerland

### Locarno International Film Festival

Via Ciseri 23
6600 Locarno
Switzerland
Tel: (41) 91 756 2121
Fax: (41) 91 756 2149
email: info@pardo.ch
Website: www.pardo.ch

**Golden Leopard:**
KHAMSOH PANI (Silent Waters)
(Pakistan/France/Germany) Dir Sabiha Sumar
**Special Jury Prize:**
MARIA (Romania/Germany/France) Dir Calin Netzer
**Silver Leopard:**
GORI VATRA (Bosnia Herzegovina/Austria) Dir Pjer
Zalica
**Silver Leopard for best first or second feature film:**
THIRTEEN (US) Dir Catherine Hardwicke
**Leopard for Best Actress:**
Holly Hunter for THIRTEEN (US) Dir Catherine
Hardwicke
Diana Dumbrava for MARIA (Romania/Germany/France)
Dir Calin Netzer
Kirron Kher for KHAMSOH PANI (Silent Water)
(Pakistan/France/Germany) Dir Sabiha Sumar
**Leopard for Best Actor:**
Serban Ionescu for MARIA (Romania/Germany/France)
Dir Calin Netzer
**Special Mentions (for Direction):**
ONNA RIHATSUSHI NO KOI (Japan) Dir Masahiro
Kobayashi
DANEHAYE RIZE BARF (Iran) Dir Alireza Amini (Iran)
**FIPRESCI Prize:**
DEPENDENCIA SEXUAL (Bolivia/US) Dir Rodrigo Bellot
**Ecumenical Jury:**
KHAMSOH PANI (Silent Waters)
(Pakistan/France/Germany) Dir Sabiha Sumar
**INTERNATIONAL FEDERATION OF CINEMA CLUBS
(FICC)**
**Don Quijote Prize:**
BOM, YEOREUM, GAEUL, GYEOWOLL, GEURIGO,
BOM (Korea/Germany) Dir Kim Ki-duk
Special Mention:
LES MARINS PERDUS Dir Claire Devers
**KHAMSOH PANI (Silent Waters)
(Pakistan/France/Germany) Dir Sabiha Sumar**
**CICAE/ARTE Prize:**
BOM, YEOREUM, GAEUL, GYEOWOLL, GEURIGO,
BOM (Korea/Germany) Dir Kim Ki-duk
**Special Mention:**
**GORI VATRA (Bosnia Herzegovina/Austria) Dir Pjer
Zalica NETPAC JURY (to promote Asian Cinema)**
BOM, YEOREUM, GAEUL, GYEOWOLL, GEURIGO,
BOM (Korea/Germany) Dir Kim Ki-duk
**CRITICS WEEK SRG SSR idée Suisse:**
THE WEATHER UNDERGROUND Dir Sam Green, Bill
Siegel
**PRIX DU PUBLIC UBS:**
DAS WUNDER VON BERN (Germany) Dir Sönke
Wortmann

**VIDEO COMPETITION**

Special Jury Prize Mention:
ERKENNEN UND VERFOLGEN (Germany) Dir Harun
Faroki
**Golden Leopard Video C.P. Company:**
CANTATA DE LAS COSAS SOLAS (Argentina) Dir Willi
Behnisch
IXIEME, JURNAL D'UN PRISONNIER (Switzerland) Dir
Pierre- Yves Borgeaux, Stephane Block

**JUNIOR JURY**
**First Prize:**
BOM, YEOREUM, GAEUL, GYEOWOLL, GEURIGO,
BOM (Korea/Germany) Dir Kim Ki-duk
**Second Prize:**
AU SUD DES NUAGES (Switzerland) Dir Jean-François
Amiguet
**Third Prize:**
GORI VATRA (Bosnia Herzegovina/Austria) Dir Pjer
Zalica
**Special Prize:**
DANEHAYE RIZE BARF (Iran) Dir Alireza Amini
**Special Mention:**
KHAMSOH PANI (Silent Waters)
(Pakistan/France/Germany) Dir Sabiha Sumar
MARIA (Romania/Germany/France) Dir Calin Netzer

**LEOPARDS OF TOMORROW - NEW SWISS TALENT**
**Golden Leopard SRG SSR idée suisse:**
L'ESCALIER Dir Frédéric Mermoud
**Silver Leopard Kodak Prize:**
LE DORMEUR Dir Richard Szotyori
**The Action Light Prize for Best Swiss Newcomer:**
MEYERS Dir Steven Hayes
**LEOPARDS OF TOMORROW - SCANDINAVIAN**
**Golden Leopard SRG SSR idée suisse:**
VIKTOR OCH HANS BRÖDER Dir Marten Klingberg
**Silver Leopard Kodak Prize:**
ONNENPELI Dir Aleksi Salmenperä
**The Film and Video Prize for Subtitles:**
HEIMAT Dir Arild Frölich
**Special Mention:**
KALA (Fish) Dir Jonathan Davies
**LEOPARDS OF TOMORROW Awarded by The Junior
Jury**
**LOT - NEW SWISS TALENT (Junior Jury):**
VIANDES Dir Bruno Deville
**Special Mention:**
SCHENGLET Dir Laurent Nègre
**LOT - SCANDINAVIAN (Junior Jury):**
REGJERINGEN MARTIN Dir Roar Uthaug
**Special Mention:**
TUNNELEN Dir Claus Schrøder Nielsen

## LONDON FILM FESTIVAL

47th Times bfi London Film Festival
Held in London, 22 October-6 November 2003

**British Film Institute
21 Stephen Street
London W1T 1LN.**
Tel: 020 7815 1322
Fax: 020 7633 0786
Website: www.lff.org.uk
**Sutherland Trophy:**
OSAMA (Afghanistan/Japan/Ireland) Dir Siddiq Barmak
**FIPRESCI Prize:**
LE MONDE VIVANT (The Living

World)(France/Belgium) Dir Eugene Green
**Satyajit Ray Award:**
EN SOM HODDER (Someone Like Hodder(Denmark)
Dir Henrik Ruben Genz
**The Satyajit Ray Foundation**
**24 Southwood Lawn Road**
**London N6 5SF.**
Website: www.rayfoundation.mistral.co.uk/foundat.htm

## 23rd LONDON CRITICS' CIRCLE FILM AWARDS
Held at Dorchester Hotel, London 12 February 2003

### Critics Circle Film Awards
51 Vartry Road
London N15 6PS
email: info@criticscircle.org.uk
Website: www.criticscircle.org.uk

**British Film Of The Year:**
ALL OR NOTHING (UK/France) Dir Mike Leigh
**Film of The Year:**
ABOUT SCHMIDT (US) Dir Alexander Payne
**British Actor of The Year:**
Hugh Grant for ABOUT A BOY
(Germany/US/France/UK) Dir Paul Weitz
**Actor of The Year:**
Michael Caine for THE QUIET AMERICAN
(US/Germany/UK) Dir Phillip Noyce
**British Actress of The Year:**
Lesley Manville  for All Or Nothing (UK/France) Dir Mike Leigh
**Actress of The Year:**
Stockard Channing for The BUSINESS OF STRANGERS
(US) Dir Patrick Stettner
**British Actor In A Supporting Role:**
Kenneth Branagh for HARRY POTTER AND THE
CHAMBER OF SECRETS (US/UK/Germany) Dir Chris
Columbus
**British Actress In A Supporting Role:**
Emily Watson for RED DRAGON (US/Germany) Dir Brett
Ratner
**British Director of The Year:**
Christopher Nolan for INSOMNIA (US)
**Director of The Year:**
Phillip Noyce for THE QUIET
AMERICAN(US/Germany/UK)
**British Screenwriter of The Year:**
Steven Knight for DIRTY PRETTY THINGS (US/UK) Dir
Stephen Frears
**Screenwriter of The Year:**
Andrew Bovell for LANTANA (Australia/Germany) Dir
Lawrence
**Foreign Language Film of The Year:**
Y TU MAMÁ TAMBIÉN (Mexico) Dir Alfonso Cuarón
**British Newcomers of The Year:**
Martin Compson for SWEET SIXTEEN
(UK/Germany/Spain/France/Italy) Dir Ken Loach
Keira Knightley for BEND IT LIKE BECKHAM
(Germany/UK) Dir Gurinder Chadha

## 75th OSCARS - ACADEMY OF MOTION PICTURE ARTS AND SCIENCES
Awarded on 23 March 2003, Kodak Theatre
Hollywood, Los Angeles
Website:www.oscar.com and www.oscars.org

**Best Film:**

CHICAGO (US/Germany) Dir Rob Marshall
**Best Director:**
Roman Polanski for THE PIANIST
(France/Poland/Germany/UK/US)
**Best Actor:**
Adrien Brody for THE PIANIST
(France/Poland/Germany/UK) Dir Roman Polanski
**Best Supporting Actor:**
Chris Cooper for ADAPTATION (US) Dir Spike Jonze
**Best Actress:**
Nicole Kidman for THE HOURS (US/UK) Dir Stephen
Daldry
**Best Supporting Actress:**
Catherine Zeta-Jones for CHICAGO (US/Germany) Dir
Rob Marshall
**Best Art Direction:**
John Myhre, Gordon Sim (Set Decoration) for CHICAGO
(US/Germany) Dir Rob Marshall
**Best Cinematography:**
Conrad L. Hall for ROAD TO PERDITION (US) Dir Sam
Mendes
**Best Costume Design:**
Colleen Atwood for CHICAGO (US/Germany) Dir Rob
Marshall
**Best Documentary Short:**
William Guttentag and Robert David Port for TWIN
TOWERS (US)
**Best Documentary Feature:**
Michael Moore for BOWLING FOR COLUMBINE
(Canada/ Germany/US)
**Best Film Editing:**
Martin Walsh for CHICAGO (US/Germany) Dir Rob
Marshall
**Best Foreign Language Film:**
nirgendwo in afrika (Germany) Dir Caroline Link
**Best Make Up:**
Beatrice DeAlba and John E. Jackson for FRIDA (US) Dir
Julie Taymor
**Best Music (Score):**
Elliot Goldenthal for FRIDA (US) Dir Julie Taymor
**Best Music (Song):**
Luis Resto, Eminen and Jeffrey Bass for 8 MILE (US) Dir
Curtis Hanson
**Best Animated Feature:**
SEN TO CHIHIRO NO KAMIKAKUSHI (Spirited Away)
(Japan) Dir Hayao Miyazaki
**Best Short - Live Action:**
Mie Andreasen and Martin Strange-Hansen for DER ER
EN YNDIG  MAND
**Best Short Animated:**
Eric Armstrong for THE CHUBBCHUBBS!
**Best Sound:**
David Lee, Michael Minkler and Dominick R. Tavella for
CHICAGO (US/Germany) Dir Rob Marshall
**Best Sound Editing:**
Michael Hopkins and Ethan van der Ryn for THE LORD
OF THE RINGS  THE TWO TOWERS (US/New Zealand)
Dir Peter Jackson
**Best Visual Effects:**
Jim Rygiel, Randall William Cook, Joe Letteri and Alex
Funke for The LORD OF THE RINGS  THE TWO
TOWERS (US/New Zealand) Dir Peter Jackson
**Best Screenplay (Adapted):**
Ronald Harwood for THE PIANIST
(France/Poland/Germany/UK/US) Dir Roman Polanski
**Best Screenplay (Original):**
Pedro Almodóvar for HABLE CON ELLA (Spain) Dir
Pedro Almodóvar

Lifetime Achievement Award:
Peter O'Toole

## SCREEN NATION FILM AND TELEVISION AWARDS

(Formerly Black Filmmakers Magazine (BFM) Film and Television Awards). Awarded 10 September, 2003 at Empire Cinema, Leicester Square, London.

Screen Nation
PO Box 43831
London NW6 5WE.
Tel: 020 7243 9846
Fax: 0709 211 0140
Website: www.screennation.com

**Best Female Performance in Film:**
Sophie Okenedo in DIRTY PRETTY THINGS (US/UK) Dir Stephen Frears
**Best Male Performance in Film:**
Chiwetel Ejiofor in DIRTY PRETTY THINGS (US/UK) Dir Stephen Frears
**Achievement in Production (Film):**
Leon Herbert and John Herbert for EMOTIONAL BACKGAMMON (UK) Dir Leon Herbert
**Winners of publicly voted People's Choice International Screen Awards -**
Best Film: CITY OF GOD (Brazil/Germany/France) Dir Fernando Meirelles
**Male Screen Personality:**
Laurence Fishbourne
**Female Screen Personality:**
Queen Latifah
**Lifetime Achievement Award:**
Spike Lee

## VENICE FILM FESTIVAL
Held in Venice, 27 August-6 September 2003

## 60th Mostra Internazionale d'Arte Cinematografica
San Marco, 1364
Ca' Giustinian
30124 Venice - Italy
Tel: (39) 041 5218878
Fax: (39) 041 5227539
email: cinema@labiennale.com
Website: www.labiennale.org

**Golden Lion for Best Film:**
VOZVRA?CENJE (The Return) (Russia) Dir Andrej Zvjagintsev
**Jury Grand Prix, Silver Lion:**
LE CERF-VOLANT (France) Dir Randa Chahal Sabbag
**Special Director's Award, Silver Lion:**
Takeshi Kitano for ZATOICHI (Japan)
**Award for an Outstanding Individual Contribution:**
Marco Bellocchio for the screenplay of BUONGIORNO, NOTTE (Italy) Dir Marco Bellocchio
**Coppa Volpi for Best Actor:**
Sean Penn in 21 GRAMS (Germany/US) Dir Alejandro González
**Coppa Volpi for Best Actress:**
Katja Riemann in ROSENSTRASSE (Germany/Belgium/Netherlands) Dir Margarethe von Trotta
**"Marcello Mastroianni" Award for Best Young Actor or**

Actress:
Najat Benssallem in RAJA (France/Morocco) Dir Jacques Doillon
**SHORT FILMS**
**Silver Lion for Best Short Film:**
NEFT (The Oil) (Russia/Azerbaijan) Dir Murad Ibragimbekov
**UIP Award for Best European Short Film:**
THE TRUMOUSE SHOW (Spain) Dir Julio Robeledo
**Special Mention:**
HOCHBETRIEB (Germany) Dir Andreas Krein
CONTROCORRENTE (UPSTREAM)
**San Marco Award:**
VODKA LEMON (France/Italy/Switzerland/Armenia) Dir Hiner Salemm
**Special Director's Award:**
Michael Schorr for SCHULTZE GETS THE BLUES (Germany)
**Upstream Prize for Best Actor:**
Asano Tadanobu for LAST LIFE IN THE UNIVERSE (Thailand/Netherlands/Hong Kong/UK) Dir Pen-ek Ratanaruang
**Upstream Prize for Best Actress:**
Scarlett Johansson in LOST IN TRANSLATION (US/Japan) Dir Sofia Coppola
**Special Mention:**
LA QUIMERA DE LOS HEROES (Argentina/France/Denmark) Dir Daniel Rosenfeld
**The International Jury of the "Luigi De Laurentiis" Award for a First Film - Lion of the Future:**
VOZVRA?CENJE (The Return) (Russia) Dir Andrej Zvjagintsev
**Special Mentions:**
POSLEDNIJ POEZD (The Last Train) (Russia) Dir Aleksej German
BALLO A TRE PASSI (Italy) Salvatore Mereu

# Film Awards 2004

This section features some of the principal film festival prizes and awards from 1 January 2004 to 30 June 2004.

## BAFTA FILM AWARDS
The Orange British Academy Film Awards
Awarded on 15 February 2004 at The Odeon, Leicester Square, London

## BAFTA
195 Piccadilly
London W1V OLN
Tel: 020 7734 0022
Fax: 020 7734 1792
Website: www.bafta.org

**Best Film:**
THE LORD OF THE RINGS  THE RETURN OF THE KING (Germany/New Zealand/US) Dir Peter Jackson
**Academy Fellowship:**
John Boorman
**Michael Balcon Award For Outstanding British Contribution to Cinema:**
Working Title Films
**Alexander Korda Award For Outstanding British Film of the Year:**
TOUCHING THE VOID (UK/US) Dir Kevin MacDonald
**David Lean Award For Achievement in Direction:**
Peter Weir for MASTER AND COMMANDER THE FAR SIDE OF THE WORLD (US)
**Best Screenplay (Original):**
Tom McCarthy for THE STATION AGENT (US) Dir Tom McCarthy
**Best Screenplay (Adapted):**
Fran Walsh, Philippa Boyens, Peter Jackson for THE LORD OF THE RINGS  THE RETURN OF THE KING (Germany/New Zealand/US) Dir Peter Jackson
**Performance by an Actress in a Leading Role:**
Scarlett Johansson in LOST IN TRANSLATION (US/Japan) Dir Sofia Coppola
**Performance by an Actor in a Leading Role:**
Bill Murray in LOST IN TRANSLATION (US/Japan) Dir Sofia Coppola
**Performance by an Actress in a Supporting Role:**
Renee Zellweger in COLD MOUNTAIN (US/UK/Romania/Italy) Dir Anthony Minghella
**Performance by an Actor in a Supporting Role:**
Bill Nighy in LOVE ACTUALLY (UK/US/France) Dir Richard Curtis
**Film Not in the English Language:**
IN THIS WORLD (UK) Dir Michael Winterbottom
**Anthony Asquith Award For Achievement in Film Music:**
Gabriel Yared/T-Bone Burnett for COLD MOUNTAIN (US/UK/Romania/Italy) Dir Anthony Minghella
**Carl Foreman Award For Special Achievement by a British Director/Producer or Writer in their First Feature Film:**
Emily Young: Director/Writer for KISS OF LIFE (UK/France/Canada)
**Best Cinematography:**
Andrew Lesnie for THE LORD OF THE RINGS  THE RETURN OF THE KING (Germany/New Zealand/US) Dir Peter Jackson
**Best Production Design:**
William Sandall for MASTER AND COMMANDER  THE FAR SIDE OF THE WORLD (US) Dir Peter Weir
**Best Costume Design:**
Wendy Stites for MASTER AND COMMANDER  THE FAR SIDE OF THE WORLD (US) Dir Peter Weir
**Best Editing:**
Sarah Flack for LOST IN TRANSLATION (US/Japan) Dir Sofia Coppola
**Best Sound:**
Richard King, Doug Hemphill,Paul Massey,Art Rochester for
MASTER AND COMMANDER  THE FAR SIDE OF THE WORLD (US) Dir Peter Weir
**Achievement in Special Visual Effects:**
Joe Letteri, Jim Rygiel, Randall William Cook, Alex Funke for THE LORD OF THE RINGS  THE RETURN OF THE KING (Germany/New Zealand/US) Dir Peter Jackson
**Best Make Up/Hair:**
Ve Neill, Martin Samuel for PIRATES OF THE CARIBBEAN: THE CURSE OF THE BLACK PEARL (US) Dir Gore Verbinski
**Best Short Film:**
BROWN PAPER BAG (UK) Dir Michael Baig Clifford
**Best Short Animation:**
JOJO IN THE STARS (UK) Dir Marc Craste
**Orange Audience Award:**
THE LORD OF THE RINGS  THE RETURN OF THE KING (Germany/New Zealand/US) Dir Peter Jackson

## 54th BERLIN INTERNATIONAL FILM FESTIVAL
Held 5-15 February 2004, Berlin
Internationale Filmfestspiele Berlin

## Berlin International Film Festival
Potsdamer Strafle 5
D-10785 Berlin
Tel: (49) 030 25 920
Fax: (49) 030 25 920 299
email: info@berlinale.de
Website: www.berlinale.de

### INTERNATIONAL JURY
**Golden Bear:**
GEGEN DIE WAND (Head On)(Germany/Turkey) Dir Fatih Akin
**Jury Grand Prix, Silver Berlin Bear:**
EL ABRAZO PARTIDO (Lost Embrace) (Argentina) Dir Daniel Burman
**Silver Berlin Bear for the Best Director:**
Kim Ki-Duk for SAMARIA (Samaritan Girl) (Korea)
**Silver Berlin Bear ex aequo for Best Actress:**
Catalina Sandino Moreno for MARIA, LLENA ERES DE GRACIA (Maria Full of Grace) (US/Colombia) Dir Joshua Marston
Charlize Theron for MONSTER (Germany/US) Dir Patty Jenkins
**Silver Berlin Bear for the Best Actor:**
Daniel Hendler for EL ABRAZO PARTIDO (Argentina) Dir Daniel Burman
**Silver Berlin Bear for an individual artistic contribution:**
The Acting Ensemble of OM JAG VANDER MIG OM (Sweden) Dir Bjorn Runge
**Silver Berlin Bear for best film music:**
Banda Osiris for PRIMO AMORE (Italy) Dir Matteo Garrone
**AGICOA  Blue Angel award for best European film:**
OM JAG VANDER MIG OM (Sweden) Dir Bjorn Runge
**The Alfred Bauer Prize for best first feature:**

MARIA, LLENA ERES DE GRACIA (Maria Full of Grace)
(US/Colombia) Dir Joshua Marston

**INTERNATIONAL SHORT FILM JURY**
**Golden Bear for Best Short Film:**
UN CARTUS DE KENT SI UN PACHET DE CAFEA
(Romania) Dir Cristi Puiu
**Jury Prize, Silver Berlin Bear:**
VET! (Netherlands) Dir Karin Junger, Brigit Hillenius
**Special Mention:**
PUBLIC/PRIVATE (Argentina) Dir Christoph Behl

**OTHER AWARDS**
**Prize of the Ecumenical Jury:**
AE FOND KISS (UK/Italy/Germany/Spain/France) Dir Ken
Loach
**Special Mention:**
SVJEDOCI (Witnesses)(Croatia) Dir Vinko Bresan
**Award for a film screened in the Panorama:**
MI PIACE LAVORARE (Italy) Dir Francesca Comencini
**Award for a film screened in the Forum:**
FOLLE EMBELLIE (France/Belgium/Canada) Dir
Dominique Cabrera
**Peace Film Prize for Best Feature:**
SVJEDOCI (Witnesses)(Croatia) Dir Vinko Bresan
**FIPRESCI prizes**
**Prize for a film screened in Competition:**
GEGEN DIE WAND (Head On)(Germany/Turkey) Dir
Fatih Akin
**Prize for a film screened in the Panorama:**
LA FACE CACHEE DE LA LUNE (Canada) Dir Robert
Lapage
**Prize for a film screened in the Forum:**
THE TIME WE KILLED (US) Dir Jennifer Reeves
**Prize of the Guild of German Art House Cinemas**
AE FOND KISS (UK/Italy/Germany/Spain/France) Dir Ken
Loach
**Readers' Prize of The Berliner Morgenpost**
25 DEGRÉS EN HIVER (Belgium/France/Spain) Dir
Stephane Vuillet
**C.I.C.A.E. Prize**
**Prize for a film screened in the Panorama:**
O OUTRO LADO DA RUA (Brazil/France) Dir Marcos
Bernstein
**Prize for a film screened in the Forum:**
B-HAPPY (Chile/Spain/Venezuela) Dir Gonzalo Justiniano
**Prix UIP Berlin**
UN CARTUS DE KENT SI UN PACHET DE CAFEA
(Cigarettes and Coffee)(Romania) Dir Cristi Puiu
**LVT – Manfred Salzberger Prize:**
WILD SIDE (France/Belgium/UK) Dir Sebastian Lifshitz
**Panorama Short Film Award**
**Best Short Film:**
TWO CARS, ONE NIGHT (New Zealand) Dir Taika
Waititi
New York Film Academy Scholarship:
FUGUE (Australia) Dir James Brown
**Special Mention:**
LE GARDE DU CORPS (France) Dir Sandrine Dumas
Panorama Audience Award:
DIE SPIELWUTIGEN (Addicted to Acting) (Germany) Dir
Andres Veiel
Panorama Audience Award – Short Film:
EN DEL AV MITT HJARTA (Sweden) Dir Johan Brisinger
**Honary Golden Bear:**
Fernando Solanas
**Berlinale Camera Awards:**
Willy Somerfield, Rgina Ziegler, Eria Rabau, Rolf Bahr
**Prizes of the Deutsches Kinderhilfswerk**

**Grand Prix for Best Feature:**
MAGNIFICO (Philippines) Dir Maryo J. de los Reyes
**Special Mention:**
DIE BLINDGÄNGER (Germany) Dir Bernd Sahling
BARBER YOSHINO (Japan) Dir Naoko Ogigami
**Special Prize for Best Short film:**
LUCIA (Germany) Dir Felix Gönnert
Special Mention:
LILLE FAR (Denmark) Dir Michael W. Horsten
CRACKER BAG (Australia) Dir Glendyn Ivin
**Crystal Bears**
**Crystal Bear for best feature film of the Kinderfilmfest:**
MAGNIFICO (Philippines) Dir Maryo J. de los Reyes
**Special Mention:**
DIE BLINDGÄNGER (Germany) Dir Bernd Sahling
LA PROPHETIE DE GRENOUILLES (Raining Cats and
Frogs) (France) Dir Jacques-Remy Girerd
**Crystal Bear for best short film:**
NUIT D'ORAGE (Stormy Night) (Canada) Dir Michele
Lemieux
**Special Mention:**
CIRCUIT MARINE (France/Canada) Dir Isabelle Favez
MAREE (Italy) Dir James Pellerito
**14plus Crystal Bear for Best Feature:**
THE WOODEN CAMERA (South Africa/France/UK) Dir
Ntshavheni Wa Luruli
**Special Mention:**
QUALITY OF LIFE (US) Dir Benjamin Morgan
**Teddy 2004**
**Teddy for Best Feature Film:**
WILD SIDE (France/Belgium/UK) Dir Sébastian Lifshitz
**Teddy for Best Documentary:**
THE NOMI SONG (Germany) Dir Andrew Horn
**Teddy for Best Short Film:**
¿CON QUÉ LA LAVARÉ? (Spain) Dir Maria Trénor
**Special Teddy:**
Edition Salzgeber
**Wolfgang Staudte Award 2004:**
FINAL SOLUTION (South Africa/US) Dir Rakesh Sharma
**Readers' Prize of The Siegessaule:**
D.E.B.S. (US) Dir Angela Robinson
**Caligari Film Prize 2004:**
DOPO MEZZANOTTE (Italy) Dir Davide Ferrario
**NETPAC Prize:**
YUNB DE NAN FANG (South of the Clouds) (China) Dir
Zhu Wen
**Special Mention:**
FINAL SOLUTION (South Africa/US) Dir Rakesh Sharma
**Don Quixote Prize of the International Federation of**
**Film Societies:**
DOPO MEZZANOTTE (Italy) Dir Davide Ferrario
**Special Mention:**
B-HAPPY (Chile/Spain/Venezuela) Dir Gonzalo Justiniano
CAMPFIRE (Israel) Dir Joseph Cedar
**Readers' Prize of The Berliner Zeitung:**
DEALER (Hungary) Dir Benedek Fliegauf
**Planet Documentary Film Award:**
GOAT WALKER (Poland) Dir Bartek Konopka, Piotr
Rosolowski
**Dialogue en Perspective Award:**
FLAMMEND' HERZ (Germany/Switzerland) Dir Andreas
Schuler, Oliver Ruts
**Special Mention:**
DER TYP (Germany) Dir Patrick Tauss
**Volkswgen Score Prize for sound designers and**
**composers:**
Tom Third
**Berlin Today Award:**
BEERLINBEIRUT (Germany) Dir Myrna Maakaron

## 57th CANNES FESTIVAL

Held in Cannes, 12-23 May 2004

### Festival de Cannes

Department Films
3, rue Amelie
F-75007 Paris
Tel: (33) 1 53 59 61 20
Fax: (3)3 1 53 59 61 24
email residence@festival-cannes.fr
Website: www.festivalcannes.org

**Feature Film Palme d'Or:**
FAHRENHEIT 9/11 (US) Dir Michael Moore
**Grand Prize:**
OLD BOY (Korea) Dir PARK Chan-wook
**Best Director Award:**
Tony Gatlif for EXILS (France)
**Jury Prize:**
SUD PRALAD (Tropical
Malady)(France/Thailand/Itlay/Germany) Dir
Apichatpong Weerasethakul
**Jury Prize:**
Irma P. Hall in THE LADYKILLERS (US) Dir Joel and
Ethan Coen
**Best Screenplay:**
Agnès Jaoui, Jean-Pierre Bacri for COMME UNE IMAGE
(France) Dir Agnes Jaoui
**Best Performance by an Actress:**
Maggie Cheung in CLEAN (France/UK/Canada) Dir
Olivier Assayas
**Best Performance by an Actor:**
Yagira Yuya in DAREMO SHIRANAI (Nobody Knows)
(Japan) Dir KORE-EDA Hirokazu
**Short Film Palme d'Or:**
TRAFIC (Romania) Dir Catalin Mitulescu
**Short Film Jury Prize:**
FLATLIFE (Belgium) Dir Jonas Geirnaert
**Prix Un Certain Regard:**
MOOLAADÉ (Senegal) Dir Ousmane Sembene
**Prix Un Regard Original:**
WHISKY (Uruguay) Dir Juan-Pablo Rebella, Pablo Stoll
**Prix Un Regard Vers L'Avenir:**
KHÂKESTAR-O-KÂK (Earth and Ashes) (Afghanistan)
Dir Atiq Rahimi
**Camera d'Or:**
OR (Mon Tresor)(Israel/France) Dir Keren YEDAYA
**Camera d'Or Special Mentions:**
LU CHENG (Passages) (China) Dir Yang Chao
KHAB É TALKH (Bitter Dream) (Iran) Dir Moshen
Amiryoussefi
**Cinéfondation Award (First Prize):**
HAPPY NOW (US) Dir Frederikke Aspöck
**Cinéfondation Award (Second Prize – Ex-æquo):**
CALATORIE LA ORAS (A Trip to the City) (Romania) Dir
Corneliu Porumboiu
99 VUOTTA ELAMASTANI (99 Years of My Life) (Finlnd)
Dir Marja Mikkonen
**Cinéfondation Award (Third Prize):**
**FAJNIE ZE JESTES (Nice to See You) (Poland)** Dir Jan
Komasa
Prix Vulcain de l'Artiste-Technicien: Eric Gautier -
Director of Photography for CLEAN (France/GB/Canada)
Dir Olivier Assayas and DIARIOS DE MOTOCICLETA
(US/France/GB/Germany) Dir Walter Salles

## 29th CÉSARS

Awarded in Paris, 21 February 2004
Selected by L'Académie des Arts et Techniques du Cinéma
19, rue Lauriston
75116 Paris
Tél. : +33 1 53 64 05 25
Fax. : +33 1 53 64 05 24
email: info@lescesarducinema.com
Website: www.lescesarducinema.com

**Best French Film:**
LES INVASIONS BARBARES (Canada/France) Dir Denys
Arcand
**Best Actor:**
Omar Sharif for MONSIEUR IBRAHIM ET LES FLEURS
DU CORAN (France)  Dir Francois Dupeyron
**Best Actress:**
Sylvie Testud for STUPEUR ET TREMBLEMENTS
(France) Dir Alain Corneau
**Best Supporting Actor:**
Darry Cowl for PAS SUR LA BOUCHE
(France/Switzerland) Dir  Alain Resnais
**Best Supporting Actress:**
Julie Depardieu for LA PETITE LILI (France/Canada) Dir
Claude Miller
**Best Director:**
Denys Arcand for LES INVASIONS BARBARES
(Canada/France)
**Best Foreign Film:**
MYSTIC RIVER (US) Dir Clint Eastwood
**Best European Union Film:**
GOOD BYE LENIN! (Germany/Spain) Dir Wolfgang Becker
**Best First Feature Film:**
DEPUIS QU'OTAR EST PARTI France/Belgium) Dir Julie
Bertucelli
**Best Short Film:**
L'HOMME SANS TÊTE (France) Dir Juan Solanas
**Best Original Screenplay:**
Denys Arcand for LES INVASIONS BARBARES
(Canada/France) Dir Denys Arcand
**Best Art Direction:**
Jacques Rouxel for BON VOYAGE (France) Dir Jean-Paul
Rappeneau
**Best Cinematography:**
Thierry Arbogast for BON VOYAGE (France) Dir Jean-
Paul Rappeneau
**Best Costume Design:**
Jackie Budin for PAS SUR LA BOUCHE
(France/Switzerland) Dir  Alain Resnais
**Best Editing:**
Ludo Troch for LA TRILOGIE  UN COUPLE
ÉPATANT/CAVALE/APRÈS LA VIE (France/Belgium) Dir
Lucas Belvaux
**Best Music:**
Benoit Charest for LES TRIPLETTES DE BELLEVILLE
(France/Belgium/Canada/UK) Dir Sylvain
**Best Sound Recordist:**
Christian Monheim for PAS SUR LA BOUCHE
(France/Switzerland) Dir  Alain Resnais
**Best Newcomer, Actor:**
Gregori Dérangère for BON VOYAGE (France) Dir Jean-
Paul Rappeneau
**Best Newcomer, Actress:**
Julie Depardieu for LA PETITE LILI (France/Canada) Dir
Claude Miller
**Honorary César:**
Micheline Presle

## EMPIRE FILM AWARDS
Awarded in London, 4 February 2004

### Empire Magazine
4th Floor
Mappin House
4 Winsley Street
London W1W 8HF
Tel: 020 7437 9011
Fax: 020 7859 8613
email: empire@ecm.emap.com
Website: www.empireonline.co.uk/magazine

**Best Film:**
THE LORD OF THE RINGS  THE RETURN OF THE
KING (Germany/New Zealand/US) Dir Peter Jackson
**Best Actor:**
Johnny Depp for PIRATES OF THE CARIBBEAN: THE
CURSE OF THE BLACK PEARL (US) Dir Gore Verbinski
**Best Actress:**
Uma Thurman in KILL BILL VOL.1 (US) Dir Quentin
Tarantino
**Best Director:**
Quentin Tarantino for KILL BILL VOL.1 (US)
**Best British Film:**
LOVE ACTUALLY (UK/US/France) Dir Richard Curtis
**Best British Actor:**
Andy Serkis in THE LORD OF THE RINGS  THE
RETURN OF THE KING (Germany/New Zealand/US) Dir
Peter Jackson
**Best British Actress:**
Emma Thompson in LOVE ACTUALLY (UK/US/France)
Dir Richard Curtis
**Best Newcomer:**
Martine McCutcheon in LOVE ACTUALLY
(UK/US/France) Dir Richard Curtis
**Empire Independent Spirit Award:**
Roger Corman
**Empire Inspiration Award:**
Ray Harryhausen
**Empire Career Achievement:**
Sigourney Weaver
**Sony Ericsson Scene of the Year:**
Ride of The Rohirrim in THE LORD OF THE RINGS
THE RETURN OF THE KING (Germany/New
Zealand/US) Dir Peter Jackson

## 31st EVENING STANDARD BRITISH FILM AWARDS
Awarded 1 February 2004, The Savoy Hotel, London,

### Evening Standard
Northcliffe House
2 Derry Street
London W8 5EE
Tel: 020 7938 600

**Best Film:**
TOUCHING THE VOID (UK/US) Dir Kevin MacDonald
**Best Actor:**
Paul Bettany in MASTER AND COMMANDER  THE FAR
SIDE OF THE WORLD (US) Dir Peter Weir/THE HEART
OF ME (UK/France) Dir Thaddeus O'Sullivan
**Best Actress:**
Emma Thompson in LOVE ACTUALLY (UK/US/France)

Dir Richard Curtis
**Best Screenplay:**
Gregor Jordan, Nora Maccoby, Eric Weiss for BUFFALO
SOLDIERS (Australia) Dir Gregor Jordan
**Peter Sellers Award for Comedy:**
Bill Nighy in LOVE ACTUALLY (UK/US/France) Dir
Richard Curtis
**Most Promising Newcomer:**
Max Pirkis for MASTER AND MASTER AND
COMMANDER  THE FAR SIDE OF THE WORLD (US)
Dir Peter Weir
**Technical Achievement:**
Seamus McGarvey for cinematography THE HOURS
(US/UK) Dir Stephen Daldry
**Alexander Walker Special Award:**
Michael Winterbottom

## 61st GOLDEN GLOBE AWARDS
Awarded 25 January 2004, Los Angeles

### Golden Globes
Hollywood Foreign Press Association
646 North Robertson Boulevard
West Hollywood
California 90069
Tel: (310) 657 1731
Fax: (310) 657 5576
email: hfpa95@aol.com
Website: www.hfpa.com

**Best Motion Picture - Drama:**
THE LORD OF THE RINGS  THE RETURN OF THE
KING (Germany/New Zealand/US) Dir Peter Jackson
**Best Motion Picture - Musical or Comedy:**
LOST IN TRANSLATION (US/Japan) Dir Sofia Coppola
**Best Director:**
Peter Jackson for THE LORD OF THE RINGS: THE
RETURN OF THE KING (Germany/New Zealand/US)
**Best Foreign Language Film:**
OSAMA Afghanistan) Dir Sedigh Barmak
**Best Performance by an Actor in a Motion Picture -
Drama:**
Sean Penn in MYSTIC RIVER (US/Australia) Dir Clint
Eastwood
**Best Performance by an Actor in a Motion Picture -
Comedy or Musical:**
Bill Murray in LOST IN TRANSLATION (US/Japan) Dir
Sofia Coppola
**Best Performance by an Actor in a Supporting Role in a
Motion Picture:**
Tim Robbins in MYSTIC RIVER (US/Australia) Dir Clint
Eastwood
**Best Performance by an Actress in a Motion Picture -
Drama:**
Charlize Theron in MONSTER Germany/US) Dir Patty
Jenkins
**Best Performance by an Actress in a Motion Picture -
Comedy or Musical:**
Diane Keaton in SOMETHING'S GOTTA GIVE (US) Dir
Nancy Meyers
**Best Performance by an Actress in a Supporting Role in
a Motion Picture:**
Renne Zellweger in COLD MOUNTAIN
(US/UK/Romania/Italy) Dir Anthony Minghella
**Best Screenplay - Motion Picture:**
Sofia Coppola for LOST IN TRANSLATION (US/Japan)

Dir Sofia Coppola
**Best Original Score - Motion Picture:**
Howard Shore for THE LORD OF THE RINGS: THE
RETURN OF THE KING (Germany/New Zealand/US) Dir
Peter Jackson
**Best Original Song - Motion Picture:**
"Into the West" Music and Lyrics by: Howard Shore, Fran
Walsh, Annie Lennox from THE LORD OF THE RINGS
THE RETURN OF THE KING (Germany/New
Zealand/US) Dir Peter Jackson
**Cecil B. DeMille Award:**
Michael Douglas

## INDIAN INTERNATIONAL FILM ACADEMY AWARDS

**Awarded 23 May 2004 in Singapore**
**5th Samsung Indian International Film Academy Awards**
Website: www.iifa.com

**Best Picture:**
KOI MIL GAYA (India) Dir  Rakesh Roshan
**Best Director:**
Rakesh Roshan for KOI MIL GAYA  (India)
**Actor in a Leading Role**
Hrithik Roshan in KOI MIL GAYA  (India) ) Dir  Rakesh
Roshan
**Actress in a Leading Role:**
Preity Zinta for KAL HO NAA HO  (India) Dir Nikhil
Advani
**Actor in a Supporting Role:**
Saif Ali Khan in  KAL HO NAA HO  (India) Dir Nikhil
Advani
**Actress in a Supporting Role:**
Jaya Bachchanan in KAL HO NAA HO  (India) Dir Nikhil
Advani
**Lyrics:**
Javed Akhtar for KAL HO NAA HO  (India) Dir Nikhil
Advani
**Performance in a Negative Role:**
J Feroz Khan in JANASHEEN (India) Dir Ferdeen Khan
**Performance in a Comic Role:**
Boman Irani in MUNNABHAI M.B.B.S (India) Dir
Rajkumar Hirani
**Male Playback Singer:**
Sonu Nigam for KAL HO NAA HO  (India) Dir Nikhil
Advani
**Female Playback Singer:**
Shreya Ghoshal  for  "Jaadu Hai Nasha Hai" from JISM
(India) Dir Amit Saxena
**Music Direction:**
Shankar-Ehsaan-Loy for KAL HO NAA HO  (India) Dir
Nikhil Advani
**Best Story:**
Karan Johar for KAL HO NAA HO  (India) Dir Nikhil
Advani
**Sound Recording:**
Jeetendra Chowdary for KOI MIL GAYA (India) )  Dir
Rakesh Roshan
**Costume Designer:**
Manish Malhotra  for KAL HO NAA HO  (India) Dir
Nikhil Advani
**Song Recording:**
Satish Gupta for KOI MIL GAYA (India) )  Dir  Rakesh
Roshan
**Art Direction:**
Sharmistha Roy  for  KAL HO NAA HO  (India) Dir
Nikhil Advani

**Choreography:**
Farah Khan for  KAL HO NAA HO  (India) Dir Nikhil
Advani
**Cinematography:**
Anil Mehta  for  KAL HO NAA HO  (India) Dir Nikhil
Advani
**Background Score:**
Shankar-Ehsaan-Loy for  KAL HO NAA HO  (India) Dir
Nikhil Advani
**Editing:**
Rajkumar Hirani for  MUNNABHAI M.B.B.S (India) Dir
Rajkumar Hirani
**Screenplay:**
Rajkumar Hirani , Lajan Joseph , Vidhu Vinod Chopra for
MUNNABHAI M.B.B.S (India) Dir Rajkumar Hirani
**Dialogue:**
Abbas Tyrewala for for  MUNNABHAI M.B.B.S (India)
Dir Rajkumar Hirani
**Sound Re - recording:**
Lesli- Anand Theatre for  L.O.C  KARGIL  (India) Dir J.P.
Dutta
**Make-up:**
Mickey Contractor  for KAL HO NAA HO  (India) Dir
Nikhil Advani
**Special Effects (Visual)**
Bimmini Special Fx , Digital Art Media for  KOI MIL
GAYA  (India) Dir  Rakesh Roshan
**Action:**
Bhiku Verma  for  L.O.C  KARGIL  (India) Dir J.P. Dutta

## 24TH LONDON CRITICS' CIRCLE FILM AWARDS

**Held at Dorchester Hotel, London 11 February 2004**

## Critics Circle Film Awards

**51 Vartry Road**
**London N15 6PS**
email: info@criticscircle.org.uk
Website: www.criticscircle.org.uk

**British Film Of The Year:**
THE MAGDALENE SISTERS (UK/Ireland) Dir Peter
Mullan
**Film of The Year:**
MASTER AND COMMANDER  THE FAR SIDE OF THE
WORLD (US) Dir Peter Weir
**British Actor of The Year:**
Paul Bettany in MASTER AND COMMANDER  THE FAR
SIDE OF THE WORLD (US) Dir Peter Weir
**Actor of The Year:**
Sean Penn in MYSTIC RIVER (US/Australia) Dir Clint
Eastwood
**British Actress of The Year:**
Anne Reid in THE MOTHER (UK) Dir Roger Michell
**Actress of The Year:**
Julianne Moore in FAR FROM HEAVEN (US/France) Dir
Todd Haynes
**British Actor In A Supporting Role:**
Bill Nighy in LOVE ACTUALLY (UK/US/France) Dir
Richard Curtis
**British Actress In A Supporting Role:**
Emma Thompson in LOVE ACTUALLY (UK/US/France)
Dir Richard Curtis
**British Director of The Year:**
Peter Mullan for THE MAGDALENE SISTERS
(UK/Ireland)
**Director of The Year:**

Clint Eastwood for MYSTIC RIVER (US/Australia)
**British Screenwriter of The Year:**
David Hare for THE HOURS (US/UK) Dir Stephen
Daldry
**Screenwriter of The Year:**
John Collee, Peter Weir for MASTER AND
COMMANDER  THE FAR SIDE OF THE WORLD (US)
Dir Peter Weir
**Foreign Language Film of The Year:**
GOOD BYE LENIN (Germany) Dir Wolfgang Becker
**British Newcomer of The Year:**
David MacKenzie for YOUNG ADAM (UK/France) Dir
David MacKenzie
**Dilys Powell Award – Excellence in Film:**
Tom Courtney
**Life Achievement Award:**
Ronald Neame
**Critics Circle Award:**
Ian McKellen

## 76th OSCARS - ACADEMY OF MOTION PICTURE ARTS AND SCIENCES

**Awarded 29 February 2004 in Hollywood, Los Angeles**
Website:www.oscar.com and www.oscars.org

**Best Picture:**
THE LORD OF THE RINGS  THE RETURN OF THE
KING (Germany/New Zealand/US) Dir Peter Jackson
**Best Director:**
Peter Jackson  for THE LORD OF THE RINGS  THE
RETURN OF THE KING (Germany/New Zealand/US)
**Best Actor:**
Sean Penn in MYSTIC RIVER (US/Australia) Dir Clint
Eastwood
**Best Supporting Actor:**
Tim Robbins in MYSTIC RIVER (US/Australia) Dir
Eastwood
**Best Actress:**
Charlize Theron in MONSTER (Germany/US) Dir Patty
Jenkins
**Best Supporting Actress:**
Renee Zellweger in COLD MOUNTAIN
(US/GB/Romania/Italy) Dir Anthony Minghella
**Best Art Direction:**
THE LORD OF THE RINGS  THE RETURN OF THE
KING (Germany/New Zealand/US) Dir Peter Jackson
**Best Cinematography:**
Russell Boyd for MASTER AND COMMANDER  THE
FAR SIDE OF THE WORLD (US) Dir Peter Weir
**Best Costume Design:**
Ngila Dickson, Richard Taylor for THE LORD OF THE
RINGS: THE RETURN OF THE KING (Germany/New
Zealand/US) Dir Peter Jackson
**Best Documentary Short:**
Maryann DeLeo for CHERNOBYL HEART (Byelarus/US)
**Best Documentary Feature:**
Errol Morris and Michael Williams for THE FOG OF WAR
(US)
**Best Film Editing:**
Jamie Selkirk for THE LORD OF THE RINGS  THE
RETURN OF THE KING (Germany/New Zealand/US) Dir
Peter Jackson
**Best Foreign Language Film:**
THE BARBARIAN INVASIONS (Canada) Dir Denys
Arcand
**Best Make Up:**

Richard Taylor, Peter King for THE LORD OF THE RINGS
THE RETURN OF THE KING (Germany/New
Zealand/US) Dir Peter Jackson
**Best Music (Score):**
Howard Shore for THE LORD OF THE RINGS: THE
RETURN OF THE KING (Germany/New Zealand/US) Dir
Peter Jackson
**Best Music (Song):**
"Into the West" Music and Lyrics by: Howard Shore, Fran
Walsh, Annie Lennox from THE LORD OF THE RINGS
THE RETURN OF THE KING (Germany/New
Zealand/US) Dir Peter Jackson
**Best Animated Feature:**
FINDING NEMO (US) Dir Andrew Stanton
**Best Short - Live Action:**
TWO SOLDIERS (US) Dir Aaron Schneider
**Best Short Animated:**
HARVIE KRUMPET (Australia) Dir Adam Elliot
**Best Sound Mixing:**
Christopher Boyes, Michael Semanick, Michael Hedges,
Hammond Peek for THE LORD OF THE RINGS  THE
RETURN OF THE KING (Germany/New Zealand/US) Dir
Peter Jackson
**Best Sound Editing:**
Richard King for MASTER AND COMMANDER  THE
FAR SIDE OF THE WORLD (US) Dir Peter Weir
**Best Visual Effects:**
Joe Letteri, Jim Rygiel, Randall William Cook, Alex Funke
for THE LORD OF THE RINGS  THE RETURN OF THE
KING (Germany/New Zealand/US) Dir Peter Jackson
**Best Screenplay (Adapted):**
Fran Walsh, Philippa Boyens, Peter Jackson for THE LORD
OF THE RINGS  THE RETURN OF THE KING
(Germany/New Zealand/US) Dir Peter Jackson
**Best Screenplay (Original):**
Sofia Coppola for LOST IN TRANSLATION (US/Japan)
Dir Sofia Coppola
**Honary Award:**
Blake Edwards

## ROTTERDAM INTERNATIONAL FILM FESTIVAL

**Held 21 January-1 February 2004**
**33rd International Film Festival Rotterdam**
**PO Box 21696, 3001 AR Rotterdam, Nethelands.**
Tel: + 31 10 890 9090
Fax: + 31 10 890 9091
Website: filmfestivalrotterdam.nl

**Tiger Awards for a first or second feature:**
BU JIAN (The Missing) (Taiwan) Dir Lee Kang-sheng
LJETO U ZLATNOJ (Summer in the Golden Valley)
(Bosnia/France) Dir Sredjan Vuletic
UNTERWEGS (En Route) (Germany) Dir Jan Krüger

## SUNDANCE FILM FESTIVAL

**Held 15-25 January 2004, Park City, Utah**
**PO Box 3630, Salt Lake City, Utah 84110, US.**
Tel: + 1 801 328 3456
Fax: +1 801 575 5175
Website: www.sundance.org

**Dramatic Grand Jury Prize:**
PRIMER (US) Dir Shane Carruth

**Documentary Grand Jury Prize:**
DIG! (US) Dir Ondi Timoner
**Dramatic Directing Award:**
Debra Grank for DOWN TO THE BONE (US)
**Documentary Directing Award:**
Morgan Spurlock for SUPER SIZE ME (US)
**Excellence in Cinematography Award – Dramatic:**
Nancy Schreiber for NOVEMBER (US) Dir Greg Harrison
**Excellence in Cinematography Award – Documentary:**
Ferne Pearlstein for IMEDLA (US)
**Dramatic Audience Award:**
MARIA FULL OF GRACE (US/Colombia) Dir Joshua
Marston
**Documentary Audience Award:**
BORN INTO BROTHELS (US) Dir Ross Kauffman, Zana
Briski
**World Cinema Dramatic Audience Award:**
SEDUCING DOCTOR LEWIS (Canada) Dir Jean-Francois
Pouliot
**World Cinema Documentary Audience Award:**
THE CORPORATION (Canada) Dir Mark Achbar,
Jennifer Abbot
**Freedom of Expression Award:**
REPATRIATION (Korea) Dir Kim Dong-won
**Waldo Salt Screenwriting Award:**
Larry Gross for WE DON'T LIVE HERE ANYMORE (US)
Dir John Curran
**Special Documentary Jury Prize:**
FARMINGVILLE (US) Dir Catherine Tambini, Carlos
Sandoval
**Special Dramatic Jury Prize:**
BROTHER TO BROTHER (US) Dir Rodney Evans
**Special Dramatic Jury Prize:**
Vera Farmiga for performance in DOWN TO THE BONE
(US) Dir Debra Granik
**Jury Prize in Short Filmmaking:**
WHEN THE STORM CAME (US) Dir Shilpi Gupta
GOWANUS, BROOKLYN (US) Dir Ryan Fleck
**Jury Prize in International Short Filmmaking:**
TOMO (UK) Dir Paul Catling
**Alfred P. Sloan Prize:**
PRIMER (US) Dir Shane Carruth

# TV Awards 2003

This section features some of the principal Television festival prizes and awards from 1 January 2003 to 31 December 2003.

## BAFTA

195 Piccadilly
London W1V OLN
Tel: 020 7734 0022
Fax: 020 7734 1792
Website: www.bafta.org

## BAFTA TELEVISION AWARDS

**Winners announced in London, Sunday 13 April 2003**
**Actress:**
Julie Walters for MURDER (Tiger Aspect for BBC2)
**Actor:**
Albert Finney for THE GATHERING STORM (Scott Free in association with HBO/BBC Films for BBC2)
**Entertainment Performance:**
Paul Merton for HAVE I GOT NEWS FOR YOU? (Hat Trick for BBC1)
**Comedy Performance:**
Ricky Gervais for The Office (BBC for BBC2)
**Single Drama:**
Production team for CONSPIRACY (HBO/BBC Films for BBC2)
**Drama Series:**
Production Team for SPOOKS (Kudos Productions for BBC1)
**Drama Serial:**
Selwyn Roberts, Charles Sturridge for SHACKLETON (Firstsight Films for C4)
**Soap:**
Kieran Roberts, Carolyn Reynolds for CORONATION STREET (Granada Television for ITV1)
**Huw Wheldon Award for Factual Series or Strand:**
Production Team for THE TRUST (Hart Ryan Productions for C4)
**The Flaherty Documentary Award:**
Roger Graef, Brian Hill for FELTHAM SINGS (Century/Films of Record for C4)
**Features:**
Stephen Lambert for FAKING IT (RDF Media for C4)
**Sport:**
Production Team for THE COMMONWEALTH GAMES (BBC for BBC1)
**News Coverage:**
Production Team for SOHAM – AUGUST 16/17 (Sky for Sky)
**Current Affairs:**
Steve Boulton, David Modell, Richard Fabb for YOUNG, NAZI & PROUD (Steve Boulton Productions for C4)
**Entertainment Programme or Series:**
Production Team for I'M A CELEBRITY – GET ME OUT OF HERE! (LWT for ITV1)
**Situation Comedy Award:**
Anil Gupta, Ash Atalla, Ricky Gervais, Stephen Merchant for THE OFFICE (BBC for BBC2)
**Comedy Programme or Series:**
Charlie Hanson, Gareth Carrick, Alistair McGowan for ALISTAIR McGOWAN'S BIG IMPRESSION (Vera for C4)
**Lew Grade Audience Award sponsored by RadioTimes**
FOYLE'S WAR (ITV1)
**Fellowship:**

David Jason
**Alan Clarke Award for Outstanding Creative Contribution to Television:**
Norma Percy and Brian Lapping

## BAFTA TELEVISION CRAFT AWARDS

**Costume Design:**
Shirley Russell for SHACKLETON (Firstsight Films for C4)
**Editing Factual:**
Peter Norrey for SAS EMBASSY SIEGE (BBC for BBC2)
**Editing Fiction/Entertainment:**
Philip Kloss for DANIEL DERONDA (BBC/WGBH Boston for BBC1)
**Graphic Design:**
Burrell Durrant Hifle for THE DINOSAUR HUNTERS (Granada for C4)
**Make Up & Hair Design:**
Daniel Parker, Frances Hannon, Stephen Rose for THE GATHERING STORM (Scott Free in association with HBO/BBC Films for BBC1)
**New Director Factual:** Alice Yglesias for DEATH (Quality Time for C4)
**New Director Fiction sponsored by Sony Pictures Television International:** Brian Hill for FALLING APART (Century Films for C4)
**New Writer sponsored by Montblanc:**
Anna Moloney for FALLING APART (Century Films for C4)
**Original Television Music sponsored by Sebastian McLean International:** Geoffrey Burgon for THE FORSYTE SAGA (Granada for ITV1)
**Photography Factual:**
Nigel Meakin for SAHARA WITH MICHAEL PALIN (Prominent Television for BBC1)
**Photography & Lighting Fiction/Entertainment:** Ivan Strasbourg for BLOODY SUNDAY (Granada for ITV1)
**Production Design:** Luciana Arrighi for THE GATHERING STORM (Scott Free in association with HBO/BBC Films for BBC2)
**Sound Factual:** Sound Team for THE QUEEN'S GOLDEN JUBILEE (BBC Events for BBC1)
**Sound Fiction/Entertainment:**
Sound Team for DANIEL DERONDA (BBC/WGBH Boston for BBC1)
**Visual Effects & Graphic Design sponsored by Oasis Television:** Max Tyrie, Tim Greenwood, Jez Gibson Harris for THE GIANT CLAW – A WALKING WITH DINOSAURS SPECIAL (Impossible Pictures for BBC1)
**Special Award:**
Carl Davis

## 43rd ROSE D'OR – FESTIVAL OF ENTERTAINMENT PROGRAMMES
**Awarded in Montreux, Switzerland. Awards 2003**

**Golden Rose:** FAKING IT (Channel 4 - UK)
**Honorary Rose :** Emil Steinberger (Switzerland)
Comedy
**Silver Rose:** THE ALL NEW HARRY HILL SHOW (Avalon Television - UK)
**Bronze Rose:** SMACK THE PONY (Channel 4/Talkback Productions - UK)
**Special Mentions:** THE RICHARD TAYLOR INTERVIEWS (Channel 4 – UK)
SHOREDITCH TW*T (Channel 4/Talkback Productions –

UK)
ALT & DURCHGEKNALLT (Brainpool – Germany)
Music
**Silver Rose:** SUSHEELA RAMAN ET CHEB MAMI
(ARTE France - France)
**Bronze Rose:** PARTY AT THE PALACE (BBC - UK)
**Sitcom : Silver Rose:** THE OFFICE (BBC - UK)
**Bronze Rose:** PUPPETS WHO KILL (PWK – CDN)
**GAMES SHOW**
**Silver Rose:** YOUR FACE OR MINE (E4/Talkback - UK)
**Bronze Rose:** INTERNATIONAL KING OF SPORTS
(Channel 5 - UK)
**VARIETY**
**Silver Rose:** DERREN BROWN – MIND CONTROL
(Channel 4 - UK)
**Bronze Rose:** PLUK DE DAG (Tros TV - NL)
**Arts & Special/ Special Prize of the City of Montreux**
**Golden Rose:** TINA IN MEXICO (Rhombus – CDN)
**Special Mention :** ROLF ON ART (BBC - UK)
**PRESS PRIZE**
**Reality Show:** FAKING IT (Channel 4 – UK)

## ROYAL TELEVISION SOCIETY AWARDS

**RTS Programme Awards**
**Awards for 2002. Presented on Tuesday 18 March 2003 by
Kirsty Young at Le Meridien, Grosvenor House, London
W1.**

**Serials & Single Drama:**
OUT OF CONTROL (BBC Films for BBC1)
**Drama Series:**
CLOCKING OFF (Red Production Company for BBC1)
**Soap:**
CORONATION STREET (Granada Television for ITV)
**Writer:**
Peter Bowker for FLESH & BLOOD (BBC Drama
Serials/Red Production Company for BBC2)
**Actor - Male:**
Christopher Eccleston for FLESH & BLOOD (BBC Drama
Serials/Red Production Company for BBC2)
**Actor - Female:**
Julie Walters for MURDER (Tiger Aspect for BBC2 )
**Network Newcomer – On Screen:**
Jimmy Carr for YOUR FACE OR MINE (Talkback for E4)
**Network Newcomer – Behind the Screen:**
David Modell (Director) for YOUNG NAZI AND PROUD
(Steve Boulton production for Channel 4)
**Regional Programme:**
AR Y STRYD (Ffilmiau'r Nant for S4C)
**Regional Presenter:**
Dewi Pws for BYD PWS (Ffilmiau'r Nant for S4C)
**Presenter (Factual):**
Susannah Constantine and Trinny Woodall for WHAT
NOT TO WEAR (BBC General Factual for BBC2)
**Entertainment Performance:**
Jonathan Ross for FRIDAY NIGHT WITH JONATHAN
ROSS/THEY THINK IT'S ALL OVER (Open Mike
Productions/Talkback Productions for BBC1)
**Entertainment:**
POP IDOL: THE FINAL & RESULTS SHOW (Thames/19
Television production for ITV)
**Comedy Performance:**
Ricky Gervais for THE OFFICE (BBC Comedy for BBC2)
**Situation Comedy & Comedy Drama:**
PHOENIX NIGHTS 2 (Ovation Entertainment for
Channel 4)

**Children's Fiction:**
DOUBLE ACT (Television Junction for 4Learning)
**Children"s Factual"**
SERIOUS JUNGLE (CBBC FOR BBC1)
**Documentary Series - General:**
THE HUNT FOR BRITAIN'S PAEDOPHILES (BBC
General Factual for BBC2)
**Single Documentary -General:**
HOUSE OF WAR (Berwick Univeral Pictures/Diverse
production for Channel 4)
**Arts:**
THE STRANGE WORLD OF BARRY WHO? (Darlow
Smithson for BBC4)
**Science & Natural History:**
SUPERFLY (Oxford Film & Television for BBC4)
**History:**
DAMBUSTERS: REVEALED (Windfall Films for Five)
**Features Primetime:**
LADS ARMY (Twenty Twenty Televsion for ITV)
**Daytime Programme:**
TODAY WITH DES (Carlton Production for ITV)
**Judges' Award:**
Peter Bazalgette
**Gold Medal:**
David Liddiment

## RTS JOURNALISM AWARDS
**Awards for 2001-2002. Presented on Thursday, 28
February 2003 by Katie Durham at London Hilton,
London**

**News – International:**
TERROR ON TAPE (CNN)
**News – Home:**
NEWSNIGHT – REPLICA GUNS (BBC2)
**Regional Daily News Magazine:**
BBC WALES TODAY: THE CLYDACH VERDICT (BBC
Wales)
**News Event:**
HOLLY AND JESSICA (Sky News)
**Camera Operator of the Year:**
Dodge Billingsley and Damien Degueldre for A HOUSE
OF WAR (Diverse Production for Channel 4)
**Presenter of the Year:**
Jon Snow, Channel 4 News
**Regional Current Affairs:**
SPOTLIGHT: PEOPLE FOR SALE (BBC Northern
Ireland)
**Current Affairs – International:**
AVENGING TERROR (A Brook Lapping production for
Channel 4)
**Current Affairs – Home:**
PANORAMA: THE CORRUPTION OF RACING (BBC1)
**Innovation:**
Virtual Reality Graphics THE BURRELL TRIAL (ITV
News)
**Television Journalist of the Year:**
Peter Taylor, BBC1/BBC2
**Young Journalist of the Year:**
Lindsey Hilsum, Diplomatic Correspondent, Channel 4
News
**News Programme of the Year:**
NEWSNIGHT (BBC2)
**News Channel of the Year:**
Sky News
**Programme of the Year:**
TONIGHT WITH TREVOR McDONALD (Granada

Television)
**JUDGES' AWARD**
David Lloyd

## RTS STUDENT TELEVISION AWARDS

Awards for 2002. Presented Thursday 1 May 2003. Hosted by Paul Watson at Centre for Magic Arts, London.

**UNDERGRADUATE**
**Animation:** Sumito Sakakibara for 3 BROTHERS (Kingston University)
**Factual:** Nathalie Berry for WHEN YOU DON'T COME HOME (Bournemouth University)
**Non-factual:** Mark Henrichsen and Jamie Goldblatt for DEAD (Edinburgh College of Art)
**POSTGRADUATE**
**Animation:** John Chorlton, Josephine Law, Jon Driscoll, Richard Overall, Bradley Miles, Toni Bates and Philippe Ciompi for LAST RUMBA IN ROCHDALE (National Film & Television School)
**Factual:** Saed Andoni for A NUMBER ZERO (Goldsmiths College)
**Non-factual:** Avie Luthra, Victoria Powell, Simon Vickery, Samantha Holgate and Simon Winter for BABY (National Film & Television School)

## RTS TELEVISION SPORTS AWARDS

Awards for 2002. Presented Monday 19 May 2003, at The London Hilton, Park Lane, London W1. Hosted by Mark Nicholas

**SPORTS PRESENTER**
Gary Linekar, BBC Sport for BBC1
**SPORTS COMMENTATOR**
Clive Tyldesley, ITV Sport for ITV1
**SPORTS PUNDIT**
Simon Hughes, Sunset + Vine Productions for Channel 4
**SPORTS NEWS REPORTER**
Gabriel Clarke, ITV Sport for ITV1
**SPORTS DOCUMENTARY**
THE GAME OF THEIR LIVES (VeryMuchSo Productions/Passion Pictures for BBC4)
**REGIONAL SPORTS PROGRAMME**
GRASPING THE THISTLE (Colour Television for BBC Scotland)
**REGIONAL SPORTS ACTUALITY PROGRAMME**
RUGBY LEAGUE RAW III (Paul Doherty International for Yorkshire Television)
**REGIONAL SPORTS PRESENTER OR COMMENTATOR**
Roger Johnson, BBC South
**LIVE OUTSIDE BROADCAST COVERAGE OF THE YEAR**
COMMONWEALTH GAMES (BBC Sport for BBC1 AND BBC2)
**SPORTS FEATURE**
HOW ARSENAL WON THE TITLE (Carlton/ISN for ITV1)
**CREATIVE SPORTS SEQUENCE OF THE YEAR**
HOW ARSENAL WON THE TITLE (Carlton/ISN for ITV1)
**SPORTS INNOVATION AWARD**
CHANNEL 4 WORLD RALLY CHAMPIONSHIP 2002 – VIRTUAL SPECTATOR (Chrysalis Television for Channel 4)
**SPORTS SHOW OR SERIES**
SKI SUNDAY: KITZBUHEL 2002 (BBC Sport for BBC2)
**SPORTS PROGRAMME OF THE YEAR**

FORMULA ONE (Chrysalis Sport/Granada Sport for ITV1
**Lifetime Achievement Award:**
Desmond Lynam

## RTS EDUCATIONAL TELEVISION AWARDS

Awards for 2002. Presented Wednesday 11 June 2003 at The Savoy, London WC2. Hosted by Reeta Chakrabarti.

**SCHOOLS TELEVISION**
**Pre School and Infants:**
STOP, LOOK, LISTEN: OKEY COKEY KARAOKE! – THE RAJA WITH BIG EARS (SFTV for 4Learning)
**Primary Arts and Language:**
LET'S WRITE A STORY: THE MASTER STORYTELLER (CBBC Education for BBC2)
**Primary Humanities:**
GEOGRAPHY JUNCTION: JAMAICA – THE LOCAL PEOPLE (Wised Up Productions for 4Learning)
**Primary and Secondary Science, Maths, Design aand ICT:**
THE MATHS CHANNEL (CBBC Education for BBC2)
**Secondary Arts and Languages:**
EXTRA (FRENCH): L'ARRIVÉE DE SAM (Double Exposure for 4Learning)
**Secondary Humanities:**
DEAD DRUNK (Hurricane Films for BBC2)
**Primary and Secondary Multimedia and Interactive:**
AROUND SCOTLAND: TECHNOLOGY – THINGS WE WEAR (BBC Scotland Commission for BBC Education Scotland)
**ADULT EDUCATIONAL TELEVISION**
**Lifelong Learning & Multimedia:**
HOW TO BE A GARDENER ONLINE COURSE (BBC Factual & Learning for BBC2 & BBCi)
**Single Programme:**
THE MAN WHO LEARNT TO SEE (Documentaries & Factual for BBC2)
**Campaigns and Seasons - RTS/NIACE Award**
SPOTLIGHT: SAVE YOURSELF FOURTUNE (Meridian Trust/Meridian Broadcasting)
**Educational Impact in the Primetime Schedule:**
GEAT BRITONS: BRUNEL (BBC Documentaries for BBC2)
**Judges' Award:**
John Richmond

## RTS CRAFT & DESIGN AWARDS

Awards for 2002-2003. Presented in London, 17 November 2003

**Costume Design - Drama:**
Odile Dicks-Mireaux for THE LOST PRINCE (A Talkback Production in association with BBC Films and a Co-Production with WGBH Boston for BBC1)
**Costume Design - Entertainment and Non Drama:**
Annie Hardinge for LITTLE BRITAIN (BBC New Comedy for BBC3 and BBC2)
**Design & Craft Innovation:**
John Downer, Michael W. Richards, Geoffrey Bell and Stuart Napier for ELEPHANTS: SPY IN THE HERD (John Downer Productions for BBC1)
**Graphic Design - Programme Content Sequence:**
Rob Hifle and Jason Mullings for SMASH HITS AWARDS (Done and Dusted for Channel 4)
**Graphic Design - Titles:**
Dimitri Kevgas for WHAT THE WORLD THINKS OF

AMERICA (BBC2)

**Judges' Award:**
I'M A CELEBRITY – GET ME OUT OF HERE! Team

**Lifetime Achievement:**
Brian Pearce

**Lighting, Photography & Camera - Lighting for Multicamera:**
Darryl Noad for RE:COVERED (Blaze Television for BBC)

**Lighting, Photography & Camera - Multicamera work:**
Camera Team for THE ABYSS – LIVE (BBC Natural History Unit for BBC)

**Lighting, Photography & Camera - Photography Documentary & Factual & Non-Drama Production:**
Roger Chapman for THE LAST PEASANTS (October Films for Channel 4)

**Lighting, Photography & Camera - Photography Drama:**
Chris Seager for STATE OF PLAY (BBC in association with Endor Productions for BBC1)

**Make up Design - Drama:**
Jessica Taylor for CUTTING IT (BBC Drama Serials for BBC1)

**Make up Design - Entertainment & Non-Drama:**
Lisa Cavalli-Green for LITTLE BRITAIN ( BBC New Comedy for BBC3 and BBC2)

**Music - Original Score**
Rob Lane for DANIEL DERONDA (BBC Drama Serials in association with WGBH Boston for BBC1)

**Music - Original Title Music**
Chris Elliot for THE BRITISH EMPIRE IN COLOUR (TWI Production in association with Carlton for ITV1)

**Production Design - Drama**
Don Taylor for DANIEL DERONDA (BBC Drama Serials in association with WGBH Boston for BBC1)

**Production Design – Entertainment & Non-Drama Productions:**
Peter Gordon for THE DAY BRITAIN STOPPED (Wall to Wall for BBC2)

**Sound - Drama:**
Ian Richardson for TOMORROW LA SCALA! (Home Movies Production for BBC Films and the Film Council)

**Sound – Entertainment & Non-Drama Productions:**
Sound Team for FIGHTING THE WAR (BBC Documentaries and Contemporary Factual for BBC2)

**Tape & Film Editing - Documentary & Factual:**
Ollie Huddleston for THE LAST PEASANTS ( October Films for Channel 4)

**Tape & Film Editing – Drama**
Tony Cranstoun for THE SECOND COMING/DANIELLE CABLE: EYEWITNESS (Red Production Company/Granada Television for ITV1)

**Tape & Film Editing – Entertainment & Situation Comedy**
Pete Hallworth for PHOENIX NIGHTS II (Ovation Entertainment Limited Production for Channel 4)

**TEAM**
Angus Macqueen, Roger Chapman, Claudia Murg and Iris Maor for THE LAS PEASANTS (October Films for Channel 4)

**Picture Enhancement**
Gerry Gedge, Phill Moss and Steve Moore for THE BRITISH EMPIRE IN COLOUR (TWI Production in association with Carlton for ITV1)

**Visual Effects – Special Effects**
Tom Harris for HORNBLOWER (Meridian Production in association with A&E Network for ITV)

**Visual Effects – Digital Effects**
The Framestore CFC Team for WALKING WITH DINOSAURS SPECIAL (Impossible Pictures for BBC1)

# TV Awards 2004

This section features some of the principal Television festival prizes and awards from 1 January 2004 to 30 June 2004.

## BAFTA

195 Piccadilly
London W1V OLN
Tel: 020 7734 0022
Fax: 020 7734 1792
Website: www.bafta.org

## BAFTA TELEVISION AWARDS

Winners announced in London, Sunday 18 April, 2004

**Actress:**
Julie Walters for THE WIFE OF BATH (CANTERBURY TALES) (BBC1)
**Actor:**
Bill Nighy for STATE OF PLAY (BBC1)
**Entertainment Performance:**
Jonathan Ross for FRIDAY NIGHT WITH JONATHAN ROSS (BBC1)
**Comedy Performance:**
Ricky Gervais for THE OFFICE CHRISTMAS SPECIAL (BBC1)
**The Richard Dimblemby Award for the Best Presenter:**
Andrew Marr
**Single Drama:**
THE DEAL (Granada Television/Channel4) Christine Langan, Stephen Frears, Peter Morgan
**Drama Series:**
BURIED (World Productions/Channel4) Production team
**Drama Serial:**
CHARLES II: THE POWER AND THE PASSION (BBC and A&E/BBC1) Kate Harwood, Adrian Hodges, Joe Wright
**Continuing Drama:**
CORONATION STREET (Granada Television/ITV1) Carolyn Reynolds, Keiran Roberts
**Features:**
WIFE SWAP (RDF Media/Channel 4)Production Team
**The Flaherty Documentary Award:**
LAGER, MUM AND ME (ONE LIFE) (BBC/BBC1) Todd Austin, Min Clough
**Huw Wheldon Award for Factual Series or Strand:**
THE NATIONAL TRUST (Oxford Film and Television/BBC4/BBC2) Claire Kavangh, Nick Kent, Patrick Forbes
**Sport:**
RUGBY WORLD CUP FINAL (ITV1) John Watts, Simon Moore, Rick Waumsley
**News Coverage:**
CHANNEL 4 NEWS – FALL OF SADDAM (ITN for Channel 4/Channel 4) Production Team
**Current Affairs:**
THE SECRET POLICEMAN (BBC/BBC1) Simon Ford, Mark Daly, Toby Sculthorpe
**Lew Grade Award for Entertainment Programme or Series:**
FRIDAY NIGHT WITH jONATHAN ROSS (Open Mike/BBC1) Addison Cresswell, Suzi Aplin, Mick Thomas
**Situation Comedy Award:**
THE OFFICE CHRISTMAS SPECIAL (BBC/BBC1) Ash Atalla, Ricky Gervais, Stephen Merchant

**Comedy Programme or Series:**
LITTLE bBRITAIN (BBC/BBC3/BBC2) Matt Lucas, David Williams, Myfanwy Moore
**Radio Times Audience Award:**
ONLY FOOLS AND HORSES
**Alan Clarke Award:**
Beryl Vertue
**Dennis Potter Award:**
Paul Abbott
**Fellowship:**
Roger Graef

## BAFTA TELEVISION CRAFT AWARDS

**Special Awards Presented to: Edward Mansell - Editor**
BBC Natural History Unit
**Costume Design sponsored by Allders:**
THE LIFE AND ADVENTURES OF NICHOLAS NICKLEBY (ITV1) Barbara Kidd
**Editing Factual:**
THE SHOW MUST GO ON (BBC2) Anna Ksiezopolska
**Editing Fiction/Entertainment sponsored by Bentley Productions:**
OTHELLO (ITV1) Nick Arthurs
**Make Up & Hair Design sponsored by Allders:**
THE WAY WE LIVE NOW (BBC1) Caroline Noble
**New Director Factual:**
WITNESS: THE TRAIN (C4) Donovan Wylie
**New Director Fiction:**
TALES FROM PLEASURE BEACH (BBC2) Edmund Coulthard
**New Writer sponsored by AKA Pictures:**
NAVIGATORS (C4) Rob Dawber
**Original Television Music sponsored by Sebastian McLean International:**
THE BLUE PLANET (BBC1) George Fenton
**Photography Factual:**
THE BLUE PLANET (BBC1) Camera Team
**Photography & Lighting Fiction/Entertainment sponsored by Kodak Entertainment Imaging:**
OTHELLO (ITV1) Daf Hobson
**Production Design sponsored by the British Studio Alliance:**
THE WAY WE LIVE NOW (BBC1) Gerry Scott
**Sound Factual:**
HELL IN THE PACIFIC (C4) Peter Eason, Craig Butters,Cliff Jones
**Sound Fiction/Entertainment:**
Clocking Off (BBC1)  Sound Team
**Visual Effects & Graphic Design  sponsored by Oasis Television:**
BANZAI (C4) Blue Source

## 44th ROSE D'OR

Held 13-18 April 2004, Lucerne, Switzerland

**Comedy:**
CREATURE COMFORTS (Aardman Animations – UK)
**Comedy Actor:**
Harry Hill in HARRY HILL'S TV BURP (UK)
**Comedy Actress:**
Anke Engelke in LADYKRACHER (Germany)
**Sitcom:**
PEEP SHOW (Channel 4 – UK)
**Sitcom Actor:**
Martin Freeman in HARDWARE (UK)
**Sitcom Actress:**

Felicitas Wolf in BERLIN, BERLIN (Germany)
**Soap:**
SAINT TROPEZ (Marathon International – France)
**Soap Actor:**
Shane Ritchie in EASTENDERS (UK)
**Soap Actress:**
Benedicte Delmas in SAINT TROPEZ (France)
**Game Show:**
MY NEW BEST FRIEND (Tiger Aspect Productions - UK)
**Game Show Host:**
Anthony McPartlin & Declan Donnelly in ANT & DEC'S
SATURDAY NIGHT TAKEAWAY (UK)
**Music:**
ONE BULLET LEFT (SF DRS/Swiss Television –
Switzerland)
**Variety:**
ANT & DEC'S SATURDAY NIGHT TAKEAWAY (Granada
Entertainment – UK)
**Arts & Specials:**
AMELIA (Rhombus International – Canada)
**Reality Show:**
WIFE SWAP (Channel 4 – UK)
**Press Prize:**
LITTLE BRITAIN (BBC – UK)
**Pilot Award:**
FUR TV (BBC – UK)
**Honorary Rose:**
John de Mol

## ROYAL TELEVISION SOCIETY AWARDS
RTS Programme Awards
**Awards for 2003. Presented in London, 16 March 2004.**

**Drama Serials:**
STATE OF PLAY (BBC in association with Endor
Productions for BBC1)
**Single Drama:**
THIS LITTLE LIFE (BBC Films & The Film Council
present a Common Features Production in association
with the Northern Production Fund and the Yorkshire
Media Production Agency/Studio of the North for BBC2)
**Drama Series:**
SPOOKS (Kudos Production for BBC1)
**Soap:**
CORONATION STREET (Granada Television for ITV)
**Writer:**
Paul Abbott for STATE OF PLAY (BBC in association with
Endor Productions for BBC1)
**Actor - Male:**
David Morrissey for THE DEAL (Granada Television for
Channel 4)
**Actor - Female:**
Kate Ashfield for THIS LITTLE LIFE (BBC Films & The
Film Council present a Common Features Production in
association with the Northern Production Fund and the
Yorkshire Media Production Agency/Studio of the North
for BBC2)
**Network Newcomer – On Screen:**
Kate Lyon for PLEASURELAND (Kudos Production for
Channel 4)
**Network Newcomer – Behind the Screen:**
Sarah Cavron (Director) for THIS LITTLE LIFE (BBC
Films & The Film Council present a Common Features
Production in association with the Northern Production
Fund and the Yorkshire Media Production Agency/Studio
of the North for BBC2)
**Regional Programme:**

CHRISTINE'S CHILDREN (Double Band Films for BBC1
Northern Ireland)
**Regional Presenter:**
Gerry Anderson for ANDERSON IN… (Green Inc. for
BBC Northern Ireland)
**Presenter (Factual):**
Melvyn Bragg for THE ADVENTURE OF ENGLISH/THE
SOUTH BANK SHOW (LWT for ITV1)
**Entertainment Performance:**
Jonathan Ross for FRIDAY NIGHT WITH JONATHAN
ROSS (Open Mike Productions for BBC1)
**Entertainment:**
LITTLE BRITAIN (BBC New Comedy for BBC3)
**EVENT**
COMIC RELIEF 2003 – THE BIG HAIR DO (BBC
Entertainment for BBC1)
**Comedy Performance:**
David Walliams and Matt Lucas for LITTLE BRITAIN
(BBC New Comedy for BBC3)
**Situation Comedy & Comedy Drama:**
THE OFFICE CHRISTMAS SPECIAL (BBC
Entertainment for BBC1)
**Children's Programme:**
UP2U (WisedUp Production for CiTV)
**Children's Drama:**
GIRLS IN LOVE (Granada Kids for CiTV)
**Documentary Series - General:**
THE LAST PEASANTS (October Film for Channel 4)
**Single Documentary -General:**
THE SECRET POLICEMAN (BBC Documentaries &
Contemporary Factual for BBC1)
**Arts:**
OPERATUNITY (Diverse Production for Channel 4)
**Science & Natural History:**
MOTHERLAND – A GENETIC JOURNEY (Takeaway
Media for BBC2)
**History:**
GEORGIAN UNDERWORLD: INVITATION TO A
HANGING (Juniper Production for Channel 4)
**Features & Factual Entertainment:**
HOLIDAY SHOWDOWN (RDF Media Production for
ITV1)
**Daytime Programme:**
BRITAIN'S SECRET SHAME (BBC Daytime/BBC Current
Affairs for BBC1)
**Judges' Award:**
Greg Dyke
**RTS International Award:**
24 (SEASON 2) (Real Time Productions and Imagine
Television in association with Twentieth Century Fox
Television for BBC2 and BBC3)

## RTS TV JOURNALISM AWARDS
**Awards for 2002-2003. Presented in London, 24 February
2004.**

**News – International:**
WELCOME TO BAGHDAD (ITV News, ITV1)
**News – Home:**
ULSTER RACISM (BBC1)
**Regional Daily News Magazine:**
MERIDIAN TONIGHT (SOUTH) (Meridian
Broadcasting)
**News Event:**
IRAQ WAR (Channel 4)
**Camera Operator of the Year:**
Darren Conway (BBC4 and BBC1)

Presenter of the Year:
John Stapleton, GMTV
**Regional Current Affairs:**
LOYALISTS AT WAR - SPOTLIGHT (BBC Northern Ireland)
**Current Affairs – International:**
IN THE LINE OF FIRE – PANORAMA (BBC1)
**Current Affairs – Home:**
COT DEATH – REAL STORY WITH FIONA BRUCE (BBC1)
**Innovation:**
REPORTING THE COURTS (Sky News)
**Specialist Journalism:**
Hilary Andersson (BBC1 and BBC4)
**Television Journalist of the Year:**
John Irvine, ITV1
**Young Journalist of the Year:**
Mark Daly – The Secret Policeman Documentaries and Contemporary Factual (for BBC1)
**News Programme of the Year:**
ITV EVENING NEWS (ITV1)
**News Channel of the Year:**
Sky News
**Programme of the Year:**
LIVING WITH MICHAEL JACKSON (Granada Television)

## RTS STUDENT TELEVISION AWARDS
**Awards for 2003. Presented in London, 7 May 2004. Hosted by Paul Watson.**

**UNDERGRADUATE**
**Animation:** Gemma Manger for THE BIRDS AND THE BEES (Southampton Institute)
**Factual:** Jean Devlin and Shona Mullen for HIGH FLYERS (Dublin Institute of Technology)
**Non-factual:** Russell Holliss and James Robinson for ROCKET BOY ROGER (Hull School of Art & Design)
POSTGRADUATE
**Animation:** Gemma Carrington, Tora Young, Sarah Barltes-Smith, Angela Feeney and Jake Roberts for COMING HOME (National Film & Television School)
**Factual:** Ditsi Carolino, Sadhana Buxani, Valerio Bonelli, Peter Marquez, Martin Jensen and Bradley Miles for RILES (National Film and Television School)
**Non-factual:** Jan Bauer, Teresa Mulqueen,Tanja Koop, Helle le Fevre and David Schweitzer for LITTLE SCARS (National Film & Television School)

## RTS TELEVISION SPORTS AWARDS AWARDS FOR 2003
**Presented 24 May 2004. Hosted by Gabby Logan at The London Hilton, Park Lane, London W1**
**Sports Presenter:**
Clare Balding, BBC TV Sport
**Sports COMMENTATOR**
Steve Cram, BBC TV Sport
**Sports PUNDIT**
Michael Johnson, BBC TV Sport
**Sports News REPORTER**
Sue Turton, ITN for Channel 4 News
**Sports Documentary**
THE REAL JOHN CURRY (Granada Television for Channel 4)
**Regional Sports Programme**
BIG SIX (BBC Northern Ireland)
**Regional Sports ACTUALITY Programme**
THE CHAMPIONSHIP (BBC Northern Ireland)
**Regional Sports Presenter or Commentator:**

Alistair Mann, Granada Television, Manchester
**Live Outside Broadcast Coverage of the year:**
CHANNEL 4 CRICKET 2003 (Sunset + Vine for Channel 4)
**Sports Feature**
GRAND NATIONAL: JOHNNY VEGAS – SUPER JOCKEY (BBC TV Sport)
**Creative Sports Sequence of the year:**
RUGBY WORLD CUP FINAL: HAPPY THE MAN (ISN/Granada Sport for ITV Sport)
**Sports  Innovation Award:**
SUNDAY GRANDSTAND: SILVERSTONE FLYING LAP (BBC TV Sport)
**Sports Show or Series:**
GRAND NATIONAL PREVIEW: THE NIGHT BEFORE THE NATIONAL (BBC TV Sport)
**Sports Programme of the year:**
THE RUGBY WORLD CUP FINAL (ISN/Granada for ITV Sport)
**Lifetime Achievement Award:**
Richie Benaud OBE
**Judges' Award:**
Martin Hopkins

## RTS EDUCATIONAL TELEVISION AWARDS
**Awards 2003. Presented 16 June 2004 at the Savoy Hotel, London.**

**SCHOOLS TELEVISION**
**Early Years (formerly Pre-School and Infants)**
SOMETHING SPECIAL: PROGRAMME 1 – FARM(CBBC Education for BBC2)
**Primary Arts and Language:**
COMING TO ENGLAND – EPISODE 3 (Floella Benjamin Productions for BBC2)
**Primary Humanities:**
LION MOUNTAIN (Resource Base and Maverick Television for BBC)
**Primary and Secondary Science, Maths, Design and ICT**
STARSHIP MATHS: PROGRAMME 4 – SHAPE, SPACE AND MEASURE (CBBC Education for BBC2)
**Secondary Arts and Languages:**
THE ENGLISH PROGRAMME: FILM FOCUS – FOOD COMMERCIALS (Double Exposure for Channel 4)
**Secondary Humanities:**
LIFE STUFF: THIS TEEN LIFE (Betty TV for Channel 4)
**Primary and Secondary Multimedia and Interactive:**
SCIENCE CLIPS: LIGHT & SHADOWS (AV Studios for BBC2)
**ADULT EDUCATIONAL TELEVISION**
**Lifelong Learning & Multimedia:**
THE HAJJ (Lion TV for Channel 4)
**Single Programme:**
REAL LIFE: BEING TERRI (Anglia Television for ITV1)
**Campaigns and Seasons - RTS/NIACE Award**
GET WRITING WITH CANTERBURY TALES (BBC Learning in Drama, Illumina Digital and Preloaded for BBC)
**Educational Impact in the Primetime Schedule:**
POMPEII: THE LAST DAY (BBC Science for BBC1)
**Judges' Award:**
Adam Hart-Davis

# British Successes in the Academy Awards 1927–2004

The following list chronicles British successes in the Academy Awards. It includes individuals who were either born, and lived and worked, in Britain into their adult lives, or those who were not born here but took on citizenship. Compiled by Erinna Mettler

### (1st) 1927/28 held in 1930

Charles Chaplin – **Special Award (acting, producing, directing and writing):** THE CIRCUS

### (2nd) 1928/29 held in 1930

Frank Lloyd – **Best Direction:** THE DIVINE LADY

### (3rd) 1929/30 held in 1930

George Arliss – **Best Actor:** THE GREEN GODDESS

### (6th) 1932/33 held in 1934

William S. Darling – **Best Art Direction:** CAVALCADE

Charles Laughton – **Best Actor:** THE PRIVATE LIFE OF HENRY VIII

Frank Lloyd – **Best Direction:** CAVALCADE

### (8th) 1935 held in 1936

Gaumont British Studios – **Best Short Subject:** WINGS OVER MT. EVEREST

Victor Mclaglen – **Best Actor:** THE INFORMER

### (11th) 1938 held in 1939

Ian Dalrymple, Cecil Lewis & W.P. Lipscomb – **Best Screenplay:** PYGMALION

### (12th) 1939 held in 1940

Robert Donat – **Best Actor:** GOODBYE MR. CHIPS

Vivien Leigh – **Best Actress:** GONE WITH THE WIND

### (13th) 1940 held in 1941

Lawrence Butler & Jack Whitney – **Special Visual Effects:**
THE THIEF OF BAGDAD

Vincent Korda – **Best Colour Set Design:** THE THIEF OF BAGDAD

### (14th) 1941 held in 1942

British Ministry of Information – **Honorary Award:** TARGET FOR TONIGHT

Donald Crisp – **Best Supporting Actor:** HOW GREEN WAS MY VALLEY

Joan Fontaine – **Best Actress:** SUSPICION

Jack Whitney & The General Studios Sound Department – **Best Sound:** THAT HAMILTON WOMAN

### (15th) 1942 held in 1943

Noel Coward – **Special Award:** IN WHICH WE SERVE

Greer Garson – **Best Actress:** MRS. MINIVER

### (16th) 1943 held in 1944

British Ministry of Information – **Best Documentary:** DESERT VICTORY

William S. Darling – **Best Art Direction:** THE SONG OF BERNADETTE

### (18th) 1945 held in 1946

The Governments of the United States & Great Britain – **Best Documentary:** THE TRUE GLORY

Ray Milland – **Best Actor:** THE LOST WEEKEND

Harry Stradling – **Best Cinematography (b/w):** THE PICTURE OF DORIAN GRAY

### (19th) 1946 held in 1947

Muriel & Sydney Box – **Best Original Screenplay:** THE SEVENTH VEIL

Clemence Dane – **Best Original Story:** VACATION FROM MARRIAGE

Olivia de Havilland – **Best Actress:** TO EACH HIS OWN

Laurence Olivier – **Special Award:** HENRY V

Thomas Howard – **Best Special Effects:** BLITHE SPIRIT

William S. Darling – **Best Art Direction (b/w):** ANNA AND THE KING OF SIAM

**(20th) 1947** held in 1948

John Bryan – **Best Art Direction:** GREAT EXPECTATIONS

Jack Cardiff – **Best Cinematography (col):** BLACK NARCISSUS

Ronald Colman – **Best Actor:** A DOUBLE LIFE

Guy Green – **Best Cinematography (b/w):** GREAT EXPECTATIONS

Edmund Gwen – **Best Supporting Actor:** MIRACLE ON 34TH STREET

**(21st) 1948** held in 1949

Carmen Dillon & Roger Furse – **Best Art Direction (b/w):** HAMLET

Brian Easdale – **Best Score:** THE RED SHOES

Roger Furse – **Best Costume Design:** HAMLET

Laurence Olivier – **Best Picture:** HAMLET

Laurence Olivier – **Best Actor:** HAMLET

**(22nd) 1949** held in 1950

British Information Services – **Best Documentary:** DAYBREAK IN UDI

Olivia de Havilland – **Best Actress:** THE HEIRESS

**(23rd) 1950** held in 1951

George Sanders – **Best Supporting Actor:** ALL ABOUT EVE

**(24th) 1951** held in 1952

James Bernard & Paul Dehn – **Best Motion Picture Story:** SEVEN DAYS TO NOON

Vivien Leigh – **Best Actress:** A STREETCAR NAMED DESIRE

**(25th) 1952** held in 1953

T.E.B. Clarke – **Best Story & Screenplay:** THE LAVENDER HILL MOB

London Films Sound Dept. – **Best Sound:** THE SOUND BARRIER

**(26th) 1954** held in 1955

British Information Services – **Best Documentary Short Subject:** THURSDAY'S CHILDREN

S. Tyne Jule – **Best Song:** THREE COINS IN THE FOUNTAIN

Jon Whitely & Vincent Winter – **Special Award (Best Juvenile Performances):** THE KIDNAPPERS

**(29th) 1956** held in 1957

George K. Arthur – **Best Short Subject:** THE BESPOKE OVERCOAT

**(30th) 1957** held in 1958

Malcolm Arnold – **Best Musical Score:** THE BRIDGE ON THE RIVER KWAI

Alec Guinness – **Best Actor:** THE BRIDGE ON THE RIVER KWAI

Jack Hildyard – **Best Cinematography:** THE BRIDGE ON THE RIVER KWAI

David Lean – **Best Director:** THE BRIDGE ON THE RIVER KWAI

Pete Taylor – **Best Editing:** THE BRIDGE ON THE RIVER KWAI

**(31st) 1958** held in 1959

Cecil Beaton – **Best Costumes:** GIGI

Wendy Hiller – **Best Supporting Actress:** SEPARATE TABLES

Thomas Howard – **Special Visual Effects:** TOM THUMB

David Niven – **Best Actor:** SEPARATE TABLES

**(32nd) 1959** held in 1960

Hugh Griffith – **Best Supporting Actor:** BEN HUR

Elizabeth Haffenden – **Best Costume Design (col.):** BEN HUR

**(33rd) 1960** held in 1961

Freddie Francis – **Best Cinematography (b/w):** SONS & LOVERS

James Hill – **Best Documentary:** GIUSEPPINA

Hayley Mills – **Special Award (Best Juvenile Performance):** POLLYANNA

Peter Ustinov – **Best Supporting Actor:** SPARTACUS

**(34th) 1961** held in 1962

Vivian C. Greenham – **Best Visual Effects:** THE GUNS OF NAVARONE

**(35th) 1962** held in 1963

John Box & John Stoll – **Best Art Direction:** LAWRENCE OF ARABIA

Anne V. Coates – **Best Editing:** LAWRENCE OF ARABIA

Jack Howells (Janus Films) – **Best Documentary:** DYLAN THOMAS

David Lean – **Best Director:** LAWRENCE OF ARABIA

Shepperton Studios Sound Dept. (John Cox Sound Director) – **Best Sound:** LAWRENCE OF ARABIA

Freddie Young – **Best Cinematography:** LAWRENCE OF ARABIA

**(36th) 1963** held in 1964

John Addison – **Best Score:** TOM JONES

John Osborne – **Best Adapted Screenplay:** TOM JONES

Tony Richardson – **Best Director:** TOM JONES

Tony Richardson (Woodfall Films) – **Best Picture:** TOM JONES

Margaret Rutherford – **Best Supporting Actress:** THE V.I.P.S

## (37th) 1964 held in 1965

Julie Andrews – **Best Actress:** MARY POPPINS

Cecil Beaton – **Best Art Direction (col):** MY FAIR LADY

Cecil Beaton – **Best Costume Design (col):** MY FAIR LADY

Rex Harrison – **Best Actor:** MY FAIR LADY

Walter Lassally – **Best Cinematography (b/w):** ZORBA THE GREEK

Harry Stradling – **Best Cinematography (col):** MY FAIR LADY

Peter Ustinov – **Best Supporting Actor:** TOPKAPI

Norman Wanstall – **Best Sound Effects:** GOLDFINGER

## (38th) 1965 held in 1966

Julie Christie – **Best Actress:** DARLING

Robert Bolt – **Adapted Screenplay:** DOCTOR ZHIVAGO

Frederic Raphael – **Original Screenplay:** DARLING

Freddie Young – **Colour Cinematography:** DOCTOR ZHIVAGO

John Box, Terence Marsh – **Best Art Direction (colour):** DOCTOR ZHIVAGO

Julie Harris – **Costume (b/w):** DARLING

Phyllis Dalton – **Costume (col):** DOCTOR ZHIVAGO

John Stears – **Special Visual Effects:** THUNDERBALL

## (39th) 1966 held in 1967

John Barry – **Best Original Score:** BORN FREE

John Barry & Don Black – **Best Song:** BORN FREE

Robert Bolt – **Best Adapted Screenplay:** A MAN FOR ALL SEASONS

Joan Bridge & Elizabeth Haffenden – **Best Costume (col):** A MAN FOR ALL SEASONS

Gordon Daniel – **Best Sound:** GRAND PRIX

Ted Moore – **Best Cinematography (col):** A MAN FOR ALL SEASONS

Ken Thorne – **Best Adapted Score:** A FUNNY THING HAPPENED ON THE WAY TO THE FORUM

Peter Watkins – **Best Documentary Feature:** THE WAR GAME

## (40th) 1967 held in 1968

Leslie Bricusse – **Best Song:** DOCTOR DOLITTLE (TALK TO THE ANIMALS)

Alfred Hitchcock – **Irving Thalberg Memorial Award**

John Poyner – **Best Sound Effects:** THE DIRTY DOZEN

## (41st) 1968 held in 1969

John Barry – **Best Original Score:** THE LION IN WINTER

Vernon Dixon & Ken Muggleston – **Best Art Direction:** OLIVER!

Carol Reed – **Best Director:** OLIVER!

Shepperton Sound Studio – **Best Sound:** OLIVER!

Charles D. Staffell – **Scientific, Class I Statuett** – for the development of a successful embodiment of the reflex background projection system for composite cinematography

John Woolf – **Best Picture:** OLIVER!

## (42nd) 1969 held in 1970

Margaret Furfe – **Best Costume:** ANNE OF THE THOUSAND DAYS

Cary Grant – **Honorary Award**

John Schlesinger – **Best Director:** Midnight Cowboy

Maggie Smith – **Best Actress:** THE PRIME OF MISS JEAN BRODIE

## (43rd) 1970 held in 1971

The Beatles – **Best Original Score:** LET IT BE

Glenda Jackson – **Best Actress:** WOMEN IN LOVE

John Mills – **Best Supporting Actor:** RYAN'S DAUGHTER

Freddie Young – **Best Cinematography:** RYAN'S DAUGHTER

## (44th) 1971 held in 1972

Robert Amram – **Best Short:** SENTINELS OF SILENCE

Ernest Archer, John Box, Vernon Dixon & Jack Maxsted – **Best Art Direction:** NICHOLAS & ALEXANDRA

Charles Chaplin – **Honorary Award**

David Hildyard & Gordon K. McCallum – **Best Sound:** FIDDLER ON THE ROOF

Oswald Morris – **Best Cinematography:** FIDDLER ON THE ROOF

## (45th) 1972 held in 1973

Charles Chaplin – **Best Original Score:** LIMELIGHT

David Hildyard – **Best Sound:** CABARET

Anthony Powell – **Best Costume Design:** TRAVELS WITH MY AUNT

Geoffrey Unsworth – **Best Cinematography:** CABARET

## (46th) 1973 held in 1974

Glenda Jackson – **Best Actress:** A TOUCH OF CLASS

## (47th) 1974 held in 1975

Albert Whitlock – **Special Achievement In Visual Effects:**

EARTHQUAKE

**(48th) 1975 held in 1976**

Ben Adam, Vernon Dixon & Roy Walker – **Best Art Direction:** BARRY LYNDON

John Alcott – **Best Cinematography:** BARRY LYNDON

Bob Godfrey – **Best Animated Short:** GREAT

Albert Whitlock – **Special Achievement In Visual Effects:** THE HINDENBERG

**(49th) 1976 held in 1977**

Peter Finch – **Best Actor:** NETWORK

**(50th) 1977 held in 1978**

John Barry, Roger Christians & Leslie Dilley – **Best Art Direction:** STAR WARS

John Mollo – **Best Costume Design:** STAR WARS

Vanessa Redgrave – **Best Supporting Actress:** JULIA

John Stears – **Best Visual Effects:** STAR WARS

**(51st) 1978 held in 1979**

Les Bowie, Colin Chilvers, Denys Coop, Roy Field & Derek Meddings – **Special Achievement In Visual Effects:** SUPERMAN

Michael Deeley, John Peverall & Barry Spikings – **Best Picture:** THE DEER HUNTER

Laurence Oilvier – **Lifetime Achievement Award**

Anthony Powell – **Best Costume Design:** DEATH ON THE NILE

Maggie Smith – **Best Supporting Actress:** CALIFORNIA SUITE

**(52nd) 1979 held in 1980**

Nick Allder, Denis Ayling & Brian Johnson – **Special Achievement In Visual Effects:** ALIEN

Alec Guinness – **Honorary Award**

Tony Walton – **Best Art Direction:** ALL THAT JAZZ

**(53rd) 1980 held in 1981**

Brian Johnson – **Special Achievement In Visual Effects:** THE EMPIRE STRIKES BACK

Lloyd Phillips – **Best Live Action Short:** THE DOLLAR BOTTOM

Anthony Powell – **Best Costume Design:** TESS

David W. Samuelson – **Scientific and Engineering Award** – for the engineering and development of the Louma Camera Crane and remote control system for motion picture production

Jack Stevens – **Best Art Direction:** TESS

Geoffrey Unsworth – **Best Cinematography:** TESS

**(54th) 1981 held in 1982**

Leslie Dilley & Michael Ford – **Best Art Direction:**

RAIDERS OF THE LOST ARK

John Gielgud – **Best Supporting Actor:** ARTHUR

Nigel Nobel – **Best Documentary Short:** CLOSE HARMONY

David Puttnam – **Best Picture:** CHARIOTS OF FIRE

Arnold Schwartzman – **Best Documentary Feature:** CLOSE HARMONY

Colin Welland – **Best Original Screenplay:** CHARIOTS OF FIRE

Kit West – **Special Achievement In Visual Effects:** RAIDERS OF THE LOST ARK

**(55th) 1982 held in 1983**

Richard Attenborough – **Best Picture:** GANDHI

Richard Attenborough – **Best Director:** GANDHI

John Briley – **Best Original Screenplay**: Gandhi

Stuart Craig, Bob Laing & Michael Seirton – **Best Art Direction:** GANDHI

Ben Kingsley – **Best Actor:** GANDHI

John Mollo – **Best Costume Design:** GANDHI

Sarah Monzani – **Best Achievement In Make Up:** QUEST FOR FIRE

Colin Mossman & Rank Laboratories – **Scientific and Engineering Award** - for the engineering and implementation of a 4,000 meter printing system for motion picture laboratories

Christine Oestreicher – **Best Live Action Short:** A SHOCKING ACCIDENT

Ronnie Taylor & Billy Williams – **Best Cinematography:** GANDHI

**(56th) 1983 held in 1984**

Gerald L. Turpin (Lightflex International) – **Scientific And Engineering Award** – for the design, engineering and development of an on-camera device providing contrast control, sourceless fill light and special effects for motion picture photography

**(57th) 1984 held in 1985**

Peggy Ashcroft – **Best Supporting Actress:** A PASSAGE TO INDIA

Jim Clark – **Best Editing:** THE KILLING FIELDS

George Gibbs – **Special Achievement In Visual Effects:** INDIANA JONES AND THE TEMPLE OF DOOM

Chris Menges – **Best Cinematography:** THE KILLING FIELDS

Peter Shaffer – **Best Adapted Screenplay:** AMADEUS

**(58th) 1985 held in 1986**

John Barry – **Best Original Score:** OUT OF AFRICA

Stephen Grimes – **Best Art Direction:** OUT OF AFRICA

David Watkin – **Best Cinematography:** OUT OF AFRICA

**(59th) 1986 held in 1987**

Brian Ackland-Snow & Brian Saregar – **Best Art Direction:** A ROOM WITH A VIEW

Jenny Beavan & John Bright – **Best Costume Design:** A ROOM WITH A VIEW

Michael Caine – **Best Supporting Actor:** HANNAH & HER SISTERS

Simon Kaye – **Best Sound:** PLATOON

Lee Electric Lighting Ltd. – **Technical Achievement Award**

Chris Menges – **Best Cinematography:** THE MISSION

Peter D. Parks – **Technical Achievement Award**

William B. Pollard & David W. Samuelson – **Technical Achievement Award**

John Richardson – **Special Achievement In Visual Effects:** ALIENS

Claire Simpson – **Best Editing:** PLATOON

Don Sharpe – **Best Sound Effects Editing:** ALIENS

Vivienne Verdon-Roe – **Best Documentary Short:** WOMEN – FOR AMERICA, FOR THE WORLD

**(60th) 1987 held in 1988**

James Acheson – **Best Costume Design:** THE LAST EMPEROR

Sean Connery – **Best Supporting Actor:** THE UNTOUCHABLES

Mark Peploe – **Best Adapted Screenplay:** THE LAST EMPEROR

Ivan Sharrock – **Best Sound:** THE LAST EMPEROR

Jeremy Thomas – **Best Picture:** THE LAST EMPEROR

**(61st) 1988 held in 1989**

James Acheson – **Best Costume Design:** DANGEROUS LIAISONS

George Gibbs – **Special Achievement In Visual Effects:** WHO FRAMED ROGER RABBIT

Christopher Hampton – **Best Adapted Screenplay:** DANGEROUS LIAISONS

**(62nd) 1989 held in 1990**

Phyllis Dalton – **Best Costume:** HENRY V

Daniel Day-Lewis – **Best Actor:** MY LEFT FOOT

Freddie Francis – **Best Cinematography:** GLORY

Brenda Fricker – **Best Supporting Actress:** MY LEFT FOOT

Anton Furst – **Best Art Direction:** BATMAN

Richard Hymns – **Best Sound Effects Editing:** INDIANA JONES AND THE LAST CRUSADE

Jessica Tandy – **Best Actress:** DRIVING MISS DAISY
James Hendrie – **Best Live Action Short:** WORK EXPERIENCE

**(63rd) 1990 held in 1991**

John Barry – **Best Original Score:** DANCES WITH WOLVES

Jeremy Irons – **Best Actor:** REVERSAL OF FORTUNE

Nick Park – **Best Animated Short:** CREATURE COMFORTS

**(64th) 1991 held in 1992**

Daniel Greaves – **Best Animated Short:** MANIPULATION

Anthony Hopkins – **Best Actor:** SILENCE OF THE LAMBS

**(65th) 1992 held in 1993**

Simon Kaye – **Best Sound:** THE LAST OF THE MOHICANS

Tim Rice – **Best Original Song:** ALADDIN (A WHOLE NEW WORLD)

Emma Thompson – **Best Actress:** HOWARDS END

Ian Whittaker – **Best Art Direction:** HOWARDS END

**(66th) 1993 held in 1994**

Richard Hymns – **Best Sound Effects Editing:** JURASSIC PARK

Nick Park – **Best Animated Short:** THE WRONG TROUSERS

Deborah Kerr – **Career Achievement Honorary Award**

**(67th) 1994 held in 1995**

Ken Adam & Carolyn Scott – **Best Art Direction:** THE MADNESS OF KING GEORGE

Peter Capaldi & Ruth Kenley-Letts – **Best Live Action Short:** FRANZ KAFKA'S IT'S A WONDERFUL LIFE

Elton John & Tim Rice – **Best Song:** THE LION KING (CAN YOU FEEL THE LOVE TONIGHT)

Alison Snowden & David Fine
-**Best Animated Short:** BOB'S BIRTHDAY

**(68th) 1995 held in 1996**

James Acheson – **Best Costume Design:** RESTORATION

Jon Blair – **Best Documentary Feature:** ANNE FRANK REMEMBERED

Lois Burwell & Peter Frampton – **Special Achievement In Make Up:** BRAVEHEART

Emma Thompson – **Best Adapted Screenplay:** SENSE & SENSIBILITY

Nick Park – **Best Animated Short:** A CLOSE SHAVE

**(69th) 1996 held in 1997**

Anthony Minghella – **Best Director:** THE ENGLISH PATIENT

Rachel Portman – **Best Original Score Musical or Comedy:** EMMA

Tim Rice & Andrew Lloyd Webber – **Best Original song:** EVITA (YOU MUST LOVE ME)

Stuart Craig & Stephanie McMillan – **Best Art Direction:** THE ENGLISH PATIENT

## (70th) 1997 held in 1998

Peter Lamont and Michael Ford – **Best Achievement In Art Direction:** TITANIC

Anne Dudley – **Best Original Score Musical or Comedy:** THE FULL MONTY

Jan Pinkava – **Best Animated Short:** GERI'S GAME

## (71st) 1998 held in 1999

David Parfitt – **Best Film:** SHAKESPEARE IN LOVE

Judi Dench – **Best Actress in a Supporting Role:** SHAKESPEARE IN LOVE

Tom Stoppard – **Best Original Screenplay:** SHAKESPEARE IN LOVE

Martin Childs and Jill Quertier – **Best Art Direction:** SHAKESPEARE IN LOVE

Sandy Powell – **Best Costume Design:** SHAKESPEARE IN LOVE

Jenny Shircore – **Best Make-up:** ELIZABETH

Stephen Warbeck – **Best Original Score Musical or Comedy:** SHAKESPEARE IN LOVE

Andy Nelson – **Best Sound:** SAVING PRIVATE RYAN

## (72nd) 1999 held in 2000

Michael Caine – **Actor in a Supporting Role:** CIDER HOUSE RULES

Peter Young – **Art Direction:** SLEEPY HOLLOW

Lindy Hemming – **Costume Design:** TOPSY-TURVY

Sam Mendes – **Directing:** AMERICAN BEAUTY

Kevin MacDonald, John Battsek, – **Documentary Feature:** ONE DAY IN SEPTEMBER

Christine Blundell, Trefor Proud – **Make up:** TOPSY-TURVY

Phil Collins – **Original Song:** TARZAN "You'll Be In My Heart"

## (73rd) 2000 held in 2001

Janty Yates – **Costume Design:** GLADIATOR

Claire Jennings – **Best Animated Short:** FATHER AND DAUGHTER

Ken Weston – **Best Sound:** GLADIATOR

Tim Burke – **Best Visual Effects:** GLADIATOR

**SPECIAL AWARDS**

Jack Cardiff – **Honorary Oscar**

Vic Armstrong – **Scientific and Technical Award**

## (74th) 2001 held in 2002

Jim Broadbent – **Actor Supporting:** IRIS

Peter Owen – **Make Up:**

Chris Munro – **Sound:**

Julian Fellowes – **Writing (Original):** GOSFORD PARK

## (75th) 2002 held in 2003

Catherine Zeta-Jones – **Actress, Supporting :** CHICAGO

Peter O'Toole – **Lifetime Achievement**

Ronald Harwood – **Adapted Screenplay:** THE PIANIST

## (76th) 2003 held in 2004

Annie Lennox (with Howard Shore, Fran Walsh) – **Best Original Song:** "Into the West" from THE LORD OF THE RINGS   THE RETURN OF THE KING

This listing does not claim to be definitive, or in any way endorse any of the booksellers listed. It aims to list as wide a variety of booksellers and services as possible (within time and space limits) that offer (or even purchase) new, out of print, second hand and rare titles on film and television. The metrocentric emphasis in the listing is purely unintentional but unfortunately inevitable. Compiled by Ayesha Khan

## Andromeda Bookshop
1 Suffolk Street,
Birmingham B1 1LT
Tel: 0121 643 1999
Website: andromedabook.co.uk
Telephone orders between 10.30-4.30, shop open: Mon-Sat 10.00-5.00
Science fiction, horror and fantasy bookshop including some titles on film and television. Mail order, Internet and shop sales

## Arnolfini Bookshop
16 Narrow Quay,
Bristol BS1 4QA
Tel: 0117 917 2300
email: bookshop@arnolfini.org.uk
Website: www.arnolfini.org.uk
Open: Tues-Sat, 11.00-5.00; Sun, 12.00-5.00
Currently undergoing some redevelopment the Arnolfini boasts one of the very best specialist arts bookshops in the country, with an exceptional range of texts on art, film, performance, design, photography, society plus relevant specialist magazines

## Bookends
108, Charing Cross Road,
London WC2H 0JN
Tel: 020 7836 3457
Website: www.bookspostfree.com
Open: Mon & Fri, 9.15-6.45, Tues-Thu, 9.00-7.15, Saturday 9.30-6.30, Sunday 9.15-4.30
General bookshop included with some film and television stock because it is a potential goldmine for that difficult to get out of print screenplay. There is also further information about shops and online service at the website

## Cinema Bookshop
13-14 Great Russell Street
London WC1B 3NH
Tel: 020 76370206
Legendary bookshop containing very large stock of new, out of print and rare books. Excellent source for the non-glossy cinema magazines. Stills and posters held too

## Cinema Store (London)
4C Orion House,
Upper St Martin's Lane,
London, WC2H 9NY
Tel: 020 7379 7895
Fax: 020 7240 7689
Shops are based on adjacent premises. This side for film books and videos.
4B Orion House,
Upper St Martin's Lane,
London, WC2H 9NY
Tel: 020 7379 7838 [general enquiries]
Tel: 020 7379 7865 [DVDs]
This half for magazines, toys, t-shirts, collectibles and DVDs

## Cinema Store (Nottingham)
Unit T2,
The Cornerhouse Leisure Complex,
Nottingham, NG1 4DB
Tel: 01159 503090
Fax: 01159 508054
Books, magazines, posters, DVDs, videos, ephemera and CD soundtracks

## Cornerhouse Bookshop
70 Oxford Street
Manchester M1 5NH
Tel: 0161 228 7621
email: info@cornerhouse.org
12 noon - 8.30pm every day (Mon - Sun)
Whereas the bookshop holds mainly film related titles, Cornerhouse Publications' book distribution service distributes contemporary visual arts, architecture, design etc. See: Website:
www.cornerhouse.org/publications (e-commerce website)

## Cusack Books
PO Box 17696
London W12 8WR
Tel: +44 (0) 20 8743 0517
Fax:f: +44 (020) 870 133 2476
email: queries@cusackbooks
Website: www.cusackbooks.com
Elaine Cusack-O'Connell
For out of print television, film and music-related books. Stock runs from Abba to Z Cars via Bagpuss, Monty Python and Truffaut. Established 1998. Mail order/Internet-based

## David Drummond at Pleasures of Past Times
11 Cecil Court
Charing Cross Road
London WC2N 4EZ
Tel: 020 7836 1142
email: Drummond @popt.fsnet.co.uk
Open: Mon-Fri 11.00 - 5.45 (Closed lunch 2.30-3.30); also open generally the first Saturday in the month (by appointment) 11.00-2.30
Books, memorabilia and other ephemera on the performing arts

## Decorum Books
24 Cloudesley Square
London N1 0HN
Tel: 020 7278 1838
Fax: 020 7837 6424
email: decorumbooks@lineone.net
Website: www.decorumbooks.co.uk
Sue Soames
Mail order only for secondhand books for film and performing arts. 150,000 approx books in stock. Occasional joint ventures with small specialist publishers on cinema and theatre architecture and design. Decorum Books 2 specialises in books on Indian cinema and performing arts, website: www.india-cinema.co.uk)

## Dress Circle
57-59 Monmouth Street
Covent Garden
London WC2H 9DG
Tel: (UK code) 020 7 240 2227
Fax: (UK code) 020 7 379 8540
email: email enquires:
info@dresscircle.co.uk
Website: www.dresscircle.co.uk

Open: Monday to Saturday, 10.00 – 6.00
Specialising in musical theatre, publications and releases

## The European Bookshop
5 Warwick Street
London W1R 5RA
Tel: 020 7734 5259
Fax: 020 7287 1720
email: direct@esb.co.uk
Website:
www.europeanbookshop.com
Open: Mon to Sat, 9:30am - 6:00pm
Foreign language stock. Services aimed at educational users. Ordering services available.
Website: www.dresscircle.co.uk

## Forbidden Planet
179 Shaftesbury Avenue
London WC2H 8JR
Tel: 020 7836 4179
email: info@forbiddenplanet.com
Website: www.forbiddenplanet.co.uk
(Branches in Birmingham, Bristol, Cambridge, Coventry, Croydon, Liverpool, London, Newcastle, Southampton).
Specialises in all aspects of science fiction, horror and fantasy. London branch has a surprisingly eclectic selection of book on film and television in spite of its specialism. Online shopping available

## Foyles
W & G Foyle Ltd,
113-119 Charing Cross Road,
London WC2H 0EB
Tel: 020 7437 5660
Fax: 020 7434 1580.
email: orders@foyles.co.uk.
Website: www.foyles.co.uk
Open: Mon-Sat 9.30-8.00, Sunday & Public Holidays, 12.00-6.00
One of the largest bookshops in the UK. Has one of the larger film and TV sections for a general bookshop. Some out of print titles held. Online ordering service via the website.

## Grant & Cutler
55-57 Great Marlborough Street,
London W1F 7AY
Tel: 020 7734 2012
Fax: 020 7734 9272
email: contactus@grantandcutler.com
Website:
www.www.grantandcutler.com
Open: Mon - Fri, 9:00 to 18:00 GMT; Thurs, 9:00 to 19:00; Sat, 9:00 to 17:30 GMT. (Please note that phone lines are not open on Sundays)
Foreign language specialists.

## Greenroom Books
Geoff Oldham
9 St James Road
Ilkley
West Yorkshire LS29 9PY
Tel: 01943 607662
email:
greenroombooks@blueyonder.co.uk
Website: www.abebooks.com/home/greenroombooks
Specialise in the performing arts: film, television, radio, theatre, opera, ballet, popular entertainment. Enquiries are welcome by e-mail, telephone and letter. Personal callers only by arrangement

## Heffers
20 Trinity Street
Cambridge CB2 1TY
Tel: 01223 568568
Fax: 01223 568591
email: artbooks@heffers.co.uk
Open: Mon-Sat, 9.00-5.30 (except Tuesday's open at 9.30), Sunday 11.00-5.00
Large bookshop, now part of the Blackwells empire. Academic/General; some secondhand. Greetings cards/post cards. Also sell and hire videos

## Henry Pordes Bookshop
58-60 Charing Cross Road
London, WC2H 0DH
Tel: 020 7836 9031
Fax: 020 7240 4232
email: henrypordes@clara.net
Website: home.clara.net/henrypordes/
Secondhand, remaindered and antiquarian booksellers

## Irish Film Centre Bookshop
The Film Institute of Ireland.
6 Eustace St.
Temple Bar
Dublin 2
Ireland
Tel:+353 1 6795744
Fax:+353 1 6778755
email: info@ifc.ie
Website: www.fii.ie/index.html
Mary Sherlock
The Irish Film Centre Shop carries a wide range of books, magazine and journals relating to film. It also stocks an extensive collection of videos, DVDs, posters and small gift items

## Kelly Books Limited
6 Redlands
Tiverton
Devon EX16 4DH
Tel: (01884) 256170
Fax: (01884) 252765

email: len@kellybooks.co.uk
Website: www.kellybooks.co.uk
Len Kelly and Lynda Kelly
Used books,magazines, pamphlets & ephemera on all aspects of the history and technology of radio, television and related subjects. Also has a small publishing arm. They also sell own publications

## National Museum of Photography, Bradford
Museum Shop
Bradford BD1 1NQ
Tel: 01274 202041
Fax:01274 202041
email: talk.nmpft@nmsi.ac.uk
Website: www.nmsi.ac.uk
Open: Tue-Sun 10.00-6.00. Entrance to the Gallery is free except for special exhibitions

## Offstage Theatre & Film Bookshop
37 Chalk Farm Road
London NW1 8AJ
Tel: 020 7485 4996
Fax: 020 7916 8046
email: offstagebookshop@aol.com
Opening hours: Mon-Fri, 10.00-6.00, Sat-Sun, 12.00-6.00
New and second hand books. Stock caters for students, academics and filmmakers. Free catalogues can be sent. Mail order available

## Peter Wood
20 Stonehill Road
Great Shelford
Cambridge CB2 5JL
Fax: Tel/fax: 01223 842419
email:
peterwoodbooks@waitrose.com
Books and memorabilia. Mail order but visitors are welcome by appointment. Free catlogue available

## Rare Discs
18 Bloomsbury Street
London WC1B 3QA
Tel: 020 7580 3516
Open: Mon - Sat, 10.00-6.30
Holds thousands of soundtracks for films, musicals, shows, films stills, posters, books, magazines etc

## Shipley Media
80 Charing Cross Road
London WC2H 0BB
Tel: 020 7240 4157
Fax: 020 7212 9939
email: sales@artbook.co.uk
Website: www.artbook.co.uk
Open: 9.30-6.30pm Mon-Fri,
New and out of print books on every

aspect of cinema, photography, fashion and textiles. International mail order service available. Shipley Media changed ownership from Zwemmer in the summer of 2003. It is now part of Shipley Specialist Art Booksellers which have 3 stores on the Charing Cross Road

### Spread Eagle Bookshop
9 Nevada Street
London SE10 9JL
Tel: 020 8305 1666
Fax: 020 8305 0447
email: books@spreadeagle.org.uk
Website: www.spreadeagle.org/cgi-bin/books.asp
Large second hand bookshop that specialises partly in cinema, design, and the performing arts

### Treasure Chest
61 Cobbold Road
Felixstowe
Suffolk IP11 7BH
Tel: 01394 270717
Open Monday to Saturday, 9.30 - 5.30pm.
Large second hand stock specialising in cinema and literature

### VinMagCo
39-43 Brewer Street
London W1R 9UD
Tel: 020 7439-0882
Fax: 020 7439-8527
email: info@vinmag.com
Website: www.vinmag.com
Open: Mon-Wed 10.00-7.00, Thursday, 10.00-8.00, Fri-Sat, 10.00-10.00, Sunday, 12.00-8.00
There are two shops in London and further stores in Brighton and Oxford. VinMagCo Ltd has been producing movie memorabilia since 1975 and supplies to retailers throughout the world. Items available include posters, photographs, postcards, t-shirts, life-size standups and mouse pads. Availability in some countries may depend on the terms under which an image is licensed. For further details or to place a wholesale order contact Paul Belchamber

## Major Chains

### Blackwells
One of the smaller but perfectly formed chains. Has online bookshop service with searchable database. The Charing Cross Road branch (100, Charing Cross Road, tel: 020 7292 5100) has a good stock of film and TV.
For other branches, see: www.bookshop.blackwells.co.uk.

### Bookcase
**138-140 Charing Cross Road**
**London WC2H**
Tel: 020 7836 8391
Bookshop chain in London that specialises in remaindered bookshops that often contain pleasant surprises for the browser and unpleasant ones for the acquisitions librarian. Sadly no website or subject listings

### Borders and Books etc.
Whether you're a fan or not, the stores usually have useful holdings on film & TV, especially in the 124 Charing Cross Road (020 7379 8877) and 203, Oxford St (020 7292 1600) branches.
See: www.borders.co.uk forwww.booksetc.co.uk for other store locations (but as yet no online service)

### Remainders Ltd
A chain trading under a variety of names, including The Works and Book Depot. As the name implies remaindered books are their speciality and they have a healthy selection of film and television books at heavily discounted prices. The website gives details of store locations, see www.theworks.gb.com

### Waterstones
Numerous stores all over the UK, usually fairly well stocked with film & TV books.
Flagship store is at in Piccadilly, London.203-206 Piccadilly, London, W1J 9LE (020 7851 2400).
Have entered strategic alliance with Amazon.co.uk for online supply and their website links directly to Amazon's searchable database and online ordering services.
For other branches information and ordering online:
www.waterstones.co.uk

## Online Services

### Advanced Book Exchange
Website: www.AbeBooks.com
Claiming to offer 40 million books from 10,000 booksellers from all over the world, this could described as the Amazon" service for used out of print and rare books. Also a useful to see judge how much your collection may be worth

### Amazon
Website: www.amazon.co.uk
The best-known online book ordering service, offering plenty of film and TV titles

### Retro Sellers
Website: www.retrosellers.com
Describing itself as the "definitive site for retro and nostalgia", covering film, TV and popular culture this comprehensive site offers features and newsletters as well as a sourcing and valuation service for those hard to find books, videos, records, CDs and stills

### UK Bookworld
Website: www.ukbookworld.com
Provides details of old and out-of-print books from British bookshops. Books mailed out and paid via credit card or cheque. Can search by title, author or subject. eg.'film' which retrieved more than 500 pages of titles. Prices range from £3.50 upwards

# CABLE, SATELLITE FILM CHANNELS

In this section the emphasis will be a selection of Cable and Satellite channels and companies which provide some kind of film elements to their programming. A full list of all the cable and satellite licences for Satellite Television Services and Licensable Programme Services can be found on the Ofcom website: www.ofcom.org.uk.

## Licensable Programme Services

Licensable Programme Services are carried to viewers in the UK over a telecommunication system. This category applies to services provided nationally to cable systems other than by satellite delivery, to community television services unique to a particular cable system and also to video-on-demand services carried over telephone networks.

Below is a list of the registered Licensable Programme Services companies.

### Arsenal AFC
Highbury
London N5 1BU
Tel: 020 7704 4000
Website: www.arsenal.co.uk
Live football screening at the Arsenal stadium

### Arts and Entertainment Broadcasting Network UK Ltd
16b Jermyn Street
London SW1Y 6ST
Tel: 020 7287 2929
Local arts and light entertainment programming for Birmingham

### Asian Television Marketing Ltd
138 Denbydale Way
Oldham OL1 1LS
Tel: 0161 627 1207
General Asian programming

### BIB (Platform) Company Ltd
Grant Way
Isleworth TW7 5QD
Tel: 0870 240 3000

### Box Television Ltd
Mappin House
4 Winsley Street
London W1W 8HF
Tel: 020 7436 1515
Music videos and information services via interactive technology

Box Television Ltd

### Breakthrough Media Group
10 Hagley Road
Stourbridge DY8 1PS
Factual food related programming
Tel: 01562 882633

### British Sky Broadcasting (BSkyB)
6 Centaurs Business Park
Grant Way, Syon Lane
Isleworth
Middlesex TW7 5QD
Tel: 0870 240 3000
Fax: 020 7705 3030
Website: www.sky.com.uk

### British Telecommunications plc
PP 4.31 Mondial House
90-94 Upper Thames St
London EC4R 3UB
Tel: 020 7469 2856

### Cable & Wireless
Caxton Way
Watford Business Park
Watford WD1 8HX
Tel: 01923 435000
Website: www.cwcom.co.uk
The Interactive Channel
Interactive entertainment, news and sport programming in Cable & Wireless's franchises

### Cable London plc
2 Stephen Street
London W1P 1PL
Tel: 020 7911 0555
Local text and graphic service for Cable London franchise

### Calderdale Television
Dean Clough
Halifax HX3 5AX
Tel: 01422 253100
Website: www.thefuse.co.uk
Local programmes for the Halifax area

### Cambridge Cable Ltd
1st Floor, Block D2
Westbrook Centre
Milton Road
Cambridge CB4 1YG
Tel: 01223 567200

email: camcable.co.uk
Interactive TV services

## CSV Media
237 Pentonville Road
London N1 9NJ
Tel: 020 7278 6601
Local programming

## Derby County Football Club Ltd
Derby County Football Club Ltd
Pride Park Stadium
Pride Park
Derby DE24 8XL
Tel: 01332 667553
News and light entertainment related to Derby Couny football club

## Flextech Television
160 Gt Portland St
London W1W 5QA
Tel: 020 7299 5000
General entertainment and programming

## Francis Mario Barbero Ltd
46 Colet Gardens
St Paul"s Court
London W14 9DL
Tel: 020 8741 7795
Lignt entertainment for London

## Hellenic Television Ltd
50 Clarendon Road
London N8 0DJ
Tel: 020 8292 7037
Greek language programming

## Homechoice
205 Holland Park Avenue
London W1
Tel: 020 7348 4000
Video on demand

## Immage 2000 Studios Ltd
Margaret Street
Immingham DN40 1LE
Tel: 01469 515151
Website: www.immage-2000.co.uk
Local programming for the Grimsby and Cleethorpes area

## IRIE TV Network
IRIE TV Network
41 Burlington Road
London N17 9HU
Tel: 0181 985 0307
General entertainment

## London News Network Ltd
The London Television Centre
Upper Ground
London SE1 9LT
Tel: 020 7827 7700
Interactive news service

## Mirus Productions Ltd
86 Adelaide Grove
London W12 0JL
Tel: 020 8740 5505
Black cultural entertainment and music programming

## Mr Mahmoud Sarabi
(Persian TV)
10 Pennine Parade
Pennine Drive
London NW2 1NT
Tel: 020 8731 9333
General entertainment. Persian language service.

## National Museum of Photography Film and Television
The Art Mill
Upper Park Gate
Bradford BD1 5DE
Tel: 01274 727488
News and local events

## ntl Group Ltd
Bartley Wood Business Park
Hook
Hants RG27 9UP
Tel: 01256 752150

## Power TV Ltd
Power TV Ltd
43 Parkhead Loan
Edinburgh EH11 4SJ
Tel: 0131 443 4642
Website: www.powertv.co.uk
Light entertainment

## Premium TV Ltd
22 Suffolk Street
London SW1Y 4HG
Tel: 020 7930 0003
Sports channel

## Rangami
PO Box 2821
London NW2 1DS
Tel: 0181 328 1084
Iranian programming on London Interconnect

## Stockwhiz Ltd
Carmelite
50 Victoria Embankment
Blackfrairs
London EC4Y 0DX
Tel: 020 7597 5113
News, information and home shopping programming

## Takerak Ltd
81 Seaford Road
London N15 5DX
Tel: 020 8802 4576
Afro-Caribbean programming

## Telewest Communications (London and South East) Ltd
5 Factory Lane
Croydon CR9 3RA
Tel: 0181 251 5151
Local programming for the Thames estuary north franchise

## Telewest Communications (Midlands and North West) Ltd
Cable Plaza, Waterfront West
Brierley Hill
West Midlands DY5 1LW
Tel: 01384 838483
Local programming for the Black Country, Telford and Worcester

## Telewest Communications (North West)
Cable House
2-8 Frenchwood Avenue
Preston PR1 4QF
Tel: 01772 902902

## Telewest Communications (Scotland and NE) Ltd
1 South Gyle
Crescent Lane
Edinburgh EH12 9EG
Tel: 0131 539 0002
Local programming for the Edinburgh franchise

## Telewest Communications Midlands and South West) Ltd
700 Waterside Drive
Aztec West
Bristol BS12 4ST
Tel: 0117 983 9000
Local programming in the Avon franchise

## Telewest Communications Networks Ltd
Genesis Business Park
Albert Drive
Woking
Surrey GU21 5RW
Tel: 01483 750 900
On Screen TV Guide

## The Adam and Eve Channel
Suite 205
Crown House
North Circular Road
London NW10 7PN
Tel: 0181 961 3335
Adult feature films

## The Dream Family Network
Christian Channel Studios

Stonehills, Shields Road
Gateshead NE10 0HW
Tel: 0191 495 2244
Christian programming on the
London Interconnect

## The Preview Channel
Penraevons Industrial Estate
Penraevon Street
Leeds LS7 2AW
Tel: 0113 239 2255
Preview forthcoming attractions on
cable networks

## Trinity and All Saints College
Brownberry Lane
Horsforth
Leeds LS18 5HD
Tel: 0113 283 7249
Local news and current affairs
Trinity and All Saints College

## TV-Africa Ltd
27 Old Gloucester Street
London WC1N 3XX
Tel: 020 7419 5012
General entertainment, African focus
Website: www.tv-africa.co.uk

## University of Sunderland

Langham Tower, Ryhope Road
Sunderland SR2 7EE
Tel: 0191 515 2452
Educational programming

## Video Networks
Rosanne House
Parkway
Welywn Garden City AL8 6HG
Tel: 01707 362500
Website: www.videonetworks.co.uk
Video-on-demand service in Hull

## Vision Broadcasting Communications
Vision Studios
Eastcott Corner
Bath Road
Swindon SN1 3LS
Tel: 01793 511244
Website: www.visionchannel.co.uk
Christian programming

## Westminster Cable
87-89 Baker Street
London W1M 1AS
Tel: 0171 935 4400
Multi-plexed promotional channel

## Yes Television (Europe) Ltd
1 Caspian Point
Caspian Way
Cardiff CF10 4DQ
Tel: 029 2046 6600

Interactive video-on-demand service

## Yorkshire Television Ltd
The Television Centre
Leeds LS3 1JS
Tel: 0113 243 8283
Local programming available on
demand

# Satellite Television Services

Satellite Television Services are
services for reception via individual
dishes or cable systems whether in
this country or in any other
provided by a companies who are
established in the UK.
Below is a list of the registered
Satellite Television Services
companies.

## 4 Ventures Ltd
124 Horseferry Road
London SW1P 2TX
Tel: 020 7396 4444
Entertainment programming, E4

## 4D Telecom Ltd
4D House
167-173 Wandsworth High St
London SW18 4JB
Tel: 0870 345 0000
Chat Box, text message service

## A & A Inform Ltd
72 New Bond Street
Mayfair
London W1S 1RR
Tel: 020 8995 1631

## ABS-CBN Europe Ltd
109 Gloucester Rd
South Kensington
London SW7 4SS
Tel: 020 7341 4447
ABS-CBN Cinema One, Films

## AC Voice TV Ltd
22 Goodwin Rd
London W12 9JW
Tel: 0870 770 2467

## Ace Television Network (ATN)
7 Peregrine Way
London SW19 4RN
Tel: 020 8947 8841

## ACTV
81 Seaford Rd
London N15 5DX
Tel: 020 8809 770

## Afghanistan Culture and Art Association
9 Ivatt Way
London N17 6PF
Tel: 020 8881 0869
Refugee TV, Community

### African Broadcasting Corporation (ABC)
3 Central Hall
Archway
London N19 3TD
Tel: 07050 202 460

### Al Mustakillah Television Ltd
49 Gorst Road
London NW10 6LS
Tel: 020 8838 2884

### Amore TV Ltd
Stonehills Complex
Shields Road
Gateshead
Tyne & Wear NE10 0HW
Tel: 0191 483 5585

### Apna TV and Radio Broadcasting
60 Aubert Park
London N5 1TS
Tel: 020 7359 6464
Website: www.apnatv.com

### Arts and Entertainment Ltd
New Pathe House
57 Jamestown Road
London NW1 7XX
Tel: 020 7424 3688
Website: ww.performancetv.co.uk

### Artsworld Channels Ltd
80 Silverthorne Road
LondonSW8 3XA
Tel: 020 7819 1160
Email: tv@artsworld.com
Website: www.artsworld.com

### Asia TV Ltd
Units 7 -9
Belvue Business Centre
Belvue Rd
Northolt,
Middlesex, UB5 5QQ
Tel: 020 8839 4000
Website: www.zeetv.co.uk
www.zeetelevision.com

### Asia World Television Ltd
17a Holland Park Gardens
London W14 8DZ
Tel: 07950 260026
Website: www.asiaworld.tv

### Asian Vision
Warton House, 3rd Floor
150 High St
Stratford
London E15 2NE
Tel: 020 8221 2115

### Asset TV Ltd
Universal Management Group

Studio 8
Church Studios
49 Camden Park Rd
London NW1 9AY
Tel: 020 7267 6345

### Auctionworld Limited
Unit 6
Elena House
IO Centre
Lea Rd
Waltham Cross EN8 7PG
Tel: 01992 760444
Website: www.auction-world.tv

### AXN Europe Ltd
Sony Pictures Europe House
25 Golden Sq
London W1F 9LU
Tel: 020 7533 1500

### B4U Network Ltd
19 Heather Park Drive
Wembley Middx HA0 1SS
Tel: 020 8795 7171
Fax: 020 8963 8445
Website: www.b4utv.com

### Bangla TV Ltd
Warton House
3rd Floor
150 High St
Stratford
London E15 2NE
Tel: 020 8519 3200

### Bazaar Television Ltd
Clerkenwell House
67 Clerkenwell Rd
London EC1R 5BL
Tel: 020 7693 8405

### BBC
80 Wood Lane
London W12 0TT
Tel: 020 8433 2722

### BBC World Ltd
Woodlands
80 Wood Lane
London W12 0TT
Tel: 020 8433 2221

### BBC Worldwide Ltd
Woodlands
80 Wood Lane
London W12 0TT
Tel: 020 8433 2000

### Best Direct (International) Ltd
167 Imperial Drive
Harrow
Middlesex HA2 7JP
Tel: 020 8868 4355

### BIZ4BIZTV Ltd
Avon House
Kensington Village
Avonmore Rd
London W14 8TS
Tel: 020 7371 5353

### BKA Network Television Ltd
391 City Rd
2nd Floor
Angel
London EC1V 1NE
Tel: 020 7837 8377

### Blockbuster Entertainment Ltd
Harefield Place
The Drive
Middlesex UB10 8AQ
Tel: 01895 866248
Video on Demand, feature films

### Bloomberg LP
City Gate House
39-45 Finsbury Square
London EC2A 1PQ
Tel: 020 7330 7500
Website: www.bloomberg.co.uk

### Box Television Ltd
Mappin House
4 Winsley Street
London W1W 8HF
Tel: 020 7436 1515
Website: www.thebox.co.uk.

### BPM Television Ltd
Po Box 5249
Brinklow
Milton Keynes
MK17 9ZH
Tel: 0870 120 5395

### British Sky Broadcasting Ltd
6 Centaurs Business Park
Grant Way
Isleworth TW7 5QD
Tel: 020 7705 3000

### Broadcasting (Gaia) Ltd
117-121 Salusbury Rd
London NW6 6RG
Tel: 020 7328 8808

### Broadcasting (UK) Ltd
33 New Cavendish St
London W1G 9TS
Tel: 020 7328 8808

### Business Information Television
11 Marlborough Place
Brighton BN1 1UB
Tel: 01273 728809

## Carlton SelecTV Cable Ltd
27 Mortimer Street
London W1N 7RJ
Tel: 020 7725 4600
Website:
www.carltonfoodnetwork.com

## Channel 208 Limited
Westbrook House
18/20 Albion Place
Maidstone
Kent ME14 5DZ
Tel: 01622 776776

## Channel 5 Broadcasting Ltd
22 Long Acre
London WC2E 9LY
Tel: 020 7550 5655
Website: www.channel5.co.uk

## Channel S Television Limited
Prestige House
Clifford Road
Walthamstow E17 4JW
Tel: 020 8253 4555

## Channel Television Ltd
Television Centre
La Pouquelaye
St Helier
Jersey JE1 3ZD
Tel: 01534 816720

## Chart Show TV Channels Ltd
37 Harwood Rd
London SW6 4QP
Tel: 020 7384 2243
Fax: 020 7384 2026
Website: www.chartshow.com

## Chelsea Digital Media Ltd
Stamford Bridge
Fulham Rd
London SW6 1HS
Tel: 020 7915 1951
Chelsea TV

## Cheltrading 370 Ltd
Third Floor
6 Cavendish Place
London W1G 9NB
The Horse Racing Channel

## Chinese News and Entertainment
Marvic House
Bishops Road
London SW6 7AD
Tel: 020 7610 3880

## Christian Communications Network Limited
14 West Kensington Mansions
Beaumont Crescent

London W14 9PE
Tel: 020 7381 4247
Website: www.ccneurope.org.uk

## Christian Television Broadcasting Ltd
Westbrook House
Albion Place
Maidstone ME14 5DZ
Tel: 01622 776 776

## CNBC Europe
10 Fleet Place
London EC4M 7QS
Tel: 020 7653 9300
Website: www.cnbceurope.com

## CNI UK Ltd
100 New Bridge Rd
London EC4V 65A
Tel: 0207 919 1000

## Crown Entertainment Ltd
234a Kings Road
London SW3 5YW
Tel: 020 7368 9100
The Hallmark Entertainment Network, Films, series and mini-series

## Cruise Control (UK) Ltd
Stanton Gate
49 Mawney Road
Romford RM7 7HL
Tel: 0870 7000 0111

## CTV (Cultural Television)
83 High Street
Rayleigh
Essex SS6 7ES
Tel: 01268 454748

## Daar Communications Ltd
3 Archway Close
Archway Rd
London N19 3TD
Tel: 0207 233 7965
Africa Independent Television

## Datel Holdings Ltd
Stafford Road, Stone
Staffordshire ST15 0DG
Tel: 01785 810800

## DBC Television Ltd
6-7 Cross Street
London EC1N 8UA
Tel: 020 7242 7770
B4U>direct, Films (Hindi)

## Definition Consultants Ltd
2-4 Hoxton Sq
London N1 6NU
Tel: 0870 744 2041

## Deshbangla Ltd
Dame Colet House

Ben Johnson Rd
Stepney Green
London E1 3NH
Tel: 020 7790 5522

## Digital Broadcasting Television Ltd
6-7 St Cross Street
London
EC1N 8UA
Tel: 020 7242 7770
u>directfilms, Filmed entertainment

## Digital Classics plc
31 Eastcastle Street
London W1W 8DL
Tel: 020 7636 1400
Fax: 020 7637 1355
Website: www.onlineclassics.com

## Digital Television Production Company Ltd
Units 6 & 7 Princes Court
Wapping Lane
London E1 9DA
Tel: 020 7942 7942

## Digital Wellbeing Ltd
Hargreaves House
20 Wollaton Street
Nottingham NG1 5FJ
Tel: 0115 968 8089

## Discovery Communications Europe
160 Great Portland Street
London W1N 5TB
Tel: 020 7462 3600
Discovery Channel

## Dovewell Communications
Dovewell Communications,
March House
Victoria Trading Estate
Victoria Rd
Acton
London W3 6GS
Tel: 020 8752 3971

## E! Entertainment Televison inc
5750 Wilshire Boulevard
Los Angeles
CA 90036
Tel: 001 323 954 2400
www.entertainment.com

## E-Music Television Ltd
33 Wyatt Drive
London SW13 8AL
Tel: 020 8741 2200
Website: www.e-musictelevision.com

## Eagle Road Studios
Moons Moat North Industrial Estate
Redditch

B98 9HF
Tel: 01527 406100

**East West Broadcast Limited.**
176 Franciscan Rd
London SW17 8HH
Tel: 020 8814 6565

**EBN (European Business News)**
10 Fleet Place
London EC4M 7RB
Tel: 020 7653 9300
Website: www.ebn.co.uk

**Eckoh Technologies (UK) Ltd**
Telford House
Corner Hall
Hemel Hempstead
Tel: 08701 107 108

**Eclipse Sat Ltd**
33 New Cavendish Street
London W1G 9TS
Tel No: 020 7224 5504
Films

**Ekushey Television (UK) Ltd**
c/o On-Air Systems Ltd
91-93 Cleveland Street
London W1T 6PL
Tel: 020 7702 4111

**Emirates Media Inc**
Po Box 63
Abu Dhabi
United Arab Emirates
Tel: 971 2 4430000

**EMMA**
37 Langford Court
Langford Place
London NW8 9DN
Tel: 020 7636 1233

**Entertainment Distribution Company Ltd**
Po Box 1011
Riyadh
11431
Saudi Arabia
Tel: 020 7935 7566
Al Qula, Movies

**ESPN Classic Sport Ltd**
McCormack House
Hogarth Business Park
London W4 2TH
Tel: 020 8233 6567

**Eternal Word Television Network Inc.**
5817 Old Leeds Road
Birmingham

Alabama 35210
USA
Tel: 00 1 205 2712 2997
Website: www.ewtn.com

**Euro Digital Corporation Ltd**
124-128 City Rd
London EC1V 2NJ
Tel: 020 7748 1500

**Europe Movieco Partners Ltd**
1 Stephen Street
London W1T 1AL
Tel: 020 7691 6960
Cinenova, Film channel with Dutch subtitles

**Extreme Motion/Urbanchillers.com**
29 Conway Street
London W1T 6BW
Tel: 020 7387 9494
Extreme Motion/Urbanchillers.com, Horror movies

**Extreme Sports Channel VOF**
The Media Centre
131-151 Great Titchfield St
London W1P 8AE
Tel: 020 7886 0760
Website: www.extreme.com

**Fans Channel plc**
Teddington Studios
Broom Rd
Teddington
Middlesex TW11 9NT
Tel: 020 8614 2675

**Finsbury Software Ltd**
123 Canfield Road
Woodford Green
Essex IG8 8JJ
Tel: 07909 593 117

**Flextech Television Ltd**
160 Gt Portland St
London W1W 5QA
Tel: 020 7299 5000
Bravo, Living

**Fox International Channels (uk) ltd**
338 Euston Road
London NW1 3AZ

**Fox Kids Europe Ltd**
338 Euston Road
London NW1 3AZ
Tel: 020 7554 9000
Website: www.foxkids.co.uk

**Fox News Channel Ltd**
1211 Avenue of the Americas

New York
NY 10036
USA
Tel: 212 301 3322

**Freedom Gospel Community Channel Ltd**
Eastern Court
182-190 Newmarket RTd
Cambridge CB5 8HE
Tel: 01223 513493

**Friendly TV Ltd**
Interxion Building
11 Hanbury St
London E1 6QR
Tel: 020 7247 8544
Website: www.friendlytv.com

**Front Row Television**
1 Stephen Street
London W1T 1AL
Tel: 020 7691 5950
Films

**Game relating entertainment**
Unit 6-7
Princes Court
Wapping Lane
London E1W 2DA
Tel: 020 7492 7492

**Gandhi Corporation Ltd**
Unit 11
Forest Business Park
South Access Rd
Walthamstow E17 8BA
Tel: 01603 660783

**Geo TV Ltd**
97 Foxwood Close
Hanworth TW13 7DW
Tel: 020 8890 3437
Website: www.geo.tv

**GMTV**
The London Television Centre
Upper Ground
London SE1 9TT
Tel: 020 7827 7009

**gobarkingmad ltd**
22 Soho Square
London W1D 4NS
Tel: 020 7070 7230

**Goldshield Group plc**
NLA Tower
12-16 Addiscombe Rd
Croydon CR0 0XT
Tel: 020 8469 8500

**Golf TV Ltd**
First Floor
1 Kingsgate

Bradford Business Park
Bradford BD1 4SJ
Tel: 01274 765111

## Golf TV Pro-Shop Ltd
1 Kingsgate
Bradford Business Park
Canal Road
Bradford BD1 4SJ
Tel: 01274 765111
Website: www.golftv.tv

## Granada Sky Broadcasting Ltd
Granada Sky Broadcasting Ltd
Franciscan Court
16 Hatfields
London SE1 8DJ
Tel: 020 7578 4040

## Gujarat Television Ltd
Unit 26
Park Royal Metro Centre
Britannia Way
Coronation Rd
London NW10 7PA
Tel: 020 8965 2100

## Gulf DTH Production
4th Floor
UK House
180 Oxford St
London W1D 1NN
Tel: 020 7478 6900
Paramount Comedy Channel

## H.O.T. Home Order Television UK Ltd
c/o De Modo Merchants
Rosemount Avenue
West Byfleet
Surrey KT14 6LJ
Tel: 0049 899250 1808

## Hallmark Entertainment Networks (UK) Ltd
234a Kings Rd
London SW3 5UA
Tel: 0207 368 9100

## HBO Communications Ltd
98 Theobalds Rd
London WC1X 8WB
Tel: 020 7984 5032

## Hi2 Ltd
Interxion Building
11 Hanbury Street
London E1 6QR
Tel: 020 7247 8544
Website: www.hollywoodtv.tv

## Hollywood Classics Movies Limited
91-93 Cleveland St

London W1T 6PL
Tel: 020 7636 7474

## Home Video Channel Ltd
Aquis House
Station Road
Hayes UB3 4DX
Tel: 020 8581 7000
Website: www.theadultchannel.co.uk

## Ice Cube TV Ltd
1 The Courtyard
Swan Centre
Fishers Lane
London W4 1RX
Tel: 0845 666 77778

## Ideal Shopping Direct Plc
Ideal Home House
Newark Rd
Peterborough PE1 5WG
Tel: 08700 777 002

## Indigo Resources Ltd
Maritime House
Basin Road North
Hove
East Sussex BN41 1WR
Tel: 01273 384969

## Indus Television Ltd
8B Newcourt Street
London NW8 7AA
Tel: 020 7722 2922

## Information TV Ltd
1 Stephen Street
London W1T 1AL
Tel: 020 7691 6302
web:www.information.tv

## International ICON Ltd
Suite 1
Lansdowne House
85 Surbiton Rd
London KT1 2JQ
Tel: 020 8549 7709

## International Shopping Network Ltd
1-4 Argyll Street
London W1V 1AD
Tel: 0171 734 7010

## Interwood Marketing Ltd
Anglers Court
33-44 Spittal St
Marlow
Tel: 0208 891 2202

## Iranian Christian Television Channel Ltd
45 Holbein House
Holbein Place
London SW18 8NJ
Tel: 020 7823 5952

## ITV News Channel Ltd
London Television Centre
Upper Ground
London SE1 9LT
Tel: 0207 620 1620

## Japan Satellite TV (Europe) Ltd (JSTV)
65 Clifton Street
London EC2A 4JE
Tel: 020 7426 7330
Website: www.jstv.co.uk

## John Mills Limited
JML House
Regis Rd
London
NW5 3EG
Tel: 020 7691 3800
Website: www.jmldirect.com

## Jones Education Company
Jones Education Company
60 Charlotte Street
London W1P 2AX
Tel: 0171 927 8427
Website: www.knowledgetv.co.uk

## Jones Infomercials
60 Charlotte St
London SW9 7XF
Tel: 0207 732 3521

## Jungle.uk.com Ltd
24 Park Royal Metro Centre
Britannia Way
London NW10 7PA
Tel: 020 8453 1120

## Kanal 5 Limited
Falcon House
115-123 Staines Rd
Hounslow TW3 3LL
Tel: 020 8814 7520

## KCK Communications Ltd
18 Teal Close
London E16 3TP
Tel: 020 7473 1996

## Khalifa Television Ltd
82 Mortimer St
London W1W 7HN
Tel: 020 8838 2959

## Kidz Sport Ltd
Walton End
Walton Lane
Bosham
West Sussex PO18 8QF
Tel: 01243 575557

## Landmark Travel Channel Ltd
66 Newman Street
London W1P 3LA

Tel: 020 7636 5401
Website: www.travelchannel.co.uk

## Landscape Channel Europe Ltd
Crowhurst
East Sussex TN33 9BX
Tel: 01424 830900
Website: www.landscapetv.com

## Life TV Media Ltd
Westbrook House
18/20 Albion Place
Maidstone
Kent ME14 5DZ
Tel: 01622 776776

## Linkchain Ltd
14-17 Wells Mews
London W1P 3FL
Tel: 020 7323 9920

## M Factory
School of Communication Design
and Media
University of Westminster
Watford Road
Harrow HA1 3TP
Tel: 0171 911 5000 ext 4036
Website: www.wmin.ac.uk

## Maidstone Broadcasting
160 Great Portland Street
London W1N 5TB
Tel: 0207 7299 5000
Website: www.challengetv.co.uk

## MAK Entertainment Ltd
3 Devonshire Street
London W1W 5BA
Tel: 020 7436 3707

## Manchester United Television
274 Deansgate
Manchester M3 4SB
Tel: 0161 834 1111
Website: www.manutd.com

## Married Couples
Po Box 4516
London SW9 7XF
Tel: 0207 732 3521

## Master Chemicals (Leeds) Ltd
Ford Street
Stockport
Cheshire SK3 0BT
Tel: 0161 429 8385
Website: www.bosun-products.com

## MBC Ltd
80 Silverthorne Road
London SW8 3XA
Tel: 020 7501 1111
Website: www.mbctvsat.com

## Media News Network Ltd
24 Ullswater Close
Bromley
Kent BR1 4JF
Tel: 020 8464 3383
Website: www.mnn.uk.com
Russian movie channel

## Mediashop Television
19 Norfolk Road
London NW8 6HG
Tel: 0171 722 0242

## Middlesex Broadcasting Corporation Ltd
MPK House
233 Belgrave Gate
Leicester LE1 3HT
Tel: 0116 253 2288

## Mobile Crazy TV
Suite 4
Kings COurt
153 High St
Watford WD17 2ER
Tel: 01923 800544

## Mrs Fran Wildish
The Vision Studios
Eastcott Corner
Bath Road
Swindon SN1 3LS
Tel: 01793 511244
Website: www.visionchannel.co.uk

## MTV Networks Europe
180 Oxford Street
London W1N 0DS
Tel: 020 7284 7777
Website: www.mtv.co.uk

## Music Choice Europe plc
57-61 Clerkenwell Rd
London EC1M 5AR
Tel: 0207 7014 8754

## Musicians Channel
75 High Street
Camberley GU15 3RB
Tel: 01622 691111

## Muslim Television Ahmadiyya
16 Gressenhall Road
London SW18 5QL
Tel: 020 8870 8517 ext 210
Website: www.alislam.org/mta

## MVI Broadcasting Ltd
Westbrook House
Albion Place
Maidstone ME14 5DZ
Tel: 01622 776776

## Mystery Channel Ltd
Templar Lodge

Edinburgh EH31 2AS
Tel: 01620 842275

## MyTravel TV plc
Parkway Two
Parkway Business Centre
300 Princess Rd
Manchester M14 7QU
Tel: 0161 232 5883
Website: www.mytravelgroup.com

## MyTV Ltd
Parkway Two
Parkway Business Centre
300 Princess Rd
Manchester M14 7QU
Tel: 0161 232 5883

## NASN
52 Haymarket
London SW1Y 4RP
Tel: 020 7389 0771

## Nation277
Units 6-7
Princes Court
Wapping Lane
London E1W 2DA
Tel: 020 7942 7942

## NGC International (UK) Ltd
Grant Way
Isleworth
Middlesex TW7 5QD
Tel: 020 7941 5073

## Nickelodeon International
180 Oxford Street
London W1N 0DS
Tel: 020 7478 5255
Website: www.nick.uk.com

## NSAT Ltd
180 Oxford Street
London W1N 0DS
Tel: 020 7478 5255
Website: www.nick.uk.com

## ntl Group Ltd
ntl House
Bartley Wood Business Park
Hook
Hants RG27 9UP
Tel: 01256 752150

## Oakhill Communications Ltd
Isleworth Studios, Studio Parade
484 London Road
Isleworth TW7 4DE
Tel: 0181 568 3511

## On Air Systems
The Media Centre
131-151 Great Titchfield St
London W1W 5BB
Tel: 020 7663 3651

**OneTV Ltd**
Station Cottage
The Street
Nacton
Ipswich IP10 0HR
Tel: 01473 659944

**Original Black Entertainment Ltd**
Bagley Studios
York Way
London N1 0AU
Tel: 0207 837 3744

**ORTV Region**
12 Skylines
Limeharbour
London E14 9TS
Tel: 020 7510 2560

**Outlook Productions Ltd**
Trafalgar House
Grenville Place
London NW7 3SA
Tel: 020 8959 3611

**P-Rock TV Ltd**
1 Bromley Lane
Chislehurst
Kent BR7 6LH
Tel: 020 8961 5456

**Pak Television Ltd**
AMC House
12 Cumberland Ave
Park Royal
London NW10 7QL
Tel: 020 8961 4911

**Pakistani Channel Ltd**
AML House
12 Cumberland Avenue
Park Royal NW10 7QL
Tel: 020 8961 4911

**Paramount UK**
Paramount British Pictures Ltd
180 Oxford Street
London W1D 1DS
Tel: 020 7478 5300

**Phoenix Chinese News and Entertainment Ltd**
7th Floor
The Chiswick Centre
414 Chiswick High Rd
London W4 5TF
Tel: 020 8987 4320

**Playboy TV UK Ltd**
Aquis House
Station Road
Hayes UB3 4DX
Tel: 020 8581 7000
Website: www.playboytv.co.uk

**Portland Enterprises (C.I.) Ltd**
Suite 14
Burlington House
St Saviour"s Rd
St Helier
Jersey JE2 4LA
Tel: 01534 703720

**Portland Television Ltd**
Suite 14
Burlington House
St Saviour"s Rd
St Helier
Jersey JE2 4LA
Tel: 01534 703720

**Power TV Ltd**
43 Parkhead Loan
Edinburgh EH11 4SJ
Tel: 0131 443 4642
Website: www.powertv.co.uk

**Praise Channel Broadcasting Network Ltd**
Po Box 46915
London E9 5DY
Tel: 020 8986 5527

**Professional Development Television Limited**
48 Tredgold Avenue
Bramhope
Leeds LS16 9BU
Tel: 0113 285 7055

**QVC**
Marco Polo House
346 Queenstown Rd
London SW8 4NQ
Tel: 020 7705 5600

**Race Track TV Ltd**
c/o The People's Net Limited
35 Park Town
Oxford 0X2 6SL
Tel:07973 313 833

**Rank Interactive Gaming Ltd**
6 Connaught Place
London W2 2EZ
Tel: 020 7535 8050

**Real Estate TV Ltd**
3rd Floor
1-6 Falconberg Court
London W1D 3AB
Tel: 020 7440 1070
Website: www.realestatetv.tv

**Reality TV Ltd**
Queens Studios
117 - 121 Salusbury Road
London NW6 6RG
Tel: 020 7328 8808

**Regal Shop**
5-7 Carnaby Street
London W1V 1PG
Tel: 0171 434 0567

**Reliant Interactive Media Corp.**
35-37 Fitzroy St
London W1T 6DX

**Revelation YV ( R TV) Ltd**
91-93 Cleveland St
London W1T 6PL
Tel: 020 7636 7474

**RHF Productions Ltd**
Suite 14
Burlington House
St Saviour"s Rd
St Helier
Jersey JE2 4LA
Tel: 01534 703720

**Romantica Ltd**
Queen"s Studios
117-124 Salusbury Rd
London NW6 6RG
Tel: 020 7328 8808

**Roudolf Aghabegian**
119 Gloucester Place
London W14 6JX
Tel: 020 7487 5858

**Russian Movie Channel**
24 Ullswater Close
Bromley
Kent BR1 4JF
Tel: 020 8464 3383
Website: www.mnn.uk.com

**S1 TV Ltd**
St. Martin's House
16 St. Martin's Le Grand
London EC1A 4RN
Tel: 020 7397 8805

**S4C2 Ltd**
50 Lambourne Crescent
Llanishen
Cardiff CF14 5GG
Tel: 029 2074 1440

**Sat-7 Media Services Ltd**
Sat - 7 Media Services Ltd
Box 100
Witney
OX8 7TD

**Satellite Entertainment Ltd**
Solarnet Media
23 Court Bushes Road
Whyteleafe
Surrey CR3 0BJ
Tel: 01883 626304

**Satellite Information Services Ltd**
17 Corsham Street
London N1 6DR
Tel: 020 7253 1232

**Satellite Television Asian Region Ltd**
8th Floor
1 Harbourfront
18 Tak Fung Street
Hungkom
Kowloon
Hong Kong
Tel: 00 852 2621 8515

**Sci-Fi Channel Europe**
5-7 Mandeville Place
London W1M 5LB
Tel: 020 7535 3500
Science fiction, fantasyand horror programming
Website: www.scifi.com

**Setanta Transmissions Scotland Ltd**
52 Haymarket
London
West Drayton SW1Y 4RP
Tel: 020 7930 8926
Website: www.setanta.com

**Shop America (Australasia) Ltd**
1st floor
1 Kingsgate
Bradford Business Park
Canal Road
Bradford BD1 4SJ

**Shop Galore**
146 Chase Side
London N14 5PP
Tel: 020 8886 1539

**Shop on the Box Ltd**
c/o Vector Direct Ltd
St Thomas House
Liston Rd
Marlow
Bucks SL7n 1DP
Tel: 01628 405119

**Shop Smart Television Ltd**
Unit 26 Metro Centre
Park Royal  NW10 7PA
Tel: 020 8453 1202

**Simply Eight Television Ltd**
150 Great Portland St
London W1W 6QD
Tel: 020 7307 6100

**Simply Nine Television Ltd**
150 Great Portland St
London W1W 6QD

Tel: 020 7307 6100

**Simply Shopping Four**
103a Oxford St
London W1D 2HG
Tel: 020 7758 3100

**Simply Television Ltd**
150 Gt Portland St
London W1W 6QD
Tel: 0207 692 1150

**Sirius Retail Television Ltd**
Chalfont Grove
Narcot Lane
Chalfont St Peter
Buckinghamshire SL9 8TW
Tel: 01494 878078

**sit-up Ltd**
4 Warple Way
London W3 0UE
Tel: 020 8600 9700

**Sky Travel Shop**
Grant Way
Isleworth
Middx TW7 5QD
Tel: 020 7705 6704

**Sony Pictures Entertainment Inc**
34 Fouberts Place
London W1B 2BH
Tel: 020 7534 7575

**SPDE Europe Ltd**
Sony Pictures Europe House
25 Golden Square
London W1F 9LU
Tel: 020 7533 1297
Interactive games channel

**STAR Television Entertainment Ltd**
8th Floor
1 Harbourfront
18 Tak Fung Street
Hunghom
Kowloon
Hong Kong
Tel: 00 852 2621 8515

**Stara Vision Limited**
54 Oswald Street
Glasgow G1 4PL
Tel: 0141 248 2495

**Starstream Ltd**
160 Great Portland Street
London W1N 5TB
Tel: 020 7299 5000
Website: www.trouble.co.uk
Programming aimed at teenagers

**Static 2358 Ltd**
Ground Floor

5 Old Street
London EC1V 9HL
Tel: 0207 250 1244

**STEP-UP**
University of Plymouth
Notte Street
Plymouth PL1 2AR
Tel: 01752 233635

**Sun 4 Sale Ltd**
Unit 8
84 Blackfriars Road
London SE1 8HA
Tel: 07770 746410

**Sun TV UK Ltd**
unit 15D
Oakcroft Rd
Chessington KT9 1RH
Tel: 020 8974 2651
Website: www.suntvuk.com

**Sunrise TV Ltd**
Sunrise House
Merrick Rd
Southall
Middx UB2 4AU
Tel: 020 8574 6666
Website: www.sunriseradio.com

**TCC**
160 Great Portland Street
London W1N 5TB
Tel: 0171 299 5000
Website: www.tcc.flextech.co.uk/

**Tel Sell UK Ltd**
Unit 5
The Robert Eliot Centre
1-1A Old Nichol St
London E2 7HR
Tel: 020 7033 0533

**Teleshopping**
4 Warple Way
London W3 0EU
Tel: 020 8600 9700
Website: www.sit-up.tv

**Teletext Holidays TV Ltd**
Building 10
Chiswick Park
566 Chiswick Park Rd
London W4 5TS
Tel: 0870 731 3553

**Teletext Ltd**
Building 10
Chiswick Park
566 Chiswick High Rd
London W4 5TS
Tel: 0870 731 3000

**Television Eighteen Mauritius Ltd**
E-1 Rani Jhansi Road

9th Floor Videocon Towers
New Delhi 100 055
India
Tel: 0091 11 353 1006

## Television In Colour
23 Cinderford Way
Bromley BR1 5PR
Tel: 020 8468 1618

## Thane Direct UK Ltd
52 Amerland Road
London SW18 1PX
Tel: 020 8870 2404

## The Advert Channel Ltd
c/o First Information
494 Midsummer Boulevard
Central Milton Keynes MK9 2EA
Tel: 01908 330747
Website: www.advertchannel.tv

## The Baby Channel Ltd
40 Claremont Road
London N6 5BY
Tel:        0870 787 7351

## The Box
Mappin House
4 Winsley Street
London W1W 8HF
Tel: 020 7436 1515
Website: www.thebox.co.uk

## The Charity Channel Television and Broadcast
3 Goldsmith Drive
Newport Pagnell
Buckinghamshire
MK16 8ED
Tel: 01908 216504

## The Chinese Channel Ltd
Teddington Studios
Broom Road
Teddington
Middlesex TW11 9NT
Tel: 020 8614 8300Website:
www.chinese-channel.co.uk
News, films and general
entertainment

## The Community Channel Ltd
3-7 Euston Centre
Regents Place
London NW1 3TG
Tel: 020 7874 7603

## The Crime Channel Ltd
Media Matrix
Lutidine House
Newark Lane
Ripley
Syrrey GU23 6BS
Tel: 01483 270480

## The Dream Family Network Ltd
Stonehills Shields Rd
Gateshead
Tyne and Wear NE10 0HW
Tel: 0191 495 2244

## The Exercise Channel Ltd
61 Eccleston Square
London SW1V 1PH
Tel: 020 7630 0225

## The Fans Channel plc
Seckloe House
101 North 13th Street
Central Milton Keynes
MK9 3NU
Tel: 020 8977 3252

## The Games Channel Ltd
61 Eccleston Square
London SW1V 1PH
Tel: 020 7630 0225

## The Gospel Channel Ltd
Gospel Channel House
Monkton Park
Chippenham SN15 3XL
Tel: 01249 446210

## The History Channel (UK)
Grant Way
Isleworth
Middlesex TW7 5QD
Tel: 0870 240 3000

## The Interactive Chart Show Channel Ltd
Solarnet Media
23 Bushes Rd
Whyteleafe
Surrey CR3 0BT
Tel: 01833 626304

## The Islam Channel Ltd
14 Bonhill Street
London EC2A 4BX
Website: www.islamchannel.tv

## The Minister for the Cabinet, HM Government
Office of the E-Envoy
Cabinet Office
Stockley House
130 Wilton Rd
London SW1V 1LQ
Tel: 020 7276 3456
Website: www.e-envoy.co.uk
Public information and Services

## The Money Channel PLC
24 Grosvenor Gardens
London SW1W 0TH
Tel: 020 7461 4400

## The Movie Channel 2
4th Floor
UK House
180 Oxford St
London W1D 1NN
Tel: 020 7478 6900
Website: www.showtimearabia.com

## The Pakistani Channel Ltd
65 North Action Road,
London, NW1D 6PS
Tel: 020 8838 6300

## The Parliamentary Channel
160 Great Portland Street
London W1N 5TB
Tel: 0171 299 5000
Website: www.parlchan.co.uk

## The Romance Channel Ltd
15 Shadwell Park Court
Leeds
West Yorkshire LS17 8TS
Tel: 07803 743948
Films and light entertainment with a
romantic theme

## The Voice TV Networks Ltd
Falcon House
115-123 Staines Road
Hounslow TW3 3LL
Tel: 020 8814 7500

## The Walt Disney Company Ltd
Building 12
566 Chiswick High Rd
London W4 5AN
Tel: 020 8222 1000

## The Weather Channel
64 Newman Street
London W1P 3PG
Tel: 0171 665 0600
Website: www.weather.com

## The Wrestling Channel Ltd
Welby House
96 Wilton Road
London SW1V 1DW
Tel: 020 7599 8904
Web: www.thewrestlingchannel.tv

## Thomas Cook TV Ltd
8 Park Place
Lawn Lane
Vauxhall
London SW8 1UD
Tel: 020 7840 7163

## TKTTV Ltd
Riverside Studios
Crisp Road
London W6 9RL
Tel: 020 8237 1075

**Toniq Entertainment Ltd**
64 The Drive
Acton
London W3 6AG
Tel: 07930 954427

**Turner Broadcasting Systems Europe Ltd**
Turner House
16 Great Marlborough St
London W1F 7HS
Tel: 020 7693 0775

**Turner Entertainment Networks International Ltd**
Turner House
16 Gt Marlborough St
London W1F 7HS
Tel: 020 7693 1000

**TV Shop Broadcasting Ltd**
Viasat Broadcast Centre
Horton Road
West Drayton UB7 8JD
Tel: 01895 431747
Website: www.tvshop.com

**TV Travel Shop Ltd**
1 Stephen St
London W1T 7AL
Tel: 020 7691 6132
Website: www.tvtravelshop.com

**TV You! plc**
1st floor
1 Kingsgate
Bradford Business Park
Canal Road
Bradford BD1 4SJ

**TV-Africa Ltd**
27 Old Gloucester Street

**London WC1N 3XX**
Tel: 020 7419 5012
Website: www.tv-africa.co.uk

**TvDanmark 1 Ltd**
Falcon House
115-123 Staines Road
Hounslow TW3 3LL
Tel: 020 8814 7550

**Tventures Ltd**
Studio 54
222 Kensal Rd
London W10 5BN
Tel: 020 7613 8660

**UC Lanka Ltd**
PO Box 5211
Milton Keynes MK5 6JZ
Tel: 01908 340139
Website: www.uclanka.com

**UK Channel Management Ltd**
160 Great Portland Street
London W1W 5QA
Tel: 020 7299 5000

**UK Gold Holdings Ltd**
160 Great Portland Street
London W1N 5TB
Tel: 020 7299 5000
Website: www.ukgold.co.uk

**UK Living Ltd**
160 Great Portland Street
London W1W 5QA
Tel: 020 7299 5000

**UK Network Sales Ltd**
211 Picadilly
London W1N 9LP
Tel: 020 7917 2731

**UKTV**
4th Floor
160 Great Portland Street
London W1N 5TB
Tel: 020 7299 5000

**UKTV New Ventures Ltd**
Unit 1
Genesis Business Park
Albert Drive
Woking
Surrey GU21 5RW
Tel: 01483 750900

**United Christian Broadcasters Ltd**
Hanchurch Christian Centre
Hanchurch
Stoke on Trent ST4 8RY
Tel: 01782 642000

**Upfront Broadcasting Ltd**
53 Davies St
Mayfair
London W1K 5JH
Tel: 020 8671 0660

**Urbanchillers Films Ltd**
9-10 Charlotte Mews
London W1T 4EF
Tel: 020 7636 2502

**V iasat Broadcastig Ltd**
Horton Rd
West Drayton UB7 8JD
Tel: 01895 433433
Website: www.viasat.co.uk

**Vectone Entertainment Holding Ltd**
58 Marsh Wall
London E14 9TP
Tel: 020 7170 0400
Website: www.vectone.com

**Vector Direct Ltd**
c/o Moorcrofts Corporate Law
Mere House
Mere Park
Dedmere Rd
Marlow
Bucks SL7 1PB
Tel: 01628 405119

**VH1**
Hawley Crescent
London NW1 8T
Tel: 020 7284 7491

**Viasat Broadcasting UK Ltd**
Viasat Broadcast Centre
Horton Road
West Drayton
Middlesex UB7 8JD
Tel: 01895 433327

**Video Interactive Television**
18 Soho Square
London W1D 3QL
Tel: 020 7025 8088

**Video Interactive Television Plc**
Studio 4
3 Lever Street
London EC1V 3QU
Tel: 020 7253 2459

**Vis iTV Ltd**
Seabraces
Perth Rd
Dundee DD1 4LN
Tel: 01382 341083

**Vis Television Media International Ltd**
405 Bondway Commercial Centre
71 Bondway
London SW18 1SQ

**Visit London Ltd**
6th Floor
2 More London Riverside
London SE1 2RR
Tel: 020 7932 2000
Website: www.visitlondon.com

**Weather Channel Europe**
64 Newman Street
London W1P 3PG
Tel: 0171 665 0600

**Westinghouse Electric Ltd**
25 James Street
London W1M 6AA
Tel: 020 7486 7000

**World Channel Ltd**
Springfield Road
Hayes UB4 0LE
Tel: 020 8573 4000

**World Health Network**
Portland House
Aldermaston Park
Aldermaston
Reading RG7 4HP

**Zone Broadcasting (EMC) Ltd**
Queens Studios
117-121 Salusbury Road
Vinters Park
Maidstone NW6 6RG
Tel: 0207 7328 8808

**Zone Broadcasting (Maximum Reality) Ltd**
Queens Studios
117-121 Salusbury Rd
London NW6 6RG
Tel: 020 7328 8808
Website: www.zonevision.co.uk

**Zone Broadcasting Showtime (Turkey) Ltd**
117-121 Salusbury Road
London NW6 6RG

**Zone Licensing Ltd**
Queens Studios
117-121 Salusbury Road
London NW6 6RG
Tel: 020 7328 8808
Website: www.zonevision.co.uk

# Channels

## Al Qula
38 Devonshire Place
London W16 6JT
Tel: 020 7935 7566
Fax: 020 7224 0964
Ownership: Entertainment Distribution Company Ltd
Programming: Movies

## Artsworld
Artsworld Channels Ltd
80 Silverthorne Road
London SW8 3XA
Tel 020 7819 1160
Fax 020 7819 1161
email: tv@artsworld.com
Website: www.artsworld.com
Ownership: BSkyB, Caledonia Investments, Guardian Media Group 20%, and private investors 60%, British Sky Broadcasting 20% (option)
Service start: 2 Dec 2000
Satellite: Astra 2 North
Programming: arts [premium]

## Asianet
PO Box 38
Greenford
Middlesex UB6 7SB
Tel: 020 8566 9000
Fax: 020 8810 5555
Website: www.asianet-tv.com
Cable only from videotape
Programming: movies and entertainment in Hindi, Punjabi and other languages

## BBC Four
BBC Television Centre
London W12 7RJ
Tel: 020 8743 8000
email: info@bbc.co.uk
Website: www.bbc.co.uk/bbcfour
Service start:2 Mar 2002
Satellite: Astra 2 South
Programming: arts

## BBC Three
BBC Television Centre
Londond W12 7RJ
Tel: 020 8743 8000
email: info@bbc.co.uk
Website: www.bbc.co.uk/bbcthree
Service start: 9 Feb 2003
Programming: general entertainment

## B4U
19 Heather Park Drive,
Wembley
HA0 1SS
Tel: 020 8795 7171
Fax: 020 8795 7181
email:b4utv@b4unetwork.comtv.com
Website: www.b4utv.com
Ownership: Bollywood Eros Network
Service start: 26 Aug 1999
Programming: mainstream Hindi feature films [subscription]

## Boomerang
Turner House
16 Great Marlborough St
London W1F 7HS
Tel: 020 7693 1000
Fax: 020 7693 1001
Website: www.cartoonnetwork.co.uk
Ownership: Turner Broadcasting
Service start: 27 May 2000
Programming: classic cartoons

## Bollywood Films
Suite 14
Burlington House
St Saviour's Rd
St Helier
Jersey JE2 4LA
Tel: 01534 703720
Fax: 01534 703760
Ownership: RHF Productions Ltd

## Bravo
160 Great Portland Street
London W1W 5QA
Tel: 020 7299 5000
Fax: 020 7299 6000
email: enquiries@bravo.co.uk
Website: www.bravo.co.uk
Ownership: Flextech Television
Service start: Sept 1985
Satellite: Astra 1C (PAL/Videocrypt)2A
Programming: old movies and television programmes general entertainment aimed at men

## Cartoon Network
Turner House
16 Great Marlborough St
London W1V 1AFF 7HS
Tel: 020 7693 1000
Fax: 020 7693 1001
email: toon.pressoffice@turner.com
Website: www.cartoon-network.co.uk
Ownership: Turner Broadcasting Systems (TBS) Inc, an AOL Time Warner Company
Service start: 17 Sept 1993
Satellite: Astra 1C, Astra 1F (PAL/clear)2A, 2B
Programming: children's animation
Also digital

## Cinenova
1 Stephen Street
London W1T 1AL
Tel: 020 7691 6960
Fax: 020 7691 5130
Ownership: Europe Movieco
Partners
Programming: Dutch movie channel

## Classic Performance
New Pathe House
57 Jamestown Road
London NW1 7XX
Tel: 020 7424 3688
Fax: 020 7424 3689
Website: www.performancetv.co.uk
Ownership: Arts & Entertainment
Ltd
Programming: arts and culture

## Classics TV
91-93 Cleveland Street
London W1T 6PL
Tel: 020 7636 7474
Fax: 020 7636 7040
Ownership: On-Air Systems Ltd
Programming: movies and general
entertainment

## The Disney Channel UK
3 Queen Caroline St
Hammersmith
London W6 9
Tel: 020 8222 1000
Fax: 020 8222 27951144
Website: www.disneychannel.co.uk
Ownership: Walt Disney Company
Ltd
Satellite: Astra 1B
(PAL/Videocrypt)2D
Programming: family entertainment
and films children's (supplied as
bonus with Sky Premier and
Moviemax)[premium]

## The European Film Channel
100 New Bridge Street
London EC4V 6JA
Tel: 020 7919 1000
Fax: 020 7919 1999
Ownership: CNI UK Ltd

## Extreme Motion/Urbanchillers.com
29 Conway Street
London W1T 6BW
Tel: 020 7387 8822
Fax: 020 7387 8822
Programming: horror movies
Extreme Sports Channel

## FilmFour
124 Horseferry Road
London SW1P 2TX
Tel: 020 7396 4444

Fax: 020 7306 8366
email:
generalfilmenquiries@filmfour.com
Website: www.filmfour.com
Ownership: Channel Four Television
4 Ventures Ltd
Programming: feature and short films
[premium][premium]
Digital

## FilmFour Weekly
see above
Programming: extreme and
challenging movies [premium]

## FilmFour World
see above
Programming: foreign movies
[premium]

## Front Row
Front Row Television
64 Newman Street
London W1P 3PG
Tel: 020 7551 5956
Ownership: NTL, Telewest
Programming: films [pay-per-view]
movies [pay-per-view]

## The Hallmark Channel Entertainment Network
3-5 Bateman Street
London W1V 5TT
Tel: 020 7368 91007439 0633
Fax: 020 7368 91017439 0644
Website:
www.hallmarkchannelint.com.uk
Service start: 1 Nov 2001
Satellite: Astra 2D
Programming: drama

## The History Channel
6 Centaurs Business Park
Grant Way,
Isleworth
Middlesex TW7 5QD
Tell: 020 7705 3000
Fax: 020 7705 3030
email:
feedback@thehistorychannel.co.uk
Website:www.thehistorychannel.
co.uk
Ownership: BSkyB 50%, Arts
&Entertainment Television Networks
50%, British Sky Broadcasting 50%
Service start: 1 Nov 1995
Satellite: Astra 1B (PAL/Videocrypt)
Programming: historical and
biographical documentaries
Also digital

## The Horror Channel
50 Riverside
South Church
Bishop Auckland

County Durham DL14 6XT
Tel: 01388 601361
Programming: films and light
entertainment with horror focus

## Hollywood Classics Movies Ltd
91-93 Cleveland Street
London W1T 6PL
Tel: 020 7636 7474
Fax: 020 7636 7040
Programming: movies and
documentaries

## ITV Select
346 Queenstown Road
London SW8 4NE
Tel: 020 7819 8000
Fax: 020 819 8100
Website: www.itv-digital.co.uk
Programming: entertainment,
movies, sport

## ITV12
200 Gray's Inn Road
London WC1X 8HF
Tel: 020 7843 8000
Fax: 020 7843 8443
email: dutyoffice@itv.co.uk
Website: www.itv.co.uk
Ownership: ITV companies
Satellite: Astra 2D
Digital; also on analogue cable

## Living
160 Great Portland St
London  W1N 5TB
Tel: 020 7299 5000
Fax: 020 7299 6000
Website: www.livingtv.co.uk
Ownership: Flextech
Service start: Sept 1993
Satellite: Astra 1C
(PAL/Videocrypt)2A
Programming: daytime lifestyle,
evening general entertainment,
particularly aimed at women

## Maximum Animatrix
Queen's Studios
117-121 Salisbury Road
London NW6 6RG
Tel: 020 7328 8808
Fax: 020 7328 8858
Ownership: Zone Licensing Ltd
Website: www.zonevision.com
Programming: Animation (some
erotic)

## Nickelodeon
15-18 Rathbone Place
London W1P 1DF
Tel: 0171 462 10000800 801 801/020
7462 1000
Fax: 0171 462 10300800 802 802/020

7462 1030
Website: www.nicktv.co.uk
Ownership: British Sky
Broadcasting 50% , MTV
NetworksViacom 50%, British Sky
Broadcasting 50%
Service start: 1 Sept 93
Satellite: Astra 1C
(PAL/Videocrypt)2B
Programming: children's

## Primemax
33 New Cavendish Street
London W1G 9TS
Tel: 0207224 5504
Fax: 020 7224 5506
Ownership: Eclipse Sat Ltd
Programming: Films

## Red Hot Films
Suite 14
Burlington House
St Saviour's Road
St Helier
Jersey JE2 4LA
Tel: 01534 703 720
Fax: 01534 703 760
Website: www.redhottv.co.uk
Ownership: RHF Productions Ltd
Programming: adult entertainment

## The Romance Channel
15 Shadwell Park Court
Leeds
West Yorkshire LS17 8TS
Tel: 07803 743948
Programming: films and
entertainment

## Russian Channel
24 Ullswater Close
Bromley
Kent BR1 4JF
Tel: 020 8464 3383
Fax: 020 8464 3381
www.mnn.uk.com
Ownership: Media News Network
Ltd
Programming: Russian movie
channel

## Sci-Fi Channel Europe
5-7 Mandeville Place
London W1M 5LB
Tel: 020 7535 3500
Fax: 020 7535 3585
Website: www.scifi.com
Ownership: Sci-Fi Channel Europe
Service start: 1 Nov 1995
Satellites: Astra 1B, Hot Bird 1
(PAL/encrypted)2A
Programming: science fiction, fantasy,
horror programming

## Showtime (The Movie Channel)
Gulf DTH Productions
117-121 Salusbury Road
London NW6 6RG
Tel: 020 7328 8808
Fax: 020 7328 8858
Programming: feature films

## Sinematurk
33 New Cavendish Street
London W1G 9TS
Tel: 020 7224 5504
Fax: 020 7224 5506
Ownership: Eclipse Sat Ltd
Programming: Turkish cinema

## Sky Box Office
6 Centaurs Business Park
Grant Way
Syon Lane
Isleworth
Middlesex TW7 5QD
Tel: 0870 240 3000020 7705 3000
Fax: 020 7705 3030
email: feedback@sky.co.uk
Website: www.sky.co.uk
Ownership: British Sky
Broadcasting
Service start: 1 Dec 97
Satellite: Eurobird, Astra 2A, 2B,
2D1E (PAL/Videocrypt)
Programming: movies, concerts,
events (pay-per-view)
Also digital

## Sky Movies Cinema
see aboveOwnership: British Sky
Broadcasting
Service start: Oct 92
Satellite: Astra 1C
(PAL/Videocrypt)2B
Programming: movies ([premium])

## Sky Movies Max
Ownership: British Sky Broadcasting
see above
Service start: Feb 1989
Satellite: Astra 12A, 2B
(PAL/Videocrypt)
Programming: movies ([premium])
Also digital

## Sky Movies Premier
see above
website: www1.sky.com/movies/premier
Satellite: Astra 2A, 2B
Programming: movies [premium]

## Sky Premier
Ownership: British Sky Broadcasting
Service start: Apr 91
Satellite: Astra 1B (PAL/Videocrypt)
Programming: movies (premium)
Also digital

## The Studio Channel
5-7 Mandeville StreetPlace
London W1U 3ARM 5JB
Tel: 020 7535 3300
Fax: 020 7535 3585
Website: www.thestudio.com
Ownership: Universal
Service start: Feb 2001
Programming: Classic Hollywood
films

## TCM (Turner Classic Movies)
Turner House
16 Great Marlborough Street
London W1F 7HS
Tel: 020 7693 1000
Fax: 020 7693 1001
email: tcmeurope@turner.com
Website: www.tcmonline.co.uk
Ownership: Turner Broadcasting
Service start: Sept 93
Satellite: Astra 1C, Astra 1F
(PAL/clear)
Programming: movies

## Urbanchillers.tv
9-10 Charlotte Mews
London W1T 4EF
Tel: 020 7636 2502
Fax: 020 7323 3307
email: studio@urbanchillers.com
Programming: horror

## Video On Demand
Harefield Place
The Drive
Middlesex UB10 8AQ
Tel: 01895 866248
Fax: 01895 866345
Ownership: Blockbuster
Entertainment Ltd
Programming: feature films

## Wizja Le Cinema
Queen's Studios
117-121 Salusbury Road
Vinters Park
Maidstone NW6 6RG
Tel: 020 7328 8808
Ownership: Zone Broadcasting
(ECM)
Programming:
Polish/Hungarian/Romanian cinema

# DIGITAL TELEVISION

## BBC Digital Services
TV Centre
Wood Lane
London W12 7RJ
Tel: 020 8743 800008700 100 123
website: www.bbc..co.uk/digital
All the BBC's digital services are
funded by the licence fee and are
therefore non-subscription

## Freeview
2nd Floor
85 Tottenham Court Road
London W1T 4DU
Tel: 08708 80 99 80
Website: www.freeview.co.uk
Freeview is marketed by DTV
Services Ltd which is a company run
by its three shareholders the BBC,
Crown Castle International and
BSkyB. DTV Services Ltd has been
established to promote Freeview by
utilising the complementary skills
and expertise of the BBC, Crown
Castle International and BSkyB
respectively. Responsibility for the
programmes shown on Freeview
however remains with the channels
providing those programmes.
**Crown Castle International**
Website: www.crowncastle.com
Crown Castle International is the
world's leading independent owner
and operator of shared wireless
communications and broadcast
infrastructure. Crown Castle
engineers, deploys, owns and operates
technologically advanced shared
wireless infrastructure, including
extensive networks of towers and
rooftops as well as analog and Digital
Radio and television broadcast
transmission systems.

## Sky Digital
6 Centaurs Business Park
Grant Way
Syon Lane
Isleworth
Middlesex TW7 5QD
Tel: 0870 240 3000
Fax: 020 7705 30300870 240 3060
email: skydigital@sky.com
Website: www.skydigital.com.uk

The cultural industries attract a large number of people every year seeking fame and fortune in this glamorous sector. Most of the websites, however, emphasise hard work, long hours, commitment, learning on the job, flexibility and especially adaptability. A love of film goes without saying. Notably, they also remind new entrants that determination should be balanced against good social skills and team working ability. This section aims to guide the reader to the main training organisations, some useful websites and some suggestions for useful books to consult. Compiled by Sean Delaney

There is good news and there is bad news. The good news is that there are probably more job opportunities and training courses than ever before. The production sector in the UK has been remarkably buoyant and has expanded significantly over the last few years creating more jobs. Most of the training organisations have created some excellent websites offering a wide range of information and advice with annotated links to other relevant websites. Informal soundings also suggest that there are plenty of openings for runners, which is the traditional foot in the door to the industry. In spite of what the industry says and does about itself, the sector will always attract the naïve and ill prepared. Sadly, this will always be to the advantage of those who have researched beyond an internet terminal.

The downside is that in spite of more opportunities, competition is as fierce as ever and it is still a very difficult sector in which to pursue (or subsidise!) a career. Skills shortages do not seem to be in 'creative' areas i.e. acting, writing, directing (where there has always been a healthy surplus) but on the technical side, although this may present some unforeseen opportunities for some people. Some fear a 'something-for-nothing' culture has evolved where some companies 'exploit' a steady stream of unpaid volunteers looking for work experience.

The Skillset Census Report 2003 did not paint a rosy picture of the industry in terms of diversity either. BFI tracking studies in the 1990s re-discovered - what was already widely known - that (close) personal contacts are vital in getting jobs in the sector. However, these barriers are being recognized and Skillset and the UK Film Council have pledged to invest £50 million over the coming years to improve and expand access and training. Knowing the right people is a fact of life of the business but the better training courses do attempt to address this.

# Two Important Websites

The two sites listed below are vital in finding out about and pursuing a career in the film (and television & media) industries. (Text in inverted commas is taken directly from official literature or websites).

## Skillset
**Prospect House**
**80-110 New Oxford Street**
**London WC1A 1HB**
Tel: 020 7520 5757
email: info@skillset.org
Website: www.skillset.org

'Skillset is the Sector Skills Council for the audiovisual industries'. Via the website and its offices in the nations & regions, Skillset is probably the first port of call for anybody interested in careers and training information in the UK.

It conducts research into skills gaps in the sector and aims to plug them with appropriate training. As well as feature films, training covers animation, commercials, corporate, facilities and post-production as well as TV, radio and interactive media.

Skillset set the standards for these courses and also provide online handy job profiles for those roles that you were too shy to ask about.

The Skillset Film Skills Fund is there to support training (and funding) for a wide range of people such as new entrants, established freelancers and even for companies with training needs. Information throughout the website is clearly linked and logically placed. There is the Skillset/BFI training courses database with over 4000 courses. There are also calendars of events and seminars from important conferences to local careers/training days.

## skillsformedia
Tel: 08080 300 900
Tel: 0808 100 8094 (Scotland)
www.skillsformedia.com

Supported by Skillset and BECTU, skillsformedia is a dedicated careers service for the film, television and media industries. There are helplines, email services and one-to-one sessions by appointment for careers advice.

The website provides a wealth of information and advice, some of which may come as a shock to creatives with poor social skills used to short working weeks. There are sections on job prospects, training, CV advice and the all-important area of funding. The Jobs section provides job factsheets and notes the areas of skills shortages. The Runners World and Case Studies sections are especially useful as they focus on how to get a foot in the door and stay there and even forge a career. The Links section is also wide ranging covering relevant organisations/sites that list jobs, funding, training or other useful information.

# Other Useful Organisations & Websites

Many national and local organisations lie beyond the scope of this chapter. It should be noted that there are a number of non-profit making and charitable organisations that exist to provide training and new opportunities at a local level. Details of these are often more likely to be found in local reference libraries. Your local government website should not be discounted as many borough councils have modest training and funding schemes and/or general information for local filmmakers. The BBC (www.bbc.co.uk/jobs/index/tips) and Channel 4 (www.channel4.com) websites are also recommended for their wide-ranging advice, information and links.

## BECTU

**BECTU Head Office**
**373-377 Clapham Road**
**London SW9 9BT**
Tel: 020 7346 0900
Fax: 020 7346 0901
email: info@bectu.org.uk
Website: www.bectu.org.uk
BECTU is the trade union for the sector. It also has a number of regional offices. Its resources pages contain useful careers advice, web links and a script registration service for members. In late 2003, BECTU organised the Move On Up event to raise issues of diversity in the cultural industries

## British Film Institute

www.bfi.org.uk
The bfi website offers a range of resources for keeping up to date with issues and themes in film. Its own services and collections, such as the *bfi* National Library, contain a wide range of materials on the UK film industry. The two sections below should also be of great use.

**BFI / Skillset Media Courses & Multimedia Courses Directory**
www.bfi.org.uk/education/courses/mediacourses/
Co-published with Skillset, and updated by the *bfi*, this database lists over 4500 courses. You can search by subject, institution or town.

**BFI Film Links Gateway**
www.bfi.org.uk/gateway
This section contains over 600 annotated links to the best websites for film and includes websites that contain jobs, training and contact information. (Enter 'job', 'career', 'training', 'contact' etc in the search field to get relevant websites).

## Film London

**20 Euston Centre**
**Regent's Place**
**London NW1 3JH**
Tel. 020 7387 8787
Fax. 020 7387 8788
email: info@filmlondon.org.uk
Website: www.filmlondon.org.uk
Opening hours: Mon-Fri: 9am to 6pm
'Film London is the strategic agency for film and media' in London. Film London has yet to announce its training initiatives so readers should look out for this in the near future. However, it has already supported the work of training providers (especially for access for new entrants from diverse backgrounds) such as: Four Corners, North Kensington Video & Drama Project (NKVDP), Connections Communications Centre (CCC Media). Film London is a partner of Working Broadband, which is aimed at black and minority ethnic people working in the cultural industries.

The FAQ's section has a good section on funding sources and runs a free to join crew database for freelancers. NB The Film London office holds subscribes to listings and journals that contains job opportunities.

## Focal

www.focal.ch/defaulte.htp
This website offers students the most up to date range of film courses available internationally. Potentially useful as the older hard copy sources seemed to have dried up.

## Ideas factory

Website: www.ideasfactory.com
email: editor@ideasfactory.com

Supported by Channel 4 and IEE, the Ideas Factory was created to help young people make the first steps in a media career. The site offers advice on careers guidance and a registration service with Worthing, a company that specialises in online recruitment. The links section looks especially useful.

## UK Film Council

**10 Little Portland Street**
**London W1W 7JG**
Tel: 020 7861 7861
Fax: 020 7861 7862
email: info@ukfilmcouncil.org.uk
Website: www.ukfilmcouncil.org.uk

The UK Film Council is the 'strategic agency for film in the UK'. As the major funding body for film in the UK, the UK Film Council offers a variety of funding for features, script development, training, completing projects, short films and the new First Light scheme, which is aimed at the 'next generation of filmmakers'.

There are also many UKFC reports, statistics and edicts available to download from its much improved website to add depth and background to applications.

# Training Organisations & Providers

Below is a listing of the bodies responsible for funding and training in the regions. Some notable training providers have also been included, which is not meant to endorse them and dismiss others. Most local providers should be listed on the BFI/Skillset Courses Directory or linked to the relevant regional body.

## ARTTS Skillcentre
**Highfield Grange**
**Bubwith**
**North Yorkshire  YO8 6DP**
Tel:  01757 288088
Fax: 01757 288253
email:  admin@artts.co.uk
Website: www.artts.co.uk
The Advanced Residential Theatre and Television Skillcentre offers one-year intensive practical diploma courses in directing, acting and production for film, television, theatre and radio. Students have constant access to the facilities and equipment.

## CYFLE
**Cyfle House**
**Gronant**
**Penrallt Isaf**
**Caernarfon**
**Gwynedd LL55 1NS**
Tel:  01286 671000
Fax: 01286 678831
email: cyfle@cyfle.co.uk
Website: www.cylfe.co.uk
Also:
**Crichton House**
**11-12 Mount Stuart Square**
**Cardiff  CF10 6EE**
Tel:  029 2046 5533
Fax: 029 2046 3344
Cyfle is the national training provider for film, television and interactive media in Wales. It has been meeting industry's training needs in Wales for 15 years. (Cyfle = Opportunity).

## FT2 - Film and Television Freelance Training
**4th Floor**
**Warwick House**
**9 Warwick Street**
**London W1B 5LY**
Tel: 020 7734 5141
Fax 020 7287 9899
email: ft2@ft2.org.uk
Website: www.ft2.org.uk

FT2 is the leading national provider of training for young people seeking to establish a freelance career in the UK film and television industry. The training programmes include a New Entrant Technical Training Programme, Setcrafts Apprenticeships and Independent Companies Researcher Training. Established in 1985, FT2 is a non-profit making company funded by Skillset and Channel 4, and has taken a lead in improving diversity in the sector.

## Global Film School
www.globalfilmschool.com
info@globalfilmschool.com
GFS is an online university that hopes to bring about the 'democratization of film education' through e-learning, seminars and events and are 'targeted at college level students'.

## Intermedia Film and Video (Nottingham)
**19 Heathcote Street**
**Nottingham. NG1 3AF**
Tel:  0115 955 6909
Fax: 0115 955 9956
email. info@intermedianotts.co.uk
Website: www.intermedianotts.co.uk
Intermedia is the leading Media Development Agency for the East Midlands with responsibility to provide services to all levels of the film, TV and new media sector in the region. This could be somebody just starting out on a production career or an established professional or company seeking development support. As well as production workshops and seminars, there are short courses covering digital camera work and desktop non-linear editing training.

## Lighthouse
**9-12 Middle Street**
**Brighton, East Sussex, BN1 1AL.**
Tel:  01273 384222
Fax: 01273 384233
email: info@lighthouse.org.uk
Website: www.lighthouse.org.uk
Lighthouse offers a wide range of courses, programmes, professional development, masterclasses, outreach projects and networking events. The Film Department focus upon developing writers, directors and producers at various stages in their careers.

## Media Training North West
**Room G082**

BBC
**Oxford Road**
**Manchester M60 1SJ**
Tel: 0161 244 4637
Fax: 0161 244 4198
email: info@mtnw.co.uk
or admin@mtnw.co.uk
Website: www.mtnw.co.uk
Regional training body for the North West. Their New Entrant schemes are to be announced in the near future. Training and development for freelancers is also available, supported with personal funding. A unique training scheme, the Game Plan, is also offered to people looking to develop their skills for a career in the digital/videogames sector.

## National Film and Television School
**NFTS Short Course Unit**
**Beaconsfield Studios**
**Station Road**
**Beaconsfield Bucks HP9 1LG**
Tel: 01494 677903
Fax: 01494 678708
email: info@nfts-scu.org.uk
Website: www.nftsfilm-tv.ac.uk/scusite/scuindex.html
NFTS has been a leading international centre for professional training for many years.
Aimed at industry professionals, wide ranges of practical hands-on short courses are offered for production, camera and lighting, sound and editing, writing and directing, art and design.

## New Producers Alliance
**9 Bourlet Close**
**London W1W 7BP**
Tel: 020 7580 2480
Fax: 020 7580 2484
email: queries@npa.org.uk
Website: www.npa.org.uk
The NPA is the UK's national membership and training organisation for independent new producers and filmmakers. Training is often free or at a nominal cost. It offers specialised training programmes and events for producers at basic/entrance and advanced levels. Its Nine Point programme begins in September and covers the industry, career development, pitching, law, finance, contracts, deals & post-production. The NPA organises internships and is usually looking for volunteers to help out. The NPA also produce a directory of members for contacts.

## Northern Film & Media

Central Square
Forth Street
Newcastle upon Tyne NE1 3PJ
Tel: 0191 269 9200
Fax: 0191 269 9213
email: annie@northernmedia.org
Website: www.northernmedia.org
(Annie Wood – Training and
Industry Development Director)
Northern Film & Media is the screen
agency for the North-East of
England. It offers training, career
development placements, graduate
retention placements, mentoring and
funding. It also offers a script
reading service, Go Back as well as
face-to-face practical careers advice
by appointment.

## Northern Ireland Film and Television Commission

Alfred House
21 Alfred Street
Belfast BT2 8ED
Tel: 028 9023 2444
Fax: 028 9023 9918
email: info@niftc.co.uk
Website: www.niftc.co.uk
The NIFTC supports a series of
training workshops throughout the
year for new entrants and established
industry professionals. Topics covered
include: pitching, Lottery funding and
application process, film financing,
basic skills for TV researchers,
budgeting and scheduling, managing
creative ideas, company start up, legal
and copyright for film.

## PACT

45 Mortimer Street
London W1W 8HJ
Tel: 020 7331 6000
Fax: 020 7331 6700
email: enquiries@pact.co.uk
Website: www.pact.co.uk
Also:

## Pact in Scotland

249 West George Street
Glasgow G2 4QE
Tel: 0141 222 4880
Fax: 0141 222 4881
'PACT is the UK trade association
that represents and promotes the
commercial interests of independent
feature film, television, animation
and interactive media companies'.
Although its website is aimed at
members already established in the
sector, the website does contain
training opportunities and a useful
FAQ's section, plus other useful

listings. PACT produce a detailed
directory of its members contact
details and productions.

## Panico London Ltd

PO Box 496
London WC1A 2WZ
Tel: 020 7485 3533
email: panico@panicofilms.com
Website: www.panicofilms.com
Panico offers a foundation course for
commercial, corporate and feature
filmmaking. The emphasis is on the
necessary and the practical, as
opposed to the 'media studies' courses.
To support this, professional contacts
are actively developed throughout:
"film work is never advertised – jobs
are filled by word of mouth". A
recruitment service through Club
Panico is also available to members.
Famous patrons include Terry Gilliam,
Terry Jones and Ben Kingsley.

## Scottish Screen

Second Floor
249 West George Street
Glasgow G2 4QE
Tel: 0141 302 1700
Fax: 0141 302 1778
email: info@scottishscreen.com
Website: www.scottishscreen.com
'Scottish Screen develops, encourages
and promotes every aspect of film,
television and new media in
Scotland'. It offers programmes such
as new entrants training, producer
development, Skills for Screen and
the Writers Factory schemes. Short
courses include: production finance,
generating creative ideas,
independent film distribution, script
development, DV camerawork and
directing, working with actors, and
script reading. It also has a First
Writes schemes aimed at younger
writers. The site has a media courses
database for Scotland.

## Screen East

1st Floor 2
Millennium Plain,
Norwich NR2 1TF
Tel: 01603 776920
Fax: 01603 767191
email: info@screeneast.co.uk
Website: www.screeneast.co.uk
Screen East is the Regional Screen
Agency for the East of England.
It is responsible for identifying
training needs and provide accredited
training courses for companies and
professionals working in the region.
(N.B. Website being redeveloped at
time of compilation).

## Screen Yorkshire

Studio 22
46 The Calls
Leeds LS2 7EY
Tel: 0113 294 4410
Fax: 0113 294 4989
email: info@screenyorkshire.co.uk
Website: www.screenyorkshire.co.uk
(Formerly Yorkshire Media Training
Consortium)
Screen Yorkshire's training
department offers training to
freelancers, new entrants and a fast
track scheme with 10-week
placements for talented people in the
region. Screen Yorkshire works with
other organisations (PACT, NFTS) to
provide training/seminars in areas
such as: generating ideas, preparing
proposals, production finance, risk
assessment, independent distribution,
DV/corporate/documentary
filmmaking and editing.

## South West Screen

St Bartholomews Court
Lewins Mead
Bristol BS1 5BT
Tel: 0117 952 9977
Fax: 0117 952 9988
email: info@swscreen.co.uk
Website: www.swscreen.co.uk
South West Screen is the film,
television and digital media agency
for the South West of England is
funded by UKFC and the SW
Regional development Agency. Its
range of courses and training include
schemes to support scriptwriters,
traineeships and research projects.
The site has useful links to regional
and national bodies.

# How to contact companies and organisations

Jobs requiring minimal experience are rarely advertised because of the cost. Therefore, the old fashioned approach of sending a CV to production companies or recruitment agencies is not without merit (see below). It is worth noting that many websites remind enquirers about relevance and length of their applications.

Getting hold of a full range of company addresses is not easy to obtain on the web. The information is far too valuable. (Try the BFI Film Links Gateway for links to the little there is). There is a well-trodden path to the hard copy directories with fat company sections. Unfortunately these are not cheap but most good reference libraries should have at least one recent edition of either the big three of the Knowledge, Kemps Production Services Handbook and Kays Production Manual, or perhaps the Production Guide. (Consult the Libraries chapter in the BFI Handbook or via: www.bfi.org.uk/facts).

The PACT Directory of UK Independent Producers is also expensive (£50+ for non-members) but many jobseekers seek out this volume as it contains detailed listings of company personnel, recent and upcoming productions with handy indexes of the types of films and programmes they make, enabling applicants to hone their CV and then forward it to relevant companies. The annotated listing of production companies in the BFI Handbook should not be overlooked either.

## Jobs sources

Although there has been a proliferation of jobs and recruitment websites, many jobs are still advertised the old fashioned way in hard copy. (Most of the sites above link to these sites, especially skillsformedia.com). There is also a range of regular commercial listings of jobs for the sector that are very expensive. These are available

(comprehensively) in the *bfi* National Library, and to some extent in the Film London office. Some organisations outside London too may offer them too. Ask nicely.

# Newspapers

Advertising space in newspapers and trade journals is expensive and therefore most jobs are likely to be for senior positions or require some proven experience and ability. However, they are always worth browsing for the exceptions. Scanning the 'Creative, Media and Sales' jobs section of the Guardian (Mondays and Saturdays) is a long observed ritual. Both trade journals Screen International (Thursday) and Broadcast (Friday) have jobs sections but may tend to be even more specialised. The BBC website also suggests scanning the Daily Telegraph (Thursday) and even the Sunday Times.

# Subscription Listings

These are a tried and trusted way of seeing what is coming up. PCR and Filmlog are well known and list upcoming job availabilities. These are the listings that might offer the openings and experience that helps to get that foot in the door. The latter two are detailed calendars of upcoming productions, which may be looking for cast and crew.

## PCR (Production and Casting Report)
**PO Box 100**
**Broadstairs**
**Kent CT10 1UJ**
Tel: 01843 860885
Web: www.pcrnewsletter.com
Part of the weekly ritual for jobseeking actors is to consult PCR every Monday. It lists upcoming film, television and theatre productions from big role in major features to low budget walk-on's. Its back page lists casting directors for film and TV. Users may need to use complementary Who's Where directory available from PCR.

## Filmlog
From PCR (as above)
Brief monthly listing of films in production and pre-production listed as seeking cast and crew. Needs to be

used in conjunction with Who's Where directory available from PCR.

## Film News
**Profile Group**
**27-29 Macklin St**
**London WC2B 5LX**
Tel: 020 7190 7777
email: info@profilegroup.co.uk
Web: www.profilegroup.co.uk
Contains two sections: A Calendar (including events, releases and birthdays) and an Index of Productions with calendar for UK based and international productions including contact details.

## Programme News (Bulletin)
Profile Group (as above)
Tel: 020 7190 7861
email: info@programmenews.co.uk
Website: www.programmenews.co.uk
Listing of upcoming TV programmes and their development stage. Contains contact details.

# Bibliography

This list is based upon the most well thumbed books in the *bfi* National Library (and the unapologetically subjective view of some of its staff) on useful works on a career and interest in filmmaking.

**Acting for film**
By Cathy Haase
Allworth Press, 2003. £14.95
ISBN 1581152523

**The art and science of screenwriting (2nd ed)**
By Philip Parker.
Intellect Books,1999. £19.95
ISBN 184500003

**The art of film acting: a guide for actors and directors**
By Jeremiah Comey
Focal Press, 2002. £18.99
ISBN 0240805070

**The art of the deal: the essential guide to business affairs for television, film and new media producers (3rd ed)**
By Dorothy Viljeon
PACT, 2002. £50.00
0952958635

**BFI Film Handbook**
Edited by Eddie Dyja
Published annually by the *bfi*. £23.99

**A Careers handbook for tv, radio, film, video and interactive media**
By Shiona Llewellyn (Recommended by Skillset)
AandC Black, 2000. £17.99
ISBN 0713656981

**Contacts: stage, television, film, radio**
Annual wide-ranging directory published annually by The Spotlight
c.£25.00

**Creative Careers: Film**
By Milly Jenkins
Trotman, 2003 (In association with Channel 4' s IDEASFACTORY)
£14.99
ISBN 085660903X

**Directing actors: creating memorable performances for film and television**
By Judith Weston
Michael Wiese Productions, 1996.
£17.99
ISBN 0941188248

**Directing single camera drama**
By Mike Crisp
Focal Press, 1998. £22.99
ISBN 0240514785

**Directing the documentary (4th ed)**
By Michael Rabiger
Focal Press, 2004. £29.95
ISBN 0240806085

**Documentary storytelling for film and videomakers**
By Sheila Curran Bernard
Focal Press, 2004. 17.99
ISBN 0240805399

**Film directing fundamentals: from script to screen**
By Nicholas T. Proferes
Focal Press, 2001. £20.99
ISBN 0240804228

**First facts 2: essential information for screenwriters, directors and producers**
By Andrea Cornwell
First Film Foundation, 2003. £16.00
ISBN 0954532600

**Getting into films and television (8th ed)**
By Robert Angell
How To Books, 2004. £10.99
ISBN 1857039742

**Get your film funded: UK film finance guide 2003/04**
By Caroline Hancock and Nic Weistreich
Shooting People Press, 2003. £17.99
ISBN 09544874400

**The guerilla film makers handbook**
By Chris Jones and Genevieve Jolliffe
Continuum, 2000. £25
ISBN 0826447139

**How to get into the film and TV business**
By Tudor Gates
Alma House, 1995. £9.95
ISBN 1899830057

**How to make money scriptwriting (2nd ed)**
By Julian Friedmann
Intellect Books, 2000. £14.95
ISBN 184150002X

**Lights, camera, action! Careers in film, television, video (2nd ed)**
By Josephine Langham
British Film Institute, 1997. £13.99
ISBN 0851705731

**Marketing and selling your film around the world: a guide for independent filmmakers**
By John Durie et. al.
Silman-James Press, 2000. £19.99
ISBN 1879505436

**Moviemakers' master class: private lessons from the world's foremost directors**
By Laurent Tiraud
Faber and Faber, 2002. £12.99
ISBN 057121102X

**Practical DV filmmaking**
By Russell Evans
Focal Press, 2002. (Includes CD-ROM) £20.99
ISBN 0240516575

**Producing and directing the short film and video (2nd ed)**
By Peter W. Rea and David K Irving
Focal Press, 2001. £34.99
ISBN 0240803949

**Research for media production (2nd ed)**
By Kathy Chater
Oxford: Focal Press, 2002. £16.99
ISBN 02405 16486

**The screenwriter's workbook**
By Syd Field

Dell, 1984. £11.00
ISBN 0440582253

**Story: substance, structure and style and the principles of screenwriting**
By McKee, Robert
Methuen, 1998. £19.99
ISBN 0413715507

**The writer's handbook: guide to writing for stage and screen**
By Barry Turner
Macmillan, 2003. £12.99
ISBN 1405000988

**The writer's journey: mythic structure for storytellers and screenwriters**
By Christopher Vogler
Pan Books, 1999. £14.99
ISBN 0330375911

**Writing, directing, and producing documentary films and videos (3rd ed)**
By Alan Rosenthal
Southern Illinois University Press, 2002. £18.50
ISBN 0809324482

**Writing the short film (2nd ed)**
By Pat Cooper and Ken Dancyger
Focal Press, 2000. £21.99
ISBN 0240803698

**You can be a movie extra: the complete guide to working as a supporting artiste in film and TV**
By Rob Martin
Titan Books, 2002. £6.99
ISBN 1840235225

Listed below are the companies who operate the major cinema chains and multiplexes in the UK, followed by the cinemas of the UK and Northern Ireland listed individually by location. Seating capacities normally exclude wheelchair spaces because of the difficulties in obtaining consistent data. Private cinemas, preview theatres, service camp cinemas and screening rooms are not listed. Many website addresses have now been added and others will follow in future editions. Revised by Allen Eyles

## KEY TO ABBREVIATIONS

P/T    Part-time screenings
S/O    Seasonal openings

# CINEMA CIRCUITS

## Apollo Cinemas
Houston House
12 Sceptre Court
Sceptre Point
Preston
Lancs PR5 6AW
Tel: 01772 323544
Fax: 01772 323545
Website: www.apollocinemas.co.uk
In summer 2004, operates 11 Apollo cinemas with 59 screens at Bangor, Barrow, Blackburn, Burnley, Crewe, Leamington, Morecambe, Paignton, Port Talbot, Rhyl and Stafford with new cinemas forthcoming at Lower Regent Street (London), Fareham, Stroud, Newbury, Altrincham and Worksop

## Artificial Eye Film Company
14 King Street
London WC2E 8HN
Tel: 020 7240 5353
Fax: 020 7240 5242
Website: www.artificial-eye.com
Film distributors operating the Chelsea Cinema and Renoir in London's West End

## Cine-UK Ltd
Chapter House
22 Chapter Street
London SW1P 4NP
Tel: 020 7932 2200
Fax: 020 7932 2222
Website: www.cineworld.co.uk
Operates 34 Cineworld multiplexes in mid-2004 with four additions scheduled at Sunderland, Bury St. Edmunds, Didcot and Cheltenham

## City Screen
Hardy House
16 -18 Beak Street
London W1F 9RD
Tel: 020 7734 4342
Fax: 020 7734 4027
Website: www.picturehouses.co.uk
Operates Picturehouses at 18 locations: Aberdeen (The Belmont), Bath (Little Theatre), Brighton (Duke of York's), Brixton (Ritzy), Cambridge (Arts), Clapham, East Grinstead, Edinburgh (Cameo), Exeter, Ely (The Maltings), Liverpool (FACT), London West End (The Other Cinema), Notting Hill (Gate), Oxford (Phoenix), Southampton (Harbour Lights), Stratford upon Avon, Stratford East (London) and York (City Screen), with a new weekend cinema opening at London's Olympia and a re-opening of the former Greenwich Cinema scheduled for next year

## Graves (Cumberland) Ltd
8 Falcon Place
Workington
Cumbria CA14 2EX
Tel: 01900 64791
Fax: 01900 601625
Four sites in Cumbria including a multiplex at Workington

## Hollywood Screen Entertainment
Anglia Square
Norwich
Norfolk
Tel: 01603 621903
Website: www.hollywoodcinemas.net
Operate cinemas in Dereham, Fakenham, Great Yarmouth, Lowestoft and Norwich

## Mainline Pictures
37 Museum Street
London WC1A 1LP
Tel: 020 7242 5523
Fax: 020 7430 0170
Website: www.screencinemas.co.uk
Operators of the Screen cinemas at Baker Street, Haverstock Hill, Islington Green, Oxted, Reigate, Walton-on-Thames and Winchester with a total of 11 screens

## Merlin Cinemas
Savoy Cinema
Causeway Head
Penzance
Cornwall
Tel: 01736 363330
Website: www.merlincinemas.co.uk
Operate cinemas in the southwest of England at Helston, Penzance, Redruth, St. Ives and Torquay

## Movie House Cinemas
Yorkgate Leisure Complex
100-150 York Street

**Belfast**
Tel: 028 9014 1404
Website: www.moviehouse.co.uk
Operates four Movie House cinemas
in Northern Ireland

## National Amusements (UK)
Showcase Cinema
Redfield Way
Lenton
Nottingham NG27 2UW
Tel: 0115 986 2508
Website: www.showcasecinemas.co.uk
Operates 19 Showcase multiplex
cinemas in mid-2004

## Northern Morris Associated Cinemas
Eller Howe Farm,
Lindale,
Grange Over Sands
Cumbria LA11 6NA
Tel/fax: 015395 35735
Website: www.nm-cinemas.co.uk
Operates the Royalty Bowness-on-
Windermere, Rex Elland, Picture
House Keighley, Regal Lancaster and
Plaza Skipton as well as booking the
Grand Clitheroe

## Odeon Cinemas
54 Whitcomb Street
London WC2H 7DN
Tel: 0207 321 0404
Fax: 0207 321 0357
Website: www.odeon.co.uk
96 cinemas with 595 screens in June
2004 with new multiplexes scheduled
for Bath and Braehead

## Reeltime Cinemas
Carlton
Westgate-on-Sea Kent
St Mildreds Road CT8 8RE
Tel: 01843 834290
Website: www.reeltime-cinemas.co.uk
Based at the Carlton Westgate-on-
Sea, Reeltime also operates Bognor
Regis Picturedrome, Bristol Orpheus,
Cosham Carlton, Dorchester Plaza,
Herne Bay Kavanagh, Margate
Dreamland, Ryde Commodore and
Sittingbourne New Century

## Scott Cinemas
Alexandra Cinemas
Market Street
Newton Abbot
Devon TQ12 2RB
Tel/fax: 01626 335432
Website: www.scottcinemas.co.uk
West Country circuit operating the
Barnstaple Central Cinemas,
Bridgwater Film Centre, Exmouth
Savoy Cinemas, Newton Abbot
Alexandra Cinemas, Lyme Regis

Regent and Sidmouth Radway

## Ster Century UK
Granite House
55-61 High Street
Frimley
Surrey GU16 7HJ
Tel: 01276 605 605
Fax: 01276 605 600
Website: www.stercentury.com
Operates multiplexes at Basingstoke,
Cardiff, Edinburgh (Leith), Leeds,
Norwich and Romford

## UCI Cinemas
7th Floor, Lee House
90 Great Bridgewater Street
Manchester M1 5JW
Tel: 0161 455 4000
Fax: 0161 455 4076
Website: www.uci-cinemas.co.uk
This American partnership between
the Paramount and Universal film
companies operates 34 purpose-built
multiplexes in the UK plus the
Empire in London's West End

## UGC Cinemas
6th Floor, Adelaide House
626 High Road, Chiswick
London W4 5RY
Tel: 020 8987 5000
Fax: 020 8742 7984
Website:
www.ugccinemas.co.uk/www.ugc.ie
The UK circuit of this leading French
film company consists of 36
multiplexes and 5 subdivided
traditional cinemas in June 2004

## Vue Entertainment
10 Chiswick Park
566Chiswick High Road
London W4 5XS
Tel: 0208 396 0100
Website: www.myvue.com
With a total of 47 sites, this combines
the former SBC (Spean Bridge)
multiplexes at Aberdeen with the
former Warner Village circuit, all of
which have been rebranded as Vue
cinemas. Expansion plans include
new multiplexes at Blackburn and
Thanet

## Ward-Anderson Cinema Group
Film House
35 Upper Abbey Street, Dublin 1
Ireland
Tel: (353) 1 872 3422/3922
Fax: (353) 1 872 3687
Leading cinema operator in Northern
and southern Ireland. Sites include
Ballymena, Belfast, Londonderry,
Lisburn and Newry

## West Coast Cinemas
Studio, John Street
Dunoon
Strathclyde
Scotland
Tel: 01369 704545
Operate cinemas in Dunoon,
Greenock and Fort William

## WTW Cinemas
Regal, The Platt
Wadebridge
Cornwall PL27 7AD
Tel: 01208 812791
Operates Wadebridge Regal, St Austell
Film Centre, Truro Plaza and Padstow
Cinedrome

# LONDON WEST END

## Baker Street
Screen on Baker Street, 96-98 Baker Street, NW1
Tel: 020 7935 2772
Website: www.screencinemas.co.uk
Seats: 1:95, 2:100

## Bayswater
UCI Whiteleys, Queensway, W2
Tel: 08700 10 20 30
Website: www.uci-cinemas.co.uk
Seats: 1:333, 2:281, 3:196, 4:178, 5:154, 6:138, 7:147, 8:125

## Bloomsbury
Renoir, Brunswick Square, WC1
Tel: 020 7837 8402
Website: www.artificial-eye.com
Seats: 1:251, 2::251

## Chelsea
Chelsea Cinema, 206 Kings Road, SW3
Tel: 020 7351 3742
Website: www.artificial-eye.com
Seats: 713

UGC, 279 Kings Road, SW3
Tel: 020 737 64744/0871 200 2000
Website: www.ugccinemas.co.uk
Seats: 1:220, 2:238, 3:122, 4:111

## City of London
Barbican Centre, Silk Street, EC2
Tel: 020 7638 8891
Website: www.barbican.org.uk/film
Seats: 1:288, 2:255

## Fulham Road
UGC, 142 Fulham Road, SW10
Tel: 0207 370 2110/0871 200 2000
Website: www.ugccinemas.co.uk
Seats: 1:348, 2:329, 3:173, 4:203, 5:218, 6:154

## Haverstock Hill
Screen on the Hill, 203 Haverstock Hill, NW3
Tel: 020 7435 3366/9787
Website: www.screencinemas.co.uk
Seats: 339

## Haymarket
UGC, Haymarket, SW1
Tel: 0207 930 6196/0871 200 2000
Website: www.ugccinemas.co.uk
Seats: 1:448, 2:200, 3:201

## Islington
Screen on the Green, 83 Upper Street, Islington, N1
Tel: 020 7226 3520
Website: www.screencinemas.co.uk
Seats: 280

Vue, 36 Parkfield Street, Islington, N1
Tel: 0870 240 6020
Website: www.myvue.com
Seats: 1:293, 2:140, 3:150, 4:103, 5:106, 6:159, 7:200, 8:198, 9:446

## Kensington
Odeon, 263 Kensington High Street, W8
Tel: 0871 22 44 007
Website: www.odeon.co.uk
Seats: 1:520, 2:66, 3:91, 4:266, 5:172, 6:204

## Leicester Square
Empire, 5-6 Leicester Square, WC2
Tel: 08700 102030
Seats: 1:1,330, 2:351, 3:77

Odeon, 24-26 Leicester Square, WC2
Tel: 0871 22 44 007
Website: www.odeon.co.uk
Seats: 1,943; Mezzanine: 1:60, 2:50, 3:60, 4:60, 5:60

Odeon, 11-18 Panton Street, SW1
Tel: 0871 22 44 007
Website: www.odeon.co.uk
Seats: 1:127, 2:143, 3:138, 4:133

Odeon, 10 Wardour Street, Swiss Centre, W1
Tel: 0871 22 44 007
Website: www.odeon.co.uk
Seats: 1:97, 2:101, 3:93, 4:108

Odeon West End, 40 Leicester Square, WC2
Tel: 0871 22 44 007
Website: www.odeon.co.uk
Seats: 1:500, 2:832

Prince Charles, Leicester Place, WC2
Tel: 020 7494 3654
Seats: 488

Vue, 3 Cranbourne Street, WC2
Tel: 08702 40 60 20/0207 437 3484
Website: www.myvue.com
Seats: 1:187, 2:126, 3:300, 4:298, 5:414, 6:264, 7:410, 8:180, 9:303

## The Mall
ICA Cinemas, The Mall, SW1
Tel: 020 7930 3647
Website: www.ica.org.uk
Seats: 185, C'théque: 45

## Marble Arch
Odeon, 10 Edgware Road, W1
Tel: 0871 22 44 007
Website: www.odeon.co.uk
Seats: 1:254, 2:119, 3:171, 4:229, 5:239

## Mayfair
Curzon Mayfair, 38 Curzon Street, W1
Tel: 020 7495 0501
Website: www.curzoncinemas.com
Seats: 1:320, 2:83

## Notting Hill
Coronet, Notting Hill Gate, W11
Tel: 020 7727 6705
Seats: 1:388, 2:147

Electric, 191 Portobello Road, W11
Tel: 020 7908 9696
Website: www.electriccinema.co.uk
Seats: 220 plus sofas

Gate, Notting Hill Gate, W11
Tel: 020 7727 4043
Seats: 240

## Olympia
Picturehouse at Olympia, Sotherby's entrance (P/T)
Website: www.picturehouses.co.uk
Seats: 448
(Opening summer 2004)

## Piccadilly Circus
Apollo West End, Lower Regent Street
Seats: 1:210, 2:140, 3:80, 4:75, 5:45
Website: www.apollocinemas.co.uk
(Opening summer 2004)

The Other Cinema, 11 Rupert Street, W1
Tel: 020 7734 1506
Website: www.picturehouses.co.uk
Seats: 1:195, 2:84

## Shaftesbury Avenue
Curzon Soho, 93-107 Shaftesbury Avenue, W1
Tel: 0207 734 2255
Website: www.curzoncinemas.com
Seats: 1:249, 2:110, 3:130

Odeon Covent Garden, 135 Shaftesbury Avenue, WC2
Tel: 0871 22 44 007
Website: www.odeon.co.uk
Seats: 1:153, 2:269, 3:167, 4:152

UGC, Shaftesbury Avenue at The Trocadero, W1
Tel: 0207 434 0032/0871 200 2000
Website: www.ugccinemas.co.uk
Seats: 1:548, 2:240, 3:146, 4:154, 5:122, 6:94, 7:89

## South Kensington
Ciné Lumière, Institut Français, 17 Queensberry Place, SW7
(P/T)

Tel: 020 7838 2144/2146
Website: www.institut-francais.org.uk
Seats: 350

Goethe Institute, 50 Princes Gate,
Exhibition Rd, SW7 (P/T)
Tel: 020 7596 4000
Seats: 170

IMAX, Science Museum, Exhibition
Road
Tel: 0870 870 4771
Seats: 450

## Tottenham Court Road
Odeon, Tottenham Court Road, W1
Tel: 0870 50 50 007
Website: www.odeon.co.uk
Seats: 1:328, 2:145, 3:137

## Waterloo
bfi London IMAX, 1 Charlie Chaplin
Walk, SE1
Tel: 020 787 2525
**Seats: 482**
National Film Theatre, South Bank,
Waterloo, SE1
Tel: 020 7928 3232
Website: www.bfi.org.uk/nft
Seats: 1:450, 2:162, 3:134

Royal Festival Hall, South Bank,
Waterloo, SE1 (P/T)
Tel: 020 7928 3002
Seats: 2,419

# OUTER LONDON

## Acton
Vue, Royale Leisure Park, Western
Avenue, Park Royal South
Tel: 020 8896 3252
Website: www.myvue.com
Seats: 1:425, 2:159, 3:205, 4:274,
5:314, 6:274, 7:205, 8:159,  9:425

## Barnet
Odeon, Great North Road
Tel: 0871 22 44 007
Website: www.odeon.co.uk
Seats: 1:532, 2:182, 3:182, 4:187, 5:155

## Beckenham
Odeon, High Street
Tel: 0871 22 44 007
Website: www.odeon.co.uk
Seats: 1:471, 2:207, 3:113. 4:190,
5:168. 6:119

## Bexleyheath
Cineworld, The Broadway
Tel: 020 8303 0015
Website: www.cineworld.co.uk
**Seats: 1:157, 2:128, 3:280, 4:244, 5:88,
6:84, 7:111, 8:168, 9:221**

## Brentford
Watermans Arts Centre, 40 High St
Tel: 020 8232 1010
Website: www.watermans.org.uk
Seats: 240

## Brixton
Ritzy, Brixton Oval,
Coldharbour Lane, SW2
Tel: 020 7733 2229
Website: www.picturehouses.co.uk
Seats: 1:353, 2:179, 3:125, 4:108, 5:84

## Bromley
Odeon, High Street
Tel: 0871 22 44 007
Website: www.odeon.co.uk
Seats: 1:392, 2:124, 3:105, 4:277

## Camden Town
Odeon, 14 Parkway, NW1
Tel: 0871 22 44 007
Website: www.odeon.co.uk
Seats: 1:403, 2:92, 3:238, 4:90, 5:103

## Clapham
Picturehouse, Venn Street, SW4
Tel: 020 7498 3323
Website: www.picturehouses.co.uk
Seats: 1:202, 2:153, 3:134, 4:115

## Croydon
(see also Purley Way)
David Lean, Clock Tower,
Katherine Street
Tel: 020 8253 1030
Seats: 68

Fairfield Halls/Ashcroft Theatre,
Park Lane (P/T)
Tel: 020 8688 9291
Seats: Fairfield: 1,552, Ashcroft: 750

Vue, Grant's, 14 High Street
Tel: 0208 688 0606
Website: www.myvue.com
Seats: 1:171, 2:194, 3:178, 4:106, 5:88,
6:398, 7:170, 8:131, 9:167, 10:224

## Dagenham
Vue, Dagenham Leisure Park, Cook
Road, off Ripple Road A13
Tel: 020 8592 1090
Website: www.myvue.com
Seats: 1:404, 2:146, 3:189, 4:252,
5:305, 6:252, 7:189

## Dalston
Rio, 107 Kingsland High Street, E8
Tel: 020 7241 9410
Website: www.riocinema.org.uk
Seats: 405

## Ealing
UGC, 59-61Uxbridge Road, W5
Tel: 0208 579 4851/0871 200 2000
Website: www.ugccinemas.co.uk
Seats: 1:576, 2:371, 3:193

## East Finchley
Phoenix, High Road, N2
Tel: 020 8444 6789
Seats: 308

## East Ham
Boleyn, Barking Road
Tel: 020 8471 4884
Seats: 1:800, 2:250, 3:250

## Elephant and Castle
Coronet, New Kent Road (P/T)
Seats: 572

## Enfield
UGC, Southbury Leisure Park, 208
Southbury Road
Tel: 0208 366 1550/0871 200 2000
Website: www.ugccinemas.co.uk
Seats: 1:156, 2: 270, 3:236, 4:186,
5:156, 6:192, 7:277, 8:522, 9:273,
10:203, 11:156, 12:270, 13:236,
14:186, 15:98

## Feltham
Cineworld, Leisure West, Browells
Lane
Tel: 020 8867 0888
Website: www.cineworld.co.uk
Seats: 1:104, 2:116, 3:132, 4:205,
5:253, 6:351, 7:302, 8:350, 9:265,
10:90, 11:112, 12: 137, 13:124, 14:99

## Finchley Road
Vue, 02 Centre, 255 Finchley Road,
NW3

Tel: 08702 40 60 20/020 7604 3066
Website: www.myvue.com
Seats: 1:359, 2:324, 3:159, 4:261,
5:376, 6:258, 7:134, 8:86

### Fulham Broadway
Vue, Unit 18, Fulham Broadway
Retail Centre, Fulham Road, SW6
Tel: 08702 40 60 20/020 7385 2025
Website: www.myvue.com
Seats: 1:127, 2:316, 3:316, 4:187,
5:163, 6:560, 7:310, 8:242, 9:136

### Greenwich
The FilmWorks, Bugsby's Way
Tel: 08700 10 20 30
Seats: 1:115, 2:138, 3:157, 4:178,
5:178, 6:157, 7:138, 8:115, 9:279,
10:338, 11:372, 12:261, 13:44, 14:44

The Greenwich Picturehouse
High Road
Seats: (5 screens)
(Scheduled to open February 2005)

### Hammersmith
UGC, 207 King Street, W6
Tel: 0208 748 2388/0871 200 2000
Website: www.ugccinemas.co.uk
Seats: 1:322, 2:322, 3:268, 4:268

Riverside Studios, Crisp Road, W6
Tel: 020 8237 1111
Seats: 200

### Hampstead
Everyman, Holly Bush Vale, NW3
Tel: 020 7431 1777
Website: www.everymancinema.com
Seats: 1:184, 2:72

### Harrow
Safari, Station Road
Tel: 020 8426 0606
Seats: 1:612, 2:133

Vue, St George's Shopping & Leisure
Centre, St. Anne's Road
Tel: 020 8427 9900
Website: www.myvue.com
Seats: 1:347, 2:288, 3:424, 4:296,
5:121, 6:109, 7:110, 8:87, 9:96

### Hayes
Beck Theatre, Grange Road (P/T)
Tel: 020 8561 8371
Seats: 518

### Holloway
Odeon, Holloway Road, N7
Tel: 0871 22 44 007
Website: www.odeon.co.uk
Seats: 1:330, 2:315, 3:72, 4:231, 5:183,
6:249, 7:92, 8:103

### Ilford
Cineworld, i-scene, Clements Road

Tel: 020 8911 2900/8553 5599
Website: www.cineworld.co.uk
Seats: 1:433, 2:362, 3:278, 4:204,
5:111.6:122, 7:180, 8:191, 9:114,
10:95, 11:146

### Kilburn
Tricycle Cinema, High Road
Tel: 020 7328 1000
Seats: 280

### Kingston-on-Thames
Odeon, Rotunda Leisure Centre,
Clarence Street
Tel: 0871 22 44 007
Website: www.odeon.co.uk
Seats: 1:199, 2:431, 3:112, 4:186,
5:178, 6:146, 7:308, 8:118, 9:161,
10:182, 11:256, 12:183, 13:339, 14:
217

### Lambeth
Imperial War Museum, Lambeth
Road, SE1 (P/T)
Tel: 020 7735 8922/7416 5320
Seats: 216

### Lee Valley
UCI, Picketts Lock Lane, Meridian
Way, Edmonton
Tel: 08700 10 20 30
Website: www.uci-cinemas.co.uk
Seats: 166 (6 screens), 208 (4 screens),
428 (2 screens)

### Mile End
Genesis, Mile End Road
Tel: 020 7780 2000
Website: www.genesiscinema.co.uk
Seats: 1:575, 2:159, 3:159, 4:101, 5:95

### Muswell Hill
Odeon, Fortis Green Road, N10
Tel: 0871 22 44 007
Website: www.odeon.co.uk
Seats: 1:400, 2:165, 3:164

### Newham
Showcase, Jenkins Lane, off A13
Tel: 020 8477 4520
Website: www.showcasecinemas.co.uk
Seats: 3,664 (14 screens)

### North Finchley
Vue, Great North Leisure Park,
Chaplin Square, N12
Tel: 020 8446 9933
Website: www.myvue.com
Seats: 1:377, 2:164, 3:219, 4:333,
5:333, 6:219, 7:164, 8:377

### Peckham
Peckham Multiplex, 95a Rye Lane
Tel: 0870 0420 299
Website: www.peckhamplex.com
Seats: 1:397, 2:255, 3:275, 4:197,
5:218, 6:112

### Purley Way
Vue, Valley Park Leisure Complex,
21 Hesterman Way, Croydon
Tel: 020 8680 1968
Website: www.myvue.com
Seats: 1:253, 2:205, 3:178, 4:396,
5:396, 6:178, 7:205, 8:253

### Putney
Odeon, High Street, SW15
Tel: 0871 22 44 007
Website: www.odeon.co.uk
Seats: 1:434, 2:315, 3:147

### Richmond
Filmhouse, Water Lane
Tel: 020 8332 0030
Seats: 150

Odeon, Hill Street
Tel: 0871 22 44 007
Website: www.odeon.co.uk
Seats: 1:406, 2:179, 3:179

Odeon Studio, Red Lion Street
Tel: 0871 22 44 007
Website: www.odeon.co.uk
Seats: 1:81, 2:78, 3:78, 4:91

### Romford
Ster Century, The Brewery, Waterloo
Road
Tel: 01708 759100
Website: www.stercentury.com
Seats: 1:160, 2:160, 3:182, 4:198,
5:198, 6:168, 7:160, 8:160, 9:108,
10:132, 11:286, 12:414, 13:464,
14:435, 15:385, 16:264

### Shepherds Bush
Vue, West 12 Shopping & Leisure
Centre, Shepherds Bush Green
Tel: 0208 749 5014/08702 40 60 20
Website: www.myvue.com
Seats: 1:127, 2:137, 3:189, 4:227,
5:287, 6:201, 7:175, 8:114, 9:387,
10:227, 11:201, 12:285

### Southall
Himalaya Palace, South Road
Tel: 020 8813 8844
Seats: 1:500, 2:150, 3:150

### Staples Corner
UGC Cinemas, Staples Corner Retail
Park, Gern Way
Tel: 0208 208 1367/0871 200 2000
Website: www.ugccinemas.co.uk
Seats: 1:455, 2:362, 3:214, 4:210,
5:166, 6:166

### Stratford
Picturehouse, Gerry Raffles Square,
Salway Road, E15
Tel: 020 8555 3366
Website: www.picturehouses.co.uk

Seats: 1:260, 2:242, 3:215, 4:151

### Streatham
Odeon, High Road, SW16
Tel: 0871 22 44 007
Website: www.odeon.co.uk
Seats: 1:451, 2:110, 3:110, 4:103,
5:237, 6:209, 7:93, 8:172

### Surrey Quays
UCI, Redriff Road, SE16
Tel: 08700 10 20 30
Website: www.uci-cinemas.co.uk
Seats: 1:401, 2:164, 3:198, 4:328,
5:198, 6:198, 7:164, 8:164, 9:411

### Sutton
UCI, St Nicholas Centre, St Nicholas
Way
Tel: 08700 10 20 30
Website: www.uci-cinemas.co.uk
Seats: 1:304, 2:296, 3:232, 4:326,
5:206, 6:326

### Swiss Cottage
Odeon, Finchley Road, NW3
Website: www.odeon.co.uk
Tel: 0871 22 44 007
Seats: 1:715, 2:111, 3:220, 4:120,
5:154, 6:156

### Wandsworth
Cineworld, Southside, Wandsworth
High Street
**Tel: 0871 220 8000**
Website: www.cineworld.co.uk
Seats: 1:206, 2:179, 3:137, 4:105,
5:136, 6:158, 7:409, 8:350, 9:261,
10:249, 11:196, 12:135, 13:185, 14:180

### West India Quay
UGC, Hertsmere Road
Tel: 0207 517 7860/0871 200 2000
Website: www.ugccinemas.co.uk
Seats: 1:111, 2:168, 3:216, 4: 275,
5:360, 6: 104, 7:164, 8: 216, 9:275,
10:359

### Willesden
Belle Vue, Willesden Green Library
Centre, NW10
Tel: 020 8830 0822
Seats: 204

### Wimbledon
Odeon, The Crescent, The Broadway,
SW19
Tel: 0871 22 44 007
Website: www.odeon.co.uk
Seats: 1:203, 2:197, 3: 217, 4:383,
5:205, 6:173, 7:378, 8:188, 9:261,
10:172, 11:232, 12:214

### Woodford
Odeon, High Road, E18
Tel: 0871 22 44 007
Website: www.odeon.co.uk

Seats: 1:207, 2:154, 3:104, 4:153,
5:161, 6:92, 7:144

### Wood Green
Cineworld, Shopping City, High
Road
Tel: 020 8829 1400
Website: www.cineworld.co.uk
Seats: 1:267, 2:315, 3:106, 4:152,
5:185, 6:111, 7:180, 8:137, 9:172,
10:140, 11:162, 12:105

Showcase, Spouters Corner,
Hollywood Green, High Road
**Tel: 0870 162 8960**
Website: www.showcasecinemas.co.uk
Seats: 1,600 (6 screens)

# ENGLAND

### Accrington – Lancashire
Vue, The Viaduct, Hyndburn Road
**Tel: 01254 306 660**
Website: www.myvue.com
Seats: 1:165, 2:265, 3:266, 4:166

### Aldeburgh - Suffolk
Aldeburgh Cinema, High Street
Tel: 01728 452996
Seats: 284

### Aldershot - Hants
West End Centre, Queens Road
(P/T)
Tel: 01252 330040
Seats: 98

### Alnwick - Northumberland
Playhouse, Bondgate Without  (P/T)
Tel: 01665 510785
Seats: 272

### Alton - Hants
Palace, Normandy Street
Tel: 01420 82303
Seats: 1:111, 2:62

### Altrincham – Greater Manchester
Apollo Cinemas
Seats: 1,800 (7 screens)
(Scheduled to open in October 2005)

### Ambleside - Cumbria
Zeffirelli's, Compston Road
Tel: 01539 431771
Seats: 1:110, 2:60

Zeffirelli's by the Park, Compston
Road
Tel: 01539 433100
Seats: 1:106, 2:63

### Ashford - Kent
Cineworld, Eureka Leisure Park,
Trinity Road
Tel: 01233 620568/622226
Website: www.cineworld.co.uk
Seats: 1:344, 2:75, 3:63, 4:89, 5:156,
6:254, 7:254, 8:156, 9:89, 10:63,
11:215, 12:345

### Ashton-under-Lyne - Greater Manchester
Cineworld, Ashton Leisure Park,
Fold Way, Off Lord Sheldon Way
**Tel: 0871 220 8000**
Website: www.cineworld.co.uk
Seats: 1:205, 2:132, 3:132, 4:247,
5:209, 6:287, 7:410, 8::287, 9:187,
10:122, 11:143, 12:148

Tameside Hippodrome, Oldham
Road (P/T)

Tel: 0161 308 3223
Seats: 1,262

### Aylesbury - Buckinghamshire
Odeon, The Exchange
Tel: 0871 22 44 007
Website: www.odeon.co.uk
Seats: 1:399, 2:283, 3:266, 4:230,
5:205, 6:194

### Banbury - Oxfordshire
Odeon, Horsefair
Tel: 0871 22 44 007
Website: www.odeon.co.uk
Seats: 1:428, 2:225

### Barnsley - South Yorkshire
Odeon, Eldon Street
Tel: 0871 22 44 007
Website: www.odeon.co.uk
Seats: 1:403, 2:438

### Barnstaple - Devon
Central Cinemas, Boutport Street
Tel: 01271 342550/370022
Website: www.scottcinemas.co.uk
Seats: 1:360, 2:80, 3:80, 4:130

### Barrow - Cumbria
Apollo, Hollywood Park, Hindpool
Road
Tel: 01229 825354
Website: www.apollocinemas.co.uk
Seats: 1:118, 2:103, 3:258, 4:258,
5:118, 6:118

### Basildon - Essex
UCI, Festival Leisure Park, Pipps
Hill
Tel: 08700 10 20 30
Website: www.uci-cinemas.co.uk
Seats: 1:361, 2:180, 3:146, 4:164,
5:220, 6:337, 7:246, 8:220, 9:164,
10:146, 11:180, 12:538

### Basingstoke - Hants
Ster Century, Festival Place
Tel: 0870 240 8984
Website: www.stercentury.com
Seats: 1:199, 2:199, 3:143, 4:275,
5:275, 6:123, 7:319, 8:248, 9:295,
10:175

Vue, Basingstoke Leisure Park,
Churchill Way West, West Ham
Tel: 01256 818 517
Website: www.myvue.com
Seats: 1:427, 2:238, 3:223, 4:154,
5:157, 6:157, 7:154, 8:223, 9:238,
10:427

### Bath - Avon
ABC, Westgate Street
Tel: 01225 461730/462959
Website: www.odeon.co.uk
Seats: 652

Little Theatre, St Michael's Place
Tel: 01225 330817
Website: www.picturehouses.co.uk
Seats: 1:192, 2:74

Odeon, James Street West
Seats: (6 screens)
(Scheduled to open late 2004)

### Bedford - Bedfordshire
Civic Theatre, Horne Lane  (P/T)
Tel: 01234 44813
Seats: 266

UGC, Aspects Leisure Park, Newham
Avenue
Tel: 01234 212826/0870 1555130
Website: www.ugccinemas.co.uk
Seats: 1:334, 2:292, 3:291, 4:289,
5:187, 6:187

### Berkhamsted – Hertfordshire
Rex, High Street (P/T)
(Not yet re-opened in summer 2004)

### Berwick - Northumberland
Maltings Art Centre, Eastern Lane
(P/T)
Tel: 01289 330999/330661
Seats: 100

Playhouse, Sandgate
Tel: 01289 307769
Seats: 650

### Bexhill - East Sussex
Curzon Picture Playhouse, Western
Road
Tel: 01424 210078
Seats: 175

### Bideford - Devon
College Theatre (P/T)
Tel: 01237 428110
Seats: 181

### Billingham - Cleveland
Forum Theatre, Town Centre  (P/T)
Tel: 01642 552663
Seats: 494

### Birkenhead - Merseyside
Vue, Europa Boulevard, Conway
Park
Tel: 0151 649 8822
Website: www.myvue.com
Seats: 1:161, 2:204, 3:429, 4:204,
5:161, 6:354, 7:311

### Birmingham - West Midlands
AMC, Broadway Plaza, Ladywood
Middleway, off Broad Street,
Edgbaston
Website: www.amccinemas.co.uk
Seats: 2,909 (12 screens)

IMAX Theatre, Millennium Point,
Curzon Street
Tel: 0121 202 2222
Seats: 385

MAC
Cannon Hill Park, Edgbaston
Tel: 0121 440 3838
Seats: 1:202, 2:144

Odeon, New Street
Tel: 0870 50 50 007
Website: www.odeon.co.uk
Seats: 1:231, 2:390, 3:298, 4:229,
5:194, 6:180, 7:130, 8:80

Piccadilly, 372 Stratford Road,
Sparkhill
Tel: 0121 773 1658

Showcase, Kingsbury Road,
Erdington
Tel: 0121 382 9779
Website: www.showcasecinemas.co.uk
Seats: 3,599 (12 screens)

UGC, Tennant Street (Broad Street)
Tel: 0121 6430631/0871 200 2000
Website: www.ugccinemas.co.uk
Seats: 1:371, 2:330, 3:269, 4:181,
5:287, 6:434, 7:341, 8:185, 9:269, 10:
240, 11:263, 12:167

Vue, 29 StarCity, Watson Road,
Nechells
Tel: 0121 326 0264
Website: www.myvue.com
Seats: 1:440, 2:138, 3:107, 4:190,
5:243, 6:243, 7:178, 8:138, 9:138,
10:119, 11:119, 12:539, 13:208,
14:208, 15:140, 16:37, 17:52, 18:52,
19:539, 20-24 currently not in use, 25:
243, 26::243, 27: 236, 28:246, 29:160,
30:338

### Bishop's Stortford - Herts
Cineworld, Anchor Street
Tel: 01279 710 000/659301
Website: www.cineworld.co.uk
Seats: 1:299, 2:104, 3:160, 4:259,
5:230, 6:185

### Blackburn - Lancashire
Apollo, King William Street
Tel: 01254 695979
Website: www.apollocinemas.co.uk
Seats: 1:295, 2:205, 3:115, 4:100, 5:95

Vue
Seats: 1,820 (10 screens)
(Scheduled to open during 2005)

### Blackpool - Lancashire
Odeon, Rigby Road
Tel: 0870 50 50 007

Website: www.odeon.co.uk
Seats: 1:417, 2:137, 3:342, 4:151, 5:198, 6:393, 7:158, 8:342, 9:376, 10:199

## Bluewater - Kent
Showcase, Upper Mall, Water Circus, Greenhithe
Tel: 0870 162 8900
Website: www.showcasecinemas.co.uk
Seats: 1:129, 2:197, 3:361, 4:464, 5:245, 6:176, 7:80, 8:139, 9:298, 10:379, 11:193, 12:132, Studio:86

## Blyth - Northumberland
Wallaw, Union Street
Tel: 01670 352504
Seats: 1:850, 2:150, 3:80
(Closed indefinitely in mid-2004)

## Bognor Regis - West Sussex
Picturedrome, Canada Grove
Tel: 01243 841015
Website: www.reeltime-cinemas.co.uk
Seats: 1:368, 2:100

ABC, Southcoast World
Tel: 0870 841916
Seats: 1:240, 2:240

## Boldon - Tyne and Wear
UGC, Abingdon Way, Boldon Leisure Park, Boldon Colliery
Tel: 0191 5360913/0870 15505512
Website: www.ugccinemas.co.uk
Seats: 1:284, 2:197, 3:80, 4:119, 5:263, 6:529, 7:263, 8:136, 9:119, 10:197, 11:284

## Bolton - Greater Manchester
Vue, Middlebrook Leisure Park, The Link Way, Off Mansel Way, Horwich
Tel: 01204 669 668
Website: www.myvue.com
Seats: 1:375, 2:124, 3:124, 4:166, 5:244, 6:269, 7:269, 8:244, 9:166, 10:124, 11:124, 12:368

UGC, Valley Entertainment, 15 Eagley Brook Way
Tel: 01204 366200/0871 200 2000
Website: www.ugccinemas.co.uk
Seats: 1: 143, 2:144, 3:118, 4:155, 5:230, 6:467, 7:635, 8:522, 9:233, 10:156, 11:156, 12:193, 13:193, 14:72, 15:72

## Borehamwood - Hertfordshire
Curzon, The Point, Shenley Road
Tel: 0208 207 2028
Seats: 1:193, 2:157, 3:121, 4:119

## Boston - Lincolnshire
Blackfriars Arts Centre, Spain Lane

(P/T)
Tel: 01205 363108
Seats: 237

West End, West Street
Tel: 01205 363634/363639
Seats: 1:360, 2::260, 3:150, 4:150, 5:110

## Bournemouth - Dorset
ABC, Westover Road
Tel: 0870 5050 007/900 7694
Seats: 1:652, 2:585, 3:223

Odeon, Westover Road
Tel: 0871 22 44 007
Website: www.odeon.co.uk
Seats: 1:757, 2:146, 3:266, 4:119, 5:119, 6:354

Sheridan IMAX Cinema, Waterfront Pier Approach
Tel: 01202 200000
Seats: 419

## Bowness-on-Windermere - Cumbria
Royalty, Lake Road
Tel: 01539 443364
Seats: 1:399, 2:100, 3:65

## Bracknell - Berkshire
South Hill Park Arts Centre
Tel: 01344 427272/484123
Seats: 1:60, 2:200

UCI, The Point, Skimpedhill Lane
Tel: 08700 10 20 30
Website: www.uci-cinemas.co.uk
Seats: 1:180, 2:193, 3:207, 4:179, 5:320, 6:320, 7:179, 8:207, 9:207, 10:179

## Bradford - West Yorkshire
Cineworld, Leisure Exchange, Vicar Lane
**Tel: 01274 387220/371941**
Website: www.cineworld.co.uk
Seats: 1:168, 2:239, 3:161, 4:301, 5:301, 6:192 7:190, 8:311, 9:166, 10:209, 11: 288, 12:106, 13:120, 14:120, 15:154, 16:259

National Museum of Photography, Film & Television
Tel: 0870 70 10 200
Website: www.nmpft.org.uk
**Seats: Pictureville: 306, Cubby Broccoli: 108, IMAX: 340**

Odeon, Gallagher Leisure Park, Thornbury
Tel: 0870 50 50 007
Website: www.odeon.co.uk
Seats: 1:126, 2:228, 3:150, 4:233, 5:384, 6:442, 7:442, 8:211, 9:257, 10:157, 11:170, 12:140, 13:148

## Braintree - Essex
Cineworld, Freeport Shopping Village
Tel: 01376 554280
Website: www.cineworld.co.uk
Seats: 1:311, 2:169, 3:93, 4:148, 5:170, 6:222, 7:222, 8:170, 9:148, 10:93, 11:207, 12:310

## Bridgnorth - Shropshire
Majestic, Whitburn Street
Tel: 01746 761815/761866
Seats: 1:500, 2:86, 3:86

## Bridgwater - Somerset
Film Centre, Penel Orlieu
Tel: 01278 422383
Website: www.scottcinemas.co.uk
Seats: 1:223, 2::232

## Bridlington - Humberside
Forum, The Promenade
Tel: 01262 676767
Seats: 1:202, 2:103, 3:57

## Brierley Hill - Staffordshire
UCI, Merry Hill Shopping Centre
Tel: 08700 10 20 30
Website: www.uci-cinemas.co.uk
Seats: 1:350, 2:350, 3:274, 4:274, 5:224, 6:224, 7:254, 8:254, 9:178, 10:178

## Brighton – East Sussex
Cinematheque, Media Centre, 9-12 Middle Street
Tel: 01273 384300
Website: www.cinematheque.org

Duke of York's Picturehouse, Preston Circus
Tel: 01273 602503
Website: www.picturehouses.co.uk
Seats: 327

Gardner Arts Centre, University of Sussex, Falmer (P/T)
Tel: 01273 685861
Seats: 354

Odeon, Kingswest, West Street
Tel: 0870 50 50 007
Website: www.odeon.co.uk
Seats: 1:389, 2: 220, 3:238, 4:238, 5: 514, 6: 286, 7:232, 8:100

UGC, Brighton Marina
Tel: 01273 818094/0870 1555145
Website: www.ugccinemas.co.uk
Seats: 1:351, 2:351, 3:251, 4:251, 5:223, 6:223, 7:202, 8:203

## Bristol – Avon
Arnolfini, Narrow Quay
Tel: 0117 929 9191
Seats: 176

Cineworld, Hengrove Leisure Park, Hengrove Way
Tel: 01275 831300
Website: www.cineworld.co.uk
Seats: 1:97, 2:123, 3:133, 4:211, 5:264, 6:343, 7:312, 8:344, 9:262, 10:88, 11:113, 12:152, 13:123, 14:98

The Cube, King Square
Tel: 0117 907 4190/4191
Seats: 124

IMAX, Canon's Marsh
Tel: 0117 915 5000
Seats: 250

Odeon, Union Street
Tel: 0871 22 44 007
Website: www.odeon.co.uk
Seats: 1:399, 2:224, 3:215

Orpheus, Northumbria Drive, Henleaze
Tel: 0117 962 1644
Website: www.reeltime-cinemas.co.uk
Seats: 1:160, 2:129, 3:125

Showcase, Avon Meads off Albert Road, St Phillips Causeway
Tel: 0117 972 3800
Website: www.showcasecinemas.co.uk
Seats: 3,408 (14 screens)

Vue, The Venue, Cribbs Causeway Leisure Complex, Merlin Road
Tel: 0117 950 0222
Website: www.myvue.com
Seats: 1:385, 2:124, 3:124, 4:166, 5:239, 6:273, 7:273, 8:239, 9:166, 10:124, 11:124, 12:385

Vue, Unit 2, Aspects Leisure Park, Avon Ring Road, Longwell Green
Tel: 0117 960 0021
Website: www.myvue.com
Seats: 1:385, 2:166, 3:124, 4:124, 5:166, 6:293, 7:337, 8:293, 9:166, 10:124, 11:124, 12:166, 13:385

Watershed, 1 Canon's Road, BS1 5TX
Tel: 0117 927 6444/925 3845
Website: www.watershed.co.uk
Seats: 1:200, 2:54
(Third screen seating 100 scheduled to open September 2004)

## Broadstairs - Kent
Windsor, Harbour Street
Tel: 01843 865726
Seats: 120

## Bromborough - Merseyside
Odeon, Wirral Leisure Retail Park, Welton Road
Tel: 0870 50 50 007

Website: www.odeon.co.uk
Seats: 1:458, 2:356, 3:238, 4:197, 5:327, 6:162, 7:162, 8:90, 9:133, 10:76, 11:120

## Bude - Cornwall
Rebel, off A39, Rainbow Trefknic Cross
Tel: 01288 361442
Seats: 120

## Burgess Hill - West Sussex
Orion, Cyprus Road
Tel: 01444 232137/243300
Website: www.orioncinema.com
Seats: 1:150, 2:121

## Burnham-on-Crouch - Essex
Rio, Station Road
Tel: 01621 782027
Seats: 1:220, 2:60

## Burnley - Lancashire
Apollo, Hollywood Park, Centenary Way, Manchester Road
Tel: 01282 456222/456333
Website: www.apollocinemas.co.uk
Seats: 1:61, 2:238, 3:93, 4:339, 5:93, 6:339, 7:93, 8:238, 9:93

## Burton-on-Trent - Staffordshire
Cineworld, Middleway Leisure Park, Guild Street
Tel: 01283 511561
Website: www.cineworld.co.uk
Seats: 1:225, 2:98, 3:136, 4:107, 5:316, 6:289, 7:203, 8:132, 9:98

## Bury - Greater Manchester
Vue, Park 66, Pilsworth Road
Tel: 08702 406020
Website: www.myvue.com
Seats: 1:559, 2:322, 3:278, 4:434, 5:208, 6:166, 7:166, 8:208, 9:434, 10:278, 11:322, 12:573

## Bury St Edmunds - Suffolk
Cineworld, Parkway
Seats: 1,500 (9 screens)
(Scheduled to open March 2005)

Odeon, Hatter Street
Tel: 0870 5050 007
Website: www.odeon.co.uk
Seats: 1:188, 2:117

## Camberley - Surrey
Camberley Theatre, Knoll Road (P/T)
Tel: 01276 707600
Seats: 338

## Cambridge - Cambridgeshire
Arts Picturehouse, St Andrews Street
Tel: 01223 504444

Website: www.picturehouses.co.uk
Seats: 1: 250, 2:150, 3:98

Cineworld, Cambridge Leisure, Clifton Way
Tel: 0871 220 8000
Website: www.cineworld.co.uk
Seats: 1:105, 2:163, 3:201, 4:129, 5:119, 6:152, 7:169, 8:285, 9:377

Vue, Grafton Centre, East Road
Tel: 01223 460 225
Website: www.myvue.com
Seats: 1:162, 2:168, 3:182, 4:205, 5:166, 6:175, 7:321, 8:442

## Cannock - Staffordshire
Picture House, Walsall Road
Tel: 01543 502226
Seats: 1:368, 2:185

## Canterbury - Kent
Odeon, St Georges Place
Tel: 0870 155 5133
Website: www.odeon.co.uk
Seats: 1:534, 2:385
Cinema 3, Gulbenkian Theatre, Cornwallis South, University of Kent, CT2 7NX
Tel: 01227 769075/764000 x4017
Seats: 300

## Canvey Island - Essex
Movie Starr Cineplex, Eastern Esplandade
Tel: 01268 699799
Seats: 1:134, 2:122, 3:104, 4:73

## Carlisle - Cumbria
Lonsdale City Cinemas, Warwick Road
Tel: 01228 514654
Seats: 1:375, 2:216, 3:54

Lonsdale City Cinemas 4 & 5, Mary Street
Tel: 01228 514654
Seats: 4:122, 5:112

Vue Cinemas, 50 Botchergate
Tel: 01228 819 104
Website: www.myvue.com
Seats: 1:148, 2::248, 3:248, 4:148, 5:301, 6:301, 7:340

## Castleford – West Yorkshire
Cineworld, Xscape, Colorado Way
Tel: 0871 220 8000
Website: www.cineworld.co.uk
Seats: 1:110, 2:134, 3:222, 4:194, 5:119, 6:265, 7:361, 8:242, 9:286, 10:103, 11:221, 12:250, 13:160, 14:87

## Chelmsford - Essex
Cramphorn Theatre, High Street (P/T)

Tel: 01245 606 505
Seats: 140

**Odeon, Kings Head Walk**
Tel: 0871 22 44 007
Website: www.odeon.co.uk
Seats: 1:339, 2:108, 3:158, 4:235,
5:171, 6:143, 7:128, 8:131

## Cheltenham - Gloucestershire
**Cineworld**
Website: www.cineworld.co.uk
**Seats: 2,000 (11 screens)**
(Scheduled to open in December
2005)

**Odeon, Winchcombe Street**
Tel: 0871 22 44 007
Website: www.odeon.co.uk
Seats: 1:261, 2:184, 3:183, 4:82, 5:129
X, 6:104 X, 7:177 X

## Chesham - Buckinghamshire
**New Elgiva Theatre, Elgiva Lane
(P/T)**
Tel: 01494 582900
Seats: 328

## Cheshire Oaks - Cheshire
**Vue, The Coliseum, Stannley Lane,
Ellesmere Port**
Tel: 0151 356 2261
Website: www.myvue.com
Seats: 1:341, 2:166, 3:124, 4:124,
5:166, 6:245, 7:272, 8:341, 9:272,
10:245, 11:166, 12:124, 13:124,
14:166, 15:341

## Chester - Cheshire
**Odeon, Northgate Street**
Tel: 0871 22 44 007
Website: www.odeon.co.uk
Seats: 1:406, 2:148, 3:148, 4:122, 5:122

**UGC, Chaser Court, Greyhound
Park, Sealand Road**
Tel: 01244 380155/0870 1555158
Website: www.ugccinemas.co.uk
Seats: 1:366, 2:366, 3:265, 4:232,
5:211, 6:211

## Chesterfield - Derbyshire
**Cineworld, Derby Road, Alma
Leisure Park**
Tel: 0246 229172/278000
Website: www.cineworld.co.uk
Seats: 1:245, 2:128, 3:107, 4:150,
5:291, 6:291, 7:150, 8:107, 9:128,
10:237

## Chichester - West Sussex
**Cineworld, Chichester Gate**
Tel: 01243 816800
Website: www.cineworld.co.uk

Seats: 1:222, 2: 222, 3:99, 4:165, 5:
295, 6: 257, 7:154, 8:125, 9:194,
10:222_

**Cinema at New Park, New Park Road**
Tel: 01243 786650
Website: www.chichestercinema.org
Seats: 120

## Chippenham - Wiltshire
**Astoria, Marshfield Road**
Tel: 01249 652498
Seats: 1:215, 2:215

## Chipping Norton - Oxfordshire
**The Theatre, Spring Street  (P/T)**
Tel: 01608 642349/642350
Seats: 213

## Christchurch - Dorset
**Regent Centre, High Street  (P/T)**
Tel: 01202 479819/499148
Seats: 485

## Cinderford - Gloucestershire
**Palace, Bellevue Road**
Tel: 01594 822555
Seats: 155
(Second auditorium under
construction in summer 2004)

## Clacton - Essex
**Flicks, Pier Avenue**
Tel: 01255 429627/421188
Seats: 1:625, 2:135

## Cleethorpes - Lincolnshire
**Parkway, Meridian Point**
Seats: (9 screens)
(Scheduled to open late 2004)

## Clevedon - Avon
**Curzon, Old Church Road**
Tel: 01275 871000
Seats: 340

## Clitheroe - Lancashire
**Grand, York Street**
Tel: 01200 423278
Seats: 400

## Colchester - Essex
**Odeon, Head Street**
Tel: 0871 22 44 007
Website: www.odeon.co.uk
Seats: 1:120, 2:168, 3:206, 4:119,
5:166, 6:305, 7:130, 8:207

## Coleford - Gloucestershire
**Studio, High Street**
Tel: 01594 833331
Website: www.circlecinemas.co.uk
Seats: 1:206, 2:82

## Consett - Co Durham
**Empire, Front Street**

Tel: 01207 218171
Seats: 535

## Cosham - Hants
**Carlton, High Street**
Tel: 023 92376635
Website: www.reeltime-cinemas.co.uk
Seats: 1:441 X, 2:118, 3:107

## Coventry - West Midlands
**Odeon, Sky Dome, Croft Road**
Tel: 0871 22 44 007
Website: www.odeon.co.uk
1:228, 2:415, 3:180, 4:359, 5:174,
6:137, 7:115, 8:163, 9:172

**Showcase, Junction 2, M6 Motorway,
Cross Point, Hinckley Road**
Tel: 0247 660 2111
Website: www.showcasecinemas.co.uk
Seats: 4,413 (14 screens)

**Warwick Arts Centre,
University of Warwick, Gibbet Hill
Road, CV4 7AL**
Tel: 0247 652 4524/3060
Website: www.warwickartscentre.co.uk
Seats: 240

## Crawley - West Sussex
**UGC, Crawley Leisure Park, London
Road**
Tel: 01293 537415/0870 9020411
Website: www.ugccinemas.co.uk
Seats: 1:236, 2:421, 3:186, 4:551,
5:186, 6:129, 7:129, 8:318, 9:173,
10:231, 11:184, 12:156, 13:173,
14:173, 15:70

## Crewe - Cheshire
**Apollo, High Street**
Tel: 01270 255708
Website: www.apollocinemas.co.uk
Seats: 1:107, 2:110, 3:91

## Cromer - Norfolk
**Regal, Hans Place**
Tel: 01263 513311
Seats: 1:129, 2:136, 3:66, 4:55

## Crosby - Merseyside
**Plaza, Crosby Road North, Waterloo**
Tel: 0151 474 4076
Seats: 1:600, 2:92, 3:74

## Darlington - Co Durham
**Arts Centre, Vane Terrace  (P/T)**
Tel: 01325 483168/483271/486555
Seats: 100

**Odeon, Northgate**
Tel: 0871 22 44 007
Website: www.odeon.co.uk
Seats: 1:579, 2:182, 3:124

## Dartington – Devon
**Barn Theatre, Arts Society, The**

Gallery, TQ9 6DE  (P/T)
Tel: 01803 865864/863073
Seats: 208

## Deal - Kent
Flicks, Queen Street
Tel: 01304 361165
Seats: 1:162, 2:99

## Derby - Derbyshire
Metro Cinema, Green Lane,
DE1 1SA
Tel: 01332 340170/347765
Seats: 128

Showcase, Forresters Park,
Osmaston Park Road at Sinfin Lane
Tel: 01332 270300
Website: www.showcasecinemas.co.uk
Seats: 2,557 (11 screens)

UCI, Meteor Centre 10, Mansfield
Road
Tel: 08700 10 20 30
**Website: www.uci-cinemas.co.uk**
Seats: 1:191, 2:188, 3:188, 4:191,
5:276, 6:276, 7:191, 8:188, 9:188,
10:191

## Dereham - Norfolk
Hollywood, Market Place
Tel: 01362 691133/691718
Website: www.hollywoodcinemas.net
Seats: 1:147, 2:95, 3:57

## Devizes - Wiltshire
Palace, Market Place
Tel: 01380 722971
Seats: 253

## Didcot – Oxfordshire
Cineworld, Station Road
**Seats: 900 (5 screens)**
(Scheduled to open in 2005)

## Didsbury – Greater Manchester
UGC, Parrs Wood Entertainment
Centre, East Didsbury
Tel: 0161 434 0909/0871 200 2000
Website: www.ugccinemas.co.uk
Seats: 1:592, 2:261, 3:181, 4:214,
5:235, 6:214, 7:186, 8:350, 9:193,
10:277, 11:145

## Doncaster - South Yorkshire
Civic Theatre, Waterdale (P/T)
Tel: 01302 62349
Seats: 547

Odeon, Hallgate
Tel: 0871 22 44 007
Website: www.odeon.co.uk
Seats: 1:975, 2:159, 3:161

Vue, Doncaster Leisure Park, Herten
Way, Bawtry Road
Tel: 01302 371020
Website: www.myvue.com
Seats: 1:224, 2:212, 3:252, 4:386,
5:252, 6:212, 7:224

## Dorchester - Dorset
Plaza, Trinity Street
Tel: 01305 262488
Website: www.reeltime-cinemas.co.uk
Seats: Premiere: 208, Century: 92

## Dorking - Surrey
Dorking Halls  (P/T)
Tel: 01306 881717
Seats: 198

## Douglas - Isle of Man
Broadway Cinema, Villa Marina,
Harris Promenade
Tel: 01624 684555
Website: www.gov.iom/villagaiety
Seats: 154

Palace Cinema
Tel: 01624 76814
Seats: 1:319, 2:120

## Dover - Kent
Silver Screen, White Cliffs
Experience, Gaol Lane
Tel: 01304 228000
Seats: 110

## Dronfield – South Yorks
Civic Hall (P/T)
Tel: 01246 418573
Seats: 200

## Dudley - West Midlands
Limelight Cinema, Black Country
Living Museum
Tel: 0121 557 9643
Seats: 100

Showcase, Castlegate Way, off
Birmingham Road
Tel: 01384 246500/246540
Website: www.showcasecinemas.co.uk
Seats: 2,850 (14 screens)

## Durham – Co Durham
Gala, Claypath
Tel: 0191 332 4041
Seats: 118
(Second part-time screen to seat
approximately 60 under construction
in summer 2004)

## Eastbourne - East Sussex
Curzon, Langney Road
Tel: 01323 731441
Seats: 1:530, 2:236, 3:236

UGC, Sovereign Harbour Retail Park
Tel: 01323 470070/0870 1555159

Website: www.ugccinemas.co.uk
Seats: 1:322, 2:312, 3:271, 4:254,
5:221, 6:221

## East Grinstead - West Sussex
King Street Picturehouse, Atrium
Building, King Street
Tel: 01342 321666
Website: www.picturehouses.co.uk
Seats: 1:240, 2:240

## Eastleigh - Hants
The Point Dance and Arts Centre,
Town Hall Centre, Leigh Road (P/T)
Tel: 023 8065 2333
Seats: 264

## Elland - North Yorkshire
Rex, Coronation Street
Tel: 01422 372140
Website: www.nm-cinemas.co.uk
Seats: 294

## Ely - Cambridgeshire
The Maltings, Ship Lane  (P/T)
Tel: 01353 666388
Website: www.picturehouses.co.uk
Seats: 200

## Epsom - Surrey
Odeon, Upper High Street
Tel: 0870 50 50 007
Website: www.odeon.co.uk
Seats: 1:320, 2:210, 3:271, 4:246,
5:172, 6:298, 7:242, 8:392

Playhouse, Ashley Avenue  (P/T)
Tel: 01372 742555/6
Seats: 300

## Esher - Surrey
Odeon, High Street
Tel: 0870 50 50 007
Website: www.odeon.co.uk
Seats: 1:524, 2:114, 3:114, 4:113

## Exeter - Devon
Northcott Theatre, Stocker Road
(P/T)
Tel: 01392 54853
Seats: 433

Odeon, Sidwell Street
Tel: 0871 22 44 007
Website: www.odeon.co.uk
Seats: 1:684, 2:120, 3:105, 4:324

Phoenix, Gandy Street (P/T)
**Tel: 01392 667080**
**Seats: 180**

Picturehouse, Bartholomew Street
West
Tel: 01392 435522
Website: www.picturehouses.co.uk
Seats: 1:220, 2:156

## Exmouth - Devon
Savoy Cinemas, Rolle Street
Tel: 01395 268220/272004
Website: www.scottcinemas.co.uk
Seats: 1:204, 2:100, 3:70

## Fakenham - Norfolk
Hollywood, The Market Place
Tel: 01328 856 466
Website: www.hollywoodcinemas.net
Seats: 1:118, 2:88, 3:60

## Falmouth - Cornwall
Arts Centre, Church Street  (P/T)
Tel: 01326 212300
Seats: 199

## Fareham - Hampshire
Apollo Cinemas
Seats: 1,600 (6 screens)
(Scheduled to open December 2004)

Ashcroft Arts Centre (P/T)
Tel: 01329 310600

Ferneham Hall, Osborn Road (P/T)
Tel: 01329 231942
Seats: 450

## Farnham - Surrey
Redgrave Theatre, Brightwell (P/T)
Tel: 01252 727 720
Seats: 362

## Faversham - Kent
New Royal, Market Place
Tel: 01795 535551
Seats: 448

## Felixstowe - Suffolk
Palace, Crescent Road
Tel: 01394 282787
Seats: 1:150, 2:90

## Folkestone - Kent
Silver Screen, Guildhall Street
Tel: 01303 221230
Seats: 1:435, 2:106

## Forest, Guernsey - Channel Islands
Mallard Cinema, Mallard Hotel, La Villiaze
Tel: 01481 64164
Seats: 1:154, 2:54, 3:75, 4:75

## Frome - Somerset
Westway, Cork Street
Tel: 01373 465685
Seats: 304

## Gainsborough - Lincolnshire
Trinity Arts Centre, Trinity Street (P/T)
Tel: 01427 810710
Seats: 210

## Gateshead - Tyne and Wear
UCI, Metro Centre
Tel: 08700 10 20 30
Website: www.uci-cinemas.co.uk
Seats: 1:200, 2:200, 3:228, 4:256, 5:374, 6:386, 7:256, 8:228, 9:200, 10:200, 11:534

## Gerrards Cross - Buckinghamshire
Odeon, Ethorpe Crescent
Tel: 0871 22 44 007
Website: www.odeon.co.uk
Seats: 1:325, 2:212

## Gloucester - Gloucestershire
Guildhall Arts Centre, Eastgate Street
Tel: 01452 505086/9
Seats: 1:120, 2:150(P/T)

New Olympus Theatre, Barton Street (P/T)
Tel: 01452 505089
Seats: 375

UGC, Peel Centre, St. Anns Way, Bristol Road
Tel: 01452 331181/0870 1555174
Website: www.ugccinemas.co.uk
Seats: 1:354, 2:354, 3:238, 4:238, 5:219, 6:219

## Godalming - Surrey
Borough Hall (P/T)
Tel: 01483 861111
Seats: 250

## Goole - Humberside
The Gate, Dunhill Road (P/T)
Tel: 01405 720219
Seats: 90

## Grantham - Lincolnshire
Paragon, St Catherine's Road
Tel: 01476 570046
Seats: 1:270, 2:160

## Grays - Essex
Thameside, Orsett Road  (P/T)
Tel: 01375 382555
Seats: 303

## Great Yarmouth - Norfolk
Hollywood, Marine Parade
Tel: 01493 842043/852600
Website: www.hollywoodcinemas.net
Seats: 1:240, 2:239, 3:193, 4:180, 5:127

## Grimsby - Lincolnshire
Odeon, Freeman Street
Tel: 01472 342878/349368
Website: www.odeon.co.uk
Seats: 1:392, 2:229, 3:126

Whitgift Film Theatre, Grimsby College (P/T)
Tel: 01472 88117
Seats: 200

## Guildford - Surrey
Odeon, Bedford Road
Tel: 0870 50 50 007
Website: www.odeon.co.uk
Seats: 1:422, 2:353, 3:269, 4:269, 5:293, 6:144, 7:108, 8:126, 9:126

## Hailsham - East Sussex
Pavilion, George Street (P/T)
Tel: 01323 841414
Seats: 203

## Halstead - Essex
Empire, Butler Road
Tel: 01787 477001
Seats: 320

## Hanley - Staffordshire
Forum Theatre,
Stoke-on-Trent City Museum,
Bethesda Street  (P/T)
Tel: 01782 232799
Seats: 300

## Harlow - Essex
Odeon, West Square
Tel: 0871 22 44 007
Website: www.odeon.co.uk
Seats: 1:399, 2:217, 3:179

Playhouse, The High (P/T)
Tel: 01279 431945
Seats: 330

UGC, Queensgate Centre, Edinburgh Way
Tel: 01279 436014/0871 200 2000
Website: www.ugccinemas.co.uk
Seats: 1:356, 2:260, 3:240, 4:234, 5:233, 6:230

## Harrogate - North Yorkshire
Odeon, East Parade
Tel: 0871 22 44 007
Website: www.odeon.co.uk
Seats: 1:298,  2:242, 3:101, 4:76, 5:329

## Hartlepool - Cleveland
Vue, The Lanyard, Marina Way
Tel: 01429 261 177
Website: www.myvue.com
Seats: 1:303, 2:345, 3:160, 4:204, 5:431, 6:204, 7:160

## Harwich - Essex
Electric Palace, King's Quay Street (P/T)
Tel: 01255 553333
Seats: 204

## Haslemere - Surrey
Haslemere Hall, Bridge Road  (P/T)

Tel: 01428 661793
Seats: 350

## Hastings - East Sussex
Electric Palace, 39a High Street (P/T)
Tel: 01424 720393
Website:
www.electricpalacecinema.com
Seats: 70

Odeon, Queens Road
Tel: 0870 50 50 007
Website: www.odeon.co.uk
Seats: 1:125, 2:172, 3:151, 4:127

## Hatfield - Herts
UCI, The Galleria, Comet Way
Tel: 08700 10 20 30
Website: www.uci-cinemas.co.uk
Seats: 1:162, 2:228, 3:263, 4:167,
5:183, 6:183, 7:260, 8:378, 9:165

## Havant - Hants
Arts Centre, East Street (P/T)
Tel: 023 92472700
Seats: 130

## Haverhill - Suffolk
Arts Centre, Town Hall, High Street
(P/T)
Tel: 01440 714140
Seats: 210

## Hayling Island - Hants
Hiads Theatre, Station Road (P/T)
Tel: 02392 466363
Seats: 150

## Haywards Heath - West Sussex
Clair Hall, Perrymount Road (P/T)
Tel: 01444 455440/454394
Website: www.midsussex.gov.uk
Seats: 350

## Heaton Moor - Greater Manchester
Savoy, Heaton Moor Road
Tel: 0161 432 2114
Seats: 476

## Hebden Bridge - West Yorkshire
Picture House, New Road
Tel: 01422 842807
Seats: 493

## Helmsley - North Yorkshire
Helmsley Arts Centre, The Old
Meeting House (P/T)
Tel: 01439 771700
Seats: 131

## Helston – Cornwall
Flora, Wendron Street
Tel: 01326 569977
Website: www.merlincinemas.co.uk
Seats: 78

## Hemel Hempstead - Herts
Odeon, Leisure World, Jarmans Park
Tel: 0871 22 44 007
Website: www.odeon.co.uk
Seats: 1:130, 2:183, 3:183, 4:317,
5:261, 6:431, 7:166, 8:161

## Henley-on-Thames - Oxfordshire
Kenton Theatre, New Street (P/T)
Tel: 01491 575698
Seats: 240

Regal, Broma Way, off Bell Street
Tel: 01491 414150
Seats: 1:152, 2:101, 3:85

## Hereford - Hereford & Worcs
Odeon, Commercial Road
Tel: 01432 272554
Website: www.odeon.co.uk
Seats: 336

The Courtyard Theatre and Arts
Centre, Edgar Street (P/T)
Tel: 01432 359252
Seats: 1:364, Studio:124

## Herne Bay - Kent
Kavanagh, William Street
Tel: 01227 362228
Website: www.reeltime-cinemas.co.uk
Seats: 1:135, 2:93

## Hexham - Northumberland
Forum, Market Place
Tel: 01434 601144
Seats: 207

## High Wycombe - Buckinghamshire
thefilmworks, Crest Road, Cressex
Website: www.uci-cinemas.co.uk
Tel: 0870 010 2030
Seats: 1:209, 2:286, 3:356, 4:356,
5:286, 6:209

## Hoddesdon - Herts
Broxbourne Civic Hall, High Street
(P/T)
Tel: 01992 441946/31
Seats: 564

## Hollinwood - Greater Manchester
Roxy, Hollins Road
Tel: 0161 681 1441/4000
Website: www.roxycinema.co.uk
Seats: 1:470, 2:130, 3:260, 4:260,
5:320, 6:96, 7:140

## Holmfirth – West Yorks
Picturedrome
Tel: 01484 689759

## Horsham - West Sussex
The Capitol, North Street
01403 750220/756080
www.thecapitolhorsham.com
Seats: 1:423 (P/T), 2:174, 3: 89

## Horwich - Lancashire
Leisure Centre, Victoria Road (P/T)
Tel: 01204 692211
Seats: 400

## Hucknall - Notts
Cineplex, High Street
Tel: 0115 963 6377
Seats: 430

## Huddersfield – West Yorkshire
UCI, McAlpine Stadium, Bradley
Mills Road
Tel: 08700 10 20 30
Website: www.uci-cinemas.co.uk
Seats: 1:142, 2:268, 3:176, 4:296,
5:371, 6:296, 7:176, 8:268, 9:142

## Hull - Humberside
Odeon, Kingston Street
Tel: 0871 22 44 007
Website: www.odeon.co.uk
Seats: 1:169, 2:169, 3:148, 4:170,
5:458, 6:272, 7:132, 8:148, 9:108,
10:88
Screen, Central Library, Albion
Street HU1 3TF
Tel: 01482 327600
Seats: 247

UCI, St Andrew's Quay, Clive
Sullivan Way
Tel: 08700 10 20 30
Website: www.uci-cinemas.co.uk
Seats: 1:166, 2:152, 3:236, 4:292,
5:292, 6:236, 7:152, 8:166

UGC, Kingswood Leisure Park,
Ennerdale Link Road
Tel: 01482 835035/0871 200 2000
Website: www.ugccinemas.co.uk
Seats: 1:165, 2:211, 3:253, 4:498,
5:253, 6:211, 7:165, 8:165, 9:98

## Hunstanton - Norfolk
Princess Theatre, The Green (P/T)
Tel: 01485 532252
Seats: 467

## Huntingdon - Cambridgeshire
Cineworld, Towerfields, Abbot's
Ripton Road
Tel: 01480 412255
Website: www.cineworld.co.uk
Seats: 1:224, 2:126, 3:90, 4:125, 5:110,
6:317, 7:284, 8:208, 9:208, 10:101

## Ilfracombe - Devon
The Landmark Theatre, Wilder Road (P/T)
Tel: 01271 324242
Seats: 175

Pendle Stairway, High Street
Tel: 01271 863260
Seats: 382

## Ilkeston - Derbyshire
Scala, Market Place
Tel: 0115 932 4612
Seats: 500

## Ipswich – Suffolk
Film Theatre, Corn Exchange, King Street, IP1 1DH
Tel: 01473 433100
Website: www.ipswich-ents.co.uk
Seats: 1:220, 2:40

Odeon, St Margaret's Street
Tel: 0871 22 44 007
Website: www.odeon.co.uk
Seats: 1:510, 2:313, 3:281, 4:210, 5:210

UGC, Cardinal Park, 11 Grafton Way
Tel: 01473 254978/0871 200 2000
Website: www.ugccinemas.co.uk
Seats: 1:168, 2:186, 3:168, 4:270, 5:179, 6:510, 7:238, 8:398, 9:186, 10:168, 11:83

## Keighley - West Yorkshire
Picture House
Tel: 01535 602561
Website: www.nm-cinemas.co.uk
Seats: 1:364, 2:95

## Kendal - Cumbria
Brewery Arts Centre, Highgate, LA9 4HE (S/O)
Tel: 01539 725133
Seats: 1:192, 2:115, Theatre (P/T) 250

## Keswick - Cumbria
Alhambra, St John Street
Tel: 017687 72195
Seats: 270

## Kettering - Northants
Odeon, Pegasus Court, Wellingborough Road
Tel: 0871 22 44 007
Website: www.odeon.co.uk
Seats: 1:173, 2:123, 3:229, 4:345, 5:103, 6:81, 7:103, 8:307

## Kingsbridge - Devon
The Reel Cinema, Fore Street
Tel: 01548 856636
Seats: 162

## King's Lynn - Norfolk
Arts Centre, King Street (P/T)
Tel: 01553 764864/765565
Seats: 314

Majestic, Tower Street
Tel: 01553 772603
Seats: 1:450, 2:123, 3:400

## Kirkby in Ashfield - Nottinghamshire
Cineplex, Kingsway
**Tel: 01623 751944**
Website: www.cineplexcinemas.com
Seats: 200

## Knutsford - Cheshire
Studio, Civic Centre, Toft Road
Tel: 01565 633005
Website: www.macclesfield.gov.uk
Seats: 174

## Lancaster - Lancashire
Regal, King Street
Tel: 01524 64141
Website: www.nm-cinemas.co.uk
Seats: 1:250, 2:246

The Dukes Cinema, Moor Lane, LA1 1QE (P/T)
Tel: 01524 598500
Seats: 307

## Leamington Spa - Warwicks
Apollo, Portland Place
Tel: 01926 427448
Website: www.apollocinemas.co.uk
Seats: 1:309, 2:199, 3:138, 4:112, 5:120, 6:120

Royal, Spa Centre, Newbold Terrace
Tel: 01926 887726/888997
Seats: 208

## Leeds - West Yorkshire
Cottage Road Cinema, Headingley
Tel: 0113 275 2001
Website: www.lounge-cinema.co.uk
Seats: 468

Hyde Park Picture House, Brudenell Road
Tel: 0113 275 2045
Website: www.leedscinema.com
Seats: 360

Lounge, North Lane, Headingley
Tel: 0113 275 2001
Website: www.lounge-cinema.co.uk
Seats: 691

Showcase, Junction 27, M62, Gelderd Road, Birstall, Batley
Tel: 01924 420 071

Website: www.showcasecinemas.co.uk
Seats: 4,250 (16 screens)

Ster Century, 22 The Light, The Headrow
**Tel: 0870 240 3696**
Website: www.stercentury.com
**Seats: 1:143, 2:142, 3:193, 4:189, 5:205, 6:236, 7:153, 8:192, 9:260, 10:260, 11:260, 12:328, 13:328**

Vue, Cardigan Fields, Kirkstall Road
Tel: 0870 240 6020/0113 279 9855
Website: www.myvue.com
Seats: 1:345, 2:124, 3:166, 4:245, 5:252, 6:245, 7:166, 8:124, 9:345

## Leicester - Leicestershire
Belle Vue, Abbey Street
Tel: 0116 262 0005
Seats: 1:250, 2:180

Odeon, Aylestone Road, Freemens Park
Tel: 0871 22 44 007
Website: www.odeon.co.uk
Seats: 1:129, 2:165, 3:154, 4:239, 5:230, 6:362, 7:332, 8:230, 9:239, 10:154, 11:165, 12:127

Phoenix Arts, 21 Upper Brown Street, LE1 5TE (P/T)
Tel: 0116 255 4854/255 5627
Seats: 274

Piccadilly, Green Lane Road
Tel: 0116 251 8880
Seats: 1:440, 2:120, 3:80

Vue, Meridian Leisure Park, Lubbesthorpe Way, Braunstone
Tel: 0116 289 4001
Website: www.myvue.com
Seats: 1:423, 2:158, 3:189, 4:266, 5:306, 6:266, 7:202, 8:158, 9:423

## Leighton Buzzard - Bedfordshire
Theatre, Lake Street (P/T)
Tel: 01525 378310
Seats: 170

## Leiston - Suffolk
Film Theatre, High Street
Tel: 01728 830549
Seats: 288

## Letchworth - Herts
Broadway, Eastcheap
Tel: 01462 681 223
Seats: 1:488, 2:176, 3:174

## Leyburn - North Yorkshire
Elite, Railway Street (P/T)
Tel: 01969 624488
Seats: 173

**Lincoln - Lincolnshire**
Odeon, Brayford Wharf
Tel: 0871 22 44 007
Website: www.odeon.co.uk
Seats: 1:169, 2:163, 3:410, 4:160,
5:169, 6:213, 7:265, 8:360, 9:102

**Littlehampton – West Sussex**
Windmill Entertainment Centre,
Church Street (P/T)
Tel: 01903 722224
Seats: 213

**Liverpool - Merseyside**
Odeon, Allerton Road
Tel: 0151 724 3550/5095
Website: www.odeon.co.uk
Seats: 490

Odeon, London Road
Tel: 0871 22 44 007
Website: www.odeon.co.uk
Seats: 1:482, 2:154, 3:157, 4:149,
5:211, 6:128, 7:132, 8:123, 9:191,
10:132

Philharmonic Hall, Hope Street
(P/T)
Tel: 0151 709 2895/3789
Seats: 1,627

Picturehouse at FACT, Wood Street
Tel: 0151 707 4450
Website: www.picturehouses.co.uk
Seats: 1:264, 2:144, 3:104, 4:50

Showcase, East Lancashire Road,
Norris Green
Tel: 0151 549 2021
Website: www.showcasecinemas.co.uk
Seats: 3,415 (12 screens)

UGC, Edge Lane Retail Park, Binns
Road
Tel: 0151 252 0551/0870 1555146
Website: www.ugccinemas.co.uk
Seats: 1:356, 2:354, 3:264, 4:264,
5:220, 6:220, 7:198, 8:200

Woolton, Mason Street
Tel: 0151 428 1919
Seats: 256

**Longridge - Lancashire**
Palace, Market Place
Tel: 01772 785600
Seats: 200

**Loughborough - Leicestershire**
Curzon, Cattle Market
Tel: 01509 212261
Seats: 1:418, 2:303, 3:199, 4:186,
5:140, 6:80

**Louth - Lincolnshire**
Playhouse, Cannon Street
Tel: 01507 603333
Seats: 1:215, 2:158, 3:78

**Lowestoft - Suffolk**
Hollywood, London Road South
Tel: 01502 588355/564567
Website: www.hollywoodcinemas.net
Seats: 1:200, 2:175, 3:65, 4:40

Marina Theatre, The Marina  (P/T)
Tel: 01502 533200/573318
Seats: 751

**Ludlow - Shropshire**
Assembly Rooms, Mill Street (P/T)
Tel: 01584 878141
Seats: 320

**Luton - Bedfordshire**
Cineworld, The Galaxy, Bridge
Street
Tel: 01582 401092/400705
Website: www.cineworld.co.uk
Seats: 1:114, 2:75, 3:112, 4:284, 5:419,
6:212, 7:123, 8:217, 9:137, 10:213,
11:240

Library Theatre, Central Library
(P/T)
Tel: 01582 547474
Seats: 238

The Hat Factory, Bute Street (P/T)
Tel: 01582 878100
Seats: 96

**Lyme Regis - Dorset**
Regent, Broad Street
Tel: 01297 442053
Website: www.scottcinemas.co.uk
Seats: 400

**Lymington - Hants**
Community Centre, New Street
(P/T)
Tel: 01590 676939
Seats: 110

**Lytham St. Annes - Lancashire**
Cinema 4, Pleasure Island, South
Promenade
Tel: 01253 780085
Seats: 1:170, 2:92, 3:117, 4:105

**Lynton – Devon**
Lynton Cinema, Lee Road
Tel: 01598 753397
Seats: 100

**Mablethorpe - Lincolnshire**
Loewen, Quebec Road
Tel: 0150 747 7040
Seats: 1:203, 2:80

**Maidenhead – Berkshire**
Nordern Farm Centre for the Arts
Tel: 01628 788997

thefilmworks, 42-44 King Street
Tel: 08700 10 20 30
Website: www.uci-cinemas.co.uk
Seats: 1:282, 2:268, 3:143, 4:115,
5:205, 6:183, 7:89, 8:130

**Maidstone - Kent**
Odeon, Lockmeadow
Tel: 0871 22 44 007
Website: www.odeon.co.uk
Seats: 1:86, 2:89, 3:127, 4:111, 5:240,
6:240, 7:398, 8:347

**Malton – North Yorkshire**
Ryedale Palace, The Lanes
Tel: 01653 600 008/698 899
Seats: 142

**Malvern - Hereford & Worcs**
Malvern Theatres, Grange Road
Tel: 01684 569256
Seats: 374, (Forum Theatre P/T) 800

**Manchester - Greater Manchester**
AMC, Great Northern Warehouse,
Deansgate & Peter Street
Tel: 0161 817 3000
Website: www.amccinemas.co.uk
Seats: 1:411, 2:476, 3:236, 4:411,
5:164, 6:164, 7:102, 8:123, 9:125,
10:157, 11:243, 12: 254, 13: 157,
14:133, 15:123, 16:102

Cornerhouse, 70 Oxford Street, M1
5NH
Tel: 0161 200 1500
Website: www.cornerhouse.org
Seats: 1:300, 2:170, 3:60

Odeon, Oxford Street
Tel: 0871 22 44 007
Website: www.odeon.co.uk
Seats: 1:617, 2:364, 3:143, 4:97, 5:201,
6:142, 7:86

Showcase, Hyde Road, Belle Vue
Tel: 0161 220 8765
Website: www.showcasecinemas.co.uk
Seats: 3,191 (14 screens)

TheFilmWorks, The Printworks,
Exchange Square
Tel: 08 700 10 20 30
Website: www.thefilmworks.co.uk
Seats: 1 (IMAX):382, 2: 222, 3:126,
4:144, 5:144, 6:144, 7:126, 8:222,
9:126, 10:144, 11:236, 12:377, 13:428,
14:168, 15:144, 16:144, 17:328,
18:570, 19:126, 20:126

UCI, Trafford Centre, The Dome,
Dumplington
Tel: 08700 10 20 30
Website: www.uci-cinemas.co.uk
Seats: 1:112, 2:112, 3:112, 4:112,
5:152, 6:152, 7:415, 8:173, 9:173,
10:173, 11:142, 12:231, 13:347,
14:283, 15:231, 16:142, 17:173,
18:173, 19:173, 20:415

## Mansfield - Notts
Odeon, Mansfield Leisure Park, Park
Lane
Tel: 0871 22 44 007
Website: www.odeon.co.uk
Seats: 1:390, 2:390, 3:246, 4:246,
5:221, 6:221, 7:193, 8:193

## March – Cambridgeshire
Hippodrome, Dartford Road
Tel: 01354 653178
Seats: 96

## Margate - Kent
Dreamland, Marine Parade
Tel: 01843 227822
Website: www.reeltime-cinemas.co.uk
Seats: 1:378, 2:376

## Marple - Greater Manchester
Regent, Stockport Road
Tel: 0161 427 5951
Seats: 285

## Market Drayton - Shropshire
Royal Festival Centre  (P/T)
Seats: 165

## Melton Mowbray - Leicestershire
Regal, King Street
Tel: 01664 562251
Seats: 226

## Middlesbrough - Cleveland
UGC, Leisure Park, Marton Road
Tel: 01642 247766/0871 200 2000
Website: www.ugccinemas.co.uk
Seats: 1:204, 2:151, 3:141, 4:271,
5:401, 6:204, 7:125, 8:141, 9:230,
10:271, 11:402

## Milton Keynes - Buckinghamshire
Cineworld, Xscape, Marlborough
Gate
Tel: 01908 230 088
Website: www.cineworld.co.uk
Seats: 1:137, 2:234, 3:205, 4:170,
5:214, 6:281, 7:304, 8:158, 9:158,
10:316, 11:281, 12: 214, 13:170, 14:
205, 15: 234, 16:135

easycinema, The Point, Midsummer
Boulevard

Website: www.easycinema.com
Seats: 1:156, 2:169, 3:250, 4:222,
5:222, 6:222, 7:222, 8:250, 9:169,
10:156

## Minehead – Somerset
ABC, Summerwest World
Tel: 0870 50 50 007
Seats: 218

## Morecambe – Lancashire
Apollo, Central Drive
Tel: 01524 426642
Website: www.apollocinemas.co.uk
Seats: 1:207, 2:207, 3:106, 4:106

## Nailsea - Avon
Cinema, Scotch Horn Leisure
Centre, Brockway (P/T)
Tel: 01275 856965
Seats: 250

## Nantwich - Cheshire
Civic Hall, Market Street  (P/T)
Tel: 01270 628633
Seats: 300

## Newark - Notts
Palace Theatre, Appleton Gate  (P/T)
Tel: 01636 655755
Seats: 351

## Newbury – Berkshire
Apollo Cinemas
Seats: 1,400 (5 screens)
(Scheduled to open July 05)

Corn Exchange, Market Place (P/T)
Tel: 01635 522733
Seats: 370

## Newcastle-under-Lyme - Staffordshire
Vue, The Square, High Street
Tel: 0178 271 4335
Website: www.myvue.com
Seats: 1:242, 2:236, 3:272, 4:319,
5:373, 6:206, 7:198, 8:241

## Newcastle-upon-Tyne - Tyne and Wear
Odeon, The Gate, Newgate Street
Tel: 0871 22 44 007
Website: www.odeon.co.uk
Seats: 1:436, 2:102, 3:273, 4:346,
5:130, 6:160, 7:199, 8:67, 9:120,
10:318, 11:157, 12: 230
Tyneside, 10-12 Pilgrim Street, NE1
6QG
Tel: 0191 232 8289
Seats: 1:296, 2:122

## Newport - Isle of Wight
Cineworld, Coppins Bridge
Tel: 01983 550800
Website: www.cineworld.co.uk
1:300, 2:96, 3:202, 4:178, 5:152, 6:101,

7:84, 8:132, 9:169, 10:195, 11:263

Medina Movie Theatre,
Mountbatten Centre, Fairlee Road
(P/T)
Tel: 01983 527 020
Seats: 419

## Newton Abbot - Devon
Alexandra Cinemas, Market Street
Tel: 01626 365368
Website: www.scottcinemas.co.uk
Seats: 1:206, 2:127

## Northampton – Northants
Forum Cinema, Lings Forum,
Weston Favell Centre, NN3 4JR
(P/T)
Tel: 01604 401006/402833
Seats: 270

Vue, Sol Central, Doddridge Street
Tel: 08712 240 240
Website: www.myvue.com
Seats: 1:444, 2:256, 3:167, 4:162,
5:198, 6:262, 7:418, 8:278, 9:181,
10:181

UGC, Sixfields Leisure Park, Weedon
Road, Upton
Tel: 01604 580880/0870 1560564
Website: www.ugccinemas.co.uk
Seats: 1:452, 2:287, 3:287, 4:207,
5:207, 6:147, 7:147, 8:147, 9:147

## Northwich - Cheshire
Regal, London Road
Tel: 01606 43130
Seats: 1:797, 2::200

## Norwich - Norfolk
Cinema City at the Playhouse, St.
George's Street
Tel: 01603 625145/622047
Website: www.cinemacity.co.uk
Seats: 308
(Temporary home - returning to St.
Andrew's Street with two additional
screens from early 2005)

Hollywood, Anglia Square
Tel: 01603 621903/767737
Website: www.hollywoodcinemas.net
Seats: 1:442, 2:197, 3:195

Ster Century, Level 4, Castle Mall
Tel: 01603 221 900
Website: www.stercentury.com
Seats: 1:170, 2:143, 3:216, 4:324,
5:313, 6:294, 7:331, 8:126

UCI, Riverside Leisure Park, Wherry
Road
Tel: 08700 10 20 30
Website: www.uci-cinemas.co.uk
Seats: 1:172, 2:349, 3:127, 4:142,

5:159, 6:272, 7:464, 8:247, 9:159, 10:142, 11:142, 12:159, 13:247, 14:212

## Nottingham - Notts
**Broadway, 14-18 Broad Street, NG1 3AL**
Tel: 0115 952 6600/952 6611
Website: www.broadway.org.uk
Seats: 1:337, 2:130
(Two additional auditoria seating approximately 100 each are scheduled to open in June 2005)

**Savoy, Derby Road**
Tel: 0115 947 2580/941 9123
Seats: 1:386, 2:128, 3:168

**Screen Room, 25 Broad Street, Hockley**
Tel: 0115 924 1133
Website: www.screenroom.co.uk
Seats: 21

**Showcase, Clifton Boulevard (A52)**
Tel: 0115 986 6766
Website: www.showcasecinemas.co.uk
Seats: 3,307 (12 screens)

**UGC, Corner House, 29 Forman Street**
Tel: 0871 2002000
Website: www.ugccinemas.co.uk
Seats: 1:368, 4:108, 5:146, 6:146, 7:130, 8:237, 9:139, 10:590, 11:108, 12:146, 13:146, 14:130
(Screens 2 & 3 not in use in summer 2004)

## Nuneaton - Warwicks
**Odeon, St. David's Way, Bermuda Park**
Tel: 0870 50 50 007
Website: www.odeon.co.uk
Seats: 1:471, 2:386, 3:314, 4:314, 5:253, 6:253, 7:210, 8:210

## Okehampton - Devon
**Carlton, St James Street**
Tel: 01837 52167
Seats: 380
(Closed at mid-2004)

## Oxford - Oxfordshire
**Odeon, George Street**
Tel: 0871 22 44 007
Website: www.odeon.co.uk
Seats: 1:252, 2:252, 3:111, 4:140, 5:239, 6:129

**Odeon, Magdalen Street**
Tel: 0871 22 44 007
Website: www.odeon.co.uk
Seats: 1:647, 2:61

**Ozone Multiplex Cinema, Ozone Leisure Park, Grenoble Road**
Tel: 0870 444 30 30
Website: www.ozonemultiplex.com
Seats: 1,800 (9 screens)

**Phoenix Picturehouse, 57 Walton Street**
Tel: 01865 512526
Website: www.picturehouses.co.uk
Seats: 1:220, 2:105

**Ultimate Picture Palace, Jeune Street**
Tel: 01865 245288
Seats: 185

## Oxted - Surrey
**The Screen, Station Road West**
Tel: 01883 722288
Website: www.screencinemas.co.uk
Seats: 442

## Padstow - Cornwall
**Cinedrome, Lanadwell Street**
Tel: 01841 532344
Seats: 183

## Paignton - Devon
**Apollo, Esplanade**
Tel: 01803 558822
Website: www.apollocinemas.co.uk
Seats: 1:360, 2:360, 3: 181, 4;181, 5:217, 6:85, 7:83, 8:77, 9:86

## Penistone - South Yorkshire
**Paramount, Town Hall**
Tel: 01226 762004
Seats: 348

## Penrith - Cumbria
**Alhambra, Middlegate**
Tel: 01768 862400
Seats: 1:167, 2:90

**Rhegel Discovery Centre**
Tel: 01768 868000
Seats: 258 (large screen format)

## Penzance - Cornwall
**Savoy, Causeway Head**
Tel: 01736 363330
Website: www.merlincinemas.co.uk
Seats: 1:200, 2:50, 3:50

## Peterborough – Cambridgeshire
**Broadway, 46 Broadway (P/T)**
Tel: 01733 316100
Seats: 1,200

**Showcase, Frank Perkins Parkway, Mallory Road, Boongate**
Tel: 01733 558 498
Website: www.showcasecinemas.co.uk
Seats: 3,365 (13 screens)

## Pickering - North Yorkshire
**Castle, 10-11 Burgate**
Tel: 01751 472622
Seats: 180

## Plymouth - Devon
**ABC, Derry's Cross**
Tel: 01752 663300/225553
Seats: 1:582, 2:380, 3:115

**Arts Centre, Looe Street**
Tel: 01752 206114
Seats: 73

**Vue, Barbican Leisure Centre, Shapters Road, Coxside**
Tel: 01752 670 084
Website: www.myvue.com
Seats: 1:167, 2:189, 3:152, 4:185, 5:187, 6:132, 7:283, 8:442, 9:479, 10:258, 11:208, 12:131, 13:126, 14:197, 15:178

## Pocklington – East Yorks
**Oak House, Pocklington Civic Arts Centre, Market Place (P/T)**
Tel: 01759 301547
Seats: 200

## Poole - Dorset
**The Cinema, Poole Centre for the Arts, Kingland Road**
Tel: 01202 685222
Seats: 103

**UCI, Tower Park, Mannings Heath**
Tel: 08700 10 20 30
Website: www.uci-cinemas.co.uk
Seats: 1:194, 2:188, 3:188, 4:194, 5:276, 6:276, 7:194, 8:188, 9:188, 10:196

## Portsmouth - Hants
**Odeon, London Road, North End**
Tel: 0871 22 44 007
Website: www.odeon.co.uk
Seats: 1:631, 2:227, 3:175, 4:259

**UCI, Port Way, Port Solent**
Tel: 08700 10 20 30
Website: www.uci-cinemas.co.uk
Seats: 1:218, 2:265, 3:342, 4:265, 5:260, 6:190

**Vue, Gunwharf Quays**
Tel: 02392 827 644
Website: www.myvue.com
1:230, 2:332, 3:430, 4:332, 5:230, 6:128, 7:110, 8:110, 9:246, 10:175, 11:193, 12:377, 13:167, 14:155

## Potters Bar - Herts
**Wyllyotts Centre, Darkes Lane  (P/T)**
Tel: 01707 645005
Seats: 345

## Preston – Lancashire
UCI, Riversway, Ashton-on-Ribble
Tel: 08700 10 20 30
Website: www.uci-cinemas.co.uk
Seats: 1:194, 2:188, 3:188, 4:194,
5:276, 6:276, 7:194, 8:188, 9:188,
10:194

Vue, The Capitol Centre, London
Way, Walton-le-Dale
Tel: 01772 882 525
Website: www.myvue.com
Seats: 1:180, 2:180, 3:412, 4:236,
5:236, 6:412, 7:192

## Quinton - West Midlands
Odeon, Hagley Road West
Tel: 0121 422 2562/2252
Website: www.odeon.co.uk
Seats: 1:300, 2:236, 3:232, 4:121

## Ramsey - Cambridgeshire
Grand, Great Whyte  (P/T)
Tel: 01487 813778
Seats: 173

## Ramsgate - Kent
Granville Premier, Victoria Parade
(P/T)
Tel: 01843 591750
**Seats: 1:210, 2:230**

## Reading - Berkshire
(see also Wokingham)

Film Theatre, Whiteknights  (P/T)
Tel: 0118 986 8497
Seats: 409

The Hexagon, South Street (P/T)
Tel: 0118 960 6060
Seats: 450

Vue, The Riverside, The Oracle
Shopping Centre
Tel: 0118 956 0047
Website: www.myvue.com
Seats: 1:134, 2:147, 3:251, 4:373, 5:191,
6:191, 7:232, 8:148, 9:118, 10:88

## Redcar - Cleveland
Regent, The Esplanade
Tel: 01642 482094
Seats: 350

## Redhill - Surrey
The Harlequin, Warwick Quadrant
(P/T)
Tel: 01737 765547
Seats: 494

## Redruth - Cornwall
Regal Film Centre, Fore Street
Tel: 01209 216278
Website: www.merlincinemas.co.uk
Seats: 1:171, 2:121, 3:600, 4:95

## Reigate - Surrey
The Screen, Bancroft Road
Tel: 01737 223200
Website: www.screencinemas.co.uk
Seats: 1:139, 2:142

## Rickmansworth - Herts
Watersmeet Theatre, High Street  (P/T)
Tel: 01923 771542
Seats: 390

## Rochdale - Greater Manchester
Odeon, Sandbrook Way, Sandbrook
Park
Tel: 0871 22 44 007
Website: www.odeon.co.uk
Seats: 1:474, 2:311, 3:311, 4:236,
5:208, 6:208, 7:208, 8:165, 9:165

## Rochester - Kent
UGC, Chariot Way, Medway Valley
Leisure Park, Strood
Tel: 01634 719963/0870 1560568
Website: www.ugccinemas.co.uk
Seats: 1:485, 2:310, 3:310, 4:217,
5:220, 6:199, 7:199, 8:92, 9:142

## Rubery - West Midlands
UGC, Great Park
Tel: 0121 4530465/0871 200 2000
Website: www.ugccinemas.co.uk
Seats: 1:165, 2:187, 3:165, 4:149,
5:288, 6:194, 7:523, 8:247, 9:400
10:149 11:187 12:165, 13:82

## Rugby - Warwicks
Cineworld, Junction One Retail &
Leisure Park, Junction One, Leicester
Road
Tel: 01788 551110
Website: www.cineworld.co.uk
Seats: 1:222, 2:95, 3:131, 4:120, 5:311,
6:290, 7:202, 8:131, 9:96

## Runcorn - Cheshire
Cineworld, Trident Park, Halton Lea
Tel: 01928 759811
Website: www.cineworld.co.uk
Seats: 1:127, 2:121, 3:94, 4:87, 5:317,
6:283, 7:164, 8:184, 9:214

## Ryde - Isle of Wight
Commodore, Star Street
Tel: 01983 564064
Website: www.reeltime-cinemas.co.uk
Seats: 1:180, 2:180, 3:180

## St Albans - Herts
Alban Arena, Civic Centre (P/T)
Tel: 01727 844488
Seats: 800

## St Austell - Cornwall
Film Centre, Chandos Place
Tel: 01726 73750
Seats: 1:274, 2:134, 3:133, 4:70, 5:70

## St Helens - Merseyside
Cineworld, Chalon Way West
Tel: 01744 616576
**Website: www.cineworld.co.uk**
Seats: 1:180, 2:139, 3:210, 4:180,
5:115, 6:103, 7:129, 8:94, 9:283,
10:302, 11:269

## St Helier Jersey - Channel Islands
Cine Centre, Lido de France, St
Saviour's Road
Tel: 01534 871611
Seats: 1:300, 2:85, 3:47, 4:400

Cineworld, Waterfront Centre
Tel: 01534 756200
Website: www.cineworld.co.uk
Seats: 1:303, 2:203, 3:189, 4:124, 5:91,
6:117, 7:139,  8:207, 9:242, 10:172

Odeon, Bath Street
Tel: 0871 22 44 007
Website: www.odeon.co.uk
Seats: 1:409, 2:247, 3:184, 4:162

## St Ives - Cornwall
Royal, Royal Square
Tel: 01736 796843
Website: www.merlincinemas.co.uk
Seats: 1:409, 2:244, 3:213, 4:171

## Salford Quays – Greater Manchester
The Red Cinema, The Designer
Outlet at the Lowry, The Quays,
Salford Quays
Tel: 08702 40 60 20/0161 872 1797
Website: www.myvue.com
Seats: 1:566, 3:318, 4:207, 5:44, 7:224,
8:314, 9:210 (Screens 2 & 6 not in use
in summer 2004)

## Salisbury - Wiltshire
Odeon, New Canal
Tel: 0871 22 44 007
Website: www.odeon.co.uk
Seats: 1:471, 2:276, 3:127, 4:111, 5:70

## Sandwich - Kent
Empire, Delf Street
Tel: 01304 620480
Seats: 130

## Scarborough - North Yorkshire
Futurist, Forshaw Road  (P/T)
Tel: 01723 370541
Seats: 1,200

Plaza, 159 North Marine Road
Tel: 01723 507567
Seats: 275

Stephen Joseph Theatre,
Westborough (P/T)

Tel: 01723 370541
Seats: 165 (McCarthy Auditorium)

YMCA Theatre, St Thomas Street
(P/T)
Tel: 01723 506750
Seats: 290

## Scunthorpe - Humberside
Screen, Central Library, Carlton
Street, DN15 6TX (P/T)
Tel: 01724 860190/860161
Seats: 253

Vue, 1 Fenton Street
Tel: 08700 10 20 30
Website: www.myvue.com
Seats: 1:251, 2:249, 3:306, 4:162,
5:175, 6:175, 7:205

## Sevenoaks - Kent
Stag Cinemas, London Road
Tel: 01732 450175/451548
Seats: 1:126, 2:108, Theatre (P/T) 450

## Shaftesbury - Dorset
Arts Centre, Bell Street  (P/T)
Tel: 01747 854321
Seats: 160

## Sheffield - South Yorkshire
The Showroom, Media and
Exhibition Centre, Paternoster Row,
S1 2BX
Tel: 0114 275 7727
Website: www.showroom.org.uk
Seats: 1:83, 2:110, 3:178, 4:282

Odeon, Arundel Gate
Tel: 0870 50 50 007
Website: www.odeon.co.uk
Seats: 1:252, 2:229, 3:248, 4:113,
5:113, 6:129, 7:171, 8:148, 9:150,
10:120

UGC, Don Valley, Broughton Lane
Tel: 0114 2421237/0870 9020420
Website: www.ugccinemas.co.uk
Seats: 1:143, 2:141, 3:164, 4:262,
5:262, 6:551, 7:691, 8:551, 9:262,
9:262, 10:262, 11:173, 12:193, 13:115,
14:197, 15:197, 16:197, 17:197, 18:93,
19:82, 20:82

Vue, Rear of the Oasis, Meadowhall
Centre
Tel: 0114 256 9825
Website: www.myvue.com
Seats: 1:200, 2:200, 3:97, 4:238, 5:200,
6:365, 7:195, 8:195, 9:73, 10:195, 11:323

## Shepton Mallet - Somerset
Amusement Centre, Market Place
(P/T)
Tel: 01749 3444688
Seats: 270

## Sheringham - Norfolk
Little Theatre, Station Road  (S/O)
Tel: 01263 822347
Seats: 198

## Shrewsbury - Shropshire
Cineworld, Old Potts Way
Tel: 01743 340726/240350
Website: www.cineworld.co.uk
Seats: 1:224, 2:157, 3:226, 4:280,
5:135, 6:100, 7:81, 8:222

The Music Hall Film Theatre, The
Square, SY1 1LH
Tel: 01743 281281
Seats: 100

## Sidmouth - Devon
Radway, Radway Place
Tel: 01395 513085
Website: www.scottcinemas.co.uk
Seats: 272

## Sittingbourne - Kent
New Century, High Street
Tel: 01795 423984/426018
Website: www.reeltime-cinemas.co.uk
Seats: 1:300, 2:110

## Skegness - Lincolnshire
ABC, Butlins Family Entertainment
Resort, Roman Bank
Tel: 0870 50 50 007
Seats: 1:120, 2:120

Tower, Lumley Road
Tel: 01754 765152
Seats: 1:165, 2:165

## Skipton - North Yorkshire
Plaza, Sackville Street
Tel: 01756 793417
Website: www.nm-cinemas.co.uk
Seats: 320

## Slough - Berkshire
UGC, 45 Queensmere Centre
Tel: 01753 511299/0871 200 2000
Website: www.ugccinemas.co.uk
Seats: 1:140, 2:130, 3:160, 4:354,
5:456, 6:194, 7:92, 8:144, 9:83, 10:74

## Solihull - West Midlands
Cineworld, Mill Lane Arcade
(Upper), Touchwood
Tel: 0121 711 5000/1025
Website: www.cineworld.co.uk
Seats: 1:100, 2:200, 3:144, 4:225,
5:155, 6:317, 7:432, 8:158, 9: 125

UCI, 120 Highlands Road,
Monkspath
Tel: 08700 10 20 30
Website: www.uci-cinemas.co.uk
Seats: 133 (6 screens), 119 (2 screens)

## South Shields - Tyne and Wear
Customs House, Mill Dam
Tel: 0191 454 1234
Seats: 1:400, 2:160

## Southampton - Hants
Harbour Lights Picturehouse, Ocean
Village SO14 3TL
Website: www.picturehouses.co.uk
Tel: 023 8033 5533
Seats: 1:325, 2:144

Odeon, Leisure World, West Quay
Road
Tel: 0871 22 44 007
Website: www.odeon.co.uk
Seats: 1:540, 2:495, 3:169, 4:111, 5:99,
6:139, 7:270, 8:318, 9:331, 10:288,
11:102, 12:102, 13:138

UGC, 4 Ocean Way, Ocean Village
Tel: 02380 232 880/0870 1555132
Website: www.ugccinemas.co.uk
Seats: 1:421, 2:346, 3:346, 4:258, 5:258

## Southend - Essex
Odeon, Victoria Circus
Tel: 0871 22 44 007
Website: www.odeon.co.uk
Seats: 1:200, 2:264, 3:145, 4:221,
5:388, 6:260, 7:260, 8:197

## Southport - Merseyside
Arts Centre, Lord Street  (P/T)
Tel: 01704 540004/540011
Seats: 400

Vue, Ocean Plaza, Marine Drive
Tel: 0870 240 4442
Website: www.myvue.com
Seats: 1:108, 2:129. 3:407, 4:155,
5:116, 6:277, 7:242

## Southwold - Suffolk
Electric Picture Palace, Blackmill
Road (P/T)
Seats: 66

## Spalding - Lincolnshire
The South Holland Centre, Market
Place  (P/T)
Tel: 01775 725031
Seats: 330

## Stafford - Staffordshire
Apollo, Newport Road
Tel: 01785 251277
Website: www.apollocinemas.co.uk
Seats: 1:305, 2:170, 3:164

## Staines - Middlesex
Vue, Two Rivers Shopping Centre,
Mustard Hill Road
Tel: 08702 406 020/01784 451331
Website: www.myvue.com

Seats: 1:139, 2:180, 3:179, 4:140, 5:269, 6:269, 7:174, 8:173, 9:318, 10:375

### Stanley - Co Durham
Lamplight Arts Centre, Front Street (P/T)
Tel: 01207 218899
Seats: 431

### Stamford - Lincolnshire
Arts Centre, St. Mary's Street
Tel: 01780 763203
Seats: 166

### Stevenage - Herts
Cineworld, Stevenage Leisure Park, Six Hills Way
Tel: 01438 740944/740310
Website: www.cineworld.co.uk
Seats: 1:357, 2:289, 3:175, 4:148, 5:88, 6:99, 7:137, 8:112, 9:168, 10:135, 11:173, 12:286, 13:247, 14:234, 15:202, 16:180

Gordon Craig Theatre, Lytton Way (P/T)
Tel: 01438 766 866
Seats: 507

### Stockport - Greater Manchester
Plaza Super Cinema, Mersey Square (P/T)
Tel: 0161 477 7779
Seats: 1,200

UGC, 4 Grand Central Square, Wellington Road South
Tel: 0161 4765996/0870 1555173
Website: www.ugccinemas.co.uk
Seats: 1:303, 2:255, 3:243, 4:243, 5:122, 6:116, 7:96, 8:120, 9:84, 10:90

### Stockton - Cleveland
The Arc, Dovecot Street
Tel: 01642 666600/666606/666669
Seats: 130

Showcase, Aintree Oval, Teeside Leisure Park (A66/A19 Junction)
Tel: 01642 633222
Website: www.showcasecinemas.co.uk
Seats: 3,400 (14 screens)

### Stoke-on-Trent - Staffordshire
Film Theatre, College Road, ST4 2DE
Tel: 01782 411188/413622
Seats: 212

Odeon, Festival Park, Etruria Road
Tel: 0871 22 44 007
Website: www.odeon.co.uk
Seats: 1:197, 2:212, 3:364, 4:158,

5:165, 6:181, 7:560, 8:158, 9:101, 10:74

### Stourport - Hereford & Worcs
Civic Centre, Civic Hall, New Street
Tel: 01562 820 505
Seats: 399

### Stowmarket - Suffolk
Regal, Ipswich Street (P/T)
Tel: 01449 612825
Seats: 234

### Stratford-on-Avon - Warwicks
Picturehouse, Windsor Street
Tel: 01789 415500
Website: www.picturehouses.co.uk
Seats: 1:208, 2:104

### Street - Somerset
Strode Theatre, Strode College, Church Road, BA16 0AB (P/T)
Tel: 01458 442846/46529
Seats: 400

### Stroud – Hampshire
Apollo Cinemas
Seats: 1,500 (5 screens)
(Scheduled to open February 2005)

### Sunderland – Tyne & Wear
Cineworld, Lampton Street
Seats: 2,200 (12 screens)
(Scheduled to open November 2004)

### Sunninghill - Berkshire
Novello Theatre, High Street (P/T)
Tel: 01990 20881
Seats: 160

### Sutton Coldfield - West Midlands
Odeon, Birmingham Road
Tel: 0871 22 44 007
Website: www.odeon.co.uk
Seats: 1:582, 2:134, 3:109, 4:327

### Swanage - Dorset
Mowlem, Shore Road (P/T)
Tel: 01929 422239
Seats: 411

### Swindon - Wiltshire
Arts Centre, Devizes Road, Old Town (P/T)
Tel: 01793 614 837
Seats: 228

Cineworld, Greenbridge Retail & Leisure Park, Drakes Way
Tel: 01793 484322/420710
Website: www.cineworld.co.uk
Seats: 1:327, 2:282, 3:170, 4:154, 5:94, 6:102, 7:134, 8:105, 9:139, 10:129, 11:137, 12:263

UGC, Shaw Ridge Leisure Park, Whitehill Way
Tel: 01793 881118/0870 1555134
Website: www.ugccinemas.co.uk
Seats: 1:349, 2:349, 3:297, 4:297, 5:272, 6:166, 7:144

Wyvern, Theatre Square (P/T)
Tel: 01793 524481
Seats: 617

### Switch Island - Merseyside
Odeon, Dunnings Bridge Road, Netherton
Tel: 0871 22 44 007
Website: www.odeon.co.uk
Seats: 1:369, 2: 228, 3:130, 4:149, 5:243, 6:156, 7:338, 8:228, 9:130, 10:149, 11:243, 12:156

### Tamworth - Staffordshire
Palace, Lower Gungate (P/T)
Tel: 01827 57100
Seats: 325

UCI, 50 Bolebridge Street
Tel: 08700 10 20 30
Website: www.uci-cinemas.co.uk
Seats: 203 (8 screens), 327 (2 screens)

### Taunton - Somerset
Odeon, Heron Gate, Riverside
Tel: 0871 22 44 007
Website: www.odeon.co.uk
Seats: 1:125, 2:372, 3:258, 4:304, 5:124

### Tavistock - Devon
The Wharf, Canal Street (P/T)
Tel: 01822 611166
Seats: 212

### Telford - Shropshire
UCI Cinemas, Telford Centre, Forgegate
Tel: 08700 10 20 30
Website: www.uci-cinemas.co.uk
Seats: 1:112, 2:106, 3:106, 4:112, 5:152, 6:154, 7:106, 8:106, 9:106, 10:196

### Tenbury Wells - Hereford & Worcs
Regal, Teme Street (P/T)
Tel: 01584 810971
Seats: 260

### Tewkesbury - Gloucestershire
Roses Theatre, Sun Street (P/T)
Tel: 01684 295074
Seats: 375

### Thanet - Kent
Vue, EuroKent Business Park
Seats: 1,820 (10 screens)
(Scheduled to open during 2005)

**Thirsk - North Yorkshire**
Ritz, Westgate
Tel: 01845 524751
Seats: 235

**Tiverton - Devon**
Tivoli, Fore Street
Tel: 01884 252157
Seats: 304

**Tonbridge - Kent**
Angel Centre, Angel Lane (P/T)
Tel: 01732 359588
Seats: 306

**Torquay - Devon**
Central, Abbey Road
Tel: 01803 380001
Website: www.merlincinemas.co.uk
Seats: 1:308, 2:122, 3:78, 4:42

Nickelodeon, Blue Walnut
Restaurant, Walnut Road, Chelston
(P/T)
Tel: 01803 605995
Seats: 25

**Torrington - Devon**
Plough Arts Centre, Fore Street
(P/T)
Tel: 01805 622552/3
Seats: 108

**Totnes - Devon**
Dartington Arts Centre, Dartington
Hall (P/T)
Tel: 01803 863073
Seats: 185

**Truro - Cornwall**
Plaza, Lemon Street
Tel: 01872 272 894
Seats: 1:300, 2:198, 3:135, 4:70

**Tunbridge Wells - Kent**
Odeon, Knights Way, Pembury
Tel: 0871 22 44 007
Website: www.odeon.co.uk
Seats: 1:437, 2:271, 3:257, 4:221,
5:138, 6:271, 7:257, 8:221, 9:139

Trinity Theatre, Church Road (P/T)
Tel: 01892 678678/678670
Seats: 294

**Uckfield - East Sussex**
Picture House, High Street
Tel: 01825 763822/764909
Website:
www.picturehouseuckfield.com
Seats: 1:150, 2:100, 3:100

**Ulverston - Cumbria**
Laurel & Hardy Museum, 4c Upper
Brook Street (P/T) (S/O)
Tel: 01229 52292/86614
Website: www.laurel-and-hardy-

museum.co.uk
Seats: 50

Cineplex, Brogden Street
Tel: 01229 53797/56211
Seats: 310

**Urmston - Greater Manchester**
Curzon, Princess Road, Flixton
Tel: 0161 748 2929
Website:
www.curzonmanchester.co.uk
Seats: 1:400, 2:134

**Uxbridge - Middlesex**
Odeon, The Chimes
Tel: 0870 50 50 007
Website: www.odeon.co.uk
Seats: 1:310, 2:414, 3:254, 4:251,
5:153, 6:193, 7:241, 8:189, 9:253

**Wadebridge - Cornwall**
Regal, The Platt
Tel: 01208 812791
Seats: 1:224, 2:98

**Wakefield - West Yorkshire**
Cineworld, Westgate Retail Park,
Colinsway
Tel: 01924 332230
Website: www.cineworld.co.uk
Seats: 1:323, 2:215, 3:84, 4:114, 5:183,
6:255, 7:255, 8:183, 9:114, 10:84,
11:215, 12:323

**Wallingford - Oxfordshire**
Corn Exchange (P/T)
Tel: 01491 825000
Seats: 187

**Wallsend – Tyne and Wear**
UCI, Osprey Drive, Silverlink Retail
Park
Tel: 08700 10 20 30
Website: www.uci-cinemas.co.uk
Seats: 1:163, 2:138, 3:127, 4:140,
5:259, 6:164, 7:152, 8:114, 9:131

**Walsall - West Midlands**
Showcase, Bentley Mill Way,
Junction 10, M6
Tel: 01922 22123
Website: www.showcasecinemas.co.uk
Seats: 2,870 (12 screens)

**Walton on Thames - Surrey**
The Screen, High Street
Tel: 01932 252825
Website: www.screencinemas.co.uk
Seats: 1:200, 2:140

**Wantage - Oxfordshire**
Regent, Newbury Street
Tel: 01235 771 155
Seats: 1:110, 2:87

**Wareham - Dorset**
Rex, West Street
Tel: 01929 552778
Seats: 151

**Warrington - Cheshire**
UCI, 100 Westbrook Centre,
Cromwell Avenue
Tel: 08700 10 20 30
Website: www.uci-cinemas.co.uk
Seats: 1:186, 2:186, 3:186, 4:186,
5:260, 6:260, 7:186, 8:186, 9:186,
10:186

**Watford - Herts**
Vue, Woodside Leisure Park, North
Orbital Road, Garston
Tel: 01923 682 886
Website: www.myvue.com
Seats: 1:249, 2:233, 3:264, 4:330,
5:221, 6:208, 7:215, 8:306

**Wellingborough - Northants**
Castle, Castle Way, Off Commercial
Way (P/T)
Tel: 01933 270007
Seats: 500

**Wellington - Somerset**
Wellesley, Mantle Street
Tel: 01823 666668/666880
Seats: 400

**Wells - Somerset**
Film Centre, Princes Road
Tel: 01749 672036/673195
Seats: 1:116, 2:113, 3:82

**Welwyn Garden City - Herts**
Campus West, The Campus, AL8
6BX (P/T)
Tel: 01707 357165
Seats: 300

**Westgate-on-Sea - Kent**
Carlton, St Mildreds Road
Tel: 01843 832019
Seats: Premiere: 297, Century: 56,
Bijou: 32

**Weston-Super-Mare - Avon**
Odeon, The Centre
Tel: 0870 50 50 007
Website: www.odeon.co.uk
Seats: 1:581, 2:104, 3:120, 4:273

Playhouse, High Street (P/T)
Tel: 01934 23521/31701
Seats: 658

**West Thurrock - Essex**
UCI, Lakeside Retail Park
Tel: 08700 10 20 30
Website: www.uci-cinemas.co.uk
Seats: 1:108, 2:130, 3:130, 4:124,
5:165, 6:165, 7:108, 8:130, 9:130,
10:138

Vue, Unit 700, Thurrock Lakeside
Shopping Centre
Tel: 01708 860 393
Website: www.myvue.com
Seats: 1:382, 2:184, 3:177, 4:237,
5:498, 6:338, 7:208

## Wetherby - West Yorkshire
Film Theatre, Caxton Street
Tel: 01937 580544
Seats: 156

## Weymouth - Dorset
Cineworld, New Bond Street
Tel: 01305 768798
Website: www.cineworld.co.uk
Seats: 1:299, 2:218, 3:265, 4:102,
5:136, 6:187, 7:139, 8:132, 9:148

## Whitby – North Yorkshire
Coliseum, Victoria Place
Tel: 01947 825000
Seats: 99

## Whitehaven - Cumbria
Rosehill Theatre, Moresby (P/T)
Tel: 01946 694039/692422
Seats: 208

## Whitley Bay - Tyne and Wear
Playhouse, Marine Avenue (P/T)
Tel: 0191 252 3505
Seats: 746

## Wigan - Greater Manchester
UGC, 4 Anjou Boulevard, Robin
Park, Robin Park Road, Newtown
Tel: 01942 218005/0870 1555150
Website: www.ugccinemas.co.uk
Seats: 1:554, 2:290, 3:290, 4:207,
5:207, 6:163, 7:163, 8:163, 9:163,
10:207, 11:129

## Wimborne - Dorset
Tivoli, West Borough (P/T)
Tel: 01202 848014
Seats: 500

## Winchester - Hants
The Screen, Southgate Street
Tel: 01962 856009
Website: www.screencinemas.co.uk
Seats: 1:214, 2:170

## Windsor - Berkshire
Arts Centre, St Leonards Road (P/T)
Tel: 01753 859336
Seats: 108

## Witney - Oxfordshire
Corn Exchange, Market Square
(P/T)
Tel: 01993 703646
Seats: 207

## Woking - Surrey
Ambassador Cinemas, Peacock
Centre off Victoria Way
Tel: 01483 761144
Seats: 1:434, 2:447, 3:190, 4:236,
5:268, 6:89

## Wokingham - Berkshire
Showcase, Loddon Bridge, Reading
Road, Winnersh
Tel: 0118 974 7711
Website: www.showcasecinemas.co.uk
Seats: 2,980 (12 screens)

## Wolverhampton - West Midlands
Cineworld, Bentley Bridge Leisure,
Wednesfield Way, Wednesfield
Tel: 01902 306922/306911
Website: www.cineworld.co.uk
Seats: 1:103, 2:113, 3:151, 4:205,
5:192, 6:343, 7:379, 8:343, 9:184,
10:89, 11:105, 12:162, 13:143, 14:98

Light House, Chubb Buildings, Fryer
Street
Tel: 01902 716055
Seats: 1:242, 2:80

## Woodbridge - Suffolk
Riverside Theatre, Quay Street
Tel: 01394 382174/380571
Seats: 280

## Woodhall Spa - Lincolnshire
Kinema in the Woods, Coronation
Road
Tel: 01526 352166
Seats: 1:290, 2:90

## Worcester – Hereford & Worcs
Odeon, Foregate Street
Tel: 0871 22 44 007
Website: www.odeon.co.uk
Seats: 1:273, 2:175, 3:172, 4:67, 5:128,
6:95, 7:202

Vue, 49-55 Friar Street
Tel: 01905 617 806
Website: www.myvue.com
Seats: 1:234, 2:254, 3:330,4:249, 5:212,
6:92

## Workington - Cumbria
Plaza, Dunmail Park Shopping
Centre, Maryport Road
Tel: 01900 870001
Seats: 1:307, 2:229, 3:174, 4:95, 5:95,
6:95

## Worksop - Notts
Apollo Cinemas
Seats: 1,800 (7 screens)
(Scheduled to open in December
2005)

Regal, Carlton Road
Tel: 01909 482896
Seats: 1:326 (P/T), 2:154

## Worthing - West Sussex
Connaught Theatre, Union Place
Tel: 01903 231799/235333
Seats: 1:512 (P/T), 2(Ritz): 220

Dome, Marine Parade
Tel: 01903 823112/200461
Website: www.worthingdome.com
Seats: 1:425, 2:110
(Scheduled to close temporarily from
January 2005 for restoration)

## Yeovil - Somerset
Cineworld, Yeo Leisure Park, Old
Station Way
Tel: 01935 381880/472042
Website: www.cineworld.co.uk
Seats: 1:168, 2:314, 3:242, 4:184, 5:97,
6:117, 7:141, 8:152, 9:278, 10:202

## York - North Yorkshire
City Screen, Coney Street
Tel: 01904 541144
Website: www.picturehouses.co.uk
Seats: 1:226, 2:142, 3:135

Odeon, Blossom Street
Tel: 0871 22 44 007
Website: www.odeon.co.uk
Seats: 1:799, 2:111, 3:111

Vue, Clifton Moor Centre, Stirling
Road
Tel: 01904 691 147
Website: www.myvue.com
Seats: 1:128, 2:212, 3:316, 4:441,
5:185, 6:251, 7:251, 8:185, 9:441,
10:316, 11::212, 12:128

# SCOTLAND

## Aberdeen - Grampian
Belmont Picturehouse, Belmont Street
Tel: 01224 343536/343534
Website: www.picturehouses.co.uk
**Seats 1:272, 2:146, 3:67**

Vue, 10 Ship Row
Tel: 084560 20266
Website: www.myvue.com
Seats: 1:319, 2:216, 3:128, 4:234, 5:214, 6:163, 7:196

UGC, Queens Link Leisure Park, Links Road
Tel: 01224 572228/0870 1550502
Website: www.ugccinemas.co.uk
Seats: 1:160, 2:86, 3:208, 4:290, 5:560, 6:280, 7:208, 8:160, 9:160

## Annan - Dumfries & Gall
Lonsdale Cinemas, Lady Street Leisure Centre, Moat Street
Tel: 01461 206901
Seats: 1:107, 2:57

## Aviemore - Highlands
Speyside, Aviemore Centre
Tel: 01479 810624/810627
Seats: 721

## Ayr - Strathclyde
Odeon, Burns Statue Square
Tel: 0871 22 44 007
Website: www.odeon.co.uk
Seats: 1:386, 2:164, 3:129, 4:449

## Campbeltown - Strathclyde
Picture House, Hall Street
Tel: 01586 553899
Seats: 265

## Clydebank - Strathclyde
UCI,
Clyde Regional Centre, Britannia Way
Tel: 08700 10 20 30
Website: www.uci-cinemas.co.uk
Seats: 1:204, 2:204, 3:232, 4:232, 5:388, 6:388, 7:256, 8:232, 9:204, 10:204

## Coatbridge - Strathclyde
Showcase, A752 Turnoff, A8
Tel: 01236 434 434
Website: www.showcasecinemas.co.uk
Seats: 3,664 (14 screens)

## Dumfries - Dumfries & Gall
Odeon, Shakespeare Street
Tel: 01387 253578
Website: www.odeon.co.uk
Seats: 360

Robert Burns Centre Film Theatre, Mill Road (P/T)
Tel: 01387 264808
Seats: 67

## Dundee - Tayside
Dundee Contemporary Arts, Nethergate
Tel: 01382 432000
Seats: 1:217, 2:77

Odeon, Eclipse Leisure Park
Tel: 0871 22 44 007
Website: www.odeon.co.uk
Seats: 1:409, 2:234, 3:317, 4:182, 5:102, 6:479, 7:256, 8:294, 9:161, 10:118

Steps Theatre, Central Library, The Wellgate, DD1 1DB
Tel: 01382 432082
Seats: 250

UGC, Camperdown Leisure Park, 6 Dayton Drive
Tel: 01382 828793/0870 9020407
Website: www.ugccinemas.co.uk
Seats: 1:263, 2: 180, 3:109, 4:224, 5:512, 6:224, 7:130, 8:109, 9:79

## Dunfermline - Fife
Odeon, Whimbrel Place, Fife Leisure Park
Tel: 0870 50 50 007
Website: www.odeon.co.uk
Seats: 1:265, 2:333, 3:265, 4:207, 5:137, 6:415, 7:265, 8:333, 9:207, 10:137

## Dunoon - Strathclyde
Studio, John Street
Tel: 01369 704545
Seats: 1:188, 2:70

## East Kilbride - Strathclyde
Arts Centre, Old Coach Road (P/T)
Tel: 01355 261000
Seats: 96

UCI, Olympia Shopping Centre, Rothesay Street, Town Centre
Tel: 08700 10 20 30
Website: www.uci-cinemas.co.uk
Seats: 1:319, 2:206, 3:219, 4:207, 5:207, 6:219, 7:206, 8:206, 9:219

## Edinburgh - Lothian
Cameo, Home Street, Tollcross
Tel: 0131 228 4141
Seats: 1:253, 2:75, 3:66

Dominion, Newbattle Terrace, Morningside
Tel: 0131 447 2660/4771
Seats: 1:586, 2:317, 322:47, 4:67

Filmhouse, 88 Lothian Road, EH3 9BZ
Tel: 0131 228 2688/6382
Seats: 1:280, 2:97, 3:73

Odeon, 118 Lothian Road
Tel: 0871 22 44 007
Website: www.odeon.co.uk
Seats: 1:295, 2:225, 3:75, 4:115

Odeon, Westside Plaza, Wester Hailes Road
Tel: 0871 22 44 007
Website: www.odeon.co.uk
Seats: 1:414, 2:317, 3:317, 4:243, 5:227, 6:211, 7:189, 8:170

Ster Century, Ocean Terminal, Ocean Drive, Victoria Dock, Leith
Tel: 0131 553 0700
Website: www.stercentury.com
Seats: 1:220, 2:155, 3:138, 4:138, 5: 155, 6: 220, 7: 372, 8: 322, 9: 145, 10:155, 11: 319, 12: 372

UCI, Kinnaird Park, Newcraighall Road
Tel: 08700 10 20 30
Website: www.uci-cinemas.co.uk
Seats: 168 (6 screens), 210 (4 screens), 314 (2 screens)

UGC, Fountain Park, 130/3 Dundee Street
Tel: 0131 2288788/0870 9020417
Website: www.ugccinemas.co.uk
Seats: 1:298, 2:339, 3:228, 4:208, 5:174, 6:159, 7:527, 8:248, 9:188, 10:194, 11:194, 12:177, 13:88

Vue, Omni Leisure Building, Greenside Place, 61/11 Leith Street
Tel: 0131 557 3964
Website: www.myvue.com
Seats: 1:348, 2:274, 3:461, 4:188, 5:148, 6:93, 7:115, 8:175, 9:175, 10:76, 11:76,12:76

## Falkirk – Central
Cineworld, Central Retail Park, Old Bison Works, off Stewart Road/Queen's Street
Tel: 01324 617860
Website: www.cineworld.co.uk
Seats: 1:311, 2:218, 3:103, 4:128, 5:171, 6:253, 7:253, 8:171, 9:128, 10:103, 11:243, 12:232

FTH Arts Centre, Town Hall, West Bridge Street (P/T)
Tel: 01324 506850

## Fort William - Highlands
Studios 1 and 2, Cameron Square

Tel: 01397 705095
Seats: 1:128, 2:76

## Galashiels - Borders
Pavilion, Market Street
Tel: 01896 752767
Seats: 1:335, 2:172, 3:147, 4:56

## Glasgow - Strathclyde
Bombay, Lorne Road, Ibrox
Tel: 0141 419 0722

Glasgow Film Theatre, 12 Rose
Street, G3 6RB
Tel: 0141 332 6535/8128
Seats: 1:404, 2:144

Grosvenor, Ashton Lane, Hillhead
Tel: 0141 339 8444
Website: www.g1group.co.uk
Seats: 1:104, 2:104

Odeon, Springfield Quay, Paisley
Road
Tel: 0871 22 44 007
Website: www.odeon.co.uk
Seats: 1:431, 2:131, 3:91, 4:200, 5:202,
6:280, 7:324, 8:131, 9:90, 10:194,
11:244, 12:258

UGC, The Forge Shopping Centre,
1221 Gallowgate, Parkhead
Tel:0141 5564282/0870 1555173
Website: www.ugccinemas.co.uk
Seats: 1:434, 2:434, 3:322, 4:262,
5:208, 6:144, 7:132

UGC, 7 Renfrew Street
Tel: 0141 353 6699/0871 200 2000
Website: www.ugccinemas.co.uk
Seats: 1:169, 2:157, 3:663, 4:192,
5:216, 6:137, 7:432, 8:195, 9:241,
10:180, 11:370, 12:195, 13:241,
14:180, 15:370, 16:83, 17:83, 18:173

## Glenrothes - Fife
Kingsway, Church Street
Tel: 01592 750980
Seats: 1:294, 2:223

## Greenock - Strathclyde
Waterfront, off Container Way
Tel: 01475 732201
Seats: 1:258, 2:148, 3:106, 4:84

## Hamilton - Strathclyde
Vue, Palace Towers, Palace Grounds
Road
Tel: 0870 240 4442
Website: www.myvue.com
Seats: 1:459, 2:180, 3:192, 4:101,
5:101, 6:93, 7:148, 8:148, 9:93

## Inverness - Highlands
Eden Court Theatre,
Bishops Road

Tel: 01463 234234
Seats: 84

Vue, Inverness Business and Retail
Park, Eastfield Way
Tel: 01463 711 175
Website: www.myvue.com
Seats: 1:314, 2:352, 3:160, 4:203,
5:430, 6:203, 7:160

## Irvine - Stathclyde
Magnum, Harbourside (S/O)
Tel: 01294 313010
Seats: 311

## Kelso - Borders
Roxy, Horse Market
Tel: 01573 224609
Seats: 260

## Kilmarnock - Strathclyde
Odeon, Queens Drive
Tel: 0870 50 50 007
Website: www.odeon.co.uk
Seats: 1:304, 2:304, 3:143, 4:183,
5:432, 6:183, 7:143, 8:199

## Kirkcaldy – Fife
Adam Smith Theatre
Bennochy Road, KY1 1ET  (P/T)
Tel: 01592 412929
Seats: 475

## Kirkwall - Orkney
New Phoenix, Pickaquoy Centre,
Muddisdale Road
Tel: 01856 879900
Seats: 244

## Largs - Strathclyde
Vikingar Cinema, Greenock Road
(S/O)
Tel: 01475 689777
Seats: 500

## Livingston – West Lothian
Vue, McArthur Glen Designer
Outlet, Almondvale Avenue
Tel: 0870 240 4442
Website: www.myvue.com
Seats: 1:402, 2:178, 3:140, 4:211,
5:254, 6:140, 7:140, 8:195

## Millport - Strathclyde
The Cinema (Town Hall), Clifton
Street  (S/O)
Tel: 01475 530741
Seats: 250

## Motherwell - Lanarkshire
Civic Theatre, Civic Centre  (P/T)
Tel: 01698 66166
Seats: 395

## Newton Stewart - Dumfries & Gall
Cinema, Victoria Street
Tel: 01671 403 333

## Oban - Strathclyde
Highland Theatre, Highland
Discovery Centre, George Street
(P/T)
Tel: 01631 563794
Seats: 1:277, 2:25

## Paisley - Strathclyde
Showcase, A761 Linwood Road, at
the Phoenix, Paisley Junction 28A
off M8/A737
Tel: 0141 887 0011
Website: www.showcasecinemas.co.uk
Seats: 3,784 (14 screens)

## Perth - Tayside
Playhouse, Murray Street
Tel: 01738 623126
Seats: 1:606, 2:56, 3:156, 4:144, 5:131,
6:113, 7:110

## Pitlochry - Tayside
Regal, Athal Road  (S/O)
Tel: 01796 2560
Seats: 400

## Portree - Highland
Aros Cinema, Viewfield Road
Tel: 01478 613750
Seats: 400

## Rothesay - Isle of Bute
MBC Cinema, Winter Gardens,
Victoria Centre, Victoria Street
Tel: 01700 505462
Seats: 98

## St Andrews - Fife
New Picture House, North Street
Tel: 01334 473509
Seats: 1:500, 2:120, 3:100

## Saltcoats - Ayrshire
Apollo, Esplanade, Winton Circus
Tel: 01294 471777
Seats: 1:144, 2:144

## Stirling - Central
Carlton, Allanpark
Tel: 01786 474137
Seats: 1:399, 2:289
MacRobert Arts Centre, University
of Stirling, FK9 4LA (P/T)
Tel: 01786 461081
Seats: 495

## Stornoway - Western Isles
Twilights, Seaforth Hotel, James
Street  (P/T)
Tel: 01851 702740
Seats: 60

## Thurso – Highland
All Star Factory, Ormlie Road
Tel: 01847 890890
Seats: 1:88, 2:152

# WALES

### Aberaman - Mid Glamorgan
Grand Theatre, Cardiff Road (P/T)
Tel: 01685 872310
Seats: 950

### Abercwmboi - Mid Glamorgan
Capitol Screen
Tel: 01443 475766
Seats: 280

### Aberdare - Mid Glamorgan
Coliseum, Mount Pleasant Street (P/T)
Tel: 01685 881188
Seats: 621

### Aberystwyth - Dyfed
Arts Centre, Penglais, Campus, University of Wales (P/T)
Tel: 01970 623232
Seats: 125

Commodore, Bath Street
Tel: 01970 612421
Seats: 410

### Bala - Gwynedd
Neuadd Buddug (P/T)
Tel: 01678 520 800
Seats: 372

### Bangor - Gwynedd
Apollo, High Street
Tel: 01248 371080
Website: www.apollocinemas.co.uk
Seats: 1:248, 2:178

Theatr Gwynedd, Deiniol Road (P/T)
Tel: 01248 351707/351708
Seats: 343

### Barry - South Glamorgan
Theatre Royal, Broad Street
Tel: 01446 735019
Seats: (two screens)

### Bethesda - Gwynedd
Ogwen, High Street (P/T)
Tel: 01286 676335
Seats: 315

### Blackwood - Gwent
Miners' Institute, High Street (P/T)
Tel: 01495 227206
Seats: 409

### Blaenavon - Gwent
Workman's Hall, High Street (P/T)
Tel: 01495 792661
Seats: 80

### Blaengarw – Mid Glamorgan
Workmen's Hall, Blaengarw Rd (P/T)
Tel: 01656 871911
Seats: 250

### Brecon - Powys
Coliseum Film Centre, Wheat Street
Tel: 01874 622501
Website: www.coliseumbrecon.co.uk
Seats: 1:164, 2:164

### Bridgend - Mid Glamorgan
Odeon, McArthur Glen Designer Outlet
Tel: 0871 22 44 007
Website: www.odeon.co.uk
Seats: 1:428, 2:324, 3:252, 4:245, 5:219, 6:176, 7:154, 8:162, 9:110

### Brynamman - Dyfed
Public Hall, Station Road
Tel: 01269 823232
Seats: 838

### Brynmawr - Gwent
Market Hall Cinema, Market Square
Tel: 01495 310576
Seats: 351

### Builth Wells - Powys
Castle Cinema, Wyeside Arts Centre, Castle Street
Tel: 01982 552555
Seats: 210

### Cardiff - South Glamorgan
Chapter, Market Road
Canton, CF5 1QE
Tel: 029 20304 400
Seats: 1:194, 2:68

St David's Hall, The Hayes (P/T)
Tel: 029 20371236/42611
Seats: 1,600

Ster Century, Millennium Plaza, Wood Street
Tel: 0870 767 2676
Website: www.stercentury.com
Seats: 1:132, 2:146, 3:273, 4:372, 5:347, 6:271, 7:191, 8:118, 9:132, 10:252, 11:324, 12:323, 13:351, 14:173

UCI, Hemingway Road, Atlantic Wharf, Cardiff Bay
Tel: 08700 10 20 30
Website: www.uci-cinemas.co.uk
Seats: 1:520, 2:353, 3:351, 4:313, 5:267, 6:267, 7:200, 8:200, 9:153, 10:153, 11:147, 12:147

UGC, Mary Ann Street
Tel: 02920 667667/0871 200 2000
Website: www.ugccinemas.co.uk

Seats: 1:132, 2:195, 3:195, 4:126, 5:155, 6:206, 7:248, 8:375, 9:478, 10:125, 11:154, 12:206, 13:248, 14:183, 15:183

### Cardigan - Dyfed
Theatr Mwldan, Bath House Road (P/T)
Tel: 01239 621200
Seats: 1:250 (P/T), 2:146

### Carmarthen - Dyfed
Lyric, King's Street (P/T)
Tel: 01267 232632
Seats: 740

### Colwyn Bay – Clwyd
Theatr Colwyn, Abergele Road (P/T)
Tel: 01492 872000
Seats: 386

### Cross Hands - Dyfed
Public Hall
Tel: 01269 844441
Seats: 300

### Cwmaman - Mid Glamorgan
Public Hall, Alice Place (P/T)
Tel: 01685 876003
Seats: 344

### Cwmbran - Gwent
Scene, The Mall
Tel: 016338 66621
Seats: 1:115, 2:78, 3:130

### Ferndale - Mid Glamorgan
Cinema, Hall, High Street (P/T)
Seats: 190

### Fishguard - Dyfed
Theatr Gwaun, West Street
Tel: 01348 873421/874051
Seats: 252

### Harlech - Gwynedd
Theatr Ardudwy, Coleg Harlech (P/T)
Tel: 01766 780667
Seats: 266

### Haverfordwest - Dyfed
Palace, Upper Market Street
Tel: 01437 767675
Website: www.palacehaverfordwest.co.uk
Seats: 1:350, 2:150

### Holyhead - Gwynedd
Empire, Stanley Street
Tel: 01407 761458
Seats: 160

Ucheldre Centre, Millbank Road (P/T)
Tel: 01407 763361
Seats: 170

**Llandudno Junction - Gwynedd**
Cineworld,
Junction Leisure Park, Off Junction Way
Tel: 01492 580503
Website: www.cineworld.co.uk
Seats: 1:228, 2:100, 3:138, 4:107, 5:322, 6:292, 7:207, 8:138, 9:100

**Llanelli - Dyfed**
Entertainment Centre, Station Rd
Tel: 07000 001234
Seats: 1:516, 2:310, 3:122

**Llantwit Major - Mid Glamorgan**
St Donat's Arts Centre, St Donat's Castle
Tel: 01446 799099
Seats: 220

**Maesteg - Mid Glamorgan**
Town Hall Cinema, Talbot Street
Tel: 01656 733269
Seats: 170

**Milford Haven - Dyfed**
Torch Theatre, St Peters Road
Tel: 01646 695267
Seats: 297

**Mold - Clwyd**
Theatr Clwyd, County Civic Centre, CH7 1YA
Tel: 01352 756331/755114
Seats: 1:530, 2:129

**Monmouth - Gwent**
Savoy, Church Street
Tel: 01600 772467
Website: www.savoytheatremonmouth.co.uk
Seats: 450

**Nantgarw – Mid Glamorgan**
Showcase, Parc Nantgarw, Treforest Industrial Estate
Tel: 01443 846 925
Website: www.showcasecinemas.co.uk
Seats: 2,604 (12 screens)

**Newport – Gwent**
City Cinema, Bridge Street
Tel: 01633 224040
Seats: 1:406, 2:171, 3:117

UGC, Retail Park, Seven Styles Avenue
Tel: 01633 274272/0870 1550516
Website: www.ugccinemas.co.uk
Seats: 1:199, 2:178, 3:123, 4:187, 5:267, 6:405, 7:458, 8:287, 9:180, 10:123, 11:211, 12:156, 13:77

**Newtown - Powys**
Regent, Broad Street
Tel: 01686 625917
Seats: 1:210, 2:40

**Pontardawe - West Glamorgan**
Arts Centre, Herbert Street
Tel: 01792 863722
Seats: 450

**Pontypool - Gwent**
Scala, Osborne Road
Tel: 0149 575 6038
Seats: 197

**Pontypridd - Mid Glamorgan**
Muni Screen, Gelliwastad Rd (P/T)
Tel: 01443 485934
Seats: 400

**Port Talbot - West Glamorgan**
Apollo, Hollywood Park, Aberavon Sea Front, Princess Margaret Way
Tel: 01639 895552
Website: www.apollocinemas.co.uk
Seats: 1:118, 2:103, 3:258, 4:258, 5:118, 6:118

**Porthcawl - Mid Glamorgan**
Grand Pavilion (S/O) (P/T)
Tel: 01656 786996
Seats: 500

**Porthmadog - Gwynedd**
Coliseum, Avenue Road
Tel: 01766 512108
Website: www.coliseum-porthmadog.co.uk
Seats: 550

**Pwllheli - Gwynedd**
Neuadd Dwyfor/Town Hall Cinema (P/T)
Tel: 01758 613371
Seats: 450

**Rhyl - Clwyd**
Apollo, Children's Village, West Promenade
Tel: 01745 353856
Website: www.apollocinemas.co.uk
Seats: 1:206, 2:206, 3:117, 4:107, 5:107

**Swansea - West Glamorgan**
Taliesin Arts Centre, University College, Singleton Park, SA2 8PZ
Tel: 01792 296883/295491
Seats: 328

UCI, Quay Parade, Parc Tawe
Tel: 08700 10 20 30
Website: www.uci-cinemas.co.uk
Seats: 1:178, 2:180, 3:186, 4:192, 5:270, 6:270, 7:192, 8:186, 9:180, 10:178

**Tenby - Dyfed**
Royal Playhouse, White Lion Street
Tel: 01834 844809
Seats: 400

**Treorchy - Mid Glamorgan**
Parc and Dare Theatre, Station Road
Tel: 01443 773112
Seats: 794

**Tywyn - Gwynedd**
The Cinema, Corbett Square
Tel: 01654 710260
Seats: 368

**Welshpool - Mid Glamorgan**
Pola, Berriew Street
Tel: 01938 555715
Seats: 1:150, 2:40

**Wrexham - Clwyd**
Odeon, Plas Coch Retail Park, Plas Coch Road
Tel: 0870 50 50 007
Website: www.odeon.co.uk
Seats: 1:351, 2:188, 3:147, 4:251, 5:110, 6:110, 7:110

**Ystradgynlais - Mid Glamorgan**
Miners' Welfare and Community Hall, Brecon Road (P/T)
Tel: 01639 843163
Seats: 345

# NORTHERN IRELAND

### Antrim - Antrim
Cineplex, Fountain Hill
Tel: 028 94 469500
Seats: 1:312, 2:232, 3:132, 4:112

### Armagh - Armagh
City Film House, Market Street
Tel: 028 37 511033
Seats: 1:225. 2:128, 3:197, 4:91

### Ballymena - Antrim
IMC, Larne Link Road
Tel: 028 25 631111
Seats: 1:342, 2:261, 3:160, 4:160, 5:109, 6:112, 7:109

### Bangor - Down
Cineplex, Valentine's Road, Castlepark
Tel: 028 91454729
Seats: 1:287, 2:196, 3:164, 4:112

### Belfast - Antrim
Cineworld, Kennedy Centre, Falls Road
Tel: 028 90 600988
Seats: 1:296, 2:190, 3:178, 4:178, 5:165

Movie House, 14 Dublin Road
Tel: 028 9024 5700/3477
Seats: 1:436, 2:354, 3:262, 4:264, 5:252, 6:272, 7:187, 8:187, 9:169, 10:118

Movie House, Yorkgate Leisure Complex
Tel: 028 975 5000/2000
Seats: 1:314, 2:264, 3:248, 4:181, 5:172, 6:97, 7:97, 8:332, 9:72, 10:67, 11:67, 12:83, 13:83, 14:475

Queen's Film Theatre, 25 College Gardens, BT9 6BS
Tel: 028 90 972600/08003 282811
Seats: 1:240, 2:120

Sheridan IMAX Cinema, Odyssey Pavilion, Queen's Quay
Tel: 028 9046 7000
Seats: 373

The Strand, Hollywood Road
Tel: 028 90 673500
Seats: 1:250, 2:193, 3:84, 4:98

Vue, The Pavilion, Odyssey, 2 Queens Quay
Tel: 02890 739134/08702 406020
Website: www.myvue.com
1:405, 2:155, 3:155, 4:155, 5:476, 6:188, 7:188, 8:267, 9:294, 10:280, 11:246, 12:246

### Carrickfergus - Antrim
Omniplex, Marina, Rogers Quay
Tel: 02893 351111
Seats: 1: 378, 2:232, 3:210, 4:153, 5:117, 6:128

### Coleraine - Londonderry
Jet Centre, Riverside Park
Tel: 028 70 329909
Seats: 1:273, 2:193, 3:152, 4:104

### Cookstown - Tyrone
Ritz, Burn Road
Tel: 02886 765182
Seats: 1:355, 2:200. 3:95, 4:100, 5:80

### Dungannon - Tyrone
Global Cinemas, Oaks Centre, Oaks Road
Tel: 02887 727733
Seats: (6 screens)

### Dungiven - Londonderry
St Canice's Hall, Main Street
Seats: 300

### Enniskillen - Fermanagh
Ardhowen Theatre, Dublin Road (P/T)
Tel: 028 66325440
Seats: 295

Omniplex, Factory Road
Tel: 02866 324777
Seats: 1:300, 2:126, 3:104, 4:154, 5:254, 6:165, 7:78

### Glengormley - Antrim
Movie House, Glenwell Road
Tel: 028 9083 3424/3410
Seats: 1:309, 2:243, 3:117, 4:110, 5:76, 6:51

### Kilkeel - Down
Vogue, Newry Road
Tel: 016937 63092
Seats: 295

### Lisburn - Antrim
Omniplex, Governors Road
Tel: 028 92 663664
Seats: 1:489, 2:219, 3:161, 4:112, 5:176, 6:234, 7:142, 8:112, 9:84, 10:66, 11:66, 12:84, 13:97, 14:148

### Londonderry - Londonderry
Orchard, Orchard Street
Tel: 028 71 267789
Seats: 1:132, 2:700 (P/T)

Strand, Quayside Centre, Strand Road
Tel: 028 71 373939/373900
Seats: 1:317, 2:256, 3:227, 4:227, 5:134, 6:124, 7:90

### Lurgan - Armagh
Euroscreen International, Portadown Road
Tel: 028 3832 1997
Seats: 1:276, 2:180, 3:110, 4:90

### Maghera - Londonderry
Movie House, 51 St Lurach's Street
Tel: 028 7964 3525/2936
Seats: 1:221, 2:117, 3:95

### Newry - Down
Omniplex, Quays Shopping Centre, Albert Basin
Tel: 028 30256098
Seats: 1:470, 2:219, 3:168, 4:203, 5:203, 6:168, 7:219, 8:333, 9:122

### Newtownards - Down
Movieland, Ards Shopping Centre, Circular Road
Tel: 028 9182 2000/01247 821000
Website: www.movieland.co.uk
Seats: 1:278, 2:238, 3:155, 4:155, 5:119, 6:119

### Omagh - Tyrone
Studios 1-6, Gillyhooley Road
Tel: 02882 242034
Seats: (six screens)

### Portrush - Antrim
Playhouse, Main Street
Tel: 028 7082 3917
Seats: 1:315, 2:65

Listed here is just a small selection of film schools, educational establishments and companies which offer courses in film and television. The duration of the courses vary from half a day to several years, and are designed for all levels from beginners to professional film-makers.

Professionals will know which specialised course they are looking for, however, for beginners, care should be taken and a good starting point would be a one-day seminar or a short introductory course in the area chosen. Students may find, that before starting a course, they need to take a preliminary, possibly part-time evening course, to allow them to make the best of a short, expensive, specialist course. For example, before going on an "Avid Film Editing Course" on a Macintosh computer, it would be advisable to be very familiar with Macintosh computers and have done some film editing.

Film-making courses are frequently 100 per cent practical and film studies courses can be 100 per cent theoretical. However, many courses are a mixture and it is always advisable, if possible, to visit the organisation before enrolling, to clearly understand what the course entails, and to see how much equipment is available for student use. For all practical courses, the ratio of equipment to students, and the quality of the equipment and facilities should be checked.

For a full and more detailed search of courses from the Skillset/bfi database of over four thousand media and multimedia courses go to the webpage:

www.bfi.org.uk/mediacourses

Please note that inclusion in this listing does not constitute a recommendation. Compiled by Lavinia Orton

## Academy of Radio, Film and Television
American Building
79A Tottenham Court Road
London W1T 4TD
Contact: Tracey Parkin
Tel: 020 8408 7158
email: help@londonacademy.co.uk
Website: www.media-courses.com
London Academy of Radio, Film & TV is aimed at people who are looking for a career and who want to update their existing skills.
Courses are run on a day, evening and weekend basis and cover a variety of the skills needed to succeed in the world of radio, film and television

## The Arts Institute at Bournemouth
School of Media
Wallisdown
Poole
Dorset BH12 5HH
Tel: 01202 363228
Fax: 01202 537729
Contact: Course Office
email: courseoffice@aib.ac.uk
Contact: Short Course Office
Tel: 01202 363 222
email: parttime@aib.ac.uk
Website: www.aib.ac.uk
Run BA Film and Animation Production Course

## BBC Training and Development
Wood Norton
Evesham
Worcs WR11 4YB
Contact: Sally Keane
Tel: 0870 122 0216
Fax: 0870 122 0145
email: training@bbc.co.uk
Website: www.bbctraining.co.uk
Run a wide range of courses covering all aspects of Television, New Media, Broadcast Technology, Radio, Journalism and Health and Safety.

## BBC Training and Development (BBC Trainees)
Room B102
Centre House
56 Wood Lane
London W12 7SB
Tel: 020 8576 8820
Fax: 020 8576 4975
Website: www.bbc.co.uk/jobs
Contact: Caroline Jackson
email: caroline.jackson.01@bbc.co.uk
Room B102
Centre House
56 Wood Lane
London W12 7SB
Tel: 020 8576 7984
Fax: 020 8576 4975
email: jessica.bone@bbc.co.uk
Contact: Jessica Bone
Website:
www.bbc.co.uk/jobs/bbctrainees
Contact: Neil Walker
Tel: 020 8576 7221
Fax: 020 8576 4975
email: neil.walker@bbc.co.uk
Room B106
Centre House
56 Wood Lane
London W12 7SB
Contact: Linda Mattock
Tel: 020 8225 8319/7344
Fax: 020 8576 4975
email: vision@bbc.co.uk
Website: www.bbc.co.uk/designvision
Room B106
Centre House
56 Wood Lane
London W12 7SB
Contact: Murray Furlong
Tel: 020 8576 7835
email: murray.furlong@bbc.co.uk
Website: www.bbc.co.uk

## Birkbeck College
University of London
School of History of Art, Film and Visual Media
43 Gordon Square
London WC1H 0PD
Tel: 020 7631 6112/6104/6102
Fax: 020 7631 6107
email: ma.cinema@bbk.ac.uk
Website: www.birkbeck.ac.uk/hafvm
Contact: Mike Allen, Ian Christie, Angela English
Offers MA courses in History of Film and Visual Media by Reasearch, History of Film and Visual Media, History of Film and Visual Media and

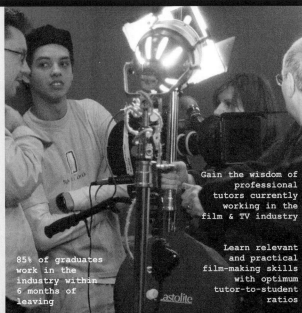

Mphil/Phd in Film and Television Studies

## BKSTS - The Moving Image Society
**Ealing Studios**
**Ealing Green**
**London W5 5EP**
Tel: 020 8584 5220
Fax: 020 8584 5230
email: training@bksts.com
Website: www.bksts.com
Contact: Training Department
The BKST mission statement is: To encourage, sustain, educate, train and represent all those who, creatively or technologically, are involved – creatively or technologically - in the business of providing moving images and associated crafts in any form and through any media.

## The Bournemouth Media School
**Bournemouth University**
**Talbot Campus**
**Fern Barrow**
**Poole, Dorset BH12 5BB**
Tel: 01202 595351
Fax: 01202 595099
email:
bmsugrad@bournemouth.ac.uk
Website: media.bournemouth.ac.uk
Contact: The Programme Administrator
The Media School at Bournemouth University is the largest centre in the UK for the study of Corporate & Marketing Communications, Journalism and Communication, Media Production and Computer Animation. It is a leading school for vocational higher education, applied research, consultancy and training - successfully preparing students for careers in the fast-growing media and communications sectors

## Brighton Film School
**Administration Office**
**13 Tudor Place**
**Dean Court Road**
**Rottingdean**
**East Sussex BN2 7DF**
Tel: 01273 302 166
Fax: 01273 302 163
email:
info@brightonfilmschool.org.uk
Website:
www.brightonfilmschool.org.uk
Contact: Franz von Habsburg
Tel: 01273 302 166
email:
franz@brightonfilmschool.org.uk

Contact: Meryl von Habsburg
Tel: 01273 302 166
Fax: 01273 302 163
email:
info@brightonfilmschool.org.uk
The Brighton Film School provides education in all aspects of motion picture production with the latest in industry developments and contacts. It encourages students to seek suitable employment

## British Universities Film and Video Council
**77 Wells Street**
**London W1T 3QJ**
Tel: 020 7393 1504
Fax: 020 7393 1555
email: events@bufvc.ac.uk
Website: www.bufvc.ac.uk
Contact: Kate Bensted
The BUFVC is a representative body which promotes the production, study and use of film and related media in higher education and research. It runs a number of one day courses throughout the year on topics such as Location Shooting, Copyright Clearance for Print, Broadcast and Multimedia Production and Production Techniques, Audio for the Web

## Cardiff University
**School of Journalism, Media and Cultural Studies**
**King Edward VII Avenue**
**Cardiff CF10 3NB**
Tel: 029 2087 4041
Fax: 029 2023 8832
email: HarrisRL@cardiff.ac.uk
Website: www.cardiff.ac.uk/jomec
Contact: Rebecca Harris
The school is one of Britain's premier centres for teaching and research in journalism, media and cultural studies

## Central Saint Martins College of Art and Design
**Short Course Office**
**Southampton Row**
**London WC1B 4AP**
Tel: 020 7514 7015
Fax: 020 7514 7016
email: shortcourse@csm.linst.ac.uk
Website: www.csm.linst.ac.uk
Contact: Chris Ball

## The Children's Film Unit
**South Way**
**Leavesden**
**Herts WD25 7LZ**
Tel: 01923 354656
Fax: 01923 354656

email: cfilmunit@aol.com
Website: www.btinternet.com/~cfu/
Contact: Carol Rennie
The Children's Film Unit is an Educational Charity, which trains young people from the ages of ten to sixteen in all aspects of film-making

## Cyfle Cyf
**Gronant**
**Penrallt Isaf**
**Caernarfon**
**Gwynedd LL55 1NW**
Tel: 01286 671000
Fax: 01286 678831
email: cyfle@cyfle.co.uk
Website: www.cyfle.co.uk
Contact: Richard Morris Jones, Iona
Cyfle is the national training provider for the Television, Film and Interactive Media industry in Wales

## University of Derby
**Film and Video Department**
**Green Lane**
**Derby DE1 1RX**
Tel: 01332 593065
Fax: 01332 622296
email:
m.m.b.thoquenne@out.derby.ac.uk
Website:
vertigo.derby.ac.uk.hitchcock
Contact: Martine Thoquenne

## Edinburgh College of Art
**School of Visual Communication**
**74 Lauriston Place**
**Edinburgh EH3 9DF**
Tel: 0131 221 6114
Fax: 0131 221 6100
email: viscom@eca.ac.uk
Website: www.eca.ac.uk
Contact: Noé Mendelle
The centre concentrates on the criticial study and analysis of visual culture and the various theories used to interpret it

## FILMU
**Leeds Metropolitan University**
**2 Queen Square**
**Leeds LS2 8AF**
Website:
www.lmu.ac.uk/hen/aad/filmu
Contact: Denise York
Tel: 0113 283 1905
Fax: 0113 283 1901
email: d.york@lmu.ac.uk

## The Film Academy
**University of Glamorgan,**
**Pontypridd, Rhondda Cynon**
**Taff, CF37 1DL**
Tel: 01443 654111
Fax: 01443 654067

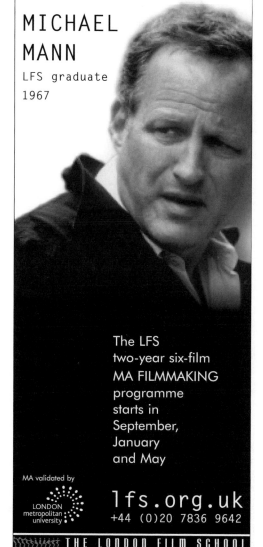

email: filmacademy@glam.ac.uk
Website:
www.glam.ac.uk/filmacademy
Contact: Rebecca Davies
The Film Academy is the only film
school in the UK dealing solely in
post-experience PhD by practice. It
provides the highest possible level of
achievement, drawing upon expertise,
resources and experience from across
the University as well as from the film
and television industry. The Film
Academy was established in order to
serve as the Academy for Dragon
International Film Studios

## The Finishing School
**National Film and Television School**
**Beaconsfield Studios**
**Station Road**
**Beaconsfield**
**Bucks HP9 1LG**
Website: www.fschool.net
Contact: St John Walker
Tel: 01494 677 022, 01494 731 462
Fax: 01494 678 708
email: sjwalker@nftsfilm-tv.ac.uk
The Finishing School is a new
industry accredited Digital Post-
Production workshop and creative
laboratory offering Effects and
Animation Courses, Short Courses
offering the latest software and
hardware equipment, reserach and
testing of new production and
training techniques

## First Film Foundation
**9 Bourlet Close**
**London W1W 7BP**
Tel: 020 7580 2111
Fax: 020 7580 2116
email: info@firstfilm.demon.co.uk
Website: www.firstfilm.co.uk
Contact: Jonathan Rawlinson
First Film Foundation was founded
to help new writers, producers and
directors to make their first film.
The programmes includes:
Information, Development and
Training, Short Film Showcasing

## Four Corners Film Workshop
**113 Roman Road**
**Bethnal Green**
**London E2 0QN**
Contact: Course Co-ordinator
Tel: 020 8981 4243/6111
Fax: 020 8983 7866
email: film@fourcorners.demon.co.uk

## ft2 - Film and Television Freelance Training
**Fourth Floor**

**Warwick House**
**9 Warwick Street**
**London W1R 5RA**
Tel: 020 7734 5141
Fax: 020 7287 9899
email: info@ft2.org.uk
Website: www.ft2.org.uk
Contact: Sharon Goode
FT2 - Film and Television Freelance
Training is the only national provider
of training for people seeking to
establish a freelance career in the
junior construction, technical and
production grades of the film and
television industry

## University of Glasgow
**Department of Theatre, Film and**
**Television Studies**
**Gilmorehill Centre**
**Glasgow  G12 8QQ**
Tel: 0141 330 3809
Fax: 0141 330 4142
email: d.eleftheriotis@tfts.arts.gla.ac.uk
Website: www.arts.gla.ac.uk/tfts
Contact: Dr Dimitris Eleftheriotis

## Goldsmiths College
**University of London**
**New Cross**
**London SE14 6NW**
Website: www.goldsmiths.ac.uk
Contact: Admissions Office
Tel: 020 7919 7060 (PG Enquiries)
email: admissions@gold.ac.uk

## Intermedia Film and Video (Nottingham) Ltd
**19 Heathcote Street**
**Nottingham NG1 3AF**
Tel: 0115 955 6909
Fax: 0115 955 9956
email: info@intermedianotts.co.uk
Website: www.intermedianotts.co.uk
Contact: Fred Broad
Intermedia is the leading Media
Development Agency for the East
Midlands. Through Production
Support, Facilities, Training and
Funding it provides
range of services for people working
at all levels of the film, television,
video and new media industries

## International Film School Wales
**University of Wales College,**
**Newport**
**School of Art, Media and Design**
**Caerleon Campus**
**PO Box 179**
**Newport NP18 1YG**
Tel: 01633 432954
Fax: 01633 432610

email:
humphry.trevelyan@newport.ac.ukW
ebsite: www.ifsw.newport.ac.uk
Contact: Humphry Trevelyan (Head
of School)
International Film School Wales
(IFSW) is the nationally recognised
institution for the promotion and
development of the audiovisual
culture of Wales through higher-level
education, research and training. The
moving image courses held at IFSW
are BA Animation, BA Film & Video,
BA Documentary and MA Film

## University of Kent at Canterbury
**School of Drama, Film and Visual**
**Arts**
**Rutherford College**
**Canterbury**
**Kent CT2 7NX**
Tel: 01227 764000 (x 3177)
Fax: 01227 827846
email: cas3@ukc.ac.uk
Website: www.ukc.ac.uk
Contact: Dr A. Wood
Tel: 01227 764000
Fax: 01227 827846
Contact: Jan Langbein
Tel: 01227 764000 (x 3177)
Fax: 01227 827846email:
j.langbein@kent.ac.uk

## University of Lincoln
**Brayford Pool**
**Lincoln LN6 7TS**
Tel: 01522 882000
email: enquiries@lincoln.ac.uk
Website: www.lincoln.ac.uk
 Head of Department of Media
Production: Barbara Cairns
Lincoln's Faculty of Media and
Humanites supports a range of
activities all designed to encourage
the growth of Lincoln as a media
production centre

## LCP (London College of Printing)
**Developments at London Institute**
**(DALI)**
**10 Back Hill**
**Clerkenwell**
**London EC1R 5LQ**
Tel: 020 7514 6562
Fax: 020 7514 6563
email: dali@lcp.linst.ac.uk
Website: www.lcptraining.co.uk
Contact: Jonathan Shaw
**Elephant and Castle**
**LondonSE1 6SB**
Website: www.lcp.linst.ac.uk
Contact: Robert Ferguson
Tel: 020 7514 6578

**CAMBRIDGE**

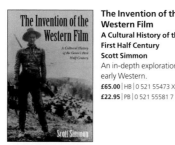

### The Invention of the Western Film
**A Cultural History of the Genre's First Half Century**
**Scott Simmon**
An in-depth exploration of the early Western.
**£65.00** | HB | 0 521 55473 X | 410pp
**£22.95** | PB | 0 521 55581 7

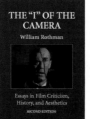

### The 'I' of the Camera
**Essays in Film Criticism, History, and Aesthetics**
**Second edition**
**William Rothman**
This second edition of William Rothman's classic includes fourteen new essays and a new foreword.
**Cambridge Studies in Film**
**£55.00** | HB | 0 521 82022 7 | 424pp
**£19.99** | PB | 0 521 52724 4

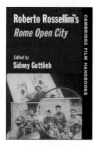

### Roberto Rossellini's *Rome Open City*
**Sidney Gottlieb**
This volume is an accessible introduction to Rossellini's *Rome Open City*.
**Cambridge Film Handbooks**
**£40.00** | HB | 0 521 83664 6 | 206pp
**£13.99** | PB | 0 521 54519 6

### British Film
**Jim Leach**
This book explores British cinema in relation to its social political and cultural contexts.
**National Film Traditions**
**£40.00** | HB | 0 521 65276 6 | 304pp
**£16.99** | PB | 0 521 65419 X

### Horror Film and Psychoanalysis
**Edited by Steven Schneider**
This volume explores the subject of psychoanalysis and film.
'Who can resist a volume which, apropos the most popular movie genre - horror, stages the debate between the main orientations of contemporary psychoanalytic film theory? And why should we resist a unique combination of top theory and fascinating topic? Everyone in cinema and cultural studies should just grab this collection, sit down and learn!'
Slavoj Zizek (University of Ljubljana, Slovenia)
'This superb collection offers its readers a roller-coaster ride through contemporary film theory and the question of horror. Psychoanalysis is the central issue for many contributors, with essays exploring not only its place in relation to the Gothic Imagination at the heart of horror but also its consequent role in both forming and analysing the horror film. Sparks fly across the pages as the philosophical and epistemological premises of theories of horror are themselves subjected to analysis and evaluation as well as, in some cases, rejection. All the while the horror film, in all its gory glory, both uncanny and irrepressible, remains centre stage throughout the wide-ranging discussions and analyses of films from Nosferatu to Scream. The essays in The Horror Film and Psychoanalysis: Freud's Worst Nightmares are exemplary philosophical and aesthetic discussions, their complex and subtle arguments are both challenging and thought-provoking.'
Elizabeth Cowie, University of Kent, Canterbury
**Cambridge Studies in Film**
**£45.00** | HB | 0 521 82521 0 | 320pp

www.cambridge.org      **CAMBRIDGE** UNIVERSITY PRESS

Fax: 020 7514 6535
email: r.ferguson@linst.ac.uk
Although the origins were in printing LCP now encompasses film and TV, digital imaging, journalism, advertising, graphic design, retailing and e-commerce, photography, publishing and many related subjects

## London College of Music and Media
Thames Valley University
St Mary's Road
Ealing
London W5 5RF
Tel: 020 8231 2304
Fax: 020 8231 2546
email: enquiries.lcm2@tvu.ac.uk
Website: elgar.tvu.ac.uk
Offers training for careers in music and media

## London Film Academy
The Old Church
52a Walham Grove
London SW6 1QR
Tel: 020 7386 7711
Fax: 020 7381 6116
email: info@londonfilmacademy.com
Website:
www.londonfilmacademy.com
Contact: Daisy Gili
LFA, a non-profit making trust founded in January 2002, is an innovative venture in professional film training for a new generation of film-makers. Students work in small groups, supported and guided by working professionals. LFA courses put theory into practice and teach principles on 16 mm film.

## London Film School
24 Shelton Street
London WC2H 9UB
Tel: 020 7836 9642 (School Secretary)
Fax: 020 7497 3718
email: film.school@lfs.org.uk
Website: www.lfs.org.uk
Contact: The Director
Formerly known as the London International Film School, the LFS remains world renowned for its professional training and its exceptional output of films and filmmakers.

## London Metropolitan University
Communication Subject Area
Sir John Cass Department of Art, Media and Design
59-63 Whitechapel High Street
London E1 7PF
Website: www.londonmet.ac.uk

Tel: 020 7320 1000/1974
Fax: 020 7320 1938
email: enqs@lgu.ac.uk
Contact: Elaine Pierson, Peter Hewitt or Course Enquiry Unit

## Metropolitan Film School
email: info@metfilmschool.co.uk,
Website: www.metfilmschool.co.uk
Tel: (0)845 658 4400
Fax: 020 7681 1819
The Metropolitan Film School aims to inspire new filmmakers, appreciators and story-tellers by delivering innovative, interactive courses in the comfort and convenience of local art house cinemas – all taught by industry professionals

## National Film and Television School
Beaconsfield Studios
Station Road
Beaconsfield
Bucks HP9 1LG
Tel: 01494 731425/731413
Fax: 01494 674042
email: admin@nftsfilm-tv.ac.uk
Website: www.nftsfilm-tv.ac.uk
Contact: The Registry
The leading international centre for professional training in the film, television and related media industries. Offers full-time MA and Diploma programmes, a part-time Script Development Diploma in partnership with The Script Factory, a Documentary Summer School and a wide range of short courses for industry professionals

## National Short Course Training Programme
National Film and Television School
Beaconsfield Studios
Station Road, Beaconsfield
Bucks HP9 1LG
Tel: 01494 677903/671234
Fax: 01494 678708
email: info@nfts-scu.org.uk
Website: www.nfts-scu.org.uk
Contact: Production Office

## Northern Visions Media Centre
4 Lower Donegall Street Place
Belfast BT1 2FN
Tel: 028 9024 5495
Fax: 028 9032 6608
email: info@northernvisions.org
Website: www.northernvisions.org
Contact: Marilyn Hyndman

## University of Nottingham
Institute of Film Studies
Nottingham NG7 2RD
Tel: 0115 951 4250
Fax: 0115 951 4270
email:
m.jancovich@nottingham.ac.uk
Website: www.nottingham.ac.uk
Contact: Professor Mark Jancovich

## Oxford Film and Video Makers
The Old Boxing Club
54 Catherine Street
Oxford OX4 3AH
Tel: 01865 792 731
email: office@ofvm.org
Website: www.ofvm.org
Contact: Richard Duriez

## PACT (Producers Alliance for Cinema and Television)
45 Mortimer Street
London W1W 8HJ
Tel: 020 7331 6000
Fax: 020 7331 6700
email: training@pact.co.uk
Website: www.pact.co.uk
Contact: Katherine Clements
Founded in 1991, Pact is the UK trade association that represents and promotes the commercial interests of independent feature film, television, animation and interactive media companies. Runs a number of traning initiatives

## Raindance Ltd
81 Berwick Street
London W1F 8TW
Tel: 020 7287 3833
Fax: 020 7439 2243
email: info@raindance.co.uk
Website: www.raindance.co.uk
Contact: Elliot Grove
Dedicated to fostering and promoting independent film in the UK and around the world, Raindance combines Film Training Courses, Rawtalent Productions, Raindance, Raindance East and Raindance Kids Film Festivals, Raindance Film Magazine, and hosts the prestigious British Independent Film Awards

## Ravensbourne College of Design and Communication
Short Course Unit
Walden Road
Chislehurst
Kent BR7 5SN
Contact: Lorraine Ceuppens
Tel: 020 8325 8323
Fax: 020 8325 8323

# THINKING OF A CAREER IN FILM AND TELEVISION?

Learn in a collaborative filmmaking environment at the National Film and Television School

## MA courses
Animation Direction
Cinematography
Composing for Film and Television
Documentary Direction
Editing
Fiction Direction
Producing
Production Design
Sound Post-Production
Screenwriting

## We also offer
Diploma in Sound Recording for Film and Television
Feature Development workshops
Advanced Programme
Short courses for professionals
Courses in Digital Compositing

## For more information, contact
The Registry
National Film and Television School
Beaconsfield Studios, Station Road
Beaconsfield, Bucks HP9 1LG
**T** 01494 731413 / 731425
**F** 01494 674042
**E** prospectus@nftsfilm-tv.ac.uk
**W** www.nftsfilm-tv.ac.uk

*Educating the best creative talent to the highest professional standard for tomorrow's screen industries*

**National Film + Television School**

email: short.courses@rave.ac.uk
Website:
www.rave.ac.uk/shortcourses/
**Walden Road**
**Chislehurst**
**Kent BR7 5SN**
Contact: Admissions Office
Tel: 020 8289 4900
Fax: 020 8325 8320
email: info@rave.ac.uk
Website: www.ravensbourne.ac.uk

## University of Reading
**Department of Film, Theatre and Television**
**Bulmershe Court**
**Woodlands Avenue**
**Earley**
**Reading RG6 1HY**
Tel: 0118 931 8878
Fax: 0118 931 8873
email: e.a.silvester@reading.ac.uk
Website: www.rdg.ac.uk/FD
Contact: Alison Butler, Alastair Phillips
The Department of Film, Theatre & Television offers film and theatre study opportunities at undergraduate and postgraduate level. Bachelor of Arts, Master of Arts in Film, Drama, Theatre, Television, Performanc

## Retford International College
**11 Grove Street**
**Retford**
**Notts DN22 6PJ**
Tel: 01777 707371
Fax: 01777 860374
email: retcol@msn.com
Contact: Jean Bryant

## University of Stirling
**Department of Film and Media Studies**
**Stirling FK9 4LA**
Tel: 01786 467520
Fax: 01786 466855
email: stirling.media@stir.ac.uk
Website: www-fms.stir.ac.uk
Contact: Dr Gillian Doyle
Founded in 1978 the Department was one of the earliest centres dedicated to the study of film and media. It has since grown into the largest of its kind in Scotland and one of the leading departments in the UK

## University of Wales, Aberystwyth
**Department of Theatre, Film and Television Studies**
**Parry-Williams Building**
**Penglais Campus**
**Aberystwyth SY23 2AJ**
Tel: 01970 621 605
Fax: 01970 622 831
email: mik@aber.ac.uk
Website: www.aber.ac.uk/tfts
Contact: Glen Creeber
Contact: Nigel Orrillard
Tel: 01970 621698
Fax: 01970 622258
email: nno@aber.ac.uk
The Department, established in 1973, offers a variety of practical, design and academic courses relating to the study of Theatre, Performance, Television, Film, Media and Communication through the medium of both English and Welsh, at undergraduate and postgraduate level

## University of Warwick
**Department of Film and Television Studies**
**Faculty of Arts**
**Coventry CV4 7AL**
Tel: 024 7652 3511
Fax: 024 7652 4757
email: E.J.Lenton@warwick.ac.uk
Website: www.warwick.ac.uk
Contact: Elaine Lenton

## University of the West of England, Bristol (Bristol, UWE)
**Faculty of Art, Media and Design**
**Bower Ashton Campus**
**Kennel Lodge Road**
**Off Clanage Road**
**Bristol BS3 2JT**
Contact: Dan Harvey, Helen Bubb
Tel: 0117 344 4721
Fax: 0117 344 4745
email: amd.enquiries@uwe.ac.uk
Website: www.uwe.ac.uk/amd

## Women's Independent Cinema House
**40 Rodney Street**
**Liverpool L1 9AA**
Tel: 0151 707 0539/8314
Fax: 0151 707 8314
email: mediawitch@hotmail.com
Contact: Ann Carney

# DISTRIBUTORS (THEATRICAL)

Compiled by Matt Ker

## Amber Films
5 & 9 Side
Newcastle-upon-Tyne NE1 3JE
Tel: 0191 232 2000
Fax: 0191 230 3217
email: amberside@btinternet.com
Website: www.amber-online.com
Distribution of films produced by
Amber

## Anchor Bay UK
6 Heddon Street
London W1B 4BT
Tel: 020 7025 7400
Fax: 020 7025 7406
email: info@anchorbay.co.uk
Website: www.anchorbay.co.uk
**Selected recent/forthcoming releases:**
The Manson Family - July 2004
Bubba Ho-Tep – Oct 2004
Toolbox Murders – Nov 2004

## Arrow Films Distributors
18 Watford Road
Radlett
Herts WD7 8LE
Tel: 01923 858306
Fax: 01923 859673
email: info@arrowfilms.co.uk
Website: www.arrowfilms.co.uk
Neil Agran
**2003 releases:**
Mrs. Caldicot's Cabbage War – 31 Jan
**Selected recent/forthcoming releases:**
Le Chagrin et la Pitié - May 2004

## Artificial Eye Film Company
14 King Street
London WC2E 8HR
Tel: 020 7240 5353
Fax: 020 7240 5242
email: info@artificial-eye.com
Website: www.artificial-eye.com
Robert Beeson
**2003 releases:**
Divine Intervention – 17 Jan
Japon – 21 Feb
The Son (Le Fils) – 14 March
Russian Ark – 4 April
Werckmeister Harmonies – 18 April
Pure – 2 May
Dolls – 30 May
Springtime in a Small Town – 13 June

Unknown Pleasures – 11 July
Sex is Comedy – 25 July
La Passion de Jeanne d'Arc – 18 July
Floating Weeds (Ukigusa) – 1 Aug
The End of Summer – 8 Aug
Van Gogh – 8 Aug
Petites Coupures – 29 Aug
Le Chignon d'Olga – 12 Sep
Time of the Wolf – 17 Oct
Waiting For Happiness – 24 Oct
Nói Albinói – 14 Nov
The Lady of Musashino – 19 Dec
The Life of Oharu – 19 Dec
**Selected recent/forthcoming releases:**
Kiss of Life – Jan 2004
Les Invasions Barbares – Feb 2004
Zatoichi – March 2004
At Five in the Afternoon – April 2004
Uzak – May 2004
Silence Between Two Thoughts – June 2004
Father and Son – Aug 2004
L'Histoire de Marie et Julien – Oct 2004
Triple Agent – Nov 2004
Koktebel – Dec 2004
Trilogy 1 – The Weeping Meadow – Jan 2005
The Holy Girl – Feb 2005

## Axiom Films
12 D'Arblay Street
London W1V 3FP
Tel: 020 7287 7720
Fax: 020 7287 7740
email: mail@axiomfilms.co.uk
Website: www.axiomfilms.co.uk
**2003 releases:**
Life and Debt - 28 Feb
El Bola - 4 April
**Selected recent/forthcoming releases:**
The Man Who Came to a Village

## bfi Distribution
21 Stephen Street
London W1T 1LN
Tel: 020 7957 8935
Fax: 020 7580 5830
email: bookings.films@bfi.org.uk
Website: www.bfi.org.uk
Margaret Deriaz/Christine Whitehouse
**2003 releases:**
Death in Venice – 14 Feb
Sunset Boulevard – 21 March

The Leopard – 2 May
Day of Wrath – 6 June
Le Cercle rouge – 4 July
Kirikou and the Sorceress – 1 Aug
Monsieur Hulot's Holiday – 8 Aug
The Great Dictator – 22 Aug
Decasia – 3 Oct
All Quiet on the Western Front – 7 Nov
Bigger than Life – 28 Nov
**Selected recent/forthcoming releases:**
Sunrise – Feb 2004
L'Age d'or/Un Chien andalou – Feb 2004
Orphee – March 2004
Performance – May 2004
I Vitelloni – July 2004
Amarcord – Sep 2004

## Blue Dolphin
40 Langham Street
London W1W 7AS
Tel: 020 7255 2494
Fax: 020 7580 7670
email: info@bluedolphinfilms.com
Website: www.bluedolphinfilms.com
Joseph D'Morais
Handle MGM/UA catalogue for theatrical distribution in the UK as well as Blue Dolphin theatrical releases.
**2003 releases:**
Fogbound – 4 April
Ten Minutes Older: The Trumpet – 3 Oct
Ten Minutes Older: The Cello – 12 Dec
**Selected recent/forthcoming releases:**
One Love – July 2004

## Blue Light
231 Portobello Road
London W11 1LT
Tel: 020 7792 9791
Fax: 020 7792 9871
email: kevan@bluelight.co.uk
Kevan Wilkinson, Alain De La Mata

## Bollywood Films
384 D Northolt Road
South Harrow
Middlesex HA2 8EX
Tel: 020 8933 6551
Fax: 020 8933 6552
**2003 releases:**

American Chai – 18 July

## Boudicca
8 Cotton's Gardens
London E2 8DN
Tel: 020 7613 5882
Fax: 020 7613 5882
email: sales@boudiccafilms.com
Website: www.boudiccafilms.com
Ray Brady

## Brian Jackson Films Ltd
39/41 Hanover Steps
St George's Fields
Albion Street
London W2 2YG
Tel: 020 7402 7543
Fax: 020 7262 5736
email: brianjfilm@aol.com
Brian Jackson
Specialising in classic feature films for
children.

## Buena Vista International (UK)
3 Queen Caroline Street
Hammersmith
London W6 9PE
Tel: 020 8222 1000
Fax is 020 8222 1534
Website: www.bvimovies.com
www.thefilmfactory.co.uk
Filmfactory is the the online home of
Buena Vista International UK and of
Buena Vista Home Entertainment
Daniel Battsek
**2003 releases:**
City of God – 3 Jan
The Hours – 14 Feb
Treasure Planet – 14 Feb
Moonlight Mile – 21 Feb
Frida – 28 Feb
Confessions of a Dangerous Mind –
14 March
The Recruit – 21 March
Shanghai Knights – 4 April
The Jungle Book 2 – 11 April
Ghosts of the Abyss – 18 April
The 25th Hour – 25 April
Dead Bodies – 25 April
Heartlands – 2 May
Hope Springs – 9 May
Full Frontal – 23 May
The Hot Chick – 23 May
Bringing Down the House – 30 May
Tadpole – 20 June
Bruce Almighty – 27 June
Piglet's Big Movie – 27 June
Veronica Guerin – 11 July
Four Feathers – 18 July
Spy Kids 3D – Game Over – 1 Aug
The Pirates of the Caribbean – 8 Aug
The Lizzie McGuire Movie – 22 Aug
Intermission – 29 Aug
Calendar Girls – 5 Sep

It Runs in the Family – 5 Sep
Once Upon a Time in Mexico – 26
Sep
Finding Nemo – 3 Oct
Holes – 10 Oct
Kill Bill – Vol.1 – 10 Oct
Seabiscuit – 31 Oct
Octane – 14 Nov
Spin the Bottle – 28 Nov
Brother Bear – 5 Dec
Freaky Friday – 19 Dec
Cold Mountain – 26 Dec
**Selected recent/forthcoming releases:**
Scary Movie 3 – Jan 2004
Starsky & Hutch – Mar 2004
Kill Bill – Vol.2 – April 2004
The Ladykillers – June 2004
King Arthur – July 2004
J.M. Barrie's Neverland – Oct 2004
Cinderella Man – Apr 2005

## Cinéfrance
12 Sunbury Place
Edinburgh EH4 3BY
Tel: 0131 225 6191
Fax: 0131 225 6971
email: info@cinefrance.co.uk
Website: www.cinefrance.co.uk
**2003 releases:**
Pot Luck (L'auberge Espagnole) – 9
May
Fluss Der Zeit
Rivers and Tides
**Selected recent/forthcoming releases:**
La Fleur du Mal – July 2004
Fear and Trembling (Stupeur et
Tremblements) – Aug 2004
Keltoum's Daughter – Sep 2004

## Circuit Films
5 Warner House
43-49 Warner Street
London EC1R 5ER
Tel: 020 8800 6440
email: kate@circuitfilms.com
Website: www.circuitfilms.com
Kate Gerova, Caroline Freeman
**2003 release:**
Rain – 27 June

## City Screen
Hardy House
16-18 Beak Street
London W1F 9RD
Tel: 020 7734 4342
Fax: 020 7734 4027
email: enquiries@picturehouses.co.uk
Website: www.picturehouses.co.uk
Maya Nakamura
Cinema operator and distributor.
**2003 releases:**
Perfume de Violetas – 10 Jan
Elling – 14 March

## Columbia TriStar Films (UK)
Europe House
25 Golden Square
London W1R 6LU
Tel: 020 7533 1111
Fax: 020 7533 1105
Website: www.sonypictures.co.uk
**2003 releases:**
The Master of Disguise – 17 Jan
I Spy – 24 Jan
Love Lisa – 31 Jan
Punch-Drunk Love – 7 Feb
Adaptation – 28 Feb
Auto Focus – 7 March
Maid in Manhattan – 7 March
Stealing Harvard – 14 March
National Security – 21 March
S Club Seeing Double – 11 April
Trapped –25 April
Half Past Dead – 2 May
Darkness Falls – 9 May
Anger Management –6 June
Identity –13 June
Crime of Father Amaro – 20 June
Cowboy Bebop – 27 June
Feardotcom – 27 June
Charlie's Angels: Full Throttle – 4 July
Daddy Day Care – 11 July
All the Real Girls – 1 Aug
Terminator 3: Rise of the Machines –
1 Aug
Hollywood Homicide – 29 Aug
Winged Migration – 5 Sep
Tears of the Sun – 12 Sep
Blind Spot: Hitler's Secretary – 26 Sep
Gigli – 26 Sep
Bad Boys 2 – 3 Oct
Laurel Canyon – 14 Nov
The Medallion – 14 Nov
S.W.A.T. – 5 Dec
**Selected recent/forthcoming releases:**
Big Fish – Jan 2004
Mona Lisa Smile – Mar 2004
Spider-Man 2 – July 2004
Envy – Aug 2004
Little Black Book – Oct 2004
Last First Kiss – Feb 2005

## Contemporary Films
24 Southwood Lawn Road
London N6 5SF
Tel: 020 8340 5715
Fax: 020 8348 1238
email:
inquiries@contemporaryfilms.com
Website:
www.contemporaryfilms.com
Eric Liknaitzky
Primarily handle archival material
and classic titles. Recent releases:
Un Chien Andalou & L'age D'or

## ContentFilm

19-21 Heddon Street
London W1B 4BG
Tel: 020 7851 6500
Fax: 020 7851 6505
Website: www.contentfilm.com
Formed in 2004 following merger of
Winchester Entertainment and
ContentFilm. See Winchester Film
Distribution below for details of their
2003 releases.
**Selected recent/forthcoming
releases:**
Scorched – July 2004
Mondays in the Sun – Aug 2004
The Night We Called It Day – Sep
2004

## Entertainment Film
## Distributors

Eagle House
108-110 Jermyn Street
London SW1Y 6HB
Tel: 020 7930 7744
Fax: 020 7930 9399
**2003 releases:**
Gangs of New York – 10 Jan
About Schmidt – 24 Jan
Final Destination 2 – 7 Feb
Far From Heaven – 7 March
A Man Apart – 4 April
Ripley's Game – 30 May
Dumb and Dumberer: When Harry
Met Lloyd – 13 June
Freddy vs. Jason – 15 Aug
The Safety of Objects – 15 Aug
Underworld – 19 Sep
Secondhand Lions – 24 Oct
The Texas Chainsaw Massacre – 31
Oct
Elf – 28 Nov
Timeline – 5 Dec
The Lord of the Rings: The Return of
the King – 19 Dec
**Selected recent/forthcoming
releases:**
Dawn of the Dead – Mar 2004
Around the World in 80 Days – July
2004
Ladies in Lavender – Oct 2004
The Libertine – Nov 2004
Blade: Trininty – Dec 2004

## Eros International

Unit 23
Sovereign Park
Coronation Road
London NW10 7QP
Tel: 020 8963 8700
Fax: 020 8963 0154
email: eros@erosintl.co.uk
Website: www.erosentertainment.com
**2003 releases:**
Dum – 24 Jan

Khushi – 7 Feb
Armaan – 16 May
Chalte Chalte – 13 June
Darna Mana Hai – 25 Jul
**Selected recent/forthcoming
releases:**
Dev – June 2004
Deewaar – June 2004
The Perfect Husband – July 2004
Feature Film Company
19-21 Heddon Street
London W1B 4BG
Tel: 020 7851 6500
Fax: 020 7851 6505
www.featurefilm.co.uk
Subsidiary of ContentFilm, see above.

## Gala

26 Danbury Street
Islington
London N1 8JU
Tel: 020 7226 5085
Fax: 020 7226 5897
Sue Porter/Lizzie Frith
**2003 releases:**
L'afrance – 14 Nov
**Selected recent/forthcoming
releases:**
The Three Marias – Jan 2004

## Guerilla Films

35 Thornbury Road
Isleworth
Middlesex TW7 4LQ
Tel: 020 8758 1716
Fax: 020 8758 9364
Website: www.guerilla-films.com
email: info@guerilla-films.com
David Wilkinson
Independent distribution company
concentrating on the release of
British films.
**2003 releases:**
Puckoon – 4 April
Nine Dead Gay Guys – 19 Sep
Taking Sides – 21 Nov
**Selected recent/forthcoming
releases:**
Silent Grace – Feb 2004
Anazapta – May 2004
Re-inventing Eddie – May 2004

## GVI (Gurpreet Video
## International)

26 Balfour Industrial Estate
Balfour Road
Southall
Middlesex
Tel: 020 8813 8059
Fax: 020 8813 8062
**2003 releases:**
Kucch To Hai – 24 Jan

## Ian Rattray

10 Wiltshire Gardens

Twickenham
Middlesex TW2 6ND
Tel: 020 8296 0555
Fax: 020 8296 0556
email: ianrattray@blueyonder.co.uk
Handles bookings on behalf of Gala,
Arrow, Revolver and releases for
Ratpack Films.

## ICA Projects

12 Carlton House Terrace
The Mall
London SW1Y 5AH
Tel: 020 7766 1416
Fax: 020 7306 0122
email: sara@ica.org.uk
Website: www.ica.org.uk
Sara Squire
**2003 releases:**
The Man Without a Past – 24 Jan
Derrida – 31 Jan
In This World – 28 March
Thomas Pynchon – 2 May
Mon-Rak Transistor – 6 June
The Clay Bird – 4 Jul
The Draughtsman's Contract – 1 Aug
Traces of a Dragon – 22 Aug
Crimson Gold – 12 Sep
Five Obstructions – 7 Nov
**Selected recent/forthcoming
releases:**
Kitchen Stories – Jan 2004
Osama – Feb 2004
All Tomorrow's Parties – April 2004
Hours of the Day – June 2004
Ping Pong – July 2004

## Icon Film Distributors

The Quadrangle, 4th Floor
180 Wardour Street
London W1F 8FX
Tel: 020 7494 8100
Fax: 020 7494 8151
Website: www.iconmovies.co.uk
Georgia Kaufman
**2003 releases:**
Rules Of Attraction – 28 Mar
Open Hearts – 4 April
Basic – 20 June
Whale Rider – 11 July
Blackball – 5 Sep
Bright Young Things – 3 Oct
The Singing Detective – 14 Nov
Wilbur Wants to Kill Himself – 5 Dec
**Selected recent/forthcoming
releases:**
Sylvia – Jan 2004
Dogville – Feb 2004
The Passion of the Christ – Mar 2004
The Butterfly Effect – April 2004
Ae Fond Kiss – Sep 2004
Mambo Italiano – Oct 2004

## Indy UK

13 Mountview

Northwood
Middlesex HA6 3NZ
Tel: 01923 820330/820518
Fax: 0870 1617339
email: ssp@indyuk.co.uk
Stuart St Paul

## Kino Kino!
24c Alexandra Road
London N8 0PP
Tel: 020 8881 9463
Fax: 020 8881 9463
Website: www.kinokino.co.uk
email: info@kinokino.co.uk

## Lux
3rd Floor
18-26 Shacklewell Lane
London E8 2EZ
Tel: 020 7503 3980
Fax: 020 7503 1606
email: info@lux.org.uk
Website: www.lux.org.uk
Distributor of artists' film and video
works

## Maiden Voyage Pictures
The Basement
18 Cleveland Street
London W1T 4HZ
Tel: 07968 005961
email: enquiries@
maidenvoyagepictures.com
Website:
www.maidenvoyagepictures.com
Bjorn Ricketts
2003 release:
La Comunidad – 4 July
Medusa Communcations &
Marketing Ltd
Regal Chambers
51 Bancroft
Hitchin
Herts SG5 1LL
Tel: 01462 421818
Fax: 01462 420393
**2003 releases:**
Ichi the Killer – 30 May
Teenage Mutant Ninja Turtles (re) –
19 Dec
**Selected recent/forthcoming
releases:**
Ju-On: The Grudge – July 2004

## Metrodome Distribution
33 Charlotte Street
London W1T 1RR
Tel: 020 7153 4421
Fax: 020 7153 4401
Website: www.metrodomegroup.com
**2003 releases:**
Lilya 4-Ever – 25 April
The Hard Word – 12 Sep
Spellbound – 10 Oct
My Life Without Me – 7 Nov

Amandla! – 19 Dec
**Selected recent/forthcoming
releases:**
Monster – April 2004
The Last Victory – June 2004
The Corporation – Oct 2004

## Millivres Multimedia
Unit M, 32-34 Spectrum House
London NW5 1LP
Tel: 020 7424 7461
Fax: 020 7424 7401
email: info@millivres.co.uk
Website:
www.millivresmultimedia.co.uk
Kim Watson
**2003 releases:**
Girls Can't Swim – 18 April
Criminal Lovers – 11 April
Gasoline – 14 Nov
**Selected recent/forthcoming
releases:**
Do I Love You? – April 2004

## Miracle Communications
38 Broadhurst Avenue
Edgware
Middx HA8 8TS
Tel: 020 8958 8512
Fax: 020 8958 5112
email:
martin@miracle63.freeserve.co.uk
Website: Martin Myers
**2003 releases:**
Trembling Before G-d – 30 May
Otherworld – 27 June
**Selected recent/forthcoming
releases:**
Almost Peaceful – June 2004

## Momentum Pictures
2nd Floor
184-192 Drummond Street
London NW1 3HP
Tel: 020 7388 1100
Fax: 020 7383 0404
email: sam.nichols@
momentumpictures.co.uk
Website:
www.momentumpictures.co.uk
Sam Nichols
**2003 releases:**
The Kid Stays in the Picture – 7 Feb
Bollywood/Hollywood – 14 Feb
The Good Thief – 28 Feb
Equilibrium – 14 March
Blue Crush – 4 April
Intacto – 11 April
Ararat – 18 April
I Capture the Castle – 9 May
The Actors – 16 May
Dirty Deeds – 6 June
Dark Blue – 4 July
Standing in the Shadows of Motown
– 25 July

Confidence – 22 Aug
Camp – 5 Sep
Raising Victor Vargas – 19 Sep
The Mother – 14 Nov
The Shape of Things – 28 Nov
Mystics – 12 Dec
Together With You – 12 Dec
Out of Time – 26 Dec
**Selected recent/forthcoming
releases:**
Lost in Translation – Jan 2004
Eternal Sunshine of the Spotless
Mind – April 2004
Nathalie – July 2004
Racing Stripes – Feb 2005

## New Line International
4th Floor
Turner House
16 Great Marlborough Street
London W1F 7HS
Tel: 020 7693 0977
Fax: 020 7693 0978
email: paul.saunter@turner.com
Website: www.newline.com
Paul Saunter
Part of Time Warner. Releases of
current New Line productions are
handled in the UK by Entertainment
Film Distributors.

## New Realm
25 Margaret Street
London W1W 8RX
Tel: 020 7436 7800
Fax: 020 7436 0690
Ancilliary distribution

## Oasis Cinemas and Film Distribution
20 Rushcroft Road
Brixton
London SW2 1LA
Tel: 020 7733 8989
Fax: 020 7733 8790
email: mail@oasiscinemas.co.uk

## Optimum Releasing
9 Rathbone Place
London W1T 1HW
Tel: 020 7637 5403
Fax: 020 7637 5408
email: info@optimumreleasing.com
Website: www.optimumreleasing.com
**2003 releases:**
Real Women Have Curves – 31 Jan
Personal Velocity – 28 Mar
Nowhere in Africa – 4 April
Mostly Martha – 16 May
Broken Wings – 6 June
Igby Goes Down – 13 June
Animal Factory – 4 July
Dragonflies – 4 July
Historias Minimas – 25 July
Le Corbeau – 25 July

Angela – 15 Aug
Roger Dodger – 15 Aug
The Man of the Year – 29 Aug
Spirited Away – 12 Sep
The Spirit of the Beehive – 19 Sep
Comandante – 3 Oct
XX/XY – 24 Oct
Blind Shaft – 7 Nov
Aileen: Life and Death of a Serial
Killer – 21 Nov
**Selected recent/forthcoming
releases:**
American Splendor – Jan 2004
Elephant – Jan 2004
Bon Voyage – May 2004
Anything Else – July 2004
Fahrenheit 9/11 – July 2004

## Orlando Pictures
**99 Susssex Way**
**London N7 6RU**
Tel: 020 7263 3555
Fax: 020 7263 3555
email: andy@orlando-pictures.com
Website: www.orlando-pictures.com
Contact: Andrew Ribeiro
Release: City of No Limits

## Palm Pictures
8 Kensington Park Road
London W11 3BU
Tel: 020 7229 3000
Fax: 020 7229 0897
Website: www.palmpictures.com
**2003 releases:**
Cremaster [The Cremaster Cycle,
parts 1-5]
Selected recent/forthcoming releases:
Stoked: The Rise and Fall of Gator –
June 2004

## Pathé Distribution Limited
**Kent House**
**14-17 Market Place**
**London W1W 8AR**
Tel: 020 7323 5151
Fax: 020 7631 3568
email : Lloyd.vanson@pathe-uk.com
Website: www.pathe.co.uk
Contact : Lloyd Vanson
**2003 releases:**
The Pianist – 24 Jan
The One and Only – 21 Feb
Evelyn – 21 March
L'Homme du Train – 21 March
Bulletproof Monk – 18 April
The Heart of Me – 2 May
To Kill a King – 16 May
Son of the Bride – 23 May
Drunk on Women and Poetry – 6
June
Max – 20 June
Wrong Turn – 27 June
Buffalo Soldiers – 18 July
Gerry – 22 Aug

Cypher – 29 Aug
Jeepers Creepers 2 – 29 Aug
Concert for George – 10 Oct
In the Cut – 31 Oct
Miranda – 7 Nov
Spun – 28 Nov
Bodysong – 5 Dec
Dead End – 12 Dec
Touching the Void – 12 Dec
**Selected recent/forthcoming
releases:**
Girl With the Pearl Earring – Jan
2004
The Emperor's New Clothes – Jan
2004
It's All About Love – Feb 2004
Bad Education – May 2004
Motorcycle Diaries – Aug 2004
Bride and Prejudice – Oct 2004
The Magic Roundabout – Feb 2005
Godsend
Two Brothers
Churchill
Bride and Prejudice
5 Children and It
Enduring Love

## Peccadillo Pictures
**3.4 Hoxton Works**
**128 Hoxton Street**
**London N1 6SH**
email: tom@pprfilm.com
Website: www.peccadillopictures.com
Tel: 020 7012 1773
Fax: 020 7012 1771
Tom Abell
Sister company of PPR.
**2003 releases:**
Ma Vie – 18 July
Food of Love – 8 Aug
**Selected recent/forthcoming
releases:**
Blue Gate Crossing – July 2004
Wild Side
Proteus
Raspberry Reich

## PPR (Parasol Peccadillo Releasing)
**3.4 Hoxton Works**
**128 Hoxton Street**
**London N1 6SH**
email: info@pprfilm.com
Website: www.pprfilm.com
Tel: 020 7012 1770
Fax: 020 7012 1771
Christian Martin
Sister company of Peccadillo Pictures.
**2003 releases:**
Le Fate Ignoranti – 25 April
Krampack – 3 Oct
**Selected recent/forthcoming
releases:**
Son Frère – Feb 2004
Best Day of My Life – May 2004

Dr Rey – August 2004
You're My Hero – September 2004
The Clan
The Ketchup Effect

## Ratpack Film Ltd
via Ian Rattray (see above)
**2003 releases:**
Jeremy Hardy Versus the Israeli Army
– 18 July

## Redbus Film Distribution
**Ariel House**
**74a Charlotte Street**
**London W1T 4QT**
Tel: 020 7299 8800
Fax: 020 7299 8801
email: ali@redbusgroup.com
Website: www.helkon-sk.com
Ali King
Formerly known as Helkon SK
**2003 releases:**
Spider – 3 Jan
Stark Raving Mad – 24 Jan
Live Forever – 7 March
That Girl From Rio – 11 April
Welcome to Colinwood – 25 April
The Hunted – 6 June
White Oleander – 19 Sep
Bollywood Queen – 17 Oct
Cabin Fever – 10 Oct
Steal – 21 Nov
**Selected recent/forthcoming
releases:**
Tooth – Feb 2004
Emile – May 2004
School for Seduction – Sep 2004

## Salvation Films
**Dewhurst House**
**Winnett Street**
**London W1D 6JY**
Tel: 020 7494 1186
Fax: 020 7287 0153
email: info@salvation-films.com
Website: www.salvation-films.com
Nigel Wingrove

## ScreenProjex
**13 Manette Street**
**London W1D 4AW**
Tel: 020 7287 1170
Fax: 020 7287 1123
email: info@screenprojex.com
Website: www.screenprojex.com
Recent releases: Chunky Monkey

## Soda Pictures
**3 Rupert Court**
**London W1D 6DX**
Tel: 020 7287 7100
Fax: 020 7287 7077
email: info@sodapictures.com
Website: www.sodapictures.com
Edward Fletcher

**2003 releases:**
Balzac and the Litle Chinese Seamstress – 9 May
El Bonaerense – 5 Sep
This is Not a Love Song – 5 Sep
Interstella 5555 – 24 Oct
The Cuckoo – 28 Nov
**Selected recent/forthcoming releases:**
The Saddest Music in the World – May 2004
Facing Windows – Sept 2004
The Shawshank Redemption – Sep 2004

## Solera Film Company Ltd
8 Great James Street
London WC1N 3DA
Tel: 020 8444961
Contact: Ana S. Martin/Jose de Esteban
email: info@solerafilm.com
Website: www.solerafilm.com
Solera specialises in the distribution of Spanish language films. Recent releases: El Abrazo Partido (Lost Embrace)

## Squirrel Films Distribution
119 Rotherhithe Street
London SE16 4NF
Tel: 020 7231 2209
Fax: 020 7231 2119
email: ostockman@sandsfilms.co.uk
Website: www.sandsfilms.co.uk

## Tartan Films
Atlantic House
5 Wardour Street
London W1D 6PB
Tel: 020 7494 1400
Fax: 020 7439 1922
Website: www.tartanvideo.com
Laura De Casto
Formerly known as Metro Tartan Distribution.
**2003 releases:**
Irreversible – 31 Jan
Persona – 31 Jan
Revenger's Tragedy – 14 Feb
Le Souffle – 11 April
Shiri – 2 May
The Happiness of the Katakuris – 16 May
Secretary – 16 May
Sympathy for Mr. Vengeance – 30 May
Dark Water – 6 June
Snake of June – 13 June
Etre et Avoir – 20 June
Fulltime Killer – 27 June
Hoover Street Revival – 4 July
Bad Guy – 11 July
Public Enemy – 25 July
Respiro – 8 Aug

Vendredi Soir – 22 Aug
Belleville Rendezvous – 29 Aug
House of 1000 Corpses – 3 Oct
Party Monster – 17 Oct
One – 14 Nov
Two – 28 Nov
Three – 5 Dec
Tattoo – 5 Dec
Dracula: Pages from a Virgin's Diary – 12 Dec
**Selected recent/forthcoming releases:**
Infernal Affairs – Feb 2004
Capturing the Friedmans – April 2004
Sixteen Years of Alcohol – July 2004
Super Size Me – Sep 2004
2046 – Oct 2004

## Twentieth Century Fox Film Co
20th Century House
31-32 Soho Square
London W1V 6AP
Tel: 020 7437 7766
Fax: 020 7734 3187
Website: www.fox.co.uk
**2003 releases:**
The Good Girl – 10 Jan
The Transporter – 17 Jan
Banger Sisters – 31 Jan
Daredevil – 14 Feb
Solaris – 28 Feb
Barbershop – 14 March
Just Married – 21 March
Life or Something Like It – 28 March
Phone Booth – 18 April
X-Men II – 2 May
Antwone Fisher – 16 May
A Guy Thing – 13 June
Nicholas Nickleby – 27 June
Brown Sugar – 18 July
Agent Cody Banks – 25 July
Legally Blonde 2 – 1 Aug
Sin Eater – 12 Sep
Le Divorce – 19 Sep
Down With Love – 3 Oct
Alien – Director's Cut – 31 Oct
The League of Extraordinary Gentlemen – 17 Oct
In America – 31 Oct
Master and Commander: The Far Side of the World – 21 Nov
Good Boy! – 19 Dec
**Selected recent/forthcoming releases:**
Stuck on You – Jan 2004
Cheaper by the Dozen- Feb 2004
The Day After Tomorrow – May 2004
Man on Fire – Sep 2004
Alien vs. Predator – Oct 2004
Star Wars Episode III – May 2005

## UGC Films UK
34 Bloomsbury Street
London WC1B 3QJ
Tel: 020 7631 4683
Fax: 020 7323 9817
email: info@ugcfilms.co.uk
Gemma Spector
**2003 releases:**
Summer Things – 20 June
Good Bye, Lenin! – 25 July
Swimming Pool – 22 Aug
**Selected recent/forthcoming releases:**
The Return – June 2004
Blueberry – July 2004

## UIP [United International Pictures (UK)]
12 Golden Square
London W1A 2JL
Tel: 020 7534 5200
Fax: 020 7636 4118
Website: www.uip.co.uk
**2003 releases:**
Star Trek X: Nemesis – 3 Jan
The Tuxedo – 10 Jan
8 Mile – 17 Jan
Catch Me If You Can – 31 Jan
Narc – 7 Feb
The Wild Thornberrys – 7 Feb
The Ring – 21 Feb
Jackass: The Movie – 28 Feb
The Life of David Gale – 14 March
The Core – 28 March
Johnny English – 11 April
How to Lose a Guy in 10 Days – 18 April
Old School – 9 May
Extreme Ops – 16 May
The Truth About Charlie – 16 May
2 Fast 2 Furious – 20 June
Biker Boyz – 27 June
Hulk – 18 July
Sinbad – 25 July
Rugrats Go Wild – 8 Aug
American Pie: The Wedding – 15 Aug
Tomb Raider 2 – 22 Aug
The Italian Job – 19 Sep
Ned Kelly – 26 Sep
Intolerable Cruelty – 24 Oct
Love Actually – 21 Nov
Thirteen – 5 Dec
The Fighting Temptations – 12 Dec
Peter Pan – 26 Dec
**Selected recent/forthcoming releases:**
Paycheck – Jan 2004
School of Rock –Feb 2004
The Cat in the Hat – April 2004
Shaun of the Dead – April 2004
Van Helsing – May 2004
Shrek 2 – July 2004
Collateral – Sep 2004
Wimbledon – Sep 2004

Bridget Jones: The Edge of Reason –
Nov 2004
Mission: Impossible 3 – May 2005
Vertigo Films
The Big Room Studios
77 Fortress Road
London NW5 1AG
Tel. 020 7428 7555
Fax. 020 7485 9713
**Selected recent/forthcoming
releases:**
The Football Factory – May 2004
It's All Gone Pete Tong – Oct 2004

## Verve Pictures
**2nd Floor**
**Kenilworth House**
**79/80 Margaret Street**
**London W1D 2JH**
Tel: 020 7436 8001
Fax: 020 7436 8002
email: giorgia@vervepics.com
Website: www.vervepics.com
**2003 releases:**
Mr In-between – 3 Oct
**Selected recent/forthcoming
releases:**
Fear x – March 2004
Carmen – July 2004
Code 46 – Sep 2004

## Warner Bros.
**98 Theobalds Road**
**London WC1X 8WB**
Tel: 020 7984 5000
Fax: 020 7984 5211
Website: www.warnerbros.co.uk
Nigel Sharrocks
**2003 releases:**
City by the Sea – 10 Jan
Ghost Ship – 24 Jan
Two Weeks Notice – 7 Feb
Analyze That – 28 Feb
Cradle 2 the Grave – 28 March
The Little Polar Bear – 11 April
Dreamcatcher – 25 April
Kangaroo Jack – 16 May
The Matrix Reloaded – 23 May
I'll Be There – 20 June
Gods and Generals – 4 July
The In-Laws – 11 July
What a Girl Wants – 8 Aug
Matchstick Men – 19 Sep
Young Adam – 26 Sep
Mystic River – 17 Oct
The Matrix: Revolutions – 7 Nov
**Selected recent/forthcoming
releases:**
The Last Samurai – Jan 2004
Something's Gotta Give – Feb 2004
Scooby-Doo 2 – April 2004
The Whole Ten Yards – June 2004
Harry Potter and the Prisoner of
Azkaban – June 2004
A Cinderella Story – Aug 2004

Ocean's Twelve – Feb 2005
Charlie and the Chocolate Factory –
July 2005

## Winchester Film Distribution see ContentFilm
**2003 releases:**
Undercover Brother – 14 Feb
The Last Great Wilderness – 9 May
The Man Who Sued God – 22 Aug
Triggermen – 26 Dec
**Selected recent/forthcoming
releases:**
Open Range – Mar 2004
Scorched – May 2004

## Winstone Film Distributors
**18 Craignish Avenue**
**Norbury**
**London SW16 4RN**
Tel: 020 8765 0240
Fax: 020 8765 0564
email: winstonefilmdist@aol.com
Mike.G.Ewin, Sara Ewin
Winstone handle theatrical
distribution of films from the former
Carlton International catalogue and
Canal + Image. Also handle releases
on behalf of Tartan Films

## Yash Raj Films International
**3rd Floor Wembley Point**
**1 Harrow Road**
**Middlesex HA9 6DE**
Tel: 0870 739 7345
Fax: 0870 739 7346
email: ukoffice@yashrajfilms.com
Website: www.yashrajfilms.com
Avtar Panesar, Apoorva Mehta
**2003 releases:**
Koi… Mil Gaya – 8 Aug

## 4MC Ltd
**142 Wardour Street**
**London W1F 8ZU**
Tel: 020 7878 7800
Fax: 020 7878 7800
Sally Hart-Ives
Telecine transfer from 35mm, Super
16mm, 16mm and Super 8mm to all
video formats with full grading,
blemish concealment and image
restoration service. Video mastering,
reformatting and duplication to and
from any format; standards conversion
service including motion compensation
via the Alchemist Ph. C. digital
converter. Also landlines for feeds to the
BT Tower and commercials playouts.
Laserdisc pre-mastering and full quality
assessment. Packaging. Duplcation,
Content Restoration, Sound Mastering,
HD editing, HD duplication and HD
conversion

## Abbey Road Studios
**3 Abbey Road**
**St John's Wood**
**London NW8 9AY**
Tel: 020 7266 7000
Fax: 020 7266 7250
email: bookings@abbeyroad.com
Website: www.abbeyroad.com
Colette Barber
Studio 1: Neve VRP 72 channel,
capacity 100 orchestra, 120 piece
choir, 44ft screen, 2 x isolation rooms,
large client lounge, shower room,
private office.
Studio 2: Neve VRP 60 channel,
capacity 55 musicians.
Studio 3: SSL 9000 J series 96 channel
mixing console. Full range
5.1monitoring. Penthouse: Neve
Capricorn Digital mixing console with
CSX film panel. 2 mobile location
recording units; Audio post
production: mastering, re-mastering,
editing, 5.1 audiopreparation and
restoration, CD preparation, copying;
Abbey Road Interactive: design and
digital video studio

## AFM Lighting Ltd
**Waxlow Road**
**London NW10 7NU**
Tel: 020 8233 7000
Fax: 020 8233 7001
email: info@afmlighting.com
Website: www.afmlighting.com
Ian Sherborn
Lighting equipment and crew hire;
generator hire

## After Image Facilities
**32 Acre Lane**
**London SW2 5SG**
Tel: 020 7737 7300
Fax: Website: www.after.arc.co.uk
email: Jane Thorburn, Mark Lucas
Website: Full broadcast sound stage -
Studio A (1,680 sq ft, black,
chromakey, blue, white cyc) and
insert studio (730 sq ft hard cyc).
Multiformat broadcast on-line post
production. Special effects -
Ultimatte/blue screen

## Air Studios
**Lyndhurst Hall, Lyndhurst Road**
**Hampstead**
**London NW3 5NG**
Tel: 020 7794 0660
Fax: 020 7794 8518
email: info@airstudios.com
Website: www.airstudios.com
Alison Burton
Lyndhurst Hall: capacity 500 sq m by
18 m high with daylight; 100 plus
musicians; four separation booths.
Full motion picture scoring facilities.
Neve 88R 96 channel console with
encore automation. 5.1monitoring.
Studio 1: capacity 60 sq m with
daylight; 40 plus musicians.
Neve/Focusrite72 channel console
with GML automation. 5.1
monitoring. Studio 2: mixing room
with SSL8000G plus series console
and Ultimation. 5.1 monitoring. Film
and TV dubbing facilities: two suites
equipped with AMS Logic II
consoles; 24 output; Audiofile SC. 5.1
monitoring. Exabyte back-up. Third
suite with AMS Logic III console.
Foley stage and ADR facilities.

## Angel Recording Studios
**311 Upper Street**
**London N1 2TU**
Tel: 020 7354 2525
Fax: 020 7226 9624
email: angel@angelstudios.co.uk
Website: www.angelstudios.co.uk
Lucy Jones

Two large orchestral studios with
Neve desks, and one small studio. All
with facilities for recording to picture

## Anvil Post Production Ltd
**Denham Studios**
**North Orbital Road, Denham**
**Uxbridge**
**Middx UB9 5HL**
Tel: 01895 833522
Fax: 01895 835006
Website: www.anvil-post.com
email: reception@anvil-post.com
Contact: Roger Beck (Director)
Sound completion service; re-
recording, ADR, post-sync, Fx
recording, transfers, foreign version
dubbing; non-linear and film editing
rooms, neg cutting, off-line editing,
production offices

## ARRI Lighting Rental
**4 Highbridge**
**Oxford Road**
**Uxbridge**
**Middx UB8 1LX**
Tel: 01895 457200
Fax: 01895 457201
email: tmoran@arrirental.com
Tim Ross
Lighting equipment hire

## Associated Press Television News
**The Interchange**
**Oval Road**
**Camden Lock**
**London NW1**
Tel: 020 7410 5410
Fax: 020 7410 5335
email: aptn_broadcast_services@
ap.org
Website: www.aptn.com
APTN Broadcast Services provides
camera crews, editing, satellite uplink,
space segment and delivery - from
anywhere in the world, direct to a
broadcaster's door

## Barcud Derwen
**Cibyn**
**Caernarfon**
**Gwynedd LL55 2BD**
Tel: 01286 684300
Fax: 01286 684379
Website: www.barcudderwen.com
email: barcud@barcudderwen.com

Video formats: 1C Beta SP
D2 OB Unit 1: up to 7 cameras 4VTR
OB Unit 2: up to 10 cameras 6VTR
DVE. Graphics Betacam units. Studio
1: 6 500 sq ft studio with audience
seating and comprehensive lighting
rig. Studio 2: 1 500 sq ft studio with
vision/lighting control gallery and
sound gallery. Three edit suites; two
graphics suites

## Bell Media
Lamb House
Church Street
Chiswick Mall
London W4 2PD
Tel: 020 8996 9960
Fax: 020 8996 9966
email: Contact Paul
Campbell(Managing Director)
Website: www.bell-media.com
email: name@bell-media.com

## Black Island Studios
Alliance Road
London W3 ORA
Tel: 020 8956 5600
Fax: 020 8956 5604
email: info@islandstudios.net
Website: www.islandstudios.net
Steve Guidici

## Blue Post Production
58 Old Compton Street
London W1D 4UF
Tel: 020 7437 2626
Fax: 020 7439 2477
email: info@bluepp.co.uk
Website: www.bluepp.co.uk
Contact: Ashley Ransen, Facilities
Manager
Digital Online Editing with Axial edit
controllers, Quantel Edit Box ,
Flame, Sound Studio with pro tools
offline/online Avid version II
Davinci Spirt, Mastergrade Suite

## BUFVC
77 Wells Street
London W1T 3QJ
Tel: 020 7393 1500
Fax: 020 7393 1555
email: ask@bufvc.ac.uk
Website: www.bufvc.ac.uk
Geoffrey O'Brien, Assistant Director
16mm video steenbeck and 16mm
viewing facilities. Seminar room for
up to 30 people with video/data
protection facilities

## Canalot Production Studios
222 Kensal Road
London W10 5BN
Tel: 020 8960 8580
Fax: 020 8960 8907

email: camalot@clara.net
Nieves Heathcote
Media business complex housing over
80 companies, involved in TV, film,
video and music production, with
boardroom to hire for meetings,
conferences and costings

## Capital FX
2nd floor 20 Dering Street
London W1S 1AJ
Tel: 0207 4939998
Fax: 0207 4939997
email: ian@capital-fx.co.uk
Website: www.capital-fx.co.uk
Contact: Ian Buckton (Managing
Director)
Graphic design and Digital VFX, laser
subtitling, opticals effects and Digital
Film Recording

## Capital Studios
13 Wandsworth Plain
London SW18 1ET
Tel: 020 8877 1234
Fax: 020 8877 0234
email: info@capitalstudios.com
Website: www.capitalstudios.com
Bobbi John Stone
Central London: 3,000 and 2,000 sq ft
fully equipped broadcast standard
television studios. 16x9/4x3
switchable, two on-line edit suites
(D3, D2, D5, Digital Betacam & Beta
SP). Avid on/off line editing. Multi
track and digital sound dubbing
facilities with commentary booth.
'Harriet' graphics suite. BT lines. All
support facilities. Car park. Expert
team, comfortable surroundings,
immaculate standards

## CFS in soho
26 Berwick Street
London W1F 8RG
Tel: 020 7734 4543
Fax: 020 7734 6600
email: cfsinsoho@colourfilmservices.co.uk
Website: www.colourfilmservices.co.uk
Ray Nunney

## Chromacolour International Ltd
Unit 5 Pilton Estate
Pitlake
Croydon
Surrey CRO 3RA
Tel: 020 8688 1991
Fax: 020 8688 1441
email: sales@chromacolour.co.uk
Website: www.chromacolour.co.uk
Contact: Joanne Hogan
Animation supplies/equipment

## Cinebuild

Studio House
Rita Road
Vauxhall
London SW8 1JU
Tel: 020 7582 8750
Fax: 020 7793 0467
Special effects: rain, snow, fog, mist,
smoke, fire, explosions; lighting and
equipment hire. Studio: 200 sq m

## Cinecontact
27 Newman Street
London W1T 1AR
Tel: 020 7323 1690
Fax: 020 7323 1215
email: lucyallen@cinecontact.co.uk
Website: www.cinecontact.co.uk
Lucy Allen
Documentary film-makers. Avid post
production facilities

## Cinesite (Europe) Ltd
Medius House
2 Sheraton Street
London W1F 8FH
Tel: 020 7973 4000
Fax: 020 7973 4040
Website: www.cinesite.com
Utilising state-of-the-art technology,
Cinesite provides expertisein visual
effects, and film scanning and
recording for feature films. Our creative
and production teams offer a full
spectrum of services from the
storyboard to the final composite,
including digital effects and shoot
supervision. Credits include King
Arthur, Sahara, Harry Potter and the
Prisoner of Azkaban, Alien vs. Predator,
Alfie and Around the World in 80 Days

## Colour Film Services
10 Wadsworth Road
Perivale
Middx UB6 7JX
Tel: 020 8998 2731
Fax: 020 8997 8738
email:
johnward@colourfilmservices.co.uk
Website: www.colourfilmservices.co.uk
D.John Ward

## Corinthian Television Facilities (CTV)
87 St John's Wood Terrace
London NW8 6PY
Tel: 020 7483 6000
Fax: 020 7483 4264
Website: www.ctv.co.uk
Website: OBs: Multi-camera and
multi-VTR vehicles. Post Production:
3 suites, 1 SP component, 2 multi-
format with 1D2 Abekas A64 A72
Aston and colour caption camera.
Studios: 2 fully equipped television

studios (1 in St John's Wood, 1 in Piccadilly Circus) 1-5 camera

## Dateline Productions
**79 Dean Street**
**London W1V 5HA**
Tel: 020 7437 4510
Fax: 020 7287 1072
email: miranda@dircon.com
Miranda Watts
Avid non-linear editing

## De Lane Lea Ltd
**75 Dean Street**
**London W11D 3PU**
Tel: 020 7432 3800
Fax: 020 7432 3838
email: info@delanelea.com
Website: www.delanelea.com
Huw Penallt-Jones, Chief Operating Officer
6 Dubbing Theatres, ADR & Foley Recording, Transfer Bay, Sound library, ISDN all formats, FTP and File Conversion, Preview Theatre licensed Cafe Bar

## Denman Productions
**60 Mallard Place**
**Strawberry Vale**
**Twickenham TW1 4SR**
Tel: 020 8891 3461
Fax: 020 8891 6413
Website: www.denman.co.uk
Anthony Gambier-Parry
Video and film production, including 3D computer animation and web design

## Depot Studios
**Bond Street**
**Coventry CV1 4AH**
Tel: 024 76 525074
Fax: 024 76 634373
email: info@depotstudios.org.uk
Website: www.depotstudios.org.uk
Contact: Anne Forgan, Matthew Taylor
A creative media centre run by Coventry City Council offering training, equipment hire, events and production support to community groups and individuals. Facilities include Avid Xpress and Adobe Premiere non linear editing, production kit including Beta SP, DVCam and Mini DV cameras, a 24 track recording studio and six workstations running Flash, Dreamweaver, Director, Photoshop and Bryce

## Digital Audio Technology
**Studio No 33**
**Shepperton Studios**
**Studios Road**
**Shepperton**
**Middlesex TW17 OQD**
Tel: 01923 593454
Fax: 01923 593613
email: ian@digitalaudiotech.com
Website: digitalaudiotech.com
Ian Silvester
Providing a one-stop solution to all your digital audio requirements for music, film, television and DVD productions

## The Digital Cinema at VTR
**64 Dean Street**
**London W1V 5HG**
Tel: 020 7437 0026
Fax: 020 7494 0059
email: alan.church@filmfactory.com
Website: www.filmfactory.com
Alan Church, Simon Giles
Digital Cinema at VTR has rapidly earned a reputation for being London's premiere digital intermediate long-form e-lab facility. VTR's colorists have justifiably been held as amongst the finest in Europe and many of the UK's top DOPs will testify to the fact. The unique combination of a dedicated team and the development of one of the fastest cutting-edge DI facilities in the UK, has made Digital Cinema at VTR one of the most popular choices among feature film producers and DOPs. The company can also offer a whole range of support services from rushes scanning, through cutting rooms to all form of TV deliverables

## Diverse Post
**6 Gorleston Street**
**London W14 8XS**
Tel: 020 7603 4567
Fax: 020 7603 2148
email: Louise@diversepost.tv
Website: www.diversepost.tv
Louise Townsend
TV post-production. Diverse Post offers a comprehensive range of post production services; from rushes dubbing, through Avid off line, online, audio dubbing, grading, subtitling and deliverables

## Dolby Laboratories
**Wootton Bassett**
**Wiltshire SN4 8QJ**
Tel: 01793 842100
Fax: 01793 842101
email: gce@dolby.co.uk
Website: www.dolby.com
Graham Edmondson
Cinema processors for replay of Dolby Digital, Dolby Digital Surround Ex and Dolby SR (analogue) film soundtracks. Sound consultancy relating to Dolby film production, distribution and exhibition. Signal processing equipment for production and broadcast of Dolby Surround, Dolby Digital and Dolby E formats for TV, DVD, and broadcast applications. Audio noise reduction equipment

## Dubbs
**25-26 Poland Street**
**London W1F 8QN**
Tel: 020 7629 0055
Fax: 020 7287 8796
email: sales@dubbs.co.uk
Website: www.dubbs.co.uk
David Wilson, Sales Manager
Lauren McCready, Business Development
Dubbs offers a complete video duplication and Digital Media facility, open 7 days a week, 24 hours a day. With a complete range of digital video duplication facilities, Dubbs provides a flexible, reliable, quality of service. Dubbs Digital Media boasts two dedicated DVD authoring systems, Sonic Solutions Creator and Fusion. In addition, Spruce and Digital Rapids allow real-time video encoding to Mpeg, Quicktime, WMV, Real, AVI, and audio formats. Dubbs also offers DVD and CD replication, and a printing and packaging service

## Dukes Island Studios
**Dukes Road, Western Avenue**
**London W3 OSL**
Tel: 0208 956 5600
Fax: 0208 956 5604
email: info@islandstudios.net
Website: www.islandstudios.net
Steve Guidici

## Edinburgh Film Productions
**Traquair House**
**Inner Leithen**
**Scottish Borders**
Tel: 01896 831188
Fax: 01896 831199

## Edinburgh Film Workshop Trust
**56 Albion Road**
**Edinburgh EH7 5QZ**
Tel: 0131 656 9123
Fax: email: post@efwt.demon.co.uk
Website: www.efwt.demon.co.uk
Website: David Halliday, Angus Ferguson
Beta SP production; 16mm Arri, 6-plates and rostrum, broadcst quality video animation and non-linear editing; off-line editing. Animation and video training, consultancy and project development. Specialists in enviornment, health and welfare

## Edric Audio-visual Hire

34-36 Oak End Way
Gerrards Cross
Bucks SL9 8BR
Tel: 01753 481400
Fax: 01753 887163
Website: www.edric-av.co.uk
James Hunter
Audiovisual and video production
facilities

## Elstree Light and Power

Millennium Studios
Elstree Way
Borehamwood
Herts WD6 1SF
Tel: 020 8236 1300
Fax: 020 8236 1333
email: elp@elstree-online.co.uk
Website: www.elstree-online.co.uk/elp
Tony Slee

## Engine Aircraft

Richmond Film Services
The Old School
Park Lane
Richmond
Surrey TW9 2RA
Tel: 020 8940 6077
Fax: 020 8948 8326
email: Sound equipment available for
hire, sales of tape and batteries, and
UK agent for Ursta recordists' trolleys
and Denecke timecode equipment

## Eon Productions Limited

Eon House
138 Piccadilly
London W1J 7NR
Tel: 020 7493 7953
Fax: 020 7408 1236
email: chris.brisley@eon.co.uk
Chrissy Brisley
22 seater screening theatre
35 mm double-head projection
multi system video/DVD equipment
Dolby Digital 5.1. Full computer
projection facility power point
presentation.Digi beta/beta SP

## Eye Film and Television

9/11a Dove Street
Norwich NR2 1DE
Tel: 01603 762551
Fax: 01603 762420
email:
production@eyefilmandtv.co.uk
Website: www.eyefilmandtv.co.uk
Lucy Bolton
Production crews, Avid Non Linear
and Final Cut Pro on and offline
systems

## Faction Films

26 Shacklewell Lane

London E8 2EZ
Tel: 020 7690 4446
Fax: 020 7690 4447
email: faction@factionfilms.co.uk
Website: www.factionfilms.co.uk
Mark Casebow
2xAvid MC1000 composer; 1 on-line,
1 off-line - for hire; Sony VX1000
digi-cam; Sony Hi-8; HHB Portadat;
Production office space available for
hire. Tape Transfer facilities

## Film Work Group

Top Floor, Chelsea Reach
79-89 Lots Road
London SW10 0RN
Tel: 020 7352 0538
Fax: 020 7351 6479
Loren Squires, Nigel Perkins
Video and Film post-production
facilities. AVID on-line (2:1) and off-
line editing. 36 gigs storage, Digital
Animation Workstations (draw, paint,
image, modification, edit). 3 machine
Hi-Band SP and mixed Beta SP/Hi-
Band with DVE. 2 machine Lo-Band
off-line with sound mixing. 6 plate
Steenbeck. Special rates for grant aided,
self-funded and non-profit projects

## FinePoint Broadcast

Hill House, Furze Hill
Kingswood
Surrey KT20 6EZ
Tel: 0800 970 2020
Fax: 0800 970 2030
email: hire@finepoint.co.uk
Website: www.finepoint.co.uk
Mark Hill, Sales Manager
Colin Smith, Hire Manager
Broadcast equipment hire. Cameras,
lenses, control units, high speed
cameras, disc recorder, cables, VTRs,
edit controllers, digital video effects,
vision mixers, monitors, sound kit

## Fisher Productions Europe Ltd

Studio House
Rita Road
Vauxhall
London SW8 1JU
Tel: 020 7793 1401
Fax: 020 7793 0467
Website: www.fishereurope.com

## Framestore CFC

9 Noel Street
London W1F 8GH
Tel: 020 7208 2600
Fax: 020 7208 2626
email:  info@framestore-cfc.com
Website: www.framestore-cfc.com
Steph Bruning
Framestore CFC was formed in

December 2001 through the union of
two of the most creative and dynamic
companies in the industry:
FrameStore and The Computer Film
Company (CFC). The company is
now the largest visual effects and
computer animation company in
Europe, with over 30 years of
combined experience in digital film
and video technology

## Frontline Television Services

35 Bedfordbury
Covent Garden
London WC2N 4DU
Tel: 020 7836 0411
Fax: 020 7379 5210
Website: www.frontline-tv.co.uk
Tracy Thomas
Extensive edit, duplication, computer
animation and multimedia facilities -
5 Avid Media Composers, Avid
Symphony, DS, Linear Digital Betacam
Suite. Low volume, low cost, quick
turnaround duplication. 2D and 3D
animation and graphics. Multimedia
facilities including encoding

## Goldcrest Post Production Facilities Ltd

Entrance 1 Lexington Street
36/44 Brewer Street
London W1F 9LX
Tel: 020 7439 7972
Fax: 020 7437 5402
email: mailbox@goldcrest-post.co.uk
Website: www.goldcrest-post.co.uk
Faye Stevens, Peter Joly
Theatre 1 with Otari Elite + consol,
Dolby SRD, Fairlight on FX3.48 DFW
film + video projection; ADR & FX
recording, built in Foley surfaces and
extensives props;
Theatre 2 with Otari Elite + consol,
Dolby SRD, video projection, ADR +
FX recording, built in Foley surfaces
& extensive props;
Theatre 3 with Protools TDM Mix +
Harrison series 12 + video projection;
ADR + FX recording, built in Foley
surfaces and extensive props;
Theatre 4 with AMS Neve, DFC2 film
consol. 35 double head, film
projection, Dolby SRD
All theatres equipped with ISDN link;
Sound Transfer Bay for all film and
video formats with Dolby SRD; Rank
Cintel MKIIC Telecine enhanced
4:2:2, Pogle and secondary colour
correction. On and offline Avid
suites, Lightworks cutting rooms,
production offices and luxury
apartments

## Hillside
**Merry Hill Road**
**Bushey**
**Herts WD23 1DR**
Tel: 020 8950 7919
Fax: 020 8421 8085
email: enquiries@hillside-studios.co.uk
Website: www.hillside-studios.co.uk
David Hillier
Production and Post-Production facilities to Broadcast standards. 1500 sq ft studio with 16 x 9 switchable cameras and Digital Mixer. Smaller studio and single camera location units available. Sounds Studios and Dubbing Suite, Non-Linear and Digital Editing. Graphics, Set Design and Construction. Offices, restaurant and parking

## Holloway Film & TV
**68-70 Wardour Street**
**London W1V 3HP**
Tel: 020 7494 0777
Fax: 020 7494 0309
email: info@hollowayfilm-co.uk
Website: www.holloway.film.co.uk
James Greenwall
BVU. Lo-Band Hi-8, Video-8 S-VHS, VHS, Standards Conversion

## The Hospital Cinema
**24 Endell Street**
**London WC2H 9HQ**
Tel: 020 7170 9134
Fax: 020 7170 9101
Website: www.thehospital.co.uk
Joe Bateman
Seating: 30 (approx)
Screen: 5 metres x 2.1metres
Film Projection: 2 x 35mm Kinoton FP 30D Projectors
Aspect Ratio: 1:1.33, 1:1.66, 1:1.85, 1:2.35
1 x 35mm Dual Magnetic double head follower
6000 ft reels
Video Facilities:
HDCam; Digi Beta/SP; IMX; DVCPro 50; Video Server (Profile); DVD; SVHS; PC/Mac with analogue and digital Interface
Standards Conversion including HD/SD up/down conversion
Audio Facilities:
Audio systems associated with film/video
14:4:2 audio mixer with Mic/Line inputs
Crown Amplifiers CTS 600; 1200; 2000
Electrovoice Front loudspeakers
Boston Acoustic surround

loudspeakers
3/6 track MTE sound followers
Dolby 650 cinema processor with Dolby Digital surround EX, Dolby A-type & SR-type analogue.
External Networking: Digital feeds direct to BT Tower. Satellite Reception; 10Mbps Internet Connection

## Hull Time Based Arts
**42 The High Street**
**Hull HU1 1PS**
Tel: 01482 586340/216446
Fax: 01482 589952
email: lab@timebase.org
Website: www.timebase.org
Walter van der Cruijsen
Avid Media Composer 9000XL non-linear editing suite with 1:1 compression, digital I/O and Commotion 2.1 compositing software, Avid Media Composer 1000 editing suite with 2:1 compression, G4 with Final Cut Pro, ProTools Audio Suite, Multimedia authoring, DVC Pro, DVCam and DV cameras, DAT recorder, Data projector and all ancillary video equipment available. Special rates for non commercial projects

## Humphries Video Services
**Unit 2, The Willow Business Centre**
**17 Willow Lane**
**Mitcham**
**Surrey CR4 4NX**
Tel: 020 8648 6111/0207 636 3636
Fax: 020 8648 5261
email: sales@hvs.co.uk
Website: www.hvs.co.uk
David Brown, Jago Michell, Richard Meredith
Video cassette duplication: all formats, any standard. Standards convertors. Macrovision anti-copy process, CD and DVD Authoring/Replication labelling, shrink wrapping, packaging and mail out services, free collections and deliveries in central London. Committed to industrial and broadcast work

## Interact Sound
**160 Barlby Road**
**London W10 6BS**
Tel: 020 8960 3115
Fax: 020 8964 3022
email: info@interact-sound.co.uk
Website: Sandie Wirtz
Spacious digital and analogue dubbing theatres. Dolby stereo, SR-D. DTS compatable. Large screen film and video projection. 5 digital audio edit suites. Rooms available for production offices. Mixers: Aad Wirtz, Lee Taylor and John Falcini

## ITN
**200 Gray's Inn Road**
**London WC1X 8XZ**
Tel: 020 7430 4134
Fax: 020 7430 4655
email: Martin Swain
Website: Martin Swain, Jenny Mazzey
2400 sq ft studio; live or recorded work; comprehensive outside source ability; audience 65; crews; video transfer; Westminster studio; graphics design service using Flash Harry, Paintbox etc; Training offered; Sound and dubbing; tape recycling; experienced staff

## Lee Lighting
**Wycombe Road**
**Wembley**
**Middlesex HAO 1QD**
Tel: 020 8900 2900
Fax: 020 8902 5500
Website: www.lee.co.uk
Website: Film/TV lighting equipment hire

## Light House Media Centre
**The Chubb Buildings**
**Fryer Street**
**Wolverhampton WV1 1HT**
Tel: 01902 716044
Fax: 01902 717143
email: raj@light-house.co.uk
Website: www.light-house.co.uk
Contact: Technical department
Three machine U-Matic edit suite (hi-band - BVE 900, lo-band BVE 600) VHS/U-Matic/Betacam/ENG kits, also animation and chroma keying

## Lighthouse
**9-12 Middle Street**
**Brighton BN1 1AL**
Tel: 01273 384222
Fax: 01273 384233
email: info@lighthouse.org.uk
Website: www.lighthouse.org.uk
Technical Department
A training and production centre, providing courses, facilities and production advice. Avid off- and online edit suites. Apple Mac graphics and animation workstations. Digital video capture & manipulation. Output to/from Betacam SP. SVHS offline edit suite. Post Production and Digital Artists equipment bursaries offered three times a year

## MAC Sound Hire
**1-2 Attenburys Park**
**Park Road**
**Altrincham**
**Cheshire WA14 5QE**
Tel: 0161 969 8311

Fax: 0161 962 9423
email: info@macsound.co.uk
Website: www.macsound.co.uk
Professional sound equipment hire

## The Machine Room
54-58 Wardour Street
London WID 4JQ
Tel: 020 7292 8506
Fax: 020 7287 3773
email: david.atkinson@
themachineroom.co.uk
Website: www.themachineroom.co.uk
David Atkinson

## Mersey Film and Video (MFV)
13 Hope Street
Liverpool L1 9BQ
Tel: 0151 708 5259
Fax: 0151 707 8595
email: info@mersey-film-video.co.uk
Website: www.mersey-film-video.co.uk
Joanne Toomey,
Producer/Development Manager
Patrick Hall (Resources Co-Ordinator)
Production facilities for: BETA SP, DVCPro, Hi8, MiniDV SVHS and VHS - full shooting kits for all. Wide range of grip and lighting equipment. All format tape duplication and tape stock. Guidance and help for funding, finance, budgets production

## Metro Broadcast
6-7 Great Chapel Street
London W1F 3FF
Tel: 020 7434 7700
Fax: 020 7434 7701
email: info@metrobroadcast.co.uk
Website: www.metrobroadcast.co.uk
Mark Cox
Broadcast Hire and Crewing:
Digital Beta, Beta SX, Beta SP, DVC Pro, DV Cam, Mini DV, Hi-Def CiniAlta, Avid: MCO, film Composers, 9000, NT or MAC
Duplication: Alchemists standards conversions from/to all formats. Technical assessment. Format include: D1, D2, D3, Digital Beta, Beta SX, DVC Pro, DV Cam, Mini DV, CD ROM, DVD

## The Mill
40/41 Great Marlborough Street
London W1F 7JQ
Tel: 020 7287 4041
Fax: 020 7287 8393
email: Contact: info@mill.co.uk
Website: www.mill.co.uk
Helen Down (PR Manager)
Post Production for commercials,

longform and music video using Spirit, Flame, Soft image, XSI and massive

## Millennium Studios
Elstree Way
Borehamwood
Herts WD6 1SF
Tel: 020 8236 1400
Fax: 020 8236 1444
email: Kate Tufano
Website: Sound stage 80'x44'x24' with 6'x44'x11' balcony flying and cyc grid. In house suppliers of: lighting; generators; rigging; photography; crew catering and fully licensed bar

## Mister Lighting Studios Ltd
2 Dukes Road
Western Avenue
London W3 0SL
Tel: 020 8956 5600
Fax: 020 8956 5604
Steve Smith
Lighting equipment/studio hire

## Molinare
34 Fouberts Place
London W1V 2BH
Tel: 020 7439 2244
Fax: 020 7734 6813
Steve Smith
Video formats: Digital Betacam, D1, D2, D3, 1 Beta SP

## Mosaic Pictures Ltd
8-12 Broadwick Street
London W1F 8HW
Tel: 020 7437 6514
Fax: 020 7494 0595
email: info@mosaicfilms.com
Website: www.mosaicfilms.com
Deborah Weavers, Managing Director
Avid Symphony, 6 Avid offline suites, DV Camera Hire, Video Transfer Suite, DV Post-Production expertise, Digibeta/16mm Aaton Cameramen, meeting room, production offices, Dubbing Studio, Commentary Booth

## The Moving Picture Company
127 Wardour Street
London W1F 0NL
Tel: 020 7434 3100
Fax: 020 7437 3951
email: mailbox@moving-picture.com
Tape Formats; D1, Digital Betacam, Betacam SP, DVCam, VHS, U-matic, DTF1, DTF 2.
Telecine; Spirit Datacine (with Mega Def), Spirit (with Pixi), Cintel DSX with Oliver, Arri Laser Recorder, FilmTel Laser, Film Cleaning, Digital Film Lab, 2 x Quantel IQ.
Duplication; U-matic, VHS, Mpeg,

CD Rom, Telestream, Playout, SohoNet,
Graphics; Maya, Renderman, Boris FX, Entropy, Mental Ray.
Special Effects; Commotion, Inferno, Infinity (Henry), Shake, Cineon, Combustion, After Effects,
On-Line Non-Linear; Fire, Inferno, Infinity (Henry), Final Cut Pro, IQ
Off-Line Non-Linear; Avid, Final Pro
Multi Media Formats; Quicktime 4, PC, Mac, MPEG 1+2, AVI, Real Player, Photoshop, Windows Media 9.
3D Hardware; Linux Based Workstations Boxx Technologies and HP, IBM Render farms.
Mac; 40 x G5's Running After Effects, Shake, Combustion, Commotion, Photoshop, Illustrator, Final Cut Pro, Design and Animation Studio, Cinema 3D, Compositing, Multimedia Compression, Hi-Res Scanning and Retouching

## Oasis Television
6-7 Great Pulteney Street
London W1F 9NA
Tel: 020 7434 4133
Fax: 020 7494 2843
email: sales@oasistv.co.uk
Website: www.oasistv.co.uk
Gareth Mullaney, Pat Gale, Darren Musgrove
Linear Onlines / Non Linear Onlines / Offline Suites / Audio Dubbing / Edit Box / Jaleo
Graphics 2D & 3D / Multimedia
Full duplication services - Aspect Ratio and Standards conversions

## Oxford Film and Video Makers (OFVM)
Centre For Film and Digital Media
54 Catherine Street
Oxford OX4 3AH
Tel: 01865 792731
Fax: 01865 792732
email: office@ofvm.org
Website: www.ofvm.org
Richard Duriez: Office Administrator
Geron Swann: Centre Director
Gary Shenton: Production Development
OFVM is an independent centre for film and digital media offering: A range of training courses Production development and support.Local screening opportunities. Post production facilities for hire

## Panavision Grips
Metropolitan Centre
Bristol Road
Greenford

Middx UB6 8UQ
Tel: 020 8839 7333
Fax: 020 8578 1536
email: enquiries@panavision.co.uk
Website: www.panavision.co.uk
Mark Furssedonn
Grip equipment and studio hire

## Peach
**Slingsby Place**
**Off Long Acre**
**London WC2E 9AB**
Tel: 020 7632 4240
Fax: 020 7632 4250
email: Tim Whitehead
Website: Andrew Swepson, Karen
Davies, Russell Parrett
Henry, Flame. Digital editing. C-
reality-Hires-Telecine. 3D Animation
with Russell Square DI tape grading.
Digital playouts and ISDN links.
Award-winning creative team

## The Pierce Rooms
**Pierce House**
**London Apollo Complex**
**Queen Caroline Street**
**London W6 9QU**
Tel: 020 8563 1234
Fax: 020 8563 1337
email: meredith@pierce-
entertainment.com
Website: www.pierce-entertainment
Meredith Leung, Studio Manager
Complete surround sound facilities:
surround sound to picture recording.
Foley and mixing. Large and accurate
main control room - Neve VR 72-60
console with flying fader automation,
recall and digital surround
automation. Dynaudio M4-surround
sound monitoring. Separate digital
preproduction room. Permanent tie
lines to Apollo theatre for studio
quality live recordings. In house team
of engineers and programmers; 24
hour maintenance; private parking

## Pinewood Shepperton Group
**Pinewood Studios**
**Sound Dept**
**Pinewood Road**
**Iver Heath**
**Bucks SL0 0NH**
Tel: 01753 656301
Fax: 01753 656014
email: graham_hartstone@pinewood-
studios.co.uk
Website:
www.pinewoodshepperton.com
Two large stereo dubbing theatres with
automated consoles, all digital release
formats. 35mm and Digital dubbing.
Akai DD8 dubbers & recorders,

Broadband connectivity, ADR & Foley
recording. Large ADR/Fx recording
theatre, 35mm or AVID
AUDIOVISION, removable drives,
Protools, ISDN Dolbyfax with
timecode in aux data. Digital dubbing
theatres with AMS/NEVE Logic 2 and
AudioFile Spectra 16. Preview theatre
115 seats. Formats 35/70mm Dolby
SR.D, DTS and SDDS. Comprehensive
transfer bay. Stereo Optical Negative
transfer including Dolby SR.D, SDDS
and DTS. Cutting rooms
**Shepperton Studios**
**Studios Road**
**Shepperton**
**Middx TW17 0QD**
Tel: 01932 572676
Fax: 01932 572396
email:
sheppertonsound@dial.pipex.com
Website:
www.pinewoodshepperton.com
Tania Robertson
Three Dubbing Theatres (16mm,
35mm, video) Post-sync, and
footsteps; effects, theatre, in-house
sound transfers

## PMPP Facilities
**69 Dean Street**
**London W1V 5HB**
Tel: 020 7437 0979
Fax: 020 7434 0386
Website: www.pmpp.dircon.co.uk
Off-line editing: BVW SP, lo-band
and VHS. Non-linear editing: 5
custom built Avid suites either self
drive or with editor. On-line editing:
Digital Betacam, D3, D2, Beta SP, 1
BVU SP and Hi-8 formats. Three
suites with Charisma effects Aston or
A72 cap gen and GVG mixers.
Graphics: Matisse Painting
Softimage 3D, Acrobat 3D
animation and T-Morph morphing
on Silicon Graphics workstations.
Sound dubbing on Avid Audiovision
or AudioFile. Voiceover studio/A-DAT
digital multi-track recording. Full
transfer duplication and standards
conversion service. Pack shot studio

## Ravenscourt Media (formerly Connections Communications Centre)
**Palingswick House**
**241 King Street**
**Hammersmith**
**London W6 9LP**
Tel: 020 8563 7184
Fax: 020 8563 1934
email:
bookings@ravenscourtmedia.co.uk

Website: www.ravenscourtmedia.co.uk
Richard Durasow
Bill Hammond (Facilities)
Production Equipment
Cameras - Sony 570, PD170,
DVX100, BVW400, Digital Pods -
include camera and portable editing
station. Wide range of sound and
lighting equipment
Post Production
Media Suite with 11 internet ready
editing stations, Final Cut Pro Editing
Stations, Final Cut Pro portable editing
facilities, Avid Media Composer,
Screening and Conference Room

## Redapple
**214 Epsom Road**
**Merrow**
**Guildford**
**Surrey GU1 2RA**
Tel: 01483 455044
Fax: 01483 455022
email: redap@msn.com
Website: Video formats: Beta SP, Beta
Sx, NTSC/PAL. Cameras: Sony DNW
90WSP, 4:3016:9, IKEGAMI, V-55
Camcorders; Transport; VW Caravelle
and Volvo Camera Cars, Twin

## Salon Ltd
**12 Swainson Road**
**London W3 7XB**
Tel: 020 8746 7611
Fax: 020 8746 7613
email: hire@salonrentals.com
Website: www.salonrentals.com
Editing Equipment rental -
Non Linear Systems from standalone
Avids and Lightworks to networked
Unity and Mediashare. Digital Sound
Editing systems including Protools
and Audiovision and a wide range of
Peripherals: Film Equipment:
35mm and 16mm Film Equipment
Hire including Steenecks, Moviolas,
Compeditors and Edit Benches
Large Linear and Non Linear West
London Edit Suites available as well
as delivery to any location

## Sheffield Independent Film
**5 Brown Street**
**Sheffield S1 2BS**
Tel: 0114 272 0304
Fax: 0114 279 5225
email: admin.sif@workstation.org.uk
Website: www.sifmediaa.org.uk
Dave Woodcock, Enquiries
Daren Eagles, General Manager
Sheffield Independent Film houses
several independent media
production companies and provides
film and video facilities including
Aaton XTR+ 16mm kit, DV and

BetaSP cameras, AVID and FCP post-production and a 1200 sq.ft studio

## Soho Images
**8-14 Meard Street**
**London W1V 3HR**
Tel: 020 7437 0831
Fax: 020 7734 9471
email: sohogroup.com
Website: www.sohoimages.com
Zahida Bacchus
Kodak endorsed laboratory offers full processing of 16/35mm film, 24 hours rushes, computerised in-house negative cutting, cinema commercials, broadcast and features bulk prints, archive and restoration. Facilities include: 8/16/35mm Telecine transfers with Wet-Gate. Spirit DataCine with POGAL Platinum, URSA Gold with DCP, Rank Cinitels' with up-grades. Sound suite using Instant Sync, InDaw and SADIE. Broadcast standards conversions, aspect ration conversions, edit suites, Avid Symphony Universal with 24P, 3D and Animation, Flame, Henry and Edit Box

## SVC
**142 Wardour Street**
**London WIF 8ZO**
Tel: 020 7734 1600
Fax: 020 7437 1854
Website: www.svc.co.uk
Website: Catherine Langley
Video Post Production including the following: Datacine, Inferno, Flame, 2 Infinitys; Henry, Computer Animation and Motion Control

## Tele-Cine
**Video House**
**48 Charlotte Street**
**London W1P 1LX**
Tel: 020 7208 2200
Fax: 020 7208 2250
email: telecine@telecine.co.uk
Website: www.telecine.co.uk
Wendy Bleazard
Digital linear and non linear editing; telecine; audio post production; DVD authoring; video compression; fibre and satellite communications; duplication

## Terry Jones PostProductions Ltd
**Goldcrest International**
**65-66 Dean Street**
**London W1D 4PL**
Tel: 020 7434 1173
Fax: 020 7494 1893
email: terryjonespost@btconnect.com
Website:
www.terryjonespostproductions.com
Terry Jones

Lightworks V.I.P. editing suites. Experiencd and creative, award winning editors handling commercials, documentaries, features and corporate work

## TVMS, TV Media
**420 Sauchiehall Street**
**Glasgow G2 3JD**
Tel: 0141 331 1993
Fax: 0141 332 9040
email: tvmsmail@aol.com
Website: Peter McNeill, Chas Chalmers
Media 100 off-line and on-line with Beta SP and Digital facilities for Broadcast, Commercials, and Corporate Productions

## Twickenham Film Studios
**St Margaret's**
**Twickenham**
**Middx TW1 2AW**
Tel: 020 8607 8888
Fax: 020 8607 8889
Website:
www.twickenhamstudios.com
Gerry Humphreys (Post Production)
Caroline Tipple (Stages)
Two dubbing theatres; ADR/Foley theatre; 40 cutting rooms; Lightworks, Avid, 16/35mm. Three stages, offices, art departments, workshop, prop rooms

## VET Training
**3rd Floor, Lux Building**
**2-4 Hoxton Square**
**London N1 6US**
Tel: 020 7505 4700
Fax: 020 7505 4800
email: facilities@vet.co.uk
Website: www.vet.co.uk
Digital media, DVD, editing, sound finishing, encoding, streaming media.

## Videolondon Sound
**16-18 Ramillies Street**
**London W1F 7LW**
Tel: 020 7734 4811
Fax: 020 7494 2553
email:
info@videolondonsoundstudios.co.uk
Website:
www.videolondonsoundstudios.co.uk
Clifford Judge
Five sophisticated sound recording studios with comprehensive digital audio postproduction facilities

## Videosonics Cinema Sound
**68a Delancey Street**
**London NW1 7RY**
Tel: 020 7209 0209
Fax: 020 7419 4470
email: info@videosonics.com

Website: www.videosonics.com
3 x All Digital THX Film Dubbing Theatres. Dolby Digital and SR 35 mm, 16mm and Super 16mm. All aspect ratios, all speeds. Video Projection if required Theatre I: AMS-Neve Logic II console (112 channels) with 24track Audiofile. Theatre II (Big Blue): AMS-Neve DFC console (224 channels) with 2 x 24 track Audio files. 3 x additional television Sound Dubbing Suites, 2 with AMS-Neve digital consoles, 1 x SSL console. 6 x Digital Audio Editing rooms, 35mm film editing, Facilities for Lightworks and Avid 2 x Foley and ADR Studios. A total of 14 AMS Audiofiles. Parking by arrangement. Wheelchair Access

## VTR Ltd
**64 Dean Street**
**London W1V 5HG**
Tel: 020 7437 0026
Fax: 020 7439 9427
email: info@vtr.co.uk
Website: www.vtr.co.uk
Anthony Frend, Rod Shelton
VTR is one of London's top digital post-production facilities specialising in feature films, commercials and promos. Facilities include 3 Spirit Datacines, Infernos, Flames, Smokes, Combustions as well as a fully dedicated 3D computer graphics and animation department. Its team of award winning colourists and effects artists are known throughout the world for their talent and creativity. VTR's new Digital Cinema division has quickly established itself as one of the leading DI (Digital Intermediate) facilities in Europe. At the heart of this operation is the 2k Specter, a non-linear telecine, offering real-time grading flexibility for features and commercials alike

## Windmill Lane Pictures
**4 Windmill Lane**
**Dublin 2**
**Ireland**
Tel: (353) 1 6713444
Fax: (353) 1 6718413
email: info@windmilllane.com
Website: www.windmilllane.com
Liz Murphy
Telecine, digital on-line, AVID off-line, Henry, Flame, Flint, EFP Crews and number 4 Audio Studio
**London W1V 3AW**
Tel: 020 7434 1121
Fax: 020 7734 0619
email: sound@worldwidegroup.ltd.uk
Website: worldwidegroup.ltd.uk

# FESTIVALS

Listed below by country of origin are a selection of international film, television and video festivals with contact names and brief synopses. Compiled by Jose De Esteban

## ARGENTINA

### Festival Internacional de Cine de Mar del Plata
11-20 March 2004
Hipólito Irigoyen 1257 2do y 3er Piso
CP 1085 Mar de Plata
Tel: 54 11 4383 5115
email: competencia.oficial@mardelplatafilmfest.com
Website: www.mdpfilmfestival.com.ar
Miguel Pereira, Director
It includes a main competition of feature films and several sections such as 'Point of View', 'Latin America XXI', 'Women & Film', 'Documentary Frame' and 'Scenes to Come', the former being a successful window for shorts films from all over the world

## AUSTRALIA

### FlickerFest International Short Festival
3-11 January 2004
Bondi Pavillion
PO BOX 7416
Bondi Beach, NSW 2026
Tel: +61 (02) 9365 6888
email: info@flickerfest.com.au
Website: www.flickerfest.com.au
Bronwyn Kidd, Festival Director
Australia's premiere international short film festival, this year celebrates its 13th edition. FlickerFest consists of a main competitive programme of international and Australian shorts, which then tour nationally to all major cities and regional centres; an Online Festival (computer generated and digital short films) and other activities including seminars and forums

### Melbourne International Film Festival
21 July-8 August 2004
PO Box 2206
Fitzroy Mail Centre
Melbourne, Vic 3065
Tel: +613 9417 2011
Fax: +613 9417 3804
email: miff@melbournefilmfestival.com.au
Website: melbournefilmfestival.com.au
James Hewison, Executive Director
A showcase for the latest developments in Australian and international filmmaking offering a wide range of features and shorts, documentaries, animation and experimental films

### Sydney Film Festival
11-26 June 2004
PO Box 96
Strawberry Hills
NSW 2012
Tel: +612 9280 0511
Fax: +612 9280 1520
email: info@sydneyfilmfest.org
Website: www.sydneyfilmfest.org
A celebration of World Cinema screening features, documentaries, shorts, animation, video, experimental work and retrospectives as well as forums and lectures with local and international industry professionals,critics and academics. Prix UIP is awarded by the audience to the best European film screened in the Contemporary World Cinema strand. Also Audience Awards for Best Documentary, Best Short and Best feature film

## AUSTRIA

### Viennale - Vienna International Film Festival
15-27 October 2004
Siebensterngasse 2
A-1070 Vienna
Tel: +431 526 5947
Fax: +431 523 4172
email: office@viennale.at
Website: www.viennale.at
Hans Hurch, Director
Festival for the general public, which premieres Austrian and international films of all genres and in all formats. FIPRESCI-Prize to a debut or follow-up film; Short Film Prize and the 'Standard Audience Jury Prize' for a film in the festival without an Austrian distribution deal

## BELGIUM

### Festival Du Film De Bruxelles
23-30 April 2004
Maliestraat 13
1050 Elsene
Tel: (32) 2 533 3420
email: info@fffb.be
Website: www.fffb.be
Dominique Janne, Director
Competitive festival promoting films from Europe and Belgium, proposes a programme consisting exclusively of first and second European works, thereby offering a real springboard to young directors.

### Festival International du Film Fantastique
11-26 March 2005
Rue de la Comptesse de Flandre 8
Gravin van Vlaanderenstraat 8
B-1020 Brussels
Tel: +32[0]2 201 1713
Fax: +32[0]2 201 1409
email:peymet@bifff.org
Webb:www.bifff.org
Competitive festival presenting over 100 features in the field of fantasy, horror, science-fiction, thrillers, cult and underground. In addition, the festival puts the spotlights on every art form related to the genre: painting, sculpture, literature, music, video, facial make-up, body painting, fashion, video games and theatre

### Flanders International Film Festival
5-16 October 2004
Leeuwstraat 40b
B-9000 Ghent
Tel: +32 9 242 8060
Fax: +32 9 221 9074
email: info@filmfestival.be
Webb: www.filmfestival.be
Jacques Dubrulle, Secretary General
Largest competitive showcase in Belgium, presenting some 190

features and 100 short films from all over the world. The festival focuses on the 'Impact of Music on Film', a fixed section in which 15 films compete for three prizes. In its 31st edition the festival celebrates South Africa

# BOSNIA and HERZEGOVINA

## Sarajevo Film Festival

20-28 August 2004
**Sarajevo Film Festival**
**Branilaca Sarajeva 5/1**
**71000 Sarajevo Bosnia and**
**Herzegovina**
Tel: 387 (33) 209-411/263-380
Fax: 387 (33) 668-186
email: info-sff@sff.ba
Website: www.sff.ba
Mirsad Purivatra, Festival Director
The festival promotes recent contemporary film production and supports the distribution of independent films in Bosnia and Herzegovina. The event also aims 'to establish Sarajevo as a new venue where film directors, actors, producers and distributors can meet, exchange ideas and initiate new projects'

# BRAZIL

## Festival do Rio BR - Rio de Janeiro Film Festival

23 September-7 October 2004
**Rua Voluntários dá Pátria 53/4th**
**Floor**
**97 Botafogo**
**Rio de Janeiro 22270-000**
Tel: +55 21 25790352
Fax: +55 21 25393580
email: films@festivaldorio.com.br
Website: www.festivaldoriobr.com.br
Ilda Santiago, Executive Director
Largest film festival in Brazil and Latin America. With prizes for Best feature, short and documentary. Also 'Premio UIP' for the best European Film voted by audiences.

## Mostra BR de Cinema -São Paulo International Film Festival

22 October- 4 November 2004
**Rua Antonio Carlos, 288-2nd andar**
**Cep 01309-010 Cerqueira Cesar-SP**
Tel: (55 11) 3141 2548/3141 1068
Fax: (55 11) 3266 7066

email: imprensa@mostra.org
Website: www.mostra.org
Leon Cakoff, Festival Director
A cultural, non-profit event for international films. The festival's main sections are: The New Filmmakers Competition and International Perspective

# BURKINA FASO

## FESPACO-Panafrican Film and TV Festival of Ouagadougou

26 February-5 March 2005
**01 BP 2505**
**Ouagadougou 01**
Tel: (226) 5030 75 38
Fax: (226) 5031 25 09
email: sg@fespaco.bf
Website: www.fespaco.bf
Baba Llama, General Delegate
The Panafrican Film and Television Festival is the largest competitive showcase in Africa.Featuring African diaspora and African filmmakers, whose work has been produced during the three years preceding the biennial festival and not shown before at FESPACO

# CANADA

## Atlantic Film Festival

12-20 September 2003
**PO Box 36139**
**5600 Sackville Street, Suit 220**
**Halifax,**
**Nova Scotia B3J 1L2**
Tel: (1) 902 422 3456
Fax: (1) 902 422 4006
email: festival@atlanticfilm.com
Website: www.atlanticfilm.com
Lia Rinaldo, Festival Director
Atlantic premieres new works from the Atlantic region and Canada. Other programmes include International Perspectives (a selection of films from Celtic and Nordic countries); Different Takes; The Late Shifts and the special children's series.

## Banff Television Festival

3-17 June 2004
**1350 Railway Avenue**
**Canmore, Alberta, T1W 3E3**
Tel: (1) 403 678 9260
Fax: (1) 403 678 9269
email: info@btvf.com
Website: www.btvf.com
Festival for television programme

makers and on-line content creators.

This year celebrating its 25th anniversary, the conference schedule features over 60 hours of workshops, plenary sessions, keynote speakers, master classes, market simulations and pitching opportunities. There is also the international Banff Rockie Awards programme competition

## Festival des Films du Monde - Montreal World Film Festival

26 August-6 September 2004
**1432, de Bleury Street**
**Montreal,Quebec H3A 2J1**
Tel: 514 848 3883
Fax: 514 848 3886
email: info@ffm-montreal.org
Website: www.ffm-montreal.org
Serge Losique, Festival President
Competitive festival with films from more than seventy countries. It includes the following sections: Cinema of Europe, Cinema of the Americas (divided in three sub-sections:Panorama Canada, Cinema of the USA, Latin American Cinema), Cinema of Asia, Cinema of Africa, Cinema of Oceania and Documentaries of the World

## Festival International de Nouveau Cinéma et des Nouveaux Médias de Montréal

14-24 October 2004
**3530 Saint-Laurent Blvd, Office 304**
**Montreal**
**Quebec H2X 2V1**
Tel: (1) 514 847 9272
email: montrealfest@fcmm.com
Website: www.fcmm.com
'Innovation and exploration are the guiding principles of the FCMM's programming'. The festival, celebrating its 33rd edition this year, is divided in four categories: Feature Film and Video, Documentary, Short and New Media.

## Hot Docs Canadian International Documentary Festival

23 April- 2 May 2004
**517 College Street**
**Suite 420,Toronto**
**Ontario, M6G 4A2**
Tel: (1) 416 203 2155
Fax: (1) 416 203 0446
email: info@hotdocs.ca
Website: www.hotdocs.ca

Hot Docs is North America's largest documentary festival with a selection of over 100 cutting-edge documentaries from Canada and the rest of the world. The festival has a reputation for providing 'a full range of professional development market and networking opportunities for documentary professionals'

### Ottawa International Student Animation Festival

22-26 September 2004
**2 Daly Avenue, Suite 120**
**Ottawa**
**Ontario K1N 6E2**
Tel: (1) 613 232 8769
Fax: (1) 613 232 6315
email: neall@magma.ca
Website: www.awn.com/ottawa
Kelly Neall, Managing Director
Presenting a special screening entitled 'Essential Viewing' featuring all the 'must see' films for any animation fan. This year highlights include a major retrospective on Animated Soviet Propaganda: 'From the October Revolution to Perestroika' and a Hayao Miyazaki Retrospective' on Fred Crippen, Robert Breer and Co Hoedeman

### Toronto International Film Festival

9-18 September 2004
**2 Carlton Street, Suite 1600**
**Toronto, Ontario M5B IJ3**
Tel: (1) 416 967 7371
Fax: (1) 416 967 9477
email: tiffg@torfilmfest.ca
Website: www.bell.ca/filmfest
Piers Handling, Festival Director
Non-competitive showcase for feature films and shorts not previously shown in Canada.The festival also includes some American premieres, retrospectives and national cinema programmes

### Vancouver International Film Festival

23 September-8 October 2004
**Suite 410, 1008 Homer Street**
**Vancouver, BC V6B 2X1**
Tel: (1) 604 685 0260
Fax: (1) 604 688 8221
email: viff@viff.org
Website: www.viff.org
Alan Franey, Festival Director
One of the largest festivals in Canada. The competitive sections include: Dragons and Tiger: The Cinemas of East Asia, Canadian Images,

Nonfictions features, Cinema of Our Time and Spotlight on France. The VIFF also presents a Trade Forum, which brings together roundtable experts on film and television for discussions and seminars

## COLOMBIA

### Festival Internacional de Cine y Television de Cartagena

27 February- 5 March 2004
**Calle San Juan de Dios**
**Baluarte de San Francisco Javier**
**A.A. 1834, Cartagena**
Tel: (57) 5664 2345
email: info@festicinecartagena.com
Website: www.festicinecartagena.com
Victor Nieto, Festival Director
The most senior film festival in Latin America. It covers: Iberoamerican short and feature films; international showcase; Colombian Television; Cinema , Television, Video and Cable markets; telefestival ; seminars and conferences

## CROATIA

### Split International Festival of New film

26 June-2 July 2004
**P.O. Box 244**
**HR-21000 Split**
Tel: +385 2134 8001
Fax: +385 2134 8002
email: split.filmfest@st.htnet.hr
Website: www.splitfilmfestival.hr
Open to all new, innovative, experimental, radical and subversive work of all genres and lengths. The festival presents screenings of selected film and videos, performances, installations, retrospectives, workshops and discussions. Prizes by international juries

### World Festival of Animated Films

14-19 June 2004
**Koncertna Direkcija Zagreb**
**Kneza Mislava 18**
**10000 Zagreb**
Tel: (385) 1 45 01 190/191/192
Fax: (385) 1 46 11 808
email: animafest@kdz.hr
Website: www.animafest.hr
Dragan Svaco, Director
Competitive showcase for animated productions of any genre made for cinema, television or internet with a

running time ranging from 30 seconds to 30 minutes.

## CUBA

### International Festival of New Latin American Cinema

1-11 December 2004
**Calle 2, no.411 e/17y19**
**10400 Vedado**
**Habana**
Tel: (53) 7 552 841
Fax: (53) 7 334 273
email: festival@icaic.inf.cu
Website: www.habanafilmfestival.com
Ivan Giroud Garate, Festival Director
A selection of Latin American films and videos, unpublished scripts and posters competing for the Coral Awards. It also includes first long feature films and videos by Latin American and Caribbean filmmakers in the category of FIRST WORKS. Other sections: Latin American Panorama, Documentary Information, Made in Cuba, Tributes, Retrospectives, Contemporary International Scene, New Latin American Film Market, seminars, books and specialised magazines launchings

## CZECH REPUBLIC

### Karlovy Vary International Film Festival

2-10 July 2004
**Film Servis Festival Karlovy Vary**
**Panská 1**
**110 00 Prague**
Tel: (420) 221 411 011/022
Fax: (420) 221 411 033
email: festival@kviff.com
Website: www.iffkv.cz
Jiri Bartoska, President
Situated in the old 19th century spa town, the festival includes a non-specialised international competition of feature films; an international competition of full-length and short documentaries; non-competitive informative film programmes and restrospectives

## DENMARK

### Copenhagen Gay & Lesbian Film Festival

15-24 October 2004
**c/o Bryggervangen 40, 2.th.**
**DK-2100 Copenhagen**

Tel: +45 2233 4424
Fax: (45) 3374 3403
email: info@cglff.dk
Website: www.cglff.dk
Simon Verheij, Organiser
Oldest film festival in Copenhagen. It
is a competitive showcase of feature,
documentary, short and experimental
works

## Odense International Film Festival

15-20 August 2005
**Vindegade 18**
**DK-5100 Odense C.**
Tel: (45) 6551 4044
Fax: (45) 6591 4318
email: off.ksf@odense.dk
Website: www.filmfestival.dk
Odense is the birthplace of the world-
famous writer of fairy-tales Hans
Christian Andersen, so it does not
come as a surprise if the film festival
there pays special tribute to fairy-tales
and artistic imagination. This year
edition celebrates the 200 anniversary
of Andersen, with a new competition
and special programmes.

## Nat Film Festival

1-15 April 2005
**St. Kannikestr, 6**
**DK 1169 Kobenhavak**
Tel: +45 3312 0005
Fax: +45 3312 7505
email: info@natfilm.dk
Website: www: natfilm.dk
The biggest international film event
in Denmark is a very successful
platform for domestic distributors,
with an Audience prize that secures
theatrical release. The festival also
provides special support for young
Danish filmmakers

# EGYPT

## Cairo International Film Festival

30 November- 10 December 2004
**17 Kasr El Nil Street**
**Cairo**
Tel: (202) 392 3962
Fax: (202) 393 8979
email: info@cairofilmfest.com
Website: www.cairofilmfest.com
Hussein Fahmi, President
The festival's competitive section is
only for films that have not competed
at other international film festivals.
Out of competition the festival
includes the following sections: Festival
of Festivals, Informative, Retrospective,
Tribute and Film Market

# FINLAND

## Midnight Sun Film Festival

16-20 June 2004
**Malminkatu 36**
**00100 Helsinki**
Tel: (358) 16 614 525
Fax: (358) 16 618 646
email: office@msfilmfestival.fi
Website: www.msfilmfestival.fi
Held in the village of Sodankylä, in
the heart of Finnish Lapland, some
120 kilometers above the Arctic
Circle, the festival can loosely be
divided into three sections: films by
the most famous film directors of all
times, Pearls of the New Cinema and
silent movies with live music. Films
are screened in three venues for 24
hours a day

## Tampere Film Festival

3-7 March 2004
**Box 305**
**33101 Tampere**
Tel: (358) 3 223 5681
Fax: (358) 3 223 0121
email: office@tamperefilmfestival.fi
Website: www.tamperefilmfestival.fi
Jukka-Pekka Laakso, Director
In addition to the short film
competitions the festival screens
several special programmes such as
Cinema Africa and Indian
Independent Documentaries made by
women

## Tough Eye International Turku Animated Film Festival

14-16 May 2004
**Linnankatu 54**
**20100 Turku**
Tel: (358) 10 553 5258
Fax: (358) 10 553 5273
email: info@tough-eye.com
Website: www.tough-eye.com
An animated film competition that
offers hundreds of short animations
from all over the world. The festival,
which takes place in every other year,
shows over forty screening
programmes, including the Timeless
Competition, the Timeless Panorama
and the Tough Eye Selection

# FRANCE

## Cinéma du Réel - International Documentary Film Festival

5-14 March 2004
**Bibliothèque Publique**

d'Information
**Centre Pompidou**
**25, rue du Renard**
**75197 Paris Cedex 04**
Tel: (33) 1 44 78 44 21
Fax: (33) 1 44 78 12 24
email: cinereel@bpi.fr
Website: www.bpi.fr
Suzette Glenadel, General Delegate
This year the International Festival of
Visual Anthropology and Social
Documentation presents an
international competition of 20 to 25
recent and previously unreleased
films, a French competition of films
shot in 2003 and a selection of non-
competitive films about Argentina

## Festival des Trois Continents

23-30 November 2004
**19 A, Passage Pommeraye**
**BP 43302**
**44033 Nantes Cedex 1**
Tel: (33) 2 40 69 74 14
Fax: (33) 2 40 73 55 22
email: festival@3continents.com
Website: www.3continents.com
Marie-Annick Ranger, General
Delegate
The Festival of the Three Continents
presents feature-length fiction films
from Africa, Asia, Latin and Black
America. The event includes a
competitive section, tributes to
directors and actors, and panoramas.

## Festival du Cinéma Américain

3-12 September 2004
**40, rue Anatole**
**92594 Levallois**
**Perret Cedex**
Tel: (33) 1 41 34 20 33
Fax: (33) 1 46 40 55 39
email: info-deauville@deauville.org
Website: www.festival-deauville.com
Competition and panorama of
American productions only.

## Festival du Court Métrage Clermont-Ferrand

28 January-5 February 2005
**La Jetée**
**6, place Michel-de-l'Hospital**
**63058 Clermont-Ferrand Cedex 1**
Tel: (33) 4 73 91 65 73
Fax: (33) 4 73 92 11 93
email: info@clermont-filmfest.com
Website: www.clermont-filmfest.com
The world's premier cinema event
dedicated to international and
national short films. The festival and
market are the most visible part of

the work of La Jetee, yet the team develops many projects related to the visual media, education and training as well as coordinating the circulation of short films at regional, national and international level

## Festival du Film Britannique de Dinard

7-10 October 2004
**2,  Boulevard Féart**
**35800 Dinard**
Tel: (33)  2 99 88 19 04
Fax: (33) 2 99 46 67 15
email:
fest.film.britain.dinard@wanadoo.fr
Website: www.festivaldufilm-
dinard.com
Competitive festival with retrospectives and exhibitions. It also promotes meetings between French and English producers

## Festival International de Films de Femmes

12-21 March 2004
**Maison des Arts**
**Place Salvador Allende**
**94000 Créteil**
Tel: (33) 1 49 80 38 98
Fax: (33) 1 43 99 04 10
email: filmsfemmes@wanadoo.fr
Website: www.filmsdefemmes.com
Jacki Buet, Programme Director
Competitive for feature films, documentaries and shorts directed by one or more women, or a mixed team

## Festival International du Film d'Amiens

5-14 November 2004
**MCA - 2, place Léon Gontier**
**80 000 Amiens**
Tel: (33) 3 2271 3570
Fax: (33) 3 2292 5304
email: contact@filmfestamiens.org
Website: www.filmfestamiens.org
Jean-Pierre Garcia, Director
The festival's goal is threefold: a quality cultural event, a meeting point for professionals and a diverse audience. It shows full-length or short films, fiction, animation, and documentaries.

## Festival International du Film d'Animation

6-11 June 2005
**JICA/MIFA**
**18 avenue du Tresum**
**BP 399**
**74013 Annecy Cédex**
Tel: (33) 04 50 10 09 00
Fax: (33) 04 50 10 09 70
email: info@annecy.org

Website: www.annecy.org
Competition for animated shorts, features, TV films and commercials produced in the previous 2 years

## Festival International du Film de Cannes

12-23 May 2004
**Departement Films**
**3, rue Amelie**
**F-75007 Paris**
Tel: (33) 1 53 59 61 71
Fax: (3)3 1 53 59 61 70
email: laurent.rivoire@festival-
cannes.fr
Website:  www.festival-cannes.org
Festival registration:
accreditation.festival.cannes.fr
Competitive section for feature films and shorts (up to 15 mins) produced in the previous year, which have not been screened outside country of origin nor been entered in other competitive festivals

## Festival International du Film Policier

8-11 April 2004
**40 Rue Anatole**
**92594 Levallois-Perret**
**Cedex**
Tel: (331) 4134 2033
Fax: (331) 4134 2077
email: sbobe@cognac.fr
Website: festival.cognac.fr
Competitive for thriller films (police movies, thrillers, film noirs, court movies, and investigations), which have not been commercially shown in France or participated in festivals in Europe

## Gérardmer-Festival du Film Fantastique

28 January-1 February 2004
**29 avenue du 19 Novembre**
**BP 105**
**88403 Gerardmer**
Tel: +03 2960 9821
Fax: +03 2960 9814
email: presse@gerardmer-
fantasticart.com
Website: www.gerardmer-
fantasticart.com
Formerly held in Avoriaz.
Competitive for international fantasy feature films (science-fiction, horror and supernatural)

## MIP-TV

11-15 April 2005
**Reed MIDEM Organisation**
**179, avenue Victor Hugo**
**75116 Paris**

Tel: (33) 1 41 90 45 84
Fax: (33) 1 44 90 45 70
email:
andre.vaillant@reedmidem.com
Website: www.miptv.com
André Vaillant, Programme Director
An international television programme market held in Cannes. It focuses on content programming for the television industry worldwide. The trade show serves professionals working in TV broadcasting, programmes production and/or distribution, video and the Internet, advertising, licensing and merchandising, consultancy, service companies and new media.

## Rencontres Cinématographiques Franco-Américaines

23-27 June 2004
**Avignon Film Festival**
**10, Montée de la Tour**
**30400 Villeneuve-les-Avignon**
Tel: +33 490 25 93 23
Fax: +33 490 25 93 24
**French-American Center of Provence**
**145 Ave. of the Americas**
**10013 NY**
Tel: +212 343 2675
Fax: +212 840 5019
email: jhr2001@aol.com
Website: www.avignonfilmfest.com
The French-American Film Workshop brings together independent filmmakers from USA and France. New independent films are celebrated. With retrospectives and round-tables.

## Sunny Side of the Doc

19-22 June 2004
**Docs Services**
**23, rue François Simon**
**13003 Marseille**
Tel: (33) 495 04 44 80
Fax: (33) 491 84 38 34
email:
contact@sunnysideofthedoc.com
Website:
www.sunnysideofthedoc.com
Yves Jeanneau, General Commissioner
International documentary market serving as an interface between professionals of the industry from 40 countries whether they be producers, distributors, broadcasters or commissioning editors

# GERMANY

## Feminale - International Women's Film Festival

6-10 October 2004
**Internationales FrauenFilmFestival**
**Maybachstr, 111**
**50670 Cologne**
Tel: (0049) 221 1300 225
Fax: (0049) 221 1300 281
email: press@feminale.de
Website: www.feminale.de
Second largest festival of this kind in the world. The Feminale offers a forum that introduces film and video productions made by women to a broad public. Its diverse programme includes the sections: Horizons-Debut Competitions, Panorama, Zoom-In, Queer Looks, Portrait, Girl's Focus and Animation

## Filmfest Hamburg

23-30 September 2004
**FilmFest Hamburg GmbH**
**Steintorweg 4**
**D-20099 Hamburg**
Tel: (49) 40 399 190 00
Fax: (49) 40 399 190 010
email: info@filmfesthamburg.de
Website: www.filmfesthamburg.de
Working in close cooperation with the Bitfilm-Festival for digital film and new media the Hamburg Film Festival has added two new sections to its programme: The Four Dimesion/DVD-Straight to Filmfest, which presents outstanding productions that did not made it to the big screen but appeared directly on DVD, and Children's Filmfest, to introduce young audience to animation films

## FilmFest München

26 June-3 July 2004
**Internationale Müenchner Filmwochen**
**Sonnenstrasse 21**
**80331 Munich**
Tel: (49) 89 3819 040
Fax: (49) 89 3819 0427
email: info@filmfest-muenchen.de
Website: filmfest-muenchen.de
The Munich International Film Festival presents new cinematic discoveries from around the world, highlights from the big studios and major companies as well as the best works by international young directors. The extensive programme of international, European and

German Premieres is rounded out with Retrospectives, Portraits, Tributes, Special Screenings and the traditional sections of World Cinema, American Independents, Made in Germany – German Films, German TV Movies and Children's Film Fest.

## Going underground International Short Film Festival

28 January-3 February 2004
**Tempelhofer Ufer 1a**
**10961 Berlin**
Tel: +49 30 2529 1322
Fax: +49 30 693  2959
email: interfilm@interfilm.de
Website: interfilm.de
An original initiative for 'Ultra Shorts' in Berlin's underground trains. Films must be silent and the narrative no more than 90 seconds long of length.

## International Film Festival Mannheim-Heidelberg

10-27 November 2004
**Collini-Center, Galerie**
**68161 Mannheim**
Tel: (49) 621 102 943
Fax: (49) 621 291 564
email: ifmh@mannheim-filmfestival.com
Website: www.mannheim-filmfestival.com
Dr Michael Koetz, Director
New talents compete in the two main sections International Competition and International Discoveries. A selection of around 35 new feature films that have never been premiered, mainly fiction films but also cinematographically interesting documentaries and short films.

## Internationale Filmfestspiele Berlin - Berlin International Film Festival

10-20 February 2005
**Potsdamer Strasse 5**
**10785 Berlin**
Tel: (49) 30 25 920 200
Fax: (49) 30 25 920 299
email: info@berlinale.de
Website: www.berlinale.de
Dieter Kosslick, Festival Director
Competition for international feature films and shorts. Includes a section, Perspektive Deutsches Kino, on current German film production and a separate competition programme for children (Kinderfilmfest),

consisting of features, shorts/animation and live action

## Internationales Leipziger Fesztival für Dokumentar- und Animationsfilm

16-24 October 2004
**DOK Filmwochen GmbH**
**Grosse Fleischergasse 11**
**04109 Leipzig**
Tel: (49) 341 980 3921
Fax: (49) 341 980 6141
email: info@dokfestival-leipzig.de
Website: www.dokfestival-leipzig.de
Fred Gehler, Director
Annual festival which under the motto 'Films of the world for human dignity' serves the promotion and circulation of international documentary and animated films

## Nordische Filmtage Lübeck - Nordic Film Days Lübeck

4-7 November 2004
**Hansestadt Lubeck-Bereich Kunst and Kultur**
**Dr. Ada Kadelbach**
**Schrildstr 12**
**23539 Lübeck**
Tel: (49) 451 122 41 00/01
Fax: (49) 451 122 41 06
email: info@filmtage.luebeck.de
Website: www.filmtage.luebeck.de
Festival of Scandinavian and Baltic films. A competition for feature, documentary and Nordic countries' films

## Oberhausen International Short Film Festival

29 april-4 May 2004
**Grillostrasse 34**
**46045 Oberhausen**
Tel: (49) 208 825 2652
Fax: (49) 208 825 5413
email: info@kurzfilmtage.de
Website: www.kurzfilmtage.de
Lars Henrik Gass, Director
With its excellent archive, distribution, publications and 'the meticulousness with which its programme is compile' the Oberhausen festival activily works to promote and ensure a lively existence for the Short Film. Special attention is paid to the shorts' position regarding social reality, cultural differences and aesthetic innovation

## Prix Europa

16-23 October 2004
**Sender Freies Berlin**
**14046 Berlin**
Tel: (49) 30 30 31 16 10
Fax: (49) 30 30 31 16 19

email: office@prix-europa.de
Website: www.prix-europa.de
Competition for fiction, non-fiction, current affairs, multicultural matters on television, documentary and drama. Open to all broadcasting organisations and producers in Europe

# GREECE

## International Thessaloniki Film Festival
November
9 Alexandras Ave.
11473 Athens
Tel: (30) 210 645 3669
Fax: (30) 210 644 8143
email: info@filmfestival.gr
Website: www.filmfestival.gr
Dedicated to the promotion of independent cinema from all over the world, the event features the International Section for first or second features (Golden Alexander for Best Film; Special Jury Award Silver Alexander); panorama on Greek films; New Horizons programme; the Balkan Survey; numerous retrospectives and tributes to leading figures in the world of films; exhibitions and special events

## Kalamata International Documentary Film Festival
October
125-127 Kifisas Avenue
11524 Athens
Tel: (30)  010 699 0660
Fax: (30) 010 699 0905
email: festival@documentary.gr
Website: www.documentary.gr
Kostas Skouras, Managing Director
The festival awards the following prizes: Golden and Silver 'Olive' Awards; Special Award; Award 'Eri Rotzokou'. It also organises a competitive Student Documentary section. Parallel events include: honorary tributes, exhibition of cinematographic giant posters, exhibition of Doc photos and music entertainment

# HONG KONG

## Hong Kong International Film Festival
22 March-6 April 2005
Film & Media Arts Office
22$^{nd}$ Floor, 181 Queen's Road Central

Hong Kong
Tel: +852 2970 3300
Hong Kong Arts Development TelT
Fax: +852 2970 3011
email: hkiff@hkiff.org.hk
Website: www.hkiff.org.hk
Non-competitive for feature films, documentaries and short films from around the world, which have been produced in the previous two years. Also a local short film and video competition; a FIPRESCI Award for Young Asian cinema and a showcase for the historical development of Hong Kong cinema

# INDIA

## International Film Festival of India
29 November- 9 December 2004
Directorate of Film Festivals
Siri Fort Auditorium Complex
August Kranti Marg, Khel Gaon
110049 New Delhi
Tel: (91) 2649 9371/9356
Fax: (91) 2649 7214/9357
email: ddiff.dff@hub.nic.in
Website: mib.nic.in/dff
With an Indian Panorama section for 21 feature and 21 non-feature films distinguised by their thematic and aesthetic excellence. The festival main objective is to promote Indian films in international film festivals in India and abroad

## International Film Festival of Kerala
December 2004
Golf Links road, Jawahar Nagar
Kowdiar, Thiruvananthapuram
695003 Kerala
Tel: +91 471 2312214/2310323
Fax: +91 471 2310322
email: chitram@md3.vsnl.net.in
Website: www.keralafilm.com
'To see to feel and to feel to think' is the motto of this festival. The competitive section is especially designed for films from Asia, Africa and Latin America whereas the non-competitive section includes Indian Cinema, World Cinema, Homages and Retrospectives

# IRAN

## International Short Film Festival
October
Iranian Young Cinema Society
Gandhi Ave, 19th Street, No 20

P.O. Box 15175-163
Tehran
Tel: (98) 21 877 3114
Fax: (98) 21 879 5675
email: info@shortfilmfest-ir.com
Website: www.shortfilmfest-ir.com
International competition with the following categories: experimental, animation, documentaries and fiction. The festival also pays tributes to short films from other countries and organises special programmes

# IRELAND

## Cork International Film Festival
October
10 Washington Street
Cork
Tel: +353 21 427 1711
Fax: +353 21 427 5945
email: info@corkfilmfest.org
Website: www.corkfilmfest.org
Michael Hannignan, Director
Ireland's oldest and biggest film event, celebrates its 50th anniversary with an international symposium on the art of the short film and Cork's role as European Capital of Culture 2005

## Dublin Lesbian and Gay Film Festival
28 August- 1 September 2004
c/o Nexus, Fumbally Court
Fumbally Lane, Dublin 8
Tel: +353 1 415 8414
Fax: +353 1 473 0597
email: dlgff@ireland.com
Website: www.gcn.ie@dlgff
Brian Sheedan, Festival Director
Presenting features, documentaries and shorts, with Audience awards for the Best film in each category

# ISRAEL

## Haifa International Film Festival
October
142 Hanassi Avenue
34633  Haifa
Tel: +97 24 835 3521/8353522
Fax: +97 24 838 4327
email: haifaff@netvision.net.il
Website: www.haifaff.co.il
Eliane Auerbach
The biggest annual meeting for professionals associated with the film industry in Israel. It is a competitive showcase for foreign and Israeli feature films, short films,

documentaries and TV dramas

## Jerusalem Film Festival

8-17 July 2004
**The Jerusalem Cinemateque**
**11, Hebron Road**
**91083 Jerusalem**
Tel: +972 2 565 4333
Fax: +972 2 565 4335/4
email: jer-cin@jer-cin.org.il
Website: www.jff.org.il
Daniel J. Cohen, Festival Director
A showcase for the finest in recent
international cinema, documentaries,
animation, avant garde,
retrospectives, special tributes and
homages, Mediterranean and Israeli
cinema. Three international awards:
Wim van Leer's In Spirit of Freedom
focused on human rights,
Mediterranean Cinema and Jewish
Theme

# ITALY

## Festival dei Popoli

26 November-2 December 2004
**Borgo Pinti 82 rosso**
**50121 Firenze**
Tel: (39) 055 244 778
Fax: (39) 055 241 364
email:
festivaldeipopoli@festivaldeipopoli.19
1.it
Website: www.festivaldeipopoli.org
Maria Bonsanti, Head of Hospitality
Office
Competitive and non-competitive
sections for documentaries on
sociological, historical, political and
anthropological subjects as well as
music, art and cinema produced
during the year preceding the festival.
The films for the competitive section
should not have been screened in
Italy before

## Festival Internazionale Cinema Giovanni - Torino Film Festival

10-20 November 2004
**Via Monte di Pietà 1**
**10121 Torino**
Tel: (39) 011 562 3309
Fax: (39) 011 562 9796
email: info@torinofilmfest.org
Website: www.torinofilmfest.org
Giulia D'Agnolo Vallan, Festival
Director
Competitive sections for
international features, shorts and
documentaries. 'Spazio Italian'
opened solely to Italian fiction and
videos and 'Spazio Torino' reserved to

filmmakers and videomakers, born or
residing in Turin and the Piedmont
region

## Festival Internazionale di Film con Tematiche Omosessuali

22-29 April 2004
**Piazza San Carlo,161**
**10123 Turin**
Tel: (39) 011 534 888
Fax: (39) 011 535 796
email: info@tglff.com
Website: www.tglff.com
Lesbian and gay themed festival.
Competitive for features, shorts and
documentaries. Also retrospectives
and special showcases for both
cinema and television work

## Giffoni Film Festival

17-24 July 2004
**C/o Cittadella del Cinema**
**84095 Giffoni Valle Piana**
Tel: (39) 089 802 3111
Fax: (39) 089 802 3210
email: info@giffoniff.it
Website: www.giffoniff.it
Claudio Gubitosi, Festival Director
Also refered to as the Giffoni's
Children Film Festival, it presents
children's films with and without
strong themes to the young. Out of
competition activities include a
debate and study section called 'Y
Generation', previews and Animated
Nights

## Le Giornate del Cinema Muto - Pordenone Silent Film Festival

9-16 October 2004
**c/o La Cineteca del Friuli**
**Via G. Bini, Palazzo Gurisatti**
**33013 Gemona**
Tel: (39) 0432 980458
Fax: (39) 0432 970542
email: info.gcm@cinetecadelfriuli.org
Website: www.cinetecadelfriuli.org
David Robinson,Festival Director
'Dziga Vertov', 'Britain's Forgotten
Men', the festival is an opportunity to
enjoy British cinema of the 1920s.
Also in this year edition 'Fort Lee: the
film town (1904-2004) a chance to
reflect on the role this community
played in the development of
American motion picture industry

## MIFED - Cinema & Television International Multimedia Market

12-16 October 2004
**Palazzina FMI,**

**Largo Domodossola 1**
**20145 Milan**
Tel: +39 02 48 5501
Fax: +39 02 48 550420
email: mifed@fmi.it
Website: www.mifed.com
International market for companies
working in the film, television, and
home videos industries.
Mostra Internazionale d'Arte

## Cinematografica - Venice International Film Festival

1-6 September 2004
**Palazzo del Cinema**
**Lungomare Marconi**
**30126 Lido de Venezia**
Tel: (39) 041 521 8711
Fax: (39) 041 522 7539
email: cinema@labiennale.org
Website: www.labiennale.org
Marco Müller, Festival Director
The oldest film Festival worldwide
(1932 - ), whose programme includes
a competition for feature film and
short films.This year's edition focuses
on the secret history of Italian cinema
from 1960 to 1980

## Mostra Internazionale del Nuovo Cinema - Pesaro Film Festival

25 June- 3 July 2004
**Via Villafranca 20**
**00185 Rome**
Tel: +39 06 445 6643
Fax: +39 06 491 163
email: info@pesarofilmfest.it
Website: www.pesarofilmfest.it
Giovanni Spagnoletti, Festival
Director
Particularly concerned with the work
of new directors, emergent cinemas
and innovation at every level. The
festival is devoted each year to an
specific country or culture. It also
organises a special event on Italian
cinema

## Noir In Festival - International Mystery Festival

A week in December
**Via Panaro, 17**
**00199 Rome**
Tel: +3906-860 3111
Fax: +3906-862 13298
email: noir@noirfest.com
Website: www.noirfest.com
With a competitive and a non-
competitive section, the festival aims
to promote and diffuse the mystery
genre (crime story, suspense, thriller,
horror, fantasy, spy story,

whodunnit…) in Italy and abroad. It presentes previews, retrospectives, meetings and seminars.

### Prix Italia

13-20 September 2003
RAI Radio Televisione Italiana
Via Monte Santo, 52
00195 Rome
Tel: (39) 06 3686 9026
Fax: (39) 06 361 2604
email: prixitalia@rai.it
Website: www.prixitalia.rai.it
Alessandro Ferodi, General Secretary
Competitive for television and radio productions from national broadcasting organisations. Prizes are awarded for quality productions in the fields of drama (single plays and serials), documentaries (culture and current affairs), performing arts (television) and music (radio)

### Taormina International Film Festival

13-20 June 2004
Palazzo Firenze
Via Pirandello 31
98039 Taormina
Tel: (39) 942 21142
Fax: (39) 942 23348
email: info@taoarte.it
Website: www.taorminafilmfest.it
Competitive for features. Emphasis on new directors and a great panorama of European, African and American films

## JAPAN

### Tokyo International Film Festival

23-31 October 2004
6F, Ginza eight Bldg.
4-14-6 Ginza, Chou-Ku
Tokyo 104-0061
Tel: +81 3 3624 1081
Fax: +81 3 3624 1087
email: info@tiff-jp.net
website: www.tiff-jp.net
The festival programme offers a competition of feature films which are either the first, second or third film by the director; Special Screenings showing 'the newest and hottest films'; Winds of Asia, focusing on Asian films and introducing works by enthusiastic Asian filmmakers; symposia with creators of game software, commercials, visual arts and Nippon Cinema Classics

### Tokyo Video Festival

14 February 2004
c/o Victor Co of Japan Ltd
1-7-1 Shinbashi
Victor Bldg, Minato-ku
Tokyo 105-0004
Tel: (81) 3 3289 2815
Fax: (81) 3 3289 2819
Website: www.jvc-tvf1@mb.kcom.ne.jp
Nobuhiko Obayashi, Director
Worldwide video contest for amateurs and professionals alike. The only requirement for a work to be accepted is that it has to be shot with a video camera and be no longer than 20 minutes. Any theme can be addressed. Past entries have dealt with personal opinions and experience, dreams, daily life and creation

### Yamagata International Documentary Film Festival

7-13 October 2005
ID Kawadacho Bldg, 3 fl.
7-6 Kawadacho
Shinjuku-Ku
Tokyo 162-0054
Tel: (81) 3 5362 0672
Fax: (81) 3 5362 0670
email: mail@tokyo.yidff.jp
Website:
www.city.yamagata.yamagata.jp/yidff
Sponsored by the city of Yamagata, this is a biennial festival whose main activities include International Competition, Jurors' Films, New Asian Currents, Japanese Panorama, Classic Japanese Film Screenings and Retrospective. The website also offers a link to Documentary Box, a journal devoted to covering recent trends in making and thinking about documentaries

## KOREA

### Pusan International Film Festival

7-15 October 2005
Yachting Center, #208
1393 Woo 1- Dong
Haeundae-Gu, Pusan
Tel: 82-51 747 3010/11
Fax: 82-51 747 3012
email: piff@piff.org
Website: www.piff.org
The first international film festival ever to be held in Korea, it acts as a window for Asian Cinema and offers a Korean Panorama in order to promote emerging talents from Asia.

The festival accepts features, experimental films, documentaries shorts and animation

## MALTA

### Golden Knight International Amateur Film & Video Festival

29 November- 1 December 2004
Malta Amateur Cine Circle
PO Box 450
Marsa, Malta
Tel: +356 412382/418387
Fax: +356 225 047
email: macc@global.net.mt
Website: www.global.net.mt/macc
The festival is divided in three sections: Amateur, Film School Student and Open. Productions should be a maximum of 30 minutes. Golden, Silver and Bronze Trophies are awarded

## MONACO

### Festival de Television de Monte Carlo

28-3 July 2004
4, Boulevard du Jardin Exotique
MC 98000 Monaco
Tel: (377) 93 10 40 60
Fax: (377) 93 50 70 14
email: info@tvfestival.com
Website: www.tvfestival.com
Sylvie Chiabant, Competition Coordinator
The Monte Carlo International Television Festival replaces the Monte Carlo Television Market & Festival previously held in February. Its aim is 'to use TV as an exceptional means of bringing people together and enriching their culture'. Prizes are awarded to short news, current affairs, 24-hour news programmes, TV films and mini-series, drama and comedy series and to a European producer

## THE NETHERLANDS

### Cinekid

17-24 October 2004
Korte Leidesedwarsstraat 12
1017 RC Amsterdam
Tel: (31) 20 531 7890
Fax: (31) 20 531 7899
email: info@cinekid.nl
Website: www.cinekid.nl
The festival provides an overview of the best international children's film,

television and new media productions. It is aimed at young people from 4 to 16, who can also try out the latest CD-Roms and participate in interactive workshops

## International Documentary Filmfestival Amsterdam
18-28 November 2004
**Kleine-Gartmanplantsoen 10**
**1017 RR Amsterdam**
Tel: (31) 20 627 3329
Fax: (31) 20 638 5388
email: info@idfa.nl
Website: www.idfa.nl
IDFA holds competitions for documentaries and videos. It also presents a Forum for co-financed European documentaries and awards the Joris Ivens prize

## International Film Festival Rotterdam
26 January-6 February 2005
**PO Box 21696**
**3001 AR Rotterdam**
Tel: (31) 10 890 9090
Fax: (31) 10 890 9091
email: tiger@filmfestivalrotterdam.nl
Website:
www.filmfestivalrotterdam.com
Simon Fiedl, Sandra den Hamer, Directors
One of the largest and most popular film festivals, its main programme includes the Tiger Awards Competition, international and European premieres. Other highlights include retrospectives on different genres and directors and World Cinema Tour

## Netherlands Film Festival
21-30 September 2005
**Stichting Nederlands Film Festival**
**PO Box 1581**
**3500 BN Utrecht**
Tel: (31) 30 230 3800
Fax: (31) 30 230 3801
email: info@filmfestival.nl
Website: www.filmfestival.nl
Screening a selection of new Dutch features, shorts, documentaries, animation and TV drama. Also retrospectives, seminars, talk-shows, Cinema Militants Lecture and Holland Film Meeting

## World Wide Video Festival
10-20 June 2004
**Keizersgracht 462**
**1016 Amsterdam GE**
Tel: (31) 20 420 7729
Fax: (31) 20 421 3828
email: wwvf@wwvf.nl

Website: www.wwvf.nl
Tom van Vliet, Director
Multi-media art festival, which accepts CD-Roms and websites. The festival is one of the pionering events in a now internationally respected field of visual arts

# NEW ZEALAND

## Auckland International Film Festival
9-25 July 2004
**The New Zealand Film Festival Trust**
**PO Box 9544**
**Marion Square**
**Wellington**
Tel: (64) 4 385 0162
Fax: (64) 4 801 7304
email: festival@nzff.co.nz
Website: www.enzedff.co.nz
The festival and its Wellington sibling (same contact) include feature and short films, documentaries, video and animation. The NZ Film Festival Trust also organises other events: Dunedin International Film Festival, Travelling Festival Circuit and Christchurch International Film Festival. Details of these can also be found on this same website

# NORWAY

## Norwegian International Film Festival
20-27 August 2004
**PO Box 145**
**5501 Haugesund**
Tel: (47) 52 743 370
Fax: (47) 52 743 371
email: info@filmfestivalen.no
Website: www.filmfestivalen.no
The festival main programme is devoted to feature films for theatrical release and its participation is reserved for film and cinema professionals, students and members of the press. The annual market, called New Nordic Films, is an opportunity for international distributors and TV companies to see new Nordic features and to meet Nordic filmmakers, producers, agents, buyers and distributors

## Oslo International Film Festival
Ten days in November
**Dronningers Gt. 16**
**N-0152 Oslo**
Tel: (47) 22 20 07 66
Fax: (47) 22 20 18 03

email: info@oslofilmfestival.com
Website: www.pluto.no/filmfestival
Tommy Lordahl, Festival Director
Regular programme includes screening of feature and short films, with special focus on American independents, new European cinema and films from Asia, documentaries on filmmaking, music, history and personal stories

# POLAND

## Crakow Film Festival
28 May-1 June 2004
**c/o Apollo-Film**
**ul. Pychowicka 7**
**30-364 Krakow**
Tel: (48) 012 427 1472
Fax: (48) 012 427 9680
email: festiwal@apollofilm.pl
Website: www.cracowfilmfestival.pl
Krzysztof Gierat, Festival Director
Also known as the International and National Documentary and Short Film Festival, the event is dedicated to documentary, animation and other short film forms. The festival grants an international life achievement award, called the Dragon of Dragons Special Prize. It also features retrospectives of national cinematography, artistic schools and directors

# PORTUGAL

## International Animated Film festival of Espinho-Cinanima
November
**Rua 62, 251**
**Apartado 743**
**4500-901 Espinho**
Tel: +351 22 734 1350
Fax: +351 22 733 1358
email: cinanima@mail.lelepac.pt
Website: www.cinanima.pt
Festival for the promotion of animation art, comprising a competitive and non-competitive programme and including retrospectives, exhibitions, debates and animation workshops

## Fantasporto-Oporto International Film Festival
21 February- 7 March 2005
**Rua Aníbal Cunha**
**84 - sala 1.6**
**4050-048 Porto**
Tel: +351 2 2207 6050
Fax: +351 2 2207 6059
email: infor@fantasporto.online.pt

Website: www.fantasporto.online.pt
Biggest film festival in Portugal and
one of the most respected in Europe
along with Sitges and Brussels. This
year the festival will pay attention to
the 'Orient Express' new section,
dedicated to Asian Cinema. The
official competition sections remain
the Fantasy Cinema and the Directors
Week, complemented by some
retrospectives and sidebars

### Festroia International Film Festival Setúbal

4-13 June 2004
**Troia International Film Festival**
**Forum Luisa Todi**
**Av. Luisa Todi, 65**
**2900-461 Setubal**
Tel: +35 1 265 525 908
Fax: +35 1 265 525 681
email: geral@festroia.pt
Website: www.festroia.pt
Presenting full-length films, the
competitive section only accepts
works from countries producing up to
thirty films per year. The Information
Section (non-competitive) includes
retrospectives distinguished by their
artistic or historic importance and
deserving public recognition

# RUSSIA

### St. Pertersburg Film Festival

23-29 June 2004
**10 Kamennoostrovsky Av.**
**St. Petersburg 197101**
Tel: (7) 812 237 0304
Fax: (7) 812 394 5870
email: info@filmfest.ru
Website: www.filmfest.ru
Russia's largest non-competitive
festival for recent outstanding works
of international and Russian origin

### Moscow International Film Festival

18-27 June 2004
**Interfest**
**10/1 Khoklhovsky per.**
**Moscow 109028**
Tel: (095) 917 2486
Fax: (095) 916 0107
email: info@miff.ru
Website: www.miff.ru
Renat Davletiarov, general Director
Although the festival has a definitive
Russian perspective, it still offers
international competition screenings,
retrospectives, films from CIS and the
Baltics, Medium Forum and Forum
for Young Filmmakers

# SINGAPORE

### Singapore International Film Festival

15 April-1 May 2004
**45A Keong Saik Road**
**Singapore 089149**
Tel: (65) 6225 7417
Fax: (65) 6738 7578
email: filmfest@pacific.net.sg
Website: www.filmfest.org.sg
Screening over 300 films consisting of
features, shorts and animations. The
festival focuses on South-east Asian
cinema as well as Indonesian and
Malaysian emerging productions

# SLOVAKIA

### Art Film Festival Trencianske Teplice

18-25 June 2004
**Art Film, n.f.**
**Konventna 8**
**81103 Bratislava**
Tel: (421) 2 5441 9481
Fax: (421) 2 5441 1679
email: artfilm@artfilm.sk
Website: www.artfilm.sk
Taking place in a spa town, the
festival views 'cinema as an art form
rather than as a commodity or
advertising tool'. Accordingly, this
event shows in competition features,
shorts and full-length documentaries
with emphasis on innovative forms
and visual means

# SOUTH AFRICA

### Cape Town International Film Festival

Three weeks in April and May or in
November
**University of Cape Town**
**Private Bag, Rondebosch**
**7700 Cape Town**
Tel: (27) 21 423 8257
Fax: (27) 21 423 8257
email: filmfest@hiddingh.uct.ac.za
Website:
www.netribution.co.uk/festivals
Trevor Steele Taylor, Director
Oldest film festival in South Africa. It
screens features, documentaries and
short films on 35mm, 16mm or
video. Emphasis on the independent,
the transgressive and the iconoclastic.
Major profile of South African
production

### Encounters South African International Documentary Festival

July-August
**925 Groove Kerk Building**
**39 Adderley Street**
**Cape Town 8000**
Tel: (27) 21 465 9289
Fax: (27) 21 465 1927
email: info@encounters.co.za
Website: www.encounters.co.za
Peter Eaton, Programmer
A joint venture with Switzerland,
aimed at promoting documentary
filmmaking and exchange between
South African and Swiss filmmakers.

### Southern African Film & Television Market

16-19 November 2004
**SABC Building**
**209 Beach Road, Sea Point**
**Cape Town**
Tel: (27) 21 430 8160
Fax: (27) 21 430 8186
email: info@sithengi.co.za
Website: www.sithengi.co.za
Michael Auret, Chief Executive
Officer
The core programmes of this media
event are the Product Market, which
deals with the buying and selling of
completed product, and The Pitching
Forum, which aims to bring about
the buying and selling of ideas. This
event includes also the Sithengi Film
Festival, showcasing films made by or
with indigenous peoples worldwide,
and RestFest, a festival of digital
filmmaking

# SPAIN

### L'Alternativa-Festival de Cine Independiente de Barcelona

12-20 November 2004
**Centre de Cultura Contemporanea**
**Montalegre 5**
**08001 Barcelona**
Tel: +34 93 306 4100
Fax: +34 93 301 8251
email: alternativa@cccb.org
Website: alternativa.cccb.org
A platform for the promotion and
distribution of films (shorts,
animations, documentaries and
features) which due to their
innovative characteristics are unable
to find a way into main exhibition
and distribution circuits

## Bilbao International Festival of Documentary & Short Films

20 November- 4 December 2004
**Colón de Larrátegui 37-4**
**Apdo. 579**
**48009 Bilbo**
Tel: +34 94 424 8698
Fax: +34 94 424 5624
email: info@zinebi.com
Website: www.zinebi.com
Competitive for animation, fiction and documentaries (up to 30 mins). The festival presents a selection of the best shorts produced in the Basque Country, Spain and Latin America

## Donostia-San Sebastian International Film Festival

15-25 September 2004
**PO BOX 397**
**20080 Donostia-San Sebastian**
Tel: +34 943 481 212
Fax: +34 943 481 218
email: films@sansebastianfestival.com
Website;
www.sansebastianfestival.ya.com
Website:
www.sansebastianfestival.ya.comMike
l Olacirequi, Festival Director
The main activities are the Official Competition and the informative section 'Zabaltegi', which presents newly released films of different formats, lengths, styles and genres. Other sections: Made in Spain, Horizontes Latinos, 'En Construccion' and Restrospectives

## Festival de Cine Español de Málaga

23 April- 1 May 2004
**Ramos Marín, 2-1C**
**29012 Málaga**
Tel: +34 952 228 242
Fax: +34 952 227 760
email: info@festivaldemalaga.com
Website: www.festivaldemalaga.com
Devotes to promote Spanish films with a clear emphasis on the development of an open market to facilitate the distribution of Spanish language films worldwide

## Huesca Film Festival

10-19 June 2004
**Avda. Parque, 1-2**
**22002 Huesca**
Tel: +34 974 212 582
Fax: +34 974 210 065
email: info@huesca-filmfestival.com
Website: www.huesca-filmfestival.com
An international short film contest

with a great deal of Iberoamerican cinema and a Sample of European Cinema to name but a couple of sections. The festival programme for 2004 includes a retrospective on French actor Jean Gabin while Chile will be the guest country

## International Film Festival For Young People

25 November- 3 December 2004
**Paseo de Begoña, 24, Entlo.**
**PO BOX 76**
**33201 Gijón**
Tel: +34 985 182 940
Fax: +34 985 182 944
email: festivalgijon@telecable.es
Website: www.gijonfilmfestival.com
Also known as the Gijon International Film Festival, its purpose is to show films featuring youngsters and their concern with life. The established programme includes the Official Sections for features and shorts, Enfants Terribles, an Informative Section for young and older spectators, comprising Outlines, Cycles and Retrospectives

## Semana Internacional de Cine de Valladolid

23-30 2 October 2004
**Teatro Calderón**
**Calle Leopoldo Cano, s/n 4th fl.**
**PO BOX 646**
**47003 Valladolid**
Tel: +34 983 426 460
Fax: +34 983 426 461
email: festvalladolid@seminci.com
Website: www.seminci.com
Fernando Lara, Director
The Valladolid International Film Festival consists of the following sections: Official, presenting a panorama of current international cinema; Meeting Point, a parallel non-competitive showcase of fiction films worthy of special attention for their subject matter or style; Time History, consisting of documentaries that deal with moments of history; and Tributes, devoted to the presentation and analysis of directors, genres, styles, schools or a national cinema. There is also the screening of almost all the Spanish films (with English subtitles) of the preceding 12 months

# ST. BARTH

## St. Barth Film Festival and 'Cinéma Caraibe'

23-28 April 2004

**BP 1017**
**St. Jean 97012**
**St Barthelemy Cedex**
Tel: (590) 27 80 11
Fax: (590) 29 74 70
email: staff@stbarthff.org
Website: www.stbarthff.org
Ellen Lampert-Gréaux, General Delegate
The festival celebrates Caribbean culture and offers a meeting place for regional filmmakers to screen and discuss their work

# SWEDEN

## Göteborg Film Festival

20 January-7 February 2005
**Olof Palmes plats**
**413 04 Göteborg**
Tel: (46) 31 339 30 00
Fax: (46) 31 41 00 63
email: goteborg@filmfestival.org
Website:
www.goteborg.filmfestival.org
Jannike Ahlund, Director
The major competitive international film event in Scandinavia (Sweden, Norway, Denmark, Finland & Iceland) and a meeting place for the Nordic film industry. The Nordic Event offers exclusive previews of the latest Nordic films with English subtitles, only open to representatives from film festivals and the film industry worldwide. The Cinemix presents a great number of seminars, lectures and debates on film, both in Swedish and English

## Stockholm International Film Festival

18-28 November 2004
**PO Box 3136**
**103 62 Stockholm**
Tel: (46) 8 677 5000
Fax: (46) 8 20 0590
email: info@filmfestivalen.se
Website: www.filmfestivalen.se
The Stockholms Trettonde Internationella is a competitive showcase for innovative feature films, with a focus on American Independents. It offers a retrospective and presents a summary of Swedish films released during the year. Also, as part of the festival, Internet users can watch ten competing international short films and vote for the best one. The winning film will receive the World Wide Winner award at the final prize ceremony in Stockholm

## Uppsala International Short Film Festival

18-24 October 2004
**Box 1746**
**751 47 Uppsala**
Tel: (46) 18 120 025
Fax: (46) 18 121 350
email: info@shortfilmfestival.com
Website: www.shortfilmfestival.com
Sofia Lindskog, Director
Sweden's premiere presents more than 200 sound and silent shorts (fiction, animation, experimental films and documentaries). The programme includes the International Competition, retrospectives, Nordic films-The Video section, Children's Film Fest and the Film School Day

# SWITZERLAND

## Festival International de Films de Fribourg

6-13 March 2005
**Rue Nicolas de Praroman 2**
**Case Postale 550**
**1701 Ribourg**
Tel: +41 26 347 42 00
Fax: +1 26 347 42 01
email: info@fiff.ch
Website: www.fiff.ch
Competition for movies and documentaries of varying lengths from Africa, Asia and Latin America. The festival also organises non-competitive sections (tributes, focus on, retrospectives) for films which have seldom or never been shown in Switzerland

## Locarno International Film Festival

6-16 August 2003
**Via Ciseri**
**6601 Locarno**
Tel: (41) 91 756 2121
Fax: (41) 91 756 2149
email: info@pardo.ch
Website: www.pardo.ch
Irene Bignardi, Artistic Director
Situated at the base of the Alps, near the Italian border, Locarno has been hosting one of the most distinguished film festivals worldwide since 1946. Its main programme consists of an International Competition (reserved for full-length features with a special focus on films which introduce new schemes and styles) and a new separate Video Competition selecting the most innovative and original video or digital productions. Other regular activities include Piazza Grande ('classic entertainement with an edge'), Filmmakers of the Present; Leopards of Tomorrow (short film output of young directors); Appellations Suisse (a bouquet of Swiss films); retrospectives and the Critics' Week (www.criticsweek.filmjournalist.ch)

## Rose d'Or Festival

13-18 April 2004
**Bigger Prix Ltd**
**PO Box 5511**
**3001 Bern**
Tel: (41) 31 318 3737
Fax: (41) 31 318 3736
email: info@rosedor.com
Website: www.rosedor.ch
George Luks, Secretary General
The Golden Rose of Montreux hosts international awards for light entertainment television programming (comedy, sitcoms, variety, music and game shows, arts and specials) from around 40 countries. It is also a business rendezvous for the onscreen entertainment community, who can attend the established conferences and choose to view TV programmes from the Videokiosk

## VIPER-International Festival for Film, Video and New Media

18-22 November 2004
**St. Alban-Rheinweg 64**
**4052 Basel**
Tel: (41) 61 283 27 00
Fax: (41) 61 283 27 05
email: information@viper.ch
Website: www.viper.ch
Conny E. Voester, Festival Director
The most important media art festival in the country. It presents new international innovative and experimental productions on films, videos, CD-ROMs and Internet. Two competitions: International Competition for Film & Video, and National Competition for Film & Video

## Visions du Réel - Nyon International Documentary Film Festival

18-24 April 2005
**Festival International de Cinéma**
**18, rue Juste Olivier**
**CP 593**
**1260 Nyon**
Tel: (41) 22 365 44 55
Fax: (41) 22 365 44 50
email: docnyon@visionsdureel.ch
Website: www.visionsdureel.ch
Jean Perret, Festival Director
International competition screening independent documentaries of all sorts: experimental films, essays, diaries, family films, major reports, historical inquiries, classic narratives and fragmentary stories

# TAIWAN

## Taipei Golden Horse Film Festival

Late November-early December
**3F, 37, Kaifeng St.**
**Taipei 100, Taiwan, ROC**
Tel: (886) 2 2388 3880
Fax: (886) 2 2370 1616
email: info@goldenhorse.org.tw
Website: www.goldenhorse.org.tw
Wei-jan Liu, Coordinator
This festival was set up by the government in an effort to stimulate and revitalise the local filmmaking industry. The event is divided in two parts: the Golden Horse Awards Chinese language Film Competition(including Mandarin, Cantonese, Taiwanese, and Shangai dialects) and the non-competitive Annual Golden Horse International Film Exhibition, featuring retrospectives and special programmes

# TANZANIA

## Festival of the Dhow Countries

27 June-4 July 2004
**ZIFF**
**PO BOX 3032**
**Zanzibar**
Tel: (255) 4 747 411499
Fax: (886) 4 747 419955
email: ziff@ziff.or.tz
Website: www.ziff.or.tz
Imruh Bakari, Festival Director
Established in 1998 as the Zanzibar International Film Festival (ZIFF), the event now promotes an extensive programme of films, music and performing arts from Africa, India, Gulf States and Indian Ocean Island-the Dhow Countries. Sidebars include women's events, chidren's panorama, workshops and seminars

# THAILAND

## Bangkok Film Festival

29 April-4 May 2004

4 Sukhumvit Soi 43
Bangkok 10110
Tel: +66 2 259 3112
Fax: +66 2 259 2987
email: bkkfest@movieseer.com
First world film festival to be born in
Bangkok, with strong commitment to
independent and unseen works. The
festival annual competition includes:
Best Feature, Best Director, Audience
Award and the Emerging Filmmaker
Award

# TURKEY

## International Istanbul Film Festival

10-25 April 2004
Istanbul Foundation for Culture and
Arts
Istiklal Caddesi Luvr Apt. No. 146
80070 Beyoglu
Istanbul
Tel: (90) 212 334 0700
Fax: (90) 212 334 0702
email: film.fest@istfest-tr.org
Website: www.istfest.org
The Istanbul Festival focuses on
features films dealing with arts
(literature, theatre, cinema, music,
dance and plastic arts). Showing over
200 films from five continents, the
festival includes popular night
screenings

# UNITED KINGDOM

## Animated Encounters

21-24 April 2005
Watershed Media Centre
1 Canon's Road
Harbourside
Bristol BS1 5TX
Tel: (44) 117 915 0185
Fax: (44) 117 930 9967
email: info@animated-
encounters.org.uk
Website: www.animated-
encounters.org.uk
Also known as the Bristol
International Animated Festival, it
consists of four days of screenings,
seminars and parties with a dedicated
Industry day, New British and
International programmes, Desert
Island Flicks and a range of special
events

## Bath Film Festival

14-31 October 2004
7 Terrace Walk
Bath BA1 1LN
Tel/Fax: (44) 1225 401149

email: info@bathfilmfestival.org
Website: www.bathfilmfestival.org
A non-competitive festival screening
titles which do not make it to the
town of Bath.It also includes a
number of classic re-releases and
participatory events (workshops,
seminars, performances) and the
Spools in Schools education
programme

## Birmingham Screen Festival

4-11 March 2004
9 Margaret Street
Birmingham B3 3BS
Tel: (44) 121 212 0777
Fax: (44) 121 212 0666
email:
bsf@birminghamscreenfestival.com
Website:
www.birminghamscreenfestival.com
The BSF celebrates the moving image
through a selection of the very best in
film, television and multimedia from
all over the world

## Bite the Mango

24-30 September 2004
National Museum of Photography,
Film & Television
Pictureville
Bradford BD1 1NQ
Tel: +44 (0)870 7010 200
Fax: +44 (0)127 4723 155
email: talk.nmpft@nmsi.ac.uk
Website: www.bitethemango.org.uk
A celebration of Asian and Black
cinema

## Bradford Film Festival

12-27 March 2004
National Museum of Photography,
Film & Television
Pictureville
Bradford BD1 1NQ
Tel: +44 (1274 203 320
email: tony.earnshaw@nmsi.ac.uk
Website:
www.bradfordfilmfestival.org.uk
Tony Earns, Festival Director
Non-competitive festival focusing on
widescreen cinemascope, IMAX,
cinerama and world cinema

## Brief Encounters: Bristol Short Film Festival

17-21 November 2004
Watershed Media Centre
1 Canon's Road
Harbourside
Bristol BS1 5TX
Tel: (44) 0117 915 0186
Fax: (44) 0117 930 9967
email: info@brief-encounters.org.uk
Website: www.brief-

encounters.org.uk
A showcase of the best in regional,
national and international short films
alongside industry seminars,
masterclasses, special events and a
Gala Awards Ceremony. Open to all
producers and directors of short films
(up to 30 mins), including animation,
documentary, drama and
experimental

## Cambridge Film Festival

8-18 July 2004
Arts Picture House
38-39 St. Andrews Street
Cambridge CB2 3AR
Tel: (44) 1223 578944
Fax: (44) 1223 578956
email: cff@picturehouses.co.uk
Website:
www.cambridgefilmfestival.org.uk
Non-competitive festival screening
new world cinema selected from
international festivals. Also featuring
director retrospectives, short film
programmes, thematic seasons and
revived classics; conference for
independent exhibitors and
distributors, public debates and post-
screening discussions

## Cardiff Screen Festival

10-20 November 2004
10 Mount Stuart SQ.
Cardiff CF10 5EE
Tel: +44 (0)2920 333 324
Fax: +44 (0)2920 333 320
email: sarah@sgrin.co.uk
Website:
www.cardiffscreenfestival.co.uk
Sarah Howells, Festival Manager
The oldest film festival in Wales offers
premiere screenings, special guest
appearances and debates on
everything from soaps to the future
of broadcasting. A celebration of film,
TV and media from Wales and
beyond

## Celtic Film and Television Festival

31 March- 3 April 2004
249 West George St.
Glasgow
Scotland G2 4QE
Tel: +44 (0) 141 302 1737
Fax: +44 )0) 141 302 1738
email: mail@celticfilm.co.uk
Website: www.celticfilm.co.uk
Competition for films, television,
radio and new media programmes
whose subject matter has particular
relevance to the Celtic regions and
countries (Brittany, Cornwall, Ireland,
Scotland and Wales).

## Chichester Film Festival

26 August-12 September 2004
**Chichester Cinema**
**New Park Road**
**Chichester**
**West Sussex PO19 1XN**
Tel: (44) 1243 786650
Fax: (44)1243 539853
email: info@chichestercinema.org
Website: www.chichestercinema.org
A non-competitive festival that
focuses on previews and
retrospectives. Special emphasis on
UK and other European productions.
There is also a five-category
international short film (up to 16
mins) competition

## Cinemagic-Northern Ireland's World Screen Festival for Young People

25 November-9 December 2004
**49 Botanic Avenue**
**Belfast BT7 1JL**
Tel: (44) 28 9031 1900
Fax: (44) 28 9031 9709
email: info@cinemagic.org.uk
Website: www.cinemagic.org.uk
Joan Burney, Festival Director
A competitive festival for
international shorts, feature films and
television programmes for young
people aged between 4 and 18. It
includes big movie premieres,
practical workshops, directors
discussions, masterclasses with
industry professionals and special
events

## Discovering Latin America Film Festival

25 November- 5 December 2004
**58 Turpin House**
**Strasburg Road**
**London SW11 5H5**
Tel: 0790 403 7358
email: alexa.dean@btinternet.com
Website: www. discovering-
latinamerica.org.uk
Alexa Dean, Art Director
The very best from Latin America,
this year in its third edition; with
retrospectives, masterclasses and last
tendencies in documentaries. The
festival's aim is not only to promote
Latin American culture, but to raise
funds to financing community
projects all over Latin America

## Edinburgh International Film Festival

18-29 August 2004
**Filmhouse**
**88 Lothian Road**
**Edinburgh EH3 9BZ**
Tel: +44 (0) 131 228 4051
Fax: +44 (0) 131 229 5501
email: info@edfilmfest.org.uk
Website: www.edfilmfest.org.uk
Shane Danielsen, Artistic Director
A unique showcase of new
international cinema with special
attention to British production.
Programme sections: Focus on British
Film; Retrospective; Gala (World,
European and British premieres);
Rosebud (first and second time
directors); Director's Focus; Reel Life
(illustrated lectures by filmmakers);
Documentary; Mirrorball (music
video); short films and animation

## Festival of Fantastic Films

20-22 August 2004
**95 Meadowgate Road**
**Salford**
**Manchester M6 8EN**
Tel: (44) 161 707 3747
Fax: (44) 161 792 0991
email: gil@glaneyoung.freeserve.co.uk
Website: www.fantastic-films.com
Tony Edwards
The Annual Convention of the
Society of Fantastic Films celebrates a
century of science fiction and fantasy
films, with guests of honour,
interviews, signing panels, dealers,
talks and a retrospective film
programme. There is also an
international competition for
independently produced feature-
length and short films

## FILMSTOCK International Film Festival

1-15 June 2004
**24 Guildford Street**
**Luton LU1 2NR**
Tel: (44) 01582 486294
Fax: (44) 01582 423347
email: contact@filmstock.co.uk
Website: www.filmstock.co.uk
Justin Doherty, Neil Fox, Festival
Directors
According to the organisers
'FILMSTOCK is more than a film
festival. It is about cinema in its
entirety and aims to fuse the joy of
movie-going with the art of
filmmaking in one simultaneous
experience'

## Foyle Film Festival

18-28 November 2004
**The Nerve Centre**
**7-8 Magazine St**
**Derry BT48 6HJ**
Tel: (44) 2871 276 432
Fax: (44) 2871 371 738
email: competition@nerve-
centre.org.uk
Website: www.foylefilmfestival.com
Northern Ireland's major annual film
event. There are four competition
categories (Best film, Best Irish short,
Best international short, and Best
animated short) plus a separate On-
Line competition for films under 10
minutes (Live Action and Flash
Animation categories)

## French Film Festival UK

12 November-1 December 2004
**12 Sunbury Place**
**Edinburgh EH4 3BY**
Tel: (44) 131 225 6191
Fax: (44) 131 225 6971
email: fff@frenchfilmfestival.org.uk
Website:
www.frenchfilmfestival.org.uk
Richard Mowe, Director
The only British festival focused
exclusively to 'le cinéma français'. The
programme falls in two categories:
Panorama, devoted to the best names
in French Cinema and New Waves,
showcasing first and second-time
directors. Held in Edinburgh,
Glasgow, Aberdeen, Dundee and
London

## Frightfest

27-30 August 2004
**C/o Ian Rattray Films**
**10 Wiltshire Gardens**
**Twickenham**
**Middlesex**
**London TW2 6ND**
Tel: 020 8296 0555
Fax: 020 8296 0556
Website: www.frightfest.co.uk
Ian Rattray
Held in London over the August
Bank Holiday at the Prince Charles
Cinema, the festival is a horror and
fantasy film event, which shows some
16 feature films from all over the
world

## Media Guardian Edinburgh International Television Festival (MGEITF)

27-29 August 2004
**1st Floor**
**17-21 Emerald Street**
**London WC1N 3QN**
Tel: (44) 207 430 1333
Fax: (44) 207 430 2299
email: info@mgeitf.co.uk
Website: www.mgeitf.co.uk
Sarah Barnett,Festival Director
Now in its 29th year, the festival is a
four-day forum featuring prominent
industry voices. Attended by over

1600 delegates, the event covers a range of topics from policy to programme-making issues

## Human Rights Watch International Film Festival
17-25 March 2004
**2ns Floor, 2-12 Pentonville Rd.**
**London N1 9HF**
Tel: +44 (0)20 7713 19 95
Fax: +44 (0)20 7713 18 00
email: hrwuk@hrw.org
Website: www.hrw.org/iff
A non-competitive festival showcasing features, shorts and documentaries with human rights themes from around the world

## Italian Film Festival
4-17 April 2004
**82 Nicolson Street**
**Edinburgh EH8 9EW**
Tel: (44) 131 668 2232
Fax: (44) 131 668 2777
email: italianinstitute@btconnect.com
Website: italcult.net/edimburgo/ici-frame_events.htm (archives)
A unique event in the UK, throwing an exclusive spotlight on 'il cinema italiano'. The festival presents documentaries, shorts, new film and new talents. It travels to Aberdeen, Dundee, Edinburgh, Glasgow and London

## IVCA Awards
One day in March
**IVCA**
**Business Communication Centre**
**19 Pepper Street, Glengall Bridge**
**London E14 9RP**
Tel: (44) 207 512 0571
Fax: (44) 207 512 0591
email: info@ivca.org
Website: www.ivca.org
The International Visual Communication Awards runs a competitive event for non-broadcast industrial/training films and videos, covering all aspects of the manufacturing and commercial world. Categories include Website, Editing, Documentary, Animation, Graphics and Special Effects, Direction, Script and Drama

## KinoFilm: Manchester's International Short Film Festival
20-26 October 2004
**42 Edge Street**
**Manchester M4 1HN**
Tel: (44) 161 288 2494
Fax: (44) 161 281 1374
email: kino.info@good.co.uk

Website: www.kinofilm.org.uk
John Wojowski, Director
Focusing on the British New Wave and International Panorama, the festival also includes: KinoLatino, Kino Horror, Going Underground and Magic Carpet. Awards for Best British and International; Best Student and Low Budget; Best Animation; Best Screenplay and Best Documentary

## Leeds International Film Festival
October 2004
**Town Hall**
**The Headrow**
**Leeds LS1 3AD**
Tel: (44) 113 247 8389
Fax: (44) 113 247 8397
email: filmfestival@leeds.gov.uk
Website: www.leedsfilm.com
Chris Fell, Director
Competition for feature films by new directors (Leeds New Directors Awards), Fiction and Animated Shorts (Louis le Prince International). Over 10 strands including Evolution (interactive and online), Eureka (European Films), Film Festival Fringe, Voices of Cinema and Cult Films

## London Lesbian and Gay Film Festival
April 2004
**National Film Theatre**
**South Bank**
**London SE1 8XT**
Tel: (44) 207 815 1323
Fax: (44) 207 633 0786
email: anna.dunwoodie@bfi.org.uk
Website: www.outuk.com/llgff
Anna Dunwoodie, Festival Administrator
Organised by the British Film Institute, the festival is not only 'a celebration of cinema and queer-maker's contribution to the art form', it is also a unique opportunity to enjoy the astounding diversity of films reflecting gay and lesbian culture. On a national tour from April to September

## Out Of Sight- International Film And Television Archive Festival
15-19 April 2004
Broadway
14-18 Broad Street
Nottingham NG1 3AL
Tel: (44) 115 952 6600
Fax: (44) 115 952 6622
email: ion@broadway.org.uk
Website: www.broadway.org.uk

An annual week-end on British Silent Cinema investigating British film production before 1930, organised by the Broadway Cinema in Nottingham and the BFI National and Television Archive

## Raindance Film Festival
October
**81 Berwick Street**
**London W1F 8TW**
Tel: (44) 207 287 3833
Fax: (44) 207 439 2243
email: festival@raindance.co.uk
Website: www.raindance.co.uk
Fostering and promoting independent film in the UK and abroad, the festival offers Film Training Courses, Rawtalent Productions, Raindance East and Raindance Kids. It also hosts the prestigious British Independent Film Awards

## Sand-Swansea Animation Days
22-27 November 2004
**Taliesin Arts Centre**
**Swansea, Wales**
Tel: +44 (0) 01792 481028
email: dmc@sihe.ac.uk
Website: www.sand2003.org.uk
Felicity Blastland, Director
International digital event, which features world leaders in 3D animation, computer games, VR and AI with their most recent work. The Sand festival is also a meeting place to exchange ideas and create new project opportunities

## Sheffield International Documentary Festival
8-14 November 2004
**The Workstation**
**15 Paternoster Row**
**Sheffield S1 2BX**
Tel: (44) 114 276 5141
Fax: (44) 114 272 1849
email: info@sidf.co.uk
Website: www.sidf.co.uk
Brent Woods, Festival Director
A platform for the best in British and international documentary film and television, the festival is both a public film event and an industry gathering, with screenings and discussions on the new developments in documentary. A selection of films travels to cinemas in the UK from November to February each year

## The Times bfi London Film Festival

20 October- 4 November 2004
**National Film Theatre**
**South Bank**
**London SE1 8XT**
Tel: (44) 207 815 1322
Fax: (44) 207 633 0786
email: sarah.lutton@bfi.org.uk
Website: www.lff.org.uk
Sarah Lutton, Programme
Coordinator
Britain's premier film festival,
presented by the British Film
Institute, it screens the best in new
cinema from all over the world. It
also includes previews of
international feature films, shorts and
videos. Selected highlights from the
festival go on tour to regional film
theatres from November to December

## Viva! Spanish Film Festival

13-23 March 2004
**Cornerhouse**
**70 Oxford Street**
**Manchester, M1 5NH**
Tel: +44 (1) 161 200 1516
email: viva@cornerhouse.org
Website: www.cornerhouse.org
The UK's only Spanish Film Festival
offers quality premieres, specially
imported new releases, special guests,
parallel events and academic
conferences. The festival tours to
major cities, among others,
Newcastle, Edinburgh, Cardiff,
Dublin and London

## Wildscreen

10-15 October 2004
**Anchor Road**
**Bristol BS1 5TT**
Tel: (44) 117 915 7100
Fax: (44) 117 915 7105
email: info@wildscreen.org.uk
Website: www.wildscreen.org.uk
Colin Butfiel, Festival Director
Biennial international festival of
moving images from the natural
world, covering all aspects of screen-
based natural history
communications, including the
Internet, interactive media and film
formats such as Imax. The festival
offers seminars, screenings,
discussions, training workshops,
trade show for delegates and the
general public. The Panda Awards
Competition is open to film, TV and
interactive productions from
anywhere in the world

## WOW! Wales One World Film Festival

12 March-24 April 2004
**Taliesin Arts Centre**
**University of Wales Swansea**
**Swansea, Wales**
Tel/Fax: +44 (0) 1239 615066
email: sa3657@eclipse.co.uk
Website: wowfilfestival.org
David Gilliam, Festival Director
Presenting films that are currently
under-represented on Welsh screens,
the festival showcases a programme
of top quality works from Africa, Asia
and Latin America

# URUGUAY

## Montevideo International Film Festival

Two weeks in April
Cinemateca Uruguaya
**Lorenzo Carnelli 1311**
**11200 Montevideo**
Tel: (598) 2 418 2460
Fax: (598) 2 419 4572
email: cinemuy@chasque.apc.org
Website: www.festival.org.uy
A competitive festival devoted to
short, feature length, documentary,
fiction, experimental, Latin American
and international films

# USA

## AFI Fest: American Film Institute Los Angeles International Film Festival

4-14 November 2004
**American Film Institute**
**2021 N. Western Avenue**
**Los Angeles, CA 90027-1657**
Tel: (1) 323 856 7600
Fax: (1) 323 467 4578
email: afifest@afi.com
Website: www.afifest.com
The festival presents over 140 films
through an International
Competition of first-and second-time
filmmakers as well as regional
showcases of international cinema:
Asian New Classics, European Film
Showcase, Latin Cinema Series and
American Directions

## American Black Film Festival

14-18 July 2004
**c/o Film Life**
**P.O. Box 688**
**New York, NY 10012**
Tel: (1) 212 219 7267

email: abff@thefilmlife.com
Website: www.abff.com
Considered as the 'Black Hollywood's
annual retreat and international film
market', the festival presents
independent film premieres,
workshops, panels, networking,
parties and Film Life Awards

## American Film Market

3-10 November 2004
**9th Floor, 10850 Wilshire Blvd**
**Los Angeles, CA 90024-4311**
Tel: (1) 310 446 1000
Fax: (1) 310 446 1600
email: AFM2004@afma.com
Website: www.afma.com/AFM
Jonathan Wolf, Managing Director
The largest motion picture trade
event in the world, held in Los
Angeles

## Asian American International Film Festival

16-24 July 2004
**Asian CineVision**
**133 W. 19th Street, Suit 300**
**New York, NY 10011**
Tel: (1) 212 989 1422
Fax: (1) 212 727 3584
email: info@asiancinevision.org
Website: www.asiancinevision.org
Diane Lee, Festival Director
Proudly known as 'The First Home to
Asian American Cinema', the festival
is a leading showcase for Asian
American film and video arts. A
selection of the festival's entries
travels on a 10-month tour to major
US cities

## Chicago International Film Festival

7-21 October 2004
**32 West Randolph St.**
**Chicago, IL 60601**
Tel: (1) 312 425 9400
Fax: (1) 312 425 0944
email: info@chicagofilmfestival.com
Website: www.chicagofilmfestival.com
Sophia Wong Boccio, Managing
Director
North America's oldest competitive
international film festival (1964 - )
presents the latest in world cinema
with new works by both veteran
masters and talented newcomers. The
highest prize for best film is the Gold
Hugo Award.

## Cleveland International Film Festival

10-20 March 2005
**Cleveland Film Society**

2510 Market Avenue
Cleveland OH 44113-3434
Tel: +1 216 623 3456
Fax: +1 216 623 0103
email: cfs@clevelandfilm.org
Website: www.clevelandfilm.org
A competitive showcase of about 80 contemporary American and international feature films plus nearly 100 shorts. The programme also includes films from Eastern Europe, American Independent, retrospectives and cinema for children

## Columbus International Film and Video Festival

Mid-October
**Film Council of Greater Columbus**
**1430 south High street, rm 322**
**Columbus, Ohio 43207**
Tel/Fax: (1) 614 841 1666
email: info@chrisawards.org
Website: www.chrisawards.org
Also known as The Chris Awards, it specialises in honouring documentary, animation, drama, CD-ROMs/Interactive, information film and video productions. The festival also includes categories for the arts, entertainment, education and business

## Fort Lauderdale International Film Festival

20 October-14 November 2004
**1314 East Las Olas Blvd. #007**
**Fort Lauderdale, FL 33301**
Tel: (1) 954 760 9898
Fax: (1) 954 760 9099
email: info@fliff.com
Website: www.fliff.com
Bonnie Leigh Adams, Senior Prog. Director
The longest festival in the world (37 days) and one of the most important regional film festivals in the US, where over 100 films (features, documentaries, art on film series, shorts, animation) are screened from Boca Raton to Miami

## Hawaii International Film Festival

21-31 October 2004
**1001 Bishop Street**
**Pacific Tower, Suite 745**
**Honolulu, Hawaii 96813**
Tel: (1) 808 528 3456
Fax: (1) 808 528 1410
email: info@hiff.org
Website: www.hiff.org
Chuck Boller, Executive Director
A State-wide event, taking place on the six Hawaiian islands, the festival presents 100 features, documentaries and shorts premieres, experimental films representing social and ethnic issues and first features by new directors. The event is also unique in discovering works from Asia made by Asians, films about the Pacific made by Pacific Islanders and films by Hawaii filmmakers presenting Hawaii in a culturally accurate way

## Human Rights Watch International Film Festival

10-24 June 2004
**350 Fifth Av.  34th Floor**
**New York, NY 10018-3299**
Tel: (1) 212 290 4700
Fax: (1) 212 736 1300
email: hrwny@hrw.org
Website: www.hrw.org/iff
A leading venue for fiction, documentary and animated films and videos, concentrating equally on artistic merit and human rights content. Screenings are usually followed by discussions with the filmmakers and Human Rights Watch (HRW) staff. The festival also awards a prize in the name of cinematographer and director Nestor Almendros, who was an active supporter of HRW's cause. In 1996, the event expanded to London (see entry under United Kingdom for details)

## Independent Feature Film Market

21-26 September 2003
**104 West 29th Street**
**12th Floor**
**New York, NY 10001-5310**
Tel: (1) 212 465 8200
Fax: (1) 212 465 8525
email: mbond@ifp.org
Website: www.ifp.org
This is the longest running market devoted to emerging American independent film talents seeking domestic and foreign distribution. It is the market for innovative projects in development, outstanding documentaries and startling works of fiction

## Miami International Film Festival

4-13 February 2005
**Film Society of Miami**
**Miami dade college**
**300 NE 2nd Av.**
**33132-2204 Miami FL**
Tel: (1) 305 237 3456
Fax: (1) 305 237 7344
email: info@miamifilmfestival.com
Website: www.miamifilmfestival.com
With its new section 'Miami Encuentros' to support Iberoamerican filmmakers, the festival has become a well-known gateway for Spanish-language films in the US

## New York Film Festival

1-17 October 2004
**Film Society of Lincoln Center**
**70 Lincoln Center Plaza**
**New York, NY 10023**
Tel: (1) 212 875 5638
Fax: (1) 212 875 5636
email: festival@filmlinc.com
Website: www.filmlinc.com
The non-competitive event, this year celebrating its 41st anniversary, screens features, shorts, documentaries, animations and experimental works

## Palm Springs International Festival of Short Films

31 August-1 September 2004
**1700 E. Tahquitz Canyon Way, #3**
**Palm Springs, CA 92262**
Tel: (1) 760 322 2930
Fax: (1) 760 322 4087
email: info@psfilmfest.org
Website: www.psfilmfest.org
Also known as the Nortel Networks PSIFF, the festival is said to have captured 'Hollywood's attention as a scouting ground for new film-making talent' and has become an 'absolute must-attend for those in the business of buying and selling short films'.

## Portland International Film Festival

13-28 February 2004
**Northwest Film Center**
**1219 SW Park Avenue**
**Portland, OR 97205**
Tel: (1) 503 228 7433
email: info@nwfilm.org
Website: www.nwfilm.org
Oregon's major film event, the festival offers approximately 100 feature and short films from over 30 countries

## San Francisco International Film Festival

15-29 April 2004
**30 Mesa St., Ste. 110**
**The Presidio**
**San Francisco, CA 94129**
Tel: (1) 415 561 5000
Fax: (1) 415 561 5099
email: info@sffs.org
Website: www.sffs.org/festival
A showcase for approximately 200

new shorts, documentaries, animation, experimental works and television productions, eligible for the Golden Gate Award competition

## San Francisco International Lesbian & Gay Film Festival

17-27 June 2004
**Frameline**
**346 Ninth St. Suit 300**
**San Francisco, CA 94103-2636**
Tel: (1) 415 703 8650
Fax: (1) 415 861 1404
email: info@frameline.org
Website: www.frameline.org
The largest and oldest festival of its kind, whose mission is 'to support, develop and promote lesbian, gay, bisexual, transgender and queer visibility through media arts'. It presents features, shorts, documentaries, videos and experimental work

## Seattle International Film Festival

20 May-13 June 2004
**911 Pine St., 6th Floor**
**Seattle, WA 98101**
Tel: (1) 206 324 9997
Fax: (1) 206 264 7919
email: SIFF_PR@seattlefilm.com
Website: www.seattlefilm.com
The biggest and most attended film Festival in the country, it includes gala premieres, new films from first-time and well-known directors, previews, special archival programmes, post-film Q&A sessions and forums

## Starz Denver International Film Festival

14-24 October 2004
**Denver Film Society**
**1725 Blake Street**
**Denver, CO 80202**
Tel: (1) 303 595 3456
Fax: (1) 303 595 0956
email: dfs@denverfilm.org
Website: www.denverfilm.org
Non-competitive event which presents over 175 films focusing on new international feature releases, independently produced fiction films and documentaries, experimental videos and children's films

## Sundance Film Festival

15-25 January 2004
**PO Box 3630**
**Salt Lake City, UT 84110**
Tel: (1) 801 328 3456
Fax: (1) 801 575 5175
email: institute@sundance.org

Website: www.sundance.org
Part of Robert Redford's Sundance Institute since 1985, the festival is recognised internationally as a showcase for the best in American Independent cinema. It is a competitive event for US and International narrative feature, full-length documentary, and short films. Its programme also includes the Native Forum section (films written and directed by Indegenous filmmakers), an Animation section, an Online Festival, special retrospectives and seminars

## Telluride Film Festival

3-6 September 2004
**379 State Street**
**Portsmouth, NH 03801**
Tel: (1) 603 433 9202
Fax: (1) 603 433 9206
email: Mail@telluridefilmfestival.org
Website: www.telluridefilmfestival.com
Although concentrating mainly on features, Telluride also organises three programmes of shorts. It is open to professional and non-professional filmmakers working in all film forms: documentary, narrative, animation and experimental

## US International Film & Video Festival

Early June
**713 S. Pacific Coast Highway, SuitA**
**Redondon beach, CA 90277-4233**
Tel: +310 540 0959
Fax: +310 316 8905
email: filmfesnfo@filmfestawards.com
Website: www.filmfestawards.com
International awards competition for television, industrial and informational productions

## WorldFest-Houston International Film Festival

16-25 April 2004
**9494SW Freeway, 5th floor**
**Houston, Texas 77074**
Tel: (1) 713 965 9955
Fax: (1) 713 965 9960
email: mail@worldfest.org
Website: www.worldfest.org
Part marketplace part film festival, the event is totally dedicated to independent feature and short films. It offers 11 major areas of competition and awards, including documentary, film & video production, TV & cable production, experimental, shorts, TV commercials, screenplays, music

video, new media, feature films and students' films

# YUGOSLAVIA

## Belgrade International Film Festival

25 February- 6 March 2005
**Majke Jevrosime 20**
**11000 Belgrade**
Tel: +381 11 334 6837
Fax: +381 11 334 6946
email: info@fest.org.yu
Website: www.fest.org.yu
Miroljub Vuckovic, Festival Director
The festival's programme consists of more than 70 films, which are shown within the following categories: Currents, USA Today, Lighthouse, Endurance, Far and Away, Fact and Puzzles

# ZIMBABWE

## Zimbabwe International Film Festival

**2 Cartenbury Road, Kensington,**
**Avondale, Harare**
Tel: +263 4 793 502
Fax: +263 4 793 502
email: zimfilmfest@zol.co.zw
Website: africafilmtv.com/ziff
Competitive for features films only, which must have been completed during the two years before the festival

# FUNDING

Check websites of organisations you wish to approach beforehand to confirm contact details.

## Funding

### ADAPT (Access for Disabled People to Arts Premises Today)
The ADAPT Trust
Wellpark
120 Sydney Street
Glasgow G31 1JF
Tel: 0141 556 2233
Fax: 0141 556 7799
email: adapt.trust@virgin.net
Website: www.adapttrust@virgin.net
Director: Stewart Coulter
Charitable trust providing advice and challenge funding to arts venues - cinemas, concert halls, libraries, heritage and historic houses, theatres, museums and galleries - throughout Great Britain. ADAPT also provides a consultancy service and undertakes access audits and assessments

### ADAPT NI
Cathedral Quarter
Managed Workspace
109-113 Royal Avenue
Belfast
Tel: 028 9023 1211
Fax: 028 9024 0878
email: info@adaptni.org
Website: www.adaptni.org
The ADAPT Fund for Northern Ireland was granted independent trust status in June 1996 by the Inland Revenue. ADAPT promotes all aspects of universal accessibility. This includes accessibility audits, technical advice, information and training on how proposed or existing premises can better accommodate people of all abilities. ADAPT has developed a programme of activities and events, which involve disabled and non-disabled people at all levels in a way, which is relevant to the objectives of the organisation. ADAPT's primary remit covers arts and community centres, theatres, concert halls, libraries, museums and public galleries, leisure centres and other buildings where arts and social

activities take place. ADAPT aims to improve accessibility in the future, not just in terms of the built environment but in the widest sense of access through projects, which encourage awareness, participation, integration and employment

### AIR (Animator In Residence)
National Museum of Photography, Film and Television
Bradford BD1 1NQ
Tel: 01274 203308
Fax: 01274 3945540
email: a.pugh@nmsi.ac.uk
Website: www.a-i-r.info
Adam Pugh
Professional animator residencies based at National Museum of Photography, Film and Television in Bradford are awarded to animators who have graduated within the last 5 years. Here they will develop their own original idea for a short animated film into a proposal for Channel 4 television's animation department, who will consider a full commission of the final production. Animators receive advice from a professional producer, £1600 materials budget, and a £3000 grant

### Awards For All
Tel: 0845 600 2040
email: info@awardsforall.org.uk
Website: www.awardsforall.org.uk
Awards for All is a grants programme supported by the Heritage Lottery Fund, the Arts Council England, Sport England, the New Opportunities Fund and the Community Fund. It funds projects that enable people to take part in art, sport, heritage and community activities, as well as projects that promote education, the environment and health in the local community. They cannot award grants to companies which aim to distribute a profit or individuals. Awards for All operates through nine regional offices in England. There are similar programmes running in Northern Ireland, Scotland and Wales. They award grants of between £500 and

£5,000. Contact 0845 600 2040 or visit the website for further information.

### Awards For All in England
Ground Floor
St Nicholas Court
25-27 Castle Gate
Nottingham NG1 7AR

### Awards for All in Scotland
Highlander House
58 Waterloo St
Glasgow G2 7DB

### British Council
Films and Literature Department
10 Spring Gardens
London SW1A 2BN
Tel: 020 7389 3166
Fax: 020 7389 3175
email: filmliteratre@britishcouncil.org
Website: www.britfilms.com, www.britishcouncil.org
Britain's International agency for cultural and educational relations. Assists in the co-ordination and shipping of films to festivals, and in some cases can provide funds for the film-maker to attend when invited. Publishers of the annual British Films Catalogue, Directory of International Film and Video Festivals and the portal website www.brit films

### Cineworks
Glasgow Media Access Centre
3rd Floor
34 Albion Street
Glasgow G1 1LH
Tel: 0141 553 2620
Fax: 0141 553 2660
email: info@cineworks.co.uk
Website: www.cineworks.co.uk
David Smith - Cineworks Co-ordinator
Cineworks is Scotland's entry level short film scheme commissioning five original projects each year in the fields of animation, documentary and drama with budgets of £10,000 or £15,000. It is run by the Glasgow Media Access Centre in partnership with the Edinburgh Mediabase and funded by Scottish Screen, The Film Council's New Cinema fund and BBC

Scotland. The five films are premiered at the Edinburgh International Film Festival before being distributed by Scottish Screen and Cineworks

## Community Fund
St Vincent House
16 Suffolk Street
London SW1Y 4NL
Tel: 020 7747 5299
email: enquiries@community-fund.org.uk
Website: www.community-fund.org.uk
Community Fund distributes money raised by the National Lottery to support charities and voluntary and community groups throughout the UK and to UK agencies working abroad. Their main aim is to help meet the needs of those at greatest disadvantage in society and to improve the quality of life in the community. See website for regional contact details and information about previously funded projects

## Edinburgh Mediabase
25a South West Thistle Street Lane
Edinburgh EH2 1EW
Tel: 0131 220 0220
Fax: 0131 220 9158
email: info@edinburghmediabase.com
Website: www.edinburghmediabase.com
Edinburgh Mediabase is a resource facility for anyone interested in film, digital video or new media. It allows budding film-makers the chance to access to good facilities Mediabase helps with everything from scriptwriting classes to broadcast quality digital cameras, professional edit suites and a monthly screening at the Cameo Cinema in Edinburgh called The Blue Room. Mediabase runs script award competitions such as: Cineworks (in partnership with Glasgow Media Access Centre), a short film production scheme designed to nurture new film-making talent, Small Wonders, a training and production scheme set up to discover new talent and Forty8ight Hours, a no-budget video production competition run in conjunction with the monthly Blue Room screening event. Mediabase also provides information and advice to members on everything from funding for their projects to careers in the creative industries

## The Isle of Man Film and Television Fund
Isle of Man Film Commission
Department of Trade & Industry
Hamilton House
Peel Road
Douglas Isle of Man
Tel: 01624 687173
Fax: 01624 687171
email: filmcomm@dti.gov.im
Website: www.gov.im/dti/iomfilm
The Isle of Man Film and Television Fund has been established to make available equity investment to film and television productions shooting wholly or partly on the Isle of Man. Offers up to 25% of the budget as direct equity investment, no upper or lower limits, and full assistance with financial structuring of budgets. Additionally, television projects will be able to apply for production credits where the project is being funded wholly or in part by a recognised broadcaster. To qualify for investment your project should be able to be filmed wholly or in part on the Isle of Man (a minimum of 50% principal photography on the Isle of Man), be capable of spending at least 20% of the below the line budget with local service providers, be otherwise fully funded, have a sales agent and/or a distributor attached and have a completion bond in place

## Kraszna-Krausz Foundation
122 Fawnbrake Avenue
London SE24 0BZ
Tel: 020 7738 6701
Fax: 020 7738 6701
email: info@k-k.org.uk
Website: www.k-k.org.uk
Andrea Livingstone, Administrator
The Foundation offers small grants to assist in the development of new or unfinished projects, work or literature where the subject specifically relates to the art, history, practice or technology of photography or the moving image (defined as film, television, video and related screen media). The Foundation also sponsors annual book awards, with prizes for books on the moving image (film, television, video and related screen media) alternating with those for books on still photography. Books that have been published in the previous two years can be submitted from publishers in any language. The prize money is around £10,000, with awards in two categories. The next awards for books on the moving imag

will be in 2005

## Nicholl Fellowships in Screenwriting
Academy of Motion Picture Arts and Sciences
1313 N. Vine St
Los Angeles, CA 90028
USA
Tel: 001 310 247 3059
email: nicholl@oscars.org
Website: www.oscars.org/nicholl
Annual Screenwriting Fellowship Awards

## The Prince's Trust
Head Office
18 Park Square East
London NW1 4LH
Tel: 020 7543 1234 Freephone: 0800 842 842
Fax: 020 7543 1200
email: info@princes-trust.org.uk
Website: www.princes-trust.org.uk
The Prince's Trust helps young people overcome barriers and get their lives working. Through practical support including training, mentoring and financial assistance, The Trust help 14-30 year olds realise their potential and transform their lives
The Arts Council of England and the English Regional Arts Boards have joined together to form a single development organisation for the arts in England. The objective is to build a national force for the arts which will deliver more funding and increased profile to artists and arts organisations, benefiting audiences everywhere. While the new structure is being set up, services continue as usual and contact details are listed below. Check www.artscouncil.org.uk for up to date information. Regional Arts Boards will fund artists' film and video. Film production funding has been delegated to the new regional screen agencies. See individual entries for contact details

# Arts Funding

The Arts Council of England and the 10 Regional Arts Boards merged to form a single organisation in April 2002, and from 17 February 2003 the organisation has been known as Arts Council England. It has a national office and nine regional offices. Between 2003 and 2006 they will invest £2 billion of public funds in the arts in England, including funding from the National Lottery.

# National Office

## Arts Council England
14 Great Peter Street
London W1P 3NQ
Tel: 020 7333 0100
Fax: 020 7973 6581
email: enquiries@artscouncil.org.uk
Website: www.artscouncil.org.uk
The National Touring Programme offers opportunities for organisations to commission and tour artists' moving image; guidelines can be requested on 020 7973 6517 or downloaded at www.artscouncil.org.uk For information about other current initiatives and opportunities, please check the website

# Regional Offices

## Arts Council England, East
Eden House
48-49 Bateman Street
Cambridge CB2 1LR
Tel: 0845 300 6200
Fax: 0870 242 1271
Website: www.artscouncil.org.uk
The Government arts development agency for East England, covering the counties of Bedfordshire, Cambridgeshire, Essex, Hertfordshire, Norfolk and Suffolk, and the unitary authorities of Luton, Peterborough and Thurrock. Aims to increase the impact of the arts by making strategic investment in professional arts companies and artists, and by providing advice and expertise to assist growth in the arts

## Arts Council England, East Midlands
St Nicholas Court
25-27 Castle Gate
Nottingham NG1 7AR
Tel: 0845 300 6200
Fax: 0115 950 2467
Areas covered: Derbyshire (including High Peak), Leicestershire, Lincolnshire, Northamptonshire, Nottinghamshire; unitary authorities of Derby, Leicester, Nottingham, and Rutland. The East Midlands now has a dedicated regional screen agency, EM Media, Which is responsible for funding film and video production in the region (see entry)

## Arts Council England, London
2 Pear Tree Court
London EC1R ODS
Tel: 0845 300 6200
Fax: 020 7608 4100
email: london@artscouncil.org.uk
Website: www.artscouncil.org.uk
Acting Regional Executive Director: Nigel Pittman
Following the merger of the regional arts boards with the Arts Council of England on 1 April 2002, London Arts is now the London Office (Greater London) of the new, single arts funding and development organisation. It has no dedicated funds for Film and Video. However, it does offer awards to individual artists working in the medium of film and video and New Media. Write to LA at the above address for funding guidelines. The London Arts Development Fund: Visual Artists strand can support visual artists working in a range of media including artists' film and video. Grants of £500-£3,000 are available towards the costs of making new work including purchase of equipment and materials, or R&D. Check website or call for deadlines. For the purposes of this scheme artists' film and video is defined as work that explores visual arts practice and is created for presentation in a visual arts context - for example as part of an installation or a gallery projection. If you are working in this area you should contact the Visual Arts unit to discuss whether your project is eligible. The screen agency London Film and Video Development Agency also runs the London Artists' Film Fund on behalf of London Arts

## Arts Council England, North East
Central Square
Forth Street
Newcastle upon Tyne NE1 3PJ
Tel: 0845 300 6200
Fax: 0191 230 1020
email: info@artscouncil
Website: www.artscouncil.org.uk
Funds artists' films and videos. Areas covered: Durham and Northumberland, and the metropolitan districts of Gateshead, Newcastle upon Tyne, North Tyneside, South Tyneside and Sunderland, and the non-metropolitan districts of Darlington, Hartlepool, Middlesbrough, Redcar and Cleveland, and Stockton-on-Tees. The North now has a dedicated regional screen agency, Northern Film & Media, Which is responsible for funding film and video production in the region

## Arts Council England North West
Manchester House
22 Bridge Street
Manchester M3 3AB
Tel: 0845 300 6200
Fax: 0161 834 6969
email: enquiries@artscouncil.org.uk
Website: www.artscouncil.org.uk
Sarah Fisher, Kathryn Hughes
Funds Artists' films and videos. Areas covered: Cheshire, Cumbria and Lancashire, and the metropolitan districts of Bolton, Bury, Knowsley, Liverpool, Manchester, Oldham, Rochdale, St. Helens, Salford, Sefton, Stockport, Tameside, Trafford, Wigan, and Wirral, and the non-metropolitan districts of Blackburn with Darwen, Blackpool, Halton, and Warrington. The North West now has a dedicated regional screen agency, North West Vision, which is responsible for funding film and video production in the region

## Arts Council England, South East
Sovereign House
Church Street
Brighton BN1 1RA
Tel: 0845 300 6200
Fax: 0870 242 1257
email: enquiries@artscouncil.org.uk
Website: www.artscouncil.org.uk
Mark Bryant
Arts Council England is the national development agency for the arts in England, distributing public money from Government and the National Lottery. Arts Council England, South east covers the following area: Buckinghamshire, East Sussex, Hampshire, Isle of Wight, Kent,

Oxfordshire, Surrey, West Susex,; and initary authorities at Bracknell Forest, Brighton and Hove, Medway Towns, Milton Keynes, Portsmouth, Reading, Slough, Southampton, West Berkshire, Windsor and Maidenhead, Wokingham

## Arts Council England, South West

Bradninch Place
Gandy Street
Exeter
Devon EX4 3LS
Tel: 0845 300 6200
Fax: 01392 229229
email: southwest@artscouncil.org.uk
Website: www.artscouncil.org.uk
Funds artists' films and videos. Areas covered: Cornwall, Devon, Dorset (excluding Borough of Christchurch), Gloucestershire, Somerset; non-metropolitan districts of Bath and North East Somerset, Bristol, North Somerset, Plymouth, South Gloucestershire, and Torbay. The South West now has a dedicated regional screen agency, South West Screen, Which is responsible for funding film and video production in the region

## Arts Council of England, West Midlands Arts

82 Granville Street
Birmingham  B11 2LH
Tel: 0121 631 3121
Fax: 0121 643 7239
email: info@west-midlands.arts.org.uk
Funds artists' films and videos. Areas covered: Shropshire, Staffordshire, Warwickshire and Worcestershire, and the metropolitan districts of metropolitan districts of Birmingham, Coventry, Dudley, Sandwell, Solihull, Walsall and Wolverhampton, and the non-metropolitan districts of Herefordshire, Stoke-on-Trent and Telford and Wrekin. The West Midlands now has a dedicated regional screen agency, Screen West Midlands, Which is responsible for funding film and video production in the region

## Arts Council of England, Yorkshire

21 Bond Street
Dewsbury
West Yorkshire WF13 1AX
Tel: 01924 455555
Fax: 01924 466522

email: yorkshire@artscouncil.org.uk
Website: www.artscouncil.org.uk
Emily Penn
Funds artists work in the moving image. Areas covered: North Yorkshire and the metropolitan districts of Barnsley, Bradford, Calderdale, Doncaster, Kirklees, Leeds, Rotherham, Sheffield, and Wakefield, and the non-metropolitan districts of the East Riding of Yorkshire, Kingston-upon-Hull, North Lincolnshire, North East Lincolnshire, and York. Yorkshire now has a dedicated regional screen agency, Screen Yorkshire, Which is responsible for funding film and video production in the region

## Arts Council of Northern Ireland

Arts Development Department
MacNeice House, 77 Malone Road
Belfast BT9 6AQ
Tel: 028 9038 5200
Fax: 028 9066 1715
email: nmckinney@artscouncil-ni.org
Website: www.artscouncil-ni.org
With effect from 1 April 2002 The Arts Council of Northern Ireland delegated its responsibility for film finance to the Northern Ireland Film & Television Commission (see separate entry). Check www.artscouncil-ni.org for details of other funds

## Arts Council of Wales

9 Museum Place
Cardiff CF10 3NX
Tel: 029 20 376500
Fax: 02920 395284
email: info@artswales.org.uk
Website: www.artswales.org.uk
The Arts Council of Wales (ACW) is responsible for funding and developing the arts in Wales. It became accountable to the National Assembly for Wales on 1 July 1998 when responsibility was transferred from the Secretary of State for Wales. Check their website for further information and funding opportunities

## Scottish Arts Council

12 Manor Place
Edinburgh EH3 7DD
Tel: 0845 603 6000/ hard of hearing prefix number with 18001
Fax: 0131 225 9833
email: help.desk@scottisharts.org.uk
Website: www.sac.org.uk
The Scottish Arts Council is one of the main channels for Government

funding for the arts in Scotland, receiving its funding from the Scottish Executive. They also distribute National Lottery funds received from the Department for Culture, Media and Sport. Check their website for details of the funds

# Public Funding

## Northern Ireland Film And Television Commission
**Third Floor Alfred House**
**21 Alfred Street**
**Belfast BT2 8ED**
Tel: 028 9023 2444
Fax: 028 9023 9918
email: info@niftc.co.uk
Website: www.niftc.co.uk
The Northern Ireland Film and Television Commission (NIFTC) offers loans to production companies for the development and production of feature films or television drama series or serials that are intended to be produced primarily in Northern Ireland. On 1 April 2002 The Arts Council of Northern Ireland delegated its responsibility for film finance to the NIIFTC. The hand-over, for a three-year pilot period will see 13 per cent of the Arts Council's National Lottery funding allocated annually to NIFTC

## Scottish Screen
**2nd Floor**
**249 West George Street**
**Glasgow  G2 4QE**
Tel 0141 302 1700
Fax 0141 302 1711
email: info@scottishscreen.com
Website: www.scottishscreen.com
Contact: Isabella Edgar, Information Manager
Scottish Screen develops, encourages and promotes every aspect of film, television and new media in Scotland. Funded by the Scottish Executive and through the National Lottery, our mission is to establish Scotland as a major screen production centre and project our culture to the world.

## Production Development
Scottish Screen currently has various film schemes in partnership with a range of other bodies.
**Cineworks**
is a new entrant production scheme partly supported by Scottish Screen to offer opportunities for filmmakers to make their first professional films. An extensive development and training programme is included. All types of work including animation and documentary are eligible. Included in the scheme is a partnership with the Film Council to produce very low budget digital shorts. For further information visit: www.cineworks.co.uk

**Tartan Shorts**
is a joint initiative with BBC Scotland to create an opportunity for Scotland's filmmaking talent to make cinematic short films. The scheme has been running for several years and each year, three projects are awarded up to a maximum of £65,000 to produce a 35 mm film. Each film should be approximately 9 minutes duration
**New Found Land**
is a collaboration with the Scottish Media Group and the National Lottery to enable new filmmakers to work on longer form drama. Six half hour projects are commissioned and shot using new digital technology, with budgets of approximately £50,000. New Found Land is now running every 2 years in conjunction with New Found Films
**New Found Films**
is a new production scheme offering emerging Scottish talent a first step into feature film production. In 2003 two 90-minute films with budgets of £200,000 went into production. Development and production finance was provided by Scottish Television, Grampian Television and the National Lottery Fund. New Found Films is now running every 2 years in conjunction with New Found Land.
**Four Minute Wonders**
is a music production scheme whereby each month around £5,000 can be won to develop and produce a video based on a new piece of music. The new track will be uploaded to the 4minutewonders.com web site at the beginning of each month.
**ALT-W**
is an initiative supporting Scotland's new media development and promotes creative entrepreneurial talent. Production grants of up to £2,500 are available for innovative digital productions that can be delivered via the web. For further details visit: www.ALT-W.com
**Tartan Smalls**
offers an opportunity for new talent to work in the children's arena, or existing talent (without previous children's experience) to enter this exciting creative genre. This scheme will create new and exciting work for an audience of 6-13 years. Three projects are shortlisted with a budget of £40,000. Projects should not exceed 9 minutes in duration.
**This Scotland**
is a documentary production scheme

for new and existing talent and will commission single documentaries within one overall strand. The scheme is co-produced by Scottish TV, Grampian TV and Scottish Screen.
**Bridging the Gap**
is a new documentary scheme aimed at Scottish based filmmakers. This scheme aims to bridge the gap between training/graduation and a first broadcast. The scheme is a collaboration between Edinburgh College of Art and Angus Digital Media Centre and is sponsored by Scottish Screen and Scottish Enterprise Tayside. Five twenty-five minute films are chosen for training and mentoring with a budget of £16,000.

## Other Funding
Outside of the various schemes, Scottish Screen occasionally will invest in one-off short film projects.

## Development
Development funding can be sought under the Seed Fund or through Script Development Funding/Project Development Funding).
**The Seed Fund**
is intended to encourage feature film projects at the early stages of development, typically where a project is insufficiently developed to be eligible for an award under the Lottery-funded Script Development scheme. It is open to both companies and individuals.
The maximum award is £5,000 and takes the form of a loan repayable if the project goes into production. Applications are considered on a monthly basis.

## Scottish Screen National Lottery Production Funding

**From 7 April 2000, Scottish Screen assumed responsibility for allocating National Lottery funds for all aspects of film production in Scotland. This represents about £3m per year for film production.**

**Other National Lottery funding programmes operated by the Scottish Arts Council remain open to film and video projects and organisations. Contact SAC for further details. The various funding programmes operated by Scottish Screen are as follows:**

**Feature Film Production Finance**
Funding is available up to £500,000 per project for feature films (including feature length documentaries) aimed at theatrical distribution.
**Short Film Production Funding**
Applications for under £25,000 are accepted on a continuous basis. Short films requesting in excess of £25,000 will be considered by the full Lottery Panel on specified dates.
Script Development Funding
Funding between £2,500 and £25,000 is available to projects which would benefit from further development of the script prior to packaging and financing. The project will be already at first draft or at the very least full treatment stage (including sample scenes where appropriate). The Scheme is aimed at projects which can make a robust case that this level of investment will materially advance the treatment or script towards the stage where it can attract the interest of financiers and/or key players.
**Project Development Funding**
Funding up to £75,000 is available for second-stage development of feature films. This is aimed at projects already at a relatively advanced stage. It will support elements such as script polish, preparation of schedule and budget, casting etc. Applications for under £25,000 are accepted on a continuous basis.
**Distribution and Exploitation Support**
Funding of up to £25,000 is available for completed feature films to support print and advertising costs associated with the commercial exploitation of the film in the UK marketplace. Funding may also be applied to overseas sales and marketing of completed features.
**Company Development Programme**
Finance of up to £75,000 is available as working capital funding into companies to support a slate of film, television and multi-media projects and to develop the commercial success of that company.
**Short Film Award Schemes**
On an annual, basis, Scottish Screen will consider applications, of up to £60,000 from outside bodies to operate short film production schemes. Previous examples included Cineworks operated by the Glasgow Media Access Centre.
**Twenty First Films - Low Budget Film Scheme**

This scheme offers support for low budget features (including feature documentaries) with budgets up to around £600,000.
Contact: Production Development Department: 0141 302 1742

## Sgrîn Cymru Wales
**The Bank, 10 Mount Stuart Square**
**Cardiff Bay**
**Cardiff CF10 5EE**
Tel: 029 2033 3300
Fax: 029 2033 3320
email: sgrin@sgrin.co.uk
Website: www.sgrin.co.uk
Head of Production - Judith Higginbottom
Short Film and New Talent Manager - Gaynor Messer Price
Lottery Manager - Anneli Jones
Sgrîn, Media Agency for Wales, is the primary organisation for film, television and new media in Wales. Sgrîn distributes lottery funding for film in Wales. Sgrin also runs short film schemes and a script reading service for those resident in Wales, and provides funding support for cinema venues, both public and private, cultural and interpretive printed and audiovisual material which complements and promotes exhibition programmes, and events. Guidelines and deadlines are available on request. The European Union Media Antenna is located at Sgrin, as is the New Media Group Wales and the Wales Screen Commission location service. For more information please visit www.sgrin.co.uk

## UK Film Council
**10 Little Portland Street**
**London W1N 7JG**
Tel: 020 7861 7861
Fax: 020 7861 7862
email: info@film.council.org.uk
Website: www.filmcouncil.org.uk
Contact: Iain Hepplewhite - Head of Communications
Tina McFarling - Head of Industry Relations
General enquiries: 020 7861 7924
www.firstlightmovies.com
The UK Film Council is the key strategic body with responsibility for advancing the film industry and film culture in the UK. Funded through the National Lottery and grant-in-aid money from the Government, It has two broad aims:
**To help develop a sustainable UK film industry; and**

**To develop film culture by improving access to, and education about, the moving image.**
The UK Film Council provides public funding for a range of initiatives supporting film development, production, training, distribution, exhibition, education and culture, which are focused on achieving these key aims.
Major initiatives include:
**The Development Fund** with £12 million over three years to support the development of a stream of high quality, innovative and commercially attractive screenplays.
**The Premiere Fund** with £24 million over three years to facilitate the production of popular, more mainstream films.
**The New Cinema Fund** with £15 million over three years to back radical and innovative filmmakers, especially new talent.
**The Distribution and Exhibition Fund** of £18 million to widen access for all to a broader range of films.
The UK Film Council is working with Skillset to deliver the first ever **comprehensive training strategy** for the British film industry. It contains a package of measures backed by an investment of around £50 million over the next five years.
**First Light** offers children and young people the opportunity to experience filmmaking using digital technology. It is supported annually by £1 million of National Lottery money.
The UK Film Council has created a £6 million a year **Regional Investment Fund** for England (RIFE) which is available to support cultural and industrial film initiatives in the English regions and works to a joined-up UK-wide agenda with the national film agencies, Scottish Screen, Sgrîn Cymru Wales and the Northern Ireland Film and Television Commission.
**Inward Investment** – the UK Film Council's International Department encourages international productions from outside the UK to come and use Britain's world-class production and facilities infrastructure and is involved in a number of export promotion initiatives.
In addition the UK Film Council also funds:
**UK Film Council US**, the UK Film Council's Los Angeles based office aims to attract inward investment into the UK from US productions.

UK Film Council US also offers a base for the UK Film Council to promote UK film exports and co-ordinate US-based training initiatives for UK industry professionals.
**The British Film Institute** (bfi), is funded by the UK Film Council. The bfi plays a key role in achieving the UK Film Council's goals and fosters public appreciation of film through improved access to cinema, film heritage and educational provision.

# Regional Screen Agencys

*These new agencies are being established to develop moving image culture in each region*

## EM-MEDIA
35 - 37 St Mary's Gate
Nottingham NG1 1PU
Tel: 0115 934 9090
Fax: 0115 950 0988
email: anna.dawson@em-media.org.uk
Website: www.em-media.org.uk
Chief Executive: Ken Hay
Head of Education and Training
Anna Dawson
EM Media is the regional screen agency for the East Midlands (Derbyshire, Leicestershire, Lincolnshire, Northamptonshire, Nottinghamshire and Rutland). It aims to develop a vibrant regional media culture and industry across a range of areas, from supporting feature and short film production, offering talent and business support, to locations advice, education initiatives, independent cinema and training. Investment funds include RIFE (Regional Investment Fund for England) Lottery and Treasury on behalf of the Film Council, and a range of European funds for production and training activities. EM Media seeks to invest in organisations and projects which meets one or more of its priorities. Further information can be found at www.em-media.org.uk

## East London Moving Image Initiative (ELMII)
This initiative builds on the successful East London Film Fund and is primarily aimed at business support and project development for companies and individuals based in the East London region.

London Borough Production Awards

## London Borough Production Awards
Also visit the site for details of London Borough production awards such as the Croydon Film And Video Awards, Enfield Film Fund, Newham Film Fund, Tower Hamlets Film Fund, Waltham Forrest Production Fund and the Wandsworth Film Fund

## North West Vision
233 Tea Factory
82 Wood Street
Liverpool L1 4DQ
Tel: 0151 708 2967
Fax: 0151 708 2984
Website: www.northwestvision.co.uk
Chief Executive: Alice Morrison
North West Vision is the media development agency for the North West region (Cheshire, Cumbria, Greater Manchester, Lancashire and Merseyside) established in April 2002 to provide a single support structure for a whole raft of cultural and industrial moving image initiatives. The agency provides funding for film and television projects and practitioners based in the North West, locations support, crewing resources, advice on post-production and facilities, support for various cultural initiatives such as arthouse cinemas and festivals, and help and advice for emerging and established filmmakers throughout the region. The fund will cover three strands: Production Development, Audience Development, and Individual & Organisational Development. Check the website for up to date details

## Northern Film & Media
Central Square
Forth Street
Newcastle upon Tyne NE1 3PJ
Tel: 0191 269 9200
Fax: 0191 269 9213
email: info@northernmedia.org
Website: www.northernmedia.org
Chief Executive: Tom Harvey
Northern Film & Media has been set up to strategically invest in the content and media industry in the North East (County Durham, Northumberland, Tees Valley and Tyne & Wear) and aims to build a vibrant and sustainable film, media and digital content industry and culture in the North. Northern Film & Media offers a range of funding

schemes covered by five strands: the development of people, content, companies, audiences, and networks. Northern Film & Media also offers advice and support on production services and locations to content production companies interested in basing their projects in the region

## Screen East
Anglia House
Norwich NR1 3JG
Tel: 0845 601 5670
Fax: 01603 767 191
email: info@screeneast.co.uk
Website: www.screeneast.co.uk
Chief Executive: Laurie Hayward
Screen East is the regional agency dedicated to developing, supporting and promoting every aspect of film, television and the moving image in the east of England (Bedfordshire, Cambridgeshire, Essex, Hertfordshire, Norfolk and Suffolk). Supported and funded by The Film Council through the Regional Investment Fund for England (RIFE) programme. RIFE is being implemented to strengthen film industry and culture in the regions, giving more opportunities to audiences, new and established filmmakers and media businesses. Production and Talent Development is a key area of Screen East's responsibilities. They offer support and finance through the National Lottery for the development of feature projects and for short film production across a variety of genres

## Screen South
Folkestone Enterprise Centre
Shearway Business Park
Shearway Road
Folkestone
Kent CT19 4RH
Tel: 01303 298 222
Fax: 01303 298 227
email: info@screensouth.org
Website: www.screensouth.org
Chief Executive: Gina Fegan
Screen South is the film and media agency for the South (Kent, Buckinghamshire, Oxfordshire, Hampshire, Surrey, Berkshire, East and West Sussex and the Isle of Wight). Screen South's funding schemes for 2002/2003 feature two sections - Strands which are aimed at the development and training of filmmakers and Open Funds which are available to those with projects that deliver Screen South's regional priorities such as film festivals, education activities, heritage projects,

film societies etc. The Strands for 2003/2003 are:

**Taped Up**

- A chance for new directors living in the Meridian region (East and West Sussex, Kent, South Essex, Surrey, Berkshire, Hampshire, the Isle of Wight) to make a short documentary or drama. Six pieces of under 10 minutes each are commissioned. This scheme is run in collaboration with Lighthouse in Brighton. Contact www.lighthouse.org.uk.

**First Cut**

- A broadcast production scheme for new filmmakers living in the Carlton region outside London to make two pieces under 10 minutes. It is open to filmmakers with no previous broadcast credit who live in Oxfordshire or Buckinghamshire. This scheme is run in collaboration with Lighthouse in Brighton. Contact www.lighthouse.org.uk.

**Free For All**

- An initiative to search for stories from those whose voices are not always heard (such as rural communities, mining communities, senior citizens, ethnic minority communities or asylum seekers) but who have a passion for visual storytelling. This scheme is for people with no experience who will be supported by mentors and encouraged to be innovative.

**One-to-One**

- For those who wish to test 'co-producing'. Working with producers from Europe, this is a chance to explore the realities of taking a short project from concept to pitch to production, whilst being mentored by those with both positive and challenging experiences of co-production. This scheme is run in collaboration with Kent Hothouse. Contact www.kenthothouse.com Check the Screen South website for further information and deadlines

## Screen West Midlands

**31-41 Bromley Street**
**Birmingham B9 4AN**
Tel: 0121 766 1470
Fax: 0121 766 1480
email: info@screenwm.co.uk
Website: www.screenwm.co.uk
Chief Executive: Krysia Rozanska
Screen West Midlands is the regional agency working to support, promote and develop all screen media in the West Midlands. Their aim is to create a sustainable screen industry throughout

the whole of the region; Birmingham and the Black Country, Herefordshire, Shropshire, Staffordshire, Warwickshire and Worcestershire. Whether film, television or new media related they can provide friendly and accurate advice for almost any enquiry and have two strands of funding: Production Development and Sector Development. Check their website, email them or call for further information

## Screen Yorkshire

**Studio 22**
**46 The Calls**
**Leeds LS2 7EY**
Tel: 0113 294 4410
Fax: 0113 294 4989
email: info@screenyorkshire.co.uk
Website: www.screenyorkshire.co.uk
Lead Officer: Jo Spreckley
Screen Yorkshire is the strategic agency for film, broadcast and the moving image sector in Yorks and the Humber. The aim is to lead the region's screen media industry to business growth and success by maximising opportunity, creating employment and promoting the vibrant creativity of the region

## South West Screen

**St Bartholomews**
**Lewins Mead**
**Bristol BS1 5BT**
Tel: 0117 952 9982
Fax: 0117 952 9988
email: cathy.gremin@swscreen.co.uk
Website: www.swscreen.co.uk
Chief Executive: Caroline Norbury
Chair: Jeremy Payne
South West Screen is the regional organisation for film, video, television and digital media in the South West (Bristol, Cornwall, Devon, Dorset, Somerset, Wiltshire, and Gloucestershire). It offers advice and funding initiatives for: low-budget short and feature-length production; experimental and cross-genre cinema; exhibition projects. Check their website or call for further information

# European and Pan-European Sources

## Eurimages

Council of Europe
**Palais de l'Europe**
**67075 Strasbourg Cédex**
**France**
Tel: (33) 3  88 41 26 40
Fax: (33) 3  88 41 27 60
Website: www.coe.int/T/E/Cultural_Co-operation/Eurimages/
Provides financial support for feature-length fiction films, documentaries, distribution and exhibition. Applications for co-production from the UK can only be accepted if a UK producer is a fourth co-producer in a tripartite co-production or the third in a bipartite, and provided the combined co-production percentage of all non-member states involved in the co-production does not exceed 30 per cent for multilateral co-productions and 20% for bi-lateral co-productions

## Europa Cinemas

**54, rue Beaubourg**
**F-75 003 Paris, France**
Tel: (33) 1 42 71 53 70
Fax: (33) 1 42 71 47 55
email: europacinema@magic.fr
Website:  www.europa-cinemas.org
Contact: Claude-Eric Poiroux, Fatima Djoumer
The objectives of this programme are to increase the programming of European film in film theatres, with European non-national films taking priority, to encourage European initiatives by exhibitors aimed at young audiences and to develop a network of theatres to enable joint initiatives at a national and European level

## FilmFörderung Hamburg

**Friedensallee 14-16**
**22765 Hamburg**
**Germany**
Tel: 00 (49) 40 39837-0
Fax: 00 (49) 40 39837-10
email: filmfoerderung@ffhh.de
Website: www.ffhh.de
Executive Director: Eva Hubert
Subsidies available for: script development; pre-production; co-production and distribution. Producers of cinema films can apply for a subsidy amounting to at most 50 per cent of the overall production

costs of the finished film. Foreign producers can also apply for this support. It is recommended to co-produce with a German partner. 150 per cent of the subsidy must be spent in Hamburg and part of the film should be shot in Hamburg. Financial support provided by the FilmFörderung Hamburg can be used in combination with other private or public funding, including that of TV networks. The FilmFörderung Hamburg also offers service and support for producers from Germany and abroad to prepare shootings in Hamburg. The film commission is a first contact on location and provides i.e. a Location Guide, a Production Guide, an internship pool.
Homepage: www.lbhh.de

# MEDIA Programme

## MEDIA Plus Programme
**European Commission, Directorate General X:**
**Education and Culture**
**rue de la Loi, 200**
**1049 Brussels, Belgium**
Tel: (32) 2 299 11 11
Fax: (32) 2 299 92 14
email: eac-media@cec.eu.int
Website:
europa.eu.int/Comm/avpolicy/media/index_en.html
Acting Head of Programme: Costas Daskalkis

**The MEDIA Plus Programme (2001 - 2006) is a European Union initiative that aims at strengthening the competitiveness of the European audiovisual industry with a series of support measures dealing with the training of professionals, development of production projects, distribution and promotion of cinematographic works and audiovisual programmes. The programme was introduced in January 2001 as a follow-up to the MEDIA 2 programme. MEDIA Plus is managed by the Directorate General for Education and Culture at the European Commission in Brussels. It is managed on a national level by a network of 38 offices called the MEDIA Desks and Antennae**

# Programme Contents

### MEDIA Training
The programme offers funding to training providers for vocational training initiatives. The Commission supports courses covering subjects including economic, financial and commercial management, use of new technologies, and scriptwriting techniques. MEDIA-supported courses are open to all MEDIA member state nationals. For details on how to participate in these courses, contact your local Desk, Antenna or Service.

### MEDIA Development
The programme offers financial support to European independent production companies to develop new fiction, documentary, animation or multimedia projects. Financial support is offered to catalogues of projects (through the "slate funding" scheme) or to single projects. The amounts awarded will not exceed 50% of development budgets. If the project co-financed by MEDIA Plus goes into production the company has an obligation to reinvest the amount awarded by MEDIA in the development of their next project or projects. Companies may apply for funding at any time within the life of a Call for Proposals, which is usually published in autumn and lasts until summer next year. Please contact your local MEDIA Desk or Antenna for details.

### MEDIA Distribution
The programme runs several schemes to support theatrical distribution and sales of European films. The Selective Scheme funds promotional campaigns of European non-national films. Distributors must apply in groupings of a minimum of five territories. The Automatic schemes for distributors and sales agents are based on their performance on the European market (admissions of European non-national films) and allow them to reinvest the funds generated through MEDIA support in minimum guarantees, co-production, and/or P&A costs for new European non-national films. A similar scheme for video/DVD publishers has recently been introduced based on net revenues from sales of non-national European films. The generated funds can then be reinvested in the cost of producing and/or promoting new non-national European works on DVD, or the costs of promoting new non-national European works on video. Non-repayable grants of up to 500,000 are available to TV producers for programmes that involve at least two European broadcasters. MEDIA Plus also provides support to networks of cinemas for the promotion and marketing of European films (e.g. Europa Cinemas). There are fixed deadlines for this funding.

### MEDIA Promotion
The programme offers financial support to encourage all kinds of promotional activities designed to facilitate European producers and distributors' access at major European and international events. It

supports European film festivals and festival networks. There are fixed deadlines running throughout the year.

**MEDIA Pilot Projects**
The programme offers support for initiatives involving the use of digital technologies for distribution. Submissions require the participation of several partners from different European countries in the form of consortia proposing business models which have potential for further development.

**MEDIA i2i Initiative**
Support for companies who raise finance through bank discounting. MEDIA Plus offers European producers 50,000 Euro per project to subsidise the costs of insurance policies, the completion guarantee and financing costs. Producers can submit several projects. The maximum contribution to one company is 100,000 Euro. Independent European production companies who either raised finance from a bank or financial institution which is a partner of the EIB Group, or received Slate Funding under the MEDIA Plus Programme are eligible.

# Contact Details

Members of the UK MEDIA team listed below should be the first point of contact for UK companies or organisations seeking information and advice on the MEDIA Plus programme. Guidelines and application forms for all schemes are available from their website: http://www.mediadesk.co.uk. However, all completed application forms should be sent directly to the MEDIA Programme office in Brussels, details of which you will find below.

## UK MEDIA Desk
Fourth Floor
66-68 Margaret Street
London W1W 8SR
Tel: 020 7323 9733
Fax: 020 7323 9747
email: england@mediadesk.co.uk
Agnieszka Moody

## MEDIA Service Northern Ireland
Third Floor
Alfred House

21 Alfred Street
Belfast BT2 8ED
Tel: 02890 232 444
Fax: 02890 239 918
email: media@niftc.co.uk
Website: www.mediadesk.co.uk
Cian Smyth

## MEDIA Antenna Scotland
249 West George Street
Glasgow G2 4QE
Tel: 0141 302 1776
Fax: 0141 302 1778
email: scotland@mediadesk.co.uk
Website: www.mediadesk.co.uk
Emma Valentine

## MEDIA Antenna Wales
The Bank
10 Mount Stuart Square
Cardiff Bay
Cardiff CF10 5EE
Tel: 02920 333 304
Fax: 02920 333 320
email: antenna@sgrin.co.uk
Gwion Owain

## MEDIA Office in Brussels
MEDIA Programme
European Commission
DG-EAC (B-100 04/22)
Rue Belliard 100
B-1049 Brussels
Belgium
Acting Head of Unit: Costas Daskalakis
Head of Development: Domenico Raneri
Head of Distribution: Hughes Becquart
Head of Training: Judith Johannes
Head of Promotion/Festivals: Elena Braun

# INTERNATIONAL SALES

Compiled by Matt Ker

## Alibi Films International
35 Long Acre
London WC2E 9JT
Tel: 020 7845 0400
Fax: 020 7836 6919
email: info@alibifilms.co.uk
Website: www.alibifilms.co.uk
CEO - Roger Holmes
Alibi is active in feature film
financing, international sales and
distribution and the production of
feature film, television drama and
children's programming. Feature titles
include: The Hard Word, South West
9 and Secretary

## APTN
(Associated Press Television News)
The Interchange
Oval Road
Camden Lock
London NW1 7DZ
Tel: 020 7482 7400
Fax: 020 7413 8327
Website: www.aptn.com
The international television arm of
The Associated Press

## AV Pictures Ltd
Caparo House
2nd floor, 103 Baker Street
London W1U 6LN
Tel: 020 7467 5012
Fax: 020 7224 5149
email: info@avpictures.co.uk
Website: www.avpictures.co.uk
Managing Director - Vic Bateman
International sales agent for
independent producers of
commercial films. Titles include: Dog
Soldiers and School For Seduction

## Axiom Films
12 D'Arblay Street
London W1V 3FP
Tel: Tel. 020 7287 7720
Fax: Fax. 020 7287 7740
email: mail@axiomfilms.co.uk
Website: www.axiomfilms.co.uk
Douglas Cummins
Features include El Bola and Life and
Debt

## BBC Worldwide
Woodlands

80 Wood Lane
London W12 0TT
Tel: 020 8433 2000
Fax: 020 8749 0538
Website: www.bbcworldwide.com
International programming
distribution, videos for education and
training, co-production and library
footage sales

## Beyond Films
3rd Floor
22 Newman Street
London W1T 1PH
Tel: 020 7636 9611
Fax: 020 7636 9622
email: films@beyond.com.au
Website: www.beyond.com.au
Hilary Davis, Stephen Kelliher, Nick
Kilcoyne
Film titles include: Strictly Ballroom,
Love & Other Catastrophes,
Paperback Hero, The Business of
Strangers, The Hard Word, Lantana,
Crackerjack, Three Blind Mice
Current titles A Good Woman, Cold
& Dark, The Oyster Farmer and
Conspiracy of Silence

## bfi Archival Footage Sales
21 Stephen Street
London W1T 1LN
Tel: 020 7957 4842
Fax: 020 7436 4014
email: footage.films@bfi.org.uk
Website:
www.bfi.org.uk/collections/afs
Jan Faull
bfi Archival Footage Sales is the
gateway for programme and filmmakers to the unrivalled materials
held in the bfi's National Film and
Television Archive. Footage available
ranges from the earliest films to
documentaries, fiction, home movies,
animation and classic and
contemporary television. Core
collections include British Transport
Films, the National Coal Board, ETV
and the silent newsreel, Topical
Budget. New collections are
constantly being added to the most
comprehensive and diverse source of
film and television in the UK

## Boudicca
8 Cotton's Gardens

London E2 8DN
Tel: 020 7613 5882
Fax: 020 7613 5882
email: sales@boudiccafilms.com
Website: www.boudiccafilms.com
Ray Brady
British independent sales and
distribution company set up by
producer/director Ray Brady

## British Film Institute Film Sales
21 Stephen Street
London W1T 1LN
Tel: 020 7957 8909
Fax: 020 7436 4014
email: sales.films@bfi.org.uk
Website: www.bfi.org.uk
Film Sales Manager - John Flahive
Film Sales Co-ordinator - Laurel
Warbrick-Keay
Sales of bfi-produced features, shorts
and documentaries, archival and
acquired titles including: early
features by Peter Greenaway and
Derek Jarman; Free Cinema; shorts
by famous directors including Ridley
Scott, Stephen Frears and Sally Potter;
shorts by new directors including
Lynne Ramsay, Sean Ellis and Tinge
Krishnan; and from the archives -
South (1919) and The Edge of the
World

## British Home Entertainment
5 Broadwater Road
Walton-on-Thames
Surrey KT12 5DB
Tel: 01932 228832
Fax: 01932 247759
email:
cw@britishhomeentertainment.co.uk
Website:
www.britishhomeentertainment.co.uk
Clive Williamson
Video distributor and sales agent.
Titles produced and owned by BHE
include An Evening with the Royal
Ballet, Othello, The Mikado, The
Soldier's Tale, Uncle Vanya, King and
Country, The Hollow Crown and The
Merry Wives of Windsor

## Buena Vista International Television
3 Queen Caroline Street
Hammersmith

London W6 9PA
Tel: 020 8222 1000
Fax: 020 8222 2795
Website: www.bvitv.com
The distribution arm of Walt Disney Television International. Also handling Buena Vista features and programming from Fox Kids Europe

## Canal + Image UK
Pinewood Studios
Pinewood Road
Iver
Bucks SL0 0NH
Tel: 01753 631111
Fax: 01753 655813
John Herron

## Capitol Films
23 Queensdale Place
London W11 4SQ
Tel: 020 7471 6000
Fax: 020 7471 6012
email: films@capitolfilms.com
Website: www.capitolfilms.com
Nicole Mackey
International film production, financing and sales company. Titles include Anything Else, The Company and Paint

## Carlton International
see Granada International

## Centre Film Sales
46 Crispin Street
London E1 6HQ
Tel: 020 8566 2388
Fax: 020 8566 2388
email: eleahy@centrefilmsales.com
Eddie Leahy

## Channel Four International
124 Horseferry Road
London SW1 2TX
Tel: 020 7396 4444
Fax: 020 7306 8363
Website: www.c4international.com
Managing Director - Paul Sowerbutts
Handles the Film Four catalogue, in addition to Channel 4 television material

## Columbia TriStar International Television
Europe House
25 Golden Square
London W1R 6LU
Tel: 020 7533 1000
Fax: 020 7533 1246
International distribution of Columbia TriStar's feature films and TV product

## Content International
19 Heddon Street

London W1B 4BG
Tel: 020 7851 6500
Fax: 020 7851 6505
Website:
www.contentinternational.com
Jamie Carmichael
Formed in 2004 following merger of Winchester Entertainment and ContentFilm. Film production and sales; television producer and sales agent of children's TV properties. Film titles handled include House of Sand and Fog and Song For a Raggy Boy

## Cumulus Distribution
Sanctuary House
45-53 Sinclair Road
London W14 0NS
Tel: 020 7300 6624
Fax: 020 7300 6529
Website: www.entercloud9.com
Subsidiary of Cloud 9 Screen Entertainment. Distributor of TV titles including The Tribe and Revelations

## Distant Horizon
61 Villiers Avenue
Surbiton
Surrey KT5 8BE
Tel: 020 8399 5126
Fax: 020 8390 5341
email: london@distant-horizon.com
Subsidiary of South African-based Videovision Entertainment. Recent features include I Capture the Castle

## DLT Entertainment UK Ltd
10 Bedford Square
London WC1B 3RA
Tel: 020 7631 1184
Fax: 020 7636 4571
email: info@dltentertainment.com
Website: www.dltentertainment.com
Specialising in comedy and drama production and sales.

## Documedia International Films Ltd
19 Widegate Street
London E1 7HP
Tel: 020 7625 6200
Fax: 020 7625 7887
Worldwide sales and distribution of drama shorts, serials, tele-movies, feature films, documentary specials and series

## Endemol UK
Shepherds Building Central
Charecroft Way
London W14 0EE
Tel: 0870 333 1700
Website: www.endemoluk.com

Licensing and distribution of Endemol programming and formats

## Entertainment Rights
Colet Court
100 Hammersmith Road
London W6 7JP
Tel: 020 8762 6200
Fax: 020 8762 6299
email:
enquiries@entertainmentrights.com
Website:
www.entertainmentrights.com
CEO – Mike Heap
Director of International Sales - Chloe van den Berg
Specialising in children's and family programming

## Fremantle International Distribution
1 Stephen Street
London W1T 1AL
Tel: 020 7691 6000
Fax: 020 7691 6060
email: fidsales@fremantlemedia.com
Website: www.fremantlemedia.com
Managing Director - Brian Harris
Executive Vice President - Joe Abrams

## Goldcrest Films International
65-66 Dean Street
London W1D 4PL
Tel: 020 7437 8696
Fax: 020 7437 4448
email: mailbox@goldcrest-films.com
Feature film production, sales and finance company. Library titles include The Mission, The Killing Fields and Name of the Rose

## Granada International
48 Leicester Square
London WC2H 7FB
Tel: 020 7491 1441
Fax: 020 7493 7677
email: int.info@granadamedia.com
Website: www.int.granadamedia.com
Managing Director - Nadine Nohr
A division of ITV plc merging the former Granada International and Carlton International operations. As well as Carlton and Granada productions, the collection incorporates: the ITC film and television library acquired by Carlton International in 1999; the Rohauer Library (classic silent films); the Korda Library (British films of the 1930s); the Romulus Library and the Rank Library (a major library of British films dating from the 1930s to the 1980s), and also incorporates the former Action Time brand

## HanWay Films

24 Hanway Street
London W1T 1UH
Tel: 020 7290 0750
Fax: 020 7290 0751
email: info@hanwayfilms.com
Website: www.hanwayfilms.com
CEO – Tim Haslam
Thierry Wase-Bailey
Specialised film sales company. Titles
include Young Adam, The Dreamers
and Besieged

## High Point

25 Elizabeth Mews
London NW3 4UH
Tel: 020 7586 3686
Fax: 020 7586 3117
email: sales@highpointfilms.co.uk
Website: www.highpointfilms.co.uk
Director - Julie Murphy-Delaney
Titles include Twin Sisters and Dead
Bodies

## Hollywood Classics

Linton House
39/51 Highgate Road
London NW5 1RS
Tel: 020 7424 7280
Fax: 020 7428 8936
email: info@hollywoodclassics.com
Website: www.hollywoodclassics.com
Melanie Tebb
Hollywood Classics has offices in
London and Los Angeles and sells
back catalogue titles of major
Hollywood studios for theatrical
release in all territories outside North
America. Also represents an
increasing library of European and
independent American titles and has
all rights to catalogues from various
independent producers

## IAC Film

23 Ransome's Dock
35/37 Parkgate Road
London SW11 4NP
Tel: 020 7801 9080
Fax: 020 7801 9081
email: general@iacholdings.co.uk
Guy Collins, Mike Ryan

## Icon Entertainment International

The Quadrangle, 4th Floor
180 Wardour Street
London W1V 3AA
Tel: 020 7494 8100
Fax: 020 7494 8151
Website: www.iconmovies.net
CEO - Nick Hill
Head of Sales - Simon Crowe
Titles include The Passion of the
Christ

## In-Motion Pictures

5 Percy Street
London W1T 1DG
Tel: 020 7467 6880
Fax: 020 7467 6890
email: sales@in-motionpictures.com
Website: www.in-motionpictures.com
VP International Sales - Alex Walton
Independent film and TV sales and
production, formerly J&M
Entertainment. Feature titles include
Break a Leg and Silent Cry

## Indigo

116 Great Portland Street
London W1W 6PJ
Tel: 020 7612 1700
Fax: 020 7612 1705
email: info@indigofilm.com
Website: www.indigofilm.com
Managing Director - David Lawley
Co-producer and distributor of film
and TV

## Lakeshore Entertainment

48 Leicester Square
London WC2H 7DB
Tel. 020 7004 7000
Fax. 020 7004 7051
email:
info@lakeshoreentertainment.com
Website:
www.lakeshoreentertainment.com
British office of US-based producer
and sales agent

## London Films

71 South Audley Street
London W1Y 5FF
Tel: 020 7499 7800
Fax: 020 7499 7994
Website: www.londonfilms.com
Andrew Luff
Founded in 1932 by Alexander Korda.
Co-productions with the BBC
include Poldark and I Claudius. More
recent series include Lady Chatterley
directed by Ken Russell and The
Scarlet Pimpernel starring Richard
E.Grant

## Myriad Pictures

Cavendish House
51-55 Mortimer Street
London W1W 8HJ
Tel: 020 7580 9200
Fax: 020 7290 0844
Website: www.myriadpictures.com
Sam Horley, Marion Pilowsky, Chris
Howard
British office of US motion pictures
and television financier, production
company and worldwide sales agent.
Recent features include Imagining
Argentina and Trauma

## NBD TV

Unit 2 Royalty Studios
105 Lancaster Road
London W11 1QF
Tel: 020 7243 3646
Fax: 020 7243 3656
email: distribution@nbdtv.com
Website: www.nbdtv.com
Specialising in music and light
entertainment programming

## Odyssey Entertainment

12 St James's Square
London SW1Y 4RB
Tel: 020 7153 3596
Fax: 020 7153 3597
sales@odyssey-entertainment.co.uk
CEO - Ralph Kamp
Feature titles include Valiant, Andrew
Lloyd Webber's The Phantom of the
Opera and The Libertine.

## Paramount Television

49 Charles Street
London W1J 5EW
Tel: 020 7318 6400
Fax: 020 7491 2086
Website: www.paramount.com
Stephen Tague
Television sales office

## Park Entertainment

4th Floor
50-51 Conduit Street
London W1S 2YT
Tel: 020 7434 4176
Fax: 020 7434 4179
email: sales@parkentertainment.com
Website:
www.parkentertainment.com
CEO - Jim Howell
Financier, distributor and sales agent
for independently produced film and
TV

## Pathe International (UK)

Kent House
14-17 Market Place
Great Titchfield Street
London W1W 8AR
Tel: 020 7462 4427
Fax: 020 7436 7891
email: internationalsales@pathe-
uk.com
Website: www.pathe-uk.com
Head of Sales - Alison Thompson

## Peakviewing Transatlantic

Suite 6, Avionics House
Quedgeley Enterprise Centre
Nass Lane
Quedgley
Gloucestershire GL2 4SN
Tel: 01452 722202
Fax: 01452 723302

email: info@peakviewing.co.uk
Website: www.peakviewing.co.uk

## Photoplay Productions
21 Princess Road
London NW1 8JR
Tel: 020 7722 2500
Fax: 020 7722 6662
Kevin Brownlow, Patrick Stanbury
TV production company. Restoration
and presentation of silent films.
Archive of silent era cinema

## Portman Film and Television
21-25 St. Anne's Court
London W1F OBJ
Tel: 020 7494 8024
Fax: 020 7494 8046
email: sales@portmanfilm.com
Website: www.portmanfilm.com
Head of Film - Tristan Whalley

## Renaissance Films
34-35 Berwick Street
London W1F 8RP
Tel: 020 7287 5190
Fax: 020 7287 5191
email: info@renaissance-films.com
Website: www.renaissance-films.com
Managing Director - Angus Finney
Head of International Sales - Claire
Taylor

## RM Associates
Shepherds West
Rockley Road
London W14 ODA
Tel: 020 7605 6600
Fax: 020 7605 6610
email: rma@rmassociates.co.uk
Website: www.rmassociates.co.uk
Distributor of music and arts
documentary and performance
programming

## S4C International
50 Lambourne Crescent
Llanishen
Cardiff CF4 5DU
Tel: 029 20 741440
Fax: 029 20 754444
email: international@s4c.co.uk
Website: www.s4ci.com
Head of International Sales -
Rhianydd Darwin
Head of Co Productions - Huw
Walters
The commercial arm of S4C, the
fourth television channel in Wales -
distribution and co-production,
including documentary and
animation titles

## Safir Films Ltd
49 Littleton Rd
Harrow
Middx HA1 3SY
Tel: 020 8423 0763
Fax: 020 8423 7963
email: lsafir@attglobal.net
Lawrence Safir
Rightsholders to numerous
Australian, US and UK features,
including Sam Spiegel's Betrayal

## Screen Ventures
49 Goodge Street
London W1T 1TE
Tel: 020 7580 7448
Fax: 020 7631 1265
email: info@screenventures.com
Website: www.screenventures.com
Managing Director - Christopher
Mould
Specialise in international film, TV
and video licensing of music, drama
and arts featuring such artists as John
Lennon, Bob Marley and Nirvana.
Worldwide sales representation for
international record companies and
independent producers. Screen
Ventures is also an independent
producer of television documentaries
and music programming

## ScreenProjex
13 Manette Street
London W1D 4AW
Tel: 020 7287 1170
Fax: 020 7287 1123
email: info@screenprojex.com
Website: www.screenprojex.com

## SMG
3 Waterhouse Square
138-142 Holborn
London EC1N 2NY
Tel: 020 7882 1000
Fax: 020 7882 1020
Website: www.smg.plc.uk
The televison division of SMG
incorporates Scottish Television,
Grampian Television, Ginger
Television and SMG TV Productions

## Southern Star
45-49 Mortimer Street
London W1W 8HX
Tel: 020 7636 9421
Fax: 020 7436 7426
Website: www.southernstargroup.com
Southern Star is an international
television rights group.

## Sullivan Entertainment
Suites 30-32, Savant House
63-65 Camden High Street
London NW1 7JL

Tel: 020 7383 5192
Fax: 020 7383 0627
email: info@sullivan-ent.co.uk
Website: www.sullivan-ent.co.uk
Muriel Thomas
International sales office of Canadian
production company and distributor

## Summit Entertainment
77 Dean Street
London W1D 3SH
Tel: 020 7494 1724
Fax: 020 7494 1725
Website: www.summit-ent.co.uk
David Garrett
British office of US feature film
producer and sales agent

## Target Entertainment
Drury House
34-43 Russell Street
London WC2B 5HA
Tel: 020 7344 1950
Fax: 020 7344 1951
Website: www.target-
entertainment.com
CEO - Alison Rayson
Distribution and licensing of TV
drama, comedy and entertainment
formats

## Twentieth Century Fox Television
31-32 Soho Square
London W1V 6AP
Tel: 020 7437 7766
Fax: 020 7439 1806
Website: www.fox.co.uk
Vice President - Stephen Cornish
Director of Sales - Randall Broman
TV sales and distribution. A News
Corporation company

## TWI
McCormack House
3 Burlington Lane
London W4 2TH
Tel: 020 8233 5300
Fax: 020 8233 5301
Website: www.imgworld.com
The world's largest independent
producer and distributor of sports
programmes, TWI is owned by IMG
Group and specialises in sports and
factual programming (including
BAFTA-winning titles). Titles
include: Trans World Sport, Futbol
Mundial, PGA European Tour
productions, ATP Tour highlights,
West Indies Test Cricket, Oddballs, A-
Z of Sport, Goal!, The Olympic
Series, Century and The Whitbread
Round The World Race

## Universal Pictures International (UPI)
Prospect House
80-110 New Oxford Street
London WC1A 1HB
Tel: 020 7079 6000
Fax: 020 7079 6500
Website: www.unistudios.com

## VCI
76 Dean Street
London W1D 3SQ
Tel: 020 7396 8888
Fax: 020 7470 6655
Website: www.vci.co.uk
Programming and Acquisitions
Director - Paul Hembury
A wholly owned subsidiary of VCI
PLC, responsible for all overseas
activities. Distributes a wide variety
of product including music, sport,
children's, fitness, documentary,
educational, special interest and
features

## Vine International Pictures
VIP House
Greenacres
New Road Hill
Downe
Orpington Kent BR6 7JA
Tel: 01689 854 123
Fax: 01689 850 990
email: info@vine-international.co.uk
Website: www.vine-
international.co.uk
Marie Vine, Barry Gill
Sale of feature films such as Rainbow,
The Pillow Book,  The Ox and the
Eye, Younger and Younger, The Prince
of Jutland, Erik the Viking, Let Him
Have It, Trouble in Mind.
Forthcoming titles include Out on a
Limb

## Warner Bros International Television
98 Theobalds Road
London WC1X 8WB
Tel: 020 7494 3710
Fax: 020 7287 9086
Website: www.wbitv.com
Richard Milnes, Donna Brett, Tim
Horan, Ian Giles
TV sales, marketing and distribution.
A division of Warner Bros
Distributors Ltd, a Time Warner
Entertainment Company

## Winchester Entertainment
see Content International
The Works
Portland House
4 Great Portland Street
London W1W 8QJ

Tel: 020 7612 1080
Fax: 020 7612 1081
Website: www.theworkslimited.com
CEO - Aline Perry
Head of Marketing - Rebecca Kearey
Head of International Sales - Joy
Wong
Formerly known as The Sales
Company, now owned by Civilian
Content.  Recent titles include Bend
It Like Beckham, In This World,
Bright Young Things, Country of My
Skull and 24 Hour Party People

# LABORATORIES

## Bucks Laboratories Ltd
714 Banbury Avenue
Slough
Berks SL1 4LR
Tel: 01753 501500
Fax: 01753 691762
Website: www.bucks.co.uk
Darren Fagg
Comprehensive lab services in Super 35mm and 35mm, Super 16mm and 16mm, starting Sunday night. West End rushes pick up unit 10.30 pm. Also day bath. Chromakopy: 35mm low-cost overnight colour reversal dubbing prints. Photogard: European coating centre for negative and print treatment. Chromascan: 35mm and 16mm video to film transfer

## CFS in soho
26 Berwick Street
London W1F 8RG
Tel: 020 7734 4543
Fax: 020 7734 6600
email:
cfsinsoho@colourfilmservices.co.uk
Website:
www.colourfilmservices.co.uk
Ray Nunney

## Colour Film Services Group
10 Wadsworth Road
Perivale
Middx UB6 7JX
Tel: 020 8998 2731
Fax: 020 8997 8738
email:
johnward@colourfilmservices.co.uk
Website:
www.colourfilmservices.co.uk
D. John Ward
Film Laboratory: full 16mm and 35mm colour processing laboratory, with Super 16mm to 35mm blow up a speciality. Video Facility: broadcastt standard wet gate telecines and full digital edit suite. Video duplication, CD mastering and archiving to various formats. Superscan: unique tape to film transfer system in both Standard Resolution and High Resolution. Sounds Studios: analogue and digital dubbing, track laying, synching, voice overs and optical transfer bay

## Deluxe Laboratories Limited
North Orbital Road
Denham
Uxbridge
Middlesex UB9 5HQ
Tel: 01895 832323
Fax: 01895 832446
Website: www.bydeluxe.com
Terry Lansbury
Deluxe London, together with Deluxe Hollywood, Deluxe Toronto and Deluxe Italia is a subsidary of the Deluxe Entertainment Services Division which forms part of The Rank Group. Comprehensive world wide laboratory services to the Motion Picture, Commercial and Television industries. London and Toronto include video transfer suites. Toronto has complete sound and dubbing suites. Part of the London operation is the well known special effects and Optical house General Screen Enterprises now with digital Cineon and Optical Effects Unit at Pinewood Studios

## Film and Photo Ltd
13 Colville Road
South Acton Industrial Estate
London W3 8BL
Tel: 020 8992 0037
Fax: 020 8993 2409
email: info@film-photo.co.uk
Website: www.film-photo.co.uk
Managing Director: Tony Scott
Post production motion picture laboratory. 16/35mm Colour & B/W reversal dupes. 16/35mm b/w neg/pos. 35mm E6 camera reversal processing. Tape to film transfers. Nitrate restoration/preservation

## Film Lab North Ltd
Croydon House
Croydon Street
Leeds LS11 9RT
Tel: 0113 243 4842
Fax: 0113 2434323
email: hnd@filmlabnorth.co.uk
Website: www.filmlabnorth.co.uk
Howard Dawson
Full service in 16mm colour Negative Processing, 16mm colour printing, 35mm colour printing video transfer.

Super 16mm a speciality - Plus 35mm colour grading and printing

## Hendersons Movie Lab
18-20 St Dunstan's Road
South Norwood
London SE25 6EU
Tel: 020 8653 2255
Fax: 020 8653 9773
email: sales@sales@themovielab.co.uk
Website: www.themovielab.co.uk
Bill Millington
Hendersons offers a comprehensive lab service in 16mm and 35mm colour and black and white. Hendersons was established in 1927 and still resides in its purpose build South London site. The company specialises in the preservation and restoration of motion picture work on behalf of many of the major feature film producers

## Sky Photographic Services Ltd
Ramillies House
Ramillies Street
London W1F 7AZ
Tel: 0207 4342266
Fax: 0207 4340828
email: info@skyphoto.demon.co.uk
Website: www.sky-photographic.co.uk
Mike Sherry, Managing Director

## Soho Images
8-14 Meard Street
London W1V 3HR
Tel: 020 7437 0831
Fax: 020 7734 9471
email: sohogroup.com
Website: www.sohoimages.com
Soho Laboratories offer day and night printing and processing of 16mm (including Super 16mm) and 35mm colour or b/w film

## Technicolor Film Services
Technicolor Ltd
Bath Road
West Drayton
Middx UB7 0DB
Tel: 020 8759 5432
Fax: 020 8759 6270
Website: www.technicolor.com
Mike Howell
West End pick-up and delivery point:

**F.M.F.**
**52 Berwick Street**
**London W1F 8SL**
Tel: 020 7287 5596
Technicolor is a worldwide film and
telecine operation, with laboratories
in Hollywood, London, Rome, New
York and Montreal. It offers a 24 hour
service covering all film formats -
16mm, 35mm and 65mm large screen
presentation. The extensive sound
service operation complements
customers' requirements by offering
transfers to all digital formats. The
newly created Technicolor Imaging is
designed to service feature,
commercial and 16mm
drama/documentary markets. Five
telecine suites accommodate two ITK
Millennium telecines, URSA and two
high grade Rank Cintel machines.
Other services include feature
mastering, drama finishing, sound
laybacks, DVD video and audio pre-
mastering all available under the
same secure roof making Technicolor
Europe's largest and most
comprehensive film processing
laboratory

## Todd-AO UK
**13 Hawley Crescent**
**London NW11 8NP**
Tel: 020 7284 7900
Fax: 020 7284 1018
Website: www.todd-ao.co.uk
Roger Harlow
Complete 35mm, Super 16 and
16mm film processing laboratory and
sound transfer service with full video
post-production facility including
Digital Wet Gate Telecines, D3,
Digital Betacam, Betacam SP and
other video formats. On-line editing,
duplication and standards
conversion. Sync sound and A+B roll
negative to tape transfer, neg cutting
service

## University of East Anglia
**East Anglian Film Archive**
**Norwich NR4 7TJ**
Tel: 01603 592664
Fax: Fax 01603 593475
email: eafa@uea.ac.uk
Website: www.uea.ac.uk/eafa
Phil Butcher
The East Anglian Film Archive
specialises in small gauge film work,
including:-
Blow up film printing of Standard
8mm, Super 8mm, and 9.5mm to
16mm. Also centre perforation
17.5mm.
Transfer to video and DVD of

Standard 8mm, Super 8mm, and
9.5mm
Conservation of Standard 8mm,
Super 8mm, 9.5mm, centre
perforation 17.5mm, and 35mm
Digital restoration service

This section provides a directory of libraries that have collections of books, periodicals, papers and other materials covering film and television. It includes a selection of libraries of academic institutions with graduate and post-graduate degree courses in the media and other organisations. Please contact the organisations directly or check websites (where available) for further details. Most of these collections are intended for student and teaching staff use: permission for access should always be sought from the Librarian first. Compiled by Ayesha Khan

### *bfi* National Library

21 Stephen Street
London W1T 1LN
Tel: 020 7255 1444
020 7436 0165 (Information)
Fax: 020 7436 2338
The bfi National Library offers access to the world's largest collection of information on film and television. As a major national research collection the main priority is to provide comprehensive coverage of British film and television, but the collection itself is international in scope.

## *bfi* National Library holdings

**Books**
Over 46,000 books covering all aspect of film and television ranging from reference books and biographies to published scripts, academic texts and broadcasting policy studies.

**Periodicals**
There are over 5,000 indexed periodical titles in the collection and over 400 are received every year from 45 countries.

**Newspaper Cuttings**
Over two million newspaper cuttings, mainly UK published, dating back to the 1930s. Most cuttings are stored on microfiche and are indexed according to film or programme title, personality, event, country and subject.

**Scripts**
Over 20,000 unpublished scripts, including production and post-

production, and a number of television scripts. Translations used for earphone commentaries at the National Film Theatre are also held.

**Publicity Materials**
A wide range of materials is available from press releases to campaign books from the turn of the century, and festival catalogues dating back to the 1934 Venice Film Festival.

**Unpublished Materials**
Extensive collections of papers donated by individuals and organisations (including the British Board of Film Classification and BECTU).

**Audio Tapes**
The Library offers three main collections; 200 interviews from on-stage events at the National Film Theatre from 1962 onwards; the Denis Gifford Collection; and a major Oral History Project organised by BECTU.

**CD-ROMs**
Along with other indexes and CD-ROMs the bfi's CD-ROM film Index International provides filmographic data and periodical references relating to over 100,000 feature films from around the world.

**SIFT (Summary of Information on Film and Television) Database**
Access to the bfi's unique and extensive database dedicated to film and television is available in the Library. SIFT users can call up information on more than 500,000 films, television programmes and videos, plus one million personalities. 150,000 organisations and 6,000 events.

## Access to the *bfi* National Library's holdings

**The Reading Room**
All of the collections are available for reference only in the Reading Room. Access to the Reading Room is available to either Day Pass holders or holders of the Library Annual Pass. The Majority of materials are stored in stacks, which are not open to users, but most can be consulted in the Reading Room. The book catalogue can be browsed in advance at

www.bfi.org.uk/library/olib. Certain categories of material can only be consulted in the Special Collection study room. Staff are on hand and full details are available in the Reading Room to support users and help them get the best out of the collections.

**Special Collections Unit**
If you wish to consult unpublished materials or originals of press book publicity then this must be done in the Special Collections Unit at Stephen Street. It is necessary to book an appointment in advance, please ring 020 7957 4772 or email speccoll@bfi.org.uk.

**Information Services**
Collection information and providing answers to enquiries and research requests is an important part of the work of the bfi National Library. Further details can be found at www.bfi.org.uk/library/services. Charges are applicable for many requests.

**Reading Room opening hours**

| | |
|---|---|
| Monday | 10.30am - 5.30pm |
| Tuesday | 10.30am - 8.00pm |
| Wednesday | 1.00pm - 8.00pm |
| Thursday | 10.30am - 8.00pm |
| Friday | 10.30am - 5.30pm |
| Closed at weekends | |

| | |
|---|---|
| Institutional pass: | £50.00 |
| Annual Library pass: | £35.00 |
| NFT Members pass: | £28.00 |
| Annual Discount passes | £22.00* |
| Weekly pass | £15.00 |
| Day pass | £ 6.00** |

*Available to Senior Citizens, Registered Disabled and Unemployed upon proof of eligibility. Students may also apply for a discounted library pass.
**Available to anyone. Spaces may be reserved by giving 48 hours notice. For more information on Institutional and Annual membership and to subscribe please call 020 7815 1374.

**Enquiry Lines**
The Enquiry Line is available for short enquiries. Frequent callers subscribe to an information service. The line is open from 10.00am-1.00pm and 2.00pm-5.00pm
Monday to Friday - 020 7255 1444.

# Aberdeen

## Aberdeen University Library
Meston Walk
Aberdeen
Grampian AB24 3UE
Tel: 01224 272580
email: library@abdn.ac.uk
Website:
www.abdn.ac.uk/diss/library/
Contact: Librarian

# Belfast

## Belfast Education and Library Board
Belfast Central Library
Royal Avenue
Belfast
Co. Antrim BT1 1EA
Tel: 012890 509150
Website: www.belb.org.uk
Contact: Librarian

## Northern Ireland Film and Television Commission (Digital Film Archive)
3rd Floor Alfred House
21 Alfred Street
Belfast BT2 8ED
Tel: 44 28 902 32 444
Fax: 44 28 902 39 918
email: info@NIFTC.co.uk
Website: www.nifc.co.uk
Contact: Information Officer
Resources: Archive of moving images about Northern Ireland 1897-2000. There is also a digital film archive of selected materials that can be viewed at various sites in Northern Ireland.

# Birmingham

## Birmingham University Library
Information Services
Main Library
Edgbaston
Birmingham B42 2SU
Tel: 0121 414 5828
Fax: 0121 471 4691
email: library@bham.ac.uk
Website: www.is.bham.ac.uk/lsd
Contact: Dean of Information Services

## University of Central England
Birmingham Institute of Art & Design
Library Services
Corporation Street
Gosta Green

Birmingham B4 7DX
Tel: 0121 331 5860
Fax: Tel: 0121 331 5877
Website: http://library.uce.ac.uk
Contact: John Ridgway, Subject Librarian

## Vivid - Birmingham's Centre for Media Arts
Unit 311F, The Big Peg
120 Vyse Street
Birmingham B18 6ND
Tel: 0121 233 4061
Fax: 0121 212 1784
email:info@vivid.org.uk
Website: www.vivid.org.uk
Contact: Marian Hall, Facilities Manager
Resources: With a focus on new media, a small archive and facilities for use by practitioners

# Bradford

## National Museum of Film and Photography
The Education Department
Bradford BD1 1NQ
Tel: 01274 202040
Fax: 01274 772325
Website: www.nmpft.org.uk
email: education.nmpft@nmsi.org.uk
Contact: Enquiries
Online resources and guides available.

# Brighton

## Brighton Public Library
Vantage Point
New England Street
Brighton BN1 2GW
Tel: 01273 290800
Fax: 01273 296965
email: blibrary@hotmail.com
Website: www.citylibraries.info
Eclectic lending collections and its advisable to contact Brighton and Hove Libraries and Museums about their Special Collections.

## University of Brighton Faculty of Art, Design and Humanities
St Peter's House Library
16-18 Richmond Place
Brighton BN2 9NA
Tel: 01273 643221
Fax: 01273 607532
email: ASKSPH@brighton.ac.uk
Website:
www.brighton.ac.uk/lis/lstpeter.shtml
Contact: Information Services Manager

# Bristol

## Bristol Central Library
Reference Library
College Green
Bristol BS1 5TL
Tel: 0117 903 7200
Fax: 0117 922 1081
email:
bristol_library_service@bristol-city.gov.uk
Contact: Kate Davenport, Head of Libraries

## University of Bristol
University Library
Tyndall Avenue
Bristol BS8 1TJ
Tel: 0117 928 9000
Fax: 0117 925 5334
email: jez.conolly@bristol.ac.uk
Website: www.bris.ac.uk/is/
Contact: Jez Conolly (Subject Librarian)

## University of Bristol Theatre Collection
Department of Drama
Cantocks Close
Bristol BS8 1UP
Tel: 0117 928 7836
Fax: 0117 928 7832
email: theatre-collection@bristol.ac.uk
Website: www.bristol.ac.uk/theatrecollection
Contact: Jo Elsworth

## University of the West of England, Bristol
Faculty of Art, Media and Design Library
Bower Ashton Campus
Kennel Lodge Road
Bristol BS3 2JT
Tel: 0117 9344 4750
email: geoff.cole@uwe.ac.uk
Website: www.uwe.ac.uk/library
Contact: Geoff Cole, Campus/Subject Librarian, Art, Media and Design

# Canterbury

## Canterbury Christ Church College Library
North Holmes Road
Canterbury
Kent CT1 1QU
Tel: 01227 767700 ext. 2514
Website: http://library.cant.ac.uk
Contact: Academic Services

**Kent Institute of Art & Design at** Canterbury
New Dover Road
Canterbury
Kent CT1 3AN
Tel: 01227 769371
Fax: 01227 817500
email: librarycant@KIAD.ac.uk
Website: www.kiad.ac.uk
Kathleen Godfrey: Campus Librarian

**Templeman Library**
University of Kent
Templeman Library
Canterbury
Kent CT2 7NU
Tel: 01227 823573
email: library-enquiry@kent.ac.uk
Website: www.ukc.ac.uk/library
Contact: Derek Whitaker, Subject Librarian

# Carlisle

**Cumbria Institute of the Arts Library**
Brampton Road
Carlisle, Cumbria CA3 9AY
Tel: 01228 400300
Fax: 01228 514491
email: info@cumbria.ac.uk
Website: www.cumbria.ac.uk
Contact: Librarian

# Cheltenham

**University of Gloucestershire**
Learning Centre, PO Box 220
The Park
Cheltenham
Gloucestershire GL50 2QF
email: kinfopark@glos.ac.uk
Website: www.glos.ac.uk

# Chester

**Chester College**
Learning Resources
Parkgate Road
Chester CH1 4BJ
Tel: 01244 375444
Fax: 01244 392820
Website: www.chester.ac.uk/lr
email: library.enquiries@chester.ac.uk
Contact: Fiona McLean (Subject Librarian)

# Chislehurst

**Ravensbourne College of**

**Design and Communication Learning Resource Centre**
Walden Road, Chislehurst
Kent BR7 5SN
Tel: 020 8289 4900
email: info@rave.ac.uk
Website: www.rave.ac.uk

# Colchester

**Colchester Institute Library Services**
Sheepen Road
Colchester CO3 3LL
Tel: 01206 518642
Website: www.colch-inst.ac.uk
Contact: Enquiries

**University of Essex**
Albert Sloman Library
Wivenhoe Park
Colchester CO4 3SQ
Tel: 01206 873192
Fax: 01206 872289
email: ewalkey@essex.ac.uk
Website:
http://libwww.essex.ac.uk/Subject_Resources/film.html
Contact: Emma Walkey, Subject Librarian

# Coventry

**Coventry Central Library**
Smithford Way
Coventry CV1 1FY
Tel: 024 7683 2314
Fax: 024 76832440
email: central.library@coventry.ac.uk
Contact: Librarian

**Lanchester Library**
Frederick Lanchester Building
Coventry University
Gosford Street
Coventry CV1 5DD
Tel: 024 7688 7542
Fax: 024 7688 7543
email: ibx032@coventry.ac.uk
Website: www.coventry.ac.uk
Contact: Anne-Marie Hayes, Subject Librarian, Arts, Design and Media

**University of Warwick Library**
Gibbet Hill Road
Coventry CV4 7AL
Tel: 024 7652 4103
Fax: 024 7652 4211
email: library@warwick.ac.uk
Website:
www2.warwick.ac.uk/services/library
Contact: Librarian

Resources: Collection of German film programme from the 1930s

# Derby

**University of Derby**
Kedleston Road Learning Centre
Kedleston Road
Derby DE22 1GB
Tel: 01332 591282
email: j.robinson@derby.ac.uk
Website:
lib.derby.ac.uk/library/homelib.html
Contact: Jane Robinson, Subject Librarian

**Nova Film and Videotape Library**
62 Ascot Avenue, Cantley
Doncaster DN4 6HE
Tel: 0870 765 1094
email: info@novaonline.co.uk
Website: www.novaonline.co.uk
Contact: Gareth Atherton
Resources: Non-fiction and archive film and contemporary videos.

# Dorking

**Surrey Performing Arts Library**
Denbies Wine Estate
London Road
Dorking, Surrey RH5 6AA
Tel: 01306 875453
email:
performing.arts@surreycc.gov.uk
lWebsite:
www.surreycc.gov.uk/libraries
Resources: Wide-ranging collection on cinema, including scripts and soundtracks.

# Douglas

**Douglas Corporation**
Douglas Public Library
10 Victoria Street, Douglas
Isle of Man IM1
Tel: 01624 696453
Fax: 01624 696400
email: j.bowring@douglas.org.im
Contact: John Bowring (Librarian)

# Dundee

**University of Dundee**
Duncan of Jordanstone College of Art and Design Library
Matthew Building
13 Perth Road
Dundee DD1 4HT

Tel: 01382 345252
Fax: 01382 229283
email: m.simmons@dundee.ac.uk
Website:
www.dundee.ac.uk/library/doj
Contact: Marie Simmons, College
Librarian
Resources: Resources aimed at the
practical rather than the theoretical.

# Edinburgh

## Edinburgh College of Art Library Service
Lauriston Place
Edinburgh
Scotland EH3 9DF
Tel: 0131 221 6034
Fax: 0131 221 6033
Website: www.lib.eca.ac.uk
Contact: Subject Librarian, Art and
Design

## Edinburgh University Library
George Square
Edinburgh EH8 9LG
Tel: 0131 650 3384
Fax: 0131 667 9780
email: library@ed.ac.uk
Website: www.lib.ed.ac.uk
Contact: Enquiries

## Napier University
Merchiston Campus Library
10 Colinton Road
Edinburgh
Scotland EH10 5DT
Tel: 0131 455 2582
Fax: 0131 455 2377
email: merchistonLC@napier.ac.uk
Website: nulis.napier.ac.uk
Contact: Sheila Barcroft, Campus
Library Manager

## National Library of Scotland
George IV Bridge
Edinburgh
Scotland EH1 1EW
Tel: 0131 226 4531
Fax: 0131 466 2804
Website: www.nls.uk

# Egham

## Royal Holloway University of London Library
Egham Hill
Egham
Surrey TW20 OEX
Tel: 01784 443823
email: library@rhul.ac.uk
Website:

www.rhul.ac.uk/information-
services/library/
Contact: Librarian

# Epsom

## Surrey Institute of Art and Design
Epsom Library and Learning
Resources Centre, Ashley Road
Epsom, Surrey KT18 5BE
Tel: 01372 202458
Fax: 01372 202457
Website: www.surrart.ac.uk
email: jseabourne@surrat.ac.uk
Contact: Jan Seabourne (site
Librarian)

# Exeter

## Exeter University
The Bill Douglas Centre for the
history of cinema and popular
culture
The Old Library
Prince of Wales Road
Exeter EX4 4SB
Tel: 01392 264321
email: info@billdouglas.org
Website: www.billdouglas.org

# Farnham

## Surrey Institute of Art & Design, University College
Farnham Campus
Falkner Road
The Hart, Farnham
Surrey GU9 7DS
Tel: 01252 722441
Fax: 01252 892616
Website: www.surrat.ac.uk
Contact: Institute Librarian
Registered users only

# Gateshead

## Gateshead Libraries and Arts Department
Gateshead Central Library
Prince Consort Road
Gateshead
Tyne and Wear NE8 4LN
Tel: 0191 477 3478
Fax: 0191 477 7454
email: enquiries@l
ibarts.gatesheadmbc.gov.uk
Website:
www.gateshead.gov.uk/libraries

# Glasgow

## Glasgow Caledonian University Library and Information Centre
Glasgow Caledonian University
Cowcaddens Road
Glasgow G4 0BA
Tel: 0141 331 3859
Website: www.lib.gcal.ac.uk
Contact: Enquiries

## Glasgow City Libraries
Mitchell Library
North Street
Glasgow G3 7DN
Tel: 0141 287 2933
Fax: 0141 287 2933
Website: www.mitchelllibrary.org
email: arts@gcl.glasgow.gov.uk
Contact: General Services Librarian

## Scottish Screen Information Service
1 Bowmont Gardens
Glasgow G12 9LR
Tel: 0141 302 1730
Fax: 0141 302 1778
email: info@scottishscreen.com
Website: www.scottishscreen.com
Contact: Isabella Edgar, Information
Manager
Resources: Production information,
press cuttings and journals. They also
provide a research service.
Access to the Shiach Script library with
over 100 feature and short film scripts

## University of Glasgow
The Library
Hillhead Street
Glasgow G12 8QE
Tel: 0141 330 6704
Fax: 0141 330 4952
Website: www.lib.gla.ac.uk
email: library@lib.gla.ac.uk
Contact: Subject Librarian

# Gravesend

## VLV - Voice of the Listener and Viewer Ltd
101 King's Drive
Gravesend
Kent DA12 5BQ
Tel: 01474 352835
Fax: 01474 351112
email: info@vlv.org
Website: www.vlv.org.uk
Contact: VLV Librarian
Resources: VLV holds archives of the
former Broadcasting Research Unit
(1980-90) and British Action for

Children's Television (1988-95). Access to these and VLV's own archive, which includes all VLV responses to government and public consultations and transcripts of most VLV conferences since 1984 is increasingly on thir website, but please contact them for further information on accessing them.

# Hatfield

## University of Hertfordshire Learning and Information Services
College Lane
Hatfield
Hertfordshire AL10 9AB
Tel: 01707 284678
Fax: 01707 284666
email: lisadmin@herts.ac.uk
Website: www.herts.ac.uk/lis/

# Huddersfield

## Kirklees Cultural Services
Huddersfield Library and Art Galllery
Princess Alexandra Walk
Huddersfield HD1 2SU
Tel: 01484 221967
Fax: 01484 221974
email: kinfo@kirkless.gov.uk
Website: www.kirklessmc.gov.uk
Contact: Reference Librarian

# Hull

## University of Lincoln
Hull School of Art and Design
Learning Support Centre
Guildhall Road
Kingston-Upon-Hull HU1 1HT
Tel: 01482 311673
Fax: 01482 311656
Website:
www.lincoln.ac.uk/ls/index.htm
Contact: Centre Manager

# Keele

## Keele Information Services
Keele University
Keele
Staffs ST5 5BG
Tel: 01782 583535
Fax: 01782 711553
Website: www.keele.ac.uk/depts/li/
email: libhelp@keele.ac.uk
Contact: Jim Linnell (Humanities subject Librarian)

# Kingston Upon Thames

## Kingston University Library Services
Knights Park Learning Resources Centre
Knights Park
Kingston Upon Thames
Surrey KT1 2QJ
Tel: 020 8547 7057
Fax: 020 8547 8039
email: library@kingston.ac.uk
Website: www.kingston.ac.uk/library
Contact: Faculty Librarian (Design)

## Kingston Museum & Heritage Service
Wheatfield Way
Kingston
Surrey KT1 2PS
Tel: 020 8547 546 5386
Website: www.kingston.gov
Contact: Paul Hill (Curator)
Resources: Holds the catalogue for the Eadweard Muybridge Collection of pre-cinema images and artefacts

# Lancaster

## Lancaster University Library
Bailrigg
Lancaster LA1 4YH
Tel: 01524 592516
email: h.clish@lancaster.ac.uk
Website: libweb.lancs.ac.uk
Contact: Helen Clish, Assistant Librarian

# Leeds

## Leeds City Libraries
Art Library
Municipal Buildings
Calverley Street
Leeds, West Yorkshire LS1 3AB
Tel: 0113 247 8247
Fax: 0113 247 8247
email: ArtLibrary@leedslearning.net
Contact: Librarian

## Leeds Metropolitan University
The Learning Centre
Leslie Silver Building
Woodhouse Lane
Leeds LS1 3HE
Tel: 0113 283 5968
email: s.mcdowell@leedsmet.ac.uk
Website: www.leedsmet.ac.uk
Contact: Sandra McDowell, Learning Advisor

# Leicester

## De Montfort University Library
Kimberlin Library, The Gateway
Leicester LE1 9BH
Tel: 0116 2551551 (x8039)
Fax: 0116 2577046
email: cneal@dmu.ac.uk
Website: www.library.dmu.ac.uk
Contact: Clifford Neal, Assistant Librarian (Media Studies)

## Leicester Reference and Information Library
Bishop Street
Leicester LE1 6AA
Tel: 0116 2995401
email:
central.eference@leicester.gov.uk
Contact: Librarian
Resources: Burchell Collection of books, journals and memorilbilia on British films from the 1920's to the late 1960's.

## University of Leicester
Centre For Mass Communication Research
University Road
Leicester LE1 7RH
Tel: 0116 2523863
Tel: Fax: 0116 2523874
email: cmcr@le.ac.uk
email: Website: www.le.ac.uk/cmcr/
Contact: Enquiries

## University of Leicester Library
PO Box 248
University Road
Leicester LE1 9QD
Tel: 0116 252 2055
Fax: 0116 252 2066
email: bem1@le.ac.uk
Website: www.le.ac.uk/library
Contact: Brian Marshall, Information Librarian
Resources:  Collection supporting Mass communication studies

# Liverpool

## Aldham Roberts Learning Resource Centre
Liverpool John Moores University
Mount Pleasant
Liverpool L3 5UZ
Tel: 0151 231 3701
Fax: 0151 707 1307
Website: http://cwis.livjm.ac.uk/lea
Contact: Senior Information Officer (Media, Critical and Creative Arts)

## Liverpool City Libraries
William Brown Street
Liverpool L3 8EW
Tel: 0151 2335835
email: refbt.central@liverpool.gov.uk
Contact: Librarian

## Liverpool Hope University College
Hope Park
Liverpool L16 9LB
Tel: 0151 291 2000
Fax: 0151 291 2037
Website: www.hope.ac.uk
Contact: Director of Learning Resources

# London

## Barbican Library
Barbican Centre
Silk Street, London EC2Y 8DS
Tel: 020 7638 0569
Fax: 020 7638 2249
email:
barbicanlib@corpoflondon.gov.uk
Website:
www.barbican.org.uk/information/library/index.shtml
Contact: Librarian

## British Universities Film & Video Council Library
77 Wells Street
London W1T 3QJ
Tel: 020 7393 1500
Fax: 020 7393 1555
email: library@bufvc.ac.uk
Website: www.bufvc.ac.uk
Luke McKernan, Head of Information
Resources: Scientific Film Association papers, BKSTS book collection, Slade Film History Register, Reuters Television newsreel documents

## Brunel University Library
Twickenham Campus
300 St Margarets Road
Twickenham Tw1 1PT
Tel: 020 8891 0121 ext. 2205
Fax: 020 8891 8240
email: library@brunel.ac.uk
Website: www.brunel.ac.uk/depts/lib
Contact: Penny Lyndon (Subject Librarian)

## Camberwell College of Arts Library
CCA
Peckham Road
London SE5 8UF
Tel: 020 7514 6349
Fax: 020 7514 6324

Website: camberwell.arts.ac.uk
Contact: College Librarian
Resources: Special Collection of original letters, papers and ephemera Camden Public Libraries

## Swiss Cottage Library
88 Avenue Road
London NW3 3HA
Tel: 020 7974 6522
Fax: 020 7974 6532
email:
swisscottagelibrary@camden.gov.uk
Website:
www.camden.gov.uk/libraries
Contact: Librarian

## Central St Martins College of Art
Library and Learning Resources
Southampton Row
London WC1B 4AP
Tel: 020 7514 7037
Fax: 020 7514 7033
Website: www.csm.linst.ac.uk
Contact: Library Manager

## English and Media Centre
18 Compton Terrace
London N1 2UN
Tel: 020 7359 8080
Fax: 020 7354 0133
email: info@englishandmedia.co.uk
Website: www.englishandmedia.co.uk
Contact: Administrator
Resources: collections aimed specifically at Secondary and FE teachers and students

## Harrow Library Services
Gayton Library
Gayton Road
Harrow
Middlesex HA1 2HL
Tel: 020 8427 6012/6986
email: gayton.library@harrow.gov.uk
Website:
www.harrow.gov.uk/council/departments/libraries/libraryhome.asp
Contact: Principal Librarian

## London Borough of Sutton
Sutton Library
St Nicholas Way
Sutton
Surrey SM1 1EA
Tel: 020 8770 4700
Fax: 020 8770 4777
email: sutton.library@sutton.gov.uk
Website: www.sutton.gov.uk
Contact: Enquiries

## Institute of Education Library (London)
Information Services

20 Bedford Way
London WC1H OAL
Tel: 020 7612 6080
Fax: 020 7612 6093
email: lib.enquiries@ioe.ac.uk
Website: www.ioe.ac.uk
Contact: Librarian

## Instituto Cervantes
102 Eaton Square
London SW1W 9AN
Tel. 020 7201 0757
Fax 020 7235 0329
email: biblon@cervantes.es
Website: www.cervantes.org.uk
Contact: Ramón Abad, Head Librarian
Instituto Cervantes in London, a Spanish government sponsored cultural center. The Library and Information Service includes among its holdings a large collection of Spanish and Latin American films and documentaries, on video and DVD, as well as a printed collection including books, magazines, film scripts, and other materials related to the Spanish-speaking world's cultural life  There are now also centres in Manchester and Leeds

## London College of Fashion Library
20 John Princes Street
London W1G 0BJ
Tel: 020 7514 7453 / 7455
Fax: 020 7514 7580
Website: www.lcf.linst.ac.uk
Contact: Library Manager

## London College of Communication Library
Elephant and Castle
London SE1 6SB
Tel: 020 7514 6527
Fax: 020 7514 6886
Website: www.arts.ac.uk/library
Contact: LIbrarian

## London Metropolitan University
Learning Centre, London North Campus
236-250 Holloway Road
London N7 6PP
Tel: 020 7133 2371
Website: www.londonmet.ac.uk
Contact: Librarian
Resources: includes London Guildhall University collections

## London Metropolitan University
Commercial Road Library
2nd Floor

41 Commercial Road
London E1 1LA
Tel: 020 7320 1869
Contact: Librarian

**Middlesex University**
Learning Resources
Cat Hill
Barnet EN4 8HT
Tel: 020 8411 5042
Fax: 020 8411 5105
Website: www.ilrs.mdx.ac.uk/
Contact: Subject Librarian

**Royal College of Art**
Kensington Gore
London SW7 2EU
Tel: 020 7590 4224
Fax: 020 7590 4500
Website: www.rca.ac.uk
email: library@rca.org.uk
Contact: Library Desk

**Royal Television Society**
Holborn Hall
100 Grays Inn Road
London WC1X 8AL
Tel: 020 7430 1000
Fax: 020 7430 0924
email: info@rts.org.uk
Website: www.rts.org.uk
Contact: Archivist
Collection: Written, photographic
and audio-visual materials on the
history of television from 1927
onwards.

**Thames Valley University**
Learning Resources Centre
St Mary's Road
Walpole House
Ealing
London W5 5RF
Tel: 020 8231 2637
Website:
www.tvu.ac.uk/lrs/index.html
Contact: Humanities Librarian

**University of East London –
School of Art and Design**
Docklands Learning Resources
Centre
4-6 University Way
London E16 2RD
Tel: 020 8223 7444
email: n.edwards@uel.ac.uk
Website: www.uel.ac.uk/lss
Contact: Nadine Edwards, Art and
Film Subject Specialist

**University of London Library**
Senate House
Malet Street
London WC1E 7HU
Tel: 020 7862 8461

Fax: 020 7862 8480
email: enquiries@ull.ac.uk
Website: www.ull.ac.uk
Contact: Enquiries

**Goldsmiths' College Library**
University of London, New Cross
London SE14 6NW
Tel: 020 7919 7150
Fax: 020 7919 7165
email: library@gold.ac.uk
Website: www.gold.ac.uk
Contact: Subject Librarian: Media &
Communications

**University of Surrey
Roehampton**
Information Services
Roehampton Lane
London SW15 5SZ
Tel: 020 8392 3770
Fax: 020 8392 3359
email:
enquiry.desk@roehampton.ac.uk
Website:
www.roehampton.ac.uk/support/info
serv/index.asp
Contact: Enquiries

**University of Westminster**
Harrow Learning Resources Centre
Watford Road
Northwick Park
Harrow HA1 3TP
Tel: 020 7911 5885
Fax: 020 7911 5952
Website: www.wmin.ac.uk/harlib
Contact: Library Manager

**Westminster Reference
Library**
35 St Martins Street
London WC2H 7HP
Tel: 020 7641 4606
Fax: 020 7641 4640
email:
reference@librarywc2@westminster.g
ov.uk
Website:
www.westminster.gov.uk/libraries/spe
cial/perform.cfm
Contact: Arts Librarian

**Wimbledon School of Art**
Learning Resources Centre
Merton Hall Road
London SW19 3QA
Tel: 020 8408 5027
Website: www.wimbledon.ac.uk
Contact: Subject Librarian

# Loughborough

**Loughborough University**

University Library
Loughborough LE11 3TU
Tel: 01509 222360
Fax: 01509 223993
Website: www.lboro.ac.uk/library/
Contact: Academic Librarian

# Luton

**University of Luton
Learning Resources**
Park Square
Luton LU1 3JU
Tel: 01582 734111 ext. 2094
Fax: 01582 489325
email: keith.daniels@luton.ac.uk
Website: lrweb.luton.ac.uk
Contact: Keith Daniels, Academic
Liaison Librarian

# Maidstone

**Kent Institute of Art &
Design at Maidstone**
Oakwood Park
Maidstone
Kent ME16 8AG
Tel: 01622 757286
Fax: 01622 62110
Website:
www.kiad.ac.uk/library/set.htm
Contact: College Librarian

# Manchester

**Manchester Arts Library**
Central Library
St Peters Square
Manchester M2 5PD
Tel: 0161 234 1974
Fax: 0116 1234 1961
Website:
www.manchester.gov.uk/libraries/cent
ral/arts/index.htm
email:
arts@libraries.manchester.gov.uk
Contact: Arts Librarian

**Manchester Metropolitan
University Library**
Sir Kenneth Green Library
All Saints Building
Oxford Road
Manchester M15 6BH
Tel: 0161 247 6116
Fax: 0161 247 6849
Website: mmu.ac.uk/services/library
email: artdesigni-lib-enq@mmu.ac.uk
Contact: Subject Librarian

**North West Film Archive**
Manchester Metropolitan University

Minshull House
47-49 Chorlton Street
Manchester M1 3EU
Tel: 0161 247 3097
Fax: 0161 247 3098
email: n.w.filmarchive@mmu.ac.uk
Website: www.nwfa.mmu.ac.uk
Contact: Enquiries
Resources: Moving image archive.
Part of the Manchester Metropolitan
University Library Service.

# Middlesbrough

## University of Teeside
Library and Information Services
Borough Road
Middlesbrough TS1 3BA
Tel: 01642 342123
email: j.burke@tees.ac.uk
Website: www.tees.ac.uk
Contact: Jane Burke, Subject
Information Team Leader

# Milton Keynes

## Open University Library
Walton Hall
Milton Keynes MK7 6AA
Tel: 01908 653138
Fax: 01908 653571
Website: oulib1.open.ac.uk
email: lib-help@open.ac.uk
Contact: Enquiries

# Newcastle upon Tyne

## University of Northumbria Library
Learning Resources
Library Building
Sandyford Road
Newcastle Upon Tyne NE1 8ST
Tel: 0191 227 4125
Fax: 0191 227 4563
email: in.ears@unn.ac.uk
Website: www.unn.ac.uk
Contact: Senior Officer, Information
Services Department

# Newport

## University of Wales College, Newport
Library and Learning Resources
Caerleon Campus
PO Box 179
Newport
Wales NP18 3YG
Tel: 01633 432102

Fax: 01633 432108
email:
angharad.evans@newport.ac.uk
Website: http://library.newport.ac.uk
Contact: Angharad Evans, Art, Media
and Design Librarian

# Northumberland

## Northumberland Library Service and Amenities Division
Gas House Lane
Morpeth
Northumberland NE61 1TA
Tel: 01670 534518
Fax: 01670 534513
email:
amenities@northumberland.gov.uk
Website:
www.northumberland.gov.uk
Contact: The Adult Services Librarian

# Norwich

## Anglia Polytechnic University
Norwich School of Art and Design
Library
St George Street
Norwich NR3 1BB
Tel: 01603 610561 ext.3073
Fax: 01603 615728
Website: www.nsad.ac.uk
email: info@nsad.ac.uk
Contact: Assistant Librarian

## East Anglian Film Archive
University of East Anglia
Norwich NR4 7TJ
Tel: 01603 592664
Fax: 01603 458553
email: eafa@uel.ac.uk
Website: www.uea.ac.uk/eafa
Contact: Assistant Archivist

## University of East Anglia Library
Norwich, Norfolk NR4 7TJ
Tel: 01603 592428
Fax: 01603 259490
email: a.noel-tod@uel.ac.uk
Website: www.lib.uea.ac.uk
Contact: Alex Noel-Tod, Film Studies
Librarian

# Nottingham

## Nottingham Central Library
The Arts Library
Angel Row
Nottingham NG1 6HP

Tel: 0115 9152811
Fax: 0115 915 2803
Website:
www.nottinghamcity.gov.uk/libraries
email:
arts.library@nottinghamcity.gov.uk
Contact: Enquiries

## Nottingham Trent University Library
Clifton Campus Library
Clifton Lane
Nottingham NG11 8NS
Tel: 0115 848 3221
Fax: 0115 848 2286
email: sian.griffiths@ntu.ac.uk
Website: www.ntu.ac.uk/llr
Contact: Sian Griffiths, Information
Specialist

## University of Nottingham
Hallward Library
University Park
Nottingham NG7 2RD
Tel: 0115 951 4561
Fax: 0115 951 4558
email: Library-Arts-
Enquiries@Nottingham.ac.uk
Website:
www.nottingham.ac.uk/library
Contact: Arts and Humanities
Librarian

# Oxford

## University of Oxford
Bodleian Library
Broad Street
Oxford OX1 3BG
Tel: 01865 277162
Fax: 01865 277112
Website: www.bodley.ox.ac.uk
Contact: Enquiries

# Plymouth

## College of St Mark and St John Library
Derriford Road
Plymouth
Devon PL6 8BH
Tel: 01752 761145
email: libraryenquiries@marjon.ac.uk
Website: www.marjon.ac.uk/library
Contact: Resources Librarian

# Poole

## Arts Institute at Bournemouth Library
Wallisdown
Poole

Dorset BH12 5HH
Tel: 01202 363256
email: cwilmot@aib.co.uk
email: library@arts-inst-
bournemouth.ac.uk/library
Contact: Charlotte Wilmot, Subject
Librarian

### Bournemouth University Library

Talbot Campus
Fern Barrow
Poole
Dorset BH12 5BB
Tel: 01202 595460
email: mholland@bournemouth.ac.uk
Website:
www.bournemouth.ac.uk/library
Contact: Matt Holland, Subject
Librarian

## Portsmouth

### Portsmouth University Library

Frewen Library
Cambridge Road
Portsmouth
Hampshire PO1 2ST
Tel: 023 9284 3243
Fax: 023 9284 3233
email: david.francis@port.ac.uk
Website: www.libr.port.ac.uk
Contact: David Francis, Subject
Librarian

## Preston

### University of Central Lancashire Library and Learning Resources Services

St Peters Square
Preston
Lancashire PR1 2HE
Tel: 01772 892285
email: aturner-bishop@uclan.ac.uk
Website: www.uclan.ac.uk
Contact: Aidan Turner-Bishop,
Subject Librarian

## Reading

### BBC Written Archives Centre

Caversham Park
Reading RG4 8T2
Tel: 0118 948 6281
Fax: 0118 946 1145
email: wac.enquiries@bbc.co.uk
Website: www.bbc.co.uk/thenandnow
Contact: Written Archivist

### Reading University Library

Whiteknights
PO Box 223
Reading RG6 6AE
Tel: 0118 931 8770
Fax: 0118 931 6636
email: library@rdg.ac.uk
Website:
www.libraries.rdg.ac.uk/home.html
Contact: Liaison Librarian for Film,
Theatre and Television

## Redhill

### Reigate School of Art, Design and Media Library

Claremont Road
Gatton Point North
Redhill
Surrey RH1 2JX
Tel: 01787 772611 ext. 1253
email: fharries@staff.es.org.uk
Website: www.esc.org.uk/rsadapp.htm
Contact: Fina Harries (Libraries and
Learning Centres Manager)

## Rochdale

### Rochdale Metropolitan Borough Libraries

Wheatsheaf Library
Wheatsheaf Centre
Baillie Street, Rochdale
Lancashire OL16 1JZ
Tel: 01706 864900
Fax: 01706 864992
email:
library.service@rochdale.gov.uk
Website: www.rochdale.gov.uk
Contact: Librarian

## Rochester

### Kent Institute of Art and Design

Rochester Campus Library
Fort Pitt
Rochester
Kent ME1 1DZ
Tel: 01634 888734
Fax: 01634 888700
Website:
www.kiad.ac.uk/library/set.htm
email: libraryroch@kiad.ac.uk
Contact: Subject  Librarian

## Salford

### University of Salford, Information Services Division (Library)

Adelphi Library
Peru Street
Salford
Greater Manchester M3 6EQ
Tel: 0161 295 6084
Website: www.isd.salford.ac.uk
Contact: Information Officer
Resources: Scripts, DVDs and
Computer Games (PC Games and
Playstation 2)

## Sheffield

### Sheffield Hallam University Learning Centre

Psalter Lane Campus
Psalter Lane
Sheffield S11 8UZ
Tel: 0114 225 2727
Fax: 0114 225 2717
email: lc-psalter@shu.ac.uk
Website: www.shu.ac.uk/
Contact: Claire Abson, Information
Specialist

### Sheffield Libraries & Information Services

Arts, Sports and Social Sciences
Section
Central Library
Surrey Street
Sheffield S1 1XZ
Tel: 0114 273 4747
Fax: 0114 2735009
email: sheffield.cas@dial.pipex.com
Website: www.sheffield.gov.uk
Contact: Frances Revel / Liz Biggins

## Southampton

### Southampton Institute

Mountbatten Library
East Park Terrace
Southampton
Hampshire SO14 0YN
Tel: 02380 319986
email: karen.garside@solent.ac.uk
Website: www.solent.ac.uk/library/
Contact: Karen Garside, Information
Librarian

### University of Southampton

Hartley Library
Highfield
Southampton S017 1BF
Tel: 02380 592 2372
email: libenqs@soton.ac.uk
Contact:  Art Section
Resources: Personal papers,
pressbooks

## Stoke-on-Trent

### Staffordshire University Library and Information Service
Thompson Library
PO Box 664
College Road
Stoke-On-Trent
Staffordshire ST4 2XS
Tel: 01782 294443
email: Isinfo@staffs.ac.uk
Website: www.staffs.ac.uk
Contact: Librarian

## Sunderland

### City Library and Art Centre
Fawcett Street
Sunderland SR1 1RE
Tel: 0191-514 1235
Fax: 0191-514 8444
email:
enquiry.desk@sunderland.gov.uk
Website: www.sunderland.gov.uk
Contact: Librarian

### University of Sunderland
Murray Library
Chester Road
Sunderland SR1 3SD
Tel: 0191 515 3149
Fax: 0191 515 2904
email:
laurie.fenwick@sunderland.ac.uk
Contact: Laurie Fenwick, Assistant
Librarian

## Wakefield

### University of Leeds
Bretton Hall Campus
National Arts Education Archive
West Bretton
Wakefield WF4 4LG
Tel: 0113 243 9132
email: l.bartle@leeds.ac.uk
Website: naea.leeds.ac.uk
Contact: Leonard Bartle, Centre
Administrator

## Winchester

### King Alfred's College
Martial Rose Library
Sparkford Road, Winchester
Hampshire SO22 4NR
Tel: 01962 827051
email: libenquires@wkac.ac.uk
Website: www.lrc.wkac.ac.uk
Contact: Librarian

### Winchester School of Art Library
Park Avenue, Winchester
Hampshire SO23 8DL
Tel: 02380 269824
Fax: 02380 269826
email: wsaenqs@soton.ac.uk
Website: www.library.soton.ac.uk
Contact: Site Librarian

## Wolverhampton

### Light House Media Centre
Media Reference Library
Chubb Buildings
Fryer Street
Wolverhampton WV1 1HT
Tel: 01902 716055
Fax: 01902 717143
email: richard@light-house.co.uk
Website: www.light-house.co.uk
Contact Richard Carr (Library
Administrator)

## University of Wolverhampton

### Harrison Learning Centre
City Campus
Wulfruna Street
Wolverhampton WV1 1SB
Tel: 01902 322300
Website: www.wlv.ac.uk/lib
Contact: Art and Design Librarian

### Wolverhampton Libraries and Information Services
Central Library
Snow Hill
Wolverhampton WV1 3AX
Tel: 01902 552026
Fax: 01902 552024
email: wolverhampton.libraries@
dial.pipex. com
Website: www.wolverhampton.gov.uk
Contact: Librarian

## York

### York St John College
Fountains Learning Centre
Lord Mayors Walk
York YO31 7EX
Tel: 01904 716699
Fax: 01904 612512
email: f.ware@yorksj.ac.uk
Website: www.yorksj.ac.uk/
Contact: Fiona Ware, Academic
Support Librarian
Resources: Holds the Yorkshire Film
Archive

# ORGANISATIONS

Listed below are the main trade/government organisations and bodies relevant to the film and television industries in the UK. This is followed by a separate list of UK Regional Film Commissions and Film Offices. Finally, a small selection of organisations from the US concludes this section

## Advertising Association
Abford House
15 Wilton Road
London SW1V 1NJ
Tel: 020 7828 2771/828 4831
Fax: 020 7931 0376
email: aa@adassoc.org.uk
Website: www.adassoc.org.uk
Philip Spink

## Advertising Producers' Association (APA)
26 Noel Street
London W1F 89Y
Tel: 020 7434 2651
Fax: 020 7434 9002
email: info@a-p-a.net
Website: www.a-p-a.net
Stephen Davies, Chief Executive
The APA represents production companies making TV and cinema commercials. It regulates agreements with agencies and with crew and provides a telephone advice service on production and legal matters and other services for members

## Advertising Standards Authority (ASA)
Brook House
2 Torrington Place
London WC1E 7HW
Tel: 020 7580 5555
Fax: 020 7631 3051
Website: www.asa.org.uk

## AFMA Europe
49 Littleton Road
Harrow
Middx HA1 3SY
Tel: 020 8423 0763
Fax: Tel: 020 8423 7963
email: lsafir@afma.com
Website: www.afma.com
Chairman: Lawrence Safir

## AIM (All Industry Marketing for Cinema)
22 Golden Square
London W1F 9JW
Tel: 020 7734 9551
Fax: 020 7734 6147
email: cea@cinemauk.ftech.co.uk
Barry Jenkins
Unites distribution, exhibition, BAFTA, UK Film Council and cinema advertising in promoting cinema and cinema going, Funds Film Education, markets cinema for sponsorship and promotional ventures and is a forum for cinema marketing ideas. AIM and the UK Film Council jointly established the Cinema Marketing Agency with a remit to increase and broaden further the UK cinema audience

## Amalgamated Engineering and Electrical Union (AEEU)
Hayes Court,
West Common Road,
Bromley,
Kent BR2 7AU
Tel: 020 8462 7755
Fax: 020 8462 4959
Website: www.aeeu.org.uk
Trade union representing - among others -people employed in film and TV lighting/electrical/electronic work

## AMPS (Association of Motion Picture Sound)
28 Knox Street
London W1H 1FS
Tel: 020 7723 6727
Fax: 020 7723 6727
email: info@amps.net
Website: www.amps.net
Brian Hickin
Promotes and encourages science, technology and creative application of all aspects of motion picture sound recording and reproduction, and seeks to promote and enhance the status of those therein engaged

## APRS - The Professional Recording Association
PO Box 22
Totnes
Devon TQ9 7YZ
Tel: 01803 868600
Fax: 01803 868444
email: info@aprs.co.uk
Website: www.aprs.co.uk
Peter Filleul, Acting Executive Director

## Arts Council England
14 Great Peter Street
London SW1P 3NQ
Tel: 0845 300 6200
Fax: 020 7973 6590
email:enquiries@artscouncil.org.uk
Website: www.artcouncil.org.uk
Chief Executive: Peter Hewitt
Chair: Professor Sir Christopher Frayling
Arts Council England is the national development agency for the arts in England, distributing public money from Government and the National Lottery. Arts Council England's main funding programme is Grants for the arts. It is open to individuals, arts organisations, national touring and other people who use the arts in their work. They are for activities that benefit people in England or that help artists and arts organisations from England to carry out their work. Arts Council England has one national and nine regional offices
**For a full listing of regional offices see Funding section**

## Arts Council of Wales
9 Museum Place
Cardiff CF10 3NX
Tel: 029 20 376500
Fax: 029 20 395284
email: info@artswales.org.uk
Website: www.artswales.org.uk
Anneli Jones, Strategic Unit
Lottery funding is available for the development and production of film projects. Responsibility for film funding is in the process of being partially delegated to Sgrin Cymru Wales

## ASIFA
International Animated Film Association
52 Old Market Street
Bristol BS2 OER
Tel: 0117 925 0187
Fax: 0117 929 9004
email: andy@eggtoons.com

Website: uk@asifa.net
Andy Wyatt
A worldwide association of individuals who work in, or make a contribution to, the animation industry, including students. Activities include involvement in UK and international events and festivals, and international children's workshops. The UK group provides an information service to members and publishes a quarterly magazine

## Association for Media Education in Scotland (AMES)

c/o D Murphy
24 Burnett Place
Aberdeen AB24 4QD
Tel: 01224 277113
email: d@murphy47.freeserve.co.uk
Des Murphy

## The Association of Independent Film Exhibitors (AIFE)

C/o City Screen
Hardy House
16-18 Beak Street
London W1F 9RD
Contact: Caroline Bull
Tel: 07968 950766
Fax: 020 7734 4027
email: caroline.b@ picturehouses.co.uk
Chairman: Tony Jones
Secretary : Dave Moutrey
Treasurer: Laraine Porter
A specialist trade association committed to the continued development of independent venues in the UK, whose primary function is to present the broadest possible range of specialised films to the general public

## Audio Visual Association

Herkomer House
156 High Street
Bushey
Herts WD2 3DD
Tel: 020 8950 5959
Fax: 020 8950 7560
email: multimedia@visual-arena.co.uk
Website: www.visual-arena.co.uk
Mike Simpson FBIPP

## Authors' Licensing & Collecting Society

Marlborough Court
14-18 Holborn
London EC1 N 2LE
Tel: 020 7395 0600
Fax: 020 7395 0660

email: alcs@alcs.co.uk
Website: www.alcs.co.uk
The ALCS is the British collecting society for all writers. Its principal purpose is to ensure that hard-to-collect revenues due to authors are efficently collected and speedily distributed. These include the simultaneous cable retransmission of the UK's terrestrial and various international channels, educational off-air recording and BBC Prime. Contact the ALCS office for more information

## BAFTA (British Academy of Film and Television Arts)

195 Piccadilly
London W1V OLN
Tel: 020 7734 0022
Fax: 020 7734 1792
Website: www.bafta.org
Amanda Berry, Chief Executive
BAFTA was formed in 1947 by Britain's most eminent filmmakers as a non-profit making company. It occupies a pivotal, unique position in the industry with a clear aim to promote excellence in film, television and interactive entertainment. BAFTA is a diverse organisation: it is a charity and a members' club; it undertakes a number of educational and training activities and has an active and successful trading arm. Membership is available to those who have a minimum of three years professional experience in the film, television or interactive entertainment industries (or any combination of these), who are able to demonstrate significant ccontribution to the industry. BAFTA has facilities for screenings, conferences, seminaars and discussion meetings. Its awards for film and television are annual televised events. There are also awards for childrens' (film and television) interactive entertainment and games. The Academy has branches in Manchester, Glasgow, Cardiff, Los Angeles and New York

## BARB (Broadcasters' Audience Research Board)

2nd Floor
18 Dering Street
London W1R 9AF
Tel: 020 7529 5531
Fax: 020 7529 5530
email: Website: www.barb.co.uk
The main source of television audience research in the United

Kingdom is supplied by BARB (Broadcasters Audience Research Board Limited). The company represents the major UK broadcasters, the British Broadcasting Corporation (BBC), the Independent Television Association (ITVA), Channels 4 and 5, BSkyB and The Institute of Practitioners in Advertising (IPA). BARB was created in August 1980 when the BBC and ITV decided to have a mutually agreed source of television audience research. BARB became operational in August 1981

## BECTU (Broadcasting Entertainment Cinematograph and Theatre Union)

373-377 Clapham Road
London SW9 9BT
Tel: 020 7346 0900
Fax: 020 7346 0901
email: info@bectu.org.uk
Website: www.bectu.org.uk
General Secretary: Roger Bolton

## BKSTS - The Moving Image Society

Suite 104, G Block
Pinewood Studios
Iver Heath
Buckinghamshire SLO ONH
Tel: 01753 656656
Fax: 01753 657016
email: info@bksts.com
Website: www.bksts.com
Wendy Laybourn
To encourage, sustain, educate, train and represent all those who, creatively or technologically, are involved – creatively or technologically - in the business of providing moving images and associated crafts in any form and through any media. The Society is dedicated to the promotion of excellence in these fields. Whilst remaining independent of all governmental and commercial organisations, it is active in fostering co-operation with other societies in the industry and in promoting its aims throughout the world.
(Formerly known as The British Kinematograph Sound and Television Society)

## British Academy of Composers and Songwriters

2nd Floor
British Music House
26 Berners Street

London W1T 3LR
Tel: 020 7636 2929
Fax: 020 7636 2212
email: info@britishacademy.com
Website: www.britishacademy.com
Fergal Kilroy

## British Amateur Television Club (BATC)
The Villa
Plas Panteidal
Aberdyfi
Gwynedd LL35 ORF
Tel: 01654 767702
Fax: email: memsec@batc.org.uk
email: Website: www.batc.org.uk
Pat Hellen
Non-profit making organisation run entirely by volunteers. BATC publish a quarterly technical publication CQ-TV which is available via subscription

## British Association of Picture Libraries and Agencies
18 Vine Hill
London EC1R 5DZ
Tel: 020 7713 1780
Fax: 020 7713 1211
email: enquiries@bapla.org.uk
Website: www.bapla.org.uk
Chief Executive: Linda Royles

## British Board of Film Classification (BBFC)
3 Soho Square
London W1D 3HD
Tel: 020 7440 1570
Fax: 020 7287 0141
email: webmaster@bbfc.co.uk
Website: www.bbfc.co.uk
Under the 1909 Cinematograph Films Act, local authorities were made responsible for safety in cinemas and also for what was shown. In 1912, the British Board of Film Censors was set up by the film industry to establish uniformity in film classification across the UK. The British Board of Film Censors became the British Board of Film Classification in 1985. The Board classifies films on behalf of local authorities and films cannot be shown in public in the UK unless they have a BBFC certificate or the relevant local authorisation. Local Authorities can, and sometimes do, overrule BBFC classification decisions. The Video Recordings Act 1984 requires that videos and video games which come under the Act must carry a BBFC classification if they are sold or rented in the UK. The BBFC is funded entirely from the

fees charged for classification.

## British Broadcasting Corporation (BBC)
Television Centre
Wood Lane
London W12 7RJ
Tel: 020 8743 8000
Website: www.bbc.co.uk
The BBC provides two national television networks, five national radio networks, as well as local radio and regional radio and television services. They are funded through the Licence Fee. The BBC is a public corporation, set up in 1927 by Royal Charter. Government proposals for the future of the BBC were published in a White Paper in July 1994. The BBC also broadcasts overseas through World Service Radio and Worldwide Television, but these are not funded through the Licence Fee

## British Cinema and Television Veterans
22 Golden Square
London W1F 9AD
Tel: 020 7436 2338
email:bctv.veterans@
btopenworld.com
An association open to all persons employed in the United Kingdom or by United Kingdom companies in the cinema and/or broadcast television industries in any capacity other than as an artiste, for a total of at least thirty years and whose career has embraced at least two years in the cinema industry. Associate Membership of the association is open to all persons who are, or have been employed in the United Kingdom or by United Kingdom companies, in the cinema, broadcast on/ and/or allied industries, in any capacity other than as artiste, for at least two years

## British Copyright Council
29-33 Berners Street
London W1T 3AB
Tel: 01986 788 122
Fax: 01986 788847
Website: www.britishcopyright.org.uk
Janet Ibbotson
Provides liaison between societies which represent the interest of those who own copyright in literature, music, drama and works of art, making representation to Government on behalf of its member societies

## The British Council

Film and Literature Department
10 Spring Gardens
London SW1A 2BN
Tel: 020 7389 3051
Fax: 020 7389 3175
Website: www.britfilms.com
The British Council is Britain's international network for education, culture and technology. It is an independent, non-political organisation with offices in over 100 countries. Film and Literature Department acts as a clearing house for international festival screenings of British short films and videos, including animation and experimental work. It also ensures British participation in a range of international feature film events. The department arranges seminars overseas on themes such as broadcasting freedom and the future of public service television. It publishes the International Directory of Film and Video Festivals (biennial) and the annual British Films Catalogue

## British Design & Art Direction (D&AD)
9 Graphite Square
Vauxhall Walk
London SE11 5EE
Tel: 020 7840 1111
Fax: 020 7840 0840
email: info@dandad.co.uk
Website: www.dandad.org
Professional association and charity representing design and advertising communities

## British Educational Communications and Technology Agency (Becta)
Milburn Hill Road
Science Park
University of Warwick
Coventry CV4 7JJ
Tel: 024 7641 6994
Fax: 024 7641 1418
email: Becta@becta.org.uk
Website: www.becta.org.uk
Becta's purpose is to support the transformation of education through the exploitation and embedding of technology in learning and teaching, in educational organisations, and in developing wider education networks and systems. We are the Governmentís key partner in the development and delivery of its Information and Communications Technology (ICT) and e-learning strategy for schools and the learning

and skills sector

## British Federation of Film Societies (BFFS)

The Ritz Building
Mount Pleasant Campus
Swansea Institute of Higher Education
Swansea SA1 6ED
Tel: 01792 481170
Fax: 01792 462219
email: bffs-admin@sihe.ac.uk
Website: www.bffs.co.uk
Adminstration Manager
BFFS-Cinema for All exists to promote the work of the voluntary exhibition sector in the UK. If you run or are thinking of starting a film society/club or other form of not-for-profit cinema exhibition BFFS-Cinema for All can provide start-up advice, equipment and financial and other support. BFFS-Cinema for All publishes the quarterly magazine 'FILM'.

## British Film Designers Guild

24 St Anslem's Place
London W1Y 1FG
Tel: 020 7499 4336
Fax: 020 7499 4336
Website: www.filmdesigners.co.uk
Promotes and encourages activities of all members of the art department. Full availability and information service open to all producers

## British Film Institute

21 Stephen Street
London W1T 1LN
Tel: 020 7255 1444
Fax: 020 7436 7950
Website: www.bfi.org.uk
Amanda Nevill, Director
Founded in 1933, the BFI was incorporated by Royal Charter in 1983; it is the UK national agency with responsibility for encouraging the arts of film and television and conserving them in the national interest

## British Institute of Professional Photography

Fox Talbot House
Amwell End
Ware
Herts SG12 9HN
Tel: 01920 464011
Fax: 01920 487056
email: info@bipp.com
Website: www.bipp.com
Company Secretary: Alex Mair

## British Interactive Multimedia Association Ltd

5/6 Clipstone Street
London W1P 7EB
Tel: 020 7436 8250
Fax: 020 7436 8251
email: enquiries@bima.co.uk
Website: www.bima.co.uk
Janice Cable, Administrator
Established in 1985, the British Interactive Media Association (BIMA) is the trade association representing the diverse interests of the UK interactive industry

## The British Phonographic Industry Ltd (BPI)

Riverside Building
County Hall
Westminster Bridge Road
London SE1 7JA
Tel: 020 7803 1300
Fax: 020 7803 1310
email: general@bpi.co.uk
Website: www.bpi.co.uk
Andrew Yeates, Director General

## British Recording Media Association

Orbital House
85 Croydon Road
Caterham
Surrey CR3 6PD
Tel: 01883 334495
Fax: 01883 334490
email: brma@admin.co.uk
Elaine Cole
Trade association for the manufacturers of blank recording media

## British Screen Advisory Council (BSAC)

13 Manette Street
London W1D 4AW
Tel: 020 7287 1111
Fax: 020 7306 0329
email:bsac@bsacouncil.co.uk
Website: www.bsac.uk.com
Director: Fiona Clarke-Hackston,
Chairman: David Elstein
BSAC brings together high level executives and specialists from both the traditional and new sectors to develop industry-wide views and to represent these views to policymakers

## British Society of Cinematographers (BSC)

PO Box 2587
Gerrards Cross
Bucks  SL9 7WZ
Tel: 01753 888052
Fax: 01753 891486
email: bscine@btconnect.com
Website: www.bscine.com
Frances Russell

## Broadcasting Press Guild

Tiverton
The Ridge
Woking
Surrey GU22 7EQ
Tel: 01483 764895 or 0208 624 9052
Fax: 01483 765882 or 0208 624 9096
email: torin.douglas@bbc.co.uk
Richard Last, Membership Secretary (01483 764895)
Torin Douglas, Lunch Secretary (0208 624 9052)

## Broadcasting Research Unit

VLV Librarian
101 King's Drive
Gravesend
Kent DA12 5BQ
Tel: 01474 352835
Fax: 01474 351112
email: vlv@btinternet.com
Website: www.vlv.org.uk
Linda Forbes
The Broadcasting Research Unit was an independent Trust researching all aspects of broadcasting, development and technologies, which operated from 1980-1991. Its publications and research are now available from the above address

## Broadcasting Standards Commission

7 The Sanctuary
London SW1P 3JS
Tel:  020 7808 1000
Fax: 020 7233 0397
email: bsc@bsc.org.uk
Website: www.bsc.org.uk
Donia Tahbaz, Communications Director

## BUFVC (British Universities Film and Video Council)

77 Wells Street
London W1T 3QJ
Tel: 020 7393 1500
Fax: 020 7393 1555
email: ask@bufvc.ac.uk
Website: www.bufvc.ac.uk
Luke McKernan, Head of Information
The BUFVC is a representative body which promotes the production, study and use of film and related media in higher education and research. It was founded in 1948 as the British Universities Film Council. The Council receives core grant support from the Joint Information Systems Committee (JISC) of the Higher Education Funding Councils via the Open University

## BVA (British Video Association)

167 Great Portland Street
London W1W 5PE
Tel: 020 7436 0041
Fax: 020 7436 0043
email: general@bva.org.uk
Website: www.bva.org.uk
Lavinia Carey
The BVA was established in 1980 to represent the interests of publishers and rights owners of pre-recorded home entertainment on video. The BVA is the most authoritative source of video industry statistical information. In April each year we publish the BVA Yearbook with detailed analysis of the previous year's VHS and DVD retail data, rental transactions, market shares and consumer usage and attitudinal feedback

## Cable Communications Association

5th Floor
Artillery House
Artillery Row
London SW1P 1RT
Tel: 020 7222 2900
Fax: 020 7799 1471
email: Chief Executive: Bob Frost
Represents the interests of cable operators, installers, programme providers and equipment suppliers.

## Campaign for Press and Broadcasting Freedom

Second Floor
23 Orford Road
Walthamstow
London E17 9NL
Tel: 020 8521 5932
Fax: 020 8521 5932
email: freepress@cpbf.org.uk
Website: www.cpbf.org.uk
A broad-based membership organisation campaigning for more diverse, accessible and accountable media in Britain, backed by the trade union movement. The CPBF was established in 1979. Its bi-monthly journal Free Press examines current ethical, industrial and political developments in media policy and practice. CPBF acts as a parliamentary lobby group on censorship and media reform

## Carlton Screen Advertising

12 Golden Square
London W1F 9JE
Tel: 020 7534 6363
Fax: 020 7534 6227

Website: www.carltonscreen.com
www.pearlanddean.com

## Celtic Film and Television Festival

249 West George Street
Glasgow G2 4QE
Tel: 0141 302 1737
Fax: 0141 302 1738
email: mail@celticfilm.co.uk
Website: www.celticfilm.co.uk
Frances Hendron, Chief Executive

## Central Office of Information (COI)

Films and Video
Hercules Road
London SE1 7DU
Tel: 020 7261 8495
Fax: 020 7261 8877
Ian Hamilton
COI Films and Video is responsible for government filmmaking on informational themes. The COI organises the production of a wide range of TV commercials and trailers, documentary films, video programmes and CD ROMs. It uses staff producers, and draws on the film and video industry for production facilities

## Children's Film and Television Foundation (CFTF)

Elstree Film and Television Studios
Borehamwood
Herts WD6 1JG
Tel: 020 8953 0844
Fax: 020 8953 0860
email: annahome@cftf.onyxnet.co.uk
Anna Home, Chief Executive
The Children's Film and Television Foundation started as the Children's Film Foundation 50 years ago. Originally it made a large number of films for Saturday morning matinees. It now finances script development for children's and family films and television projects. Funding is on a loan basis. Films from the Foundation's library are available for hiring at a nominal charge in 35mm, 16mm and video formats

## Cinema Advertising Association (CAA)

12 Golden Square
London W1F 9JE
Tel: 020 7534 6363
Fax: 020 7534 6227
email: Website: www.adassoc.org.uk
Website: www.pearlanddean.com
www.carltonscreen.com

## Cinema Exhibitors' Association (CEA)

22 Golden Square
London W1R 3PA
Tel: 020 7734 9551
Fax: 020 7734 6147
email: cea@cinemauk.ftech.co.uk
Contact : John Wilkinson, Annette Bradford and Elaine Pearce
Exhibition was the first sector of the film industry to organise nationally, in 1912. Following a merger with the Association of Independent Cinemas (AIC) it became the only association representing cinema exhibition. CEA members comprise over 90% of UK commercial cinemas, including independents, regional film theatres and cinemas in local authority ownership. CEA represents its members' interests with the industry and to local, national and European Government. It is closely involved in legislation which could affect exhibitors (current and proposed) emanating from UK Government and the European Commission. CEA produces guidelines for its members in areas such as Disability Access & Employment and Fire Risk. Its Executive Board meets regularly to decide on CEA policy and CEA Branches around the UK, which also meet regularly, relay feedback and comment to the Board.

## Cinema & Television Benevolent Fund (CTBF)

22 Golden Square
London W1F 9AD
Tel: 020 7437 6567
Fax: 020 7437 7186
email: infor@ctbf.co.uk
Website: www.ctbf.co.uk
Gayle Gover - Director of Development.

## Cinema Theatre Association

44 Harrowdene Gardens
Teddington
Middx TW11 0DJ
Tel: 020 8977 2608
Fax: Website: www.cinema-theatre.org.uk
Adam Unger
The Cinema Theatre Association was formed in 1967 to promote interest in Britain's cinema building legacy, in particular the magnificent movie palaces of the 1920s and 1930s. It is the only major organisation committed to cinema preservation in the UK. It campaigns for the protection of architecturally

important cinemas and runs a comprehensive archive. The CTA publishes a bi-monthly bulletin and the magazine Picture House

## Commonwealth Broadcasting Association
17 Fleet Street
London EC4 1AA
Tel: 020 7583 5550
Fax: 020 7583 5549
email: cba@cba.org.uk
Website: www.cba.org.uk
Elizabeth Smith, Secretary General

## Critics' Circle
51 Vartry Road,
London N15 6PS
Website: www.criticscircle.org.uk
Hon. Secretary: Charles Hedges

## Deaf Broadcasting Council
70 Blacketts Wood Drive
Chorleywood, Rickmansworth
Herts WD3 5QQ
Tel: 01923 284538
Fax: 01923 283127
email: rmyers@waitrose.com
Website: deafbroadcastcouncil.org.uk
Ruth Meyers

## Defence Press and Broadcasting Advisory Committee
Room G27, Ministry of Defence
Metropole Building
Northumberland Avenue
London WC2N 5BP
Tel: 020 7218 2206
Fax: 020 7218 5857
Website: www.dnotice.org.uk
Secretary: Rear Admiral Nick Wilkinson
The Committee is made up of senior officials from the Ministry of Defence, the Home Office and the Foreign & Commonwealth Office and representatives of the media. It issues guidance, in the form of DA Notices, on the publication of information which it regards as sensitive for reasons of national security

## Department for Culture, Media and Sport (DCMS)
2-4 Cockspur Street
London, SW1Y 5DH
Tel: 020 7211 6200
email: enquires@gov.uk
Website: www.culture.gov.uk
Secretary of State for Culture, Media & Sport: Rt Hon Tessa Jowell MP
Minister for the Arts: Rt Hon Estelle Morris MP

## Department for Education and Employment (DFEE)
Sanctuary Buildings
Great Smith Street
London SW1P 3BT
Tel: 020 7925 5000 Public enquiries: 0171 925 5555
Fax: 020 7925 6000
email: info@dfee.gov.uk
Website: www.dfee.gov.uk

## The Directors' and Producers' Rights Society
Victoria Chambers
16-18 Strutton Ground
London SW1P 2HP
Tel: 020 7227 4757
Fax: 020 7227 4755
email: info@dprs.org
Website: www.dprs.org
Suzan Dormer, Chief Executive
The Directors' and Producers' Rights Society is a collecting society which administers authorials rights payments on behalf of British film and television Directors

## Draft Zero
Medius House (LG Floor)
2 Sheraton Street
London W1F 8BH
Tel:  0870 366 6966
Fax:  07092 371 565
email: info@draft zero.com
Website: www.draftzero.com.
Nick Crittenden
A training and consultancy organisation that focuses on screenplay development for film, TV, radio and multimedia projects.  It provides a development programme for screenwriters and modular short courses for industry personnel working in development aimed at producers, directors, development executives, script readers, script editors as well as screenwriters

## Em Media – The regional film and media agency for the East Midlands
35-37 St Mary's Gate
Nottingham NG1 1PU
Tel: 0115 934 9090
Fax: 0115 950 0988
email: info@em-media.org.uk
Website: www.em-media.org.uk
Ken Hay, Chief Executive

## Equity
Guild House
Upper St Martin's Lane
London WC2H 9EG
Tel: 020 7379 6000
Fax: 020 7379 7001
email: info@equity.org.uk
Website: www.equity.org.uk
General Secretary: Ian McGarry

## European Captioning Institute
Thurston House
80 Lincoln Road
Peterborough PE1 2SN
Tel: 0207 323 4657
Fax: 0207 323 4658

## Federation of Entertainment Unions (FEU)
1 Highfield
Twyford, Nr Winchester
Hants SO21 1QR
Tel: 01962 713134
Fax: 01962 713134
email: harris.s@btconnect.com
Steve Harris
The FEU represents 170,000 people working across the media and entertainment industries in the UK. It is a lobbying and campaigning group which meets regularly with statutory bodies and pressure groups ranging from the BBC, Ofcom, and the Film Council through to the Voice of the Listener and Viewer. The Federation comprises Equity, Broadcasting Entertainment Cinematograph and Theatre Union, Musicians' Union, National Union of Journalists, the Professional Footballers' Association, Writers' Guild of Great Britain and Amicus (Electricians Section). It has three standing committees covering Film and Electronic Media, European Affairs and Training

## The Feminist Library
5a Westminster Bridge Road
London SE1 7XW
Tel: 020 7928 7789
Fax: email: feministlibrary@beeb.net
Website: www.gn.apg.org/womeninlondon
The Feminist Library provides information about women's studies, courses, and current events. It has a large collection of fiction and non-fiction books, pamphlets, papers etc. It holds a wide selection of journals and newsletters from all over the world and produces its own quarterly newsletter

## Film Archive Forum
c/o British Universities Film & Video Council (BUFVC)
77 Wells Street
London W1T 3QJ
Tel: 020 7393 1500
Fax: 020 7393 1555

email: faf@bufvc.ac.uk
Website: www.bufvc.ac.uk
Luke McKernan, Chair

## Film Artistes' Association (FAA)

373-377 Clapham Road
London SW9 9BT
Tel: 020 7436 0900
Fax: 020 7436 0901
email: smacdonald@bectu.org.uk
Spencer MacDonald
The FAA represents extras, doubles,
stand-ins. Under an agreement with
PACT, it supplies all background
artistes in the major film studios and
within a 40 mile radius of Charing
Cross on all locations

## Film Distributors' Association (FDA)

22 Golden Square
London W1F 9JW
Tel: 020 7437 4383
Fax: 020 7734 0912
email: info@fda.uk.net
Website: www.launchingfilms.com
Chief Executive: Mark Batey
Film Distributors' Association is the
trade body for UK theatrical film
distributors. It promotes the generic
interests of distributors and offers a
range of services to its member
companies and others.

## Film Education

2nd Floor
21-22 Poland Street
London W1V 3DD
Tel: 020 7851 9450
Fax: 020 7439 3218
email: postbox@filmeducation.org
Website: www.filmeducation.org
Ian Wall

## Film London

20 Euston Centre
Regent's Place
London NW1 3JH
Tel: 020 7387 8787
Fax: 020 7387 8788
email: info@filmlondon.org.uk
Website: www.filmlondon.org.uk
Adrian Wooton, Chief Executive
Officer
Gill Henderson, Head of Industry
and Cultural Development
Sue Hayes, Film Commissioner
Daniela Kirchner, Head of
Information and Strategy
Andy Cole, Head of Communications
In April 2003 the London Film
Commission (LFC) and the London
Film and Video Development Agency
(LFVDA) were brought together to

form Film London, the single
strategic agency for the development
of film and the screen sector in
London. Film London is an
independent company supported by
the UK Film Council and the London
Development Agency. It has a board
chaired by the film producer Sandy
Lieberson. Film London provides an
integrated service in production and
business support, training, film
locations, cinema education and
exhibition

## The Film Office

The Old Town Hall
Patriot Square
Bethnal Green
London E2 9NP
Tel: 020 8980 8771
Fax: 020 8981 2272
email: info@thefilmoffice.fsnet.co.uk
Website: www.filmoffice.co.uk
Works in association with local
authorities in London to assist with
filming in London locations

## Film Unit Drivers Guild

136 The Crossways
Heston
Middlesex TW5 OJR
Tel: 020 8569 5001
Fax: 020 8569 6001
email: letstalk@fudg.uk.com
Website: www.fudg.com
L. Newell

## First Film Foundation

9 Bourlet Close
London W1P 7PJ
Tel: 020 7580 2111
Fax: 020 7580 2116
email: info@firstfilm.demon.co.uk
Website: www.firstfilm.co.uk
First Film Foundation is a charity
that exisits to help new British
writers, producers and directors make
their first feature film by providing a
range of unique, educational and
promotional programmes. FFF also
provides impartial practical advice on
how to develop a career in the film
industry

## FOCAL International Ltd (Federation of Commercial Audio-Visual Libraries)

Pentax House, South Hill Avenue
South Harrow
Middx HA2 ODU
Tel: 020 8423 5853
Fax: 020 8933 4826
email: info@focalint.org
Website: www.focalint.org
Commercial Manager: Anne Johnson

## Gaelic Media Service

see Seirbheis nam Meadhanan
Gàidhlig

## German Federal Film Board and Export Union of Germany Cinema

Top Floor
113-117 Charing Cross Road
London W2H ODT
Tel: 020 7437 2047
Fax: 020 7439 2947
Iris Ordonez
UK representative of the German
Federal Film Board
(Filmförderungsanstalt), the
government industry organisation,
and the German Film Export Union
(Export Union des Deutschen Films),
the official trade association for the
promotion of German films abroad.
For full details see entries under
Organisations (Europe)

## Grierson Memorial Trust

c/o Ivan Sopher & co
5 Elstree Gate
Elstree Way
Borehamwood
Herts WD6 1JD
Tel: 020 8207 0602
Fax: 020 8207 6758
email: admin@greirsontrust.org
Website: www.griersontrust.org
Jeanette Lipscombe, Trust
Adminstrator

## Guild of British Camera Technicians

Panavision Building
Metropolitan Centre
Bristol Road
Greenford
Middlesex UB5 8GD
Tel: 020 8813 1999
Fax: 020 8813 2111
email: admin@gbct.org
Website: www.gbct.org
Christine Henwood, Office Manager

## Guild of British Film Editors

72 Pembroke Road
London W8 6NX
Tel: 020 7602 8319
Fax: 020 7602 8319
email:
secretarygbfe@btopenworld.com
Sally Fisher, Secretary

## Guild of Stunt and Action Co-ordinators

72 Pembroke Road
London W8 6NX
Tel: 020 7602 8319
Fax: 020 7602 8319

email: stunts.uk@btinternet.com
Sally Fisher
To promote the highest standards of safety and professionalism in film and television stunt work

## Guild of Television Cameramen
1 Churchill Road
Whitchurch, Tavistock
Devon PL19 9BU
Tel: 01822 614405
Fax: 01822 615785
Website: www.gtc.org.uk
Sheila Lewis
The Guild was formed in 1972 'to ensure and preserve the professional status of the television cameramen and to establish, uphold and advance the standards of qualification and competence of cameramen'. The Guild is not a union and seeks to avoid political involvement

## Guild of Vision Mixers
147 Ship Lane
Farnborough
Hants GU14 8BJ
Tel: 01252 514953
Fax: 01252 514953
email: guild@visionmixers.tv
Website: visionmixers.tv
Peter Turl
The Guild aims to represent the interests of vision mixers throughout the UK and Ireland, and seeks to maintain the highest professional standards in vision-mixing

## The Hospital
24 Endell Street
London WC2H 9HQ
Tel: 020 7170 9134
Fax: 020 7170 9101
Website: www.thehospital.co.uk
Joe Bateman
The Hospital is developing an environment and services that bring together creative and like-minded people to create, collaborate and play. Our 60,000 sqft building located in central London consists of state-of-the-art TV and music studios, a gallery, public restaurant and private members club.
(See The Hospital Cinema in Facilities)

## IAC (Institute of Amateur Cinematographers)
24c West Street
Epsom
Surrey KT18 7RJ
Tel: 01372 739672
Fax: 01372 739672

email: iacfilmvideo@compuserve.com
Website: www.theiac.org.uk
Janet Smith, Admin Secretary

## Imperial War Museum Film and Video Archive
Lambeth Road
London SE1 6HZ
Tel: 020 7416 5299
Fax: 020 7416 5379
email: film@iwm.org.uk
Website: www.iwm.org.uk
See entry under Archives and Film Libraries

## Incorporated Society of British Advertisers (ISBA)
44 Hertford Street
London W1J 7AE
Tel: 020 7499 7502
Fax: 020 7629 5255
email: info@isba.org.uk
Website: www.isba.org.uk
Joe Lamb, Communications Manager

## Incorporated Society of Musicians (ISM)
10 Stratford Place
London W1C 1AA
Tel: 020 7629 4413
Fax: 020 7408 1538
email: membership@ism.org
Website: www.ism.org
Chief Executive: Neil Hoyle

## The Independent Cinema Office
2nd Floor
Kenilworth House
79-80 Margaret Street
London W1W 8TA
Tel: 020 7636 7120
Fax: 020 7636 7121
email: info@independentcinemaoffice.org.uk
Website: www.independentcinemaoffice.org.uk
Established in July 2003, the Independent Cinema Office is a new national organisation that aims to develop and support independent film exhibition throughout Britain. The ICO works in association with independent cinemas, film festivals, film societies and the regional and national screen agencies.
Every cinema has different ambitions, different expectations and different audiences. The ICO works with film exhibitors, helping them to create unique, commercially viable programmes that appeal to the most diverse range of local audiences. The

ICO's clients range from the internationally acclaimed Watershed Media Centre in Bristol to local authority-run cinemas such as Hull Screen to part time cinemas such as the Kino in Middlesborough. We also work with film festivals and film societies. The ICO curates and organises touring programmes of films that would not otherwise receive a national release. Projects for 2004 included ¡Viva! Spanish Film Festival on Tour, UK Jewish Film Festival on Tour and Model Behaviour, a touring programme of model animation by award-winning animators Adam Elliot and Pjotr Sapegin.
The ICO also organises training initiatives for film exhibitors including an annual 2-week course in cultural film exhibition

## Institute of Practitioners in Advertising (IPA)
44 Belgrave Square
London SW1X 8QS
Tel: 020 7235 7020
Fax: 020 7245 9904
email: Website: www.ipa.co.uk
Website: The representative body for UK advertising agencies. Represents the collective views of its member agencies in negotiations with Government departments, the media and industry and consumer organisations

## Intellect
Russell Square House
10 - 12 Russell Square
London WC1B 5EE
Tel: 020 7331 2000
Fax: 020 7331 2040/56
email: info@intellect.org
Website: www.intellectuk.org
Intellect is the trade body for the UK based information technology, telecommunications and electronics industry

## International Association of Broadcasting Manufacturers (IABM)
Broad Oaks
Parish Lane
Farnham Common
Slough SL2 3JW
Tel: 01753 645682
Fax: 01753 645682
email: info@iabm.org.uk
Website: www.iabm.org.uk
Secretariat: Brenda White

## International Federation of

## the Phonographic Industry (IFPI)

IFPI Secretariat
54 Regent Street
London W1R 5PJ
Tel: 020 7878 7900
Fax: 020 7878 7950
email: info@ifpi.org
Website: www.ifpi.org
Director General: Nicholas Garnett

## International Institute of Communications

Regent House
24-25 Nutford Place
London W1Y 5YN
Tel: 020 7323 9622
Fax: 020 7323 9623
email: enquiries@iicom.org
Website: www.iicom.org

## International Intelligence on Culture

4 Baden Place
Crosby Row
London SE1 1YW
Tel: 020 7403 7001
Fax: 020 7403 2009
email: enquiry@intelculure.org
Website: www.intelculture.org
Information Service
International Intelligence on Culture
is a dynamic consultancy which
brings together a highly-experienced
multi-national group of experts to
work with and for the international
cultural sector. Our activities include:
policy intelligence; research;
consultancy; training; and
information services. Our email,
journal and web-based subscriber
service International Cultural
Compass will keep you up-to-date
with international developments,
policies and programmes relating to
culture. Meanwhile our training
sessions and information service can
develop your awareness of existing
opportunities, and how to access
them and of key issues in the field

## ITV Network Ltd

200 Gray's Inn Road
London WC1X 8HF
Tel: 020 7843 8000
Fax: 020 7843 8160
email: dutyoffice@itv.co.uk
Website: www.itv.co.uk
Director of Programmes: J.Nigel
Pickard

## IVCA (International Visual Communication Association)

Business Communication Centre
19 Pepper Street
Glengall Bridge
London E14 9RP
Tel: 020 7512 0571
email: info@ivca.org
Chief Executive: Wayne Drew
The IVCA is the largest European
Association of its kind, representing a
wide range of organisations and
individuals working in the established
and developing technologies of
corporate visual communication.
With roots in video, film and
business events industries, the
Association has also developed
significant representation of the new
and fast growing technologies,
notably business television,
interactive television, multimedia,
interactive software and the internet.
It holds the biggest Award ceremony
of its kind in the world to promote
the sector and provides business
services for its members. These
include: legal help, internet service,
insurance, arbitration etc. The IVCA
also holds events/seminars for
training, networking and for all
industry related topics

## Kraszna-Krausz Foundation

122 Fawnbrake Avenue
London SE24 0BZ
Tel: 020 7738 6701
Fax: 020 7738 6701
email: info@k-k.org.uk
Website: www.k-k.org.uk
Andrea Livingstone, Administrator
The Foundation offers small grants to
assist in the development of new or
unfinished projects, work or literature
where the subject specifically relates
to the art, history, practice or
technology of photography or the
moving image (defined as film,
television, video and related screen
media). The Foundation also
sponsors annual book awards, with
prizes for books on the moving image
alternating with those for books on
still photography

## Lux

3rd Floor
18 Shacklewell Lane
London E8 2EZ
Tel: 020 7503 3980
Fax: 020 7503 1606
email: ben@lux.org.uk
Website: www.lux.org.uk
LUX is a not-for-profit organisation
established to promote and support
artists' moving image work both in
the UK and internationally. While
LUX represents the collection of the
former Lux Centre, it does not run a
cinema, a gallery, offer equipment
hire, post-production facilities or
training courses

## Mechanical-Copyright Protection Society (MCPS)

29/33 Berner Street
London W1T 3AB
Tel: 020 8664 4500
Fax: 020 7306 4380
email: first name . last name @
mcps.co.uk
Website: www.mcps.co.uk
Contact: The Media Licensing
Department
The Mechanical-Copyright
Protection Society Ltd currently
represents around 16,300 composers,
songwriters and music publishers
whenever their copyright musical
works are recorded. Acting as an
agent on behalf of its members,
MCPS negotiates agreements with
those who wish to record and
distribute product containing
copyright musical works. MCPS
collects and then distributes
"mechanical" royalties generated
from the copying of music onto many
different formats (CD, video,
computer games etc). MCPS is a
wholly owned subsidiary of the Music
Publishers Association.

## Medialex - Legal & Business Training

15 Sandycombe Road
Kew
Richmond
Surrey TW9 2EP
Tel: 020 8940 7039
Fax: 020 8758 8647
email: info@medialex.co.uk
Industry approved Media Law
seminars designed for the film and
television industry including
copyright, contracts, industry
agreements, music copyright, internet
and new media

## Mediawatch-uk

3 Willow House
Kennington Road
Ashford
Kent TN24 0NR
Tel: 01233 633936
Fax: 01233 633836
email: info@mediawatchuk.org
Website: www.mediawatchuk.org
Director: John C Beyer

## Mental Health Media

356 Holloway Road

London N7 6PA
Tel: 020 7700 8171
Fax: 020 7686 0959
email: info@mhmedia.com
Website: www.mhmedia.com
Mental Health Media produces and
sells videos and multimedia resources
which educate and inform about
mental health and distress. We also
provide media skills training and
support to users and professionals

## Metier
Glyde House
Glydegate
Bradford BD5 0BQ
Tel: 01274 738 800
Fax: 01274 391 566
email: Chief Exec: Duncan Sones
A National Training Organisation,
developing National and Scottish
Vocational Qualifications for
occupations in performing and visual
arts, arts administration, front-of-
house, arts development &
interpretation and technical support
functions in the arts and
entertainment sector. It is responsible
for strategic action to improve the
quality, availability and effectiveness
of vocational training within its
industrial sector

## Music Publishers Association Ltd
3rd Floor
20 York Buildings
London WC2N 6JU
Tel: 020 7389 0665
Fax: 020 7839 7776
email: pbrindley@mpaonline.org.uk
Website: www.mpaoline.org.uk
Paul Brindley, Communications
Consultant

## Music Video Producers' Association (MVPA)
26 Noel Street
London W1F 8GT
Tel: 020 7434 2651
Fax: 020 7434 9002
email: michael@a-p-a.net
Website: www.a-p-a.net
Stephen Davies
The MFVPA represents production
companies making music promos. It
advises on agreements and provides a
telephone advice service to members
on production and legal matters

## Musicians' Union (MU)
60-62 Clapham Road
London SW9 0JJ
Tel: 020 7582 5566
Fax: 020 7582 9805

email: info@musiciansunion.org.uk
Website: www.musiciansunion.org.uk
Howard Evans: Asst General Secretary
(Media):
The Musicians' Union was established
in 1893 and represents over 31,000
musicians working in all sectors of
the music business. As well as
negotiating on behalf of its members
with all the major employers in the
industry, the MU offers a portfolio of
services tailored for the self-employed
by providing assistance for full-time
professional, semi-pro and student
musicians of all ages. The Union also
has a specialist Media Dept which
deals with a wide range of music
related issues in film and TV,
including the implementation and
interpretation of the MU/PACT
agreement, the synchronisation of
audio recordings, EPKs and rights
clearances.

## National Association for Higher Education in the Moving Image (NAHEMI)
Sir John Cass Department of Art
London Metropolitan University
59-63 Whitechapel High Street
London E1 7PY
Tel: 020 8840 2815
Fax: email: yossibal@aol.com
Website: Yossi Balanescu-Bal
A forum for debate on all aspects of
film, video and animation production
in Higher Education.The Association
has links with industry and
government bodies and represents
courses in the UK and the Republic
of Ireland that offer a major study in
film, video, television, animation and
new media practice. NAHEMI's
cultural programme includes
contributions to the Bristol Brief
Encounters Short Film Festival, to
Ffresh, the Welsh Students' Film
Festival and to the Scottish Students
on Screen festival in Dundee.
Two prestigious yearly student filmmaking awards are offered by
NAHEMI in collaboration with
Kodak UK and a third award is
selected specifically by NAHEMI
Wales. Every year, NAHEMI organises
the Eat Our Shorts Expo of student
film and animation at the National
Film Theatre in London. This event
brings together member schools in a
two days long celebration of film
students' innovation and creativity
through a series of screenings and
debates with industry professionals

## National Campaign for the Arts
Pegasus House
37-43 Sackville Street
London W1S 3EH
Tel: 020 7333 0375
Fax: 020 7333 0660
email: nca@artscampaign.org.uk
Website: www.artscampaign.org.uk
Director: Victoria Todd

## National Film and Television School
Beaconsfield Studios, Station Road
Beaconsfield
Bucks HP9 1LG
Tel: 01494 671234
Fax: 01494 674042
email: admin@nftsfilm-tv.ac.uk
Website: www.nftsfilm-tv.ac.uk
Director Nik Powell
The National Film and Television
School provides advanced training
and retraining to professional
standards in all major film and TV
programme-making disciplines.
Graduates are entitled to BECTU
membership on entering
employment. It is an autonomous
non-profit making organisation
funded by the Department for
Culture, Media and Sport and the
film and television industries.
See also under Courses.

## National Film Trustee Company Limited (NFTC)
4th Floor
66-68 Margaret Street
London W1W 8SR
Tel: 020 7580 6799
Fax: 020 7636 6711
email: louisa@nftc.co.uk
Website: www.nftc.co.uk
Louisa Bewley (Managing Director)

## National Museum of Photography Film & Television
Bradford BD1 1NQ
Tel: 0870 7010200
Fax: 01274 723155
email: talk.nmpt@nmsi.ac.uk
Website: www.nmpft.org.uk
Bill Lawrence, Head of Film
The world's only museum devoted to
still and moving pictures, their
technology and history. Host to three
annual film festivals - Bradford Film
Festival, Bite the Mango and BAF! -
and home to three cinemas, including
the world's only public Cinerama and
Europe's first IMAX film system. TV
Heaven offers 700 landmark

programmes for viewing on demand while Insight: Collections and Research Centre is home to the national coollection of TV receivers and cameras, cinematography and a library of television commercials and film posters

## National Screen Service
Unit 1
Perivale Industrial Park
Horsenden Lane South
Greenford
Middlesex UB6 7RU
Tel: 020 8991 2121
Fax: 020 8991 5757
Pat Walton, Jane Plunkett

## National Union of Journalists
Headland House
308-312 Grays Inn Road
London WC1X 8DP
Tel: 020 020 7843 3726
Fax: 020 0207 833 5830
email: paulm@nuj.org.uk
Paul McLaughlin, National Broadcasting Organiser
Represents more than 5,000 journalists working in broadcasting in the areas of news, sport, current affairs and features. It has agreements with all the major broadcasting companies and the BBC. It also has agreements with the main broadcasting agencies, APTN, Reuters Television and PACT

## NESTA (The National Endowment for Science, Technology and the Arts)
Fishmongers' Chambers,
110 Upper Thames Street
London, EC4R 3TW
Tel: Tel 020 7645 9500 Enquiry Line: 020 7645 9538
Fax: 020 7645 9501
email: nesta@nesta.org.uk
Website: www.nesta.org.uk
Chief Executive: Jeremy Newton

## New Producers Alliance (NPA)
9 Bourlet Close
London W1W 7BP
Tel: 020 7580 2480
Fax: 020 7580 2484
email: queries@npa.org.uk
Website: www.npa.org.uk
The NPA is the national membership and training organisation for independent new producers and filmmakers. It provides access to contacts, information and advice regarding film production to over

1,000 members, ranging from film students and first timers to highly experienced feature filmmakers, major production companies and industry affiliates. Members services include; specialised producer training programmes from entrance' to advanced' levels; ongoing events, masterclasses, seminars, networking evenings, practical workshops and preview screenings; free advice services including legal and tax & accountancy; monthly newsletter and online members' directory

## Nielsen EDI
Sixth Floor
Endeavour House
189 Shaftesbury Avenue
London WC2H 87J
Tel: 020 7105 5200
Fax: 020 7170 5201
Website: www.nielsenedi.com
Dave Thurston, Managing Director
Nielsen EDI provides the film industry with official box office information. The London office currently tracks all films for all distributors from 865 theatres, covering 4,600 playdates per week across the U.K. and Ireland

## Northern Ireland Film and Television Commission
3rd Floor
Alfred House
21 Alfred Street
Belfast BT2 BED
Tel: 01232 232444
Fax: 01232 239918
email: info@nifc.co.uk
Website: www.nifc.co.uk
The Northern Ireland Film Commission promotes the growth of film and television culture and the industry in Northern Ireland
**For further details see Funding**

## no.w.here
Studio 38, Buzzer A
110-116 Kingsgate Rd
London NW6 2JG
Tel: 020 7372 3925
email: courses@nowhere-lab.org
no.w.here film lab is a new centre for artist film production in London. It runs workshops and convenes critical debates about experimental film's dialogue with contemporary culture

## Ofcom
Office of Communications
Riverside House
2A Southwark Bridge House
London SE1 9HA

Tel: 0845 456 3000
Fax: 0845 456 3333
email: contact@ofcom.org.uk
Website: www.ofcom.org.uk
Ofcom is the regulator for the UK communications industries, with responsibilities across television, radio, telecommunications and wireless communications services. Ofcom exists to further the interests of citizen-consumers as the communications industries enter the digital age

## Office for National Statistics
1 Drummond Gate
London SW1V 2QQ
Tel: 0845 601 3034
Fax: 01633 652747
email: Website: www.statistics.gov.uk
Website: email: info@statistics.gov.uk
The Office for National Statistics (ONS) is the government department that provides statistical and registration services. ONS is responsible for producing a wide range of key economic and social statistics which are used by policy makers across government to create evidence-based policies and monitor performance against them. ONS also builds and maintains data sources both for itself and for its business and research customers. It makes statistics available so that everyone can easily assess the state of the nation, the performance of government and their own position

## Office of Fair Trading
Fleetbank House
2-6 Salisbury Square
London EC4Y 8JX
Tel: 08457 22 44 99
email: enquires@oft.gsi.gov.uk
Website: www.oft.gov.uk
The Office of Fair Trading (OFT) currently enforces UK competition legislation in the film and television sectors. It also has a specific role relating to the supply of films for exhibition in cinemas. Following a report by the Monopolies and Mergers Commission (MMC) in 1994, the OFT is responsible for ensuring that the adverse public interest findings of the MMC are remedied. Under the Broadcasting Act 1990, the OFT also has three specific roles in relation to the television industry. In his report published in December 1992, the Director General of Fair Trading

assessed the Channel 3 networking arrangement. The OFT also has a role in reviewing news provision for ITV and since January 1993 the OFT has had to monitor the BBC's progress towards a statutory requirement to source 25 per cent of its qualifying programming from independent producers.

## The Official UK Charts Company

4th Floor
58/59 Great Marlborough Street
London W1F 7JY
Tel: 020 7478 8500
Fax: 020 7436 8519
email: info@theofficialcharts.com
Website: www.theofficialcharts.com
Omar Maskatiya

## PACT (Producers Alliance for Cinema and Television)

45 Mortimer Street
London W1W 8HJ
Tel: 020 7331 6000
Fax: 0020 7331 6700
email: enquiries@pact.co.uk
Website: www.pact.co.uk
Chief Executive: John McVay

## Pearl & Dean

3 Waterhouse Square
138-142 Holborn
London EC1N 2NY
Tel: 020 7882 1100
Fax: 020 7882 1111
Website: www.pearlanddean.com

## Performing Right Society (PRS)

29-33 Berners Street
London W1T 3AB
Tel: 020 7580 5544
Fax: 020 7306 4455
Website: www.prs.co.uk
PRS collects licence fees for the public performance and broadcast of musical works. It distributes this money to its members - writers and publishers of music

## Phonographic Performance (PPL)

1 Upper James Street
London W1F 9DE
Tel: 020 7534 1000
Fax: 020 7534 1111
Jill Drew
PPL (Phonographic Performance Limited) represents over 3,000 record companies - 14,000 labels and licenses the broadcast and public performance of their repertoire - recordings in every genre of music.

We collect and distribute revenues from radio stations, pubs, clubs and thousands of users of sound recordings on behalf of member companies as well as some 25,000 performers

## The Production Guild of Great Britain

Pinewood Studios
Pinewood Road
Iver Heath
Bucks SL0 0NH
Tel: 01753 651767
Fax: 01753 652803
email: info@productionguild.com
Website: www.productionguild.com
Lynne Hames (Administrator)

## Production Managers Association (PMA)

Ealing Studios
Ealing Green
Ealing
London W5 5EP
Tel: 020 8758 8699
Fax: 020 8758 8658
Website: www.pma.org.uk
C.Fleming

## Radio, Electrical and Television Retailers' Association (RETRA)

Retra House
St John's Terrace
1 Ampthill Street
Bedford MK42 9EY
Tel: 01234 269110
Fax: 01234 269609
email: retra@tetra.co.uk
Website: www.retra.co.uk
Fred Round

## The Research Centre for Television and Interactivity

4th Floor
227 West George Street
Glasgow G2 2ND
Tel: 0141 568 7113
Fax: 0141 568 7114
email: admin@researchcentre.co.uk
Website: www.researchcentre.co.uk
Carol Sinclair Organisations Director:
The Research Centre for television and interactivity works with broadcasters, producers and others in the creative industries to develop business and talent in the sector. It is a knowledge bank, training centre, ideas factory, business and consultancy

## The Royal Photographic Society

Milsom Street

Bath, Avon BA1 1DN
Tel: 01225 462841
Fax: 01225 448688
email: rps@rps.org
Website: www.rps.org
Judi O'Brien, Director General
President: Roger Reynolds, Hon FRPS
A learned society founded 150 years ago for the promotion and enjoyment of all aspects of the art and science photography. Contains a specialist Film and Video Group, secretary John Tarby, FRPS, with a regular journal, meetings and the opportunity to submit productions for the George Sewell Trophy and the Hugh Baddeley Trophy; and an Audiovisual group, secretary Eddie Spence, FRPS, offering an extensive programme of events, seminars and demonstrations, and the bi-monthly magazine AV News. Membership open to both amateur and professional photographers.

## Royal Television Society

Holborn Hall
100 Grays Inn Road
London WC1X 8AL
Tel: 020 7430 1000
Fax: 020 7430 0924
email: info@art.org.uk
Website: www.rts.org.uk
Dep. Exec. Director: Claire Price
The Television Society was formed on 7 September 1927, nine years before the first public service broadcast from Alexandra Palace. The Society was granted its Royal title in 1966 and now represents over 4,000 members from the entire spectrum of the broadcasting industry. No longer just an engineering society, RTS members can now be found in all parts of the ever widening industry. In order to serve its members nationwide, the Society has Regional Centres, each running its own programme of lectures and social functions throughout the year

## Scottish Arts Council

12 Manor Place
Edinburgh EH3 7DD
Tel: 0131 226 6051
Fax: 0131 225 9833
email: help.desk@scottisharts.co.uk
Website: www.sac.org.uk
Director: Graham Berry
The Scottish Arts Council is an executive non-departmental public body (NDPB) which is one of the main channels for Government funding for the arts in Scotland,

receiving its funding from the Scottish Executive. It distributes National Lottery funds received from the Department for Culture, Media and Sport.
**For further details see Funding**

## Scottish Screen
Second Floor
249 West George Street
Glasgow G2 4QE
Tel: 0141 302 1700
Fax: 0141 302 1711
email: info@scottishscreen.com
Website: www.scottishscreen.com
Chief Executive: Steve McIntyre
**For further details see Funding**

## Screenwriters' Workshop
Suffolk House
1-8 Whitfield Place
London W1T 5JU
Tel: 020 7387 5511
Fax: 020 7387 5511
email: screenoffice@tiscali.co.uk
Website: www.lsw.org.uk
Katharine Way

## The Script Factory
Welbeck House
66/67 Wells Street
London W1T 3PY
Tel: 020 7323 1414
Fax: 020 7323 9464
email: general@scriptfactory.co.uk
Website: www.scriptfactory.co.uk
Briony Hanson, Co-Director
The Script Factory is a filmmakers' organisation which works to fill the gap between screenwriters and the film industry. It runs UK-wide screenwriter, producer and development training in partnership with the UK Film Council; stages SCENE Insiders, a major MEDIA-funded international development programme across Europe; presents performed readings of screenplays in development which have included Dirty Pretty Things and Lawless Heart; and produces a high profile series of masterclasses with filmmakers who have included Spike Lee, Thomas Vinterberg, Mira Nair, Robert Altman and Lynne Ramsay

## Seirbheis nam Meadhanan Gàidhlig (Gaelic Media Service)
Taigh Shĺphoirt,
Seaforth Road
Stornoway
Isle of Lewis HSI 2SD
Tel: 01851 705550
Fax: 01851 706432

email: calum@ccg.org.uk
Website: www.ccg.org.uk
Comataidh Telebhisein Gàidhlig (the Gaelic Television Committee) was set up in 1990 to channel Government funding into the production of Gaelic programmes. It became Comataidh Craolaidh Gaidhlig (the Gaelic Broadcasting Committee) as a result of the 1996 Broadcasting Act, when its mandate was extended to include responsibilities for radio and to undertake a consultative role in relation to Gaelic programmes on digital television. Under the 2003 Communications Act, Comataidh Craolaidh Gàidhlig became known as Seirbheis nam Meadhanan Gàidhlig (the Gaelic Media Service) and was given a wider remit including the power to commission programmes and to apply for a broadcast licence.

## Sgrîn Cymru Wales
(Media Agency for Wales)
The Bank, 10 Mount Stuart Square
Cardiff Bay
Cardiff CF10 5EE
Tel: 029 2033 3300
Fax: 029 2033 3320
email: sgrin@sgrin.co.uk
Website: www.sgrin.co.uk
Chief Executive: J. Berwyn Rowlands
**For further details see Funding**

## The Short Film Bureau
74 Newman Street
London, W1T 3EL
Tel: 020 7207 636 2400
Fax: 020 7207 636 8558
email: info@shortfilmbureau.com
Website: www.shortfilmbureau.com
Contact: Kim Leggatt

## SKILLSET
The Sector Skills Council for the Audio Visual Industries
80-110 New Oxford Street
London WC1A 1HB
Tel: 020 7520 5757
Fax: 020 7520 5758
email: info@skillset.org
Website: www.skillset.org
www.sillsformedia.com
**For further details see Careers and Training**

## The Society for Screen-Based Learning
9 Bridge Street
Tadcaster LS24 9AW
North Yorkshire
Tel: 01937 530520
Fax: 01937 530520
email: josie.key@learningonscreen.u-

net.com
Website: www.learningonscreen.org.uk
The Society is a meeting place, a skills forum, a resource for all those who want to exploit screen-based media in their roles as managers, trainers, lecturers, teachers, producers and communicators in the field of education, training, government and commerce

## Society of Authors' Broadcasting Group
84 Drayton Gardens
London SW10 9SB
Tel: 020 7373 6642
Fax: 020 7373 5768
email: jhodder@societyofauthors.org
Website: www.societyofauthors.org
Jo Hodder
Specialities: Radio, television and film scriptwriters

## Society of Cable Telecommunication Engineers (SCTE)
Fulton House Business Centre
Fulton Road, Wembley Park
Middlesex HA9 0TF
Tel: 020 8902 8998
Fax: 020 8903 8719
email: office@scte.org.uk
Website: www.scte.org.uk
Mrs Beverley K Allgood

## Society of Television Lighting Directors
Longwall
Crayburne
Betsham
Kent DA13 9PB
email: secretary@stld.org.uk
Website: www.stld.org.uk
The Society provides a forum for the exchange of ideas in all aspects of the TV profession including techniques and equipment. Meetings are organised throughout the UK and abroad. Technical information and news of members' activities are published in the Society's magazine

## TAC (Welsh Independent Producers)
Gronant
Caernarfon
Gwynedd LL55 1NS
Tel: 01286 671123
Fax: 01286 678890
email: email post@teledwyr.com
Website: www.teledwyr.com
Dafydd Hughes

## UK Film Council

10 Little Portland Street
London W1N 7JG
Tel: 020 7861 7861
Fax: 020 7861 7862
email: info@film.council.org.uk
Website: www.filmcouncil.org.uk
Contact: Iain Hepplewhite - Head of Communications
Tina McFarling - Head of Industry Relations
General enquiries: 020 7861 7924
www.firstlightmovies.com
The UK Film Council is the key strategic body with responsibility for advancing the film industry and film culture in the UK. Funded through the National Lottery and grant-in-aid money from the Government, It has two broad aims:
**To help develop a sustainable UK film industry;** and
**To develop film culture by improving access to, and education about, the moving image.**
The UK Film Council provides public funding for a range of initiatives supporting film development, production, training, distribution, exhibition, education and culture, which are focused on achieving these key aims.
Major initiatives include:
**The Development Fund** with £12 million over three years to support the development of a stream of high quality, innovative and commercially attractive screenplays.
**The Premiere Fund** with £24 million over three years to facilitate the production of popular, more mainstream films.
**The New Cinema Fund** with £15 million over three years to back radical and innovative filmmakers, especially new talent.
**The Distribution and Exhibition Fund** of £18 million to widen access for all to a broader range of films.
The UK Film Council is working with Skillset to deliver the first ever **comprehensive training strategy** for the British film industry. It contains a package of measures backed by an investment of around £50 million over the next five years.
**First Light** offers children and young people the opportunity to experience filmmaking using digital technology. It is supported annually by £1 million of National Lottery money.
The UK Film Council has created a £6 million a year **Regional Investment Fund** for England (RIFE) which is available to support cultural

and industrial film initiatives in the English regions and works to a joined-up UK-wide agenda with the national film agencies, Scottish Screen, Sgrîn Cymru Wales and the Northern Ireland Film and Television Commission.
**Inward Investment** – the UK Film Council's International Department encourages international productions from outside the UK to come and use Britain's world-class production and facilities infrastructure and is involved in a number of export promotion initiatives.
In addition the UK Film Council also funds:
**UK Film Council US**, the UK Film Council's Los Angeles based office aims to attract inward investment into the UK from US productions. UK Film Council US also offers a base for the UK Film Council to promote UK film exports and co-ordinate US-based training initiatives for UK industry professionals.
**The British Film Institute** (bfi), is funded by the UK Film Council. The bfi plays a key role in achieving the UK Film Council's goals and fosters public appreciation of film through improved access to cinema, film heritage and educational provision

## Variety Club of Great Britain
Variety Club House
93 Bayham Street
London NW1 OAG
Tel: 020 7428 8100
Fax: 020 7428 8111
email: info@varietyclub.org.uk
Website: www.varietyclub.org.uk
Ginny Martin

## The Video Standards Council
Kinetic Business Centre
Theobald Street
Borehamwood
Herts WD6 4PJ
Tel: 0208 387 4020
Fax: 0208 387 4004
Website: www.videostandards.org.uk
The VSC was established in 1989 as a non-profit making body set up to develop and oversee a Code of Practice and Code of Practice Rules designed to promote high standards within the video industry. The Code and Rules have subsequently been expanded to promote high standards within the computer and video games industry

### Videola (UK)
Paramount House
162/170 Wardour Street
London W1V 3AT
Tel: 020 7437 2136
Fax: 020 7437 5413

### VLV - Voice of the Listener and Viewer Ltd
101 King's Drive
Gravesend
Kent DA12 5BQ
Tel: 01474 352835
Fax: 01474 351112
email: vlv@btinternet.com
Website: www.vlv.org.uk
Linda Forbes

### Women in Film and Television (UK)
6 Langley Street
London WC2H 9JA
Tel: 020 7240 4875
Fax: 020 7379 1625
email: info@wftv.org.uk
Website: www.wftv.org.uk
Emily Compton

### Writers' Guild of Great Britain
15 Britannia Street
London WC1X 9JN
Tel: 020 7833 0777
Fax: 020 7833 4777
email: admin@writersguild.org.uk
Website: www.writersguild.org.uk
Bernie Corbett, General Secretary

### Yorkshire/Yorkshire Media Industries Partnership
Yorkshire Screen Commission
The Workstation
15 Paternoster Row
Sheffield S1 2BX
Tel: 0114 279 6511
Fax: 0114 279 6511
email: liz.ysc@workstation.org.uk
Liz Rymer, Acting CEO

# UK Film Commissions and Film Offices

### Bath Film Office
Abbey Chambers
Abbey Church Yard
Bath BA1 1LY
Tel: 01225 477711
Fax: 01225 477221
email: bath_filmoffice@
bathnes.gov.uk
Website: www.visitbath.co.uk
Maggie Ainley, Film Commissioner

### East Midlands Screen Commission
Broadway Media Centre
14-18 Broad Street
Nottingham NG1 3AL
Tel: 011 5910 5564
Fax: 011 5910 5563
email: emsc@emsc.org.uk
Website: Webite: www.emsc.org.uk
Contacts: Phil Nodding, Emily
Lappin, Kath Anderson

### Edinburgh Film Focus
Castlecliff
25 Johnston Terrace
Edinburgh EH1 2NH
Tel: 0131 622 7337
Fax: 0131 622 7338
email: info@edinfilm.com
Website: www.edinfilm.com
George Carlaw, Ros Davis, Heather
MacIntyre, Lucy Quinton

### Glasgow Film Office
City Chambers
Glasgow G2 1DU
Tel: 0141 287 0424
Fax: 0141 287 0311
email: film.office@drs.glasgow.gov.uk
Website: www.glasgowfilm.org.uk
Lenny Crooks, Director

### Isle of Man Film Limited
First Floor, Hamilton House
Peel Road, Douglas
Isle of Man 1M1 5EP
Tel: 01624 687173
Fax: 01624 687171
email: iomfilm@dti.gov.im
Website: www.isleofmanfilm.com
Hilary Dugdale, Project Manager

### Lanarkshire Screen Locations
Dept of Planning & Environment
Fleming House - 4th Floor
1 Tryst Road
Cumbernauld G67 1JW
Tel: 01236 616559
Fax: 01236 616283
email: gibsonl@northlan.gov.uk
Linda Gibson
Covers North Lanarkshire, South
Lanarkshire

### Lancashire Film Office
Lancashire County Developments Ltd
1st Floor Robert House
Starkie Street
Preston PR1 3LU
Tel: 01772 551 876
Fax: 01772 886 513
email: lyndab@northwestvision.co.uk
Website: www.northwestvision.co.uk
Lynda Banister

### Liverpool Film Office
4th Floor, Pioneer Buildings
67 Dale Street
Liverpool L2 2NS
Tel: 0151 291 9191
Fax: 0151 291 9199
email: lfo@liverpool.gov.uk
Website: filmliverpool.com
Lynn Saunders, Film Office Manager

### North West Vision
233 Tea Factory
82 Wood Street
Liverpool L1 4DQ
Tel: 0151 708 2967
Fax: 0151 708 2984
Website: www.northwestvision.co.uk
Area: Cheshire, Greater Manchester,
Lancashire, Merseyside and Cumbria

### Northern Film and Media
Central Square
Forth Street
Newcastle Upon Tyne NE1 3PJ
Tel: 0191 269 9212
Fax: 0191 269 9213
email: locations@northernmedia.org
Gayle Mason, Dave Watson
Area: Durham, Teesside, Tyne &
Wear, Northumberland

### Scottish Highlands & Islands Film Commission Comisean Fiolm na Gaidhealtachd's nan Eilean Alba
Inverness Castle
Inverness 1V2 3EG
Tel: 01463 710221
Fax: 01463 710848
email: trish@scotfilm.org
Website: www.scotfilm.org
Trish Shorthouse, Jenny Yeomans

### Screen East
1st Floor
2 Millennium Plain
Norwich NR2 1TF
Tel: 01603 776920
Fax: 01603 767191
email: info@screeneast.co.uk
Website: www.screeneast.co.uk
Nicky Dade
Screen East is the screen agency
dedicated to developing, supporting
and promoting a thriving and
successful film and media industry
and culture in the counties of
Bedfordshire, Cambridgeshire, Essex,
Hertfordshire, Norfolk and Suffolk.
This is done through Screen East's
Production, Enterprise and Skills, and
Audiences and Education
departments. Screen East is funded by
the UK Film Council and by the East
of England Development Agency
(EEDA). It allocates Lotttery funding
on behalf of the UK Film Council
through the Regional Investment
Fund for England (RIFE).

### Screen South
Folkestone Enterprise Centre
Shearway Business Park
Shearway Road
Kent CT19 4RH
Tel: 01303 851 320
email: firstname@screensouth.org
Gina Fegan, Chief Executive
Graham Benson, Chair

### Screen West Midlands
31-41 Bromley Street
Birmingham B9 4AN
Tel: 0121 766 1470
Fax: 0121 766 1480
email: info@screenwm.co.uk
Website: www.screenwm.co.uk
Chief Executive: Krysia Rozanska

### Screen West Screen
59 Prince Street
Bristol BS1 4QH
Tel: 0117 377 6066
Fax: 0117 377 6067
email:
firstname.surname@swscreen.co.uk
Caroline Norbury, Chief Executive
Jeremy Payne, Chair

### South West Scotland Screen Commission
Gracefield Arts Centre
28 Edinburgh Road
Dumfries DG1 1JQ
Tel: 01387 263666
Fax: 01387 263666
email: screencom@dumgal.gov.uk
Website: www.sw-scotland-
screen.com
Belle Doyle

## Southern Screen Commission
Town Hall
Bartholomew Square
Brighton BN1 1JA
Tel: 01273 384211
Fax: 01273 384211
email: southernscreen@pavilion.co.uk
Website: Philippe Chandless
Southern Screen promotes and
markets locations, personnel and
services in the South East to the film
and television industries

## Tayscreen.com
Dundee Contemporary Arts
152 Nethergate
Dundee DD1 4DY
Tel: 01382 432321
Fax: 01382 432252
email: info@tayscreen.com
Website: www.tayscreen.com
Julie Craike

## Wales Screen Commission
Central Office
Unit 6G Science Park
Cefn Llan
Aberystwyth
Ceredigion SY23 3AH
Tel:  01970 627186
Fax: 01970 617942
email: enquiry
@walesscreencommission.co.uk
Website:
www.walesscreencommission.co.uk
The Wales Screen Commission seeks
to promote the use of Wales' facilities
and locations for the production of
films, television programmes and
commercials. Offices in Cardiff,
Llandeilo, Aberystwyth, Bangor and
Wrexham

## Yorkshire Screen Commission
The Workstation
15 Paternoster Row
Sheffield S1 2BX
Tel: 0114 279 9115
Fax: 0114  2798593
email: ysc@workstation.org.uk
Website: www.ysc.co.uk
Liz Rymer, Commissioner

# US Organisations

## American Film Institute
2021 North Western Avenue
Los Angeles, CA 90027
Tel:  (323) 856-7600
Fax: Fax (323) 467-4578
email: Website: www.AFI.com
Website: Communications Office

Tel: (323) 856 7667

## AMPAS (Academy of Motion Picture Arts & Sciences)
8949 Wilshire Boulevard
Beverly Hills
CA 90211
Tel: (1) 310 247 3000
Fax: (1) 310 859 9619
Organisation of producers, actors and
others which is responsible for widely
promoting and supporting the film
industry, as well as for awarding the
annual Oscars

## Hollywood Foreign Press Association
292 S. La Cienega Blvd, #316
Beverly Hills
CA 90211
Tel: (1) 310 657 1731
Fax: (1) 310 657 5576
Journalists reporting on the
entertainment industry for non-US
media. Annual event: Golden Globe
Awards - awarding achievements in
motion pictures and television

## The Museum of Television and Radio
25 West 52 Street
New York, NY 10019
Tel: (1) 212 621 6600
Fax: (1) 212 621 6715
Website: www.mtr.org
The Museum of Television & Radio
465 N. Beverly Drive
Beverly Hills, CA 90210
Tel: (310) 786-1000
The Museum of Television & Radio is
the premier trust of radio and
television's heritage, making available
to the public the finest collection of
programs and promoting a greater
appreciation for the artistic value,
social impact, and historic
importance of the medium. The
Museum of Television and Radio
offers something for everyone with
over 120,000 television and radio
programs that are available at
individual consoles. The Museum
also presents theater screenings,
seminars, and listening series
throughout the year.

# ORGANISATIONS (EUROPE)

The following is a list of some of the main pan–European film and television organisations, entries for countries of the European Union. Compiled by Natalie Sergent

## Pan-European Organisations

### Association de Gestion Internationale Collective des Oeuvres Audiovisuelles
26, rue de St-Jean
1203 Geneva
Switzerland
Tel: (41) 22 340 32 00
Fax: (41) 22 340 34 32
email:info@agicoa.org
Website: www.agicoa.org
The Association of International Collective Management of Audiovisual Works was set up in 1981 as a non-governmental organisation to defend audiovisual producers' copyrights, especially in the area of cable TV and similar retransmission means

### CARTOON
European Association of Animation Film
314 Boulevard Lambermont
1030 Brussels
Tel: (32) 2 245 1200
Fax: (32) 2 245 4689
email: cartoon@skynet.be
Website: www.cartoon-media.be
European animation network which organises the annual CARTOON FORUM, co-ordinates the grouping of animation studios and runs specialist training courses in animation

### Eurimages
Council of Europe
Avenue de l'Europe
67075 Strasbourg Cédex
France
Tel: (33) 3 88 41 20 33
Fax: (33) 3 88 41 27 45
email: Euroimages@coe.int
Website:
www.coe.int/T/E/Cultural_Co-operation/Eurimages/ages

Euroimages is the Council of Europe fund for the co-production, distribution and exhibition of European cinematographic work. Set up as a  Partial Agreement it currently has 30 Member States. Its aim is to promote the European film industry by encouraging the production and distribution of films and fostering co-operation between professionals

### Europa Cinemas
54, rue Beaubourg
75 003 Paris
Tel: (33) 1 42 71 53 70
Fax: (33) 1 42 71 47 55
email: europacinema@magic.fr
Website: www.europa-cinemas.org
Encourages screenings and promotion of European and Mediterranean films in a network of cinemas in European and Mediterranean cities. It offers financial support for screening European and Mediterranean films, for promotional activities and for special events

### European Academy for Film & Television
69, rue Verte
1210 Brussels
Belgium
Tel: (32) 2 218 66 07
Fax: (32) 2 217 55 72
The purpose of the Academy, a non-profit making association, is the research, development and disclosure of all matters relating to cinema and television chiefly in the European continent, taking into account artistic, commercial, cultural, economic, financial, historical, institutional, pedagogical, trade union and technical aspects. Quarterly newsletter, ACANEWS

### European Audiovisual Observatory
76, allée de la Robertsau
67000 Strasbourg
France
Tel: (33) 3 88 144 400
Fax: (33) 3 88 144 419
email: obs@obs.coe.int
Website: www.obs.coe.int

Set up in 1992, this institution gathers and circulates information on the audiovisual industry in Europe in the fields of broadcasting (TV/radio), film, video, DVD and multimedia/Internet, media law and policy, and advertising/sponsorship

### European Broadcasting Union/Union Européenne de Radio-Télévision
17a Ancienne Route
1218 Grand-Saconnex
Geneva
Switzerland
Tel: (41) 0 22 717 2111
Fax: (41) 0 22 747 4000
email: ebu@ebu.ch
Website: www.ebu.ch
Working on behalf of its Members in the European area, the EBU/UER negotiates broadcasting rights for major sports events, operates the Eurovision and Euroradio networks, stimulates and co-ordinates productions. At its office in Brussels, it represents the interests of public service broadcasters before the European institutions

### European Coordination of Film Festivals
64, rue Philippe le Bon
1000 Brussels
Belgium
Tel: (32) 22 801 376
Fax: (32) 22 309 141
email: cefc@skypro.be
Website: www.eurofilmfest.org
Marie José  Carta, Executive Secretary
A network of 200 audio-visual festivals in Europe to promote the diversity of the European moving image through collaboration projects such as touring programmes, staff exchanges, research and conferences on the socio-economic impact of film festivals, electronic subtitling and sponsorship, and the quarterly newsletter (EuroFilmFest)

### European Film Academy
Kurfurstendamm 225
10719 Berlin
Germany
Tel: (49) 30 887 167 - 0
Fax: (49) 30 887 167 77

email: efa@europeanfilmacademy.org
Website:
www.europeanfilmacademy.org
Founded in 1989 under the name of
European Cinema Society (renamed
European Film Academy in 1991) by
its first president Ingmar Bergman
and 40 filmmakers to advance the
interests of the European film
industry through conferences and
workshops. Wim Wenders acts as its
President since 1996

## European Film College
Carl Th. Dreyers Vej 1
8400 Ebeltoft
Denmark
Tel: (45) 86 34 0055
Fax: (45) 8634 0535
email: administration@efc.dk
Website: www.efc.dk
Founded in 1993 with the overall goal
of contributing to a vibrant film
culture and a successful film industry
in Europe. It provides education and
training in all aspects of the
audiovisual media to undergraduates,
professionals and the general public

## European Institute for the Media
Zollhof 2A
40221 Düsseldorf
Germany
Tel: (49) 211 90 10 40
Fax: (49) 211 90 10 456
email: info@eim.org
Website: www.eim.org
A think tank for research and strategy
concerning developments in
European media and
communications, based in Düsseldorf
and Paris. Its main areas of research
are the impact of convergence on the
media, cross-border developments in
the media and their role in the
process of European integration, the
public interest aspects of (new)
media developments and the growth
of the Information Society

## Euroscript
Suffolk House
1-8 Whitfield Place
London W1T 5JU
Tel/Fax: 020 7387 5880
email: info@euroscript.co.uk
Website: www.euroscript.co.uk
Originally funded for five years by the
European Union's MEDIA II
programme, Euroscript provides
tailor-made development support for
screenwriters, producers, production
companies worldwide. They also run
international workshops and a bi-

annual Film Story Competition
encouraging original new screen and
TV ideas from new and established
writers

## EUTELSAT
70, rue Balard
75502 Paris Cédex 15
France
Tel: (33) 1 53 98 47 47
Website: www.eutelsat.com
The European Telecommunications
Satellite Organisation operates a
satellite system for intra-European
communications of all kinds. Traffic
carried includes Television and Radio
channels, programme exchanges,
satellite newsgathering, telephony and
business communications

## Fédération Européenne des Industries Techniques de l'Image et du Son
50, avenue Marceau
75008 Paris
France
Tel: (33) 1 45 05 72 55
A federation of European
professional organisations
representing those working in film
and video services and facilities in all
audio-visual and cinematographic
markets

## Fédération Internationale de la Presse Cinématographique (FIPRESCI)
Schleissheimer Str 83
80797 Munich
Germany
Tel: (49) 89 18 23 03
Fax: (49) 89 18 47 66
email: info@fipresci.org
Website: www.fipresci.org
International Federation of Film
Critics. See About Us section on their
website for European contact details

## Institut de l'Audiovisuel et des Télécommunications en Europe
BP 4167
34092 Montpelier Cédex 5
France
Tel: (33) 4 67 14 44 44
Fax: (33) 4 67 14 44 00
email: info@idate.fr
Website: www.idate.org
IDATE specialises in analysis of the
information and communications
technologies sectors and provides an
operational consultancy (surveys and
expert missions), a world observatory

for the communications sectors, and
a forum for discussion and debate

## Institut de Formation et d'Enseignement pour les Métiers de l'Image et du Son (FEMIS)
6, rue Francoeur
75018 Paris
France
Tel: (33) 1 53 41 21 00
Fax: (33) 1 53 41 02 80
email: femis@femis.fr
Website: www.femis.fr
High level technical training in the
audio-visual field for French
applicants and those from outside
France with a working knowledge of
French. Organises regular student
exchanges with other European film
schools

## International Federation of Actors
Guild House
Upper St Martin's Lane
London WC2H 9EG
Tel: 020 7379 0900
Fax: 020 7379 8260
email: info@fia-actors.com
Website: www.fia-actors.com
International body which represents
the trade unions and associations of
actors, dancers and other performers
throughout the world

## Media Entertainment International
Rue de l'Hopital, 31
1000 Brussels
Belgium
Tel: (32) 2 234 56 50
Fax: (32) 2 235 08 61
Website: www.union-
network.org/UNIsite/Sectors/MEI/M
EI.html
Formerly known as International
Secretariat for Arts, Mass Media and
Entertainment Trade Union (-1995),
MEI caters to the special concerns of
unions and similar associations
whose members are engaged in mass
media, entertainment and the arts

## Telefilm Canada/Europe
5, rue de Constantine
75007 Paris
France
Tel: (33) 1 44 18 35 30
Fax: (33) 1 47 05 72 76
email: laurec@telefilm.gc.ca
Website: www.telefilm.gc.ca
Canadian government organisation
financing film and television
productions. European office

provides link between Canada, UK and other European countries

## Union Internationale des Cinémas

15, rue de Berri
75008 Paris
France
Tel: (33) 1 42 89 31 50
Fax: (33) 1 42 89 31 40
email: unicine@club-internet.fr
UNIC defends the interests of cinema exhibitors worldwide, particularly in matters of law and economics. It publishes UNIC News and a Bulletin. Also provides statistical information and special studies concerning the exhibition sector to members and others

# AUSTRIA

## Austrian Film Commission

Stiftgasse 6
1070 Vienna
Tel: (43) 1 526 33 23-0
Fax: (43) 1 526 68 01
email: office@afc.at
Website: www.afc.at
Promotes Austrian cinema throughout the world

## Fachverband der Audiovisions und Filmindustrie Österreichs

Wiedner Haupstrafle 63
1045 Vienna
Tel: (43) 5 90 900 3010
Fax: (43) 5 90 900 276
email: krenmayr@fafo.at
Website: www.fafo.at
Association of Audiovisual and Film Industry

## Fachverband der Lichtspieltheater und Audiovisionsveranstalter

Wiedner Hauptstraße 63
1045 Vienna
Tel: (43) 1 5 90 900 3471
Fax: (43) 1 5 90 900-3526
email: kinos@wko.at
Website: www.diekinos.at
Austrian Professional Audiovisual Organisers and Movie Theatres Association

## Österreichisches Filminstitut

Spittelberggasse 3
1070 Wien
Tel: (43) 1 526 97 30
Fax: (43) 1 526 97 30/400
email: office@filminstitut.at
Website: www.filminstitut.at

## Österreichisches Filmmuseum

Augustinerstrasse 1
1010 Vienna
Tel: (43) 1 533 70 54 29
Fax: (43) 1 533 70 56 25
email: office@filmmuseum.at
Website: www.filmmuseum.at

# BELGIUM

## Flanders Image

Handelskaai 18/3
1000 Brussels
Tel: (32) 2 226 06 30
Fax: (32) 2 219 19 36
email: flandersimage@vaf.be
Website: www.flanders-image.com
A division of the Flemish Audiovisual Fund (VAF), Flanders Image promotes Flemish audiovisual products abroad

## Ministère de la Communauté Française de Belgique

Service Général de l'Audiovisuel et des Multimédias
Espace 27 Septembre
Boulevard Léopold II 44
1080 Brussels
Tel: (32) 2 413 35 02
Fax: (32) 2 413 20 68
email: daav@cfwb.be
Website: www.cfwb.be/av
Assistance given to the production of documentaries, short and long features by independent producers

## Musée du Cinéma/Filmmuseum

Palais des Beaux-Arts
9, rue Baron Horta
1000 Brussels
Tel: (32) 2 507 83 70
Fax: (32) 2 513 12 72
email: filmmuseum@ledoux.be
Website: www.ledoux.be

## Radio-Télévision Belge de la Communauté Française (RTBF)

Service Médiation
Local 9 M 51
1044 Brussels
Tel: (32) 2 737 39 30
Website: www.rtbf.be
Public broadcaster responsible for French language services

## Vlaams Audiovisueel Fonds

Handelskaai 18/3
1000 Brussels
Tel: (32) 2 226 06 30
Fax: (32) 2 219 19 36
email: info@vaf.be
Website: www.vaf.be
The Flemish Audiovisual Fund (VAF) supports audiovisual production in, as well as international co-productions with Flanders. Its aims are to develop a sustainable Flemish audiovisual industry, to encourage and support upcoming audiovisual talent and to promote productions

## Vlaamse-Radio- en Televisieomroep (VRT)

Reyerslaan 52
1043 Brussels
Tel: (32) 2 741 3111
Fax: (32) 2 734 9351
email: info@vrt.be
Website: www.vrt.be
Public television and radio station serving Dutch speaking Flemish community in Belgium

# CYPRUS

## Cyprus Broadcasting Corporation

CyBc street
2120 Nicosia
Tel: (357) 2286 2000
Fax: (357) 2231 4050
Website: www.cybc.com.cy
Cyprus' public broadcasting service, transmitting island-wide on three radio and two television channels (RIK1 and RIK2)

## Ministry of Education and Culture

Corner Thoucydides and Kimon
1434 Lefkosia (Nicosia)
Tel: (357) 228 00607
Fax: (357) 2230 5974
email: moec@moec.gov.cy
Website: www.cyprus.gov.cy
The Cultural Services of the Ministry of Education and Culture are involved with the promotion and organisation of exhibitions, festivals and international cultural events (festivals, symposia, Biennale of Arts)

## Ministry of the Interior - Press and Information Office

Apellis St.
1456 Lefkosia (Nicosia)
Tel: (357) 228 01119
Fax: (357) 226 66123
email: communications@pio.moi.gov.cy
Website: www.moi.gov.cy
The Cinema and Audio-Visual

Productions Section of the Ministry of the Interior acts as the Secretariat of the Cinema Advisory Committee (CAC), which examines proposals submitted by film directors and producers and are funded by the government on CAC's recommendation. It also has responsibility for the Film Classification Board

## CZECH REPUBLIC

### Audiovisual Producers' Association

Narodni Trida 28
110 00 Prague 1
Tel: (420) 2 2110 5302
Fax: (420) 2 2110 5303
email: apa@iol.cz
Website: www.apa.iol.cz
Founded in 1994, APA protects and promotes producers' interests by solving legal and tax issues dealing with film production and takes part in making legislative norms

### Czech Television

Kavci hory
140 70 Prague
Tel: (420) 2 6113 1111
email: info@czech-tv.cz
Website: www.czech-tv.cz
The public service television broadcasting CT1 and CT2 both nationwide

### State Fund for the Support and Development of Czech Cinematography

Website: www.mkcr.cz

## DENMARK

### CultureNet Denmark

Slotsholmsgade 1
1216 Copenhagen
Tel: (45) 72 26 51 80
email: kulturnet@kulturnet.dk
Website: www.kulturnet.dk
Soren Krogh, Project Manager
A portal to Danish culture on the Internet featuring a Culture Guide to Danish cultural institutions, Cultural News containing news articles and essays, and a daily updated Calendar of activities and events. Managed by the Ministry of Culture

### Danmarks Radio (DR)

Morkhojvej 170
2860 Soborg
Tel: (45) 35 20 30 40
Fax: (45 ) 35 20 26 44
email: dr@dr.dk

Website: www.dr.dk
Founded in 1925 as a public service organisation, the Danish Broadcasting Corporation is Denmark's oldest and largest electronic media enterprise providing radio and television programmes

### Det Danske Filminstitut

Gothersgade 55
1123 Copenhagen
Tel: (45) 33 74 34 00
Fax: (45) 33 74 34 01
email: dfi@dfi.dk
Website: www.dfi.dk
The Danish Film Institute is the national agency responsible for supporting and encouraging film and cinema culture and for conserving these in the national interest. The Institute's operations extend from participation in the development and production of feature films, shorts and documentaries, over distribution and marketing, to managing the national film archive and the cinematheque

### Film- og TV-Arbejderforeningen

Kongens Nytorv 21
Baghuset 3. sal
1050 Copenhagen
Tel: (45) 33 14 33 55
Fax: (45) 33 14 33 03
email: faf@filmtv.dk
Website: www.filmtv.dk
The Danish Film and Television Workers Trade Union organises film, video and television workers, and maintains the professional, social, economic and artistic interests of its members. Negotiates collective agreements for feature films, documentaries, commercials, negotiating contracts, copyright and authors' rights

### Producentforeningen

Bernhard Bangs Alle 25
2000 Frederiksberg
Tel: (45) 33 86 28 80
Fax: (45) 33 86 28 88
email: info@pro-f.dk
Website:
www.producentforeningen.dk
Association of Danish film and TV producers producing short film and documentaries, feature films, TV programmes, film and TV commercials, educational films, multimedia productions, and corporate profile videos

## ESTONIA

### Eesti Filmi Sihtasutsus

Vana Viru 3
Tallinn 10111
Tel: (372) 0 627 6060
Fax: (372) 0 627 6061
email: film@efsa.ee
Website: www.efsa.ee
The Estonian Film Foundation was established in 1997 by the Government of Estonia as a private legal institution with the task of financing Estonian film production, establishing and developing international film contacts, promoting Estonian films at home and abroad, supporting the training of Estonian filmmakers and audiovisual professionals, and creating and maintaining Estonian film databases

## FINLAND

### AVEK

Hietaniemenkatu 2
00100 Helsinki
Tel: (358) 9 431 521
Fax: (358) 9 431 523 77
email: avek@avek.kopiosto.fi
Website: www.kopiosto.fi/avek
The Promotion Centre for Audiovisual Culture was established in 1987 by the Finnish copyright organisaton Kopiosto to promote cinema, video tapes and television culture. It collects copyright entitlements for levies on blank video tapes, distributes funds to independent producers, and subsidies the production of short films/documentaries and training

### Suomen Elokuvasaatio

Kanavakatu 12
00160 Helsinki
Tel: (358) 9 6220 300
Fax: (358) 9 6220 3050
email: keskus@ses.fi
Website: www.ses.fi
The Finnish Film Foundation is an independent foundation supervised by the Department for Cultural Policy in the Ministry of Education. Its task is to support and develop Finnish film production, distribution and exhibition

## FRANCE

### Bibliothèque du Film (BIFI)

100, rue du Faubourg Saint-Antoine
75012 Paris
Tel : (33) 1 53 02 22 30
Fax: (33) 153 02 22 39
email: cid@bifi.fr

Website: www.bifi.fr

## Centre National de la Cinématographie

12, rue de Lübeck
75016 Paris
Tel: (33) 1 44 34 34 40
Fax: (33) 1 47 55 04 91
Website: www.cnc.fr
A government institution, under the auspices of the Ministry of Culture. Its areas of concern are: the economics of cinema and the audio-visual industries; film regulation; the promotion of the cinema industries and the protection of cinema heritage. Offers financial assistance in all aspects of French cinema (production, exhibition, distribution etc). In 1986, the CNC was made responsible for the system of aid offered to the production of films made for television. These include fiction films, animated films and documentaries

## Chambre Syndicale des Producteurs et Exportateurs de Films Français

5, rue du Cirque
75008 Paris
Tel: (33) 1 53 89 01 30
Fax: (33) 1 42 25 94 27
email: cspeff@wanadoo.fr
National federation of French cinema production

## Cinémathèque Française - Musée du Cinéma

4, rue de Longchamp
75016 Paris
Tel: (33) 1 53 65 74 57
Fax: (33) 1 53 65 74 97
email: contact@cinemathequefrancaise.com
Website: www.cinemathequefrancaise.com
Founded in 1936 by Henri Langlois and Georges Franju, with the financial help of Paul-Auguste Harlé, to save, conserve and show films. Now houses screening theatres, library and stills and posters library. Its Musée du Cinéma, created by Langlois in 1972, closed down in 1997. It will reopen in 2006 in the former American Center building, Bercy

## Fédération Nationale des Distributeurs de Films

74, avenue Kléber
75116 Paris

Tel: (33) 1 56 90 33 00
Fax: (33) 1 56 90 33 01
email: films.fndf@fndf.org
Website: www.fndf.org
National federation of film distributors

## Fédération Nationale des Industries Techniques du Cinéma et de l'Audiovisuel

36, rue Washington
75008 Paris
Tel: (33) 1 43 59 11 70
email: fitca@wanadoo.fr
Website: www.fitca-france.com
A federation of technical trade associations which acts as intermediary between its members and their market. Maintains a database on all technical aspects of production, and helps French and European companies find suitable partners for research and development or commercial ventures

## Forum des images

Forum des Halles
Porte Saint-Eustache
75001 Paris
Tel: (33) 1 44 76 62 00
Fax: (33) 1 40 26 40 96
email: contact@forumdesimages.net
Website: www.forumdesimages.net

## France 2

22, avenue Montaigne
75008 Paris
Tel: (33) 1 44 21 42 42
Fax: (33) 1 44 21 51 45
Website: www.france2.fr
Main public service terrestrial television channel. Along with France 3 and France 5 part of the France Televisions Group

## Institut National de l'Audiovisuel

4, avenue de l'Europe
94366 Bry-sur-Marne Cédex
Tel: (33) 1 49 83 20 00
Fax: (33) 1 49 83 25 80
email: international@ina.fr
Website: www.ina.fr
INA conserves and provides programmes from the public radio and television channels for professional use. Since 1995, all radio and television programme broadcasts, including commercials and video clips have been listed in the Inatheque databases

## TF1

1, Quai du Point du Jour
92656 Boulogne Cédex
Tel: (33) 1 41 41 12 34

Fax: (33) 1 41 41 29 10
Website: www.tf1.fr
Privatised national television channel

# GERMANY

## Arbeitsgemeinschaft der öffentlich rechtlichen Rundfunkanstalten der Bundesrepublik Deutschland

Programme Directorate of Deutsches Fernsehen
Arnulfstrasse 42
Postfach 20 06 22
80335 Munich
Tel: (49) 89 59 00 01
Fax: (49) 89 59 00 32 49
email: info@daserste.de
Website: www.daserste.de
ARD is one of the two public service broadcasters in Germany, consisting of 9 independent broadcasting corporations

## Beauftragter der Bundesregierung für Anglelengesheiten der Kultur und de Medien

Postfach 170290
53108 Bonn
Tel: (49) 1888 681 3594
Fax: (49) 1888 681 3885
Website: www.bundesregierung.de/en/News-by-subject/Culture-,11696/Film-policy.htm
Federal Government for Cultural and Media Affairs' film policy

## Bundesverband Deutscher Fernsehproduzenten

Brienner Strasse 26
80333 Munich
Tel: (49) 89 286 28 385
Fax: (49) 89 286 28 247
email: post@tv-produzentent.de
Website: www.tv-produzenten.de
Trade association for independent television producers

## Deutsches Filmmuseum

Schaumainkai 41
60596 Frankfurt am Main
Tel: (49) 692 123 88 30
Fax: (49) 692 123 78 81
email: info@deutsches-filmmuseum.de
Website: www.deutsches-filmmuseum.de

## Export-Union des Deutschen Films

Sonnenstr. 21

80331 Munich
Tel: (49) 895 997 87-0
Fax: (49) 895 997 87-30
email: export-union@german-cinema.de
Website: www.german-cinema.de
Official trade association for the promotion of German Cinema

## Filmförderungsanstalt
Grosse Präsidentenstrasse 9
10178 Berlin
Tel: (49) 302 757 7-0
Fax: (49) 302 757 7-111
email: presse@ffa.de
Website: www.ffa.de
German Federal Film Board

## Filmmuseum Berlin - Deutsche Kinemathek
Potsdamer Strasse 2
10785 Berlin
Tel: (49) 303 009 03-0
Fax: (49) 303 009 03-13
email: info@filmmuseum-berlin.de
Website: www.filmmuseum-berlin.de

## Freiwillige Selbstkontrolle der Filmwirtschaft
Kreuzberger Ring 56
65205 Wiesbaden
Tel: (49) 611 778 910
Fax: (49) 611 7789 139
email: info@spio-fsk.de
Website: www.spio-fsk.de
Film industry voluntary self-regulatory body. Activities are to examine together with official competent representatives which films can be shown to minors under 18 year olds and under; to discuss the examination of films with youth groups, and to organise seminars on the study of film, videos and new media

## Kunsthochschule für Medien Köln
Peter-Welter-Platz 2
50676 Cologne
Tel: (49) 221 20 189 0
Fax: (49) 221 201 891 7
email: presse@khm.de
Website: www.khm.de
The Academy of Media Arts offers an Audio-visual Media graduate programme concentrating on the areas of television/film, media art, media design and art and media science

## ZDF Germany Television
ZDF-Zuschauerservice
55100 Mainz
Tel: (49) 613 170 2060

Fax: (49) 613 170 2170
email: info@zdf.de
Website: www.zdf.de
National public service television broadcaster

# GREECE

## ERT SA (Hellenic Broadcasting Corporation)
Messoghion 402
15342 Aghia Paraskevi
Athens
Tel: (30) 1 639 0772
Fax: (30) 1 639 0652
Website: www.ert.gr
National public television and radio broadcaster for information, education and entertainment

## Greek Film Centre
10 Panepistimiou Str
10671 Athens
Tel: (30) 210 36 34 586
Fax: (30) 210 36 30 970
email: info@gfc.gr
Website: www.gfc.gr
Finances film productions; promotes and supports film distribution both domestically and internationally in commercial and parallel circuits; organises retrospectives and film weeks abroad; participates in festivals; organises seminars aimed at providing professional training; and issues publications on the history of Greek cinema

# HUNGARY

## Magyar Filmunio
Varosligeti Fasor 38
1068 Budapest
Tel: (361) 351 7760
Fax: (361) 352 6734
email: filmunio@filmunio.hu
Website: www.filmunio.hu
Established in 1992 by the Motion Picture Public Foundation of Hungary, it acts as a switchboard between Hungarian industry professionals and their partners abroad and organises film festivals at home and on the international scene

## Magyar Mozgokep Kozalapitvany
Varosligeti fasor 38
1068 Budapest
Tel: (361) 351 76 96
Fax: (361) 352 87 89
email: info@mmka.hu
Website: www.mmka.org
Motion Picture Public Foundation of Hungary

## National Cultural Fund
Bajza u. 32
1062 Budapest
Tel: (361) 352 72 30
Fax: (361) 352 72 30
email: elnok@nka.hu
Website:
www.nka.hu/index_noflash.html
Operating under the supervision of the Ministry of Cultural Heritage, the NCF supports the creation and preservation of Hungarian cultural values and their propagation domestically and abroad

## ORTT (Orszagos Radio es Televizio Testulet Kozlemenyei)
Reviczky u 5
1088 Budapest
Tel: (361) 267 2590
Fax: (361) 267 2612
Website: www.ortt.hu
National Radio and Television Commission

# IRELAND

## An Chomhairle Ealaíon
70 Merrion Square
Dublin 2
Tel: (353) 1 618 0200
Fax: (353) 1 676 1302
email: info@artscouncil.ie
Website: www.artscouncil.ie
The Arts Council promotes creative experiment through support to filmmakers through various bursaries, awards and schemes. It also supports the film production organisations (FilmBase, Cork Film Centre, Galway Film Centre), who encourage training, short film production and information provision, especially for the emerging filmmaker

## Bord Scannán na hÉireann
Rockfort House
St. Augustine Street
Galway
Tel: (353) 91 561 398
Fax: (353) 91 561 405
email: info@filmboard.ie
Website: www.filmboard.ie
Irish Film Board

## Film Censor's Office
16 Harcourt Terrace
Dublin 2
Tel: (353) 1 799 6100
Fax: (353) 1 676 1898
email: info@ifco.gov.ie
The Official Film Censor is appointed by the Irish Government to consider

and classify all feature films and videos distributed in Ireland

### Irish Film Institute
6 Eustace Street
Temple Bar
Dublin 2
Tel: (353) 1 679 5744
Fax: (353) 1 677 8755
email: fii@ifc.ie
Website: www.fii.ie
Preserves, presents and promotes film culture in Ireland

### RTE (Radio Telefis Eireann)
Donnybrook
Dublin 4
Tel: (353) 1 208 3111
Fax: (353) 1 208 3080
email: info@rte.ie
Website: www.rte.ie
Public service national broadcaster

## ITALY

### ANICA (Associazione Nazionale Industrie Cinematografiche Audiovisive e Multimediali)
Viale Regina Margherita 286
00198 Rome
Tel: (39) 06 4425961
email: anica@anica.it
Website: www.anica.it
Trade association for television and movie producers and distributors, representing technical industries (post-production companies/dubbing/studios/labs); home video producers and distributors; television and radio broadcasters

### Fininvest Television
Viale Europa 48
20093 Cologno Monzese, Milan
Fax: (39) 2 251 47031
Major competitor to RAI, running television channels Canale 5, Italia Uno and Rete Quattro

### Fondazione Cineteca Italiana
Palazzo Dugnani
Via Daniele Manin, 2
20121 Milan
Tel: (39) 2 29 00 56 59
Fax: (39) 2 29 00 37 06
email: info@cinetecamilano.it
Website: www.cinetecamilano.it
Includes Archives of the History of Film and Museum of Cinema

### Museo Nazionale del Cinema

**Fondazione Maria Adriana Prolo**
Via Montebello 20
10124 Turin
Tel: (39) 11 812 56 58
Fax: (39) 11 812 57 38
Website:
www.museonazionaledelcinema.org
Archives of cinema photography and images

### RAI (Radiotelevisione Italiana)
Viale Mazzini 14
00195 Rome
Tel: (39) 6 361 3608
Fax: (39) 6 323 1010
Website: www.rai.it
Italian state broadcaster

## LATVIA

### Latvia State Radio and Television Centre
Str. Erglu 7
1012 Riga
Tel: (371) 710 8704
Fax: (371) 710 8740
email: lvrtc@lvrtc.lv
Website: www.lvrtc.lv/English

### National Film Centre of Latvia
Elizabetes iela 49
1010 Riga
Tel: (371) 750 5074
Fax: (371) 750 5077
email: nfc@nfc.gov.lv
Website: www.nfc.lv/ffl/html/nfc.html
Established in 1991 as a state institution under the Ministry of Culture, the organisation's main objectives are to administer the Government's financial support to Latvian films; prepare legal acts securing the functioning of filmmaking in Latvia; preserve the national audio-visual heritage; promote Latvian films abroad; co-operate with relevant international and national organisations; register films and videos; issue licences to video distribution companies in Latvia; and form a database of Latvian films and filmmakers. It also closely co-operates with the Latvian Filmmakers Union (same postal address)

### Riga Film Museum
Smerla iela 3
1006 Riga
Tel/Fax: (371) 754 5099
email: kinomuz@latnet.lv
Website:
www.nfc.lv/ffl/html/museum.html
Inga Perkone, Director

Located in the Riga Film Studios building, the museum contains a rich collection of items related to the national cinema (including production during WWII and under the Soviet Occupation) – about 70,000 units of films, photographs, promotional materials, documents, keepsakes, sketches of set designs and costumes. Use of the library materials is free of charge

## LITHUANIA

### Lietuvos Radijo ir Televizijos Komisija
Vytenio 6/23
03113 Vilnius
Tel: (370) 5 233 0660
Fax: (370) 5 264 7125
emai: rtk@rtk.lt
Website: www.rtk.lt
The Radio and Television Commission of Lithuania is an independent institution with powers of regulation and supervision of activities of commercial radio and television broadcasters, which is accountable to the Seimas of he Republic

### Lithuania Theatre, Music and Cinema
Cinema Department and Collections
4 Vilniaus str.
2001 Vilnius
Tel: (370) 226 224 06
emai: ltmkm@takas.lt
Website:
teatras.mch.mii.lt/Kinas/Kinas.en.htm

## LUXEMBOURG

### Centre National de l'Audiovisuel
5, rue de Zoufftgen
3598 Luxembourg
Tel: (352) 52 24 241
Fax: (352) 52 06 55
email: info@cna.etat.lu
Website: www.cna.lu

### Cinémathèque Municipale - Ville de Luxembourg
10, rue Eugène Ruppert
2453 Luxembourg
Tel: (352) 47 96 26 44
Fax: (352) 40 75 19
email: cinematheque@vdl.lu
Website: www.luxembourg-city.lu/culture/cinematheque/index.php
Official film archive, preserving international film heritage

## Film Fund Luxembourg

Fonds national de soutien a la production audiovisuelle
5, rue Large
1917 Luxembourg
Tel: (352) 478 20 65
Fax: (352) 22 09 63
email: info@filmfund.etat.lu
Website: www.filmfund.lu
The Audiovisual Production Support provides discretionary loans to local producers to finance development/scriptwriting, distribution and production, repayable from the finished work's receipt. Co-operates closely with the Union of Luxembourg Audiovisual Producers (ULPA), which represents specialists production companies. The Fund also assists supervisory ministers in areas such as the drafting of regulations and legislation, compiles statistics relating to the sector, determines the award of 'Luxembourg nationality' for audiovisual works and maintains a national register of productions

## RTL Group

45, boulevard Pierre Frieden
1543 Luxembourg
Tel: (352) 2486 5130
Fax: (352) 2486 5139
email:
andrew.buckhurst@rtlgroup.com
Website: www.rtlgroup.com
Andrew Buckhurst, External Communications
Europe's largest TV, radio and production company with 26 TV channels and 24 radio stations in 9 countries. Produces television content such as game shows and soaps, including 'Pop Idol' and 'The Bill'

# MALTA

## Malta Film Commission

The Trade Centre
San Gwann, SGN 09
Tel: (356) 21 497970
Fax: (356) 21 499568
email: info@mfc.com.mt
Website: www.mfc.com.mt
Oliver Mallia, Film Commissioner
MFC is a non-profit making organisation and offers its services free of charge to foreign film and television productions. Its aims are to create international awareness about Malta's unlimited potential as a film location, serve to facilitate and assist film crews before and during their stay on the island. Set up in 1999 under the auspices of the Ministry for Economic Services, the Commission now forms part of the Ministry of Foreign Affairs and Investment Promotion

## Public Broadcasting Services

75, St. Luke's Road
G'Mangia MSD 09
Tel: (356) 21 225051
Fax: (357) 2231 4050
Website: www.pbs.com.mt
PBS operates two TV stations: TVM (Television Malta) and Community Channel 12

# NETHERLANDS

## Film museum

PO Box 74782
1071 AA Amsterdam
Tel: (31) 20 589 1400
Fax: (31) 20 683 3401
email: info@filmmuseum.nl
Website: www.filmmuseum.nl
Film museum with three public screenings each day, permanent and temporary exhibitions, library, film café and film distribution

## Ministerie van Onderwijs, Cultuur en Wetenschap

Film Department
PO Box 16375
25000BJ Den Haag
Tel: (31) 704 123 456
Fax: (31) 704 123 450
email: info@minocw.nl
Website: www.minocw.nl
The film department of the Ministry of Education, Culture and Science is responsible for the development and maintenance of Dutch film policy. Subsidises various different organisations for production, distribution, promotion and conservation of film

## Nederlands Fonds voor de Film

Jan Luykenstraat 2
1071CM Amsterdam
Tel: (31) 20 570 7676
Fax: (31) 20 570 7689
email: info@filmfund.nl
Website: www.filmfund.nl/

## Netherlands Public Broadcasting

Webredactie Omroep.nl
PO Box 26444
1202 JJ Hilversum
Tel: (31) 35 677 1993
Fax: (31) 35 677 2497
Website: www.portal.omroep.nl

Public corporation co-ordinating three-channel public television (plus five radio channels and internet activities)

## Stichting Coproductiefonds Binnenlandse Omroep

CoBO-fonds
Postvak M.54
PO Box 26444
1202 JJ Hilversum
Tel: (31) 35 677 53 48
Fax: (31) 35 677 19 55
Website:sites.omroep.nl/cobofonds/index.html
The Dutch Co-production Fund for Broadcasting Companies

# POLAND

## Panstowa Wyzsza Szkola Filmova Telewizyjna I Teatralna

Ul. Targowa 61/63
90-323 Lodz
Tel: (48) 42 6743943
Fax: (48) 42 6748139
email: swzfilm@mazurek.man.lodz.pl
Website: www.szkola.filmowa.lodz.pl
Founded in 1948 the National Film, Television and Theatre School of Lodz has been an important education centre for Polish film-makers with Wajda, Polanski and Kieslowski at the head, and a pivotal cultural centre for the whole country. It holds an Archive with a large collection of all the past student films and the films used for the practical exercises; a Library with one of the largest collections of film books in Poland, enriched by a collection of CD's

## Telewijza Polska

J.P. Woronicza 17
00 999 Warsaw ul.
email: TVP@tvp.pl
Website: www.tvp.com.pl

# PORTUGAL

## Cinemateca Portuguesa – Museu do Cinemateca

Rua Barata Salgueiro, 39
1269-059 Lisbon
Tel: (351) 21 359 62 00
Fax: (351) 21 352 31 80
email: cinemateca@cinemateca.pt
Website: www.cinemateca.pt
Portuguese Film Archive – Film Museum, preserving, restoring and showing films. Includes a public documentation centre, a stills and posters archive

## Instituto do Cinema, Audiovisual e Multimedia
Rua San Pedro de Alcantara, 45-1
1269-138 Lisbon
Tel: (351) 21359 62 00
Fax: (351) 21 323 08 00
email: mail@icam.pt
Website: www.icam.pt
ICAM assists with subsidies, improvement, regulation of the television and film industry

## RadioTelevisao Portuguesa
Avenida Marechal Gomes da Costa, 37
1849-030 Lisbon
Tel: (351) 21 794 70 00
Fax: (351) 21 794 75 70
Website: www.rtp.pt

# SLOVAK REPUBLIC

## Slovenska Televizia
Mlynska Dolina
84545 Bratislava
Tel: (421) 2 606 11111
Fax: (421) 352 6734
email: riaditel@stv.sk
Website: www.stv.sk
Slovak public television

## Slovensky Filmovy Ustav
Slovak Film Institute
Grosslingova 32
81109 Bratislava
Tel: (421) 571 015 25
Fax: (21) 527 332 14
email: filmsk@sfu.sk
Website: www.filmsk.sk
www.sfu.sk

# SLOVENIA

## Drustvo Slovenskih Filmskih Ustvarjalcev
Miklosiceva 26
1000 Ljubljana
Tel: (386) 1 438 16 40
Fax: (386) 1 438 16 45
email: dsfu@guest.arnes.si
Website: www.drustvo-dsfu.si
Association of Slovenian Filmmakers

## Radio Televizija Slovenija
Kolodvorska 2
1550 Ljubljana
Tel: (386) 1 475 21 11
Website: www.rtvslo.si
Public service broadcasting 2 national TV channels, 3 national radio channels, airing one radio and TV channel for the Italian and Hungarian national community respectively, and producing radio and TV programmes for Slovene national minorities in the neighbouring countries

## Slovenian Cinematheque
Miklosiceva 38
1000 Ljubljana
Tel: (386) 1 434 25 20
Fax: (386) 1 439 65 40
Website: www.kinoteka.si
Founded as an autonomous cultural institution in 1996 to set up and preserve a library collection of international films. Its other important task is to enrich its modest film collection of classic and contemporary world film masterpieces and equip it with Slovenian subtitles. Holds original prints of Ernst Lubitsch's first preserved feature Als ich tot war (When I was dead, 1916), Franz Hofer's first preserved film Des Alters erste Spuren (The first sign of getting old) and the short film Le Jongleur (Pathe, 1913)

# SPAIN

## Academia de las Artes y de las Ciencias Cinematográficas de España
General Oraá 68
28006 Madrid
Tel: (34) 1 563 33 41
Fax: (34) 1 563 26 93
Website: www.sie.es/acacine

## Filmoteca Española
Magdalena 10
28012 Madrid
Tel: (34) 91 467 26 00
Fax: (34) 91 467 26 11
email: filmoteca@filmoteca.mcu.es
Website:
www.cultura.mecd.es/cine/film/filmot
eca.jsp

## Instituto de la Cinematografia y de las Artes Audio-visuales
Ministerio de Cultura
Plaza del Rey 1
28071 Madrid
Tel: (34) 91 701 71 56
Fax: (34) 91 701 73 52
Website:
www.mcu.es/cine/index.html
Promotes, protects and diffuses cinema and audiovisual activities in production, distribution and exhibition. Gives financial support in these areas to Spanish companies. Also involved in the promotion of Spanish cinema and audio-visual arts, and their influence on the different communities within Spain

## Radio Television Española
Edificio Prado del Rey - 3a planta
Office 3/014,
Prado Del Rey
28223 Madrid
email: consultas@rtve.es
Website: www.rtve.es
National public service broadcaster, film producer and distributor

# SWEDEN

## Oberoende Filmares Förbund
Box 27 121
Borgvägen 1
102 52 Stockholm
Tel: (46) 8 665 12 21
Fax: (46) 8 663 66 55
email: kansliet@off.se
Website: www.off.se
Independent Film Producers Association

## Statens biografbyrå
Box 7728
103 95 Stockholm
Tel: (46) 8 24 34 25
Fax: (46) 8 21 01 78
email: registrator@sb.se
Website: www.sb.se
Swedish National Board of Film Classification

## Svenska Filminstitutet
Box 27 126
Filmhuset
Borgvägen 1-5
10252 Stockholm
Tel: (46) 8 665 11 00
Fax: (46) 8 661 18 20
email: info@sfi.se
Website: www.sfi.se

## Sveriges Biografägareförbund
Box 1147
171 23 Solna
Tel: (46) 8 735 97 80
Fax: (46) 8 730 25 60
Swedish Exhibitors Association

## Sveriges Filmuthyrareförening upa
Box 23021
10435 Stockholm
Tel: (46) 8 441 55 70
Fax: (46) 8 34 38 10
Swedish Film Distributors Association

# PR COMPANIES

## Avalon Public Relations
4a Exmoor Street
London W10 6BD
Tel: 020 7598 7222
Fax: 020 7598 7223
email: edt@avalonuk.com
Edward Thomson
Specialist entertainment based pr
agency providing services from pr
and unit publicity to transmission
publicity and media launches

## The Associates
39-41 North Road
London N7 9DP
Tel: 020 7700 3388
Fax: 020 7609 2249
email: info@associates.co.uk
Website: www.the-associates.co.uk
Lisa Richards - Director
Film and video publicity specialists
Richard Larcombe - Managing
Director
Lisa Richards - Executive Director
Lisa DeBell - Account Manager
Almar Haflidason - Account Manager
Taryn Anderson - Financial
Controller
Mike Brennan - Writer/researcher

## Blue Dolphin PR and Marketing
40 Langham Street
London W1N 5RG
Tel: 020 7255 2494
Fax: 020 7580 7670
email: traceyhislop@
bluedolphinfilms.com
Website: www.bluedolphinfilms.com
PR and marketing arm of Blue
Dolphin Films that specialises in key
areas, such as film, video, television
and music

## The Braben Company
18b Pindock Mews
London W9 2PY
Tel: 0207 289 1616
Fax: 0207 289 1166
email: firstname@braben.co.uk
Website: Web: www.braben.co.uk
CEO: Ms. Sarah Braben
Managing Director: Matt Bourn
Braben Company was launched in
1994 and is a leading PR consultancy
for the media and entertainment

industries. Today the company has an
extensive portfolio of clients in
television, film and video, publishing,
radio and new media, providing
corporate, trade and consumer
communications

## Byron Advertising, Marketing and PR
Byron House
Wallingford Road
Uxbridge
Middx UB8 2RW
Tel: 01895 252131
Fax: 01895 252137
Les Barnes

## Emma Chapman Publicity
2nd Floor
18 Great Portland Street
London W1W 8QP
Tel: 020 7637 0990
Fax: 020 7637 0660
email: emma@ecpub.com
Contact: Emma Chapman

## CJP Public Relations Ltd
Park House
8 Grove Ash
Mount Farm
Milton Keynes MK 1B2
Tel: 01908 275271
Fax: 01908 275 272
email: t.chalmers@cjppr.co.uk
Website: www.cjppr.co.uk
Theo Chalmers

## Max Clifford Associates
109 New Bond Street
London W1Y 9AA
Tel: 020 7408 2350
Fax: 020 7409 2294
Max Clifford

## DDA Public Relations Ltd
192-198 Vauxhall Bridge Rd
London SW1V 1DX
Tel: 020 7932 9800 0
Fax: 020 7932 4950
email: info@ddapr.com
Website: www.ddapr.com
Dennis Davidson, Julia Finn, Graham
Smith

## emfoundation
the Old Truman Brewery
91-95 Brick Lane
London E1 6QN

Tel: 020 7247 4171
Fax: 020 7247 4170
email: info@emfoundation.co.uk
Website: emfoundation.co.uk
Keeley Naylor
emfoundation is a publicity & events
management consultancy which was
founded in 1998

## FEREF Limited
14-17 Wells Mews
London W1A 1ET
Tel: 020 7580 6546
Fax: 020 7631 3156
email: robinbehling@feref.com
Website: www.feref.com
Robin Behling, Chris Kinsella

## Lynne Franks PR
327-329 Harrow Road
London W9 3RB
Tel: 020 7724 6777
Fax: 020 7724 8484
Website: www.lynnefranks.com
Julian Henry

## freud communications
19-21 Mortimer Street
London W1T 3DX
Tel:  020 7291 6386
F:ax 020 7637 2626
email:
Johanna.fernihough@freud.com
Website: www.freud.com
Jo Fernihough

## HPS-PR Ltd
Park House
Desborough Park Road
High Wycombe
Bucks, HP 123 DJ
Tel: 01494 684353
Fax: 01494 440952
email: r.hodges@hps-pr.co.uk
Ms Ray Hodges, MCam MIPR

## Sue Hyman Associates
St. Martin's House
59 St. Martin's Lane
London WC2N 4JS
Tel: 020 7379 8420/9944
Fax: 020 7379 4944
email: sue.hyman@btinternet.com
Sue Hyman

## JAC Publicity
1st Floor, Playhouse Court
64 Southwark Bridge Road

London SE1 0AS
Tel: 020 7261 1211
Fax: 020 7261 1214
email: susie@jac-ltd.com
Claire Forbes

## Richard Laver Publicity
3 Troy Court
Kensington High Street
London W8 7RA
Tel: 020 7937 7322
email: richardlaver@btconnect.com
Richard Laver

## McDonald and Rutter (M+R)
34 Bloomsbury Street
London WC1B 3QJ
Tel: 020 7637 2600
Fax: 020 7637 3690
email: info@mcdonalddrutter.com
Website: www.mcdonaldrutter.com
Charles McDonald, Jonathan Rutter

## Optimum Communications
34 Hanway Street
London W1P 9DE
Tel: 020 7580 5352
Fax: 020 7636 3945
Nigel Passingham

## Porter Frith Publicity & Marketing
26 Danbury Street
London N1 8JU
Tel: 020 7359 3734
Fax: 020 7226 5897
Sue Porter, Liz Frith

## The PR Contact
Garden Studio
32 Newman Street
London, W1T 1PU
Tel: 020 7323 1200
Fax: 020 7323 1070
email: info@theprcontact.com
Directors:  Phil Symes, Ronaldo Mourao

## Premier Public Relations
91 Berwick Street
London W1 F 8QQ
Tel: 020 7292 8330
Fax: 020 7734 2024
email: (firstname)@prempr.co.uk
Website: www.prempr.co.uk
Lawrence Atkinson (Film)
Lawrence Atkinson (director - Film)
Melissa Hall-Smith (director - Television)
Laura Aron (director - Personal)
Abigal Ault (director - Busness Affairs)
James Knox (Home Entertainment)
Jane Gibbs (International)

Chris Paton (Managing Director)
Ginger Corbett (Managing Director)
Sara Keene (CEO)

## SSA Public Relations
Chesham House
150 Regent Street
London W1B 5ST
Tel: 020 7432 0336
Fax: 020 7432 0342
email: kfouchestssa@aol.com
Website: www.ssapr.com
Karine Fouchet
S.S.A Public Relations is a full service public relations firm that provides trade and consumer publicity for a wide range of corporate and entertainment clients. The company specialises in key areas, representing television and theatrical film production and distribution companies

## Peter Thompson Associates
12 Bourchier Street
London W1D 4HZ
Tel: 020 7439 1210
email: info@ptassociates.co.uk
Peter Thompson, Amanda Malpass

## Town House Publicity
45 Islington Park Street
London N1 1QB
Tel: 020 7226 7450
Fax: 020 7359 6026
email: thp@townhousepublicity.co.uk
Website: www.townhousepublicty.co.uk
Mary Fulton

## UpFront Television Ltd
39-41 New Oxford Street
London WC1A 1BN
Tel: 020 7836 7702
Fax: 020 7836 7701
email: info@celebritiesworldwide.com
Website: www.celebritiesworldwide.com
Claire Nye , Richard Brecker, Joint Managing Directors:
Established in 1991, Upfront Television has developed a reputation as England's leading independent production company, specialising in celebrity booking with credits including 'The Lord of the Rings: The Return Of The King' UK premiere, the Elle Style Awards 1998-2004, the Mobo Awards 2003, the 2002 Kerrang! Awards, the 2000 Maxim Women of the Year and the Brit Awards. Paul Chowdhry, Jimmy Gulzar, Victoria Silvstedt

## Stella Wilson Publicity
130 Calabria Road
London N5 1HT
Tel: 020 7354 5672
Fax: 020 7354 2242
email: stella@starmaker.demon.co.uk
Stella Wilson

# PRESS CONTACTS

**Archive Zones**
*(Quarterly)*
FOCAL
Pentax House
South Hill Avenue
Harrow
Middlesex HA2 ODU
Tel: 020 78423 5853
Fax: 020 7933 4826
email: info@focalint.org
Website: www.focalint.org
Editor: Michael Archer
Journal of FOCAL International

**Arena**
*(Monthly)*
Endeavour House,
189 Shaftsbury Avenue,
London WC2H 8JD
Tel: 020 7437 9011
Fax: 020 7208 3709
Website: www.emapmagazines.co.uk
Magazine for men covering general
interest, film, literature, music and
fashion.
Lead time: 6-8 weeks
Circulation: 100,000

**Ariel**
*(Weekly, Tues)*
MC2 A1 Media Centre
Media Village,
2001 Wood Lane
London W12 7TQ
Tel: 020 7765 3623
Fax: 020 7765 3646
email: claire.barrett@bbc.co.uk
Editor: Andrew Harvey
Deputy Editors: Sally Hillier and
Cathy Loughran
BBC staff magazine.
Lead time: Tuesday before
publication
Circulation: 24,000

**Art Monthly**
Britannia Art Publications Ltd.
4th Floor
28 Charing Cross Road
London WC2H 0DB
Tel: 020 7240 0389
Fax: 020 7497 0726
email: info@artmonthly.co.uk
Website: www.artmonthly.co.uk
Editor: Patricia Bickers
Deputy Editor: Andrew Wilson
Aimed at artists, art dealers, teachers,
students, collectors, arts
administrators, and all those
interested in contemporary visual art.
Includes a review section covering
exhibitions and books.
Lead time: 4 weeks
Circulation: 4,000 plus

**Asian Times**
*(Weekly, Tues)*
Ethnic Media Group
Whitchapel Technical Centre,
Unit 2
65 Whitechapel Road
London E1 1DU
Tel: 020 7650 2000
Fax: 020 7650 2001
email: asiantimes@easterneyeuk.co.uk
Website: www.ethnicmedia.co.uk
Editor: Isaac Hamza
National weekly newspaper for
Britain's English-speaking Asian
Community.
Press Day: Friday
Circulation: 30,000

**The Big Issue**
*(Weekly, Mon)*
1-5 Wandsworth Road
Vauxhall
London SW8 2LN
Tel: 020 7526 3200
Fax: 020 7526 3201
email: editorial@bigissue.com
Website: www.bigissue.com
Editor: Matt Ford
Deputy Editor (Arts): Charles
Howgego
Film: Leslie Felperin
General interest magazine, with
emphasis on homelessness. Sold by
the homeless.
Lead time: Tues, 3 weeks before
Circulation: ABC figure 122,059

**Black Filmmaker**
Suite 13
5 Blackhorse Lane
London E17 6DS
Tel: 020 85319111
email: bfm@teleregion.co.uk
Website:
www.blackfilmmakermag.com
Editor: Menelik Shabazz
Deputy Editor: Marsha Prescod
Magazine focusing on black film and
television.

**The Bookseller**
VNU Entertainment Media UK Ltd
Endeavour House
189 Shaftesbury Avenue
London WC2H 8TJ
Tel: 020 7420 6103
Fax: 020 74200 6103
Editor: Nicholas Clee
Website: www.thebookseller.com

**Bollywood**
*(Weekly, Tues)*
Ethnic Media Group
Whitchapel Technical Centre,
Unit 2
65 Whitechapel Road
London E1 1DU
Tel: 020 7650 2000
Fax: 020 7650 2001
Website: www.ethnicmedia.co.uk
Annual publication featuring the best
films and the superstars from the
world's most prolific film industry

**British Cinematographer**
Incorporating Eyepiece
Pinewood Studios
Iver Heath
Buckinghamshire SL0 ONH
Tel: 01753 650101
Fax: 01753 650111
Editor: Ron Prince

**Broadcast**
*(Weekly, Fri)*
EMAP Media
33-39 Bowling Green Lane
London EC1R 0DA
Tel: 020 7505 8000
Fax: 020 75058504
Editor: Conor Dignam
email: bcasted@media.emap.co.uk
Website: www.broadcastnow.co.uk
Broadcasting industry news magazine
with coverage of TV, radio, cable and
satellite, corporate production and
international programming and
distribution.
Press day: Wed.
Lead time: 2 weeks  C
irculation: 13,556

**The Business of Film**
*(Monthly)*
41-42 Berners Street
London W1T 3NB
Tel: 020 7372 9992

Fax: 020 73729993
email:
elspeth@thebusinessoffilm.com
Website: www.thebusinessoffilm.com
Publisher/Editor: Elspeth Tavares
Aimed at film industry professionals -
producers, distributors, exhibitors,
investors, financiers.
Lead time: 2 weeks

## Caribbean Times
*(Weekly, Mon)*
**Ethnic Media Group**
**Whitchapel Technical Centre,**
**Unit 2**
**65 Whitechapel Road**
**London E1 1DU**
Tel: 020 7650 2000
Fax: 020 7650 2001
email:
caribbeantimes@ethnicmedia.co.uk
Website: www.ethnicmedia.co.uk
Editor: Ron Shillingford
Editorial Director: Michael Eboda
Tabloid dealing with issues pertinent
to community it serves.
Press day: Fri
Circulation: 25,000

## Cinema Business
*(10 issues per year)*
**Quadrant House, 250 Kennington**
**Lane, London, SE11 5RD.**
Tel: 0845 226 7982
email: mark.moran@landor.co.uk
Subscription based trade magazine
for the exhibition and distribution
sector

## City Life
*(Fortnightly)*
**164 Deansgate**
**Manchester M60 2RD**
Tel: 0161 211 2708
Fax: 0161 839 1488
email:  editorial@citlife.co.uk
Website: www.citylife.co.uk
Editor: David Alan Lloyd
Cinema: Danny Moran
What's on in and around Greater
Manchester.
Circulation: 20,000

## Company
*(Monthly)*
**The National Magazine Company**
**National Magazine House**
**72 Broadwick St.**
**London, W1F 9EP**
Tel: 020 7439 5000
Fax: 020 7437 6886
email: company.mail@natmags.co.uk
Website: www.natmags.co.uk and
www.company.co.uk
Editior: Victoria White

Glossy magazine for women aged 18-30.
Lead time: 10 weeks
Circulation: 330,373

## Cosmopolitan
*(Monthly)*
**National Magazine House**
**72 Broadwick Street**
**London W1V 2BP**
Tel: 020 7439 5000
Fax: 02074376886
email: cosmo.mail@natmags.co.uk
Website: www.natmags.co.uk and
www.cosmopolitan.co.uk
Editor: Sam Baker
Lyifestyle magazine for women aged
18-35.
Lead time: 12 weeks
Circulation: 463,058

## Creation International
*(Monthly)*
**Hardware Creations Ltd.**
**48 The Broadway**
**Maidenhead**
**Berkshire SL6 1PW**
Tel: 01628773935
email: dick@hardwarecreations.tv
Website: www.broadcast-
hardware.com
Editor: Dick Hobbs
Film, television, new media publication.
Circulation: 12,000

## Creative Review
*(Monthly)*
**Centaur Publishing, St. Giles House**
**50 Poland Street**
**London W1V 4AX**
Tel: 020 79704000
Fax: 020 7970 4099
Website: www.mad.co.uk/cr/index.asp
Editor: Patrick Burgoyne
Publisher: Jess MacDermot
Trade paper for creative people covering
film, advertising and design. Film
reviews, profiles and technical features.
Lead time: 4 weeks
Circulation: 19,000

## Cult Times
**Visual Imagination Limited**
**9 Blades Court, Deodar Road**
**London SW15 2NU**
Tel: 020 8875 1520
Fax: 020 8875 1588
email: culttimes@visimag.com
Website: www.www.visimag.com
/culttimes
Editor: Paul Spragg
Guide to Cult TV

## Daily Mail
**Associated Newspaper Holdings**
**Northcliffe House**
**2 Derry Street**

**London W8 5TT**
Tel: 020 7938 6000
Showbusiness Dpt.: 020 79386362
Fax: 020 79384890
Website: www.dailymail.co.uk
Editor: Paul Dacre
Managing Director: Guy Zitter
Entertainment Collumnist: Baz
Bamigboye
Film: Christopher Tookey
TV: Peter Paterson
National daily tabloid newspaper.
Circulation: 2,163,676

## The Daily Star
**Express Newspapers PLC**
**Ludgate House**
**245 Blackfriars Road**
**London SE1 9UX**
Tel: 020 792227373
Fax: 020 7922 7962
email: dailystarnewsdesk@dailystar.co.uk
Website: www.dailystar.co.uk
Editor: Peter Hill
National tabloid daily newspaper.
Circulation: 672,949

## Daily Telegraph
**Telegraph Group Ltd.**
**1 Canada Square**
**Canary Wharf**
**London E14 5DT**
Tel: 020 7538 5000
Fax: 020 7538 6242
Website: www.telegraph.co.uk
Editor: Charles Moore
Film critic: Sukdev Sandhu
Arts Editor: Sarah Crompton
Media Correspondent: Tom Leonard
TV & Entertainment Editor: Marsha
Dunstan
National broadsheet daily newspaper.
Lead time: 1 week
Circulation: 1,214,000

## Diva
*(Monthly)*
**Diva Magazine, Unit M**
**Spectrum House**
**32-34 Gordon House Road**
**London NW5 1LP**
Tel: 020 7424 7400
Fax: 020 7424 7401
email:  edit@divamag.co.uk
Website: www.divamag.co.uk
Editor: Gillian Rodgerson
Magazine on lesbian news and culture.
Lead times: 4-6 weeks
Circulation: 35,000

## Eastern Eye
*(Weekly,Thurs)*
**Ethnic Media Group**
**Whitchapel Technical Centre,**
**Unit 2**

65 Whitechapel Road
London E1 1DU
Tel: 020 7650 2000
Fax: 020 7650 2001
Editor: Amar Singh
Community news and perspectives on British Asian culture. Includes media reviews and indepth features on sports, music, and the arts.
Circulation: 35,000

## The Economist
(Weekly)
25 St James's Street
London SW1A 1HG
Tel: 020 7830 7000
Fax: 020 79300458
email: inquires@economist.com
Website: www.economist.com
Editor: Bill Emmott
Culture Correspondant: Edmund Fawcett
International coverage of major political, social and business developments with arts section.
Press day: Wed
Circulation: 838,030

## Elle
(Monthly)
Covden House, Langley Street,
London WC2H 9JA
Tel: 020 71507000
Fax: 020 71507001
email: sarahbailey@hf-uk.com
Website: www.hachettefilipacchi.co.uk
Editor: Sarah Bailey
General Manager: Julie Harris
Glossy magazine aimed at 18-35 year old career women.
Lead time: 3 months
Circulation: 220,000

## Empire
(Monthly)
Empire Magazine
4th Floor
Mappin House
4 Winsley Street
London W1W 8HF
Tel: 020 74361515
Fax: 020 73438703
email: empire@emap.com
Website: www.empireonline.co.uk
Editor: Colin Kennedy
Quality film monthly incorporating features, interviews and movie news as well as reviews of all new movies and videos.
Lead time: 3 weeks
Circulation: 161,503

## Evening Standard
(Mon-Fri)
*Associate Newspaper Holdings Plc.*

Northcliffe House
2 Derry Street
Kensington
London W8 5TT
Tel: 020 7938 6000
Fax: 02079372648
Website: www.eveningstandard.co.uk
Editor: Veronica Wadley
Film: Neil Norman
Media editor: Victor Sebestyen
London weekday evening paper.
Circulation: 438,136

## The Express
Express Newspapers Ltd.
Hamilton House
1 Temple Avenue
London EC4
Tel:020 7928 8000
Fax: 020 7620 1654
email: editor@express.co.uk
Website: www.express.co.uk
National daily tabloid newspaper
Circulation: 941,790

## The Express on Sunday
Express Newspapers Ltd.
Hamilton House
1 Temple Avenue
London EC4
Tel:020 7928 8000
Fax: 020 7620 1654
email: editor@express.co.uk
Website: www.express.co.uk
Editor: Rosie Boycott
Film: Chris Peachment
TV: Nigel Billen
National Sunday tabloid newspaper.
Circulation: 894,204

## The Face
(Monthly)
Endeavour House
189 Shaftesbury Avenue
London WC2H 8JG
Tel: 02072955000
email: editorial@theface.co.uk
Website: www.theface.co.uk
Film: Alex Rainer
Visual-orientated youth culture magazine: emphasis on music, fashion and films.
Lead time: 4 weeks
Circulation: 100,744

## FHM
(Monthly)
Mappin House,
4 Winsley Street,
London, W1W 8HF
Tel: 020 7859 8657
Fax: 020 78598670
email: jacqui.tangney@emap.com
Website: www.fhm.co.uk
Editor: David Davies

Deputy Editor: David Moynihan
Men's lifestyle magazine.
Lead time: 6 weeks
Circulation: 755,000

## Film Review
(Monthly + 4 specials)
Visual Imagination Ltd.
9 Blades Court, Deodar Road
London SW15 2NU
Tel: 020 8875 1520
Fax: 020 8875 1588
email: filmreview@visimag.com
Website: www.visimag.com/filmreview
Editor: Grant Kempster
Reviews of films on cinema screen and video; star interviews and profiles; book and CD reviews.
Lead time: 1 month
Circulation: 50,000

## Film Waves
(Quarterly)
Obraz Productions Ltd
PO Box 420 Edgware HA8 0XA
Tel: 020 8951 1681
email: filmwaves@filmwaves.co.uk
Website: www.filmwaves.co.uk
Editor/Publisher: Marco Zee-Jotti
Magazine for low/no-budget filmmakers

## Financial Times
1 Southwark Bridge
London SE1 9HL
Tel: 020 7873 3000
Fax: 020 7873 3076
Website: www.ft.com
Editor: Andrew Gowers
Deputy Editor: Chrystia Freeland
National Broadsheet Newspaper giving financial information.
Circulation: 316,578

## Gay Times
(Monthly)
Milliveres Prowler Ltd
Spectrum House
32-34 Gordon House Road
London NW5 1LP
Tel: 020 7424 7400
Fax: 020 7424 7401
email: edit@gaytimes.co.uk
Website: www.gaytimes.co.uk
Arts editor: James Cary Parkes
Britain's leading gay magazine. Extensive film, television and arts coverage
Lead time: 6-8 weeks
Circulation: 65,000

## The Guardian
119 Farringdon Road
London EC1R 3ER
Tel: 020 7278 2332
Fax: 020 7837 2114
email: userhelp@guardian.co.uk

Website: www.guardian.co.uk
Editor: Alan Rusbridger
Media Editor: Charlie Burgess
National broadsheet daily newspaper.
Circulation: 407,870

## Harpers & Queen
(Monthly)
National Magazine House
72 Broadwick Street
London W1F 9EP
Tel: 020 7439 5000
Fax: 020 7439 6886
email:
rebecca.broadley@natmags.co.uk (PA
to Editor)
Website: www.harpersandqueen.co.uk
Editor: Lucy Yeomans
Arts & Films: Sarah Buys
Glossy magazine for women.
Lead time: 12 weeks
Circulation: 88, 049

## Heat
Endeavour House
189 Shaftsbury Avenue
London WC2H 8JG
Tel: 020 7859 8657
Fax: 020 7598670
Website: www.emap.com
email: heat@ecm.emap.com
Editor: Mark Frith

## The Herald
200 Renfield Street
Glasgow
Scotland
G2 3QB
Tel: 01413027000
Fax: 01413027171
email: arts@theherald.co.uk
Website: www.theherald.co.uk
Editor: Harry Reid
Film critic: William Russell
TV editor: Ken Wright
Scottish daily newspaper
Circulation: 107,527

## The Hollywood Reporter
(Daily and Weekly international, Tues)
US Office:
VNU Business Publications
5055 Wilshire Blvd
Los Angeles
CA 90036-4396
UK Office:
50-51 Bedford Row
London WC1R 4LR
Tel: 020 78228301
Fax: 020 72429137
email:
hollywoodreporter@galleon.co.uk
Website: www.hollywoodrepoter.com
Editor-in-Chief/Publisher: Robert J.
Dowling

Editor: Howard Burns
TV Editor: Andrew Grossman
Film Editor: Gregg Kiday
Showbusiness trade paper.
Circulation: 39,000

## Home Entertainment Week
(Weekly, Fri)
Bleeding Edge
3rd Floor, Jordon House
47 Brunswick Place
London N1 6EB
Tel: 020 7608 6767
Fax: 020 7608 6768
email: jhayward@columbus-
group.co.uk
Website: www.heweek.co.uk
Editor: Peter Dodd
Video trade publication for rental
and retail.
Lead time: Monday before
publication
Circulation: 7,613

## i-D Magazine
(Monthly)
US Office:
116 East 27th Street/ Floor 6
New York
NY 10016
Tel: 212 4471400
Fax: 212 4475231
UK Office:
Universal House
124 Tabbernacle Street
London EC2A 4SA
Tel: 020 7490 9710
Fax: 020 7251 2225
email: idedit@fwpubs.com
Website: www.idonline.com
Editor: Julie Lasky
Film & TV: David Cox
Youth/fashion magazine with film
features
Lead time: 6-8 weeks
Circulation: 65,000

## Illustrated London News
(2 pa)
20 Upper Ground
London SE1 9PF
Tel: 020 7805 5555
Fax: 020 7805 5911
email: iln@ilng.co.uk
Website: www.ilng.co.uk
Editor: Alison Booth
News, pictorial record and
commentary, and a guide to coming
events
Lead time: 8-10 weeks
Circulation: 30,000

## In Camera
(Quarterly)
Kodak House

Entertainment Imaging
P.O Box 9b
Thanmes Ditton
Surrey KT7 OBR
Tel: 01442 844875
Fax: 01442 844987
Website: www.kodak.com
Editor: Martin Pearce
Business editor: Elisabete Perazzi
Journal for motion picture industry,
primarily for cinematographers, but
also for other technicians and anyone
in the industry
Lead time: 4 weeks
Circulation: 45,000

## The Independent on Sunday
Independent House
191 Marsh Wall
London E14 9RS
Tel: 020 7005 2000
Fax: 020 7005 2627
email: newseditor@independent
.co.uk
Website: www.independent.co.uk
National broadsheet Sunday
newspaper.
Lead time: 2 weeks
Circulation: 227,959

## The Independent
Independent House
191 Marsh Wall
London E14 9RS
Tel: 020 7293 2000
Fax: 020 7293 2047
email: newseditor@independent.co.uk
Website: www.independent.co.uk
Editor(s): Simon Kelner & Janet
Street-Porter
National broadsheet daily newspaper.
Circulation: 224,897

## International Connection
Brave New World International Ltd.
Orchardton House
Auchencairn
Dumfries & Galloway
DG7 1QL
Tel: 08451306249
Fax: 08456588329
email: susan@bnw.demon.co.uk
Website: www.filmtvdir.com
Editor: Lauren Courtney
Publisher: Susan Foster
Film and TV industry business
magazine.

## Interzone
(Monthly)
David Pringle
C/o Interzone
217 Preston Drove
Brighton BN1 6FL
Tel: 01273 504710

email: interzone@cix.co.uk
Website: www.sfsite.com/interzone
Editor/Publisher: David Pringle
Film: Nick Lowe
Science-fiction and fantasy magazine.
Lead time: 8 weeks
Circulation: 10,000

### The List
(Fortnightly, Thur)
14 High Street
Edinburgh EH1 1TE
Tel: 0131 550 3050
Fax: 0131 557 8500
email: mail@list.co.uk
Website: www.list.co.uk
Film editor: Paul Dale
TV: Brian Donaldson
Glasgow/Edinburgh events guide
Lead time: 1 week
Circulation: 18,000

### Mail on Sunday
Associated Newspaper Holdings Ltd.
Northcliffe House
2 Derry Street
London  W8 5TT
Tel: 020 7938 6000
Fax: 020 79384890
Website: www.mailonsunday.co.uk
Editor: Peter Wright
Film: Sebastian Faulks
TV critic: Jaci Stephen
National Sunday tabloid newspaper.
Press day: Fri/Sat
Circulation: 2,325,618

### Marie Claire
(Monthly)
13th Floor Kings Reach Tower
Stamford Street
London SE1 9LS
Tel: 020 704445000
Fax: 020 7261 5277
Website: www.ipcmedia.com
Editor: Marie O'Riordan
Women's magazine
Lead time: 3 months
Circulation: 457,034

### Media Week
(Weekly, Thur)
Quantum House
19 Scarbrook Road
Croydon CR9 ILX
Tel: 020 85654326
Fax: 020 8565 4394
email: mweeked@mediaweek.co.uk
Website: www.mediaweek.co.uk
Editor: Tim Burrowes
Deputy Editor: Mike Butcher
News magazine aimed at the
advertising and media industries.
Press day: Wed
Circulation: 13,209 ABC

### The Mirror
Mirror Group Newspapers Ltd.
1 Canada Square
Canary Wharf
London E14 5AP
Tel: 020 7293 3000
Fax: 020 72932435
email: feedback@mirror.co.uk
Website: www.mirror.co.uk
Editor: Piers Morgan
Film/TV Editor: Nicola Methuen
Film Critic: Kevin O'Sullivan
National tabliod daily newspaper
with daily/weekly film and television
column.
Circulation: 1,841,000
incorporating The Daily Record
(Scottish daily newspaper)

### Mojo
Mappin House
4 Winsley Street
London W1W 8HF
Tel: 020 7436 1515
Circulation: 104,437

### Movie Club News
Orchardton House
Auchencairn
Dumfries & Galloway
DG7 1QL
Tel: 0845 1306249
Fax: 0845 658 83429
email:  edit@bnw.demon.co.uk
Website: www.review.uk.com
Circulation: 60,000

### Movie Idols
Visual Imagination Limited
9 Blades Court
Deodar Road
London SW15 2NU
Fax: 020 8875 1588
email: movieidolss@visimag.com
Website: www.visimag.com
/movieidols
Film Review's poster magazine with
film facts and pictures from
blockbusters.

### New Musical Express
(Weekly, Wed)
25th Floor
King's Reach Tower
Stamford Street
London SE1 9LS
Tel: 08704445000
Fax: 020 7261 5185
Website: www.nme.com
Editor: Conor McNicholas
Film/TV editor: John Mulvey
Rock music newspaper
Lead time: Mon, 1 week before press

day
Circulation: 72,557

### New Statesman and Society
(Weekly, Fri)
7th Floor,
Victoria Station House
191 Victoria Street
London SW1E 5NE
Tel: 020 7828 1232
Fax: 020 7828 1881
email:  info@newstatesman.co.uk
Website: www.newstatesman.co.uk
Editor: Peter Wilby
Art Director: David Gibbons
Independent radical journal of
political, social and cultural
comment.
Press day: Mon
Circulation: 26,000

### News of the World
News Group Newspapers Ltd.
1 Virginia Street
London E1 9XR
Tel: 020 77824000
Fax: 020 75839504
email: ricky.sutton@news-of-the-
world.co.uk
Website: www.newsoftheworld.co.uk
Editor: Ricky Sutton
Films: Johnathon Ross
TV critic: Charles Catchpole
National Sunday tabloid newspaper.
Press day: Sat
Circulation: 4,003,000

### The Observer
(Weekly, Sun)
119 Farringdon Road
London EC1R 3ER
Tel: 020 7278 2332
Fax: 020 7713 4250
email: media@guardian.co.uk
Website: observer.guardian.co.uk
Arts editor: Jane Ferguson
Film critic: Philip French
TV: Mike Bradley
National daily broadsheet newspaper.
Lead time: 1 week
Press day: Fri
Circulation: 450,831

### The PACT Magazine
Producers Alliance for Cinema and
Television
C21 Media
Top Floor, 25 Phipp Street
London EC2 A4NP
Tel: 020 7729 7460
Fax: 020 7729 7461
email: Louise@c21media.net
Website: www.pact.co.uk
Editor: Louise Bateman

PACT members' monthly.
Circulation: 2,000

### The People
(Weekly, Sunday)
1 Canada Square
Canary Wharf
London E14 5AP
Tel: 020 7510 3000
Fax: 020 7293 3280
Website: www.people.co.uk
Editor: Mark Thomas
National Sunday newspaper.
Press day: Sat
Circulation: 1,400,000

### Picture House
(Annual)
Cinema Theatre Association
c/o Neville C Taylor
Flat 1, 128 Gloucester Terrace
London W2 6HP
Tel: 01444 246893
email: nevtaylor@freeuk.com
Editor: Allen Eyles
Documents the past and present
history of cinema buildings.
Lead time: 8 weeks
Circulation: 2,000

### Pink Paper The
(Weekly, Thur)
2n Floor Medius House
63-69 New Oxford Street
London WC1A 1DG
Tel: 020 7845 4300
Fax: 020 78454309
email: editorial@pinkpaper.co.uk
Website: www.pinkpaper.com
Editor: Tristan Reid Smith
Assistant Editor: Simon Swift
Film/TV: Simon Swift
Britain's national lesbian and gay
newspaper.
Lead time: 14 days
Circulation: 53,780[d]

### PIX
c/o BFI Publishing
21 Stephen Street
London W1T 1LN
Tel: 020 7957 4789
Fax: 020 7636 2516
Editor/Designer: Ilona Halberstadt
A counterpoint of images and critical
texts, PIX brings together
experimental, independent and
commercial cinema from all over the
world and explores its relation to
other arts.

### Pocket Films
Rosedale House
Rosedale Road
Richmond
Surrey TW9 2SZ

Tel: 020 8939 9017/07931741419
email: pocketfilms@yahoo.com
Editor: Tony Franks
Two publications: The London
Cinema Map (published quarterly)
and Pocket Films (published weekly,
scheduled re-launch Autumn 2002).
The London Cinema Map is a visual
guide to the location of the capital's
100-plus cinemas.
Circulation: Up to 200,000

### Press Gazette
19 Scarbrook Road
Croydon
Surrey CR9 1LX
Tel: 020 8565 4473
Fax: 020 8565 4395
email: pged@app.co.uk
Website: www.pressgazette.co.uk
Editor: Ian Reeves
Weekly magazine covering all aspects
of the media industry: journalism;
advertising; broadcast; freelance.
Press day: Thurs
Circulation: 8,500

### Q
(Monthly)
1st Floor
Mappin House
4 Winsley Street
London W1W 8HF
Tel: 020 74361515
Fax: 020 73479305
email: Qmagazine@Q4music.com
Website: www.qonline.co.uk
Editor: Paul Rees
Specialist music magazine for 18-45
year olds. Includes reviews of new
albums, films and books
Lead time: 2 months
Circulation: 212,607

### Radio Times
(Weekly, Tues)
80 Wood Lane
London W12 0TT
Tel: 0870 6084455
Fax: 020 8433 3923
email: radio.times@bbc.co.uk
Website: www.radiotimes.com
Editor: Gill Hudson
Films: Barry Norman
Weekly guide to UK television, radio
and satellite programmes.
Lead time: 14 days
Circulation: 1,157,481

### Regional Film & Video
(Monthly)
Flagship Publishing
48-50 York Street
Belfast BT15 1AS
Tel: 028 9031 9008

Fax: 028 9072 7800
email:
rfvnewscopy@flagshipmedia.co.uk
Website: www.4rfv.co.uk
Editor: Gavin Bell
Film and Video Trade Newspaper.
Circulation: 12,000

### Satellite TV Europe
Highbury – WV
53-79 Highgate Road
London NW5 1TW
Tel: 020 73311000
Fax: 020 73311273
email: mail@satellitetvtoday.com
Website: www.satellitetvtoday.com
Editor: Paul Hirons
Circulation: 100,000

### The Scotsman
The Scotsman Publications Ltd.
Barclay House
108 Holyrood Road
Edinburgh EH8 8AS
Tel: 0131 620 8620
Fax: 0131 620 8616
email: Jmcgurk@scotsman.com
Website: www.scotsman.com
Editorial Director: John McGurk
Assistant Editor: Charlotte Ross
Arts Editor: Andrew Eaton
Film Editor: Alistair Mackay
Scottish daily newspaper.
Circulation: 77,057

### Scotland on Sunday
The Scotsman Publications Ltd.
Barclay House
108 Holyrood Road
Edinburgh EH8 8AS
Tel: 0131 620 8620
Fax: 0131 620 8616
Website: www.scotsman.com
email: Jmcgurk@scotsman.com
Arts & Film Editor: Fiona Leith
Scottish Sunday newspaper.
Lead time: 10 days
Circulation: 110,000

### Screen Digest
(Monthly)
Lyme House Studios
38 Georgiana Street
London NW1 0EB
Tel: 020 7424 2820
Fax: 020 7580 0060
email: editorial@screendigest.com
Website: www.screendigest.com
Managing director: Allan Hardy
Editor: David Fisher
Executive editor: Ben Keen
Deputy editor: Mark Smith
International industry news digest
and research report covering film,
television, cable, satellite, video and

other multimedia information. Has a centre page reference system every month on subjects like law, statistics or sales.

## Screen Finance
*(Fortnightly)*
**Informa Media**
**Mortimer House**
**37-41 Mortimer Street**
**London W1T 3JH**
Website: www.infomamedia.com
Tel: 020 70174248
Fax: 020 7017 4289
Editor: Tim Adler
Detailed analysis and news coverage of the film and television industries in the UK and Europe
Lead time: 1-3 days

## Screen International
*(Weekly, Thur)*
**EMAP Media**
**33-39 Bowling Green Lane**
**London EC1R 0DA**
Tel: 020 7505 8000
Fax: 020 7505 8117
email:
Leo.Barraclough@media.emap.co.uk
Website: www.screendaily.com
Managing Editor: Leo Barraclough
UK Film Editor: Adam Minns
Features Editor: Louise Tutt
News & Analysis Editor: Tim Dams
International trade magazine for the film, television, video, cable and satellite industries. Regular news, features, production information from around the world
Press day: Tue
Features lead time: 3 months
Circulation: 10,000

## Screen
*(Quarterly)*
**The Gilmorehill Centre**
**University of Glasgow**
**Glasgow G12 8QQ**
Tel: 0141 330 5035
Fax: 0141 330 3515
email: screen@arts.gla.ac.uk
Website: www.screen.arts.gla.ac.uk
Editorial Assistant: Caroline Beven
Journal of essays, reports, debates and reviews on film and television studies. Organises the annual Screen Studies Conference
Circulation: 1,400

## SFX
**Future Publishing**
**99 Baker Street**
**London W1M 1FB**
Tel: 0207 3172600
Fax: 0207 4865678

email: sfx@futurenet.co.uk
Website: www.sfx.co.uk
Editor: Dave Golder
Circulation: 39,603

## Shivers
*(Monthly)*
**Visual Imagination Ltd**
**9 Blades Court**
**Deodar Road**
**London SW15 2NU**
Website: www.visimag.com
Tel: 020 8875 1520
Fax: 020 8875 1588
Editor: David Miller
Horror film reviews and features.
Lead time: 1 month
Circulation: 30,000

## Sight and Sound
*(Monthly)*
**British Film Institute**
**21 Stephen Street**
**London W1T 1LN**
Tel: 020 7255 1444
Fax: 020 7436 2327
Editor: Nick James
Incorporating 'Monthly Film Bulletin'. Includes regular columns, feature articles, a book review section and review/synopsis/credits of every feature film theatrically released, plus a brief listing of every video
Copy date: 4th of each month
Circulation: 25,000

## South Wales Argus
**Cardiff Road**
**Maesglas**
**Newport**
**Gwent NP20 3QN**
Tel: 01633 810000
Fax: 01633 777202
email: kevin.ward@gwent-wales.co.uk
Website: www.thisisgwent.co.uk
Editor: Gerry Keighley
Deputy Editor: Kevin Ward
Film & TV editor: Lesley Williams
Regional evening newspaper
Lead time: 2 weeks
Circulation: 32,569

## The Spectator
*(Weekly, Thur)*
**56 Doughty Street**
**London WC1N 2LL**
Tel: 020 7405 1706
Fax: 020 7242 0603
email: editor@spectator.co.uk
Website: www.spectator.co.uk
Editor: Boris Johnson
Arts editor: Elizabeth Anderson
Film: Mark Steyn
TV: James Delingpole and Simon Hoggart

Independent review of politics, current affairs, literature and the arts.
Press day: Wed
Circulation: 60,000

## Stage Screen & Radio
*(10 issues a year)*
**BECTU**
**373-377 Clapham Road**
**London SW9 9BT**
Tel: 020 73460900
Fax: 020 73460901
email: info@bectu.org.uk
Website: www.bectu.org.uk
Editor: Janice Turner
Journal of the film, broadcasting, theatre and entertainment union BECTU. Reporting and analysis of these industries and the union's activities plus coverage of technological developments.
Lead time: 4 weeks
Circulation: 34,600

## The Stage
*(Weekly, Thurs)*
**The Stage Newspaper Ltd.**
**47 Bermondsey Street**
**London SE1 3XT**
Tel: 020 7403 1818
Fax: 020 7357 9287
email: editor@thestage.co.uk
Website: www.thestage.co.uk
Editor: Brian Atwood
Weekly trade paper covering all aspects of entertainment.
Circulation: 40,198 ABC

## Starburst
*(Monthly + 4 Specials + German language version)*
**Visual Imagination**
**9 Blades Court**
**Deodar Road**
**London SW15 2NU**
Tel: 020 8875 1520
Fax: 020 8875 1588
email: starburst@visimag.com
Website: www.visimag.com/starburst
Group Editor: Stephen Payne
Editor: Gary Gillat
Magazine covering science fiction, fantasy and horror films, television and video.
Lead time: 1 month
Circulation: 45,000

## Stardust
*(Monthly)*
**Magna Publishing Co. (UK) Ltd.**
**1st Floor**
**1 Blandford Street**
**London W1U 3DA**
Tel: 0207 224 2600
Fex: 0207 224 2699

email: stardustmag@aol.com
Editor: Ashwin Varde
Magazine focusing on Indian cinema.
Circulation: 207,787

### Stills Audio Motion
SAM Publications
15 Marden Road
Staplehurst
Kent TN12 0NF
Tel: 0158 089 1683
Fax: 0158 089 0143
email: stillsaudiomotion@talk21.com
Editor: Steve Bergson

### The Sun
PO Box 481
1 Virginia Street
London E1 9XP
Tel: 020 7782 4000
Fax: 020 7488 3253
Website: www.thesun.co.uk
Editor: Rebecca Wade
Showbiz Editor: Victoria Newton
TV Features: Beth Adams
National daily tabloid newspaper
Circulation: 3,875,329

### Sunday Mirror
Mirror Group Newspapers Ltd.
1 Canada Square
Canary Wharf
London E14 5AP
Tel: 020 7293 3000
Fax: 020 72932435
email: feedback@mirror.co.uk
Website: www.mirror.co.uk
Film critic: Quentin Falk
TV: David Rowe, Pam Francis
National Sunday tabloid newspaper.
Circulation: 2,268,263

### Sunday Telegraph
Telegraph Group Ltd.
1 Canada Square
Canary Wharf
London E14 5AP
Tel: 020 7538 5000
Fax: 020 7538 6242
email: starts@telegraph.co.uk
Website: www.telegraph.co.uk
Arts: Susannah Herbert
Film: Jenny McCartney
TV: John Preston
National Sunday broadsheet
newspaper.
Circulation: 886,377

### Sunday Times
1 Pennington Street
London E98 1TT
Tel: 020 7782 5000
Website: www.the-times.co.uk
Editor: John Witherow
National broadsheet Sunday
newspaper.

Press day: Wed
Circulation: 1,314,576

### Talking Pictures
(Quarterly)
1 Orchard Cottages
Colebrook
Plympton
Plymouth PL7 4AJ
Tel: 01752 347200
email: valis23a@aol.com
Website: www.talkingpix.co.uk
Editor: Nigel Watson
Online magazine (formerly Talking
Pictures) devoted to a serious yet
entertaining look at film, computer
entertainment, television and
video/DVD.

### Tatler
(Monthly)
Vogue House
1 Hanover Square
London W1S 1JU
Tel: 020 7499 9080
Fax: 020 74931345
Website: www.tatler.co.uk
Editorial Director: Vassi Chamberlain
Arts Editor: Camila Long
Features Editor: Kate Bernard
Smart society magazine favouring
profiles, fashion and the arts.
Lead time: 3 months
Circulation: 88,235

### Telegraph Magazine
Telegraph Group Ltd.
1 Canada Square
Canary Wharf
London E14 5DT
Tel: 020 7538 5000
Fax: 020 75386242
Website: www.telegraph.co.uk
TV films: Jessamy Calkin
Supplement to Saturday edition of
the Daily Telegraph
Lead time: 6 weeks
Circulation: 1,300,000

### Television
(10 p.a.)
Royal Television Society
Holborn Hall
100 Gray's Inn Road
London WC1X 8AL
Tel: 020 7430 1000
Fax: 020 7430 0924
email: info@rts.org.uk
Website: www.rts.org.uk
Editor: Steve Clarke
Television trade magazine
Lead time: 2 weeks
Circulation: 4,000

### Televisual
(Monthly)

St. Giles House
50 Poland Street
London W1F 7AX
Tel: 020 7970 6446
Fax: 020 7970 6733
email: tvlcirc@centaur.co.uk
Website: www.televisual.com
Editor: Mundy Ellis
Features Editor: James Hamilton
Monthly business magazine for
production professionals in the
business of moving pictures
News lead time: 1 month
Features lead time: 2 months
Circulation: 6,000

### Time Out
(Weekly, Tues)
Universal House
251 Tottenham Court Road
London W1P 7AB
Tel: 020 7813 3000
Fax: 020 7813 6001
Website: www.timeout.co.uk
Editor: Laura Lee Davis
Film: Geoff Andrew, Tom Charity
TV: Alkarim Jivani
London listings magazine with
cinema and television sections.
Listings lead time: 8 days
Features lead time: 1 week
Circulation: 100,000 plus

### The Times Educational Supplement Scotland
(Weekly, Fri)
Scott House
10 South St Andrew Street
Edinburgh EH2 2AZ
Tel: 0131 557 1133
Fax: 0131 558 1155
email: scoted@tes.co.uk
Website: www.tes.co.uk/scotland
Editor: Olga Wojtas
Press day: Wed
Circulation: 10,000

### The Times Educational Supplement
(Weekly, Fri)
Admiral House
66-68 East Smithfield
London E1 1BX
Tel: 020 7782 3000
Fax: 020 7782 3333
email: editor@tes.co.uk
Website: www.tes.co.uk
Editor: Bob Doe
Deputy Editor: David Budge
Review editor, Friday magazine:
Geraldine Brennan
Press day: Tuesday
Lead itme for reviews: copy 14-21
days
Circulation: 157,000

## The Times Higher Educational Supplement

(*Weekly, Fri*)
**Admiral House**
**66-68 East Smithfield**
**London E1 1BX**
Tel: 020 7782 3000
Fax: 020 7782 3333
email: editor@thes.co.uk
Editor: John O'leary
Deputy Editor: Gerard Kelly
Press day: Wed
Lead time for reviews: copy 10 days
before publication
Circulation: 26,666

## The Times Literary Supplement

(*Weekly, Fri*)
**Admiral House**
**66-68 East Smithfield**
**London E1W 1BX**
Tel: 020 7782 3000
Fax: 020 7782 3100
email: lettersethe-tls.co.uk
Website: www.the-tls.co.uk
Arts editor: Will Eaves
Press day: Tues
Lead time: 2 weeks
Circulation: 35,000

## The Times

**1 Pennington Street**
**London E98 1TT**
Tel: 020 7782 5000
Website: www.the-times.co.uk
Editor: Robert Tomson
Film/video critic: Geoff Brown
Film writer: David Robinson
TV: Matthew Bond
National daily newspaper
Circulation: 747,054

## Total Film

**Future Publishing**
**99 Baker Street**
**London W1M 1FB**
Tel: 020 7317 2600
Fax: 020 74865678
email: totalfilm@futurenet.co.uk
Website: www.futurenet.co.uk
Editor: Matt Mueller

## Tribune

(*Weekly, Fri*)
**9 Arkwright Road**
**London NW3 6AN**
Tel: 020 7433 6410
Fax: 020 74336419
email: mail@tribuneweekly.com
Website: www.tribuneweekly.com
Editor: Mark Seddon
Review editor: Caroline Rees

Political and cultural weekly that
covers issues concerning the labour
and trade union movements.
Lead time: 14 days
Circulation: 10,000

## TV Choice

**H. Bauer Publishing**
**Academic House,**
**24-28 Oval Road,**
**London NW1 7DT**
Tel: 020 7241 8000
Circulation: 1,017,468

## TV & Satellite Week

(*Weekly, Tues*)
**IPC Media**
**King's Reach Tower**
**Stamford Street**
**London SE1 9LS**
Website: www.tvandsatelliteweek.com
Editor: Jonathan Bowman
Circulation: 224,003

## TV Times

(*Weekly, Tues*)
**IPC Media**
**King's Reach Tower**
**Stamford Street**
**London SE1 9LS**
Website: www.ipcmedia.com
Tel: 020 7261 7000
Fax: 020 7261 7777
Editor: Mike Hollinsworth
Film editor: David Quinlan
Weekly magazine of listings and
features serving viewers of trestrial,
satellite and radio programmes.
Lead time: 6 weeks
Circulation: 524,131

## TV Quick

**H. Bauer Publishing**
**Academic House,**
**24-28 Oval Road,**
**London NW1 7DT**
Tel: 020 7241 8000
Circulation: 375,780

## TV Zone

(Monthly + 4 specials)
**Visual Imagination Limited**
**9 Blades Court**
**Deodar Road**
London SW15 2NU
Tel: 020 8875 1520
Fax: 020 8875 1588
email: tvzone@visimag.com
Website: www.visimag.com/tvzone
Editor: Tom Spilsbury
Magazine of cult television, past,
present and future, with emphasis on
science fiction and fantasy
Lead time: 1 month
Circulation: 45,000

## Ultimate DVD

**Visual Imagination Limited**
**9 Blades Court**
**Deodar Road**
**London SW15 2NU**
Tel: 020 8875 1520
Fax: 020 8875 1588
email: ultimatedvd@visimag.com
Website:
www.visimag.com/ultimatedvd
Magazine for DVD buyers

## Uncut

**IPC Magazines Ltd**
**King's Reach Tower**
**Stamford Street**
**London SE1 9LS**
Tel: 020 7261 6992
Fax: 020 7261 5573
Website: www.uncut.net
Editor: Allan Jones
Art Editor: Kerrin Hands
Circulation: 111,167

## Variety

(*Weekly, Mon*) *and Daily* (*Mon-Fri*)
**7th Floor**
**88 Theobalds Road**
**London WC1X 8RR**
Tel: 020 7611 4580
Fax: 020 7611 4591
email: news@reedbusiness.com
Website: www.variety.com
International Sales Director: Lionel
O'Hara
European editor: Adam Dawtrey
International showbusiness
newspaper
Press day: Thurs
Circulation: 36,000

## Viewfinder

(*4 p.a.*)
**BUFVC**
**77 Wells Street**
**London W1T 3QJ**
Tel: 020 7393 1500
Fax: 020 7393 1555
email: ask@bufvc.ac.uk
Website: www.bufvc.ac.uk
Editor: Hetty Malcom-Smith
Periodical for people in higher
education and further education and
research, includes articles on the
production, study and use of film,
television and related media. Also
includes supplement Media Online
Focus Deadlines: 25 January, 24 April,
24 August, 25 October
Lead time: 6 weeks
Circulation: 5,000

## Vogue

(*Monthly*)
*Conde Nast Publications Ltd.*

Vogue House
Hanover Square
London W1R 0AD
Tel: 020 7499 9080
Fax: 020 7493 1345
email: voguemagaizne@codenast.com
Website: www.vogue.com
Editor: Alexandra Shulman
Films: Susie Forbes
Glossy magazine for women
Lead time: 12 weeks
Circulation: 201,187

## The Voice

*(Weekly, Monday)*
Vee Tee Ay (Media) Resources Ltd.
Nu Vox House
Coldharbour Lane
London SW9 8PL
Tel: 020 7737 7377
Fax: 020 7274 8994
email: mail@the-voice.co.uk
Website: www.voice-online.net
Editor in chief: Mike Best
Arts: Diedre Forbes
Britain's leading black newspaper
with mainly 18-35 age group
readership. Regular film, television
and video coverage. Supplements
include W2W and Young Voices.
Press day: Friday
Circulation: 40,000

## Webuser

IPC Media
King's Reach Tower
Stamford Street
London SE1 9LS
Website: web-user.co.uk
Editor: Richard Clark

## What's On In London

*(Weekly, Tues)*
180 Pentonville Road
London N1 9LB
Tel: 020 7278 4393
Fax: 020 7837 5838
Website:
www.whatsoninlondon.co.uk
Editor: Michael Darvell
Films & Video: Rachel Holdsworth
Publisher: E G Shaw
London based weekly covering
cinema, theatre, music, arts, books,
entertainment and video
Press day: Friday
Lead time: 10 days
Circulation: 35,000

## What's On TV

*(Weekly, Tues)*
King's Reach Tower
London SE1 9LS
Tel: 020 7261 7769
Fax: 020 7261 7739

email: colin.touch@ipcmedia.com
Editor: Colin Tough
Publisher: Rachel Pearce
TV listings magazine
Lead time: 3 weeks
Circulation: 1,654,843

## Xposé

Visual Imagination Limited
9 Blades Court
Deodar Road
London SW15 2NU
Tel: 020 8875 1520
Fax: 020 8875 1588
email: expose@visimag.com
Website: www.visimag.com/expose
Explores the world of fantastic films
and TV programmes

# BBC Radio

## 1Xtra

Broadcasting House
London W1A 1AA
Tel: 020 7224 2424
email: 1xtra@bbc.co.uk
Website: www.bbc.co.uk/1xtra
Radio Station playing Hip Hop, RnB,
Garage,Dance Hall, Drum & Bass ect.

## BBC Radio 1

London W1N 4DJ
Tel: 08700 100 100
Text: 81199
email: one.world@bbc.co.uk
Website: www.bbc.co.uk/readio1

## BBC Radio 2

Broadcasting House
London W1A 1AA
Tel: 020 7224 2424
Website: www.bbc.co.uk/radio2

## BBC Radio 3

Broadcasting House
London W1A 1AA
Tel: 020 7224 2424
Website: www.bbc.co.uk/radio3

## BBC Radio 4

Broadcasting House
London W1A 1AA
Tel: 020 7224 2424
Website: www.bbc.co.uk/radio4
Controller: Helen Boaden
Talk shows including Women's Hour.

## BBC Radio 5 Live

Room 2605
Television Centre
Wood Lane
London W12 7RJ
Tel: 08700 100 500
Website: www.bbc.co.uk/fivelive
BBC's sport station.

## BBC 6 Music

BBC Western House
London W1A 1AA
Tel: 020 7224 2424
email: 6music@bbc.co.uk
Website: www.bbc.co.uk/6music
Pop and rock music from the
contemporary to the classic.

## BBC 7

Room 1003
BBC Broadcasting House
London W1A 1AA
Tel: 0207 7224 2424
email: bbc7@bbc.co.uk
Website: www.bbc.co.uk/bbc7
One of the BBC's new digital radio
networks.

## BBC Asian Network
PO Box 869
Birmingham B5 7ZA
Tel: 08459440445
Website:
www.bbc.co.uk/asiannetwork
See website for contacts for individual
presenters/shows
BBC's station for UK Asian
communities.

## BBC Radio Berkshire
PO Box 104.4
Reading
Berkshire RG4 8TZ
Tel: 0118 946 4200
Fax: 0118 946 4555
email: radio.berkshire@bbc.co.uk
Website: www.bbc.co.uk/berkshire
Editor: Marianne Bell

## BBC Radio Bristol
Broadcasting House
Whiteladies Road
Bristol BS8 2LR
Tel: 0117 973 2211
email: radio.bristol@bbc.co.uk
Website: www.bbc.co.uk/bristol

## BBC Radio Cambridgeshire
104 Hills Road
Cambridge
CB2 1LD
Tel: 01223259696
Fax: 01223589870
email: cambs@bbc.co.uk
Website:
www.bbc.co.uk/cambridgeshire
Editor: David Martin

## BBC CWR (Coventry & Warwickshire)
Hold Court
1 Greyfriars Road
Coventry CV1 2WR
Tel: 024 7686 0086
email:
coventry.warwickshire@bbc.co.uk
Website:
www.bbc.co.uk/coventrywarwickshire
Editor: Keith Beech

## BBC Radio Cleveland
Broadcasting House
Newport Road
Middlesbrough TS1 5DG
Tel: 01642 225211
Fax: 01642 219 837
email: bbcradiocleveland@bbc.co.uk
Website: www.bbc.co.uk/cleveland
Managing Editor: Andrew Glover

## BBC Radio Cornwall
Phoenix Wharf
Truro
Cornwall TR1 1UA
Tel: 01872 275421
Fax: 01872 240679
email: radio.cornwall@bbc.co.uk
Website: www.bbc.co.uk/cornwall
Managing Editor: Pauline Causey

## BBC Radio Cumbria
Annetwell Street
Carlisle
Cumbria CA3 8BB
Tel: 01228 592 444
Fax: 01228 640 079
email: radio.cumbria@bbc.co.uk
Website: www.bbc.co.uk/cumbria
Editor: Nigel Dyson

## BBC Radio Derby
PO Box 104.5
Derby DE1 3HL
Tel: 01332 361111
Fax: 01332 290794
email:  radio.derby@bbc.co.uk
Website: bbc.co.uk/radioderby
Managing Editor: Simon Cornes

## BBC Radio Devon
Broadcasting House
Seymour Road
Mannamead
Plymouth PL3 5YQ
Tel: 01752 260323
Fax: 01752 234599
email:  john.lilley@bbc.co.uk
Website: www.bbc.co.uk/devon
Editor: John Lilley

## BBC Radio Foyle
Northland Road
Derry/Londonderry  BT48 7GD
Tel: 028 7137 8600
email: foyle@bbc.co.uk
Website:
www.bbc.co.uk/northernierland
Manager: Ana Leddy

## BBC Essex
PO Box 765
Chelmsford
Essex  CM2 9XB
Tel: 01245 616000
Fax: 01245 492983
email:  essex@bbc.co.uk
Website: www.bbc.co.uk/essex
Station Manager: Margaret Hyde

## BBC Radio Gloucester
London Road
Gloucester
GL1 1SW
Tel: 01452 308 585
Fax: 01452 309 491
email: radio.gloucester@bbc.co.uk
Website: www.bbc.co.uk/gloucester
Editor: Mark Hurrell

## BBC GMR
PO Box 951
Oxford Road
Manchester M60 1SD
Tel: 0161 200 2000
Fax: 0161 228 6110
email: gmr@bbc.co.uk
Website: www.bbc.co.uk/gmr
Editor: Steve Taylor

## BBC Radio Guernsey
Broadcasting House
Bulwer Avenue
St. Sampson's
Guernsey GY2 4LA
Tel: 01481 200 600
Fax: 01481 200 373
email: radio.guernsey@bbc.co.uk
Website: www.bbc.co.uk/guernsey
Editor: Rod Holms

## BBC Hereford & Worcester
Hylton Road
Worcester WR2 5WW
Tel: 01905 748485
43 Broad Street
Hereford HR4 9WW
Tel: 01432355252
email: bbch@bbc.co.uk
Website:
www.bbc.co.uk/herefordandworcester

## BBC Radio Humberside
9 Chapel Street
Hull HU1 3NU
Tel: 01482 323232
Fax: 01482 226409
email: radio.humberside@bbc.co.uk
Website: www.bbc.co.uk/humberside
Editor: Helen Thomas

## BBC Radio Jersey
18 Parade Road
St Helier
Jersey JE2 3PL
Tel: 01534 87000
email: radio.jersey@bbc.co.uk
Website: www.bbc.co.uk/jersey
Editor: Denzil Dudley

## BBC Radio Lancashire
20-26 Darwen Street
Blackburn
Lancs  BB2 2EA
Tel: 01254 262411
Fax: 01254 680821
email: radio.lancashire@bbc.co.uk
Website: www.bbc.co.uk/lancashire
Editor: John Clayton

## BBC Radio Leeds
Broadcasting House
Woodhouse Lane
Leeds LS2 9PN
Tel: 0113 224 7300
Fax: 0113 242 0652

email: radio.leeds@bbc.co.uk
Website: www.bbc.co.uk/leeds
Editor: Richard Whitaker

### BBC Radio Leicester
Epic House/9th Floor
Charles Street
Leicester LE1 3SH
Tel: 0116 251 6688
Fax: 0116 251 1463
email: radioleicester@bbc.co.uk
Website:
www.bbc.co.uk/leicester@bbc.co.uk
Editor: Liam McCarthy

### BBC Radio Lincolnshire
PO Box 219
Lincoln LN1 3BQ
Tel: 01522 511411
Fax: 01522 511058
email: radio.lincolnshire@bbc.co.uk
Website: www.bbc.co.uk/lincolnshire
Editor: Charlie Partridge

### BBC Radio London
PO Box 94.9
Marylebone High Street
London W1A 6FL
Tel: 020 7224 2424
email: yourlondon@bbc.co.uk
Website: www.bbc.co.uk/london
Editor: David Robey

### BBC Radio Kent
The Great Hall
Mount Pleasant Road
Tunbridge Wells
Kent TN1 1QQ
Tel: 01892 670 000
Fax: 01892 675 644
email: radio.kent@bbc.co.uk
Website: www.bbc.co.uk/kent

### BBC Radio Merseyside
55 Paradise Street
Liverpool L1 3BP
Tel: 0151 708 5500
Fax: 0151 794 0988
email: radio.merseyside@bbc.co.uk
Website: www.bbc.co.uk/merseyside
Editor: Mick Ord

### BBC Radio Newcastle
Broadcasting Centre
Barrack Road
Newcastle Upon Tyne NE99 1RN
Tel: 0191 232 4141
Fax: 0191 232 5082
email: radio.newcastle@bbc.co.uk
Website: www.bbc.co.uk/newcastle
Editor: Sarah Drummond

### BBC Radio Norfolk
Norfolk Tower
Surrey Street
Norwich NR1 3PA

Tel: 01603 617411
Fax: 01603 633692
email: radionorfolk@bbc.co.uk
Website: www.bbc.co.uk/norfolk
Editor: David Clayton

### BBC Radio Northampton
Broadcasting House
Abington Street
Northampton NN1 2BH
Tel: 01604 239100
Fax: 01604 230709
email:
radionorthhampton@bbc.co.uk
Website:
www.bbc.co.uk/northhampton
Editor: David Clargo

### BBC Radio Nottingham
London Road
Nottingham NG2 4UU
Tel: 0115 955 0500
Fax: 0115 955 0501
email: radio.nottingham@bbc.co.uk
Website: www.bbc.co.uk/nottingham
Editor: Mike Bettison

### BBC Radio Oxford
269 Banbury Road
Oxford OX2 7DW
Tel: 01865889092
Fax: 08459311555
email: oxford.online@bbc.co.uk
Website: www.bbc.co.uk/oxford
Editor: Phil Ashworth

### BBC Radio Scotland
Queen Margaret Drive
Glasgow G12 8DG
email: enquiries.scot@bbc.co.uk
Website: www.bbc.co.uk/scotland
/radioscotland

### BBC Radio Sheffield
54 Shoreham Street
Sheffield S1 4RS
Tel: 0114 2731177
Fax: 0114 2675454
email: radio.sheffield@bbc.co.uk
Website: www.bbc.co.uk/sheffield
Editor: Gary Keown

### BBC Radio Shropshire
2-4 Boscobel Drive
Harlescott
Shrewsbury SY1 3TT
Tel: 017143 248484
Fax: 01743 271702
email: radio.shropshire@bbc.co.uk
Website: www.bbc.co.uk/shropshire
Editor: Tim Pemberton

### BBC Radio Solent
Havelock Road
Southhampton SO14 7PW
Tel: 02380632811

Fax: 02380339648
email: radio.solent@bbc.co.uk
Website: www.bbc.co.uk/solent
Editor: Mia Costello

### BBC Radio Stoke
Cheapside
Hanley
Stoke-on-Trent ST1 1JJ
Tel: 01782 208080
Fax: 01782 289115
email: radio.stoke@bbc.co.uk
Website: www.bbc.co.uk/stoke
Editor: Sue Owen

### BBC Southern Cournties Radio
Broadcasting House
Guildford
Surrey GU2 7AP
Tel: 01483 306306
Fax: 01483 304952
email:
southerncounties.radio@bbc.co.uk
Website:
www.bbc.co.uk/southerncounties
Editor: Mike Hapgood

### BBC Somerset Sound
Broadcasting House
Park Street, Taunton
Somerset TA1 4DA
Tel: 01823 348920
Fax: 01823 332539
email: somerset.sound@bbc.co.uk
Website: www.bbc.co.uk/somerset
Assistant Editor: Simon Clifford

### BBC Radio Suffolk
Broadcasting House
St. Matthew's Street
Ipswich
Suffolk IP1 3EP
Tel: 01473250000
Fax: 01473210997
email: radiosuffolk@bbc.co.uk
Website: www.bbc.co.uk/suffolk
Managing Editor: Gerald Main

### BBC Radio Swindon
PO Box 1234
Swindon
Tel: 01793 513626
Fax: 01793 513650
email: radio.swindon@bbc.co.uk
Website: www.bbc.co.uk/swindon
Editor: Tony Worgan

### BBC Three Counties Radio
1 Hastings Street
Luton LU1 5XL
Tel: 01582 637400
Fax: 01582 401467
email: 3cr@bbc.co.uk
Website: www.bbc.co.uk/3cr
Editor: Mark Norman

## BBC Radio Ulster
PO Box 1116
Belfast BT2 7AJ
Tel: 08700100222
Website:
www.bbc.co.uk/northernireland/radi
oulster

## BBC Radio Wales
Broadasting House
Llandaff
Cardiff CF2 2YQ
Tel: 02920322000
email: radiowales@bbc.co.uk
Website: www.bbc.co.uk/radiowales

## BBC Radio Wiltshire
PO Box 1234
Trowbridge & Salisbury
Tel: 01793 513626
Fax: 01793 513650
email: radio.wiltshire@bbc.co.uk
Website: www.bbc.co.uk/wiltshire
Editor: Tony Worgan

## BBC Radio WM
PO Box 206
Birmingham B5 7SD
Tel: 0121 432 8888
Fax: 0121 414 8817
email: radio.wm@bbc.co.uk
Website: www.bbc.co.uk/wm
Editor: Keith Beech

## BBC World Service
231CB Bush House
Strand
London W12 O2Y
Tel: 020 7557 2941
Fax: 020 7557 1912
email: worldservice.press@bbc.co.uk
Website: www.bbc.co.uk/worldservice

## BBC Radio York
20 Bootham Row
York YO30 7BR
Tel: 01904641351
email:
northyourkshire.radio@bbc.co.uk
Website: www.bbc.co.uk/york
Editor: Matt Youdale

# Independent Radio

## Capital FM Network
30 Leicester Square
London WC2H 7LA
Tel: 0207 766 6000
Fax: 0207 7666 1000
email: nicky.tranter@capitalradio.com
Website: www.capitalfm.com
Managing Director: Andria Vidler
Including Stations for London,
Birmingham, Hampshire, South
Wales, Sussex, Manchester and Kent.

## Capital Gold Network
30 Leicester Square
London WC2H 7LA
Tel: 0207 766 6000
Fax: 0207 7666 1000
Website: www.capitalgold.com
Managing Director: Lyn Long

## Century FM Network
Century House
Waterfront Quays
Salford Quays
Manchester M5 2XW
Tel: 0161 400 0105
Fax: 0161 400 1105
Managing Director: Nick Davidson
Including stations in Nottingham,
Manchester, Gateshead and Fareham.

## Classic FM
7 Swallow Place
Oxford Circus
London W1B 2AG
Tel: 0207 343 9000
Website: www.classicfm.co.uk

## Virgin 1215 AM
1 Golden Square
London W1F 9DJ
Tel: 020 7434 1215
Fax: 020 7434 1197
Website: www.virgin.com

## Xfm Network
30 Leicester Square
London WC2H 7LA
Tel: 0207 766 6000
Fax: 0207 766 6100
Website: www.xfm.com
Managing Director: Graham Bryce

# Independent Television Companies

## Anglia Television
Anglia House
Norwich NR1 3JG
Tel: 01603 615151
Fax: 01603 761245
email: dutyoffice@angliatv.co.uk
Website: www.anglia.tv.co.uk
Includes regional centres in
Cambridge, Chelmsford, Ipswich,
Nothampton, Luton, Peterborough
and Milton Keynes.

## Border Television
Television Centre
Carlisle CA1 3NT
Tel: 01228 525101
Fax: 01228 541384
Website: www.border-tv.com

## Carlton Television
35-38 Portman Square
London W1H 6NU
Tel: 020 7486 6688
Fax: 020 7486 1132
email: dutyoffice@carltontv.vo.uk
Website: www.carlton.com

## Central Independent Television (East)
Carlton Studios
Lenton Lane
Nottingham NG7 2NA
Tel: 0115 986 3322
Fax: 0115 964 5018
Website: www.carlton.com

## Central Independent Television (South)
9 Windrush Court
Abingdon Business Park
Abingdon
Oxon OX14 1SA
Tel: 01235 554123
Fax: 01235 524024
Website: www.carlton.com

## Channel Five Broadcasting
22 Long Acre
London WC2E 9LY
Tel: 020 7550 5555
Fax: 020 7550 5554
email: dutyoffice@channel5.co.uk
Website: www.five.tv

## Channel Four Television
124 Horseferry Road
London SW1P 2TX
Tel: 020 7396 4444
Fax: 020 7306 8353
Website: www.channel4.co.uk

## Channel Television
Guernsey Office:
Television House
Bulwer Avenue
St Sampsons
Guernsey GY2 4LA
Tel: 01481 41888
Fax: 01481 41889
email: broadcast.gsy@channeltv.co.uk
Jersey Office:
The Television Centre
La Pouquelaye
St Helier
Jersey JE1 3ZD
Tel: 01534 816816
Fax: 01534 816817
email: broadcast@channeltv.co.uk
London Office:
Channel Television Ltd.
Unit 16A/3rd Floor
Enterprise House
59-65 Upper Ground
London SE1 9PQ
Tel: 020 7633 9902
Fax: 020 7401 8982
Website: www.channeltv.co.uk
Managing Director: Michael Lucas

## GMTV
London Television Centre
Upper Ground
London SE1 9LT
Tel: 020 7827 7000
Fax: 020 7827 7249
email: malcolm.douglas@gmtv.co.uk
Website: www.gmtv.co.uk

## Grampian Television
The Television Centre
Craigshaw Business Park
West Tullos AB12 3QH
Tel: 01224 848848
email:
viewer.enquiries@grampiantv.co.uk
Website: www.grampiantv.co.uk
North Tonight; Crossfire; News
Programmes

## Granada Television
Quay Street
Manchester M60 9EA
Tel: 0161 832 7211
Fax: 0161 827 2029
Albert Dock
Liverpool L3 4BA
Tel: 0151 709 9393
White Cross
Lancaster LA1 4XQ
Tel: 01524 606688
36 Golden Square
London W1R 4AH
Tel: 0171 734 8080
Bridgegate House
5 Bridge Place
Lower Bridge Street

Chester CH1 1SA
Tel: 01244 313966
email: duty.office@granadatv.co.uk
Website: www.granadatv.co.uk

## HTV Wales
Television Centre
Culverhouse Cross
Cardiff CF5 6XJ
Tel: 01222 590590
Fax: 01222 590759
Website: www.htvwales.com

## HTV West
Television Centre
Bath Road
Bristol BS4 3HG
Tel: 0117 9722722
Fax: 0117 972 3122
Website: www.htvwest.com
HTV News; The West This Week,
West Eye View

## Independent Television News (ITN)
200 Gray's Inn Road
London WC1X 8XZHF
Tel: 020 7833 3000
Fax: 020 7430 4868
Website: www.itn.co.uk

## Meridian Broadcasting
TV Centre
Northam Road
Southampton SO14 0PZ
Tel: 023 8022 2555
Fax: 023 8071 2081
email: dutyoffice@meridiantv.com
Website: www.meridiantv.com

## S4C
Parc Ty Glas
Llanishen
Cardiff CF4 5DU
Tel: 01222 747444
Fax: 01222 754444
email: s4c@s4c.co.uk
Website: www.S4c.co.uk
Head of Press and Public Relations:
David Meredith

## Scottish TV
200 Renfield Street
Glasgow G2 3PR
Tel: 0141 300 3000
Fax: 0141 332 9274
email:
viewer.enquiries@scottishtv.co.uk
Website: www.scottishtv.co.uk

## Tyne Tees Television
The Television Centre
City Road
Newcastle upon Tyne NE1 2AL
Tel: 0191 261 0181
Fax: 0191 232 2302

Website: www.tynetees.tv

## Ulster Television
Havelock House
Ormeau Road
Belfast BT7 1EB
Tel: 01232 328122
Fax: 01232 246695
Website: www.utvlive.com

## Westcountry Television
Western Wood Way
Language Science Park
Plymouth PL7 5BQ
Tel: 01752 333333
Fax: 01752 333033
Website: www.itv.com/westcountry

## Yorkshire Television
The Television Centre
Kirkstall Road
Leeds LS3 1JS
Tel: 0113 243 8283
Fax: 0113 243 3655
Website: www.yorkshire-television.tv

# BBC Television

## British Broadcasting Corporation
Television Centre
Wood Lane
London W12 7RJ
Tel: 020 8743 8000
Website: www.bbc.co.uk/tv
Direector General: Greg Dyke

## BBC East Midlands Today
London Road
Nottingham NG2 4UU
Tel: 0115 955 0500
Fax: 0115 902 1984
email: emt@bbc.co.uk
Website:
www.bbc.co.uk/midlandstoday

## BBC Look East
St. Catherine's Close
All Saints Green
Norwich NR1 3ND
Tel: 01603 619331
Fax: 01603 284455
104 Hill Road
Cambridge CB2 1LD
Tel: 01223 259696
Fax: 01223 460823
email: look.east@bbc.co.uk
Website: www.bbc.co.uk/lookeast

## Look North
Broadcasting Centre
Barrack Road
Newcastle Upon Tyne NE99 2NE
Tel: 0191 232 1313
email:

looknorth.notheast.cumbria@bbc.co.uk
Editor: Andrew Lambert
Broadcasting House
Woodhouse Lane
Leeds LS2 9PX
Tel: 0113 244 1188
Fax: 0113 244 2131
email: look.north@bbc.co.uk
Website: www.bbc.co.uk/looknorth
Editor: Jake Fowler

## Midlands Today

BBC West Midlands
Pebble Mill
Brimingham B5 7QQ
Tel: 0121 432 8888
email: midlandstoday@bbc.co.uk
Website:
www.bbc.co.uk/midlandstoday
Head of regional and local
programmes: David Holdsworth
Editor: Chas Watkins

## North West Tonight

New Broadcasting House
Oxford Road
ManchesterM60 1SJ
Tel: 0161 200 2020
email: nwt@bbc.co.uk
Website:
www.bbc.co.uk/northwesttonight
Head of regional and local
programmes: Martin Brooks

## Points West

Broadcasting House
Whiteladies Road
Bristol BS8 2LR
Tel: 0117 973 2211
Fax: 0117 974 1537
email: pointswest@bbc.co.uk
Website: www.bbc.co.uk/pointswest
Editor(s): Jane Kinghorn & Stephanie
Marshall

## South East Today

The Great Hall
Mount Pleasant Road
Tunbridge Wells TN1 1QQ
Tel: 01892 675580
Fax: 01892 549118
email: southeasttoday@bbc.co.uk
Website:
www.bbc.co.uk/southeasttoday
Acting Editor: Graham Majin

## South Today

Havelock Road
Southhamption SO14 7PU
Tel: 02380 226201
Fax: 02380 339931
email: south.today@bbc.co.uk
Website: www.bbc.co.uk/southtoday
Editor: Lee Desty

## Spotlight

BBC South West
Broadcasting House
Seymour Road
Plymouth PL3 5BD
Tel: 01752 229201
Fax: 01752 234595
email: spotlight@bbc.co.uk
www.bbc.co.uk/spotlight
Editor: Simon Read

# News and Photo Agencies

## Associated Press

12 Norwich Street
London EC4A 1BP
Tel: 020 7353 1515
Fax: 020 7583 0196
email: info@ap.org
Website: www.ap.org

## Central Office of Information

Hercules House
London SE1 7DU
Tel: 020 7928 2345
Fax: 020 7928 5037
Website: www.coi.gov.uk

## Central Press Features

5th Floor
BUP Building
Temple Way
Bristol BF99 7HD
Tel: 0117 934 3604
Fax: 0117 934 3642
email: sam.bush@central-press.co.uk
Website: www.central-press.co.uk

## Fleet Street News Agency

68 Exmouth Market
London EC1R 4RA
Tel: 020 7278 5661
Fax: 020 7278 8480

## News Team International

Stratford House
Stratford Place
Camp Hill
Birmingham B12 0HT
Tel: 0121 246 5511
Fax: 0121 246 5100
Provides material from the West
Midlands and Manchester Region.

## Press Association

292 Vauxhall Bridge Road
London SW1V 1AE
Tel: 020 7963 7000
Northern Headquarters:
The Bishop's Manor, Market Place
Howden
E. Yorks DN14 7BL
email: information@pa.press.net
Website: www.pa.press.net/

## Reuters Ltd

85 Fleet Street
London EC4P 4AJ
Tel: 020 7250 1122
Fax: 020 7542 7921
Website: www.reuters.com
Chief Executive: Tom Glocer
Incompassing Bridge News for
business information.

## Scotland News and Features
TFI
8 Rossie Place
Edinburgh EH7 5SG
Tel: 0131 244 2709

## Solo
49 Kensington High Street
London W8 5ED
Tel: 020 7376 2166
Fax: 020 7938 3165
Feature and news material from
Associated Newspapers and IPC
Magazines.

## Wales News Service
Womanby Street
Cardiff CF1 2UD
Tel: 01222 666 366
Fax: 01222 664181

## United Press International
Prince Consort House
27-29 Albert Embankment
London SE1 7TJ
Tel: 020 7820 4180
Fax: 0207 8204 4190
Website: www.upi.com
UPI London Editor: Dr. Hussain
Hindawi

# PREVIEW THEATRES

**BAFTA**
195 Piccadilly
London W1J 9LN
Tel: 020 734 0022
Fax: 020 7734 1009
email: pollyc@bafta.org
Website: www.bafta.org
Polly Collins
Formats: Twin 35mm all aspect
ratios. Dolby A, SR, SRD, DTS sound.
35 Double head mono, twin/triple
track stereo plus Dolby Matrix.
16mm and super 16mm, 16 double
head stereo plus Dolby Matrix.
BARCO G-10 ELM Data Video
Projector VHS, Lo Band U-matic,
Beta, Beta SP, Digi Beta + DVD.
Interfaces for most PC outputs,
SVGA, MAC etc. 35mm slides single,
with a remote control, Audio, RGB
Video Tie Lines in Theatre. ISDN 3.
Catering by Roux Fine Dining. Seats:
Princess Anne Theatre, 213 Run Run
Shaw Theatre, 30 (not all formats
available), Function Room, up to 200
Disabled access: ramp, lift and other
facilities

**British Film Institute**
21 Stephen Street
London W1P 2LN
Tel: 020 7957 8976
Fax: 020 7436 7950
email: roger.young@bfi.org.uk
Website: www.bfi.org.uk
Picture Formats: All aspect ratios
Film Speeds: 16fps-30fps
Formats: 35mm: Mono/Dolby
A/SR/SRD+EX
16mm: Mono/Dolby A/SR
Video Projection: VHS/SVHS/U-
Matic/Beta SP/DVD/Laserdisc
Hospitality Room
Disabled Access
Seats: 1: 36, 2: 36

**BUFVC**
77 Wells Street
London W1T 3QJ
Tel: 020 7393 1500
Fax: 020 7393 1555
email: services@bufvc.ac.uk
Website: bufvc.ac.uk
Geoffrey O'Brien, Assistant Director
Formats: Viewing rooms equipped
with 16mm double-head, Betacam,
SVHS, VHS, lo-band and hi-band U-
Matic, Betamax, Phillips 1500
Seats: 20-30 max

**Century Preview Theatres**
31-32 Soho Square
London W1V 6AP
Tel: 020 7753 7135
Fax: 020 7753 7138
email: projection@foxinc.com
Nick Ross
Picture Formats: 1.1:37, 1.1:66,
1.1:85, Super 35, Scope
Sound Formats: (CP 500) Mono,
Dolby A, SR, SR-D+EX. DTS. Double
Head 6 TRK (Magnetic) 2000 ft. Also:
Spotlighting, microphones, lecturns,
for conventions. Most video formats
using DLP
Seating Capacity: 73

**Chapter Cinema**
Market Road
Canton
Cardiff CF5 1QE
Tel: 01222 311050
Fax: 01222 313431
email: tony.whitehead@chapter-
online.co.uk
Website: www.chapter.org.uk
Tony Whitehead, Cinema
Programmer
Formats: 35mm optical, 16mm
optical/sep mag, high quality video
projection, U-Matic/VHS - all
standards. Beta SP PAL2 Channel
infra-red audio
amplification/simultaneous
translation system in both screens.
Reception space, bars and restaurant
Seats: 1:194, 2:68

**Columbia TriStar Films UK**
Sony Pictures Europe House
25 Golden Square
London W1R 6LU
Tel: 020 7533 1095
Fax: 020 7533 1105
Formats: 35mm optical (SDDS,
Dolby SR" + "A" type)/double head
SVA Mag

**Computer Film Company**
19-23 Wells Street
London W1P 3FB
Tel: 020 7344 8000
Fax: 020 7344 8001

email: charlie.dodiya@framestore-
cfc.com
Website: www.framestore-cfc.com
Charlie Dodiya
Picture Formats: 1.1:33, 1.1:66,
1.1:85, Super 35, Scope. Variable
speeds, reverse projection if required.
Sound Formats: Mono, Dolby A, SR,
SRD. Video VHS + Beta + DVD. Bar
area

**Curzon Soho**
93-107 Shaftesbury Avenue
London W1D 5DY
Tel: 020 7734 2255
Fax: 020 7734 1977
email:
rob.kenny@curzoncinemas.com
Website: www.curzoncinemas.com
Robert Kenny
Picture Formats: 1.1:33, 1.1:66,
1.1:85, Scope. Kodak slide projection,
Video Projection: Beta SP, Digi-Beta,
Powerpoint Capable, Analogue
Projector, PA on request, all theatres
to THX standard

**De Lane Lea**
75 Dean Street
London W11D 3PU
Tel: 020 7432 3800
Fax: 020 7432 3838
email: info@delanelea.com
Website: www.delanelea.com
Picture Formats: 35mm. 1.1:33,
1.1:66, 1.1:85. Super 35, Scope
Sound Formats: Mono, Dolby, A + SR
with double-head capacity
(magnetic) 6,4,3 track stereo

**Edinburgh Film & TV
Studios**
Nine Mile Burn
Penicuik EH26 9LT
Tel: 01968 672131
Fax: 01968 672685
Website:
www.edinburghfilmstudios.co.uk
Formats: 16mm and 35mm double-
head stereo, U-Matic, VHS
Seats: 100

**Eon Productions Limited**
Eon House
138 Piccadilly
London W1J 7NR
Tel: 020 7493 7953

Fax: 020 7408 1236
email: chris.brisley@eon.co.uk
Chrissy Brisley
35mm Projection, 1.1:33 & 1.1:85
scope, Dolby digital 5.1 sound, VHS
pal/ntsc, DVD multi region, Digit
beta / beta sp, powerpoint
presentation, 22 seater

## Filmhouse
**88 Lothian Road**
**Edinburgh EH3 9BZ**
Tel: 0131 228 6382
Fax: 0131 229 6482
email: admin@filmhousecinema.com
Website: www.ffilmhousecinema.com
Gwen Orr

## Foresight Preview Theatre
**Beaumont House**
**Kensington Village**
**Avonmore Road**
**London W14 8TS**
Tel: 020 7348 1065
35mm Optical (Dolby A, SR, SRD),
35mm Sep Mag (Monon & Stereo)
VHS, Umatic, Betacam, DVD Large
Screen Television, Slides, OHP and
Multimedia presentation
Seats: 55-70

## ICA
**The Mall**
**London SW1Y 5AH**
Tel: 020 7766 1413
Fax: 020 7306 0122
email: hires@ica.org.uk
Website: www.ica.org.uk
Cinema 1: 185 seats
35mm film changeover projection.
Beta sp pal, VHS pal, DVD pal/ntsc
multiregion, LD pal/ntsc.
Playback in Dolby Pro-logic, stereo or
mono.
Data projection up to SXGA, native
XGA resolution.
CD and cassette playback/recording.
Stage area with 2 point lighting
Facilities available with notice:
Vocal pa from table mics for
conference.
35mm slide projection.
Radio mic
Lecturn
Additional video formats
Cinema 2: 45 seats.
35mm film projection from tower.
16mm film projection.
1:33 1:66 1:85 2:35 combined
optical prints only
Video projection.
Barco cine 7 CRT projector. Flat or
anamorphic video
Beta sp pal, VHS pal/ntsc/secam,
DVD pal/ntsc multi region (No

recordable DVD's playable)
CD & cassette playback
Infra red hearing support with
induction loop
Facilities available with notice:
35mm slide projection
Additional video formats
Data projection using LCD projector
brought in.

## Imperial War Museum
(Corporate Hospitality)
**Lambeth Road**
**London SE1 6HZ**
Tel: 020 7416 5293
Fax: 020 7416 5229
email: film@iwm.org.uk
Website: www.iwm.org.uk
Toby Haggith
Formats: 35mm and 16mm; Betacam,
U-Matic, SVHS and VHS. Catering by
arrangement. Large Exhibit Hall,
capacity: 1,000 Disabled access
Seats: Cinema: 200

## King's Lynn Arts Centre
**27/29 King Street**
**King's Lynn**
**Norfolk PE30 1HA**
Tel: 01553 765565
Fax: 01553 762141
Website: www.kingslynnarts.co.uk
Formats: 16mm, 35mm
Seats: 349

## Mr Young's Screening Rooms
**14 D'Arblay Street**
**London W1V 3FP**
Tel: 020 7437 1771
Fax: 020 7734 4520
email: enquires@mryoungs.com
Website: www.mryoungs.com
Contact: Reuben
Formats: 35mm, Super 35mm, U-
Matic, VHS, Betacam SP, Dolby stereo
double-head optical and magnetic
Dolby SR. Large screen video
projection. Bar area, catering by
request. Theatres non-smoking
Seats: 1: 42, 2: 25, 3:45

## Picture Production Company
**19-20 Poland Street**
**London W1F 8QF**
Tel: 020 7439 4944
Fax: 020 7434 9140
email: sales@theppc.com
Website: www.theppc.com

## Pinewood Shepperton Group
**Pinewood Studios**
**Sound Department - Preview**

**Theatres**
**Pinewood Road**
**Iver Heath**
**Bucks SL0 0NH**
Tel: 01753 656296
Fax: 01753 656014
email: helen_wells@
pinewoodshepperton.com
Website: www.pinewood-studios.com
Contact: Helen Wells
Formats: 35mm, 70mm, Dolby SR,
SR.D, DTS, SDDS. Compot,
Commag, Sepmag. Separate timecode
digital sound screening by
arrangement. Screen width 34ft.
Disabled access. Lounge available.
Seats: 118 seats
**Shepperton Studios**
**Studios Road**
**Shepperton**
**Middx TW17 0QD**
Tel: 01932 562611/572350
Fax: 01932 568989
email:
sheppertonstudios@dial.pipex.com
Formats: 35mm double-head and
married, Dolby A + SR,
Seats: (35mm) 17

## Planet Hollywood
**13 Coventry Street**
**London W1**
Tel: 020 7437 7827
Fax: 020 7439 7827
Website: www.planet-
hollywood.demon.co.uk
Formats: 35mm, 70mm, SVHS/VHS,
U-Matic, Laser Disc, Lucasfilm Ltd
THX Sound Sytem, Dolby CP200 +
SRD/DTS digital stereo. Super 35mm
with separate magnetic tracks and
remote volume control. Microphone
facilities. Lifts for the disabled
available
Seats: Cinema: 75, Dining area: 85,
120 (standing)
Refurbished members bar with the
screening room.
The Rex Cinema and Bar
**21 Rupert Street**
**London W11V 7FE**
Tel: 020 7287 0102
Fax: 020 7478 1501

## RSA
**8 John Adam Street**
**London WC2N 6EZ**
Tel: 020 7839 5049
Fax: 020 7321 0271
email: Conference@rsa-
uk.demon.co.uk
Website: www.rsa.org.uk
The Great Room
Video Formats: SVHS, Beta SP. Other
formats by arrangement.

Barcographics 8100 Projector for Video and Data Projection. Loop system for hard of hearing, disabled access to all rooms. Full catering available: Seats: 202

## Screen West

**John Brown Publishing**
**136-142 Bramley Road**
**London W10 6SR**
Tel: 020 7565 3102
Fax: 020 7565 3077
email: sarah.alliston@jbcp.co.uk
Website: www.screenwest.co.uk
Sarah Alliston
Enquiries: Sarah Alliston
State of the art preview theatre with luxury seating for 74 people. Formats: 35mm, Super 35mm, Double Head, Beta, VHS, PC. Surround Sound: Optical, Magnetic, Digital (SRD and DTS). and full catering Beta SP, Digi beta on request facilities in the adjoining function room.

## The Curzon Minema

**45 Knightsbridge**
**London SW1X 7NL**
Tel: 020 7235 4226
Fax: 020 7235 3426
email:info@minema.com
Website: www.minema.com
Formats: 35mm and 16mm, video and AV presentations

## The Screening Room at MPC

**The Moving Picture Company**
**127 Wardour Street**
**London W1V 0NL**
Tel: 020 7494 7879
Fax: 020 7287 9698
email: screening@moving-picture.co.uk
Website: www.moving-picture.co.uk
Contact: Paul Roberts, Chief Film Technician
Mark Wiseman, Senior Film Technician
74 Seat wheelchair accessible professional Screening Room and reception foyer.
35mm Sondor Film Projectors, all aspect ratios inc. Super 35.
Split screen comparisons and interlocking projectors possible. Variable speed playback ( 2fps - 30fps) with full auditorium control. Magnetic 6track,3track,SVA with or without SR noise reduction.
DLP digital projection from all formats by arrangement.
HD projection available by arrangement for additional charge.

## Twentieth Century Fox

**Executive Theatre**
**31-32 Soho Square**
**London W1V 6AP**
Tel: 020 7735 7135
Fax: 020 7735 7138
email: projection@foxinc.com
Peter Holland
Picture formats: 1.1:85, 1:1:66 Scope, Super 35 + DLP Video Projection - Digitbeta
Sound formats (CP500) Mono, Dolby A, SR, SR-D-EX, 3 Track Mag
Seating 37

## Twickenham Film Studios

**St Margaret's**
**Twickenham**
**Middx TW1 2AW**
Tel: 020 8607 8888
Fax: 020 8607 8889
Website: www.twickenhamstudios.com
Gerry Humphreys
Formats: 35mm.
Seats: 31

## UIP International Theatre

**UIP House**
**45 Beadon Road**
**Hammersmith**
**London**
Tel: 0208 563 4336 (Nina Carter bookings) Tel: 0208 563 4143 (George Frith Projectionists)
email: george-frith@uip.com email: nina-carter@uip.com
George Frith, Chief Projectionist
Picture Formats: 1.1:33, 1.1:66, 1.1:85, Scope
Sound Formats: Mono, Dolby, A+SR, SRD +EX, DTS, SDDS, Double head (magnetic). Mono, SVA, 6 Track Video: VHS, U-Matic, Beta SP. Digi Beta

## Warner Bros

**98 Theobalds Road**
**London WC1X 8WB**
Tel: 020 7984 5272
email: Website: www.warnerbros.co.uk

## Watershed

**1 Canons Road**
**Harbourside**
**Bristol BS1 5TX**
Tel: 0117 9276444
Fax: 0117 9213958
email: info@watershed.co.uk
Website: www.watershed.co.uk
Madeleine Probst - Exhibitions Co-ordinator
35mm, Super 8mm, Super 16mm double-head, Digi Beta, Beta SP

Screening rooms
The following is a selection of cinemas and preview theatres available for hire, principally in the London region. Contact the individual venues for details of their technical facilities and screening capacities.

The following section provides a tip of the iceberg view of some UK film and TV production companies. Film production companies in particular are often hard to tie down, as many companies are created and exist for one film only. Other companies prefer to retain some anonymity in order to stem the tide of unsolicited scripts from would-be hopefuls. However, there are some useful places to check for listings of production companies.

Perhaps the best online resource is www.britfilms.co.uk which tracks current UK films in production and often gives useful contact details of the production companies involved.

There are three useful publications which provide information about Production companies.

They are: the Knowledge published by Miller Freeman (www.theknowledgeonline.com) the PACT Directory published by The Producers Alliance for Cinema and Television (www.www.pact.co.uk) and Who's Where published by PCR (www.pcrnewsletter.com)

It is also worth contacting the bfi's Information Line 020 7255 1444 (ask for the Information Line) since the bfi Information Officers have all the above publications at their fingertips and can often help out with details on some specific companies.

## Aardman Animations
Gas Ferry Road
Bristol BS1 6UN
Tel: 0117 984 8485
Fax: 0117 984 8486
Website: www.aardman.com

## Absolutely Productions
Craven House
Suite 226
121 Kingsway
London WC2B 6PA
Tel: 00 44 (0)20 7930 3113
Fax: 00 44 (0)20 7930 4114
email: info@absolutely-uk.com
Website: www.absolutely-uk.com

## Acacia Productions Ltd
80 Weston Park
London N8 9TB
Tel: 020 8341 9392
Fax: 020 8341 4879
email: acacia@dial.pipex.com
Website:
www.acaciaproductions.co.uk
Edward Milner

## Action Time
Wrendal House
2 Whitworth Street
West Manchester M15WX
Tel: 0161 236 8999
Fax: 0161 236 8845

## Addictive TV
The Old House
39a North Road
London N7 9DP
Tel: 020 7700 0333
Fax: 020 7700 0303
email: mail@addictive.com
Website: www.addictive.com
Jim Walters

## Adventure Pictures
6 Blackbird Yard
Ravenscroft Street
London E2 7RP
Tel: 020 7613 2233
Fax: 020 7256 0842
email: mail@adventurepictures.co.uk
Website: www.sallypotter.com

## After Image Ltd
32 Acre Lane
London SW2 5SG
Tel: 020 737 7300
Website: www.after.arc.co.uk
Jane Thornburn

## Agenda Film
Castell Close
Enterprise Park
Swansea SA7 9FH
Tel: 01792 410510
Fax: 01792 775469

## Alibi Productions
35 Long Acre
London WC2E 9JT
Tel: 020 7845 0420
Fax: 020 7379 7039
email: rogerholmes@alibifilms.co.uk
Website: www.alibifilms.co.uk
Roger Holmes

## Alive Productions
37 Harwood Road
London SW6 4QP
Tel: 020 7384 2243
Fax: 020 7384 2026
email: alive@alivetelevision.com
Website: alivetelevision.com

## Alomo Productions Ltd
c/o FremantleMedia Ltd
1 Stephen Street
London W1P 1PJ
Tel: 020 7434 3060
Website: www.fremantlemedia.com

## Amber Films
5 & 9 Side
Newcastle-upon-Tyne NE1 3JE
Tel: 0191 232 2000
Fax: 0191 230 3217
email: amberside@btinternet.com
Website: www.amber-online.com
Pat McCarthy
Amber was established in 1969 with the specific intention of creating a film and photographic practice in relation to the working class communities of the North East of England. From its foundation it has pursued a policy of integrating production, exhibition and distribution. Throughout its 30 year history, it has pioneered experimental partnerships between film makers, photographers, writers and local communities in the North East of England. Distribution of films produced by Amber, recent titles

include Like Father, Eden Valley and
The Scar

## Amy International Productions
PO Box 55
Minehead
Somerset TA24 7WA
Tel: 01398 371270
Fax: 01398 371428
email: simon@amyinternational.
demon.co.uk
Simon Maccorkindale

## Angelic Pictures Ltd
No 1
23 Belgrave Gardens
Islington
London NW8 0QY
Tel:  020 7624 7774
Fax:  020 7624 7774
email: rslw1@hotmail.com
Website: www.angelicpictures.co.uk
Rebecca Wilson

## Anglia Television Limited
Anglia House
Norwich NR1 3JG
Tel: 01603 615151
Fax: 01603 631032
Website: www.anglia.tv.com

## Anglo American Pictures
Ealing Studios
Ealing Green
London W5 5EP
Tel: 07802 666 693
email: admin@anglo-ap.com
Website:
www.angloamericanpictures.com
Chris Barfoot
Current features in development:
Beansidhe (Curse of the Black Witch)
Fall of the Roman Empire

## Anglo/Fortunato Films
170 Popes Lane
London W5 4NJ
Tel: 020 8932 7676
Fax: 020 8932 7491
Luciano Celentino

## The Animation Station
Leisure and Tourism Department
Cherwell District Council
Bodicote House
Bodicote, Banbury
Oxon OX15 4AA
Tel: 01295 221730
Fax: 01295 270797
email: animation.station@cherwell-
dc.gov.uk
Website: www.animationstation.co.uk
ClintonOsborne.  Multimedia Arts
Development Officer

## Animha Productions
121 Roman Road
Linthorpe
Middlesbrough TS5 5QB
Tel: 01642 813 137
email: info@animha.com
Website: www.animha.com
Dave Brunskill

## Antelope South Ltd
Drounces, White Chimney Row
Westbourne
Emsworth PO10 8RS
Tel: 01243 370 806
Fax: 01243 376 985
email: mick.csaky@antelope.co.uk
Website: www.antelope.co.uk
Mick Csáky

## Arcane Pictures
46 Wetherby Mansions
Earl Court Square
London SW5 9DI
Tel: 020 7244 6590
Fax: 020 7565 4495
email: info@arcanepictures.com
Website: www.arcanepictures.com
Meg Thomson

## Archer Street Ltd
Studio 5
10/11 Archer Street
London W1D 7AZ
Tel: 020 7439 0540
Fax: 020 7437 1182
email: films@archerstreet.com
Andy Paterson, Producer

## Ariel Productions Ltd
46 Melcoub Regis Court
59 Weymouth Street
London W1G 8NT
Tel: 020 7935 6636
email:ottoplaschtes@lycos.co.uk
Otto Plaschkes

## Arlington Productions Ltd
Cippenham Court
Cippenham Lane
Cippenham, Nr Slough
Berkshire SL1 5AU
Tel: 01753 516767
Fax: 01753 691785

## Ashford Entertainment Corporation Ltd
20 The Chase
Coulsdon
Surrey CR5 2EG
Tel: 020 8660 9609
email: info@ashford-
entertainment.co.uk
Website: www.ashford-
entertainment.co.uk
Frazer Ashford

## Assembly Film & Television Ltd
Riverside Studios
Crisp Road, Hammersmith
London W6 9RL
Tel: 020 8237 1075
Fax: 020 8237 1071
email:
judithmurrell@riversidestudios.co.uk
Website: www.chrysalis.co.uk
William Burdett-Coutts

## Richard Attenborough Productions,
Twickenham Studios
St Margaret's
Twickenham TW1 2AW
Tel: 020 8607 8873
Fax: 0208744 2766
Judy Wasdell

## AV Pictures Ltd
102 Dean Street
3rd London W1D 3TQ
Tel: 020 7758 1484
Fax: 020 7758 1491
email: info@avpictures
Vic Bateman, Jane Carolan

## Avalon Television
4a Exmoor Street
London W10 6BD
Tel: 020 7598 7280
Fax: 020 7598 7281
email: edt@avalonuk.com
Website: www.avalonuk.com

## Basilisk Communications
3rd Floor
26 Shacklewell Lane
London E8 2EZ
Tel: 020 7690 0117
Fax: 020 7690 4333
email: daybreak@prontomail.com

## Peter Batty Productions
Claremont House, Renfrew Road
Kingston
Surrey KT2 7NT
Tel: 020 8942 6304
Fax: 020 8336 1661

## Bazal
46-47 Bedford Square
London WC1B 3DP
Tel: 0870 3331700
Fax: 020 7462 9998

## BBC Films Ltd
1 Mortimer Street
London W1T 3JA
Tel: 0207 7650251
Fax: 0207 7650278
Website: www.bbc.co.uk/bbcfilms
Corin Long

## The Big Group
91 Princedale Road
London W11 4HS
Tel: 020 7229 8827
Fax: 020 7243 146
email: ed.riseman@biggroup.co.uk
Website: www.biggroup.co.uk
Ed Riseman

## Black Coral Productions
2nd Floor
241 High Street
London E17 7BH
Tel: 020 8520 2881
Fax: 020 8520 2358
email: bcp@coralmedia.co.uk
Lazell Daley, Managing Director,
Producer

## Black & White Pictures
Teddington Studios
Teddington TW11 9NT
Tel: 020 8614 2344
Fax: 020 8614 2500
email: production@
blackandwhitepictures.co.uk
Joy Mellins - Sean Blowers
(Producers)

## Blue Dolphin Film & Video
40 Langham Street
London W1N 5RG
Tel: 020 7255 2494
Fax: 020 7580 7670
Website: www.bluedolphinfilms.com

## Blue Heaven Productions Ltd
45 Leather Lane
London EC1N 7TJ
Tel: 020 7404 4222
Fax: 020 7404 4266

## Braunarts
The Beehive
226a Gipsy Road
London SE27 9RB
Tel: 020 8670 9917
Fax: 020 8670 9917
email: terry@braunarts.com &
gabi@braunarts.com
Website: www.braunarts.com
Contact: Gabi Braun & Terry Braun

## BreakThrufilms Ltd
2nd Floor
Highgate Business Centre
33 Greenwood Place
London NW5 1LB
Tel: 020 7428 3974
Fax: 020 7428 3963
email: hugh@breakthrufilms.co.uk
Website: www.breakthrufilms.co.uk
Libby Mourant - Production
Manager

Alan Dewhurst, Producer
HughWelchman, Producer
Tom Truscott
Feature films/Animation production
company

## Bronco Films
The Producer's Centre
61 Holland Street
Glasgow G2 4NJ
Tel: 0141 287 6817
Fax: 0141 287 6817
email: broncofilm@btinternet.com
Website: www.broncofilms.co.uk
Peter Broughan

## Brook Lapping Productions
6 Anglers Lane
London NW5 3DG
Tel: 020 7482 3100
Fax: 020 7284 0626
Anne Lapping

## Buena Vista Productions
Centre West
3 Queen Caroline Street
Hammersmith
London W4 9PE
Tel: 020 8222 1000
Fax: 020 8222 2795

## John Burder Films
37 Braidley Road
Meyrick Park
Bournemouth BH2 6JY
Tel: 01202 295 395
email: burderfilms@aol.com
Website: www.johnburder.co.uk

## Buxton Raven Productions Ltd
102 Clarence Road
London E5 8HB
Tel: 020 8986 0063
Fax: 020 8986 2708
email: jb@buxtonraven.com
Website: buxtonraven.com
Jette Bonnevie, Jens Ravn

## Cabalva Studios
Whitney-on-Wye
Herefordshire HR3 6EX
Tel: 01497 831 800
Fax: 01497 831 808
email: mail@transatlanticfilms.com
Website: www.transatlanticfilms.com
Revel Guest
Studio 1
3 Brackenbury Road
London W6 OBE

## Capitol Films
23 Queensdale Place
London W11 4SQ
Tel: 020 7471 6000
Fax: 020 7471 6012

email: films@capitolfilms.com
Website: www.capitolfilms.com

## Carey Films Ltd
5 Henshaw Lane
Yeadon
Leeds LS19 7RW
Tel: 00 44 (0)113 250 6411
Fax: 00 44 (0)113 210 9426
email: owen@careyfilms.com
Website: www.careyfilms.com

## Carnival (Films and Theatre) Ltd
12 Raddington Road
Ladbroke Grove
London W10 5TG
Tel: 020 8968 0968
Fax: 020 8968 0155
email: info@carnival-films.co.uk
Website: www.carnival-films.co.uk

## Cartwn Cymru
32 Wordsworth Avenue
Roath
Cardiff CF24 3FR
Tel: 02920 463556
email: production@cartwn-
cymru.com
Naomi Jones

## Catalyst Television
Brook Green Studios
186 Shepherd's Bush Road
London W6 7LL
Tel: 020 7603 7030
Fax: 020 7603 9519

## Celador Films
39 Long Acre
London WC2E 9LG
Tel: 020 7845 6998
Fax: 020 7836 1117
email: Imackinnon@celador.co.uk
Website: celador.co.uk
ivana MacKinnon

## Celador Productions
39 Long Acre
London WC2E 9JT
Tel: 020 7240 8101
Fax: 020 7836 1117
Paul Smith

## CF1 CYF
Uppercliff House
Uppercliff Close
Penarth CF64 1BE
Tel: 02920 400820
Fax: 02920 400821
email: CF1CYF@hotmail.com
Website: www.fearmovie.com

## Channel X
22 Stephenson Way
London NW1 2HD

Tel: 020 7387 3874
Fax: 020 7387 0738
email: mail@channelx.co.uk

### Charisma Films
507 Riverbank House
1 Putney Bridge Approach
London SW6 3JD
Tel: 020 7610 6830
Fax: 020 7610 6836
email: charismafi@aol.com
Alan Balladur, Head of Development

### Chatsworth Television
97-99 Dean Street
London W1D 3DE
Tel: 020 7734 4302
Fax: 020 7437 3301
email: television@chatsworth-tv.co.uk
Website: www.chatsworth-tv.co.uk
Malcolm Heyworth, Managing Director

### The Children's Film Unit
South Way
Leavesden
Herts WD25 7LZ
Tel: 01923 354656
Fax: 01923 354656
email: cfilmunit@aol.com
Website: www.childrensfilmunit.com
Carol Rennie

### Chrysalis Visual Entertainment
The Chrysalis Building
13 Bramley Road
London W10 6SP
Tel: 020 7221 2213
Fax: 020 7465 6159
Website: www.chrysalis.co.uk
Charlotte Boundy

### Cinema Verity Productions Ltd
11 Addison Avenue
London W11 4QS
Tel: 020 7460 2777
Fax: 020 7371 3329
email: cinemaverity@aol.com
Verity Lambert

### Circus Films Ltd
Shepperton Studios
Shepperton
Middlesex TW17 OQD
Tel: 01932 572680/1
Fax: 01932 568989

### Civilian Content plc
4th Floor
Portland House
4 Great Portland Street
London W1W 8QJ
Tel: 020 7612 0050
Fax: 020 7612 0031

email: contact@civilancontent.com
Website: www.civilancontent.com
Chris Auty, Managing Director

### Colstar International Television Limited
78 York Street
London W1H 1DP
Tel: 020 7625 6200
email: media@colstar.tv
Website: www.colstar.tv
Steve Goddard, Executive Producer Film sales into world television and multimedia markets, coproductions and independent film making new-author publishing, rights licensing and merchandising. Feature films, HD - television films, drama serials and documentaries, short drama, new author publishing. Colstar International Television Limited represent innovative output from writers, directors, producers and their production companies, as well as its own films

### Company Pictures
Suffolk House
1/8 Whitfield Place
London W1T 5JU
Tel: 020 7380 3900
Fax: 020 7380 1166
email:
enquiries@companypictures.co.uk
Website: www.companypictures.co.uk

### Connections Communications Centre Ltd
Palingswick House
241 King Street
Hammersmith
London W6 9LP
Tel: 020 8741 1766
Fax: 020 8563 1934
email: @cccmedia.co.uk
Website: www.cccmedia.co.uk
Jacqueline Davis

### Cosgrove Hall Films
8 Albany Road
Chorlton-cum-Hardy
Manchester M21 0AW
Tel: 0161 882 2500
Fax: 0161 882 2555
email: animation@chf.co.uk
Website: www.chd.uk.com
Susan Ennis, Head of Production

### Judy Couniham Films Ltd
12a Newburgh Street
London W1V 1LG
Tel: 020 7287 4329
Fax: 020 7287 2303

### Covent Garden Films
67 Palfrey Place
London SW8 1AR
Tel: 00 44 (0)20 7820 7555
Fax: 00 44 (0)20 7820 7591
email: simon@coventgardenfilms.com
Website: www.coventgardenfilms.com

### Crowfoot Films
82 Berwick Street
London WC1N 1AP
Tel: 020 7287 5040
Fax: 020 7734 0544
email: info@crowfootfilms.com
Beth Sanders

### Dakota Films
4a Junction Mews
London W2 1PN
Tel: 020 7706 9407
Fax: 020 7402 6111
email: info@dakota-films.demon.co.uk

### Dan Films Ltd
32 Maple Street
London W1T 6HB
Tel: 020 7916 4771
Fax: 020 7916 4773
email: office@danfilms.com
Website: www.danfilms.com
Jason Newmark (Producer)

### Dazed Film & TV
112 - 116 Old Street
London EC1V 9BG
Tel: 020 7549 6840
Fax: 020 7336 0966
email: laura@confused.co.uk
Website: www.dazedfilmtv.com
Contact: Laura Hastings-Smith, Company Director/Executive Producer
Dazed Film & TV is part of the Dazed group which also comprises Dazed & Confused magazine, Another Magazine, Dazed Books and Rankin Photography

### De Warrenne Pictures Ltd
St. Anne's House
Diadem Court
Soho
London W1D 3EF
Tel: 020 7734 7648
Fax: 070 9236 7853
email: info@dewarrenne.com
Website: www.dewarrenne.com
Tom Waller

### Different Films
P.O. Box 564
London WC2H 8Lz
Tel: 0845 4 58 57 90
Fax: 0845 4 58 57 91

email: info@differentfilms.co.uk
Website: www.differentfilms.co.uk
Douglas M Ray

## Dirty Hands Productions
2nd Floor
2-4 Noel Street
London W1F 8GN
Tel: 020 7287 7410
Fax: 020 7734 7131

## Diverse Productions
6 Gorleston Street
London W14 8XS
Tel: 020 7603 4567
Fax: 020 7603 2148
email: info@diverse.tv
Website: www.diverse.co.uk

## DLT Entertainment UK Ltd
10 Bedford Square
London WC1B  3RA
Tel: 020 7631 1184
Fax: 020 7636 4571
John Bartlett,J ohn Reynolds, Gary
Mitchell
Specialising in comedy and drama
production and sales. Recent titles
include: My Family (5 series), Meet
My Folks and As Time Goes By for
BBC Television

## DNA Films
First Floor
15 Greek Street
London W1D 4DP
Tel: 020 7292 8700
Fax: 020 7292 8701
email: info@dnafilms.com
Website: www.dnafilms.com
Joanne Smith

## Domino Films
7 King Harry Lane
St Albans AL3 4AS
Tel: 01727 750153
email: Jo@dominofilms.co.uk
Joanna Mack

## The Drama House
Coach Road Cottages
Little Saxham
Bury St Edmunds 1P29 5LE
Tel: 01284 810521
Fax: 01284 811425
email: jack@dramahouse.co.uk
Website: www.dramahouse.co.uk
Jack Emery

## Dramatis Personae
19 Regency Street
London SW1P 4BY
Tel: 020 7834 9300
email: nathansilver@btconnect.com
Nathan Silver

## Ecosse Films
Brigade House
8 Parsons Green
London SW6 4TN
Tel: 020 7371 0290
Fax: 020 7736 3436
email: info@ecossefilms.com
Website: www.ecossefilms.com
Sophie Grumbar, Assistant to
Managing Director
Jessica Amory, Office Manager

## Edinburgh Film & Video Productions
Traquair House
Innelleithen
Peeblessairl EH44 6PW
Tel: 01896 831188
Fax: 01896 831198
Robin Crichton

## Edric Audio Visual
34-36 Oak End Way
Gerrards Cross
Buckinghamshire SL9 8BR
Tel: 01753 481416
Fax: 01753 887163
email: robin@edic-av.co.uk
Website: www.edric-av.co.uk
Robin Congdon, Managing Director

## Endboard Productions
114a Poplar Road
Bearwood
Birmingham B66 4AP
Tel: 0121 429 9779
Fax: 0121 429 9008
email: Sunandan@endboard.com
Website: www.endboard.com
Sunandan Walia, Director

## Eon Productions Limited
Eon House
138 Piccadilly
London W1J 7NR
Tel: 020 7493 7953
Fax: 020 7408 1236
email: chris.brisley@eon.co.uk
Website: www.jamesbond.com
Katherine McCormack
Recent Prod:  Die Another Day

## Equilibrium Films
28 Sheen Common Drive
Richmond TW10 5BN
Tel: 020 7602 1989/07930
Fax: 020 7602 1989
John Miles

## Extreme International
The Coach House
Ashford Lodge
Halstead
Essex C09 2RR
Tel: 01787 479000

Fax: 01787 479111
email: xdream@dream.co.uk
Website:
www.extremeinternational.com
Alistair Gosling

## Festival Film and Television Ltd
Festival House, Tranquil Passage
Blackheath Village
London SE3 OBJ
Tel: 020 8297 9999
Fax: 020 8297 1155
email: info@festivalfilm.com
Website: www.festivalfilm.com
Ray Marshall

## Figment Films Ltd
1st Floor
15 Greek Street
London W1D 4DP
Tel: 020 7291 8700
Fax: 020 7292 8701
email: figment@globalnet.co.uk
Website: www.figmentfilms.com

## Film and General Productions
4 Bradbrook House
Studio Place
London SW1X 8EL
Tel: 020 7235 4495
Fax: 020 7245 9853
email: cparsons@filmgen.co.uk
Clive Parsons

## The Film Consortium
6 Flitcroft Street
London WC28H 8DJ
Tel: 020 7691 4440
Fax: 020 7691 4445

## FilmFair Animation
Unit 8
Silver Road
White City Industrial Park
London W12 7SG
Tel: 020 8735 1888
Fax: 020 8743 9591
email: info@film.co.uk

## FilmFour Ltd
124 Horseferry Road
London SW1P 2TX
Tel: 020 7396 4444
Website: www.channel4.com/film
Tessa Ross, Head of FilmFour

## Firedog Films
20 The Chase
Coulsdon
Surrey,  CR5 2EG
Tel: 020 8660 9609
email: email  info@firedogfilms.co.uk
Website: www.firedogfilms.co.uk
Jonathan Martin

## The First Film Company
38 Great Windmill Street
London W1V 7PA
Tel: 020 7439 1640
Fax: 020 7437 2062

## Flashback Television Ltd
9-11 Bowling Green Lane
London EC1R OBG
Tel: 020 7490 8996
Fax: 020 7490 5610
email: mailbox@flashbacktv.co.uk
Website: www.flashbacktv.co.uk

## Flashlight Films
10 Golden Square
London W1R 3AF
Tel: 020 7436 6060
Fax: 020 7287 4232
email: kate@flashlightfilms.com
Website: www.flashlightfilms.com
Kate Hagar, Aaron Simpson

## Focus Films
The Rotunda Studios
Rear of 116-118 Finchley Road
London NW3 5HT
Tel: 020 7435 9004
Fax: 020 7431 3562
email: focus@focusfilms.co.uk
Website: www.focusfilms.co.uk
David Pupkewitz, Producer
Malcolm Kohll, Head of Development
Lucinda Van Rie Head of Production,
co-producer, Cigal Kaplan, Assistant
to Head of Development

## Mark Forstater Productions Ltd
27 Lonsdale Road
London NW6 6RA
Tel: 020 7624 1123
Fax: 020 7624 1124

## Fox Searchlight Pictures
Twentieth Century-Fox Film Co Ltd
Twentieth Century House
31-32 Soho Square
London W1D 3AP
Tel: 020 7437 7766
Fax: 020 7734 2170
Website: www.fox.co.uk

## Fragile Films
95-97 Dean Street
London W1N 3XX
Tel: 020 7287 6200
Fax: 020 7287 0069
email: fragile@fragilefilms.com

## Freedom Pictures
10 Rylett Crescent
Shepherds Bush
London W12 9RL
Tel: 0468 855746

Fax: 020 8743 6981
email:
timewhite@freedompictures.co.uk
Tim White

## Front Page Films
507 Riverbank House
1 Putney Bridge Approach
London SW6 3JD
Tel: 020 7736 4534
Fax: 020 7610 6836
email: charismafi@aol.com
Alan Balladur, Head of Development

## Fugitive Films
2 1/2  Gate Street
London WC2A 3HP
Tel: 020 7242 6969
Fax: 020 7242 6970
email: john@fugitivemusic.f9.co.uk

## Fulcrum TV
254 Goswell Road
London EC1V 7RE
Tel: 020 7253 0353
Fax: 020 7490 0206
email: info@FulcrumTV.com
Website: www.FulcrumTV.com
Sandra Leeming, Production
Manager

## Gainsborough (Film & TV) Productions
The Groom Cottage
Pinewood Studios
Pinewood Lane
Iver Heath
Iver Bucks SLO ONH
Tel: 020 7409 1925
Fax: 020 7408 2042

## Global Vision Network
Elstree Film Studios
Borehamwood
Hertfordshire WD6 1JG
Tel: 020 8324 2333
Fax: 020 8324 2700
email: info@gvn.co.uk
Website: www.gvn.co.uk

## Bob Godfrey Films
199 Kings Cross Road
London WC1X 9DB
Tel: 020 7278 5711
Fax: 020 7278 6809
email: mhayes@BGFilms.fsnet.co.uk

## Goldcrest Films International
65-66 Dean Street
London W1D 4PL
Tel: 020 7437 8696
Fax: 020 7437 4448

## Granada Film
4th Floor

48 Leicester Square
London WC2H 7FB
Tel: 020 7389 8555
Fax: 020 7930 8499
email: granada.film@
granadamedia.com
Jacky Fitt

## GranadaWild
1-5 Whiteladies Road
Clifton
Bristol BS8 1NU
Tel: 0117 9745800
Fax: 0117 9733531
email: rosemary.ballingall@
granadamedia.com
Contact  Rosemary Ballingall

## Greenpoint Films
7 Denmark Street
London WC2H 8LZ
Tel: 020 7240 7066
Fax: 020 7240 7088
email: info@greenpointfilms.co.uk
Website: greenpointfilms.co.uk
Ann Scott

## Gruber Films
4th Floor
Portland House
London W1W 8QJ
Tel: 020 7612 0070
Fax: 020 7612 0033
email: gruber@civiliancontent.com
Neil Peplow

## Gullane Entertainment PLC
Stoneham Gate
Stoneham Lane
Eastleigh S050 9NW
Tel: 023 8064 9200
Fax: 023 8064 9201
Website: www.gullane.com

## HAL Films Ltd
45a Brewer Street
London W1R 3FD
Tel: 020 7434 4408

## Halas & Batchelor
The Halas & Batchelor Collection Ltd
Southerham House
Southerham
Lewes
East Sussex BN8 6JN
Tel: 01273 488 322
Fax: 01273 488 322
email: vivien@haba.demon.co.uk
Website: www.halasandbatchelor.com
Vivien Halas

## Hammer Film Productions Ltd
92 New Cavendish Street
London W1W 6XJ
Tel: 020 7637 2322

Fax: 020 7323 2307
email: firstname@hammerfilms.com
Website: www.hammerfilms.com
Terry Ilott

## Harbour Pictures
11 Langton Street
London SW10 OJL
Tel: 020 7351 7070
Fax: 020 7352 3528
email: info@harbourpictures.com
Website: www.harbourpictures.com
Nick Barton, Suzanne Mackie

## Harcourt Films
58 Camden Square
London NW1 9XE
Tel: 020 7267 0882
Fax: 020 7267 1064

## Hartswood Films
Twickenham Studios
The Barons
St Margarets
Twickenham
Middx TW1 2AW
Tel: 020 8607 8736
Fax: 020 8607 8744
Debbie Vertue

## Hat Trick Productions
10 Livonia Street
London W1F 8AF
Tel: 020 7434 2451
Fax: 020 7287 9791
Website: www.hattrick.com
Denise O'Donoghue

## Jim Henson Productions
30 Oval Road, Camden
London NW1 7DE
Tel: 020 7428 4000
Fax: 020 7428 4001

## Holmes Associates
38-42 Whitfield Street
London W1P 5RF
Tel: 020 7813 4333
Fax: 020 7637 9024

## Hurll Television Michael
3rd Floor
Beaumont House
Kensington Village
Avonmore Road
London W14 8TS
Tel: 020 7605 1200
Fax: 020 7605 1201

## IBT Productions Ltd
3-7 Euston Centre
Regent's Place
London NW1 3JG
Tel: 020 7874 7650
Fax: 020 7874 7644
email: mail@ibt.org.uk

Website: www.ibt.org.uk

## Icon Entertainment International Ltd
The Quadrangle , 4th Floor
180 Wardour Street
London W1V 3AA
Tel: 020 7494 8100
Fax: 020 7494 8151

## Illuminations Films/Koninck
19-20 Rheidol Mews
Rheidol Terrace
London N1 8NU
Tel: 020 7288 8400
Fax: 020 7359 1151
email: griff@illumin.co.uk
Website: www.illumin.co.uk
Keith Griffiths, Simon Field

## Illuminations Television
19-20 Rheidol Mews
Rheidol Terrace
London N1 8NU
Tel: 020 7226 0266
Fax: 020 7359 1151
email: illuminations@illumin.co.uk
Website: www.illumin.co.uk

## Imaginary Films
75 East Road
London N1 6AH
Tel: 020 7490 1724
Fax: 020 7490 1764
email: anna@boudiccafilms.com
Website: boudicafilms.com
Ray Brady

## Impact Pictures Ltd
3 Percy Street
London W1T 1DE
Tel: 020 7636 7716
Fax: 020 7636 7814
email: production@impactpix.com
Jeremy Bolt, Judy Goldberg

## InFilm Productions Ltd
37 Arteslan Road
London W2
Tel: 020 7792 5152
Fax: 020 7792 5153
email: infilm@infilmproductions.com
Website: www.infilmproductions.com
Dorothy Berwin, Paul Augarde

## Intermedia
9-13 Grosvenor Street
London W1X 9FB
Tel: 020 7495 3322
Fax: 020 7495 3993
email: info@intermediafilm.co.uk
Website: www.intermediafilm.co.uk
Gavin James

## J&M Entertainment Ltd

2 Dorset Square
London NW1 6PX
Tel: 020 7723 6544
Fax: 020 7724 7541
email: sales@jment.com
Website: ww.jment.com
Julia Palau

## Jigsaw Films
5th Floor
83-84 Berwick Street
London W1F 8TS
Tel: 020 7437 3128
Fax: 020 7437 3129
Sarah Radclyffe, Bill Godfrey,
Courtney Pledger

## Kai Film & TV Productions
1 Ravenslea Road
London SW12 8SA
Tel: 020 8673 4550
Fax: 020 8675 4760
email: mwallington@btinternet.com

## Kaos Films
Pinewood Studios
Tel: 020 8455 1385
Fax: 020 8201 9904
email: enquiries@kaosfilms.co.uk
Website: www.kaosfilms.co.uk
Arif Hussen, Piers Jackson

## Bill Kenwright Films
BKL House
106 Harrow Road
London W2 1RR
Tel: 020 7446 6200
Fax: 020 7446 6222
email: info@kenwright.com
Website: www.kenwright.com
Bill Kenwright, Liz Holford

## Kinetic Pictures
Video and Broadcast Production
The Chubb Buildings
Fryer Street
Wolverhampton WV1 1HT
Tel: 01902 716055
Fax: 01902 717143
email: urmalajassal@light-house.co.uk
Website: www.light-house.co.uk
Urmala Jassal - Kinetic Producer

## King Rollo Films
Dolphin Court
High Street
Honiton
Devon EX14 1HT
Tel: 01404 45218
Fax: 01404 45328
email: admin@kingrollofilms.co.uk
Clive Juster

## Kismet Film Company Ltd
27-29 Berwick Street

London W1V 3RF
Tel: 020 7734 9878
Fax: 020 7734 9871
Michele Camarda

## Landseer Productions
140 Royal College Street
London NW1 0TA
Tel: 020 7485 7333
Fax: 020 7485 7573
email: mail@landseerfilms.com
Website: www.landseerfilms.com

## Large Door Productions
3 Shamrock Street
London SW4 6HF
Tel: 020 7627 4218
email: ldoor@demon.co.uk
John Ellis

## Little Bird Co
9 Grafton Mews
London W1P 5LG
Tel: 020 7380 3980
Fax: 020 7380 3981
email: info@littlebird.co.uk
Website: www.littlebird.ie

## Little Dancer Films
61 Benthal Road
London SE19 3JJ
Tel: 0208 806 7504
email: littledancerfilm@aol.com
Robert Smith

## London Films
71 South Audley Street
London W1K 1JA
Tel: 020 7499 7800
Fax: 020 7499 7994
email: luff@londonfilms.com
Website: www.londonfilms.com
Andrew Luff

## M W Entertainments Ltd
48 Dean Street
London W1V 5HL
Tel: 020 7734 7707
Fax: 020 7734 7727

## Malachite Productions
East Kirkby House
Spilsby
Lincolnshire PE23 4BX
Tel: 01790 763538
Fax: 01790 763409
email: info@malachite.co.uk
Website: www.malachite.co.uk
Charles Mapleston

## Malone Gill Productions Ltd
27 Campden Hill Road
London W8 7DX
Tel: 020 7937 0557
Fax: 0207 376 1727
email: malonegill@aol.com

Georgina Denison

## Manuel Productions Ltd Jo
11 Keslake Road
London NW6 6DG
Tel: 020 8930 0777
Fax: 020 8933 5475

## Maya Vision International Ltd
43 New Oxford Street
London WC1A 1BH
Tel: 020 7836 1113
Fax: 020 7836 5169
email: info@mayavisionint.com
Website: www.mayavisionint.com
John Cranmer

## Media 19
21 Foyle Street
Sunderland SR1 1LE
Tel: 0191 565 5709
Fax: 0191 565 6288
email: media19@media19.co.uk
Website: www.media19.co.uk
Nick Oldman, Belinda Williams

## Media Darlings Ltd
2/78 Greencroft Gardens
London NW6 3JQ
Tel: 020 7372 5020
Fax: 020 7372 0407
email: enquiries@mediadarlings.net
Michelle Kastly

## The Media Trust
3-7 Euston Centre
Regent's Place
Off Euston Road
London NW1 3JG
Tel: 020 7874 7600
Fax: 020 7874 7644
email: info@mediatrust.org
Website: www.mediatrust.org

## Mentorn Barraclough Carey
43 Whitfield Street
London W1P 67G
Tel: 020 7258 6800
Fax: 020 7258 6888
email: mentorn@mentorn.co.uk
Website: www.mentorn.co.uk

## Merchant Ivory Productions
46 Lexington Street
London W1R 3LH
Tel: 020 7437 1200/439 4335
Fax: 020 7734 1579
email:
miplondon@merchantivory.demon.c
o.uk
Website: www.merchantivory.com
Paul Bradley

## The Mersey Television Company

Campus Manor
Childwall Abbey Road
Liverpool L16 0JP
Tel: 0151 722 9122
Fax: 0151 722 6839
email: admin@merseytv.com
Website: www.merseytv.

## Millennium Pictures
Suite 77
2 Landsdowne Row
Berkley Square
London W1J 6HL
Tel: 020 7413 9171
Fax: 020 7493 4935
email: daniel@figuero.freeserve.co.uk
Website: www.figuero.co.uk

## Mirage Films Ltd
5 Wardour Mews
London W1V 8AL
Tel: 020 7734 3627
Fax: 020 7734 3735
email: production@miragefilms.co.uk
Ian Llande/Thomas Ritter

## Miramax International
Elsey House
24-30 Great Titchfield Street
London W1W 8BF
Tel: 020 7535 8300
Fax: 020 7535 8301
Website: www.miramax.com
David Aukin

## Momentum Productions
Century House
351 Richmond Road
Twickenham TW1 2ER
Tel: 020 8843 8300
Fax: 020 8538 9568
email: production@momentum.co.uk
Website: www.momentum.co.uk
Guy Meyer/Darren Cavanagh

## Mosaic Films Ltd
2nd Floor
8-12 Broadwick Street
London W1V 1FH
Tel: 020 7437 6514
Fax: 020 7494 0595
email: info@mosaicfilms.com
Website: www.mosaicfilms.com
Contact: Colin Luke (London)

## MW Entertainments
48 Dean Street
Soho
London W1D 5BF
Tel: 020 7734 7707
Fax: 020 7734 7727
email: contact@michaelwhite.co.uk

## Noel Gay Television
Shepperton Studios
Studios Road

Shepperton
Middx TW17 OQD
Tel: 01932 592575
Fax: 01932 592172

## Nova Productions
62 Ascot Avenue
Cantley
Doncaster DN3 6HE
Tel: 0870 765 1021
Fax: 0870 125 7917
email: info@novaonline.co.uk
Website: www.novaonline.co.uk
Andrew White, Maurice White,
Gareth Atherton
Film, television and graphics
production company, specialising in
documentary, entertainment, special
event and music promo production.
Producer of programmes released on
sell-through video on its own label
via subsidiary Nova Home
Entertainment and on other labels.
Game Show format development and
graphic production. Also training,
promotional and multi-camera OB
production for broadcast and non-
broadcast.

## Nunhead Films plc
Pinewood Studios
Pinewood Road
Iver Heath
Bucks SL0 0NH
Tel: 01753 650075
Fax: 01753 655 700
email: info@nunheadfilms.com
Carol Lemon, John Stewart

## Orbit Media Ltd
80a Dean Street
London W1D 3SN
Tel: 020 7287 4264
Fax: 020 7287 0984
Website: www.orbitmedia.co.uk
Jordan Reynolds

## Orlando TV Productions
Up-the-Steps
Little Tew
Chipping Norton
Oxon OX7 4JB
Tel: 01608 683218
Fax: 01608 683364
email: info@orlandodigital.co.uk
Website: www.orlandodigital.co.uk
Mike Tomlinson,

## Oxford Film and Video Makers
Centre For Film and Digital Media
54 Catherine Street
Oxford OX4 3AH
Oxford OX3 9HY
Tel: 01865 792731 or 01865 792732

Fax: 01865 742901
email: office@ofvm.org
Website: www.ofvm.org
Richard Duriez

## Oxford Film & Television
6 Erskine Road
London NW3 3AJ
Tel: 020 7483 3637
Fax: 020 7483 3567
email: email@oftv.co.uk
Website: www.oftv.co.uk
Annie Lee, Head of Productions

## Oxford Scientific Films
Oxford Scientific Films Ltd
Network House
Ground Floor
Station Yard, Thame
Oxon OX9 3UH
Tel: 01844 262 370
Fax: 01844 262 380
email: film.library@osf.uk.com
Website: www.osf.uk.com
Jane Mulleneux

## Pagoda Film & Television Corporation Ltd
Twentieth Century House
31-32 Soho Square
London W1V 6AP
Tel: 020 7534 3500
Fax: 020 7534 3501
email: pag@pagodafilm.co.uk
Head of Development

## Paladin Invision Ltd
8 Barb Mews
London W6 7PA
Tel: 0207 371 2123
Fax: 0207 371 2160
Website: www.pitv.com
Clive Syddall
A multi Emmy-Award winning
company specialising in Anglo-
American co-productions of quality,
popular factual programming
including history, science, current
affairs, religion and music and arts
programming

## paradogs Ltd
1st floor
17 - 25 Cremer St
London E2 8HD
Tel: 020 7613 3001 (Mobile 07970
107592)
email:
paradogs@pinkpink.demon.co.uk
Website: www.ofcamera.org.uk
Steven Eastwood, Director/producer

## Parallax Pictures
7 Denmark Street
London WC2H 8LS

Tel: 020 7836 1478
Fax: 020 7497 8062
email: info@parallaxpictures.co.uk
Website: www.parallaxpictures.co.uk
Sally Hibbin

## Paramount-British Pictures Ltd
Paramount House
162-170 Wardour Street
London W1V
Fax: 020 7734 0387

## Paranoid Celluloid
Keepers Cottage
Wennington
Abbots Ripton
Huntingdon
Cambridgeshire PE18 0JB
Tel: 00 44 (0)1487 773 255
Fax: 00 44 (0)1487 773 640
email: adammason@paranoid-
celluloid.com
Website: www.paranoid-celluloid.com

## Pathé Pictures
Kent House
Market Place
London W1N 8AR
Tel: 020 7323 5151
Fax: 020 7636 7594

## Peakviewing Transatlantic
The Wheelhouse
Bonds Mill
Stonehouse
Gloucestershire GL10 3RF
Tel: 01453 826300
Fax: 01453 826303
email: info@peakviewing.co.uk
Website: www.peakviewing.co.uk

## Persistent Vision Productions
299 Ivydale Road
London SE15 3DZ
Tel: 020 7639 5596
Carol Lemon, John Stewart

## Photoplay Productions
21 Princess Road
London NW1 8JR
Tel: 020 7722 2500
Fax: 020 7722 6662

## Picture Palace Films Ltd
13 Egbert Street
London NW1 8LJ
Tel: 020 7586 8763
Fax: 020 7586 9048
email: info@picturepalace.com
Website: www.picturepalace.com
Malcolm Craddock, Katherine
Hedderly

## Pilton Pictures

30 Ferry Road Avenue
Edinburgh EH4 4BA
Tel: 0131 343 1151
Fax: 0131 343 2820
email: info@piltonvideo.org
Website: www.piltonvideo.org.uk

## Planet 24 Productions
35-38 Portman Square
London W1H ONU
Tel: 020 7486 6268
Fax: 020 7612 0679
Website: www.planet24.com
Ed Forsdick

## Portman Productions
167 Wardour Street
London W1V 3TA
Tel: 020 7468 3400
Fax: 020 7468 3499

## Praxis Films
PO Box 290
Market Rasen
Lincs LN3 6BB
Tel: 01472 399976
Fax: 01472 399976
email: info@praxisfilms.com
Website: www.praxisfilms.com
Sue Waterfield

## Pretty Clever Pictures
Shepperton Studios
Shepperton
Middx TW17 0QD
Tel: 01932 592047
Fax: 01932 592454
email: pcpics@globalnet.co.uk
Gelly Morgan, Managing Director

## Prominent Features
34 Tavistock Street
London WC2E 7PB
Tel: 020 7497 1100
Fax: 020 7497 1133
email: 101322.552@compuserve.com
Website: www.palinstravels.co.uk
Steve Abbott

## Prominent Television
34 Tavistock Street
London WC2E 7PB
Tel: 020 7497 1100
Fax: Fax; 020 7497 1133
email: paulbird@prominent-tv.co.uk
Anne James/Steve Abbott

## Sarah Radclyffe Productions
10/11 St George's Mews
London NW1 8XE
Tel: 020 7483 3356
Fax: 020 7586 8063
email: mail@srpltd.co.uk
Sarah Radclyffe, Bill Godfrey

## Ragdoll Limited
Pinewood Studios
Pinewood Road
Iver Heath
Bucks SL0 0NH
Tel: 01753 631800
Fax: 01753 631831
email: pinewood@ragdoll.co.uk
Website: ragdoll.co.uk
Liz Queenan

## Raw Charm
Ty Cefn
Rectory Road
Cardiff CF1 1QL
Tel: 029 20 641511
Fax: 029 20 668220
email: pam@rawcharm.co.uk
Website: www.rawcharm.tv
Pamela Hunt

## Recorded Picture Co
24 Hanway Street
London W1T 1UH
Tel: 020 7636 2251
Fax: 020 7636 2261
email: rpc@recordedpicture.com
Website: www.recordedpicture.com
Karin Padgham

## Redwave Films (UK) Ltd
31-32 Soho Square
London W1D 3AP
Tel: 020 7753 7200
Fax: 020 7753 7201

## The Reel Thing Ltd
20 The Chase
Coulsdon
Surrey CR5 2EG
Tel: 020 8668 8188
email: info@reelthing.tv
Website: www.reelthing.tv
Frazer Ashford

## Revere Enterainment Company Limited
91 Berwick Street
London W1F 0NE
Tel: 020 7292 8370
Fax: 020 7292 8372
John Goldstone, Producer

## Revolution Films
c/o The Works
4 Great Portland Street
London W1W 8QJ
Tel: 020 7612 1080
Fax: 020 7612 1081
Website: www.theworksltd.com
Merryn Conaway

## Richmond Light Horse Productions Ltd
3 Esmond Court

Thackeray Street
London W8
Tel: 020 7937 9315
Fax: 020 7938 4024
Euan Lloyd

## Riverchild Films
2nd floor, 26 Goodge St
London W1T 2QG
Tel: 020 7636 1122
Fax: 020 7636 1133
email:
riverchild@riverchild.demon.co.uk

## RM Associates
46 Great Marlborough Street
London W1V 1DB
Tel: 020 7439 2637
Fax: 020 7439 2316
email: rma@rmassociates.co.uk
Neil Mundy (Director of Programmes)

## Roadshow Productions
11 Elvaston Place
London SW7 5QG
Tel: 020 7584 0542
Fax: 020 7584 1549
email: dzuhot@hotmail.com
Daniel Unger

## Rocket Pictures
1 Blythe Road
London W14 OHG
Tel: 020 7603 9530
Fax: 020 7348 4830
Luke Lloyd Davies

## Rodney Read
45 Richmond Road
Twickenham
Middx TW1 3AW
Tel: 020 8891 2875
Fax: 020 8744 9603
email:
Rodney_Read@blueyonder.co.uk
R.J.D. Read

## RSPB Film
The Lodge, Sandy
Bedfordshire SG19 2DL
Tel: 01767 680551
Fax: 01767 683262
email: mark.percival@rspb.org.uk
Website: www.rspb.org.uk
Mark Percival

## Samuelson Productions
13 Manette Street
London W1D 4AW
Tel: 020 7439 4900
Fax: 020 7439 4901

## Scala Productions
4th Floor, Portland House
London W1W 8QJ

Tel: 020 7612 0060
Fax: 020 7612 0031
email: scalaprods@aol.com
Nik Powell, Ian Prior

## Scottish Television Enterprises
Cowcaddens
Glasgow G2 3PR
Tel: 0141 300 3000
Fax: 0141 300 3030
Darrel James, Managing Director

## Screen Ventures
49 Goodge Street
London W1T 1TE
Tel: 020 7580 7448
Fax: 020 7631 1265
email: infro@screenventures.com
Website: www.screenventures.com

## September Films Ltd
Glen House
22 Glenthorne Road
London W6 ONG
Tel: 020 8563 9393
Fax: 020 8741 7214
email:
september@septemberfilms.com
Website: www.septemberfilms.com

## Shine Limited
108 Palace Gardens Terrace
London W8 4RT
Tel: 020 7313 8000
Fax: 020 7313 8041
email: info@shinelimited.com
Website: www.shinelimited.com
Marc Boothe

## Siren Film and Video Ltd
5 Charlotte Square
Newcastle-upon-Tyne NE1 4XF
Tel: 0191 232 7900
email: sirenfilms@aol.com
Website: childhoodstudies.com

## Siriol Productions
Phoenix Buildings
3 Mount Stuart Square
Butetown
Cardiff CF10 5EE
Tel: 02920 488400
Fax: 02920 485962
email: robin.lyons@siriol.co.uk
Website: www.siriolproductions.com
Robin Lyons, Managing Director

## Sirius Pictures
12 Elmley Street
Plumstead
London SE18 7NT
Tel: 00 44 (0)20 8854 1206
Fax: 00 44 (0)20 8854 1206
email: info@siriuspictures.co.uk
Website: www.siriuspictures.co.uk

## Sixteen Films
2nd Floor
187 Wardour Street
London W1F 8ZB
Tel: 020 7734 0168
Fax: 020 7439 4196
email: info@sixteenfilms.co.uk

## SKA Productions Ltd
1 Horse and Dolphin Yard
London W1V 7LG
Tel: 020 7434 0869
Fax: 020 7437 3245

## Skreba
Union Hall
29 Union Street
London SE1 1SC
Tel: 020 7357 9924
Fax: 020 7357 9920

## Sky Pictures
BSky B, 6 Centaurs Park
Grant Way, Syon Lane
Isleworth
Middlesex TW7 5QD
Tel: 020 7941 5588
Fax: 0207 941 5599

## Skyline Films
PO Box 821U
London W41 1WH
Tel: 0836 275584
Fax: 020 8354 2219
Steve Clark-Hall, Mairi Bett

## Sly Fox Films Limited
6 York Buildings
London WC2N 6JN
Tel: 020 7839 1000
Fax: 020 7839 6486
email: linfo@slyfoxfilms.com
Website: www.slyfoxfilms.com
Linda James

## Smoking Dogs Films
26 Shacklewell Lane
London E.8 2EZ
Tel: 020 7249 6644
Fax: 020 7249 6655
email: info@smokingdogsfilms.com
John Akomfrah, Lina Gopaul, David
Lawson

## Soho Communications
2 Percy Street
London W1T 1DD
Tel: 020 7637 5825
Fax: 020 7436 9740
email: Jstaton@dircon.co.uk
Website: sohocommunications.com
Jon Staton

## Sonnet Films
2-3 Duck Lane
London W1F OHX

Tel: 020 7292 4700
Fax: 020 7434 1531

## Sony Pictures Europe UK Ltd
Sony Pictures Europe House
25 Golden Square
London W1R 6LU
Tel: 020 7533 1111
Fax: 020 7533 1105

## Specific Films
25 Rathbone Street
London W1T 1NQ
Tel: 020 7580 7476
Fax: 020 7494 2676
email: info@specificfilms.com
Michael Hamlyn

## Spice Factory
81 The Promenade
Peacehaven
Brighton
East Sussex BN10 8LS
Tel: 01273 585275
Fax: 01273 585304
email: info@spicefactory.co.uk
Alex Marshall/Emily Kyriakides

## Stagescreen Productions
12 Upper St Martin's Lane
London WC2H 9JY
Tel: 020 7497 2510
Fax: 020 7497 2208
email: stagescreenprods@aol.com
Jeffrey Taylor

## Sterling Pictures
53 Great Portland Street
London W1W 7LG
Tel: 020 7323 6810
Fax: 020 7323 6811
email: admin@sterlingpictures.com
Website: www.sterlingpictures.com

## Talent Television
2nd Floor Regent House
235 Regent Street
London W1B 2EH
Tel: 020 7434 1677
Fax: 020 7434 1577
email: entertainment@talenttv.com
John Kaye Cooper, Managing
Director

## Talisman Films Limited
5 Addison Place
London W11 4RJ
Tel: 020 7603 7474
Fax: 020 7602 7422
email: email@talismanfilms.com
Richard Jackson, Andrew Lawton

## TalkBack Productions
36 Percy Street
London W1P 0LN
Tel: 020 7323 9777

Fax: 020 7637 5105

## Richard Taylor Cartoon Films
River View, Waterloo Drive
Clun, Craven Arms
Shropshire SY7 8JD
Tel: 01588 640 073

## Telescope Pictures Ltd
Twickenham Film Studios
Saint Margarets
Twickenham
Middlesex TW1 2AW
Tel: 020 8607 8888
Fax: 020 8607 8889
email: telescopepics@aol.com

## Teliesyn
Chapter Arts Centre
Market Road
Cardiff CF5 1QE
Tel: 029 2030 0876
Fax: 029 2030 0877
email: ebost:tv@teliesyn.demon.co.uk
Website: www.teliesyn.co.uk

## Tempest Films
33 Brookfield
Highgate West Hill
London N6 6AT
Tel: 020 8340 0877
Fax: 020 8340 9309
email: man@temp-films.demon.co.uk
Jacky Stoller

## Testimony Films
12 Great George Street,
Bristol BS1 5RS
Tel: 0117 925 8589
Fax: 0117 925 7668
email:
stevehumphries@testimonyfilms.com
Website: www.testimonyfilms.com
Steve Humphries

## The Illuminated Film Company
115 Gunnersbury Lane
Acton
London W3 8HQ
Tel: 020 8896 1666
Fax: 020 8896 1669
email: info@illuminatedfilms.com
Website: www.illuminatedfilms.com
Iain Harvey

## Thin Man Films
9 Greek Street
London W1D 4DQ
Tel: 020 7734 7372
Fax: 020 7287 5228
Claire Broughton

## Think TV
47 Dean Street

London W1
Tel: 07802 666 693
email: info@thinktv.co.uk
Website: www.thinkcompanies.com
Chris Barfoot/Terry Eckersley/Barry Upton
Current productions in development:
'Against All Odds', 'Play It Forward',
'The Albert Atkins Diet Book'.

## Tiger Aspect Productions
5 Soho Square
London W1V 5DE
Tel: 020 7434 0672
Fax: 020 7287 1448
email: pictures@tigeraspect.co.uk
Website: www.tigeraspect.co.uk

## TKO Communications
PO Box 130, Hove
East Sussex BN3 6QU
Tel: 01273 550088
Fax: 01273 540969
email: jkruger02@aol.com

## Toledo Productions
First Floor, 15 Greek Street
London W1D 4DP
Tel: 020 7292 8715
Fax: 020 7292 8701
email:
duncan.kenworthy@dnafilms.com

## Topaz Productions Ltd
Manchester House
46 Wormholt Road
London W12 0LS
Tel: 020 8749 2619
Fax: 020 8749 0358
email:
prints@topazprods.freeserve.co.uk

## Trademark Films
Phoenix Theatre
110 Charing Cross Road
London WC2H 0JP
Tel: 020 7240 5585
Fax: 020 7240 5586
email: mail@trademarkfilms.co.uk

## Trans World International
TWI House
23 Eyot Gardens
London W6 9TR
Tel: 020 8233 5400
Fax: 020 8233 5401

## Transatlantic Films
Studio 1
3 Brackenbury Road
London W6 0BE
Tel: 020 8735 0505
Fax: 020 8735 0605
email: mail@transatlanticfilms.com
Website: www.transatlanticfilms.com
Corisande Albert, Revel Guest

## Tribune Productions Ltd
22 Bentley Way
Stanmore
Middlesex HA7 3RP
Tel: 020 8420 7230
Fax: 020 8420 7230

## Trijbits Productions
14 -16 Great Pulteney Street
London W1R 3DG
Tel: 020 7439 4343
Fax: 020 7434 4447
email: trijbits@globalnet.co.uk
Julia Caithness

## Try Again Limited
Leigh Grove Farmhouse
Leigh Grove
Bradford on Avon
Wilts BA15 2RF
Tel: 01225 862 705
Fax: 01225 862 205
Michael Darlow, Rod Taylor, Chris Frederick

## Turn On TV
Warehouse 4
121 Princess Street
Manchester M1 7AG
Tel: 0161 247 7700
Fax: 0161 247 7711
email: mail@turnontv.co.uk
Website: www.turnontv.co.uk
Dee Hamid

## TV Cartoons
39 Grafton Way
London W1P 5LA
Tel: 020 7388 2222
Fax: 020 7383 4192
John Coates, Norman Kauffman

## Twentieth Century-Fox Productions Ltd
20th Century House
31-31 Soho Square
London W1V 6AP
Tel: 020 7437 7766
Fax: 020 7734 3187

## Twenty Twenty Television
Suite 2, Grand Union House
29 Kentish Town Road
London Nw1 9NX
Tel: 020 7284 2020
Fax: 020 7284 1810

## Tyburn Film Productions Ltd
Cippenham Court
Cippenham Lane
Cippenham, Nr Slough
Berkshire SL1 5AU
Tel: 01753 516767
Fax: 01753 691785

## UBA (United British Artists)
21 Alderville Road
London SW6 3RL
Tel: 01984 623619
Fax: 01984 623733

## Universal Pictures International
Oxford House
76 Oxford Street
London W1N 0H9
Tel: 020 7307 1300
Fax: 020 7307 1301

## Universal Pictures Ltd
1 Hamilton Mews
London W1V 9FF
Tel: 020 7491 4666
Fax: 020 7493 4702

## Upfront Television Ltd
39-41 New Oxford Street
London WC1A 1BN
Tel: 020 7836 7702
Fax: 020 7836 7701
email: info@celebritiesworldwide.com
Website: www.celebritiesworldwide.com
Claire Nye , Richard Brecker, Joint
Managing Directors:
Established in 1991, Upfront
Television has developed a reputation
as England's leading independent
production company, specialising in
celebrity booking with credits
including 'The Lord of the Rings: The
Return Of The King' UK premiere,
the Elle Style Awards 1998-2004, the
Mobo Awards 2003, the 2002
Kerrang! Awards, the 2000 Maxim
Women of the Year and the Brit
Awards. Paul Chowdhry, Jimmy
Gulzar, Victoria Silvstedt

## Vera Productions Ltd
3rd Floor
66/68 Margaret Street
London W1W 8SR
Tel: 020 7436 6116
Fax: 020 7436 6117/6016
email: racheail@vera.co.uk
Contact: Elaine Morris

## Vine International Pictures
VIP House, Greenacres
New Road Hill, Downe
Orpington Kent BR6 7JA
Tel: 01689 854 123
Fax: 01689 850 990
email: vine@easynet.co.uk
Website: www.vine-
international.co.uk

## Vixen Films
13 Aubert Park

Highbury
London N5 1TL
Tel: 020 7359 7368
Fax: 020 7359 7368
email: tg@tgraham.demon.co.uk

## Viz
4 Bank Street
Inverkeithing
Fife KY11 1LR
Tel: 01383 412811
Fax: 01383 418103
email: grigorfilm@aol.com
Murray Grigor

## Walsh Bros Ltd
24 Redding House, Harlinger Street
King Henry's Wharf
London SE18 5SR
Tel: 020 8858 6870/020 8854 5557
Fax: 020 8858 6870
email: info@walshbros.co.uk
Website: Website;
www.walshbros.co.uk
John Walsh

## Warner Bros International Television
Warner House
7th Floor
98 Theobalds Road
London WC1X 8WB
Tel: 020 7984 5439
Fax: 020 7984 5421

## Warner Bros. Productions Ltd
Warner Suite,, Pinewood Studios
Pinewood Road
Iver Heath
Buckinghamshire SL0 ONH
Tel: 01753 654545
Fax: 01753 655703

## Warner Sisters Film & TV Ltd, Cine Sisters Ltd
The Cottage
Pall Mall Deposit
124 Barlby Road
London W10 6BL
Tel: 020 8960 3550
Fax: 020 8960 3880
email: sisters@warnercine.com

## David Wickes Productions
10 Abbey Orchard Street
Westminster
London SW1P 2JP
Tel: 020 7222 0820
Fax: 020 7222 0822
email: wickesco@aol.com
David Wickes, Heide Wilsher

## Winchester Entertainment plc
19-21 Heddon Street
London, W1B 4BG

Tel: 020 7851 6500
Fax: 020 7851 6506
email: gsmith@winchesterent.co.uk
Website: www.winchesterent.com
Chief Executive: Gary Smith

## Working Title Films
Oxford House
76 Oxford Street
London W1D 1BS
Tel: 020 7307 2212
Fax: 020 7307 3002
Website: www.workingtitlefilms.com

## World Productions Limited
Eagle House
50 Tiarshall Street
London W1F 9BQ
Tel: 020 7734 3536
Fax: 020 7758 7070
email: info@world-productions.com
Website: www.world-
productions.com
Helen Saunders

## The Worldmark Production Company Ltd
7 Cornwall Crescent
London W11 1PH
Tel: 020 7792 9800
Fax: 020 7792 9801
David Wooster

## Zenith Entertainment plc
43-45 Dorset Street
London W1H 4AB
Tel: 020 7224 2440
Fax: 020 7224 3194
email: general@zenith.tv.co.uk

## Zenith North
11th Floor
Cale Cross House
156 Pilgrim Street
Newcastle upon Tyne NE1 6SU
Tel: 0191 261 0077
Fax: 0191 222 0271
email: zenithnorth@dial.pipex.com

## Zephyr Films
33 Percy Street
London W1T 2DF
Tel: 020 7255 3555
Fax: 020 7221 3777
email: chris@zephyrfilms.co.uk
Contact: Phil Robertson or Chris
Curling.

## Zooid Pictures Limited
66 Alexander Road
London N19 5PQ
Tel: 020 7281 2407
Fax: 020 7281 2404
email: pictures@zooid.co.uk
Website: www.zooid.co.uk

# PRODUCTION STARTS

With the advent of digital technology it is getting increasingly difficult to track and trace Production Starts. The list here is made up of the available informaton on feature-length films intended for theatrical release with a significant British involvement (whether creative, financial or UK-based) which went into production between January and December 2003. Additionally, production start date, distributor and release information is given where known up to 1 August 2004.

**Category A –**
Feature films where the cultural and financial impetus is from the UK and where the majority of personnel are British.

**Category B –**
Majority UK Co-Productions. Films in which, although there are foreign partners, there is a UK cultural content and a significant amount of British finance and personnel.

**Category C –**
Minority UK Co-productions. Foreign (non US) films in which there is a small UK involvement in finance or personnel.

**Category D –**
American financed or part-financed films made in the UK. Most titles have a British cultural content.

**Category E –**
American Films with some British financial involvement.

## Ae Fond Kiss...
16 June
Production Companies: **Sixteen Films, Bianca Films (Italy), EMC (Germany), Tornasol (Spain)**
Subsidy: **Scottish Screen**
Sales Agents: **The Works, Icon Entertainment, Diaphana (France), Tornasol (Spain), BIM (Italy)**
Other Finance: **Azure, Glasgow Film Office**
Budget: £3m
Dir: **Ken Loach**
with Atta Yaquib, Eva Birthistle, Riaz Ahmad, Shabana Baksh, Shamshad Akhtar, Ghizala Avan, Gary Lewis, David McKay
Country: UK/Italy/Germany/Spain/France
Distributor: **Icon Film Distribution**
Release date: Scheduled UK theatrical release on 17 September 2004
**Category B**

## Agent Cody Banks 2 Destination London
1 June
Production Companies: **Splendid Pictures (USA), Maverick Film Co (USA), Dylan Sellers Prod (USA),**
Sales Agents: **MGM/UA (USA)**
Budget: £16m
Dir: **Kevin Allen**
with Frankie Muniz, Anthony Anderson, Hannah Spearritt, Cynthia Stevenson, Daniel Roebuck, Anna Chancellor
Country: US/UK
Distributor: **20th Century Fox International (UK)**
Release date: 26 March 2004
Box office: £1,010,311
**Category D**

## Alexander
22 September
Production Companies: **Intermedia, Pacifica Film (USA)**
Sales Agents: **IS Film Distribution (USA), Warner Bros (USA), Constantin Film (USA), Golden Harves (HK), Shani Film (Israel)**
Budget: £100m
Dir: **Oliver Stone**
with Colin Farrel, Angelina Jolie, Anthony Hopkins, Jared Leto, Rosario Dawson, Val Kilmer
Country: US/UK
**Category E**

## Alfie
9 September
Production Companies: **Paramount Pictures (UK)**
TV backing: **BBC Films**
Sales Agents: **Paramount Pictures**
Budget: £20m
Dir: **Charles Shyer**
with Jude Law, Susan Saradndon, Marisa Tomei
Country: US/UK
**Category D**

## Asylum
18 August
Production Companies: **Seven Arts, Woodfall Films, Samson Films**
Sales Agents: **Seven Arts Inter (USA), Paramount Classics (USA)**
Other Finance: **Blue Ride (USA), Future Film Group**
Budget: £15m
Dir: **Nigel Roffe-Barker**
with Nabil Elouahabi, Dai Bradley, Furman Dar
Country: UK
**Category B**

## Being Julia
16 June
Production Companies: **Serendipity Point Films (Canada), ISL Films (Hungary), Myriad Pictures**
Sales Agents: **Myriad Pictures, Sony Pic Classics (USA), THINKFilm (Canada)**
Other Finance: **First Choice, Astral Media (Canada), Corus Entertainment, Greenberg Fund (Canada), Telefilm Canada (USA)**
Budget: £11m
Dir: **István Szabó**
with Annette Bening, Jeremy Irons
Country: UK/Canada/Hungary
**Category C**

## Beyond the Sea
10 November
Production Companies: **Archer Street, Quality International (Germany), Trigger Street Prod (USA)**
Sales Agents: **VisionView, Lions Gate**

Ent (Canada)
Budget: £14m
Dir: Kevin Spacey
with Kevin Spacey, Kate Bosworth,
John Goodman, Bob Hoskins, Brenda
Blethyn, Greta Scacchi
Country: UK/US/Germany
Category B

## Blackout Journey

Production Companies: **Towers of London, FilmLine**
Budget: £n/a
Dir: Siegfried Kamml
with Arno Frisch, Traute Furthner,
Marek Harloff, Mavie Hörbiger,
Proschat Madani, Antoine Monot Jr.
Marion Rottenhofer
Country: UK/**Austria/Germany**
Category C

## Blind Flight

6 January
Production Companies: **Parallax Independent, Partisan Films, Makar Productions, Samson Films (Ireland), Network Movie (Germany)**
TV backing: **ZDF/Arte (Germany)**
Subsidy: **Irish Film Board, Glasgow Film Office, Scottish Screen, UK Film Council, Arts Council of Northern Ireland**
Sales Agents: **Moviehouse Entertainment, Optimum Releasing**
Other Finance: **Matrix, Royal Bank of Scotland**
Budget: £2.3m
Dir: John Furse
with Ian Hart, Linus Roache
Country: UK/Germany/Ireland
Distributor: Optimum Releasing
Release date: 20 February 2004
Box office: £105,458
Category B

## Bride & Prejudice

14 July
Production Companies: **Bride Productions**
Sales Agents: **Pathé International/Miramax (USA)**
Other Finance: **Inside Track**
Budget: £15m
Dir: Gurinder Chadha
with Aishwarya Rai, Namrata Shirodkar
Country: UK
Category D

## The Bridges of San Luis Rey

3 April
Production Companies: **Pembridge Pictures, Spice Factory, Kanzaman (Spain), Davis Film (France)**

Sales Agents: **Senator Inter (Germany)**,
Other Finance: **Movision, Scion Film Financing**,
Budget: £13.4m
Dir: Mary McGuckian
with Robert De Niro, Kathy Bates,
Harvey Keitel, Gabriel Byrne
Country: UK/Spain/Ireland/France
Category B

## Bridget Jones: The Edge of Reason

12 October
Production Companies: **Working Title Films**
Sales Agents: **Universal**
Budget: £18m
Dir: Beeban Kidron
with Renée Zellweger, Colin Firth,
Hugh Grant
Country: UK
Category D

## Bride of Ice

13 February
Production Companies: **Marloo Media (Germany)**
Sales Agents: **Lightning**
Other Finance: **UKI Films**
Budget: £0.63m
Dir: Polly Steele
with Valentina Cervi, Ciarán McMenamin, William Armstrong,
James Purefoy
Country: UK
Category C

## Bullet Boy

Production Companies: **Shine Limited**
Sales Agents: **Portman Film and Television Ltd**
Dir: Saul Dibb
with Leon Black, Claire Perkins,
Ashley Walters
Country: UK
Category A

## Bye Bye Blackbird

25 October
Production Companies: **Samsa (Luxembourg), Reverse Angle Factory (germany), Dor Films (Australia), Ipso Facto Films**
Sales Agents: **Samsa Distribution (Luxembourg), Movihouse Ent**
Subsidy: **Film Fund Lux (Luxembourg), Osterreiche Film (Germany), MFG (Germany), NRW (Germany)**
Other Finance: **Great British Films**
Budget: £4.7m
Dir: Robinson Savary
with James Thierrée, Derek Jacobi,

Izabella Miko, Jodhi May
Country: UK/Germany/Luxembourg
Category C

## Chasing Liberty

25 May
Production Companies: **Alcon Entertainment (USA)**
Sales Agents: **Warner Bros (USA)**
Budget: £14m
Dir: Andy Cardiff
with Mandy Moore, Stark Sands,
Annabella Sciorra, Mark Harmon,
Jeremy Piven
Country: UK/US
Category D

## Churchill The Hollywood Years

23 March
Production Companies: **Little Bird**
TV backing: BSkyB
Subsidy: **UK Film Council**
Sales Agents: **Pathé International**
Other Finance: **IoM Film & TV Fund**
Budget: £10m
Dir: Peter Richardson
with Christian Slater, Neve Campbell,
Vic Reeves, Bob Mortimer, Leslie
Phillips, MacKenzie Crook, James
Dreyfus, Steve Pemberton, Harry
Enfield, Antony Sher
Country: UK/Ireland
Category B

## Closer to the Sun

Production Companies: **Global Films, Mnemoics, Edgelimagebank**
Budget: £0.6m
Category A

## Code 46

6 January
Production Companies: **Revolution Films**
TV backing: **BBC Films**
Subsidy: **UK Film Council**
Sales Agents: **The Works**
Other Finance: **United Artists (USA)**
Budget: £4.50m
Dir: Michael Winterbottom
with Tim Robbins, Samantha Morton
Country: UK/US
Category D

## Cold & Dark

18 November
Production Companies: **Cold Films, Future Film Group**
Sales Agents: **Beyond Films (Australia)**
Other Finance: **Paradigm Hyde**
Budget: £2.40m
Dir: Andrew Goth
with Luke Goss, Kevin Howarth,

Carly Turnbull, Matt Lucas, David Gant
Country: UK
Category A

## Compleat Female Stage Beauty
See Stage Beauty

## Country of My Skull
28 March
Production Companies: **Studio Eight, Merlin Films (Ireland), Chartoff Productions (USA), Phoenix Pictures (USA), Morula Pictures (South Africa), Film Afrika Worldwid (South Africa)**
Sales Agents: **The Works**
Other Finance: **Ingenious/Ind Dev. Corp of S.Africa**
Budget: £9.39
**Dir:** John Boorman
with Samuel L. Jackson, Juliette Bincoche, Brendan Gleeson, Menzi Ngubane, Nick Boraine
Country: UK/Ireland/Zaire/US
Category D

## Creep
20 October
Production Companies: **Artisan Ent (USA), Dan Films, Zero West (Germany)**
Subsidy: **UK Film Council, Filmstiftung NRW (Germany)**
Sales Agents: **Captitol Films, Pathé International, X-Filme (Germany)**
Budget: £3.3m
**Dir:** Chris Smith
with Franka Potente
Country: UK/Germany
Category B

## Curse of the Wererabbit
24 October
Production Companies: **Aardman Animation**
Sales Agents: **Dreamworks Distributors (USA)**
Budget: £25m
**Dir:** Nick Park
with the voice of Helena Bonham Carter, Ralph Fiennes
Country: UK/US
Category D

## Danny the Dog
22 January
Production Companies: **Europa Corp (France), Current Ent (USA)**
Sales Agents: **20th Century Fox (USA)**
Budget: £26.25m
**Dir:** Louis Leterrier
with Li Jet, Morgan Freeman, Bob

Hoskins
Country: UK/France/US
Category D

## De-Lovely
5 May
Production Companies: **Winkler Films (USA), Cloud Nine Films**
Sales Agents: **MGM/UA (USA)**
Budget: £15m
**Dir:** Irwin Winkler
with Kevin Kline, Ashley Judd, Kevin McNally, Allan Corduner, sandra Nelson, Keith Allen
Country: UK/US/Luxembourg
Category D

## Dead Fish
10 October
Production Companies: **SE8 Group, Orange Pictures (Germany), IMF (Germany)**
Sales Agents: **Franchise Pictures (USA)**
Budget: £8m
**Dir:** Charley Stadler
with Gary Oldman, Robert Carlyle, Terence Stamp, Elena Anaya
Country: UK/US/Germany
Category B

## Deadline: Beirut
Production Companies: **Psychology News, Film Consortium, UK Film Council, Baker Street MediaRaphael Films, Cinetelefilms,**
Country: UK/France/Tunisia
Category C

## Dead Man's Shoes
7 May
Production Companies: **Warp Films**
TV backing: FilmFour
Subsidy: **East Midlands Media Inv.**
Sales Agents: **Optimum Releasing**
Budget: £1.5m
**Dir:** Shane Meadows
with Paddy Considine, Gary Stretch, Toby Kebbell
Country: UK
Category A

## Dear Frankie
17 March
Production Companies: **Scorpio films**
Subsidy: **UK Film Council/Scottish Screen**
Sales Agents: **Pathé International**
Other Finance: **Inside Track**
Budget: £3.20
**Dir:** Shona Auerbach
with Emily Mortimer, Gerard Butler
Country: UK
Category A

## Dear Wendy
26 September
Production Companies: **Lucky Punch (Denmark), Liberator 2 (France), Pain Unlimited (Germany), Zoma Films**
TV backing: **TV2/Denmark (Denmark), Arte/ZDF (Germany), Canal Plus (France), Arte France (France)**
Subsidy: **Dan Filminstiute (Denmark), Nord Film and TV Fund (Denmark)**
Sales Agents: **Trust Film Sales (Denmark)**
Other Finance: **Nordisk Film SVT Sweden, Filmstiftung NRW (Germany)**
Budget: £4.6m
**Dir:** Thomas Vinterberg
with Jamie Bell
Country: UK/France/ Denmark/Germany
Category C

## A Different Loyalty
28 April
Production Companies: **Forum Films (Canada), Spice Factory**
Sales Agents: **Arclight Pictures (Australia), Lions Gate (South Africa)**
Other Finance: **Movision**
Budget: £9.5m
**Dir:** Marek Kanievska
with Sharon Stone, Rupert Everett
Country: UK/Canada
Category C

## Enduring Love
17 September
Production Companies: **Free Range Films**
TV backing: **FilmFour**
Subsidy: **UK Film Council**
Sales Agents: **Pathé International**
Other Finance: **Inside Track**
Budget: £3m
**Dir:** Roger Michell
with Samantha Morton, Rhys Ifans, Daniel Craig
Country: UK
Category A

## Fat Slags
10 August
Production Companies: **Artists Independent Network**
Sales Agents: **Pathé International**
Budget: £3.5m
**Dir:** Ed Bye
with Sophie Thompson, Fiona Allen, Jerry O'Connell, Geri Halliwell
Country: UK
Category A

## Fateless

aka Sorstalanság
15 December
Production Companies: **Magic Media
(Hungary), EuroArts (Germany),
Renegade Films**
Subsidy:**Hungarian Ministry,
Cultural Her, Hungarian Motion
Picture Found, MDR (Germany),
MDM (Germany) MFG (Germany)**
Budget: £7m
Dir: **Lajos Koltai**
with János Bán, Judit Schell
Country: UK/Germany/Hungary
Category C

## Five Children and It

30 June
Production Companies: **Captiol
Films, Engame Ent (USA), Jim
Henson Co (USA)**
Subsidy: **UK Film Council**
Other Finance: **IoM Film & TV Fund**
Budget: £12.3m
Dir: **John Stephenson**
with Eddie Izzard, Kenneth Branagh,
Zoë Wanamaker, Freddie Highmore,
Tara Fitzgerald, John Sessions, Alex
Jennings, Jonathan Bailey, Jessica
Claridge, Poppy Rogers
Country: UK/US
Category D

## Frozen

16 August
Production Companies: **Liminal
Films, RS Productions, Shoreline
Films, Freedonia Films**
Sales Agents: **Trust Film Sales**
Other Finance: **Zentorpa**
Budget: £1.40m
Dir: **Juliet McKoen**
with Shirely Henderson, Roshan Seth,
Ralf Little, Kerry Fox, Sean Harris
Country: UK
Category A

## A Good Woman

3 November
Production Companies: **Meltemi
Entertainment, International Arts
Ent (USA), Lighthouse Ent (USA),
Buskin Film (Italy), Kanzaman
(Spain)**
Sales Agents: **Beyond Films
(Australia)**
Other Finance: **Magic Hour Finance,
Thema Productions (Luxembourg),
Matrix Film Finance**
Budget: £7m
Dir: **Mike Barker**
with Helen Hunt, Scarlett Johansson,
Tom Wilkinson, Mark Umbers
Country: UK/US

Category D

## Harry Potter and the Prisoner of Azkaban

24 February
Production Companies: **Heyday
Films**
Sales Agents: **Warner Bros (USA**
Budget: £100m
Dir: **Alfonso Cuarón**
with Daniel Radcliffe, Rupert Grint,
Emma Watson, Julie Christie, Robbie
Coltrane, Michael Gambon, Gary
Oldman, Alan Rickman, Fiona Shaw
Country: UK/US
Distributor: Warner Bros
Release date: 4th June 2004
Box office: £45,217,254
Category D

## Head in the Clouds

19 March
Production Companies: **Remstar
(Canada), Dakota, Tusk**
Sales Agents: **Arclight Pictures (Aus)**
Other Finance: **Movision**
Budget: £11.6m
Dir: **John Duigan**
with Charlize Theron, Penélope Cruz,
Stuart Townsend, Thomas
Kretschmann, Karin Vanasse
Country: UK/Canada
Category C

## Hello You

1 August
Production Companies: **Fecund
Films**
Other Finance: Private Investors
Budget: **£0.6m**
Dir: **John Keates**
Country: UK
Category A

## The Hillside Strangler

21 June
Production Companies: **Tartan
Films, Constant Howling Prod
(USA)**
Sales Agents: **Tartan Films
Distribution**
Budget: £1.2m
Dir: **Chuck Parello**
with Thomas C. Howell, Nicholas
Turturro, Allison Lange, Tricia
Dickson, Roz Witt
Country: UK/US
Category E

## Hollywood Files

Production Companies:
**Studio Eight, GFT, Movieweb,**
Budget: £3.28m
Country: UK/Italy/Canada
Category C

## How to Film Your Neighbour

25 April
Production Companies: **Mad As Hell
Films**
Other Finance: Private Investors
Budget: £1m
Dir: **Steve Kitt**
with Nik Renouf, Heriette Nelson,
Eric Redman, Steve Dineen, Simon
Roberts
Country: UK
Category A

## In My Father's Den

8 September
Production Companies: **T.H.E. Film
(New Zealand)**
Subsidy: **UK Film Council**
Sales Agents: **Element X, NZ Film
Commission, Optimum Releasing,
Icon Film Distribution**
Other Finance: **Visionview, NZ On
Air**
Budget: £3m
Dir: **Brad McGann**
with Matthew MacFadyen, Emily
Barclay, Colin Moy, Miranda Otto
Country: UK/New Zealand
Category C

## Innocence

Production Companies:
**Blue Light, UK Film Council, Ex
Nihilo, Love Streams**
Country: UK/France
Category C

## Inside I'm Dancing

20 October
Production Companies: **WT2,
Octagon Films (Ireland)**
Subsidy: **Irish Film Board**
Sales Agents: **Universal Pictures
(USA)**
Other Finance: Private Investors
Budget: £3.6m
Dir: **Damien O'Donnell**
with James McAvoy, Steven
Robertson
Country: UK/Ireland
Category B

## Jet Lag

12 October
Production Companies: **Visionary
Films (Cha), Balagan Productions**
Sales Agents: **Visionary (Cha)**
Budget: £2.6m
Country: UK/China
Category C

## Jonjo Mickeybo

15 October
Production Companies: **WT2, New**

Moon Pictures (Ireland)
Subsidy: **Irish Film Board, N.Ireland Film and TV Commission**
Sales Agents: **Universal Pictures (USA)**
Budget: £3m
Dir: Terry Loane
with Niall Wright, John Joe McNeil, Gina McKee, Adrain Dunbar, Julie Walters
Country: UK/Ireland
**Category B**

## Ladies in Lavender
15 September
Production Companies: **Scala Productions**
Subsidy: **UK Film Council**
Sales Agents: **Lakeshore Ent (USA)/Entertainment**
Other Finance: **Baker Street Media Finance, Paradigm Hyde Films**
Budget: £3.6m
Dir: Charles Dance
with Judi Dench, Maggie Smith,
Country: UK
**Category A**

## Last Sign
Production Companies:
**Spice Factory, Transfilm, Carrere**
Budget: £7.2m
Dir: Douglas Law
with Andie MacDowell, Tim Roth, Samuel Le Bihan, Mimi Kuzyk, Tyler Hynes, Margot Kidder
Country: UK/France/Canada
**Category C**

## Layer Cake
30 June
Production Companies: **Ska Films**
Sales Agents: **Columbia Tristar (USA), Sony Pictures Ent (USA)**
Budget: £5m
Dir: Matthew Vaughn
with Daniel Craig, Michael Gambon, Tom Hardy, Colm Meaney, Jamie Foreman, Sienna Miller
Country: UK
**Category D**

## The Life and Death of Peter Sellers
14 April
Production Companies: **HBO (USA)**
TV backing: **HBO (USA)**
Other Finance: **Aurelio De Laurentis (Italy)**
Budget: £15m
Dir: Anthony Hopkins
with Geoffrey Rush, Charlize Theron, Emily Watson, Sonia Aquino
Country: UK/US
**Category D**

## Lila Says
Production Companies:
**Passion Pictures, UK Film Council, Huit et Demi, Zeal, France 2, Pyramide**
**Category C**

## Man About Dog
Production Companies:
**Pot Boiler Productions, Treasure Entertainment,Irish Film Board, Section 481**
Budget: £1.50
Dir: Paddy Brethnach
with Alan Leech, Ciaran Nolan, Tom Murphy, Sean McGinley, Fiona Flanagan
Country: UK/Ireland
**Category B**

## Map of the Universe 2 The Memos
15 August
Production Companies: **Global Films**
Sales Agents: **Global Films**
Other Finance: **Barclays Bank**
Budget:
Dir: Nick Peterson
with Dolly Di Rosso, John Watehouse, Stewart Timings
Country: UK
**Category A**

## Map of the Universe 3 In & Out of Planet Earth
19 October
Production Companies: **Global Films**
Sales Agents: **Global Films**
Other Finance: **Barclays Bank, Mnemonics Studios**
Dir: Nick Peterson
with Dolly Di Rosso, John Watehouse, Stewart Timings
Country: UK
**Category A**

## The Merchant of Venice
23 November
Production Companies: **Movision, Spice Factory, Avenue Pictures (USA), Navidi-Wilde Productions (Italy)**
Subsidy: **UK Film Council/Instituto Luce (Italian)**
Sales Agents: **Arclight Pictures (Australia)**
Other Finance: **Scotts Atlantic (USA), Studios DeLux (Luxembourg)**
Budget: £18m
Dir: Michael Radford
with Al Pacino, Lynn Collins, Ian McKellen, Joseph Fiennes
Country: UK

**Category D**

## Millions
5 May
Production Companies: **Mission Pictures**
TV backing: **BBC Films**
Budget: £5m
Dir: Danny Boyle
with James Nesbitt, Daisy Donovan, Lewis McGibbon, Alex Etel
Country: UK
**Category A**

## Mother Theresa
Production Companies:
**Spice Factory -Blue Spice, Lux Vide**
Budget: £8.10
Country: UK/Italy/Sri Lanka
**Category C**

## Mouth to Mouth
5 May
Production Companies: **MJW Productions**
Dir: Alison Murray
with August Diehl
Country: UK/Germany
**Category C**

## My Brother is a Dog
1 October
Production Companies: **Tradewind Pictures (Germany), Bos Bros (Germany), Film & TV Production (Neth), F&ME**
TV backing: **WDR (Germany)**
Subsidy: **BRW (Germany), MDM (Germany), FFA (Germany) BKM (Germany) Dutch Film Fund (Netherlands)**
Sales Agents: **Bavaria Films Intl (Germany)**
Other Finance: **Invicta Capital**
Budget: £3.1m
Country: UK/Germany/Netherlands
**Category C**

## My Summer Love
4 August
Production Companies: **Apocalypso Pictures**
TV backing: **BBC Films**
Subsidy: **Film Consortium**
Sales Agents: **TheWorks**
Other Finance: **BS Media Finance**
Budget: £1.6m
Dir: Paul Pawlikowski
with Paddy Considine, Emily Blunt, Nathalie Press
Country: UK
**Category A**

## Niceland
21 July

Production Companies: **Zik Zak Filmworks (Iceland), Tradewind Pictures (Germany), Nimbus Films (Denmark) F&ME**
Subsidy: **NRW (Germany), Nord. Film & TV Fund, Dan Film Institute (Denmark), Ice. Film Fund, Ham. Film Fund, Eurimages**
Sales Agents: **Bavaria Films International**
Other Finance: **Invicta Capital**
Budget: £1.75m
**Dir:** Fridrik Thór Fridriksson
Country:
UK/Iceland/Germany/Germany/Denmark/ Norway
Category C

## Nine Songs

Production Companies: **Revolution Films**
**Dir:** Michael Winterbottom
with Kieran O'Brien, Georgina Burke, Margo Stilley
Country: UK
Category A

## Oh Happy Days!

Production Companies:
**Ugly Duckling, Fine and Mellow, Nordisk, Matrix Film Finance, Danish Film Institute**
Country: UK/Denmark
Budget: £1.88
Category C

## Omagh

Production Companies: **Izenda Productions Limited**
**Tiger Aspect, Channel 4, Hell's Kitchen/Irish Film Board, RTE**
**Dir:** Pete Travis
with Gerard McSorley, Michelle Forbes, Brenda Fricker, Stuart Graham, Peter Balance, Pauline Hutton, Fiona Glascott
Country: UK/Ireland
Category B

## Out on a Limb

Production Companies:
**Theta Films, Out on a Limb**
Country: UK/South Africa
Budget £1.0m
**Dir:** Robert Heath
with Henry Goodman, Neil Stuke
Category B

## The Oyster Farmer

Production Companies: **Anthony Buckley Films (Australia), Oyster Farmer Films**
Subsidy: **Film Finance Corp (Australia), New S. Wales Film, TV Off**

Sales Agents: **Beyond Films (Australia)**
Other Finance: **Showtime (Australia), Ocean/Dendy (Australia), Little Wing Films, Future Film Group**
Budget: £3m
**Dir:** Anna Reeves
with Alex O'Lachlan, Jim Norton, Diana Glenn
Country: UK/Australia
Category C

## The Preacher

8 September
Production Companies: **Theorema Films (Netherlands), Samsa Films (Luxembourg), Davd P. Kelly Productions**
TV backing: **Vara TV (Netherlands), NOS (Netherlands)**
Other Finance: **Dutch, Dutch Cobo Fund (Netherlands)**
Budget: £2.3m
Country: UK/Netherlands
Category C

## Phantom of the Opera

15 September
Production Companies: **Really Useful Films, Scion Films**
Sales Agents: **Odyssey Ent (USA), Warner Bros (USA)**
Budget: £48m
**Dir:** Joel Schumacher
with Gerard Butler, Emmy Rossum, Patrick Wilson, Mirander Richardson, Minnie Driver
Country: UK/US
Category A

## Piccadilly Jim

24 November
Production Companies: **Mission Pictures**
Subsidy: **Isle of Man Film Ltd**
Sales Agents: **Myriad Pictures (USA), Universal Pictures (USA)**
Other Finance: **Inside Track**
Budget: £9m
**Dir:** John McKay
with Sam Rockwell, Tom Wilkinson, Brenda Blethyn, Hugh Bonneville, Frances O'Connor, Allison Janney
Country: UK/US
Category D

## Proof

24 September
Production Companies: **Hart Sharp Ent (USA)**
Sales Agents: **Miramax (USA),**
Other Finance: **Endgame Ent**
Budget: £12m
**Dir:** John Madden

with Anthony Hopkins, Gwyneth Paltrow, Jake Gyllenhall, Hope Davis
Country: UK/US
Category D

## The Purifiers

2003
Production Companies: **Bill Kenwright Films Ltd., S2S Post, Vestry Films**
Sales Agents: **Park Entertainment Ltd**
**Dir:** Richard Jobson
with Kevin McKidd, Dominic Monaghan, Amber Sainsbury, Rachel Grant, Gordon Alexande
Country: UK
**Distributor**: Working Title (UK)
Release date:
Category A

## Queen of Sheba's Pearls

Production Companies:
**AKA Pictures, Sweetwater, Swedish Film Institute, TV4**
Country: UK/Sweden
Category B

## Rabbit on the Moon

17 November
Production Companies: **Beanca Films (Germany), Calle Cruzada (Spain), Headgear Films**
Other Finance: **Fidicine Fund (Spain), Gussi Distribution (Mexico), Private Investors**
Budget: £1.8m
**Dir:** Jorge Ramîrez Suárez
with Bruno Bichir, Jesus Ochoa, Alvaro Guerrero
Country: UK/Germany/Spain
Category C

## Red Light Runners

28 August
Production Companies: **Nu Creation Film Group (Ireland)**
Sales Agents: **Miramax (USA)**
Other Finance:  Private Investors
Budget:
**Dir:** Nick Egan
with Michael madsen, Harvey Keitel, Crispin Glover, Kate Ashfield
Country: UK
Category B

## Red Rose

14 June
Production Companies: **Palm Tree UK**
Sales Agents: **Eagle Rock UK**
Other Finance: Private Investors
Budget: £2.50
**Dir:** Robbie Moffat
with Michael E. Rodgers, Lucy Russell, Rebecca R. Palmer

Country: UK
Category A

## Resident Evil
**11 August**
Production Companies: **Davis Films (France)**, **Constantin Film (Germany)**, **Impact Pictures**
Sales Agents: **Sony Pictures Ent (USA)**, **Screen Gems (USA)**
Budget: £25m
**Dir:** Alexander Witt
Country: UK
Category C

## The Rulers, the Dealers and the Losers
**13 July**
Production Companies: **RDL Productions**
Other Finance: Private Investors
Budget: £0.7m
**Dir:** Stephen Jackson
with Terrance Anderson, Moshe Dennis, Richard Field, Ricky Hards, Edward Bryant
Country: UK
Category A

## School For Seduction
**30 March**
Production Companies: **Ipso Facto Films**
Sales Agents: **AV Pictures, Helkon, Telepool (Germany)**
Other Finance: **Her Films, UK Films Services**
Budget: £3m
**Dir:** Sue Heel
with Kelly Brook, Dervla Kirwan, Margi Clarke, Emily Woof, Tim Healy, Jessica Johnson
Country: UK
Category A

## Sex Lives of the Potato Men
**28 April**
Production Companies: **Devotion Film**
Subsidy: **UK Film Council**
Sales Agents: **Entertainment**
Budget: £1.8m
**Dir:** Andy Humphries
with Johnny Vegas, MacKenzie Crook, Mark Gatiss
Country: UK
**Distributor**: Entertainment
Release date: 20 February 2004
Category A

## Shaun of the Dead
**11 May**
Production Companies: **WT2, Big Talk Productions**

Sales Agents: **Universal Pictures (USA)**
Budget: £3.76m
**Dir:** Edgar Wright
with Simon Pegg, Kate Ashfield, Nick Frost, Lucy Davis, Dylan Moran
Country: UK/US
Distributor: UIP
Release date: 9 April 2004
Box office: £6,557,247
Category A

## Sky Captain and the World of Tomorrow
**10 March**
Production Companies: **Brooklyn (USA)**, **Natural Nylon**
Sales Agents:
**Dir:** Kerry Conran
with Jude Law, Gwyneth Paltrow, Angelina Jolie
Country: UK/US
Category D

## Sons of the Wind
**17 March**
Production Companies: **Dan Films, UGC Images (France), Mate Productions (Spain)**
Sales Agents: **UGC Images (France)**
Other Finance: **Ingenious**
Budget: £12.9m
**Dir:** Julien Seri
with Burt Kwouk
Country: UK/France/Spain
Category B

## Something Borrowed
Production Companies:
**Gold Circle Films, 26 Films, Something Borrowed Ltd**
**Dir:** Clare Kilner
with Debra Messing, Dermot Mulroney
Country: UK/US
Category D

## Spivs
**31 March**
Production Companies: **Carnaby Productions**
Sales Agents: **Content International**
Budget: £2.4m
**Dir:** Colin Teague
with Ken Stott, Nick Moran, Kate Ashfield, Dominic Monaghan, Jack Dee, Linda Bassett, Elizabeth Berrington, Roshan Seth, Paul Kaye
Country: UK
Category A

## Stage Beauty
**27 June**
Production Companies: **Qwerty Films, Ni European Filmprod**

**(Germany), Tribeca Productions**
TV backing: **BBC Films**
Sales Agents: **Icon Ent. Momentum Pictures**
Budget: £9m
**Dir:** Richard Eyre
with Billy Crudup, Claire Danes, Rupert Everett, Tom Wilkinson, Ben Chaplin, Hugh Bonneville, Richard Griffiths
Country: UK/Germany/US
**Distributor**: Momentum Pictures
Release date: Scheduled UK theatrical release on 3 September 2004
Category B

## The Statement
**31 March**
Production Companies: **Serendipity P. Films (Canada), Odessa Films (France), Company Pictures, Spice Factory**
Sales Agents: **Summit Ent (USA), Sony Pic Classics (USA)**
Other Finance: **Movision**
Budget: £11.2m
**Dir:** Norman Jewison
with Michael Caine, Tilda Swinton, Jeremy Northam, Alan Bates, John Boswall, Matt Craven, Frank Finlay, Ciarán Hinds, William Hutt, Noam Jenkins
Country: UK
Category C

## Strings
**4 August**
Production Companies: **Bald films (Denmark), Bob Film (Sweden), Nordisk Film (Norway), F&ME**
Sales Agents: **Trust Film Sales (Den)**
Other Finance: **Sandrew Metronome (Denmark)**
Budget: £2.4m
**Dir:** Anders Ronnow-Klarlund
Country: UK/Denmark/Sweden/Norway
Category C

## That Touch of Pink
**28 April**
Production Companies: **Sienna Films (Canada), Martin Pope Productions**
TV backing: **Chum TV (Canada), Movie Central (Canada), Movie Network (Canada)**
Subsidy: **Canada TV Fund (Canada), Astral Media (Canada)**
Sales Agents: **Alliance Atlantis (Canada), Redbus,, Mongrel Media (Canada)**
Other Finance: **Telefilm Canada (Canada), Greenberg Fund (Canada), Invicta Film Partnership**
Budget: £3m

**Dir:** Ian Iqbal Rashid
with Jimi Mistry, Kyle MacLachlan, Kristen Holden-Reid, Suleka Mathew
Country: UK/Canada
Category C

## Things to Do Before You're 30
7 September
Production Companies: **Samuelson Productions**
Sales Agents: **Alliance Atlantis (USA), Momentum Pictures**
Other Finance: **IoM Film and TV Fund, First Choice, Royal Bank of Scotland**
Budget: £3m
**Dir:** Simon Shore
with Dougray Scott, Emilia Fox, Jimi Mistry, Billie Piper, Shaun Parkes
Country: UK
Category A

## Thunderbirds
6 March
Production Companies: **Working Title**
Sales Agents: **Universal Pictures (USA)**
Other Finance: Private Investors
Budget: £41m
**Dir:** Jonathan Frakes
with Bill Paxton, Anthony Edwards, Sophia Myles, Ron Cook, Brady Corbet, Soren Fulton, Vanessa Anne Hudgens, Rose Keegan
Country: UK/US/France
Distributor: UIP
Release date: 23 July 2004
Box office: £2,866,922
Category D

## Tooth
28 April
Production Companies: **Redbus Pictures, Archangel Productions**
Sales Agents: **Lakeshore Ent (USA)**
Budget: £7.5m
**Dir:** Edward Nammour
with Harry Enfield, Vinnie Jones, Stephen Fry, Jim Broadbent, Tim Dutton, Sally Phillips, Jerry Hall, Richard E. Grant, Phyllida Law, Anna Wing
Country: UK/US
Distributor: Redbus Film Distribution
Release date: 13 February 2004
Category D

## Trauma
30 April
Production Companies: **Ministry of Fear**
TV backing: **BBC Films**

Subsidy: **IoM Film and TV Fund**
Sales Agents: **Myriad Pictures (USA), Warner Bros (USA), Filmax (Spain), Nordisk (Sweden)**
Other Finance: **First Choice**
Budget: £8m
**Dir:** Marc Evans
with Colin Firth, Mena Suvari
Country: UK/Ireland/US
Category D

## Tristan & Isolde
3 September
Production Companies: **Scott Free Productions**
Sales Agents: **Franchise Pictures, 20th Century Fox (USA)**
Other Finance: **Matrix Film Finance**
Budget: £30m
**Dir:** Kevin Reynolds
with Rufus Sewell, Dexter Fletcher, Sophia Myles, James Franco, David O'Hara
Country: UK/Czech Republic/Germany
Category B

## Troy
22 April
Production Companies: **Warner Bros (USA), Village Roadshow (USA),**
Sales Agents: **Warner Bros (USA)**
Other Finance: £62m
Budget:
**Dir:** Wolfgang Petersen
with Brad Pitt, Eric Bana, Orlando Bloom, Peter O'Toole, Rose Byrne
Country: UK/US/MT/Australia
Distributor:
Release date: 14 May 2004
Box office: £17,964,967
Category D

## Upside of Anger
Production Companies:
**Sun-Lite Pictures**
**Dir:** Jack Binder
with Kevin Costner, Joan Allen, Erika Christensen
Category D

## Valiant
15 September
Production Companies: **Vanguard Animation, Ealing Studios**
Subsidy: **UK Film Council**
Sales Agents: **Odyssey Ent, Entertainment, Buena Vista (USA)**
Other Finance: **BS Media Finance**
Budget: £27.5m
**Dir:** Gary Chapman
with the voices of Ewan McGregor, Hugh Laurie, Rupert Everett, Jim Broadbent, Ricky Gervais, John Hurt, Ben Kingsley, Olivia Williams, John

Cleese
Country: UK/US
Category A

## Vanity Fair
19 May
Production Companies: **Granada Films, Tempesta Films (USA)**
Sales Agents: **Focus Features (USA)**
Budget: **£14.2m**
**Dir:** Mira Nair
with Reese Witherspoon, Eileen Atkins, Jim Broadbent, Gabriel Byrne, Romola Garai, Duglas Hodge, Bob Hoskins, Rhys Ifans
Country: UK/US
Box office:
Category D

## Vera Drake
30 September
Production Companies: **Thin Man Films**
Subsidy: **UK Film Council**
Sales Agents: **Studio Canal (France)**
Budget: £5m
**Dir:** Mike Leigh
with Imedlda Staunton, Jim Broadbent, Philip Davis, Fenella Woolgar, Daniel Mays
Country: UK
Category A

## A Way of Life
1 September
Production Companies: **Awol Films**
TV backing: **HTV**
Subsidy: **UK Film Council/Arts Council of Wales**
Sales Agents: **Portman Films/Verve Pictures**
Budget: £2m
**Dir:** Amma Asante
with Brenda Blethyn, Oliver Haden, Stephanie James, Gary Sheppeard, Dean Wong, Sara Gregory
Country: UK
Category A

## A Way Through the Woods
8 September
Production Companies: **Celador**
Sales Agents: **Fox Searchlight (USA)**
Other Finance: **DNA Films**
Budget: £5m
**Dir:** Julian Fellowes
with Emily Watson, Rupert Everett
Country: UK
Category D

## White on White
29 June
Production Companies: **Cinerenta (Germany)**
Sales Agents: **Lakeshore Ent (USA)**

Budget: £12.5m
**Dir:** Roger Spottiswoode
with Barry Pepper, Willem Dafoe,
Claire Forlani, Jacinda Barrett, Alan
Cumming, Ian Hart, Tom Wilkinson
Country: UK/Germany/US
**Category D**

## Wild Side

Production Companies:
**Maïa Films, Aligator Films, Zephyr
Films, Lancelot Films**
**Dir:** Sébastien Lifshitz
with Stephanie Michelini, Edouard
Nikitne, Yasmine Belmadi, Josiane
Stoléu, Fabrice Rodriguez
Country: UK/France/Belgium
**Category C**

## Wimbledon

**14 July**
Production Companies: **Working
Title**
Sales Agents: **Universal Pictures
(USA)**
Other Finance: **Inside Track,
Miramax (USA)**
Budget: £25m
**Dir:** Richard Loncraine
with Paul Bettany, Kirsten Dunst,
Sam Neil, Jon Favreau, Bernard Hill
Country: UK/US
**Category D**

## The Wooden Camera

Production Companies: **Richard
Green and Associates, Odelion, Tall
Stories**
Other Finance: **European
Commission, UK Film Council**
**Dir:** NtshaveniWa Luruli
with Junior Singo, Innocent
Msimango, Dana De Agrella, Lisa
Petersen, Jean-Pierre Cassel
Country: UK/US
**Category C**

## Yes

**14 April**
Production Companies: **Adventure
Pictures**
Subsidy: **UK Film Council**
Sales Agents: **Green Street Films
(USA)**
Budget: £1.4m
**Dir:** Sally Potter
with Simon Abkarian, Joan Allen,
Samantha Bond, Shirley Henderson
Country: UK
**Category A**

Listed here are feature-length films, both British and foreign which had a theatrical release in the UK between January and December 2003. Films released during the latter half of 2002 and still on release in 2003 are shown italicised.

Entries quote the title, distributor, UK release date, certificate, country of origin, director/s, leading players, production company/ies, duration, gauge (other than 35 mm) and the Sight and Sound reference (or Film Monthly Bulletin reference in the case or re-releases) if available.

Box office totals are provided and also take into account films still on release in 2004 (ie those released in November or December 2002). Opening weekend information is also included.

Films with some or total UK involvement are highlighted with monetary symbols representing the nations of the co-producers. * denotes re-release

Credits are taken from the SIFT database compiled by Filmographic Services of the bfi National Film Library. Additional research by Elena Marcarini

## 2 Fast 2 Furious
United International Pictures – 20 June
12A (US/Germany) 2003
Director:  John Singleton
Producer: Neal H. Moritz
Screenplay: Michael Brandt, Derek Haas
Story: Michael Brandt, Derek Haas Gary Scott Thompson
Based on characters created by Gary Scott Thompson
Director of Photography: Matthew F. Leonetti
Editors: Bruce Cannon, Dallas Puett
Production Designer: Keith Brian Burns
Music:  David Arnold
Cast:
Paul Walker – Brian O'Conner
Tyrese – Roman 'Ro' Pearce
Eva Mendes – Monica Fuentes
Cole Hauser – Carter Verone
Chris 'Ludacris' (C) Bridges – Tej
James Remar – Agent Markham
Thom Barry –Agent Bilkins
Michael Ealy – Slap Jack
Junior, Mark Boone – Detective Whitworth
Devon Aoki – Suki
© Mikona Productions GmbH & Co. KG.
Production Companies:
Universal Pictures presents a Neal H. Moritz production of a John Singleton film
In association with Mikona Productions GmbH & Co. KG.
107 minutes 32 seconds (11 seconds cut)
Locations: Miami (Florida, USA)
Sight and Sound. v13.n8.August 2003 p.62-63
Box Office: £7,570,861
Opening Weekend: £2,747,875
Screens: 424

## 8 Mile
United International Pictures – 17 January
15 USA/Germany 2002
Director: Curtis Hanson
Producers:  Brian Grazer
Curtis Hanson
Jimmy Iovine
Screenplay: Scott Silver

Director of Photography: Rodrigo Prieto
Editor: Jay Rabinowitz
Craig Kitson
Production Designer: Philip Messina
Music/Music Arrangers: Eminem
Luis Resto
Cast:
Eminem – Jimmy Smith Jr
Kim Basinger – Stephanie
Mekhi Phifer – Future
Brittany Murphy – Alex
Evan Jones – Cheddar Bob
Omar Benson Miller – Sol George
De'Angelo Wilson – DJ Iz
Eugene Byrd – Wink
Taryn Manning – Janeane
© Mikona Productions GmbH & Co. KG
Production Companies:
Universal Pictures and Imagine Entertainment present
a Brian Grazer/ Curtis Hanson production
In association with Mikona Productions GmbH & Co. KG
110 minutes 23 seconds
Location: Detroit (USA)
Sight  and Sound: v.13, n.2, February 2003, p. 36-37, 42
Box Office: £13,254,845
Opening Weekend: £4,440,334
Screens: 423

## The 25th Hour
Buena Vista International – 25 April
15 USA 2002
Director: Spike Lee
Producers: Spike Lee, Jon Kilik, Tobey Maguire, Julia Chasman
Screenplay: David Benioff
Based on his novel
Director of Photography: Rodrigo Prieto
Editor: Barry Alexander Brown
Production Designer:  James Chinlund
Music/Music Conductor:  Terence Blanchard
Cast:
Edward Norton –  Monty Brogan
Philip Seymour Hoffman –  Jacob Elinsky
Barry Pepper –  Francis Xavier Slaughtery
Rosario Dawson –  Naturelle Riviera

Anna Paquin – Mary D'Annunzio
Brian Cox – James Brogan
Tony Siragusa – Kostya Novotny
Levani – Uncle Nikolai
Misha Kuznetsov – Senka Valghobek
Isiah Whitlock Jr – Agent Flood
Michael Genet – Agent Cunningham
Patrice O'Neal – Khari
Al Palagonia – Salvatore Dominick
Aaron Stanford – Marcuse
Marc H. Simon – Schultz
Armando Riesco – Phelan
© Touchstone Pictures
Production Companies:
Touchstone Pictures presents
a 40 Acres and a Mule
Filmworks/Industry
Entertainment/Gamut Films
production
134 minutes 36 seconds
Location: **New York (NY, USA)**
Sight and Sound: **v.13, n.3, March
2003, p.58**
Box Office: **£831,902**
Opening Weekend: **£198,341**
Screens: **114**

## Aapke Pehle Bhi Kahin Dekha...
**Gurpreet Video International – 10
January**
Box Office: **£12,529**
Opening Weekend: **£5,257**
Screens: **5**

## About Schmidt
**Entertainment – 24 January
15 USA 2002**
Director: **Alexander Payne**
Producers: **Harry Gittes, Michael
Besman**
Screenplay: **Alexander Payne
Jim Taylor**
Based on the novel by **Louis Begley**
Director of Photography: **James
Glennon**
Editor:**Kevin Tent**
Production Designer:**Jane Ann
Stewart**
Music: **Rolfe Kent**
Cast:
Jack Nicholson – Warren Schmidt
Hope Davis – Jeannie Schmidt
Dermot Mulroney – Randall Hertzel
Len Cariou – Ray Nichols
Howard Hesseman – Larry Hertzel
Kathy Bates – Roberta Hertzel
June Squibb – Helen Schmidt
Matt Winston – Gary Nordin,
Warren's replacement – Harry
Groener – John Rusk – Connie
Ray – Vicki Rusk
© New Line Productions, Inc.
Production Company

New Line Cinema presents
a Michael Besman/
Harry Gittes production
125 minutes 14 seconds
Location: **Omaha (Nebraska, USA)**
Sight and Sound: **v.13, n.3, p. 34**
Box Office: **£3,854,737**
Opening Weekend: **£757,325**
Screens: **220**

## The Actors
**Momentum Pictures – 16 May
15 United
Kingdom/Ireland/USA/Germany
2002**
Director: **Conor McPherson**
Producers: **Stephen Woolley, Neil
Jordan, Redmond Morris**
Screenplay: **Conor McPherson**
From an original story by Neil
Jordan
Director of Photography: **Seamus
McGarvey**
Editor: **Emer Reynolds**
Production Designer: **Mark Geraghty**
Music/Music Conductor:
**Michael Nyman**
Cast
Michael Caine – Anthony O'Malley
Dylan Moran – Tom
Michael Gambon – Barreller
Lena Headey – Dolores Barreller
Miranda Richardson – Mrs Magnani
Michael McElhatton – Jock
Aisling O'Sullivan – Rita
Ben Miller – Clive ©
FilmFour/Company of Wolves
Production Companies:
FilmFour, Miramax Films and
Senator Film present in association
with Bord Scannán na hÉireann/The
Irish Film Board
a Company of Wolves production
in association with Four Provinces
Films
Produced with the support of
investment incentives for the Irish
Film Industry provided by the
Government of Ireland
91 minutes 42 seconds
Location: **Dublin (Ireland)**
Sight and Sound: **v.13, n.5, p. 38**
Box Office: **£458,220**
Opening Weekend: **£226,860**
Screens: **270**

## Adaption.
**Columbia TriStar – 28 February
15 USA 2002**
Director: **Spike Jonze**
Producers: **Edward Saxon, Vincent
Landay, Jonathan Demme**
Screenplay: **Charlie Kaufman,
Donald Kaufman**
Based on the book **The Orchid Thief**

by **Susan Orlean**
Director of Photography: **Lance
Acord**
Editor: **Eric Zumbrunnen**
Production Designer: **K.K. Barrett**
Music: **Carter Burwell**
Cast
Nicolas Cage – Charlie Kaufman/
Donald Kaufman
Meryl Streep – Susan Orlean
Chris Cooper – John Laroche
Tilda Swinton – Valeria
Cara Seymour – Amelia
Brian Cox – Robert McKee
Judy Greer – Alice the waitress
Maggie Gyllenhaal – Caroline
Ron Livingston – Marty
Jay Tavare – Matthew Osceola
G. Paul Davis – Russell
Roger Willie – Randy
© Columbia Pictures Industries, Inc
Production Companies:
Columbia Pictures presents in
association with Intermedia Films
a Magnet/Clinica Estetico
production
114 minutes and 42 seconds
Sight and Sound: **v.13, n.3, p.34**
Box Office: **£1,280,860**
Opening Weekend: **£238,958**
Screens: **94**

## Agent Cody Banks
**20th Century Fox – 25 July
12A USA 2003**
Director: **Harald Zwart**
Producers: **David C. Glasser
Andreas Klein, Guy Oseary, Dylan
Sellers, David Nicksay**
Screenplay: **Ashley Edward Miller,
Zack Stentz, Scott Alexander, Larry
Karaszewski**
Story: **Jeffrey Jurgensen**
Director of Photography: **Denis
Crossan**
Editor: **Jim Miller**
Production Designer: **Rusty Smith**
Music: **John Powell**
Cast:
Frankie Muniz – Cody Banks
Hilary Duff – Natalie Connors
Angie Harmon – Ronica Miles
Keith David – CIA director
Cynthia Stevenson – Mrs Banks
Arnold Vosloo – Molay
Ian McShane – Brinkman
Daniel Roebuck – Mr Banks
Darrell Hammond – Earl
Martin Donovan – Dr Connors
© Metro-Goldwyn-Mayer Pictures,
Inc.
Production Companies::
Metro-Goldwyn-Mayer Pictures
presents

a Splendid Pictures, Maverick Films, Dylan Sellers production
102 minutes 14 seconds
(7 seconds cut)
Location: **Vancouver (Canada)**
Sight and Sound: **vol.13, n.9, p.36**
Box Office: **£1,444,146**
Opening Weekend: **£534,312**
Screens: **363**

### Aileen: Life and Death of a Serial Killer

Optimum Releasing – 21 November 2003
15 UK 2003
Directors: **Nick Broomfield, Joan Churchill**
Producer: **Jo Human**
Camera: **Joan Churchill**
Editor: **Claire Ferguson**
Music: **Rob Lane**
Cast:
Aileen Wuornos, Nick Broomfield, Joe Hobson, Steve Glazer aka 'Dr.Legal', Dawn Botkins, Tyria Moore, Arlene Pralle, Danny Caldwell, Michelle Showan, Jerry Moss
© **Lafayette Film Ltd**
Production Companies::
A Lafayette Film produced for Channel 4
92  minutes and 52 seconds
Sight and Sound: **vol.14, n.1, p.36**
Box Office: **£12,702**
Opening Weekend: **£4,294**
Screens: **3**

### Alien - Director's Cut

Twentieth Century Fox – 31 October
Box Office: **£542,950**
Opening Weekend: **£208,081**
Screens: **134**

### All Quiet on the Western Front (re)

BFI – 7 November
Box Office: **£13,092**
Opening Weekend: **£2,778**
Screen: **1**

### All the Real Girls

Columbia TriStar – 01 August
15 USA 2002
Director: **David Gordon Green**
Producers:  **Lisa Muskat, Jean Doumanian**
Screenplay: **David Gordon Green**
Story: **David Gordon Green, Paul Schneider**
Director of Photography: **Tim Orr**
Editors: **Zene Baker, Steven Gonzales**
Production Designer:  **Richard Wright**
Music/Original Score

Performed/Recorded by: **David Wingo, Michael Linnen**
Cast:
Patricia Clarkson – Elvira Fine
Maurice Compte – Bo
Zooey Deschanel – Noel
Danny McBride – Bust-Ass
Ben Mouton – Uncle Leland
Paul Schneider – Paul
Shea Whigham – Tip
John Kirkland – Justin
Maya Ling Pruitt – Feng-Shui
Heather McComb – Mary-Margaret
James Marshall Case – Judge Harvey
© **Jean Doumanian Productions Inc.**
Production Companies::
**Sony Pictures Classics presents a Jean Doumanian production
This film was produced with the assistance of the Mark Silverman Fellowship for New Producers/The Sundance Insititute
This film was developed with the assistance of the Sundance Institute**
107 minutes and 24 seconds
Location: **Marshall (North Carolina, USA), Asheville (North Carolina, USA)**
Sight and Sound: **v. 13, n. 9, p.37**
Box Office: **£80,820**
Opening Weekend: **£18,829**
Screens: **9**

### Amandla! A Revolution in Four Part Harmony

Metrodome Distributors – 19 December
12A USA/South Africa 2002
Director: **Lee Hirsch**
Producers:  **Lee Hirsch, Sherry Simpson Dean**
Cinematographers:  **Clive Sacke
Ivan Leathers
Brand Jordaan**
Editor: **Johanna Demetrakas**
Featuring – African Devoted Artists – The Anc National Choir – Gerhard Botes – Audrey Brown – Jeremy Cronin – The Community of Diepkloof, Soweto – Peter 'Commissar' Dimba – Abdullah Ibrahim – Ronnie Kasrils – Peter Khumalo – Sibongile Khumalo – Big Voice Jack Lerole – Sibusiso Lerole – Andile Magengefele – Itumeleng MMal Adrianne de la Rosa – Gail Smith – Johan Steinberg – Vincent Vena – Nkosana Xulu – Lindiwe Zulu – © **Kwela Productions
Production Productions**
Production Companies::
**Kwela Productions in association with Bomb Films, HBO/Cinemax Documentary Films, The Ford**

Foundation and the South African Broadcasting Corporation
102 minutes 56 seconds
Sight and Sound: **v.14, n. 2, p. 34**
Box Office: **£11,673**
Opening Weekend: **£3,024**
Screens: **2**

### American Chai

Bollywood Films – 18 July
Box Office: **£4,813**
Opening Weekend: **£2,782**
Screens: **6**

### American Cousins

Bard – 28 November
15 United Kingdom 2002
Director: **Donald Coutts**
Producer: **Margaret Matheson**
Screenplay: **Sergio Casci**
Director of Photography: **Jerry Kelly**
Editor: **Lindy Cameron**
Production Designer:  **Andrew Harris**
Music: **Donald Shaw**
Cast:
Danny Nucci – Gino
Shirley Henderson – Alice
Gerald LepkSight – Roberto
Vincent Pastore – Tony
Dan Hedaya – Settimo
Russell Hunter – Nonno
Stevan Rimkus – JoJo
Stephen Graham – Henry
Jake Abraham – Vince
Alan McQueen – Ostap
© **Unblinking Eye Partnership/Unblinking Eye No. 2 Partnership**
Production Companies::
**Little Wing Films
A Bard Entertainments production developed with financial assistance from Scottish Screen and from the Scottish Screen National Lottery Fund
in association with The Glasgow Film Office
Script Factory**
93 minutes 8 seconds
Scotland
Sight and Sound: **v. 14, n.1, p. 36-37**
Box Office: **£21,323**
Opening Weekend: **£7,633**
Screens: **6**

### American Pie: The Wedding

United International Pictures – 15 August
15 USA/Germany 2003
Director: **Jesse Dylan**
Producers: **Warren Zide, Craig Perry, Chris Moore, Adam Herz, Chris Bender**
Screenplay: **Adam Herz**

Based on characters created by himself
Director of Photography: **Lloyd Ahern**
Editor: **Stuart Pappé**
Production Designer: **Clayton Hartley**
Music/Score Producer: **Christophe Beck**
Cast:
**Jason Biggs – Jim Levenstein
Molly Cheek – Mrs Levenstein, Jim's mom
Alyson Hannigan – Michelle Flaherty
January Jones – Cadence Flaherty
Thomas Ian Nicholas – Kevin Myers
Seann William Scott – Steve Stifler
Eddie Kaye Thomas – Paul Finch
Fred Willard – Harold Flaherty
Eugene Levy – Mr Levenstein, Jim's dad
Deborah Rush – Mary Flaherty**
© **Loumolo GmbH & Co KG**
Production Companies:
**Universal Pictures presents a Zide/Perry - LivePlanet production
In association with Loumolo GmbH & Co KG
96 minutes and 10 seconds**
Sight and Sound: **vol. 13, n.10, p. 44**
Box Office: **£17,011,925**
Opening Weekend: **£4,151,788**
Screens: **426**

## Analyze That

**Warner Bros – 28 February
15 USA/Australia 2002**
Director: **Harold Ramis**
Producers: **Paula Weinstein, Jane Rosenthal**
Screenplay: **Peter Steinfeld, Harold Ramis, Peter Tolan**
Based on characters created by –
**Kenneth Lonergan, Peter Tolan**
Director of Photography: **Ellen Kuras**
Editor: **Andrew Mondshein**
Production Designer: **Wynn Thomas**
Music: **David Holmes**
Cast:
**Robert De Niro – Paul Vitti
Billy Crystal – Dr Ben Sobel
Lisa Kudrow – Laura Sobel
Joe Viterelli – Jelly
Reg Rogers – Raoul Berman
Cathy Moriarty-Gentile – Patti LoPresti
John Finn – Richard Chapin
Kyle Sabihy – Michael Sobel
Callie Thorne – Agent Cerrone
Pat Cooper – Salvatore Masiello
Frank Gio – Lou Rigazzi**
© **Warner Bros. (US, Canada, Bahamas, Bermuda)**

© Village Roadshow Films (BVI) Limited (all other territories)
Production Companies::
**Warner Bros Pictures presents in association with Village Roadshow Pictures and NPV Entertainment
a Baltimore Spring Creek Pictures, Face/Tribeca production
95 minutes and 38 seconds**
Location: **New York (NY, USA), New Jersey (NY, USA)**
Sight and Sound: **vol.13, n.3, p.35**
Box Office: **£1,323,773**
Opening Weekend: **£575,278**
Screens: **290**

## Andaaz

**Tip Top Entertainment – 23 May**
Box Office: **£317,530**
Opening Weekend: **£101,504**
Screens: **32**

## Angela

**Optimum Releasing – 15 August
15 Italy 2001**
Director: **Roberta Torre**
Producers: **Lierka Rusic, Rita Rusic**
Screenplay/Story: **Roberta Torre**
Director of Photography: **Daniele Ciprì**
Editor: **Roberto Missiroli**
Art Director: **Enrico Serafini**
Music: **Andrea Guerra**
Cast:
**Donatella Finocchiaro – Angela Parlagreco
Andrea Di Stefano – Masino
Mario Pupella – Saro Parlagreco
Tony Gambino – Santino
Erasmo Lo Bello – Mimmo
Maria Mistretta – Minica
Giuseppe Pettinato – Raffaele Santangelo**
© **Rita Rusic Company/Movieweb**
Production Companies::
**Rita Rusic Company and Movieweb present
91 minutes 4 seconds**
Location: **Palermo (Italy), Sicily (Italy)**
Sight and Sound: **v.13, n.9, p. 37, 38.**
Box Office: **£2,243**
Opening Weekend: **£724**
Screen: **1**

## Anger Management

**Columbia TriStar – 06 June
15 USA 2003**
Director: **Peter Segal**
Producers: **Jack Giarraputo, Barry Bernardi**
Screenplay: **David Dorfman**
Director of Photography: **Donald M. McAlpine**

Editor: **Jeff Gourson**
Production Designer: **Alan Au**
Music: **Teddy Castellucci** — Cast:
**Jack Nicholson – Dr Buddy Rydell
Adam Sandler – Dave Buznik
Marisa Tomei – Linda
Luis Guzmán – Lou
Allen Covert – Andrew
Lynne Thigpen – Hon. Brenda Daniels, the judge
Kurt Fuller – Frank Head
Jonathan Loughran – Nate
Krista Allen – Stacy
January Jones – Gina**
© **Revolution Studios Distribution Company LLC**
Production Companies::
**Revolution Studios presents a Happy Madison production
104 minutes 53 seconds**
Location: **Los Angeles (CA, USA)**
Sight and Sound: **v.13, n. 7, p.36**
Box Office: **£5,772,351**
Opening Weekend: **£ 1,768,335**
Screens: **431**

## Animal Factory

**Optimum Releasing – 04 July
15 USA 2000**
Director: **Steve Buscemi**
Producers: **Elie Samaha, Andrew Stevens, Julie Yorn, Steve Buscemi**
Screenplay: **Edward Bunker John Steppling**
Based on the novel – The Animal Factory by
**Edward Bunker**
Director of Photography: **Phil Parmet**
Editor: **Kate Williams**
Production Designer: **Steve Rosenzweig**
Music: **John Lurie**
Cast:
**Willem Dafoe – Earl Copen
Edward Furlong – Ron Decker
Danny Trejo – Vito
Mark Boone Junior – Paul Adams
Seymour Cassel – Lieutenant Seeman
Mickey Rourke – Jan the Actress
Tom Arnold – Buck Rowan
John Heard – James Decker
Chris Bauer – Bad Eye
Rockets Redglare – Charles 'Big Rand' Rand**
© **Animal Productions LLC**
Production Companies::
**Franchise Pictures presents Phoenician Entertainment/ Industry Entertainment/ Artists Production Group production
94 minutes 26 seconds**

Location: **Philadelphia (PA, USA)**
Sight and Sound: **v.13, n.9, p.40**
Box Office: £59,405
Opening Weekend: £8,801
Screens: **5**

## Antwone Fisher

**Twentieth Century Fox – 16 May**
**15 USA 2002**
Director: **Denzel Washington**
Producers: **Todd Black, Randa**
**Haines, Denzel Washington**
Screenplay: **Antwone Fisher**
Director of Photography: **Philippe**
**Rousselot**
Editor: **Conrad Buff**
Production Designer: **Nelson Coates**
Music: **Mychael Danna**
Cast:
**Derek Luke – Antwone Fisher**
**Joy Bryant – Cheryl Smolley**
**Denzel Washington – Jerome**
**Davenport**
**Salli Richardson – Berta**
**Earl Billings – James**
**Kevin Connolly – Slim**
**Viola Davis – Eva**
**Rainoldo Gooding – Grayson**
**Novella Nelson – Mrs Tate**
**Yolanda Ross – Nadine**
**Kenté Scott – Kansas City**
**Stephen Snedden – Berkley**
© Twentieth Century Fox Film
Corporation [all territories except
Brazil, Italy, Korea, Japan, Spain]
© TCF Hungary Film Rights
Exploitation Limited Liability
Company/Twentieth
Century Fox Film Corporation
[Brazil, Italy, Korea, Japan, Spain]
Production Companies::
**Fox Searchlight Pictures presents a**
**Mundy Lane/Todd Black production**
— 119 minutes 46 seconds
Location: **Cleveland (Ohio, USA),**
**San Diego (CA, USA)**
Sight and Sound: **v.13, n. 6, p.36**
Box Office: £174,618
Opening Weekend: £59,976
Screens: **46**

## Ararat

**Momentum Pictures – 18 April**
**15 Canada/France  2002**
Director: **Atom Egoyan**
Producers: **Robert Lantos**
**Atom Egoyan**
Screenplay: **Atom Egoyan**
The historical events in this film are
based on Clarence Ussher's eye-
witness account of the Armenian
genocide of 1915, published as An
American Physician in Turkey
Director of Photography: **Paul**

Sarossy
Editor: **Susan Shipton**
Production Designer: **Phillip Barker**
Music/Score Producer: **Mychael**
**Danna**
Cast:
**David Alpay – Raffi**
**Charles Aznavour – Edward Saroyan**
**Eric Bogosian – Rouben**
**Brent Carver – Philip**
**Marie-Josée Croze – Celia**
**Bruce Greenwood – Clarence**
**Ussher/Martin**
**Arsinée Khanjian – Ani**
**Elias Koteas – Ali/Jevdet Bay**
**Christopher Plummer – David**
**Simon Abkarian – Arshile Gorky**
© Serendipity Point Films/Ego Film
Arts
Production Companies::
**Alliance Atlantis and Serendipity**
**Point Films present**
**in association with Ego Film Arts**
**and ARP**
**a Robert Lantos production**
**Produced with the participation of**
**Telefilm Canada, The Movie**
**Network, Super Ecran, Astral Media,**
**The Harold Greenberg Fund/Le**
**Fonds Harold Greenberg**
**Produced with the**
**assistance/participation of Canada**
**The Canadian Film or Video**
**115 minutes 26 seconds**
Location: **Alberta (Canada), Toronto**
**(Canada)**
Sight and Sound: **v.13, n. 5, p.38-39.**
Box Office: £39,375
Opening Weekend: £4,656
Screens: **6**

## Armaan

**Eros International Ltd – 16 May**
Box Office: £316,524
Opening Weekend: £111,124
Screens: **27**

## Asmali Konak

**Rio Distribution – 5 December**
Box Office: £ 39,273
Opening Weekend: £2,350
Screens: **2**

## Auto Focus

**Columbia TriStar – 07 March**
**18 USA 2002**
Director: **Paul Schrader**
Producers: **Scott Alexander, Larry**
**Karaszewski, Todd Rosken, Pat**
**Dollard, Alicia Allain**
Screenplay: **Michael Gerbosi**
Based on the book **The Murder of**
**Bob Crane by Robert Graysmith**
Director of Photography: **Fred**
**Murphy**

Editor: **Kristina Boden**
Production Designer: **James**
**Chinlund**
Music: **Angelo Badalamenti**
Cast:
**Greg Kinnear – Bob Crane**
**Willem Dafoe – John Carpenter**
**Rita Wilson – Anne Crane**
**Kurt Fuller – Werner Klemperer**
**Maria Bello – Patricia Olsen Crane**
**Ron Leibman – Lenny**
**Ed Begley Jr – Mel Rosen**
**Michael Rodgers – Richard Dawson**
**Michael McKean – video executive**
**Christopher Neiman – Robert Clary**
**Bruce Solomon – Edward H.**
**Feldman, the producer**
**Lyle Kanouse – John Banner**
**Donnamarie Recco –**
**Melissa/Mistress Victoria**
**Cheryl Lynn Bowers – Cynthia Lynn**
© Focus Puller, Inc
Production Companies::
**Sony Pictures Classics**
**in association with**
**Propaganda Films and Good**
**Machine**
**105 minutes 25 seconds**
Location: **Arizona (USA), New York**
**City (NY, USA)**
Sight and Sound: **v.113, n.3, p. 32-33,**
36
Box Office: £39,341
Opening Weekend: £15,117
Screens: **19**

## Baaz

**Spark Entertainment – 07 February**
Box Office: £26,306
Opening Weekend: £8,571
Screens: **8**

## Bad Boys 2

**Columbia TriStar – 03 October**
**15 USA 2003**
Director: **Michael Bay**
Producer: **Jerry Bruckheimer**
Screenplay: **Ron Shelton, Jerry Stahl**
Story: **Marianne Wibberley, Cormac**
**Wibberley, Ron Shelton**
Based on characters created by
**George Gallo**
Director of Photography: **Amir**
**Mokri**
Editors: **Mark Goldblatt**
**Thomas A. Muldoon**
**Roger Barton**
Production Designer: **Dominic**
**Watkins**
Music: **Trevor Rabin**
Cast:
**Martin Lawrence  – Detective**
**Marcus Burnett**
**Will Smith  – Detective Mike Eugene**

Lowrey
Gabrielle Union – Sydney 'Syd'
Burnett
Jordi Mollà – Hector Juan Carlos
'Johnny' Tapia
Peter Stormare – Alexei
Theresa Randle – Theresa Burnett
Joe Pantoliano – Captain Howard
Michael Shannon – Floyd Poteet
Jon Seda – Roberto
Otto Sanchez – Carlos
© Columbia Pictures Industries, Inc.
Production Companies:
Columbia Pictures presents
a Don Simpson/Jerry Bruckheimer
production
146 minutes 37 seconds
Location: Miami (Florida, USA)
Puerto Rico
Sight and Sound: v. 13, n. 11, p. 32
Box Office: £8,686,047
Opening Weekend: £3,175,258
Screens: 383

## Bad Guy
Metro Tartan – 11 July
18 Republic of Korea 2001
Director: **Kim Ki-deok**
Producer: **Lee Seung-jae**
Screenplay: **Kim Ki-duk**
Director of Photography: **Hwang
Chul-hyun**
Editor: **Hahm Sung-won**
Art Directors: **Kim Sun-joo
Kim Hyun-ok**
Music: **Park Ho-joon**
Cast:
Cho Jae-hyun – Han-ki
Seo Won – Sun-hwa
Kim Yoon-tae – Jung-tae
Choi Duk-moon – Myoung-soo
Kim Jung-young – Eun-hye
Choi Yoon-young – Hyun-ja
Shin Yoo-jin – Min-jung
NamGoong Min – Hyun-soo
Lee Han-wee – Dal-soo
© LJ Film
Production Companies::
Tube Entertainment,
LJ Film, Light & Joy — 102 minutes
29 seconds
Sight and Sound: v.13, n.8, p.36
Box Office: £11,375
Opening Weekend: £2,979
Screens: 3

## Baghban
Eros International Limited – 03
October
Box Office: £748,028
Opening Weekend: £118,528
Screens: 29

## Balzac and the Little
## Chinese Seamstress

Soda Pictures – 09 May
12A France/China 2002
Director: **Dai Sijie**
Producer: **Lise Fayolle**
Screenplay: **Dai Sijie, Nadine Perront**
Based on the novel by
Dai Sijie
Director of Photography: **Jean-Marie
Dreujou**
Editors: **Julia Gregory
Luc Barnier**
Art Director: **Cao Jiuping**
Music: **Wang Pujian**
Cast:
**Zhou Xun** – little Chinese
seamstress
**Liu Ye** – Ma
**Chen Kun** – Luo
**Wang Shuangbao** – village chief
**Cong Zhijun** – old tailor
**Wang Hongwei** – Four Eyes
**Xiao Xiong** – Four Eyes' mother
**Tang Zuohul** – miller
**Chen Wei** – village chief's wife
**Chen Tianlu** – commune head
**Fan Qing-Yun** – doctor
© Les Productions Internationales "Le
Film"/Les Films de la
Suane/StudioCanal France/France 3
Cinéma/TF1 International
Production Companies::
**Lise Fayolle presents
in association with Philippe
Rousselet
a production of Productions
Internationale "Le Film"
in co-production with Le
StudioCanal, France 3 Cinéma, Les
Films de la Suane and TF1
International
with the participation of Canal+,
Bac Films,
Le Centre Natonal de la
Cinématographie
in collaboration with China Films,
Forbidden City Studios Inc, Beijing
110 minutes 41 seconds**
Location: **China, Paris (France)**
Sight and Sound: v.13, n. 5, p.39, 40
Box Office: £79,607
Opening Weekend: £9,791
Screens: 4

## Banger Sisters
20th Century Fox – 31 January
Director: **Bob Dolman**
Producers: **Mark Johnson, Elizabeth
Cantillon**
Screenplay: **Bob Dolman**
Director of Photography: **Karl Walter
Lindenlaub**
Editor: **Aram Nigoghossian**
Production Designer: **Maia Javan**
Music/Orchestrations: **Trevor Rabin**

Cast:
Goldie Hawn – Suzette
Susan Sarandon – Lavinia 'Vinnie'
Kingsley
Geoffrey Rush – Harry Plumber
Erika Christensen – Hannah
Robin Thomas – Raymond
Eva Amurri – Ginger
Matthew Carey – Jules
Andre Ware – Jake the bartender
Adam Tomei – club owner
Sal Lopez – pump attendant
Kohl Sudduth – hotel clerk
© Twentieth Century Fox Film
Corporation
Production Companies::
**Fox Searchlight presents
a Gran Via/Elizabeth Cantillon
production
97 minutes 40 seconds**
Location: **Los Angeles**
Sight and Sound: vol. 13, n. 2, p. 38
Box Office: £409,523
Opening Weekend: £201,731
Screens: 181

## Barbershop
20th Century Fox – 14 March
12A USA 2002
Director: **Tim Story**
Producers: **Robert Teitel, George
Tillman Jr, Mark Brown**
Screenplay: **Mark Brown, Don D.
Scott, Marshall Todd**
Story: **Mark Brown**
Director of Photography: **Tom
Priestley**
Editor: **John Carter**
Production Designer: **Roger Fortune**
Music/Music Conductor: **Terence
Blanchard**
Cast:
Ice Cube – Calvin Palmer
Anthony Anderson – JD
Sean Patrick Thomas – Jimmy James
Eve – Terri Jones
Troy Garity – Isaac Rosenberg
Michael Ealy – Ricky Nash
Leonard Earl Howze – Dinka
Keith David – Lester
Lahmard Tate – Billy
Jazsmin Lewis – Jennifer Palmer
Tom Wright – Detective Williams
Jason George – Kevin
© Metro-Goldwyn-Mayer Pictures
Inc.
Production Companies:
**Metro-Goldwyn-Mayer Pictures
presents
a State Street Pictures/Cube Vision
production
102 minutes 42 seconds**
Location: **Chicago (Illinois, USA)**
Sight and Sound: v. 13, n. 2, p. 38-39

Box Office: **£347,755**
Opening Weekend: **£145,741**
Screens: **100**

## Basic

Icon Film Distributors – 20 June
15 Germany/USA/United Kingdom
2002
Director: **John McTiernan**
Producers: **Mike Medavoy, Arnie
Messer, James Vanderbilt, Michael
Tadross**
Screenplay: **James Vanderbilt**
Director of Photography: **Steve
Mason**
Editor: **George Folsey Jr**
Production Designer: **Dennis
Bradford**
Music: **Klaus Badelt**
Cast:
John Travolta – Tom Hardy
Connie Nielsen – Captain Julia
Osborne
Samuel L. Jackson – Sergeant
Nathan West
Giovanni Ribisi – Kendall
Brian Van Holt – Dunbar
Taye Diggs – Pike
Cristián de la Fuente – Castro
Dash Mihok – Mueller
Tim Daly – Colonel Bill Styles
Roselyn Sanchez – Nunez
Harry Connick Jr – Vilmer
© IM Filmproduktions- und
Vertriebs GmbH & Co. KG
Production Companies:
**Columbia Pictures and InterMedia
Films present
a Phoenix Pictures production — 98
minutes 27 seconds**
Location: **Florida (USA), Panama**
Sight and Sound: **v.13, n.8, p.36-37**
Box Office: **£608,492**
Opening Weekend: **£248,088**
Screens: **311**

## Belleville Rendezvous

Metro Tartan – 29 August
12A France/Canada/Belgium/United
Kingdom 2002
Director: **Sylvain Chomet**
Producers: **Didier Brunner, Les
Armateurs: Didier Brunner**
Vivi Film:
**Viviane Vanfleteren**
RGP France:
**Régis Ghezelbash**
Conceived/Written by
**Sylvain Chomet**
Editors: **Chantal Colibert Brunner,
Alain Dumais**
Art Director: **Evgeni Tomov**
Music/Music Arranger/Musical
Director: **Benoît Charest**

Voice Cast:
**Jean-Claude Donda – General de
Gaulle/race commentators/public
address at the Tour de France/tramp
Dirk Denoyelle – race
commentators/tramp
Monica Viegas – Graziella de Vila –
Madame Souza
Michel Robin – Noël Baye –
Champion**
© Les Armateurs/Production
Champion Inc/Vivi Film/France 3
Cinéma/RGP France
Production Companies::
**Presenting a Les Armateurs
production
in association with Production
Champion, Vivi Film, France 3
Cinéma, RGP France
in partnership with Canal+, sofica
Gimages 3 and Cofimage 12
a co-production with Téléfilm
Canada and SODEC - Société de
développement des enterprises
culturelles, Québec
supported by Centre National de la
Cinématographie, Cartoon, Media
Programme of the European Union,
Procirep, BBC Bristol and BBC
Worldwide
with assistance from Fonds Film in
Vlaanderen and National Loterij
Produced with the participation of
the Canadian Television Fund
created by the Government of
Canada and the Canadian Cable
Industry
with the participation of the Poitou-
Charentes Region
with the participation of the
Département, with the support from
Conseil Général de la Charente
in association with BBC Bristol and
BBC Worldwide
with the participation of the
Ministère de la Culture et de la
Communication
et du Centre National de la
Cinématographie
with the support from European
Union Media Programme and
Cartoon for The Old Lady and the
Pigeons, Cartoon d'Or 97
with the support from Fonds Film in
Vlaanderen and the National Loterij
produced with Téléfilm Canada in
the scope of a Canada-France
co-production
SODEC - Société de développement
des enterprises culturelles, Québec
produced in association with The
Movie Network and Super Ecran
Quebec Film and Television Tax
Credit**

**Canada, The Canadian Film and
Video Production Tax Credit
80 minutes 50 seconds**
Sight and Sound: **v.13, n.8, p.40-41**
Box Office: **£664,333**
Opening Weekend: **£20,813**
Screens: **3**

## Benzina (Gasoline)

Millivres – 14 November
15 Italy 2001
Director: **Monica Lisa Stambrini**
Producer: **Galliano Juso**
Screenplay: **Monica Lisa Stambrini
Elena Stancanelli, Anneritte Ciccone**
Based on the novel Benzina by  –
**Elena Stancanelli**
Director of Photography: **Fabio
Cianchetti**
Editor: **Paola Freddi**
Art Director: **Alessandro Rosa**
Music: **Massimo Zamboni
Luca Rossi, Simone Filippi**
Cast:
Maya Sansa – Stella
Regina Orioli – Lenni
Mariella Valentini – Mamma
Chiara Conti – Pippi
Marco Quaglia – Sandro
Pietro Ragusa – Filippo
Osvaldo Livio Alzari – cashier
Production Companies::
**Galliano Juso presents with the
participation of Tele + a film by
Monica Lisa Stambrini
Produced by Galiano Juso for
Digital Film srl
This film was made witharticipation
of Tele + a film by Monica Lisa
Stambrini produced by Galiano Juso
for Digital Film srl
This film was made with the
contribution of Ministero per i Beni
e le Attività Culturali
88 minutes 5  seconds**
Sigth and Sound: **v.14, n. 1, p. 44**
Box Office: **£1,763**
Opening Weekend: **£931**
Screens: **1**

## Bhoot

Spark Entertainment – 30 May
Box Office: **£80,461**
Opening Weekend: **£27,361**
Screens: **14**

## Bigger than Life (re)

BFI – 28 November
Box Office: **£14,139**
Opening Weekend: **£4,723**
Screen: **1**

## Biker Boyz

United International Pictures – 27
June

12A USA 2003
Director: **Reggie Rock Bythewood**
Producers: **Stephanie Allain, Gina Prince-Bythewood, Erwin Stoff**
Screenplay: **Craig Fernandez Reggie Rock Bythewood**
Based on the New Times article by **Michael Gougis**
Director of Photography: **Gregory Gardiner**
Editors: **Terilyn A. Shropshire Caroline Ross**
Production Designer: **Cecilia Montiel**
Music/Orchestrations :**Camara Kambon**
Cast:
**Laurence Fishburne – Smoke**
**Derek Luke – Kid**
**Orlando Jones – Soul Train**
**Djimon Hounsou – Motherland**
**Lisa Bonet – Queenie**
**Brendan Fehr – Stuntman**
**Larenz Tate – Wood**
**Kid Rock – Dogg**
**Rick Gonzalez – Primo**
**Meagan Good – Tina**
© **DreamWorks LLC**
Production Companies:
**DreamWorks Pictures presents a 3 Arts Entertainment production**
111 minutes
Location: **California (USA)**
Sight and Sound: **v.13, n.9, p.42**
Box Office: **£133,292**
Opening Weekend: **£65,412**
Screens: 139

## Blackball

Icon Film Distributors – 05 September
15 United Kingdom 2003
Director: **Mel Smith**
Producer: **James Gay-Rees**
Screenplay: **Tim Firth**
Director of Photography: **Vernon Layton**
Editor: **Christopher Blunden**
Production Designer: **Grenville Horner**
Music: **Stephen Warbeck**
Cast:
**Paul Kaye – Cliff Starkey**
**James Cromwell – Ray Speight**
**Alice Evans – Kerry**
**Bernard Cribbins – Mutley**
**Johnny Vegas – Trevor**
**Imelda Staunton – Bridget**
**Vince Vaughn – Rick Schwartz**
**James Fleet – Alan the Pipe**
**David Ryall – Giles Wilton**
**Ian McNeice – Hugh the Sideburns**
**Kenneth Cranham – Chairman Collins**
**Terry Alderton – Bouncer Jonno**

© **Blackball Distribution**
Production Companies:
**Icon Entertainment International presents
in association with
The Isle of Man Film Commission and Inside Track Films
a Midfield Films production
Developed with the assistance of Working Title Films**
96 minutes 52 seconds
Location: **London (UK), Torquay (UK), Isle of Man (UK)**
Sight and Sound: **v.13, n.11, p.33**
Box Office: **£882,669**
Opening Weekend: **£376,233**
Screens: 304

## Blind Shaft

Optimum Releasing – 7 November 2003
15 China/Hong Kong 2003
Director: **Li Yang**
Producer: **Li Yang**
Screenplay: **LI Yang**
Adapted from Liu Qingbang's novel Shenmu/Sacred Wood – **Liu Qingbang**
Director of Photography: **Liu Yonghong**
Editors: **Li Yang, Karl Riedl**
Art Director: **Yang Jun**
Cast:
**Li Yixiang – Song Jinming**
**Wang Shuangbao – Tang Zhaoyang**
**Wang Baoqiang – Yuan Fengming**
**An Jing – Xiao Hong**
**Bao Zhenjiang – Boss Huang**
**Sun Wei – Tang Zhaoxia**
**Zhao Junzhi – Miss Ma**
**Wang Yining – Mamasan**
**Liu Zhenqi – Lao Li**
**Zhang Lulu – waitress**
© **Li Yang/Tang SSplendour Films Limited**
Production Companies::
**The Film Library
Li Yang presents Li Yang, Tang Splendour Films Limited production in association with Bronze Age Films Co. Ltd.
A Li Yang film**
92 minutes 19 seconds
Sight and Sound: **v. 14, n. 1, p. 38**
Box Office: **£14,024**
Opening Weekend: **£4,703**
Screens: 3

## Blind Spot; Hitler's Secretary

Columbia Tristar – 26 Sept
PG Austria 2002
Directors: **André Heller, Othmar Schmiderer**

Producers: **Danny Krausz, Kurt Stocker**
Camera: **Othmar Schmiderer**
Editor: **Daniel Pöhacker**
With
**Traudl Junge**
© **Dor Film**
Production Companies:
**Dor Film presents
a Dor Film production in association with the Heller Werkstatt**
90 minutes 33 seconds
Sight and Sound: **v.13, n.10, p.44-45**
Box Office: **£7,828**
Opening Weekend: **£1,914**
Screen: 1

## Blue Crush

Momentum Pictures – 04 April
12A USA/Germany 2002
Director: **John Stockwell**
Producers: **Brian Grazen, Karen Kehela**
Screenplay: **Lizzy Weiss, John Stockwell**
Story: **Lizzy Weiss**
Based on the magazine article Surf Girls of Maui by **Susan Orlean**
Director of Photography: **David Hennings**
Editor: **Emma E. Hickox**
Production Designer: **Tom Meyer**
Music: **Paul Haslinger**
Cast:
**Kate Bosworth – Anne Marie**
**Michelle Rodriguez – Eden**
**Matthew Davis – Matt Tollman**
**Sanoe Lake – Lena**
**Mika Boorem – Penny**
**Faizon Love – Leslie**
**Chris Taloa – Drew**
**Kala Alexander – Kala**
**Ruben Tejada – JJ**
**Kaupena Miranda – Kaupena**
© **Mikona Productions GmbH & Co. KG**
Production Companies::
**Universal Pictures and Imagine Entertainment present a Brian Grazer production
In association with Mikona Productions GmbH & Co. KG**
104 minutes 35 seconds
Location: **Hawaii (USA)**
Sight and Sound: **v.13, n. 6, p. 37**
Box Office: **£1,451,646**
Opening Weekend: **£491,419**
Screens: 319

## Bodysong

Pathe Distribution Ltd
18 United Kingdom 2002
Director: **Simon Pummell**
Producer: **Janine Marmot**

Screenplay: **Simon Pummell**
Editor: **Daniel Goddard**
Music: **Jonny Greenwood**
© **FilmFour/Film Council**
Production Companies::
**FilmFour and the Film Council
present a Hot Property
productiooooon
Made with the support of the Film
Council New Cinema Fund
Developed with the support of the
MEDIA Programme of the European
Union**
81 minutes 35 seconds
Sight and Sound: v.14, n. 1, p. 39
Box Office: £10,344
Opening Weekend: £2,808
Screens: 3

## Bollywood/Hollywood
Momentum Pictures – 14 February
12A  Canada 2002
Director: **Deepa Mehta**
Producer: **David Hamilton**
Screenplay: **Deepa Mehta**
Director of Photography: **Doug Koch**
Editor: **Barry Farrell**
Production Designer: **Tamara
Deverell**
Music: **Sandeep Chowta**
Additional Background Music
Composed/Arranged/Programmed:
**Pravin Mani**
Lyrics: **Ajay Virmani, Taabish
Romani, Jaideep**
Cast:
**Rahul Khanna** – Rahul Seth
**Lisa Ray** – Sue (Sunita) Singh
**Rishma Malik** – Twinky
**Jazz Mann** – Bobby
**Moushumi Chatterjee** – Mummy ji
**Dina Pathak** – Grandma ji
**Kulbushan Kharbanda** – Mr Singh
**Ranjit Chowdhry** – Rocky
**Leesa Gaspari** – Lucy
**Arjun Lombardi-Singh** – Go
(Govind)
**Neelam Mansingh** – Mrs Singh
© **Bollywood/Hollywood
Productions, Inc.**
Production Companies:
**Produced with the participation of
Telefilm Canada and Canadian
Television Fund created by the
government of Canada and the
Canadian cable industry
CTF: License Fee Program
and Astral Media The Harold
Greenberg Fund
and produced with the participation
of The Movie Network and Super
Ecran
a film produced in participation
with Movie Central and Corus**

**Produced in association with Chum
Television**
105 minutes 13 seconds
Location: **Toronto, Tornhill (Canada)**
Sight and Sound: v.13, n.4, p.34 – Box
Office: £248,898
Opening Weekend: £59,316
Screens: 35

## Bollywood Queen
Redbus – 17 October
PG United Kingdom/Australia 2002
Director: **Jeremy Wooding**
Producers: **Michael Lionello Cowan,
Jason Piette, Jeremy Wooding,
Michelle Turner**
Screenplay: **Neil Spencer
Jeremy Wooding**
Director of Photography: **Jono Smith**
Editor: **Ben Yeates**
Production Designer: **Jeffrey Sherriff**
Music: **Steve Beresford**
Cast:
**Preeya Kalidas** – Geena
**James McAvoy** – Jay
**Ciarán McMenamin** – Dean
**Ray Panthaki** – Anil
**Kat Bhathena** – Anjali
**Karen Shenaz David** – Neeta
**Amerjit Deu** – Sanjay
**Ronny Jhutti** – Dillip
**Matt Bardock** – Facer
**Ian McShane** – Frank, Jay & Dean's
father
© **Investing in Enterprise
Limited/BQ Films Limited**
Production Companies::
**Arclight Films presents a Great
British Films/Spice Factory/Stretch
Limo
Productions film
in association with Enterprise Films
and Dreamfish Productions**
89 minutes 33 seconds
Location: **London's East End (UK)**
Sight and Sound: v.13, n.12, p.28
Box Office: £50,246
Opening Weekend: £27,020
Screens: 34

## Boom
Bollywood Films – 19 September
Box Office: £69,550
Opening Weekend: £35,302
Screens: 24

## The Boy David Story
Ratpack – 12 September
PG United Kingdom 2002
Director: **Alex McCall**
Producers: **Desmond Wilcox, Alex
McCall**
Screenplay: **Desmond Wilcox, Alex
McCall**
Film Camera:men: **Andrew Dunn**

**Denis Borrow, Alex Scott
John McNeil, Dick Johnstone, Chic
Cecchini**
Editor: **Sarah Böszörményi**
**Music/Music
Conductor/Orchestrator –
Christopher Gunning
With** – David L. Jackson – Ian
Jackson – Marjorie Jackson –
Andrew Jackson – Linda Jackson –
Sarah Jackson – Susan Jackson –
Mary Rodriguez – Father Severino –
Sister Sita – Mother Amalia – Father
Castillo – Santos López – Eva López
– Señora Violetta de Belaundi – Elli
Griffis de Zuniga – Norma Calderon
– Katie Till – Paula Pugliese –
Martine Schopfer – Tony Anderanin
– Joey Nibras – Mr Lee – © Armac
Films Limited
Production Companies::
**Armac Films
in association with Scottish Screen**
— 99 minutes 33 seconds
Sight and Sound: v.13, n.11, p.34
Box Office: £1,444
Opening Weekend: £375
Screen: 1

## Bright Young Things
Icon Films Distribution – 03
October
15 United Kingdom 2003
Director: **Stephen Fry**
Producers: **Gina Carter
Miranda Davis**
Screenplay: **Stephen Fry**
Based on the novel Vile Bodies by
**Evelyn Waugh**
Director of Photography: **Henry
Braham**
Editor: **Alex Mackie**
Production Designer: **Michael
Howells**
Music/MusicConductor/
Orchestrator: **Anne Dudley**
Cast:
**Emily Mortimer**  – Nina
**Stephen Campbell Moore**  – Adam
**Dan Aykroyd**  – Lord Monomark
**Jim Broadbent**  – the drunken major
**Stockard Channing**  – Mrs Melrose
Ape
**Guy Henry** – Archie
**James McAvoy** – Simon Balcairn
**Michael Sheen** – Miles
**David Tennant** – Ginger
**Fenella Woolgar** – Agatha
**Peter O'Toole** – Colonel Blount
**Simon McBurney** – Sneath (Photo-
rat)
© **Bright Young Films Limited/The
Film Consortium Limited**
Production Companies:

The Film Consortium presents in association with UK Film Council and Visionview and Icon Film Distribution
a Revolution Films/Doubting Hall production
Developed with the support of the MEDIA Programme of the European Union
Developed with the assistance of Jay Pond Jones, Piers Thompson
Production Finance provided by DZ Bank with special thanks to Bernard Traynor
Produced in association with the Second Close Film Fund Partnerships
Supported by the National Lottery through UK Film Council
106 minutes 14 seconds
Sight and Sound: v.13, n.11, p.36 –
Box Office: £1,084,776
Opening Weekend: £327,293
Screens: 192

## Bringing Down the House
Buena Vista International – 30 May
12A USA 2003
Director: **Adam Shankman**
Producers: **David Hoberman, Ashok Amritraj**
Screenplay: **Jason Filardi**
Director of Photography: **Julio Macat**
Editor: **Jerry Greenberg**
Production Designer: **Linda Descenna**
Music: **Lalo Schifrin**
Cast:
**Steve Martin – Peter Sanderson**
**Queen Latifah – Charlene Morton**
**Eugene Levy – Howie Rottman**
**Joan Plowright – Mrs Arness**
**Jean Smart – Kate**
**Kimberly J. Brown – Sarah Sanderson**
**Angus T. Jones – Georgey Sanderson**
**Missi Pyle – Ashley**
**Michael Rosenbaum – Todd Gendler**
**Betty White – Mrs Kline**
© Touchstone Pictures
Production Companies:
**Touchstone Pictures present in association with Hyde Park Entertainment**
**a David Hoberman/Ashok Amritraj production**
105 minutes 7 seconds
Sight and Sound: v. 13, n. 6, p. 38-39
Location: **Los Angeles (CA, USA)**
Box Office: £3,537,660
Opening Weekend: £1,133,139
Screens: 388

## Broken Wings
Optimum Releasing – 06 June

15 Israel 2002
Director: **Nir Bergman**
Producer: **Assaf Amir**
Screenplay: **Nir Bergman**
Director of Photography: **Valentin Belonogov**
Editor: **Einat Glaser Zahrhin**
Art Director:
**Ido Dolev**
Music: **Avi Belleli**
Cast:
**Orly Zilberschatz-Banai – Dafna Ulman**
**Maya Maron – Maya Ulman**
**Nitai Gvirtz – Yair Ulman**
**Eliana Magon – Bar Ulman**
**Daniel Magon – Ido Ulman**
**Dana Ivgy – Iris**
**Vladimir Freedman – Dr Valentin Goldman**
**Mooki (Danny Niv) – Yoram**
**Nimrod Cohen – Gaga**
**Yarden Bar-Kochva – Flora, school counselor**
© Norma Productions
Production Companies:
**Assaf Amir & Norma Productions present**
**The film was produced with the support of The Israel Film Fund, The Ministry of Science, Culture and Sport,**
**The Israel Film Council**
**The film was produced in association with DBS Satellite Services (1998) Ltd**
**Israel Fund for Film Production**
**The Haifa Art, Culture and Sport Company**
83 minutes 41 seconds
Location: **Haifa (Israel), Tel-Aviv (Israel)**
Sight and Sound: v.13, n. 7, p. 37
Box Office: £55,323
Opening Weekend: £20,840
Screens: 10

## Brother Bear
Buena Vista Intl – 5 December
U USA 2003
Directors: **Aaron Blaise**
**Robert Walker**
Producer: **Chuck Williams**
Screenplay: **Tab Murphy, Lorne Cameron, David Hoselton, Steve Bencich, Ron J. Friedman**
Story: **Nathan Greno, Stevie Wermers-Skelton, Kevin Deters, Woody Woodman, Thom Enriquez, Kevin Harkey, Broose Johnson, John Norton, John Puglisi**
Editor: **Tim Mertens**
Art Direction: **Robh Ruppel**
Music: **Mark Mancina Phil Collins**

Songs: **Phil Collins**
Voice Cast:
**Joaquin Phoenix – Kenai**
**Jeremy Suarez – Koda**
**Jason Raize – Denahi**
**Rick Moranis – Rutt**
**Dave Thomas – Tuke**
**D.B. Sweeney – Sitka**
**Joan Copeland – Tanana**
**Michael Clarke Duncan – Tug**
**Harold Gould – old Denahi**
**Paul Christie – Daniel Mastrogiorgio – rams**
© Disney Enterprises, Inc.
**Production Company – Walt Disney Pictures presents**
85 minutes 4 seconds
Sight and Sound: v. 14, n.1, p. 39-40
Box Office: £4,445,123
Opening Weekend: £887,321
Screens: 340

## Brown Sugar
20th Century Fox – 18 July
12A USA 2002
Director: **Rick Famuyiwa**
Producer: **Peter Heller**
Screenplay: **Michael Elliot, Rick Famuyiwa**
Story: **Michael Elliot**
Director of Photography: **Enrique Chediak**
Editor: **Dirk Westervelt**
Production Designer: **Kalina Ivanov**
Music/Score Conductor/Orchestrator:
**Robert Hurst**
Cast:
**Taye Diggs – Dre**
**Sanaa Lathan – Sidney**
**Mos Def – Chris**
**Nicole Ari Parker – Reese**
**Boris Kodjoe – Kelby**
**Queen Latifah – Francine**
**Wendell Pierce – Simon**
**Erik Weiner – Ren**
**Reggi Wyns – Ten**
**Melissa Martinez – Meghan**
© Twentieth Century Fox Film Corporation
Production Companies:
**Fox Searchlight Pictures presents**
**a Heller Highwater/Magic Johnson Entertainment production**
109 minutes 9 seconds
Location: **New York (NY, USA)**
Sight and Sound: v. 13, n. 8, p. 37-38
– Box Office: £314,436
Opening Weekend: £90,877
Screens: 84

## Bruce Almighty
Buena Vista International – 27 June
12A USA 2003
Director: **Tom Shadyac**
Producers: **Tom Shadyac, Jim**

Carrey, James D. Brubaker, Michael Bostick, Steve Koren, Mark O'Keefe
Screenplay: **Steve Koren, Mark O'Keefe. Steve Oedekerk**
Story: **Steve Koren, Mark O'Keefe**
Director of Photography: **Dean Semler**
Editor: **Scott Hill**
Production Designer: **Linda DeScenna**
Music: **John Debney**
Cast:
**Jim Carrey – Bruce Nolan**
**Morgan Freeman – God**
**Jennifer Aniston – Grace Connelly**
**Philip Baker Hall – Jack Keller**
**Catherine Bell – Susan Ortega**
**Lisa Ann Walter – Debbie**
**Steven Carell – Evan Baxter**
**Nora Dunn – Ally Loman**
**Eddie Jemison – Bobby**
**Paul Satterfield – Dallas Coleman**
**Mark Kiely – Fred Donohue**
**Sally Kirkland – Anita**
© Universal Studios
Production Companies:
**Spyglass Entertainment and Universal Pictures present a Shady Acres/**
**Pit Bull production**
**101 minutes 4 seconds**
**Los Angeles (CA, USA), Buffalo (NY, USA), San Diego (CA, USA)**
Sight and Sound: **v. 13, n. 8, p. 38-39**
Box Office: **£23,609,015**
Opening Weekend: **£7,260,467**
Screens: **446**

## Buffalo Soldiers

Pathé Distribution – 18 July
15 United Kingdom/USA/Germany 2001
Director: **Gregor Jordan**
Producers: **Rainer Grupe, Ariane Moody**
Screenplay: **Gregor Jordan Eric Axel Weiss, Nora Maccoby**
Based on the book **by Robert O'Connor**
Director of Photography: **Oliver Stapleton**
Editor: **Lee Smith**
Production Designer: **Steven Jones-Evans**
Music/Music Supervisor: **David Holmes**
Cast:
**Joaquin Phoenix – Ray Elwood**
**Ed Harris – Colonel Berman**
**Scott Glenn – Sergeant Lee**
**Anna Paquin – Robyn Lee**
**Gabriel Mann – Knoll**
**Leon Robinson – Stoney**
**Sheik Mahmud-Bey – Sergeant Saad**

**Michael Peña – Garcia**
**Glenn Fitzgerald – Hicks**
**Dean Stockwell – General Lancaster**
**Elizabeth McGovern – Mrs Berman**
© Film Four Limited/Grosvenor Park Productions UK
Production Companies:
**FilmFour and Good Machine International present**
**with Odeon Pictures**
**in association with Miramax Films and Grosvenor Park**
**a Gorilla Entertainment/Strange Fiction production**
**Supported by MFG Medien-und Filmgesellschaft Baden Württemberg mbH**
**98 minutes 2 seconds**
Location: **Southern Germany**
Sight and Sound: **v.13, n.8, p.40-41**
Box Office: **£1,079,140**
Opening Weekend: **£113,664**
Screens: **37**

## Bulletproof Monk

Pathé Distribution – 18 April
12A USA 2003
Director: **Paul Hunter**
Producers: **Charles Roven, Douglas Segal, Terence Chang, John Woo**
Screenplay: **Ethan Reiff, Cyrus Voris**
Based on The Flypaper Press comic book
Director of Photography: **Stefan Czapsky**
Editor: **Robert K. Lambert**
Production Designer: **Deborah Evans**
Music: **Eric Serra**
Cast:
**Chow Yun-Fat – Monk with No Name**
**Seann William Scott – Kar**
**Jaime King – Jade/bad girl**
**Karel Roden – Struker**
**Victoria Smurfit – Nina**
**Marcus Jean Pirae – Mr Funktastic**
**Mako – Mr Kojima**
**Roger Yuan – Master Monk**
**Chris Collins – Sax**
**Sean Bell – Diesel**
© Metro-Goldwyn-Mayer Pictures Inc
(in the United States, Canada, France and their territories and protectorates)
© Lakeshore Entertainment Group LLC
(throughout the world other than in the United States, Canada, France and their territories and protectorates)
Production Companies:
**Metro-Goldwyn-Mayer Pictures presents**

in association with Lakeshore Entertainment and Mosaic Media Group
**a Lion Rock production**
**a Flypaper Press production**
**103 minute 46 seconds**
Location: **Toronto (Ontario, Canada)**
Sight and Sound: **v.13, n.6, p.39-40**
Box Office: **£2,041,378**
Opening Weekend: **£607,839**
Screens: **322**

## Cabin Fever

Redbus – 10 October
15 USA 2002
Director: **Eli Roth**
Producers: **Eli Roth, Lauren Moews Sam Froelich, Evan Astrowsky**
Screenplay: **Randy Pearlstein, Eli Roth**
Story: **Eli Roth**
Director of Photography: **Scott Kevan**
Editor: **Ryan Folsey**
Production Designer: **Franco Giacomo Carbone**
Music: **Nathan Barr, Angelo Badalamenti**
Cast:
**The Kids**
**Rider Strong – Paul**
**Jordan Ladd – Karen**
**Joey Kern – Jeff**
**Cerina Vincent – Marcy**
**James DeBello – Bert**
**The Neighbours**
**Arie Verveen – the hermit**
**Christy Ward – the hog lady**
**Michael Harding – Shotgun Casey**
© Cabin Pictures, LLC
Production Companies:
**Black Sky Entertainment in association with Deer Path Films presents a DownHome Entertainment/Tonic Films production**
**92 minutes 18 seconds**
Location: **North Carolina (USA), Los Angeles (CA, USA)**
Sight and Sound: **v. 13, n. 12, p. 28-29**
Box Office: **£2,888,563**
Opening Weekend: **£1,056,338**
Screens: **277**

## Calcutta Mail

Venus Entertainment – 05 September
Box Office: **£32,059**
Opening Weekend: **£12,929**
Screens: **13**

## Calendar Girls

Buena Vista International – 05 September
12A United Kingdom/USA 2003

Director: **Nigel Cole**
Producers: **Suzanne Mackie, Nick Barton**
Screenplay: **Juliet Towhidi, Tim Firth**
Director of Photography: **Ashley Rowe**
Editor: **Michael Parker**
Production Designer: **Martin Childs**
Music: **Patrick Doyle**
Cast:
**Helen Mirren** – Chris
**Julie Walters** – Annie
**John Alderton** – John
**Linda Bassett** – Cora
**Annette Crosbie** – Jessie
**Philip Glenister** – Lawrence
**Ciarán Hinds** – Rod
**Celia Imrie** – Celia
**Geraldine James** – Marie
**Penelope Wilton** – Ruth
**George Costigan** – Eddie
**Graham Crowden** – Richard
© Buena Vista International
Production Companies:
**Touchstone Pictures presents a Harbour Pictures production**
108 minutes 11 seconds
Location: **Yorkshire (UK), London (UK), Los Angeles (CA, USA)**
Sight and Sound: v. 13, n. 11, p. 37-38
Box Office: £20,336,222
Opening Weekend: £74,150
Screen: 1

## Camp

**Momentum Pictures** – 05 September
12A USA 2003
Director: **Todd Graff**
Producers: **Todd Graff, Katie Roumel, Christine Vachon, Pamela Koffler, Danny DeVito, Michael Shamberg, Stacey Sher, Jonathan Weisgal**
Screenplay: **Todd Graff**
Director of Photography: **Kip Bogdahn**
Editor: **Myron Kerstein**
Production Designer: **Dina Goldman**
Music: **Stephen Trask**
Cast:
**Daniel Letterle** – Vlad
**Joanna Chilcoat** – Ellen
**Robin De Jesus** – Michael
**Steven Cutts** – Shaun
**Vince Rimoldi** – Spitzer
**Kahiry Bess** – Petie
**Tiffany Taylor** – Jenna
**Sasha Allen** – Dee
**Alana Allen** – Jill
**Anna Kendrick** – Fritzi
**Don Dixon** – Bert
© Elsie Films Inc.
Production Companies:
**IFC Films presents**

an IFC production
a Jersey Films/Killer Films/Laughlin Park Pictures production
111 minutes 24 seconds
Sight and Sound: v.13, n. 9, p.44
Box Office: £548,770
Opening Weekend: £245,183
Screens: 215

## Catch Me If You Can

**United International Pictures** – 31 January
12A USA 2002
Director: **Steven Spielberg**
Producers: **Steven Spielberg, Walter F. Parkes**
Screenplay: **Jeff Nathanson**
Based on the book by
**Frank W. Abagnale with Stan Redding**
Director of Photography: **Janusz Kaminski**
Editor: **Michael Kahn**
Production Designer: **Jeannine Oppewall**
Music: **John Williams**
Cast:
**Leonardo DiCaprio** – Frank William Abagnale Jr
**Tom Hanks** – Carl Hanratty
**Christopher Walken** – Frank William Abagnale Sr
**Martin Sheen** – Roger Strong
**Nathalie Baye** – Paula Abagnale
**Amy Adams** – Brenda Strong
**James Brolin** – Jack Barnes, club president
**Brian Howe** – Tom Fox
**Frank John Hughes** – Earl Amdursky
**Steve Eastin** – Paul Morgan
**Chris Ellis** – Special Agent Witkins
© DreamWorks LLC
Production Companies:
**DreamWorks Pictures presents a Kemp Company and Splendid Pictures production**
**a Parkes/MacDonald production**
**Amblin' Entertainment**
141 minutes 5 seconds
Location: **Los Angeles (CA, USA)**
Sight and Sound: v. 13, n. 2, p. 39-40
Box Office: £15,065,226
Opening Weekend: £3,720,957
Screens: 459

## Chalte Chalte

**Eros International Limited** – 13 June
Box Office: £775,552
Opening Weekend: £289,883
Screen: 37

## Charlie's Angels: Full Throttle

**Columbia TriStar** – 04 July

12A USA 2003
Director: **McG**
Producers: **Leonard Goldberg, Drew Barrymore, Nancy Juvonen**
Screenplay: **John August, Cormac Wibberley, Marianne Wibberley**
Story: **John August**
Based on the TV series created by
**Ivan Goff, Ben Roberts**
Director of Photography: **Russell Carpenter**
Editor: **Wayne Wahrman**
Production Designer: **J. Michael Riva**
Music: **Edward Shearmur**
Cast:
**Cameron Diaz** – Natalie Cook
**Drew Barrymore** – Dylan Sanders
**Lucy Liu** – Alex Munday
**Bernie Mac** – Jimmy Bosley
**Crispin Glover** – thin man
**Justin Theroux** – Seamus O'Grady
**Robert Patrick** – Ray Carter
**Demi Moore** – Madison Lee
**Rodrigo Santoro** – Randy Emmers
**Shia LaBeouf** – Max
**John Forsythe** – voice of Charlie Townsend
**Matt LeBlanc** – Jason Gibbons
© Columbia Pictures Industries, Inc
Production Companies:
**Columbia Pictures presents a Leonard Goldberg production in association with Flower Films and Tall Trees Productions/Wonderland Sound and Vision**
105 minutes 43 seconds
Location: **Los Angeles (CA, USA)**
Sight and Sound: v.13, n.8, p.41-42
Box Office: £12,355,642
Opening Weekend: £3,273,078
Screens: 473

## Chori Chori

**21st Century Film** – 01 August
Box Office: £151,987
Opening Weekend: £48,913
Screens: 16

## Chura Liya Hai Tumne

**Bollywood Films** – 21 March
Box Office: £48,210
Opening Weekend: £13,293
Screens: 8

## Cinemania

**Park Circus Films** – 05 September
12A Germany/USA 2002
Directors: **Angela Christlieb, Stephen Kijak**
Producer: **Gunter Hanfgarn**
Camera: **Angela Christlieb**
Editors: **Angela Christlieb, Stephen Kijak**
Music: **Stereo Total, Robert Drasnin**
With

Jack Angstreich – Eric Chadbourne
Bill Heidbreder – Roberta Hill
Harvey Schwartz – and
Richard Aidala – projectionist
Tia Bonacore – usher
David Schwartz – curator
Michael Slipp – neighbour
© Hanfgarn & Ufer
Production Companies:
Hanfgarn & Ufer Film und TV
Produktion present an Angela
Christlieb & Stephen Kijak film
A Hanfgarn & Ufer Film-und TV
Produktion film
Supported by Filmboard Berlin-
Brandenberg, Filmstiftung NRW
in co-production with Bayerischer
Rundfunk, Westdeutscher Rundfunk
in association with Loop Filmworks,
Winstar Film & Video
83 minutes 16 seconds
Sight and Sound: v.13, n.12, p.29-30
Box Office: £1,134
Opening Weekend: £491
Screens: 2

## Citizen Verdict

Georgia Films – 12 September
15 United Kingdom/Germany/USA
2003
Director: **Philippe Martinez**
Producers:  **Philippe Martinez,
Helmut Breuer**
Screenplay: **Tony Clarke, Frank
Rehwaldt, Kristina Hamilton,
Philippe Martinez**
Director of Photography: **Michael
Brierley**
Editor: **Kristina Hamilton**
Production Designer: **Zack Grobler**
Cast:
Armand Assante – Sam Patterson
Roy Scheider – Governor Bull Tyler
Jerry Springer – Marty Rockman
Justine Mitchell – Jessica Landers
Raffaello Degruttola – Ricky Carr
Dorette Potgieter – Carlene Osway
Clive Scott – Judge Halvern
Lynn Blades – Tawny Scott
André Jacobs – Jack Hamilton
© The Aquarius Film Company
LLP/Exactlord Ltd/Lucky Select
GmbH
Production Companies:
Bauer Martinez Studios presents an
Aquarius Film Company production
in co-production with Exactlord a
Lucky 7 Productions Company &
Lucky Select
in association with Curzon Motion
Pictures
with the participation of
Entertainment Guarantors
funded with the participation of

Scotts Atlantic (London)
97 minutes 58 seconds
Location: **Cape Town (South Africa),
Johannesburg (South Africa), New
Brunswick (Canada), Clearwater
(Florida, USA), Tampa (Florida,
USA)**
Sight and Sound: v. 13, n. 11, p. 10-11
Box Office: £9,593
Opening Weekend: £5,819
Screens: 32

## City By the Sea

Warner Bros – 10 January
15 USA 2001
Director: **Michael Caton-Jones**
Producers:  **Brad Grey, Elie Samaha
Michael Caton-Jones, Matthew Baer**
Screenplay: **Ken Hixon**
Based on an article entitled Mark of
a Murderer by Michael McAlary
Director of Photography: **Karl Walter
Lindenlaub**
Editor: **Jim Clark**
Production Designer: **Jane Musky**
Music: **John Murphy**
Cast:
Robert De Niro – Lieutenant
Vincent LaMarca
Frances McDormand – Michelle
James Franco – Joseph Howard
'Joey' LaMarca
Eliza Dushku – Gina
William Forsythe – Spyder
Patti LuPone – Maggie, Joey's
mother
Anson Mount – Dave Simon
John Doman – Chief Henderson
Brian Tarantina – Snake
Drena De Niro – Vanessa Hansen
Michael P. Moran – Herb, Vincent's
neighbour
Nestor Serrano – Rossi
© Seabreeze Productions Inc
Production Companies:
Warner Bros. Pictures presents a
Brad Grey Pictures production
Franchise Pictures
108 minutes 16 seconds
New York (NY, USA)
Sight and Sound: v.13, n.1 p. 37-38
Box Office: £149,915
Opening Weekend: £77,936
Screens: 53

## City of God

Buena Vista Intl – 3 January
18 Brazil/Germany/France 2002
Director: **Fernando Meirelles**
Producers:  **Andréa Barata Ribeiro,
Mauricio Andrade Ramos**
Screenplay: **Braulio Mantovani**
Based on the novel by
Paulo Lins
Director of Photography: **Cesar**

Charlone
Editor: **Daniel Rezende**
Art Director:  **Tulé Peake**
Music: **Antônio Pinto, Ed Côrtes**
Cast:
Alexandre Rodrigues – Buscapé
Leandro Firmino da Hora – Ze
Pequeño
Phellipe Haagensen – Bené
Douglas Silva – Dadinho
Jonathan Haagensen – Cabeleira
Matheus Nachtergaele – Sandro
Cenoura
Seu Jorge – Mané Galinha
Jefechander Suplino – Alicate
Aiice Braga – Angélica
Emerson Gomes – Barbantinho
© O2 Filmes Curtos Ltda/Hank
Levine Film GmbH
Production Companies:
Walter Salles and Donald K.
Ranvaud present
an O2 Filmes and VideoFilmes
production
in co-production with Globo Filmes,
Lumière and Wild Bunch
129 minutes 40 seconds
Location: **Rio de Janeiro (Brasil)**
Sight and Sound: v. 13, n. 1, p. 38-39
Box Office: £2,372,951
Opening Weekend: £307,177
Screens: 76

## The Clay Bird

ICA Projects – 04 July
PG France/Bangladesh 2002
Director: **Tareque Masud**
Producer: **Catherine Masud**
Screenplay: **Tareque Masud,
Catherine Masud**
Story/Dialogue: **Tareque Masud**
Director of Photography: **Sudheer
Palsane**
Editor: **Catherine Masud**
Art Directors: **Sylvain Nahmias, Kazi
Rakib, Tarun Ghosh, Uttam Guha**
Cast:
Nurul Islam Bablu – Anu
Russell Farazi – Rokon
Jayanto Chattopadhyay – Kazi
Rokeya Prachy – Ayesha
Soaeb Islam – Milon
Lameesa R. Reemjheem – Asma
Moin Ahmed – Ibrahim
Md. Moslemuddin – Bakiullah,
headmaster
Abdul Karim – Halim Mia
Shah Alam Dewan – Karim,
boatman
© MK2 sa/Audiovision
Production Companies:
Marin Karmitz presents
an MK2/Audiovision production
With the support of 'Fonds Sud',

French Ministry of Culture and Communication,
CNC and Ministry of Foreign Affairs
98 minutes 38 seconds
Sight and Sound: v.13, n.8, p.42-43
Box Office: £39,757
Opening Weekend: £6,204
Screens: 3

## Cold Mountain
Buena Vista Intl – 26 December
15 USA/United
Kingdom/Romania/Italy 2003
Director: **Anthony Minghella**
Producers: **Sydney Pollack, William Horberg, Albert Berger, Ron Yerxa**
Screenplay: **Anthony Minghella**
Based on the book by – **Charles Frazier**
Director of Photography: **John Seale**
Editor: **Walter Murch**
Production Designer: **Dante Ferretti**
Music: **Gabriel Yared**
Cast:
Jude Law – W.P. Inman
Nicole Kidman – Ada Monroe
Renée Zellweger – Ruby Thewes
Eileen Atkins – Maddy
Brendan Gleeson – Stobrod Thewes
Philip Seymour Hoffman – Reverend Veasey
Natalie Portman – Sara
Giovanni Ribisi – Junior
Donald Sutherland – Reverend Monroe
Ray Winstone – Teague
© Miramax Film Corp.
Production Companies::
Miramax Films presents a Mirage Enterprises/Bona Fide production
An Anthony Minghella film
Romanian Production Services
152 minutes 19 seconds
Location: **Romania, South Carolina (USA), Virginia/North Carolina (USA)**
Sight and Sound: v. 14, n. 2, p. 32-33, 38
Box Office: £1,779,132
Opening Weekend: £380,994
Screens: 135

## Comandante
Optimum Releasing – 03 October
PG Spain/USA 2003
Director: **Oliver Stone**
Producers: **Oliver Stone, Fernando Sulichin**
Original Idea – **José Ibañez Álvaro Longoria**
Directors of Photography:
**Rodrigo Prieto, Carlos Marcovich**
Editors: **Alex Márquez, Elisa Bonora**
Music: **Alberto Iglesias**
With

Fidel Castro  – Oliver Stone
Juanita Vera  – Fidel Castro Jr
Fidel Castro III  – Juan Almeída
© Media Producción, Spain
Production Companies:
**Pentagrama Films and Morena Films present**
**an Oliver Stone film**
**a presentation of Home Box Office**
99 minutes 17 seconds
Sight and Sound: v.13, n.11, p.39
Box Office: £26,312
Opening Weekend: £6,664
Screens: 5

## Concert for George
Pathé Distribution – 10 October
PG United Kingdom/Australia/USA 2003
Director: **David Leland**
Producers: **Ray Cooper, Olivia Harrison, Jon Kamen**
Director of Photography: **Chris Menges**
Editor: **Claire Ferguson**
Production Design: **Eve Stewart**
Musical Director: **Eric Clapton**
Featuring
Joe Brown, Eric Clapton, Jools Holland, Sam Brown, Jeff Lynne, Paul McCartney, Tom Petty and the Heartbreakers, Billy Preston, Ringo Starr
© Oops Publishing Ltd.
Production Companies:
**Warner Music Group presents a @radical.media production**
97 minutes 24 seconds
Location: **Royal Albert Hall (London, UK)**
Sight and Sound: v.13, n.12 p.30
Box Office: £11,138
Opening Weekend: £3,635
Screens: 5

## Confessions of a Dangerous Mind
Buena Vista International – 14 March
15 USA/Germany/United Kingdom 2002
Director: **George Clooney**
Producer: **Andrew Lazar**
Screenplay: **Charlie Kaufman**
Based on the book by
**Chuck Barris**
Director of Photography: **Newton Thomas Sigel**
Editor: **Stephen Mirrione**
Production Designer: **James D. Bissell**
Music: **Alex Wurman**
Cast:
Sam Rockwell – Chuck Barris

Drew Barrymore – Penny Pacino
George Clooney – Jim Byrd
Julia Roberts – Patricia
Rutger Hauer – Keeler
Maggie Gyllenhaal – Debbie
Robert John Burke – Instructor Jenks
Jennifer Hall – Georgia
Kristen Wilson – Loretta
J. Todd Anderson – stud bachelor
Carlos Carrasco – Brazioni
Emilio Rivera – Benitez
© JVS GmbH & Co
Production Companies:
**a Mad Chance production**
**in association with Section Eight**
**a Miramax Films presentation**
**in association with Renaissance Films**
**In association with JVS GmbH & Co**
113 minutes 22 seconds
Location: **Montreal (Canada), California (USA)**
Sight and Sound: v.13, n.3, p.36-37
Box Office: £1,457,769
Opening Weekend: £356,623
Screens: 201

## Confidence
Momentum Pictures – 22 August
15 USA/Germany 2003
Director: **James Foley**
Producers: **Marc Butan, Michael Paseornek, Michael Burns, Michael Ohoven**
Screenplay: **Doug Jung**
Director of Photography: **Juan Ruiz Anchía**
Editor: **Stuart Levy**
Production Designer: **William Arnold**
Music/Music Conductor/Score Producer:
**Christophe Beck**
Cast:
Edward Burns – Jake Vig
Rachel Weisz – Lily
Andy Garcia – Gunther Butan
Paul Giamatti – Gordo
Luis Guzmán – Manzano
Donal Logue – Whitworth
Brian Van Holt – Miles
Franky G. – Lupus
Robert Forster – Morgan Price
Morris Chestnut – Travis
Dustin Hoffman – King
Leland Orser – Lionel Dolby
Louis Lombardi – Big Al
© Lions Gate Films, Inc.
Production Companies:
**Lions Gate Films**
**in association with Cinerenta**
**present an Ignite Entertainment and Cinewhite production**

97 minutes 15 seconds
New York (NY, USA)
Sight and Sound: **v.13, n.10, p.45-46**
Box Office: **£1,189,939**
Opening Weekend: **£325,685**
Screens: **251**

### The Core
United International Pictures – 28
March
12A USA/Germany/Canada 2003
Director: **Jon Amiel**
Producers:  **David Foster, Cooper Layne**
**Sean Bailey**
Screenplay: **Cooper Layne, John Rogers**
Director of Photography: **John Lindley**
Editor: **Terry Rawlings**
Production Designer: **Philip Harrison**
Music: **Christopher Young**
Cast:
**Aaron Eckhart – Josh Keyes**
**Hilary Swank – Major Rebecca 'Beck' Childs**
**Delroy Lindo – Dr Ed 'Braz' Brazzelton**
**Stanley Tucci – Dr Conrad Zimsky**
**D.J. Qualls – Rat**
**Richard Jenkins – General Thomas Purcell**
**Tchéky Karyo – Dr Serge Leveque**
**Bruce Greenwood – Commander Richard Iverson**
**Alfre Woodard – Stickley**
**Christopher Shyer – Dave Perry**
© MFP Munich Film Partners New
Century GmbH & Co. Core
Productions KG
Production Companies:
**Paramount Pictures presents
a David Foster Cooper Layne Sean
Bailey production
In association with MFP Munich
Film Partners New Century GmbH
& Co. Core Productions KG
With the participation of the
Province of British Columbia**
135 minutes
Location: **Vancouver (Canada), Utah (USA)**
Sight and Sound: **v. 13, n. 5, p. 40-41**
Box Office: **£1,580,762**
Opening Weekend: **£583,238**
Screens: **395**

### Cowboy Bebop
Columbia TriStar – 27 June
12A Japan 2001
Director: **Shinichiro Watanabe**
Producers:  **Masuo Ueda, Masahiko
Minami, Minoru Takanashi**

Screenplay: **Keiko Nobumoto**
Based on the story by
**Hajime Yatate**
Director of Photography: **Yoichi Ogami**
Editor: **Shuichi Kakesu**
Art Director: **Atsushi Morikawa**
Music: **Yoko Kanno**
Voice Cast:
**Koichi Yamader – Spike Spiegel**
**Unsho Ishizuka – Jet Black**
**Megumi Hayashibara – Faye Valentine**
**Aoi Tada – Ed**
**Yasuku Yara – Hoffman**
**Kazuhiko Inoue – Shadkins**
**Jyurouta Kosugi – Harris**
**Kinryu Arimoto – captain**
**Hidekatsu Shibata – colonel**
**Yuji Ueda – Lee**
© Sunrise/Bones/Bandai Visual
Production Companies:
**a production of Sunrise, Bones,
Bandai Visual Film**
114 minutes 59 seconds
Sight and Sound: **v.13, n.9, p.44-45**
Box Office: **£4,863**
Opening Weekend: **£907**
Screen: **1**

### Cradle 2 The Grave
Warner Bros – 28 March
15 USA 2003
Director: **Andrzej Bartkowiak**
Producer: **Joel Silver**
Screenplay: **John O'Brien, Channing Gibson**
Story:  **John O'Brien**
Director of Photography: **Daryn Okada**
Editor: **Derek G. Brechin**
Production Designer: **David F. Klassen**
Music: **John Frizzell, Damon 'Grease' Blackman**
Cast:
**Jet Li – Su**
**DMX – Tony Fait**
**Anthony Anderson – Tommy**
**Kelly Hu – Sona**
**Tom Arnold – Archie, the fence**
**Mark Dacascos – Ling**
**Gabrielle Union – Daria**
**Michael Jace – Odion**
**Drag-On – Miles**
**Paige Hurd – Vanessa**
**Paolo Seganti – Christophe**
**Richard Trapp – Douglas**
© Warner Bros.
Production Companies:
**Warner Bros. Pictures presents a
Silver Pictures production** – 101
minutes 9 seconds
Location: **Los Angeles (CA, USA)**

Sight and Sound: **v.13, n.  5, p. 41-42**
Box Office: **£1,192,431**
Opening Weekend: **£374,938**
Screens: **201**

### Cremaster Cycle
Palm Pictures – 17 October
Box Office: **£12,632**
Opening Weekend: **£3,323**
Screen: **1**

### Crimson Gold
ICA Projects – 12 September
12A Iran 2003
Director: **Jafar Panahi**
Producer: **Jafar Panahi**
Screenplay: **Abbas Kiarostami**
Director of Photography: **Hossain Jafarian**
Editor:  **Jafar Panahi**
Art Director: **Iraj Raminfar**
Music: **Peyman Yazdanian**
Cast:
**Hossein Emadeddin  – Hussein**
**Kamyar Sheisi – Ali**
**Azita Rayeji  – the bride**
**Shahram Vaziri  – the jeweller**
**Pourang Nakhaei  – Pourang**
**Kaveh Najmabadi  – Saber Safaei**
**Yadollah Samadian  – Ramin Rastad**
© Jafar Panahi Productions.
96 minutes 26 seconds
Sight and Sound: **v.13, n. 11, p.40**
Box Office: **£37,683**
Opening Weekend: **£2,939**
Screen: **1**

### Crime of Father Amaro
Columbia TriStar – 20 June
15 Mexico/Spain/Argentina/France
2002
Director: **Carlos Carrera**
Producers:  **Alfredo Ripstein, Daniel
Birman Ripstein**
Screenplay: **Vicente Leñero**
Based on the novel by  **José María Eça
de Queiroz**
Director of Photography: **Guillermo Granillo**
Editor: **Óscar Figueroa**
Art Director: **Carmen Giménez Cacho**
Music:  **Rosino Serrano**
Cast:
**Gael García Bernal – Father Amaro**
**Ana Claudia Talancón – Amelia**
**Sancho Gracia – Father Benito**
**Angélica Aragón – Sanjuanera**
**Luisa Huertas – Dionisia**
**Pedro Armendáriz – mayor**
**Ernesto Gómez Cruz – bishop**
**Gastón Melo – Martín**
**Damián Alcázar – Father Natalio**
© D.R. Alameda Films
S.A./Foprocine/Imcine/Wanda Visión

Production Companies:
**Alfredo Ripstein, Alameda Films, Wanda Visión, Blu Films, Fondo para la Producción Cinematográfica de Calidad, Instituto Mexicano de Cinematografía, Cinecolor México, Cinecolor Argentina, Videocolor Argentina, Artcam - Francia, Daniel Birman Ripstein, Gobierno del Estado de Veracruz - Llave, with the support of the Ibermedia program present a Carlos Carrera film Made with the support of Fonds-Sud Cinéma Ministerio de Asuntos Extranjeros de Francia, Centre National de la Cinématographie 118 minutes 29 seconds**
Location: **Mexico**
Sight and Sound: v. 13, n. 8, p. 44-45
Box Office: **£86,606**
Opening Weekend: **£14,886**
Screens: **12**

## Cypher
**Pathé Distribution Ltd – 29 August 15 USA 2002**
Director: **Vincenzo Natali**
Producers: **Hunt Lowry, Paul Federbush, Casey LaScala, Wendy Grean**
Screenplay: **Brian King**
Director of Photography: **Derek Rogers**
Editor: **Bert Kish**
Production Designer: **Jasna Stefanovic**
Music: **Michael Andrews**
Cast:
**Jeremy Northam – Morgan Sullivan
Lucy Liu – Rita
Nigel Bennett – Finster
Timothy Webber – Callaway
David Hewlett – Dunn
Kari Matchett – Diane
Kristina Nicoll – Amy
Joseph Scoren – Digicorp
technicians – Stephen Brown
Arnold Pinnock – pilot in mensroom –**
© **Pandora**
Production Companies:
**Pandora presents a Gaylord Films production 95 minutes 17 seconds**
Sight and Sound: v.13, n.10, p.46-47
Box Office: **£293,459**
Opening Weekend: **£34,084**
Screen: **7**

## Cuckoo
**Soda Pictures – 28 November 12A Russia 2002**
Director: **Aleksandr Rogozhkin**
Producer: **Sergei Selianov**
Screenplay: **Aleksandr Rogozhkin**
Director of Photography: **Andrei Zhegalov**
Editor: **Iuliia Rumiantseva**
Production Designer: **Vladimir Svetozarov**
Music: **Dmitrii Pavlov**
Cast:
**Ville Haapasalo – Veiko
Anni-Kristina Juuso – Anni
Viktor Bychkov – Ivan Psholty
Mikhail Korobochkin – Aleksei
Kashnikov – Denis Aksenov –
Aleksei Panzheev – Aleksandr
Kuikka – Vladimir Matveev –**
Production Companies:
**STV Film Company (St Petersburg), with the support of the Cinema Service of the Ministry of Culture of the Russian Federation 107 minutes 32 seconds**
Sight and Sound: **v.14, n.14, p. 41-42**
Box Office: **£19,177**
Opening Weekend: **£6,522**
Screen: **4**

## Daddy Day Care
**Columbia TriStar – 11 July PG USA 2003 – Director Steve Carr**
Producers: **John Davis, Matt Berenson, Wyck Godfrey**
Screenplay: **Geoff Rodkey**
Director of Photography: **Steven Poster**
Editor: **Christopher Greenbury**
Production Designer: **Garreth Stover**
Music: **David Newman**
Cast:
**Eddie Murphy – Charlie Hinton
Jeff Garlin – Phil
Steve Zahn – Marvin
Regina King – Kim Hinton
Kevin Nealon – Bruce
Jonathan Katz – Mr Dan Kubitz
Siobhan Fallon Hogan – Peggy
Lisa Edelstein – Crispin's mom
Lacey Chabert – Jenny
Laura Kightlinger – Sheila**
© Revolution Studios Distribution Company LLC
Production Companies:
**Revolution Studios present a Davis Entertainment production 92 minutes 10 seconds**
Location: **Los Angeles (CA, USA)**
Sight and Sound: **v.13, n.9, p.48-49**
Box Office: **£5,365,402**
Opening Weekend: **£796,259**

Screens: **404**

## Daredevil
**20th Century Fox – 14 February 15 USA 2003 – Director: Mark Stephen Johnson**
Producers: **Arnon Milchan, Gary Foster, Avi Arad, Kathleen Courtney**
Screenplay: **Mark Steven Johnson**
Director of Photography: **Ericson Core**
Editors: **Dennis Virkler Armen Minasian**
Production Designer: **Barry Chusid**
Music: **Graeme Revell**
Cast:
**Ben Affleck – Matt Murdock, 'Daredevil' – Jennifer Garner
Elektra Natchios – Michael Clarke Duncan
Wilson Fisk, 'Kingpin' – Colin Farrell
Bullseye – Joe Pantoliano
Ulrich – Jon Favreau
Franklin Nelson – David Keith
Jack 'The Devil' Murdock – Scott Terra
young Matt – Ellen Pompeo
Karen Page – Leland Orser
Wesley**
© Twentieth Century Fox Film Corporation/Regency Entertainment (USA) Inc [USA only]
© Twentieth Century Fox Film Corporation/Monarchy Enterprises S.a.r.l. [all other territories except Brazil, Italy, Korea, Japan, Spain]
© TCF Hungary Film Rights Exploitation Limited Liability Company/Twentieth Century Fox Film Corporation/Monarchy Enterprises S.a.r.l. [Brazil, Italy, Korea, Japan, Spain]
Production Companies:
**Twentieth Century Fox and Regency Enterprises present in association with Marvel Enterprises, Inc. a New Regency/Horseshoe Bay production 103 minutes 5 seconds**
Location: **Los Angeles (CA, USA)**
Sight and Sound: v. 13, n. 4, p. 34-35
Box Office: **£5,635,119**
Opening Weekend: **£1,953,136**
Screens: **384**

## Dark Blue
**Momentum Pictures – 04 July 15 Germany/United Kingdom/USA 2002**
Director: **Ron Shelton**
Producers: **Caldecot Chubb, David Blocker, James Jacks, Sean Daniel**
Screenplay: **David Ayer**
Story: **James Ellroy**
Director of Photography: **Barry**

Peterson
Editor: **Paul Seydor**
Production Designer: **Dennis Washington**
Music/Orchestrator: **Terence Blanchard**
Cast:
**Kurt Russell – Eldon Perry**
**Brendan Gleeson – Jack Van Meter**
**Scott Speedman – Bobby Keough**
**Michael Michele – Beth Williamson**
**Lolita Davidovich – Sally Perry**
**Dash Mihok – Gary Sidwell**
**Jonathan Banks – James Barcomb**
**Graham Beckel – Peltz**
**Khandi Alexander – Janelle Holland**
**Kurupt – Darryl Orchard**
© IM Filmproduktion und Vertriebs GmbH & Co KG
Production Companies:
**Intermedia and United Artists present**
**in association with**
**IM Filmproduktion**
**an Alphaville production**
**in association with Cosmic Pictures**
**118 minutes 8 seconds**
Location: **Los Angeles (CA, USA)**
Sight and Sound: **v.13, n.5, p.43-44**
Box Office: **£256,352**
Opening Weekend: **£70,049**
Screens: **62**

## Dark Water

Metro Tartan – 06 June
15 Japan 2002
Director: **Hideo Nakata**
Producer: **Taka Ichise**
Screenplay: **Yoshihiro Nakamura, Ken-ichi Suzuki**
Based on the novel by **Kôji Suzuki**
Director of Photography: **Junichirô Hayashi**
Editor: **Nobuyuki Takahashi**
Art Director:
**Katsumi Nakazawa**
Music: **Kenji Kawai**
Cast:
**Hitomi Kuroki – Itsumi Matsubara**
**Rio Kanno – Ikuko aged 6**
**Mirei Oguchi – Mitsuko Kawai**
**Asami Mizukawa – Ikuko Hamada aged 16**
Production Companies:
**Dark Water Film Partners present an Oz production**
**101 minutes 9 seconds**
Sight and Sound: **v.13, n.7, p.39**
Box Office: **£215,370**
Opening Weekend: **£34,978**
Screens: **15**

## Darkness Falls

Columbia TriStar – 9 May
15 USA 2003

Director: **Jonathan Liebesman**
Producers: **John Hegeman, John Fasano, William Sherak, Jason Shuman**
Screenplay: **John Fasano, James Vanderbilt, Joe Harris**
Story: **Joe Harris**
Director of Photography: **Dan Laustsen**
Editors: **Steve Mirkovich, Tim Alverson**
Production Designer: **George Liddle**
Music: **Brian Tyler**
Cast:
**Chaney Kley – Kyle Walsh**
**Emma Caulfield – Caitlin Green**
**Lee Cormie – Michael Greene**
**Grant Piro – Larry**
**Sullivan Stapleton – Officer Matt Henry**
**Steve Mouzakis – Dr Peter Murphy**
**Peter Curtin – Dr Travis**
**Kestie Morassi – Nurse Lauren**
**Jenny Lovell – Nurse Alex**
**John Stanton – Captain Thomas Henry**
© Revolution Studios Distribution Company, LLC
Production Companies:
**Revolution Studios presents a Distant Corners/Blue Star Pictures production**
**84 minutes 34 seconds**
Melbourne (Australia), Sidney (Australia), Gold Coast (Australia)
Sight and Sound: **v.13, n.6, p.41**
Box Office: **£1,737,676**
Opening Weekend: **£483,739**
Screens: **295**

## Darna Mana Hai

Eros International Ltd – 25July
Box Office: **£33,035**
Opening Weekend: **£17,557**
Screens: **13**

## Day of Wrath (re)

BFI – 06 June
Box Office: **£10,935**
Opening Weekend: **£3,320**
Screen: **1**

## Dead Bodies

Buena Vista International – 25 April
Box Office: **£74,131**
Opening Weekend: **£26,648**
Screen: **29**

## Dead End

Pathe Distribution Ltd. – 12 December
15 France  2003
Directors: **Jean-Baptiste Andrea, Fabrice Canepa**
Producers: **James Hutt, Gabriella**

Stollenwerck
Screenplay: **Jean-Baptiste Andrea, Fabrice Canepa**
Director of Photography: **Alexander Buono**
Editor: **Antoine Vareille**
Production Designer: **Bryce Holtshousen**
Music/Music Supervisor: **Greg De Belles**
Cast:
**Ray Wise – Frank Harrington**
**Alexandra Holden – Marion Harrington**
**Lin Shaye – Laura Harrington**
**Mick Cain – Richard Harrington**
© Captain Movies/Sagittaire Films/Sagittaire Distribution/Studio Canal Plus
Production Companies::
**Captain Movies and Sagittaire Films present in association with Studio Canal Plus and 3.2.1. Films a James Huth, Gabriella Stollenwerck, Yves Chevalier production**
**A film by Jean-Baptiste Andrea and Fabrice Canepa**
**83 minutes 17 seconds**
Location: **Los Angeles County (CA, USA)**
Sight and Sound: **v. 14, n. 2, p. 40**
Box Office: **£134,932**
Opening Weekend: **£52,130**
Screen: **35**

## Death in Venice (re)

BFI – 14 February
Box Office: **£40,811**
Opening Weekend: **£6,006**
Screen: **2**

## Devil's Gate

Indy UK – 7 November
Box Office: **£2,908**
Opening Weekend: **£922**
Screen: **2**

## Dil Ka Rishtaa

Venus Entertainment – 17 January
Box Office: **£446,480**
Opening Weekend: **£108,120**
Screen: **23**

## Dirty Deeds

Momentum Pictures – 06 June
18 Australia/United Kingdom 2002
Director: **David Caesar**
Producers: **Bryan Brown, Debbie Balderstone**
Screenplay: **David Caesar**
Director of Photography: **Geoffrey Hall**
Editor: **Mark Perry**
Production Designer: **Chris Kennedy**
Music: **Paul Healy**

Cast:
Bryan Brown – Barry Ryan
Toni Collette – Sharon Ryan
John Goodman – Tony Testano
Sam Neill – Detective Sergeant Ray Murphy
Sam Worthington – Darcy
Kestie Morassi – Margaret
William McInnes – Tom 'Hollywood' Reilly
Andrew S. Gilbert – Norm
Gary Waddell – Freddie Kelly
Felix Williamson – Sal Cassela
© Australian Film Finance Corporation Limited/Macquarie Film Corporation Limited/Nine Films and Television Pty Limited/New South Wales Film and Television Office/Dirty Deeds Productions Pty Limited
Production Companies:
a New Town Film in association with Haystack Productions
a Dirty Deeds production in association with Alliance Atlantis Motion Picture Distribution in association with Momentum Pictures
Financed with the assistance of Nine Films and Television
Produced with the assistance of New South Wales Film and Television Office
Financed with the assistance of Macquarie Film Corporation
Financed with the assistance of Australian Film Finance Corporation
97 minutes 41 seconds
Location: Sidney (Australia), Broken Hill (Australia)
Sight and Sound: v.13, n.7, p. 40
Box Office: £42,141
Opening Weekend: £18,787
Screen: 33

### Divine Intervention
Artificial Eye – 17 January
15 France/Germany/Morocco/Netherlands/USA 2002
Director: Elia Suleiman
Producer: Humbert Balsan
Screenplay: Elia Suleiman
Director of Photography: Marc-André Batigne
Editor: Véronique Lange
Art Directors: Miguel Markin
Denis Renault
Music Supervisor: Serge Guillerme
Cast:
Elia Suleiman – E.S.
Manal Khader – the woman
Nayef Fahoum Daher – father
George Ibrahim – Santa Claus

Jamal Daher – Jamal
Amer Daher – Auni
Lutuf Nuweiser – neighbour with American van
Riad Masarweh – Abu Basil
Bassem Loulou – Abu Amer
© Ognon Pictures/Arte France Cinéma/Gimages Films/Lichtblick
Production Companies:
Humbert Balsan presents an Ognon Pictures, Arte France Cinéma, Gimages Film, Soread 2M, Lichtblick co-production with the participation of Centre National de la Cinématographie, Filmstiftung Nordrhein-Westfalen, Fonds Sud, Hubert Bals Fund and The Ford Foundation, The European Commission (East Jerusalem Office), The French General Consulate (Cultural Service East Jerusalem Office)
93 minutes 4 seconds
Sight and Sound: v.13, n.1, p.42-43
Box Office: £106,702
Opening Weekend: £20,593
Screen: 5

### Dolls
Artificial Eye – 30 May
12A Japan 2002 – Director: Takeshi Kitano
Producers: Masayuki Mori
Takio Yoshida
Screenplay: Takeshi Kitano
Director of Photography: Katsumi Yanagijima
Edited by – Takeshi Kitano
Production Designer: Norihiro Isoda
Music: Joe Hisaishi
Cast:
Miho Kanno – Sawako
Hidetoshi Nishijima – Matsumoto
Tatsuya Mihashi – Hiro, the boss
Chieko Matsubara – the woman in the park
Kyoko Fukada – Haruna Yamaguchi, the pop star
Tsutomu Tageshige – Nukui, the fan
© Bandai Visual/Tokyo FM/Television Tokyo/Office Kitano
Production Companies:
Produced by Bandai Visual/Tokyo FM/Television Tokyo/Office Kitano
113 minutes 38 seconds
Sight and Sound: v.13, n.6, p.42
Box Office: £83,914
Opening Weekend: £11,207
Screen: 6

### Double Whammy
Winchester Films – 18 July

15 USA/Germany 2001
Director: Tom DiCillo
Producers: David Kronemyer, Larry Katz, Marcus Viscidi, Jim Serpico
Screenplay: Tom DiCillo
Director of Photography: Robert Yeoman
Editor: Camilla Toniolo
Production Designer: Michael Shaw
Music: Jim Farmer
Cast:
Denis Leary – Ray Pluto
Elizabeth Hurley – Doctor Ann Beamer
Luis Guzmán – Juan Benitez
Victor Argo – Lieutenant Spigot
Chris Noth – Chick Dimitri
Donald Faison – Cletis
Keith Nobbs – Duke
Steve Buscemi – Jerry Cubbins
Maurice Compte – Jo Jo
Otto Sanchez – Ping Pong
Melonie Diaz – Maribel Benitez
© Gold Circle Films
Production Companies:
Gold Circle Films and Myriad Pictures present a Lemon Sky/Apostle production in association with IN-motion AG Movie & TV Productions (and the World Media Fund)
100 minutes 20 seconds
Location: New York (USA), New Jersey (USA)
Sight and Sound: v.13, n.10, p.48
Box Office: £33,830
Opening Weekend: £9,221
Screen: 10

### Down With Love
Twentieth Century Fox – 03 October
12A USA/Germany 2003
Director: Peyton Reed
Producers: Bruce Cohen, Dan Jinks
Screenplay: Eve Ahlert, Dennis Drake
Director of Photography: Jeff Cronenweth
Editor: Larry Bock
Production Designer: Andrew Laws
Music: Marc Shaiman
Cast:
Renée Zellweger – Barbara Novak
Ewan McGregor – Catcher Block
David Hyde Pierce – Peter McMannus
Sarah Paulson – Vicki Hiller
Tony Randall – Theodore Banner
Rachel Dratch – Gladys
Jack Plotnick – Maurice
John Aylward – E.G.
Warren Munson – C.B.
Matt Ross – J.B.
Michael Ensign

© Mediastream Dritte Dilm GmbH & Co. Beteiligungs KG/Twentieth Century Fox Film Corporation
Production Companies:
**Fox 2000 Pictures and Regency Enterprises present
in association with Mediastream III
a Jinks/Cohen Company production**
101 minutes 28 seconds
Location: **Los Angeles (CA, USA)**
Sight and Sound: **v. 13, n. 11, p. 41-42**
Box Office: **£2,053,348**
Opening Weekend: **£599,047**
Screens: **298**

## Dracula: Pages from a Virgin's Diary
Tartan Films 12 December
Box Office: **£3,186**
Opening Weekend: **£1,466**
Screens: **1**

## Dragonflies
Optimum Releasing – 04 July
15 Norway/Sweden 2002
Director: **Marius Holst**
Producer: **Sigve Endresen**
Screenplay: **Nikolaj Frobenius**
In collaboration with
**Marius Holst**
Based on the short story: Natt til mørk morgen by **Ingvar Ambjørnsen**
Director of Photography: **John Christian Rosenlund**
Editor: **Sophie Hesselberg**
Art Directors: **Lotte Wallin, Katrin Lea Tag**
Music: **Magne Furuholmen, Kjetil Bjerkestrand**
Cast:
**Kim Bodnia – Eddie
Maria Bonnevie – Maria
Mikael Persbrandt – Kullmann
Tord Peterson – Sven
Thomas Skarpjordet – Thomas
Tintin Anderzon – Birger's wife
Shanti Roney – lover
Anastasios Soulis – Birger's son
Willy Karlsson – shop owner
Ulla-Britt Norrman-Olsson – Eline
Tilda Wrange – baby**
© 41/2/Motlys/Final Cut Entertainment
Production Companies:
**41/2 and Motlys
in co-production with Final Cut
presents
Supported by Norsk Filminstitutt
(Harry Guttormsen), Svenska
Filminstitutet (Feature Film
Consultant: Lena Hansson-Varhegyi), Nordisk Film & TV Fond
In co-operation with NRK-Drama,
TV-4 Sverige, Canal+ Scandinavia**

and Diopter A/S
109 minutes 25 seconds
Sight and Sound: **v.13, n.9, p. 46**
Box Office: **£8,703**
Opening Weekend: **£1,030**
Screen: **1**

## The Draughtman's Contract (re)
ICA Projects – 01 August
Box Office: **£1,741**
Opening Weekend: **£1,284**
Screen: **1**

## Dreamcatcher
Warner Bros – 25 April
15 USA/Australia 2003
Director: **Lawrence Kasdan**
Producers: **Lawrence Kasdan, Charles Okun**
Screenplay: **William Goldman Lawrence Kasdan**
Based on the book by **Stephen King**
Director of Photography: **John Seale**
Editors: **Carol Littleton, Raul Davalos**
Production Designer: **Jon Hutman**
Music: **James Newton Howard**
Cast:
**Morgan Freeman – Colonel Abraham Curtis
Thomas Jane – Dr Henry Devlin
Jason Lee – Beaver
Damian Lewis – Jonesy
Timothy Olyphant – Pete
Tom Sizemore – Owen Underhill
Donnie Wahlberg – Duddits
Mikey Holekamp – young Henry
Reece Thompson – young Beaver
Giacomo Baessato – young Jonesy
Joel Palmer – young Pete
Andrew Robb – young Duddits**
© Warner Bros.
(US, Bahamas, Bermuda)
© Village Roadshow Films (BVI) Limited
(all other territories)
Production Companies:
**Castle Rock Entertainment presents
in association with Village
Roadshow Pictures and
NPV Entertainment
a Kasdan Pictures production**
133 minutes 34 seconds
Location: **Vancouver (Canada)**
Sight and Sound: **v.13, n.6, p.44**
Box Office: **£1,896,579**
Opening Weekend: **£729,525**
Screens: **344**

## Drunk on Women and Poetry
Pathé Distribution Ltd – 06 June
15 Republic of Korea
Director: **Im Kwon-taek**

Producer: **Lee Tae-won**
Screenplay: **Kim Young-oak, Im Kwon-taek, Kang Hea-yun**
Director of Photography: **Jung Il-sung**
Editor: **Park Soon-duk**
Production Designer: **Ju Byoung-do**
Music: **Kim Young-dong**
Cast:
**Choi Min-sik – Jang Seung-ub
Ahn Sung-ki – Kim Byung-moon
You Ho-jeong – Mae-hyang
Kim Yeo-Jin – Jin-hong
Son Ye-jin – So-woon
Han Myoung-gu – Lee Eung-heon
Jung Tae-woo – Jang Seung-ub as a teenager
Choi Jong-sung – Jang Seung-ub as a boy
Ki Jung-soo – Master Yoo-sook
Park Ji-il – Scholar Gwak Sung-min**
Production Companies:
**Cinema Service presents
a Taehung Pictures production
in association with MVP Capital,
TeraSource Venture Capital
(i pictures) and SBS
Sponsored by Hana Bank**
116 minutes 48 seconds
Sight and Sound: **v.13, n.6, p.40-41**
Box Office: **£29,725**
Opening Weekend: **£6,201**
Screens: **3**

## Dum
Eros International Ltd – 24 January
Box Office: **£30,484**
Opening Weekend: **£14,178**
Screens: **13**

## Dumb and Dumberer: When Harry Met Lloyd
Entertainment – 13 June
12A USA/Germany 2003
Director: **Troy Miller**
Producers: **Oren Koules, Charles B. Wessler, Brad Krevoy Steve Stabler, Troy Miller**
Screenplay: **Robert Brener, Troy Miller**
Story: **Robert Brener**
Based on characters created by
**Peter Farrelly, Bennett Yellin, Bobby Farrelly**
Director of Photography: **Anthony Richmond**
Editor: **Lawrence Jordan**
Production Designer: **Cecilia Montiel**
Music: **Eban Schletter**
Cast:
**Eric Christian Olsen – Lloyd Christmas
Derek Richardson – Harry Dunne
Rachel Nichols – Jessica Matthews**

Cheri Oteri – Ms Heller
Luis Guzmán – Ray
Elden Henson – Turk
William Lee Scott – Carl
Mimi Rogers – Mrs Dunne
Eugene Levy – Pricipal Collins
Lin Shaye – Margie
© MIKADO Verwaltungsgesellschaft
mbH & Co. Produktions KG
Production Companies:
New Line Cinema presents
a Brad Krevoy/Charles B.
Wessler/Steve Stabler production
a Burg/Koules and Dakota Pictures
production
in association with MIKADO
Verwaltungsgesellschaft mbH & Co.
Produktions KG
84 minutes 50 seconds
Location: **Atlanta (GA, USA)**
Sight and Sound: **v.13, n. 9,p.47-48**
Box Office: **£1,702,461**
Opening Weekend: **£673,202**
Screen: **350**

## Ek Aur Ek Gyarah
Eros International Ltd – 28 March
Box Office: **£125,180**
Opening Weekend: **£36,470**
Screens: **16**

## El Bola
Axiom Films – 04 April
15 Spain 2000
Director: **Achero Mañas**
Screenplay: **Achero Mañas**
With the collaboration of
Verónica Fernández
Director of Photography: **Juan Carlos
Gómez**
Editor: **Nacho Ruiz Capillas**
Production Designers:
**D. Goldstein
R. Steinberg**
Music: **Eduardo Arbide**
Cast:
Juan José Ballesta – Bola
Pablo Galán – Alfredo
Alberto Jiménez – José Manuel
Morón
Mariano Wagener – Laura
Nieve de Medina – Marisa
Gloria Muñoz – Aurora
Javier Lago – Alfonso
Omar Muñoz – Juan
Soledad Osorio – grandmother
© TESELA S.R.L.
Production Companies:
a TESELA P.C. production with the
participation of TVE
and Canal + (España)
With the collaboration of I.C.A.A.,
Ministerio de Educación, Cultura y
Deportes
Developed with the support of the

MEDIA programme of the European
Union
87 minutes 9 seconds
Location: **Madrid**
Sight and Sound: **v.13, n.6, p.38**
Box Office: **£10,665**
Opening Weekend: **£1,228**
Screen: **1**

## El Bonaerense
Soda Pictures – 05 September
15
Argentina/Netherlands/France/Chile
2002
Director: **Pablo Trapero**
Screenplay: **Pablo Trapero**
Director of Photography: **Guillermo
Nieto, Suipacha, Cobi Migliora**
Editor: **Nicolás Goldbart**
Production Designer: **Sebastian
Roses**
Music: **Damas Gratis, Pablo Lescano**
Cast:
Jorge Román – 'Zapa', Enrique
Orlando Mendoza
Dario Levy – Deputy Inspector Gallo
Mimi Arduh – Mabel
Hugo Anganuzzi – Polaco
Victor Hugo Carrizo – Inspector
Molinari
Graciana Chironi – Graciana, Zapa's
mother
Roberto Posse – Uncle Ismael
Mendoza
Luis Vicat – Pellegrino
Anibal Barengo – Caneva
Gerardo Maffoni – Officer Osario
Liliana de Maria – Officer Marina
© Pablo Trapero
Production Companies:
Instituto Nacional de Cine y Artes
Audiovisuales (INCAA Argentina);
Festival
Internacional de Cine de Rotterdam
Hubert Bals Fund, Holanda;
Programa Ibermedia; Fonds Sud,
Ministerio Franc´es de la Cultura y
de la Comunicación,
Centro Nacional de la
Cinematografía (CNC), Ministerio
Francés de Asuntos Extranjeros
Francia, + Studio Canal Francia;
Andres Wood Producciones, Chile;
Pablo Trapero, Argentina present
101 minutes 99 seconds
Sight and Sound: **v.13, n.11, p.33-34**
Box Office: **£23,068**
Opening Weekend: **£5,865**
Screens: **3**

## Elf
Entertainment – 28 November
PG Germany/USA 2003
Director: **Jon Favreau**
Producers: **Jon Berg, Todd**

Komarnicki, Shauna Robertson
Screenplay: **David Berenbaum**
Director of Photography: **Greg
Gardiner**
Editor: **Dan Lebental**
Production Designer: **Rusty Smith**
Music: **John Debney**
Cast:
Will Ferrell – Buddy
James Caan – Walter
Zooey Deschanel – Jovie
Mary Steenburgen – Emily
Daniel Tay – Michael
Edward Asner – Santa
Bob Newhart – Papa Elf
Faizon Love – Gimbels manager
Peter Dinklage – Miles Finch
Amy Sedaris – Deb
© Munich Carlyle Productions
GmbH & Co. KG/New Line
Productions, Inc.
Production Companies::
New Line Cinema presents a Guy
Walks into a Bar production
in association with Munich Carlyle
Productions GmbH & Co. KG
A film by Jon Favreau
96 minutes 34 seconds
Sight and Sound: **v. 14, n. 1, p.42-43**
Box Office: **£15,834,316**
Opening Weekend: **£4,538,440**
Screens: **392**

## Elling
City Screen – 14 March
15 Norway 2001
Director: **Petter Næss**
Producer: **Dag Alveberg**
Screenplay: **Axel Hellstenius**
Based on the novel Brødre i blodet by
**Ingvar Ambjørnsen**
Director of Photography: **Svein
Krøvel**
Editor: **Inge-Lise Langfeldt**
Art Director:
**Harald Egede-Nissen**
Music: **Lars Lillo Stenberg**
Cast:
Per Christian Ellefsen – Elling
Sven Nordin – Kjell Bjarne
Marit Pia Jacobsen – Reidun
Nordsletten
Jørgen Langhelle – Frank Åsli
Per Christensen – Alfons Jørgensen
Hilde Olausson – Gunn
Ola Otnes – Hauger
Eli-Anne Linnestad – Johanne
Cecilie Mosli – Cecilie Kornes
Haakon Rafaelsen – Haakon
Willum
© Maipo
Production Companies:
Maipo Film- & TV Produksjon
presents

Produced with support from
Audiovisuelt Produksjonsfond (Elin
Erichsen) and – 88 minutes 35
seconds
Sight and Sound: v.13, n.3, p. 38-39
Box Office: £53,460
Opening Weekend: £11,298
Screens: 13

## Emotional Backgammon
Buccaneer – 29 August
15 United Kingdom 2003
Director: **Leon Herbert**
Producers:  **John Herbert, Leon
Herbert**
Screenplay: **Leon Herbert, Matthew
Hope**
Director of Photography: **Koutaiba
Al-Janabi**
Editor: **Oxford Bird**
Production Designer: **John Herbert**
Score: **Paul Foss, Chris Nicholaides**
Soundtrack: **Trevor Shakes**
Cast:
**Wil Johnson**  – John
**Daniela Lavender**  – Mary
**Leon Herbert**  – Steve
**Jacqueline De Peza**  – Jane
**Bob Mercer**  – Paul
**Steve Weston**  – cab driver
**Steve Edwin**  – psychiatrist
**Catherine Coyne**  – Jane's house
party
**Dee Cannon**  – theatre director
© Emotional Backgammon Limited
Production Companies:
**Buccaneer Film Distribution**
**Odeon Cinema presents an Emotion
Backgammon production**
**in association with**
**Big H Productions**
**and The Film Council**
93 minutes 41 seconds
Sight and Sound; v.13, n.11, p.42-43
Box Office: £1,046
Opening Weekend: £1,046
Screen: 1

## The End of Summer
Artificial Eye – 08 August
Box Office: £14,118
Opening Weekend: £3,230
Screen: 1

## Equilibrium
Momentum Pictures – 14 March
15 USA 2002
Director: **Kurt Wimmer**
Producers:  **Jan De Bont, Lucas
Foster**
Screenplay: **Kurt Wimmer**
Director of Photography: **Dion Beebe**
Editors: **Tom Rolf, William Yeh**
Production Designers:  **Wolf Kroeger**
Music/Score Producer: **Klaus Badelt**

Cast:
**Christian Bale**  – John Preston
**Emily Watson**  – Mary O'Brien
**Taye Diggs**  – Brandt
**Angus MacFadyen**  – Dupont
**Sean Bean**  – Partridge
**Sean Pertwee**  – father
**Matthew Harbour**  – Robbie Preston
**William Fichtner**  – Jurgen
**Dominic Purcell**  – Seamus
**Christian Kahrmann**  – officer in
charge
© Miramax Film Corp.
Production Companies:
**Dimension Films presents  a Blue
Tulip production created by
Miramax Film Corp.**
106 minutes 53 seconds
Location: Berlin (Germany)
Sight and Sound: v.13, n.4, p.35-36
Box Office: £1,448,396
Opening Weekend: £548,043
Screens: 292

## Etre et Avoir
Tartan Films – 20 June
U France 2002
Director: **Nicolas Philibert**
Producer: **Gilles Sandoz**
Directors of Photography: **Katell
Djian, Laurent Didier**
Editor: **Nicolas Philibert**
Music:  **Philippe Hersant**
With
**George Lopez**  – the teacher
**Alizé – Axel – Guillaume – Jessie –
Johan (Jojo) – Johann – Jonathan –
Julien – Laura – Létitia –**
© Maïa Films/ARTE France
CINEMA/
les Films d'Ici/CNDP - France
Production Companies:
**Maïa Films presents in co-
production with ARTE France
CINEMA, les Films d'Ici and
le Centre National de
Documentation Pédagogique
with the participation of CANAL+,
Centre National de la
Cinématographie,
GIMAGES 4,
and the support of le Ministère de
l'Education Nationale, Conseil
Régional d'Auvergne, Procirep**
104 minutes 29 seconds
Sight and Sound: v.13, n.8, p.45
Box Office: £704,582
Opening Weekend: £33,314
Screens: 10

## Evelyn
Pathé Distribution Ltd – 21 March
PG Germany/USA/Ireland 2002
Director: **Bruce Beresford**
Producers:  **Pierce Brosnan, Beau St.**

Clair, Michael Ohoven
Screenplay: **Paul Pender**
Director of Photography: **André
Fleuren**
Editor: **Humphrey Dixon**
Production Designer: **John Stoddart**
Music/Musical Director/
Orchestrations: **Stephen Endelman**
Cast:
**Pierce Brosnan**  – Desmond Doyle
**Aidan Quinn**  – Nick Barron
**Julianna Margulies**  – Bernadette
Beattie
**Stephen Rea**  – Michael Beattie
**John Lynch**  – Senior Counsel Mr
Wolfe
**Sophie Vavasseur**  – Evelyn Doyle
**Alan Bates**  – Tom Connolly
**Niall Beagan**  – Dermot Doyle
**Hugh MacDonagh**  – Maurice Doyle
–**Mairead Devlin**  – Charlotte Doyle
**Frank Kelly**  – Henry Doyle
© CineEvelyn Internationale
Filmproduktionsgesell-schaft mbH &
Co. 1Beteiligungs-KG
Production Companies:
**First Look Media and Cinerenta
present**
**in association with United Artists
an Irish DreamTime production
Produced in association with
CineEvelyn
Produced with the support of
investment incentives for the Irish
film industry provided by the
government of Ireland
Developed in association with ACE
With the assistance of the European
Co-production Fund Limited,
London, England
Developed with financial assistance
from Scottish Screen**
94 minutes 45 seconds
Location: Ireland
Sight and Sound: v.13, n.4, p.36-37
Box Office: £1,445,396
Opening Weekend: £344,270
Screens: 293

## Extreme Ops
United International Pictures – 16
May
12A United
Kingdom/Germany/USA/
Luxembourg/Austria/Canada 2002
Director: **Christian Duguay**
Producers: **Moshe Diamant, Jan
Fantl**
Screenplay: **Michael Zaidan**
Story: **Timothy Scott Bogart, Mark
Mullin**
Director of Photography: **Hannes
Hubach**
Editors: **Clive Barrett, Sylvain Lebel**

Production Designer: **Philip Harrison**
Music: **Normand Corbeil, Stanislas Syrewicz**
Cast:
**Devon Sawa** – Will
**Bridgette Wilson-Sampras** – Chloe
**Rupert Graves** – Jeffrey
**Rufus Sewell** – Ian
**Heino Ferch** – Mark
**Joe Absolom** – Silo
**Jana Pallaske** – Kittie
**Jean-Pierre Castaldi** – Zoran
**Liliana Komorowska** – Yana
**Klaus Löwitsch** – Pavlov
© Extreme Productions Ltd/ApolloMedia GmbH & Co. 4. Filmproduktion KG
Production Companies:
**MDP Worldwide and Diamant Cohen Productions present an ApolloMedia, Extreme Productions production in association with The Carousel Picture Company
With the support of Cine Tirol
With the participation of the Province of British Columbia
Production Service Tax Credit**
93 minutes 26 seconds
Sight and Sound: **v.13, n.7, p.41**
Box Office: **£27,394**
Opening Weekend: **£14,751**
Screens: **24**

## Far From Heaven
Entertainment – 07 March
12A USA/France 2002
Director: **Todd Haynes**
Producers: **Jody Patton, Christine Vachon**
Screenplay: **Todd Haynes**
Director of Photography: **Edward Lachman**
Editor: **James Lyons**
Production Designer: **Mark Friedberg**
Music: **Elmer Bernstein**
Cast:
**Julianne Moore** – Cathy Whitaker
**Dennis Quaid** – Frank Whitaker
**Dennis Haysbert** – Raymond Deagan
**Patricia Clarkson** – Eleanor Fine
**Viola Davis** – Sybil
**James Rebhorn** – Doctor Bowman
**Celia Weston** – Mona Lauder
**Michael Gaston** – Stan Fine
**Ryan Ward** – David Whitaker
**Lindsay Andretta** – Janice Whitaker
© Focus Features/Vulcan Productions
Production Companies:
**TF1 International and Vulcan Productions
in association with Focus Features**

presents
**a Killer Films, Jon Wells, Section Eight production**
107 minutes 22 seconds
Location: **New Jersey (USA), New York (NY, USA)**
Sight and Sound: **v. 13, n. 3, p. 40-41**
Box Office: **£1,853,941**
Opening Weekend: **£452,369**
Screens: **195**

## Fausto 5.0
Soda Pictures – 06 June
18 Spain 2001 – Directors
**Isidro Ortiz
Álex Ollé
Carlos Padrissa**
Producers: **Ramón Vidal
Eduardo Campoy**
Screenplay: **Fernando León de Aranoa**
Story:
**Fernando León de Aranoa
Isidro Ortiz
Álex Ollé
Carlos Padrissa
From an original idea by Lola Becaria, Isidro Ortiz,
Álex Ollé, Carlos Padrissa, Fernando León de Aranoa**
Dialogue
**Fernando León de Aranoa**
Director of Photography: **Pedro del Rey**
Editor: **Manel G. Frasquiel**
Art Director:
**Leo Casamitjana**
Music: **Josep Sanou
Toni M. Mir**
Cast:
**Miguel Ángel Solá**
Fausto
**Eduard Fernández**
Santos Vella
**Najwa Nimri**
Julia
**Raquel González**
Margarita
**Juan Fernández**
Quiroga
**Irene Montalà**
Marta
**Carmen Contreras**
old lady
**Cristina Piaget**
haggard woman
**Pep Molina**
Bielsa
**Oscar Borràs**
Fierro
**Keke Creixems**
presenter
© **Fausto P.C., S.L.**
Production Companies:

**With the participation of TVE Televisión Española, Vía Digital, Televisió de Catalunya, MEDIA
a Fausto P.C. and Cartel production in association with 42nd Street Productions
a film by Isidro Ortiz and la Fura dels Bals
With the collaboration of I.C.A.A. (Instituto de las Ciencias y Artes Audiovisuales)
I.C.I.C. (Institut Catalá de Industries Culturals)
I.C.F. (Insitut Catalá de Finances)**
94 minutes 18 seconds
Sight and Sound: **v.13, n.7, p.42**
Box Office: **£5,151**
Opening Weekend: **£2,077**
Screens: **8**

## Feardotcom
Columbia TriStar – 27 June
18 United Kingdom/Germany/ Luxembourg/USA 2002
Director: **William Malone**
Producers: **Moshe Diamant, Limor Diamant**
Screenplay: **Josephine Coyle**
Story: **Moshe Diamant**
Director of Photography: **Christian Sebaldt**
Editor: **Alan Strachan**
Production Designer: **Jérôme Latour**
Music/Music Conductor: **Nicholas Pike**
Cast:
**Stephen Dorff** – Detective Mike Reilly
**Natascha McElhone** – Terry Huston
**Stephen Rea** – Alistair Pratt
**Udo Kier** – Polidori
**Amelia Curtis** – Denise
**Jeffrey Combs** – Styles
**Nigel Terry** – Turnbull
**Gesine Cukrowski** – Jeannine
**Michael Sarrazin** – Frank Bryant
**Jana Güttgemanns** – little girl
© Fear.com Productions Ltd./ApolloMedia GmbH & Co. 4. Filmproduktion KG/The Carousel Film Company, SA
Production Companies:
**MDP Worldwide presents an ApolloMedia/Fear.com Productions/Carousel Film Company
co-production
with the support of the Film Fund Luxembourg**
101 minutes 19 seconds
Location: **Luxembourg, Montreal (Canada)**
Sight and Sound: **v. 13, n. 7, p. 43**
Box Office: **£53,284**

Opening Weekend: £23,025
Screens: 78

## The Fighting Temptations
United Intl. Pictures – 12 December
PG USA 2003
Director: **Jonathan Lynn**
Producers: **David Gale, Loretha
Jones, Jeff Pollack**
Screenplay: **Saladin K. Patterson,
Elizabeth Hunter**
Story: **Elizabeth Hunter**
Director of Photography: **Affonso
Beato**
Editor: **Paul Hirsch**
Production Designer: **Victoria Paul**
Music: **Jimmy Jam, Terry Lewis,
James 'Big Jim' Wright**
Cast:
**Cuba Gooding Jr – Darrin Hill
Beyoncé Knowles – Lilly
Mike Epps – Lucius
Steve Harvey – Miles Smoke
LaTanya Richardson – Paulina
Pritchett
Nigel Washington – little Darrin
Chloe Bailey – little Lilly
Demetress Long – church usher
Ann Nesby – Aunt Sally Walker
Faith Evans – Maryann Hill**
© Paramount Pictures
Production Companies::
**Paramount Pictures presents an
MTV Films production in
association with Handprint Films
A Jonathan Lynn film**
123 minutes
Location: **Atlanta (GA, USA)**
Sight and Sound: v. 14, n. 2, p. 44, 46
Box Office: £335,127
Opening Weekend: £151,994
Screens: 157

## Final Destination 2
Entertainment – 07 February
15 USA 2003
Director: **David R. Ellis**
Producers: **Warren Zide
Craig Perry**
Screenplay: **J. Mackye Gruber
Eric Bress**
Story: **J. Mackye Gruber, Eric Bress
Jeffrey Reddick**
Director of Photography: **Gary Capo**
Editor: **Eric Sears**
Production Designer: **Michael Bolton**
Music: **Shirley Walker**
Cast:
**Ali Larter – Clear Rivers
A.J. Cook – Kimberly Corman
Michael Landes – Thomas Burke
T.C. Carson – Eugene Dix
Jonathan Cherry – Rory
Keegan Connor Tracy – Kat**

**Sarah Carter – Shaina
Lynda Boyd – Nora Carpenter
David Paetkau – Evan Lewis
Justina Machado – Isabella Hudson
James Kirk – Tim Carpenter**
© New Line Productions, Inc.
Production Companies:
**New Line Cinema presents a
Zide/Perry production**
90 minutes 3 seconds
Location: **Vancouver (Canada)**
Sight and Sound: v. 13, n. 4, p. 37
Box Office: £5,679,816
Opening Weekend: £1,675,057
Screens: 330

## Finding Nemo
Buena Vista International – 03
October
U USA 2003
Director: **Andrew Stanton**
Producer: **Graham Walters**
Screenplay: **Andrew Stanton, Bob
Peterson, David Reynolds**
Original Story: **Andrew Stanton**
Directors of Photography: **Sharon
Calahan, Jeremy Lasky**
Editor: **David Ian Salter**
Production Designer: **Ralph
Eggleston**
Music: **Thomas Newman**
Voice Cast:
**Albert Brooks – Marlin
Ellen DeGeneres – Dory
Alexander Gould – Nemo
Willem Dafoe – Gill
Brad Garrett – Bloat
Allison Janney – Peach
Austin Pendleton – Gurgle
Stephen Root – Bubbles
Vicki Lewis – Deb/Flo
Joe Ranft – Jacques**
© Disney Enterprises Inc/Pixar
Animation Studios
Production Companies:
**Walt Disney Pictures presents a
Pixar Animation Studios film**
97 minutes 17 seconds
Sight and Sound: v.13, n.11, p.43-44
Box Office: £37,333,799
Opening Weekend: £152,793
Screens: 2

## The Five Obstructions
ICA Projects – 7 November
15 Denmark/Belgium/Switzerland/
France/Sweden/Finland/United
Kingdom/Norway 2003
Directors: **Jørgen Leth, Lars von
Trier**
Producer: **Carsten Holst**
Idea: **Lars von Trier**
Based on The Perfect Human (1967)
by Jørgen Leth

Director of Photography: **Dan
Holmberg**
Editors: **Camilla Skousen, Morten
Højbjerg**
With:
**Jørgen Leth – the director
Lars von Trier – the obstructor
Carsten Holst – the Producer**
© Zentropa Real ApS/Almaz Film
Productions SA/Wajnbrosse
Productions/Panic Productions
Production Companies:
**Zentropa Real, Wajnbrosse
Productions, Almaz Film
Productions, Panic Productions
present a film by Jørgen Leth & Lars
von Trier
Produced by Zentropa Real ApS,
Wajnbrosse Productions, Almaz
Film Productions SA, Panic
Productions
Supported by
Eurimages /Danish Film Institute
(Jakob Høgel)
In co-production with DR TV,
Memfis Film International, Centre
du Cinéma et de
l'Audiovisuel de la Communauté
Française de Belgique
In association with Nordic Film- &
TV Fund (Kristin Ulseth/Eva
Færevaag/Svend
Abrahamsen), Swedish Film
Institute (Göran Olsson), SVT
(Björn Arvas), YLE TV1**
Co-Productions, Channel 4, Canal+
Scandinavia, Loterie Nationale
90 minutes 59 seconds
Location: **Havana (Cuba), Bombay
(India), Avedore and Copenhagen
(Denmark), Port-au-Prince (Haiti)**
Sight and Sound: v. 13, n. 12, p. 34
Box Office: £21,928
Opening Weekend: £3,214
Screens: 2

## Floating Weeds (re)
Artifical Eye – 01 August
Box Office: £15,444
Opening Weekend: £4,211
Screen: 1

## Fogbound
Blue Dolphin – 04 April
18 Netherlands/United Kingdom
2001
Director: **Ate de Jong**
Producers: **Ate de Jong , Angela
Roessel**
Screenplay: **Michael Lally , Ate de
Jong**
Director of Photography: **Erwin
Roodhart**
Editor: **Nigel Galt**

Production Designer: **Ben van Os**
Music: **Frank Fitzpatrick**
Cast:
**Luke Perry** – Bob
**Ben Daniels** – Leo
**Orla Brady** – Ann
**Jeroen Krabbé** – Dr Duff
**Ali Hames** – Gloria
**Meg Kubota** – Shiny
**Stella Tanner** – Nanny Moses
**Kevin Moore** – vicar
© MeesPierson Film C.V.
Production Companies:
a **Mulholland Pictures/MeesPierson
Film C.V. production
in association with InterMedia Films**
This film was made financially
possible by private investors in
MeesPierson Film C.V., Dutch Film
Fund, Cobo Fund
Developed with support of the
Media Programme of the European
Union
98 minutes 45 seconds
Sight and Sound: v.13, n.5, p.44-45
Box Office: £1,033
Opening Weekend: £1,033
Screens: 2

## Four Feathers
Buena Vista International – 18 July
15 USA 2002
Director: **Shekhar Kapur**
Producers: **Paul Feldsher, Marty
Katz, Stanley R. Jaffe, Robert D. Jaffe**
Screenplay: **Michael Schiffer,
Hossein Amini**
Based on the novel by **A.E.W Mason**
Director of Photography: **Robert
Richardson**
Editor: **Steven Rosenblum**
Production Designer: **Allan Cameron**
Music/Music
Conductor/Orchestrations: **James
Horner**
Cast:
**Heath Ledger** – Harry Feversham
**Wes Bentley** – Jack Durrance
**Kate Hudson** – Ethne
**Djimon Hounsou** – Abou Fatma
**Michael Sheen** – Trench
**Mohamed Bouich** – Sudanese story-
teller
**Campbell Brown** – Dervish Ansar
**Daniel Caltagirone** – Gustave
**James Cosmo** – Colonel Sutch
**Andy Coumbe** – Colonel other
regiment
**Angela Douglas** – Aunt Mary
© Miramax Film Corp./Paramount
Pictures Corporation
Production Companies:
**Paramount Pictures and Miramax
Films present**

a **Jaffilms production**
131 minutes 20 seconds
Location: **UK, Morocco**
Sight and Sound: v. 13, n. 9, p. 48-49
Box Office: £164,725
Opening Weekend: £61,800
Screens: 143

## Freaky Friday
Buena Vista International – 19
December
PG USA 2003
Director: **Mark Waters**
Producer: **Andrew Gunn**
Screenplay: **Heather Hach, Leslie
Dixon**
Based on the book by Mary Rodgers
Director of Photography: **Oliver
Wood**
Editor: **Bruce Green**
Production Designer: **Cary White**
Music: **Rolfe Kent**
Cast:
**Jamie Lee Curtis** – Doctor Tess
Coleman
**Lindsay Lohan** – Anna Coleman
**Mark Harmon** – Ryan, Tess' fiancé
**Harold Gould** – grandfather
**Chad Michael Murray** – Jakee
**Stephen Tobolowsky** – Mr Bates
**Christina Vidal** – Maddie
**Ryan Malgarini** – Harry Coleman
**Haley Hudson** – Peg
**Rosalind Chao** – Pei-Pei
© Disney Enterprises, Inc.
Production Companies
**Walt Disney Pictures presents a
GUNNFilms production**
96 minutes 57 seconds
Location: **Los Angeles (CA, USA)**
Sight and Sound: v. 14, n. 1, p. 43-44
Box Office: £4,530,548
Opening Weekend: £1,214,559
Screens: 348

## Freddy vs Jason
Entertainment – 15 August
18 USA 2003
Director: **Ronny Yu**
Producer: **Sean S. Cunningham**
Screenplay: **Damian Shannon, Mark
Swift**
Based on characters created by **Wes
Craven, Victor Miller**
Director of Photography: **Fred
Murphy**
Editor: **Mark Stevens**
Production Designer: **John Willett**
Music: **Graeme Revell**
Cast:
**Monica Keena** – Lori Campbell
**Kelly Rowland** – Kia
**Jason Ritter** – Will
**Christopher George Marquette** –
Linderman

**Lochlyn Munro** – Deputy Stubbs
**Katharine Isabelle** – Gibb
**Brendan Fletcher** – Mark
**Zacharias Ward** – Mark's brother
**Ken Kirzinger** – Jason Voorhees
**Robert Englund** – Freddy Krueger
**Tom Butler** – Dr Campbell
© New Line Productions, Inc
**Production Company**
**New Line Cinema presents
a Sean S. Cunningham production**
97 minutes 17 seconds
Location: **Vancouver (Canada)**
Sight and Sound: v.13, n.11, p.44-45
Box Office: £2,730,294
Opening Weekend: £785,870
Screens: 237

## Frida
Buena Vista International – 28
February
15 USA 2002
Director: **Julie Taymor**
Producers: **Sarah Green, Salma
Hayek, Jay Polstein, Lizz Speed,
Nancy Hardin, Lindsay Flickinger
Roberto Sneider**
Screenplay: **Clancy Sigal, Diane Lake,
Gregory Nava, Anna Thomas**
Based on the book by **Hayden
Herrera**
Director of Photography: **Rodrigo
Prieto**
Editor: **Françoise Bonnot**
Production Designer: **Felipe
Fernández del Paso**
Music: **Elliot Goldenthal**
Cast:
**Salma Hayek** – Frida Kahlo
**Alfred Molina** – Diego Rivera
**Valeria Golino** – Lupe Marín
**Mia Maestro** – Cristina Kahlo
**Roger Rees** – Guillermo Kahlo
**Diego Luna** – Alejandro 'Alex'
Gómez Arias
**Patricia Reyes Spíndola** – Matilde
Kahlo
**Margarita Sanz** – Natalia Sedova
Trotsky
**Geoffrey Rush** – Leon Trotsky
**Amelia Zapata** – maid
**Alejandro Usigli** – professor
© Miramax Film Corp.
Production Companies:
**Miramax Films presents
in association with Margaret Rose
Perenchio
a Ventanarosa production
in association with
Lions Gate Films**
122 minutes 38 seconds
Location: **Mexico City (Mexico),
Paris (France), New York (NY, USA)**
Sight and Sound: v. 13, n. 3, p. 41-42
Box Office: £580,795

Opening Weekend: 54,278
Screens: 16

## Full Frontal
Buena Vista International – 23 May
18 USA 2002
Director: Steven Soderbergh
Producers: Scott Kramer, Gregory
Jacobs
Screenplay: Coleman Hough
Director of Photography: Peter
Andrews
Editor: Sarah Flack
Cast:
David Duchovny – Gus Delario
Nicky Katt – 'Hitler'
Catherine Keener – Lee Bright,
Carl's wife
Mary Mccormack – Linda Sharp,
Lee's sister
David Hyde Pierce – Carl Bright
Julia Roberts – Francesca
Davis/'Catherine'
Blair Underwood – Calvin
Cummings/'Nicholas'
Enrico Colantoni – Arty/Ed
Erika Alexander – Lucy Morgan
Tracy Vilar – Heather, the vet
Brandon Keener – Francesca's
assistant
Jeff Garlin – Harvey, probably
David Alan Basche – Nicholas'
agent
Terence Stamp – Wilson, man on
plane/himself
Nancy Lenehan – woman on plane
© Miramax Film Corp/Populist
Pictures
Production Company
a Miramax Films presentation
100 minutes 43 seconds
Location: Los Angeles (CA, USA)
Sight and Sound: v.13, n.7, p.44
Box Office: £59,931
Opening Weekend: £18,262
Screens: 28

## Fulltime Killer
(Metro) Tartan Films – 27 June
18 Hong Kong 2001
Directors: Johnnie To, Wai Ka-fai
Producers: Johnnie To, Wai Ka Fai
Andy Lau
Screenplay: Wai Ka Fai, Joey O'Bryan
Based on the novel by Edmond Pang
Director of Photography: Cheng Siu
Keung
Editor: David Richardson
Art Directors: Silver Cheung, Jerome
Fung
Music: Guy Zerafa
Co-composed by Alex Khaskin
Cast:
Andy Lau – Tok
Takashi Sorimachi – O

Simon Yam – Lee
Kelly Lin – Chin
Cherrie Ying – Gigi
Lam Suet – Fat Ice
Teddy Lin – C7
© Teamwork Motion Pictures
Limited
Production Companies:
Teamwork Motion Pictures Limited
presents
in association with CMC Magnetics
Corporation
a Milkyway Image (Hong Kong)
Limited, Teamwork Motion Pictures
Limited production
100 minutes 20 seconds
Sight and Sound: v.13, n.7, p.44-45
Box Office: £15,103
Opening Weekend: £3,287
Screen: 3

## Gangaajal
Venus Entertainment – 29 August
Box Office: £13,263
Opening Weekend: £7,052
Screens: 7

## Gangs of New York
Entertainment – 10 January
18 USA 2002
Director: Martin Scorsese
Producers: Alberto Grimaldi,
Harvey Weinstein
Screenplay: Jay Cocks, Steven
Zaillian, Kenneth Lonergan
Story: Jay Cocks
Director of Photography: Michael
Ballhaus
Editor: Thelma Schoonmaker
Production Designer: Dante Ferretti
Music: Howard Shore
Cast:
Leonardo DiCaprio – Amsterdam
Vallon
Daniel Day-Lewis – Bill 'The
Butcher' Cutting
Cameron Diaz – Jenny Everdeane
Jim Broadbent – Boss Tweed
John C. Reilly – Happy Jack
Henry Thomas – Johnny Sirocco
Brendan Gleeson – Walter 'Monk'
McGinn
Gary Lewis – McGloin
Stephen Graham – Shang
Eddie Marsan – Killoran
Alec McCowen – Reverend Raleigh
David Hemmings – Mr
Schermerhorn
Larry Gilliard Jr – Jimmy Spoils
© Miramax Film Corp.
Production Companies:
Initial Entertainment Group
presents
Miramax Films presents
a Martin Scorsese picture

an Alberto Grimaldi production
167 minutes 40 seconds
Location: Rome (Italy), New York
(NY, USA)
Sight and Sound: v.13, n.2, p.44-45
Box Office: £10,563,616
Opening Weekend: £2,622,748
Screens: 385

## Gerry
Pathé Distribution – 22 August
15 USA 2001
Director: Gus Van Sant
Producer: Dany Wolf
Screenplay: Casey Affleck, Matt
Damon, Gus Van Sant
Director of Photography: Harris
Savides
Music: Arvo Pärt
Cast:
Casey Affleck – Gerry
Matt Damon – Gerry
© My Cactus, Inc.
102 minutes 46 seconds
Sight and Sound: v.13, n.10, p.50-51
Box Office: £9,638
Opening Weekend: £3,262
Screen: 4

## Ghost Ship
Warner Bros – 24 January
18 USA/Australia 2002
Director: Steve Beck
Producers: Joel Silver, Robert
Zemeckis, Gilbert Adler
Screenplay: Mark Hanlon, John
Pogue
Story: Mark Hanlon
Director of Photography: Gale
Tattersall
Editor: Roger Barton
Production Designer: Graham
'Grace' Walker
Music: John Frizzell
Cast:
Julianna Margulies – Maureen Epps
Ron Eldard – Technician Dodge
Desmond Harrington – Jack
Ferriman
Isaiah Washington – First Mate
Greer
Gabriel Byrne – Captain Sean
Murphy
Alex Dimitriades – Technician
Santos
Karl Urban – Technician Munder
Emily Browning – Katie
Francesca Rettondini – Francesca
© Warner Bros.
(US, Canada, Bahamas, Bermuda)
© Village Roadshow Films (BVI)
Limited
(all other territories)
Production Companies:
Warner Bros Pictures presents in

association with Village Roadshow Pictures and NPV Entertainment a Dark Castle Entertainment production
90 minutes 38 seconds
Location: **Brisbane (Australia), Moreton Bay (Queensland, Australia)**
Sight and Sound: **v. 13, n.1, p. 46**
Box Office: **£2,130,692**
Opening Weekend: **£784,565**
Screens: **282**

## Ghosts of the Abyss (LSF)
Buena Vista International – 18 April
PG USA 2003
Director: **James Cameron**
Producers: **James Cameron, Chuck Comisky, Gig Rackauskas, Janace Tashjian**
Director of Photography: **Vince Pace**
Editors: **Ed W. Marsh**
**Sven Pape, John Refoua**
Production Designer Ghost Unit: **Martin Laing**
Music/Music
Conductor/Orchestrator: **Joel McNeely**
Cast:
**Bill Paxton** – himself, observer
**Dr John Broadwater** – himself, NOAA marine archaeologist
**Lori Johnston** – Dr Charles Pellegrino
themselves, microbiologists – **Don Lynch**
**Dr Charles Pellegrino** – themselves, historians
**Ken Marschall** – himself, visual historian
**Jim Cameron** – Mike Cameron
**Jeffrey N. Ledda** – themselves, ROV pilots
© Walden Media LLC
Production Companies:
**Walt Disney Pictures presents in association with Walden Media an Earthship production**
60 minutes 50 seconds
Location: **North Atlantic Ocean**
Sight and Sound: **v. 13, n. 6, p. 45-46**
Box Office: **£1,688,766**
Opening Weekend: **£75,227**
Screens: **5**

## Gigli
Columbia TriStar – 26 September
15 USA 2003
Director: **Martin Brest**
Producers: **Casey Silver, Martin Brest**
Screenplay: **Martin Brest**
Director of Photography: **Robert Elswit**
Editors: **Billy Weber**

Julie Monroe
Production Designer: **Gary Frutkoff**
Music: **John Powell**
Cast:
**Ben Affleck** – Larry Gigli
**Jennifer Lopez** – Ricki
**Justin Bartha** – Brian
**Lainie Kazan** – Larry's mother
**Missy Crider** – Robin
**Al Pacino** – Starkman
**Terrance Camilleri** – man in dryer
**David Backus** – laundry customer
© Revolution Studios Distribution Company, LLC
Production Companies:
**Revolution Studios presents a City Lights/Casey Silver production**
121 minutes 13 seconds
Location: **Los Angeles (CA, USA)**
Sight and Sound: **v. 13, n. 11, p. 46-47**
Box Office: **£24,451**
Opening Weekend: **£14,687**
Screens: **73**

## Girls Can't Swim
Millivres – 18 April
15 France 2000
Director: **Anne-Sophie Birot**
Producer: **Philippe Jacquier**
Screenplay: **Anne-Sophie Birot, Christophe Honoré**
Director of Photography: **Nathalie Durand**
Editor: **Pascale Chavance**
Production Designer: **Yvon Moreno**
Cast:
**Isild Le Besco** – Gwen
**Karen Alyx** – Lise
**Pascal Elso** – Alain, Gwen's father
**Marie Rivière** – Lise's mother
**Pascale Bussières** – Celine, Gwen's mother
**Julien Cottereau** – Frédo
**Yelda Reynaud** – Solange
**Sandrine Blancke** – Vivianne
**Dominique Lacarrière** – Rose
© Sépia production/ YMC Productions
Production Companies:
**Philippe Jacquier presents a production of Sépia production, YMC Productions with the participation of Centre National de la Cinématographie and the aid of Conseil Régional de Bretagne**
**Film produced with the support of Procirep**
101 minutes 41 seconds
Sight and Sound: **v.13, n.7, p. 45-46**
Box Office: **£750**
Opening Weekend: **£750**
Screen: **1**

## Gods and Generals
Warner Bros – 04 July
12A USA 2002
Director: **Ronald F. Maxwell**
Producer: **Ronald F. Maxwell**
Screenplay: **Ronald F. Maxwell**
Based on the book by **Jeff Shaara**
Director of Photography: **Kees van Oostrum**
Editor: **Corky Ehlers**
Production Designer: **Michael Z. Hanan**
Music: **John Frizzell, Randy Edelman**
Cast:
**Jeff Daniels** – Lieutenant Colonel Joshua Lawrence Chamberlain
**Stephen Lang** – General Stonewall Jackson
**Robert Duvall** – General Robert E. Lee
**Mira Sorvino** – Fanny Chamberlain
**Kevin Conway** – Sergeant Buster Kilrain
**C. Thomas Howell** – Sergeant Thomas Chamberlain
**Matt Letscher** – Colonel Adelbert Ames
**Frankie Faison** – Jim Lewis
**Jeremy London** – Alexander 'Sandie' Pendleton
**William Sanderson** – General A.P. Hill
© Ted Turner Film Properties, LLC
Production Companies:
**An Antietam Filmworks production in association with Esparza/Katz Productions, Rehme Productions, Inc., Mace Neufeld Productions**
231 minutes 3 seconds
Location: **Virginia (USA), Maryland (USA)**
Sight and Sound: **v. 13, n. 9, p. 50-51**
Box Office: **£9,872**
Opening Weekend: **£2,837**
Screen: **3**

## Goldfish Memory
Eclipse Pictures – 05 September
Box Office: **£53,101**
Opening Weekend: **£12,325**
Screens: **7**

## Good Boy!
Twentieth Century Fox – 19 December
U USA 2003
Director: **John Hoffman**
Producers: **Lisa Henson, Kristine Belson**
Screenplay: **John Hoffman**
Screen story by **Zeke Richardson, John Hoffman**
Based on Dogs from Outer Space by

Zeke Richardson
Director of Photography: **James Glennon**
Editor: **Craig P. Herring**
Production Designer: **Jerry Wanek**
Music: **Mark Mothersbaugh**
Cast:
**Molly Shannon – Mrs Baker**
**Liam Aiken – Owen Baker**
**Kevin Nealon – Mr Baker**
**Brittany Moldowan – Connie Fleming**
**George Touliatos – Mr Leone**
**Patti Allan – Ms Ryan**
**Hunter Elliot – Frankie**
**Mikhael Speidel – Fred**
**Benjamin Ratner – Wilson's dad**
**Peter Flemming – Wilson's other dad**
© Metro-Goldwyn-Mayer Pictures Inc.
Production Companies::
**Metro-Goldwyn-Mayer Pictures presents a Jim Henson Pictures production**
87 minutes 35 seconds
Location: **Vancouver (British Columbia, CA)**
Sight and Sound: v. 14, n. 1, p. 45-46
Box Office: £604,963
Opening Weekend: £146,354
Screens: 255

## Good Bye Lenin!

UGC Films – 25 July
15 Germany 2003
Director: **Wolfgang Becker**
Producer: **Stefan Arndt**
Screenplay: **Bernd Lichtenberg**
Director of Photography: **Martin Kukula**
Editor: **Peter R. Adam**
Production Designers: **Lothar Holler**
Shoot 2: **Daniele Drobny, Anina Diener**
Music/Music Arranger: **Yann Tiersen**
Cast:
**Daniel Brühl – Alexander 'Alex' Kerner**
**Katrin Sass – Christiane Kerner, Alex's mother**
**Maria Simon – Ariane Kerner**
**Chulpan Khamatova – Lara**
**Florian Lukas – Denis**
**Alexander Beyer – Rainer**
**Burghart Klaussner – Robert Kerner, Alex's father**
**Michael Gwisdek – Mr Klapprath, the principal**
**Christine Schorn – Mrs Schäfer**
**Jürgen Holtz – Mr Ganske**
**Jochen Stern – Mr Mehlert**
© X Filme Creative Pool GmbH
Production Companies:

a co-production of X Filme Creative Pool GmbH with Westdeutschen Rundfunk, Köln and ARTE
Supported by Filmstiftung NRW, Filmboard Berlin-Brandenburg, Filmförderungsanstalt, BKM, MEDIA
Distribution supported by Filmstiftung NRW, Filmförderungsanstalt, Filmboard Berlin-Brandenburg, FilmFernsehFonds Bayern
121 minutes 8 seconds
Sight and Sound: v.13, n.9, p.51-52
Box Office: £1,119,521
Opening Weekend: £135,311
Screens: 26

## The Good Girl

20th Century Fox – 10 January
15 USA/Germany/Netherlands 2001
Director: **Miguel Arteta**
Producer: **Matthew Greenfield**
Screenplay: **Mike White**
Director of Photography: **Enrique Chediak**
Editor: **Jeff Betancourt**
Production Designer: **Daniel Bradford**
Music: **Joey Waronker, Tony Maxwell, James O'Brien, Mark Orton**
Cast:
**Jennifer Aniston – Justine Last**
**Zooey Deschanel – Cheryl**
**Jake Gyllenhaal – Holden Worther**
**John Carroll Lynch – Jack Field, your store manager**
**Tim Blake Nelson – Bubba**
**John C. Reilly – Phil Last**
**Deborah Rush – Gwen Jackson**
**Mike White – Corny**
**Jacquie Barnbrook – heavy set woman**
**Annie O'Donnell – haggard woman**
© Die Sechste World Media Productions GmbH & Co Medien und Musik KG
Production Companies:
**Fox Searchlight Pictures and Myriad Pictuires present in association with IN-Motion AG, WMF V and Hungry Eye Lowland Pictures**
a Flan de Coco film
93 minutes 13 seconds
Sight and Sound: v.13, n.1, p.47
Box Office: £496,248
Opening Weekend: £114,235
Screens: 28

## The Good Thief

Momentum Pictures – 28 February
15 United Kingdom/France/Ireland 2002

Director: **Neil Jordan**
Producers: **Stephen Woolley, John Wells, Seaton McLean**
Screenplay: **Neil Jordan**
Based on Bob Le Flambeur by **Jean Pierre Melville and the screenplay by Auguste Le Breton and Jean Pierre Melville**
Director of Photography: **Chris Menges**
Editor: **Tony Lawson**
Production Designer: **Anthony Pratt**
Music: **Elliot Goldenthal**
Cast:
**Nick Nolte – Bob**
**Tchéky Karyo – Roger**
**Saïd Taghmaoui – Paulo**
**Gérard Darmon – Raoul**
**Emir Kusturica – Vladimir**
**Mark Lavoine – Remi**
**Ouassini Embarek – Said**
**Mark Polish – Albert**
**Michael Polish – Bertram**
**Nutsa Kukhianidze – Anne**
**Patricia Kell – Yvonne**
**Julien Maurel – Philippe**
© Double Down Productions Limited/T.N.V.O., S.A.R.L./Metropolitan Film Productions Limited
Production Companies:
**Alliance Atlantis presents a Stephen Woolley, John Wells, Alliance Atlantis production**
**Produced with the support of investment incentives for the Irish Film Industry provided by the Government of Ireland**
108 minutes 44 seconds
Location: **Nice (France), Monte Carlo, Ventimiglia (Italy)**
Sight and Sound: v. 13, n. 3, p. 42, 44
Box Office: £325,514
Opening Weekend: £39,122
Screens: 20

## The Great Dictator  (re)

BFI – 22 August
Box Office: £34,321
Opening Weekend: £5,714
Screens: 2

## Green Card Fever

Tip Top Entertainment – 29 August
Box Office: £35,389
Opening Weekend: £16,125
Screens: 26

## A Guy Thing

20th Century Fox – 13 June
12A USA 2002
Director: **Chris Koch**
Producers: **David Ladd, David Nicksay**
Screenplay: **Greg Glienna, Pete**

Schwaba, Matt Tarses, Bill Wrubel
Story: **Greg Glienna**
Director of Photography: **Robbie Greenberg**
Editor: **David Moritz**
Production Designer: **Dan Davis**
Music/Bird Call Solos: **Mark Mothersbaugh**
Cast:
**Jason Lee** – Paul
**Julia Stiles** – Becky
**Selma Blair** – Karen
**James Brolin** – Ken
**Shawn Hatosy** – Jim
**Lochlyn Munro** – Ray
**Diana Scarwid** – Sandra
**Julie Hagerty** – Dorothy
**David Koechner** – Buck
**Thomas Lennon** – Pete
© Metro-Goldwyn-Mayer Pictures Inc
Production Companies:
**Metro-Goldwyn-Mayer Pictures presents**
**a David Ladd Films production**
**101 minutes 50 seconds**
Location: **Vancouver (Canada)**
Sight and Sound: v. 13, n. 5, p. 45-46
Box Office: £346,735
Opening Weekend: £134,956
Screens: 196

## Half Past Dead
Columbia TriStar – 02 May
15 USA/Germany 2002
Director: **Don Michael Paul**
Producers: **Andrew Stevens, Elie Samaha, Steven Seagal**
Screenplay: **Don Michael Paul**
Director of Photography: **Michael Slovis**
Editor: **Vanick Moradian**
Production Designer: **Albrecht Konrad**
Music: **Tyler Bates**
Cast:
**Steven Seagal** – Sasha Petrosevitch
**Morris Chestnut** – 49er One
**Ja Rule** – Nick
**Nia Peeples** – 49er Six
**Tony Plana** – El Fuego
**Kurupt** – Twitch
**Michael Taliferro** – Little Joe
**Claudia Christian** – Williams
**Linda Thorson** – Jane McPherson
**Bruce Weitz** – Lester
© Half Dead Productions Inc
Production Companies:
**Screen Gems and Franchise Pictures present**
**in association with Modern Media Filmproduktion**
**98 minutes 24 seconds**
Location: **Berlin (Germany)**

Sight and Sound: v. 13, n. 7, p. 46-47
Box Office: £101,172
Opening Weekend: £45,708
Screens: 73

## Happiness of the Katakuris
Metro Tartan – 16 May
15 Japan 2001
Director: **Takashi Miike**
Producers: **Tetsuo Sasho Hirotsugu Yoshida**
Screenplay: **Kikumi Yamagishi**
Based on the Korean movie Joyonghan Kajon/Quiet Family
Director of Photography: **Akio Nomura**
Editor: **Taiji Shimamura**
Production Designer: **Tetsuo Harada**
Music: **Koji Makaino, Kôji Endô**
Cast:
**Kenji Sawada** – Masao Katakuri
**Keiko Matsuzaka** – Terue Katakuri
**Shinji Takeda** – Masayuki Katakuri
**Naomi Nishida** – Shizue Katakuri
**Tamaki Miyazaki** – Yurie Katakuri
**Tetsuro Tanba** – Nihei Katakuri, Masao's father
**Kiyoshiro Imawano** – Richard Sagawa
**Gatapishi** – Pochi the dog
Production Companies:
**Produced by Shochiku, Mainichi Broadcasting, Eisei Gekijo, Spike, Sedic International, Dentsu, Gentosha, Little Garage, Ganmo**
**112 minutes 42 seconds**
Sight and Sound: v.13, n.6, p. 47-48
Box Office: £17,894
Opening Weekend: £5,010
Screens: 3

## The Hard Word
Metrodome Dist – 12 September
18 Australia/United Kingdom 2002
Director: **Scott Roberts**
Producer: **Al Clark**
Screenplay: **Scott Roberts**
Director of Photography: **Brian Breheny**
Editor: **Martin Connor**
Production Designer: **Paddy Reardon**
Music: **David Thrussell**
Cast:
**Guy Pearce** – Dale Twentyman
**Rachel Griffiths** – Carol Twentyman
**Robert Taylor** – Frank Malone
**Joel Edgerton** – Shane Twentyman
**Damien Richardson** – Mal Twentyman
**Rhondda Findleton** – Jane Moore
**Kate Atkinson** – Pamela
**Vince Colosimo** – Detective Mick Kelly
**Paul Sonkkila** – Detective Jack O'Riordan

**Kim Gyngell** – Paul
**Dorian Nkono** – Tarzan
© Australian Film Finance Corporation Limited/Wildheart Films Pty Limited
Production Companies:
**Metrodome Distribution in association with Alibi Films International and Australian Film Finance Corporation present a Wildheart production**
**Produced with the assistance of the Melbourne Film Office and Film Victoria**
**Produced with the assistance of the Australian Film Commission**
**Financed with the assistance of the Australian Film Finance Corporation**
**103 minutes 41 seconds**
Location: **Melbourne (Australia), Sidney (Australia)**
Sight and Sound: v.13, n.11, p.47
Box Office: £67,912
Opening Weekend: £27,283
Screens: 27

## Hason Raja
Rafu Miah – 25 april
Box Office: £282
Opening Weekend: £55
Screen: 1
Hawa
Eros International Limited – 4 July
Box Office: £7,099
Opening Weekend: £3,313
Screens: 6

## Hawayien
Movie Box – 22 August
Box Office: £40,631
Opening Weekend: £11,670
Screens: 5

## Heart of Me
Pathé Distribution – 02 May
15 United Kingdom/France 2002
Director: **Thaddeus O'Sullivan**
Producer: **Martin Pope**
Screenplay: **Lucinda Coxon**
Based on the novel The Echoing Grove by **Rosamond Lehmann**
Director of Photography: **Gyula Pados**
Editor: **Alex Mackie**
Production Designer: **Michael Carlin**
Music: **Nicholas Hooper**
Cast:
**Helena Bonham Carter** – Dinah
**Olivia Williams** – Madeleine
**Paul Bettany** – Rickie
**Eleanor Bron** – Mrs Burkett
**Luke Newberry** – Anthony
**Tom Ward** – Jack

Gillian Hanna – Betty
Andrew Havill – Charles
Alison Reid – Bridie
Kathryn Tennant-Maw – Sylvia
© Arch Enterprises
Limited/BBC/Take 3 Partnership
Production Companies:
BBC Films presents in association
with Take 3, Isle of Man Film
Commission and Pandoraan MP
productionDeveloped by BBC Films
95 minutes 28 seconds
Location: **London (UK)**
Sight and Sound: v. 13, n. 5, p. 46-47
Box Office: £234,137
Opening Weekend: £52,466
Screens: 41

## Heartlands

Buena Vista International – 02 May
12A USA/United Kingdom 2002
Director: **Damien O'Donnell**
Producers: **Gina Carter, Richard
Jobson**
Screenplay: **Paul Fraser**
Story: **Paul Fraser, Richard Jobson
Andrew Keyte**
From an original idea by **Paul Fraser**
Director of Photography: **Alwin
Küchler**
Editor: **Frances Parker**
Production Designer: **Tom Conroy**
Featuring the Songs/Music of: **Kate
Rusby, John McCusker**
Cast:
Michael Sheen – Colin
Mark Addy – Ron
Jim Carter – Geoff
Celia Imrie – Sonja
Ruth Jones – Mandy
Phillipa Peak – Sarah
Jane Robbins – Sandra
Paul Shane – Zippy
Mark Strong – Ian
Joseph Dempsie – Craig
© Miramax Film Corp.
Production Companies:
Miramax Films and DNA Films
present
in association with the Film Council
a Vestry and Revolution Films
production
90 minutes 56 seconds
Location: **Peak District, Liverpool
(UK)**
Sight and Sound: v. 13, n. 5, p. 47
Box Office: £72,228
Opening Weekend: £26,493
Screens: 31

## Hejar

Rio Distribution – 07 February
PG Turkey/Greece/Hungary 2000
Director: **Handan Ipekçi**
Producer: **Handan Ipekçi**

Screenplay: **Handan Ipekçi**
Director of Photography: **Erdal
Kahraman**
Editor: **Nikos Kanakis**
Production Designers: **Mustafà Ziya
Ülkenciler, Natali Yares**
Music: **Serdar Yalçin
Mazlum Cimen**
Cast:
Sukran Güngör – Rifat Bey
Dilan Erçetin – Hejar
Füsun Demirel – Sakine
Ismail Hakki Sen – Abdülkadir
Evdo
Yildiz Kenter – Müzeyyen Hanim
Production Companies:
Yeni Yapim Film, Istanbul
Hyperion S.A., Athens
Focus Film Ltd
Tivoli-Filmproductions, Budapest
Supported by Motion Picture Public
Foundation of Hungary (Magyar
Mozgókép Közalapítvány), TV2,
Eurimages (Council of Europe),
Cultural Ministry of Turkey, Greek
Film Centre
119 minutes 44 seconds
Sight and Sound: v.13, n.4, p.38
Box Office: £1,099
Opening Weekend: £1,099
Screen: 1

## Henry: Portrait of a Serial Killer (Uncut)

Optimum Releasing – 02 May
Box Office: £2,563
Opening Weekend: £687
Screen: 1

## Hero: Love Story of a Spy The

Venus Entertainment – 11 April
Box Office: £236,274
Opening Weekend: £40,655
Screens: 17

## Historias Minimas

Optimum Releasing – 25 July
15 Argentina/Spain 2002
Director: **Carlos Sorín**
Screenplay: **Pablo Solarz**
From an idea by **Carlos Sorín, Pablo
Solarz**
Director of Photography: **Hugo
Colace**
Editor: **Mohamed Rajid**
Art Director: **Margarita Jusid**
Music: **Nicolas Sorín**
Cast:
Javier Lombardo – Roberto
Antonio Benedicti – Don Justo
Javiera Bravo – María Flores
Julia Solomonoff – Julia
Laura Vagnoni – Estela
Enrique Otranto – Carlos

Mariela Diaz – Rosa
María Rosa Cianferoni – Ana
María del Carmén Jiménez – baker's
assistant 1
Magin Cesar García – García
© Guacamole Films/Wanda Visión
Production Companies:
Guacamole and Wanda Visión
present
a Carlos Sorín film
91 minutes 32 seconds
Sight and Sound: v.13, n.8, p. 51-52
Box Office: £9,949
Opening Weekend: £2,254
Screens: 2

## Holes

Buena Vista International – 10
October
PG USA 2003
Director: **Andrew Davis**
Producers: **Mike Medavoy, Andrew
Davis, Teresa Tucker-Davies
Lowell Blank**
Screenplay: **Louis Sachar**
Based on his novel – Director of
Photography: **Stephen St. John**
Editors: **Thomas J. Nordberg, Jeffrey
Wolf, ProductiiiWolf**
Production Designer: **Maher Ahmad**
Music/Score Producer: **Joel McNeely**
Cast:
Sigourney Weaver – the warden
Jon Voight – Mr Sir
Tim Blake Nelson – Doctor
Pendanski
Shia LaBeouf – Stanley Yelnats IV
Khleo Thomas – Hector 'Zero'
Zeroni
Jake M. Smith – Squid
Byron Cotton – Armpit
Brenden Jefferson – X-Ray
Miguel Castro – Magnet
© Walden Media, LLC
Production Companies::
Walt Disney Pictures presents in
association with Walden Media
a Chicago Pacific
Entertainment/Phoenix Pictures
production
117 minutes 21 seconds
Location: **California (USA)**
Sight and Sound: v. 14, n. 1, p. 46-47
Box Office: £1,374,279
Opening Weekend: £1,202
Screens: 5

## House of 1000 Corpses

Tartan Films – 3 October
18 USA 2000
Director: **Rob Zombie**
Producer: **Andy Gould**
Screenplay: **Rob Zombie**
Directors of Photography:
**Tom Richmond**

Alex Poppas
Editors: **Kathryn Himoff, Robert K. Lambert, Sean Lambert**
Production Designer: **Gregg Gibbs**
Music: **Rob Zombie, Otis, Sheri Moon, Baby, Karen Black, Mother Firefly, Chris Hardwick, Jerry Goldsmith, Erin Daniels, Denise Willis, Jennifer Jostyn, Mary Knowles, Rainn Wilson, Bill Hudley Walton Goggins, Steve Naish**
© Universal Studios
Production Companies:
**A Rob Zombie film**
88 minutes 38 seconds
Sight and Sound: **v.13, n.12, p.36**
Box Office: **£106,892**
Opening Weekend: **£42,721**
Screens: **42**

## Hollywood Homicide
Columbia TriStar – 29 August
12A USA 2003
Director: **Ron Shelton**
Producers: **Lou Pitt, Ron Shelton**
Screenplay: **Robert Souza, Ron Shelton**
Director of Photography: **Barry Peterson**
Editor: **Paul Seydor**
Production Designer: **Jim Bissell**
Music: **Alex Wurman**
Cast:
**Harrison Ford** – Joe Gavilan
**Josh Hartnett** – K.C. Calden
**Lena Olin** – Ruby
**Bruce Greenwood** – Lt Bennie Macko
**Isaiah Washington** – Antoine Sartain
**Lolita Davidovich** – Cleo
**Keith David** – Leon
**Master P** – Julius Armas
**Gladys Knight** – Olivia Robidoux
**Lou Diamond Phillips** – Wanda
© Revolution Studios Distribution Company LLC
Production Companies:
**Revolution Studios presents a Pitt/Shelton production**
115 minutes 48 seconds
Location: **Los Angeles (CA, USA)**
Sight and Sound: **v. 13, n. 11, p. 48**
Box Office: **£925,055**
Opening Weekend: **£352,445**
Screens: **291**

## Hoover Street Revival
(Metro) Tartan Films – 04 July
15 United Kingdom/France 2002 –
Director: **Sophie Fiennes**
Producer: **Sophie Fiennes**
Camera: **Sophie Fiennes, Benito Strangio, Jennifer Lane, Dan Kozman, Blaine Davidson**

Editor: **Brian Tagg**
With:
**Noel Jones** – pastor
**Patrick Bolton** – organ
**Stan Lewis** – keyboards
**John Hayes** – bass guitar
**Chris Johnson** – drums
**Masa Kohama** – lead guitar
**Levern Greenwood** – praise team leader
**Alvin Jones** – blues guitarist
**Jonathan T. Grier** – director, The Voices of Judah
© Amoeba Film Ltd/Film Council/Idéale Audience
Production Companies:
**The Film Council, Idéale Audience, France 2, BBC present an Amoeba film**
**Made with the support of the Film Council New Cinema Fund with the support of the Centre National de la Cinématographie**
103 minutes 27 seconds
Sight and Sound: **v.13, n. 8, p.46**
Box Office: **£14,075**
Opening Weekend: **£3,423**
Screens: **9**

## Hope Springs
Buena Vista International – 09 May
12A United Kingdom/USA 2002
Director: **Mark Herman**
Producer: **Barnaby Thompson**
Screenplay: **Mark Herman**
Based on the novel New Cardiff by **Charles Webb**
Director of Photography: **Ashley Rowe**
Editor: **Michael Ellis**
Production Designer: **Don Taylor**
Music/Music Conductor/Arranger: **John Altman**
Cast:
**Colin Firth** – Colin Ware
**Heather Graham** – Mandy
**Minnie Driver** – Vera
**Oliver Platt** – Doug Reed
**Frank Collison** – Fisher
**Mary Steenburgen** – Joanie Fisher
**Mary Black** – Mrs Peterson
**Ken Kramer** – Mr Peterson
**Chad Faust** – Rob
**Tony Alcantar** – Webster
© Buena Vista International
Production Companies:
**Touchstone Pictures presents a Fragile Films production**
92 minutes 3 seconds
Location: **Vancouver (Canada)**
Sight and Sound: **v. 13, n. 5, p. 48**
Box Office: **£1,062,100**
Opening Weekend: **£366,352**
Screens: **303**

## The Hot Chick
Buena Vista International – 23 May
12A USA 2002
Director: **Tom Brady**
Producers: **John Schneider Carr D'Angelo**
Screenplay: **Tom Brady Rob Schneider**
Director of Photography: **Tim Suhrstedt**
Editor: **Peck Prior**
Production Designer: **Marc Fisichella**
Music: **John Debney**
Cast:
**Rob Schneider** – Jessica
**Anna Faris** – April
**Matthew Lawrence** – Billy
**Eric Christian Olsen** – Jake
**Robert Davi** – Stan
**Melora Hardin** – Carol
**Alexandra Holden** – Lulu
**Rachel McAdams** – Jessica
**Maritza Murray** – Keecia
**Fay Hauser** – Mrs Thomas
**Jodi Long** – Korean mother
© Touchstone Pictures
Production Companies:
**Touchstone Pictures present a Happy Madison production**
104 minutes 16 seconds
Location: **Los Angeles (CA, USA)**
Sight and Sound: **v.13, n. 6, p. 48-49**
Box Office: **£487,389**
Opening Weekend: **£169,452**
Screens: **218**

## The Hours
Buena Vista International – 14 February
12A USA 2002
Director: **Stephen Daldry**
Producers: **Scott Rudin, Robert Fox**
Screenplay: **David Hare**
Based on the novel by **Michael Cunningham**
Director of Photography: **Seamus McGarvey**
Editor: **Peter Boyle**
Production Designer: **Maria Djurkovic**
Music: **Philip Glass**
Cast:
**Nicole Kidman** – Virginia Woolf
**Julianne Moore** – Laura Brown
**Meryl Streep** – Clarissa Vaughan
**Stephen Dillane** – Leonard Woolf
**Miranda Richardson** – Vanessa Bell
**George Loftus** – Quentin Bell
**Charley Ramm** – Julian Bell
**John C. Reilly** – Dan Brown
**Jack Rovello** – Richie
**Toni Collette** – Kitty
**Ed Harris** – Richard Brown
**Allison Janney** – Sally Lester

Claire Danes – Julia Vaughan
© Miramax Film Corp./Paramount
Pictures Corporation
Production Companies:
**Paramount Pictures and Miramax
Films present
a Scott Rudin/Robert Fox
production
114 minutes 38 seconds
Sight and Sounds: v. 13, n. 3, p. 45
Box Office: £4,697,689**
Opening Weekend: £616,573
Screens: **209**

## How to Lose A Guy in 10 Days

**United International Pictures – 18
April**
12A USA/Germany 2003
Director: **Donald Petrie**
Producers: **Lynda Obst, Robert
Evans, Christine Peters**
Screenplay: **Kristen Buckley
Brian Regan, Burr Steers**
Based on the book by **Michele
Alexander, Jeannie Long**
Director of Photography: **John Bailey**
Editor: **Debra Neil-Fisher**
Production Designer: **Thérèse
DePrez**
Music/Music Conductor: **David
Newman**
Cast:
**Kate Hudson** – Andie Anderson
**Matthew McConaughey** –
Benjamin 'Ben' Barry
**Kathryn Hahn** – Michelle
**Annie Parisse** – Jeannie
**Adam Goldberg** – Tony
**Thomas Lennon** – Thayer
**Michael Michele** – Spears
**Shalom Harlow** – Green
**Robert Klein** – Phillip Warren
**Bebe Neuwirth** – Lana Jong
© MMP Moviemakers Production
GmbH & Co KG
Production Companies:
**Paramount Pictures presents
a Robert Evans/Christine Peters
production and a Lynda Obst
production
Produced in association with W2
Flm Production GmbH and MMP
Verwaltungsgesellschaft MbH
115 minutes 32 seconds**
Location: **New York (NW, USA),
Toronto (Canada)**
Sight and Sound: v. 13, n. 5, p. 49-50
Box Office: £6,890,861
Opening Weekend: £1,247,975
Screens: **361**

## The Hulk

**United International Pictures – 18**
July
12A USA 2003
Director: **Ang Lee**
Producers: **James Schamus, Larry
Franco, Gale Anne Hurd
Avi Arad**
Screenplay: **John Turman, Michael
France, James Schamus**
Story: **James Schamus**
Based on the Marvel comic book
character created by **Stan Lee,
Jack Kirby**
Director of Photography: **Frederick
Elmes**
Editor: **Tim Squyres**
Production Designer: **Rick Heinrichs**
Music/Score Producer: **Danny
Elfman**
Cast:
**Eric Bana** – Bruce Banner
**Jennifer Connelly** – Betty Ross
**Sam Elliott** – General
'Thunderbolt' Ross
**Josh Lucas** – Glenn Talbot
**Nick Nolte** – David Banner, Bruce's
father
**Paul Kersey** – young David Banner
**Cara Buono** – Edith Banner
**Todd Tesen** – young Ross
**Kevin Rankin** – Harper
**Celia Weston** – Mrs Krenzler
© Universal Studios
Production Companies:
**Universal Pictures presents in
association with Marvel Enterprises
a Valhalla Motion Pictures/Good
Machine production
138 minutes 7 seconds**
Location: **Arizona (USA)**
Sight and Sound: v. 13, n. 8, p. 46-47
Box Office: £8,364,049
Opening Weekend: £3,529,440
Screens: **500**

## Hungama

**Venus Entertainment – 01 August**
Box Office: £58,213
Opening Weekend: £15,277
Screens: **13**

## The Hunted

**Redbus – 06 June**
15 USA 2003
Director: **William Friedkin**
Producers: **Ricardo Mestres, James
Jacks**
Screenplay: **David Griffiths, Peter
Griffiths, Art Monterastelli**
Director of Photography: **Caleb
Deschanel**
Editor: **Augie Hess**
Production Designer: **William Cruse**
Music/Orchestra Conductor: **Brian
Tyler**
Cast:

**Tommy Lee Jones** – L.T. Bonham
**Benicio Del Toro** – Aaron Hallam
**Connie Nielsen** – Special Agent
Abby Durrell
**Leslie Stefanson** – Irene Kravitz
**John Finn** – Ted Chenoweth
**José Zúñiga** – Moret
**Ron Canada** – Van Zandt
**Mark Pellegrino** – Dale Hewitt
**Lonny Chapman** – Zander
© Paramount Pictures
Production Companies:
**Paramount Pictures presents
in association with Lakeshore
Entertainment
a Ricardo Mestres/Alphaville
production
94 minutes 27 seconds**
Sight and Sound: v. 13, n. 8, p. 47-48
Box Office: £1,160,000
Opening Weekend: £394,122
Screens: **280**

## I Capture the Castle

**Momentum Pictures – 09 May**
PG United Kingdom/South Africa
Director: **Tim Fywell**
Producer: **David Parfitt**
Screenplay: **Heidi Thomas**
Based on the novel by **Dodie Smith**
Director of Photography: **Richard
Greatrex**
Editor: **Roy Sharman**
Production Designer: **John-Paul
Kelly**
Music/Music Conductor/
Orchestrator: **Dario Marianelli**
Cast:
**Marc Blucas** – Neil Cotton
**Rose Byrne** – Rose Mortmain
**Sinéad Cusack** – Mrs Elspeth
Cotton
**Tara Fitzgerald** – Topaz
**Romola Garai** – Cassandra
Mortmain
**Bill Nighy** – James Mortmain
**Henry Thomas** – Simon Cotton
**David Bamber** – vicar
**Henry Cavill** – Stephen
**James Faulkner** – Aubrey Fox-
Cotton
© Trademark (Castle) Ltd/BBC
Films/Distant Horizon Ltd/Take 3
Partnership
Production Companies:
**Distant Horizon
BBC Film present
in association with The Isle of Man
Film Commission
and Baker Street/
Take 3 Partnerships
a Trademark Films/
BBC Films production
Developed by BBC Films and**

Trademark Films
in association with 50 Cannon
Entertainment
112 minutes 58 seconds
Location: **Manobler Castle (Pembs,
UK), Eltham Palace, Isle of Man
(UK), London (UK)**
Sight and Sound: **v. 13, n. 5, p. 50-51**
Box Office: **£1,043,230**
Opening Weekend: **£138,142**
Screens: **76**

## I Spy

Columbia TriStar – 24 January
12A USA 2002
Director: **Betty Thomas**
Producers: **Jenno Topping, Betty
Thomas, Mario Kassar, Andy Vajna**
Screenplay: **Marianne Wibberley
Cormac Wibberley, Jay Scherick,
David Ronn**
Story: **Marianne Wibberley, Cormac
Wibberley**
Based on characters created by
**Morton Fine, David Friedkin**
Director of Photography: **Oliver
Wood**
Editor: **Peter Teschner**
Production Designer: **Marcia Hinds-
Johnson**
Music: **Richard Gibbs**
Cast:
**Eddie Murphy** – Kelly Robinson
**Owen Wilson** – Alex Scott
**Famke Janssen** – Rachel Wright
**Malcolm McDowell** – Arnold
Gundars
**Gary Cole** – Carlos
**Phill Lewis** – Jerry
**Viv Leacock** – T.J.
**Keith Dallas** – Lunchbox
**Tate Taylor** – Lieutenant Percy
**Lynda Boyd** – Edna
© Columbia Pictures Industries, Inc.
Production Companies:
**Columbia Pictures presents a Tall
Trees/C-2 Pictures production
in association with Sheldon Leonard
Productions
96 minutes 31 seconds**
Location: **Budapest (Hungary)**
Sight and Sound: **v. 13, n. 2, p. 46-47**
Box Office: **£2,206,393**
Opening Weekend: **£878,229**
Screens: **273**

## I'll Be There

Warner Bros – 20 June
12A USA 2002
Director: **Craig Ferguson**
Producer: **James G. Robinson**
Screenplay: **Craig Ferguson, Philip
McGrade**
Director of Photography: **Ian Wilson**
Editors: **Sheldon Kahn, Doc McGhee**

Sheldon Kahn
Production Designer: **Tim Harvey**
Music/Synthesizers Performed by
**Trevor Jones**
Cast:
**Craig Ferguson** – Paul Kerr
**Jemma Redgrave** – Rebecca
Edmonds
**Ralph Brown** – Digger
**Ian McNeice** – Graham
**Imelda Staunton** – Dr Bridget
**Anthony Stewart Head** – Sam
Gervasi
**Joss Ackland** – Evil Edmonds
**Charlotte Church** – Olivia
Edmonds
**Stephen Noonan** – Gordano
**Joseph Alessi** – Enzo
© Morgan Creek International
Limited
Production Companies:
**James G. Robinson presents
a Morgan Creek production
In association with Immortal
Entertainment
105 minutes 13 seconds**
Location: **London (UK)**
Sight and Sound: **v. 13, n. 8, p. 50-51**
Box Office: **£28,293**
Opening Weekend: **£14,829**
Screens: **78**

## Identity

Columbia TriStar – 13 June
15 USA 2003
Director: **James Mangold**
Producer: **Cathy Konrad**
Screenplay: **Michael Cooney**
Director of Photography: **Phedon
Papamichael**
Editor: **David Brenner**
Production Designer: **Mark
Friedberg**
Music/Music Conductor: **Alan
Silvestri**
Cast:
**John Cusack** – Ed
**Ray Liotta** – Rhodes
**Amanda Peet** – Paris
**John Hawkes** – Larry
**Alfred Molina** – doctor
**Clea Duvall** – Ginny
**John C. McGinley** – George
**William Lee Scott** – Lou
**Jake Busey** – Robert Maine
**Pruitt Taylor Vince** – Malcolm
Rivers
© Columbia Pictures Industries, Inc.
Production Companies:
**Columbia Pictures presents
a Konrad Pictures production
89 minutes 56 seconds**
Los Angeles (CA, USA)
Sight and Sound: **v. 13, n. 8, p.50**

Box Office: £3,367,288
Opening Weekend: £719,468
Screens: 342

## Igby Goes Down

Optimum Releasing – 13 June
15 USA/Germany 2002
Director: **Burr Steers**
Producers: **Lisa Tornell, Marco
Weber**
Screenplay: **Burr Steers**
Director of Photography: **Wedigo von
Schultzendorff**
Editor: **William Anderson**
Production Designer: **Kevin
Thompson**
Music: **Uwe Fahrenkrog Petersen**
Cast:
**Kieran Culkin** – Jason 'Igby'
Slocumb
**Claire Danes** – Sookie Sapperstein
**Jeff Goldblum** – D.H. Baines
**Jared Harris** – Russel
**Amanda Peet** – Rachel
**Ryan Phillippe** – Oliver 'Ollie'
Slocumb
**Bill Pullman** – Jason Slocumb
**Susan Sarandon** – Mimi Slocumb
**Rory Culkin** – Igby aged 10
**Peter Tambakis** – Oliver aged 13
**Bill Irwin** – Lieutenant Ernest
Smith
© Atlantic Streamline Film
Productions LLC
Production Companies:
**United Artists and Atlantic
Streamline present
in association with
Helkon International Pictures and
Crossroads Films
a Marco Weber Lisa Tornell
production
97 minutes 59 seconds**
Location: **New York (NY, USA)**
Sight and Sound: **v. 13, n. 7, p. 47**
Box Office: £481,527
Opening Weekend: £86,581
Screens: 47

## In America

Twentieth Century Fox – 31 October
15 USA/Ireland/United Kingdom
2003
Director: **Jim Sheridan**
Producers: **Jim Sheridan, Arthur
Lappin**
Screenplay: **Jim Sheridan, Naomi
Sheridan, Kirsten Sheridan**
Director of Photography: **Declan
Quinn**
Editor: **Naomi Geraghty**
Production Designer: **Mark Geraghty**
Music/Music Arrangers/Producers:
**Gavin Friday, Maurice Seezer**
Cast:

Samantha Morton – Sarah
Paddy Considine – Johnny
Djimon Hounsou – Mateo
Sarah Bolger – Christy
Emma Bolger – Ariel
Neal Jones – immigration officers
Randall Carlton – immigration officers
Ciaran Cronin – Frankie
Juan Hernandez – Papo
© Twentieth Century Fox Film Corporation (all territories except Brazil,
Italy, Korea, Japan, Spain)
© TCF Hungary Film Rights Exploitation Limited Liability Company/Twentieth
Century Fox Film Corporation (Brazil, Italy, Korea, Japan, Spain)
Production Companies:
**Fox Searchlight Pictures presents a Jim Sheridan film**
**A Hell's Kitchen production**
**A Hell's Kitchen Limited/East of Harlem (UK) Limited co-production**
**Produced with the support of investment incentives for the Irish film industry provided by the government of Ireland**
105 minutes 29 seconds
Location: **New York (NY, USA), Dublin (Ireland)**
Sight and Sound: **v. 13, n. 12, p. 36-37**
Box Office: **£1,886,049**
Opening Weekend: **£284,259**
Screens: **87**

## In the Cut

Pathé Distribution – 31 October
18 United Kingdom 2003
Director: **Jane Campion**
Producers: **Laurie Parker, Nicole Kidman**
Screenplay: **Jane Campion, Susanna Moore**
Based on the novel by **Susanna Moore**
Director of Photography: **Dion Beebe**
Editor: **Alexandre De Franceschi**
Production Designer: **David Brisbin**
Music/Music Arranger
Producer: **Hilmar Örn Hilmarsson**
Cast:
Meg Ryan – Frannie Avery
Mark Ruffalo – Detective James Malloy
Jennifer Jason Leigh – Pauline
Nick Damici – Detective Richard Rodriguez
Sharrieff Pugh – Cornelius Webb
Michael Nuccio – Frannie's young father
Alison Nega – young father's fiancée
Dominick Aries – attentive husband

Susan Gardner – perfect wife
Heather Litteer – Angela Sands
© Pathé Productions Limited
Production Companies:
**Pathé Productions Ltd presents a Laurie Parker production**
**A Jane Campion film**
118 minutes 38 seconds
Location: **New York City (NY, USA)**
Sight and Sound: **v. 13, n. 12, p. 37-38**
Box Office: **£1,039,473**
Opening Weekend: **£279,068**
Screens: **117**

## In the Name of Buddha

Miracle Communications – 16 May
18 Sri Lanka 2002
Director: **Rajesh Touchriver**
Producers: **K. Shanmughathas, Sai George**
Screenplay: **Rajesh Touchriver**
Story conceived by **Sai George**
Directors of Photography:
**Jain Joseph, Rajaratnam**
Editor: **Ranjan Abraham**
Production Designer: **Sunil Babu**
Music: **Rajamani**
Cast:
Shiju – Siva
Soniya – Geetha
Jyothi Lal – leader
Amit – Mikara
Jayasoorya – doctor
Sunil Kudavathoor – Sri Lankan officer 1
Jinesh – Stengun boy
Pamela – immigration officer
Biju Sreedharan – agent
Padmasree – suicide bomber
© Da' Sai Films International Limited/Sai Ann Films
Production Companies:
**Da' Sai Films International presents in association with Sai Ann Films**
146 minutes 20 seconds
Sight and Sound: **v.13, n. 7, p.47-48**
Box Office: **£50,500**
Opening Weekend: **£9,402**
Screens: **5**

## In This World

ICA Projects – 28 March
15 United Kingdom 2002
Director: **Michael Winterbottom**
Producers: **Andrew Eaton, Anita Overland**
Screenplay: **Tony Grisoni**
Director of Photography: **Marcel Zyskind**
Editor: **Peter Christelis**
Music/Music Conductor: **Dario Marianelli**
Cast:
Jamal Udin torabi – Jamal
Enayatullah – Enayat

Imran Paracha – travel agent
Hiddayatullah – Enayat's brother
Hossain Baghaeian – Behrooz
Yaaghoob Nosraj Poor – Kurdish father
Kerem Atabeyoglu – policeman
Erham Sekizcan – factory boss
Nabil Elouahabi – Yusif
Paul Popplewell – voice over
© The Film Consortium/Dallington Films Limited/BBC Films
Production Companies::
**The Film Consortium and BBC Films**
**in association with**
**The Film Council,**
**The Works present**
**a Revolution Films production**
**Made with the support of The Film Council**
89 minutes 59 seconds
Location: **Pakistan, Iran, Turkey, Italy, France, England**
Sight and Sound: **v. 13, n. 4, p. 40**
Box Office: **£147,623**
Opening Weekend: **£12,153**
Screens: **5**

## The In-Laws

Warner Bros – 11 July
12A USA/Germany/Canada 2003
Director: **Andrew Fleming**
Producers: **Bill Gerber, Elie Samaha Bill Todman Jr, Joel Simon**
Screenplay: **Nat Mauldin, Ed Solomon**
Based on the screenplay by **Andrew Bergman**
Director of Photography: **Alexander Gruszynski**
Editor: **Mia Goldman**
Production Designer: **Andrew McAlpine**
Music Supervisor: **James Sall**
Cast:
Michael Douglas – Steve Tobias
Albert Brooks – Jerry Peyser
Robin Tunney – Angela Harris
Ryan Reynolds – Marc Tobias
David Suchet – Jean-Pierre Thibodoux
Lindsay Sloane – Melissa Peyser
Russell Andrews – Agent Will Hutchins
Maria Ricossa – Katherine Peyser
Candice Bergen – Judy Tobias
Michael Bodnar – Cherkasov's bodyguard
© MHF Film Academy
Production Companies:
**Franchise Pictures presents**
**a Gerber Pictures production**
**in association with Furthur Films**
**and MHF Erste Academy Film**

GmbH & Co. Produktions KG
With assistance from
the Ontario Media Development
Corporation
97 minutes 40 seconds
Location: Toronto (Canada), Chicago
(Illinois, USA)
Sight and Sound: v. 13, n. 9, p. 54
Box Office: £314,926
Opening Weekend: £108,031
Screens: 237

## Indian Babu
Himalayan Motion Pictures – 07
March
Box Office: £46,461
Opening Weekend: £17,613
Screens: 12

## Innocence
Capers Matcine – 10 January
12 Australia/Belgium 2000
Director: **Paul Cox**
Producers: **Paul Cox**
**Mark Patterson**
Screenplay: **Paul Cox**
Director of Photography: **Tony Clark**
Editor: **Simon Whitington**
Production Designer: **Tony Cronin**
Music: **Paul Grabowsky**
Cast:
**Julia Blake**
Claire
**Charles Tingwell**
**Andreas Borg**
**Terry Norris**
John, Claire's husband
**Robert Menzies**
David, Claire's son
**Marta Dusseldorp**
Monique
**Kristine van Pellicom**
young Claire
**Kenny Aernouts**
young Andreas
**Chris Haywood**
minister
**Norman Kaye**
Gerald
© Strand/New Oz Productions LLC,
The Premium Movie Partnership,
The South Australian Film
Corporation, Cinemedia
Corporation and Paul Cox
Production Companies:
**Strand/New Oz Productions,
Showtime Australia** in association
with South Australian Film
Corporation and Illumination Films
in association with CinéTé
present
a film by Paul Cox
In association with The Premium
Movie Partnership
Produced with the financial

assistance of the South Australian
Film Corporation
Produced with the assistance of Film
Victoria a division of Cinemedia
Produced in association with
Strand/New Oz Productions LLC
Script developed with the assistance
of the Australian Film Commission
With the financial support of Het
Fonds Film in Vlaanderen and the
Grand Prix of the 19th Flanders
International Film Festival, Ghent,
supported by the Flemish Ministry
of Economic Affairs
95 minutes 8 seconds
Location: South Australia, Belgium
Sight and Sound: v. 13, n. 3, p. 46
Box Office: £6,058
Opening Weekend: £6,058
Screens: 9

## Intacto
Momentum Pictures – 11 April
15 Spain 2001
Director: **Juan Carlos Fresnadillo**
Screenplay: **Andrés Koppel, Juan
Carlos Fresnadillo**
Dialogue: **Walter Leonard**
Director of Photography: **Xavier
Giménez**
Editor: **Nacho Ruiz Capillas**
Art Director: **César Macarrón**
Music: **Lucio Godoy**
Cast:
**Leonardo Sbaraglia** – Tomás
**Eusebio Poncela** – Federico
**Mónica López** – Sara
**Antonio Dechent** – Alejandro
**Max von Sydow** – Sam
**Guillermo Toledo** – Horacio
**Alber Ponte** – Sara's husband
**Andrea San Vicente** – Sara's
daughter
**Jesús Noguero** – Ramón Serrada
captives – **Marisa Lull**
nurse
© Sociedad General de Cine, S.A.
Production Companies:
a **Sogecine** production for Telecinco
with the participation of Canal+
and the collaboration of Tenerife
Film Commission
108 minutes 41 seconds
Sight and Sound: v. 13, n. 5, p. 51-52
Box Office: £299,743
Opening Weekend: £59,898
Screens: 20

## Intermission
Buena Vista International – 29
August
18 Ireland/United Kingdom/USA
2003
Director: **John Crowley**
Producers: **Stephen Woolley, Neil**

Jordan, **Alan Moloney**
Screenplay: **Mark O'Rowe**
Director of Photography: **Ryszard
Lenczewski**
Editor: **Lucia Zucchetti**
Production Designer: **Tom Conroy**
Music: **John Murphy**
Cast:
**Colin Farrell** – Lehiff
**Shirley Henderson** – Sally
**Kelly Macdonald** – Deirdre
**Colm Meaney** – Detective Jerry
Lynch
**Cillian Murphy** – John
**Kerry Condon** – café waitress
**Johnny Thompson** – old man in café
**Emma Bolger** – child with ice cream
**Deirdre Molloy** – woman in
shopping mall
**Brían F. O'Byrne** – Mick
© Company of Wolves
(Intermission) Limited
Production Companies:
**Buena Vista International** presents
in association with Bord Scannán na
hÉireann/The Irish Film Board, The
Film Council, IFC Films and Invicta
Capital Limited
a Company of Wolves production
nán na hÉireann/The Irish Film
Board, The Film Council, IFC Films
and Invicta Capital Limited a
Company of Wolves production
in association with Parallel Film
Productions and Portman Film
A John Crowley film
Produced with the support of
investment incentives for the Irish
film industry provided by the
government of Ireland
Made with the support of the Film
Council New Cinema Fund
Distributed by Portman Film
105 minutes 42 seconds
Location: Dublin (Ireland)
Sight and Sound: v. 14, n. 1, p. 47
Box Office: £2,082,523
Opening Weekend: £146,220
Screens: 28

## Interstella 5555
Soda Pictures – 24 October
PG Japan/France 2003
Directors: **Kazuhisa Takenouchi,
Hirotoshi Nissen, Oaisuke Nishio**
Produced by **Thomas Bangalter,
Guy-Manuel de Homem-Christo**
Producers: **Shinji Shimizu, Hiroyuki
Sakurada**
Screenplay: **Thomas Bangalter,
Cedric Hervet, Guy-Manuel de
Homem-Christo**
Director of Photography: – **Fumio
Hirokawa**

Editors: **Shigeru Nishiyama**
**Olivier Gajan**
Production Companies::
**Virgin Music presents**
**a Daft Life Ltd production in**
**association with Toei Animation**
**Co-production: Toei Animation**
**Phils Inc, M.S.J.**
**Musashinoseisakujo, Kaguna, Taure**
**— 68 minutes 10 seconds**
Sight and Sound: v. 14, n. 1, p. 48
Box Office: £17,390
Opening Weekend: £1,860
Screens: 3

## Intolerable Cruelty
**United International Pictures – 24**
**October**
**12A USA 2003**
Director: **Joel Coen**
Producers: **Ethan Coen, Brian**
**Grazer**
Screenplay: **Robert Ramsey, Matthew**
**Stone, Ethan Coen, Joel Coen**
Story: **Robert Ramsey, Matthew**
**Stone, John Romano**
Director of Photography: **Roger**
**Deakins**
Editor: **Roderick Jaynes**
[**i.e. Joel Coen**
**Ethan Coen**]
Production Designer: **Leslie**
**McDonald**
Music/Music Conductor:
**Carter Burwell**
Cast:
**George Clooney** – Miles Longfellow
Massey
**Catherine Zeta-Jones** – Marylin
Rexroth
**Geoffrey Rush** – Donovan Donaly
**Cedric The Entertainer** – Gus Petch
**Edward Herrmann** – Rex Rexroth
**Paul Adelstein** – Wrigley
**Richard Jenkins** – Freddy Bender
**Billy Bob Thornton** – Howard
Drexler Doyle
**Julia Duffy** – Sarah Batista
O'Flanagan Sorkin
**Jonathan Hadary** – Heinz, the
Baron Krauss von Espy
**Tom Aldredge** – Herb Myerson
© Universal Studios.
Production Companies:
**Universal Pictures and Imagine**
**Entertainment present**
**a Brain Grazer production**
**in association with Alphaville**
**99 minutes 41 seconds**
Location: **Los Angeles (CA, USA)**
Sight and Sound: v. 13, n. 11, p. 30-
31, 49
Box Office: £6,599,772
Opening Weekend: £1,555,684

Screens: **380**

## Irreversible
**Metro Tartan – 31 January**
**18 France 2002**
Director: **Gaspar Noé**
Producers: **Christophe Rossignon,**
**Richard Grandpierre**
Screenplay: **Gaspar Noé**
Director of Photography: **Benoît**
**Debie**
Editors: **Gaspar Noé, Araud, Cauchy**
Art Directors:
**Alain Juteau, Soler, Bayart,Castello**
Cast:
**Monica Bellucci** – Alex
**Vincent Cassel** – Marcus
**Albert Dupontel** – Pierre
**Jo Prestia** – Le Tenia
**Philippe Nahon** – Philippe, ex-
butcher
**Stéphane Drouot** – Stéphane
**Jean-Louis Costes** – Maso, man
beaten to death in club
**Gondouin** – Mike
**Mourad Khima** – Mourad
**Hellal** – Layde
© Nord-Ouest
Production/StudioCanal France/120
Films/Les Cinémas de la Zone
Production Companies:
**Produced by Nord-Ouest**
**Production and Eskwad in co-**
**production with StudioCanal, 120**
**Films and Les Cinémas de la Zone**
**with the participation of Canal+**
**97 minutes 24 seconds**
Location: **Paris (France)**
Sight and Sound: v. 13, n. 3, p. 46, 48
Box Office: £173,016
Opening Weekend: £36,165
Screens: 16

## Ishq Vishk
**Venus Entertainment – 09 May**
Box Office: £17,027
Opening Weekend: £8,109
Screens: 7

## It Runs in the Family
**Buena Vista International – 05**
**September**
**12A USA 2002**
Director: **Fred Schepisi**
Producer: **Michael Douglas**
Screenplay: **Jesse Wigutow**
Director of Photography: **Ian Baker**
Editor: **Kate Williams**
Production Designer: **Patrizia von**
**Brandenstein**
Music/MusicConductor/
Orchestrator: **Paul Grabowsky**
Cast:
**Michael Douglas** – Alex Gromberg

**Kirk Douglas** – Mitchell Gromberg
**Rory Culkin** – Eli Gromberg
**Cameron Douglas** – Asher
Gromberg
**Diana Douglas** – Evelyn Gromberg
**Michelle Monaghan** – Peg Maloney
**Geoffrey Arend** – Malik
**Sarita Choudhury** – Suzie
**Irene Gorovaia** – Abby Staley
**Annie Golden** – Deb
**Mark Hammer** – Stephen
Gromberg
© Metro-Goldwyn-Mayer Pictures
Inc.
© Buena Vista International, Inc.
© Family Films, LLC
Production Companies:
**Metro-Goldwyn-Mayer Pictures and**
**Buena Vista International present**
**a Furthur Films production**
**109 minutes 25 seconds**
Location: **New York (NY, USA)**
Sight and Sound: v. 13, n. 11, p. 49-50
Box Office: £8,956
Opening Weekend: £7,166
Screen: 1

## Italian Job
**United International Pictures – 19**
**September**
**12A USA 2003**
Director: **F. Gary Gray**
Producer: **Donald De Line**
Screenplay: **Donna Powers, Wayne**
**Powers**
Based on the film written by
**Troy Kennedy Martin**
Director of Photography: **Wally**
**Pfister**
Editors: **Richard Francis-Bruce**
**Christopher Rouse**
Production Designer: **Charles Wood**
Music: **John Powell**
Cast:
**Mark Wahlberg** – Charlie Croker
**Charlize Theron** – Stella Bridger
**Edward Norton** – Steve
**Seth Green** – Lyle
**Jason Statham** – Handsome Rob
**Mos Def** – Left Ear
**Franky G** – Wrench
**Donald Sutherland** – John Bridger
**Fausto Callegarini** – Italian guard
© Paramount Pictures
Production Companies:
**Paramount Pictures presents a De**
**Line Pictures production**
**110 minutes 37 seconds**
Location: **Venice (Italy), Los Angeles**
**(CA, USA)**
Sight and Sound: v.13, n12, p.38-39
Box Office: £7,713,411
Opening Weekend: £2,294,027
Screens: 428

## Jaal - The Trap

Venus Entertainment – 18 July
Box Office: £28,590
Opening Weekend: £12,366
Screens: **9**
Janasheen
Venus Entertainment – 28
November
Box Office: £45,162
Opening Weekend: £28,416
Screens: **12**

## Jackass: The movie

United International Pictures – 28
February
18 USA 2002
Director: **Jeff Tremaine**
Producers: **Jeff Tremaine, Spike
Jonze, Johnny Knoxville**
Director of Photography: **Dimitry
Elyashkevich**
Editors: **Liz Ewart, Mark Hansen,
Kristine Young**
Music Supervisor: **Karen Glauber**
With
**Johnny Knoxville, Bam Margera,
Steve-O, Chris Pontius, Ryan Dunn
Jason 'Wee Man' Acuña, Preston
Lacy, Dave England, Ehren
McGhehey, Brandon DiCamillo,
April Margera, Phil Margera, Jess
Margera, Chris Raab, Rake Yohn**
© Paramount Pictures/MTV
Networks
Production Companies:
**Paramount Pictures and MTV Films**
present
a Dickhouse production
in association with Lynch Siderow
productions
85 minutes 4 seconds
Sight and Sound: **v. 13, n. 3, p. 49**
Box Office: £4,017,537
Opening Weekend: £1,314,740
Screens: **340**

## Japon

Artificial Eye – 21 February
18 Mexico/Spain/Netherlands/
Germany 2001
Director: **Carlos Reygadas C**
Producer: **Carlos Reygadas C**
Screenplay: **Carlos Reygadas C**
Director of Photography: **Diego
Martinez Vignatti**
Editors: **Daniel Melguizo, Carlos
Serrano Azcona, David Torres
Labansat**
Art Director: **Alejandro Reygadas**
Cast:
**Alejandro Ferretis** – the man
**Magdalena Flores** – Ascen
**Carlos Reygadas Barquín** – the
hunter

**Martín Serrano** – Juan Luis
**Rolando Hernández** – the judge
**Yolanda Villa** – Sabina
**'El Gordo' (Bernabé Pérez)** –
singing peasant
**Pablo Gil Sánchez Mejorada** –
**Alejandro Sánchez Mejorada** –
hunting boys
**Ernesto Velázquez** – hunter
unloading
**Pablo Tamariz** – puzzled hunter
© Carlos Reygadas Castillo
Production Companies:
**NoDream Cinema presents
with the collaboration of
Mantarraya Producciones
and with the participation of Solaris
Film and Fondo Hubert Bals Festival
Internacional de Rótterdam,
ZDF/arte
With the contribution of el Instituto
Mexicano de Cinematografía**
132 minutes 54 seconds
Sight and Sound: **v. 13, n. 3, p. 49-50**
Box Office: £51,609
Opening Weekend: £8,043
Screens: **3**

## Jeepers Creepers 2

Pathé Distribution – 29 August
15 USA 2002
Director: **Victor Salva**
Producer: **Tom Luse**
Screenplay: **Victor Salva**
Based on characters created by
himself
Director of Photography: **Don E.
Fauntleroy**
Editor: **Ed Marx**
Production Designer: **Peter Jamison**
Music/Music Conductor: **Bennett
Salvay**
Cast:
**Ray Wise** – Taggart
**Eric Nenninger** – Scott Braddock
**Garikayi Mutambirwa** – Deaundre
'Double D' Davis
**Nicki Aycox** – Minxie Hayes
**Marieh Delfino** – Rhonda Truitt
**Diane Delano** – Betty Borman, the
bus driver
**Thom Gossom Jr** – Coach Charlie
Hanna
**Billy Aaron Brown** – Andy 'Bucky'
Buck
**Lena Cardwell** – Chelsea Farmer
**Al Santos** – Dante Belasco
© Jeepers Crepers II, LLC
Production Companies:
**United Artists presents
in association with Myriad Pictures
an American Zoetrope production**
103 minutes 58 seconds
Sight and Sound: **v.13, n10, p.51**

Box Office: £3,546,737
Opening Weekend: £1,069,346
Screens: **341**

## Jism

Bollywood Films – 17 January
Box Office: £12,933
Opening Weekend: £5,173
Screens: **7**

## Jogger's Park

Bollywood Films – 12 September
Box Office: £3,578
Opening Weekend: £2,551
Screens: **6**

## Johnny English

United International Pictures – 11
April
PG USA/France/UK 2003
Director: **Peter Howitt**
Producers: **Tim Bevan, Eric Fellner,
Mark Huffam**
Screenplay: **Neal Purvis, Robert
Wade, William Davies**
Director of Photography: **Remi
Adefarasin**
Editor: **Robin Sales**
Production Designer: **Chris Seagers**
Music/Music Conductor:
**Edward Shearmur**
Cast:
**Rowan Atkinson** – Johnny English
**Natalie Imbruglia** – Lorna
Campbell
**Ben Miller** – Bough
**John Malkovich** – Pascal Sauvage
**Tim Pigott-Smith** – Pegasus
**Kevin McNally** – prime minister
**Oliver Ford Davies** – Archbishop of
Canterbury
**Douglas McFerran** – Carlos
Vendetta
**Tasha De Vasconcelos** – exotic
woman
**Greg Wise** – Agent One
© Universal Studios
Production Companies:
**Universal Pictures and StudioCanal**
present
a Working Title production
87 minutes 34 seconds
Location: **London (UK)**
Sight and Sound: **v. 13, n. 5, p. 52, 54**
Box Office: £19,634,179
Opening Weekend: £3,435,342
Screens: **445**

## Jungle Book 2

Buena Vista International – 11 April
U USA 2002
Director: **Steve Trenbirth**
Producers: **Mary Thorne, Chris
Chase**
Screenplay: **Karl Geurs**

Editors: **Peter Lonsdale, Christopher Gee**
Art Director: **Michael Peraza**
Music/Music Conductor: **Joel McNeely**
Voice Cast:
**John Goodman** – Baloo
**Haley Joel Osment** – Mowgli
**Mae Whitman** – Shanti
**Connor Funk** – Ranjan
**Bob Joles** – Bagheera
**Tony Jay** – Shere Khan
**John Rhys-Davies** – Ranjan's father
**Jim Cummings** – Kaa/Colonel Hathi/M.C. Monkey
**Phil Collins** – Lucky
© Disney Enterprises, Inc
Production Companies:
**Walt Disney Pictures presents**
**Produced by Disney Toon Studios**
**72 minutes 25 seconds**
Sight and Sound: v.13, n. 7, p. 48-49
Box Office: £8,276,027
Opening Weekend: £1,436,730
Screens: 478

## Just Married

**20th Century Fox – 21 March**
12A USA/Germany 2003
Director: **Shawn Levy**
Producer: **Robert Simonds**
Screenplay: **Sam Harper**
Director of Photography: **Jonathan Brown**
Editors: **Don Zimmerman, Scott Hill**
Production Designer: **Nina Ruscio**
Music: **Christophe Beck**
Cast:
**Ashton Kutcher** – Tom Leezak
**Brittany Murphy** – Sarah McNerney
**Christian Kane** – Peter Prentiss
**David Moscow** – Kyle
**Monet Mazur** – Lauren McNerney
**David Rasche** – Mr McNerney
**Thad Luckinbill** – Willie McNerney
**David Agranov** – Paul McNerney
**Taran Killam** – Dickie McNerney
**Raymond J. Barry** – Mr Leezak
© Mediastream 1, Productions GmbH/Twentieth Century Fox Film Corporation
Production Companies:
**Twentieth Century Fox presents in association with Mediastream 1, Productions a Robert Simonds production**
**94 minutes 38 seconds**
Location: **Los Angeles (CA, USA), Venice (Italy), France**
Sight and Sound: v.13, n. 5, p. 54-55
Box Office: £3,695,213
Opening Weekend: £973,468
Screens: 331

Kal Ho Naa Ho
Yash Raj Films – 28 November
Box Office: £1,549,839
Opening Weekend: £436,790
Screens: 37

## Kangaroo Jack

**Warner Bros – 16 May**
PG USA 2003
Director: **David McNally**
Producer: **Jerry Bruckheimer**
Screenplay: **Steve Bing, Scott Rosenberg**
Story: **Steve Bing, Barry O'Brien**
Director of Photography: **Peter Menzies Jr**
Editors: **John Murray, William Goldenberg, Jim May**
Production Designer: **George Liddle**
Music: **Trevor Rabin**
Cast:
**Jerry O'Connell** – Charlie Carbone
**Anthony Anderson** – Louis Booker
**Estella Warren** – Jessie
**Michael Shannon** – Frankie Lombardo
**Bill Hunter** – Blue
**Christopher Walken** – Sal Maggio
**Marton Csokas** – Mr Smith
**David Ngoombujarra** – Mr Jimmy
**Dyan Cannon** – Anna Carbone
**Mark Sellitto** – Blasta
**Damien Fotiou** – Baby J
**Christopher Baker** – Crumble
**Ryan Gibson** – Hoon
**Denise Roberts** – Tansy
**Antonio Vitiello** – Toot
**Mario Di Ienno** – Tommy
© Warner Bros.
Production Company:
**Castle Rock Entertainment presents a Jerry Bruckheimer production**
**88 minutes 59 seconds**
Location: **Sidney (Australia), Cooper Pedy & Alice Springs (Australia)**
Sight and Sound: v. 13, n. 7, p. 49-50
Box Office: £3,249,457
Opening Weekend: £764,917
Screens: 373

## Kash Aap Hamare Hote

**Gurpreet Video International – 14 February**
Box Office: £8,746
Opening Weekend: £3,862
Screen: 6

## Khel

**Venus Entertienment – 3 October**
Box Office: £23,512
Opening Weekend: £7,754
Screens: 8

## Khushi

**Eros International Ltd – 07 February**

Box Office: £186,005
Opening Weekend: £53,576
Screens: 22

## The Kid Stays in the Picture

**Momentum Pictures – 07 February**
15 USA 2002
Directors: **Brett Morgan, Nanette Burstein**
Producers: **Brett Morgan, Nanette Burstein, Graydon Carter**
Adapted for the Screen by **Brett Morgan**
Based on the book by **Robert Evans**
Director of Photography: **John Bailey**
Editor: **Jun Diaz**
LA Production Designer: **Mark W. Harper**
Music: **Jeff Danna**
With
**Robert Evans**
**Dustin Hoffman**
© Woodland Pictures, LLC
Production Companies:
**USA Films presents a Highway Films and Ministry of Propaganda Films production**
**93 minutes 36 seconds**
Sight and Sound: v. 13, n. 1, p. 49-50
Box Office: £67,690
Opening Weekend: £17,660
Screens: 16

## Kill Bill - volume 1

**Buena Vista International – 10 October**
18 USA 2003
Director: **Quentin Tarantino**
Producer: **Lawrence Bender**
Screenplay: **Quentin Tarantino**
Based on the character of 'The Bride' created by **Q&U**
Director of Photography: **Robert Richardson**
Editor: **Sally Menke**
Production Designers:
**Yohei Taneda, David Wasco**
Music: **The RZA**
Cast:
**Uma Thurman** – the bride
**Julie Dreyfus** – Sofie Fatale
**Michael Bowen** – Buck
**Jun Kunimura** – Boss Tanaka
**Kenji Oba** – bald guy
**Yuki Kazamatsuri** – proprietor
**James Parks** – Edgar McGraw
**Akaji Maro** – Boss Ozawah
**Kazuki Kitamura** – Crazy 88 #2
**Goro Daimon** – Boss Honda
© Supercool Manchu, Inc.
Production Companies:
**Miramax Films presents a Band Apart production**
**The 4th film by Quentin Tarantino**
**110 minutes 30 seconds**

Location: **Los Angeles (CA, USA), Mexico, Tokyo (Japan), Beijing (China)**
Sight and Sound: **v. 13, n. 12, p. 39-40, 42**
Box Office: **£11,548,157**
Opening Weekend: **£162,857**
Screen: **1**

## Kirikou and the Sorceress

BFI – 01 August
U France/Belgium/Luxembourg 1998
Directors: **Michel Ocelot**
in collaboration with
**Raymond Burlet**
Producers: **Didier Brunner, Jacques Vercruyssen, Violette Vercruyssen-Wacha, Paul Thiltges**
Screenplay: **Michel Ocelot**
in collaboration with
**Raymond Burlet**
Editor: **Dominique Lefever**
Production Designers:
**Anne-Lise Koehler
Thierry Million**
Music: **Youssou N'Dour**
Voice Cast:
**Doudou Gueye Thiaw – Kirikou as a baby
Maimouna N'Diaye – Kirikou's mother
Awa Sène Sarr – Karaba the sorceress
Robert Lionsol – wise man of the mountain
William Nadylam-Yotnda
Sébastien Hébrant – Kirikou as a young man
Tshilombo Lubambu – Kirikou's uncle
Marie Augustine Diatta – strong woman
Mouhamadou Moustapha Diop – Fetish on the roof
Isseu Niang – thin woman**
© Les Armateurs/ODEC Kid Cartoons/Monipoly Productions/France 3 Cinéma/R.T.B.F. (Télévision Belge)
Production Companies:
**Les Armateurs/ODEC Kid Cartoons/Monipoly Productions/France 3 Cinéma/R.T.B.F. (Télévision Belge)**
present
a film by Michel Ocelot
a Les Armateurs/ODEC Kid Cartoons/Monipoly Productions/Trans Europe Film/Studio O/France 3 Cinéma/R.T.B.F. (Télévision Belge)/Exposure co-production
with the support of Fonds

Eurimages du Conseil de l'Europe, Centre National de la Cinématrographie, Programme Média de l'Union Européenne et de Cartoon, Centre du Cinéma et de l'Audiovisuel de la Communauté Française de Belgique, l'Agence de Coopération Culturelle et Technique (ACCT)
with the participation of Canal+, Fonds National de Soutien à la Production Audiovisuelle, Luxembourg
With the support of Procirep
73 minutes 51 seconds
Sight and Sound: **v.13, n. 11, p.50, 52**
Box Office: **£20,482**
Opening Weekend: **£2,185**
Screens: **9**

## Koi...Mil Gaya

Yash Raj Films – 08 August
Box Office: **£647,035**
Opening Weekend: **£177,100**
Screens: **36**

## Krampack

PPR – 03 October
15 Spain 2000
Director: **Cesc Gay**
Producers: **Gerardo Herrero, Marta Esteban**
Screenplay: **Cesc Gay, Tomás Aragay**
Based on the play by
**Jordi Sánchez**
Director of Photography: **Andreu Rebés**
Editor: **Frank Gutiérrez**
Art Director: **Llorenç Miquel**
Music: **Riqui Sabatés, Joan Díaz, Jordi Prats**
Cast:
**Fernando Ramallo – Danì
Jordi Vilches – Nico
Marieta Orozco – Elena
Esther Nubiola – Berta
Chisco Amado – Julián Quintana
Ana Gracia – Sonia
Myriam Mézières – Marianne
Mingo Ràfols – Arturo
Pau Durà – Marío
Muntsa Alcañiz – Dani's mother**
© Messidor Films, S.L.
Production Companies:
**A Messidor Films production with the participation of TVE Television Española+, Canal+ and the collaboration of Televisió de Catalunya**
94 minutes 28 seconds
Location: **Garraf (Barcelona, Spain), Castelldefels (Barcelona, Spain)**
Sight and Sound: **v. 13, n. 12, p. 42**
Box Office: **£36,042**
Opening Weekend: **£6,413**

Screens: **4**

## Kuch To Hai

Gurpreet Video International – 24 January
Box Office: **£17,331**
Opening Weekend: **£7,908**
Screens: **7**

## Kuch Naa Kaho

Eros International Ltd – 05 September
Box Office: **£266,705**
Opening Weekend: **£76,708**
Screens: **28**

## Kung Phooey!

Mandrake Media – 24 October
12A USA 2002
Director: **Darryl Fong**
Producer: **Darryl Fong**
Screenplay: **Darryl Fong**
Director of Photography: **Cliff Traiman**
Editors: **Steven S. Liu, Rick LeCompte**
Production Designer: **Mulan Chanrandel**
Music: **Ryan Kallas, Kent Carter**
Cast:
**Michael Chow – Art Chew
Joyce Thi Brew – Helen Hu
Colman Domingo – Roy Lee
Karena Davis – Sue Shee
Wallace Choy – Uncle Wong
Robert Wu – Lo Fat
Fred Salvallon – One Ton
Stuart Yee – Non Fat**
© Kung Phooey Productions, LLC
Production Companies::
**Nakota Films in association with Kung Phooey Productions presents a film by Darryl Fong**
87 minutes 16 seconds
Sight and Sound: **v. 14, n. 1, p. 49-50**
Box Office: **£3,367**
Opening Weekend: **£1,747**
Screens: **4**
L.O.C. (Kargil)
Eros International Ltd – 26 December
Box Office: **£141,318**
Opening Weekend: **£59,086**
Screens: **27**

## L'Afrance

Gala – 14 November
Box Office: **£1,932**
Opening Weekend: **£1,310**
Screen: **1**

## L'Homme du Train

Pathé Distribution – 21 March
12A France/United Kingdom/Germany/Japan 2002

Director: **Patrice Leconte**
Producer: **Philippe Carcassonne**
Scenario/Dialogues: **Claude Klotz**
Director of Photography: **Jean-Marie Dreujou**
Editor: **Joëlle Hache**
Art Director: **Ivan Maussion**
Music: **Pascale Estève**
Cast:
**Jean Rochefort** – **Manesquier**
**Johnny Hallyday** – **Milan**
**Jean-François Stévenin** – **Luigi**
**Charlie Nelson** – **Max**
**Pascal Parmentier** – **Sadko**
**Isabelle Petit-Jacques** – **Viviane**
**Édith Scob** – **Manesquier's sister**
**Maurice Chevit** – **barber**
**Riton Liebman** – **tough guy**
**Olivier Fauron** – **schoolboy**
**Véronique Kapoian** – **bakery salesgirl**
© Ciné B/Zoulou Films/Rhône-Alpes Cinéma/FCC/Film Council/Pandora Film Produktion/Cinéma Parisien/Media Suits
Production Companies:
a Ciné B, Zoulou Films, Rhône-Alpes Cinéma, FCC, Tubedale Films, Pandora Film Produktion, Cinéma Parisien, Media Suits
co-production
in association with Film Council
with the participation of Région Rhône-Alpes, Centre National de la Cinématographie and Canal+
this film was supported by Eurimages
in association with sofica Sofinergie 5, Natexis Banques Populaires Images 2
Made with the support of the Film Council Premiere Fund
90 minutes 15 seconds
Location: **Rhône-Alpes (France)**
Sight and Sound: **v. 13, n. 4, p. 39**
Box Office: **£430,958**
Opening Weekend: **£43,734**
Screens: **18**

## La Comunidad
Maiden Voyage Pictures – 04 July
15 Spain 2000
Director: **Alex de la Iglesia**
Producer: **Andrés Vicente Gómez**
Screenplay: **Jorge Guerricaechevarría Alex de la Iglesia**
Director of Photography: **Kiko de la Rica**
Editor: **Alejandro Lázaro**
Art Directors: **Arturo García Otaduy 'Biaffra', José Luis Arrizabálaga**
Music: **Roque Baños**
Cast:
**Carmen Maura** – **Julia García**

**Eduardo Antuña** – **Charly**
**María Asquerino** – **Encarna**
**Jesús Bonilla** – **Ricardo**
**Marta Fernández Muro** – **Paquita**
**Paca Gabaldón** – **Hortensia**
**Ane Gabarain** – **Karina**
**Sancho Gracia** – **Castro**
**Emilio Gutiérrez Caba** – **Emilio**
**Kiti Manver** – **Dolores**
© Lola Films, S.A.
Production Companies:
A Lolafilms S.A. production
with the participation of Antena 3 and the participation of Vía Digital
108 minutes 58 seconds
Location: **Spain**
Sight and Sound: **v. 13, n. 7, p. 37-38**
Box Office: **£50,351**
Opening Weekend: **£9,550**
Screens: **4**

## The Lady of Musashino (re)
Artificial Eye – 19 December
Box Office: **£3,056**
Opening Weekend: **£1,164**
Screen: **1**

## Larki Punjaban
Bollywood Films – 21 November
Box Office: **£26,054**
Opening Weekend: **£4,243**
Screens: **16**

## The Last Great Wilderness
Feature Film Company – 09 May
18 United Kingdom/Denmark 2002
Director: **David Mackenzie**
Producer: **Gillian Berrie**
Screenplay: **Michael Tait, Alastair Mackenzie, Gillian Berrie, David Mackenzie**
With thanks to the Cast for contributions
Director of Photography: **Simon Dennis**
Editor: **Jake Roberts**
Production Designer: **Tom Sayer**
Music: **The Pastels**
Cast:
**Alastair Mackenzie** – **Charlie**
**Jonny Phillips** – **Vincente**
**Ewan Stewart** – **Magnus**
**David Hayman** – **Ruaridh**
**Victoria Smurfit** – **Claire**
**Louise Irwin** – **Morag**
**Jane Stenson** – **Flora**
**John Comerford** – **Paul**
**Ford Kiernan** – **Eric**
© Sigma Films
Production Companies:
Sigma Films present
in association with Scottish Screen, Monkeypuzzle, Zentropa, Serious Facilities and Feature Film Company
Development funded by Scottish

Screen
95 minutes 56 seconds
Sight and Sound: **v. 13, n. 6, p. 49**
Box Office: **£27,672**
Opening Weekend: **£8,589**
Screens: **8**

## The Late Twentieth
Timeless Picture – 5 December
18 United Kingdom 2002
Director: **Hadi Hajaig**
Producer: **Hadi Hajaig**
Screenplay: **Hadi Hajaig**
Director of Photography: **Peter Ellmore**
Editors: **Hadi Hajaig, John Bovenizer**
Art Directors: **Josh Grace, Kate Piper**
Music/Music Score Conductor: **Simon Lambros**
Cast:
**John Webber** – **Ali, the man**
**Justin Allder** – **Tom**
**Sam Loggin** – **Jane**
**Camilla Heaney** – **Margaret**
**Markus Napier** – **Dave**
**Paula Jennings** – **Eve**
**Robin Hellier** – **policeman**
**Phil Campbell** – **robber**
**Neil D'Souza** – **shopkeeper**
© Timeless Pictures PLC
Production Company –
Presented/Made by Timeless Pictures PLC
79 minutes 36 seconds
Location: **London, Hastings, Brighton (UK)**
Sight and Sound: **v. 14, n. 2, p. 50, 52**
Box Office: **£4,442**
Opening Weekend: **£2,910**
Screens: **3**

## Laurel Canyon
Columbia Tristar – 14 November
12A USA 2002
Director: **Lisa Cholodenko**
Producers: **Jeffrey Levy-Hinte, Susan A. Stover**
Screenplay: **Lisa Cholodenko**
Director of Photography: **Wally Pfister**
Editor: **Amy E. Duddleston**
Production Designer: **Catherine Hardwicke**
Music: **Craig Wedren**
Cast:
**Frances McDormand** – **Jane**
**Christian Bale** – **Sam**
**Kate Beckinsale** – **Alex**
**Natascha McElhone** – **Sara**
**Alessandro Nivola** – **Ian**
**Louis Knox Barlow** – **Fripp**
**Russell Pollard** – **Rowan**
**Imaad Wasif** – **Dean**
**Mickey Petralia** – **Mickey**
**Melissa De Sousa** – **Claudia**

© Kuleshov Productions, LLC.
Production Companies::
A Sony Pictures Classics release in association with Good Machine International
An Antidote Films production
A film by Lisa Cholodenko developed with the assistance of the Sundance Institute
Developed in association with HeadQuarters Inc.
103 minutes 2 seconds
Location: Los Angeles (CA, USA)
Sight and Sound: v. 14, n. 1, p. 50
Box Office: £50,701
Opening Weekend: £21,562
Screens: 15

### Le Cercle Rouge  (Re)

BFI – 04 July
Box Office: £85,655
Opening Weekend: £18,701
Screens: 4

### Le Chignon D'Olga

BFI – 12 September
15 France/Belgium 2001
Director: **Jérôme Bonnell**
Producers  Artcam International:
**Joël Farges Élise Jalladeau**
AT-production: **Arnaud de Battice, Sylvain Goldberg**
Screenplay: **Jérôme Bonnell**
Director of Photography: **Pascal Lagriffoul**
Editor: **Ludo Troch**
Art Director:  **Benoît Béchet**
Cast:
**Hubert Benhamdine  – Julien**
**Nathalie Boutefeu  – Alice**
**Florence Loiret-Caille  – Emma**
**Serge Riaboukine  – Gilles**
**Marc Citti  – Pascal**
**Antoine Goldet  – Basile**
**Valérie Stroh  – Nicole**
**Clotilde Hesme  – Marion**
**Jean-Michel Portal  – Grégoire**
**Bernard Blancan  – Yves**
© Artcam/AT-production/StudioCanal/France 3 Cinéma
Production Companies:
**Joël Farges, Élise Jalladeau, Arnauld de Battice and Sylvain Golberg present**
in coproduction with StudioCanal, France 3 Cinéma
with the participation of Canal+ and Studio Images 8
a co-production of Artcam International,
AT-production
with the support of Procirep
with the participation of Centre National de la Cinématographie

95 minutes 13 seconds
Sight and Sound: **v. 13, n.10, p. 42-43, 45**
Box Office: £40,440
Opening Weekend: £6,036
Screens: 2

### Le Corbeau

Optimum Releasing – 25 July
Box Office: £20,885
Opening Weekend: £5,024
Screen: 1

### Le Divorce

Twentieth Century Fox – 19 September
12A USA/United Kingdom
Director: **James Ivory**
Producers: **Ismail Merchant, Michael Schiffer**
Screenplay: **Ruth Prawer Jhabvala, James Ivory**
Based on the novel by **Diane Johnson**
Director of Photography: **Pierre Lhomme**
Editor: **John David Allen**
Production Designer: **Frédéric Bénard**
Music: **Richard Robbins**
Cast:
**Jean-Marc Barr – Maître Bertram**
**Leslie Caron – Suzanne de Persand**
**Stockard Channing – Margreeve Walker**
**Glenn Close – Olivia Pace**
**Romain Duris – Yves**
**Stephen Fry – Piers Janely**
**Kate Hudson – Isabel Walker**
**Samuel Labarthe – Antoine de Persand**
**Thomas Lennon – Roger Walker**
**Thierry Lhermitte – Edgar Cosset**
**Daniel Mesguich – Louvre expert**
© Twentieth Century Fox Film Corporation [all territories except Brazil, Italy, Korea, Japan, Spain]
© TCF Hungary Film Rights Exploitation Limited Liability Company/Twentieth Century Fox Film Corporation [Brazil, Italy, Korea, Japan, Spain]
Production Companies:
**Fox Searchlight presents**
**a Merchant Ivory/Radar Pictures production**
117 minutes 10 seconds
Location: **Paris (France)**
Sight and Sound: **v. 13, n. 10, p. 47**
Box Office: £288,287
Opening Weekend: £93,061
Screen: 75

### Le Fate Ignoranti

Parasol Peccadillo Releasing – 25

April
15 Italy/France 2001
Director: **Ferzan Özpetek**
Producers:  **Tilde Corsi, Gianni Romoli**
Screenplay: **Gianni Romoli Ferzan Özpetek**
from their own story:
Director of Photography: **Pasquale Mari**
Editor: **Patrizio Marone**
Art Director:  **Bruno Cesari**
Music/Orchestrator: **Andrea Guerra**
Cast:
**Margherita Buy – Antonia**
**Stefano Accorsi – Michele**
**Serra Yilmaz – Serra**
**Gabriel Garko – Ernesto**
**Andrea Renzi – Massimo**
**Rosaria Del Cicco – Luisella**
**Koray Candemir – Emir**
**Lucrezia Valia – Mara**
**Filippo Nigro – Riccardo**
**Ivan Bacchi – Luciano**
© R&C Produzioni/
Les Films Balenciaga
Production Companies:
**Tilde Corsi & Gianni Romoli present**
**a co-production of**
**R&C Produzioni (Rome) - Les Films Balenciaga (Paris)**
**with the support of MEDIA**
109 minutes 33 seconds
Location: **Rome (Italy)**
Sight and Sound: **v. 13, n.  6, p. 45**
Box Office: £8,202
Opening Weekend: £5,766
**Screen: 1**

### Le Souffle

Metro Tartan – 11 April
15 France 2001
Director: **Damien Odoul**
Producers/Executive Producers:
**Gérard Lacroix, Gérard Pont Edgard Tenenbaum**
Scenario/Dialogue: **Damien Odoul**
Director of Photography: **Pascale Granel**
Editor: **Gwénola Heaulme**
Art Director:  **Hélène Melani**
Cast:
**Pierre-Louis Bonnetblanc – David**
**Dominique Chevallier – Jacques**
**Maxime Dalbrut – Paul**
**Jean-Claude Lecante – Jean-Claude**
**Jean Milord – M'sieur Milord**
**Stéphane Terpereau – Stef**
**Thierry Benoîton – Kangourou**
**Pierre Lasvaud – Pierrot**
**Laurent Simon – Matthieu**
**Laure Magadoux – Aurore**
© Morgane Production
Production Companies:

Morgane Production (Gérard Lacroix) and Centre National de la Cinématographie
with the support of Région Limousin present
77 minutes 30 seconds
Sight and Sound: v. 14, n. 5, p. 36-37, 62
Box Office: £19,561
Opening Weekend: £2,735
Screens: 3

## The League of Extraordinary Gentlemen

Twentieth Century Fox – 17 October
12A Germany/USA 2003
Director : **Stephen Norrington**
Producers: **Don Murphy, Trevor Albert**
Screenplay: **James Dale Robinson**
Based upon the comic books/graphic novel by **Alan Moore, Kevin O'Neill**
Director of Photography: **Dan Laustsen**
Editor: **Paul Rubell**
Production Designer: **Carol Spier**
Music: **Trevor Jones**
Cast:
Sean Connery – Allan Quatermain
Naseeruddin Shah – Captain Nemo
Peta Wilson – Mina Harker
Tony Curran – Rodney Skinner, the invisible man
Stuart Townsend – Dorian Gray
Shane West – Tom Sawyer
Jason Flemyng – Doctor Henry Jekyll/Edward Hyde
Richard Roxburgh – M
Max Ryan – Dante
Tom Goodman-Hill – Sanderson Reed
David Hemmings – Nigel
© Mediastream Dritte Film GmbH & Co. Beteiligungs KG/Twentieth Century Fox Film Corporation
Production Companies:
**Twentieth Century Fox presents in association with Mediastream III a Don Murphy production**
110 minutes 4 seconds
Location: **UK, Prague (Czech Republic), Malta,**
Sight and Sound: v. 13, n. 11, p. 53
Box Office: £7,358,166
Opening Weekend: £2,005,435
Screens: 365

## Legally Blonde: 2 Red, White

20th Century – 01 August
PG USA 2003
Director: **Charles Herman-Wurmfeld**
Producers:  **Marc Platt, David**
Nicksay
Screenplay: **Kate Kondell**
Story: **Eve Ahlert, Dennis Drake, Kate Kondell**
Based on the characters created by **Amanda Brown**
Director of Photography: **Elliot Davis**
Editor: **Peter Teschner**
Production Designer: **Missy Stewart**
Music: **Rolfe Kent**
Cast:
Reese Witherspoon – Elle Woods
Sally Field – Congresswoman Rudd
Regina King – Grace Rossiter
Jennifer Coolidge – Paulette Parcelle
Bruce McGill – Stanford Marks
Dana Ivey – Libby Hauser
Mary Lynn Rajskub – Rena Gulani
Jessica Cauffiel – Margot
Alanna Ubach – Serena
J. Barton – Timothy McGinn
© Metro-Goldwyn-Mayer Pictures Inc.
Production Companies:
**Metro-Goldwyn-Mayer Pictures presents a Marc Platt production in association with Type A Films**
96 minutes 18 seconds
Location: **Los Angeles (CA, USA)**
Sight and Sound: v.13, n. 9, p.55-56
Box Office: £5,283,911
Opening Weekend: £1,546,483
Screens: 351

## The Leopard  (Re)

BFI – 02 May
Box Office: £344,520
Opening Weekend: £39,102
Screens: 5

## Life and Debt

Axiom Films – 28 February
PG USA 2001
Director: **Stephanie Black**
Producer: **Stephanie Black**
Narration Written by  **Jamaica Kincaid**
Based on her non-fiction text A Small Place
Cinematography:  **Malik Sayeed, Kyle Kibbe, Richard Lannaman, Alex Nepomniaschy**
Editor: **John Mullen**
With
**Michael Manley, Stanley Fischer, Dr Michael Witter, David Coore, Jean Bertrand Aristide, Buju Banton Yami Bolo**
© Stephanie Black
Production Companies:
**a Tuff Gong Pictures production**
This film was made possible by the generous funding of:
**ITVS, The Soros Documentary**
Fund, John Simon Guggenheim Film Fellowship, The National Endowment for the Arts, The Rockefeller Foundation, New York State Council on the Arts, The Samuel Rubin Foundation, The Paul Robeson Fund, Edelman Family Fund, The Solidago Foundation
85 minutes 52 seconds
Sight and Sound: v.13, n. 5, p. 55-56
Box Office: £9,723
Opening Weekend: £1,793
Screens: 2

## Matchstick Men

Warner Bros – 19 September
12A USA/United Kingdom 2003
Director: **Ridley Scott**
Producers:  **Jack Rapke**
Ridley Scott
Steve Starkey
Sean Bailey
Ted Griffin
Screenplay: **Nicholas Griffin**
Ted Griffin
Based on the book **by**
Eric Garcia
Director of Photography: **John Mathieson**
Editor: **Dody Dorn**
Production Designer: **Tom Foden**
Music: **Hans Zimmer**
Cast:
Nicolas Cage
Roy Waller
Sam Rockwell
Frank Mercer
Alison Lohman
Angela
Bruce Altman
Dr Harris Klein
Bruce McGill
Chuck Frechette
Sheila Kelley
Kathy the cashier
Beth Grant
laundry lady
Jenny O'Hara
Mrs Schaffer
Steve Eastin
Mr Schaffer
Fran Kranz
slacker boyfriend
© Warner Bros. Entertainment Inc.
Production Companies:
**Warner Bros. Pictures presents an ImageMovers/Scott Free production in association with Rickshaw Productions and LivePlanet**
115 minutes 57 seconds
Location: **Los Angeles (CA, USA)**
Sight and Sound: v. 13, n. 11, p. 54
Box Office: £1,388,620

Opening Weekend: £53,128
Screens: **10**

## The Life of David Gale

United International Pictures – 14
March
15 USA/United Kingdom/Germany
2002
Director: **Alan Parker**
Producers: **Alan Parker, Nicolas
Cage**
Screenplay: **Charles Randolph**
Director of Photography: **Michael
Seresin**
Editor: **Gerry Hambling**
Production Designer: **Geoffrey
Kirkland**
Music: **Alex Parker, Jake Parker**
Cast:
**Kevin Spacey – David Gale
Kate Winslet – Bitsey Bloom
Laura Linney – Constance Harraway
Gabriel Mann – Zack Stemmons
Matt Craven – Dusty Wright
Leon Rippy – Braxton Belyeu
Rhona Mitra – Berlin
Melissa McCarthy – goth girl, 'Nico'
Jim Beaver – Duke Grover
Cleo King – Barbara Kreuster**
© Mikona Productions GmbH & Co.
KG
Production Companies:
**Universal Pictures and InterMedia
Films present
a Saturn Films/Dirty Hands
production
In association with Mikona
Productions GmbH & Co. KG**
130 minutes 21 seconds
Location: **Austin, Taylor (Texas,
USA), Huntsville (Texas, USA),
Barcelona (Spain)**
Sight and Sound: **v. 13, n. 4, p. 41-42**
Box Office: **£2,469,489**
Opening Weekend: **£725,698**
Screens: **343**

## Life of Oharu (Re)

Artificial Eye – 19 December
Box Office: **£11,593**
Opening Weekend: **£1,747**
Screens: **1**

## Life or Something Like it

20th Century Fox – 28 March
12A USA 2002
Director: **Stephen Herek**
Producers: **Arnon Milchan
John Davis, Wong Chi-Li, Toby Jaffe**
Screenplay: **John Scott Shepherd
Dana Stevens**
Story: **John Scott Shepherd**
Director of Photography: **Stephen H.
Burum**
Editor: **Trudy Ship**

Production Designer: **Bill Groom**
Music/Music Conductor: **David
Newman**
Cast:
**Angelina Jolie – Lanie Kerrigan
Edward Burns – Pete
Tony Shalhoub – Prophet Jack
Christian Kane – Cal
James Gammon – Lanie's father
Melissa Errico – Andrea
Stockard Channing – Deborah
Connors
Lisa Thornhill – Gwen
Greg Itzin – Dennis
Max Baker – Vin**
© Regency Entertainment (USA) Inc.
[in the US]
© Monarchy Enterprises S.a.r.l [in the
rest of the world]
Production Companies:
**Regency Enterprises presents a
Davis Entertainment/New Regency
production
In association with Epsilon Motion
Pictures**
103 minutes 31 seconds
Location: **Vancouver (British
Columbia, Canada), Seattle
(Washington, NY), New York (NY,
USA)**
Sight and Sound: **v. 13, n. 6, p. 50**
Box Office: **£3,063**
Opening Weekend: **£1,604**
Screens: **10**

## Lilya 4-Ever

Metrodome Distributors – 25 April
18 Sweden/Denmark 2002
Director: **Lukas Moodysson**
Producer:
**Lars Jönsson**
Screenplay: **Lukas Moodysson**
Director of Photography: **Ulf Brantås**
Editor: **Michal Leszczylowski, Oleg
Morgunov, Bernhard Winkler**
Art Director: **Josefin Åsberg**
Music: **Nathan Larson**
Cast:
**Oksana Akinshina – Lilya
Artiom Bogucharskij – Volodya
Ljubov Agapova – Lilya's mother
Lilia Sinkarjova – Aunt Anna
Elina Benenson – Natasha
Pavel Ponomarjov – Andrei
Tomas Neumann – Witek
Anastasia Bedredinova – neighbour
Tönu Kark – Sergei
Nikolai Bentsler – Natasha's
boyfriend**
© Memfis Film Rights
Production Companies:
**Produced by Memfis Film in co-
production with Zentropa
Entertainment5 ApS, Film i Väst,**

Sveriges
Television Göteborg, Nordic Film- &
TV Fund/Svend Abrahamsen
and with support from Swedish Film
Institute/Lena Hansson-Varhegyi,
Danish
Film Institute, Vinca Wiedemann
109 minutes 2 seconds
Sight and Sound: **v. 13, n. 5, p. 56, 58**
Box Office: **£219,895**
Opening Weekend: **£38,800**
Screens: **13**

## The Little Polar Bear

Warners Bros – 11 April
U Germany/Switzerland/USA 2001
Directors: **Thilo Graf Rothkirch
Piet de Rycker**
Producers: **Thilo Graf Rothkirch
Willi Geike**
Screenplay: **Bert Schrickel, Thomas
Wittenburg, Piet de Rycker**
Based on the books by **Hans de Beer**
English Adaptation: **Steve Kramer**
Music/Music Producers: **Nigel
Clarke, Michael Csányi-Wills**
Voice Cast:
**Mijail Verona – Lars
Maximilian Artjo – Robby
Jochen Busse – Kalle
Mike Krüger – Nalle
Bernd Stelter – Palle
Ingolf Lück – Mika
Vanessa Petruo – Manili
Jeanette Biedermann – Greta
Dirk Bach – Caruso
Sandro Blᴏmel – Pieps**
© Rothkirch/Cartoon-Film/Warner
Bros. Film GmbH
Production Companies:
**a Rothkirch/Cartoon-Film and
Warner Bros. Film GmbH
production
in co-operation with Kringel Medien
AG, Motion Works GmbH,
Animationsstudio Ludewig GmbH,
Animagix Media AG,
Animationsfabrik GmbH, Comet
Film GmbH, BB-Film GmbH,
Westdeutscher Rundfunk, Nord-Süd
Verlag (Switzerland)
Supported by Filmstiftung
Nordrhein-Westfalen GmbH,
Filmboard
Berlin-Brandenburg GmbH,
FilmFörderung Hamburg GmbH,
Mitteldeutsche
Medienförderung GmbH,
Filmförderungsanstalt, Beauftragter
der Bundesregierung
für Angelegenheiten der Kultur und
der Medien, Kuratorium junger
deutscher Film
English Language Version**

Warner Bros. Pictures presents
a Rothkirch/Cartoon-Film
production
in co-production with Warner Bros.
Filmproduktion GmbH
77 minutes 5 seconds
Sight and Sound: v.13, n.6, p. 52
Box Office: £749,475
Opening Weekend: £71,408
Screens: 235

## Live Forever

Redbus – 7 March
15 United Kingdom
Director: **John Dower**
Producer:  **John Battsek**
Director of Photography: **Frédéric
Fabre**
Editor:  **Jake Martin**
With – Noel Gallagher – Liam
Gallagher – Damon Albarn – Jarvis
Cocker – Kevin Cummins – Toby
Young – Ozwald Boateng – Damien
Hirst – Robert Del Naja – Jon Savage
– Louise Wener – James Brown –
Peter Mandelson – Phil Savidge
© Passion Pictures
Limited/Horsebridge Productions
Limited/Film Council/BBC
Production Companies::
**Helkon SK presents a Passion
Pictures production for the BBC,
Film Council and
Horsebridge Productions**
86 minutes 25 seconds
Sight and Sound: v. 13, n.  2, p. 48
Box Office: £22,066
Opening Weekend: £5,796
Screens: 12

## The Lizzie McGuire Movie

Buena Vista International – 22
August
U USA 2003
Director: **Jim Fall**
Producers:  **Stan Rogow**
Screenplay: **Susan Estelle Jansen, Ed
Decter, John J. Strauss**
Director of Photography: **Jerzy
Zielinski**
Editors:  **Margie Goodspeed
Margaret Guinee, Wilt Henderson**
Production Designer: **Douglas
Higgins**
Music/Music Conductor:  **Cliff
Eidelman**
Cast:
**Hilary Duff – Lizzie
McGuire/Isabella
Adam Lamberg – David 'Gordo'
Gordon
Hallie Todd – Jo McGuire
Robert Carradine – Sam McGuire
Jake Thomas – Matt McGuire
Ashlie Brillault – Kate**

Clayton Snyder – Ethan
Alex Borstein – Miss Ungermeyer
Yani Gellman – Paolo
Brendan Kelly – Sergei
© Disney Enterprises, Inc.
Production Company
Walt Disney Pictures presents
a Stan Rogow production
**93 minutes 45 seconds**
Location: **Rome (Italy), Vancouver
(Canada)**
Sight and Sound: v. 13, n. 11, p. 53-54
Box Office: **£1,857,502**
Opening Weekend: £39,772
Screens: 70

## The Lord of the Rings: The Return of the King

Entertainment – 19 December
12A Germany/New Zealand/USA
2003
Director: **Peter Jackson**
Producers: **Barrie M. Osborne, Peter
Jackson, Fran Walsh**
Screenplay: **Fran Walsh**, Philippa
Boyens, Peter Jackson
Based on the book by J.R.R. Tolkien
Director of Photography: **Andrew
Lesnie**
Editors: **Jamie Selkirk, Annie Collins**
Production Designer:  **Grant Major**
Music/Music
Conductor/Orchestrator:  **Howard
Shore**
Cast:
**Elijah Wood – Frodo Baggins
Ian McKellen – Gandalf
Liv Tyler – Arwen
Viggo Mortensen – Aragorn
Sean Astin – Samwise 'Sam' Gamgee
Cate Blanchett – Galadriel
John Rhys-Davies – Gimli
Bernard Hill – King Theoden of
Rohan
Billy Boyd – Peregrin 'Pippin' Took
Dominic Monaghan – Meriadoc
'Merry' Brandybuck**
© Lord Dritte Productions
Deutschland Filmproduktion GmbH
& Co. KG
**Production Companies::
New Line Cinema presents a
Wingnut Films production
In association with Lord Dritte
Productions Deutschland
Filmproduktion GmbH & Co. KG
200 minutes 54 seconds**
Sight and Sound: v. 14, n. 2, p. 52-54
Box Office: £41,841,702
Opening Weekend: £15,021,761
Screens: 494

## The Lord of the Rings: The Fellowship of the Ring (re)

Entertainment – 5 December
Box Office: £41,884
Opening Weekend: £19,004
Screens: 21

## The Lord of the Rings: The Two Towers

Entertainment – 12 December
Box Office: £54,290
Opening Weekend: £42,378
Screens: 16

## Love Actually

United International Pictures – 21
November
15 United Kingdom/USA/France
2003
Director: **Richard Curtis**
Producers:  **Tim Bevan, Eric Fellner,
Duncan Kenworthy**
Screenplay: **Richard Curtis**
Director of Photography: **Michael
Coulter**
Editor: **Nick Moore**
Production Designer: **Jim Clay**
Music/Music Producer/Arranger:
**Craig Armstrong**
Cast:
**Alan Rickman – Harry
Bill Nighy – Billy Mack
Colin Firth – Jamie
Emma Thompson – Karen
Hugh Grant – David, The Prime
Minister
Laura Linney – Sarah
Liam Neeson – Daniel
Martine McCutcheon – Natalie
Andrew Lincoln – Mark
Chiwetel Ejiofor – Peter
Gregor Fisher – Joe
Heike Makatsch – Mia
Keira Knightley – Juliet
Kris Marshall – Colin Frissell
Lucia Moniz – Aurelia Barros**
© WT Venture LLC.
Production Companies:
**Universal Pictures and StudioCanal
present
a Working Title production in
association with
DNA Films ─ 134 minutes 56
seconds**
Location: **London (UK), Provence
(France)**
Sight and Sound: v. 13, n. 12, p. 44, 46
Box Office: £31,948,206
Opening Weekend: £6,657,479
Screens: 477

## Love at Times Square

Gurpreet Video – 14 February
Box Office: £595
Opening Weekend:  £128
Screens: 2

## Love Liza

Columbia TriStar – 31 January
15 Germany/USA/France 2002
Director: **Todd Louiso**
Producers: **Chris Hanley, Fernando Sulichin, Ruth Charny, Jeff Roda**
Screenplay: **Gordy Hoffman**
Director of Photography: **Lisa Rinzler**
Editors: **Katz, Anne Stein**
Production Designer: **Stephen Beatrice**
Music: **Jim O'Rourke**
Cast:
**Philip Seymour Hoffman – Wilson Joel**
**Jack Kehler – Denny**
**Stephen Tobolowsky – Tom Bailey**
**Erika Alexander – Brenda**
**Shannon Holt – Angela Ryan from Bailey Federated**
**Kevin Breznahan – Jim**
**Daniel Farber – Huffer boy**
**Kelli Garner – Huffer girl**
**Chris Ellis – Patriot Model Aeronautics clerk**
**Wayne Duvall – gas station cashier**
© Kinowelt/Wild Bunch/Love Liza Inc
Production Companies:
**Kinowelt Filmproduktion GmbH and Wild Bunch present in association with Studio Canal a Muse/Blacklist Production in association with Ruth Charny and Jeff Roda**
89 minutes 42 seconds
Sight and Sound: v. 13, n. 2, p. 51-52
Box Office: £11,817
Opening Weekend: £2,523
Screens: 3

## Ma Vie

Peccadillo Pictures – 18 July
15 France 2002
Directors: **Olivier Ducastel, Jacques Martineau**
Producer: **Nicolas Blanc**
Screenplay: **Olivier Ducastel Jacques Martineau**
Directors of Photography: **Matthieu Poirot-Delpech, Pierre Milon**
Editor: **Sabine Mamou**
Art Director: **Juliette Chanaud**
Music: **Philippe Miller**
Cast:
**Ariane Ascaride – Caroline**
**Jonathan Zaccaœ – Laurent**
**Hélène Surgère – grandmother**
**Lucas Bonnifait – Ludovic**
**Frédéric Gorny – man on the cliff**
**Jimmy Tavares – Étienne**
**Nicolas Pontois – skating friend**
**Frédéric Sendon – bookshop**

customer
**Marcelle Lamy – Madame Langrune**
**Frédéric Voldman – trainer**
© Agat Films & Cie
Production Companies:
**Agat Films & Cie present with the participation of Canal+ a production of Agat Film & Cie with the participation of Canal+**
105 minutes 7 seconds
Sight and Sound: v. 13, n. 9, p. 56, 58
Box Office: **£2,042**
Opening Weekend: £2,042
Screens: 1

## Maid in Manhattan

Columbia TriStar – 07 March
PG USA 2002
Director: **Wayne Wang**
Producers: **Elaine Goldsmith-Thomas, Deborah Schindler, Paul Schiff**
Screenplay: **Kevin Wade**
Story: **Edmond Dantes [i.e. John Hughes]**
Director of Photography: **Karl Walter Lindenlaub**
Editor: **Craig McKay**
Production Designer: **Jane Musky**
Music/Music Conductor: **Alan Silvestri**
Cast:
**Jennifer Lopez – Marisa Ventura**
**Ralph Fiennes – Christopher Marshall**
**Natasha Richardson – Caroline Lane**
**Stanley Tucci – Jerry Siegel, campaign manager**
**Tyler Garcia Posey – Ty Ventura**
**Frances Conroy – Paula Burns**
**Chris Eigeman – John Bextrum, hotel manager**
**Marissa Matrone – Stephanie Kehoe**
**Amy Sedaris – Rachel Hoffberg**
**Priscilla Lopez – Veronica Ventura, Marisa's mother**
© Revolution Studios Distribution Company, LLC.
Production Companies:
**Revolution Studios presents a Red Om Films production**
105 minutes 10 seconds
Location: **New York (NY, USA)**
Sight and Sound: v. 13, n.3, p. 52-53
Box Office: **£8,240,828**
Opening Weekend: £2,424,584
Screens: 422

## Main Prem Ki Diwani Hoon

Yash Raj Films – 27 June
Box Office: **£547,245**
Opening Weekend: £159,003
Screens: 34

## Man Apart

Entertainment – 04 April
18 USA/Germany 2003
Director: **F. Gary Gray**
Producers: **Tucker Tooley, Vincent Newman, Joseph Nittolo, Vin Diesel**
Screenplay: **Christian Gudegast Paul Scheuring**
Director of Photography: **Jack N. Green**
Editors: **Bob Brown William Hoy**
Production Designer: **Ida Random**
Music/Score Orchestrator/Conductor: **Anne Dudley**
Cast:
**Vin Diesel – Sean Vetter**
**Larenz Tate – Demetrius Hicks**
**Timothy Olyphant – Hollywood Jack**
**Geno Silva – Memo Lucero**
**Jacqueline Obradors – Stacy Vetter**
**Steve Eastin – Ty Frost**
**Juan Fernández – Mateo Santos**
**Jeff Kober – Pomona Joe**
**Marco Rodriguez – Hondo**
**Mike Moroff – Gustavo Leon**
© "DIA" Productions GmbH & Co. KG
Production Companies:
**New Line Cinema presents a Vincent Newman & Tucker Tooley production and Joseph Nittolo Entertainment production In association with "DIA" Productions GmbH & Co. KG**
109 minutes 26 seconds
Location: **Los Angeles (CA, USA), New Mexico (USA)**
Sight and Sound: v. 13, n. 6, p. 53
Box Office: **£1,298,976**
Opening Weekend: £527,730
Screens: 329

## The Man of the Year

Optimum Releasing – 29 August
15 Brasil/USA 2003 – Director: **José Henrique Fonseca**
Producers: **Flávio R. Tambellini, José Henrique Fonseca Leonardo Monteiro de Barros**
Screenplay: **Rubem Fonseca**
Based on the novel O matador by **Patrícia Melo**
Director of Photography: **Breno Silveira**
Editor: **Sérgio Mekler**
Production Designer: **Toni Vanzolini**
Music: **Dado Villa-Lobos**
Cast:
**Murilo –Benício Máiquel Jorge**
**Cláudia Abreu Cledir**
**Natália Lage – Érica**
**Jorge Dória – Dr Carvalho**
**André Gonçalves – Galego**

Lázaro Ramos – Marcão
Perfeito Fortuna – Robinson
Moska – Enoque
Wagner Moura – Suel
André Barros – Marlênio
© Conspiração Filmes
Entretenimento S/A, Rio de
Janeiro/Quanta Centro de Produções
Ltda./Megacolor Ltda./Mega Finish
S/C Ltda., São Paulo/Warner Bros.
International, Burbank CA
Production Companies:
Conspiração Filmes, Warner Bros
Pictures
in association with Estudiosmega
and Mégacolor present
112 minutes 43 seconds
Sight and Sound: v.13, n.10, p. 54-55
Box Office: £9,234
Opening Weekend: £2,980
Screens: 3

## The Man Who Sued God
Winchester Films – 22 August
15 Australia 2001
Director: **Mark Joffe**
Producer: **Ben Gannon**
Screenplay: **Don Watson**
Based on an original screenplay by
**John Clarke**
Based on an original idea by **Patrick
McCarville**
Director of Photography: **Peter James**
Editor: **Peter Barton**
Production Designer: **Luigi Pittorino**
Music: **David Bridie**
Cast:
Billy Connolly – Steve Myers
Judy Davis – Anna Redmond
Colin Friels – David Myers
Wendy Hughes – Jules Myers
Bille Brown – Gerry Ryan
John Howard – Edward Piggott
Emily Browning – Rebecca Myers
Blair Venn – Les
Vincent Ball – cardinal
Tim Robertson – Judge Bonaface
© Australian Film Finance
Corporation Limited/View Films Pty
Ltd/The Premium Movie
Partnership/New South Wales Film
and Television Office
Production Companies:
Australian Film Finance
Corporation
in association with the New South
Wales Film & Television Office
and Showtime Australia presents
a Gannon Films/Empress Road
production
Developed with the assistance of
Film Victoria
Produced in association with The
Premium Movie Partnership for

Showtime Australia
101 minutes 57 seconds
Location: **Sidney (Australia)**,
**Bermagu (Australia)**
Sight and Sound: v. 13, n. 10, p. 55-56
Box Office: £1,106,354
Opening Weekend: £195,418
Screens: 123

## Man Without a Past
ICA Projects – 24 January
12A Finland/Germany/France 2002
Director: **Aki Kaurismäki**
Producer: **Aki Kaurismäki**
Screenplay: **Aki Kaurismäki**
Director of Photography: **Timo
Salminen**
Editor: **Timo Linnasalo**
Art Directors: **Markku Pätilä, Jukka
Salmi**
Cast:
Markku Peltola – M, man without a
past
Kati Outinen – Irma
Juhani Niemelä – Nieminen
Kaija Pakarinen – Kaisa Nieminen
Sakari Kuosmanen – Anttila
Annikki Tähti – flea market
manageress
Anneli Sauli – bar owner
Elina Salo – docks office clerk
Outi Mäenpää – bank official
Esko Nikkari – bank robber
© Sputnik Oy
Production Companies:
Sputnik Oy presents
Produced by Sputnik Oy (Aki
Kaurismäki)
in co-production with YLE TV-1
(Eila Werning), Pandora Film in
collaboration
with ZDF/ARTE and Network
Movie, Pyramide Productions in
collaboration with
Arte France Cinéma, Canal+ and
Centre National de la
Cinématographie
Supported by Suomen
elokuvasäätiö, Nordic Film and
Television Fund
96 minutes 50 seconds
Location: **Helsinki (Finland)**
Sight and Sound: v. 13, n. 2, p. 53
Box Office: £200,288
Opening Weekend: £33,257
Screens: 10

## Master and Commander:
the Far Side of the World
Twentieth Century Fox – 21
November
12A USA 2003
Director: **Peter Weir**
Producers: **Peter Weir, Duncan**

Henderson, Samuel Goldwyn Jr
Screenplay: **Peter Weir**
**John Collee**
Based upon the novels Master and
Commander and The Far Side of the
World by **Patrick O'Brian**
Director of Photography: **Russell
Boyd**
Editor: **Lee Smith**
Production Designer: **William
Sandell**
Music: **Iva Davies, Christopher
Gordon, Richard Tognetti**
Cast:
Russell Crowe – Captain Jack Aubrey
Paul Bettany – Doctor Stephen
Maturin, ship's surgeon
Billy Boyd – Barrett Bonden,
Coxswain
James D'Arcy – 1st Lieutenant
Thomas Pullings
Lee Ingleby – Midshipman Hollom
George Innes – Joe Plaice, Able
Seaman
Mark Lewis Jones – Mr Hogg,
Whaler
Chris Larkin – Captain Howard,
Royal Marines
Richard McCabe – Mr Higgins,
Surgeon's Mate
© Twentieth Century Fox Film
Corporation/Universal
Studios/Miramax Film Corp.
(all territories except Brazil, Italy,
Korea, Japan & Spain)
© TCF Hungary Film Rights
Exploitation Limited Liability
Company/Twentieth Century Fox
Film Corporation and Universal
Studios/Miramax Film Corp. (Brazil,
Italy, Korea, Japan & Spain)
Production Companies:
Twentieth Century Fox, Universal
Pictures and Miramax Films present
a Samuel Goldwyn Films production
138 minutes 11 seconds
Location: **Baja (Mexico), The
Galápagos Islands**
Sight and Sound: v. 14, n. 1, p. 53-54
Box Office: £6,495,832
Opening Weekend: £61,056
Screens: 1

## Master of Disguise
Columbia TriStar – 17 January
PG USA 2002
Director: **Perry Andelin Blake**
Producers: **Sid Ganis, Alex Siskin,
Barry Bernardi, Todd Garner**
Screenplay: **Dana Carvey, Harris
Goldberg**
Director of Photography: **Peter Lyons
Collister**
Editors: **Peck Prior, Sandy Solowitz**

Production Designer: **Alan Au**
Music: **Marc Ellis**
Cast:
**Dana Carvey – Pistachio Disguisey**
**Brent Spiner – Devlin Bowman**
**Jennifer Esposito – Jennifer**
**Harold Gould – Grandfather**
**Disguisey**
**James Brolin – Frabbrizio Disguisey**
**Maria Canals – Sophia**
**Mark Devine – Trent**
**Edie McClurg – Mama Disguisey**
**Austin Wolff – Barney**
**Robert Machray – Texas man**
© Revolution Studios Distribution
Company LLC
Production Companies:
**Revolution Studios presents a Happy**
**Madison production**
**in association with Out of the Blue**
**Entertainment**
**80 minutes 10 seconds**
Location: **Los Angeles (CA, USA)**
Sight and Sound: **v. 13, n. 2, p. 53-54**
Box Office: **£109,729**
Opening Weekend: **£60,077**
Screens: **75**

## The Matrix Reloaded
Warner Bros – 23 May
15 USA/Australia 2003
Directors: **The Wachowski Brothers**
**[i.e. Andy Wachowski**
**Larry Wachowski]**
Producer: **Joel Silver**
Screenplay: **The Wachowski Brothers**
Director of Photography: **Bill Pope**
Editor: **Zach Staenberg**
Production Designer: **Owen Paterson**
Music/Music Conductor: **Don Davis**
Cast:
**Keanu Reeves – Thomas 'Neo'**
**Anderson**
**Laurence Fishburne – Morpheus**
**Carrie-Anne Moss – Trinity**
**Hugo Weaving – Agent Smith**
**Jada Pinkett Smith – Niobe**
**Gloria Foster – The Oracle**
**Harold Perrineau – Link**
**Monica Bellucci – Persephone**
**Harry Lennix – Commander Lock**
**Lambert Wilson – Merovingian**
© Warner Bros. Entertainment Inc
(US, Canada, Bahamas, Bermuda)
© Village Roadshow Films (BVI)
Limited
(all other territories)
Production Companies:
**Warner Bros Pictures presents**
**in association with Village**
**Roadshow Pictures and NPV**
**Entertainment**
**a Silver Pictures production**
**138 minutes 9 seconds**

Location: **Australia, Alameda (CA,**
**USA)**
Sight and Sound: **v. 13, n. 7, p. 50, 52-**
53
Box Office: **£32,292,898**
Opening Weekend: **£12,165,276**
Screens: **481**

## The Matrix Revolutions
Warner Bros – 7 November
15 USA/Australia 2003
Directors: **The Wachowski Brothers**
**[i.e. Andy Wachowski**
**Larry Wachowski]**
Producer: **Joel Silver**
Screenplay: **The Wachowksi Brothers**
Director of Photography: **Bill Pope**
Editor: **Zach Staenberg**
Production Designer: **Owen**
**Paterson**
Music: **Don Davis**
Cast:
**Keanu Reeves – Thomas 'Neo'**
**Anderson**
**Laurence Fishburne – Morpheus**
**Carrie-Anne Moss – Trinity**
**Hugo Weaving – Agent Smith**
**Jada Pinkett Smith – Niobe**
**Mary Alice – The Oracle**
**Tanveer K. Atwal – Sati**
**Helmut Bakaitis – The Architect**
**Kate Beahan – coat check girl**
**Francine Bell – Councillor Grace**
**Monica Bellucci – Persephone**
(c)Warner Bros. (US, Canada,
Bahamas, Bermuda)
(c)Village Roadshow Films (BVI)
Limited
(all other territories)
Production Companies::
**Warner Bros Pictures presents in**
**association with Village Roadshow**
**Pictures and NPV Entertainment a**
**Silver Pictures production**
**128 minutes 48 seconds**
Location: **Australia, Alameda (CA,**
**USA), California (USA)**
Sight and Sound: **v. 14, n. 1, p. 54-55**
Box Office: **£17,829,237**
Opening Weekend: **£8,712,350**
Screens: **467**

## Max
Pathé Distribution Limited – 20
June
15 Hungary/Canada/United
Kingdom 2002
Director: **Menno Meyjes**
Producer: **András Hámori**
Screenplay: **Menno Meyjes**
Director of Photography: **Lajos**
**Koltai**
Editor: **Chris Wyatt**
Production Designer: **Ben van Os**
**Composer, Dan Jones**

Cast:
**John Cusack – Max Rothman**
**Noah Taylor – Adolf Hitler**
**Molly Parker – Nina Rothman**
**Ulrich Thomsen – Captain Mayr**
**David Horovitch – Max's father**
**Janet Suzman – Max's mother**
**Peter Capaldi – George Grosz**
**Kevin McKidd – George Grosz**
**John Grillo – Nina's father**
**Caroleen Feeney – saleslady**
**Judit Hernádi – Frau Schmidt**
© JAP Films Kft/AAMP 1
Inc/Natural Nylon II Production Ltd
Production Companies:
**Pathé Pictures presents in**
**association with Film Council**
**and in association with Aconit**
**an H2O Motion Pictures production**
**Made with the support of the Film**
**Council**
**With the participation of Canada**
**The Government of Ontario**
**Ontario Film and Television Tax**
**Credit Program**
**a JAP Films, AAMP 1, Natural Nylon**
**II**
**co-production**
**108 minutes 26 seconds**
Location: **Budapest (Hungary)**
Sight and Sound: **v. 13, n. 7, p. 53-54**
Box Office: **£128,296**
Opening Weekend: **£20,469**
Screens: **14**

## The Medallion
Columbia Tristar – 14 November
PG Hong Kong/USA 2003
Director: **Gordon Chan Ka-Seung**
Producer: **Alfred Cheung Kin-Ting**
Screenplay: **Bennett Joshua Davlin,**
**Alfred Cheung Kin-Ting, Gordon**
**Chan Ka-Seung, Paul Wheeler**
**Bey Logan**
Story: /Original Characters: **Alfred**
**Cheung Kin-Ting**
Director of Photography: **Arthur**
**Wong Ngok-Tai**
Editor: **Chan Ki-Hop**
Production Designer:
**Joseph C. Nemec III**
Music: **Adrian Lee**
Cast:
**Jackie Chan – Eddie Yang**
**Lee Evans – Arthur Watson**
**Claire Forlani – Nicole James**
**Julian Sands – Snakehead**
**John Rhys-Davies – Commander**
**Hammerstock-Smythe**
**Anthony Wong Chau-Sang – Lester**
**Wong**
**Christy Chung Lai-Tai – Charlotte**
**Watson**
**Johann Giscard Myers – Giscard –**

Alexander Bao – Jay
Lau Siu-Ming – antiquarium dealer
© Golden Port Productions Ltd
Production Companies:
**Tristar Pictures Presents in
association with Emperor
Multimedia Group
a Golden Port Productions Limited
production
A Jackie Chan production
88 minutes 20 seconds**
Location: **Hong Kong, Dublin
(Ireland), Australia**
Sight and Sound: v. 14, n. 3, p. 49
Box Office: £241,700
Opening Weekend: £106,797
Screens: 104

## Metropolis (Re)
Arrow Films – 17 January
Box Office: £1,079
Opening Weekend: £1,079
Screen: 1

## Miranda
Pathe Distribution Ltd – 7
November
15 United Kingdom/Germany 2002
Director: **Marc Munden**
Producer: **Laurence Bowen**
Screenplay: **Rob Young**
Director of Photography: **Ben Davis**
Editor: **Bill Diver**
Production Designer: **Alice
Normington**
Music: **Murray Gold**
Cast:
Christina Ricci – Miranda
John Simm – Frank
Kyle MacLachlan – Nailor
John Hurt – Christian
Julian Rhind-Tutt – Rod
Cavan Clerkin – Gerry
Matthew Marsh – Charles
Pik-Sen Lim – Mrs Wang
Joanne Froggatt – Jacquie
Tamsin Greig – receptionist
© **FilmFour Limited/
Film Council**
Production Companies::
**Film Four presents in association
with Film Council and Senator
Films production
A Feelgood Films production for
FilmFour made with the support of
the Film Council Premiere Fund
92 minutes 34 seconds**
Location: **London, Scarborough
(UK) , North of England**
Sight and Sound: v. 14, n. 1, p. 55-56
Box Office: £8,552
Opening Weekend: £3,553
Screens: 13

## Mon-Rak Transistor
ICA Projects – 06 June
15 Thailand 2002
Director: **Pan-ek Ratanaruang**
Producers: **Nonzee Nimibutr,
Duangkamol Limcharoen**
Screenplay: **Pen-ek Ratanaruang**
Based on the novel by
**Wat Wanlayangkoon**
Director of Photography: **Chankit
Chamniwikaipong**
Editor: **Patamanadda Yukol**
Production Designer: **Saksiri
Chuntarangsri**
Music: **Amornbhong
Methakunavudh, Chartchai
Pongprapapan**
Cast:
Suppakorn Kitsuwan – Pan
Siriyakorn Pukkavesa – Sadaw
Black Pomtong – Yod
Somlek Sakdikul – Suwat
Porntip Papanai – Dao
Ampol Rattanawong – Siew
Prasit Wongrakthai – Chuey,
Sadaw's father
Chartchai Hamnuansak – prison
guard
Akarat Nitipon – Kiattisak
Sawang Rodnuch – Yen
Production Companies:
**Cinemasia and Five Star
Productions present
a Pen-ek Ratanaruang film
120 minutes 46 seconds**
Sight and Sound: V.13, n.8 p. 52
Box Office: £658
Opening Weekend: £658
Screen: 1

## Monsieur Hulot's Holiday (re)
BFI – 08 August
Box Office: £75,190
Opening Weekend: £6,538
Screens: 3

## Moonlight Mile
Buena Vista International – 21
February
15 USA 2002
Director: **Brad Silberling**
Producers: **Mark Johnson, Brad
Silberling**
Screenplay: **Brad Silberling**
Director of Photography: **Phedon
Papamichael**
Editor: **Lisa Zeno Churgin**
Production Designer: **Missy Stewart**
Music: **Mark Isham**
Cast:
Jake Gyllenhaal – Joe Nast
Dustin Hoffman – Ben Floss
Susan Sarandon – JoJo Floss

Holly Hunter – Mona Camp
Ellen Pompeo – Bertie Knox
Richard T. Jones – Ty
Allan Corduner – Stan Michaels
Dabney Coleman – Mike Mulcahey
Aleksia Landeau – Cheryl
Richard Messing – rabbi
© Touchstone Pictures
Production Companies:
**Touchstone Pictures and Hyde Park
Entertainment present
a Reveal Entertainment/Gran
Via/Punch production
Created by Sticky Productions Inc
116 minutes 48 seconds**
Location: **Los Angeles (CA, USA),
Boston (MA, USA)**
Sight and Sound: v. 13, n. 4, p. 42, 44
Box Office: £31,273
Opening Weekend: £13,264
Screens: 24

## Most Fertile Man in Ireland
Ian Rattray Films – 20 June
15 United Kingdom/Ireland 2000
Director: **Dudi Appleton**
Producer: **David Collins**
Screenplay: **Jim Keeble**
Director of Photography: **Ronan Fox**
Editor: **Emer Reynolds**
Production Designer: **Tom Conroy**
Music: **James Johnston**
Cast:
Kris Marshall – Eamonn Manley
Kathy Kiera Clarke – Rosie
Bronagh Gallagher – Millicent
James Nesbitt – Mad Dog Billy
Wilson
Tara Lynn O'Neill – Mary Mallory
Kenneth Cranham – Da
Marc O'Shea – Raymond
Olivia Nash – Ma
Mary Black – Mrs O'Riordan
Toyah Willcox – Dr Johnson
© British Sky Broadcasting/Samson
Films
Production Companies:
**Alibi Films International/
Sky Pictures present
in association with Bord Scannán na
hÉireann/The Irish Film Board
and the Northern Ireland Film
Commission
a Samson Films/Hot Film
production
Produced with the support of
incentives for the Irish Film
industry provided by the
Government of Ireland
96 minutes 26 seconds**
Sight and Sound: v.13, n.10, p.56
Box Office: £4,799
Opening Weekend: £4,799
Screens: 13

## Mostly Martha

Optimum Releasing – 16 May
PG
Germany/Austria/Switzerland/Italy
Director: **Sandra Nettelbeck**
Producers: **Karl Baumgartner,
Christoph Friedel**
Kinowelt: **Christine Berg**
Screenplay: **Sandra Nettelbeck**
Director of Photography: **Michael
Bertl**
Editor: **Mona Bräuer**
Art Director: **Thomas Freudenthal**
Cast:
**Martina Gedeck** – Martha
**Maxime Foerste** – Lina
**August Zirner** – therapist
**Ulrich Thomsen** – Sam
**Sibylle Canonica** – Frida
**Katja Studt** – Lea
**Idil Üner** – Bernadette
**Oliver Broumis** – Jan
**Antonio Wannek** – Carlos
**Sergio Castellitto** – Mario
© Pandora Film Produktion
GmbH/Prisma Film/T&C
Film/Palomar
Production Companies:
**Pandora Film Produktion GmbH**
(Köln)
in co-production with Prisma Film
(Wien), T&C Film AG (Zürich),
Palomar (Rome), Kinowelt
Filmproduktion (München) present
in collaboration with SWR/WDR,
ARTE, ORF, SF DRS/SRG SSR idée
suisse, Teleclub, RAI Cinema,
Bavaria Film International
with support of
Filmförderung Hamburg,
Filmstiftung Nordrhein-Westfalen,
Filmförderungsanstalt, Eurimages,
Kuratorium junger deutscher Film,
Österreichisches Filminstitut, ORF
(Austria), Bundesamt für Kultur des
Eidgenössischen Departementes des
Innern (Switzerland)
**106 minutes 48 seconds**
Location: **Hamburg (Germany), Italy**
Sight and Sound: **v. 13, n. 6, p. 54**
Box Office: **£154,296**
Opening Weekend: **£38,309**
Screens: **14**

## The Mother

Momentum Pictures – 14 November
15 United Kingdom 2003
Director: **Roger Michell**
Producer: **Kevin Loader**
Screenplay: **Hanif Kureishi**
Director of Photography: **Alwin
Küchler**
Editor: **Nicolas Gaster**
Production Designer: **Mark Tildesley**

Music: **Jeremy Sams**
Cast:
**Anne Reid** – May
**Cathryn Bradshaw** – Paula
**Daniel Craig** – Darren
**Steven Mackintosh** – Bobby
**Oliver Ford Davies** – Bruce
**Anna Wilson Jones** – Helen
**Peter Vaughan** – Toots
**Danira Govich** – au pair
**Harry Michell** – Harry
**Rosie Michell** – Rosie
© BBC Films
Production Companies:
**BBC Films presents
in association with Renaissance
Films a Free Range Films production**
112 minutes 1 second
Location: **London (UK)**
Sight and Sound: **v. 13, n. 12, p. 46**
Box Office: **£256,972**
Opening Weekend: **£59,077**
Screens: **21**

## Mr. and Mrs. Iyer

Tip Top Entertainment – 11 April
Box Office: **£7,864**
Opening Weekend: **£2,132**
Screen: **4**

## Mr In-Between

Verve Picture – 3 October
15 United Kingdom 2001
Director: **Paul Sarossy**
Producers: **Michael Lionello Cowan,
Jason Piette, Andreas Bajohra,
Yvonne Michael, Bob Portal**
Screenplay: **Peter Waddington**
From the novel by **Neil Cross**
Director of Photography: **Haris
Zambarloukos**
Editor: **Eddie Hamilton**
Production Designer: **Matthew
Davies**
Music: **Jennie Muskett**
Cast:
**Andrew Howard** – Jon
**Geraldine O'Rawe** – Cathy
**Andrew Tiernan** – Andy
**Mark Benton** – Phil
**Saeed Jaffrey** – Mr Basmati
**Clive Russell** – Mr Michaelmas
**Clint Dyer** – Rickets
**Peter Waddington** – the priest
**Gina Yashere** – dancing woman
**Brian Hibbard** – Gordon
© Zoefilm Ltd.
Production Companies:
**Fusion International Sales
Corporation presents a Great British
Films and Phantom Pictures/Spice
Factory production in association
with Enterprise Films**
98 minutes 27 seconds
Location: **London (UK), Eastbourne**

(UK)
Sight and Sound: **v. 13, n.12, p. 47**
Box Office: **£7,864**
Opening Weekend: **£2,132**
Screen: **4**

## Mrs. Caldicot's Cabbage War

Arrow Films – 31 January
12 United Kingdom 2001
Director: **Ian Sharp**
Producer: **Andy Birmingham**
Screenplay: **Malcolm Stone**
Based on the book by
**Vernon Coleman**
Director of Photography: **Sue Gibson**
Editor: **Gerry Hambling**
Production Designer: **Malcolm Stone**
Music: **Alan Lisk**
Cast:
**Pauline Collins** – Thelma Caldicot
**Peter Capaldi** – Derek Caldicot, her
son
**Anna Wilson-Jones** – Veronica
Caldicot
**Gwenllian Davies** – Audrey
**Sheila Reid** – Joyce
**Frank Mills** – Leslie
**Frank Middlemass** – Bernard
**John Alderton** – Hawksmoor
**Isla Blair** – matron
**Paul Freeman** – Jenkins
© Evolution Films Limited
Production Companies:
**Evolution Films presents
a Cabbage film**
110 minutes 26 seconds
Location: **UK**
Sight and Sound: **v. 12, n. 12, p. 54-55**
Box Office: **£16,415**
Opening Weekend: **£4,702**
Screens: **11**

## Mumbai Matinee

Eros International Limited – 26
September
Box Office: **£1,686**
Opening Weekend: **£1,058**
Screens: **4**

## Mumbai Se Aaya Mera Dost

Gurpreet Video International – 22
August
Box Office: **£58,797**
Opening Weekend: **£24,961**
Screens: **19**

## Munnabhai Mbbs

Eros International Ltd – 19
December
Box Office: **£133,117**
Opening Weekend: **£31,760**
Screens: **13**

## My Life Without Me

Metrodome Dist. – 7 November
15 Spain/Canada 2002
Director: **Isabel Coixet**
Producers: **Esther García, Gordon McLennan**
Screenplay: **Isabel Coixet**
Based on Pretending the Bed is a Raft by **Nanci Kincaid**
Director of Photography: **Jean Claude Larrieu**
Editor: **Lisa Jane Robison**
Production Designer: **Carol Lavallee**
Music: **Alfonso de Vilallonga**
Cast:
**Sarah Polley** – Ann
**Amanda Plummer** – Laurie
**Scott Speedman** – Don, Ann's husband
**Leonor Watling** – Ann's neighbour
**Deborah Harry** – Ann's mother
**Maria de Medeiros** – the hairdresser
**Mark Ruffalo** – Lee
**Julian Richings** – Doctor Thompson
**Kenya Jo Kennedy** – Patsy
**Jessica Amlee** – Penny
© El Deseo D.A. S.L.U./Milestone Productions Inc.
Production Companies::
**Focus Features**
**El Deseo present an**
**El Deseo D.A. S.L.U. and Milestone Productions Inc. co-production in association with Antena 3 Televisión, Vía Digital, Alliance Atlantis**
**A film by Isabel Coixet produced with the participation of The Province of British Columbia Film Incentive**
**with the participation of the Canadian Film or Video Tax Credit in association with The Movie Network, Super Écran, Movie Central, Corus, Miss Wasabi**
105 minutes 59 seconds
Location: **British Columbia (Canada)**
Sight and Sound: **v. 14, n. 1, p. 56**
Box Office: **£143,572**
Opening Weekend: **£35,166**
Screens: **23**

## Mystic River

Warners Bros – 17 October
15 USA/Australia 2003
Director: **Clint Eastwood**
Producers: **Robert Lorenz, Judie G. Hoyt, Clint Eastwood**
Screenplay: **Brian Helgeland**
Based on the novel by **Dennis Lehane**
Director of Photography: **Tom Stern**
Editor: **Joel Cox**
Production Designer: **Henry Bumstead**
Music: **Clint Eastwood**
Cast:
**Sean Penn** – Jimmy Markum
**Tim Robbins** – Dave Boyle
**Kevin Bacon** – Sean Devine
**Laurence Fishburne** – Whitey Powers
**Marcia Gay Harden** – Celeste Boyle
**Laura Linney** – Annabeth Markum
**Kevin Chapman** – Val Savage
**Thomas Guiry** – Brendan Harris
**Emmy Rossum** – Katie Markum
**Spencer Treat Clark** – Silent Ray Harris
© Warner Bros. (US, Canada, Bahamas, Bermuda)
© Village Roadshow Films (BVI) Limited (all other territories)
Production Companies:
**Warner Bros. Pictures presents in association with Village Roadshow Pictures and NPV Entertainment a Malpaso production**
137 minutes 24 seconds
Location: **Boston (MA, USA), Los Angeles (CA, USA)**
Sight and Sound: **v. 13, n. 12, p. 47-48**
Box Office: **£1,819,480**
Opening Weekend: **£295,135**
Screens: **119**

## Mystics

Momentum Pictures – 12 December
Box Office: **£12,594**
Opening Weekend: **£5,864**
Screens: **15**

## Narc

United International Pictures – 07 February
18 USA 2002
Director: **Joe Carnahan**
Producers: **Diane Nabatoff , Ray Liotta, Michelle Grace, Julius R. Nasso**
Screenplay: **Joe Carnahan**
Director of Photography: **Alex Nepomniaschy**
Editor: **John Gilroy**
Production Designers:
**Greg Beale, Taavo Soodor**
Music: **Cliff Martinez**
Cast:
**Jason Patric** – Nick Tellis
**Ray Liotta** – Lieutenant Henry Oak
**Busta Rhymes** – Darnell 'Big D Love' Beery
**Chi McBride** – Captain Cheevers
**Dan Leis** – Elvin Dowd
**Lloyd Adams** – Walter Dandridge
**Meagan Issa** – little girl
**Lina Felice** – Jeanine Mueller
**Alan C. Peterson** – Freeman Franks
**Karen Robinson** – Liz Delmer

© Paramount Pictures
Production Companies:
**Paramount Pictures and Lions Gate Films present a Cruise/Wagner production in association with Splendid Pictures, Emmett Furla Films a Julius R. Nasso production and Tiara Blu Films** – 105 minutes 21 seconds
Location: **Toront o(Canada)**
Sight and Sound: **v. 13, n. 2, p. 54, 56**
Box Office: **£196,486**
Opening Weekend: **£70,805**
Screens: **40**

## National Security

Columbia TriStar – 21 March
12A USA/United Kingdom 2003
Director: **Dennis Dugan**
Producers: **Bobby Newmyer, Jeff Silver, Michael Green**
Screenplay: **Jay Scherick David Ronn**
Director of Photography: **Oliver Wood**
Editor: **Debra Neil-Fisher**
Production Designer: **Larry Fulton**
Music: **Randy Edelman**
Cast:
**Martin Lawrence** – Earl Montgomery
**Steve Zahn** – Hank Rafferty
**Colm Feore** – Detective Frank McDuff
**Bill Duke** – Lieutenant Washington
**Eric Roberts** – Nash
**Timothy Busfield** – Charlie Reed
**Robinne Lee** – Denise
**Brett Cullen** – Heston
**Ken Lerner** – Hank's lawyer
**Matt McCoy** – Robert Barton
© Columbia Pictures Industries, Inc.
Production Companies:
**Columbia Pictures presents an Outlaw, Intermedia, Firm Films production**
88 minutes 13 seconds
Location: **Los Angeles (CA, USA)**
Sight and Sound: **v.13, n. 4, p. 44-45**
Box Office: **£1,051,388**
Opening Weekend: **£426,698**
Screens: **261**

## Ned Kelly

United International Pictures – 26 September
15 Australia/United Kingdom/USA/France 2003
Director: **Gregor Jordan**
Producers: **Nelson Woss, Lynda House**
Screenplay: **John Michael McDonagh**
Based on the novel Our Sunshine by

Robert Drewe
Director of Photography: **Oliver Stapleton**
Editor: **Jon Gregory**
Production Designer: **Steven Jones-Evans**
Music: **Klaus Badelt**
Cast:
Heath Ledger – Ned Kelly
Orlando Bloom – Joe Byrne
Naomi Watts – Julia Cook
Joel Edgerton – Aaron Sherritt
Laurence Kinlan – Dan Kelly
Philip Barantini – Steve Hart
Kerry Condon – Kate Kelly
Kris McQuade – Ellen Kelly
Geoffrey Rush – Superintendent Francis Hare
Kiri Paramore – Fitzpatrick
© Kelly Gang Films Pty Limited/Sunshine Films Limited
Production Companies:
**Universal Pictures, StudioCanal, Working Title Films present an Endymion Fims Production in association with WTA With the assistance of The Melbourne Film Office**
109 minutes 56 seconds
Location: **Victoria (Australia)**
Sight and Sound: v. 13, n. 11, p. 56
Box Office: £509,728
Opening Weekend: £211,643
Screens: 213

## Nine Dead Gay Guys
Guerilla Films – 19 September
18 United Kingdom 2002 – Director:
**Lab Ky Mo**
Producer:
**Lamia Nayeb-St.Hilaire**
Screenplay: **Lab Ky Mo**
Director of Photography: **Damien Elliott**
Editors: **Christopher Blunden Jonathon Braman**
Production Designer: **Nik Callan**
Music: **Stephen W. Parsons**
Cast:
Glenn Mulhern
Kenny
Brendan Mackey
Byron
Steven Berkoff
Jeff
Michael Praed
The Queen
Vas Blackwood
Donkey-Dick Dark
Fish
Old Nick
Simon Godley
Golders Green
Carol Decker

Jeff's wife
Raymond Griffiths
The Desperate Dwarf
Abdala Keserwani
Dick-Cheese Deepak
© **9 Men Partnership**
Production Companies:
**Little Wing Films presents in assocation with 9 Films a Lab Ky Mo film Park Entertainment/Little Wing Films**
82 minutes 45 seconds
Location: **London (UK)**
Sight and Sound: v.13, n. 11 p. 57
Box Office: £12,685
Opening Weekend: £4,457
Screens: 5

## Nicholas Nickleby
20th Century Fox – 27 June
PG USA/United Kingdom 2002
Director: **Douglas McGrath**
Producers: **Simon Channing Williams, John N. Hart, Jeffrey Sharp**
Screenplay: **Douglas McGrath**
Based on the novel by
**Charles Dickens**
Director of Photography: **Dick Pope**
Editor: **Lesley Walker**
Production Designer: **Eve Stewart**
Music/Music Produced: **Rachel Portman**
Cast:
Jamie Bell – Smike
Jim Broadbent – Wackford Squeers
Tom Courtenay – Newman Noggs
Alan Cumming – Mr Folair
Edward Fox – Sir Mulberry Hawk
Romola Garai – Kate Nickleby
Anne Hathaway – Madeline Bray
Barry Humphries – Mr Leadville
Charlie Hunnam – Nicholas Nickleby
Nathan Lane – Vincent Crummles
Christopher Plummer – Ralph Nickleby
Timothy Spall – Charles Cheeryble
Juliet Stevenson – Mrs Squeers
© United Artists Films Inc
Production Companies:
**United Artists presents a Hart Sharp Entertainment production in association with Cloud Nine Films**
132 minutes 19 seconds
Location: **London, Liverpool (UK)**
Sight and Sound: v. 13, n. 8, p. 54
Box Office: £1,115,052
Opening Weekend: £222,376
Screens: 204

## Noi Albinoi
Artificial Eye – 14 November
15 Iceland/Germany/United Kingdom/Denmark 2002 – Director:
**Dagur Kári Petursson**
Producers: **Philippe Bober, Kim Magnusson, Skúli Fr. Malmqvist Thorir Snaer Sigurjonsson**
Screenplay: **Dagur Kári**
Director of Photography: **Rasmus Videbæk**
Editor: **Daniel Dencik**
Production Designer: **Jón Steinar Ragnarsson**
Music: **Slowblow**
Cast:
Tómas Lemarquis – Nói
Thröstur Leó Gunnarsson – Kiddi Beikon
Elin Hansdóttir – Íris
Anna Fridriksdóttir – Lina
Hjalti Rögnvaldsson – Óskar
Petur Einarsson – priest
Kjartan Bjargmundsson – Gylfi
Thorsteinn Gunnarsson – Thorarinn school master
Gudmundur Ólafsson – teacher
Haraldur Jónsson – psychiatrist
© ZikZak Kvikmyndir/Essential Filmproduktion/The Bureau/M&M Productions
Production Companies:
**Zik Zak Kvikmyndir, Essential Filmproduktion, The Bureau, M&M Productions supported by Danske Filminstitut, Film Council, Filmboard Berlin-Brandenburg, Filmstiftung Nordrhein-Westfalen, Kvikmyndasjódur Íslands in co-operation with ZDF Das Kleine Fernsehspiel/ARTE**
92 minutes 44 seconds
Sight and Sound: v.13, n. 12, p. 48-49
Box Office: £101,339
Opening Weekend: £13,877
Screens: 5

## Nowhere in Africa
Optimum Releasing – 04 April
15 Germany 2001
Director: **Caroline Link**
Producer: **Peter Herrmann**
Screenplay: **Caroline Link**
Based freely on the novel by
**Stefanie Zweig**
Director of Photography: **Gernot Roll**
Editor: **Patricia Rommel**
Production Designers: **Susann Bieling, Uwe Szielasko**
Music: **Niki Reiser**
Cast:
Juliane Köhler – Jettel Redlich
Merab Ninidze – Walter Redlich

Sidede Onyulo – Owuor
Matthias Habich – Süßkind
Lea Kurka – Regina Redlich, younger
Karoline Eckertz – Regina Redlich, older
Gerd Heinz – Max
Hildegard Schmahl – Ina
Maritta Horwarth – Liesel
Regina Zimmermann – Käthe
© MTM GmbH/Constantin Film GmbH/Bavaria Film GmbH
Production Companies:
**Constantin Film presents an MTM Medien & Television München Produktion in co-production with Constantin Film Produktion, Bavaria Film, MC One Supported by FilmFernsehFonds Bayern, Filmförderungsanstalt, Bayerischer Banken Fonds and Bundesbeauftragter für Kultur und Medien Screenplay development supported by Mediterranean Film Institute (MFI), an initiative of Media II of the European Union**
141 minutes 27 seconds
Location: **Bavaria (Germany), Kenya**
Sight and Sound: **v. 13, n. 4, p. 45-46**
Box Office: **£257,679**
Opening Weekend: **£27,382**
Screen: **4**

## Octane

Buena Vista Intl – 14 November
15 Luxembourg/United Kingdom 2003
Director: **Marcus Adams**
Producers: **Alistair MacLean Clark, Basil Stephens**
Screenplay: **Stephen Volk**
Director of Photography: **Robin Vidgeon**
Editor: **Trevor Waite**
Production Designer: **Max Gottlieb**
Music: **Orbital**
Cast:
**Madeleine Stowe – Senga
Norman Reedus – recovery man
Bijou Phillips – backpacker
Mischa Barton – Nat
Jonathan Rhys-Meyers – the father
Leo Gregory – joyrider
Gary Parker – vacation man
Amber Batty – vacation woman
Jenny Jules – Highway Patrol sergeant
Patrick O'Kane – trucker**
© Harvest Pictures PLC/Harvest Pictures II Limited/Random Harvest Pictures Limited/The Take 4

Partnerships/High Octane Productions Limited/Delux Productions SA
Production Companies:
**Four Horsemen Films presents a Random Harvest/Harvest Pictures Plc/Harvest Pictures II/ Take 4 Partnerships production A High Octane Productions/Delux Productions co-production in association with the Film Fund Luxembourg A Marcus Adams film**
90 minutes 34 seconds
Location: **Luxembourg**
Sight and Sound: **v. 13, n. 12, p. 49**
Box Office: **£19,061**
Opening Weekend: **£9,910**
Screens: **24**

## Okay

Metropolis Films – 17 October
15 Denmark/Norway/Germany 2002
Director: **Jesper Westerlin Nielsen**
Producer: **Peter Bech**
Screenplay: **Kim Fupz Aakeson**
Director of Photography: **Erik Zappon**
Editor: **Morten Giese**
Art Director: **Peter de Neergaard**
Score: **Halfdan E**
Cast:
**Paprika Steen – Nete
Ole Ernst – Nete's father
Troels Lyby – Kristian
Nicolaj Kopernikus – Martin, Nete's brother
Molly Blixt Egelind – Katrine, the daughter
Laura Drasbæk – Tanja
Trine Dyrholm – Trisse
Lotte Merete Andersen – Janni
Jesper Christensen – doctor
Henrik Prip – Nete's boss**
© Bech Film ApS
Production Companies:
**Bavaria Film International presents Bech Film presents Produced by Peter Bech Productions ApS in association with Danske Fiminstitut/TV2 Danmark (Marianne Christensen/Adam Price/Camilla Hammerich)**
96 minutes 55 seconds
Location: **Copenhagen (Denmark)**
Sight and Sound: **v. 13, n. 11, p. 57-58**
Box Office: **£6,263**
Opening Weekend: **£1,816**
Screen: **1**

## Old School

United International Pictures – 9 May
15 USA 2002
Director: **Todd Phillips**

Producers: **Daniel Goldberg, Joe Medjuck, Todd Phillips**
Screenplay: **Todd Phillips, Scot Armstrong**
Story: **Court Crandall, Todd Phillips Scot Armstrong**
Director of Photography: **Mark Irwin**
Editor: **Michael Jablow**
Production Designer: **Clark Hunter**
Music: **Theodore Shapiro**
Cast:
**Luke Wilson – Mitch
Will Ferrell – Frank
Vince Vaughn – Beanie
Ellen Pompeo – Nicole
Juliette Lewis – Heidi
Leah Remini – Lara
Perrey Reeves – Marissa
Craig Kilborn – Mark
Jeremy Piven – Gordon Pritchard, the dean
Elisha Cuthbert – Darcie**
© DreamWorks LLC
Production Companies:
**DreamWorks Pictures presents a Montecito Picture Company production**
90 minutes 36 seconds
Location: **Los Angeles (CA, USA)**
Sight and Sound: **v. 13, n. 7, p. 54**
Box Office: **£2,299,855**
Opening Weekend: **£742,478**
Screens: **316**

## Once Upon a Time in Mexico

Buena Vista International – 26 September
15 USA 2003
Director: **Robert Rodriguez**
Producers: **Elizabeth Avellán, Carlos Gallardo, Robert Rodriguez**
Screenplay: **Robert Rodriguez**
Director of Photography: **Robert Rodriguez**
Editor: **Robert Rodriguez**
Art Director: **Melo Hinojosa**
Music: **Robert Rodriguez**
Cast:
**Antonio Banderas – El Mariachi
Salma Hayek – Carolina
Johnny Depp – Agent Sands
Mickey Rourke – Billy
Eva Mendes – Ajedrez
Danny Trejo – Cucuy
Enrique Iglesias – Lorenzo
Marco Leonardi – Fideo
Cheech Marin – Belini
Rubén Blades – Jorge FBI**
© Columbia Pictures Industries, Inc.
Production Companies:
**Columbia Pictures and Dimension Films present a Troublemaker Studios production**

101 minutes 34 seconds
Location: **Mexico**
Sight and Sound: **v. 13, n. 11, p. 58-59**
Box Office: **£2,632,597**
Opening Weekend: **£846,100**
Screens: **313**

### [One] Cavale

**Metro Tartan Distributors – 14 November**
**15 France/Belgium 2002**
Director: **Lucas Belvaux**
Producers: **Patrick Sobelman, Diana Elbaum**
Screenplay: **Lucas Belvaux**
Director of Photography: **Pierre Milon**
Editor: **Valérie Loiseleux**
Art Director: **Frédérique Belvaux**
Music/Music Director/Orchestrator: **Riccardo Del Fra**
Cast:
**Ornella Muti – Cécile François Morel – Alain
Dominique Blanc – Agnès
Gilbert Melki – Pascal
Valérie Mairesse – Claire
Bernard Mazzinghi – Georges
Raphaële Godin – Louise
Catherine Frot – Jeanne
Lucas Belvaux – Pierre
Patrick Depeyra – Vincent**
© Agat Films & Cie/Entre Chien et Loup/RTBF/Rhône-Alpes Cinéma
Production Companies:
**Agat Films & Cie and Entre Chien et Loup present in co-production with Rhône-Alpes Cinéma and RTBF (Télévision Belge) with the participation of Centre National de la Cinématographie, Eurimages, Centre du Cinéma et de l'Audiovisuel de la Communauté Française de Belgique, Télédistributeurs Wallons, Region Rhône-Alpes, La Loterie Nationale de Belgique
in association with Cofimage 12, Gimages 5, Natexis Banques Populaires Images
2 and with the participation of Canal+
a film by Lucas Belvaux**
113 minutes 49 seconds
Location: **Grenoble (France)**
Sight and Sound: **v. 13, n. 12, p. 26-27, 50**
Box Office: **£97,944**
Opening Weekend: **£20,981**
Screens: **9**

### The One and Only

**Pathé Distribution Ltd – 21 February**
**15 United Kingdom/France 2002**
Director: **Simon Cellan Jones**
Producer: **Leslee Udwin**
Screenplay: **Peter Flannery**
Based on Den eneste ene produced by **Sandrew Metronome,**
Associate Producer: **Bo Christensen,** and based on an original screenplay by **Kim Fupz Aakeson and an original idea by Susanne Bier**
Director of Photography: **Remi Adefarasin**
Editor: **Pia Di Ciaula**
Production Designer: **Zoë MacLeod**
Music/Orchestrations: **Gabriel Yared**
Cast:
**Justine Waddell – Stevie
Richard Roxburgh – Neil
Jonathan Cake – Sonny
Patsy Kensit – Stella
Michael Hodgson – Stan
Aisling O'Sullivan – Jenny
Kerry Rolfe – Sharon
Donna Air – Donna
Angel Thomas – Mgala
Charlie Hardwick – doctor**
© Assassin Films Limited/TF1 International Pictures/Pathé Fund Limited
Production Companies:
**Pathé Pictures, TF1 International & Sky present
in association with The Film Council
an Assassin Films production
Made with the support of the Film Council
Made with financial support from the Northern Production Fund and One North East**
91 minutes 20 seconds
Location: **Newcastle (UK)**
Sight and Sound: **v. 13, n. 3, p. 53-54**
Box Office: **£113,150**
Opening Weekend: **£61,413**
Screens: **136**

### Oops!

**Venus Entertainment – 14 November**
Box Office: **£3,188**
Opening Weekend: **£2,133**
Screens: **6**

### Open Hearts

**Icon Film Distribution – 04 April**
**15 Denmark 2002**
Director: **Susanne Bier**
Producer: **Vibeke Windelöv**
Screenplay: **Anders Thomas Jensen**
Story: **Susanne Bier**
Director of Photography: **Morten Søborg**
Editors: **Pernille Bech Christensen, Thomas Krag**

Music: **Jesper Winge Leisner**
Cast:
**Mads Mikkelsen – Niels
Sonja Richter – Cecilie, 'Cille'
Nikolaj Lie Kaas – Joachim
Paprika Steen – Marie
Stine Bjrregaard – Stine
Birthe Neumann – Hanne
Niels Olsen – Finn
Ulf Pilgaard – Thomsen
Ronnie Hiort Lorenzen – Gustav
Pelle Bang Sørensen – Emil**
© Zentropa Entertainments4
Production Companies:
**Zentropa Entertainments4 presents
Produced by Zentropa Entertainments4
in collaboration with DR TV-Drama (Ditte Christiansen, Marianne Moritzen) and supported by The Danish Filminstitute**
113 minutes 20 seconds
Location: **Copenhagen (Denmark)**
Sight and Sound: **v. 13, n. 4, p. 46**
Box Office: **£89,849**
Opening Weekend: **£19,710**
Screens: **11**

### Otherworld

**Miracle Communications – 27 June**
**12A United Kingdom 2002**
Director: **Derek Hayes**
Live Action Director: **Marc Evans**
Producer: **Naomi Jones**
Screenplay: **Martin Lamb, Penelope Middelboe**
Directors of Photography
Live Action: **Nina Kellgren, Peter Thornton, Tony Yates**
Editor: **William Oswald**
Designed by **Derek Hayes**
Production Designers:
Live Action: **Hayden Pearce, Jon Henson**
Music/Music Arranger: **John Cale**
Voice Cast:
**Daniel Evans – Dan
Jenny Livsey – Rhiannon
Matthew Rhys – Lleu
Sue Jones Davies – Siân
Ioan Gruffudd – King Bendigeidfran
Peter Gruffydd – Math
Robert Gwyndaf – Llwyd
Mali Harries – Cigfa
Aneirin Hughes – Gronw
Clare Isaac – Branwen**
© S4C
Production Companies:
**S4C Films & S4C International present
a Cartwn Cymru production
in association with The Arts Council of Wales and BBC Cymru/Wales**

with the participation of British
Screen and BSkyB
supported by the National Lottery
through The Arts Council of Wales
108 minutes 32 seconds
Sight and Sound: v. 13, n. 9, p. 58-59
Box Office: £1,272
Opening Weekend: £433
Screens: 3

## Out of Control
Tip Top Entertainment – 21
November
Box Office: £70,812
Opening Weekend: £26,201
Screens: 20

## Out of Time
Momentum Pictures – 26 December
12A USA 2003
Director: **Carl Franklin**
Producers: **Neal H. Moritz, Jesse
B'franklin**
Screenplay: **Dave Collard**
Director of Photography: **Theo van
de Sande**
Editor: **Carole Kravetz**
Production Designer: **Paul Peters**
Music: **Graeme Revell**
Cast:
**Denzel Washington** – Matt Lee
Whitlock
**Eva Mendes** – Alex Diaz Whitlock
**Sanaa Lathan** – Ann Merai Harrison
**Dean Cain** – Chris Harrison
**John Billingsley** – Chae
**Robert Baker** – Tony Dalton
**Alex Carter** – Cabot
**Antoni Corone** – Deputy Baste
**Terry Loughlin** – Agent Stark
**Nora Dunn** – Dr Donovan
© Metro-Goldwyn-Mayer Pictures
Inc.
Production Companies::
Metro-Goldwyn-Mayer Pictures
presents an Original Film, Monarch
Pictures production
105 minutes 23 seconds
Location: **Miami (Florida, USA)**
Sight and Sound: v. 14, n. 1, p. 57
Box Office: £988,096
Opening Weekend: £311,508
Screens: 236

## Party Monster
Tartan Films – 17 October
18 USA/Netherlands 2003
Directors: **Fenton Bailey, Randy
Barbato**
Producers: **Fenton Bailey, Randy
Barbato, Jon Marcus, Bradford
Simpson, Christine Vachon**
Screenplay: **Fenton Bailey
Randy Barbato**
Based on the book

Disco Bloodbath by
**James St. James**
Director of Photography: **Teodoro
Maniaci**
Editor: **Jeremy Simmons**
Production Designer: **Andrea Stanley**
Music: **Jimmy Harry**
Cast:
**Macaulay Culkin** – Michael Alig
**Seth Green** – James St. James
**Chloë Sevigny** – Gitsie
**Natasha Lyonne** – Brooke
**Wilmer Valderrama** – DJ Keoki
**Wilson Cruz** – Angel Melendez
**Diana Scarwid** – Elke Alig,
Michael's mother
**Dylan McDermott** – Peter Gatien
**Marilyn Manson** – Christina
**Dillon Woolley** – young James
© Skrink Inc.
Production Companies:
a ContentFilm presentation
in association with Fortissimo Film
Sales
a Killer Films/John Wells production
a World of Wonder production
98 minutes 46 seconds
New York City (NY, USA)
Sight and Sound: v. 13, n. 11, p. 59-60
Box Office: £73,260
Opening Weekend: £18,714
Screens: 11

## Parwana
Eros International Ltd – 12
September
Box Office: £26,890
Opening Weekend: £12,045
Screens: 11

## Passion of Joan of Arc (Re)
Artificial Eye – 18 July
Box Office: £14,473
Opening Weekend: £2,897
Screen: 1

## Perfume de Violetas
City Screen – 10 January
15 Mexico/USA/Netherlands 2000
Director: **Marysa Sistach**
Producer:**José Buil**
Screenplay: **José Buil**
Story: **José Buil, Marysa Sistach**
Director of Photography: **Servando
Gajá**
Editors: **José Buil, Humberto
Hernández**
Art Director: **Guadalupe Sánchez**
Music Supervisor: **Annette Fradera**
Cast:
**Ximena Ayala** – Yessica
**Nancy Gutiérrez** – Miriam
**Arcelia Ramírez** – Miriam's mother
**Luis Fernando Peña** – Yessica's
stepbrother

**Gabino Rodríguez** – Héctor
**Pablo Delgado** – Juan
**Rosario Zúñiga** – prefect
**Soledad González** – director
**Eligio Meléndez** – Yessica's
stepfather
© Producciones Tragaluz S.A. de C.V.
Production Companies:
Consejo Nacional para la Cultura y
las Artes, Fondo para la Producción
Cinematográfica de Calidad,
Instituto Mexicano de
Cinematografía
Producciones Tragaluz present
a film by Maryse Sistach and José
Buil
Palmera Films
with the support of John Simon
Guggenheim Memorial Foundation,
Hubert Bals Fund, Fondo Nacional
para la Cultura y las Artes
Centro de Capacitación
Cinematográfica, Filmoteca de la
UNAM and TV UNAM
88 minutes 19 seconds
Location: **Mexico City (Mexico)**
Sight and Sound: v. 13, n. 2, p. 56-57
Box Office: £2,378
Opening Weekend: £2,378
Screens: 2

## Persona (Re)
Metro Tartan – 31 January
Box Office: £44,683
Opening Weekend: £8,480
Screens: 2

## Personal Velocity
Optimum Releasing – 28 March
15 USA 2001
Director: **Rebecca Miller**
Producers: **Gary Winick, Alexis
Alexanian, Lemore Syvan**
Screenplay: **Rebecca Miller**
Based on her book Personal Velocity
Director of Photography: **Ellen Kuras**
Editor: **Sabine Hoffman**
Production Designer: **Judy Becker**
Music: **Michael Rohatyn**
Cast:
**Kyra Sedgwick** – Delia Shunt
**Parker Posey** – Greta Herskovitz
**Fairuza Balk** – Paula
**David Warshofsky** – Kurt Wurtzle
**Leo Fitzpatrick** – Mylert
**Tim Guinee** – Lee Schneeweiss
**Patti D'Arbanville** – Celia
**Ben Shenkman** – Max
**Joel De La Fuente** – Thavi Matola
**Marceline Hugot** – Pam
© Trilogy Filmworks Inc
Production Companies:
The Independent Film Channel
Productions presents
an InDigEnt production

in association with Goldheart/Blue
Magic Pictures
86 minutes 21 seconds
New York City (NY, USA)
Sight and Sound: v. 13, n. 4, p. 47
Box Office: £82,260
Opening Weekend: £19,012
Screens: 14

## Peter Pan

United International Pictures – 26
December
PG USA/United Kingdom/Australia
Director: **P.J. Hogan**
Producers: **Lucy Fisher, Douglas
Wick, Patrick McCormick**
Screenplay: **P.J. Hogan
Michael Goldenberg**
Based upon the original stageplay and
books written by **J.M. Barrie**
Director of Photography:
**Donald M. McAlpine**
Editors: **Garth Craven, Michael Kahn**
Production Designer: **Roger Ford**
Music: **James Newton Howard**
Cast:
Jason Isaacs – Mr George
Darling/Captain Hook
Jeremy Sumpter – Peter Pan
Rachel Hurd-Wood – Wendy
Darling
Olivia Williams – Mrs Darling
Ludivine Sagnier – Tink
Richard Briers – Smee
Lynn Redgrave – Aunt Millicent
Geoffrey Palmer – Sir Edward
Quiller Couch
Harry Newell – John Darling
Freddie Popplewell – Michael
Darling
© Columbia Pictures Industries
Inc/Universal Studios/Revolution
Studios Distribution Company LLC
Production Companies::
**Universal Pictures/Columbia
Pictures/Revolution Studios
Present a Douglas Wick-Lucy Fisher
production
An Allied Stars Production
A P.J.Hogan film
Produced with the assistance of
Pacific Film and Television
Commission**
113 minutes 8 seconds
Location: **Queensland (Australia)**
Sight and Sound: v. 14, n. 3, p. 56-57
Box Office: £4,866,710
Opening Weekend: £1,359,372
Screens: 439

## Petites Coupures

Artificial Eye – 29 August
15 France/United Kingdom 2002
Director: **Pascal Bonitzer**
Producers: **Jean-Michel Rey,**

Philippe Liégeois
Screenplay: **Pascal Bonitzer**
Director of Photography: **William
Lubtchansky**
Editor: **Suzanne Koch**
Production Designer: **Emmanuel de
Chauvigny**
Music/Orchestra Conductor: **John
Scott**
Cast:
Daniel Auteuil – Bruno Beckmann
Kristin Scott Thomas – Béatrice
Pascale Bussières – Mathilde
Ludivine Sagnier – Nathalie
Catherine Mouchet – Anne Sermain
Emmanuelle Devos – Gaëlle
Beckmann
Hanns Zischler – Etienne Verekher
Jean Yanne – Gérard Sermain
Aladin Reibel – Fromager
Jeremie Lippman – Simon Sermain
© Rezo Productions/Axiom Films
Ltd/France 2 Cinéma/Rhônes Alpes
Cinéma
Production Companies:
**Rezo Productions presents
a co-production of Rezo
Productions and Axiom Films
with France 2 Cinéma and Rhônes
Alpes Cinéma
in association with sofica Sofinergie
5, France Télévision Images 2, Rezo
Films
with the participation of Région
Rhône Alpes, Centre National de la
Cinématographie, Canal+
with the support of Procirep**
95 minutes 35 seconds
Location: **Paris, Lyon, Grenoble
(France)**
Sight and Sound: v. 13, n. 10, p. 58
Box Office: £73,897
Opening Weekend: £13,275
Screens: 4

## Phone Booth

20th Century Fox – 18 April
15 USA 2002
Director: **Joel Schumacher**
Producers: **Gil Netter, David Zucker**
Screenplay: **Larry Cohen**
Director of Photography: **Matthew
Libatique**
Editor: **Mark Stevens**
Production Designer: **Andrew Laws**
Music: **Harry Gregson-Williams**
Cast:
Colin Farrell – Stu Shepard
Kiefer Sutherland – the caller
Forest Whitaker – Captain Ramey
Radha Mitchell – Kelly Shepard
Katie Holmes – Pamela McFadden
Paula Jai Parker – Felicia
Arian Ash – Corky

Tia Texada – Asia
John Enos III – Leon
Richard T. Jones – Sergeant Cole
© Twentieth Century Fox Film
Corporation
Production Companies:
**Fox 2000 Pictures presents a
Zucker/Netter production**
80 minutes 58 seconds
Nw York (NY,USA)
Sight and Sound: v. 13, n. 4, p. 48
Box Office: £6,669,724
Opening Weekend: £1,385,040
Screens: 254

## The Pianist

Pathé Distribution – 24 January
15 France/Poland/Germany/United
Kingdom/USA 2002
Director: **Roman Polanski**
Producers: **Roman Polanski, Robert
Benmussa, Alain Sarde**
Screenplay: **Ronald Harwood**
Based on the book by **Wladyslaw
Szpilman**
Director of Photography: **Pawel
Edelman**
Editor: **Hervé de Luze**
Production Designer: **Allan Starski**
Music: **Wojciech Kilar**
Cast:
Adrien Brody – Wladyslaw
Szpilman
Thomas Kretschmann – Captain
Wilm Hosenfeld
Frank Finlay – Mr Szpilman, the
father
Maureen Lipman – Mrs Szpilman,
the mother
Emilia Fox – Dorota
Ed Stoppard – Henryk Szpilman,
the brother
Julia Rayner – Regina Szpilman, the
sister
Jessica Kate Meyer – Halina
Szpilman, the sister
Michal Zebrowski – Jurek
Wanja Mues – SS officer who slaps
father
© R.P. Productions/Heritage
Films/Studios Babelsberg/Runteam
Ltd.
Production Companies:
**R.P. Productions, Heritage Films,
Studio Babelsberg, Runteam Ltd.
With the participation of Canal+
and Studio Canal+
Bac Films, Canal+ Poland, Telewizja
Polska S.A., Agencja Produkcji
Filmowej
Filmboard Berlin-Brandenburg
(FBB), Filmfernsehfonds Bayern
(FFF),
Filmförderungsanstalt (FFA)**

148 minutes 42 seconds
Location: **Warsaw (Poland), Berlin ,
Jüteborg (Germany)**
Sight and Sound: **v. 13, n. 2, p. 57-58**
Box Office: **£2,965,030**
Opening Weekend: **£195,222**
Screens: **64**

### Piglet's Big Movie

Buena Vista International – 27 June
U USA 2003
Director: **Francis Glebas**
Producer: **Michelle Pappalardo-
Robinson**
Screenplay: **Brian Hohfeld**
Adapted from/Inspired by the works
of **A.A. Milne**
Art Director:  **Fred Warter**
Music/Music Conductor:  **Carl
Johnson**
Voice Cast:
**John Fiedler  – Piglet**
**Jim Cummings  – Winnie the
Pooh/Tigger**
**Andre Stojka  – Owl**
**Kath Soucie  – Kanga**
**Nikita Hopkins  – Roo**
**Peter Cullen  – Eeyore**
**Ken Sansom  – Rabbit**
**Tom Wheatley  – Christopher Robin**
© Disney Enterprises, Inc.
Production Companies:
**Walt Disney Pictures presents
Produced by DisneyTOON Studios
Burbank - Sidney - Tokyo**
74 minutes 53 seconds
Sight and Sound: **v.13, n.10, p. 57-58**
Box Office: **£4,357,495**
Opening Weekend: **£22,787**
Screens: **25**

### Pinjar

**Gurpreet Video Int – 24 October**
Box Office: **£65,202**
Opening Weekend: **£14,013**
Screens: **12**

### Pirates of the Caribbean

Buena Vista International  – 08
August
12A USA 2003
Director: **Gore Verbinski**
Producer: **Jerry Bruckheimer**
Screenplay: **Ted Elliott, Terry Rossio**
Screen Story: **Ted Elliott, Terry
Rossio, Stuart Beattie, Jay Wolpert**
Based on Walt Disney's Pirates of
the Caribbean
Director of Photography: **Dariusz
Wolski**
Editors: **Craig Wood, Stephen Rivkin
Arthur Schmidt**
Production Designer: **Brian Morris**
Music: **Klaus Badelt**
Cast:

**Johnny Depp  – Captain Jack
Sparrow**
**Geoffrey Rush  – Captain Barbossa**
**Orlando Bloom  – Will Turner**
**Keira Knightley  – Elizabeth Swann**
**Jack Davenport  – Commodore
Norrington**
**Kevin R. McNally  – Joshamee Gibbs**
**Zoë Saldana  – Anamaria**
**Jonathan Pryce  – Governor
Weatherby Swann**
**Treva Etienne  – Koehler**
**David Bailie  – Cotton**
© Disney Enterprises, Inc./Jerry
Bruckheimer, Inc.
Production Companies:
**Walt Disney Pictures presents
in association with Jerry
Bruckheimer Films**
142 minutes 55 seconds
Location: **Caribbean, Los Angeles
(CA, USA)**
Sight and Sound: **v. 13, n. 9, p. 59-60**
Box Office: **£28,171,721**
Opening Weekend: **£3,765,450**
Screens: **452**

### Pot Luck

**Cinefrance – 09 May**
15 France/Spain 2002
Director: **Cédric Klapisch**
Producer: **Ce Qui Me Meut, Bruno
Levy**
Screenplay: **Cédric Klapisch**
Director of Photography: **Dominique
Colin**
Editor: **Francine Sandberg**
Art Directors: **François Emmanuelli**
Spanish Crew: **Rosa Ros**
Music: **Kouz-1, Loïk Dury, Mathieu
Dury**
Cast:
**Romain Duris  – Xavier**
**Judith Godrèche  – Anne Sophie**
**Audrey Tautou  – Martine**
**Cécile de France  – Isabelle**
**Keilly Reilly  – Wendy**
**Cristina Brondo  – Soledad**
**Federico D'Anna  – Alessandro**
**Barnaby Metschurat  – Tobias**
**Christian Pagh  – Lars**
**Kevin Bishop  – William**
© CQMM/France 2/Studio Canal
Cinéma/Bac Films/Mate
Production/Castelao Productions
Production Companies:
**Ce Qui Me Meut presents
Ce Qui Me Meut, StudioCanal,
France 2 Cinéma, Bac Films, Mate
Production and Castelao
Productions**
with the participation of Canal+,
France 2, Vía Digital
121 minutes 55 seconds

Location: **Paris (France), Barcelona
(Spain)**
Sight and Sound: **v. 13, n. 7, p. 55**
Box Office: **£9,471**
Opening Weekend: **£9,471**
Screens: **8**

### Public Enemy

Metro Tartan – 25 July
18 Republic of Korea 2002
Director: **Kang Woo-suk**
Producers: **Kang Woo-suk, Ji Mee-
hyang, Lee Min-ho**
Screenplay: **Baek Seung-jae, Jung
Yoon-seup, Kim Hyun-jung, Chae
Yoon-suk**
Story: **Gu Bon-han**
Director of Photography: **Kim Sung-
bok**
Editor: **Ko Im-pyo**
Production Designer: **Choi Byung-
geun**
Art Director:  **Bae Moo-chul**
Cast:
**Sul Kyung-gu  – Kang Chul-joong**
**Lee Sung-jae  – Cho Gyu-hwan**
**Kang Shin-il  – Captain Uhm**
**Kim Jung-hak  – Detective Kim
Yeong-Su**
**Doh Yong-gu  – Detective Nam**
**Ahn Na-sang  – Detective Lee**
**Lee Moon-shik  – Lee Ahn-soo,
'Math'**
**Sung Ji-roo  – Dae-gil**
**Yoo Hae-jin  – Y oung-man**
**Lee Jung-hun  – pesky inspector**
© Cinema Sevice
Production Companies:
**Presented by Cinema Service in
association with SBS**
138 minutes 18 seconds
Sight and Sound: **v.13, n. 8, p. 55**
Box Office: **£6,951**
Opening Weekend: **£2,142**
Screens: **3**

### Puckoon

**Guerilla Films – 04 April**
PG United
Kingdom/Germany/Ireland 2002
Director: **Terence Ryan**
Producers: **Ken Tuohy, Terence Ryan**
Screenplay: **Terence Ryan**
Based on the book by
**Spike Milligan**
Director of Photography: **Peter
Hannan**
Editor: **Dermot Diskin**
Production Designer: **John Bunker**
Music:  **Richard Hartley, Pól
Brennan**
Cast:
**Sean Hughes  – Dan Madigan**
**Elliott Gould  – Dr Sean Goldstein**
**Richard Attenborough  –**

writer/director
Daragh O'Malley – Father Patrick
Rudden
John Lynch – O'Brien
Griff Rhys Jones – Colonel Stokes
Nickolas Grace – Foggerty
B.J. Hogg – Thomas Rafferty
David Kelly – O'Toole
Milo O'Shea – Sergeant
McGillikuddie
© Y2K/MPB
Production Companies:
MPB Production, Y2K Film
Productions Ltd
Supported by the National Lottery
through the Arts Council of
Northern Ireland and the Northern
Ireland Film Commission
Completed with the help of Bord
Scannán na hÉireann/The Irish Film
Board
Development and
pre-production financing provided
by Freewheel International
Developed in association with
Riverjam Ltd
Pre-production financing provided
by Susan Morrall, Helen Morrall
Developed in association with
Cheltenham Studios Ltd
Developed in association with
Fairholme Ltd
UK production company: Insight
Ventures Ltd
Irish co-production company:
Distinguished Features Ltd
Made with the assistance of the
Northern Ireland Film Commission
(Richard Taylor, Andrew Reid)
83 minutes 37 seconds
Location: **Northern Ireland (UK),
Ireland**
Sight and Sound: v. 13, n. 5, p. 58-59
Box Office: **£5,991**
Opening Weekend: **£3,796**
Screens: **8**

### Punch-Drunk Love
Columbia TriStar – 07 February
15 USA 2002
Director: **Paul Thomas Anderson**
Producers:  **JoAnne Sellar, Daniel
Lupi, Paul Thomas Anderson**
Screenplay: **Paul Thomas Anderson**
Director of Photography: **Robert
Elswit**
Editor: **Leslie Jones**
Production Designer: **William
Arnold**
Music: **Jon Brion**
Cast:
Adam Sandler – Barry Egan
Emily Watson – Lena Leonard
Philip Seymour Hoffman – Dean

Trumbell
Luis Guzmán – Lance
Mary Lynn Rajskub – Elizabeth
Lisa Spector – Susan
Julie Hermelin – Karen Hermelin
Kathleen –
Hazel Mailloux – Rhonda
Nicole Gelbard – Nicole
© Revolution Studios Distribution
Company LLC
Production Companies:
**Revolution Studios/New Line
Cinema present
a JoAnne Sellar/Ghoulardi Film
Company production
a P.T. Anderson picture**
95 minutes 3 seconds
Sight and Sound: v.13, n. 2, p. 58, 60
Box Office: **£480,854**
Opening Weekend: **£151,494**
Screens: **82**

### Pure
Artificial Eye – 02 May
18 United Kingdom 2002
Director: **Gillies MacKinnon**
Producer: **Howard Burch**
Screenplay: **Alison Hume**
Director of Photography: **John de
Borman**
Editor: **Pia Di Ciaula**
Production Designer: **Jon Henson**
Music: **Nitin Sawhney**
Cast:
Molly Parker – Mel
David Wenham – Lenny
Geraldine McEwan – Nanna
Kate Ashfield – Helen
Gary Lewis – Detective Inspector
French
Karl Johnson – granddad
Keira Knightley – Louise
Nitin Ganatra – Abu
Marsha Thomason – Vicki
Harry Eden – Paul
© A Bad Way Ltd
Production Companies:
**Little Wing Films present
a Kudos production**
96 minutes 45 seconds
Location: **East End (London, UK)**
Sight and Sound: v. 13, n. 5, p. 59
Box Office: **£26,947**
Opening Weekend: **£6,136**
Screens: **8**

### Qayamat
Venus Entertainment – 11 July
Box Office: **£74,690**
Opening Weekend: **£22,086**
Screens: **13**

### Rain
Circuit Film – 27 June
15 New Zealand 2001

Director: **Christine Jeffs**
Producer: **Philippa Campbell**
Screenplay: **Christine Jeffs**
Adaptation: **Philippa Campbell**
Based on the novel by **Kirsty Gunn**
Director of Photography: **John Toon**
Editor: **Paul Maxwell**
Art Director: **Kirsty Clayton**
Music/Music Producers:  **Neil Finn,
Edmund McWilliams**
Cast:
Alicia Fulford-Wierzbicki – Janey
Sarah Peirse – Kate
Marton Csokas – Cady
Alistair Browning – Ed
Aaron Murphy – Jim
David Taylor – Sam
Chris Sherwood – Ron
Claire Dougan – Joy
Alison Routledge – Heather
Pino Scopas – Pino
© Rain Film Productions Ltd
Production Companies:
**Rose Road, Communicado
in association with
the New Zealand Film
Commission present**
91 minutes 37 seconds
Sight and Sound: v.13, n. 8, p. 55-56
Box Office: **£9,026**
Opening Weekend: **£5,152**
Screens: **2**

### Raising Victor Vargas
Momentum Pictures – 19 September
15 France/USA 2002
Director: **Peter Sollett**
Producers:  **Alain de la Mata, Peter
Sollett, Robin O'Hara, Scott
Macaulay**
Screenplay: **Peter Sollett**
Story:  **Peter Sollett, Eva Vives**
Director of Photography: **Tim Orr**
Editor: **Myron Kerstein**
Production Designer: **Judy Becker**
Music: **Roy Nathanson, Bill Ware**
Cast:
Victor Rasuk – Victor Vargas
Judy Marte – Judy Ramirez
Melonie Diaz – Melonie
Altagracia Guzman – grandma
Silvestre Rasuk – Nino Vargas
Krystal Rodriguez – Vicki Vargas
Kevin Rivera – Harold
Wilfree Vasquez – Carlos
Donna Maldonado – Donna
Matthew Roberts – Hector
© StudioCanal
Production Companies:
**a StudioCanal production
in association with Forensic Films
Developed with the assistance of the
Sundance Institute
This film has been supported by La**

Cinéfondation and La Résidence du Festival de Cannes
87 minutes 49 seconds
Sight and Sound: v. 13, n. 11, p. 60, 62
Box Office: £238,339
Opening Weekend: £50,672
Screens: 22

## Raja Bhaiya

Spark Entertainment – 24 October
Box Office: £5,002
Opening Weekend: £3,152
Screens: 4

## Real Women Have Curves

Optimum Releasing – 31 January
12A USA 2002
Director: **Patricia Cardoso**
Producers:  **George LaVoo, Effie T. Brown**
Screenplay: **George LaVoo, Josefina Lopez**
Based on the play by
**Josefina Lopez**
Director of Photography: **Jim Denault**
Editor: **Sloane Klevin**
Production Designer: **Brigitte Broch**
Music: **Heitor Pereira**
Cast:
**America Ferrera**  – Ana García
**Lupe Ontiveros**  – Carmen, Ana's mother
**Ingrid Oliu**  – Estela
**George Lopez**  – Mr Elias Guzman, Ana's English teacher
**Brian Sites**  – Jimmy
**Jorge Cervera Jr**  – Raul
**Felipe de Alba**  – grandfather
**Soledad St. Hilaire**  – Pancha
**Lourdes Perez**  – Rosali
**José Gerardo Zamora Jr**  – Juan José
© Home Box Office
Production Companies:
**HBO Films in association with Newmarket Films
presents
a LaVoo production**
86 minutes 17 seconds
Sight and Sound: v.13, n. 2, p. 60-61
Box Office: £63,749
Opening Weekend: £17,745
Screens: 14

## The Recruit

Buena Vista International – 21 March
12A USA 2003
Director: **Roger Donaldson**
Producers:  **Roger Birnbaum, Jeff Apple, Gary Barber**
Screenplay: **Roger Towne, Kurt Wimmer, Mitch Glazer**
Director of Photography: **Stuart Dryburgh**

Editor: **David Rosenbloom**
Production Designer: **Andrew McAlpine**
Music/Score Conductor/Producer: **Klaus Badelt**
Cast:
**Al Pacino**  – Walter Burke
**Colin Farrell**  – James Clayton
**Bridget Moynahan**  – Layla Moore
**Gabriel Macht**  – Zach
**Karl Pruner**  – Dennis Slayne
**Mike Realba**  – Ronnie
**Dom Fiore**  – instructor 1
**Ron Lea**  – Bill Rudolph, Dell rep
**Jeanie Calleja**  – co-ed 1
**Jessica Greco**  – brunette at Blue Ridge
© Spyglass Entertainment Group L.P.
Production Companies:
**Touchstone Pictures and Spyglass Entertainment present a Birnbaum/Barber production**
114 minutes 52 seconds
Location: **Toronto (Canada), Washington (USA)**
Sight and Sound: v. 13, n. 4, p. 48-49
Box Office: £4,524,792
Opening Weekend: £34,928
**Screen: 1**

## Respiro

Metro Tartan – 08 August
12A Italy/France 2002
Director: **Emanuele Crialese**
Producer: **Domenico Procacci**
Screenplay: **Emanuele Crialese**
Director of Photography: **Fabio Zamarion**
Editor: **Didier Ranz**
Art Director:  **Beatrice Scarpato**
Cast:
**Muzzi Loffredo**  – grandmother
**Elio Germano**  – Pier Luigi
**Valeria Golino**  – Grazia
**Vincenzo Amato**  – Pietro
**Francesco Casisa**  – Pasquale
**Veronica D'Agostino**  – Marinella
**Filippo Pucillo**  – Filippo
**Avy Marciano**  – French cyclist
**Elio Germano**  – Pier Luigi
© Fandango/Les Films des Tournelles/Roissy Film
Production Companies:
**Domenico Procacci presents an Italian-French co-production of Fandango, Les Films des Tournelles, Roissy Films
in collaboration with Medusa Films and Tele+
supported by Eurimages
and with the participation of TPS Cinéma**
95 minutes 43 seconds
Location: **Lampedusa (Sicily, Italy)**

Sight and Sound: v.13, n. 9, p. 60, 62
Box Office: £359,413
Opening Weekend: £52,327
Screens: 38

## Revenger's Tragedy

Metro Tartan – 14 February
15 United Kingdom 2002
Director: **Alex Cox**
Producers:  **Margaret Matheson, Tod Davies**
Screenplay: **Frank Cottrell Boyce**
Based on the play by **Thomas Middleton**
Director of Photography: **Len Gowing**
Editor: **Ray Fowlis**
Production Designers:  **Cecilia Montiel, Remi Vaughan-Richards**
Music: **Chumbawamba**
Cast:
**Christopher Eccleston**  – Vindici
**Eddie Izzard**  – Lussurioso
**Derek Jacobi**  – Duke
**Kevin Knapman**  – Firework
**Michael Ryan**  – Kristopher Lundon
**Gary McKenna**  – thugs
**Joseph Cottrell Boyce**  – thugs
**Jean Butler**  – Gloriana
**Andrew Schofield**  – Carlo
**Paul Reynolds**  – Junior
**Justin Salinger**  – Ambitioso
© Revengers Ltd
Production Companies:
**The Film Council and Northcroft Films present
a Bard Entertainments production
an Exterminating Angel film
Developed with the assistance of British Screen Finance Limited
Made with the support of the Film Council New Cinema Fund**
109 minutes 24 seconds
Location: **Liverpool (UK)**
Sight and Sound: v. 13, n. 2, p. 61
Box Office: £42,278
Opening Weekend: £8,167
Screens: 7

## The Ring

United International Pictures – 21 February
15 USA 2002
Director: **Gore Verbinski**
Producers:  **Walter F. Parkes, Laurie MacDonald**
Screenplay: **Ehren Kruger**
Based on the novel by **Kôji Suzuki**
and the motion picture by
**The Ring/Spiral Production Group**
Director of Photography: **Bojan Bazelli**
Editor: **Craig Wood**
Production Designer: **Tom Duffield**
Music: **Hans Zimmer**

Cast:
Naomi Watts – Rachel Keller
Martin Henderson – Noah
David Dorfman – Aidan
Brian Cox – Richard Morgan
Jane Alexander – Dr Grasnik
Lindsay Frost – Ruth
Amber Tamblyn – Katie
Rachael Bella – Becca
Daveigh Chase – Samara
Shannon Cochran – Anna Morgan
© DreamWorks LLC
Production Companies:
**DreamWorks Pictures presents a MacDonald/Parkes production a Bender-Spink, Inc. production 115 minutes 19 seconds**
Location: **Los Angeles (CA, USA), Seattle (Washington, USA)**
Sight and Sound: **v. 13, n. 4, p. 49-50**
Box Office: **£9,675,766**
Opening Weekend: **£2,200,084**
Screens: **396**

## Ripley's Game
Entertainment – 30 May
15 USA/Italy/United Kingdom 2002
Director: **Liliana Cavani**
Producers: **Ileen Maisel, Simon Bosanquet, Riccardo Tozzi**
Screenplay: **Charles McKeown Liliana Cavani**
Based on the novel by **Patricia Highsmith**
Director of Photography: **Alfio Contini**
Editor: **Jon Harris**
Production Designer: **Francesco Frigeri**
Music: **Ennio Morricone**
Cast:
John Malkovich – Tom Ripley
Dougray Scott – Jonathan Trevanny
Ray Winstone – Reeves
Lena Headey – Sarah Trevanny
Chiara Caselli – Luisa Ripley
Sam Blitz – Matthew Trevanny
Evelina Meghnagi – Maria
Paolo Paoloni – Franco
Maurizio Luca – Franco's assistant
Yurij Rosstalnyi – Guleghin
© New Line Productions Inc
Production Companies:
**Fine Line Features present a Baby Films/Cattleya/Mr. Mudd production Pre-production financing by Freewheel International 110 minutes 19 seconds**
Location: **Hamburg (Germany), Asolo and Padua (Italy), Rome (Italy)**
Sight and Sound: **v. 13, n. 7, p. 55-56**
Box Office: **£1,011,364**

Opening Weekend: **£244,457**
Screens: **252**

## Roger Dodger
Optimum Releasing – 15 August
15 USA 2002
Director: **Dylan Kidd**
Producers: **Anne Chaisson, Dylan Kidd, George Van Buskirk**
Screenplay: **Dylan Kidd**
Director of Photography: **Joaquin Baca-Asay**
Editor: **Andy Keir**
Production Designer: **Stephen Beatrice**
Music: **Craig Wedren**
Cast:
Jennifer Beals – Sophie
Elizabeth Berkley – Andrea
Jesse Eisenberg – Nick
Isabella Rossellini – Joyce
Campbell Scott – Roger Swanson
Mina Badie – Donna
Ben Shenkman – Donovan
Chris Stack – Chris
Morena Bacarin – Rachel, girl in bar
Lisa Emery – Regina, woman in bar
© Roger Dodger, LLC
Production Company
**Holedigger Films presents 105 minutes 46 seconds**
Location: **New York (NY, USA)**
Sight and Sound: **v. 13, n. 9, p. 62-63**
Box Office: **£255,692**
Opening Weekend: **£46,319**
Screens: **15**

## Rugrats Go Wild
United International Pictures – 08 August
U USA 2003
Directors: **Norton Virgien, John Eng**
Producers: **Arlene Klasky, Gabor Csupo**
Screenplay: **Kate Boutilier**
Based on Rugrats characters created by **Arlene Klasky, Gabor Csupo, Paul Germain**
Based on the Wild Thornberrys characters created by **Arlene Klasky, Gabor Csupo, Steve Pepoon, David Silverman, Steve Sustarsic**
Editors: **John Bryant Kimberly Rettberg**
Production Designer: **Dima Malanitchev**
Music: **Mark Mothersbaugh**
Voice Cast:
E.G. Daily – Tommy Pickles
Nancy Cartwright – Chuckie Finster
Kath Soucie – Phil DeVille
Kath Soucie – Lil DeVille
Dionne Quan – Kimi Finster

Cheryl Chase – Angelica Pickles
Tim Curry – Nigel Thornberry
Joe Alaskey – Grandpa Lou
Tress MacNeille – Charlotte Pickles
Michael Bell – Drew Pickles
© Paramount Pictures Corporation/Viacom International Inc
Production Companies:
**Paramount Pictures and Nickelodeon Movies present a Klasky Csupo production 80 minutes 56 seconds**
Sight and Sound: **v.13, n. 10, p. 60, 62**
Box Office: **£3,191,900**
Opening Weekend: **£360,005**
Screens: **368**

## Rules of Attraction
Icon Film Distribution – 28 March
18 USA/Germany 2002
Director: **Roger Avary**
Producer: **Greg Shapiro**
Screenplay: **Roger Avary**
Based on the novel by **Bret Easton Ellis**
Director of Photography: **Robert Brinkmann**
Editor: **Sharon Rutter**
Production Designer: **Sharon Seymour**
Music: **Tomandandy**
Cast:
James Van Der Beek – Sean Bateman
Shannyn Sossamon – Lauren Hynde
Kip Pardue – Victor
Jessica Biel – Lara
Ian Somerhalder – Paul Denton
Clifton Collins Jr – Rupert
Thomas Ian Nicholas – Mitchell
Swoosie Kurtz – Mrs Jared
Faye Dunaway – Mrs Denton
Eric Szmanda – NYU film student
© Lions Gate Films, Inc
Production Companies:
**Lions Gate Films presents a Kingsgate Films production in association with Roger Avary Filmproduktion 110 minutes 34 seconds (original US release 24 seconds shorter)**
Location: **Southern California (USA)**
Sight and Sound: **v. 13, n. 4, p. 50, 52**
Box Office: **£1,115,711**
Opening Weekend: **£227,531**
Screens: **103**

## Rules: Pyaar Ka Superhit
Hyde Park Pictures Ltd – 19 September
Box Office: **£901**
Opening Weekend: **£359**
Screens: **3**

## Russian Ark

Artificial Eye – 04 April
U
Russia/Germany/Japan/Canada/Finl
and/Denmark
Director: **Aleksandr Sokurov**
Producers: **Andrey Deryabin, Jens
Meurer, Karsten Stöter**
Screenplay: **Anatoli Nikiforov,
Alexander Sokurov**
Dialogues: **Boris Khaimsky,
Alexander Sokurov, Svetlana
Proskurina**
Director of Photography: **Tilman
Büttner**
Editor: **Sergey Ivanov**
Visual Concept/ – Principal Image
Design: **Alexander Sokurov**
Music: **Mikhail Glinka, Peter
Tchaikovsky, G. Persella, Georg
Philipp Telemann**
Arranged/Interpreted/ – Original
Music: **Sergey Yevtushenko**
Cast:
**Sergei Dreiden** – the stranger
**Maria Kuznetsova** – Catherine the
Great
**Leonid Mozgovoy** – the spy
**Mikhail Piotrovsky** – himself
**David Giorgobiani** – Orbeli
**Alexander Chaban** – Boris
Piotrovsky
**Lev Yeliseyev** – Oleg Khmelnitsky
**Alla Osipenko** – themselves
© Hermitage Bridge Studio/Egoli
Tossell Film AG
Production Companies:
**The State Hermitage Museum
presents
a Hermitage Bridge Studio and Egoli
Tossell Film AG production
in association with
Ministry of Culture of the Russian
Federation, Department of the State
Support for Cinematography,
Mitteldeutsche Medienförderung,
Filmboard Berlin
Brandenburg,
Kulturelle Filmförderung des
Bundes, Filmförderung Hamburg,
Filmbüro Nordrhein-Westfalen,
Kulturelle Filmförderung Sachsen-
Anhalt,
WDR/ARTE, Fora-Film M, Kopp
Media, NHK, Seville Pictures Inc,
YLE/TV1, DR 1,
AST Studio,
The Mariinsky Theatre
Financial Support:
Boje Buck Production
Development supported by Media
Programme of the European Union
and Eureka**
'Twinnings'

Sponsored by Studio Babelsberg,
Pulkovo Aviation Enterprise,
Lufthansa Airlines, Hotel Astoria
(St. Petersburg)
99 minutes 12 seconds
Sight and Sound: v. 13, n. 4, p. 52-53
Box Office: £471,505
Opening Weekend: £42,463
Screens: 8

## S Club Seeing Double

Columbia TriStar – 11 April
PG United Kingdom/Spain 2003
Director: **Nigel Dick**
Producers: **Simon Fuller, Alan
Barnette**
For Media Pro: **Josep Ma. Puigvert**
Screenplay: **Kim Fuller, Paul
Alexander**
Director of Photography: **Joan Benet**
Editor: **Mark Henson**
Production Designer: **Laia Colet**
Music: **Jim Meacock**
Cast:
**Tina Barrett** – Tina
**Jon Lee** – Jon
**Bradley McIntosh** – Bradley
**Jo O'Meara** – Jo
**Hannah Spearritt** – Hannah
**Rachel Stevens** – Rachel
**David Gant** – Victor
**Joseph Adams** – Alistair
**Cristina Piaget** – Susan Sealove
**Meritxell Santamaría** – Natalie
© Double Vision Film Ltd/Media Pro
Production Companies:
**Columbia Pictures present
a 19 Entertainment production
Produced by Double Vision Film Ltd
and Media Pro**
91 minutes 6 seconds
Sight and Sound: v.13, n. 6, p. 55-56
Box Office: **£2,306,944**
Opening Weekend: £ 338,383
Screens: 395

## S.W.A.T.

Columbia Tristar – 5 December
12A USA 2003
Director: **Clark Johnson**
Producers: **Neal H. Moritz, Dan
Halsted, Chris Lee**
Screenplay: **David Ayer, David
McKenna**
Story: **Ron Mita, Jim McClain**
Based on characters created by
**Robert Hamner**
Director of Photography: **Gabriel
Beristain**
Editor: **Michael Tronick**
Production Designer: **Mayne Berke**
Music: **Elliot Goldenthal**
Cast:
**Samuel L. Jackson** – Sergeant Dan
'Hondo' Harrelson

**Colin Farrell** – Jim Street
**Michelle Rodriguez** – Chris Sanchez
**James Todd Smith aka LL Cool J** –
Deacon 'Deke' Kaye
**Josh Charles** – T.J. McCabe
**Jeremy Renner** – Brian Gamble
**Brian Van Holt** – Michael Boxer
**Olivier Martinez** – Alex Montel
**Reginald E. Cathey** – Lieutenant
Greg Velasquez
**Larry Poindexter** – Captain Thomas
Fuller
© Columbia Pictures Industries,
Inc.
Production Companies::
**Columbia Pictures presents an
Original Film /Camelot
Pictures/Chris Lee production**
117 minutes 6 seconds
Location: **LosAngeles (CA, USA)**
Sight and Sound: v. 14, n. 1, p. 60, 62
Box Office: **£5,149,101**
Opening Weekend: £1,960,281
Screens: 379

## Saaya

Spark Entertainment – 04 July
Box Office: **£10,177**
Opening Weekend: £4,420
Screens: 5

## The Safety of Objects

Entertainment – 15 August
15 United Kingdom/USA 2001
Director: **Rose Troche**
Producers: **Dorothy Berwin,
Christine Vachon**
Screenplay: **Rose Troche**
Based on the book of stories by **A.M.
Homes**
Director of Photography: **Enrique
Chediak**
Editor: **Geraldine Peroni**
Production Designer: **Andrea Stanley**
Music/Music Arranged/Performed by
**Emboznik: Barb Morrison, Charles
Nieland, Nance Nieland**
Cast:
**Glenn Close** – Esther Gold
**Dermot Mulroney** – Jim Train
**Jessica Campbell** – Julie Gold
**Patricia Clarkson** – Annette
Jennings
**Joshua Jackson** – Paul Gold
**Moira Kelly** – Susan Train
**Robert Klein** – Howard Gold
**Timothy Olyphant** – Randy
**Mary Kay Place** – Helen
Christianson
**Kristen Stewart** – Sam Jennings
© an InFilm/Killer Films production
for Renaissance Films
Production Companies:
**Renaissance Films and Clear Blue
Sky Productions present**

an InFilm/Killer Films production
120 minutes 26 seconds
Location: **Toronto (Canada), New York (NY, USA)**
Sight and Sound: **v. 13, n. 9, p. 63- 64**
Box Office: **£8,231**
Opening Weekend: **£3,682**
Screens: **4**

### Seabiscuit

Buena Vista International – 31 October
PG USA 2003
Director: **Gary Ross**
Producers: **Kathleen Kennedy, Frank Marshall, Gary Ross, Jane Sindell**
Screenplay: **Gary Ross**
Based on the book by
**Laura Hillenbrand**
Director of Photography: **John Schwartzman**
Editor: **William Goldenberg**
Production Designer: **Jeannine Oppewall**
Music: **Randy Newman**
Cast:
**Tobey Maguire** – Johnny 'Red' Pollard
**Jeff Bridges** – Charles Howard
**Chris Cooper** – Tom Smith
**Elizabeth Banks** – Marcela Howard
**Gary Stevens** – George 'The Iceman' Woolf
**William H. Macy** – 'Tick-Tock' McGlaughlin
**Kingston DuCoeur** – Sam
**Eddie Jones** – Samuel Riddle
**Ed Lauter** – Charles Strub
**Michael O'Neill** – Mr Pollard
© Universal Studios/DreamWorks LLC/Spyglass Entertainment Group, L.P.
Production Companies:
**Spyglass Entertainment, Universal Pictures, DreamWorks Pictures present a Larger Than Life, Kennedy/Marshall production
A Gary Ross film**
140 minutes 39 seconds
Location: **California (USA), New York (NY, USA), Kentucky (USA)**
Sight and Sound: **v. 13, n. 12, p. 50-51**
Box Office: **£3,029,887**
Opening Weekend: **£62,242**
Screens: **15**

### Secondhand Lions

Entertainment – 24 October
PG USA 2003
Director: **Tim McCanlies**
Producers: **David Kirschner, Scott Ross, Corey Sienega**
Screenplay: **Tim McCanlies**
Director of Photography: **Jack Green**
Editor: **David Moritz**

Production Designer: **David J. Bomba**
Music: **Patrick Doyle**
Cast:
**Michael Caine** – Garth McCann
**Robert Duvall** – Hubbard 'Hub' McCann
**Haley Joel Osment** – Walter
**Nicky Katt** – Stan
**Kyra Sedgwick** – Mae, Walter's mother
**Michael O'Neill** – Ralph
**Deirdre O'Connell** – Helen
**Christian Kane** – young Hub
**Eric Balfour** – Sheik's grandson
**Emmanuelle Vaugier** – Jasmine
© New Line Productions, Inc.
Production Companies:
**New Line Cinema presents a David Kirschner production in association with Digital Domain Productions**
108 minutes 39 seconds
Location: **Austin (Texas)**
Sight and Sound: **v. 13, n. 12, p. 51-52**
Box Office: **£766,704**
Opening Weekend: **£200,851**
Screens: **260**

### Secretary

Metro Tartan – 16 May
18 USA 2002
Director: **Steven Shainberg**
Producers: **Steven Shainberg, Andrew Fierberg, Amy Hobby**
Screenplay: **Erin Cressida Wilson**
Story adapted by **Steven Shainberg Erin Cressida Wilson**
Based on the short story by **Mary Gaitskill**
Director of Photography: **Steven Fierberg**
Editor: **Pam Wise**
Production Designer: **Amy Danger**
Music: **Angelo Badalamenti**
Cast:
**James Spader** – E. Edward Grey
**Maggie Gyllenhaal** – Lee Holloway
**Jeremy Davies** – Peter
**Patrick Bauchau** – Dr Twardon
**Stephen McHattie** – Burt Holloway
**Oz Perkins** – Jonathan
**Jessica Tuck** – Tricia O'Connor
**Amy Locane** – Lee's sister
**Lesley Ann Warren** – Joan Holloway
**Mary Joy** – Sylvia
© Secretary Productions, LLC
Production Companies:
**The Slough Pond Company presents a double A films production in association with TwoPoundBag Productions**
111 minutes 11 seconds
Sight and Sound: **v. 13, n. 6, p. 54-55**
Box Office: **£1,063,088**

Opening Weekend: **£165,318**
Screens: **30**

### Sex is Comedy

Artificial Eye – 25 July
18 France 2002
Director: **Catherine Breillat**
Producer: **Jean-François Lepetit**
Screenplay: **Catherine Breillat**
Director of Photography: **Laurent Machuel**
Editor: **Pascale Chavance**
Art Director: **Frédérique Belvaux**
Music Supervisors :
**Pascale Chavance, Pedro Marques**
Cast:
**Anne Parillaud** – Jeanne
**Grégoire Colin** – the actor
**Roxane Mesquida** – the actress
**Ashley Wanninger** – Léo
**Dominique Colladant** – Willy
**Bart Binnema**
Director of Photography: **Yves Osmu**
Sound engineer: **Francis Seleck**
Production manager **Elisabete Piecho**
Continuity girl Diane Scapa
Art Director:
© Flach Film/CB Films/Arte France Cinéma
Production Companies:
**a Flach Film - CB Films production an Arte France Cinéma co-production in association with France Télévision Images 2 with the participation of Canal+ and the Centre National de la Cinématographie**
94 minutes 43 seconds
Location: **Portugal**
Sight and Sound: **v. 13, n. 8, p. 56, 58**
Box Office: **£24,865**
Opening Weekend: **£6,690**
Screens: **5**

### Shanghai Knights

Buena Vista International – 04 April
12A USA 2003
Director: **David Dobkin**
Producers: **Roger Birnbaum
Gary Barber, Jonathan Glickman**
Screenplay: **Alfred Gough, Miles Millar**
Based on characters created by
**Alfred Gough, Miles Millar**
Director of Photography: **Adrian Biddle**
Editor: **Malcolm Campbell**
Production Designer: **Allan Cameron**
Music/Orchestra Conductor:
**Randy Edelman**
Cast:
**Jackie Chan** – Chon Wang
**Owen Wilson** – Roy O'Bannon
**Aaron Johnson** – Charlie
**Thomas Fisher** – Artie Doyle

Aidan Gillen – Rathbone
Wong Fann – Chon Lin
Donnie Yen – Wu Chan
Oliver Cotton – Jack the Ripper
Alissa King – prostitute
Constantine Gregory – the mayor
© Spyglass Entertainment Group L.P.
Production Companies:
**Touchstone Pictures and Spyglass
Entertainment present a
Birnbaum/Barber production
in association with
A Jackie Chan Films Limited
production**
114 minutes 23 seconds
Location: **London (UK)**
Sight and Sound: v. 13, n. 5, p. 60
Box Office: £2,310,348
Opening Weekend: £749,655
Screens: 371

## Shape of Things

Momentum Pictures – 28 November
15 USA/France 2003
Director: **Neil LaBute**
Producers: **Neil LaBute, Gail
Mutrux, Philip Steuer, Rachel Weisz**
Screenplay: **Neil LaBute**
Based on his stage play
Director of Photography: **James L.
Carter**
Editor: **Joel Plotch**
Art Direction: **Lynette Meyer**
Music Supervisor: **Nick Angel**
Cast:
Gretchen Mol – Jenny
Paul Rudd – Adam
Rachel Weisz – Evelyn
Frederick Weller – Philip
William Calvert – Thomas Brunelle
– Moosie Drier – Jennifer Crystal
Foley – Sierra French-Myerson –
Lara Harris – Jessie S. Marion –
voice-overs
Production Companies:
**Focus Features and StudioCanal
present a Working Title production
in association with Pretty Pictures**
96 minutes 59 seconds
Location: **New York (NY, USA)**
Sight and Sound: v. 14, n. 1, p. 57-58
Box Office: £52,484
Opening Weekend: £17,986
Screens: 15

## Shiri

Metro Tartan – 02 May
18 Republic of Korea 1999
Director: **Kang JeGyu**
Producers: **Lee Kwan-hak, Byun
Moo-rim**
Screenplay: **P`ark Je-hyun
Paek Woon-hak, Jeon Yoon-soo**
Original Story: **Kang JeGyu**
Director of Photography: **Kim Sung-**

bok
Editor: **Park Kok-ji**
Art Directors: **Park Il-ryun, Oh Sang-
man**
Music: **Lee Dong-jun**
Cast:
Han Suk-kyu – Ryu Jung-won
Choi Min-sik – Park Mu-young
Song Kang-ho – Lee Jung-gil
Kim Yun-jin – Lee Myung-hyun
Yun Ju-sang – Ko Jung-suk
Park Yong-woo – Er Sung-sik
Park Eun-sook – Lee Bang-hee
Cho Duck-hyun – Lee Won-doo
Park Jong-moon – Bae Won-sik
Jung Jin-oh – Park Yong-snag
Production Companies:
**Samsung Pictures present a
KangJeGyu Films production
Co-investor KTFC**
125 minutes
Sight and Sound: v. 13, n. 6, p. 56
Box Office: £16,797
Opening Weekend: £3,516
Screens: 3

## Shoreditch

Georgia Films – 28 November
15 United Kingdom 2002
Director: **Malcolm Needs**
Producer: **Malcolm Needs**
Screenplay: **Malcolm Needs**
Director of Photography: **Zoran
Veljkovic**
Editor: **Henry Richardson**
Production Designers: **– Andrea
Christelis, Johnny Hawkins**
Jazz Club:**Tracy Ann-Baines**
Music: **Rick Taylor, Steve Brown**
Cast:
Joely Richardson – Butterfly
Shane Richie – Thomas Hickman
Glen Murphy – Albert Challis
John Standing – Jenson Thackery
Natasha Wightman – Maisie
Hickman
Jonathan Coy – Karl
Adam Ross – Tom Hickman
Brian Bovell – Chad
Joe Shaw – William Nichols
Claire Tyler – Abigail
© Aquarius Film Company/Mother
Meighan Productions
Limited/Movietrack
Pictures Limited
Production Companies::
**Aquarius Film Company
in co-production with Mother
Meighan Productions Limited and
Movietrack Pictures Limited
presents
a film by Malcolm Needs**
100 minutes 35 seconds
Sight and Sound: v.14, n. 2, p. 58-59

Box Office: £2,272
Opening Weekend: £1,240
Screens: 2

## Sin Eater

Twentieth Century Fox – 12
September
15 Germany/USA 2003
Director: **Brian Helgeland**
Producers: **Brian Helgeland, Craig
Baumgarten**
Screenplay: **Brian Helgeland**
Director of Photography: **Nicola
Pecorini**
Editor: **Kevin Stitt**
Production Designer: **Miljen 'Kreka'
Kljakovic**
Music: **David Torn**
Cast:
Heath Ledger – Alex Bernier
Shannyn Sossamon – Mara Sinclair
Mark Addy – Thomas Garrett
Benno Fürmann – William Eden,
the sin eater
Peter Weller – Cardinal Driscoll
Francesco Carnelutti – Dominic
Mattia Sbragia – apathetic bishop
Mirko Casaburo
little boy
Giulia Lombardi – little girl
Richard Bremmer – bookstore
owner
© N1 European Film Produktions
GmbH & Co. KG/Twentieth Century
Fox Film Corporation
Production Companies:
**Twentieth Century Fox presents a
Baumgarten Merims production
In association with
N1 European Film Produktions
GmbH & Co. KG**
102 minutes 12 seconds
Location: **Italy**
Sight and Sound: v. 13, n. 11, p. 62-63
Box Office: £321,517
Opening Weekend: £161,779
Screens: 160

## Sinbad

United International Pictures – 25
July
U USA 2003
Directors: **Tim Johnson, Patrick
Gilmore**
Producers: **Mireille Soria, Jeffrey
Katzenberg**
Screenplay: **John Logan**
Story:
**Éric `Bibo' Bergeron, Serguei
Kouchnerov,Sharon Bridgeman,
Denise Nagisa Koyama, Jurgen Gross
Rob Porter, Rodolphe Guenoden,
Jeff Snow, Simon Wells**
Editor: **Tom Finan**
Production Designer: **Raymond**

Zibach
Music: **Harry Gregson-Williams**
Voice Cast:
**Brad Pitt** – Sinbad
**Catherine Zeta-Jones** – Marina
**Michelle Pfeiffer** – Eris
**Joseph Fiennes** – Proteus
**Dennis Haysbert** – Kale
**Timothy West** – Dymas
**Adriano Giannini** – Rat
**Raman Hui** – Jin
**Jim Cummings** – Luca
**Conrad Vernon** – Jed
© DreamWorks LLC
Production Company
DreamWorks Pictures presents
**85 minutes 15 seconds**
Sight and Sound: v. 13, n. 10, p. 62-63
Box Office: £2,784,261
Opening Weekend: £828,550
Screens: **392**

## The Singing Detective
Icon Film Distribution – 14
November
15 USA 2003
Director: **Keith Gordon**
Producers: **Mel Gibson**
**Steven Haft**
**Bruce Davey**
Screenplay: **Dennis Potter**
Based upon the television series by
Dennis Potter
Director of Photography: **Tom Richmond**
Editor: **Jeff Wishengrad**
Production Designer: **Patricia Norris**
Music Supervisor: **Ken Weiss**
Cast:
**Robert Downey Jr** – Dan Dark
**Robin Wright Penn** –
Nicola/Nina/blonde
**Jeremy Northam** – Mark Binney
**Katie Holmes** – Nurse Mills
**Carla Gugino** – Betty Dark/hooker
**Adrien Brody** – 1st hood
**Jon Polito** – 2nd hood
**Saul Rubinek** – skin specialist
**Amy Aquino** – Nurse Nozhki
**David Dorfman** – young Dan Dark
© Icon Distribution, LLC
Production Companies:
**Icon Productions presents a Haft
Entertainment production
Annction**
**108 minutes 51 seconds**
Location: **Los Angeles (CA, USA)**
Sight and Sound: v. 14, n. 1, p. 58-59
Box Office: £61,728
Opening Weekend: £24,958
Screens: **30**

## Snake of June
Metro Tartan – 13 June
18 Japan 2002

Director: **Shinya Tsukamoto**
Producer: **Shinya Tsukamoto**
Screenplay: **Shinya Tsukamoto**
Director of Photography: **Shinya Tsukamoto**
Editor: **Shinya Tsukamoto**
Set Designer: **Shinya Tsukamoto**
Music: **Chu Ishikawa**
Cast:
**Asuka Kurosawa** – Rinko
**Yuji Koutari** – Shigehiko
**Shinya Tsukamoto** – Iguchi
**Susumu Terajima** – Mansaku Fuwa
**Tomoro Taguchi**
© Kaijyu Theater/Tsukamoto Shinya
Production Company
**a Kaijyu Theatre production**
**76 minutes 54 seconds**
Sight and Sound: v. 13, n. 7, p. 56-57
Box Office: £15,219
Opening Weekend: £3,628
Screens: **3**

## Solaris
20th Century Fox – 28 February
12A USA 2002
Director: **Steven Soderbergh**
Producers: **James Cameron, Rae Sanchini, Jon Landau**
Screenplay: **Steven Soderbergh**
Based on the book by
**Stanislaw Lem**
Director of Photography: **Peter Andrews**
[i.e. Steven Soderbergh]
Editor: **Mary Ann Bernard**
[i.e. Steven Soderbergh]
Production Design: **Philip Messina**
Music: **Cliff Martinez**
Cast:
**George Clooney** – Chris Kelvin
**Natascha McElhone** – Rheya
**Jeremy Davies** – Snow
**Viola Davis** – Gordon
**Ulrich Tukur** – Gibarian
**John Cho** – DBA emissaries
**Morgan Rusler** – DBA emissaries
**Shane Skelton** – Gibarian's son
**Michael Ensign** – Elpidia Carrillo
friends
**Kent D. Faulcon** – Lauren M. Cohn
patients
© Twentieth Century Fox Film
Corporation [all territories except
Brazil, Italy, Korea, Japan, Spain]
© TCF Hungary Film Rights
Exploitation Limited Liability
Company/Twentieth Century Fox
Film Corporation [Brazil, Italy,
Korea, Japan, Spain]
Production Companies:
**a Twentieth Century Fox
presentation**
**a Lightstorm Entertainment**

production
**98 minutes 26 seconds**
Location: **Los Angeles (CA, USA)**
Sight and Sound: v. 13, n. 3, p. 54-55
Box Office: £910,591
Opening Weekend: £313,804
Screens: **153**

## The Son  (Le Fils)
Artificial Eye – 14 March
12A Belgium/France 2002
Directors: **Jean-Pierre Dardenne, Luc Dardenne**
Producers: **Jean-Pierre Dardenne, Luc Dardenne, Denis Freyd**
Screenplay: **Jean-Pierre Dardenne, Luc Dardenne**
Director of Photography: **Alain Marcoen**
Editor: **Marie-Hélène Dozo**
Art Director: **Igor Gabriel**
Cast:
**Olivier Gourmet** – Olivier
**Morgan Marinne** – Francis Thirion
**Isabelle Soupart** – Magali
**Nassim Hassaïni** – Omar
**Kevin Leroy** – Raoul
**Félicien Pitsaer** – Steve
**Remy Renaud** – Philippo
**Annette Closset** – Catherine,
training centre director
**Fabian Marnette** – Rino
© Les Films du Fleuve/Archipel
35/RTBF (Télévision belge)
Production Companies:
**Jean-Pierre and Luc Dardenne,
Denis Freyd present
Les Films du Fleuve, Archipel 35,
RTBF (Télévision belge)**
with the support of Centre du
Cinéma et de l'Audiovisuel de la
Communauté française de Belgique
and Télédistributeurs wallons,
Eurimages, la Loterie nationale de
Belgique
with the participation of Canal+,
Centre National de la
Cinématographie,
Wallimage
**103 minutes 45 seconds**
Sight and Sound: v. 13, n. 3, p. 55
Box Office: £39,716
Opening Weekend: £5,457
Screens: **2**

## Son of the Bride
Pathé Distribution – 23 May
15 Argentina/Spain 2001
Director: **Juan José Campanella**
Producers: **Gerardo Herrero, Adrián Suar**
Screenplay: **Fernando Castets, Juan José Campanella**
Director of Photography: **Daniel Shulman**

Editor: **Camilo Antolini**
Art Director: **Mercedes Alfonsín**
Music: **Ángel Illarramendi**
Cast:
**Ricardo Darín** – Rafael Belvedere
**Héctor Alterio** – Nino Belvedere
**Norma Aleandro** – Norma
Belvedere
**Eduardo Blanco** – Juan Carlos
**Natalia Verbeke** – Naty
**Gimena Nobile** – Vicky
**David Masajnik** – Nacho
**Claudia Fontán** – Sandra
**Atilio Pozzobón** – Francesco
**Salo Pasik** – Daniel
© Pol-Ka Producciones
S.A./Patagonik Film
Group/JEMPSA/Tornasol Films
Production Companies:
**a Pol-Ka Producciones, Jempsa,**
**Patagonik Film Group, Tornasol**
**Films production**
**with the collaboration of Vía Digital**
**Supported by INCAA and ICAA**
125 minutes 7 seconds
Sight and Sound: **v. 13, n. 6, p. 57**
Box Office: **£138,433**
Opening Weekend: **£23,955**
Screens: **16**

## Song for a Raggy Boy
**Abbey Home Entertainment** – 17
October
15 Ireland/Denmark/Spain/United
Kingdom2003
Director: **Aisling Walsh**
Producers: **Tristan Orpen-Lynch,**
**Dominic Wright, John McDonnell**
**Kevin Byron-Murphy**
Based on the book and screenplay by
**Patrick Galvin**
Director of Photography: **Peter**
**Robertson**
Editor: **BryanOates**
Production Designer: **John Hand**
Music/Music
Conductor/Orchestrator: **Richard**
**Blackford**
Cast:
**Aidan Quinn** – William Franklin
**Iain Glen** – Brother John
**Marc Warren** – Brother Mac
**Dudley Sutton** – Brother Tom
**Alan Devlin** – Sather Demian
**Stuart Graham** – Brother Whelan
**John Travers** – Liam Mercier 636
**Chris Newman** – Patrick Delaney
743
**Andrew Simpson** – Gerard Peters
458
**Mark Butler** – Downey 913
© Subotica
Entertainment/Moviefan/Lolafilms/Z
oma

Production Companies::
**Lolafilms presents a Subotica**
**Entertainment productionin**
**association with**
**Moviefan (Denmark), Zoma (UK),**
**Lolafilms (Spain) and Bord Scánnan**
**na hhÉireann/The Irish Film Board,**
**Eurimages, Danish Film Institute,**
**Fantastic Films, Titan Red Pictures**
**In association with Invicta Limited**
**and AngloIrish Bank**
**Produced with the support of**
**investment incentives for the Irish**
**Film Industry provided by the**
**Government of Ireland**
**Developed with the support of the**
**MEDIA Programme of the European**
**Union**
**Supported by Bord Scannán na**
**hÉireann/The Irish Film Institute**
**(Morten Grunwald)**
**A film by Aisling Walsh**
97 minutes 28 seconds
Location: **Ballyvourney, Co. Cork**
**(Ireland), Co. Kerry (Ireland)**
Sight and Sound: **v. 14, n. 5, p. 73**
Box Office: **£479,243**
Opening Weekend: **£88,324**
Screens: **37**

## Spellbound
**Metrodome Distributors** – 10
October
U USA 2002
Director: **Jeffrey Blitz**
Producers: **Jeffrey Blitz, Sean Welch**
Camera: **Jeffrey Blitz**
Editor: **Yana Gorskaya**
Music: **Daniel Hulsizer**
With
**Angela Arenivar** – Ubaldo Arenivar
– Angela's father
**Jorge Arenivar** – Angela's brother
**Mr & Mrs McGarraugh** ranch
owners
**Concepción** – Arenivar Angela's
mother
**Mrs Slaughter** – Angela's teacher
**Neelima** – Potter County Champion
© Jeff Blitz
Production Companies:
**a Blitz/Welch picture**
**major funding for Spellbound**
**provided by The Pacific Pioneer**
**Fund, Andy Blitz**
**this project sponsored by**
**International Documentary**
**Association**
**Film Arts Foundation (San**
**Francisco)**
96 minutes 40 seconds
Sight and Sound: **v. 13, n. 11, p. 63**
Box Office: **£440,505**
Opening Weekend: **£57,735**

Screens: **13**

## Spider
**Redbus** – 03 January
15 Canada/United Kingdom/Japan
2002
Director: **David Cronenberg**
Producers: **David Cronenberg,**
**Samuel Hadida, Catherine Bailey**
Screenplay: **Patrick McGrath**
Based on his novel
Director of Photography: **Peter**
**Suschitzky**
Editor: **Ronald Sanders**
Production Designer: **Andrew**
**Sanders**
Music/Music
Conductor/Orchestrator: **Howard**
**Shore**
Cast:
**Ralph Fiennes** – Spider
**Miranda Richardson** – Yvonne/Mrs
Cleg/
Mrs Wilkinson
**Gabriel Byrne** – Bill Cleg
**John Neville** – Terrence
**Bradley Hall** – Boy Spider
**Lynn Redgrave** – Mrs Wilkinson
**Gary Reineke** – Freddy
**Philip Craig** – John
**Cliff Saunders** – Bob
**Tara Ellis** – Nora
© Spider Productions Limited/Spider
Films Limited
Production Companies:
**Capitol Films and Artists**
**Independent Network present in**
**association with Odeon Films and**
**Media Suits**
**a Catherine Bailey/**
**Davis Films/Artists Independent**
**Network/Grosvenor Park**
**production**
**Produced with the participation of**
**Telefilm Canada**
**With the assistance of Canada  The**
**Canadian Film or Video Production**
**Tax Credit**
**Pre-production financing provided**
**by Freewheel International**
98 minutes 29 seconds
Location: **London (UK), Toronto**
**(Canada)**
Sight and Sound: **v. 13, n. 1, p. 52-53**
Box Office: **£326,414**
Opening Weekend: **£64,083**
Screens: **19**

## Spin the Bottle
**Buena Vista International** – 28
November
Box Office: **£339,001**
Opening Weekend: **£95,533**
Screens: **37**

## The Spirit of the Beehive (Re)
Optimum Releaseing – 19 September
Box Office: £17,933
Opening Weekend: £4,624
Screen: 1

## Spirited Away
Optimum Releasing – 12 September
PG Japan 2001
Director: Hayao Miyazaki
Producer: Toshio Suzuki
Screenplay: Hayao Miyazaki
Editor: Takeshi Seyama
Art Director: Yoji Takeshige
Music/Music Conductor/Piano Solos
Joe Hisaishi
Voice Cast:
Rumi Hiiragi – Chihiro
Miyu Irino – Haku
Mari Natsuki – Yubaba/Zeniba
Takashi Naito – Akio, Chihiro's father
Yasuko Sawaguchi – Yugo, Chihiro's mother
Tatsuya Gashuin – Frog man
Yumi Tamai – Lin
Yo Oizumi – foreman of the frog men
Koba Hayashi – River God
Tsunehiko Kamijo – school principal
© Nibariki TGNDDTM
Production Companies:
Tokuma Shoten, Studio Ghibli, Nippon Television Network, Dentsu, Buena Vista Home Entertainment, Tohokushinsha Film and Mitsubishi present
124 minutes 53 seconds
Sight and Sound: v. 13, n. 9, p. 34-35, 64
Box Office: £932,453
Opening Weekend: £152,504
Screens: 51

## Springtime in a Small Town
Artificial Eye – 13 June
PG China/Hong Kong/France 2002
Director: Tian Zhuangzhuang
Producers: Li Xiaowan, Bill Kong, Ting Yatming
Screenplay: Ah Cheng
Based on the story: by
Li Tianji and on the 1948 screenplay by Fei Mu
Director of Photography: Mark Lee Pingbin
Editor: Xu Jianping
Production Designer: Cheng Guangming
Music: Zhao Li
Cast:

Hu Jingfan – Yuwen, the wife
Wu Jun – Dai Liyan, the husband
Xin Baiqing – Zhang Zhichen, the visitor
Ye Xiaokeng – Lao Huang, the retainer
Lu Sisi – Dai Xiu, the sister
© Glory Top Properties
Production Companies:
Produced by China Film Group Corporation-Beijing Film Studio, Beijing ROSAT
Film-TV Production Co. Ltd, Glory Top Properties Limited, Beijing Beida
Culture Development Co., Ltd
In association with Fortissimo Film Sales, Paradis Films, Orly Films
116 minutes 33 seconds
Sight and Sound: v. 13, n. 7, p. 57
Box Office: £138,197
Opening Weekend: £14,631
Screens: 5

## Spun
Pathe Distribution Ltd – 28 November
18 USA/United Kingdom/France 2002
Director: Jonas Åkerlund
Producers: Chris Hanley, Fernando Sulichin, Timothy Wayne Peternel
Danny Vinik
Screenplay: Will De Los Santos
Creighton Vero
Director of Photography: Eric Broms
Editors: Jonas Åkerlund
with
Johan Söderberg
Production Design: Richard Lassalle
Music: Billy Corgan
Cast:
Jason Schwartzman – Ross
John Leguizamo – Spider Mike
Mena Suvari – Cookie
Patrick Fugit – Frisbee
Peter Stormare – mullet cop
Alexis Arquette – moustache cop
Deborah Harry – neighbour
Eric Roberts – the man
Chloe Hunter – April Love
Nicholas Gonzalez – Angel
© Spun Productions Inc.
Production Companies::
Silver Nitrate presents in association with Amuse Pictures/Little Magic Films & Sagittaire Films a Muse/Blacklist production in association with Brink Films, Petterson Akerlund & Stone Canyon Entertainment
101 minutes 3 seconds
Sight and Sound: v. 14, n. 1, p. 59-60
Box Office: £126,142

Opening Weekend: £50,201
Screens: 48

## Spy Kids 3D Game Over
Buena Vista International – 01 August
U USA 2003
Director: Robert Rodriguez
Producers: Elizabeth Avellán, Robert Rodriguez
Screenplay: Robert Rodriguez
Director of Photography: Robert Rodriguez
Editor: Robert Rodriguez
Art Director: : Jeanette Scott
Music: Robert Rodriguez
Cast:
Antonio Banderas – Gregorio Cortez
Carla Gugino – Ingrid Cortez
Alexa Vega – Carmen Cortez
Daryl Sabara – Juni Cortez
Ricardo Montalban – grandfather
Holland Taylor – grandmother
Mike Judge – Donnagon Giggles
Matt O'Leary – Gary Giggles
Emily Osment – Gerti Giggles
Cheech Marin – Felix Gumm
© Miramax Film Corp.
Production Company
a Robert Rodriguez digital file
84 minutes 15 seconds
Sight and Sound: v. 13, n. 10, p. 63-64
Box Office: £7,259,036
Opening Weekend: £979,374
Screens: 377

## Ssshhh
Eros International Ltd – 24 October
Box Office: £6,134
Opening Weekend: £1,186
Screens: 3

## Standing in Shadows of Motown
Momentum Pictures – 25 July
PG USA 2002
Director: Paul Justman
Producers: Sandy Passman
Allan Slutsky, Paul Justman
Narration Written by Walter Dallas, Ntozake Shange
Inspired by the book by
Allan 'Dr. Licks' Slutsky
Directors of Photography:
Doug Milsome, Lon Stratton
Editor: Anne Erikson
Production Designer: Rolfe Bergsman
Underscore Composers:
Evan Solot, Mick Rossi, Allan Slutsky
Cast:
Alex Alexander – young Marvin Gaye
Donald Becks Jr – young Uriel

Jones
Gary Bosek – young Bob Babbitt
Michael Ellison – young Benny Benjamin
Otis Lockhart – young Robert White
Brian Marable – young James Jamerson
Antoine McKay – young Jack Ashford
Mark Mutafian – young studio musician
Antonio Ramirez – young Eddie Willis
Kevin Smith – young Joe Hunter
© Elliott Scott Productions LLC
Production Companies:
Artisan Entertainment presents an Elliott Scott/Rimshot production
108 minutes 3 seconds
Sight and Sound: v. 13, n. 8, p. 58-59
Box Office: £78,165
Opening Weekend: £9,444
Screens: 5

## Star Trek X: Nemesis

United International Pictures – 03 January
12A USA 2002
Director: **Stuart Baird**
Producer: **Rick Berman**
Screenplay: **John Logan**
Story:
**John Logan, Rick Berman, Brent Spiner**
Based on Star Trek created by
**Gene Roddenberry**
Director of Photography: **Jeffrey L. Kimball**
Editor: **Dallas Puett**
Production Designer: **Herman Zimmerman**
Music/Orchestra Conductor:
**Jerry Goldsmith**
Cast:
Patrick Stewart – Jean-Luc Picard
Jonathan Frakes – William Riker
Brent Spiner – Data/B-4
LeVar Burton – Geordi La Forge
Michael Dorn – Worf
Marina Sirtis – Deanna Troi
Gates McFadden – Beverly Crusher
Tom Hardy – Shinzon
Ron Perlman – Viceroy
Shannon Cochran – Senator Tal'aura
© Paramount Pictures
Production Company
Paramount Pictures presents a Rick Berman production
116 minutes 31 seconds
Location: **Losa Angeles (CA, USA)**
Sight and Sound: v. 13, n. 2, p. 61-62
Box Office: £4,776,455

Opening Weekend: £1,957,845
Screens: 426

## Stark Raving Mad

Redbus – 24 January
15 USA 2002
Directors: **Drew Daywalt, David Schneider**
Producer: **John Baldecchi**
Screenplay: **Drew Daywalt, David Schneider**
Concept: **Drew Daywalt, Patrick Kiely, David Schneider**
Director of Photography: **Chuck Cohen**
Editor: **Hughes Winborne**
Production Designer: **Keith Brian Burns**
Music: **John Digweed**
**Nick Muir**
Cast:
Seann William Scott – Ben McGewan
Patrick Breen – Jeffrey Jay
Terry Chen – Jin Sun
John Crye – Jake Nealson
Dave Foley – Roy
Paul Hungerford – Scott
Monet Mazur – Vanessa
Suzi Nakamura – Betty Shin
Reagan Dale Neis – Kitten
Timmi Sharp – Rikki Simms
© Raving Mad Productions, LLC
Production Companies:
Newmarket presents in association with Summit Entertainment
a Lawrence Bender production
a Dave & Drew film
100 minutes 51 seconds
Location: **Vancouver (British Columbia, Canada)**
Sight and Sound: v. 13, n. 4, p. 53-54
Box Office: £621
Opening Weekend: £351
Screen: 1

## Steal

Redbus – 21 November
15 Canada/France/United Kingdom 2002
Director: **Gérard Pirès**
Producers: **Éric Altmayer, Nicolas Altmayer, Claude Léger, Jason Piette**
**Michael Lionello Cowan**
Screenplay: **Mark Ezra**
Director of Photography: **Tetsuo Nagata**
Editor: **Véronique Lange**
Production Designer: **Guy Lalande**
Music: **Andy Gray**
Cast:
Stephen Dorff – Slim
Natasha Henstridge – Karen
Bruce Payne – Lieutenant Magruder
Steven Berkoff – Surtayne

Karen Cliche – Alex
Clé Bennett – Otis
Steven McCarthy – Frank
Tom McCamus – creep
Alain Goulem – Pandelis
Andreas Apergis – Nixdorfer
© Filmguard Productions (Heist) Inc./Mandarin S.A./Spice Factory (Heist) Limited
Production Companies::
A Transfilm-Mandarin-Spice Factory production
in association with Future Film Financing Limited and Téléfilm Canada
A Gerard Pirès film
84 minutes 15 seconds
Location: **Montreal (Canada)**
Sight and Sound: v. 14, n. 2, p. 59-60
Box Office: £40,331
Opening Weekend: £23,372
Screens: 51

## Stealing Harvard

Columbia TriStar – 14 March
12A USA 2002
Director: **Bruce McCulloch**
Producer: **Susan Cavan**
Screenplay: **Peter Tolan**
Story: **Martin Hynes, Peter Tolan**
Director of Photography: **Ueli Steiger**
Editor: **Malcolm Campbell**
Production Designer: **Gregory Keen**
Music/Score Producer: **Christophe Beck**
Cast:
Tom Green – Duff
Jason Lee – John Plummer
Leslie Mann – Elaine
Megan Mullally – Patty
Dennis Farina – Mr Warner
Richard Jenkins – Mr Cook
John C. McGinley – Detective Charles
Chris Penn – David Loach
Seymour Cassel – Uncle Jack
Tammy Blanchard – Noreen
© Revolution Studios Distribution Company LLC
Production Companies:
Revolution Studios and Imagine Entertainment present
85 minutes 19 seconds
Location: **Los Angeles (CA,USA)**
Sight and Sound: v. 13, n. 5, p. 62
Box Office: £16,754
Opening Weekend: £11,690
Screens: 48

## Summer Things

UGC Films – 20 June
15 France/United Kingdom/Italy 2002
Director: **Michel Blanc**
Producer: **Yves Marmion**

Scenario/Adaptation/ – Dialogue:
**Michel Blanc**
Based on the novel Summer
Things/Vacances anglaises **by Joseph
Connolly**
Director of Photography: **Sean
Bobbitt**
Editor: **Maryline Monthieux**
Art Director: **Benoît Barouh**
Music/Music Arranger/ –
Orchestrator: **Mark Russell**
Cast:
**Charlotte Rampling** – Elisabeth
Lannier
**Jacques Dutronc** – Bertrand
Lannier
**Carole Bouquet** – Lulu
**Michel Blanc** – Jean-Pierre
**Karin Viard** – Véronique, 'Véro'
**Denis Podalydès** – Jérôme
**Clotilde Courau** – Julie
**Vincent Elbaz** – Maxime
**Lou Doillon** – Emilie
**Sami Bouajila** – Kevin
© UGC YM/UGC Images/Mercury
Film Productions/Alia Film/France 2
Cinéma
Production Companies:
**UGC presents**
**UGC YM, UGC Images, Mercury
Film Productions, Dan Films, Alia
Film, France 2 Cinéma**
This film was supported by
Eurimages
With the participation of Canal+,
sofica
Sofinergie 5
In partnership with Le Conseil
Général du Pas de Calais
and with the aid of CRRAV de la
Région Nord/Pas de Calais
With the participation of
TPS/Multivision, Kiosque
103 minutes 26 seconds
Location: **Le Touquet and Paris
(France)**
Sight and Sound: v. 13, n. 7, p. 58
Box Office: £132,238
Opening Weekend: £27,609
Screens: **13**

## Sunset Boulevard (Re)
BFI – 14 March
Box Office: £51,231
Opening Weekend: £6,906
Screens: **2**

## Supari
Bollywood Films – 20 June
Box Office: £6,853
Opening Weekend: £3,971
Screens: **6**

## Swimming Pool
UGC Films – 22 August

15 France/United Kingdom 2002
Director: **François Ozon**
Producers: **Olivier Delbosc, Marc
Missonnier**
Screenplay: **François Ozon**
With the collaboration of
**Emmanuèle Bernheim**
Director of Photography: **Yorick Le
Saux**
Editor: **Monica Coleman**
Art Director: **Wouter Zoon**
Music/Original Score
Conductor/Orchestrator: **Philippe
Rombi**
Cast:
**Charlotte Rampling** – Sarah
Morton
**Ludivine Sagnier** – Julie
**Charles Dance** – John Bosload
**Marc Fayolle** – Marcel
**Jean-Marie Lamour** – Franck
**Mireille Mossé** – Marcel's daughter
**Michel Fau** – men
**Jean-Claude Lecas** – men
**Emilie Gavois Kahn** – waitress at
café
**Erarde Forestali** – old man
**Lauren Farrow** – Julia
© Fidélité/Headforce Limited/France
2 Cinéma/Gimages Films/Foz
Production Companies:
**Fidélité presents**
**a co-production with France 2
Cinéma, Gimages Films, Foz
in association with Headforce
Limited
with the participation of Canal+**
102 minutes 41 seconds
Sight and Sound: v. 13, n. 10, p. 64, 66
Box Office: £713,821
Opening Weekend: £119,092
Screens: **37**

## Sympathy For Mr. Vengeance
Tartan Films – 30 May
18 Republic of Korea 2002 –
Director: **Park Chan-wook**
Producer: **Lee Jae-soon**
Screenplay: **Lee Moo-young, Lee
Yong-jong, Park Ridame**
Director of Photography: **Kim
Byung-il**
Editor: **Kim Sang-Beom**
Production Designer: **Choi Jung-hwa**
Music: **Pae Hyun-jin**
Cast:
**Song Kang-ho** – Park Dong-jin
**Shin Ha-gyun** – Ryu
**Bae Du-na** – Cha Yeong-mi
**Im Ji-eun** – Ryu's sister
**Han Bo-bae** – Yu-sun
**Kim Se-dong** – chief os staff
**Lee Dae-yeon** – Choe

Production Companies:
**CJ Entertainment present
a Studio Box production**
121 minutes 8 seconds
Sight and Sound: v. 13, n. 7, p. 58-59
Box Office: £13,829
Opening Weekend: £3,264
Screens: **3**

## Tadpole
Buena Vista International – 20 June
15 USA 2002
Director: **Gary Winick**
Producers: **Alexis Alexanian, Gary
Winick, Dolly Hall**
Screenplay: **Heather McGowan, Niels
Mueller**
Story: **Heather McGowan, Niels
Mueller, Gary Winick**
Director of Photography: **Hubert
Taczanowski**
Editor: **Susan Littenberg**
Production Designer: **Anthony
Gasparro**
Music: **Renaud Pion**
Cast:
**Sigourney Weaver** – Eve Grubman
**John Ritter** – Stanley Grubman
**Bebe Neuwirth** – Diane
**Robert Iler** – Charlie
**Adam LeFevre** – Phil
**Peter Appel** – Jimmy
**Alicia van Couvering** – Daphne
Tisch
**Kate Mara** – Miranda Spear
**Ron Rifkin** – Professor Tisch
**Paul Butler** – Professor Sherman
**Hope Chernov** – Samantha
**Debbon Ayer** – Jean
**Aaron Stanford** – Oscar Grubman
© Gladpole Productions Inc
Production Companies:
**Miramax Films and IFC Productions
present
an InDigEnt production
in association with Dolly Hall
Productions**
78 minutes 23 seconds
Location: **New York (NY, USA)**
Sight and Sound: v. 13, n. 8, p. 59-60
Box Office: £71,235
Opening Weekend: £20,191
Screens: **26**

## Taj Mahal: An Eternal Love
Eros International Ltd – 21
November
Box Office: £2,504
Opening Weekend: £534
Screens: **4**

## Taking Sides
Guerilla Films – 21 November
15 Germany/France/United
Kingdom/Austria 2001

Director: **István Szabó**
Producer: **Yves Pasquier**
Screenplay: **Ronald Harwood**
**Based on his play**
Director of Photography: **Lajos Koltai**
Editor: **Sylvie Landra**
Production Designer: **Ken Adam**
Music Supervisor: **Musikverlag Vuvag GmbH, Ulrich Trimborn**
Cast:
**Harvey Keitel** – **Major Steve Arnold**
**Stellan Skarsgård** – **Doctor Wilhelm Furtwängler**
**Moritz Bleibtreu** – **Lieutenant David Wills**
**Birgit Minichmayr** – **Emmi Straube**
**Ulrich Tukur** – **Helmuth Rode**
**Hanns Zischler** – **Rudolf Werner**
**Armin Rhode** – **Schlec**
**August Zirner** – **Captain Ed Martin**
**Thomas Thieme** – **Reischsminister**
**Robin Renucci** – **Captain Vernay**
© MBP International Medien Beteiligungs-Film und TV-Produktions Gesellschaft/Maecenas Film und Fernseh GmbH/Studio Babelsberg GmbH/Paladin Production S.A./France 2 Cinéma/Satel Fernseh und Filmproductionsges GmbH/Jeremy Isaccs Productions/TwanPix
Production Companies:
**MBP, Maecenas Film, Paladin Production and Studio Babelsberg present a Little Bear production of an István Szabó film in association with Jeremy Isaccs Productions, TwanPix, Satel Film, BR - Bayerischer Rundfunk, MDR, ORF and France 2 Cinéma with the participation of Canal+, FFA, Filmboard, MDM with the support of Eurimages Developed with the support of MEDIA Supported by Centre National de la Cinématographie In association with The Spice Factory, Enterprise Films**
110 minutes 55 seconds
Location: **Dresden, Berlin, Brandenberg (Germany),**
Sight and Sound: v. 13, n. 12, p. 52-53
Box Office: **£9,576**
Opening Weekend: **£4,375**
Screens: **6**

## Talaash
**Tip Top Entertainment** – **03 January**
Box Office: **£125,385**
Opening Weekend: **£63,765**
Screens: **25**

## Tattoo
**Tartan Films** – **5 December**
**18 Germany 2002**
Director: **Robert Schwentke**
Producers: **Jan Hinter, Roman Kuhn**
Screenplay: **Robert Schwentke**
Director of Photography: **Jan Fehse**
Editor: **Peter Przygodda**
Production Designer: **Josef Sanktjohanser**
Music: **Martin Todsharow**
Cast:
**August Diehl** – **Marc Schrader**
**Christian Redl** – **Detective Minks**
**Nadeshda Brennicke** – **Maya Kroner**
**Johan Leysen** – **Frank Schoubya**
**Fatih Cevikkollu** – **Dix**
**Monica Bleibtreu** – **Inspector Roth**
**Ilknur Bahadir** – **Meltem**
**Joe Bausch** – **Günzel**
**Florian Panzner** – **Poscher**
**Jasmin Schwiers** – **Marie Minks**
© Lounge Entertainment AG/StudioCanal Filmproduktion GmbH & Co. KG, B.A. Produktion
Production Companies::
**StudioCanal Produktion presents Lounge Entertainment Produktion in
co-production with StudioCanal Filmproduktion and B.A. Produktion
A film by Robert Schwenrtke
Made with the support of Filmförderung in Berlin-Brandenburg, Forderverein Filmstadt Berlin, FilmFernsehFonds Bayern, Filmförderungsanstalt**
108 minutes 52 seconds
Sight and Sound: v. 14, n. 2, p. 62-63
Box Office: **£4,751**
Opening Weekend: **£1,653**
Screens: **1**

## Tears of the Sun
**Columbia TriStar** – **12 September**
**15 USA 2003**
Director: **Antoine Fuqua**
Producers: **Michael Lobell, Arnold Rifkin, Ian Bryce**
Screenplay: **Alex Lasker Patrick Cirillo**
Director of Photography: **Mauro Fiore**
Editor: **Conrad Buff**
Production Designer: **Naomi Shohan**
Music: **Hans Zimmer**
Cast:
**Bruce Willis** – **Lieutenant A.K. Waters**
**Monica Bellucci** – **Dr Lena Kendricks**
**Cole Hauser** – **James 'Red' Atkins**
**Eamonn Walker** – **Ellis 'Zee'**

**Pettigrew**
**Nick Chinlund** – **Michael 'Slo' Slowenski**
**Fionnula Flanagan** – **Sister Grace**
**Malick Bowens** – **Colonel Idris Sadick**
**Tom Skerritt** – **Captain Bill Rhodes**
**Johnny Messner** – **Kelly Lake**
**Paul Francis** – **Danny 'Doc' Kelley**
© Revolution Studios Distribution Company, LLC
Production Companies:
**Revolution Studios presents a Michael Lebell production a Cheyenne Enterprises production**
120 minutes 50 seconds
Location: **Hawaii (USA)**
Sight and Sound: v. 13, n. 10, p. 66-67
Box Office: **£842,590**
Opening Weekend: **£406,324**
Screens: **297**

## Tere Naam
**Eros International Limited** – **15 August**
Box Office: **£142,629**
Opening Weekend: **£42,591**
Screens: **21**

## Teenage Mutant Ninja (Re)
**Medusa 19 December**
Box Office: **£18,489**
Opening Weekend: **£3,687**
Screens: **31**

## Ten Minutes Older: Cello
**Blue Dolphin** – **12 December**
**15 Germany/United Kingdom/USA 2002**
Directors: **various**
Producers: **Nicolas McClintock, Nigel Thomas, Ulrich Felsberg**
Director of Photography: Links
Shoot:**Yang Shu**
Editor: **Peter Christelis**
Music: **Paul Englishby**
© Road Movies Filmproduktion GmbH
Production Companies::
**Made by Ten Minutes Older Ltd, London
Road Sales presents an Odyssey Films, London/Matador Pictures and Road Movies production in association with AtomFilms**
106 minutes
Sight and Sound: v. 14, n. 1, p. 62-63
Box Office: £ **1,615**
Opening Weekend: **£1,615**
Screen: **1**

## Terminator 3: Rise of Machines
**Columbia TriStar** – **01 August**
**12A Germany/USA 2003**

Director: **Jonathan Mostow**
Producers: **Hal Lieberman, Colin Wilson, Mario F. Kassar, Andrew G. Vajna, Joel B. Michaels**
Screenplay: **John Brancato, Michael Ferris**
Story: **John Brancato, Michael Ferris Tedi Sarafian**
Director of Photography: **Don Burgess**
Editors: **Neil Travis, Nicolas de Toth**
Production Designer: **Jeff Mann**
Music: **Marco Beltrami**
Cast:
**Arnold Schwarzenegger** – Terminator
**Nick Stahl** – John Connor
**Claire Danes** – Kate Brewster
**David Andrews** – Robert Brewster
**Kristanna Loken** – TX
**Mark Famiglietti** – Scott Petersen
**Earl Boen** – Dr Peter Silberman
**Moira Harris** – Betsy
**Chopper Bernet** – chief engineer
**Chris Lawford** – Brewster's aide
© IMF Internationale Medien und Film GmbH & Co. 3 Produktions KG
Production Companies:
**Mario F. Kassar and Andrew G. Vajna present
an Intermedia/IMF production
in association with
C2 Pictures and Mostow/Lieberman Productions**
108 minutes 56 seconds
Los Angeles (CA, USA)
Sight and Sound: **v. 13, n. 10, p. 67-68**
Box Office: **£18,909,904**
Opening Weekend: **£6,080,369**
Screens: **478**

## Texas Chainsaw Massacre
Entertainment – 31 October
18 USA 2003
Director: **Marcus Nispel**
Producers: **Michael Bay, Mike Fleiss**
Screenplay: **Scott Kosar**
Based on a screenplay by **Kim Henkel, Tobe Hooper**
Director of Photography: **Daniel C. Pearl**
Editor: **Glen Scantlebury**
Production Designer: **Gregory Blair**
Music: **Steve Jablonsky**
Cast:
**Jessica Biel** – Erin
**Jonathan Tucker** – Morgan
**Erica Leerhsen** – Pepper
**Mike Vogel** – Andy
**Eric Balfour** – Kemper
**David Dorfman** – Jedidiah
**R. Lee Ermey** – Sheriff Hoyt
**Andrew Bryniarski** – Thomas Hewitt

**Lauren German** – teenage girl
**Terrence Evans** – Old Monty
© Chainsaw Productions, LLC.
Production Companies:
**Focus Features and Michael Bay present in association with Radar Pictures a Platinum Dunes/Next Entertainment production**
98 minutes 11 seconds
Location: **Austin (Texas, USA), Taylor (Texas, USA)**
Sight and Sound: **v. 13, n. 12, p. 54-55**
Box Office: **£3,916,647**
Opening Weekend: **£1,357,534**
Screens: **327**

## That Girl From Rio
Redbus – 11 April
15 Spain/United Kingdom2000
Director: **Christopher Monger**
Producers: **Andrés Vicente Gómez, Muir Sutherland**
Screenplay: **Christopher Monger**
Based on a script by **Francisco Lara, Julián Ibáñez** and an idea by
**Juan Carlos Guerrero Torres**
Director of Photography: **José Luis Alcaine**
Editor: **Nicholas Wentworth**
Production Designer: **Charles Garrad**
Music: **Roque Baños**
Cast:
**Hugh Laurie** – Raymond
**Vanessa Nunes** – Orlinda
**Santiago Segura** – Paulo
**Lia Williams** – Cathy
**Patrick Barlow** – Strothers
**Nelson Xavier** – Bichero
**Hugh Lloyd** – Albert
**John Junkin** – Mr Bigelow
**Julio Levi** – Copacabana concierge
**Paul Jerricho** – inspector
© Lolafilms S.A./Casanova Pictures Production
Production Companies:
**a Lolafilms and Casanova Pictures production with the participation of Antena 3 Televisión
and the participation of Vía Digital
developed with the support of the MEDIA programme of the European Union**
103 minutes 17 seconds
Location: **Rio de Janeiro (Brasil), London (UK)**
Sight and Sound: **v. 13, n. 6, p. 46-47**
Box Office: **£488**
Opening Weekend: **£488**
Screen: **1**

## thirteen
United International Pictures – 5 December
18 USA/United Kingdom 2003
Director: **Catherine Hardwicke**

Producers: **Jeffrey Levy-Hinte, Michael London**
Screenplay: **Catherine Hardwicke Nikki Reed**
Director of Photography: **Elliot Davis**
Editor: **Nancy Richardson**
Production Designer: **Carol Strober**
Music/Music Producer: **Mark Mothersbaugh**
Cast:
**Holly Hunter** – Melanie
**Evan Rachel Wood** – Tracy
**Nikki Reed** – Evie Zamora
**Jeremy Sisto** – Brady
**Brady Corbet** – Mason
**Deborah Kara Unger** – Brooke
**Kip Pardue** – Luke
**Sarah Clarke** – Birdie
**D.W. Moffett** – Travis
**Vanessa Anne Hudgens** – Noel
© Venice Surf Club LLC
Production Companies:
**Universal Pictures and Studio Canal present in association with Michael London Productions and Working Title Films
an Antidote Films production**
99 minutes 57 seconds
Sight and Sound: **v. 13, n. 12, p. 55-56**
Box Office: **£235,036**
Opening Weekend: **£53,553**
Screens: **26**

## This is Not a Love Song
Soda Pictures – 05 September
18 United Kingdom/USA 2002
Director: **Billie Eltringham**
Producer: **Mark Blaney**
Screenplay: **Simon Beaufoy**
With additional development by
**Bille Eltringham, Michael Colgan, Kenny Glenaan**
Director of Photography: **Robbie Ryan**
Editor: **Ewa J. Lind**
Production Designer: **Jon Henson**
Music: **Adrian Johnston**
Cast:
**Michael Colgan** – Spike
**Kenny Glenaan** – Heaton
**David Bradley** – Mr Bellamy
**John Henshaw** – Arthur
**Adam Pepper** – William
**Keri Arnold** – Gerry
**Chris Middleton** – policeman
© This is Not a Company Ltd.
Production Companies:
**Soda Pictures presents
in association with This Is Not a Company
a Footprints Films production
in association with Strange Dog/UK Film Council and Longfellow Productions**

made with the support of The Film Council Development Fund and New Cinema Fund
91 minutes 23 seconds
Location: **Aberfoyle and Glasgow (Scotland, UK)**
Sight and Sound: **v. 13, n. 11, p. 63-64**
Box Office: **£1,709**
Opening Weekend: **£867**
Screens: **4**

## Thomas Pynchon: A Journey into the Mind of <p.>

ICA Projects – 02 May
No certificate Germany/Switzerland 2001
Directors: **Fosco Dubini, Donatello Dubini**
Screenplay: **Fosco Dubini, Donatello Dubini**
Director of Photography: **Donatello Dubini**
Editors: **Fosco Dubini,Donatello Dubini**
Music: **The Residents**
With
Richard Lane – webmaster
George Plimpton – critic
Jules Siegel – writer
Chrissie Wexler – painter
Richard Roland – bookseller
Irwin Corey – comedian
Tim Ware – webmaster
Steve Tomaske – librarian
Allen Rush – webmaster
James Bone – journalist
John Levine – writers
Melvin Boukhiet – writers
© Dubini Filmproduktion Köln/Tre Valli Filmproduktion Zürich
Production Companies: **Dubini Filmproduktion Köln**
**Tre Valli Filmproduktion Zürich**
**ZDF/ARTE**
Financial support: **ZFD/ARTE, Beauftragter der Bundesregierung für Kultur und Medien (BKM), Filmbüro NW, Eidgenössisches Departement des Innern (EDI), Migros Kulturprozent**
96 minutes
Sight and Sound: **v. 13, n. 6, p. 57-58**
Box Office: **£230**
Opening Weekend: **£230**
Screen: **1**

## [Three] After Life

Tartan Films – 5 December
15 France/Belgium 2002
Director: **Lucas Belvaux**
Producers: **Patrick Sobelman, Diana Elbaum**
Screenplay: **Lucas Belvaux**
Director of Photography: **Pierre**

Milon
Editor: **Danielle Anezin**
Art Director: **Frédérique Belvaux**
Music/Music Director/Orchestrator: **Riccardo Del Fra**
Cast:
Dominique Blanc – Agnès Manise
Gilbert Melki – Pascal Manise
Ornella Muti – Cécile Coste
Catherine Frot – Jeanne Rivet
François Morel – Alain Coste
Valérie Mairesse – Claire
Patrick Descamps – Jaquillat
Bernard Mazzinghi – Georges Colinet
Alexis Tomassian – Banane
Pierre Gérard – Olivier
© Agat Films & Cie, Entre Chien et Loup, RTBF, Rhône-Alpes Cinéma
Production Companies: **Agat Films & Cie and Entre Chien et Loup present in co-production with Rhône-Alpes Cinéma and RTBF (Télévision Belge) with the participation of Centre National de la Cinématographie, Eurimages, Centre du Cinéma et de l'Audiovisuel de la Communauté Française de Belgique, Télédistributeurs Wallons, Region Rhône-Alpes, La Loterie Nationale de Belgique in association with Cofimage 12, Gimages 5, Natexis Banques Populaires Images 2 and with the participation of Canal+**
a film by Lucas Belvaux
124 minutes 59 seconds
Location: **Grenoble (France)**
Sight and Sound: **v. 13, n. 12, p. 26-27, 56**
Box Office: **£27,702**
Opening Weekend: **£5,957**
Screens: **8**

## Time of the Wolf

Artificial Eye – 17 October
15 France/Austria/Germany
Director: **Michael Haneke**
Producers: **Margaret Ménégoz Veit Heiduschka**
Screenplay: **Michael Haneke**
Director of Photography: **Jürgen Jürges**
Editors: **Monika Willi, Nadine Muse**
Art Director: **Christoph Kanter**
Cast:
Isabelle Huppert – Anne
Anaïs Demoustier – Eva
Lucas Biscombe – Ben
Hakim Taleb – the young runaway
Patrice Chéreau – Thomas Brandt
Béatrice Dalle – Lise Brandt
Olivier Gourmet – Koslowski

Brigitte Roüan – Béa
Daniel Duval – Georges
Branko Samarovski – policeman
© Les Films du Losange/Wega-Film/Bavaria Film/ARTE France Cinéma/France 3 Cinéma
Production Companies: **Les Films du Losange, Wega Film, Bavaria Film present with France 3 Cinéma, ARTE France Cinéma, Österreichischer Rudnfunk Fernsehen, Bayerischer Rundfunk, Arte With the participation of Canal+, Centre National de la Cinématographie, Österreichisches Filminstitut, Filmfonds Wien, FilmFernsehFonds Bayern With the support of Eurimages**
A production of Margaret Menegoz (Paris), Veit Heiduschka (Vienna)
113 minutes 29 seconds
Sight and Sound: **v. 13, n. 11, p. 64-65**
Box Office: **£36,377**
Opening Weekend: **£6,972**
Screens: **6**

## Timeline

Entertainment – 5 December
12A USA 2003
Director: **Richard Donner**
Producers: **Lauren Shuler Donner, Jim Van Wyck, Richard Donner**
Screenplay: **Jeff Maguire George Nolfi**
Based on the novel by **Michael Crichton**
Director of Photography: **Caleb Deschanel**
Editor: **Richard Marks**
Production Designer: **Daniel T. Dorrance**
Music/Orchestra Conductor: **Brian Tyler**
Cast:
Paul Walker – Chris Johnston
Frances O'Connor – Kate Ericson
Gerard Butler – Andre Marek
Billy Connolly – Professor Edward Johnston
Anna Friel – Lady Claire
Neal McDonough – Frank Gordon
Ethan Embry – Josh Stern
David Thewlis – Robert Doniger
Matt Craven – Steven Kramer
Michael Sheen – Lord Oliver
© Paramount Pictures Corporation
Production Companies:: **Paramount Pictures, Mutual Film Company and Cobalt Media Group present a Donners' Company/Artists Production Group production A Richard Donner film**

115 minutes 22 seconds
Location: **Montreal (Canada)**
Sight and Sound: **v. 14, n. 2, p. 64**
Box Office: **£629,376**
Opening Weekend: **£279,505**
Screen: **270**

## To Kill a King
Pathé Distribution – 16 May
12A United Kingdom/Germany 2003
Director: **Mike Barker**
Producer: **Kevin Loader**
Screenplay: **Jenny Mayhew**
Director of Photography: **Eigil Bryld**
Editor: **Guy Bensley**
Production Designer: **Sophie Becher**
Music/Score Arranger/Producer:
**Richard G. Mitchell**
Cast:
**Tim Roth** – Oliver Cromwell
**Dougray Scott** – Lord General
**Thomas Fairfax**
**Olivia Williams** – Lady Anne
Fairfax
**James Bolam** – Denzil Holles,
Speaker of the House
**Corin Redgrave** – Lord de Vere,
Lady Anne's father
**Finbar Lynch** – Cousin Henry
**Julian Rhind-Tutt** – James
**Adrian Scarborough** – Sergeant
Joyce
**Jeremy Swift** – The Earl of Whitby
**Rupert Everett** – King Charles I
© Fairfax Films Limited
Production Companies:
**FilmFour presents**
**In association with HanWay**
**In association with Rockwood Edge**
**and Future Film Financing**
**a Natural Nylon**
**Entertainment/Screenland**
**Movieworld production**
84 minutes 15 seconds
Sight and Sound: **v. 13, n. 6, p. 34-35,**
**58**
Box Office: **£256,002**
Opening Weekend: **£59,701**
Screens: **53**

## Together With You
Momentum Pictures – 12 December
PG China 2002
Director: **Chen Kaige**
Producers: **Tong Gang, Chen Hong**
Screenplay: **Chen Kaige, Xue Xiaolu**
Director of Photography: **Kim**
**Hyungkoo**
Editor: **Zhou Ying**
Production Designers:
**Cao Jiuping, Liu Luyi**
Music: **Zhao Lin**
Cast:
**Liu Peiqi** – Liu Cheng
**Chen Hong** – Lili

**Wang Zhiwen** – Professor Jiang
**Chen Kaige** – Professor Yu Shifeng
**Tang Yun** – Liu Xiaochun
**Cheng Qian** – Hui, Lili's lover
**Liu Bing** – Debao
**Kim Hairi** – Professor Yu's wife
**Li Chuanyun** – Tang Rong
**Zhang Qing** – Lin Yu
Production Companies:
**Fourth Production Company of**
**China Film Group Corporation,**
**Century Hero Film Investment Co.**
**Ltd., China Movie Channel, 21st**
**Century Shengkai Film Company**
**a Chen Kaige film**
118 minutes 26 seconds
Sight and Sound: **v. 13, n. 12, p. 56-57**
Box Office: **£35,552**
Opening Weekend: **£13,288**
Screens: **14**

## Tomb Raider 2
United International Pictures – 22
August
12A USA/United
Kingdom/Germany/Japan 2003
Director: **Jan De Bont**
Producers: **Lawrence Gordon, Lloyd**
**Levin**
Screenplay: **Dean Georgaris**
Story: **Steven E. De Souza, James V.**
**Hart**
Based on the Eidos Interactive game
series developed by **Core Design**
Director of Photography: **David**
**Tattersall**
Editor: **Michael Kahn**
Production Designer: **Kirk M.**
**Petruccelli**
Music/Music Conductor: **Alan**
**Silvestri**
Cast:
**Angelina Jolie** – Lara Croft
**Gerard Butler** – Terry Sheridan
**Noah Taylor** – Bryce
**Ciarán Hinds** – Jonathan Reiss
**Djimon Hounsou** – Kosa
**Til Schweiger** – Sean
**Christopher Barrie** – Hillary
**Simon Yam** – Chen Lo
**Terence Yin** – Xien
**Daniel Caltagirone** – Nicholas
**Petraki**
© Paramount Pictures
Production Companies:
**Paramount Pictures presents**
**in association with Mutual Film**
**Company & BBC, Tele-München,**
**Toho-Towa**
**a Lawrence Gordon/Lloyd Levin**
**production**
**in association with Eidos Interactive**
**Limited**
117 minutes 7 seconds

Location: **London (UK), Kenya,**
Hong Kong, Greece
Sight and Sounds: **v. 13, n. 10, p. 52,**
54
Box Office: **£5,253,709**
Opening Weekend: **£1,524,676**
Screens: **449**

## Touching the Void
Pathe Distribution Ltd – 12
December
15 United Kingdom/USA 2003
Director: **Kevin Macdonald**
Producer: **John Smithson**
Based on Touching the Void by **Joe**
**Siimpson**
Director of Photography: **Mike Eley**
Editor: **Justine Wright**
Art Direction – **Patrick Bill**
Music: **Alex Heffes**
With – Joe Simpson – Simon Yates –
Richard Hawking –
Reconstruction Cast:
**Brendan Mackey** – Joe Simpson
**Nicholas Aaron** – Simon Yates
**Ollie Vargas** – Richard Hawking
© **FilmFour Limited/Film Council**
Production Companies::
**Film Four and the Film Council**
**present in association with Channel**
**4 and PBS**
**a Darlow Smithson production**
**co-financed by Channel 4 Television,**
**co-financed by PBS**
**Made with the support of the Film**
**Council New Cinema Fund**
**a Darlow Smithson production for**
**FilmFour**
106 minutes 13 seconds
Location: **Peru and the Alps**
Sight and Sound: **v.14, n. 1, p. 63-64**
Box Office: **£619,011**
Opening Weekend: **£115,332**
Screens: **29**

## The Transporter
20th Century Fox – 17 January
15 France/USA 2002
Director: **Corey Yuen**
Producers: **Luc Besson**
**Steven Chasman**
Screenplay: **Luc Besson**
**Robert Mark Kamen**
Director of Photography: **Pierre**
**Morel**
Editor: **Nicolas Trembasiewicz**
Production Designer: **Hugues**
**Tissandier**
Music: **Stanley Clarke**
Cast:
**Jason Statham** – Frank Martin
**Shu Qi** – Lai
**Matt Schulze** – Wall Street
**François Berléand** – Tarconi
**Ric Young** – Mr Kwai

Doug Rand – leader
Didier Saint Melin – boss
Tonio Descanvelle – Laurent
Desponds
Matthieu Albertini – thugs
Vincent Nemeth – pilot
© Europacorp/
TF1 Films Production
Production Companies:
Twentieth Century Fox presents
a Europacorp production
in co-production with TF1 Films
Production
in association with Current
Entertainment and Canal+
92 minutes 1 second
Location: **Paris and South of France**
Sight and Sound: **v.13, n. 1, p. 55-56**
Box Office: **£712,283**
Opening Weekend: **£388,420**
Screens: **208**

## Trapped
Columbia TriStar – 25 April
15 USA/Germany 2002
Director: **Luis Mandoki**
Producers: **Mimi Polk Gitlin**
**Luis Mandoki**
Screenplay: **Greg Iles**
Based on his novel 24 hours
Directors of Photography: **Frederick**
**Elmes, Piotr Sobocinski**
Editor: **Jerry Greenberg**
Production Designer: **Richard**
**Sylbert**
Music: **John Ottman**
Cast:
Charlize Theron – Karen Jennings
Courtney Love – Cheryl Hickey
Stuart Townsend – Will Jennings
Kevin Bacon – Joe Hickey
Pruitt Taylor Vince – Marvin
Dakota Fanning – Abby Jennings
Steve Rankin – Hank Ferris
Garry Chalk – Agent Chalmers
Jodie Markell – Mary McDill
Matt Koby – Peter McDill
© 24 Hours Productions Inc
Production Companies:
Columbia Pictures presents in
association with Senator
Entertainment and
The Canton Company
a Mandolin
Entertainment/Propaganda Films
production
101 minutes 29 seconds
Location: **Vancouver (Canada)**
Sight and Sound: **v. 13, n. 5, p. 63**
Box Office: **£55,298**
Opening Weekend: **£30,302**
Screens: **84**

## Treasure Planet
Buena Vista International – 14

February
U USA 2002
Directors: **John Musker, Ron**
**Clements**
Producers: **Roy Conli, John Musker,**
**Ron Clements**
Screenplay: **Ron Clements, John**
**Musker, Rob Edwards**
Adapted from the novel Treasure
Island by **Robert Louis Stevenson**
Animation Story: **Ron Clements,**
**John Musker, Ted Elliott, Terry**
**Rossio**
Editor: **Michael Kelly**
Production Designers: **Steven Olds,**
**Frank Nissen**
Music/Score Producer: **James**
**Newton Howard**
Original Songs Written/Performed by
**John Rzeznik**
Voice Cast:
Joseph Gordon-Levitt – Jim
Hawkins
Brian Murray – John Silver
Emma Thompson – Captain Amelia
David Hyde Pierce – Doctor
Doppler
Martin Short – B.E.N.
Dane A. Davis – Morph
Michael Wincott – Scroop
Laurie Metcalf – Sarah
Roscoe Lee Browne – Mr Arrow
Patrick McGoohan – Billy Bones
© Disney Enterprises, Inc.
Production Company
Walt Disney Pictures presents
95 minutes 31 seconds
Location: **Los Angeles (CA, USA)**
Sight and Sound: **v. 13, n. 2, p. 64-65**
Box Office: **£6,713,835**
Opening Weekend: **£888,084**
Screens: **409**

## Trembling Before G-D
Miracle Communications – 30 May
15 USA/Israel/France 2000
Sandi Simcha Dubowski
Producers: **Sandi Dubowski**
**Marc Smolowitz**
Cinematographers USA:
Donna Binder, Sandra Chandler,
Mik Cribben, Jim Denault, Ken
Druckerman, Sandi Dubowski,
Kirsten Johnson, Kevin Keating,
Karen Kramer, Jennifer Lane, David
Leitner, Marie Pederson, Ben Speth,
Fawn Yacker, Andrew Yarme
UK:
Noski Deville, Sandi Dubowski
Israel:
Nili Aslan, Sandi Dubowski, Issa
Freij, Jackie Matithau, Yoram Milo,
Yitzhak Portal, Abigail Sperber
Editor: **Susan Korda**

Composer: **John Zorn**
With
Dr Yaakov Meir Weil – David from
Los Angeles – Rabbi Aharon
Feldman – Rabbi Shlomo Riskin –
Rabbi Steve Greenberg – 'Malka'
from Miami – 'Leah' from Miami –
Michelle from Brooklyn – Shlomo
Ashkinazy – Naomi Mark – 'Tamar'
from Jerusalem – Mark from
London – Israel from Brooklyn –
'Devorah' from Israel – Rabbi
Nathan Lopes Cardozo – Rabbi Meir
Fund – © Simcha Leib Productions
Production Companies:
Simcha Leib Productions and
Turbulent Arts present
in association with Keshet
Broadcasting, Ltd. (Israel)
in co-production with Pretty
Pictures (Paris) and Cinephil Ltd.
(Tel Aviv)
84 minutes 15 seconds
Sight and Sound: **v.13, n. 6, p. 58**
Box Office: **£31,256**
Opening Weekend: **£6,288**
Screens: **4**

## Triggermen
Winchester Films 26 December
15 Canada/Germany 2001
Director: **John Bradshaw**
Producers: **Deborah Kiss, Sabine**
**Mueller, Mark Thomas**
Screenplay: **Tony Johnston**
Director of Photography: **Barry**
**Stone**
Editor: **Lisa Grootenboer**
Production Designer: **Tim Boys**
Music: **Terence M. Gowan, Blair**
**Packham**
Cast:
Neil Morrissey – Pete Maynard
Donnie Wahlberg – Terry Malloy
Adrian Dunbar – Andy Jarrett
Claire Forlani – Emma Cutler
Amanda Plummer – Penny Archer
Michael Rapaport – Tommy O'Brian
Louis Di Bianco – Franco D'Amico
Shawn Lawrence – Roger
Deschamps
Bill MacDonald – Boots
Saul Rubinek – Jazzer
© T-Men Productions Inc.
Production Companies:
First Look Media presents in
association with
International Pictures and Now
Entertainment Group
a Trimuse Entertainment and
Gemini Film production
A John Bradshaw film
96 minutes 3 seconds
Sight and Sound: **v. 14, n. 3, p. 69-70**

Box Office: £32,789
Opening Weekend: £11,721
Screens: 34

## The Truth About Charlie

United International Pictures – 16
May
12A USA/Germany 2002
Director: Jonathan Demme
Producers: Jonathan Demme
Peter Saraf, Edward Saxon
Screenplay: Jonathan Demme, Steve
Schmidt, Peter Joshua
[i.e. Peter Stone], Jessica Bendinger
Based on the motion picture Charade
screenplay by Peter Stone
Director of Photography: Tak
Fujimoto
Editor: Carol Littleton
Production Designer: Hugo Luczyc-
Wyhowski
Music/Music Producer: Rachel
Portman
Cast:
Mark Wahlberg – Lewis
Bartholomew
Thandie Newton – Regina 'Reggie'
Lambert
Tim Robbins – Carson J. Dyle
Park Joong-hoon – Lee Il-sang
Ted Levine – Emil Zadapec
Lisa Gay Hamilton – Lola Jansco
Christine Boisson – Commandant
Dominique
Stephen Dillane – Charlie
Frédérique Meininger – Madame du
Lac
Magali Noël – mysterious woman in
black
© Mediastream Zweite Film GmbH &
Co.l Productions KG
Production Companies:
Universal Pictures presents a Clinica
Estetico production
104 minutes 4 seconds
Location: Paris (France)
Sight and Sound: v. 13, n. 8, p. 60, 62
Box Office: £66,057
Opening Weekend: £37,015
Screens: 75

## The Tuxedo

United International Pictures – 10
January
12A USA 2002
Director: Kevin Donovan
Producers: Adam Schroeder, John H.
Williams
Screenplay: Michael J. Wilson,
Michael Leeson
Story: Phil Hay, Matt Manfredi,
Michael J. Wilson
Director of Photography: Stephen F.
Windon
Editor: Craig P. Herring

Production Designers: Paul Denham
Austerberry, Monte Fay Hallis
Music: John Debney, Christophe
Beck
Cast:
Jackie Chan – Jimmy Tong
Jennifer Love Hewitt – Del Blaine
Jason Isaacs – Clark Devlin
Debi Mazar – Steena
Ritchie Coster – Diedrich Banning
Peter Stormare – Doctor Simms
Mia Cottet – Cheryl
Romany Malco – Mitch
Daniel Kash – Rogers
Jody Racicot – Kells
Boyd Banks – Vic
© DreamWorks LLC
Production Companies:
DreamWorks Pictures presents a
Vanguard Films production
a Parkes/MacDonald production
98 minutes 45 seconds
Location: Toronto (Ontario, Canada)
Sight and Sound: v. 13, n. 3, p. 56
Box Office: £3,502,823
Opening Weekend: £1,080,504
Screens: 258

## [Two] On the Run

Tartan Films – 28 November
PG France/Belgium 2002
Director: Lucas Belvaux
Producers: Patrick Sobelman, Diana
Elbaum
Screenplay: Lucas Belvaux
Director of Photography: Pierre
Milon
Editor: Ludo Troch
Art Director: Frédérique Belvaux
Music/Music Performer: Riccardo
Del Fra
Cast:
Catherine Frot – Jeanne Rivet
Lucas Belvaux – Bruno Le Roux
Dominique Blanc – Agnès Manise
Ornella Muti – Cécile Coste
Alexis Tomassian – Banane
Olivier Darimont – Francis Rivet
Patrick Descamps – Jaquillat
Yves Claessens – Freddy
Gilbert Melki – Pascal
Christine Henkart – Madame Guiot
© Agat Films & Cie, Entre Chien et
Loup, RTBF, Rhône-Alpes Cinéma
Production Companies:
Agat Films & Cie and Entre Chien et
Loup present in co-production with
Rhône-Alpes Cinéma and RTBF
(Télévision Belge)
with the participation of Centre
National de la Cinématographie,
Eurimages, Centre du Cinéma et de
l'Audiovisuel de la Communauté
Française de Belgique,

Télédistributeurs Wallons, Region
Rhône-Alpes, La Loterie Nationale
de Belgique
in association with Cofimage 12,
Gimages 5, Natexis Banques
Populaires Images 2 and with the
participation of Canal+ un film de
Lucas Belvaux
97 minutes 24 seconds
Location: Grenoble (France)
Sight and Sound: v. 13, n. 12, p. 26-
27, 50, 56, 58
Box Office: £37,854
Opening Weekend: £9,569
Screens: 9

## Two Weeks Notice

Warner Bros – 07 February
12A USA/Australia 2002
Director: Marc Lawrence
Producer: Sandra Bullock
Screenplay: Marc Lawrence
Director of Photography: Laszlo
Kovacs
Editor: Susan E. Morse
Production Designer: Peter Larkin
Music: John Powell
Cast:
Hugh Grant – George Wade
Sandra Bullock – Lucy Kelson
Alicia Witt – June Carter
Dana Ivey – Ruth Kelson
Robert Klein – Larry Kelson
Heather Burns – Meryl Brooks
David Haig – Howard Wade
Dorian Missick – Tony
Joseph Badalucco – construction
foreman
Jonathan Dokuchitz – Tom
© Warner Bros. [US, Bermuda,
Bahamas]
© Village Roadshow Films (BVI)
Limited [All other territories]
Production Companies:
Castle Rock Entertainment presents
in association with Village
Roadshow Pictures and NPV
Entertainment
a Fortis Films production
101 minutes 8 seconds
Location: New York (NY, USA)
Sight and Sound: v. 13, n. 4, p. 55-56
Box Office: £13,524,795
Opening Weekend: £2,636,050
Screens: 414

## Undercover Brother

Winchester Films – 14 February
12 USA 2002
Director: Malcolm D. Lee
Producers: Brian Grazer, Michael
Jenkinson, Damon Lee
Screenplay: John Ridley, Michael
McCullers
Based on the Internet series created

by **John Ridley**
Story: **John Ridley**
Director of Photography: **Tom Priestley**
Editor: **William Kerr**
Production Designer: **William Elliott**
Music: **Stanley Clarke**
Cast:
**Eddie Griffin** – Undercover Brother
**Chris Kattan** – Mr Feather
**Denise Richards** – White She Devil
**Dave Chappelle** – Conspiracy Brother
**Aunjanue Ellis** – Sistah Girl
**Chi McBride** – the chief
**Neil Patrick Harris** – Lance
**Jack Noseworthy** – Mr Elias
**Gary Anthony Williams** – Smart Brother
**Jim O'Connor** – Chad
© Universal Studios
Production Companies:
**Universal Pictures and Imagine Entertainment present**
85 minutes 52 seconds
Location: **Toronto** (Canada)
Sight and Sound: **v. 13, n. 3, p. 59**
Box Office: **£789,884**
Opening Weekend: **£235,527**
Screens: **130**

## Underworld
**Entertainment** – 19 September
15 United
Kingdom/Germany/Hungary/USA
2003
Director: **Len Wiseman**
Producers: **Tom Rosenberg**
**Gary Lucchesi**
Screenplay: **Danny McBride**
Story: **Kevin Grevioux, Len Wiseman, Danny McBride**
Director of Photography: **Tony Pierce-Roberts**
Editor: **Martin Hunter**
Production Designer: **Bruton Jones**
Music/Score Producer: **Paul Haslinger**
Cast:
**Kate Beckinsale** – Selene
**Scott Speedman**
Michael
**Michael Sheen** – Lucian
**Shane Brolly** – Kraven
**Bill Nighy** – Viktor
**Erwin Leder** – Singe
**Sophia Myles** – Erika
**Robbie Gee** – Kahn
**Wentworth Miller** – Doctor Adam
**Kevin Grevioux** – Raze
© Subterranean Productions LLC
Production Companies:
**Lakeshore Entertainment and Screen Gems presents a Lakeshore**

**Entertainment production**
**A Subterranean Productions UK Limited, Underworld Produktions GmbH, Laurenfilm KFT and Subterranean Productions LLC co-production**
121 minutes 4 seconds
Location: **Budapest** (Hungary)
Sight and Sound: **v. 13, n. 12, p. 58-59**
Box Office: **£4,391,553**
Opening Weekend: **£1,487,839**
Screens: **348**

## Unknown Pleasures
**Artificial Eye** – 11 July
12A Japan/France/Republic of Korea/China 2002
Director: **Jia Zhang Ke**
Producers: **Shozo Ichiyama, Li Kit-ming**
Screenplay: **Jia ZhangKe**
Director of Photography: **Yu Lik Wai**
Editor: **Chow Keung**
Art Director: **Liang Jiang Dong**
Cast:
**Zhao Tao** – Qiao Qiao
**Zhao Wei Wei** – Bin Bin
**Wu Qiong** – Xiao Ji
**Li Zhu Bin** – Qiao San
**Zhou Qing Feng** – Yuan Yuan
**Wang Hong Wei** – Xiao Wu
**Bai Ru** – Bin Bin's mother
**Liu Xi An** – Xiao Ji's father
**Xu Shou Lin** – Sister Zhu
**Ren Ai Jun** – hairdresser
© Office Kitano/Lumen Films/E-Pictures
Production Companies:
**Office Kitano, Lumen Films, E-Pictures present**
**a T-Mark Inc., Hu-Tong Communication production**
**in association with Bitters End**
112 minutes 30 seconds
Sight and Sound: **v. 13, n. 7, p. 34-35, 59**
Box Office: **£3,483**
Opening Weekend: **£1,217**
Screen: **1**

## Van Gogh (Re)
**Artificial Eye** – 08 August
Box Office: **£10,005**
Opening Weekend: **£2,387**
Screen: **1**

## Vendredi Soir
**Metro Tartan** – 22 August
15 France 2002
Director: **Claire Denis**
Producer: **Bruno Pesery**
Screenplay: **Emmanuèle Bernheim**
**Claire Denis**
Based on the novel by
**Emmanuèle Bernheim**

Director of Photography: **Agnès Godard**
Editor: **Nelly Quettier**
Art Director: **Katia Wyszkop**
Music: **Dickon Hinchcliffe**
Cast:
**Valérie Lemercier** – Laure
**Vincent Lindon** – Jean
**Grégoire Colin** – young man in parka
**Hélène Fillières** – tired young woman
**Hélène de Saint-Père** – Marie
**Florence Loiret-Caille** – young woman at pin-ball machine
**Micha Lescot** – hotel receptionist
**Nicolas Struve** – man at collision
**Jérôme Pouly** – another man at collision
**Conception Pires** – concierge
© Arena Films/France 2 Cinéma
Production Companies:
**Arena Films presents**
**a co-production of Arena Films, France 2 Cinéma, France Télévision Images**
**with the participation of Canal+**
**and with the support of Centre National de la Cinématographie**
89 minutes 19 seconds
Sight and Sound: **v. 13, n. 10, p. 68, 70**
Box Office: **£76,686**
Opening Weekend: **£8,447**
Screen: **3**

## Veronica Guerin
**Buena Vista International** – 11 July
18 USA/United Kingdom/Ireland
2003
Director: **Joel Schumacher**
Producer: **Jerry Bruckheimer**
Screenplay: **Carol Doyle, Mary Agnes Donoghue**
Story: **Carol Doyle**
Director of Photography: **Brendan Galvin**
Editor: **David Gamble**
Production Designer: **Nathan Crowley**
Music: **Harry Gregson-Williams**
Cast:
**Cate Blanchett** – Veronica Guerin
**Gerard McSorley** – John Gilligan
**Ciarán Hinds** – John Traynor
**Brenda Fricker** – Bernie Guerin
**Don Wycherley** – Chris Mulligan
**Barry Barnes** – Graham Turley
**Simon O'Driscoll** – Cathal Turley
**Emmet Bergin** – Aengus Fanning
**Charlotte Bradley** – Ann Harris
**Mark Lambert** – Willy Kealy
© Touchstone Pictures/Jerry Bruckheimer, Inc.
Production Companies:

Touchstone Pictures and Jerry Bruckheimer Films present
Produced with the support of investment incentives for the Irish film industry provided by the Government of Ireland
A co-production of Persevere Productions Limited (UK) and World 2000 Entertainment Limited (Ireland)
98 minutes 8 seconds
Location: **Ireland**
Sight and Sound: v. 13, n. 10, p. 70-71
Box Office: **£3,304,231**
Opening Weekend: **£271,996**
Screens: **53**

## Virgil Bliss

P-Kino – 14 March
15 USA 2001
Director: **Joe Maggio**
Producers: **John Maggio, Joe Maggio**
Screenplay: **Joe Maggio**
Director of Photography: **Harlan Bosmajian**
Editor: **Elizabeth Downer**
Music: **Greta Gaines, Clint Jordan, Anthony Gorman**
Cast:
**Clint Jordan** – Virgil Bliss
**Kirsten Russell** – Ruby
**Anthony Gorman** – Manny Alvarez
**Greg Amici** – Gilette
**Marc Romeo** – Devo
**Anthony Hayden** – Lester
**Tom Brangle** – captain
**Whitney Hamilton** – Virgil's boss
**Denny Bess** – Lombardo
**Alejandra Leon** – prostitute 2
© P-Kino Films, Inc/Concrete Films
Production Companies:
**P-Kino Films and Concrete Films present**
93 minutes 52 seconds
Sight and Sound: v. 13, n. 5, p. 63-64
Box Office: **£285**
Opening Weekend: **£285**
Screen: **1**

## Waiting For Happiness

Artificial Eye – 24 October
U
France/Switzerland/Netherlands/Cz ech Republic 2002
Director: **Abderrahmane Sissako**
Screenplay: **Abderrahmane Sissako**
Director of Photography: **Jacques Besse**
Editor: **Nadia Ben Rachid**
Art Directors: **Joseph Kpobly, Laurent Cavero**
Cast:
**Khatra Ould Abdel Kader** – Khatra
**Maata Ould Mohamed Abeid** – Maata

**Mohamed Mahmoud Ould Mohamed** – Abdallah
**Fatimetou Mint Ahmeda** – the mother
**Nana Diakite** – Nana
**Makanfing Dabo** – Makan
**Santha Leng** – Tchu
**Baba Ould Mini** – Sidi
**Mickaël Onoimweniku** – Mickaël
**Diallo Ibrahima Sory** – Diallo
© Duo Films/ARTE France
Production Companies:
**ARTE France presents an ARTE France/Duo Films co-production with the support of Commission Européenne, Fonds Européen de Développement, Ministère Français des Affaires Etrangères, Fonds Francophone de Production Audiovisuelle du Sud, Agence intergouvernementale de la Francophonie, CIRTEF**
a Duo Films and ARTE France co-production
with the support of la Commission Européenne, Fonds Européen de Développement, Centre National de la Cinématographie, Ministère Français des Affaires Étrangères,
Fonds Francophone de Production Audiovisuelle du Sud,
Agence Intergouvernementale de la Francophonie and CIRTEF, Fondation Montecinema Verità and Direction du Développement et de la Coopération, Département Fédéral des Affaires Étrangères, Fonds Hubert Bals/Cinemart, Festival International de Rotterdam
Procirep
and Programme Média de l'Union Européenne
95 minutes 38 seconds
Sight and Sound: v. 13, n. 11, p. 65
Box Office: **£25,204**
Opening Weekend: **£4,048**
Screens: **2**

## Welcome to Collinwood

Redbus – 25 April
15 USA/Germany 2002
Directors: **Anthony Russo, Joe Russo**
Producers: **George Clooney, Steven Soderbergh**
Screenplay: **Anthony Russo, Joe Russo**
Based on the film I soliti ignoti written by
**Suso Cecchi d'Amico, Mario Monicelli, Agenore Incrocci Furio Scarpelli**
Directors of Photography: **Lisa Rinzler, Charles Minsky**

Editor: **Amy E. Duddleston**
Production Designer: **Tom Meyer**
Music: **Mark Mothersbaugh**
Cast:
**William H. Macy** – Riley
**Isaiah Washington** – Leon
**Sam Rockwell** – Pero
**Michael Jeter** – Toto
**Luis Guzmán** – Cosimo
**Patricia Clarkson** – Rosalind
**Andrew Davoli** – Basil
**George Clooney** – Jerzy
**Jennifer Esposito** – Carmela
**Gabrielle Union** – Michelle
© Gaylord Films LLC.
Production Companies:
**Warner Bros. Pictures presents in association with Pandora and H5B5 Media AG a Section Eight production**
85 minutes 58 seconds
Location: **Cleveland (Ohio, USA)**
Sight and Sound: v. 13, n. 5, p. 64
Box Office: **£2,000,030**
Opening Weekend: **£688,465**
Screens: **288**

## Werckmeister Harmonies

Artificial Eye – 18 April
12A Hungary/Germany/France/ Switzerland/Italy 2000
Director: **Béla Tarr**
Producers: Goëss Films: **Franz Goëss Miklós Szita, Von Vietinghoff Filmproduktion GmbH: Joachim von Vietinghoff**
13. Production:
**Paul Saadoun**
Screenplay: **László Krasznahorkai, Béla Tarr**
Based on the novel Az ellenállás melankóliája/Melancholy of Resistance by **László Krasznahorkai**
Photographed by **Gábor Medvigy, Jörg Widmer, Patrick de Ranter, Rob Tregenza, Emil Novák, Erwin Lanzensberger, Miklós Gurbán**
Editor: **Ágnes Hranitzky**
Artistic Consultant: **Gyula Pauer**
Music: **Mihály Víg**
Cast:
**Lars Rudolph** – János Valuska
**Peter Fitz** – György Eszter
**Hanna Schygulla** – Tünde Eszter
**János Derzsi** – man in broad-cloth coat
**Djoko Rossich** – man in Western boots
**Tamás Wichmann** – man in the sailor-cap
**Ferenc Kállai** – director
**Mihály Kormos** – factotum
**Dr Putyi Horváth** – porter
**Éva Almási Albert** – Aunt Piri

© Goëss Film/
Von Vietinghoff Filmproduktion/
13. Production
Production Companies:
**Goëss Film (Budapest), Von
Vietinghoff Filmproduktion (Berlin)
and 13. Production (Marseille)**
present
**a László Krasznahorkai, Ágnes
Hranitzky and Béla Tarr film**
This film was made with the support
of Magyar Mozgókép Közalapítvány/
Hungarian Motion Picture Fund,
Országos Rádió és Televízió
Testület/National Radio and
Television Association, Magyar
Televízió/Hungarian
Television, Nemzeti Kulturális
Alapprogram/National Cultural
Programme, ZDF
(Christoph Holch), ARTE (Meinolf
Zurhorst), Eurimages, Fondazione
Montecinemaverità (Locarno) and
RAI 3
**145 minutes 26 seconds**
Sight and Sound: v. 13, n. 4, p. 32-33,
56
Box Office: **£18,560**
Opening Weekend: **£2,921**
Screen: **1**

## Whale Rider
Icon Film Distribution – 11 July
PG New Zealand/Germany 2002
Director: **Niki Caro**
Producers: **Tim Sanders, John
Barnett, Frank Hübner**
Screenplay: **Niki Caro**
Based on the book  The Whale Rider
by **Witi Ihimaera**
Director of Photography: **Leon
Narbey**
Editor: **David Coulson**
Production Designer: **Grant Major**
Music: **Lisa Gerrard**
Cast:
**Keisha Castle-Hughes – Paikea
Rawiri Paratene – Koro
Vicky Haughton – Flowers
Cliff Curtis – Porourangi
Grant Roa – Rawiri
Mana Taumaunu – Hemi
Tyronne White – Jake
Taupuru Whakataka-Brightwell –
Ropata
Tenia McClutchie-Mita – Wiremu
Rachel House – Shilo**
© **South Pacific Pictures
Productions Ltd./ApolloMedia
GmbH & Co. 5. Filmproduktion KG**
Production Companies:
**South Pacific Pictures, ApolloMedia,
Pandora Film
in association with The New**

Zealand Film Production Fund, The
New Zealand Film Commission, NZ
on Air and sponsored by
Filmstiftung Nordrhein-Westfalen
GmbH present
**101 minutes 25 seconds**
Location: **New Zealand**
Sight and Sound: v. 13, n. 8, p. 63
Box Office: **£1,436,152**
Opening Weekend: **£121,610**
Screens: **56**

## What a Girl Wants
Warner Bros – 08 August
PG USA 2003
Director: **Dennie Gordon**
Producers:  **Denise Di Novi, Bill
Gerber, Hunt Lowry**
Screenplay: **Jenny Bicks, Elizabeth
Chandler**
Based on the screenplay by **William
Douglas Home** based on his play The
Reluctant Debutante
Director of Photography: **Andrew
Dunn**
Editor: **Charles McClelland**
Production Designer: **Michael Carlin**
Music: **Rupert Gregson-Williams**
Cast:
**Amanda Bynes – Daphne Reynolds
Colin Firth – Henry Dashwood
Kelly Preston – Libby Reynolds
Eileen Atkins – Jocelyn Dashwood
Anna Chancellor – Glynnis Payne
Jonathan Pryce – Alistair Payne
Oliver James – Ian Wallace
Soleil McGhee – young Daphne
Peter Reeves – Sir John Dashwood
James Greene – Percy**
© Warner Bros/Gaylord Films LLC
Production Companies:
**Warner Bros Pictures presents
in association with Gaylord Films
a Di Novi Pictures/Gerber Pictures
production
104 minutes 49 seconds**
Location: **London (UK)**
Sight and Sound: v. 13, n. 10, p. 71
Box Office: **£865,399**
Opening Weekend: **£220,217**
Screens: **250**

## White Oleander
Redbus – 19 September
12A USA 2002
Director: **Peter Kosminsky**
Producers: **John Wells, Hunt Lowry**
Screenplay: **Mary Agnes Donoghue**
Based on the novel by
**Janet Fitch**
Director of Photography: **Elliot Davis**
Editor: **Chris Ridsdale**
Production Designer: **Donald
Graham Burt**
Music: **Thomas Newman**

Cast:
**Alison Lohman  – Astrid Magnussen
Robin Wright Penn – Starr
Michelle Pfeiffer – Ingrid
Magnussen
Renée Zellweger – Claire Richards
Billy Connolly – Barry Kolker
Svetlana Efremova – Rena
Patrick Fugit – Paul Trout
Cole Hauser – Ray
Noah Wyle – Mark Richards
Amy Aquino – Miss Martinez**
© Warner Bros. (US, Canada,
Bahamas & Bermuda)
© Gaylord Films LLC (all other
territories)
Production Companies:
**Warner Bros. Pictures presents in
association with Pandora a John
Wells production
109 minutes 26 seconds**
Los Angeles (CA, USA)
Sight and Sound: v. 13, n. 12, p. 59-60
Box Office: **£4,732**
Opening Weekend: **£2,673**
Screens: **15**

## Wilbur Wants to Kill Himself
Icon Film Distribution – 5
December
15 Denmark/United
Kingdom/Norway/France 2002
Director: **Lone Scherfig**
Producer: **Sisse Graum Olsen**
Screenplay: **Lherfig
Anders Thomas Jensen**
Director of Photography: **Jørgen
Johansson**
Editor: **Gerd Tjur**
Production Designer: **Jette Lehmann
Mone Scherfig, Anders Thomas
Jensen**
Director of Photography: **Jørgen
Johansson**
Editor: **Gerd Tjur**
Production Designer: **Jette Lehmann**
Music: **Joachim Holbek**
Cast:
**Jamie Sives – Wilbur
Adrian Rawlins – Harbour
Shirley Henderson – Alice
Lisa McKinlay – Mary
Mads Mikkelsen – Doctor Horst
Julia Davis – Moira
Susan Vidler – Sophie
Robert McIntosh – Taylor
Lorraine McIntosh – Ruby
Gordon Brown – Wayne**
© Zentropa Entertainments6
ApS/Wilbur Ltd.
Production Companies::
**Produced by Zentropa
Entertainments 6, Wilbur Ltd. in**

association with Scottish Screen, Sigma Films Ltd., TV2/Danmark (Adam Price/Camilla Hammerich), Glasgow Film Office, Sveriges Television AB, SVT Fiktion Supported by Danish Film Institute (Vinca Wiedemann), Nordic Film- & TV Fund (Svend Abrahamsen) Distributed in conjunction with Trust Film Sales2, Les Films du Losange, Nordisk Film Biografdistribution, Nordisk Film Developed with the support of the MEDIA programme of the European Union
109 minutes 1 second
Location: Glasgow (Scotland, UK)
Sight and Sound: v. 14, n. 1, p. 64
Box Office: £120,645
Opening Weekend: £37,461
Screens: 31

### The Wild Thornberrys
United International Pictures – 07 February
U USA 2002
Directors: **Jeff McGrath, Cathy Malkasian**
Producers: **Arlene Klasky, Gabor Csupo**
Screenplay: **Kate Boutilier**
Based on characters created by – **Arlene Klasky, Gabor Csupo Steve Pepoon, David Silverman, Stephen Sustarsic**
Editor: **John Bryant**
Production Designer: **Dima Malanitchev**
Music: **Drew Neumann**
Voice Cast:
**Brenda Blethyn** – Mrs Fairgood
**Rupert Everett** – Sloan Blackburn
**Lynn Redgrave** – Cordelia Thornberry
**Marisa Tomei** – Bree Blackburn
**Alfre Woodard** – Akela, cheetah mother
**Flea** – Donnie Thornberry
**Jodi Carlisle** – Marianne Thornberry
**Lacey Chabert** – Eliza Thornberry
**Tim Curry** – Nigel Thornberry
**Danielle Harris** – Debbie Thornberry
© Paramount Pictures/Viacom International Inc
Production Companies:
**Paramount Pictures and Nickelodeon Movies present a Klasky Csupo production**
85 minutes 18 seconds
Location: Los Angeles (CA, USA)
Sight and Sound: v.13, n. 3, p. 60
Box Office: **£6,199,827**

Opening Weekend: £1,430,610
Screens: 330

### Winged Migration
Columbia TriStar – 05 September
U France/Germany/Spain/Italy/ Switzerland 2001
Director: **Jacques Perrin**
Producer: **Jacques Perrin**
Screenplay: **Jacques Perrin, Stéphane Durand**
in collaboration with **Jean Dorst, Guy Jarry, Francis Roux**
Based on an idea by **Valentine Perrin**
Camera:men: **Pierre Bec, Pierre Berthier, Alain Ducousset, Benoît Nicoulin, Lee Parker, Christophe Pottier, Zhang Yuan**
Editor: **Marie-Josèphe Yoyotte**
Art Director: **Régis Nicolino**
Music/Music Director: **Bruno Coulais**
© Galatée Films/France 2 Cinéma/France 3 Cinéma/Bac Films/ Les Films de la Guéville/Pandora Film/Wanda Vision S.A./Eyescreen S.R.L./JMH Productions
Production Companies:
**Galatée Films presents a France 2 Cinéma, France 3 Cinéma, Les Productions de la Guéville, Bac Films co-production with participation of Canal+ and Pandora Films (Germany) in association with WDR and Filmstiftung NRW, JMH Productions (Switzerland) in association with the Television Suisse Romande, Wanda Vision S.A (Spain), Eyescreen S.R.L. (Italy) With the support of Liliane Bettencourt in the name of the Bettencourt Schueller Foundation, Lufthansa, Electricité de France, Crédit Agricole, Primagaz, The Aveyron General Council, The Languedoc-Roussillon Regional Council, The Calvados Regional Council, The Basse Normandie Regional Council, The Lozère Regional Council and The French National Centre for Cinematography, the European Commission, Eurimages (the Council of Europe support funds), the Procirep (Film and Television Producers' Association), the GAN Foundation for Cinema**
89 minutes 11 seconds
Sight and Sound: v. 13, n. 7, p.60
Box Office: **£92,624**
Opening Weekend: **£7,667**
Screens: **6**

### Wrong Turn
Pathé Distribution – 27 June
18 Germany/USA/Canada 2003
Director: **Rob Schmidt**
Producers: **Stan Winston, Brian Gilbert, Erik Feig, Robert Kulzer**
Screenplay: **Alan McElroy**
Director of Photography: **John S. Bartley**
Editor: **Michael Ross**
Production Designer: **Alicia Keywan**
Music/Electronic Score Performer: **Elia Cmiral**
Cast:
**Desmond Harrington** – Chris Flynn
**Eliza Dushku** – Jessie Burlingame
**Emmanuelle Chriqui** – Carly
**Jeremy Sisto** – Scott
**Lindy Booth** – Francine
**Julian Richings** – Three Finger
**Garry Robbins** – Saw-Tooth
**Ted Clark** – One-Eye
**Kevin Zegers** – Evan
**Yvonne Gaudry** – Halley
**Joel Harris**
© **Constantin Film International GmbH/Constantin International B.V.**
Production Companies:
**Summit Entertainment and Constantin Film present a Constantin Film, Summit Entertainment, McOne, Stan Winston production in association with Newmarket Capital Group Produced with the participation of The Canadian Film or Video Production Tax Credit, The Government of Ontario - The Ontario Film & Television Tax Credit**
84 minutes 24 seconds
West Virginia (USA)
Sight and Sound: v. 13, n. 8, p. 64
Box Office: **£1,568,699**
Opening Weekend: **£370,562**
Screens: **253**

### X-Men 2
20th Century Fox – 02 May
12 A USA 2003
Director: **Bryan Singer**
Producers: **Lauren Shuler Donner, Ralph Winter**
Screenplay: **Michael Dougherty, Dan Harris, David Hayter**
Story: **Zak Penn, David Hayter, Bryan Singer**
Director of Photography: **Newton Thomas Sigel**
Editor: **John Ottman**
Production Designer: **Guy Hendrix Dyas**

Music: **John Ottman**
Cast:
**Patrick Stewart** – **Professor Charles Xavier**
**Hugh Jackman** – **Logan/Wolverine**
**Ian McKellen** – **Eric Lensherr/Magneto**
**Halle Berry** – **Ororo Munroe/Storm**
**Famke Janssen** – **Doctor Jean Grey**
**James Marsden** – **Scott Summers/Cyclops**
**Rebecca Romijn-Stamos** – **Raven Darkholme/Mystique/Grace**
**Brian Cox** – **Colonel William Stryker**
**Alan Cumming** – **Kurt Wagner/Nightcrawler**
**Bruce Davison** – **Senator Kelly**
© Twentieth Century Fox Film Corporation [all territories except Brazil, Italy, Korea, Japan, Spain]
© TCF Hungary Film Rights Exploitation Limited Liability Company/Twentieth Century Fox Film Corporation [Brazil, Italy, Korea, Japan, Spain]
Production Companies:
**Twentieth Century Fox presents in association with Marvel Enterprises, Inc.**
**The Donners' Company/Bad Hat Harry production**
**133 minutes 24 seconds**
Location: **Vancouver (Canada)**
Sight and Sound: **v. 13, n. 6, p. 59-60**
Box Office: **£20,604,154**
Opening Weekend: **£7,037,861**
Screens: **449**

### XX/XY

Optimum Releasing – 24 October
15 USA 2001
Director: **Austin Chick**
Producers: **Mitchell B. Robbins, Isen Robbins, Aimee Schoof**
Screenplay: **Austin Chick**
Director of Photography: **Uta Briesewitz**
Editor: **William A. Anderson**
Production Designer: **Judy Becker**
Music: **The Insects**
Cast:
**Mark Ruffalo** – **Coles**
**Kathleen Robertson** – **Thea**
**Maya Stange** – **Sam**
**Petra Wright** – **Claire**
**Kel O'Neill** – **Sid**
**Joshua Spafford** – **Jonathon**
**Zach Shaffer** – **Nick**
**Joey Kern** – **Tommy**
**Evan Neuman** – **guy who asks for his $ back**
**John A. McKay** – **Mitchell**
© Robbins Entertainment.

Production Companies:
**a Robbins Entertainment production**
**An Austin Chick film**
**in association with Intrinsic Value/7th Floor/Natural Nylon, NYC**
**90 minutes 56 seconds**
Location: **New York (NY, USA)**
Sight and Sound: **v. 13, n. 12, p. 60**
Box Office: **£7,695**
Opening Weekend: **£2,891**
Screens: **1**

### Yeh Dil

Bollywood Films – 04 April
Box Office: **£15,283**
Opening Weekend: **£5,324**
Screens: **9**

### Young Adam

Warner Bros – 26 September
18 United Kingdom/France
Director: **David Mackenzie**
Producer: **Jeremy Thomas**
Screenplay: **David Mackenzie**
Based on the novel by
**Alexander Trocchi**
Director of Photography: **Giles Nuttgens**
Editor: **Colin Monie**
Production Designer: **Laurence Dorman**
Music: **David Byrne**
Cast:
**Ewan McGregor** – **Joe**
**Tilda Swinton** – **Ella**
**Peter Mullan** – **Les**
**Emily Mortimer** – **Cathie**
**Jack McElhone** – **Jim Gault**
**Therese Bradley** – **Gwen**
**Ewan Stewart** – **Daniel Gordon**
**Stuart McQuarrie** – **Bill**
**Pauline Turner** – **Connie**
**Alan Cooke** – **Bob M'bussi**
© Young Adam Productions Limited/StudioCanal
Production Companies:
**a Warner Bros. Pictures release of a Recorded Picture Company, Hanway, Film Council, Scottish Screen and Sveno Media presentation**
**a Jeremy Thomas production**
**Made with the support of the National Lottery through the Film Council Premiere Fund and Scottish Screen**
**Developed in association with Sigma Films**
**97 minutes 37 seconds**
Location: **Glasgow (Scotland), United Kingdom, Ireland**
Sight and Sound: **v. 13, n. 10, p. 72**
Box Office: **£835,117**

Opening Weekend: **£228,692**
Screens: **133**

### Zameen

Venus Entertainment – 26 September
Box Office: **£29,717**
Opening Weekend: **£15,975**
Screens: **9**

# SPECIALISED GOODS AND SERVICES

This section has been divided into four parts. The first part features services specialising in actors, audiences and casting. The second lists costume, make-up and prop services. The third section is a general section of specialised goods and services for the film, television and video industries including such items as film stock suppliers, effects units and music services. The final section combines legal and business services for the industry

## Actors, Audiences and Casting

### Avalon Publicity Limited
4a Exmoor Street
London W10 6BD
Tel: 020 7598 7222
Fax: 020 7598 7223
email: edt@avalonuk.com
Edward Thomson

### Bromley Casting (Film & TV Extras Directory)
77 Widmore Road
Bromley BR1 3AA
Tel: 020 8466 8239
Fax: 020 8466 8239
email: admin@bromleycasting.tv
Website: www.bromleycasting.tv
Simon Allen
Providing quality background artisits to the UK film and TV industry

### Celebrities Worldwide Ltd
39-41 New Oxford Street
London WC1A 1BN
Tel: 020 7836 7702/3
Fax: 020 7836 7701
email: info@celebritiesworldwide.com
Website:
www.celebritiesworldwide.com
Claire Nye , Richard Brecker, Joint Managing Directors
Website providing 30,000 celebrity contacts (available on subscription), for UK & international stars from the worlds of: Film, TV, Music, Sport, Fashion, Comedy, Arts, News, Business, and Politics.  Contacts are updated and added daily.  Details are comprehensive and where applicable:

Publicists, Agents, PA's, Personal Managers, Record Companies, Production Companies and Lawyers.

### Downes Agency
96 Broadway
Bexleyheath
Kent DA6 7DE
Tel: 020 8304 0541
Fax: 020 8301 5591
email: downes@presentersagency.com
Website: www.presentersagency.com
Agents representing presenters and actors experienced in the fields of presentations, documentaries, commentaries, narrations, television dramas, feature films, industrial videos, training films, voice-overs, conferences and commercials

### Lip Service Casting Ltd
60-66 Wardour Street
London W1F 0TA
Tel: 020 7734 3393
Fax: 020 7734 3373
email: bookings@lipservice.co.uk
Website: www.lipservice.co.uk
Susan Mactavish
Voiceover agency for actors, and voiceover casting agency

## Costumes, Make-up and Props

### Angels - The Costumiers
1 Garrick Road
London NW9 6AA
Tel: 020 8202 2244
Fax: 020 8202 1820
email: angels@angels.uk.com
Website: www.angels.uk.com
Richard Green
World's largest Costume Hire Company. Extensive ranges covering every historical period, including contemporary clothing, civil and military uniforms. Full in-house ladies and men's making service, millinery department, jewellery, glasses and watch hire. Branches also in Shaftesbury Avenue and Paris. Additional services:- experienced personal costumiers, designers office space, reference library and shipping department

### Angels Wigs
40 Camden Street
London NW1 0EN
Tel: 020 7 387 0999
Fax: 020 7 383 5603
email: wigs@angels.uk.com
Ben Stanton
All types of styles of wigs and hairpieces in either human hair bespoke or synthetic ready-to-wear. Large stocks held, ready to dress, for hire including legal wigs. In house craftsmen to advise on style or period. Facial hair made to order for sale

### Cabervans
Caberfeidh
Cloch Road
Gourock
Nr. Glasgow  PA19 1BA
Tel: 01475 638775
Fax: 01475 638775
Make-up and wardrobe units, dining coaches, motorhomes, 3 & 4 bay American artistes Unit cars, minibuses and 77 seat coaches

### Hirearchy Classic & Contemporary Costume
45-47 Palmerston Road

Boscombe
Bournemouth
**Dorset BH1 4HW**
Tel: 01202 394465
email: hirearchy@aol.com
Website: www.hirearchy.co.uk
Paul Tarrant
Specialising in the hire of ladies and
gents costumes from medieval to
present day. Also accessories, make-
up, wigs, militaria jewellery, textiles
and luggage

## Hothouse Models & Effects
10 St Leonard's Road
Park Royal
**London NW10 6SY**
Tel: 020 8961 3666
Fax: 020 8961 3777
email: info@hothousefx.co.uk
Website: www.hothousefx.co.uk
Jez Clarke, Greg Lawrence
Special effects, mechanical rigs,
models, sculpture and atmospherics
for film and television

## Image Co, The
**Pinewood Studios**
**Iver Heath**
**Buckinghamshire SLO ONH**
Tel: 01753 630066
Fax: 01753 639900
email: mail@image-company.com
John Prentice
Wardrobe costume badging service,
prop and promotional clothing

## Kevin Jones, Freelance Costume Assistant & Designer
32 Austen Walk
West Bromwich
**West Midlands B71 1RD**
Tel: (0121) 588 6801 Mobile: 07775
623738
Fax: (0121) 588 6801
email: KJ58@vodafone.net
Costume Assistant, Designer, dresser
for films television, commercials, pop
videos, promotions, product
launches, fashion shows, theatre,
tours

## Neal Scanlan Studio
Elstree Film Studios
Borehamwood
**Hertfordshire WD6 1JG**
Tel: 0208 324 2620
Fax: 0208 324 2774
Animatronics and special makeup
effects

## Robert Hale Flowers
Interior and Flower Designers
8 Lovell Street

**York YO123 1BO**
Tel: 01904 613044
Contact: Robert Hale
Suppliers and designers of interior
flower decoration

## Ten Tenths
106 Gifford Street
**London N1 0DF**
Tel: 020 7607 4887
Fax: 020 7609 8124
email: mike@tentenths.co.uk
Website: www.tentenths.co.uk
Mike Hallowes

## Woodbridge Productions Ltd
PO Box 123
Hounslow
**London TW4 7EX**
Tel: 020 8574 7778
Fax: 0208 574 7778
email:
info@woodbridgeproductions.co.uk
Website:
woodbridgeproductions.co.uk
John Woodbridge

## 3rd Generation Sets
Manygate Lane
Shepperton
**Middx TW17 9EG**
Tel: 01932 226341
Fax: 01932 246336
email: Callum@hallifordstudios.com
Website:
www.hallifordfilmstudios.com
Contact: Callum Andrews/Studio
manager

# Film Services

## Aerial Cameras Systems Ltd
Innovation House
Douglas Drive
Godalming
**Surrey GU7 1JX**
Tel: 01483 426 767
Fax: 01483 413 900
email: info@aerialcamerasystems.com
Website:
www.aerialcamerasystems.com
Matt Coyde

## Agfa-Gevaert
Motion Picture Division
27 Great West Road
Brentford
**Middx TW8 9AX**
Tel: 020 8231 4301
Fax: 020 8231 4315
Philip Hill

## Any Effects
B2 Ochham Park Barns
Ochham
**Surrey GU23 6NG**
Tel: 0800 2983484
Fax: 01483 223 233
email: jules@anyeffects.com
Website: www.anyeffects.com
Mechanical (front of camera) special
effects. Pyrotechnics: simulated
explosions, bullet hits. Fine models
for close up camera work. Weather:
rain, snow, fog, wind. Breakaways:
shatterglass, windows, bottles, glasses,
collapsing furniture, walls, floors.
Specialised engineering rigs and
propmaking service

## Art
66 Josephine Avenue
**London SW2 2LA**
Tel: 07976 294 985
Fax: 07970 455 956
email: h_artstar@hotmail.com
Website: www.artstar.clara.net
Henrietta Cartwright
Small art consultancy supplying
clients, including the BBC,
advertising companies and interior
decorators, with paintings and
sculpture to meet their requirements

## Riky Ash Falling For You
c/o 65 Britania Avenue
**Nottingham NG6 OEA**
Tel: 0115 849 3470 (Mobile 07850
471227)
Website: www.fallingforyou.tv
Television and Film Stuntman, Stunt
Coordinator, with over 300 television
and film credits. Extensive work for

TV, feature films, commercials, non-broadcast video, promotions and advertising

## Audio Interactive Ltd
Pinewood Studios
Iver Heath
Buckinghamshire SLO ONH
Tel: 01753 651700
Dick Joseph

## Bennett Underwater Productions, Charlie
114 Addison Gardens
West Kensington
London W14 0DS
Tel: 020 7263 952
email: chazben@aol.com

## Bionic Productions Ltd
Pinewood Studios
Pinewood Road
Iver
Bucks SLO ONH
Tel: 01753 653456
Fax: 01753 654507

## Bonded Services
Aerodrome Way
Cranford Lane
Hounslow
Middx TW5 9QB
Tel: 020 8897 7973
Fax: 020 8897 5541
email: info@ftsbonded.com
Website: www.ftsbonded.com
Kim Erin Cowley, Head of Business Development

## Boulton-Hawker Films
Hadleigh
near Ipswich
Suffolk IP7 5BG
Tel: 01473 822235
Fax: 01473 824519

## C I Travel
Shepperton Studios
Shepperton, Studio 16
Middx TW17 0QD
Tel: 01932 592323
Fax: 01932 592417
email: steve.garner@citravel.co.uk
Website: www.citravel.co.uk
Steve Garner/Debbie Hunter

## Camera Associates Ltd
Pinewood Studios
Iver Heath
Buckinghamshire SLO ONH
Tel: 01753 631007
Dave Cooper

## Cinetron Desgin
Shepperton Studios
Shepperton

Middx TW17 0QD
Tel: 01932 572611
Fax: 01932 568989

## Concept 2 Media Ltd
Consett
Brays Lane
Hyde Heath
Amersham
Bucks HP6 5RU
Tel: 01494 772518
email: info@concept2media.co.uk
Website: www.concept2media.com
Stephen Lofthouse

## Concert Lights UK
c/o Elstree Film Studios
Borehamwood
Herts WD6 1JG
Tel: 020 8953 1600
Work on Who Wants to be a Millionnaire for Celador Productions and a number of TV shows

## Connections Communications Centre Ltd
Palingswick House
241 King Street
Hammersmith
London W6 9LP
Tel: 020 8741 1766
Fax: 020 8563 1934
email: @cccmedia.co.uk
Website: www.cccmedia.co.uk
Jacqueline Davis
A registered charity producing promotional and educational videos for the voluntary sector. Currently in production Travelling Forward a 25 minute documentary commissioned by the Thalidomide Society

## Cool Million
Mortimer House
46 Sheen Lane
London SW14 8LP
Tel: 020 8878 7887
Fax: 020 6878 8687
Promotional merchandising, launch parties and roadshows

## De Wolfe Music
Shropshire House
2nd Floor East
11/20 Capper Street
London WC13 6JA
Tel: 020 7631 3600
Fax: 020 7631 3700
email: warren@dewolfemusic.co.uk
Website: www.dewolfemusic.co.uk
Warren De Wolfe, Alan Howe
World's largest production music library. Represents 40 composers for commissions, television and film scores. Offices worldwide, sound FX

department, 3 x 24-track recording studios all with music to picture facilities, also digital editing

## Digital Works
Tel: 07957 568139
email: info@digitise.info
Website: www.digitise.info
Raj Chahal
Live video production within large and small venue's NIA, Wembly Arena. Expertise in web streaming, web video technolgies.

## Dynamic Mounts International
Shepperton Studios
Shepperton
Middx TW17 0QD
Tel: 01932 592348
Fax: 01932 592138
email: dmi@mega3.tv
Website: www.mega3.tv
Dan Gillham
Camera equipment

## EOS Electronics AV
EOS House
Weston Square
Barry
South Glamorgan CF63 2YF
Tel: 01446 741212
Fax: 01446 746120
Specialist manufacturers of video animation, video time laspsing and video archiving equipment. Products: Supertoon Low Cost School Animation System, AC 580 Lo-band Controller, BAC900 Broadcast Animation Controller, LCP3 Compact Disc, Listening Posts

## ETH Screen Music
17 Pilrig Street
Edinburgh EH6 5AN
Tel: 0131 553 2721
Harald Tobermann

## Film Game, The
Unit 30
Metropolitan Centre
3 Taunton Road
Greenford
Middlesex, UB6 8UQ
Tel: 020 7494 9922
Fax: 020 7494 9944
email : email : sales@filmgame.co.uk
James Rowlands/Nick Flynn
Leading supplier of motion picture film stock (available on sale or return) and an extensive range of consumables to compliment your every production requirement

## The Film Stock Centre Blanx
68-70 Wardour Street
London W1F OTB
Tel: 020 7494 2244
Fax: 020 7287 2040
email: sales@fscblanx.co.uk
Rob Flood
A "Kodak @" reseller of motion
picture film stock and stills film, Sony
and all major brands of professional
video tape stock, film consumables,
professional audio products and data
media. Open weekdays 8.30am to
7pm. Emergency callout service 0831
701407

## Film Vault Search Service
Unit 7
The Boundary
Wheatley Road
Garsington
Oxford OX44 9EJ
Tel: 01865 361 000
Fax: 01865 361 500
email: mail@filmvault.co.uk
Website: www.filmvault.co.uk
Steve Cummings
The largest deleted video search
service in the country. No charges for
deposit or 'search fees'. Every video
sold is checked against faults and is
professionally cleaned, comes with
the correct copyright, BBFC
certificate and full guarantee.

## Focus International Transport Ltd
Shepperton Studios
Shepperton
Middx TW17 0QD
Tel: 01932 572339
Fax: 01932 568989

## Formatt Filters
Unit 30
Metropolitan Centre
3 Taunton Road
Greenford
Middlesex, UB6 8UQ
Tel: 020 8570 7701
Fax: 020 8570 7702
email: info@formatt.co.uk
Website: www.format.co.uk
Mark Blaker
Camera filters that match the
precision of your finest lenses.
Formatt Filters is renowed for the
high quality and technical excellence
of its camer filters and lighting gels

## FSC Blanx
68 - 70 Wardour Street
London, W1F 0TB

Tel: Tel : 020 7494 2244
Fax: Fax : 020 7287 2040
email: email : sales@fscblanx.co.uk
Contact : Jessica Finisterre/ Lisa
Renton/ Anna O'Leary
Friendly shop and sales team in th
heart of Soho, selling every kind of
broadcast video tape, professional
audio tape, data media stock and
consumables. Open at weekends

## Fully Equipped & Formatt Filters
Unit 30
Metropolitan Centre
3 Taunton Road
Greenford
Middlesex, UB6 8UQ
Tel: 020 8578 7701
Fax: 020 8578 7702
email: info@fullyequipped.co.uk
Website: www.format.co.uk
Mark Blaker/John Sears/Rob Flood
Premier choice for all new and used
equipment. Products include
cameras, tripods, grip, lighting, sound
& editing equipment. Our sales team
combines 100 years of experience in
the film & video industry

## Harkness Hall Ltd
Unit A
Norton Road
Stevenage
Herts SG1 2LX
Tel: 020 8953 3611
Fax: 020 8207 3657
email: sales@harknesshall.com
Website: www.harknesshall.com
Andrew Robinson, Tony Dilley
Screens for cinemas, screening rooms,
foyers, multi-purpose venues; front,
rear and 3D projection; frames,
masking and roller screens; portable
screens for inside and outside use

## Heliphotos Aerial Photography
Elstree Aerodrome
Elstree
Hertfordshire
Tel: 0208 207 6042

## Kodak Limited
Entertainment Imaging
PO Box 66, Station Road
Hemel Hempstead
Herts HP1 1JU
Tel: 01442 845945
Fax: 01442 844458
Website: www.kodak.com/go/motion
Customer Service
Suppliers of the full range of Kodak
colour negative and print films,
including the new family of Vision

colour negative films

## Little Cinema Company Limited
72 New Bond Street
London W1S 1RR
Tel: 020 7385 5521
Fax: 020 7385 5524
email: sales@littlecinema.co.uk
Joanne van Praagh
Suppliers and installers of digital
projection, sound, and control
systems for screening rooms and
private cinemas worldwide.

## Marine Bio-images
1 Orchard Cottages
Coombe Barton
Shobrooke, Crediton
Devon EX17 1BS
Tel: 01363 775 278
Fax: 01363 775 278
email: email colin-m@marine-bio-
images.com
Website: www.marine-bio-
images.com
Contact: Colin Munro

## Midland Fire Protection Services
101 Lockhurst Lane
Coventry CV6 5SF
Tel: 024 7668 5252 (mobile) 07836
651408
Fax: 024 7663 7575
email: info@midlandrire.co.uk
Website: midlandfire.co.uk
Robin Crane

## Moving Image Touring Exhibition Service (MITES)
Foundation For Art & Creative
Technology (FACT)
88 Wood Street
Liverpool L1 4DX
Tel: 0151 707 4435
Fax: 0151 707 4432
email: mites@fact.co.uk
Website: www.mites.org.uk
Simon Bradshaw

## Oxford Scientific Films (OSF)
Lower Road
Long Hanborough
Oxford OX8 8LL
Tel: 01993 881 881
Fax: 01993 882 808/883969
email: enquires@osf.uk.com
Website: www.osf.uk.com
Sean Morris
ndependent production company
specialising in blue-chip natural
history documentaries for broadcast.
30 years of experience and

innovation in specialist camera techniques. Extensive stills and stock footage libraries

## Pirate Motion Control
St Leonards Road
London NW10 6ST
Tel: 020 8930 5000
Fax: 020 8930 5001
email: help@pirate.co.uk
Website: www.pirate.co.uk
Michael Ganss
Motion Control Studio for 16mm film and video. 12 axis rig & 3 motion controlled lighting dimmer circuits. Call for showreel

## ProDigital Audio Services
3 George Street
West Bay
Dorset DT6 4EY
Tel: 01308 422 866
Sound equipment, service and maintenance. Specialises in location sound equipment for the film and television industry - particularly DAT recorders

## Radcliffes Transport Services
3-9 Willow Lane
Willow Lane Industrial Estate
Mitcham
Surrey CR4 4NA
Tel: 020 8687 2344
Fax: 020 8687 0997
Specialist transport specifically for the film and television industry, both nationally and internationally. Fleet ranges from transit vans to 40' air ride articulated vehicles with experienced staff

## The Screen Company
182 High Street
Cottenham
Cambridge CB4 8RX
Tel: 01954 250139
Fax: 01954 252005
email: thescreencompany@onetel.net.uk
Website: www.thescreencompany.co.uk
Pat Turner
Manufacture, supply and installation of all types of front and rear projection screens for video, slide, film and OHP

## The Screenwriters Store
The Screenwriter's Store Ltd.
Suite 121, Friars House
157-168 Blackfriars Road
London SE1 8EZ
Tel: 020 7261 1908

Fax: 020 7261 1909
email: bfi@thesws.com
Website: www.thesws.com
Rinaldo Quacquarini/Johanna Reder
Opening Hours: Mon- Fri, 9.30am - 6pm (callers by prior arrangement please)
Europe's largest authorised reseller and distributor of screenwriting and production software, also selling seminars, consultancy. The website has over 1000 popular screenplays in proper script format available for free downloading

## Simmons Aerofilms Limited
32-34 Station Close
Potters Bar
Hertfordshire EN6 1TL
Tel: 01707-648390
Fax: :01707-648399
email:library@aerofilms.com
Website: www.simmonsaerofilms.com
Chris Mawson, Library Manager
Simmons Aerofilms is the world's first commercial aerial photography company with over 80 years experience capturing aerial images of the UK and overseas for both the professional and home user

## Snow-Bond
37 Oakwood Drive
Heaton
Bolton BL1 5EE
Tel: 01204 841285
Fax: 01204 841285

## Studio Art
Elstree Film Studios
Boreham Wood
Hertfordshire WD6 1JG
Tel: 0208 324 2600
Fax: 0208 324 2601
Danny Rogers

## The National Research Group
Tel: 020 7351 4370
Lucy McDonald

## Visionworks Internet Ltd
13 Chartfield Avenue
London SW15 6DT
Tel: 020 8789 4254
Fax: 020 8785 0520
Website: www.visionworksinternet.com
Sandy Knight
Web design from basic level up to e-commerce

## Workspace Management Limited
Canalot Production Studios

222 Kensal Road
London W10 5BN
Tel: 020 89608580
Fax: 020 89608907
email: sarah.charrington@workspacegroup.co.uk
Andrea Kolakasi, Studio Manager
Sarah Charrington, Assistant Manager
Large Media business complex housing over 90 companies

## Zooid Pictures Limited
66 Alexander Road
London N19 5PQ
Tel: 020 7281 2407
Fax: 020 7281 2404
email: pictures@zooid.co.uk
Website: www.zooid.co.uk
Richard Philpott
For over 20 years, Zooid has been a one-stop media resources supplier and researcher for all copyright materials including film/video, stills, illustration, animation and sound, from archives, libraries, agencies, private collections and museums worldwide, for use in film, television, book publishing, CD-Rom, multimedia, presentations and on-line services. Zooid manage all aspects from first briefing through to licensing. Zooid use advanced digital technologies and license their management system, Picture Desk, to leading international publishers

# Legal and Business Services

## Ashurst Morris Crisp
Broadwalk House
5 Appold Street
London EC2A 2HA
Tel: 0207 638 1111
Fax: 0207 972 7990
email: film.tv@ashursts.com
Website: www.ashursts.com
Tony Ghee, Charlotte Douglas, Vanessa Bertelli, Sergei Ostrovsky, Monica Keightley
Leading City law firm with a young and progressive media and telecommunications team. Advice is provided on all aspects of the film and television industry, including corporate, employment, property and tax issues. Clients include leading national broadcasters, cable network operators and a number of small independents

## Barclays Bank Media Banking Centre
27 Soho Square
London W1A 4WA
Tel: 020 7445 5773
Fax: 020 7445 5802
email: tony.tozzi@barclayscorporate.com
Tony Tozzi
Large business centre providing a comprehensive range of banking services to all aspects of the film and television industry

## Deloitte & Touche
Hill House
1 Little New Street
London EC4A 3TR
Tel: 020 7936 3000
Fax: 020 7583 8517
Website: www.deloitte.co.uk
Gavin Hamilton-Deeley
Advisors to film, television and broadcasting organisations. Business plans and financial models for companies, tax planning and business advice for individuals, and information on legal and regulatory developments affecting the sector

## Dorsey & Whitney
21 Wilson Street
London EC2M 2TD
Tel: 020 7588 0800
Fax: 020 7588 0555

## Film Finances
14/15 Conduit Street
London W1R 9TG
Tel: 020 7629 6557
Fax: 020 7491 7530
Website: www.filmfinances.com
Provide completion guarantees for the film and television industry

## Henry Hepworth
Media Law Solicitors
5 John Street
London WC1N 2HH
Tel: 020 7242 7999
Fax: 020 7242 7988
A new specialist media and intellectual property practice with a distinctive high quality client base which is active across the entire spectrum of the copyright and intellectual property industries

## The Media Law Partnership,
33 Prospect Road
London NW2 2JU
Tel: 020 7435 7127
Fax: 0870 1307486
email: as@medialaw.uk.com
Adam Sutcliffe
Offers experience in all aspects of the negotiation and drafting of agreements for film production, film financing and international co-productions, with an emphasis on concise and effective documents, and a practical 'business affairs' approach to legal matters for all those involved in the film-making and distribution process

## Olswang
90 Long Acre
London WC2E 9TT
Tel: 020 7208 8888
Fax: 020 7208 8800
email: olsmail@olswang.co.uk
Website: www.olswang.co.uk
One of the UK's leading entertainment and media law firms. It provides specialist advice in all aspects of broadcasting, satellite, cable, multimedia, IT & telecommunications, media convergence and music law, to the European and US markets

## Richards Butler
110 Cannon Street
London EC4N 6AR
Tel: 020 7772 5763
Selina Short, Communications
Richards Butler is an international law firm which has been associated with the media and entertainment industry for over 60 years

# STUDIOS

## 3 Mills Studios
Three Mill Lane
London E3 3DU
Tel: 020 7363 3336
Fax: 020 8215 3499
email:
candice.macdonald@3mills.com
Website: www.3mills.com
Candice McDonald (Bookings/PR Manager)
16 Stages, 6 Rehearsal Rooms,
Production Offices, Restaurant/Bar
Recent features:
Corpse Bride, The Yank, Code 46,
Spivs, 28 Days Later,
Recent television:
Bad Girls, Footballer's Wives, Ny-
Lon, 15 Storeys High, The Mighty
Boosh, Dream Team, Mile High, 24
Hour Quiz

## BBC Television Centre Studios
Wood Lane
London W12 7RJ
Tel: 020 8700 100 883
email: bbcresources.co.uk
Website: bbcresources.com
National Call Centre
8 full-facility television studios
TC1   10,250 sq ft
TC3   8,000 sq ft
TC4 and TC8   8,000 sq ft (digital and widescreen capable)
TC6   8,000 sq ft (digital)
TC2, TC5 and TC7 3,500 sq ft

## Bray Studios
Down Place
Water Oakley
Windsor Road
Windsor SL4 5UG
Tel: 01628 622111
Fax: 01628 770381
email: b.earl@tiscali.co.uk
Studio manager: Beryl Earl
STAGES
1 (sound) 955 sq metres
2 (sound) 948 sq metres
3 (sound) 238 sq metres
4 (sound) 167 sq metres
FILM
Revelation
TELEVISION
Born and Bred II and III
Fimbles I and II

## De Lane Lea Dean Street Studio
75 Dean Street
London W1V 5HA
Tel: 020 7432 3800
Fax: 020 7432 3838
email: info@delanelea.com
Website: www.delanelea.com
Huw Penallt-Jones, Chief Operating Officer

## Ealing Studios
Ealing Studios
Ealing Green
London W5 5EP
Tel: 020 8567 6655
Fax: 020 8758 8658
email: info@ealingstudios.com
Website: www.ealingstudios.com
Bookings Office
STAGES:
1 (silent) = area 232m2
2 (sound) = 864m2
3A (sound) = 530m2
3B (sound) = 530m2
3A/B combined = 1,080m2
4 (model stage silent) = 390m2
5 (sound) = 90m2
FILMS:
Shaun Of The Dead
Bride and Prejudice
Just One Of Those Things
Notting Hill
TELEVISION:
Rodger Rodger (BBC)
Spooks (Kudos)
Red Cap (Stormy Film Productions)
The Royle Family (Granada)

## Halliford Studios
Manygate Lane
Shepperton
Middx TW17 9EG
Tel: 01932 226341
Fax: 01932 246336
email: sales@hallifordstudios.com
Website:
www.hallifordfilmstudios.com
Contact: Callum Andrews/Studio manager
Stages:
A stage 60'*60' (18.27*18.27m) 334sq metres, 18'6" HIGH (5.63m)
B stage 60'*40' (18.27*12.18m) 223sq metres, 18'6" HIGH (5.63m)

## Holborn Studios
49/50 Eagle Wharf Road
London N1 7ED
Tel: 020 7490 4099
Fax: 020 7253 8120
email: reception@holborn-studios.co.uk
Website: www.holbornstudios.com
Ian Barker, Studio manager
STAGES
4  2,470 sq feet
6  2,940 sq feet
7  2,660 sq feet
18 roomsets  3,125 sq feet
Also eight fashion studios, set
building, E6 lab, b/w labs, Calumet in
house, canal-side restaurant and bar.

## Lamb Studios
Lamb House
Church Street
Chiswick
London W4 2PD
Tel: 020 89969961
Fax: 020 89969966
Website: www.bell.com
Address Lamb House
Church StreetChiswick
London
England
W4 2PD
Telephone 020 89969961
Fax 020 89969966
Website www.bell.com
Lamb Studios

## Leavesden Studios
PO Box 3000
Leavesden
Herts WD2 7LT
Tel: 01923 685 060
Fax: 01923 685 061
Studio Manager: Daniel Dark
STAGES
A 32,076sq feet
B 28,116 sq feet
C 11,285 sq feet
D 11,808 sq feet
F 15,427 sq feet
G 14,036 sq feet
Flight Shed 1 35,776
Effects 15,367 sq feet
Back Lot      100 acres
180 degrees of clear and
uninterrupted horizon
Further 200,000 sq.ft of covered space

available
FILMS
GoldenEye, Mortal Kombat,
Annihilation; Sleepy Hollow, Star
Wars: Episode One - The Phantom
Menance, An Ideal Husband

## Magic Eye Film Studios

Magic Eye Film Studios
20 Lydden Road
London SW18 4LR
Tel: 020 8877 0800
Fax: 020 8874 7274
Website: www.magiceye.co.uk
email: info@magiceye.co.uk
Magic Eye offers five fully operational
stages, ranging from 900 to 4,500
square feet. They all include
production offices and make-up
rooms. Several of the stages are also
fully coved

## Millennium Studios

Elstree Way
Herts WD6 1SF
Tel: 020 8236 1400
Fax: 020 8236 1444
Website: www.elstree-online.co.uk
Contact: Ronan Willson
'X' Stage: 327 sq metres sound stage
with flying grid and cyc. Camera
room, construction workshop,
wardrobe, dressing rooms, edit
rooms, hospitality suite and
production offices are also on site.
Recent productions: Carnivl Films
'Bug' Series

## Pinewood Shepperton Group

Pinewood Studios
Pinewood Road
Iver Heath
Bucks SL0 0NH
Tel: 01753 651700
Fax: 01753 656844
email: bookings@
pinewoodshepperton.com
Website:
www.pinewoodshepperton.comMana
ging
STAGES
A 1,685 sq metres
(Tank: 12.2m x 9.2m x 2.5m)
B 827 sq metres
C 827 sq metres
D 1,685 sq metres
(Tank: 12.2m x 9.2m x 2.5m)
E 1,685 sq metres
(Tank: 12.2m x 9.2m x 2.5m)
F 698 sq metres
(Tank: 6.1m x 6.1m x 2.5m)
G 247 sq metres
H 300 sq metres
J 824 sq metres - dedicated TV Studio

K 824 sq metres
L 880 sq metres
M 880 sq metres
N/P 767 sq metres
R 1,780 sq metres
S 1,789 sq metres
South Dock (silent)
1,547 sq metres
Albert R Broccoli 007 (silent) 4,223
sq metres (Tank: 90.5m x 22.3m x
2.7m Reservoir: 15.3m x 28.7m x
2.7m)
Large Process 454 sq metres
Exterior Lot 50 acres, comprising
formal gardens and lake, woods,
fields, concrete service roads and
squares
Exterior Tank 67.4m narrowing to
32m wide, 60.4 long, 1.06m deep.
Capacity 764,000 gallons. Inner Tank:
15.5m x 12.2m x 2.7m. Backing
73.2m x 18.3m
Largest outdoor tank in Europe
FILMS
Die Another Day, Quills, Proof of
Life, Tomb Raider, Revelation,
Charlotte Gray, The Hours, Below,
the World is Not Enough, the
Mummy Returns
TELEVISION
Dinotopia, Jack and the Beanstalk -
the Real Story, Wit, Hornblower,
Thursday the 12th, Sam's Game, My
Family
**Shepperton Studios**
**Studio Road**
**Shepperton**
**Middx TW17 0QD**
Tel: 01932 562 611
Fax: 01932 568 989
email:
bookings@pinewoodshepperton.com
Website:
www.pinewoodshepperton.com
Paul Olliver
STAGES
A 1,668 sq metres
B 1,115 sq metres
C 1,668 sq metres
D 1,115 sq metres
E 294 sq metres
F 294 sq metres
G 629 sq metres
H 2,660 sq metres
I 657 sq metres
J 1,394 sq metres
K 1,114 sq metres
L 604 sq metres
M 259 sq metres
T 261 sq metres
R 948 sq metres
S 929 sq metres
FILMS
Dirty Pretty Things, Just Visiting,

Possession, Killing Me Softly, Two
Men Went To War, Shakespeare in
Love; Elizabeth, Hilary & Jackie;
Sliding Doors; Notting Hill; Love's
Labour's Lost; End of the Affair

## Riverside Studios

Crisp Road
Hammersmith
London W6 9RL
Tel: 020 8237 1000
Fax: 020 8237 1011
email:
jonfawcett@riversidestudios.co.uk
Website: www.riversidestudios.co.uk
Jon Fawcett
Studio One 529 sq metres
Studio Two 378 sq metres
Studio Three 130 sq metres
Plus preview cinema, various dressing
rooms, offices, café
TELEVISION
T.F.I. Friday, 'Collins & McConies
Movie Club', Channel 4 Sitcom
Festival, 'This Morning with Richard
Not Judy', Top of the Pops (2001)

## Rotherhithe Studios/Sands Films Studios

119 Rotherhithe Street
London SE16 4NF
Tel: 020 7231 2209
Fax: 020 7231 2119
email: ostockman@sands.films.co.uk
Website: sandsfilms.co.uk
O Stockman, C Goodwin
STAGES
1 Rotherhithe 180 sq metres
Pre-production, construction, post-
production facilities, period costume
making, props
FILMS
The Children's Midsummer Night's
Dream
The Lost Prince
Peter Pan
Touching the Void
Vanity Fair
Nouvelle France

## South West Film Studios

St Agnes
Cornwall TR5 0LA
Tel: (0)1872 554131
Fax: (0)1872 552880
email:
info@southwestfilmstudios.com
Website:
www.southwestfilmstudios.com
Kate Hughes
South West Film Studios is a new
purpose built studio facility, located
on the stunning north coast of
Cornwall. It offers a complete
package

for film productions, including sound stages, water stage, workshop and office spaces, all set in beautiful landscaped gardens. South West Film Studios offers a flexible approach, whether you require a production base for a location shoot or fully sound proofed stage facilities.
Stages
1A - 24m x 18m x 12m
1B - 24m x 18m x 12m including water tank 3 x 3 x 2.5m
1A/B combined 36m x 24m x 12m
Stage 2 - 21m x 21m x 11.5m

## Stonehills Studios
Shields Road
Gateshead
Tyne and Wear NE10 0HW
Tel: 0191 495 2244
Fax: 0191 495 2266
Studio Manager: Nick Walker
STAGES
1 1,433 sq feet
2   750 sq feet
The North's largest independent television facility comprising of Digital Betacam Edit Suite with the BVE 9100 Edit Controller, and Abekas ASWR 8100 mixer, A57 DVE and four machine editing, including two DVW 500s. Also three Avid off-line suites, 2D Matador and 3D Alias graphics and a Sound Studio comprising a Soundtracs 6800 24-track 32 channel desk and Soundscape 8-track digital editing machine
TELEVISION
Germ Genie, BBC 2; The Spark, Border; Come Snow Come Blow, Granada

## Teddington Studios
Broom Road
Teddington
Middlesex TW11 9NT
Tel: 020 8977 3252
Fax: 020 8943 4050
email: sales@teddington.co.uk
Website: www.teddington.co.uk
Sales and Client Liaison
STUDIOS
1 653 sq metres
2 372 sq metres
3 120 sq metres
TELEVISION
This is Your Life; Des O'Connor Tonight; Harry Hill; Brian Conley Show; Alistair McGowan, My Hero, Beast, Coupling

## Twickenham Film Studios
St Margaret's
Twickenham

Middx TW1 2AW
Tel: 020 8607 8888
Fax: 020 8607 8889
Website: www.twickenhamstudios.com
Gerry Humphreys, Caroline Tipple (Stages)
STAGES
1 702 sq metres
with tank 37 sq metres x 2.6m deep
2 186 sq metres
3 516 sq metres
2 x dubbing theatres; 1 x ADR/Foley theatre; 40 x cutting rooms; Lightworks, Avid 35/16mm
Films include
Brothers Grimm
Dead Fish

## Westway Studios
8 Olaf Street
London W11 4BE
Tel: 020 7221 9041
Fax: 020 7221 9399
Steve/Kathy
STAGES
1 502 sq metres (Sound Stage)
2 475 sq metres
3 169 sq metres
4 261 sq metres

# TELEVISION COMPANIES

Below are listed all British terrestrial television companies. A more comprehensive listing of programmes, producers and cast members can be found via the web pages of each company. It is also worth exploring the *bfi* Television Handbook for a thorough look into the TV industry

## BBC Television

### British Broadcasting Corporation
Television Centre
Wood Lane
Shepherds Bush
London W12 7RJ
Tel: 020 8743 8000
Website: www.bbc.co.uk
BBC Broadcasting House
Potrland Place
London W1A 1AA
Tel: 020 7580 4468
BBC Drama
Television Centre
Wood Lane
London W12 7RJ
Tel: 020 8743 8000
Tel: 020 85761 1861 (publicity dept)
BBC Resources
Television Centre
Wood Lane
London W12 7RJ
Tel: 08700 100 883
Fax: 08700 100 884
email: bbcresources@bbc.co.uk
Website: www.bbcresources.co.uk

### BBC Worldwide
Woodlands
80 Wood Lane
London W12 0TT
Tel: 020 8433 2000
Fax: 020 8749 0538
email: bbcworldwide@bbc.co.uk
Website: www.bbcworldwide.com
Online Catalogue:
www.bbcworldwidetv.com

### BBC Broadcast Programme Acquisition
BBC TV Centre
Wood Lane
London W12 7RJ
Tel: 020 8225 6721

Fax: 020 8749 0893
Controller, Programme Acquisition: George McGhee
Head of Films: Steve Jenkins
Responsible for feature film acquisition.
Head of Series: Sue Deeks
Responsible for fiction series acquisition.
Business Development Manager: Paul Eggington
Responsible for short fiction film acquisition.
Head of Legal and Business Affairs: Paul Fagan
Responsible for acquisitions business issues.

## Regional Television

### BBC East (Look East)
St Catherine's Close
All Saint's Green
Norwich, Norfolk NR1 3ND
moving Autumn 2003 to
The Forum
Millennium Plain
Norwich, Norfolk NR2 1TF
Tel: 01603 619331
Fax: 01603 667865
email: look.east@bbc.co.uk
Head, Regional & Local Programmes: Tim Bishop

### BBC East Midlands
East Midlands Broadcasting Centre,
London Road,
Nottingham NG2 4UU
Tel: 0115 955 0500
Fax: 0115 902 1984
email: emt@bbc.co.uk
Head of Regional & Local Progs: Alison Ford

### BBC London
35c Marylebone High Street
London W1U 4QA
Tel: 020 7224 2424
email: yourlondon@bbc.co.uk
Head of Regional & Local Programmes: Michael MacFarlane

### BBC North
Broadcasting Centre
Woodhouse Lane
Leeds LS2 9PX

Tel: 0113 244 1188
Fax: 0113 243 9387
email: look.north@bbc.co.uk
Head of Regional & Local Programmes: Colin Philpott

### BBC North East & Cumbria
Broadcasting Centre
Barrack Road
Newcastle upon Tyne NE99 2NE
Tel: 0191 232 1313
Fax: 0191 221 0112
email:
look.north.northeast.cumbria@bbc.co.uk
Head of Regional & Local Programmes: Wendy Pilmer

### BBC North West
New Broadcasting House
Oxford Road
Manchester M60 1SJ
Tel: 0161 200 2020
Fax: 0164 236 1005
email: nwt@bbc.co.uk
Head of Regional & Local Programmes: Martin Brooks

### BBC Northern Ireland
Broadcasting House
Ormeau Avenue
Belfast BT2 8HQ
Tel: 028 9033 8000
Fax: 028 9033 8800
email: ni@bbc.co.uk
Controller: Anna Carragher

### BBC Scotland
Broadcasting House
Queen Margaret Drive
Glasgow G12 8DG
Tel: 0141 338 2000
Fax: 0141 334 0614
email: enquiries.scot@bbc.co.uk
Controller, BBC Scotland: John McCormick
Edinburgh
Broadcasting House
Queen Street
Edinburgh EH2 1JF
Tel: 0131 225 3131
Aberdeen
Broadcasting House
Beechgrove Terrace
Aberdeen AB9 2ZT
Tel: 01224 625233

## BBC South
Broadcasting House
Havelock Road
Southampton SO14 7PU
Tel: 0238 022 6201
email: south.today@bbc.co.uk
Head of Regional & Local
Programmes: Eve Turner

## BBC South East
The Great Hall
Mount Pleasant Road
Tunbridge Wells
Kent TN1 1QQ
Tel: 01892 670 000
email: southeasttoday@bbc.co.uk
Head of Regional & Local
Programmes: Laura Ellis

## BBC South West
Broadcasting House
Seymour Road
Plymouth PL3 5BD
Tel: 01752 229201
Fax: 01752 234595
email: spotlight@bbc.co.uk
Head of Regional & Local
Programmes: Leo Devine

## BBC Wales
Broadcasting House
Llandaff
Cardiff CF5 2YQ
Tel: 029 2032 2000
email: feedback.wales@bbc.co.uk
Controller, BBC Wales: Menna
Richards
Broadcasting House
Meirion Road
Bangor
Gwynedd LL57 3BY
Tel: 01248 370880
Fax: 01248 351443

## BBC West
Broadcasting House
Whiteladies Road
Bristol BS8 2LR
Tel: 0117 973 2211
email: pointswest@bbc.co.uk
Head of Regional & Local
Programmes: Andrew Wilson

## BBC West Midlands
BBC Pebble Mill
Birmingham B5 7QQ
moving late 2003 to
The Mailbox
Royal Mail Street
Birmingham B1 1XL
**Tel: 0121 567 6767**
Tel: 0121 432 8888
email: midlands.today@bbc.co.uk
Head of Regional & Local Progs:
David Holdsworthy

# Independent Television Companies

## Anglia Television
Anglia House
Norwich NR1 3JG
Tel: 01603 615151
Fax: 01603 631032
Website: www.anglia.tv.co.uk
Email: pr@angliatv.co.uk
Fax: 01603 761245 (Press Office)
Regional Offices:
**Cambridge**
26 Newmarket Road
Cambridge CB5 8DT
Tel: 01223 357676
**Chelmsford**
64-68 New London Road
Chelmsford CM2 0YU
Tel: 01245 357676
**Ipswich**
Hubbard House
Civic Drive
Ipswich IP1 2QA
Tel: 01473 226157
**Luton**
16 Park Street
Luton LU1 2DP
Tel: 01582 729666
**Milton Keynes**
ADMAIL 3222
Milton Keynes MK2 2NA
Tel: 01908 691660
**Northampton**
77b Abington Street
Northampton NN1 2BH
Tel: 01604 624 343
**Peterborough**
6 Bretton Green Village
Rightwell, Bretton
Peterborough PE3 8DY
Tel: 01733 269440
Part of the Granada Media Group
and covering the east of England,
Anglia Television produces around 8
hrs of news and other programmes
per week for its own transmission.
Anglia also produces programmes for
the ITV Network and other
broadcasters such as Channel 4.

## Border Television
The Television Centre
Carlisle CA1 3NT
Tel: 01228 525101
Fax: 01228 541384
Website: www.border-tv.com
Covering 288,000 homes in Cumbria,
Border Television's broadcast
coverage extends from Peebles in the
North, down to Seascale in the south
and includes the Isle of Man., and

viewers in the Border Television
region watch more television than the
national average. Border Television
renewed its licence in 2001 and is
required to produce/commission a
minimum of 294 hrs of regional
programming annually. It also
producers material for the ITV
Network, such as the award-winning
series Innovators and other
broadcasters including Channel 4.

## Carlton Television
101 St Martin's Lane
London WC2N 4RF
Tel: 020 7240 4000
Fax: 020 7240 4171
Website: www.carlton.com
Carlton Television holds 5 ITV
franchises: Carlton London Region
(weekdays), Carlton Central Region,
Carlton West Country Region, HTV
Wales and HTV West. Most Carlton
commissioning is now channeled
through its subsidiary Carlton
Productions - see below

## Carlton Productions
35-38 Portman Square
London W1H 0NU
Tel: 020 7486 6688
Fax: 020 7486 1132
Supplier of popular programming
across all genres. It includes
entertainment producer Planet 24
(www.planet24.com) and game show
format supplier Action Time
(www.action-time.com).

## Carlton Broadcasting Central Region
Website: www.itv.com/carltoncentral
**West Midlands:**
**Central Court**
**Gas Street**
**Birmingham B1 2JT**
Tel: 0121 643 9898
Fax: 0121 643 4897
**East Midlands:**
**Carlton Studios,**
**Lenton Lane**
**Nottingham NG7 2NA**
Tel: 0115 986 3322
Fax: 0115 964 5552
**South Midlands:**
**9 Windrush Court**
**Abingdon Business Park**
**Abingdon OX14 1SA**
Tel: 01235 554123
Fax: 01235 524024
**Outside Broadcasting Facilities:**
**Carlton 021**
**Units 11-13 Gravelly Industrial Park,**
**Gravelly Hill,**

Birmingham B24 8HZ
Tel: 0121 327 2021
Fax: 0121 327 7021
Website: www.carlton021.net
email: 021info@carltontv.co.uk
**Carlton Studios**
Lenton Lane,
Nottingham NG7 2NA
Tel: 01159 863 322**Carlton
Broadcasting London
Region**
101 St Martin's Lane,
London WC2N 4RF
Tel: 020 7240 4000
Fax: 020 7240 4171
Tel: 020 7347 3611 (Press Office)
email: dutyoffice@carltontv.co.uk
Website: www.itv.com/carltonlondon
**London Television Centre
Upper Ground
London SE1 9LT
Tel: 020 7620 1620**
Fax: 020 7827 7500
Holds the weekday ITV licence for
the areas of London and the South-
East. Carlton Television London is
required to produce/commission a
minimum of 419 hours of regional
programming annually. It also
produces material for the ITV
Network and other broadcasters.

## Carlton Broadcasting West Country Region
**Western Wood Way
Langage Science Park
Plymouth PL7 5BQ**
Tel: 01752 333333
Fax: 01752 333444
email: dutyoffice@carltontv.co.uk
Website:
www.itv.com/carltonwestcountry
Owned by Carlton, Westcountry
Television has a network of seven
regional studios together with the
main studio and headquarters in
Plymouth and broadcasts to Cornwall
and Devon and to much of Dorset
and Somerset.The company transmits
to 1.7 million people who live in one
of the most diverse regions in the
UK, and WT is strongly committed to
reflecting this diversity in its regional
coverage. Westcountry Television is
required to produce/commission a
minimum of 628 hours of regional
programming. The company also
produces material for the ITV
network and other broadcasters such
as Channel 4

## Central Television
see Carlton Broadcasting Central
Region

## Channel Four Television
**124 Horseferry Road
London SW1P 2TX**
Tel: 020 7396 4444
Fax: 020 7306 8353
Website: www.channel4.com
Channel 4 is a national service set up
by Act of Parliament in 1982 as a non
profit making corporation, funded
principally by its revenue from
advertising. Its remit is to: have a
distinctive character of its own, and
cater for interests not served by other
channels; provide a diverse service
including news, current affairs,
education, religion and multicultural
programming, all of which are to be
an integral part of the peak-time
programming strategy, reflect and
respond to disability issues; place
educational material at the heart of
the schedule; play a central role in the
UK film industry; and encourage a
large and diverse independent
production industry, within and
outside London. With a handful of
exceptions, C4 does not make
programmes itself - it both
commissions new material from
production companies and buys in
already completed programmes. In
2002, 67% of broadcast hours were
made up of new programming, and
C4 achieved 10% share of all viewing.
In this year a reorganisation also took
place to face financial challenges.
FilmFour was restructured and
production absorbed back into the
main channel.

## Channel Television
**Television Centre, La Pouquelaye
St Helier
Jersey JE1 3ZD**
Tel: 01534 816816
Fax: 01534 816817
email: broadcast@channeltv.co.uk
**Television House, Bulwer Avenue
St Sampson
Guernsey GY2 4LA**
Tel: 01481 241888
Fax: 01481 241866
email: broadcast.gsy@channeltv.co.uk
**Unit 16A, 3rd floor
Enterprise House
59-65 Upper Ground
London SE1 9PQ**
Tel: 020 7633 9902
Fax: 020 7401 8982
email: broadcast@channeltv.co.uk
Website: www.channeltv.co.uk
Owned by Yattendon Investment
Trust and covering the Channel
Islands (principally the Islands of

Jersey, Guernsey, Alderney, Herm and
Sark) with a population of 150,000,
Channel Television produced 124
hours of regional programming over
2002. The regional programme
service is centred around local events
and current affairs and the station's
main studios are based in Jersey with
additional studios in Guernsey

## five
**22 Long Acre
London WC2E 9LY**
Tel: 020 7550 5555
Fax: 020 7550 5554
Website: www.channel5.co.uk
(www.five.tv)
email: dutyoffice@channel5.co.uk
Channel 5 launched on 30 March
1997, as the UK's fifth terrestrial
broadcaster. Before broadcasting
could begin, however, 5 was faced
with the Herculean task of retuning 9
million homes across the UK.
Coverage has now extended to 86.6%
of homes with a share average for
2002 of 6.3%. Channel 5 is owned by
two shareholders, RTL Group
64.625% and United Business Media
35.375%. Under its remit, 51% of
programming must be original, 51%
must be of European origin, 25%
must be independent commissions,
there must a minimum of 11 hours
news programming; and 62 hours per
week of programming must be
subtitled. In 2002 Channel 5 changed
its name to five.

## GMTV
**London Television Centre
Upper Ground
London SE1 9LT**
Tel: 020 7827 7000
Fax: 020 7827 7001/020 7827 7100
Website: gm.tv (or www.gmtv.co.uk)
Owned by Carlton, Disney, Granada
and the Scottish Media Group, each
holding a 25% share, GMTV
broadcasts nationally news and
magazine programming, with
features on life style and show
business, on the ITV network from
6.00 am to 9.25 am. Weekday
programming share for 2002 was
30.4%.

## Grampian Television
**Queen's Cross
Aberdeen AB15 4XJ**
Tel: 01224 846846
Fax: 01224 846800
email:
viewer.enquiries@grampian.co.uk
Website: www.grampiantv.co.uk

Part of the Scottish Media Group and covering the North of Scotland, including Aberdeen, Dundee and Inverness, Grampian TV broadcasts to an audience of 1.2 million viewers. During 2002, Grampian gained a 32% peak-time audience share. Grampian also produces material for the ITV Network and other broadcasters such as BBC1, Channel 4, and Nickelodeon.

## Granada Media

**Main offices:**
**Granada Television Centre**
**Quay Street**
**Manchester M60 9EA**
Tel: 0161 832 7211
Fax: 0161 827 2029
email: officers.duty@granadamedia.com
Website: www.granadamedia.com
News centres:
**London**
**4th Floor**
**48 Leicester Square**
**London WC2H 7FB**
Tel: 020 7389 8555
Fax: 020 7930 8499
**Granada News Centre**
**Albert Dock, Liverpool L3 4BA**
Tel: 0151 709 9393
Fax: 0151 709 3389
**Chester**
**Bridgegate House**
**5 Bridge Place**
**Lower Bridge Street**
**Chester CH1 1SA**
Tel: 01244 313966
Fax: 01244 320599
**Lancaster**
**White Cross, Lancaster LA1 4XQ**
Tel: 01524 60688
Fax: 01524 67607
**Blackburn**
**Daisyfield Business Centre**
**Appleby Street**
**Blackburn BB1 3BL**
Tel: 01254 690099
Fax: 01254 699299
**Granada Film**
**The London Television Centre**
**Upper Ground**
**London SE1 9LT**
**Tel: 020 7620 1620**
Granada is the largest company in the UK commercial television sector, providing programmes for UK and international broadcasters. It currently owns seven ITV licenses – Granada TV, LWT (London Weekend Television), Yorkshire TV, Tyne Tees TV, Meridian Broadcasting, Anglia TV and Border Television, covering

15 million homes. In 2001 it restructured into two distinct divisions: Enterprises and Content. Granada TV has held the ITV franchise for the North of England since the start of commercial television in the UK in 1956. Its transmission area includes Manchester and Liverpool, and stretches from the Lake District to Shropshire, and from the North Wales coast to the Pennines, serving a population of 6.2 million. During 2002, Granada TV broadcasted 491 hours of regional programming. It also makes programmes for the ITV Network and other broadcasters such as Channel 4

## HTV Wales

**The Television Centre**
**Culverhouse Cross**
**Cardiff CF5 6XJ**
Tel: 02920 590 590
Fax: 02920 597 183
email: info@htv.co.uk
Website: www.htvwales.com; www.itv1wales.com
**Carmarthen Office:**
**Top Floor**
**19-20 Lammas Street**
**Carmarthen SA31 3AL**
Tel: 01267 236 806
Fax: 01267 238 228
email: giles.smith@itv1wales.co.uk
**Colwyn Bay Office:**
**Celtic Business Centres**
**Plas Eirias**
**Heritage Gate, Abergele Road,**
**Colwyn Bay LL29 8BW**
Tel: 01492 513888
Fax: 01492 513888
email: colwyn@itv1wales.co.uk
**Swansea Office:**
**21 Walter Road**
**Swansea SA1 5NQ**
Tel: 029 20 590746
email: richard.nosworthy@itv1wales.co.uk
**Newtown Office:**
**St. David's House**
**Newtown**
**Powys SY16 1RB**
Tel: 01686 623381
Fax: 01686 624816
email: rob.shelly@itv1wales.co.uk
**Wrexham Office:**
**HTV Wales**
**Crown Buildings**
**31 Chester Street**
**Wrexham**
Tel: 01978 261 462
email: paul.mewies@itv1wales.co.uk
Part of the Carlton Group and

covering Wales, during 2001 HTV Wales broadcasted 615 hours of regional programming. It also makes programmes for the ITV Network and other broadcasters and S4C. The company is committed to producing range of its programmes in the Welsh language.

## HTV West

**Television Centre**
**Bath Road**
**Bristol BS4 3HG**
Tel: 0117 972 2722
Fax: 0117 971 7685
email: reception@htv-west.co.uk
Website: www.htvwest.com; www.itv1west.com
Owned by Carlton and covering the West of England.

## Independent Television News

**200 Gray's Inn Road**
**London WC1X 8XZ**
Tel: 020 7833 3000
Fax: 020 7430 4868
Website: www.itn.co.uk
Chairman: Mark Wood
Chief Executive: Stewart Purvis
Finance Director: Andrew Whitaker
ITN is the news provider nominated by the Independent Television Commission to supply news programme for the ITV network. Subject to review, this licence is for a ten year period from 1993. ITN also provides news for Channel 4, Channel 5 and for the Independent Radio News (IRN) network. ITN is recognised as one of the world's leading news organisation whose programmes and reports are seen in every corner of the globe. In addition to its base in London, ITN has permanent bureaux in Washington, Moscow, South Africa, the Middle East, Hong Kong, and Brussels as well as at Westminster and eight other locations around the UK. Other business concerns are ITN Archive, ITN Factual, and ITN International.

## ITV Network Centre

**200 Gray's Inn Road**
**London WC1X 8HF**
Tel: 020 7843 8000
Fax: 020 7843 8158
Website: www.itv.com
ITV is a federation of regional broadcasters. National coverage is achieved by 15 licensees, broadcasting in 14 regional areas : Anglia, Border, Carlton London, Carlton Central,

Carlton West Country, Channel, Grampian, Granada, HTV, LWT, Meridian, Scottish Television, Ulster Television, Tyne Tees, Yorkshire. (London has two licencees, one for the weekday - Carlton and one for the weekend - LWT) In May 2002 the ITV licensees agreed a Charter for the Nations and the Regions with its regulator, the ITC. In autumn 2002 ITV1 was adopted as the lead channel brand in most ITV regions.

## LWT (London Weekend Television)
**The London Television Centre**
**Upper Ground**
**London SE1 9LT**
Tel: 020 7620 1620
Website: www.lwt.co.uk
Part of the Granada Media Group, LWT has the London Franchise for the weekend, beginning 17.15 on Fridays and ending 06.00 Mondays, As LWT can be picked up well beyond the London area, it serves a population of around 11 million. LWT is also a major supplier of programmes to the ITV Network and other broadcasters such as Channel 4, Channel 5 and BSkyB. LWT and Carlton TV are joint owners of the London News Network.

## Meridian Broadcasting Ltd
**Television Centre**
**Northam Road**
**Southampton SO14 0PZ**
Tel: 023 8022 2555
Fax: 023 8033 5050
email: dutyoffice@meridiantv.com
Website: www.meridiantv.com
Regional news centres:
**Maidstone**
**West Point**
**New Hythe**
**Maidstone**
**Kent ME20 6XX**
Tel: 01622 882244
Fax: 01622 714000
**Newbury**
**1-3 Brookway**
**Hambridge Lane**
**Newbury, Berks RG14 5UZ**
Tel: 01635 522322
Fax: 01635 522620
Part of the Granada Media Group, Meridian covers the South and South East of England, broadcasting to a population of 5.5 million. Meridian Broadcasting's main studio complex is in Southampton with additional studios at Maidstone, Newbury and Brighton. During 2002, the company

broadcast more than 630 hrs of new programmes and also supplied material to other networks including Channel 4, Channel 5 and BBC.

## S4C
**Parc Ty Glas**
**Llanishen**
**Cardiff CF14 5DU**
Tel: 029 2074 7444
Fax: 029 2075 4444
**Lôn Ddewi**
**Caernarfon LL55 1ER**
Tel: 01286 674622
email: s4c@s4c.co.uk
Website: www.s4c.co.uk
Channel Four Wales) was established under the Broadcasting Act, 1980 and is responsible for providing a service of Welsh and English programmes on the Fourth Channel in Wales, with a remit that the majority of programmes shown between 18.30 and 22.00 should be in Welsh. In 2002 it broadcast roughly 40 hours of Welsh language programming per week. The remainder of its output, is provided by Channel 4 and is in English. 10 hours per week of Welsh programmes are provided by the BBC and the rest are commissioned/purchased from independent producers. Since 1993 S4C has been directly funded by the Treasury and is responsible for selling its own advertising. In November 1998 S4C Digital was launched, which provides over 80 hours a week of Welsh language programming.

## Scottish Television
**200 Renfield Street**
**Glasgow G2 3PR**
Tel: 0141 300 3000
Fax: 0141 300 3030
email: viewer.enquiries@scottishtv.co.uk
Website: www.scottishtv.co.uk
Part of the Scottish Media Group, Scottish TV has held the ITV licence for Central Scotland since commercial television started in 1957. It remains the most watched station in Scotland, broadcasting to 3.4 million viewers. In addition to programmes for its own region, ST also makes programmes for the ITV Network and other broadcasters such as Channel 4.

## Tyne Tees Television
**The Television Centre**
**City Road**
**Newcastle Upon Tyne NE1 2AL**
Tel: 0191 261 0181

Fax: 0191 261 2302
Becoming part of the Granada Media Group in 1997 and covering the North East of England, TTTV has a transmission area stretching from Berwick in the North to Selby in the South and across to Alston in the West. Operating from studios and offices in Newcastle, Sunderland, Billingham, York, and Westminster, the company provides more than 11.5 hours of regional output each week. TTTV also produces material for the ITV network and other broadcasters such as Channel 4.

## Ulster Television
**Havelock House**
**Ormeau Road**
**Belfast BT7 1EB**
Tel: 028 90328122
Fax: 028 90246695
email: info@u.tv
Website: www.utv.co.uk
Covering Northern Ireland, during 2002 UTV produced/commissioned 568 hours of local programmes for its own transmission.

## Westcountry Television
**see Carlton Broadcasting West Country Region**

## Yorkshire Television
**The Television Centre**
**Kirkstall Road**
**Leeds LS3 1JS**
Tel: 0113 243 8283
Fax: 0113 242 3867
Website: www.yorkshiretv.com
**Regional offices:**
**Sheffield**
**Charter Square**
**Sheffield S1 4HS**
Tel: 0114 272 3262
Fax: 0114 275 4134
**Hull**
**23 Brook Street**
**The Prospect Centre**
**Hull HU2 8PN**
Tel: 01482 24488
Fax: 01482 586028
**Lincoln**
**88 Bailgate**
**Lincoln LN1 3AR**
Tel: 01522 530738
Fax: 01522 514162
**Immingham**
**Immage Studios**
**Margaret Street**
**Immingham**
**NE Lincs DN40 1LE**
Tel: 01469 510 661
Fax: 01469 510 662
**York**

**8 Coppergate**
**York YO1 1NR**
Tel: 01904 610066
Fax: 01904 610067
Yorkshire Television broadcasts to a
population of 5.7 million.  The main
studio complex is in Leeds but there
are regional offices in Sheffield, Hull,
Grimsby, Lincoln, and York.  Each
year the regional programmes
department produces over 900 hours
of regional programmes for its own
transmission.  It also produces
programmes for  the ITV network and
other channels, such as Channel 4

# VIDEO/DVD LABELS

These companies acquire the UK rights to all or specialised forms of audio-visual product and arrange for its distribution on video or DVD at a retail level. Examples of titles released on each label are also listed. A listing of currently available titles, and also those available for hire only, can be found in the trade catalogue Videolog (published by Trade Service Information) which is updated on a monthly basis. Videolog is used by most retailers - so check with your local store first - and may also be held by your local reference library. Check the Film Links Gateway at www.bfi.org.uk for online sources of deleted videos and DVDs.

## Abbey Home Media
435-437 Edgware Road
London W2 1TH
Tel: 020 7563 3910
Fax: 020 7563 3911
*Action Man*
*Bump*
*Butt-Ugly Martians*
*Postman pat*
*Redwall*
*Superted*
*Tweenies*

## Academy Video
See bfi Video

## American Independence
see Winchester Entertainment

## Arrow Film Distributors
18 Watford Road
Radlett
Herts WD7 8LE
Tel: 01923 858306
Fax: 01923 869673
email: neil@arrowfilms.co.uk
Website: www.arrowfilms.co.uk
Neil Agran
*Cinema Paradiso*
*La Bonne Annee*
*Rififi*
*Would I Lie to You*

## Art House Productions
39-41 North Road
Islington
London N7 9DP

Tel: 020 7700 0068
Fax: 020 7609 2249
*Les Biches*
*Bicycle Thieves*

## Artificial Eye Film Company
14 King Street
London WC2E 8HR
Tel: 020 7240 5353
Fax: 020 7240 5242
email: video@artificial-eye.com
Website: www.artificial-eye.com
Robert Beeson
**2004 Video Releases**
Unknown Pleasures/Xiao Wu (2 discs) - 23 Feb 2004
The Decline of the American Empire - 23 Feb 2004
Le Chignon D'Olga - 29 March 2004
Waiting for Happiness - 29 March 2004
Noi Albinoi - 26 April 2004
Pure - 26 April 2004
Kiss of Life - May 2004
Time of the Wolf - May 2004
The Barbarian Invasions - June 2004
Zatoichi - July 2004
**2004 DVD Releases**
Unknown Pleasures/Xiao Wu (2 discs) - 23 Feb 2004
The Decline of the American Empire - 23 Feb 2004
Wreckmeister Harmonies/Damnation (2 discs) - 23 Feb 2004
Le Chignon D'Olga - 29 March 2004
Waiting for Happiness - 29 March 2004
The Life of O'Haru - 29 March 2004
Noi Albinoi - 26 April 2004
Pure - 26 April 2004
The Three Colours Trilogy (4 disc box set) - 26 April
Kiss of Life - May 2004
Time of the Wolf - May 2004
The Barbarian Invasions - June 2004
Zatoichi - July 2004
At Five in the Afternoon - August 2004
The Apple - August 2004
Uzak - September 2004
Silence Between Two Thoughts - October 2004
Last Life in the Universe - November 2004

## BBC Worldwide Publishing
Woodlands

80 Wood Lane
London W12 0TT
Tel: 020 8433 2000
Fax: 020 8749 0538
*Abigail's Party*
*Absolutely Fabulous*

## *bfi* Video
21 Stephen Street
London W1T 1LN
Tel: 020 7957 8957
Fax: 020 7957 8968
email: video.films@bfi.org.uk
Website: www.bfi.org.uk
bfi Video, incorporating Connoisseur and Academy, releases over 300 titles (including DVDs) covering every decade of cinema, from the 1890s to the present. New releases are under the bfi Video label.
*La Belle Et La Bete*

## Blue Dolphin Film & Video
40 Langham Street
London W1W 7AS
Tel: 020 7255 2494
Fax: 020 7580 7670
Website: www.bluedolphinfilms.com
*Blonde Fist*
*Crystal Voyager*

## Blue Light
231 Portobello Road
London W11 1LT
Tel: 020 7792 9791
Fax: 020 7792 9871
*Festen*
*Ma Vie En Rose*

## BMG Music Programming
Bedford House
69-79 Fulham High Street
London SW6 3JW
Tel: 020 7384 7500
Fax: 020 7384 8010
*Dawn of the Dead*
*The Harder They Come*

## Buena Vista International (UK)
3 Queen Caroline Street
Hammersmith
London W6 9PE
Tel: 020 8222 1000
Fax is 020 8222 1534
Website: www.bvimovies.com
www.thefilmfactory.co.uk

Filmfactory is the the online home of Buena Vista International UK and of Buena Vista Home Entertainment. Distribute and market Walt Disney, Touchstone, and Hollywood Pictures product on video and DVD

## Carlton Visual Entertainment
5th Floor
35-38 Portman Square
London W1H 0NU
Tel: 020 7486 6688
Fax: 020 7612 7257
Gerry Donohoe, Managing Director
Carlton Visual Entertainment is a leading independent video and DVD distributor specialising in classic film, TV, children's and special interest genres. As part of the Carlton Group it has access to the largest British owned film catalogue (encompassing the Rank, Korda, Rohauer, Romulus and ITC collections)

## Channel 5
Universal Pictures Video
1st Floor, 1 Sussex Place
Hammersmith
London W6 9XS
Tel: 020 8910 5000
Fax: 020 8910 5404
*Babar*
*The Herbs*

## Channel Four Video
124 Horseferry Road
London SW1P 2TX
Tel: 020 7306 3675
Fax: 020 7306 8044
Lyndsey Bartlett
*Black Books*
*Brass Eye*

## Cherry Red Films
Unit 17
1st Floor
Elysium Gate West
126-128 New Kings Road
London SW6 4LZ
Tel: 020 7371 5844
Fax: 020 7384 1854
email: ian@cherryred.co.uk
Website: www.cherryred.co.uk
Ian McVay, Matt Bristow
Release DVD versions of certain
Visionary Film titles.
*James Dean - The Rare Movies*
*Groupies*
*The Man, His World, His Music -*
*Johnny Cash Documentary*
*UK/IDK - A Film About Pnk and*
*Skinheads*
*Momus - Man of Letters - Docmentary*
And over 50 music titles revealed on

DVD

## Cinema Club
76 Dean Street
London W1D 3SQ
Tel: 020 7316 4488
Fax: 020 7316 4489
email: info@cinemaclub.co.uk
Website: www.cinemaclub.co.uk
Cinema Club is the low price DVD and VHS publishing division of Video Collection International

## Classic Pictures Entertainment
Shepperton Film Studios
Studios Road
Shepperton TW17 0QD
Tel: 01932 592016
Fax: 01932 592046
History and Nostalgia titles such as:
*The Battle Of Britain*

## Clear Vision
36 Queensway
Ponders End
Enfield
Middx EN3 4SA
Tel: 020 8805 1354
Fax: 020 8805 9987
Website: www.clearvision.co.uk
Ian Allan
Wrestling and TV Drama titles, including:
*The Bill*
*Minder*
*Callan*
*World Wrestling Entertainment*

## Columbia TriStar Home Video
Sony Pictures Europe House
25 Golden Square
London W1R 6LU
Tel: 020 7533 1200
Fax: 020 7533 1015
*The Basketball Diaries*
*Charlie's Angels*

## Connoisseur Video
see bfi video

## Contender Entertainment Group
48 Margaret Street
London W1W 8SE
Tel: 020 7907 3773
Fax: 020 7907 3777
Joan Lofts, Director of TV
*Tractor Tom*
*Peppa Pig*

## Dreamworks Home Entertainment
UIP House

45 Beadon Road
London W6 OEG
Tel: 020 8563 4160
Fax: 020 8748 0734
*American Beauty*
*Antz*

## Entertainment in Video
108-110 Jermyn Street
London SW1Y 6HB
Tel: 020 7930 7766
Fax: 020 7930 9399
*Ali*
*Gosford Park*

## Eros International
Unit 23
Sovereign Park
Coronation Road
London NW10 7PA
Tel: 020 8963 8700
Fax: 020 8963 0154
email: eros@erosintl.co.uk
*Chori Chori Chupke Chupke*
*Dhadkan*

## Film Four Video
Distributed through VCI

## Firefly Entertainment Limited
Suite 5
3rd Floor
9 North Audley Street
London W1K 6WF
Tel: 020 7659 0840
Fax: 020 7659 0850
email:
garethw@fireflyentertainment.co.uk
Gareth Watson, Managing Director
Distributor, publisher & producer of sell-through video. Genres include sport, fitness, special interest, music, film & TV

## Fremantle Home Entertainment
1 Stephen Street
London W1T 1AL
Tel: 020 7691 6000
Fax: 020 7691 6079
Website:
www.fremantlemedia.com/homeentertainment.com
Julia Katharina Ohle
Pete Kalhan, Snr Vice President
*History of Football*
*Arsenal*
*Celtic FC*
*Manchester City FC*
*World at War*
*Men Behaving Badly*
*Goodness Gracious Me (Series 1-3)*
*Monkey*
*The Water Margin*

*Rainbow*
*Chorlton and the Wheelies*
*Rafifi*
*Straw Dogs*
*World War 1 in Colour*
*Really Bend It Like Beckham*

## Granada Media
**Commercial Ventures**
**200 Gray's Inn Road**
**London WC1X 8XZ**
Tel: 020 7316 6000
Fax: 020 7316 3222
Website: www.granadavideo.com
Nathalie Roussety, Granada
Productions

## Green Umbrella Sport & Leisure
**4 The Links**
**Old Woking Road**
**Old Woking**
**Surrey GU22 8BF**
Tel: 01483 726969
Fax: 01483 721188
email: sales@greenumbrella.co.uk
Website: www.greenumbrella.co.uk
Jules Gammond
Sports and special interest videos and
DVDs

## guerilla films
**35 Thornbury Road**
**Iselworth**
**Middlesex TW7 4LQ**
Tel: 020 8758 1716
Fax: 020 8758 9364
Website: www.guerilla-films.com
Includes films by Eric Rohmer, Barbet
Shroeder, Jacques Rivette
Fully independent distribution
company. Since 1999 it has
concentrated on only releasing British
films. Recent releases include -
*Beginner's Luck, Two Men Went to
War, Puckoon, Nine Dead Gay Guys*

## ICA Projects
**12 Carlton House Terrace**
**London SW1Y 5AH**
Tel: 020 7766 1416
Fax: 020 306 0122
email: Saras@ica.org.uk
Website: www.ica.org.uk
Sara Squire
*Abouna*
*All About Lily Chou Chou*
*Ten*
*Atanarjuat*
*The Man Without a Past*
*In This World*
*Mon-rak Transistor*
*The Clay Bird*

## Icon Home Entertainment
**180 Wardour Street**
**London W1F 8FX**
Tel: 020 7494 8100
Fax: 020 7494 8141
*The Dish*
*Felicia's Journey*

## Manga Entertainment
**8 Kensington Park Road**
**London W11 3BU**
Tel: 020 7229 3000
Fax: 020 7221 8899
Website: www.manga.co.uk
Kim McCauley
*Akira*
*Ghost in the Shell*
*Ninja Scroll*

## Medusa Communications & Marketing
**Regal Chambers**
**51 Bancroft**
**Hitchin**
**Herts SG5 1LL**
Tel: 01462 421818
Fax: 01462 420393
Video and DVD distributors for:
Playboy; Hong Kong Legends;
Medusa Pictures; Adult Channel,
Danielle Steele titles
*Cannonball Run*

## Metrodome Distribution
**5th Floor**
**33 Charlotte Street**
**London W1T 1RR**
Tel: 020 7408 2121
Fax: 020 7409 1935
*Chopper*
*Dagon*

## MGM Home Entertainment (Europe) Ltd
**5 Kew Road**
**Richmond**
**London TW9 2PR**
Tel: 020 8939 9300
Fax: 020 8939 9314
*The Great Escape*
*The Magnificent Seven*
*Four Weddings And A Funeral*
*The Good, The Bad and The Ugly*

## Millivres Multimedia
**Unit M**
**Spectrum House**
**32-34 Gordon House Road**
**London NW5 1LP**
Tel: 020 7424 7400
Fax: 020 7424 7401
Website: www.millivres.co.uk

## Momentum Pictures
**2nd Floor,**

**184-192 Drummond St**
**London NW1 3HP**
Tel: 020 7391 6900
Fax: 020 7383 0404
*Crossroads*
*CSI - Crime Scene Investigation*
*Amélie*

## Nova Productions
**62 Ascot Avenue**
**Cantley**
**Doncaster DN3 6HE**
Tel: 0870 765 1094
Fax: 0870 125 7917
email: library@novaonline.co.uk
Website: www.novaonline.co.uk
Contact Andrew White, Gareth
Atherton
Sell-through video distributor, a
subsidiary of Nova Productions, with
a catalogue of specialist & local
interest documentaries and nostalgia
programming. Britain's leading
transport label, with releases on
trains, trams, bus, cars, motorbikes
and trolleybuses

## Odyssey Video
**PO Box 32889**
**London N1 2WP**
Tel: 020 7704 6355
Fax: 020 7704 6365
*Ambush in Waco*
*A Place for Annie*

## Optimum Releasing
**22 Newman Street**
**London W1T 1PH**
Tel: 020 7637 5403
Fax: 020 7637 5408
email: info@optimumreleasing.com
Website: www.optimumreleasing.com

## Orbit Media Ltd
**80a Dean Street**
**London W1D 3SN**
Tel: 020 7287 4264
Fax: 020 7727 0515
email: chris@orbitmedia.co.uk
Website: www.orbitmedia.co.uk
Screen classics label, feature films and
documentaries
Sherlock Holmes Library

## Paramount Home Entertainment
**180 Oxford St**
**London W1N 0DS**
Tel: 020 7478 6866
Fax: 020 7478 6868
*Breakfast At Tiffany's*
*Chinatown*

## Pathé Distribution
**Kent House**

14-17 Market Place
**London W1W 8AR**
Tel: 020 7323 5151
Fax: 0207 323 1773
email: Lloyd.vanson@pathe-uk.com
Website: www.pathe.co.uk
Contact: Lloyd Vanson
*Jeepers Creepers 2*
*Wrong Turn*
*In The Cut*
*Girl With A Pearl Earring*
*Godsend*
*Bad Education*
*Two Brothers*

## Quantum Leap
**1a Great Northern Street**
**Huntingdon**
**Cambridgeshire PE29 7HJ**
Tel: 01480 450006
Fax: 01480 456686
email: quantumleap@ukonline.co.uk
Website: www.qleap.co.uk
Kim Lyon
Special interest titles with subjects
such as gardening, alternative health,
sport. Titles include:
*Crop Circles - The Cosmic Connection*

## Redbus
**Ariel House**
**74a Charlotte Street**
**London W1T 4QJ**
Tel: 020 7299 8800
Fax: 020 7299 8801
Website: www.redbus.com
*The Gift*
*Jeepers Creepers*

## Screen Edge
**St. Annes house**
**329 Clifdon Drive South**
**Lytham St. Annes**
**Lancashire FY8 1LP**
Tel: 01253 781994
Fax: 01253 712453
email: johnbeoutlaw23.com
Website: www.screenedge.com
Incorporates Screen Edge, Screen
Edge Pink Japan, and the Visionary
Labels

## Tartan Video
**28 Poland Street**
**London W1F 8QW**
Tel: 020 7292 0523
Fax: 020 7292 0521
email: info@tartanvideo.com
Website: www.tartanvideo.com
Contact: Matthew Hamilton
*Audition*
*Irreversible*
*Secretary*
*Belleville Rendez-vous*

## Thames Video Home Entertainment
**Twentieth Century House**
**31-32 Soho Square**
**London W1D 3AP**
Tel: 020 7753 8686
Fax: 020 7434 1625
Now Fremantle Home Entertainment
Twentieth Century Fox Home
Entertainment

## Universal Pictures Video
**1 Sussex Place**
**Hamersmith**
**London W6 9XS**
Tel: 020 8910 5000
Fax: 020 8910 5404
Labels include Playback (nostalgia), 4
Front Video (low price), Electric
Pictures Video (specialist feature
films) and Channel 5 (low price
children's)
*Bagpuss*

## Video Collection International
**76 Dean Street**
**London W1D 3SQ**
Tel: 020 7396 8888
Fax: 020 7396 8996/7
VCI runs as a label as well as a
distributor. They cover feature films,
television, children's programming,
sport, music etc.
Ali G titles

## Visionary Film
Incorporates Visionary Film,
Visionary Documentary, Visionary
Art Experimental and Visionary
Music Video.
see Screen Edge

## Warner Home Video
**Warner House**
**98 Theobald's Road**
**London WC1X 8WB**
Tel: 020 7984 6400
Fax: 020 7984 5001
*Annie Get Your Gun*
*Bend It Like Beckham*

## Warner Vision
**35-38 Portman Square**
**London W1H 6LR**
Tel: 020 7467 2566
Fax: 020 7467 2564
*Big Brother*
*The Sopranos*

## Winchester Entertainment
**19 Heddon Street**
**London W1B 4BG**
Tel: 020 7851 6500
Fax: 020 7851 6505

Labels include: Feature Film
Company, American Independence
and Winchester.
*Another Life*

## Yash Raj Films
**3rd Floor Wembley Point**
**1 Harrow Road**
**Middlesex HA9 6DE**
Tel: 0870 739 7345
Fax: 0870 739 7346
email: ukoffice@yashrajfilms.com
Website: www.yashrajfilms.com
Hindi language titles
*Daag*

# WEBSITES

This section contains a small selection of useful websites which coincide with most of the sections in this book. For more detailed information visit the gateway film links section on the *bfi* website.
www.bfi.org.uk/gateway

## Archive and Film Libraries

Alexandra Palace TV Society
www.apts.org.uk

ARKive
www.arkive.org.uk

BFI National Film and TV Archive
www.bfi.org.uk/collections

British Association of Picture Libraries and Agencies (BAPLA)
www.bapla.org.uk

British Movietone News
movietone.com

British Pathe
www.britishpathe.com

British Universities Film and Video Council
www.bufvc.ac.uk/

Contemporary Films Archive
contemporaryfilms.com/archives/arc_set.htm

East Anglian Film Archive
www.uea.ac.uk/eafa/

FIAF: The International Federation of Film Archives
www.cinema.ucla.edu/FIAF/

FIAT: International Federation of Television Archives
camilla.nb.no/fiat

FOCAL
www.focalint.org

Footage.net
www.footage.net

France - La Vidéoteque de paris
www.vdp.fr/

Getty Images Creative
www.imagesbank.com

Hulton Archive
www.archivefilms.com

Huntley Film Archives
www.huntleyarchives.com

Imperial War Museum Film and Video Archive
iwm.org.uk/lambeth/film.htm

National Archive of Film Shorts
www.nafs.co.uk

National Museum of Photography Film & Television
www.nmsi.ac.uk/nmpft

North West Film Archive
www.nwfa.mmu.ac.uk

Scottish Film and Television Archive
www.scottishscreen.com

SEAPAVAA
members.nbci.com/archives/

South East Film and Video Archive
shs.surreycc.gov.uk/sefva.html

Tanmedia
www.tanmedia.co.uk

UK Film Archive Forum
www.bufvc.ac.uk/faf/html

Wales Film and Television Archive Archif Ffilm a Theledu Cymru
www.sgrinwales.demon.co.uk/filmarchive.htm

Wessex Film and Sound Archive
www.hants.gov.uk/record-office/film.html

## Awards

BAFTA
www.bafta.org

Berlin
www.berlinale.de

British Independent Film Awards
www.bifa.org.uk

Cannes
www.festival-cannes-fr

Edinburgh International Film Festival
www.edfilmfest.org.uk/

Emmys
www.emmys.org/

Emmys International
www.intlemmyawards.com/

European Film Awards
www.europeanfilmacademy.org

Alex Fung's Film Page
www.ncf.carleton.ca/~aw220/

Golden Globes
www.hfpa.com

Golden Rose of Montreux
www.rosedor.ch

Golden Rasberry Awards
www.razzies.com

Grierson Trust Awards
www.editor.net/griersontrustrman

International Film Academy
www.iifa.com

Karlovy Vary
www.iffkv.cz

Locarno
www.pardo.ch

Oscars
www.oscars.org/awards

Monte Carlo TV Festival
www.tvfestival.com/

Royal Television Society Awards
www.rts.org.uk/

## Books

*bfi* Publishing
www.bfi.org.uk/bookvid

Oxford University Press
www.oup.co.uk

Routledge
www.routledge.com

*bfi* Film and Television Handbook
www.bfi.org.uk/handbook

## Booksellers

Amazon
www.amazon.co.uk

Blackwell's
www.blackwell.co.uk/bookshops

Cinema Store
www.atlasdigital.com/cinemastore

Reel Posters
www.reelposter.com

Retro Sellers
www.retrosellers.com

Waterstones
www.waterstones.co.uk

UK BookWorld
www.ukbookworld.com

## Cable, Satellite and Digital

Cable/Satellite Guide
www.sceneone.co.uk/s1/TV

BSkyB
www.sky.co.uk

Freeview
www.freeview.co.uk

NTL
www.ntl.co.uk

SkyDigital
www.skydigital.co.uk

Telewest Communications
www.telewest.co.uk

## Careers and Training

British Council Training and Careers
Advice
www.britfilms.com/training

Film Education
www.filmeducation.org

Focal
www.focal.ch

Global Film School
www.globalfilmschool.com

Ideas factory
www.ideasfactory.com

Institut National de l'Audiovisual
www.ina.fr

Moving Image Gateway
www.bufvc.ac.uk/gateway

National Film and Television School
www.nftsfilm-tv.ac.uk

Skillset
www.skillset.org

skillsformedia
www.skillsformedia.com

## Cinemas

Apollo Cinemas
www.apollocinemas.co.uk

Artificial Eye Film Company
www.artificial-eye.com

Caledonian Cinemas
www.caledoniancinemas.co.uk

Cinema Admissions
www.dodona.co.uk

Cinemas in the UK
www.aber.ac.uk/~jwp/cinemas

The Cinema Theatre Association
cinema-theatre.org.uk

Cineworld
www.cineworld.co.uk

City Screen
www.picturehouses.co.uk

Film Finder
www.yell.co.uk/yell/ff/

Fox Movies
www.foxmovies.com

Free Tickets
www.freecinematickets.co.uk/

Hollywood Screen Entertainment
www.hollywoodcinemas.net

Mainline
www.screencinemas.co.uk

Merlin Cinemas
www.merlincinemas.co.uk

National Amusements (UK)
www.showcasecinemas.co.uk

Northern Morris Associated
Cinemas
www.nm-cinemas.co.uk

Odeon
www.odeon.co.uk

Picturehouse
www.picturehouse-cinemas.co.uk

Reeltime Cinemas
www.reeltime-cinemas.co.uk

Scoot
www.cinema.scoot.co.uk

Ster Century
www.stercentury.co.uk

Showcase Cinemas
www.showcasecinemas.co.uk

UCI (UK) Ltd
www.uci-cinemas.co.uk

UCG
www.ucg.fr

Vue Entertainment Group
www.myvue.com

Warner Village
warnervillage.co.uk

## Courses

Academy of Radio, Film and
Television
www.media-courses.com

The American Intercontinental
University
www.aiulondon.ac.uk

University of Bath
www.bath.ac.uk

BBC Training and Development
www.bbctraining.co.uk

Birkbeck College University of
London
www.birkbeck.ac.uk

University of Birmingham
www.birmingham.ac.uk

Bournemouth University
www.bournemouth.ac.uk

University of Bradford
www.bradford.ac.uk

Brighton Film School
www.brightonfilmschool.org.uk

Bristol Animation Course
www.mediaworks.org.uk/animate

University of Bristol
www.bristol.ac.uk

British Universities Film and Video
Council
www.bufvc.ac.uk

Brunel University
www.brunel.ac.uk

Canterbury Christ Church College
www.cant.ac.uk

Cardiff University
www.cardiff.ac.uk/jomec

Coventry University
www.alvis.coventry.ac.uk

Cyber Film School
www.cyberfilmschool.com

De Montfort University Bedford
**www.dmu.ac.uk/Bedford**

De Montfort University Leicester
**www.dmu.ac.uk/Leicester**

University of Derby
**www.derby.ac.uk**

University of East Anglia
**www.uea.ac.uk**

University of East London
**www.bradford.ac.uk**

University of Exeter
**www.ex.ac.uk**

First Film Foundation
**www.firstfilm.co.uk**

University of Glasgow
**www.arts.gla.ac.uk/tfts/**

Glasgow Caledonian University
**www.gcal.ac.uk**

Global Film School
**www.globalfilmschool.com**

Goldsmiths College
**www.goldsmiths.ac.uk**

Kent Institute of Art and Design
**www.kiad.ac.uk**

University of Kent
**www.ukc.ac.uk**

King Alfred's College Winchester
**www.wkac.ac.uk**

Kingston University
**www.kingston.ac.uk**

University of Leicester
**www.le.ac.uk**

University of Liverpool
**www.liv.ac.uk**

Liverpool John Moores University
**www.livjm.ac.uk**

London Guildhall University
**www.lgu.ac.uk**

London Film Academy
**www.londonfilmacademy.com**

London Film School
**www.lifs..org.uk**

London School of Economics and
Political Science
**www.lse.ac.uk**

University of Manchester
**www.man.ac.uk**

Middlesex University
**www.mddx.ac.uk**

Napier University
**www.napier.ac.uk**

National Film and Television School
**www.nftsfilm-tv.ac.uk**

National Short Course Training
Programme
**www.nfts-scu.org.uk**

University of Newcastle upon Tyne
**www.ncl.ac.uk/ncrif**

Northern School of Film and
Television
 **www.lmu.ac.uk**

University of Northumbria at
Newcastle
**www.unn.ac.uk**

Nova Camcorder School
 **www.novaonline.co.uk**

University of Portsmouth
**www.port.ac.uk**

University of Reading
**www.reading.ac.uk**

College of Ripon and York St John
**www.ucrysj.ac.uk**

Raindance Ltd
**www.raindance.co.uk**

Roehampton Institute
**www.roehampton.ac.uk**

**Royal College of Art**
www.rca.ac.uk/Design

University of Salford
**www.salford.ac.uk**

University of Sheffield
**www.sheffield.ac.uk**

Sheffield Hallam University
**www.shef.ac.uk**

South Bank University
**www.sbu.ac.uk**

Staffordshire University
**www.staffs.ac.uk**

University of Stirling:Film and Media
Studies Department
**www-fms.stir.ac.uk**

The University of Sunderland
**www.sunderland.ac.uk**

University of Sussex
**www.sussex.ac.uk**

Thames Valley University
**www.tvu.ac.uk**

Trinity and All Saints College
 **www.tasc.ac.uk**

University of Wales College, Newport
**http;//www.newport.ac.uk**

University College Warrington
**www.warr.ac.uk**

University of Warwick
**www.warwick.ac.uk**

University of Westminster
**www.wmin.ac.uk**

University of Wolverhampton
**www.wolverhampton.ac.uk**

## Databases/film reviews

625 Television Room
**www.625.uk.com**

All Movie Database
**allmovie.com**

Animation World Network
**www.awn.com**

Baseline
**www.pkbaseline.com**

Bib Online
**www.bibnet.com**

Box Office
**www.entdata.com**

Box Office Guru
**www.boxofficeguru.com/**

Brit Movie
**www.britmovie.co.uk**

Castnet
**castnet.com**

Classic Movies
**www.geocities.com/Hollywood/9766**

Classic TV
**www.classic-tv.com**

Cult TV
**www.metronet.co.uk/cultv**

European Cinema On-Line Database
**www.mediasalles.it**

FilmUnlimited
**www.filmunlimited.co.uk**

Film TV
**www.film-tv.co.uk/**

Highangle
**www.highangle.co.uk**

Hollywood Online
**www.hollywood.com**

InDevelopment
**www.indevelopment.co.uk**

Internet Movie Database
**www.uk.imdb.com**

The Knowledge
www.theknowledgeonline.com

The Location guide
www.thelocationguide.com

Media UK Internet Directory
www.mediauk.com/directory

Mandy's International Film and TV
Production Directory
www.mandy.com

Moving Image Gateway
www.bufvc.ac.uk/gateway

Movie Map
www.visitbritain.com/moviemap/

Movie Page
www.movie-page.com

National Filmographies
www.rosland.freeserve.co.uk/filmbo
oks.htm

Netribution
www.netribution.co.uk

Popcorn
www.popcorn.co.uk

Production Base
www.productionbase.co.uk

Spotlight
www.spotlightcd.com
www.players-guide.com

TV Guide - Movies
www.tvguide.com/movies

TV Cream
tv.cream.org

UKTV
www.uktv.com

World Wide Box Office
www.worldwideboxoffice.com

## Distributors (Theatrical)

Arrow Films Distributors
www.arrowfilms.co.uk

Artificial Eye Film Company
www.artificial-eye.com

BFI
www.bfi.org.uk

Blue Dolphin Film & Video
www.bluedolphinfilms.com

Blue Light
www.bluelight.co.uk

Boudicca
www.boudiccafilms.com

Buena Vista International (UK)
www.bvimovies.com

Cinefrance
www.cinefrance.co.uk

City Screen
www.picturehouses.co.uk

Columbia TriStar Films (UK)
www.columbiatristar.co.uk

Contemporary Films
www.contemporaryfilms.com

ContentFilm
www.contentfilm.com

Eros International
www.erosentertainment.com

Film Distributors Association
www.launchingfilms.com

Guerilla Films
www.guerilla-films.com

ICA Projects
www.ica.org.uk

Icon Film Distributors
www.iconmovies.co.uk

Metro Tartan Distribution Ltd
www.tartanvideo.com

Metrodome Distribution
www.metrodomegroup.com

Millivres Multimedia
www.millivresmultimedia.co.uk

Momentum Pictures
www.momentumpictures. co.uk

New Line International
www.newline.com

Optimum Releasing
www.optimumreleasing.com

Pathé Distribution
www.pathe.co.uk

Redbus
www.helkon-sk.com

Salvation Films
www.salvation-films.com

ScreenProjex
www.screenprojex.com

Soda Pictures
www. sodapictures.com

Twentieth Century Fox Film Co
www.fox.co.uk

UIP (United International Pictures)
www.uip.com

Universal Studios
universalstudios.com

Warner Bros
www.warnerbros.com

Winchester Film Distribution
www.winchesterent.com

Yash Raj Films International Ltd
www.yashrajfilms.com

## Facilities

Abbey Road Studios
www.abbeyroad.co.uk/

Cinesite (Europe) Ltd
www.cinesite.com

Communicopia Ltd
www.communicopia.co.uk

Connections Communications
Centre
www.cccmedia.demon.co.uk

Dubbs
www.dubbs.co.uk

Edinburgh Film Workshop Trust
www.efwt.demon.co.uk

The Film Factory at VTR
www.filmfactory.com

FrameStore
www.framestore.co.uk

Hillside Studios
www.ctvc.co.uk

Hull Time Based Arts
www.htba.demon.co.uk

Lee Lighting
www.lee.co.uk

PMPP Facilities
www.pmpp.dircon.co.uk

Salon Post-Productions
www.salon.ndirect.co.uk

Tele-Cine
www.telecine.co.uk

VTR Ltd
www.vtr.co.uk

## Festivals

Edinburgh International Film Festival
**www.edfilmfest.org.uk**

Film Festivals Servers
**www.filmfestivals.com**

Berlin
**www.berlinale.de**

Cannes
**www.festival-cannes-fr**

London Film Festival
**www.lff.org.uk**

Karlovy Vary International Film
Festival
**www.iffkv.cz**

Sundance Film Festival
**www.sundance.org**

## Film Societies

Film Societies
**www.bffs.org.uk**

## Funding

Arts Council of England
**www.artscouncil.org.uk**

Arts Council of Northern Ireland
**www.artscouncil-ni.org**

Arts Council of Wales
**www.ccc-acw.org.uk**

British Council
**www.britfilms.com**

Kraszna-Krausz Foundation
**www.k-k.org.uk**

Scottish Screen
**www.scottishscreen.com**

Sgrin, Media Agency for Wales
**www.sgrinwales.demon.co.uk**

UK Media
**www.mediadesk.co.uk**

The UK Film Council
**www.ukfilmcouncil.org.uk**

English Regional Arts Boards
**www.arts.org.uk**

Northern Ireland Film Commission
**www.nifc.co.uk/**

Shooting people
**shootingpeople.org**

Scottish Screen
**www.scottishscreen.com/**

Sgrîn
**www.sgrinwales.demon.co.uk**

## International Sales

BBC Worldwide
**www.bbc.worldwide.com**

BRITE (British Independent
Television Enterprises)
**www.brite.tv.co.uk**

London Television Service
**www.londontv.com**

Pearson Television International
**www.pearsontv.com**

Twentieth Century Fox Television
**www.fox.co.uk**

Vine International Pictures
**www.vineinternational.co.uk**

## Libraries

*bfi* National Library
**www.bfi.org.uk/library**

British Library
**www.bl.uk/**

COPAC
**copac.ac.uk/copac/**

Film Libraries - International
**www.unesco.org/webworld/portal_b
ib/Library_Websites/Special/Film_L
ibraries/**

Library Association
**www.la-hq.org.uk**

Public Libraries - Online Information
and Queries answered online.
**www.earl.org.uk**

## Organisations

American Film Institute
**www.afionline.org/**

Arts Council of England
**www.artscouncil.org.uk**

Authors Licensing and Collecting
Society
**www.alcs.co.uk**

BBC
**www.bbc.co.uk**

British Council - British films
**www.britfilms.com**

British Film Commission
**www.britfilmcom.co.uk**

British Film Institute
**www.bfi.org.uk**

BKSTS - The Moving Image Society
**www.bksts.demon.co.uk**

BUFVC(British Universities Film and
Video Council
**www.bufvc.ac.uk**

Department for Culture, Media and
Sport (DCMS)
**www.culture.gov.uk/**

Directors' Guild of Great Britain
**www.dggb.co.uk**

EDI
**www.entdata.com**

Equity
**www.equity.org.uk/**

National Museum of Photography,
Film and Television
**www.nmsi.ac.uk/nmpft**

Federation Against Copyright Theft –
FACT
**www.fact-uk.org.uk/**

Film London
**www.filmlondon.org.uk**

New Producer's Alliance
**www.npa.org.uk**

PACT - Producers Alliance for
Cinema and Television
**www.pact.co.uk**

Shooting People
**www.shootingpeople.org**

Scottish Screen
**www.scottishscreen.com**

Skillset
**www.skillset.org**

Women in Film and TV - the
Organisation
**www.wftv.org.uk**

## Organisations (Europe)

Association of European Film
Institutes
**www.filmeurope.co.uk**

Cordis
**www.cordis.lu**

European Association of Animation
Film
**www.cartoon-media.be**

European Audio-visual Observatory
**www.obs.coe.int**

EURIMAGES
**www.culture.coe.fr/eurimages**

Europa
**www.europa.eu.int**

European Broadcasting Union (EBU)
**www.ebu.ch/**

The European Coordination of Film
Festivals EEIG
**www.eurofilmfest.org**

European Documentary Network
**www.edn.dk**

European Film Academy
**www.europeanfilmacademy.org**

EUTELSAT (European
Telecommunications Satellite
Organisation)
**www.eutelsat.org**

Idea
**www.europa.eu.int/idea**

Austrian Film Commission
**www.afc.at**

Belgium - The Flemish Film Institute
**www.vfi-filminsituutbe**

Denmark - Danish Film Institute
**www.dfi.dk**

Estonia – Eesti Filmi Sihtasutsus
**www.efsa.ee**

Finland - AVEK - The Promotion
Centre for Audio-visual Culture in
Finland
**www.kopiostofi/avek**

Finnish Film Archive
**www.sea.fi**

The Finnish Film Foundation
**www.ses.fi/ses**

France - Bibliothèque du Film (BIFI)
**www.bifi.fr**

TV France International
**www.tvfi.com**

Germany - Filmf`rderungsanstalt
**www.ffa.de**

Greek Film Centre
**www.gfc.gr**

Hungary – Magyar Filmunio
**www.filmunio.hu**

Iceland - Icelandic Film Fund
**www.centrum.is/filmfund**

Ireland - Bord Scann·n na
hÉ.ireann/Irish Film Board
**www.iol.ie/filmboard**

Film Institute of Ireland
**www.iftn.ie/ifc**

Italy – Museo Nazionale del Cinema
**www.museonazionaledelcinema.org**

National Film Centre of Latvia
**www.nfc.lv/ffl/html/nfc.html**

Netherlands – Flm museum
**www.filmmuseum.nl**

Poland - Panstowa Wyzsza Szkola
Filmova Telewizyjna I Teatralna
**www.szkola.filmowa.lodz.pl**

Poland - Polish Cinema Database
**info.fuw.edu.pl/Filmy/**

Portugal - Portuguese Film and
Audiovisual Institute
**www.nfi.no/nfi.htm**

Slovak Film Institute
**www.filmsk.sk**

Slovenian Cinematheque
**www.kinoteka.si**

Scottish Screen
**www.scottishscreen.com**

Spain – Filmoteca Española
**www.cultura.mecd.es/cine/film/film
oteca.jsp**

## Press Contacts

6degrees.co.uk
**www.6degrees.co.uk**

Empire
**www.empireonline.co.uk**

Filmwaves
**www.filmwaves.co.uk**

Film Unlimited
**filmunlimited.co.uk**

Flicks
**www.flicks.co.uk**

Guardian online
**www.guardian.co.uk/guardian**

Inside Out
**www.insideout.co.uk**

Movie Club News
**www.movieclubnews.co.uk**

Premiere
**www.premieremag.com**

Radio Times
**www.radiotimes.beeb.com**

Screen
**www.arts.gla.ac**

Screendaily
**screendaily.com**

Screen Digest
**www.screendigest.com**

Sight and Sound
**www.bfi.org.uk/sightandsound**

Sunday Times
**www.sunday-times.co.uk**

Talking Pictures
**www.filmcentre.co.uk**

Television
**www.rts.org.uk**

Time Out
**www.timeout.co.uk/**

Total Film
**www.futurenet.co.uk**

UK Government press releases
**www.open.gov.uk/**

Uncut
**www.uncut.net**

Variety
**www.variety.com**

Visimag
**visimag.com**

## Preview Theatres

BAFTA
**www.bafta.org**

The Curzon Minema
**www.minema.com**

Mr Young's Screening Rooms
**www.mryoungs.com**

RSA
**www.rsa.org.uk**

The Screening Room
**www.moving-picture.co.uk**

## Production Companies

Aardman Animations
**www.aardman.com**

British Film Commission
**www.britfilmcom.co.uk**

British Films Catalogue
**www.britfilms.com/**

Fox Searchlight Pictures
**www.fox.co.uk**

guerilla films
**www.guerilla.u-net.com**

Hammer Film Productions Limited
**www.hammerfilms.com**

imaginary films
**www.imagfilm.co.uk**

Mosiac Films Limited
**www.mosaicfilms.com**

New Producers Alliance
**www.npa.org.uk**

PACT
**www.pact.co.uk**

Zooid Pictures Limited
**www.zooid.co.uk**

## Specialised Goods and Services

Ashurst Morris Crisp
**www.ashursts.com**

Bromley Casting (Film & TV Extras Agency)
**www.showcall.co.uk**

Hothouse Models & Effects
**www.hothousefx.co.uk**

MBS Underwater Video Specialists
**www.eclipse.co.uk.mbs**

Moving Image Touring Exhibition Service (MITES)
**www.mites.org.uk**

Olswang
**www.olswang.co.uk**

## Studios

Capital FX
**www.capital.fx.co.uk**

Ealing Studios
**www.ealingstudios.co.uk**

Elstree Film Studios
**www.elstreefilmstudios.co.uk**

Hillside Studios
**www.ctvc.co.uk**

Millennium Studios
**www.elstree-online.co.uk**

Pinewood Studios
**www.pinewood-studios.co.uk**

## Television Companies

625 Television Room
**www.625.uk.com**

TV Commissions
**www.tvcommissions.com**

TV Guides
**www.link-it.com/TV**
**www.sceneone.co.uk/s1/TV**

Episode Guides Page
**epguides.com/**

Anglia Television
**www.anglia.tv.co.uk/**

BBC
**www.bbc.co.uk/**

Border Television
**www.border-tv.com/**

Carlton Television
**www.carltontv.co.uk/**

Channel Four
**www.channel4.com**

Granada Television
**www.granada.co.uk**
HTV
**www.htv.co.uk/**

London Weekend Television (LWT)
**www.lwt.co.uk/**

Meridian Broadcasting Ltd
**www.meridan.tv.co.uk/**

S4C
**www.s4c.co.uk/**

Scottish Television
**www.stv.co.uk/**

Ulster Television
**www.utvlive.com**

## Video Labels

British Videogram Association
**www.bva.org.uk**

Blockbuster Entertainment
**www.blockbuster.com**

DVD rental
**www.movietrak.com**

MovieMail
**www.moviem.co.uk**

Movies Unlimited
**www.moviesunlimited.com**

Videolog
**www.videolog.co.uk**

## Workshops

City Eye
**www.city-eye.co.uk**

Edinburgh Film Workshop Trust
**www.efwt.demon.co.uk**

Hull Time Based Arts
**www.htba.demon.co.uk**

Pilton Video
**www.piltonvideo.co.uk**

The Place in the Park Studios
**www.screenhero.demon.co.uk**

Real Time Video
**www.rtvideo.demon.co.uk**

Vera Media
**www.vera-media.co.uk**

Vivid
**www.wavespace.waverider.co.uk/~vivid/**

The selection of workshops listed below are generally non-profit distributing and subsidised organisations. Some workshops are also active in making audio-visual products for UK and international media markets

## Amber Side Workshop
5-9 Side
Newcastle upon Tyne NE1 3JE
Tel: 0191 232 2000
Fax: 0191 230 3217
Website: www.amber-online.com
Murray Martin

## Belfast Film Workshop
37 Queen Street
Belfast BT1 6EA
Tel: 01232 648387
Fax: 01232 246657

## Black Media Training Trust (BMTT)
Workstation
15 Paternoster Row
Sheffield S12 BX
Tel: 01142 492207
Fax: 01142 492207
Contact: Carl Baker

## Blaze the Trail Limited (Film & Television Training)
2nd Floor
241 High Street
London E17 7BH
Tel: 020 8520 4569
Fax: 020 8520 2358
email: bctraining@coralmedia.co.uk
Website: www.blaze-the-trail.com
The Course Coordinator

## British Deaf Association
1-3 Worship Street
London EC2A 2AB
Tel: 020 7614 3142 (voice) Tel: 0171 588 3528 (text)
Fax: 020 7588 3526
email: lucyf@bda.org.uk
Website: www.bda.org.uk
Lucy Franklin, Film Festival Coordinator

## Caravel Media Centre
The Great Barn Studios
Cippenham Lane
Slough SL1 5AU

Tel: 01753 534828
Fax: 01753 571383
email: caraveltv@aol.com
Website: www.caravelstudios.com
Anita See

## Chapter MovieMaker
Chapter Arts Centre
Market Road
Canton
Cardiff CF5 1QE
Tel: 029 2031 1050
Fax: 029 2031 3431
email: tony.whitehead@chapter-online.co.uk
Website: www.chapter.org
Tony Whitehead

## Children's Film Unit The
South Way
Leavesden
Herts WD25 7LZ
Tel: 01923 354656
Fax: 01923 354656
email: cfilmunit@aol.com
Website: www.childrensfilmunit.com
Carol Rennie, Adminstrator

## City Eye
Swaythling Neighbourhood Centre
Rear 200 Burgess Road
Swaythling
Southampton SO16 3AY
Tel:  023 80677167
Fax: 023 80 677267
email: admin@city-eye.co.uk
Website: www.city-eye.co.uk
David White, Susan Beckett

## Connections Communications Centre
Palingswick House
241 King Street
Hammersmith
London W6 9LP
Tel: 020 8741 1766
Fax: 020 8563 1934
email: connections@cccmedia.demon.co.uk
Website: www.cccmedia.demon.co.uk
Jacqueline Davis

## cre8 studios
Town Hall Studios
Regent Circus
Swindon SN1 1QF
Tel: 01793 463224

Fax: 01793 463223
email: keith@cre8studios.org.uk
Website: www.swindon.gov.uk//index/leisure/artsandculture/cre8.htm
Keith Phillips

## Cultural Partnerships
90 De Beauvoir Road
London N1 4EN
Tel: 020 7254 8217
Fax: 020 7254 7541
Heather McAdam, Lol Gellor, Inge Blackman

## Depot Studios
Bond Street
Coventry CV1 4AH
Tel: 024 76 525074
Fax: 024 76 634373
email: info@depotstudios.org.uk
Website: www.depotstudios.org.uk
Contact: Anne Forgan, Matthew Taylor

## Edinburgh Film Workshop Trust
29 Albion Road
Edinburgh EH7 5QZ
Tel: 0131 656 9123
email: post@efwt.demon.co.uk
Website: www.efwt.demon.co.uk
David Halliday

## Edinburgh Mediabase
25a SW Thistle Street Lane
Edinburgh EH2 1EW
Tel: 0131 220 0220
Fax: 0131 220 9158
email: info@edinburghmediabase.com
email: training@edinburghmediabase.com
Website: www.edinburghmediabase.com
Paul Ryan

## Exeter Phoenix
Media Centre
Bradninch Place
Gandy Street
Exeter
Devon EX4 3LS
Tel: 01392 667066
Fax: 01392 667596
email: media@exeterphoenix.org.uk
Website: www.exeterphoenix.org.uk
Jonas Hawkins

## Film Work Group
Top Floor, Chelsea Reach
79-89 Lots Road
London SW10 0RN
Tel: 0171 352 0538
Fax: 0171 351 6479
Loren Squires, Nigel Perkins

## First Take
Merseyside Innovation Centre
131 Mount Pleasant
Liverpool L3 5TF
Tel: 0151 708 5767
Fax: 0151 707 0230
email: all@first-take.demon.co.uk
Website: www.first-take.demon.co.uk
Mark Bareham, Lynne Harwood

## Four Corners Film Workshop
113 Roman Road
Bethnal Green
London E2 0QN
Tel: 020 8981 6111
Fax: 020 8983 4441
email: film@fourcorners.demon.co.uk
Website: www.fourcornersfilm.org
Lyn Turner

## Fradharc Ur
11 Scotland Street
Stornoway
Isle of Lewis PA87
Tel: 01851 703255

## Glasgow Media Access Centre
3rd Floor
34 Albion Street
Glasgow G1 1LH
Tel: 0141 553 2620
Fax: 0141 553 2660
email: contactgmac@aol.com
Website: www.g-mac.co.uk /
www.cineworks.co.uk
Alice Stilgoe, David Smith, Kirsty
Kyle, William Summers

## Hull Time Based Arts
42 The High Street
Hull HU1 1PS
Tel: 01482 216446
Fax: 01482 589952
email: timebase@htba.demon.co.uk
Website: www.timebase.org
Annabel McCourt, Dan Van Heeswyk

## Intermedia Film and Video
19 Heathcote Street
Nottingham NG1 3AF
Tel: 0115 955 6909
Fax: 0115 955 9956
email: info@intermedianotts.co.uk
Website: intermedianotts.co.uk
Ceris Morris, Director

## Knew productions
The Place in the Park Studios,
Bellevue Road
Wrexham
North Wales LL13 7NH
Tel: 01978 358522
email: studio@knewmedia.co.uk
Website: www.knewmedia.co.uk
Richard Knew

## Leeds Animation Workshop (A Women's Collective)
45 Bayswater Row
Leeds LS8 5LF
Tel: 0113 248 4997
Fax: 0113 248 4997
Website:
www.leedsanimation.demon.co.uk
Jane Bradshaw, Terry Wragg,
Stephanie Munro, Janis Goodman,
Milena Dragic

## Media Production Facilities
Bon Marche Centre
Ferndale Road
London SW9 8BJ
Tel: 020 7737 7152
Fax: 020 7738 5428
email: mpf@media-
production.demon.co.uk
Website: www.media-
production.demon.co.uk

## The Media Workshop
City Museum and Art Gallery
Priestgate
Peterborough PE1 1LF
Tel: 01733 343119
Fax: 01733 341928
email: mediaworkshop@
peterborough.gov.uk
Clifton Stewart, Media Development
Coordinator

## Mersey Film and Video (MFV)
13 Hope Street
Liverpool L1 9BQ
Tel: 0151 708 5259
Fax: 0151 707 8595
email: info@mersey-film-video.co.uk
Website: www.mersey-film-
video.co.uk

## Migrant Media
Studio 401
Greenhealth Centre
31 Three Colts Lane
London EZ 6JB
Tel: 020 7729 9109
Fax: 020 7729 6909
email: info@injusticefilm.co.uk
Website: www.injusticefilm.co.uk
Ken Fero, Yesim Deveci

## Moving Image Touring Exhibition Services (MITES)
Foundation For Art & Creative
Technology (FACT)
88 Wood Street
Liverpool L1 4DX
Tel: 0151 707 4435
Fax: 0151 707 4432
email: mites@fact.co.uk
Website: www.mites.org.uk
Simon Bradshaw

## Nerve Centre
7/8 Magazine Street
Derry BT48 6HJ
Northern Ireland
Tel: 02871 260562
Fax: 02871 371738
Website: www.nerve-centre.org.uk
Bernie McLaughlin, Aisling McGill

## The Old Dairy Studios
156b Haxby Road
York YO3 7JN
Tel: 01904 641394
Fax: 01904 692052
Website: www.olddairystudios.co.uk

## Oxford Film and Video Makers
Centre For Film and Digital Media
54 Catherine St
Oxford OX4 3AH
Tel: 01865 792731 or 01865 792732
Fax: 01865 742901
email: office@ofvm.org
Website: www.ofvm.org
Richard Duriez

## Panico London Ltd
PO Box 496
London WC1A 2WZ
Tel: 020 7485 3533
Fax: 020 7485 3533
email: panico@panicofilms.com
Website: www.panicofilms.com

## Picture This Moving Image
40 Sydney Row
Spike Island Studios
Bristol BS1 6UU
Bristol BS2 0QL
Tel: 0117 925 7010
Fax: 0117 925 7040
email: office@picture-this.org.uk
Website: www.picture-this.co.uk
Josephine Lanyon, Director

## Pilton Video
30 Ferry Road Avenue
Edinburgh EH4 4BA
Tel: 0131 343 1151
Fax: 0131 343 2820
email: info@piltonvideo.org
Website: www.piltonvideo.org

Hugh Farrell, Joel Venet, Eleanor Hill, Graham Fitzpatrick, Graham Drydale

## Platform Films and Video
Unit 14, Pennybank Chambers
33-35 St Johns Square
London EC1M 4DS
Tel: 020 7278 8394
Fax: 020 7278 8394
email: platform.films@virgin.net
Chris Reeves

## Real Time Video
The Arts and Media Centre
21 South Street
Reading RG1 4QU
Tel: 0118 901 5205
Fax: 0118 901 5206
email: info@real-time.org.uk and info@real-time.fsnet.co.uk
Website: www.real-time.org.uk
Clive Robertson

## Screenwriters' Workshop
Suffolk House
1-8 Whitfield Place
London W1T 5JU
Tel: 0171 387 5511
Fax: 020 7387 5511
email: screenoffice@tiscali.co.uk
Website: www.lsw.org.uk
Katharine Way

## Sheffield Independent Film
5 Brown Street
Sheffield S1 2BS
Tel: 0114 272 0304
Fax: 0114 279 5225
email: admin.sif@workstation.org.uk
Gloria Ward

## Signals Media Arts
Victoria Chambers
St Runwald Street
Colchester CO1 1HF
Tel: 01206 560255
Fax: 01206 369086
email: admin@signals.org.uk
Website: signals.org.uk
Anita Belli

## Swingbridge Video
Norden House
41 Stowell Street
Newcastle upon Tyne NE1 4YB
Tel/Fax: 0191 232 3762
email: Swingvid@aol.com
Contact: Hugh Kelly

## The Public
Unit 1 Overend Street
West Bromwich
West Midlands  B70 6EY
Tel: 0121 525 6861
Fax: 0121 525 6475
email: @jubart.demon.co.uk

Website: www.c-plex.co.uk
Caroline Manders

## Trilith
Corner Cottage, Brickyard Lane
Bourton, Gillingham
Dorset SP8 5PJ
Tel: 01747 840750/840727

## Valley and Vale Community Arts Ltd
Valley and Vale Community Arts
Sardis Media Centre
Heol Dewi Sant
Betws
Bridgend CF32 8SU
Tel: 01656 729246/871911
Fax: 01656 729185/870507
Website: valleyandvale.co.uk
Alex Bowen, Director

## Vera Media
30-38 Dock Street
Leeds LS10 1JF
Tel: 0113 2428646
Fax: 0113 242 8739
email: vera@vera-media.co.uk
Website: www.vera-media.co.uk
Al Garthwaite, Catherine Mitchell

## VET (Video Engineering & Training)
Lux Building
2-4 Hoxton Square
London N1 6NU
Tel: 020 7505 4700
Fax: 020 7505 4800
email: post@vet.co.uk
Website: www.vet.co.uk

## Vivid
Birmingham's Centre for Media Arts ltd
Unit 311
The Big Peg
120 Vyse Street, Jewellery Quarter
Birmingham B18 6ND
Tel: 0121 233 4061
Fax: 0121 212 1784
email: info@vivid.org.uk
Website: www.vivid.org.uk
Yasmeen Baig-Clifford

## Welfare State International (WSI)
The Ellers
Ulverston
Cumbria LA12 0AA
Tel: 01229 581127
Fax: 01229 581232

## West Yorkshire Media Services
Hall Place Studios
3 Queen Square

Leeds LS2 813U
Tel: 0113 283 1906
Fax: 0113 283 1906
email: m.spadafora@lmu.ac.uk
Website: www.hallplacestudios.com
Maria Spadafora

## WFA
Media and Cultural Centre
9 Lucy Street
Manchester M15 4BX
Tel: 0161 848 9785
Fax: 0161 848 9783
email: wfa@timewarp.co.uk
Website: www.wfamedia.co.uk
Chloe Beattie

# A